BLOOD AND SOIL

OTHER BOOKS BY BEN KIERNAN

Peasants and Politics in Kampuchea, 1942–1981 (coauthor)

Revolution and Its Aftermath in Kampuchea (coeditor)

How Pol Pot Came to Power: Colonialism, Nationalism, and Communism in Cambodia, 1930–1975

Burchett: Reporting the Other Side of the World, 1939–1983 (editor)

Pol Pot Plans the Future: Confidential Leadership Documents from Democratic Kampuchea, 1976–1977 (coeditor)

Genocide and Democracy in Cambodia: The Khmer Rouge, the United Nations, and the International Community (editor)

The Pol Pot Regime: Race, Power, and Genocide in Cambodia under the Khmer Rouge, 1975–1979

Le génocide au Cambodge, 1975–1979: Race, idéologie et pouvoir

Conflict and Change in Cambodia (editor)

The Specter of Genocide: Mass Murder in Historical Perspective (coeditor)

Genocide and Resistance in Southeast Asia: Documentation, Denial, and Justice in Cambodia and East Timor

BLOOD AND SOIL

A World History of

Genocide and Extermination

from

Sparta to Darfur

Ben Kiernan

Yale University Press New Haven & London

The author has made his best efforts to secure permission for the use of all copyrighted images and material. Any rightsholders with questions are encouraged to contact the author care of Yale University Press.

Published with assistance from the Kingsley Trust Association Publica-tion Fund established by the Scroll and Key Society of Yale College. Also published with assistance from the Mary Cady Tew Memorial Fund.

Designed by James J. Johnson and set in Minion Roman types by Tseng Information Systems, Inc., Durham, North Carolina. Printed in the United States of America by R.R. Donnelley, Harrisonburg, Virginia.

Library of Congress Cataloging-in-Publication Data

Kiernan, Ben.
Blood and soil : a world history of genocide and extermination from Sparta to Darfur / Ben Kiernan.
p. cm.
Includes bibliographical references and index.
ISBN 978-0-300-10098-3 (cloth : alk. paper)

1. Genocide 2. Crimes against humanity. I. Title.
HV6322.7.K54 2007
304.6'63—dc22
2007001525

A catalogue record for this book is available from the British Library.

The paper in this book meets the guidelines for permanence and durability of the Committee on Production Guidelines for Book Longevity of the Council on Library Resources.

10 9 8 7 6 5 4 3 2 1

For Glenda Elizabeth Gilmore

Contents

Part Three. **Twentieth-Century Genocides**

Illustrations follow pages 86, 246, 374, and 438

Maps

Introduction

"At the beginning of the world," said the Portuguese Jesuit Manuel de Nóbrega in 1559, "all was homicide."[1] This was a suspect but significant statement. From the sixteenth century, many Europeans began looking to ancient precedents, even for genocide, a phenomenon that had become more frequent after European expansion accelerated in 1492. A cult of antiquity inspired those on the brink of modernity even as they took up technological innovations, including some that facilitated mass murder.

Nóbrega's claim contained more than a grain of truth. Mass killing was no New World novelty. Some prehistorians suspect that ancestors of modern humans exterminated Europe's archaic Neanderthal population. Later archaeological evidence suggests that during the Stone Age, "competing local communities may have resorted even to annihilation of one another." Over 5,000 years ago, for example, Mesolithic hunter-gatherers in a region of what is now Germany carefully positioned the skulls of 34 men, women, and children in a cave. Archaeologists found these "trophy" skulls arranged in groups "like eggs in a basket." Most bore evidence of multiple blows with stone axes.[2]

The rise of agriculture in the Neolithic era supplied a surplus that could sustain systematic warfare. If Europe's first farmers were more civilized than prehistoric hunters, ironically, well-provisioned agricultural societies may also have been more prone to mass killing. Evidence exists of the destruction of entire communities. Excavation at the early Neolithic site of Talheim in Germany revealed that 7,000 years ago, a group of killers armed with six axes massacred 18 adults and 16 children, then threw their bodies into a large pit. A late Neolithic site in France, dating from 2,000 B.C.E., yielded evidence of the hasty burial of 100 people of all ages and both sexes, many with arrowheads embedded in their skeletons. While some archaeologists date the origins of war earlier, in the Mesolithic era, others argue that armed conflicts began only when prehistoric hunters became farmers, settled down, and fought over land. Palisades and ditches defended many Neolithic villages.[3]

The prominence in genocidal ideology of cults of antiquity and a fetish for agriculture are two of the four major themes of *Blood and Soil*. Some ancient precedents reveal early preoccupations with land use. According to the Bible, for example, extreme violence often accompanied conflicts over land and sometimes pitted prospective farmers against ethnically alien town dwellers. While God promised the Israelites "a good and spacious land, a land flowing with milk and honey" (Exodus 3:8), the book of Deuteronomy added: "Of the cities . . . which the Lord thy God doth give thee for an inheritance, thou shalt save alive nothing that breatheth" (20:16). The book of Joshua (6–10) describes Israelite massacres of the entire populations of seven cities, including Jericho and three Amorite kingdoms. "Joshua smote all the country of the hills, and of the south, and of the vale, and of the springs," and "utterly destroyed all that breathed" (10:40; see fig. 1).

Animosity toward nonagriculturalists—nomadic, pastoral, or urbanized— may have fueled some of the conflicts described in the Old Testament. One target of Deuteronomy were the Amorites, whom the Sumerians termed a pastoral people who "do not grow grain." In more urbanized Canaan, the Israelite arrival apparently brought agricultural terracing and sedentarization to previously sparsely settled areas. The new devotion of the Israelites—heretofore pastoralists themselves—to agriculture may have intensified their ideological hostility to other pastoral peoples even as they clung to their own pastoral traditions.[4]

Yet the biblical association of agriculture with righteousness was never pervasive; the pastoral image of the shepherd and flock remained more common until the fifteenth century. In the book of Genesis, Cain offered "fruits of the soil," but God "did not look with favor" on them, accepting only Abel's new lamb (4:3–4). Expelled from Eden for killing Abel, Cain became "the first peasant" of ancient and medieval Christianity. Far from being favored, as historian Paul Freedman has shown, Cain signified the "ur-peasant"—deformed, rustic, and wicked.[5] Biblical pastoralism and the medieval model of a pristine, idyllic garden both rejected the cultivator. Farming found relative ideological favor only in the modern era.

Some ancient sources also suggest a third recurring theme of genocide and thus of this book: ethnic enmity. The Old Testament is replete with examples. Deuteronomy trumpets hatred and violence: "But thou shalt utterly destroy them—the Hittites, Amorites, Canaanites, Perizzites, Hivites and Jebusites—as the LORD your God has commanded you" (20:17). Listing these same ethnic groups, the book of Exodus adds: "I will wipe them out" (23:23). Again in Deuteronomy we read: "[T]hou shalt smite them, and utterly destroy them; thou shalt make no covenant with them, nor shew mercy unto them. . . . Thou shalt consume all the people which the Lord thy God shall deliver thee; thine eye shall have no pity upon them" (7:2, 16). Whatever this might reveal of actual biblical events, such extremism is neither limited to nor representative of Jewish texts, any more than the Koran's injunction to "slay the idolaters wherever you find them" (9:5) is representative of Islamic texts. Jews in particular have long been major victims of ethnic persecution and slaughter; during the second millennium, it was often professed Christians who appealed to violent biblical injunctions as precedents for the mass murder of other groups.

Imperial and territorial conquests compose the fourth major theme of this book. Ancient empires set their own genocidal precedents. The dispersal of the Jews began with Nebuchadnezzar's conquest of Jerusalem in 586 B.C.E. and the deportation of its inhabitants to Babylon. After Rome's destruction of Carthage in 146 B.C.E., its annexation of Egypt in 6 C.E. excluded Alexandria's large Jewish community from the privileges accorded to citizens, and Jews suffered two expulsions from Rome itself. Indeed, "the first pogrom in Jewish history" shook Alexandria in 38 C.E. when Romans herded Jews into a ghetto as rioters burned synagogues and looted shops. [6] Like other diaspora populations, Jews became increasingly vulnerable.

Blood and Soil focuses on the six centuries since 1400, the period historians term "the modern era." The main features of modern genocidal ideology emerged then, from combinations of religious or racial hatred with territorial expansionism and cults of antiquity and agriculture. This book charts the slow development of modern genocidal racism against a background of sectarian warfare, ancient models, and worldwide conquest of new territory with accompanying visions of its idealized cultivation. When agrarian idealism shaded into antiurban or monopolist thinking, genocide was occasionally associated with rising hostility to cities or commercial centers.

The modern era gave prominence to these notions. At first, drawing upon the Bible, European medieval culture had considered agricultural serfs to be

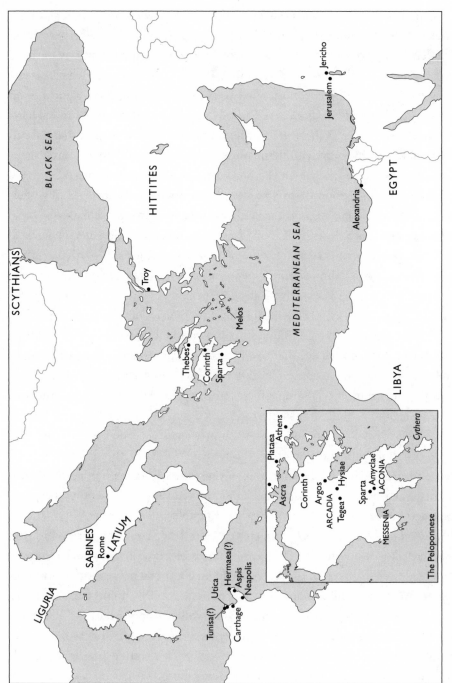

MAP 1. The ancient eastern Mediterranean

descendants of Ham, cursed by Noah and doomed to their subordinate status. Their mundane assignment precluded them from any ideological role in the domination of others. But then, during the Middle Ages in the Islamic world, and later in early modern Europe and America, Cain's image as the archetypal peasant merged with the racialist symbol of a black African Ham as the archetypal slave. The two concepts fused in Europe in the sixteenth century and influenced America until the nineteenth. As the curse of Ham became slowly racialized, it migrated from European serfs to haunt Africans and Native Americans.[7] From the sixteenth century, liberated from Ham's curse and enlisted in the settlement of the New World, European peasants and farmers became a symbol of superiority to Indians rather than of subordination to other Europeans.

Modern expansion thus saw the emergence of a complementary ideology of cultivation. Farming as an occupation came to be considered superior to hunter-gathering, to pastoral herding, even to the newly burgeoning city life that depended upon agricultural supply. Promoting the culture and utility of a yeomanry more than farmers' material needs, a novel emphasis on the importance of cultivation lent legitimacy to the brutal seizure of lands occupied until then by progeny of both Cain and Ham. This new agrarian vision, together with emerging racism, helped fuel early modern Europe's enclosures, land clearances, and colonial expansion. Most colonial encounters in particular were at least initially violent. Catastrophes multiplied with conquests from the West Indies to the East Indies.

The technological imbalance of forces that made modern genocide feasible was rarer in the ancient and medieval worlds. Only from the fifteenth century, the dawn of the modern era, did advances in transportation and firepower frequently bring into collision societies separated by the requisite technology chasm. Genocide sometimes resulted—from the expansionism of Asian powers as well as in the New World. In both Europe and Asia, the early modern era also saw the rise of cults of antiquity and of agriculture, which strengthened emerging notions of racial superiority.

Genocides were nevertheless exceptional, emerging from specific social conditions and individual human decisions. However, if each was unique, and some were extreme, historical connections and consistent themes appeared. The long history of genocidal violence multiplying across the globe therefore has but one redeeming feature—but it is of inestimable importance. With hindsight, it is now possible to discern patterns in the development of genocidal movements and regimes. Because they emerged in different centuries in a range of societies with varying cultures, they might seem to have been provoked by different historical crises in no apparent sequence, perpetrated by diverse political groups with a multiplicity of ideological labels, targeting a vast spectrum of victims. Yet these genocides do have much in common. Six hundred years of evidence helps us detect their essential elements not only in retrospect but, by analysis of common causes, potentially in advance, which increases the possibility of preventing future genocides with timely action.

Perpetrators and Dissenters

Much of this book documents genocides by European perpetrators, but it also shows that they hold no monopoly on the crime. Rebelling Indians in Peru and African slaves in Haiti, for instance, committed genocidal massacres of European settlers and planters. Elsewhere, mass killing occurred in the absence of colonialism. Consider the Fifth Dalai Lama's instructions to repress Tibetan rebels, issued in 1660:

> Make the male lines like trees that have had their roots cut;
> Make the female lines like brooks that have dried up in winter;
> Make the children and grandchildren like eggs smashed against rocks;
> Make the servants and followers like heaps of grass consumed by fire; . . .
> In short, annihilate any traces of them, even their name.[8]

Although more extensive written sources survive for Western history, adequate evidence from other regions shows that European conquest of most of the globe sprang from no inherently greater cultural propensity for violence. The roots of genocide lie elsewhere, if not everywhere.

Moreover, in the Judeo-Christian tradition, violent domination also provoked internal dissent. In the first book of Samuel (15:1–16:1), God recalled that Amalekites had "lain in wait" for the Israelites on their journey from Egypt, and he told Saul: "Now go and smite Amalek, and utterly destroy all that they have, and spare them not; but slay both man and woman, infant and suckling, ox and sheep." The Israelites then "utterly destroyed all the people with the edge of the sword," but Saul spared Agag, king of Amalek, and his kingdom's best stock. When God found that Saul "hath not followed my commandments," Samuel "hewed Agag in pieces before the Lord." God punished Saul for refusing to "utterly destroy the sinners the Amalekites" by denying Saul's descendants the throne of Israel. Along with its genocidal injunction, this episode provided a biblical precedent for Jewish and Christian (and Islamic) dissent: the recalcitrant who would not complete a genocide paid a heavy price, yet not a mortal one. Demands for obedience and genocide recur in Judeo-Christian scripture, but so do models of dissent and nonviolence.

Many Christians took such lessons to heart. "We dispute in schools," Englishman John Bulwer wrote in *Anthropometamorphosis* in 1653, "whether, if it were possible for man to do so, it were lawful for him to destroy any one species of God's creatures, though it were but the species of toads and spiders, because this were taking away one link of God's chain, one note of his harmony." Bulwer was contesting calls for extermination of vermin in the English countryside, authorized by a 1566 act of Parliament allowing bounties for killing foxes, polecats, weasels, otters, and hedgehogs. Bulwer was defending animal species, yet his text certainly also implied a religious injunction against what we today would call genocide.[9]

Some English settlers committed that crime in parts of North America and later in Australia, but they were not the only ones. Virginia Indians perpetrated genocidal massacres of white settlers in 1622 and again in 1644. In the founding years of the colony of New South Wales, local Aboriginal leader Bennelong repeatedly requested British support to "exterminate" rival groups. Governor Arthur Phillip did not oblige. An elderly Aboriginal warrior from Victoria's Westernport tribe told an Englishman in 1844 of the near annihilation of his people several years earlier. "Wild blacks" had surrounded the tribe at night, "killed nearly all the men, stole the females and destroyed the children, so that few escaped." The man asked: "Where are all my brothers? do you see any old men? I am the only one." His people were lying "about the country like dead kangaroos." That same year an Aborigine showed Chief Protector George Augustus Robinson the site where a "Whole Tribe" had recently been "destroyed by the Yattewittongs and their Allies," and "blanched human bones strewed the surface and marked the spot where the slaughter happened."[10]

Some English colonists in both Australia and America tried to stop genocidal massacres of indigenous people. Besides Phillip in Sydney, Roger Williams in Rhode Island and Governor Edmund Andros in New York, as well as Americans Benjamin Franklin in Pennsylvania and Sam Houston in Texas, not to mention the sixteenth-century Spanish missionary Bartolomé de Las Casas, all made genuine and effective efforts to conciliate or assist indigenous people. At regional and local levels, at least, the most shocking European violence was deplored, restrained, or resisted by such people, or was even rivaled by that of perpetrators from opposing cultures, which in turn possessed their own conciliators and dissenters.

The same is true of the even darker twentieth century, when all continents produced perpetrators of genocide as well as dissenters. The technology, scale, and intensity of this violence were all new. At least 30 million people perished in genocides across the globe. Some were sudden or concentrated outbursts of mass murder, like those committed by the Young Turks in 1915, the Nazis in World War II, the Khmer Rouge in 1975–79, or Rwanda's Hutu Power regime in just three months in 1994 (chapters 10, 11, and 15).

Other genocides were gradual and prolonged. In the USSR, Stalin's regime of terror rose and fell incrementally, over nearly three decades, before and after his homicidal frenzy of the 1930s (chapter 13). Maoism, along with its Chinese and Japanese enemies, subjected China to intermittent cycles of deadly violence from the 1920s to the 1970s, peaking in a regime-made famine that killed tens of millions in the 1950s (chapters 12 and 14). Third world populations suffered long and hard under smaller, but equally relentless, killer regimes like that of Kim Il-sung in North Korea, where repression and starvation escalated under his son, Kim Jong-il. After a U.S.-sponsored coup ended a democratic era in Guatemala in 1954, murderous political repression plagued that country until 1996, persisting even after its intense genocidal phase of 1981–83.[11] Extermination in East Timor began with the Indonesian invasion of 1975, reached its zenith in 1978–80, and continued sporadically until Jakarta's violent withdrawal in 1999. Mass killing in Sudan has gathered pace since 1982, with its Islamist regime taking 2 million victims by 2006, first Christians and animists, then black Muslims in Darfur.

The twenty-first century could be just as bleak. After the cold war ended in 1989, new flashpoints emerged. Multinational Communist regimes like the USSR, Yugoslavia, and Czechoslovakia collapsed in ethnic division, as did their allies Afghanistan and Ethiopia. Armed territorial secession threatened other large multiethnic states like Indonesia and Congo. Following the 1994 genocide in Rwanda, ethnic violence spread to Burundi and to Congo, where a new genocide erupted. Ethnic cleansing campaigns in the Caucasus and Chechnya cleared ground for new conflicts that seem to resist solution. Vicious Al-Qaeda terrorism targets civilians from Manhattan to Madrid, from Morocco to the Moro region of the Philippines. Muslim-Christian violence has erupted in Indonesia, Nigeria, Pakistan, and Iraq. Threats loom in rising anti-immigrant, nativist, and religious fundamentalist movements from western Europe to East

Asia. A deepening divide in China, Islamic rebellions in southern Thailand and the Philippines, murderous insurgency and repression in Iraq, international and domestic crisis in North Korea, continuing ethnopolitical dissension in Afghanistan and suppression in Burma, and brutal national-religious conflicts in Kashmir and Sri Lanka all bode ill for twenty-first-century ethnic concilia-tion.

Countervailing trends offer grounds for hope but not complacency. The end of the colonial era and of the cold war, the spread of democracy and inter-national law, and the rise of U.N. peacekeeping all reduced the number of inter-state wars, internal coups, and crises. (Less reassuringly, mass flight reduced the death rate, too: the number of refugees and displaced people quadrupled from 10 to 40 million between 1970 and 1992.) According to the 2005 *Human Secu-rity Report,* even the number of genocides, after "nearly five decades of inexo-rable increase," became fewer in the late 1990s, when "more people were being killed in sub-Saharan Africa's wars than the rest of the world put together." Yet new conflicts have broken out since: "That the world is getting more peace-ful is no consolation to people suffering in Darfur, Iraq, Colombia, Congo or Nepal."[12] As genocide prevention has become more feasible, it remains urgent. It requires prediction of likely outbreaks, which in turn demands a prescient understanding of common features of genocide that often emerge early in the process.

Historical and Legal Definitions

The first step in identifying the essential and thus the predictable elements of genocides is to adopt a consistently defined term for use in comparison. One such term has been *holocaust,* originally a biblical Greek word for a reli-gious offering sacrificed completely by fire. From the late fifteenth century, it began to acquire overtones of mass murder. Bishop John Alcock's description in *Mons Perfeccionis* in 1497 of "an holocauste of martyrdom made to Cryste" includes the original meaning but may also have coined the word's modern English usage as a metaphor for religious violence. The Spanish missionary Las Casas employed the term in his sixteenth-century exposé of conquistador brutality, *The Devastation of the Indies.* In their "butchery" in Guatemala in 1524–30, Las Casas wrote, "[w]henever the Spaniards captured an important noble or chieftain, they did him the honor of burning him at the stake. . . . You can judge what would be the number of victims that were swallowed up in the holocaust." Bishop George Berkeley had in mind violent cultural suppression when he wrote in 1732, "Druids would have sacrificed many a holocaust of free-thinkers." American missionaries in Turkey in 1896 denounced Ottoman massacres of Armenian Christians as a "holocaust." Writing in 1941, Sean O'Faolain used the same term for the violent English conquest and devastation of Ireland's Munster province in the 1580s.[13]

Those authors might not choose that word now. The 1941–45 Nazi genocide of the Jews did not just constitute the most extensive case of genocide; it differed from most others in an important respect. The Holocaust was one of the first historical examples of attempted *physical* "racial" extermination, a campaign to murder an entire people. Yet it was not the only one. Part 2 of this book demonstrates that earlier, on a smaller scale, such a fate had already befallen some indigenous peoples, while later, ethnic Vietnamese in Cambodia and Tutsi in Rwanda suffered similar devastation (chapter 15).

The term *genocide* emerged in the early 1940s as the Nazis carried out their crime. In October 1943, a year after O'Faolain had publicized a sixteenth-century "holocaust," the Polish Jewish jurist Raphael Lemkin coined "genocide." He put it into print in November 1944 in his classic *Axis Rule in Occupied Europe*. By the time he died in 1959, Lemkin had nearly completed a magisterial analysis of a long list of historical cases and themes of genocide, which remains unpublished. He thought that genocide should be understood to include the attempted destruction not only of ethnic and religious groups but of political ones, and that the term should also encompass systematic cultural destruction.[14]

Lemkin was the major force behind the 1948 United Nations Convention on the Prevention and Punishment of Genocide. This treaty gave his new term a legal meaning, narrower than he intended yet still much broader than the colloquial sense of total, state-organized, physical extermination. The convention defines the crime of genocide as an *attempt* at extermination, whether *partial or complete:* "acts committed with the intent to destroy, in whole or in part, a national, racial, ethnical, or religious group, as such." Genocide need not be state planned or even violent. Among the acts it prohibits, the convention lists the nonviolent destruction of a protected group. While excluding, to Lemkin's disappointment, cultural destruction and political extermination, the convention specifically covers the forcible removal of children from their families, the imposition of living conditions that make it difficult to sustain a group's existence, and the infliction of physical or mental harm with the intent to destroy a group "as such." The legal definition of genocide applies, then, to the removals of Aboriginal children from their parents to "breed out the colour"—as an Australian official put it in 1933. Thus a new legal discipline of international criminal law emerged from the convention and the Nuremberg trials. It has since overseen what one writer calls "the rapid evolution of the crime from an academic concept to a firmly-established principle of international law."[15] This legal process has expanded significantly on the narrower popular understanding of genocide based on the Nazi Holocaust.

By 2007, 140 states had ratified the 1948 U.N. convention. The recourse now available to victims under international law is sufficient cause to accept its definition of genocide. To be sure, the new legal field lacks "a wide body of supporting theoretical structure," and some nonlegal scholars of genocide employ the term more broadly to cover the destruction of political groups. Yet whether we find the convention conceptually coherent, or narrow or broad enough, it has the force of international law, binding on nearly all U.N. member states. A recent legal study terms the Genocide Convention "one of the most widely accepted" treaties.[16] Since 1998, special International Criminal Tribunals have convicted perpetrators for acts of genocide committed in both the former Yugoslavia and Rwanda. The convention's definition is also enshrined in the statute of the first permanent International Criminal Court, created in 2002 and ratified by 104 states as of 2007.

The U.N. Genocide Convention is a product of twentieth-century events and the legal response to them. Legally, it cannot be applied retroactively to events before 1951, when it came into force. *Nullem crimen sine lege* (no crime without law) prevents prosecution of any genocidists for crimes committed before their state became a party to the convention in force. Thus the Nuremberg Tribunal convicted no Nazis of the distinct crime of genocide. Yet it is clear that Hitler's regime did perpetrate genocide, and that surviving perpetrators could have been prosecuted for it at Nuremberg, had the 1948 convention been applicable international law before the Holocaust. Indeed, in 1948–49, other Allied courts convicted 15 Nazis for genocide as a crime against humanity (not as a distinct crime).[17] Many aspects of the convention's definition of genocide were written specifically to outlaw the very kinds of events that had taken place during World War II and during the Armenian genocide in World War I.

This book, a comparative study of the social, political, and intellectual history of genocidal violence, applies the 1948 U.N. definition to earlier as well as later events. There is no conceptual reason to avoid applying it to pre-1900 catastrophes to assess whether they fit that definition. Only a consistent survey of centuries of ethnopolitical violence can determine similarities and differences between cases. Equally, even though states ignored the 1948 convention for decades afterward, it is also useful to apply it to subsequent events. The United States acceded to the convention only in 1988.[18] Until as late as 1995, when the new Ad Hoc International Criminal Tribunal for the Former Yugoslavia (ICTY) issued its first indictments, no international forum had ever prosecuted a genocide perpetrator for breaching the convention—despite its status as statutory international criminal law. It took exactly 50 years, from 1948 to 1998, to register the first international judicial conviction for genocide, the finding of the International Criminal Tribunal for Rwanda (ICTR) that that country's former prime minister, Jean Kambanda, was guilty of the crime. Until the late 1990s, then, perpetrators contemplating genocide could have easily dismissed the prospect of any such legal action against them. The convention's first half century of existence probably did not practicably deter genocide nor alter the decision-making climate for those tempted to commit it.

Consistent conceptual categories transcend the terms used to label them. But let me anticipate two objections. Some find application of the term *genocide* to earlier centuries an anachronistic deployment of a twentieth-century notion. Yet to reach a conclusion on whether twentieth-century genocide was distinctive, we must first adopt a single definition and consistently apply it to earlier and later events. A different objection is that genocide did occur before 1900 but that it was then more common, failed to invoke the moral opprobrium it does now, and therefore should not be placed in the same category. A major conclusion of this book is that genocide indeed occurred commonly before the twentieth century. I leave the moral distinction to the reader.

Article 2 of the 1948 Genocide Convention sets out the three main components of the crime. It first defines the groups that may become *victims* of genocide: all or part of "a national, ethnical, racial or religious group." The convention then lists various *acts* meeting its definition of genocide, if committed against all or part of such a group with the *intent* to destroy it, "as such."

Acts of Genocide

The convention's article 2 (sections a–e) places acts of genocide into five legal categories. These could form a moral hierarchy, but I will suggest a more conceptual classification. Sections a–c describe *physical* genocide, not just killing but also violence "causing serious bodily or mental harm to members of the group," or the use of other force "deliberately inflicting on the group conditions of life calculated to bring about its physical destruction in whole or in part." Courts have found that these acts could include "placing a group on a subsistence diet, reducing required medical services below a minimum, [and] withholding sufficient living accommodations." Sections d and e describe *biological* genocide, which need not involve physical destruction, but destruction by the employment or threat of force against a group to prevent it from reproducing: "imposing measures intended to prevent births within the group" or "forcibly transferring children of the group to another group." In addition to these five specified categories of acts, the international criminal law definition evolving from legal judgments based on the convention has incorporated a sixth, not explicitly listed in it: rape/death camps that target the women of a group. What is sometimes called *gendercide* therefore now legally constitutes an act of genocide.[19]

Not covered by the convention, though, is *cultural* genocide, or "ethnocide"—imposing a new culture on a group, for instance, by the enforcement of educational or linguistic restrictions, without necessarily causing physical destruction or biological disappearance. Nor does the convention cover the destruction of a *political* party or group.

Genocidal Massacres and Extermination

In addition to these legal categories, Leo Kuper, the pioneering sociologist of genocide, identified a more widespread phenomenon that he called "genocidal massacres." This seventh category, unspecified in the 1948 convention, comprises shorter, limited episodes of killing directed at a specific local or regional community, targeted because of its membership in a larger group. Genocidal massacres often serve as object lessons for other members of the group.[20] They may occur in three forms: state organized, communal, or a combination of the two.

First, imperial powers have often employed genocidal massacres, for example, during the Jewish revolt against Roman rule of ancient Palestine. The historian Flavius Josephus recorded precisely how in Alexandria in 68 C.E., the city's Roman governor, Tiberius Julius Alexander, ordered the 3rd and 22nd Legions to conduct, and then to break off, a genocidal massacre of Jews.

Josephus wrote: "Because the governor now understood that those who were most riotous would not be pacified unless some great calamity would overtake them, he sent out the two Roman legions that were in the city, together with 5,000 other soldiers, who had recently arrived from Libya, to punish the Jews. They were permitted not only to kill them, but to plunder them." Roman soldiers then "rushed violently" into Alexandria's Jewish quarter "and did as they were ordered." The Jews resisted fiercely, Josephus went on, but "they were unmercifully and completely destroyed.... The Romans showed no mercy to the infants, had no regard for the aged, and went on in the slaughter of persons of every age, until all the place was overflowed with blood, and 50,000 Jews lay dead. And the remainder would have perished as well, had they not put themselves at the mercy of Alexander. He felt pity and gave orders to the legionaries to retire. Being accustomed to obey orders, the soldiers left off killing immediately." [21]

Second, like genocide itself, genocidal massacres are not limited to killings carried out by a state or its representatives. They may be outbreaks of local communal strife, limited in place and time to what some call "genocidal moments." These included probably the two worst massacres of the Clan Wars in early modern Scotland. In 1577, a party of the MacLeod clan from Skye raided the island of Eigg by sea, forcing its entire population, 395 members of the MacDonald clan, to flee and hide in St. Francis' Cave, under a waterfall. The MacLeods discovered the cave, diverted the flow of the waterfall, built large fires at the mouth of the cave, and deliberately suffocated to death every man, woman, and child on Eigg. The next year, MacDonalds from the nearby island of Uist staged a retaliatory raid. One Sunday morning in May 1578, they quietly drew their galleys up on the beach near Trumpan Church on Skye. The MacDonald attackers rapidly surrounded the church and incinerated its entire congregation of MacLeods by barricading them inside and setting fire to its thatched roof. One woman survived. [22]

Finally, in the twenty-first century, communal conflict and state policy, often in coordination, have continued to generate genocidal massacres and moments. In the Indian state of Gujarat in 2002, a Muslim mob reportedly attacked a train carrying Hindu activists. Two carriages burned, killing 59 people. The next day a newspaper in Gujarat, a state governed by a Hindu nationalist party, proclaimed: "Avenge blood for blood." Gujarati police then helped nationalist gangs kill 800–2,000 local Muslims in three days. They raped, mutilated, and murdered scores of women and girls, setting fire to Muslim homes, shops, and mosques, while Gujarat's government imposed what Human Rights Watch called "a massive cover-up of the state's role in the massacres." A former chief justice of the Delhi High Court denounced what he called "the communalisation of the State authorities," and Indian lawyers and human rights activists urged the passage of legislation to "treat communal violence as genocide."[23]

In some genocidal massacres, however, it is unclear that intent existed to destroy a protected group "as such," even in part, and so the 1948 U.N. convention does not apply. Those cases of localized "genocidal massacre," collective murder of people for their membership in a larger group, remain subject to other key international criminal prohibitions that outlaw crimes against humanity. The latter are defined as "a widespread or systematic attack directed against a civilian population."[24] They include the murder of political or social groups unprotected by the Genocide Convention.

The meaning of "extermination," like "holocaust," has changed over the millennia. The classical Latin *exterminare,* Old French *exterminer,* and Middle English *exterminen* all meant simply "to drive out, expel, or banish." However, in the Vulgate Latin version of the Hebrew and Greek scriptures, composed in the third and fourth centuries, the term *exterminare* first took on the additional sense of "abolish, extirpate, destroy." This became its meaning in medieval Latin. In Britain, twelfth-century Latin texts also used the term *exterminium* for "destruction" and *exterminator* for "destroyer." Those two meanings resurfaced in mid-fifteenth-century Latin and first appeared in English writings in the seventeenth century. For instance, Hobbes wrote in *The Leviathan* in 1651: "A People coming into possession of a Land by warre, do not always exterminate the antient Inhabitants." Thus, the primary meaning of "extermination" became "total extirpation, utter destruction," although the secondary, obsolescent sense, "driving out by force," remained in use in the eighteenth century.[25]

Since the Nazi Holocaust, the crime of "extermination" has been a crime against humanity, and its definition includes not only massacres but also "the intentional infliction of conditions of life, inter alia the deprivation of access to food and medicine, calculated to bring about the destruction of part of a population." Enslavement and deportation are also crimes against humanity. The purpose of these persecutions is not relevant to guilt, nor do charges of crimes against humanity require proof of specific "intent to destroy" a group "in whole or in part."[26]

Under the 1948 convention, genocide itself may be partial. Indeed, it usually falls far short of the total extinction of a group. Conversely, sometimes even extinction is not genocide (when intent is lacking). Terms like *genocide, extinction, extermination, civil war, ethnic "cleansing," war crimes,* and *biological warfare* all represent independent and often overlapping concepts, neither synonymous nor mutually exclusive. For instance, in wartime, killing soldiers in combat is routine and distinct from the prohibited mass murder of civilians. Such mass murder, even if it ends once all resistance stops, is a war crime and may also qualify as either genocide or genocidal massacres if it targets protected groups. With or without an ethnic element, mass murder of civilians is more frequent in war than in peacetime, but it is not the same as the killing of armed combatants.

Other Acts Facilitating Genocide

Article 3 of the Genocide Convention also prohibits other criminal acts, separate from genocide, as punishable violations of the 1948 treaty. They include conspiracy, incitement, and attempt to commit genocide, and complicity in genocide. These distinct legal categories are useful for historical analysis as well.

Government actions, policies, prohibitions, and, in the case of a responsibility to protect, even deliberate *inaction* in a crisis could fall into the category of complicity in genocide. In colonial Australia, for example, British authorities rarely set out to exterminate Aborigines, as some settlers and police units did. Nor did U.S. federal officials deliberately plan to eliminate Native Americans in California in the 1850s or later in parts of the West, as some U.S. army officers, state governments, and bounty-hunting posses did. Yet on both continents, official policies and their deliberate, sustained enforcement facilitated or resulted in a predictable outcome: genocide of Aboriginal and Native American peoples. Authorities in Australia prohibited Aborigines from testifying in court, even in their own defense, until 1876 in New South Wales (1884 in Queensland), and U.S. legal prohibitions barring Indian witnesses or dismissing their testimony applied until 1847 (in California until 1872), while at the same time other laws in both countries often prevented indigenous people from acquiring firearms with which they could defend themselves from repeated attack.[27] Thus governments discriminating against these ethnic groups outlawed their judicial and military self-defense, even against genocide. Under the 1948 convention, such official discrimination and refusal to protect subjects or citizens from genocide does not comprise that crime itself but might be evidence of complicity in it or one of the other violations: conspiracy, attempt, or incitement to commit genocide. The distinct crime of genocide, to repeat, requires the act of "killing," or another of the specified acts, committed with "intent to destroy" at least part of a protected group.

Genocidal Intent

A perpetrator's premeditation may be located somewhere along a spectrum of mental states ranging from more to less heinous: from a genocidal motive for the act to a purposefulness in its execution to knowledge of the certain result of the act to awareness of a predictable or probable outcome from it. In criminal law, the word *intent* includes all of these possible meanings, but under the 1948 convention, genocidal intent does not extend to a simple disregard of the risk of likely harm from an act or to criminal negligence or accident. The perpetrator must commit the act deliberately, but even this "general intent," as lawyers call it, is inadequate. Genocide also requires "specific intent," that is, the act must be specifically committed to accomplish complete or partial destruction of a group. The International Law Commission says "a general awareness of the *probable* consequences of such an act . . . is not sufficient." A judgment of the ICTY's Appeals Chamber adds: "The specific intent requires that the perpetrator, by one of the prohibited acts, . . . seeks to achieve the destruction, in whole or in part, of a national, ethnical, racial or religious group, as such."[28] Comparable acts committed even deliberately but in a reckless manner do not constitute genocide. The crime requires the perpetrator's conscious desire.

This is a higher threshold than that for the separate crime of *complicity* in genocide and for other violations of international criminal law, such as extermination or other crimes against humanity and war crimes. The ICTY found in 1997 that an accomplice in a common purpose, even if he personally "did not intend to bring about a certain result," demonstrated complicity simply by being "aware that the actions of the group were most likely to lead to the result but nevertheless willingly took that risk." Such a mental state, though "more than mere negligence," is inadequate for a genocide conviction. Moreover, the 1948 convention requires more than the 1998 Treaty of the International Criminal Court, which describes intent as present when a person "means to cause that consequence or is aware that it will occur in the ordinary course of events." International tribunals have ruled that genocide must be consciously desired, not simply negligently caused or recklessly risked. A perpetrator's awareness

of it as the act's likely or even certain consequences may not meet this requirement of conscious desire.[29]

On the other hand, like criminal law generally, the Genocide Convention
requires no specific *motive.* Indeed, that term is absent from the convention. A
proposed motive requirement, that genocide must be committed "on grounds
of" the national or racial origin, religious belief, or political opinion of a group's
members was deliberately removed from the convention's text during the 1948
negotiations. The substituted compromise phrase, intent to destroy a group "as
such," retains a suggestion of motive, so that genocide must be a desired result
of the act, but it does not require genocide to be the perpetrator's motive for
it. The "specific intent" to destroy a group requires only intentional action and
a purposefulness or conscious desire to accomplish the act: as the ICTR put it
in a 1998 judgment, "the perpetrator clearly seeks to produce the act charged."
This remains distinct from the motive for it. In 2001 the ICTY Appeals Chamber stressed "the necessity to distinguish specific intent from motive," adding:
"The personal motive of the perpetrator of the crime of genocide may be, for
example, to obtain personal economic benefits, or political advantage or some
form of power."[30] Destruction of an ethnic group, then, need not be a motive
for subjecting the group to genocide. Conscious desire does not require single-
minded purpose.

The more colloquial understanding, that the crime requires a genocidal
motive from the start, has no legal basis. Proof of a genocidal motive certainly
establishes genocidal intent, but it is not the only possible method of doing
so. The International Law Commission defines the acts prohibited by the 1948
convention as "intentional or volitional acts which an individual could not
usually commit without knowing that certain consequences would result."[31]
Genocide is not necessarily their motive; it could instead be a consciously accepted consequence of such acts perpetrated in the service of a variety of motives or goals. One of Hitler's motives for establishing Auschwitz was specifically to destroy Jews, but over the centuries other perpetrators have pursued
different goals—conquest, ethnic "cleansing," dictatorship, "national security,"
communism—resulting in genocidal outcomes that were not the perpetrator's original motive. Genocide (and especially genocidal massacre) may be a
means, rather than an end in itself. Many perpetrators bent on another purpose—such as forcing the surrender, dispossession, or departure of a victim
group—have threatened genocide, committing it only when the threat alone

failed to achieve those goals, or desisting once they are fulfilled. That is still genocide, if consciously desired, despite the nongenocidal motive.

In removing the motive requirement, the drafters of the convention also recognized the practical question of proof. Lawyers, like historians, have limited ability to divine psychological states such as intent or planning, let alone motive. As legal scholar William Schabas has pointed out, proof of intent to commit genocide does not necessarily require a courtroom revelation or confession of motive from the accused, nor do prosecutors often call psychiatrists to testify as to what the accused intended. Instead, a court may infer proof of the "intent to destroy a group, in whole or in part, as such" from a pattern of actions to that effect. For instance, the Trial Chamber of the ICTR ruled in 1998 that "in the absence of a confession from the accused, his intent can be inferred from a certain number of presumptions of fact." These include "all acts or utterances of the accused," or "the general context of the perpetration of other culpable acts systematically directed against that same group . . . the scale of atrocities committed, their general nature, in a region or a country, or furthermore, the fact of deliberately and systematically targeting victims on account of their membership of a particular group, while excluding the members of other groups." The ICTY Trial Chamber also ruled: "The number of the victims selected only because of their membership in a group would lead one to the conclusion that an intent to destroy the group, at least in part, was present." Or as the ICTY Appeals Chamber put it, proof of specific intent "may, in the absence of direct explicit evidence, be inferred from a number of facts and circumstances, such as the general context, the perpetration of other culpable acts systematically directed against the same group, the scale of atrocities committed, the systematic targeting of victims on account of their membership of a particular group, or the repetition of destructive and discriminatory acts." [32]

The ICTY added that the intent requirement demands no proof of a genocidal *plan,* either: "The Appeals Chamber is of the opinion that the existence of a plan or policy is not a legal ingredient of the crime. However, in the context of proving specific intent, the existence of a plan or policy may become an important factor in most cases. The evidence may be consistent with the existence of a plan or policy, or may even show such existence, and the existence of a plan or policy may facilitate proof of the crime." [33] Under contemporary international law, then, genocide demands both intentionality and purposefulness, but it requires neither a genocidal motive nor a "smoking gun" blueprint of an extermination project.

Genocide Studies

Genocide proliferated between the 1948 Nuremberg judgments and 1993–94, when the U.N. established the first international tribunals, those for Bosnia and Rwanda. Academic as well as legal scholarship on the crime arose in response. From the 1970s, a few pioneering sociologists, political scientists, and historians, inspired by Lemkin and provoked to action by genocidal recurrences after the Holocaust, by the impunity of their perpetrators, and by denial of the Holocaust and the Armenian genocide, began to broaden our understanding of the phenomenon ʋeyond Nazi crimes.[34] The interdisciplinary field of comparative genocide studies, newer than that of international criminal law, has produced theories, academic definitions, typologies of genocide, and mathematical approaches to its prediction and prevention. These scholars have enlarged the conceptual toolkit for "early warning" and intervention. For bureaucratic reasons, however, this new science is often under pressure to deliver "late warning," that is, alerting governments only at the time of most pressing danger, frequently the sole point at which news of dire developments can finally force politicians to focus on needed counteraction. Longer-term predictive capacities must strengthen the case for intervention in the process well before that point.

Moreover, the post–cold war advances in international legal scholarship and jurisprudence, and prosecutions of genocidists for new outbreaks, have also brought about new possibilities for confronting genocide. Since the early 1990s saw the first applications of the convention, the trend toward imposing human rights accountability has continued. Culminating in the establishment of the permanent International Criminal Court in 2002, this trend has also resulted in U.N. commissions of inquiry on El Salvador, Yugoslavia, Guatemala, Cambodia, East Timor, and Darfur, as well as the South African Truth Commission on apartheid, the Pinochet legal cases in London and Santiago, and various international and national tribunals from Europe (Kosovo) to Latin America (Argentina and Brazil), Africa (Ethiopia and Sierra Leone), and Asia (East Timor and Cambodia). And in The Hague, in contrast to the 1980s when no state agreed to file a genocide case against Pol Pot's Khmer Rouge regime at the International Court of Justice (ICJ), which hears only disputes between states, the ICJ in 2006 heard Bosnia's case charging Serbia with state responsibility for genocide in the 1990s, and in 2007 it found Serbia guilty of violations of the convention. Turkey's bid for admission to the European Community has even renewed international scrutiny of the Armenian genocide. Legal pressure and research has thus made the evidence and documentation of twentieth-century genocide available on an unprecedented scale, enabling a thorough historical accounting. Formerly secret archives with truckloads of incriminating documents have surfaced from Phnom Penh to Paraguay.[35]

Legal institutions set up to review and punish genocides after they occur strengthen the case for action to prevent future ones. But early and effective intervention also requires an understanding of the past patterns of the phenomenon and the obsessions propelling its perpetrators. If a criminal conviction provides a still snapshot of a crime, historical footage can capture the motion that led up to it. The prehistory of a genocide, from social background to ideological formulation, decision-making processes, and the first genocidal massacres, reveals a series of detectable warning signs.

Common Ideological Features of Genocides

Informed deterrence or timely prevention are more feasible if common features of perpetrators' genocidal thinking can be identified in advance of their rise to power. This book examines philosophical outlooks and obsessions, often harmless in themselves yet invidiously related, that have long supplied lethal ideological ammunition to projects of violent militarism and territorial expansion. They include not only racial and religious hatreds but also other idealist cults of ancient glory or pristine purity, more modern conceptions of biological contamination, and varied historical forms of agrarian romanticism and other obsessions with land use.

Racism

Genocidal thinking usually involves idealized conceptions of the world, utopian or dystopian, divorced from reality but capable of being forcefully imposed upon it. Racism is a prime example. Anthropologists have long seen "race" as a social construction and have made no distinction between it and cultural attributes such as ethnicity. Race, like skin color, is not a useful predictor of behavior or abilities. The world is not meaningfully classified into "races," for instance, the five "great" ones—Caucasian, Mongoloid, Semitic, Negroid, and Australoid—any more than it is into right- and left-handers or those of various hair colorations. Yet many people believe in five great races or think that a subgroup like Jews, Vietnamese, or Tutsi displays certain fixed characteristics. Racism involves prejudice against a race or subgroup on the grounds of its imagined inferiority or threat. When racists act to destroy all or some members of a race or subgroup, they commit genocide. More often, people have harbored cultural prejudices against a group—say, Americans—or adherents of a certain religion. Though there is no "American race," it is possible to be prejudiced against such a national or ethnic group and act to destroy it: also genocide. And it is possible to do the same to a subgroup, such as a "tribe" or an ethnolinguistic community of Native Americans or Aborigines. Racism, then, is discriminatory but does not require prejudice against one of the great "races." It may exist independently of races, or of any belief in biology or in innate inferiority. Racism is an ideology, an idealist concept lacking material basis.

Yet racism may include a sense of historical change. Prejudice against a "fallen race" might not extend to its noble ancestors. Perpetrators persecuting a "backward" ethnic group may allow that its surviving descendants could yet progress after many centuries, or that their own ancestors were once equally primitive. Prejudice promoting genocide may thus arise from suppositions of a victim group's innate *inferiority* (in a static view of history) or its historical *anteriority* (in a progressive view) or even from a perceived threat of domination by a group possessing alleged *superiority*.

Even when sparked by real fear, racism is often accompanied by dominating ambition. Usually expressed as a phobia of contamination, political racism also disguises a forceful demand on all members of one's own group to maintain distance from another group. Nonconformers, then, expose differences between racists and their race. Disseminating the ideology usually requires disciplining the dissenters. Racist practitioners must enforce domination not just on their racial targets but on both sides of the purported racial divide. For instance, racism demands domestic gender domination, too. Preventing "contamination" of women of a group by men of another race requires restricting women's personal choices.

Moreover, racism need not be adopted by a whole group for genocide to occur. The crime requires no domestic consensus, no "race war" pitting an entire people against another in a contest for supremacy. Genocide frequently happens when only a small part of one group conspires and acts. That such plots usually lack participation from most of the conspirators' race—indeed, they often provoke dissidence and accentuate intraracial conflict—underscores the material unreality of race and racism.

The Ideal, the Irrational, the Nostalgic, and the Technology

Racism becomes genocidal when perpetrators imagine a world without certain kinds of people in it. A similar metaphysic marks some other forms of idealist thinking and action: the rejection of a real historical community or a retreat from everyday life in favor of an imagined vision or idea. Pastoralism is a related ideal in that it often eliminates inhabitants from a landscape. Agrarianism, too, as historian Keith Thomas notes in the case of "the cult of the countryside" in early modern England, is "a mystification and an evasion of reality." Woodruff Smith puts it another way, discussing Wilhelmine Germany: "The idea that farmers achieved, through effort, a balance among natural forces gave the agrarian image part of its appeal to people with little first hand experience with actual agriculture." In the absence of much evidence, many also believed that farmers' sons made excellent soldiers.[36] Later in the twentieth century, similar "ideals" inspired mass murderers of both right and left, from Hitler to Mao and Pol Pot. This is not to equate pastoral romance, agrarian ideals, or historical myth with violent racism or expansionism, but the frequent combination of them all in genocidal ideology is striking. They share a basis in the utopian, the intangible, the irrational.

Historians acknowledge the role of emotional or even irrational motivation. In his book *Feelings in History,* Ramsay MacMullen quotes leading British, German, and French scholars who all stressed the importance of emotion over calm calculation in the making of history. Lewis Namier wrote that "men's actions are mostly conditioned by factors other than reason." G. W. F. Hegel argued that "nothing great in the world has been accomplished without passion." Hippolyte Taine saw *sentiments* as "the true cause of human action, while the parading about of politics is quite secondary." MacMullen comes closer to the truth when he links specific emotions to certain actions, pointing out that *anger* gives "the most, and most long-lasting, force to our actions," while "violence displays emotions so obviously at work, they can hardly be ignored."[37] Such nonmaterial or even irrational factors are most evident of all in mass murder.

Yet Carthage wasn't destroyed in a day. Idealization, mythmaking, and anger are insufficient. Genocide requires material power over a sizable population. Over the centuries, whatever destructive means diverse perpetrators have employed, their technology always had to overwhelm that of the victims. Usually this material or organizational superiority is relatively recent, either the result of startling new economic developments or the cause of unsettling social rearrangements. Moreover, within the dominating society, such rapid changes often provoke nostalgic romanticism for a threatened and increasingly idealized or pristine tradition. A new political culture grows in reaction and proportion to the unfamiliar sources of social power. In cases of genocide, the new ideology of tradition even reinforces that advancing power by adding heightened social intolerance at home to military dominance abroad. This uneasy historical amalgam of technological advancement, new social or political relations, and feared loss of a romanticized past characterizes genocidal regimes. The inverse interplay between socioeconomic and ideological forces is crucial.

Even where ideology does reflect material developments, there is a significant time lag between prevailing ideal and changed reality. From era to era, ideology often outlives the changes promoting it by a generation or more. Historical factors that fostered a particular worldview are sometimes long gone by the time the view prevails.[38]

Moreover, the ideological outcome often contradicts its cause, producing paradoxical juxtapositions. Rapid change or modernization provokes not only new thinking but also a revival of tradition. For example, intensive agriculture displaces herdsmen, yet nourishes a pastoral nostalgia on the part of their dispossessors. The *Eclogues,* Virgil's first pastoral poems, contrast the farmers' very idyll with their displacement by soldier colonists. Virgil begins: "You, Tityrus, under the spread of a beech, lie practicing country songs. We, exile-bound, are forced to say good-bye to our native ground, our ancestral fields. You, leaf-shaded, lounge there and with little reed-pipe teach the woodlands all around us to resound." The empty glades owed their carefree lure to sad exile. Virgil's idyllic landscapes are "sunny, but they have long sloping shadows," as Gilbert Highet put it. The pastoral is an "escape, from brutal reality into an ideal," where "fact and fancy constantly merge." The harsher the reality, the brighter the ideal. For Virgil's shepherds and goatherds, "the harder, longer, less romantic work of ploughing, sowing and reaping the grain is scarcely mentioned." Virgil turned to agriculture only in his next work, the *Georgics,* which opened:

"What makes the cornfields happy, under what constellation it's best to turn the soil."[39]

Other pathbreaking social changes, such as commercial agriculture, urban development, or seaborne colonization, not only opened up new horizons but again fostered nostalgia for an irretrievable untroubled calm on the land—if not pastoral romance, then agrarian subsistence or a combination of the two. The ancient Greek poet Hesiod cautioned farmers against trade, for merchant ships had to "till the surly grey," the sea instead of the soil. When urbanization first developed in northern Italy during the Renaissance, it brought a new cult of the countryside, with its *villeggiatura,* the elegant rural summer retreat. Then overseas colonization provoked an escalation to a more intense pastoral romance. Sir Walter Ralegh styled himself "Shepherd of the Ocean."[40]

Burgeoning urbanization, even as it depopulated country areas, also fueled a more intense agrarian ideology, just as in a much later escalation, industrialization fostered another cult of the wilderness. The sloping shadows lengthened with the day. The literary scholar Raymond Williams recalled that "Sidney's *Arcadia,* which gives a continuing title to English neo-pastoral, was written in a park which had been made by enclosing a whole village and evicting the tenants." Distance from social reality is a common feature of agrarian as well as pastoral ideology. Historian Richard Hofstadter remarked that in the early United States, agrarianism was less a farmer's cause than "a preoccupation of the upper classes, of those who enjoyed a classical education, read pastoral poetry, experimented with breeding stock, and owned plantations or country estates." However, "[t]he more commercial this society became . . . the more reason it found to cling to the noncommercial, agrarian values. . . . And the more rapidly the farmers' sons moved into the towns, the more nostalgic the whole culture became about its rural past." In Germany, too, Woodruff Smith adds, agrarian ideas could unite "social groups whose only significant similarity in outlook was an animus against modernity," while "[r]omantic agrarianism was often used in politics to justify proposed policies that would primarily benefit groups other than small farmers."[41] Communist visions of industrialization, too, mixed with images of rural bounty while Stalinist urbanization starved peasants.

In genocidal thinking the appeal of cultivation often shades into that of pastoralism. Bloodthirsty hunters, when finally nearing "extinction," become ancient warriors tragically doomed to yield to progress. Real farm and ideal forest each demand purification. Neither process—imagined or implemented—

allows space for the defeated community to subsist; combined idealization of sylvan scenery and peasant cultivation has often proved lethal. Arcadian romanticism excludes people, just as the spread of intensive agriculture leaves no land for actual pastoralists, let alone forest-dwellers.

In different eras, the fetish of cultivation can be a frontiersman's rallying cry against the pastoralist and hunter-gatherer or an urban diversion from the industrial machine. It may be strengthened by pastoral ideology or by agrarianism. The ideology may bear an inverse relation to the socioeconomic situation or none at all. An insistence on dispossession of highlanders or indigenous people on grounds that they did not cultivate their land has been applied just as forcefully in cases where they were practicing agriculture as when they weren't. The source of that insistence lay in neither the rural reality nor the behavior of the colonized, but in the ideology arriving from the metropolis.

The drumbeat of reaction quickens loudest when the advance accelerates over new ground. The more rapid the move toward modernity, the greater the potential destabilization, the more the change requires a mask of tradition, and the more powerful the demands for restoration. Historian Victor Lieberman writes that "all pre-modern cultures *ipso facto* valued received wisdom over innovation, and for that reason masked innovation which was often quite substantial." The pressure increased in the modern era. As historian Stephen Vlastos puts it, "tradition is what modernity *requires* to prevent society from flying apart."[42] Socioeconomic modernization needs the cloak of continuity, which also heightens its appeal. Tradition thrives on rapid change. The more drastic the revolution, the deeper the reaction.

The effect is geometric in the case of genocide, which militarily requires a quantum leap in technological advancement and superiority over its victims. Such change provokes a concomitant ideological reaction, and so antimodern thinking, whether politically invented by leaders or authentically summoned by supporters, accompanies genocide and fuels it. Neotraditional ideologies, not based on material progress but reacting to it and masking it, reinforce the potential for genocide that exists in the idealist nature of racism. The combination of military power and social tension between new and old, ambition and reaction, domestic and foreign, reality and revival, is explosive.

Over the centuries, these strange social landscapes—hills of technological progress cut by ravines of ideological reaction—are littered with apparently contradictory signposts that nevertheless help trace the historical path to genocide. For example, slaveholding landlords idealize the sturdy, independent peasant. An efficient new agricultural economy fertilizes the pastoral imagination. The fetish for cultivation produces a romanticization of pristine forest. Urban growth fosters a desire to return to the countryside. Modern military metaphors invoke the destruction of farm vermin. Industrial development provokes awe for barren wilderness. Scientific racism incorporates parables about ancient human bloodlines, breeding, and pest extermination. The contradictions are consistent. In early-twentieth-century Japan, for instance, its leaders determined that "in order to maintain opposition to Europe, it was also necessary to incorporate Western utilitarian civilization."[43] Once again, however, contorted combinations of ideals and matériel are insufficient for genocide.

The ideals themselves are more complementary. Genocidal intent requires a predilection for massive violence and the targeting of an unarmed or relatively poorly armed victim group. That mindset usually comes with an expansionist territorial drive, bolstered by a sense of historical loss and racial or religious resentment. Those notions in turn connect to concepts of superior land use and inferior occupants. As idealist predilections, there is much in common between racism or religious prejudice and notions of biological purity, historical decline, and rural romanticism. Yet each is also much more widespread than genocide and on its own may not lead to violence or conquest. Only roped together can they scale the heights of partial or total ethnic extermination. Genocide requires not just brutal force and racial hatred, but most often also a cult of antiquity glorifying a lost history, a vision of ideal land use, and its deployment as justification for territorial aggression. We shall now examine these three themes in turn.

Cults of Antiquity

Even as they require technological dominance, genocide and extermination betray a preoccupation with restoring purity and order. In racial or geographical terms, this often demands eradication of foreign contamination and return to an imagined pure origin. In the perpetrators' historical consciousness, it usually implies arresting a perceived decline, restoring a lost utopia, or inscribing a purportedly ancient model on someone else's land.

Cults of antiquity have provided genocidists with political models that span millennia and link continents. Precedents went beyond the biblical. Hitler considered classical Sparta a model racialist state, and the fate of Carthage served as a metaphor for mass killing and planned destruction in the minds of perpetrators from the conquistadors to the Nazis. Early modern Dutch and English imperialists, some of whom committed genocidal massacres in North America, commonly invoked ancient Roman precedent.[44] From Ireland to New South Wales, colonialists saw the ancient Scythian barbarian rematerialize in the guise of their new native subjects or victim groups.

Like racism, cults of antiquity also fit snugly into an ideal agrarian landscape. Cultivation became a symbol or modern incarnation of lost ancient power. A "revival of antiquity" accompanied urbanization in Renaissance Italy as well as the new cult of the countryside. Forty years after fetching a newly bound copy of Livy for his father, Niccolò Machiavelli added a political dimension to the rising rural ideology: "Unhealthy countries can become healthy if a vast number of men occupies them suddenly, cultivating the soil to improve it. . . . Since the system of planting colonies has lapsed, it is more difficult to keep conquered territories, empty spaces are not filled, and overpopulated areas are not relieved. As a result, many parts of the world are deserted in comparison with ancient times."[45]

Occurring precisely at the onset of European transatlantic conquests, the Renaissance rediscovery of classical antiquity nourished as much mythology as scholarship about the past. It spread in all directions. For instance, as Russian expansion began around 1450, Moscow's grand prince, Ivan III, sent a delegation to the Holy Roman Empire. Drawing on Polish or Lithuanian influences, a Russian court manuscript composed around 1510 traced the tsar's descent from Augustus Caesar. Sixteenth-century Europe, writes historian Paul Freedman, "yielded to no other period in its fondness for ingenious, circular, and spectacularly erroneous historical theorizing."[46]

Along with Roman models, calls to reestablish mythical pasts of rural harmony soon proliferated as well. Seventeenth-century English writers urged a "Restauration" of the Garden of Eden. Its imagined meadows and fields of corn and fruit trees, and "curious groves and walks," symbolized both "beauty and order." The Fall of Adam and Eve, they believed, had ushered in an invasion of thorns and briars, turning fertile fields to barren heaths. Much later, Hitler's vision of reconstructing Eastern Europe as a new "Garden of Eden" differed greatly in content, but it shared the notion of historical decline from Nature's original perfection and the imperative to recover it.[47]

Pristine purity also attracted Asians of various political hues. Pol Pot's youthful Cambodian mentor in Paris, Keng Vannsak, considered Buddhism and Hinduism to be longtime Indian contaminants of the ancient Khmer "original Culture." In 1952 Pol Pot even called himself "the original Khmer." Cambodia, Vannsak reiterated later, needed to rediscover its indigenous, non-Indic, "Khmer Cultural Base" and reject the contemporary "Indo-Cambodian bastardy." Similarly, the architects of Japan's late-nineteenth-century Meiji Restoration aimed in part to "restore" its original mythical era that predated Japan's corruption by Buddhist and Sinic culture. Like racism itself, such xenophobic notions were often almost metaphysical, explicitly contesting materialist influences. One Japanese early-twentieth-century idealist saw a parallel with ancient Greek culture, destroyed by Roman "materialism," while another preached a "farewell to realism."[48]

The purity and power of the ancient model can also sponsor beliefs in a racial or ethnocultural superiority transcending time and place. Cults of antiquity encourage a sense of victimization at perceived historical loss and even justify restitution by conquest of those perceived to be misusing lands to which they have inadequate claim.

Cults of Cultivation

Genocidal conquerors legitimize their territorial expansion by racial superiority or glorious antiquity at the same time as they claim a unique capacity to put the conquered lands into productive agricultural use. It is of course unsurprising that genocidal regimes emphasize the importance of land and farm life, since most regimes of any kind have always done so. Cultivating food crops has been called "the oldest profession." Worldwide, agriculture has long been the largest economic sector. Even in early modern England, one of the most urbanized countries by 1700, three quarters of its population remained rural. Towns with more than 5,000 inhabitants housed a mere 13 percent of the English, constituting a majority only as late as 1851. Even in the 1950s, as few as 30 percent of the world's people lived in urban settings. Only in the twenty-first century, writes Deane Neubauer, director of the Globalization Research Network, "for the first time in human history, more people live in cities than do not."[49] During the previous millennia in which the peasantry composed the world's largest social class, genocide was not a common element of traditional rural cultures. The rise of agriculture simply provided surpluses that could be extracted to support soldiers, without necessarily transforming farmers into killers, let alone planners of genocide, whose ideological sources lay beyond the villages: among warrior elites, settlers, cities, and governments. Genocide arose when, among other things, such groups idealized their peasantry from afar or coveted land they thought other groups were misusing.

The romance of agrarianism easily escapes farming communities themselves. The grinding poverty and backbreaking labor of rural life has rarely moved peasants to recommend it as a social ideal. In the view of historian Richard Hofstadter, even the early American farmer was usually "inspired to make money, and such self-sufficiency as he actually had was usually forced upon him." Hofstadter's farmers were quite distinct from their protagonists, "the articulate people who talked and wrote about farmers and farming," those who especially admired its "noncommercial, nonpecuniary, self-sufficient aspects."[50]

This distant idealization of agriculture is mostly modern. Explicit statements that all society rests upon agricultural labor are documented from 1000 C.E., but among medieval elites they coexisted with a nonideological ambivalence that considered peasants to be as lowly as they were productive, as alien as they were Christian. Historian Liana Vardi writes that in the Middle Ages and until as late as the eighteenth century, most elite Europeans saw peasants as "the very antithesis of culture." The uncultivated, even unpopulated, pastoral idyll of Virgil's *Eclogues* still dominated the high cultural imagination. The land itself, empty, was the ideal. That began to change in the early modern era. From the late fourteenth century, Paul Freedman writes, "praise for the peasant poured out." After 1500, according to Vardi, "cultural paradigms that sought to redefine the nature of man, stressing life in the world, also came to celebrate the peasants' daily activities. Peasants were shown in command of the fields." In this sharp midmillennium break, "[s]ixteenth century art and poetry turned the countryside over to the peasants, while elites retreated to imaginary pastoral landscapes." Increasing interest in "real agricultural work," the classical cultural revival, new interest in Virgil's agriculturalist *Georgics,* and "the Renaissance fascination with the human body" all elevated the peasant to "a heroic and martial status." In the seventeenth century, European wars and social unrest briefly created demand for sheltered vistas of the aristocratic estate, again driving the peasant from rural landscapes, which now featured "cultivated nature without people." Yet as order returned, Vardi continues, eighteenth-century art "reintegrated the peasant within the rural landscape" to portray "virtuous householders . . . in harmony with the elites."[51]

More ideology than experience or observation was at work here. As historian Keith Thomas comments, a conventional theme of seventeenth- and eighteenth-century English literature held that "country-dwellers were not just healthier, but morally more admirable" than urban dwellers: "It had little justification in social fact, for agriculture was the most ruthlessly developed sector of the economy, small husbandmen were declining in number, wage-labour was universal, and the vices of avarice, oppression and hypocrisy were at least as prominent in the countryside as in the town." That only brought lost pastoral harmony and virtue into ever greater demand. It also assigned utility to conservative ideology, which held, as Woodruff Smith writes of late-nineteenth-century Germany, that "peasants deserved special consideration because of the manifold benefits that they conferred on society simply by being the way they were."[52] Meanwhile, as the agrarian romance blossomed, it was also transplanted to new soil in the colonies.

Agriculture and Expansion

Views of nature in England, to take an important case, passed through several phases, as Thomas shows. First, in the sixteenth and seventeenth centuries, agriculture expanded into previously uncultivated areas. The tamers of that natural world saw it as flawed, "hopeless sterility," "Nature's *pudenda*," a "deformed chaos" requiring man's mastery and symmetrical imprint. A spreading agricultural grid, according to prominent writers of this period, had to take "precedency before meadows, pastures, woods, mines." Land, in this view, should not remain wilderness but "should by culture and husbandry yield things necessary for man's life." God had "committed the earth to man to be by him cultivated and polished." Fruit orchards won praise if they seemed under control, "as if they had been drawn through one mould," or "uniform . . . in straight lines every way." Agriculture now expressed power and domination. By 1700 the challenge itself became a mathematical calculation: uncultivated heaths, mountains, wasteland, forests, parks, and commons still accounted for 13 million of England's 37 million acres. The same commentators saw poetic beauty in the transformation of agriculture, "the russet heath turn'd into greenest grass." As one put it, "Beauty requires that the hedges should be in straight lines." Another could conceive "no idea of picturesque beauty separate from fertility of soil."[53] Pastoralism retreated before the agricultural imperatives of investors and improvers, plowing over the known globe.

By the mid-eighteenth century, however, a new and different urban reaction set in. Where English agriculture had tamed nature and fed cities, now excessive urbanization of the countryside was deplored. The rapid expansion and "de-ruralization" of London and other towns also caused many of their inhabitants to view pristine nature not as degenerate but as mystical and elevating. The earth now offered a spontaneous "natural pulchritude" involving "asymmetries and a wild variety." Thomas writes also of a new "rage for mountain scenery." Thus, as much of the countryside began to approach a geometrical grid, pastoral visions returned to rival the agricultural. Highlanders were no longer barbarians but simple innocents. A visitor in 1810 found rural England "too much chequered with enclosures for picturesqueness." Gardens now attempted to imitate the "irregularity of nature."[54] Disillusion with mundane material progress also dispatched the romance further afield. Thus the noble savage arrived in the colonies, providing an ideological but only a brief practical respite for indigenous peoples there.

Nineteenth-century European nationalism marked a third phase in which agricultural ideology intersected with ethnic, historical, and expansionist predilections. As Vardi points out: "In the nationalist revivals of the nineteenth century, peasants . . . came to embody the nation, its traditions and mores, unsullied by modern concepts."[55] Chapters 7 to 9 show that new imperial and industrial might engendered not only scientific racism but also more pastoral and agrarian myths, to the double detriment and even destruction of the colonized.

The romance of agrarianism heated up as urbanization escalated in the twentieth century, as part 3 of this book shows. Nostalgia for a lost rural world could spread still wider in the twenty-first, with 60 percent of the earth's population living in towns. As many as 411 cities each house more than a million people. "All the demographic data point ineluctably to the 21st century emerging as the urban century," Neubauer writes, while large areas of the world's biggest cities "will be infested by 19th-century-style poverty." Given their inverse relationships to urbanization, agrarian or even pastoral ideals may yet flourish again. As the poet and author Percy Bysshe Shelley wrote in 1815, "[W]hen we are surrounded by human beings and yet they sympathise not with us, we love the flowers, the grass, the waters and the sky."[56] Antisocial romanticism, if combined with racist thinking, has especially threatened diasporic ethnic groups that are urbanized or historically barred from living on the land, such as Jews and Gypsies.

Moreover, cults of agriculture have not only flourished in urban settings but have often proved resilient enough to dismiss actual cultivation performed by targeted ethnic groups. Mass killing has complemented a drive for settler monopoly of new land even when settlers and natives *both* pursued agriculture, or despite settlers' need for native labor. In seventeenth-century Virginia and nineteenth-century Tasmania, English settlers found Indians and Aborigines who used fire to facilitate shifting agriculture and the growth of wild fruits, nuts, and new grasses to lure game. Virginia Indians had converted extensive woodland into large meadows and cornfields. Setting out from Jamestown in 1607, a newly arrived Englishman reported finding the countryside "all flowing over with fair flowers of sundry colours and kinds, as though it had been in any garden or orchard in England." Forests were so free of undergrowth that the English reported being able to see a mile ahead and drive a carriage through the glades. Historian Edmund Morgan has written that "there was probably more open land in Indian Virginia than there is in Virginia today."[57] Yet settlers rarely acknowledged this indigenous land management, even when new-growth forests spread alongside English cultivation of the land after displacement of its previous occupants. The myth that Indians lacked agriculture prevailed anyway. With further disregard for reality, the Virginia and New England colonists' need for Indian assistance and farm labor also failed to deter them from perpetrating genocidal massacres of local Indians. Even to the detriment of agriculture, colonial officials usually preferred laborers they could totally control. They sometimes marched against Indians simply in order to deny absconding white laborers any refuge with them.

Indigenous agriculture, when acknowledged, engaged an additional factor: fear of economic competition. Later settlers in North Carolina and Georgia, encountering the skilled Indian farmers of the Five Civilized Tribes, took over their farms as the United States banished the Indians to Oklahoma. In New South Wales, some Aborigines learned to cultivate corn and other crops, only to be driven from their farms as late as the 1920s.[58] In combination with doctrinal assumptions of racial superiority and the imperative of territorial expansion, the yeoman cultivator vision demanded monopoly of the land, and would brook neither physical challenge from the prior occupants nor competition from any of them who took up farming.

Genocidal Pragmatism

Genocidal enterprises, ambitious by definition, require an ideological inflexibility so severe that, ironically, pragmatic skill is required to implement them.

To succeed, the necessary political resolve demands both apocalyptic vision and prudent compromise. The rapid new technological developments that make genocide possible ignite explosive ideological compounds in the minds of perpetrators and set off competing visions within their society. Interests in the destruction of other groups vary. Usually undertaken by radical, unstable regimes, genocide rarely emerges from sociopolitical consensus but often includes an attempt to silence domestic differences by focusing attention on an external, supposedly common threat. Or the violence itself provokes dissent as some domestic opponents react while others are silenced. To proceed toward their goal or simply to retain power, perpetrators frequently contract entangling or temporary alliances that confuse the clarity and finality of their thought. To defuse dissent, divide opposition, or concentrate maximum force, selected members or groups from a targeted community may be spared, singled out for preferential treatment, or even enlisted in the cause. The huge endeavor of mass killing requires mobilization of enormous human, material, and administrative resources. It demands perpetrators and bystanders and creates victims and survivors. It needs incitement, organization, guile, and denial, often simultaneously. The very variety of audiences requires a mixture of messages, often contradictory. To defuse potential protest, or turn bystanders into perpetrators, some members of this varied audience may be informed that, say, the territory being seized is an uninhabited pastoral idyll, others that its inhabitants fail to exploit its agricultural potential. The political culture of genocide is by nature incoherent, inconsistent, and partial. It is difficult to identify except as a whole, a combination of crosscutting signals and disguises.

The goals of radical utopian regimes, even professedly materialist ones like Communist states, share this heterogeneity with explicitly genocidal enterprises. The more all-encompassing the project, the more its instigators must adopt pragmatic, contradictory tactics. Regimes pursuing idealist fantasies, such as the Communist vision of a classless society or "new man," or ambitious transformational schemes like crash industrial or agricultural modernization, have often resorted to concomitant racist or violent methods, even on a mass scale, up to or including genocide. This is true of the two giant Communist regimes, Stalin's USSR and Mao's China.

Such stratagems rarely fully succeed, even in the case of a centralized, state-planned genocide. The extremism commonly provokes divisions in both the perpetrator and victim societies. Genocide perpetrators thus face extensive social and political challenges inherent in the enterprise itself. Implementing far-reaching visions of all-out class-on-class or race-on-race confrontations is difficult. Such massive violence and destruction cannot be carried out without major ideological detours and deceptions. The challenge of predicting and then preventing genocide is to identify in advance the obsessions that drive domination and violence and the ideological predilections that overrule their own inherent tensions and pragmatic impossibilities.

In focusing on genocide, extermination, and genocidal massacres in heterogeneous historical landscapes, this book cannot offer a history of the spread of disease, war, aggression, colonialism, racism, agrarianism, or the misuse of history itself. Many of those phenomena, especially in combination, do facilitate genocidal outcomes, but individually, they are far more complex and varied. Even their deadliest depredations, for instance, the spread of colonial epidemics, must be distinguished from genocide. Yet they should not distract us from it. It is no answer to evidence of genocidal killing to state, often correctly, that it was overshadowed by a greater toll from unwittingly introduced diseases. Whether genocide accounted for more or fewer deaths than other causes is irrelevant to identifying and preventing it. Nor should larger, unplanned tragedies like epidemics obscure lesser crimes, even if unconnected, that lead to the extinction of a population also ravaged by disease. In other words, it is possible neither to convict microbes of genocide nor to present their great destruction as a defense exhibit for perpetrators. If microbes cannot stand trial, people are responsible for their actions. The Genocide Convention provides for the prosecution of individuals as well as states. It is again no answer to evidence of genocide on part of a colonial frontier, say, to note its absence elsewhere on that frontier or a lack of state involvement. Perpetrators may act as agents for, accomplices in, or conspirators against state policies. Whether genocide is a typical or uncommon product of a specific historical process or regime is again irrelevant. This book seeks simply to examine those cases where genocide and extermination have occurred and to explain why.

Historical Connections

Genocides not only exhibit similarities, many are actually related events. Their relationships are often personal and generational. For example, we can identify the German precursors of individual Holocaust perpetrators. Heinrich Göring, father of the future Nazi leader Hermann Göring, served in 1885–91 as *Reichskommissar* of German Southwest Africa (now Namibia). There, German participants in the 1904–8 genocide of the Herero and Nama peoples included the future Nazi governor of Bavaria, Franz Ritter von Epp, who during World War II presided over the liquidation of virtually all Bavaria's Jews and Gypsies. At the Nazis' 1931 Nuremberg rally, von Epp and Hermann Göring stood together in front of Hitler.[59]

Personal connections linked these genocides even in the cultural sphere. Another future Nazi, Eugen Fischer, carried out his racialist research in German Southwest Africa, on miscegenation among the mixed Dutch/Hottentot "Rehoboth Bastards." In a 1913 study, Fischer advocated protecting "an inferior race . . . only for so long as they are of use to us—otherwise . . . in my opinion, destruction." He became head of Germany's Kaiser Wilhelm Institute for Anthropology, Human Heredity, and Eugenics, denounced "coloured, Jewish, and Gypsy hybrids," and provided Hitler with a copy of his work while the latter was writing *Mein Kampf.* After taking power in 1933, Hitler appointed Fischer rector of the University of Berlin, where he set about removing Jewish professors. Fischer's institute later trained and sponsored pseudo-scientific research by Nazi doctors who included the notorious Josef Mengele.[60]

German racial annihilation in colonial Southwest Africa was not the only precursor to the Holocaust. Vahakn Dadrian has detailed the role of Germany alongside its Ottoman ally in the 1915 genocide of Armenians in Turkey. Max Erwin von Scheubner Richter, co-commander of a joint Turko-German expeditionary force, who reported in 1915 that "the Armenians of Turkey for all practical purposes have been exterminated," died at Hitler's side during the Nazis' abortive putsch in Munich in 1923. Launching his invasion of Poland in 1939, Hitler reportedly dismissed a question about its international legality by remarking, "Who after all is today speaking of the destruction of the Armenians?" In command at Auschwitz, the Nazi regime appointed Rudolf Höss, who had also fought in the German army in Turkey during the Armenian genocide.[61]

Along with the affirmative precedents of successful genocide and perpetrator impunity, negative lessons from one outbreak may also spark another. From Beijing in 1965, Cambodian Communist Party leader Pol Pot observed as Indonesia's dictator General Suharto slaughtered half a million Communists after the military takeover in Jakarta. The Cambodian later wrote: "If our analysis had failed, we would have been in greater danger than the communists in Indonesia."[62] Avoiding that fate for Cambodian Communism would be one of

Pol Pot's motives for his own mass murders. The earlier Indonesian massacre cannot excuse a possibly even greater crime, but may help explain it.

Similarities have also linked dissenters and opponents of genocide through time and space. During the English settlers' conflict with Tasmanian Aborigines in the 1820s, one settler critically labeled Thomas Gregson, a political reformer and government opponent, as a "modern Las Casas." The critic complained that despite "the barbarous aggressions of an ungrateful and treacherous race," Gregson had gone so far as "to question the justice and policy of attacking the Blacks," terming it a "usurpation on the part of the English to take possession of this island," and adding that "the one who would kill a black man would also kill a white man." The Spanish precedent came up again in Sydney a decade later. The Chief Protector of Aborigines, George Augustus Robinson, wondered why New South Wales colonists were "so anxious to exterminate the original and lawful proprietors of the soil," citing what he was reading in "the newspapers of the colony" in 1838. Robinson went on: "[A]nd they may exterminate them. The Spaniards did so in Hispaniola; it took only thirty years to accomplish it, but an odium rests and ever will rest upon the name of a Spaniard."[63]

Recognizing Genocide

During the twentieth century, genocide implicated the entire political spectrum, from Nazis to Communists to pro–U.S. regimes. Even discounting alliances based on realpolitik, the phenomenon transcends political labels. Genocide has been associated with expanding colonialism, shrinking empires, religious communalism, atheistic dictatorships, unfettered capitalism, National Socialism, Communist revolution, post-Communist nationalism, National Security militarism, and Islamist terror. A few genocidists have even been elected. Fewer have been reelected.

Yet its multifarious guises do not make genocide unsusceptible to analysis or too disparate for consistent description. Certain historical and social conditions—war, economic depression, political destabilization—predictably nourish budding genocidists. The underlying features of their ideologies, though often irrational, can be identified, defined, detected, and addressed. As in the past, racism, religious prejudices, revivalist cults of antiquity, territorial expansionism, an obsession with contesting and cultivating land, and the idealization of social classes such as the peasantry are equally likely to mark many of the tragedies of this century. These telltale philosophical features can help track the most dangerous ideologies in times of turbulence. Whatever the government, political party label, or insurgent acronym, these signal characteristics, as well as the elements of the crime embodied in its U.N. definition, have marked almost every historical case. Often evident at initial stages of incitement or planning of the crime, these traits can serve as indicators of its likelihood and of perpetrator intent. In future cases, spotted early, these warning signs can help to identify emerging tragedies and to mobilize intervention to prevent them.

Political scientist Daniel Chirot and psychologist Clark McCauley point out that "genocidal events have been common enough to suggest that they cannot be explained as some kind of deviant behavior," and Benjamin Valentino writes that "if we hope to anticipate mass killing, we must begin to think of it in the same way its perpetrators do."[64] This history of genocide focuses on the mindset of the killers as much as the experiences of their victims. Inside information from perpetrators becomes public only rarely and with time. *Blood and Soil* includes some older cases that inflicted smaller tolls yet yielded richer evidence than more recent crimes whose perpetrators have so far enjoyed greater success in hiding their plans from view. Speaking for themselves, especially in secret, perpetrators have uncovered what they believed or claimed they were doing. Where the two are different, even their lies may reveal useful indication of their priorities.

Central to this book are four recurring ideological preoccupations of the perpetrators of genocide, extermination, and genocidal massacres: racism, expansionism, agrarianism, and antiquity. The presence of these four obsessions often seems sufficient for genocidal violence, though not all four are necessary conditions. For space reasons, this study cannot be comprehensive. It excludes some cases of mass murder that deserve more attention, from the Mongols' slaughter of the inhabitants of Baghdad in 1258 to the conquistador destruction of the Inca civilization in sixteenth-century Peru to the Congo Free State of Belgium's King Leopold, who took a personal interest in the conquistador precedent and set up an extractive regime that presided over possibly 10 million Congolese deaths from murder, overwork, and disease between 1880 and 1910. Also excluded are catastrophes lacking more than one of the four major features of genocide I have identified. When a million Irish people died under British rule in the 1845–51 Great Famine, the prime cause was a potato blight, and though the British authorities' refusal to supply aid after October 1847 or stop food exports from Ireland betrayed both ethnic animus and ideological rigidity, that was not a case of mass murder, nor was it inspired by agrarian thinking or ancient models. Much the same applies to the even larger famine that ravaged Persia under British occupation after World War I, when possibly 10 million people perished.[65] Yet some of the cases examined in this book are also exceptional. Stalin's mass killings included ethnic purges, yet they lacked any agrarian rationale—unlike Mao's Chinese regime, which caused millions more deaths. For its part, Mao's Great Leap Forward famine in China in 1958–61 involved neither mass murder, ethnic targeting, nor a cult of antiquity, but it is included here with Mao's campaigns of political murder because of the famine's toll of possibly 30 million dead.

The first two parts of this book detail some of the genocidal consequences of imperial and colonial expansion of both European and Asian states and their dispossessions of indigenous peoples, from ancient times to the early twentieth century. In part 1, "Early Imperial Expansion," chapter 1 examines classical genocide and its memory in the medieval world. Chapter 2 shows the debts to and departures from classical and agrarian models on the part of Spanish Catholic conquistadors in the New World. Chapters 3 and 4 examine a half dozen cases of genocide and mass murder in East and Southeast Asia between 1400 and 1800. Then, in part 2, "Settler Colonialism," chapter 5 examines the English Protestant conquerors of sixteenth-century Ireland and their responses to classical and agrarian models, chapters 6 and 7 cover colonial genocides and genocidal massacres in North America and nineteenth-century Australia, and chapter 8 discusses cases of genocide, extermination, and genocidal massacres in the United States after independence from Britain. Chapter 9 compares colonial catastrophes in Africa under French and German settler regimes.

Part 3 of *Blood and Soil* examines the multiplicity of genocides in the twentieth century, including the postcolonial era. Chapters 10 to 12 analyze the cases perpetrated by national chauvinist regimes: the Young Turks, the Nazis, and imperial Japan. Chapters 13 and 14 examine the crimes of the major Communist leaders Lenin, Stalin, and Mao in the USSR and China from the Bolshevik Revolution of 1917 to Mao's death in 1976. Chapter 15 and the epilogue then survey the global record from 1965 to 2006, involving genocidal regimes that span the political spectrum, from Cambodia and Rwanda to Indonesia and East Timor, Bangladesh, Guatemala, Iraq, Bosnia, and the crisis in Darfur.

The book ends with the case of Al-Qaeda, a genocidal group of contemporary origin yet displaying key characteristics shared by most of its precursors. The persistent recurrence among genocide perpetrators of ideological obsessions with violent ethnic prejudice, whether racial or religious, with cults of antiquity and agriculture, and with territorial expansionism, reveals possibilities for predicting and hopefully preventing further cases of genocide in the twenty-first century.

Part One

EARLY IMPERIAL EXPANSION

MAP 2. The ancient western Mediterranean

CHAPTER 1

Classical Genocide and
Early Modern Memory

The cults of classical antiquity and of agriculture that emerged during and after the Renaissance, along with new religious and racial thinking, made key intellectual contributions to the outbreaks of genocidal violence that accompanied Europe's early modern expansion. From the turn of the sixteenth century, as leaders and thinkers began to build new empires, they looked for lessons and inspiration from antiquity. At their classical height, Sparta and Rome stood out as martial models of successful longevity. Rome's internal decay and corruption by exotic luxuries also served as a cautionary tale, and the legendary annihilations of Troy and Carthage provided precedents for harsh treatment of new enemies. As empires grew, so did cultural and racial prejudices. Newly uncovered and occasionally inaccurate, ancient models and agricultural roles helped define conquered peoples and even justify their destruction.

Writing of his native village of Ascra in central Greece in the eighth century b.c.e., the poet Hesiod composed two of the first texts that idealized agricultural "fair husbandry." He also criticized commerce and set down notions of race and gender hierarchy, but he lacked an obsession with domination or violence that later appeared in the writings of some of his classical successors.[1] Celebrating "the rich-pastured earth" with advice to farmers in *Works and Days*, Hesiod praised the "rich man who hastens to plough and plant and manage his household." In his view, the "wheat fields of the fortunate" require a disciplined "sturdy man" to "drive a straight furrow" and make grain "nod towards the earth with thickness." Only to "straight-judging men" who "feast on the crops they tend" would "womenfolk bear children that resemble their parents." Such farmers earned a lyrical pastoral life: "When the golden thistle is in flower, and the noisy cicada sitting in the tree pours down its clear song thick and fast, . . . then goats are fattest and wine is best, women are most lustful, but men are weakest." Yet "the trouble women cause" made them "a calamity for men who live by bread." Hesiod warned: "No arse-rigged woman must deceive your wits with her wily twitterings when she pokes into your granary." He compared men to productive bees, and women to "drones" who "pile the toil of others into their own bellies."[2]

His idealization of the patriarchal rural hearth carried a similar prejudice against trade and travel. While "profit deludes men's minds," commerce takes them from the land to brave "the violet-dark sea." The prudent, happily self-sufficient farmer does not "ply on ships," but should store "all your substance under lock inside the house." "If now the desire to go to sea (disagreeable as it is) has hold of you," then "come home again as quickly as you can." Only the gods could stop a farmer growing enough in one day "to provide you for a whole year without working. Soon you would stow your rudder" and live on the fruit of "the grain-giving ploughland."[3]

Hesiod combined his notions of the sturdy farmer, devious woman, and deluded merchant with an emerging theory of race.[4] Early Greeks took the Near Eastern myth of five successive "ages" or "races" of mankind, symbolized by different metals, and elaborated a concept of racial hierarchy and repeated extinctions. Hesiod's first "race of men" lived in the golden age, when "the grain-giving soil bore its fruits of its own accord in unstinted plenty," and they "harvested their fields in contentment." Their demise was not final: "Since the earth covered up that race, they have been divine spirits." But the succeeding, "much inferior" silver race was short-lived and soon exterminated. Unable to "restrain themselves from crimes against each other," they were "put away by Zeus." Likewise, their successors, "a terrible and fierce race" of bronze, "were laid low by their own hands, and they went to chill Hades' house of decay leaving no names . . . dark death got them." Next, in turn, the "demigods" were destroyed, as at Troy, by "ugly war and fearful fighting." Survivors live in the Isles of the Blessed where "the grain-giving soil bears its honey-sweet fruits." Last, there came a fifth "race of iron," which Hesiod lamented was his own. He predicted: "Zeus will destroy this race of men also. . . . Nor will father be like children nor children to father." Among this race, Hesiod distinguished Greeks from "the black men," but he assigned no hierarchy or prejudice.[5]

Possibly for the first time, Hesiod connected cultivation, gender, "race," and extinction. Yet he disapproved of the aggression essential to genocide. He advised his brother to "hearken to Right" and "not promote violence. For violence is bad for a lowly man; not even a man of worth can carry it easily.... Right gets the upper hand over violence in the end." People who "occupy themselves with violence," not its victims, are the ones whose "womenfolk do not give birth, and households decline." Hesiod's legendary "bronze age" men were prone to "acts of violence," in his view perhaps precisely because they were nonagricultural, "no eaters of corn." Though he innovatively linked race and agriculture, he did not foster militarism. That was the role of a powerful state emerging to the south of his homeland, a state that in Hesiod's lifetime "committed herself to an almost purely agricultural future."[6] Sparta's combination of agrarianism and violence against its enemies made it a precursor of genocidal regimes.

Sparta and Its Neighbors

Ancient Sparta was a society without cities. It prohibited the circulation of money and domestic trade, carefully controlled external commerce, and made a "concerted effort to depreciate family life."[7] Based on an unpaid subject labor force, it was a secretive, militaristic, expansionist state that practiced frequent expulsions of foreigners and demonstrated a capacity for mass murder.[8]

Sparta's "uniquely military society," in the words of historian Paul Cartledge, was "a conquest-state," a "workshop of war."[9] Its expansion, he writes, probably began in the eighth century B.C.E., with the "conquest and annihilation of Aigys," a town in its own region, Lakonia. Fifty years later, Sparta launched an invasion of the neighboring region of Messenia. This conquest, completed in a 20-year war of pacification, doubled Lakonia's population base and made Sparta the wealthiest state in Greece, facing no foreign invasions of its territory for three and a half centuries.[10] Sparta dominated and exploited Messenia from 735 to 370 B.C.E., repressing local revolts like the seventh-century Second Messenian War, and another in the fifth century. Messenia's population made up most of Sparta's Helots, its serf-like labor force whose name denoted "capture."[11] In the sixth century, Sparta conquered Tegea and took control of Arcadia.[12] Its defeat of Argos in 546 led to the subjugation, Herodotus wrote, of "most of the Peloponnese." By 500, Sparta dominated its neighbors and controlled the "Peloponnesian League." It reached the zenith of its power with its key role in the Greek victories over Persia in 480–479 and its defeat of Athens in the Peloponnesian War of 431–403.[13]

Sparta based its lasting power partly on ethnic domination, maintained by violence. A minority of Sparta's Helots were domestic serfs from Lakonia, but most were Messenian in origin and these, historian G. E. M. de Ste. Croix writes, "never lost their consciousness of being Messenians." Thus, the Spartans feared that they could rebel at any time, as they successfully did, with Theban help, in 369, when they reestablished the polis of Messene.[14] Sparta's ruling ephors had long ritually declared war on the Helots, in what Cartledge calls a unique but "typically Spartan expression of politically calculated religiosity designed to absolve in advance from ritual pollution any Spartan who killed a Helot."[15] Thucydides describes a case where the Spartans had "raised up some Helot suppliants from the temple of Poseidon at Taenarus [in Lakonia], led them away and slain them." A great earthquake then struck Sparta, in c. 465. Over 20,000 people perished, and Lakonian Helots rose up alongside Messenians in a revolt that raged for much of the next decade.[16]

One ethnic conflict led to another. Sparta called on Athens for aid in fighting the Helots. However, Thucydides tells us, when their combined assault on the Helot stronghold at Mt. Ithome failed, the Spartans were not only disheartened, but worse: they were "apprehensive of the enterprising and revolutionary character of the Athenians, and further *looking upon them as of alien extraction*," the Spartans feared both political challenge and a potential Helot-Athenian alliance. They sent the Athenians home. Insulted, Athens allied itself with Sparta's enemy Argos. The Messenian rebels on Mt. Ithome finally surrendered, on Sparta's conditions: "that they should depart from the Peloponnese under safe conduct, and should never set foot in it again; any one who might hereafter be found there was to be the slave of his captor."[17]

War crimes compounded Sparta's domestic brutality and xenophobia. From the outbreak of the Peloponnesian War, the Spartans "butchered as enemies all whom they took on the sea, whether allies of Athens or neutrals," Thucydides wrote. After Spartan troops took Plataea they cold-bloodedly "massacred . . . not less than two hundred" of its men, "with twenty-five Athenians who had shared in the siege." In 419, Spartans captured the town of Hysiae, "killing all the freemen that fell into their hands."[18]

The subjugated Messenian and Lakonian Helots made up Sparta's agricultural workforce. Their servitude released every Spartan "from all productive labour," freeing them for war.[19] Bound to a plot of land, the Helots performed this labor "under pain of instant death"; even Lakonian Helots were often expendable. Ste. Croix writes that Spartans could "cut the throats of their Helots at will, provided only that they had gone through the legal formality of declaring them 'enemies of the state.'"[20] Cartledge adds that Helots were even "culled" by Spartan youth as part of their training. The Krypteia, or Secret Service Brigade, a group of select 18-year-olds assigned to forage for themselves in the countryside, was specifically commissioned "to kill, after dark," any Helots "whom they should accidentally-on-purpose come upon." Besides these random executions, some Spartan massacres of Helots were organized on a large scale. Around 423, Thucydides informs us, 2,000 Helots who had served creditably in their army in the Peloponnesian War were invited to request emancipation. When they did, Spartan forces massacred them, "as it was thought that the first to claim their freedom would be the most high-spirited and the most apt to rebel."[21]

The Perioikoi, a category of people practicing trade, fishing, and crafts (particularly weaponry) in the service of the Spartans, from whom they were segregated, occupied the rung of the social ladder above the Helots. These were the town dwellers of Lakonia and Messenia, "free men but subjected to Spartan suzerainty and not endowed with citizen-rights at Sparta." The Lakonian Perioikoi were "indistinguishable ethnically, linguistically and culturally from the Spartans."[22]

Finally, the citizens of Sparta formed an elite cadre. Only a tenth of the population, fewer than 10,000 people, were full citizens. These Spartiates, the male inhabitants of Sparta's four original villages and the village of Amyklai, lived and trained there but were barred from agricultural labor. "Their sole skill and their major preoccupation was warfare." Spartiate citizenship depended on payment of common mess dues from the produce delivered to the Spartiates by the individual Helots permanently tied to working their private plots. This system evolved to "perpetuate Spartan control over the Helots and Perioikoi without abolishing the wide and growing disparities within the citizen body itself." Spartiates had to adopt "a simple and uniform attire."[23]

Traditional "land-oriented values" dominated the polity. Thucydides reported that Sparta was not "brought together in a single town ... but composed of villages after the old fashion of Greece." Its "closed and archaic" system contrasted with the Greek city-states. Favoring autarchy, Sparta discouraged both trade and towns and approached Hesiod's ideal of the self-sufficient, near-subsistence farmer, spurning the commercial producer and merchant. Laws barred Spartiates from engaging in trade or "expenditures for consumption and display." Cartledge writes that Lakonia "was extraordinarily autarchic in essential foodstuffs" and had abundant deposits of iron ore. Sparta decided

around 550 not to import silver, and coined none until the third century, unlike other Greek states in their prime. Iron spits apparently figured in Spartan
exchanges, but Cartledge finds the evidence "unclear whether they are monetary or purely functional." Plutarch asserted that the early Spartan lawgiver
Lycurgus had "introduced a large iron coin too bulky to carry off in any great
quantity." Seneca wrote that Spartans had to pay debts "in gold or in leather
bearing an official stamp." Coins, presumably permitted among the Perioikoi,
"have been found on only two Perioikic sites."[24] Sparta seems to have been one
of history's few states without a widely circulating currency.

Sparta was a collective under strict state control. In a "social compromise
between rich and poor citizens," the Spartiates or Homoioi (Peers) submitted
to state interests. From the age of seven, they underwent "an austere public
upbringing (the *agoge*) followed by a common lifestyle of participation in the
messes and in military training and service in the army."[25] The state, not the
individual landowners, owned the Helots working the Spartiates' private landholdings. Only the state could emancipate them. It enforced communal eating
and simple uniformity of attire and, according to Thucydides, "did most to assimilate the life of the rich to that of the common people" among the Spartiate
citizens. The state even prohibited individual names on tombstones.[26]

Communal living facilitated state supervision. Xenophon tells us that
Lycurgus had deliberately arranged for the Spartans to eat their meals in common, "because he knew that when people are at home they behave in their
most relaxed manner." A Spartiate who married before age 30 was not allowed
to live with his wife: "[H]is infrequent home visits were supposed to be conducted under cover of darkness, in conspiratorial secrecy from his messmates
and even from the rest of his own household." Fathers who had married after
30 lived most of their lives communally and publicly with male peers, while
"the Spartan boy left the parental household for good" at age seven.[27]

The links between Sparta's agrarian ideology, domestic repression, ethnic
domination, and expansionist violence highlight its role as a precursor of genocide. Agrarianism was common in Greek thought and influenced later civilizations. Writing during the fourth century, Aristotle stated in *Politics*: "Hesiod
was right when he wrote, 'First and foremost a house and a wife and an ox for
the ploughing.'" Aristotle preferred agriculturalists to "idle" pastoralists, and
he, too, denigrated trade and usury.[28] An early pupil of his, writing in *Oeconomica*, termed cultivation the prime "natural" vocation that was "attendant
on our goods and chattels." For, "by Nature's appointment all creatures receive

sustenance from their mother, and mankind like the rest from the common mother the earth." Moreover, "Agriculture is the most honest of all such occupations; seeing that the wealth it brings is not derived from other men," distinguishing it from trade and wage employment. Finally, "agriculture contributes notably to the making of a manly character." Cultivation, "unlike the mechanical arts," Aristotle's pupil wrote, does not "weaken" men but inures them "to exposure and toil and invigorates them to face the perils of war. For the farmer's possessions, unlike those of other men, lie outside the city's defenses."[29] Historian Victor Davis Hanson argues that the "ethos of the land" represented "a near-religious feeling among the Greeks that yeoman agriculture, manual work on one's own farm, was morally uplifting." The very term for landed property, *ousia,* also meant "essence." Even in an urban polis like Athens, agrarian ideology was pervasive if not as influential as in Sparta; in an exceptional episode of violence that has been described as genocide, Athenian forces murdered all the men they captured on the island of Melos, at the height of their city's maritime power during the Peloponnesian War. However, Hanson distinguishes "urban, democratic and imperialist Athens" from the "ten-acre farmer" who provided the Greek hoplite infantry.[30] Sparta's agrarianism produced a territorial, land-based expansion distinct from that of commercial, maritime Athens. The first classical genocide would combine agrarian ideology with both sea power and territorial imperialism.

Rome and Carthage

The most famous incitement to genocide is probably *Delenda est Carthago,* or "Carthage must be destroyed!" the words of the second-century B.C.E. Roman official Marcus Porcius Cato, the Censor.[31] Plutarch tells us that this injunction ended every speech Cato made in the Senate "on any matter whatsoever," from 153 to his death at 85 in 149. Scipio Nasica—son-in-law of Scipio Africanus, conqueror of Hannibal in the Second Punic War (218–202 B.C.E.)—would always reply: "Carthage should be allowed to exist." Ultimately, Cato silenced such challenges.[32] Rome decided on war "long before" it launched the Third Punic War in 149.[33] Cato even denounced Carthage in front of its delegation to the Senate, in one of his last Senate speeches: "Who are the ones who have often violated the treaty? . . . Who are the ones who have waged war most cruelly? . . . Who are the ones who have ravaged Italy? The Carthaginians. Who are the ones who demand forgiveness? The Carthaginians. See then how it would suit them to get what they want." The Senate forbade a response from the Carthaginian delegates. Just before Cato's death, Rome began a siege of the world's wealthiest city.[34]

Unaware that the Senate had secretly decided "to destroy Carthage for good, once the war was ended," the Carthaginians quickly complied with the Roman demand to surrender their 200,000 individual weapons and 2,000 catapults.[35] Then came the surprise demand that they abandon their city, deserting its shrines and religious cults.[36] To this, the Carthaginians said no, and a brutal three-year war ensued. Appian described one battle in which "70,000, including non-combatants" were killed, probably an exaggeration. But Polybius, who participated in the campaign, confirmed that "the number of deaths was incredibly large," and that the Carthaginians were "utterly exterminated."[37]

In 146, the Roman legions led by Scipio Aemilianus, Cato's ally and the brother-in-law of his son, finally broke through the city's walls. Appian recounts its end:

> All places were filled with groans, shrieks, shouts, and every kind of agony. Some were stabbed, others were hurled alive from the roofs to the pavement, some of them falling on the heads of spears, or other pointed weapons, or swords. No one dared to set fire to the houses on account of those who were still on the roofs, until Scipio reached Byrsa. Then he set fire to the three streets all together, and gave orders to keep the passage-ways clear of burning material so that the charging detachments of the army might move back and forth freely.
>
> Then came new scenes of horror. The fire spread and carried everything down, and the soldiers did not wait to destroy the buildings little by little, but pulled them all down together. So the crashing grew louder, and many fell with the stones into the midst dead. Others were seen still living, especially old men, women, and young children who had hidden in the inmost nooks of the houses, some of them wounded, some more or less burned, and uttering horrible cries. Still others, thrust out and falling from such a height with the stones, timbers, and fire, were torn asunder into all kinds of horrible shapes, crushed and mangled.

To keep the streets open for their attacks, Roman soldiers threw "the dead and the living together into holes in the ground, sweeping them along like sticks and stones or turning them over with their iron tools, and man was used for filling up a ditch. Some were thrown in head foremost, while their legs, sticking out of the ground, writhed a long time. Others fell with their feet downward and their heads above ground. Horses ran over them, crushing their faces and skulls, not purposely on the part of the riders, but in their headlong haste. . . . Six days and nights were consumed in this kind of turmoil, the soldiers being changed so that they might not be worn out with toil, slaughter, want of sleep, and these horrid sights." The next day the remaining Carthaginians surrendered, including their commander, Hasdrubal. Then his wife appeared at the burning temple of Asclepius.[38] Polybius saw her there, "dressed like a great lady, but holding her children, who wore nothing but their smocks, by each hand and wrapping them in her cloak." She reproached Hasdrubal for his surrender, adding, "this fire will entomb me and my children." Then, Appian writes, "she slew her children, flung them into the fire, and plunged in after them." As flames consumed the rest of the city, Scipio turned to Polybius, grasped his hand, and said: "A glorious moment, Polybius; but I have a dread foreboding that some day the same doom will be pronounced upon my own country."[39]

Of Carthage's population of 200,000 to 400,000, at least 145,000 had perished, and Scipio dispersed into slavery all 55,000 survivors, including 25,000 women.[40] "The Senate sent ten of the noblest of their own number as deputies to arrange the affairs of Africa," Appian wrote. "These men decreed that if anything was still left of Carthage, Scipio should raze it to the ground, and that nobody should be allowed to live there." The Senators also "decided to destroy, to the last one," all the African towns "that had allied themselves consistently with the enemy." Roman troops duly demolished at least six cities of Punic culture. They spared seven other towns that had defected to them.[41] This was no *Kulturkrieg*, nor a war of racial extermination; the Romans did not massacre the survivors, or the adult males, as the Athenians had at Melos.[42] Yet Rome had decided on "the destruction of the nation."[43] Its policy of "extreme violence," the "annihilation of Carthage and most of its inhabitants," ruining "an entire culture," fits the definition in the 1948 UN Genocide Convention: intentional destruction "in whole or in part, [of] a national, ethnical, racial or religious group, as such."[44]

Cato's policy had overcome spirited opposition in Rome. As Plutarch concluded: "The annihilation of Carthage . . . was primarily due to the advice and counsel of Cato."[45] The Censor ultimately won a Senate majority, but the depth of his personal preoccupation was unusual. Cato's catalogue of Punic atrocities resonated with his audience, who remembered the suffering Hannibal's army had visited on Italy. Badian writes that "hatred and resentment towards [Carthage] seem to have smouldered in the minds of the Senate, although right down to the fifties there was never any reasonable doubt of Carthaginian loyalty."[46] Cato's purported list of Carthaginian treaty breaches was not only legalistic—no other writer "put such emphasis on the topic"—but historically flimsy.[47]

What ideology demanded the disappearance of a disarmed mercantile city? Whatever the military reasons for pursuing the siege after 149, the socio-political motivation of the destruction's leading proponent is significant. Cato liked to claim for himself Spartan descent, and his broader thinking recalled features of Sparta at its zenith: militaristic expansionism, the idealization of cultivation, notions of gender and social hierarchy, and cultural prejudices.

Despite "the amazing regularity with which Rome went to war" in this era, its preplanned and well-executed policy to destroy Carthage totally was also unusual. Historians differ on the threat the city posed to Rome, and whether Rome's demands were calculated to minimize it or stemmed from "extreme power hunger."[48] But to Cato, the danger was as much internal. In his view, Roman society suffered from domestic flaws that made it inadequately resilient to the threat of Carthage's existence.

A distinguished Roman administrator and orator, man of letters and action ("Stick to the point; the words will follow"), Cato was a veteran of the Second Punic War, when he had first criticized Scipio Africanus for profligacy. With relentless corruption allegations, Cato hounded Scipio to his death in 183. Pliny noticed that Cato's history of the first two Punic Wars "removed the names" of several Scipios and other commanders, caustically naming only Hannibal's elephant.[49] Cato considered fame a dangerous temptation, while domestic "avarice and extravagance . . . have been the destruction of all great empires."[50] He insisted on Roman military domination. "The Carthaginians are already our enemies; for he who prepares everything against me, so that he can make war at whatever time he wishes, is already my enemy even though he is not yet using arms."[51]

Elected consul in 195, Cato took command in formerly Carthaginian-ruled Spain, where he put down major rebellions. A courageous and effective general, he was noted "for his cruelty towards his defeated enemies."[52] The Roman historian Livy sympathized: "Cato had more difficulty subduing the enemy . . . because he had, as it were, to reclaim them, like slaves who had asserted their freedom." Cato commanded his officers in Spain "to force this nation . . . to accept again the yoke which it has cast off." In one battle, Livy cites an estimate of 40,000 enemies killed. When seven towns rebelled, "Cato marched his army against them and brought them under control without any fighting worth recording," but after they again revolted, he ensured that "the conquered

were not granted the same pardon as before. They were all sold by public auc-
tion." Plutarch said Cato subdued some tribes by force, others by diplomacy.
"Cato himself claims that he captured more cities in Spain than he spent days
there. Nor is this an idle boast, if indeed it is true that they numbered more
than four hundred." Nevertheless, Cato "stayed in Spain rather too long," and
one of the Scipios tried to relieve him of his command. In response, Cato took
"five companies of infantry and five hundred horse and subdued the tribe of
the Lacetani by force of arms. In addition, he recovered and put to death six
hundred of those who had gone over to the enemy."[53] Like other commanders,
Cato was murderous against military opposition and tolerant of societies who
offered surrender. His military career ended in 191 after a fearless feat of arms
that clinched Rome's victory in Greece.

After all his efforts in Spain and the eastern Mediterranean, he took a close
interest in subsequent events. Rebellions in Spain in 154, in Macedonia in 151,
and in the Peloponnese two years later probably troubled him. But a crowning
blow may have come when Cato actually saw Carthage. On a mission there in
152 at age 81, he was shocked by the city's recovery from its defeat a half century before. Unburdened of overseas territories, Carthage was again a thriving
mercantile metropolis, "burgeoning with an abundance of young men, brim-
ming with copious wealth, teeming with weapons." He returned to Rome with
a sense of assault. While "he was rearranging the folds of his toga in the senate,
Cato by design let fall some Libyan figs and then, after everyone had expressed
admiration for their size and beauty, he said that the land that produced them
was but three days' sail from Rome."[54] This threat had to be destroyed.

Cato was posturing. His figs could not have come from Carthage, more
than a six-day voyage even in the summer's fine sailing weather. His audience
of "senatorial gentlemen farmers" probably knew the figs came from Cato's
own estate near Rome. Some may even have read his advice on how to plant
African figs in Italy.[55] Carthage was not an economic threat; its products barely
penetrated the Italian market, and its annihilation would have helped few of
Rome's merchants. In fact, Cato cared little for traders, Roman or Carthaginian.
Questioned about moneylending, he replied: "You might as well ask me what I
think about murder."[56]

Cato idealized farmers, not merchants. His only extant work, *De Agri Cultura,* began by contrasting the trader with his ideal citizen—the farmer: "It is
true that to obtain money by trade is sometimes more profitable, were it not so
hazardous; and likewise money-lending, if it were as honourable. Our ancestors

held this view and embodied it in their laws. . . . And when they would praise a worthy man their praise took this form: 'good farmer' and 'good settler'; one so praised was thought to have received the greatest commendation. The trader I consider to be an energetic man, and one bent on making money; but, as I said above, it is a dangerous career and one subject to disaster." "On the other hand," Cato went on, "it is from the farming class that the bravest men and the sturdiest soldiers come, their calling is most highly respected, their livelihood is most assured and is looked on with the least hostility, and those who are engaged in that pursuit are least inclined to be disaffected."[57]

Cato saw the loyal peasant farmer, often using slave labor captured in foreign campaigns, as the foundation of Roman power at home and abroad. According to Polybius, "Cato once declared in a public speech that anybody could see the republic was going downhill when a pretty boy could cost more than a plot of land and jars of fish more than ploughmen."[58] Yet rhetorically idealizing the peasantry and lauding its utility did not necessarily mean advancing peasant interests. From an old plebeian family, Cato cultivated "fondly the life of simplicity and self-discipline" even as he owned "great plantations" of slaves and "preferred to buy those prisoners of war who were young and still susceptible, like puppies." Moreover, Plutarch asserts, Cato practiced "the most disreputable branch of moneylending."[59]

Cato's alleged hypocrisy is less important than his romanticization of peasants in opposition to merchants, its pervasive ideological influence, and its military significance for his Carthaginian policy. After Rome disarmed the Carthaginians in 149, the consul Censorinus had commanded them to move 10 miles from the sea, "for we are resolved to raze your city to the ground." He explained that proximity to the sea had tempted and corrupted Carthage: "The sea made you invade Sicily and lose it again . . . [it] always begets a grasping disposition by the very facilities which it offers for gain. . . . Naval prowess is like merchants' gains—a good profit today and a total loss tomorrow. . . . Believe me, Carthaginians, life inland, with the joys of agriculture and quiet, is much more equable. Although the gains of agriculture are, perhaps, smaller than those of mercantile life, they are surer and a great deal safer . . . an inland city enjoys all the security of the solid earth." But the Carthaginians refused this injunction, and were slaughtered. W. V. Harris points out that the Romans may have recalled Plato's advice that "if a city was to avoid being full of trade and the moral consequences of trade, it must be 80 stades (ten miles) from the sea."[60] Rome itself is 16 miles inland.

Cato wanted women kept in their place, like peasants and traders: "There is the greatest danger from any class of people, once you allow meetings and conferences and secret consultations." Cato opposed the repeal in 195 of a wartime law denying women the right to "possess more than half an ounce of gold, or wear parti-coloured clothing, or ride in a horse-drawn vehicle in a city or town." Clamoring for repeal of this law, increasing numbers of women "came in from the towns and rural centres [and] beset all the streets of the city and all the approaches to the Forum," Livy wrote. Cato was outraged: "Are you in the habit of running out into the streets, blocking the roads, addressing other women's husbands?" he asked. "Or are you more alluring in the street than in the home, more attractive to other women's husbands . . . ? And yet, even at home, . . . it would not become you to be concerned about the question of what laws should be passed or repealed in this place," he scolded. Cato denounced the female throng as an "untamed animal," a "secession of the women." He compared it to a plebeian riot, but he also made an example of "that rich woman over there" who simply wanted to flaunt her wealth. Perhaps invoking the Spartan model, he preferred that "the dress of all [be] made uniform." He saw politicized women, like any dissenters, as an internal threat to the republic: "Our liberty, overthrown in the home by female indiscipline, is now being crushed and trodden underfoot here, too, in the Forum. It is because we have not kept them under control individually that we are now terrorized by them collectively. . . . But we (heaven preserve us) are now allowing them even to take part in politics, and actually to appear in the Forum and to be present at our meetings and assemblies! What they are longing for is complete liberty, or rather . . . complete license. . . . The very moment they begin to be your equals, they will be your superiors. Good heavens!"[61]

For Cato, women out of place threatened social control. According to Plutarch, "since he believed that, among slaves, sex was the greatest cause of delinquency, he made it a rule that his male slaves could, for a set fee, have intercourse with his female slaves, but no one of them was allowed to consort with another woman." After Cato's wife died, a prostitute "would come to see him without anyone's knowing of it." In public life he was more severe. In Spain, one of his officers hanged himself after Cato discovered he had bought three captive boys. "Cato sold the boys and returned the price to the treasury." He once banished from the Senate a man who "had kissed his own wife in broad daylight and in sight of his daughter." Cato joked publicly that he had "never embraced his wife except after a loud thunderclap"—Jupiter's blessing.[62]

Controlling gender roles preoccupied Rome's rulers. Women were not the only domestic group whose independent activities raised fears of external threats or justified external expansion. In 186, Roman magistrates uncovered and prosecuted an alleged conspiratorial Bacchic cult that sponsored illicit sexual acts, violating a ban on secrecy and male priests. The main purpose of the cult, formerly composed of women, had become male homosexual activity. The magistrates "convicted a large number of men and women of foul sexual acts" in the service of a cult they labeled "alien" and "un-Roman." The Senate launched an invasion of Dalmatia in 156 largely "because they did not want the men of Italy to become womanish through too lengthy a spell of peace."[63]

A warrior abroad, Cato feared Romans were becoming soft at home. In civilian life he "never stopped taking on feuds," becoming a pugnacious prosecutor and "vigorous opponent of the nobility, of luxurious living, and of the invasion into Italy of Greek culture." As Roman nobles adopted "Greek luxury and refinement," Cato saw it as exotic corruption, a threat to Rome's culture: "We have crossed into Greece and Asia (regions full of all kinds of sensual allurements) and are even laying hands on the treasures of kings—I am the more alarmed lest these things should capture us instead of our capturing them." At that time, explained Plutarch, "Rome was, on account of its size, unable to preserve its purity; because of its domination over many lands and peoples it was coming into contact with various races and was exposed to patterns of behavior of every description." Its "urban life was half imported," as Ramsay MacMullen has shown. Romans used Greek terms not only for domestic architecture, equipment, containers, and food, but also for cosmetics, "little embellishments and treats, the things one would enjoy at evening parties or in the performing arts, technical terms of science and mechanics, cult acts and items, the terminology of maritime travel and commerce." Members of the aristocracy "were surrounded by, they floated upon, a sea of products and artifacts and daily usages that had originated in the east." There were "two schools of thought among the upper classes, at war over the right style of life."[64]

Cato devoted himself to preserving Roman culture. He produced the first historical work in Latin. His innovation was a statement of conservative ideology, since previous Roman historians had written in Greek. Its seven books do not survive, but an outline by Cornelius Nepos reveals the preoccupations of Cato's "didactic moralizing and pioneer ethnography." One book told of the early Roman kings, and four dealt with "the origins of all the communities of Italy" and the Punic Wars.[65] Cato focused on Rome's lineage, as distinct from those of its enemies, and on the secrets of its success—husbandry, morals, and discipline. Racial prejudice, as we know it, was relatively uncommon in the ancient world.[66] Yet Cato wrote that Rome followed the mores of the Sabines, his own forebears, who claimed descent from hardy Spartans. He found the Ligurians, by contrast, to be "illiterate and liars." The Greeks of his day were "an utterly vile and unruly race."[67] He admired aspects of their history and even learned their language late in life, but he condemned "all Greek literature across the board" and promoted a series of repressive measures, including expulsion of teachers of Epicureanism and destruction of Greek philosophical works. Cato's hostility toward Greek rhetoric led to another crackdown against philosophers and teachers in 161.[68] At age 79, he expelled the visiting Greek skeptic Carneades, whose brilliant rhetoric was attracting young Romans to philosophy. Cato "resolved to exorcize all the philosophers from the city," says Plutarch. "Disturbed by this passion for words . . . he had come to blows with philosophical pursuits in general and was zealously trying to discredit Greek civilization and culture as a whole."[69] He attacked a political foe for singing and performing Greek verse. Greek "luxury and laxity," even culture, like colored clothing and Libyan figs, fostered Roman extravagance and decline. Cato was convinced that "the city was in need of a great purgation."[70] Indeed, just seven years after the destruction of Carthage came the first expulsion of Jews from Rome, in 139.

Cato's view of Carthage represented his most sustained response to a panorama of perils. His perception of combined foreign and domestic subversion of Roman culture helps explain Cato's determination to destroy Carthage. Plutarch speculated that Scipio Nasica, for his part, preferred to keep the threat handy, "like a bridle, to serve as a corrective to the impudence of the masses, since he felt that Carthage was not so powerful that it could prevail over Rome, nor yet so weak that it could be treated with contempt. But, as far as Cato was concerned, it was precisely this that seemed to be a cause for alarm, that a city that had always been great and had now, in addition, been sobered and chastened by hardships was threatening the Roman people at a time when they were to a great extent intoxicated and staggering as a result of the authority that they now possessed. Rather, he felt, they should eliminate altogether the foreign threats to their supremacy and give themselves an opportunity to mend their domestic faults." Indeed, Rome's destruction of Carthage and its sack of Corinth occurred in the same year.[71] One scholar speculates that in harping on Carthage, Cato had aimed "to launch Rome into a long and difficult war in the

West" against a traditional enemy, fearing that further involvement in Greece and the East would threaten Rome's cultural identity.[72] Cato's broader notions of culture and politics fostered a violent, vindictive hostility toward Carthage not applied to other regions.

Carthage's threat to Rome paled before Cato's threat to Carthage. His ideal of the controlled, militarized ethnic rural community, corruptible by external influences and weakened by others' successes, provided a formula for genocide. His vision also threatened the rights of citizens of Rome, which he consistently patrolled for signs of weakness. Cato's thinking underlines the connections between the domestic and transnational aspects of genocidal policies, ancient and modern.

History and Memory

The destruction of Carthage set a precedent for genocide. Rome ruled the Mediterranean, and its legions marched into northern Europe, occasionally employing genocidal massacres against enemies. Campaigning in what is now the Netherlands in 55 B.C.E., Julius Caesar almost annihilated two German tribes, the Usipetes and the Tencteri, which he claimed numbered 430,000, probably an exaggeration. After initial clashes, the tribes had requested a truce. "A large number of Germans, including all their chiefs and elders[,] came to visit me in my camp," Caesar wrote:

> I ordered that they should be detained. I led the whole of my army out of the camp . . . reaching the enemy camp before the Germans could realize what was happening. . . . They were given no time to make plans or arm themselves. . . . [T]those Germans able to arm themselves fast enough resisted our men for a short time, fighting among their carts and baggage wagons. But because the Germans had brought everything they had with them when they left their homes and crossed the Rhine, there was also a great crowd of women and children and these now began to flee in all directions. I sent the cavalry to hunt them down. When the Germans heard cries behind them and saw that their own people were being killed, they threw away their weapons, abandoned their standards, and rushed out of the camp. . . . A large number of them were killed and the rest flung themselves into the river, where they perished overcome by panic, exhaustion, and the force of the current. Our men returned to camp without a single fatal casualty.

Caesar crossed the Rhine in relentless pursuit of the survivors, who were sheltered by a third tribe, the Sugambri. "I stayed a few days in their territory, burning all their villages and buildings and cutting down their crops."[73] When a fourth group, the Eburones, destroyed a Roman legion, Caesar annihilated them. He described his "intention" as to "overwhelm the Eburones with a huge force of men, and so wipe out that tribe and its very name, as a punishment for the great crime it had committed." Soon, "[e]very part of the territory of the Eburones was now being plundered."[74] They vanished from the historical record, but the Sugambri fought on, defeating another legion in 17 B.C.E. After a decade of military retaliations, Rome deported 40,000 surviving Sugambri west of the Rhine, setting another precedent. A half century later, during the Roman conquest of south Wales, Tacitus reported: "Conspicuous above all in stubborn resistance were the Silures, whose rage was fired by words rumoured to have been spoken by the Roman general, to the effect, that as the Sugambri had been formerly destroyed or transplanted into Gaul, so the name of the Silures ought to be blotted out." One historian writes that only the death of that general "saved the Silures from extinction."[75]

As civil wars wracked the Roman republic itself from 49 B.C.E., some of its men of letters immortalized genocidal massacres even as others evoked idyllic rural scenes. It was in these troubled times that Virgil began composing pastoral poetry in Latin. His fourth *Eclogue* recalled Hesiod, as it foreshadowed "a new race" descending from the skies to "end the iron race and bring in the golden all over the world." In the *Georgics,* which appeared in 29, Virgil took up a more agricultural theme:[76]

> The husbandman
> With hooked ploughshare turns the soil; from hence
> Springs his year's labour; hence, too, he sustains
> Country and cottage homestead, . . .
> Meanwhile about his lips sweet children cling;
> His chaste house keeps its purity.

Virgil traced this agrarian bliss to the Italian heritage that gave Rome its glory: "Such life of yore the ancient Sabines led, such Remus and his brother . . . and Rome became the fair world's fairest."[77] The civil wars ended in 30 B.C.E. with Octavian's defeat of Anthony and Cleopatra in Egypt. The next year Octavian returned to Rome, becoming the emperor Augustus in 27.

Such a splendid empire merited a complete explanation and celebration. Virgil spent his final decade (29–19) composing his imperial epic, the *Aeneid,* having set down a view of history: "I shall lead the Muses home as captives in a triumphal procession."[78] In Virgil's ideal, women were seen rather than heard. Ellen Oliensis writes, "In the world of Virgilian pastoral, girls are not singers; they do not perform, and while they are sometimes quoted, we never hear them speak."[79] In the *Aeneid,* recalling Cato, women are "alarming and violent creatures, prone to the making of terrible scenes," even embodying a "clash between Western civilization and the barbaric glitter and animal deities of the East." When Cleopatra commanded her warships, "Anubis barked and all manner of monstrous gods leveled their weapons."[80]

The *Aeneid* traced Rome's and Octavian's glory to the city's putative founder, a survivor of the Greek destruction of Troy. Cato had written of Aeneas's Trojans and their legendary arrival in Latium, when they killed its king, Latinus, in battle. Now Virgil transformed Latinus into an ally of Aeneas, nationalizing Aeneas just as he had called the hardworking bees of the *Georgics* "little Romans." Octavian claimed descent from Aeneas's son Iulus.[81] And just as Octavian had conquered Cleopatra, Virgil pits Aeneas's destiny against that of another North African queen—Dido of Carthage.

The story of the *Aeneid* begins: "There was an ancient city . . ." Virgil's readers might have thought of Rome, or Troy. But he is referring to Carthage, "held by colonists from Tyre, opposite Italy . . . a city of great wealth and ruthless in the pursuit of war. . . . Juno is said to have loved it more than any other place. . . . But she had heard that there was rising from the blood of Troy a race of men who in days to come would overthrow this Tyrian citadel . . . [and] sack the land of Libya."[82]

Book 2 of the *Aeneid* offers an astonishing literary depiction of genocide— the destruction of Troy. Aeneas narrates the city's calamitous fall and his own narrow escape. "Who could speak of such slaughter? Who could weep tears to match that suffering? . . . The bodies of the dead lay through all its streets and houses and the sacred shrines of its gods. . . . Everywhere there was fear, and death in many forms." Aeneas recounts an "orgy of killing" near King Priam's palace, adding: "I saw Hecuba with a hundred women, her daughters and the wives of her sons. I saw Priam's blood all over the altar. . . . Down fell the fifty bedchambers with all the hopes for generations yet to come. . . . Hecuba and her daughters were sitting flocked round the altar, like doves driven down in a black storm. . . . So ended the destiny of Priam, . . . a corpse without a name." He perished "with Troy ablaze," while Aeneas's men "had all deserted and thrown themselves from the roof or given their suffering bodies to the flames"[83]—just as the wife of Carthage's last commander, Hasdrubal, would plunge with her children into the flames of her city centuries later. Vivid description of a legendary genocide substituted for the unstated historical one.

The dramatic irony is that Aeneas is telling his story to Dido, Carthage's founder. Virgil's readers all knew, and he had just reminded them, of the fate of Carthage itself. When Aeneas lands in North Africa before reaching Italy, he finds Dido, herself a refugee from Tyre, founding her new city. But Jupiter has promised that Aeneas's Rome will be "an empire that will know no end" (*imperium sine fine*). Jupiter subdues the Carthaginians' "fiery temper," lest Dido, "in her ignorance of destiny, should bar her country" to the Trojan antecedents of the Romans destined to destroy it. Virgil's ironies come thick and fast. "The Tyrians were working with a will; some of them were laying out the line of walls or rolling up great stones for building the citadel; others were choosing sites for building . . . drawing up laws and electing magistrates and a senate. . . . They were like bees at the beginning of summer, busy in the sunshine all through the flowery meadows, bringing out the young of the race." Waiting to meet Dido, Aeneas sees them erecting a temple. Then a "strange sight . . . allayed his fears," giving him "better confidence for the future." Painted on the new temple's walls were scenes from battles recently fought at Troy! Aeneas wept: "Is there anywhere now on the face of this earth that is not full of the knowledge of our misfortunes? Look at Priam. Here too . . . there are tears for suffering and men's hearts are touched by what man has to bear. . . . We are known here."[84] Virgil built the destruction of Carthage into its very creation.

As Aeneas "stood gazing" at the murals, even recognizing himself "in the confusion of battle," Dido arrives. Roman readers must have gasped. Heightening the drama, a Trojan even assures Dido that "we have not come to Libya to pillage your homes." Dido unwittingly tells them: "The city which I am founding is yours. Draw your ships up on the beach." Aeneas says: "We are the remnants left by the Greeks . . . whatever survives of the Trojan race, scattered as it is over the face of the wide earth. May the gods bring you the reward you deserve, if there are any gods who have regard for goodness, if there is any justice in the world." Dido then tells of her own wanderings, adding: "Through my own suffering, I am learning to help those who suffer."[85]

Not everyone thinks Dido is going to be helpful. Aeneas's mother, Venus, fears "the treacherous house of Carthage and the double-tongued people of Tyre." The goddess learns that Aeneas is sending to Carthage his son Iulus, ancestor of its eventual Roman conquerors, bearing "gifts which have survived the burning of Troy"—a cloak brought there by Helen and the scepter of Priam's daughter. Venus sends Cupid with the gifts, disguised as Iulus. And so Cupid makes Dido fall in love with Aeneas. Unadvised to beware Trojans bearing gifts and "doomed to be the victim of a plague that was yet to come," Dido toasts this "day of happiness for the Tyrians and the men of Troy, and may our descendants long remember it." Attended, like the unfortunate Hecuba, by 100 female slaves, Dido asks "question after question about Priam." It is at her insistence that Aeneas tells his tale of "the doomed Priam" and "the last day of a doomed people." She hears how, as the survivors crept from the city, "[h]orror was everywhere and the very silence chilled the blood.... Troy lay smoking on the ground."[86]

The dramatic power of Virgil's multiple ironies came from Roman readers' knowledge of the similar, much more recent fate of Carthage. It is forecast to Dido unwittingly by Aeneas's narration of the fall of Troy. Virgil acknowledges that Romans needed no reminder of Carthage's destruction, passing over it with a silence that compounds the drama, but indeed chills the blood. Aeneas's decision to leave Carthage and found Rome brings Dido an ominous nightmare, "looking for her Tyrians in an empty land." Wishing she had destroyed "father and son and all their race," she curses Aeneas: "May he ... see his innocent people dying.... As for you, my Tyrians, you must pursue with hatred the whole line of his descendants ... shore against shore, sea against sea, sword against sword. Let there be war between the nations and between their sons forever." Dido's suicide by fire as Aeneas's ships depart not only recounts the legendary beginning of Carthage but, as Virgil's audience knew, also foreshadows its end, when Hasdrubal's wife followed Dido's example.[87]

Later, Aeneas meets Dido on his journey to the underworld. Weeping, he asks: " 'Was I the cause of your dying?' ... Her features moved no more when he began to speak than if she had been a block of flint or Parian marble," like the razed stones of Carthage. "Then at last she rushed away, hating him, into the shadows.... Aeneas was no less stricken by the injustice of her fate, and long did he gaze after her, pitying her," as if Virgil himself was silently contemplating the more recent disappearance of her city. Then the shade of Aeneas's father, Anchises, shows him the future, "the glory that lies in store ... for the men of Italian stock who will be our descendants." Romulus, Caesar, "and all the sons of Iulus" parade by. "Who would leave you unmentioned, great Cato? ... or the two Scipios, both of them thunderbolts of war, the bane of Libya?"[88]

The *Aeneid* depicts centuries of deadly mutual enmity between Rome and

Carthage and links them both to Troy. Virgil's dramatic metaphor of Rome's "empire without end" as the product of genocides a millennium apart still reverberates through Western civilization two millennia later. Along with the *Georgics,* which Dryden termed "the best poem of the best poet," the *Aeneid* guaranteed Virgil an "unbroken ascendancy of eighteen centuries."[89]

In the three decades after Virgil's death, Livy (64 B.C.E.–17 C.E.) completed a massive 142-book *History of Rome from Its Foundation.* In the first third of this work, covering the period up to 167 B.C.E., Livy praised Cato "far above" his peers for his "force of character" and "versatile genius." The Censor was "the bravest soldier in a fight," an "outstanding general," the "most skilled" lawyer, and "the most eloquent advocate" whose words were "preserved inviolate in writings of every kind." To Livy, Cato was "a man of iron constitution, in body and in mind," with "a rigid integrity and a contempt for popularity and riches."[90] Along with Virgil's subtle relocation of the Carthaginian tragedy in Trojan legend and Roman glory, Livy's assessment of the early Cato guaranteed his historical reputation as a model leader of the republic.

However, Livy's account of the Third Punic War was lost sometime after St. Augustine read it in the early fifth century. Its loss played a key part in a prolonged erasure of Carthage from history, compounding its physical annihilation. The disappearance of all of Livy's books 46–142 ended his extant account of Rome's history in the year 167.[91] For part of his narrative of the Punic Wars, Livy had relied on the Greek writer Polybius, an eyewitness to the fate of Carthage.[92] Yet the major part of Polybius's works was also subsequently lost, along with much of the entire classical corpus. A thirteenth-century writer even attributed Homer's *Iliad* and *Odyssey* to Sophocles.[93]

The medieval world thus had little knowledge of what had happened to Carthage. Apart from brief passages of Cicero and Sallust, the only extant classical descriptions of the city's destruction were the Greek texts of Polybius, the second-century historian Appian, who had read Polybius, and Strabo. Less accessible in western Europe, these were republished only in the late fifteenth century. Fragments survived of Polybius's books 7–40, including excerpts on the Third Punic War. Books 1–5 were first translated into Latin only in 1454. Book 6 and other excerpts first appeared in various European languages in the second quarter of the sixteenth century. The first English translation, of book 1, appeared only in 1568.[94] The most detailed extant account of the Third Punic War, that of Appian, was first published in Latin in 1452. Strabo's account in his *Geography* appeared in Italy in 1423, was translated into Latin in the 1450s, and first published in 1469.[95] Even Livy's book 44, with its clipped prediction of "the destruction of Carthage," was rediscovered and printed as late as 1531. Only then did the story of Rome's annihilation of the city become widely known, as western Europe's own expansion began.[96]

Meanwhile, Virgil's pastoral had become the poetry of new empires modeled on Roman antiquity. Court poetry of the Holy Roman Empire likened an official in Bavaria to the shepherd of the *Eclogues,* "coming from his apple-rich estate."[97] Imperial expansion was brutal, but medieval warfare rarely reached the level of genocide. Charlemagne, who inherited the Frankish territories in 768, soon launched a 30-year war against the Saxons. After they almost destroyed a Frankish army, Charlemagne had 4,500 Saxon prisoners "beheaded on a single day," according to the Royal Frankish Annals. Posing as Israelites in a new promised land, Charlemagne's army had apparently drawn inspiration from the biblical massacres of Amalekites and Moabites. Yet deportation was more common than extermination in the Middle Ages. Other annals recorded that "the Franks slew a multitude of men," but also "led back many Saxons into Francia in fetters." The Royal Annals reported that as many as "7070 were taken away" from Saxony in 795, and later another "1600 leading men." Then, in 804, Charlemagne "transported all the Saxons who dwelt beyond the Elbe and in Wihmodia . . . together with their wives and children into Francia." The Saxons, his ninth-century biographer wrote, were thus "made one people with the Franks."[98]

Later medieval writers drew upon Virgil to depict Aeneas's founding of Rome, its destruction of Carthage, and the forging of an empire as events that occurred according to God's plan. Bocccaccio told the tale as part of a journey "to establish Christianity as a universal religion with Rome as its seat."[99] Others, such as the twelfth-century French author of the *Roman d'Eneas,* ignored the *Aeneid*'s religious and national, dynastic ethos, simply preserving the love story, recast into a medieval court setting.[100]

In Europe, as in Cato's Rome, domestic division accompanied imperial conquest. In his study *The Making of Europe,* historian Robert Bartlett traces a "hardening of anti-Jewish feeling" over the first half of the second millennium, accompanying European expansion.[101] In the "first great slaughter of Europe's Jews by Christians," errant Crusader bands massacred possibly 8,000 Jews in eight German cities in May–June 1096. Marching into Jerusalem three years later, according to the archbishop of Tyre, Crusaders murdered "about ten thousand infidels"—both Muslims and Jews—in the Temple enclosure. They burned more Jews alive in the synagogue and butchered thousands of Muslims in the al-Aqsa mosque.[102]

Meanwhile, England's Norman conquerors were expanding into Wales. Contemporaneous Norman historians wrote that the invaders "caused the ruin and wretched deaths of many thousands" and subjected the native Britons to "unrestrained plunder and slaughter."[103] Medieval Welsh chronicles, too, accused "the French" (i.e., the Normans) of imposing "tyranny and injustice" upon Wales, using "law and judgments and violence." By these means, one chronicle asserted, "the French seized all the lands of the Britons" and in several regions, "drove away all the inhabitants from the land." It added that in the twelfth century, King Henry I of England dispatched an army to Wales to fight the Britons: "And out of hate for them they set their minds upon exterminating all the Britons, so that the name of the Britons should never more be called to mind from that time forth."[104] Yet these worst fears proved unfounded. As elsewhere in medieval Europe, repression rarely extended to genocide.[105]

Racial thinking was yet to appear in either Christian or Jewish writing. The first Jewish text to mention "the black slaves, the sons of Ham," the twelfth-century commentary of Benjamin of Tudela, also referred to honest black merchants, among whom lived black Jews.[106] In the thirteenth to fifteenth centuries, the vague medieval European term *barbarian* gradually came to mean non-Christian peoples and races of any creed who were savage or "uncivil" in their behavior. In Italy and Spain, translations of Aristotle's writings from Greek and Arabic had started to appear, and the Dominican William of Moerbeke translated Aristotle's *Politics* in 1260.[107] Europeans could now consider the term *barbarian* as used in Aristotle's discussion of "natural slavery" and could note its ramifications for a new racial division of the world.

Still far short of genocide, this amounted to further elision of ethnicity and agriculture. Aristotle had prefigured some of Cato's agrarian views, though not other positions Cato espoused, and he now played an ambiguous role in their slow reemergence. *Oeconomica,* a work that depicted agriculture as "a natural occupation" and "the most honest," was in fact written by Aristotle's pupil, but was long incorrectly attributed to him after its first translation into Latin in 1295. However, Aristotle had romanticized neither cultivation nor an ethnic community of farmers. He wrote in *Politics:* "Those who are to cultivate the soil should best of all, if the ideal system is to be stated, be slaves ... but as a second best they should be alien serfs."[108]

Aristotle had coined the term *natural slavery. Politics* began with his assertion, "Every state . . . is a sort of partnership," based initially, he wrote, on "those who are unable to exist without one another," like men and women, and "the union of natural ruler and natural subject for the sake of security," in which "master and slave have the same interest." Aristotle added that, in contrast to the Greeks, "barbarians have no class of natural rulers, but with them the conjugal partnership is a partnership of female slave and male slave. Hence the saying of the poets, 'Tis meet that Greeks should rule barbarians,' implying that barbarian and slave are the same in nature."[109]

Aristotle aired various views on whether all barbarians were "natural slaves." Thus, "some maintain that for one man to be another man's master is contrary to nature . . . and there is no difference between them by nature, and that therefore it is unjust, for it is based on force." Aristotle considered "whether or not anyone exists who is by nature" a slave, "or whether on the contrary all slavery is against nature." He did find it "natural and expedient for the body to be governed by the soul," so "all men that differ as widely as the soul does from the body and the human being from the lower animal . . . are by nature slaves," and he added that "there are cases of people of whom some are freemen and the others slaves by nature." Yet Aristotle conceded that "those who assert the opposite are also right in a manner." He wrote that "many jurists" denounced the enslavement of war captives and "say that it is monstrous if the person powerful enough to use force, and superior in power, is to have the victim of his force as his slave." And those of the opposing view "do not mean to assert that Greeks themselves if taken prisoners are slaves, but that barbarians are. Yet when they say this they are merely seeking for the principles of natural slavery," that some people "are essentially slaves everywhere." This was a view Aristotle rejected, "for they assume that just as from a man springs a man and from a brute springs a brute, so also from good parents comes a good son, but as a matter of fact nature frequently while intending to do this is unable to bring it about." Aristotle barely endorsed the view of "barbarian" races as natural slaves but opted for a compromise: "in some instances it is not the case that one set are slaves and the other freemen by nature," while in other cases "such a distinction does exist." His conclusion—"the just acquiring of slaves, being like a sort of warfare or hunting. Let this then stand as our definition of slave and master"—was no resounding legitimation of either "natural slavery" or racial division. He even recommended that "all slaves should have their freedom set before them as a reward."[110] Nevertheless, his term "natural slavery," with its racialist connotations, later proved useful to expanding empires.

Racial thinking gained ground only slowly. Another thirteenth-century Dominican, Albertus Magnus (c. 1206–80), refined the concept of "barbarian" with a Christian adaptation of Aristotelian categories of human difference. He asserted that "the man who does not observe the laws concerning the ordering of social participation is most certainly a *barbarus.*" Yet this was no genetic trait: "Bestial men, however, are rare, since it is a rare man who has no spark of humanity. It does, however, occur, and usually from two causes: physical handicap and deprivation, or from disease." Albertus Magnus's pupil St. Thomas Aquinas (1225–74), in his commentary on Aristotle, gave the term *barbarian* further attention by investigating the conditions under which some races remain barbaric and others become civilized.[111] While he asserted the biological and psychological unity of mankind, Aquinas, also a Dominican, became the first Christian author to revive the doctrine of "natural slavery."[112] The underlying tensions in Aristotle had reappeared and now began to escalate, pitting concepts of human commonality against emerging notions of racial difference, compounding the contradictions between sectarianism and religious universalism.

Notions of individual, religious, and cultural properties, stirring in a new convection of classical learning, slowly distilled into emerging ethnic precipitations. The thirteenth century, Bartlett writes, saw the accentuation of English-Welsh divisions "in unmistakably racial terms." A medieval Czech chronicle, too, tells of a prince who paid in silver "anyone who brought him a hundred noses cut off from the Germans." In the later Middle Ages came a new biological racism. From 1323, admission to the Brunswick guild of tailors required proof of German descent. The cobblers of Beeskow rejected Slavs, and the bakers' guild there accepted "[n]o one of Wendish stock"—only applicants of "German blood and tongue." Riga bakers prohibited members from marrying "illegitimate or non-German" women. Anglo-Norman guilds in Drogheda excluded the Irish. The Statutes of Kilkenny in 1366 denounced "the manners, fashion and language of the Irish enemies." In 1395, Richard II of England coined the term *wild Irish* with his formula "irrois savages, nos enemis."[113]

In the late fourteenth century the term *race* appeared in European languages.[114] Fifty years later authorities in Limerick held that "[n]o one of Irish blood or birth" could obtain a civic office or apprenticeship; Dublin apprentices had to be "of Englis berthe." Bartlett concludes that now, "[b]iological descent replaced cultural identity as the first criterion of race," epitomized by English rulers' use of "the term 'blood' in fifteenth century Irish discriminatory rules,"

which fostered ghettoization, as in "all the newly settled, conquered or converted peripheries" of Europe.[115] Only in the sixteenth century did the medieval French term *nation* and Low German *natie* (birth, origin, descent group)
begin to assume their broader modern political meanings and the connotation
of *Volk*.[116]

From their divergent intellectual roots, these political notions thrived. Ex-
pounding on Aquinas's theory of Aristotle's "natural slavery," the Scottish theologian John Mair applied it in 1519 to the Caribbean Indians, who "live like
beasts on either side of the equator." He added that "the first person to conquer
them, justly rules over them because they are by nature slaves." Mair incorrectly quoted Aristotle as stating that "the Greeks should be masters over the
barbarians because, by nature, the barbarians and slaves are the same." A contemporaneous counternarrative sprang from the Thomist doctrine of universal
humanity, producing the Renaissance notion of "the republic of all the world"
(*respublica totius orbis*), in the words of the Spanish theologian Francisco de
Vitoria (c. 1492–1546). Jean Bodin even wrote in 1650: "All men surprisingly
work together in a world state as if it were one and the same city state." By that
time, writes historian Anthony Pagden, such thoughts were "commonplace."[117]
A concept of universal monarchy, too, could justify world conquest.

Meanwhile, Virgil's corpus, especially the *Aeneid,* had entered "the life
blood of English readers."[118] Geoffrey of Monmouth opened his *History of the
Kings of Britain,* composed in 1136, with the story of Aeneas's great-grandson:
"Brutus Occupies the Island of Albion." It begins on a double note of agrarian
nationalism and Virgilian pastoral: "Britain, the best of islands . . . has broad
fields and hillsides which are suitable for the most intensive farming . . . [and]
flowers of every hue which offer their honey to the flitting bees."[119] Sir Walter
Ralegh's five-volume *History of the World,* published in 1614, often quoted the
Aeneid and included almost an entire book on the Punic Wars.[120] Ralegh wrote
that history had left no trace of "Carthage, Rome and the rest, no fruit, flower,
grasse, nor leafe, springing upon the face of the Earth, of those seedes: No, their
very roots and ruines doe hardly remaine." Rome, he said, had deliberated in
"good leysure to devise upon the ruine of Carthage; after which, the race of
[Carthage's neighbor] Masanissa himselfe was shortly by them rooted up," just
as the Carthaginians had been.[121] From the sixteenth century on, advocates of
religious or ethnic violence often cited the Carthaginians as a prime precedent
of an exterminated people.

Perpetrators even quoted Cato directly. During the English conquest of the Scottish Highlands, London's secretary of state for Scotland, Sir John Dalrymple, wrote in 1691 of the MacDonald clan of Glencoe: "[T]here is no reckoning with them; *delenda est Carthago.*" Dalrymple meant what he said. He described the Catholic MacDonalds as "the only popish clan in the kingdom, and it will be popular to take a severe course with them." He instructed the authorities in Scotland to use "fire and sword and all manner of hostility; to burn their houses, . . . and to cut off [kill] the men." Dalrymple termed this "rooting out the damnable sept [clan]." King William signed orders to attack the clan leader MacIain of Glencoe "and that tribe" and "to extirpate that band of thieves." Dalrymple urged "that the thieving tribe in Glencoe may be rooted out in earnest." These genocidal orders passed down the chain of command. When they reached Scotland, the commander in chief there, Sir Thomas Livingstone, knew that MacIain had surrendered two weeks earlier and sworn an oath of loyalty. Yet Livingstone told Lieutenant Colonel James Hamilton that "the orders are so positive from Court to me not to spare any of them that have not timely come in," that he should "begin with Glencoe, and spare nothing which belongs to him, but do not trouble the Government with prisoners." Dalrymple insisted that despite its surrender, the "thieving tribe" must be "rooted out and cut off. It must be quietly done." Hamilton informed Major Robert Duncanson: "The orders are that none be spared." Duncanson instructed Captain Robert Campbell "to put to the sword all under seventy." It was "the King's special command" that "these miscreants be cut off root and branch." Attacking Glencoe in a snowstorm, troops killed MacIain and 37 of his men in their homes, and some women and children, but most of the clan escaped. Days later, when Hamilton reported taking prisoners, Livingstone ruled it "a mistake that these villains were not shot," and he ordered all prisoners "dispatched . . . where they are found." Dalrymple wrote: "All I regret is, that any of the sept got away."[122]

Continued conflict and territorial expansion brought cumulative assaults on subject cultures, as rising racism fortified religious conquest. Spain deprived the Muslims of Castille of their jural autonomy in 1412, and of their Arabic schools by 1462. After the Turkish capture of Constantinople in 1453, Pope Nicholas empowered the Portuguese monarch to enslave "all Saracens and pagans whatsoever, and all other enemies of Christ wheresoever," and to seize their lands and property.[123] In 1483, Spain enslaved captives taken in its "just war" against Muslims in Valencia, and six years later the Catholic crown approved the enslavement of Canary Islanders, who were allegedly heretics, though in fact Christians.[124]

The year 1492 heralded Spain's expansion into the New World, but also the expulsion of its Jews and the conquest of the last Muslim state on the Iberian Peninsula. Reporting on his first voyage, Christopher Columbus wrote to King Ferdinand and Queen Isabella:"On 2 January in the year 1492, when your Highnesses had concluded their war with the Moors who reigned in Europe, I saw your Highnesses' banners victoriously raised on the towers of the Alhambra.... Therefore having expelled all the Jews from your domains in that same month of January, your Highnesses commanded me to go with an adequate fleet to these parts of India." Historian Lisa Jardine writes that the Spanish crown now "announced an official policy" of "ethnic and doctrinal purity," rejecting not only the "vigorous and heterogeneous trade throughout the known world" but also the contribution of specialist artisanal manufactures produced by ethnic and religious communities. In its new westward search for commodities free of the "network of Christian, Jewish and Islamic agents, merchants and middlemen," Spain sought "an ethnically cleansed 'new world.'"[125]

At home, forcible conversion of all Spanish Muslims neared completion by 1526, but racialist thinking outstripped religious persecution. Now even their practice of Christianity failed to protect these converted "Moriscos." Madrid banned Moorish costumes, veils, and the use of Arabic and even imposed Spanish names, in what Bartlett calls "a policy of cultural genocide." In the sixteenth century, race became a prominent feature of human categorization. By the seventeenth, Spain was demanding "purity of blood"—no Jewish or Muslim forbears. In 1609–14, Madrid deported up to a third of a million Moriscos.[126]

The first biological racial theories arose in the New World, inspired by a pastoral vision and justifying agricultural colonization. From the sixteenth century, Creole thinkers in the Americas considered the hemisphere a pastoral Paradise, the Garden of Eden. Accepting the biblical doctrines of Creation and common human descent from Adam and Eve, they avoided the heresy of polygenesis and instead traced what they considered the inferiority of Native Americans to Noah's curse on Ham. This enabled Spanish intellectuals from the New World to rebut metropolitan critics of the colonies by asserting that virtue lay in "lands, not peoples," and to abandon the hitherto influential environmental determinism that, in the case of a paradise, precluded Indian inferiority. In Mexico City in 1591, the émigré Spanish physician Juan de Cárdenas published *Problemas y secretos maravillosos de las Indias,* which the historian Jorge Cañizares Esguerra calls possibly "the first modern treatise on racial physiology." Predating modern scientific racism by two centuries, Cárdenas distinguished Europeans from Indians by contrasting "the composition and organization of our [body] and theirs." The colonial intellectual Enrico Martínez wrote in 1606 that Indians and blacks had mental "abilities far inferior to that of the Spaniards," as each group was made of different "matter" and possessed its own "temperament, disposition of the brain and body organs." Racial distinctions assumed agricultural import by the mid-seventeenth century, when a Jesuit in the Indies asserted that Indians were "phlegmatic by nature," whereas "[i]n Spain a single man does more work in his fields than four Indians will do here."[127]

Spain also imported antiquity to the New World. In what is now Colombia, conquistadors founded Cartagena in 1533, naming it after the town Hannibal's brother-in-law Hasdrubal had established in Spain, "New Carthage," in 227 B.C.E. Construction of Cartago itself began in Costa Rica in 1564.[128] Meanwhile, Hernán Cortés, having conquered Mexico, returned to Spain and sailed with the putative heir of Aeneas, Holy Roman Emperor Charles V, in his unsuccessful attack on Algiers in 1541.[129] Thirty years later, Charles V's illegitimate son, the Spanish commander Don John of Austria, captured Tunis. Don John "went to hunt lions and wild bulls on the very site of Carthage."[130] The imperial and the pastoral had returned to the scene of a classical crime.

CHAPTER 2

The Spanish Conquest of the New World, 1492–1600

I f Christopher Columbus's discovery of the New World recharted the globe, the ensuing Spanish conquest of the Caribbean basin and Mexico transformed it. Heavily armed columns of troops devastated the most populous islands and destroyed the most powerful kingdom of the New World, dispatched massive quantities of plunder back to the Old, opened up the Americas to other European powers and settlers, and established grim new precedents for their murder of indigenous peoples. This in turn sparked lasting controversies in Spain and abroad. Domestic critics like Bartolomé de Las Casas called the Spanish record into question, provoking apologists to defend it and laying the first groundwork for a modern discourse of human rights.

The arrival of Columbus in the Caribbean in 1492 quickly led to one bloody conquest after another. In 20 years the islands of Hispaniola, Jamaica, Puerto Rico, and Cuba all fell into Spanish hands. Their large indigenous populations declined dramatically at the hands of the conquistadores and the enslavement, deportations, and diseases that came with them. The conquests of Mexico from 1519 and Guatemala from 1523 inflicted even more catastrophic losses on much larger populations, though in each of these cases many indigenous people survived, unlike on some of the islands, whose populations soon disappeared forever.

From the Old World to the New

Ancient Rome's republic and empire offered many models for the expanding power of early modern Spain. Its explorers and conquistadores, their apologists and opponents—all cited classical precedents for their actions and arguments. While planning his voyages of discovery, Columbus drew on ancient, medieval, and more contemporary sources. These included not only a 1477 work by Aeneas Sylvius (Pope Pius II) and a Latin edition of Marco Polo's *Travels*, but also another item in Columbus's small personal library: the 1491 Castilian translation of Plutarch's *Lives*, including his biography of Cato the Censor.[1]

Columbus was not unique in consulting such sources. By the time Hernán Cortés, conqueror of Mexico, left for the New World in 1504, he may have read Caesar's *Commentaries*, which had appeared in Spanish by 1498. A battlefield command he gave his troops in Mexico resembled an order of Caesar's.[2] Cortés had studied Latin and, according to his soldier Bernal Díaz del Castillo, had a law degree.[3] He was familiar with Castilian legal codes, which referred frequently to Aristotle and antiquity. A leading scholar has suggested that Cortés had also read Livy.[4] Another, skeptical, still finds in Cortés "Latinate constructions and even distant echoes of Roman historians."[5] Twenty years after Livy's text that briefly noted the destruction of Carthage was first printed in 1531, his complete extant corpus appeared in Spanish translation.[6] In the 1560s, Diaz wrote, "the name of Cortés is as famous in our day as was that of Caesar among the Romans, or of Hannibal among the Carthaginians."[7]

Before marching inland to conquer Mexico in 1519, Cortés told his men to "rely on our own good swords and stout hearts," and then "went on to draw many comparisons and relate the heroic deeds of the Romans." Diaz added: "One and all we answered him that we would obey his orders, that the die was cast for good fortune, as Caesar said when he crossed the Rubicon." In one of his Mexican battles, Cortés again addressed his troops: "As for your observation, gentlemen, that the most famous Roman captains never performed deeds equal to ours, you are quite right."[8] The night before his attack on the Aztec capital, Tenochtitlan, Cortés once more recounted to his men the achievements of the Romans "to encourage them in their deeds."[9] In his sixteenth-century study of the Conquest, Bernardino de Sahagún pursued Cortés's comparison in reference to other Mexican cities: "This famous and great city of Tula, so rich and fine, so wise and brave, ultimately suffered the wretched fate of Troy," while for their part, "[t]he Tlaxcaltecs seem to have succeeded the Carthaginians."[10]

Mexico became the stakes in what historian Anthony Pagden calls "a competition for universal monarchy."[11] The Spanish king Charles V became the Holy Roman Emperor in June 1519. In a letter to him the next year, Cortés portrayed his captive Moteucçoma (Moctezuma) as handing over a second empire to Charles, on the model of the Emperor Constantine's putative "dona-

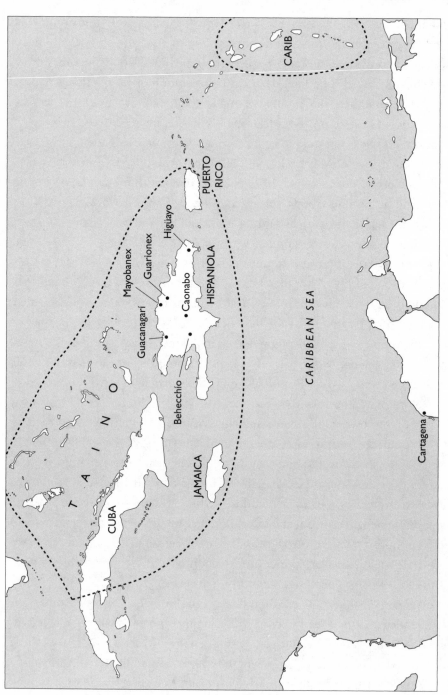

MAP 3. The Spanish conquest of the Caribbean

tion" of Rome's western empire to the pope. Cortés addressed Charles V as "the Most High and Powerful Caesar."[12] Of course, the classicisms served the contemporary cause and its geographical ambition. Cortés frequently compared the Aztecs not only to ancient barbarians but also to Spain's closer enemies, the Moors.[13] Indeed, with Spain in the role of Rome, the term *Barbaria* came to specify Islamic North Africa, playing the part of its ancient overlord, Carthage.[14]

But the cult of antiquity plumbed intellectual depths. The Spanish overseer of Indian labor in the mines of Hispaniola, Gonzalo Fernández de Oviedo, portrayed the Indians as descendants of the barbarian Visigoths, comparing them with ancient Thracians and Ethiopians, and adding that God "consented to their extermination."[15] The major intellectual apologist for Spain's conquests, the Córdoba rhetorician Juan Ginés de Sepúlveda (1490–1573), argued that Indians were barbarians because unlike the Romans they had failed to preserve "any monument to their history." Sixteenth-century European accounts of supposed Indian cannibalistic rituals resemble Livy's portrayal of the Bacchanalia and compared Caribbean Indians with Homer's Laestrygones, who ate Ulysses' men.[16]

Sepúlveda deployed Aristotelian concepts of superiority and "natural slavery" to argue that Spanish offensives against Indians were just wars. The thousands of natives "who scattered in flight like women before Spaniards so few" were inferior even to those other cannibals, the Scythian barbarians of Rome's ancient frontiers.[17] Only the more courageous Mexicans, "the most human" of the Indians, bore comparison even to the Scythians, traditional enemies of the church.[18] Sepúlveda added that "the Romans justly subjugated the other nations of the world," just as, for their sins, "the Amorites and Perizzites and other inhabitants of the Promised Land were exterminated by the Children of Israel."[19] Yet Sepúlveda also condemned the Jews, whose "extermination God desired because of their crimes and idolatry."[20] A just war, Sepúlveda argued, can be undertaken "to punish evil-doers," like "the many wars waged by the Greeks and Romans for this reason, with much approval from the people, whose consensus must be considered to be a law of nature."[21] Sepúlveda concluded of the Indians: "And if they refuse our rule, they may be compelled by force of arms to accept it. Such a war will be just according to natural law. Such a war would be far more just than even the war that the Romans waged against all the nations of the world in order to force them to submit to their rule."[22]

Sepúlveda's nemesis, Bartolomé de Las Casas (1484–1566), the major proponent of the view that Spanish treatment of the Indians was unjust, cited further examples from antiquity, in his case not to justify but rather to denounce the Spanish practices they had prefigured. He called Aristotle "a pagan now burning in hell."[23] Choosing a local precedent calculated to impress his audience, Las Casas highlighted Rome's mistreatment of Spaniards following its victory over Carthage. Thus, "after the Romans had defeated Spain, they bought a great number of slaves to send to the mines (in all likelihood many, if not all, were Spaniards) and they were an incredible source of wealth, although at the cost of anguish and calamities suffered from excessive work and only the strongest could survive the labor and the blows: otherwise death was a more desirable state, as Diodorus says." Terming gold "the cause of death," Las Casas added with irony that similar calamities now "occur wherever the Spaniards send Indians to the mines." Another defender of Indian rights, the theologian Francisco de Vitoria (c. 1492–1546), cited the *Aeneid* to highlight the barbarity of—the Italians who had initially refused welcome to Aeneas's ships.[24]

To some extent, then, the two sides in the Spanish debate over who the Indians were and how to treat them both shared the premise of classical precedent. By the sixteenth century, Aristotle in particular enjoyed widespread popularity in Europe. The second quarter of that century alone saw the publication of 116 editions of his works.[25] Many scholars speciously attributed to Aristotle the notion that "barbarians and slaves are by nature one," following the thirteenth-century revival by St. Thomas Aquinas of Aristotle's theory of natural slavery. But in sixteenth-century Spain, identifying the "natural slaves" proved intellectually fraught since Aristotle had not only failed to nominate the "barbarians" for this title, but he had even advocated freedom for "all slaves" who worked well.[26]

Moreover, though Aristotle had anticipated some of the agrarianist views of Cato the Censor, his progressive vision of freedom envisaged the city-state not as a danger or as prone to corruption, but as a development of cultivator communities, a "partnership finally composed of several villages," which "has attained the limit of virtually complete self-sufficiency." To Aristotle, town and country were complementary. The city was not a peril but the pinnacle of human achievement. At first the city-state, as he put it, "comes into existence for the sake of life," and then "it exists for the good life."[27]

Conquistadors who thought to bring European agriculture to the New World would gape at the cities they found there. Cortés described at length "the magnificence, the strange and marvelous things of this great city," Tenochtitlan, with its flourishing markets, temples, and "many large and beautiful houses." He compared it to Córdoba and Seville, asserting that "these people live almost like those in Spain, and in as much harmony and order as there."[28] No reading of Aristotle would help to justify destroying all that. Nevertheless, by the early seventeenth century Spanish Dominican and Franciscan authors propounded theories that the Indians of the Americas were descended from the Carthaginians.[29] At any rate, they had met a similar fate.

Conquest and Cultivation in the Caribbean

Estimates of the native population of the island of Hispaniola when the Spanish arrived in 1492 range from under 500,000 to more than 1 million.[30] Bartolomé de Las Casas, who landed there a decade later, initially suggested the 1492 population was "more than three million."[31] But in his *Historia de las Indias* (1560), Las Casas said the archbishop of Seville "told me one day" that Columbus claimed to have counted 1,100,000 "heads."[32] In 1535, Las Casas's opponent Gonzalo Fernández de Oviedo offered the same apparently official estimate for 1492 in his *Historia general y natural de las Indias*. Just 17 years later, only 60,000 natives remained alive on Hispaniola.[33] Both Spanish writers agreed that by 1510, only 46,000 Indians survived there, a figure also apparently derived from the colonial authorities.[34]

Las Casas estimated that by 1542, "our Spaniards" in the Caribbean, Mexico, and Central America had "devastated the land and exterminated the rational people who fully inhabited it," killing "more than twelve million men, women, and children." Their methods included "unjustly waging cruel and bloody wars," killing "all the native rulers and young men," and enslaving the survivors. The five indigenous kingdoms on Hispaniola, Las Casas wrote, were the first victims. There the Spanish "began their subjection of the women and children, taking them away from the Indians to use them and ill use them. . . . They attacked the towns and spared neither the children nor the aged."[35]

Direct killing caused only a minority of the Indian deaths, however. From the outset a major goal of their oppressors was enslavement. On the first day of his landfall, October 12, 1492, Columbus predicted in his journal that the Indians "should be good servants." Two days later, he reported to the king and queen of Spain: "When your Highnesses so command, they can all be carried off to Castile or held captive in the island itself, since with fifty men they would all be kept in subjection and forced to do whatever may be wished." Likening the Indians to cattle, Columbus ordered his men to capture "seven head of women, young ones and adults, and three small children." On December 16, he repeated that the Taino people of the island "are fit to be ordered about and made to work, to sow and do everything else."[36]

Columbus had in mind agriculture and precious metals. Writing to the Spanish king and queen on March 4, 1493, he said that "the trees and fruits and grasses are extremely beautiful" on the many islands he had discovered, including fertile Hispaniola and Cuba, "delectable lands for all things, and for sowing and planting and raising livestock." While Cuba had "large valleys and meadows and fields," Columbus wrote, Hispaniola had "the advantage in every respect," with its "very fruitful and broad" trees and "marvelous meadows and fields incomparable to those of Castile." Jamaica, for its part, had "gold in immeasurable quantities."[37] Hispaniola, Columbus went on, would also provide Spain's sovereigns with "so many slaves that they are innumerable; and they will come from the idolaters." He envisaged enslaving the inhabitants of the island of Caribo as well. "And when Your Highnesses give the order for me to send slaves, I hope to bring or send these for the most part."[38]

Columbus's other goals included territorial and military expansion. Having befriended Guacanagarí, ruler of Marién, one of the five kingdoms on Hispaniola, "who prided himself in calling me and having me for a brother," Columbus sailed back to Spain with about 20 Taino captives. He informed the Spanish sovereigns that in their names he had taken possession of "innumerable people and very many islands." He had left a garrison in Hispaniola adequate "to subjugate the entire island." Columbus assured the monarchs that "this beginning of the taking of the Indies and all that they contain" would bring him such wealth that within 10 years, he would "be able to pay Your Highnesses" for 10,000 cavalry and 100,000 infantry, all to be deployed "for the war and conquest of Jerusalem."[39]

Columbus was also the first in a long line of colonists to advance the claim that indigenous Americans failed to farm the land. Noting the suitability of the Caribbean archipelago for both agriculture and stock raising, he quickly added, "of which I have not seen any kind on any of these islands."[40] The bishop of Santa Marta in Colombia later described Indians as "not men with rational souls but wild men of the woods."[41] The view that "these are men" was espoused by the theologian Francisco de Vitoria, who actually omitted agriculture from his modified list of Aristotle's features of a civilization. Vitoria's more positive judgment of the Indians was that although they lacked "a diligent system of agriculture," nevertheless "they have properly organised cities, a recognizable form of marriage, magistrates, rulers, laws, industry, commerce ... [and] a form of religion."[42]

Most upholders of Spain's lawful conquest denied or denigrated Indian agriculture, but those defending Indian rights and capacities rarely accorded such importance to cultivation.[43] Las Casas, the major opponent of Spanish colonial practice, did hope to establish farming colonies in the Indies,[44] and he used agrarian metaphors to condemn opposing commentators on the treatment of Indians: having "failed to till the field of this dangerous material with the rake of Christian discretion and prudence, they sowed an arid seed, wild and unfruitful."[45] Yet when Las Casas discussed "barbarians," like Vitoria he did not dwell on their supposed failure to cultivate the land. Indeed, he wrote, "a people can be called barbarians and still be wise, courageous, prudent and lead a settled life."[46] By contrast, Las Casas's early opponent Palacios Rubios, who considered Indians natural slaves, stressed their lack of property and their small communal plots, which failed to qualify as authentic agriculture.[47] Juan Ginés de Sepúlveda admitted in 1547 that the peoples of Mexico "have cities" and "carry on commercial activities in the manner of civilized peoples," but argued that this was a secondary matter. It "only serves to prove that they are not bears or monkeys." Mexicans' real inferiority lay in their lack of private property and yeoman agriculture, revealed by the fact that "no one possesses anything individually, neither a house nor a field."[48]

When Columbus returned to Hispaniola in November 1493, he brought seeds from Spain to plant new crops. He discovered that warriors of the kingdom of Maguana, apparently responding to Spanish attacks on their property and women, had killed his garrison and destroyed the fort.[49] Employing a ruse, Spanish soldiers arrested Maguana's king, Caonabo, whom Columbus dispatched to Spain. Caonabo died en route. More chiefs from Maguana revolted in March 1495. In a Spanish offensive, 200 heavily armed soldiers and cavalry attacked and routed tens of thousands of warriors. The Maguana chiefs were killed. Columbus sent a shipload of their followers to Spain as slaves, but the crown freed them and returned them to Hispaniola.[50]

The largest of the island's five kingdoms, Maguá, occupied the central region of Hispaniola from its northern to its southern coast.[51] According to Las Casas, "The Christians fell upon them suddenly, at midnight ... [with no] time to get their weapons ... [and] did them great damage. The Christians captured the King Guarionex and many others; they killed many of the captured leaders

... burning them alive."[52] They put the chained captive Guarionex on a ship bound for Spain, which went down in the Atlantic. Meanwhile, King Guacana-garí of Marién, who Columbus noted in 1493 had offered him "much friend-ship," died in the hills, according to Las Casas, after "fleeing to escape the cruel persecutions meted out to him and his people by the Christians."[53]

With Columbus on his 1493 voyage was Las Casas's father, who had left the nine-year-old Bartolomé behind in Seville. Columbus gave the father land in the New World, and he established a provisioning business.[54] At the age of 18, Bartolomé joined him, arriving in the fleet of Hispaniola's new governor, Nico-lás de Ovando (1502–9).[55] Ovando had instructions from the Spanish queen Isabella that the Indians were "to be well treated as our subjects."[56] However, that same year a Spanish fighting dog killed a chief of the island's fourth king-dom, Higüey, provoking Indians there to revolt. "Ovando rounded up six or seven hundred of them, put them in a chief's *bohío,* or house, and had them knifed to death. He then ordered their bodies to be dragged into the adjoining plaza and publicly counted." Spaniards hanged the elderly queen of Higüey. Then, in 1503, Ovando set out with 300 troops and 60 horses, according to Las Casas, to attack the fifth kingdom, Xaraguá, "the best ordered and the most circumspect" on the island. Ovando's forces hanged the queen of Xaraguá, burned alive "three hundred Indian nobles," and killed "a countless number of the common people." Some nobles who had briefly escaped to an offshore island were sold into slavery. "I had one given me as a slave," Las Casas wrote later.[57]

Spain's Queen Isabella decreed in 1504 that should any Caribbean Indians "continue to resist," refusing either to "receive my captains and men," to be in-structed in Catholicism, or "to be in my service and obedience, they may be captured and are to be taken to these my Kingdoms and Domain and to other parts and places to be sold." Historian Neil Whitehead notes "the wide-ranging license given for the hunting down of *caribes.*"[58] When Isabella died in late 1504, she left a will calling for the Indians to be "well and justly treated" and compensated for their losses, but King Ferdinand maintained the crown's right to enslave them. Las Casas, who lived in Hispaniola until 1506, asserted that "the worst depredations" against Indians followed the news of Isabella's death. "And there were countless people that I saw burned alive or cut to pieces or tor-tured. . . . They also made slaves of many Indians."[59] Las Casas wrote that "the Spaniards, their slave-drivers and masters did not care, treating them like some stupid animals. Natives perished, working in the gold mines as well as in agricultural work. The colonists exploited them without compassion or consideration, and the iron discipline, oppression and fatigue killed native workers."[60] After returning to Europe in 1506, Las Casas was back within four years, having entered the priesthood in Rome and obtained degrees in canon law.[61] Meanwhile, Juan Garcés, a Spanish settler in Hispaniola who had "slaughtered and tortured natives," also murdered his own wife, a native chief. Las Casas wrote that Garcés, fearing retribution, "took to the hills for three or four years."[62]

Meanwhile, in 1509 the Spanish launched their conquests of the neighboring islands of Puerto Rico and Jamaica. Their population, Las Casas wrote, numbered "more than six hundred thousand souls, it has been stated." This may have been an official figure; Las Casas himself estimated "more than one million." After initial massacres, the conquistadors forced these Indians into "hard labour of the mines, thus eradicating them from the earth." Survivors numbered "no more than two hundred" in 1552.[63]

In what is now Panama, a small Spanish settlement run from 1511 by Vasco Núñez de Balboa initially coexisted with local Indians. But Balboa turned to a ruthless search for gold.[64] On January 20, 1513, he wrote to the king advocating genocide: "These Indians of Caribana have well deserved death a thousand times, because they are very bad people and have at other times killed many Christians and some of ours at the time we lost the ship there, and I do not say make them slaves according to their evil breed but even order them burnt to the last, young and old, so that no memory remains of such evil people."[65] During Balboa's march to the Pacific, an Indian village defied his forces, who opened fire. "More than six hundred Indians were slain, along with the cacique Torecha, who is said to have had his head torn off by a dog." Occupying the village on September 23, 1513, the Spaniards found over 40 "male patricians attired as females," led by Torecha's brother. Condemning them for sodomy, Balboa loosed his dogs on the whole group—all were quickly torn to pieces.[66] Returning from his discovery of the Pacific, Balboa tortured and murdered Indian chiefs who denied possessing any gold. Oviedo added that "the cruelties were not stated, but there were many." The crown later withdrew its support for such violence by distinguishing wars against Indians from those against Moors. The region's Spanish governor had Balboa executed in 1519.[67]

The struggle for justice was many-sided, like the motives of the perpetrators. Las Casas implicated even the first missionaries in the New World, the Franciscans who landed in Hispaniola in 1502, in the ill-treatment of natives. He described an official grant of land and labor to the Franciscans, which they assigned to a Spaniard in return for daily supplies of food for their friars. Using this Indian labor, the Spanish settler mined 22,750 grams of gold, "not to mention his profits from husbandry," while "incidentally killing his natives in the process."[68] Here and elsewhere Las Casas makes clear that the motive of the Spanish slave drivers was generally not to exterminate the Indians but to exploit their labor. "I do not say that they want to kill the Indians directly, because of the hatred they bear for them. They kill them because they want to be rich and get a lot of gold, which is their sole aim, through the labor and the sweat of the tortured and the unfortunate."[69] Yet these "incidental" deaths were not accidental, but clearly intentional. In the modern legal sense, regardless of their aim or motive, the colonists possessed intent to destroy the Indians, at least in part.

Strong dissension over the treatment of Indians emerged under Columbus's son Diego de Colón, who served as governor of the Indies from 1508 to 1515. On returning there from Spain, Las Casas celebrated his inaugural High Mass in Hispaniola in 1510, becoming the first priest to do so in the New World. In the same year, the first Dominican missionaries arrived on the island. According to Las Casas, the Dominican friar Pedro de Córdoba soon delivered the first sermon ever addressed to Indians on Hispaniola. At his request the Spanish settlers sent their servants and workers to his church to hear the sermon. Las Casas, who was in the audience, wrote that Indian "men and women, old and young, saw the friar sitting on a bench, a crucifix in his hands," preaching to them through interpreters.[70] This impressed both Indians and settlers.

Meanwhile, the Dominicans received an inside account from a perpetrator of atrocities against Indians. Stealing down from his refuge in the hills, the former killer Juan Garcés secretly visited the friars, repented, asked to join their order, and then, according to Las Casas, "gave the brethren detailed information of the cruelties committed against innocent natives in peace and in war." The Dominicans also received other "reports of the deaths of so many natives and witnessed the decrease of the native population." So they "decided to go public with their feelings in the pulpits."[71]

In December 1511, the friars invited Governor Colón and all Spanish residents of Santo Domingo to attend Sunday Mass.[72] With the blessing of the other 12 Dominicans on the island, Fray Antonio de Montesinos preached a pre-Christmas sermon that outraged both the Spanish authorities and the settler community. Montesinos became "the first friar to accuse the conquistadors and settlers of the exploitation, nay even destruction of the native population."[73] In his *Historia de las Indias,* which Las Casas began writing a decade later, he praised Montesinos as "a fine friar and excellent preacher."[74] In the sermon to the Spaniards, Montesinos denounced "the cruelty and tyranny you practice on these innocent natives," and their "atrocious and horrible slavery," with their masters "not even feeding them properly." He added: "They once flourished in large communities, but a great many are now dead and forgotten as a result of your actions. They die as a result of the dreadful burdens you impose on them ... you kill them by compelling them to work in gold mines."[75] Again, this comprised not outright slaughter, but the intentional infliction of life-threatening conditions, informed by knowledge of the previous outcome of such practices.

Diego de Colón and the colony's leading officials met immediately and demanded a retraction, saying that "these Indians had been granted to them by the Crown, and the monarch was the owner of all the Indies." But the next Sunday, Montesinos reiterated his charges, and "the members of the congregation left the Church in utter fury."[76] They complained to the king of Spain, dispatching a Franciscan to make their case to him. Montesinos followed him back and was able to present the king with a memorandum. Las Casas records: "Fray Antonio carried a file containing a document, divided into chapters and listing the atrocities in war and peace inflicted on the Indians of the island, all well authenticated and all perpetrated by Spanish colonists. The document listed everything: the destruction of the Indians, the war against them, the slavery and death in the mines."[77]

The king appointed a commission to investigate the charges. The opinions of only two of its dozen members have survived. One was written by "the king's preacher," Don Gil Gregorio. He quoted Aristotle's *Politics,* "where it appears that through the barbarity and wicked disposition of the people of the Antilles they may, and should be, governed as slaves." Gregorio recommended what he called "qualified slavery," apparently referring to their continued virtual serfdom in the system of Spanish-run estates known as *encomiendas.* "It is beneficial for them," he wrote, "to serve their lord without any payment or reward, for total liberty is harmful to them." Tyranny was required to govern "these Indians, who it is said, are like talking animals."[78]

Perhaps because of his royal position, Don Gregorio's view carried weight. The full commission recommended in 1512 that the Indians "should be treated as free citizens," but added six further recommendations, beginning: "Your Majesty should order the natives to work." They should have convenient "rest periods" and receive "an adequate wage," possibly "in clothing and/or objects." The Indians' labor must not impede their "instruction in our faith." The authorities should provide the natives "proper housing" and allow them to "own plots of land," and they "should be allowed sufficient time to till their own land."[79] Dissatisfied with this ruling, Montesinos returned to Hispaniola in 1513. His pessimism proved justified, for in that year the new Laws of Burgos proclaimed that the Indians were to be rounded up and concentrated near the Spanish towns, and their homes destroyed so they could not avoid "communication with the Christians and flee into the jungle." These new laws denounced the Indians, whose "sole aim and pleasure in life is to have the freedom to do with themselves exactly as they pleased."[80] Las Casas would later write that the commission's recommendation of continued servitude without eliminating the prevalent "despotic" conditions "led, inevitably, to the extinction of the Indians."[81]

By then Las Casas had already participated as a chaplain in the invasion of Cuba in 1511. He witnessed "such terrible cruelties done there as I had never seen before nor thought to see." In one unprovoked massacre, he wrote, Spanish forces led by Diego de Velásquez and Pánfilio de Narváez "put to the sword more than three thousand souls." Another Spaniard whom Las Casas knew, Roderige Albuquerque, worked 270 Indians to death in three months, and then another 500.[82]

Agricultural slavery was a major cause of the death toll, as Las Casas later explained: "The men were sent to the mines as far as eighty leagues away while their wives remained to work the soil, not with hoes or ploughshares drawn by oxen, but with their own sweat and sharpened poles that were far from equaling the equipment used for similar work in Castile. They had to make silo-like heaps for cassava plants, by digging 12 square feet 4 palms deep and 10,000 or 12,000 of such hills—a giant's work—next to one another. . . . As for the newly born, they died early because their mothers, overworked and famished, had no milk to nurse them, and for this reason, while I was in Cuba, 7,000 children died in three months." Massive death tolls could only have been a predictable result of the intentional removal of parents from children and the dispersal of entire communities. Anthony Pagden writes: "The dissolution of tribal unity and of the group's sense of social cohesion . . . contributed, of course, to the dramatic decline of the native population of the Antilles after the Spanish occupation."[83]

Las Casas broke with this system of death only gradually. For his service in Cuba, he received land and was able to exploit its conquered people as servants, "sending his share of Indians to work fields and gold mines," which he later regretted. But around 1513, he became disillusioned with the conquistador regime. He later traced his conversion to reading Ecclesiasticus (34:21–22): "The bread of the needy is their life. He that defraudeth him thereof is a man of blood. He that taketh away his neighbour's living slayeth him."[84] Las Casas had neatly identified the responsibility of the Spanish for the Indians' destruction. In modern legal terms, the conquistadors demonstrated criminal *intent,* even though in many cases their *motive* was theft rather than murder. In some cases, this deliberate, purposeful violence rose to the level of genocide; in others, genocidal massacres and extermination. After a year of misgivings, Las Casas "went public." In his sermon on Pentecost Sunday, 1514, Las Casas condemned the ill-treatment of Indians and freed his own slaves soon afterward. He began a lifelong career dedicated to exposing injustices of the Spanish colonial system.[85]

However, opponents of Las Casas's views were gathering strength. In Spain the previous year, Martí Fernández de Enciso, a prospective settler in the New World, presented a memorial to the king's confessor and the secretary of the Royal Council. Enciso argued that "when the people of Jericho did not give up their land Joshua surrounded them and killed them all except one woman who had protected his spies." On this precedent, therefore, he argued, idolatrous Indians could be required to "hand over their land," which the pope had given the king of Spain. "If the Indians would not do this, he might justly wage war against them, kill them and enslave those captured in war." The king ordered the drawing up of a proclamation stating these principles, to be read to Indians before hostilities commenced. This document, known as the Requirement (*requerimiento*), warned Indians who did not acknowledge their new masters: "We shall take you and your wives and your children, and shall make slaves of them . . . and shall do all the harm and damage that we can, as to vassals who do not obey . . . and we protest that the deaths and losses which shall accrue from this are your fault."[86] Spain could then blame its genocidal activities on the victims.

In 1514, Spain imposed a *repartimiento,* dividing the native lands and peoples among settlers and forcing the Indians to remain on their lands as virtual serfs in encomiendas.[87] This apparently formalized the status quo. At that time, just 32,000 Indians survived on Hispaniola. Over 90 percent had perished in just 22 years. A Spanish census revealed that only 22,726 were able to work.[88] According to Las Casas: "After the wars and the killings ended, when usually there survived only some boys, some women, and some children, these survivors were distributed among the Christians to be slaves." The higher the rank of the Spaniard, the more Indians were assigned: hundreds in some cases. The settlers put men to work in gold mines and sent women "into the fields of the big ranches to hoe and till the land," preventing them from cohabiting and having children. Men and women died "from the same causes, exhaustion and hunger."[89] Cruelty, violent greed, and the imposition of agricultural serfdom all took their continuing genocidal toll.

Mexico

Hernán Cortés arrived in the Indies in 1504, two years after Las Casas. He had been heading off to a military career in the Italian wars when he learned of Columbus's discovery of a New World. Making his way to Hispaniola, Cortés became a notary there. Along with Las Casas, he participated in the conquest of Cuba in 1511 and acquired gold mines on the island.[90]

In April 1519, Cortés landed a small Spanish army on the coast of Mexico, to begin the conquest of the kingdom then known as Anahuac, which was ruled by the Mexica monarch Moteucçoma (Moctezuma) from his inland capital, Tenochtitlan.[91] Anahuac was a relatively recent political empire, whose religious rituals demanded human sacrifice of infants, foreign victims, and, in most cases, captured prisoners of war. After repressing a Huaxtec revolt on the northern coast in 1487, for instance, Mexica authorities brought back to the slaughter four processions of sacrificial captives, possibly 20,000 victims.[92] Mexica domination provoked enmity among groups like the Tlaxcalans, whom the Spaniards would recruit.

A Nahua account, composed 20 years after the conquest, records the first indigenous contact with the Spanish invaders, "who came to the seashore . . . going along by boat." Five local officials "went out on the water; the water folk paddled for them. When they approached the Spaniards, they made the earth-eating gesture at the prow of the boat(s). . . . They went as if to sell them things, so that they could spy on them and contemplate them. They gave them precious cloaks, precious goods, the very cloaks pertaining to Moteucçoma which no one else could don."[93]

In Tenochtitlan, according to the Nahua account, lord Moctezuma soon

Fig. 1 *Joshua's Victory over the Amorites* (study), by Nicolas Poussin (1594–1665). The Fitzwilliam Museum, University of Cambridge. Photo © Fitzwilliam Museum. See p. 2.

Fig. 2 Cortés's troops massacre Cholulans, Mexico, October 1519 (Lienzo de Tlaxcala). From Miguel Leon-Portilla, ed., *The Broken Spears: The Atzec Account of the Conquest of Mexico* (Boston, 1992), 42. See pp. 89–90.

Fig. 3   The Spanish massacre of Aztec nobility in the main temple of Tenochtitlan, May 1520 (Codex Duran). From Miguel Leon-Portilla, ed., *The Broken Spears: The Atzec Account of the Conquest of Mexico* (Boston, 1992), 75. See p. 91.

Imprinted at London for Edward White, dwelling at the little North
doore of Paules Church, at the signe of the Gunne.

Fig. 4 Lord Arthur Grey de Wilton orders the Smerwick massacre of surrendered
Papal troops, Dingle, Ireland, November 1580. "I put in certain bands, who straight fell
to execution. There were 600 slain." Woodcut from A.M. [Anthony Munday?], *The true
reporte of the prosperous successe which God gaue vnto our English soldiours against the
forraine bands of our Romaine enemies, lately ariued, (but soone inough to theyr cost) in
Ireland, in the yeare 1580* (London, 1581). Courtesy University of Cambridge Library
and Vincent Carey. In this pamphlet, its author reported as *Newes out of Ireland* that
"five hundred and five were slaine, and seventeen hanged," with "onely two hurt of our
men. . . . Thus may we see how God fighteth for us." A.M. also asserted that the Papal
troops had received their "just desarts . . . incited by a blasphemous Antichristian Prel-
ate," and added that "the Popes holines forsoothe followed the footesteps and example
of his Predecessors, which have beene ever sowers of sedition, raisers of Rebellion,
mainteyners of disobedience, Authors of infinite bloudshedding, which is even growne
to be the Badge of their Catholike (or rather Cacolike) profession." See p. 204.

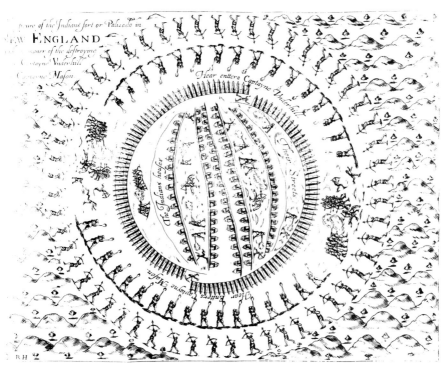

Fig. 5   The massacre of the Pequots, Mystic, Connecticut, May 26, 1637. Depicted in "The Figure of the Indians Fort or Palizado in New England and the Maner of the Destroying It by Captayne Underhill and Captayne Mason," from John Underhill, *Newes from America* (London, 1638). See pp. 230–31.

Fig. 6 "Agriculture: Plowing." From Diderot's *Encyclopédie* (Paris, 1754–72).

Fig. 7 "Agriculture: Sugar Cultivation." From Diderot's *Encyclopédie* (Paris, 1754–72).

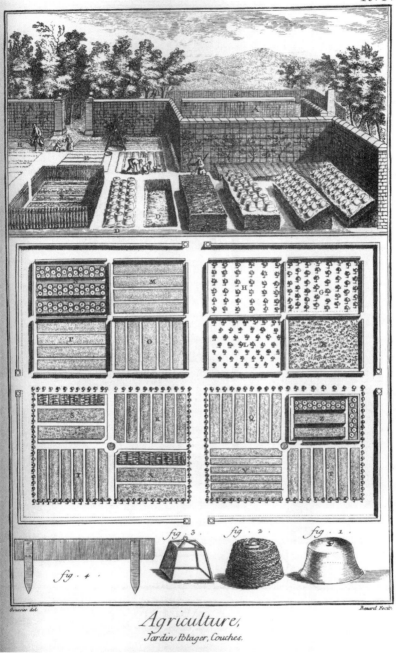

Fig. 8 "Agriculture: Kitchen Garden and Seedbeds." From Diderot's *Encyclopédie* (Paris, 1754–72).

Fig. 9 Lieutenant Colonel David Williamson's western Pennsylvania militia massacred
90 Moravian Delaware Indians, including 61 women and children, at Gnadenhutten
on March 8, 1782. Sketch from William D. Howells, *Stories of Ohio* (New York, 1897),
courtesy Beinecke Library, Yale University.

Fig. 10 *The Residence of David Twining, 1787,* by Edward Hicks (American,
1780–1849), 1845–47. Abby Aldrich Rockefeller Folk Art Museum, Colonial Williamsburg Foundation, Williamsburg, Va. Photo by Colonial Williamsburg.

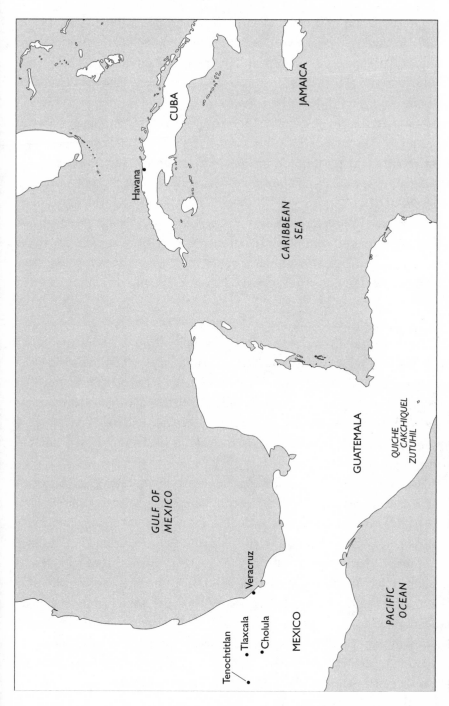

MAP 4. The Spanish conquest of Mexico and Guatemala

grew "greatly afraid and taken aback" when officials reported news of this meeting to him. "It especially made him faint when he heard how the guns went off at [the Spaniards'] command, sounding like thunder, causing people actually to swoon, blocking the ears. And when it went off, something like a ball came out from inside, and fire went showering and spitting out." The ball could make a hill seem "to crumble," or turn "a tree to dust." The Spaniards rode "deer that carried them," which were "as tall as the roof," and their huge dogs "went about panting, with their tongues hanging down," and "eyes like coal." Hearing all this, Moctezuma "seemed to faint away, he grew concerned and disturbed."[94]

The future was indeed ominous. The contemporary population of what is now Mexico has been estimated at 12 million. After Cortés's conquistadores took over Anahuac in 1519–21, that population fell by 85 percent, to as low as 1 million by 1600, in what historians call "one of history's greatest holocausts."[95]

Cortés pursued his conquest of Anahuac by means of what Pagden calls "spectacularly brutal campaigns." First, marching inland in August 1519, Cortés's army of 400 Spaniards and their coastal Indian allies confronted the Otomi people. The Nahua account composed two decades later records that "the Otomis met them with hostilities and war. But they annihilated the Otomis of Tecoac, who were destroyed completely. They lanced and stabbed them, they shot them with guns, iron bolts, crossbows. Not just a few but a huge number of them were destroyed."[96]

Cortés next faced a large opposing force in the province of Tlaxcala, which had rebelled against the Mexica of Tenochtitlan. Bernal Díaz describes several fierce battles with the Tlaxcalans, including an engagement on September 5, in which "we were killing many of them."[97] Cortés later represented to Charles V that at first he had attempted to read the royal proclamation of conquest: "I began to deliver the formal *requerimiento* through the interpreters who were with me and before a notary, but the longer I spent in admonishing them and requesting peace the more they pressed us."[98] The Indians withdrew after a day of fighting. "I had done them much harm without receiving any," Cortés reported. The next day he rode ahead with cavalry and infantry: "I burnt five or six small places of about a hundred inhabitants." The violence quickly escalated. The following day, Cortés went on, "I burnt more than ten villages, in one of which there were more than 3,000 houses, where the inhabitants fought with us, although there was no one there to help them." Several days later, Cortés reported: "I attacked two towns where I killed many people, but I did not burn the houses, lest the fires should alert the other towns nearby. At dawn I came upon another large town. . . . As I took them by surprise, they rushed out unarmed, and the women and children ran naked through the streets, and I began to do them some harm."[99]

The brutality was succeeded by a credible threat of genocide. Cortés now sent messengers to the rulers of Tlaxcala urging a peace. According to Díaz, the messengers were ordered "to say that if they did not now come to terms, we would slay all their people." Another message soon followed, announcing that unless peace was concluded "within two days we should go and kill them all and destroy their country."[100] The Tlaxcalans naturally sued for peace, and 5,000 of them joined the Spanish campaign against their enemies in Tenochtitlan.[101] The eventual victory of Cortés owed much to his success in enlisting rebel Indians to fight the Mexica. In this major case, he did so by threatening genocide.

A convincing threat required demonstration of its seriousness. The Spaniards reached the city of Cholula, a rival of Tlaxcala, in October. Cortés claimed he soon learned of a plot to destroy his army encamped there. "I decided to forestall an attack," he later informed Charles V.[102] A Nahua account, by contrast, ascribes treachery to the Spaniards: "When they arrived, there was a general summons and cry that all the noblemen, rulers, subordinate leaders, warriors, and commoners should come, and everyone assembled in the temple courtyard. . . . They did not meet the Spaniards with weapons of war." However, "[w]hen they had all come together," the Spanish "blocked the entrances."[103] In his account Cortés wrote: "I sent for some of the chiefs of the city, saying that I wished to speak with them. I put them in a room and meanwhile warned our men to be prepared, when a harquebus was fired, to fall on the many Indians who were outside our quarters and on those who were inside. And so it was done." Cortés shackled the chiefs and told them, according to Díaz, "that the royal laws decreed that such treasons as those should not remain unpunished and that for their crime they must die."[104] Cortés's captain, Andrés de Tapia, quoted him as telling the 30 Cholulan dignitaries in his custody, "you shall all die, and as a sign that you are traitors I shall destroy your city so that no edifice remains." Díaz continued: "Then he ordered a musket to be fired, which was the signal that we had agreed upon for that purpose, and a blow was given to them which they will remember for ever, for we killed many of them."[105] The Nahua account blames the Tlaxcalans for inciting the Spanish to attack the

Cholulans. "Thereupon people were stabbed, struck, and killed . . . stealthily and treacherously" (see fig. 2).[106]

Tapia confirms that Cortés "ordered most of those lords killed, leaving a few of them fettered, and ordered the signal given the Spaniards to attack the men in the courtyards and kill them all, and so it was done. They defended themselves . . . [but] most of them died anyway. . . . This done, the Spaniards and Indians in our company went out in squads to different parts of the city, killing warriors and burning houses." Cortés, who attacked on horseback, claimed that the Cholulans were "well prepared" but "easy to disperse," as they were taken by surprise without their leaders. The result was a massacre. Cortés wrote: "We fought so hard that in two hours more than three thousand men were killed."[107]

At this point the Tlaxcalan allies arrived, having fought their way into the city. Some 5,000 of them now joined the Spanish.[108] Tapia reported that they "looted the city and destroyed everything possible." Díaz described the Tlaxcalans "plundering and making prisoners and we could not stop them."[109] Cortés continued the assault on the Cholulans: "I ordered some towers and fortified houses from which they were attacking us to be set on fire. And so I proceeded through the city fighting for five hours or more."[110] Many Cholulan priests who refused to surrender were incinerated when the Spanish burned down what Tapia called their "principal idol's tower." Tapia concluded: "So everything possible was done to destroy this city, but [Cortés] ordered us to refrain from killing women and children. The destruction took two days, during which many of the inhabitants went to hide in the hills and fields." Years later Cortés's secretary Francisco López de Gómara wrote that the Spaniards "were dripping with blood and walked over nothing but dead bodies."[111] Most estimates put the Cholulan death toll at 6,000, some as high as 20,000.[112]

Cortés allowed the city to be repopulated and freed surviving chiefs. The terror had had its desired effect. The Nahua account states: "And all the common people went about in a state of excitement; there were frequent disturbances, as if the earth moved and (quaked), as if everything were spinning before one's eyes. People took fright."[113] Díaz concurred. "This affair and punishment at Cholula," he wrote, "became known throughout the provinces of New Spain and if we had a reputation for valour before, from now on they took us for sorcerers." Cortés blamed Moteucçoma for the conflict. He informed Mexica royal envoys that "now I intended to enter his land at war doing all the harm I could as an enemy, though I regretted it very much as I had always wished rather to be his friend and ask his advice on all the things that must be done in this land."[114]

Hoping to awe the Spaniards with the magnificence of his capital, Moteucçoma admitted them to Tenochtitlan. Cortés surprised his host, arresting him as a hostage and taking over the city in his name.[115] When a rival Spanish force approached, however, Cortés marched out to confront it, leaving Pedro de Alvarado in command of Tenochtitlan. In early May 1520, Alvarado attacked and murdered a large number of the Mexica nobility during a ceremonial feast (see fig. 3).[116] This provoked an uprising in the city. In the eyes of the population, Moteucçoma had by now lost his authority. Cortés returned to a maelstrom of Mexica opposition. A crowd assaulted and killed Moteucçoma, whose brother assumed the throne. The Spaniards had to retreat from the city.

In January 1521, Cortés's troops approached Tenochtitlan once again. They attacked the lakeside town of Ixtapalapa. Cortés considered that city's 10,000 inhabitants "ill-disposed to us" and, he reported, "I determined to march against them." He went on: "[W]e drove them back into the water, some up to their chests and others swimming, and we took many of the houses on the water. More than six thousand of them, men, women, and children, perished that day, for our Indian allies, when they saw the victory which God had given us, had no other thought but to kill, right and left."[117]

The toll escalated in the battles for the capital itself, in part because of relentless Indian attempts to capture Spanish soldiers alive for ritual torture or sacrifice rather than kill them on the battlefield. Massive numbers of Indians perished in these asymmetrical engagements, ideologically and militarily unequal. The Spaniards enjoyed the clear advantage of a preparedness to kill indiscriminately. They destroyed much of the city and reduced its people to "human wreckage."[118] Inga Clendinnen writes of the end of the Mexica capital: "As they filed out of the wreckage which had been Tenochtitlan, the Spaniards were waiting. They took the prettier women and the young boys, branding them on the face to mark them as possessions, and set the men to raising a Spanish city on the ruins of their own." They had Aztec priests torn apart by dogs. In 1523, Cortés hanged the defeated emperor Cuauhtemoc, along with the lords of his allied kingdoms. A Mexica lament begins:

> Broken spears lie in the roads,
> We have torn our hair in our grief.
> The houses are roofless now, and their walls
> Are red with blood ... our inheritance, our city, is lost and dead.[119]

A new militaristic, agrarian slave state succeeded the Mexica empire. His secretary Gómara wrote that Cortés quickly imported from the Caribbean both warhorses and draft horses as well as brood stock and agricultural items: "sugar cane, mulberry trees for silk, vine cuttings, and other plants." Cortés sent to Spain "for arms, iron, guns, powder, tools, forges for fabricating implements, and for olive pits, seeds, and nuts, which do not yield in the islands."[120] By October 1524 he was able to report to Charles V: "In the whole territory, from one sea to another, the natives serve without complaint." But there were two exceptions, the provinces Zapotecas and Mixes, "very rich in mines." Cortés sent two expeditions against them. The second, comprising 150 Spaniards with four artillery pieces, set out in February 1524. Cortés wrote to the king: "When these people have been conquered, the men who are going there say they will lay waste the country and enslave the inhabitants for having been so rebellious." Cortés concurred with this ambition. "I ordered that those who were taken alive should be branded with Your Highness's mark, and that once those belonging to Your Majesty had been set aside the rest should be distributed amongst the men on the expedition."[121]

Like Columbus in Hispaniola before him, Cortés not only sought precious metals and slaves but also made efforts to foster agriculture in Mexico, even during the height of his war of conquest. As he recalled in a letter written in 1520 to Charles V: "According to the Spaniards who went there, that province of Malinaltebeque was very well provided for setting up farms. I therefore asked Mutezuma [Moteucçoma] to have a farm built there for Your Majesty; and he was so diligent in all this that in two months about ninety-five bushels of maize were sown, and fifteen of beans and two thousand cacao plants." Cortés informed the emperor that the new farm included four houses and a water tank, 2,000 ducks and chickens, "and other things for dairy farming, which the Spaniards who saw them many times valued at twenty thousand pesos de oro."[122] These agricultural projects multiplied, but after Moteucçoma's death local rebellions brought them to an end, as Cortés told the emperor in 1522. "I ordered, as I informed Your Majesty in a previous account, that certain farms should be built for Your Majesty, in two or three of the most suitable provinces, and that each farm should produce grain and other things." For this purpose Cortés had sent Spaniards to various provinces. With one exception, he now wrote, "all those provinces were in revolt." Rebels had "killed the Spaniards on the farms."[123] In April 1521, the two survivors in the single pacified province wrote for help, stating that "it is time to harvest the cacao and the Culuans hinder us with the fighting."[124]

Agriculture remained "a matter of great concern for Cortés," according to Pagden. Cultivation was a key aspect of his vision for Mexico.[125] A member of Cortés's household became one of the first farmers in New Spain and built one of the first sugar mills near Mexico City. Each Spanish cavalryman who had brought his own horse received enough land to plant 100 "hills" of potatoes.[126] Cortés reported to Charles V in 1524 that many indigenous people "have their own plantations where they grow all the vegetables grown in Spain of which we have been able to obtain seeds. I assure Your Caesarean Majesty that if they could but be given plants and seeds from Spain, and if your Highness were pleased to command them to be sent to us, as I requested in my earlier report, there would in a very short time be a great abundance of produce, for these Indians are much given to cultivating the soil and planting orchards."[127] He reiterated "the need we have of plants of all sorts, for this land is well suited to all kinds of agriculture." Yet, Cortés complained, "until now nothing has been sent." He implored the Spanish sovereign to ensure "that every ship shall bring a certain number of plants and shall be forbidden to sail without them." He issued ordinances to Spaniards in Mexico to "oblige them to settle on the land." They were also to marry or to bring their wives from Spain within 18 months. From the beginning, Cortés had set out to "people" (*poblar*) the new land with Spanish colonists. As Pagden writes, he aimed "to establish a European agricultural economy." Thus, as well as a victim of genocide, Mexico became the New World's first European settlement.[128]

Guatemala and Colombia

As noted in the introduction, Las Casas called the conquest of Guatemala a "holocaust."[129] In late 1523, Cortés dispatched his lieutenant Pedro de Alvarado, butcher of the Mexica nobility, to subjugate the kingdoms to the south. Alvarado took 120 cavalry, 300 infantry, and four artillery pieces.[130] *The Annals of the Cakchiquels*, composed in the 1570s by a Mayan noble who witnessed the ensuing campaigns, corroborate many of Las Casas's accusations. For instance, Las Casas claimed in 1552 that the Quiché monarch and nobles of Ultatlán "came out to welcome" Alvarado, "borne in litters, accompanied by trumpets." But the next day, Alvarado unsuccessfully demanded gold from them, and in "a great massacre," he "had them burnt alive without trial or sentencing."[131] The annals, written later in Cakchiquel Maya, stated that in February 1524, "all the Quiché who had gone out to meet the Spaniards were exterminated. Then the Quichés were destroyed before Xelahub." According to the annals, Alvarado "tortured" and then "burned" the Quiché kings.[132] He confirmed this in his own report to Cortés: "And seeing that by occupying their land and burning it, I could bring them into the service of His Majesty, I decided to burn the lords … for the good and benefit of this country, I burned them and ordered that the city be burned to its foundations."[133]

The annals also report that Alvarado quickly summoned the Cakchiquel Maya to "come to kill the Quichés" and collect their tribute for him. In April–May 1524, Alvarado marched against and "destroyed" the Zutuhils, then turned and "killed those of Atacat." He returned in two months, demanding that the Cakchiquel lords pay him 1,200 gold pesos: "If you do not bring with you all of the money of the tribes, I will burn you." At this the Cakchiquel lords demurred, and they later wrote: "Half of the money had already been delivered when we escaped. . . . Ten days after we fled from the city, [Alvarado] began to make war upon us." In September 1524, "they began to make us suffer. We scattered ourselves under the trees, under the vines, oh, my sons. All our tribes joined in the fight." More Spanish attacks in 1525 "killed many brave men." Seizing Yximché, the Cakchiquel capital, Alvarado "burned the city" on February 7, 1526.[134]

Cortés wrote to Charles V in 1526 that the regions of "Utlatan and Guatemala" had "rebelled on account of certain ill treatment they received, [and] have never again been pacified." Pedro de Alvarado, Cortés continued, "makes constant war against them" with 700 Spanish troops, and "at times as many as ten thousand of our Indian allies," but still he had not defeated the Guatemalans: "rather each day they grow stronger through the people who come to join them."[135] On March 27, 1527, according to *The Annals of the Cakchiquels,* "our slaughter by the Spaniards began. The people fought them, and they continued to fight a prolonged war. Death struck us anew, but none of the people paid the tribute." Finally, in 1528, some Cakchiquels began to submit. The next year their monarchs surrendered, after five years of resistance "under the trees, under the vines." Alvarado imposed "heavy tribute," including gold; "four hundred men and four hundred women were delivered to him to be sent to wash gold. All the people extracted the gold." A Cakchiquel king died in 1532 while "washing gold." Alvarado put 800 more men and women to work building Guatemala City. Meanwhile, Spanish forces conquered Honduras and Nicaragua as well.

Alvarado marched into Honduras and "destroyed . . . the people of Tzutzampan and those of Choloma," along with other towns.[136] Pagden writes that enslavement of Indians now became "the chief economic activity of the otherwise impoverished region of Nicaragua."[137]

For Guatemalans, at least, some relief was in sight. The Royal Audience of Mexico sent Alonso de Maldonado in May 1536 to head the Municipal Council of Guatemala and to impeach Alvarado, who fled to Spain. The Cakchiquels welcomed this. "Soon there was no more washing of gold; the tribute of boys and girls was suspended. Soon also there was an end to the deaths by fire and hanging, and the highway robberies of the Spaniards ceased. Soon the people could be seen travelling on the roads again as it was before the tribute commenced."[138] However, in September 1539, Alvarado arrived back from Spain, unimpeached. Maldonaldo left "at once." On May 19 the next year, fearing another revolt, the Municipal Council of Guatemala asked Alvarado to deal with the imprisoned Cakchiquel and Quiché monarchs: "to take them away in your fleet or, if they have given cause, to punish them." Alvarado quickly hanged the kings, and executed other lords in 1541. He died in July of that year.[139] The death toll during his rule remains unknown. According to Las Casas, Alvarado had described Guatemala in 1524 as "even more populous than Mexico," which had 12 million inhabitants. Las Casas estimated that by 1540 "he and his brothers and other Spaniards have slain four or five million souls."[140] That would almost constitute a holocaust in scale as well as in name. The death toll in Mexico did exceed half its population, while Alvarado's depredations in Guatemala seem yet more brutal, but there is no way to establish an accurate figure.

Meanwhile, in South America, in what is now Colombia, other settlers had founded the town of Cartagena, naming it for the Spanish city established by the ancient Carthaginians. Cristóbal Guerra initiated conflict there by staging what Las Casas called "particularly fierce" attacks that provoked bitter Indian resistance. Then, in 1504, Queen Isabella had named Cartagena in her decree that authorized "capture" and sale into slavery of those who "continue to resist."[141] Then, Las Casas added, "the king gave permission to declare an all-out war against them and capture them as slaves." According to the writer Cristóbal de la Tovilla, as quoted by Las Casas, the slave-trading Spanish governor Alonso de Hojeda dropped anchor in Cartagena "at the King's order to make war against the Indians" for their retaliation against Spanish slave raiders.[142] Las Casas wrote that Hojeda attacked the village of Calamar, "knifing, killing and capturing right and left," burned eight Indians alive, and carried off 60 in his slave ships. He then raided the town of Turbaco, whose inhabitants fled but "ran straight into the Spaniards who disemboweled them and cut them to pieces. If they fled to their huts, the Spaniards burned them alive. . . . [They] committed incredible slaughter there, sparing neither women nor children, old nor young." Hojeda was thus "the first to assault the continent and kill, plunder and enslave."[143]

He set a 30-year pattern there. The bishop of Cartagena, Fray Tomás de Toro, wrote to the king on May 31, 1535: "The whole land is in turmoil and the Indians greatly aroused because of the cruelties and maltreatment of the Christians. . . . Their hands are bloody with slaying and cleaving asunder children, hanging Indians, cutting off hands, and roasting to death certain Indian men and women . . . all because they will not tell them where to find gold."[144]

In the Wake of Genocide

The genocide in Mexico ended only gradually, beginning with the crown's appointment in 1535 of the first viceroy of New Spain, Antonio de Mendoza, who became known as "the good viceroy" during his term in office (1535–51). Gómara reported Mendoza establishing "several towns, after the fashion of Roman colonies."[145] Violence persisted, and on several occasions, Mendoza allegedly had Indians thrown to dogs as he watched. In 1546 the report of a secret inquiry into his conduct stated: "After the capture of the hill of Mixtón, many of the Indians seized in its conquest were put to death in his presence and by his orders. Some were placed in line and blown into bits by cannon fire; others were torn to pieces by dogs, and others were given to Negroes to be put to death, and these killed them with knife thrusts while others were hung."[146]

Placed in context, however, this was only one of a list of charges inspired by Cortés and leveled at his successor, Mendoza. In most of their complaints recorded by the 1546 inquiry, conquistadores accused the viceroy of "favoring some more than others" in his assignment of the ownership of land and its inhabitants. Legal suits proliferated over the transfer of estates, including their Indian populations. Mendoza allegedly "had not seen fit to provide the present keeper of the arsenal," a Cortés partisan, "with Indian districts." In one case, "he should have given all the Indians in *encomienda* to the said Juan Enríquez." Another complaint asserted that "the viceroy gave the said Indians in *encomienda* to Juan Guerrero, who married a bastard mestiza." Mendoza was in fact exonerated of these charges and advised his successor: "Treat the Indians like any other people and do not make special rules and regulations for them."[147]

Pope Paul III's papal bull of 1537 had reiterated that Native Americans were rational beings with souls whose lives and property should be protected. Two years later, the leading Spanish theologian Francisco de Vitoria (c. 1492–1546) noted reports of "so many massacres, so many innocent men despoiled and robbed."[148] The Cortés of Valladolid appealed to the king of Spain in 1542 to "order an end to the cruelties committed in the Indies against the Indians, for God will be served thereby and the Indies preserved instead of being depopulated as is happening at present."[149] Spain passed the New Laws in 1542, to abolish Indian slavery and the encomienda system.[150]

But the damage was done. As Las Casas and others made clear, without access to the modern term, genocide had occurred, as well as extermination. Despite some exaggerations, Las Casas's main charges had been proved substantially correct.[151] Other contemporary sources concurred. In 1541, even his critic Toribio de Motolinía wrote: "He alone Who counts the drops of rain water and the sands of the sea can count all the deaths and the devastated lands" of the Caribbean. In the Bahamas, for instance, "[m]any of these people the Spaniards killed and consigned to perdition. . . . I have seen and known many in this land and have confessed some of its people, who are very intelligent and conscientious. Now, why would not the others have proved to be the same, if the Spaniards had not been in such a hurry to kill them and get them out of the way?"[152] In Hispaniola, only 200 Indians survived in 1542, and the population decline continued. Gerónimo de Mendieta wrote in his *Historia Eclesiástica Indiana* that by 1595 the natives of the Caribbean had been "completely wiped out."[153] While this was not totally accurate, and although most of the Spanish had no genocidal motive to exterminate the Indians, they nonetheless for extractive purposes deliberately and consciously imposed violent measures that they knew would have that deadly effect.

Just three years after the New Laws abolished encomienda in 1542, a counteroffensive by *encomenderos* threatened the laws' enforceability and convinced the emperor to repeal most of their provisions. In this atmosphere, in 1544, Juan Ginés de Sepúlveda wrote his dialogue *Democrates secundus sive de justis causis belli apud Indios*. Having previously urged Charles V to launch a new crusade against the Turks, Sepúlveda now advocated "solid glory" for Spain in "just wars" against Indians.[154] He added a strong voice to Spanish chauvinism. "More than any other country," Sepúlveda wrote, Spain "hates and detests depraved individuals." He proclaimed "the absence of gluttony and lasciviousness among the Spaniards. Is there any nation in Europe that can compare with Spain in frugality and sobriety?" Like Cato the Censor in republican Rome, Sepúlveda feared that mercantile activity would corrupt Spain's ethnic purity: "through commercial dealings with foreigners extravagance has invaded the tables of the mighty . . . one must hope that in a short time will be reestablished the pure and innate parsimony of our native customs."[155]

As much as Spanish superiority, Sepúlveda emphasized Indian inferiority. He wrote in Ciceronian Latin, with his literary mouthpiece Democrates speaking "the language of a Roman moralist"—to a Lutheran interlocutor.[156] One modern author has defended Sepúlveda against charges of "recommending enslavement and destruction of the Indians," asserting that he favored only their "serfdom" rather than slavery; he notes that Sepúlveda's refusal to depart from classical Latin prevented him distinguishing "slave" from "serf." His classical term *servus* (slave) had to encompass both meanings. It had come to clearly denote "serf" only in the medieval Latin that Sepúlveda abjured, in which *esclavus* meant "slave."[157] He avoided the latter term, but apparently considered it more important to write only in classical Latin than to make this distinction (which Aristotle made).[158] Sepúlveda's thinking is nevertheless clear. He considered the Indians slaves or serfs "by nature" (*natura servus*). He described them as "barbarous and inhuman peoples abhorring all civil life, customs, and virtue." They were "as inferior to Spaniards as children are to adults, women are to men, . . . and finally, I shall say, almost as monkeys are to men." Distinguishing "beasts" and "barbarians" from "human men" (*humani*), Sepúlveda termed Indians *homunculi,* a Latin term denoting biologically unnatural creatures of magic origin, "in whom hardly a vestige of humanity remains." He likened Indians to "pigs with their eyes fixed always on the ground." Only with "the passage of time," rule by "our laws and customs," and Christianity, could they "become more human."[159]

The two sides of Sepúlveda's argument merged in his discussion of Indian and Spanish violence. In the case of the Mexica, Sepúlveda was right to denounce their "prodigious sacrifice of human victims, the extreme harm that they inflicted on innocent persons, their horrible banquets of human flesh."[160] Yet given what he must have known of Spain's record in Mexico by 1544, Sepúlveda's claim that unlike the Indians, "our soldiers, even in their personal vices and sins, are not accustomed to act contrary to the laws of nature" constituted a cover-up and deliberate denial. He preferred to praise the sack of Rome by a mixed European force in 1527: "There was scarcely a single Spaniard among those who died from the plague who did not order all the goods he had stolen from the Roman citizens returned in his last will and testament." Neither Italian nor German troops did that, Sepúlveda claimed. Nor would Indians merit compensation, he went on to assert, given "the gentleness and humanity of our soldiers, who, even in battle, after the attainment of victory, expressed great concern and care in saving the greatest possible number of the conquered."[161] Questioned by members of the Council of the Indies and condemned by two Spanish universities, Sepúlveda's book was not published.

However, the contending claims of Sepúlveda and Las Casas led to their famous debate at Valladolid in 1550. Las Casas argued that "impious bandits" had devastated the Indies, leaving them "by the death of thousands of peoples almost like a desert." The majority of the judges agreed with him but declined to make their verdict public.[162] Though proven wrong, Sepúlveda deployed his scholarship and stature to minimize both public debate and remedial action.

The Franciscan missionary Pedro de Gante predicted in 1552 that deportations of Indians from their homes would destroy them all within 40 years. The Council of the Indies received detailed reports of significant population losses that followed the deportations.[163] Mexico's demographic decline reached such a rate that by 1600 only 1 million Indians survived, a loss of about 11 million in 80 years of Spanish rule. Yet Luis Sánchez, a colonist of Nueva Granada who had participated in five expeditions of conquest during his 18 years in Spanish America, suggested that other regions may have suffered even more than Mexico. In 1566, Sánchez wrote to the president of the Council of Castile deploring the "destruction and extinction, which has been and is going on daily" in the New World. He charged that Spaniards "have for the greater part left not a living creature [in] lands which were once full of Indians," where "millions of people . . . have been killed." In an ominous comparison, Sánchez added: "I do not speak of Mexico, for I understand that there has always been in Mexico a show of justice and favor toward the Indians."[164]

Despite Las Casas's efforts, his victory in the Valladolid debate, and the outcry from other missionaries, the cult of antiquity, imperial ideology, and race prejudice of Spanish court intellectuals like Sepúlveda helped legitimize extraordinary colonial cruelty, contributing to the genocidal outcome. But so had the expansionist aims of the crown and the agrarian impositions of the settler regime. In 1534 the crown attempted to reconcile Spanish interests with those of the Indians by urging Cortés to import more cattle into Mexico, so that the Indians "may have meat to eat."[165] But the Spanish judge (*oidor*) Alonso de Zorita summed up the situation in Mexico 30 years later: "The Indians have also been laid low by the labor of making sheep, cattle and pig farms, of fencing these farms, of putting up farm buildings, and by their labor on roads, bridges, water courses, stone walls, and sugar mills. For this labor, in which they were occupied for many days and weeks, they were taken away from their homes, their accustomed tempo of work and mode of life were disrupted; and on top of everything else they had to supply the materials for these projects at their own cost and bring them on their own backs without receiving any pay or even food. Now they are paid, but so little that they cannot buy enough to eat."[166] Zorita also revealed that even a fellow judge could mingle blood and soil: "I knew an *oidor* who said publicly from his dais in a loud voice, that if water were lacking to irrigate the Spaniards' farms, it would be done with the blood of the Indians."[167]

Though the conquistadores were brutal, the major killers were the new diseases they brought—measles, influenza, typhus, pneumonia, tuberculosis, diphtheria, pleurisy and, in 1518, smallpox. Spaniards did not deliberately spread these diseases to destroy Indians. Yet their massacres, enslavement, separation of families, and forced labor not only took their own toll but also made the Indian population far more vulnerable to the introduced diseases than if their societies had been left intact. Tzvetan Todorov explains that the deliberate mass murder, the maltreatment, and the "microbe shock" were by no means discrete causes, but mutually reinforcing. Of sixteenth-century Mexico, Todorov writes: "If the word genocide has ever been applied accurately to a case, this is it."[168]

CHAPTER 3

Guns and Genocide in East Asia,
1400–1600

As in fifteenth-century Spain and other monarchies of early modern continental Europe, ethnic allegiances also remained fluid in the large, regionalized, multiethnic kingdoms of early modern Southeast Asia. Historian Victor Lieberman points out that Southeast Asia's heterogeneous courts and hinterlands still made "no formal demand that rulers be of the same ethnicity as their subjects." In *Strange Parallels,* his study of a millennium of state formation and integration in Southeast Asia, Lieberman shows how "projects of ethnic differentiation" proceeded only fitfully there, enlisting "universal religions" like Confucianism and Buddhism as well as emerging cults of antiquity associated with each. The pretensions of competing Southeast Asian dynasties to universal rule and responsibility fostered the slow ethnopolitical consolidation of the early modern kingdoms of Vietnam, Cambodia, Burma, and Thailand.[1] Increasingly centralized Confucian and Buddhist states emerged in Southeast Asia along with intensification of agriculture, demographic growth, and, after the establishment of China's Ming dynasty in 1368, the diffusion of new technology. All this brought the region unprecedented wealth, new territorial expansionism, and ethnic conflict, which threatened the survival of its smaller polities.[2]

From the fourteenth to the eighteenth centuries, as in Europe, new notions of ethnic difference and a heightened sense of both ancient and agrarian models combined explosively with the introduction of firearms to exacerbate ethnoreligious conflicts. The next two chapters analyze cases of both genocide and more limited genocidal massacres in Asian states during the four centuries to 1800. Vietnam's new Confucian civilizational mission against its neighbors, Japan's territorial unification and invasions of Korea, an Iberian conquistador assault on Cambodia, the expansion of Java's powerful new Mataram dynasty and its brutal purge of Javanese Islam, and, in Burma and Cambodia, increasingly exclusive ethnoreligious identities based on Buddhism all produced outbursts of unprecedented mass killing.

The Vietnamese Destruction of Champa, 1390–1509

When Columbus set out on his last voyage in 1503, he still thought that Central America was eastern Asia. He suspected he had located Marco Polo's "Ciamba," the Southeast Asian kingdom of Champa.[3] Polo had passed through that realm in 1295, when the Cham people, mostly Hinduized, dominated what is now the central coast of Vietnam. However, by the time Columbus imagined he was nearing Champa in 1503, it had endured catastrophic destruction.

From the eleventh century, the intermittent campaigns for southward expansion of soldiers and settlers from the Vietnamese Buddhist kingdom of Dai Viet, based in the Red River basin of what is now northern Vietnam, provoked bitter wars with Chams. Until the fifteenth century, Champa gave as good as it got. Supplied with weapons by China's Sung dynasty, it was a formidable military and naval opponent, deploying cavalry and archery, Chinese-style crossbows, and ballistas. When the Mongols briefly invaded Champa in 1282, its defenders deployed 100 "Muslim three-component arm trebuchets."[4]

The initial military goals of both Champa and Dai Viet, in the words of historian John K. Whitmore, were reciprocal: "political subordination and loot, not territorial conquest or the reformulation of the local civilization."[5] After one eleventh-century war, Dai Viet deported its Cham captives north and resettled them in the Vietnamese heartland. A Cham community survived there and remained recognizably foreign to a Vietnamese visitor to the district two centuries later.[6] Meanwhile, economic and demographic expansion doubled the population of Dai Viet's Red River delta to an estimated 2.4 million between 1200 and 1340. A school of Confucian literati slowly emerged from a new agrarian class of modestly wealthy "lower landlords" farming private holdings with hired laborers and tenants rather than the serfs used by the Buddhist aristocracy.[7]

Interstate conflict escalated with the pressures on the land frontier in the fourteenth century. By 1400 Cham attacks had combined with falling land pro-

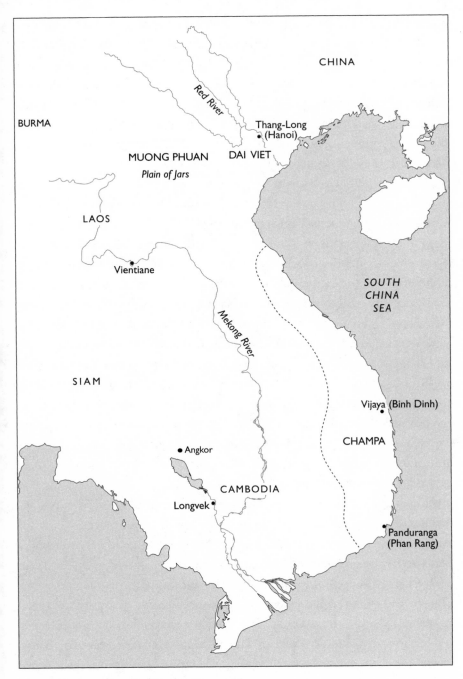

CHINA

Red River

BURMA

Thang-Long
(Hanoi)

MUONG PHUAN

Plain of Jars

DAI VIET

LAOS

Vientiane

SOUTH
CHINA
SEA

Mekong River

SIAM

Vijaya (Binh Dinh)

Angkor

CHAMPA

CAMBODIA

Longvek

Panduranga
(Phan Rang)

MAP 5. Early modern Dai Viet and its neighbors

ductivity and average farm sizes, along with drought, disease, and domestic rebellions, to cause a one-third reduction in the Red River delta population, to 1.6 million. Cham armies repeatedly invaded Dai Viet from 1360 to 1390 and requested aid from China, but the new Ming dynasty (1368–1644) declined to intervene.[8] Champa's fleet sacked the Vietnamese capital Thang-long (Hanoi) in 1371. Cham troops burned down the royal palace and archives and ransacked the treasury, plunging Dai Viet into "an era of crises." Six years later, Dai Viet's king fell in battle besieging the Cham capital.[9] Vietnamese annals record that the Chams captured a Vietnamese prince, forcing him to marry a Cham princess. They took Hanoi again in 1379 and once more in 1383. Dai Viet considered Cham armies "a perpetual threat to the kingdom."[10]

The sense of crisis in Dai Viet nourished a new intellectual movement with ominous implications for Champa. What Whitmore calls "the rise of 'antiquity'" in Dai Viet began among its Confucian literati, in the very era of Europe's own classical revival.[11] Around 1340, the year before Petrarch became Rome's poet laureate, the ruler of Dai Viet summoned the Confucian scholar Chu Van An (1292–1370) to the Hanoi court. Skilled in the Chinese language and classical texts, Chu Van An served for the next two decades as royal tutor and director of the National Academy. Whitmore calls him "the top textual specialist and ideologue of that world." Urging a reduction in Buddhist influence and "direct confrontation with the ills of existing society," Chu Van An "looked to connect his age with that of the sage rulers" of ancient China by "returning to antiquity" (Ch. fu-ku; Viet. phuc-co), re-creating "the ideals of that past in the present." He fostered what he called "ancient writing" (Ch. ku-wen; Viet. co-van) and a new school of "socially conscious poetry among the Vietnamese elite." An's core teachings were, in Whitmore's words: "[U]se the Chinese texts, concentrate on Antiquity and how it applies to the present day, be aware of the problems of the Buddhist present . . . and know the need for such local institutions of textual study as his own." One of his students wrote: "I have studied the texts. I focused on (the questions of) Antiquity and today, as well as the dao of the sages by which they transformed their people."[12]

In the early 1360s, Chu Van An demanded the execution of seven "treacherous" courtiers, the new king's "powerful favourites." His advice was rejected, and An "resigned from public life."[13] From a hilltop east of Hanoi, he pronounced caustically: "Fish splash the pond—but where have dragons gone?"[14] During his "exemplary retirement," An's influence persisted; he returned to court in 1370 for the next king's coronation. When he died he became the first

Vietnamese scholar admitted into the Temple of Literature. During the next decade, at the height of the Cham wars, An's students completed the reconstruction of a Vietnamese mythic history and an aggressive new ideology based on the metaphor "writing and chariots." The new school of thought indigenized China's ancient "sage rulers" by Vietnamizing the classical realm of Van-lang mentioned in Chinese records. As Whitmore puts it: "This Antiquity of the Sinic world became a Vietnamese Antiquity." A new ancient ethnic model took shape. Chu Van An's student Pham Su Manh praised the "pure, simple customs" of the primordial Viet people of Van-lang. An official edict warned Vietnamese in 1374 not to "dress in the fashion of northerners [Chinese] or copy the speech of the Chams and Lao countries."[15] Historian Nguyen The Anh considers this "the first sign" of Dai Viet unease at Cham cultural influence.[16] Still, Whitmore finds a continuing equilibrium between the Cham and Vietnamese courts, neither yet "viewing the other as culturally inferior."[17]

At the same time, the advent of the Ming dynasty in China in 1368 ushered in a military revolution. Chinese troops now possessed "the most advanced firearms in the early modern world." From the late fourteenth century, the new weapons spread to mainland Southeast Asia, with "far-reaching implications." Dai Viet in particular, whose armies had long deployed catapults, scaling ladders, and other siege techniques, quickly acquired and mastered the technology of "war rockets," cannon (using bamboo tubes rather than iron), and other gunpowder weaponry. In 1390, Vietnamese infantry cut down the Cham warrior-monarch Che Bong Nga (r. 1360–90) in a volley of fire from handheld muskets, a new weapon that sparked chaos among the Cham troops. Severing Che Bong Nga's head, the victorious Vietnamese then routed his navy, saving Dai Viet from destruction and finally shifting the balance of power against Champa.[18] Whitmore considers Che Bong Nga "the last great king of classical Southeast Asia." A new era was beginning.[19]

Responding in part to the shock of the 1371 Cham invasion, the Vietnamese intellectual current that in the 1380s began to merge indigenous thought with classical now grew ever more vigorous and ambitious. The rising usurper Ho Quy Ly carried out a series of violent purges and came to dominate the Dai Viet court. He moved to strengthen the state against both the Cham threat and domestic disintegration. By 1395, Quy Ly was presenting himself in the role of China's ancient Duke of Chou. He claimed descent from a mythical Chinese emperor whom Confucius had praised for governing "efficiently without exertion." Quy Ly favored the Five Classics of Confucianism over the more recent

Four Books of the Neo-Confucians, enforced sharp distinctions of rank, and placed a maximum limit on landholdings.[20] Soon, Whitmore writes, "[c]lassical Chinese learning had grown in influence to the point where the head of state made use of it in a rather eccentric way for his own purposes." These purposes included Quy Ly's aim "to thrust central power and control throughout Vietnamese territory." He had the reigning king murdered, provoking a coup attempt that Quy Ly repressed by executing 370 dissidents, seizing their possessions, enslaving their female relatives, and burying alive or drowning the males of all ages. Ho Quy Ly's reign of terror extended as "the search for the guilty dragged on for years," along with new purges. Quy Ly also launched four new attacks on Champa in 1400–1403, conquering half of its territory despite Chinese warships helping to defend it. "For the first time," Whitmore writes, "the Vietnamese made a specific attempt to carve out new territory and fill it with their own people." Quy Ly dispatched brigades of landless peasants south to cultivate and patrol the new frontier. He urged a border official in 1405 not to relent but to give priority to military and agricultural tasks: "Instruct the soldiers and the farmers diligently. . . . Pulling out the border soldiers, what kind of harvest is that?" Vietnamese forces developed a new fire lance, superior even to those of the Ming. Ho Quy Ly's son, the "left grand councilor" of his court, was an expert at manufacturing this weapon.[21]

A cult of antiquity, an expansionist drive, advanced military technology, and a fetish of cultivation were by now all in place. Ethnic hostility, however, remained blurred. Ho Quy Ly still tried to assimilate captured Cham leaders and woo defectors by giving them Vietnamese names and appointments. Dai Viet continued "to treat the Chams as legitimate competitors and potential allies."[22]

The Ming invasion of 1407 ended Quy Ly's rule and temporarily eclipsed the independence of Dai Viet. The Chinese invaders imposed a traumatic 20-year annexation of the country, which had three major long-term effects. It ensured a comprehensive transfer to Dai Viet of the new Ming military technology, it appears to have strengthened ethnic distinctions all round, and it implanted the Chinese model of bureaucratic government.

The Ming emperor initially took care to ensure that Vietnamese forces would not obtain the new weapons technology, including the Chinese musket known as the "magic handgun." The emperor ordered all firearms counted, "and not a single piece is allowed to be missing." Two "Magic Gun Generals" commanded possibly 21,000 riflemen in a Chinese invading force of 215,000.

Breaking into a Vietnamese citadel, the invading Chinese troops fired muskets, cannon, and rockets at defenders mounted on elephants. The Vietnamese had lacked cannon but quickly learned the technique, killing a Ming general with cannon fire within a year. From 1418, the burgeoning guerrilla forces of the emerging resistance leader Lê Loi captured quantities of Ming weaponry and began to challenge the Chinese, using cannon again from 1425. The Ming brought in reinforcements of 10,000 sharpshooters, from whom victorious Vietnamese captured "countless" weapons. By 1427, Chinese prisoners furnished the Vietnamese with siege techniques, "primitive tanks," "flying horse carts," Muslim trebuchets, and possibly the Chinese "thousand-ball thunder cannon."[23]

A successful attack on a Chinese-held fortress ended the war. Vietnamese troops "built earth-hills from which they shot into the city," tunneled under it, and carried out assaults with captured weapons such as fire lances, rocket arrows, cannon, and the turtle-colored "Duke Lü's overlook and assault carts." After this victory, the Vietnamese repatriated 80,000 Ming prisoners to China and confiscated all their weapons. The next year Lê Loi's new dynasty began building up the Dai Viet navy. Each main general commanded 10 large warships and a unit headed by an "associate administrator of strong crossbows and flame-throwers," including one supersized weapon and 100 large, medium, and small "flame-throwers." The new dynasty redoubled the collection of saltpeter and banned its sale in 1428. Records of the smuggling of copper from the Chinese province of Yunnan for firearms manufacture in Dai Viet date from 1429. Lê Loi's new dynasty launched a military buildup that made Dai Viet "the first gunpowder empire in Southeast Asia."[24]

The war had also polarized ethnic distinctions. A Vietnamese writer rejoiced: "The soil is again the soil of the Southern kingdom. The people are again the people of the Viet race. Coats and skirts and customs are in agreement with those of the past. The moral and political order is re-established as of old."[25] Ethnicity and classical antiquity were now securely intertwined. The leading thinker of the early Lê dynasty, the scholar Nguyen Trai, was a product of the Confucian examinations held under Ho Quy Ly in 1400. According to Whitmore, Trai's cohort was a legacy of Chu Van An, representing "the culmination of the intellectual development of the 1380s and of Quy Ly's own peculiar brand of classical thought." Trai himself had reputedly memorized all the Confucian *Classics* and the *Histories*. Alongside this, an indigenous sense of ethnic identity was intensifying. He and others believed in the 1430s: "We

Vietnamese cannot follow the languages and clothing styles of the Chinese, the Chams, the Lao, the Siamese, or the Cambodians and thereby create chaos among our own customs."[26]

Yet a Chinese-style bureaucratic administration began to dominate Dai Viet from the 1430s. The rising generation of Vietnamese literati educated in the Ming era came to power with the coronation of Lê Loi's grandson, Lê Thanh-tong, in 1460. Administrative rationality soon replaced aristocratic rule. Thanh-tong's court pursued the Chinese model of Six Ministries, established triennial examinations on the Confucian texts for appointees, and "brought the Vietnamese government for the first time into the villages." It also disdained trade and discouraged visits by foreign merchants.[27]

Equally in conformity with Confucian precepts, agriculture came to the forefront of Vietnamese official preoccupations. By the second half of the fifteenth century, as elsewhere in Southeast Asia, a new period of prosperity reigned. Attending to its ritual responsibilities, the Lê court "frequently prayed for rain." Rulers issued edicts on cultivation, irrigation, land reclamation, and farm labor. Historian Sun Laichen writes: "For example, in 1498, an edict was issued to the effect that officials should inspect irrigation works, select officials to be in charge of agriculture, and officials both outside and inside the capital should report on the situation of agriculture." The new Lê legal code protected agriculture and banned the killing of farm cattle. Dai Viet's Confucian historian, Ngo Si Lien, wrote: "Our founding father sprang from the posterity of the Divine Farmer Ruler"—Shen-nung, the legendary Chinese emperor said to have invented the plow.[28]

Along with its enhanced administrative reach, Dai Viet's claim to be the inheritor of not only classical Chinese antiquity but also its alleged agricultural superiority implied a heightened threat to its neighbor Champa. In its foreign relations, the court of Lê Thanh-tong (r. 1460–97) emphasized "the moral question" and the difference between the "civilized" and the "barbarian." As Whitmore puts it, "In both his own villages and other countries, the ruler of Dai Viet now theoretically held the responsibility to tell the occupants how they ought to live."[29]

Conflict had already begun as the Dai Viet state strengthened. Its forces took the Cham capital Vijaya (modern Binh Dinh) in 1446, and in the accustomed fashion, looted and abandoned it.[30] The Vietnamese captured the Cham king and took him to Hanoi, then invaded Champa again in 1450 and carried off 33,500 captives. Lagging behind Dai Viet in military technology, Champa

apparently still possessed no firearms.[31] In 1460, the year Lê Thanh-tong as-
sumed the throne, Cham envoys visiting China protested that "Annam [Dai
Viet] had aggressed against them," and four years later "again complained that
Annam had attacked them, and extorted a white elephant." The envoys asked
China to send officials "to pacify" the Vietnamese "and to erect border stelae, in
order to end their aggression."[32]

However, Dai Viet was building up to a major campaign. In 1465 Lê Thanh-
tong held maneuvers of his land and sea forces, which totaled 100,000 troops.
He set down detailed operational rules for the navy, elephant corps, cavalry,
and infantry. The next year he organized the armed forces along Ming lines.
Each of the five divisions was assigned 10 warships, one major "fire tube," 10
large and 80 small "fire tubes." Dai Viet was now importing large quantities of
copper to make guns and cannon. In 1467 Lê Thanh-tong ordered the manufacture of new types of weapons and prohibited the use of saltpeter for fire-
works.[33] He personally oversaw six naval maneuvers along the Red River and
had maps made of the 12 Vietnamese provinces, with military needs in mind. In
1469 Champa protested to China once more that "Annam was extorting from
Champa rhinoceroses and elephants." Dai Viet had demanded that Champa
accept tributary status and "serve Annam" as it did China.[34]

Rejecting such status, a Cham army marched north in 1470. Lê Thanh-tong
declared war on the Cham king, Ban-la Tra-toan (r. 1460–71), stating confidently that Dai Viet possessed more troops and superior weapons.[35] "Your last
hour has come," he announced; he was ready to "annihilate" his Cham enemies.
Thanh-tong's edicts declared that Champa and its threat were to be destroyed
"for good." Whitmore comments: "For the first time, the Vietnamese armed
forces were activated for a moral purpose—the destruction of evil and the
establishment of civilization in a foreign land."[36]

The war was short and brutal. Lê Thanh-tong mobilized a large force of
reserves, taking personal command of an army now mustering 200,000–
300,000 troops, at a reputed daily cost to the Dai Viet treasury of 1,000 gold
liang (taels). They swept south and defeated the Cham forces of fewer than
100,000, including a large elephant corps that had marched to meet them. King
Tra-toan "immediately sought terms, but Thang-tong refused negotiations and
pressed on with the offensive." The Vietnamese army employed cannons, firearms, and scaling ladders to besiege Vijaya. Deployment of firepower against
its east gate enabled the attacking troops to break in to the Cham capital.[37] Dai
Viet chronicles record that they put 40,000–60,000 Chams to the sword.[38]

China's *Ming shi* annals add that the Vietnamese forces "smashed" Champa: "Annam sacked their country [with] massive burning and looting, and subsequently occupied their territory." Cham officials later told the Chinese court: "Annam destroyed our country."[39]

The Vietnamese captured 50 members of the Cham royal family. Troops brought King Tra-toan kneeling before his conqueror. Dai Viet chronicles record his interrogation by Lê Thanh-tong: "Are you the lord of Champa? I am. Who do you think I am? Just from your face I know you are the Emperor. How many children do you have? More than ten." Thanh-tong spared Tra-toan and let him keep two wives. As Dai Viet soldiers bundled him away, Thanh-tong ordered them to observe the decorum befitting a former "lord of the country." But the Vietnamese deported the royal family and 20,000–30,000 prisoners to the north.[40] Tra-toan died of illness aboard a Vietnamese junk; his head was severed and fastened to the prow.[41] The royal family were assigned quarters beside the palace in Hanoi, where they lived for 30 years. Some of the Cham prisoners were enslaved on the estates of Vietnamese dignitaries and others ordered to adopt Vietnamese names, marry Vietnamese, and start "correcting themselves."[42] But local opposition to their assimilation grew.

The annexed northern and central regions of Champa now became Dai Viet's thirteenth province.[43] Resistance continued in the "mountain valleys" of the south. Chinese annals recorded in 1485 that "Champa is a distant and dangerous place, and Annam is still employing troops there." Cham envoys told the imperial court four years later that "Annam remains unbridled in its encroachments and violence."[44]

Lê Thanh-tong's expansionism also looked west. In 1448, Dai Viet had annexed land from Muong Phuan, in what is today the Plain of Jars in northeastern Laos. Thanh-tong made this territory a prefecture of Dai Viet in 1471 and, after conquering Champa, he launched a new western campaign against both the Phuan realm and the Lao kingdom of Lan Xang in 1479. Whitmore writes: "Citing the Chinese classics (the *Books of Changes* and *of Poetry* and the *Rituals of Zhou*), he called on his forces to spread righteousness and virtue through the mountains." Vietnamese and Tai chronicles concur that over 180,000 Dai Viet troops marched west in the fall of 1479.[45] Advancing on several fronts and "seizing the enemy by the throat," they burned the capital of Muong Phuan and took the Lao capital, Luang Prabang, the next year. Casualties were high. Vietnamese records assert that in Muong Phuan, "70,000 out of 90,000 households were starved to death," probably a severe exaggeration.[46] By September

1480, according to Chinese spies, Dai Viet forces took 20 of Lan Xang's strong-points and killed "over 20,000" Lao. They pushed on, defeating Tai resistance all the way to the upper Irrawady River, even briefly invading the Burmese kingdom of Ava. The Vietnamese forces retreated back to Dai Viet only after being driven out of Lan Xang in late 1484. Tai chronicles of the era reflect a "sudden surge of Dai Viet power" across the northern mainland of Southeast Asia. In the South China Sea, Dai Viet also clashed with shipping from as far afield as Malacca and the Ryuku Islands.[47]

The era's major Dai Viet chronicle summarized Lê Thanh-tong's extraordinary 38-year reign. He "fixed official ranks, promoted rites and music, chose clean and able officials, sent expeditions to the four directions, expanded the territories; Tra Toan was captured, Laos collapsed, Ryukyu was defeated . . . the barbarians in the four directions surrendered, . . . the country was peaceful and well governed. How spectacular was this!"[48]

Lê Thanh-tong's son Hien-tong, succeeding him on his death in 1497, saw no reason to alter policy. One of the court's literati quoted Lê Hien-tong as often saying: "Our Sainted Ancestors originated the civilized world; Our Father [Thanh-tong] reformed inside [the country] and rejected [the barbarians] outside. The model has been set, we have nothing at all to change!"[49] However, official ethnic discrimination increased. In 1499, a new ruling forbade Vietnamese of all ranks from marrying Cham women.[50] This order may have been a response to an internal crisis in Dai Viet, as events threatened to spin out of control. King Tra-Toan's son escaped back to Champa, taking his father's remains. Then the Vietnamese "devil king," Lê Uy Muc, seized the throne of Dai Viet in 1505, murdering his grandmother and two ministers and ushering in an era of instability.[51] According to his successor, "court members interfered in the government, the maternal side seized power, laws and restrictions annoyed and embittered the people, rules led to trouble and revolt, agriculture went into decline."[52] Cham slaves on Vietnamese estates staged a mass escape to the south, and those who remained were distrusted. Finally, the annals of Dai Viet record that in 1509, apparently after uncovering a plot, "the king gave the order to massacre all the Cham" who remained in the neighborhood of the capital. That autumn, in the eighth month of 1509, "on the king's order, all the Cham prisoners in custody were executed."[53] While intermittently pursuing genocidal policies against Chams from 1471 to 1509, Dai Viet had vastly expanded its territory. It annexed 22 of Champa's 27 regions and partitioned the remaining five, its southern rump, into three small principalities.[54]

The aftermath of the conquest proved ironic. Partly because of the difficulty of administering its new far-flung territories, Dai Viet itself fell apart in the sixteenth and seventeenth centuries. The northern Vietnamese heartland lost control of the southern frontier region, now called Dang Trong, which annexed more territory along the coast after a 1611 Cham attack. A 50-year north-south Vietnamese civil war began in 1627. Dang Trong emerged as a commercial power and became Japan's largest trading partner.[55] The region's Nguyen lords continued to impose conquest, expulsion, and assimilation on the Chams. In a battle with northern forces in 1648, Dang Trong took 30,000 prisoners and resettled them on appropriated Cham lands whose inhabitants had fled its incursions. Dang Trong proclaimed that "previously, this land was of Cham barbarians. Now the population is small but land is large." The Nguyen put their fellow Vietnamese captives to work clearing new land among the cultivated plots.[56]

Dang Trong's war with the north ended in stalemate in 1672. The Nguyen turned south to crush the last principality of the Chams, whose attempts to retake lost territory had resumed. After Champa attacked in 1692, Dang Trong seized its remaining port, Panduranga (Phan Rang). A Cham rebellion the next year secured Panduranga recognition as a tributary kingdom, with Vietnamese magistrates in charge of the increasing numbers of new settlers. Nguyen lords instructed captured Cham leaders to "change their clothes and to follow the customs" of the Vietnamese, "in order to govern their people" in the Confucian manner. Dang Trong recruited only ethnic Vietnamese for its armies.[57] Champa's surviving royalty and 5,000 others fled to Cambodia.[58] About 50,000 unassimilated Chams remained in the small, powerless principality on Vietnam's southern coast.[59]

Japan's Unification and Its Invasions of Korea, 1567–98

Blown off course in a typhoon, a Chinese junk landed on a small southern Japanese island in 1543. Aboard were three Portuguese carrying muskets, which "caused considerable excitement among the rescuers." The Japanese were soon fabricating the new firearms and employing them in local warfare. Musket-wielding infantrymen now brought deadlier violence to the civil wars that had wracked Japan since 1467. They soon created havoc against cavalry, which in one generation almost disappeared from Japanese battlefields.[60]

It took a brutal military machine to eventually vanquish the array of contending forces in these civil wars. Japan was divided into 120 regional domains, eclipsing the influence of both the emperor and the shogun in much of the country. Regional *daimyo* recruited rival armies among provincial landholders by exercising their power to adjudicate land disputes, assign property, and defer taxation.[61] Buddhist sects, too, possessed vast landholdings, fortresses, and armies.[62] Now Portuguese ships brought Jesuit missionaries to southern Japan, and the Christian conversion of several daimyo on the island of Kyushu from the 1550s led to more conflict there.[63] Historian James Murdoch described Japan in that era as "one wild welter of seething intestine strife from end to end." According to Mary Elizabeth Berry, "violence had become the law," while "patricide, ruthless marriage politics, the murder of allies and the ruin of religious institutions were common. Many families splintered, and premature death threatened all."[64] Conrad Totman notes the disintegration of "society's muscle, money, and myth."[65]

Out of all this came a new Japanese polity. A year before Elizabeth I's coronation in London in 1558, Emperor Ōgimachi ascended the throne in Kyoto, but his role proved ephemeral. It was the warlord Toyotomi Hideyoshi who rose to dominate Japan through his forceful military and administrative unification of the country by the 1590s, laying the groundwork for his further attempted conquests in Korea and even China. The new militaristic, centralizing regime brandished a cult of Japanese antiquity, an ideology that stressed the role of peasant farmers in the largely rice-growing society of Japan's three most populous islands, and an obsession with territorial expansion.

By the time Hideyoshi launched his first invasion of Korea in 1592, Japan had suffered a century of continuous domestic warfare, and its armies had decades of experience with muskets.[66] They comprised tens of thousands of battle-hardened fighters, some of them well equipped with firearms. Generals deployed "long lines of musketeers" who "mowed down their adversaries with no pretense of chivalry." Korea, by contrast, lacked firearms, effective conscription, and recent experience of warfare.[67] The imbalance of forces was even greater than that between Dai Viet and Champa in the previous century. Once a brutal militarism had succeeded in unifying Japan, the stage was set for catastrophic violence in Korea.

Japanese unification had begun in earnest in 1567. In Owari province east of Kyoto, the expanding forces of the regional daimyo Oda Nobunaga broke through to Mino province. His commander Toyotomi Hideyoshi stormed a fortress, which Nobunaga renamed Gifu, after the starting point of a twelfth-

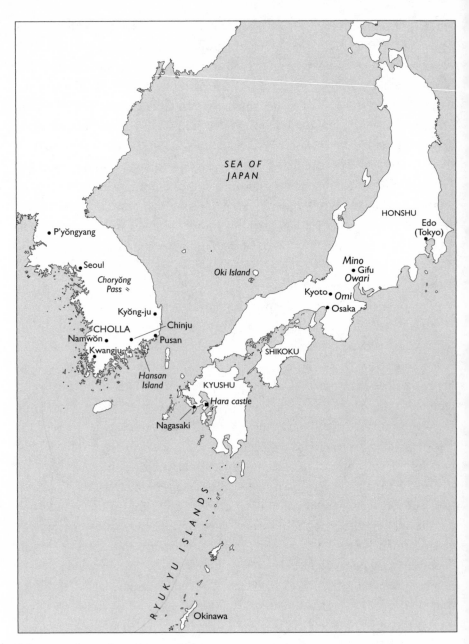

MAP 6. Early modern Japan and Korea

century B.C.E. campaign to unify China. The indigenization of antiquity proceeded as in Dai Viet (and in England in this period—see chapter 5). In Japan, Hideyoshi would later succeed Nobunaga and even aim to excel the country's first shogun, who took power in the twelfth century C.E. Meanwhile, Emperor Ōgimachi requested Nobunaga's assistance in "the recovery of the imperial holdings in your two provinces of Mino and Owari," and even in repairing his palace.[68] The imperial family was in dire straits.

The office of the shogun was troubled, too. Its full title, Berry writes, meant "the great general who subdues the barbarians," hailing back to eighth-century battles against the indigenous people of the Japanese islands. Now the shogunate was disputed among Ashikaga descendants, who had held the office since 1338. An attack on the palace in 1565 killed the incumbent shogun and most of his family. Three years later, Oda Nobunaga threw his support behind a claimant and marched into Kyoto in triumph to install the new shogun.[69]

To expand his domain and "order the state under a single sword," Nobunaga commenced a reign of terror and annihilation of opponents that "immersed Japan in a bloodbath it would never forget." In 1570–73, Nobunaga's army, including Hideyoshi's 3,000-strong field command, fought seven campaigns—against the shogun he had put in power, two armed Buddhist sects, and three regional military houses. Hideyoshi reported on a battle against the Asai house and Honganji monks: "[W]e caught the Asai as they approached. . . . We cut through them and many were taken. . . . I do not know how many were lost. We lay in wait at Hachiman for our final vengeance. Three times we met them, pursuing and crushing them. We took the heads of the dead. The others we chased into the lake."[70]

Brutalities increased as Nobunaga launched an "avowed war" against the political-military power of Japan's armed Buddhist monkhood. The fortified eighth-century monastery of Enryakuji had sheltered Asai forces. Nobunaga told his officers: "Surround their dens and burn them, and suffer none within them to live!"[71] The attack began on September 29, 1571. Nobunaga's first biographer wrote: "Although the troops of the monastery contested every inch of the hill, they were not equal to the occasion. Everything, everywhere, from the central cathedral to the twenty-one shrines of the Mountain King, the bell tower, and the library, were burned to the ground." In this attack Nobunaga's army destroyed hundreds of the buildings of one of Japan's three holiest Buddhist institutions, and burned to death or slaughtered several thousand monks. His soldiers killed everyone else they captured: servants, concubines, and children.[72] One Japanese wrote: "It was miserable to see [the temple] completely reduced to ashes. . . . Several thousand corpses lay scattered around." A court diarist described the sack as "the ruin of the Buddhist law. I cannot explain it, I cannot. What will happen to the Imperial law?" Another denounced "this disaster for the realm. Words cannot describe it."[73]

Oda Nobunaga turned and drove the shogun into exile in 1573, seizing Kyoto and the port of Sakai. He burned and razed the capital's eight-centuries-old political center.[74] Nobunaga then had several of its monasteries demolished and "all the stone idols in Kyoto and the neighborhood" broken up for use in the construction of new palaces. "It was then a common sight to see the erstwhile tutelary divinities of the capital dragged through the mud of the streets with ropes around their necks, while Nobunaga made mock of all the futile clamour of the *bonzes* [monks]." Wearing a tiger skin and carrying a scimitar, Nobunaga supervised the 14,000–25,000 construction workers, guarded by thousands of soldiers. Following his example, "everyone wore skins and no one dared to appear before him in court dress."[75] He had the heads of the defeated chiefs of rival military houses lacquered and gilded, and executed his nephew who had married into the Asai house. Nobunaga ordered his men to treat the defeated provincial samurai "with courtesy" but added that "samurai who cannot be trusted should be banished or forced to commit suicide." Berry cites "reports from vanquished houses" confirming that "exile or forced suicide of much of the resident military population followed Oda victories." In 1574, Nobunaga besieged two fortresses defended by 20,000 armed members of the Ikko Buddhist sect. "When their food supplies had given out and they were weakened from hunger, he torched their stockades, burning the defenders within and slaying those who tried to escape."[76]

In the late 1570s, Nobunaga escalated his massacres, extermination of powerful families, and attacks on Buddhist fortresses, departing only occasionally from what Berry calls a "pattern of total reprisal." He overran four sectarian strongholds in 1574–77.[77] Then, in 1579, Nobunaga agreed to adjudicate a debate between Buddhist monks of the Jodo and Nichiren sects, on condition that the losers would be decapitated. When the Nichiren monks acknowledged defeat, Nobunaga imposed the death penalty, "seized most of the other leading priests of the sect and deported them to a desert island," and forced the membership into exile. According to a Jesuit report, all Nichiren temples "in the four kingdoms around Kyoto were promptly ruined, destroyed and burned. . . . The temples ruined formerly and during the last few days by Nobunaga appear infinite." This campaign vanquished "the only really aggressive Buddhist sect in Japan."[78]

Next, in 1579–80, Nobunaga's army of 60,000 besieged the Honganji sect's temple fortress in Osaka. After thousands of old men, women, and children tried to escape, "a junk with a gruesome load of human ears and noses" floated back downstream to let the castle's defenders know their fate. The slaughter on both sides produced a smell of burning flesh everywhere. In late 1580, Nobunaga permitted Osaka to negotiate its surrender, possibly because of the Honganji sect's nationwide influence. By 1581–82, Hideyoshi, too, was negotiating truces with armed opponents in his western provincial fiefs. But not all. He later recalled, "Bessho of Miki [castle] plotted rebellion and caused me great trouble. . . . But finally I took Bessho's head. Thereupon our lord [Nobunaga] repeatedly sent me rewards and letters of gratitude, granting me gold mines in Tajima and utensils for the tea ceremony."[79]

Instead, trouble brewed. Nobunaga wrote Hideyoshi's wife: "I particularly looked with admiration upon your features and your appearance which seemed doubly [beautiful] since we last met. That [Hideyoshi] is said to be ceaselessly dissatisfied is a great wrong, beyond words. However far he searches, this bald rat will never find again anyone like yourself. . . . Please show this letter to [Hideyoshi]." A Jesuit resident added that Nobunaga "despises all the other Japanese kings and princes and speaks to them over his shoulder as if they were lowly servants," and speculated that he planned to proclaim himself a god.[80]

Nobunaga may even have seen Christians as allies against his religious enemies. Another Jesuit reported in 1582 that Nobunaga "has little respect for the *Kami* [Shintō deities] and the *Hotoke* [Buddhas], whom the Japanese worship with such devotion." Responding in particular to the Buddhists' military challenge, Nobunaga "aims at their total ruin," the Jesuit report stated. And "in proportion to the intensity of his enmity to the *bonzes* and their sects, is his good will towards our Fathers who preach the law of God, whence he has shown them so many favours that his subjects are amazed."[81]

A vassal assassinated Oda Nobunaga in 1582. The warlord had set "a pattern of aggressive national rule," controlling one-third of Japan, including many of its wealthiest and most strategic areas. His general Toyotomi Hideyoshi now picked up the momentum. He set about conquering the remainder of the country's 66 provinces, controlled by a dozen great houses with extensive domains. For the next decade, however, Hideyoshi largely eschewed Nobunaga's terror tactics. He preferred to exercise military dominance and neutralize resistance by diplomatically conceding regional autonomy to rival daimyo and potential allies, confirming their control of their fiefdoms. In a spectacularly successful series of campaigns, Hideyoshi pacified all of Japan by 1591.[82]

There were premonitions of the cruelty to come. First, Hideyoshi faced internal Oda rivals, including two sons of Nobunaga. In 1582 he wrote to a mistress: "I will have the investitures in Omi reviewed and its castles destroyed. When there is time I shall recover Osaka and shall station my men there. I shall order them to level the castles of the whole land to prevent further rebellions and to preserve the nation in peace for the next fifty years." Hideyoshi pursued Shibata Katsuie's rival army of 30,000 to a castle in Omi, and then described what happened: "Katsuie climbed to the ninth floor of his keep, . . . and declared his intention to kill himself. . . . His men, deeply moved, shed tears which soaked the sleeves of their armor. When all was quiet to the east and the west, Katsuie stabbed his wife, children, and other members of his family, and then cut [open] his stomach." In a mass suicide, over 80 of his retainers followed suit.[83]

By 1583–84, Hideyoshi fielded an army of 50,000 soldiers, including 5,000 musketeers. He proclaimed: "The government of Japan will be superior to anything since Yoritomo," its twelfth-century first shogun. In 1585 Hideyoshi took the office of regent, the highest a subject of the emperor could occupy.[84] He led 40,000 men against Japan's two most sacred surviving Buddhist institutions. The Shingon monks of Negoro were leading arms producers, former suppliers of the Honganji sect. Hideyoshi razed the monastery's scores of structures, warning its supreme temple at Koya against "manufacture or retention of senseless weapons" by monks who neglected "their religious studies," and threatening them to "be discerning in this matter" now that the Negoro temple had been "finally destroyed."[85]

Hideyoshi turned to Japan's two southerly islands. He took Shikoku first, then invaded Kyushu with 250,000 men in late 1586. Nagasaki and other Kyushu port cities, Japan's gateway to the outside world, were in turmoil. After Christian missionaries had arrived in 1549 and converted three daimyo, one had handed Nagasaki over to Jesuits, who sold shares in Portuguese cargoes and brokered precious metal deals. Daimyo had their retainers forcibly baptized, authentic mass conversions spread in the countryside, and religious warfare erupted. Buddhist exactions provoked Christians to widespread destruction of Buddhist and Shintō shrines. Hideyoshi's armies enlisted both Honganji Buddhists and a local Christian daimyo, and overcame the debilitated resistance by mid-1587. As in Shikoku, while recalcitrants suffered "human losses and devastation," Hideyoshi divided Kyushu among local supporters and defeated enemies, rewarding loyalists and winning new allies. He took elders and children as hostages.[86]

Given the local strength of Christianity, Hideyoshi's policy toward it was pragmatic. At the close of this campaign, Hideyoshi published a critical edict: "Japan is the Land of the Gods. Diffusion here from the Kirishitan [Christian] Country of a pernicious doctrine is most undesirable. . . . To approach the people of our provinces and districts and, making them into sectarians, cause them to destroy the shrines of the gods and temples of the Buddhas, is a thing unheard of in previous ages." He complained that Christian padres, who "by means of their clever doctrine, amass parishioners as they please," were violating the Buddhist law and therefore "can hardly be allowed to remain on Japanese soil." Yet he acted cautiously, saying: "Whether one desires to become a follower of the padre is up to that person's own conscience."[87] Hideyoshi took over Nagasaki but exempted traders from punishment and did not enforce expulsion of Europeans. Instead, he welcomed Franciscans to Kyoto in 1593, allowing them to build a monastery and church. He promoted several Christians in his ranks. The Franciscan leader wrote: "While this king lives we can enjoy much security." But sectarian wounds were opened.[88] Hideyoshi destroyed churches and convents in the Kinki region. He had abandoned Nobunaga's more militaristic policy of "the realm subjected to military power," but he had also reversed his predecessor's more pro-Christian antagonism to Shintō and Buddhist influence.[89] The long-term future of Japanese Christianity was grim.

Looming closer was another conflict, which also emerged in the campaign for Kyushu. As early as 1578, Hideyoshi had predicted to Nobunaga: "When Kyushu is ours, . . . I will prepare ships of war and supplies and go over and take Korea . . . to enable me to make still further conquests. . . . I intend to bring the whole of China under my sway. When that is effected the three countries (China, Korea, and Japan) will be one. I shall do it all as easily as a man rolls up a piece of matting and carries it under his arm." Again in 1586 Hideyoshi predicted "the conquest of Korea and China, for which enterprise he was issuing orders for the sawing of planks to make two thousand vessels in which to transport his army." He forecast to a daimyo: "I shall extend my conquest to China." Now, having conquered Kyushu, Hideyoshi wrote home to his wife in

1587: "By fast ships I have dispatched [orders] to Korea to serve the throne of Japan. Should [Korea] fail to serve [our throne], I have dispatched [the message] by fast ships that I will punish [it] next year. Even China will enter my grip. I will command it during my lifetime."[90] By the time he pacified eastern Honshu in 1591, Hideyoshi had forged modern Japan in just eight years, and was ready to take on China.[91]

Accompanying Hideyoshi's militarism and expansionism was a traditional conception of agricultural order that reinforced Japanese ethnic identity and exacerbated the genocidal violence of his coming attacks on Korea. With the introduction of a wet rice economy in the fourth century B.C.E., Japan's emerging polity had developed its own agrarian cosmology that depicted deities as the ear of the rice plant. According to the earliest written Japanese document, the Shintō creation myth *Kojiki* (712 C.E.), the country was founded when the Sun Goddess sent her grandson there with seeds from heaven to turn the wilderness into rich rice land. The ancient Japanese emperors were shamans, responsible for timing the rituals required to guarantee the rice crop.[92] From medieval times, the shogun had assumed the emperor's political and military powers, but the imperial polity remained based on agriculture, not only economically but culturally.

Rice is "*the* marker of Japanese identity," writes anthropologist Emiko Ohnuki-Tierney. The Deity of Rice Paddies, representing the ancestors of the Japanese, was embodied in an icon of the indigenous soul, the cherry blossom, spring's "symbolic equivalent" of its autumn counterpart, the rice plant. With Mt. Fuji, cherry blossoms and rice paddies became "the symbols of unchanging Japan." Ohnuki-Tierney adds that "even today, the core imperial rituals officiated by the emperor . . . are all related to rice-harvesting." Hideyoshi took power across Japan at a time when the dominance of this agrarian cosmology reached new heights, compounded by the influence of Buddhism and Shintoism. Rice was sacred, and the consumption of meat even became prohibited as impure. Butchering was by now an "abominable" profession, suitable only for the country's "outcaste" population.[93]

Control of agriculture was vital to political power. In 1568, Nobunaga's forces began to register the lands under their expanding control. The first cadastral survey was in Omi, which became Hideyoshi's fief in 1574. He founded a castle on Lake Biwa, expanded the port town, exempted its residents from taxation, and began local land surveys.[94] Historian George Sansom adds that Nobunaga and Hideyoshi restrained Japan's growing free cities: "Both can be charged with suppressing the rise of an independent urban class of tradesmen and artisans."[95] In their agrarian model, farmers were to remain in their place as "a subservient peasantry."[96] In mid-1588, on the verge of unifying Japan, Hideyoshi decreed that its farmers were "strictly forbidden" to possess swords "or any other form of weapon." He feared that "the paddies and dry fields of the places concerned will not be cultivated and the fiefs will be wasted." Swords were to be collected and melted down for use "in the forthcoming construction of the Great Buddha. This will be an act by which the farmers will be saved in this life, needless to say, and in the life to come." Furthermore, "If farmers possess agricultural tools alone and engage completely in cultivation, they shall [prosper] into eternity, even to their children and grandchildren. It is with compassion for the farmers that we rule in this manner . . . the farmers shall invest their energies in agriculture."[97]

Hideyoshi meant to bind peasants to the soil and separate them "from all other classes." In a second edict in 1591, he attempted to further police armed opposition and freeze the social order. He forbade soldiers from joining farmers or townspeople. Samurai must remain attached to their lords. Should escaped samurai be harbored or concealed, "all in that neighborhood and in that place shall be brought to judgment." This meant execution. Any lord who employed another's samurai had to provide three innocents' severed heads in expiation or "be brought to judgment without inquiries." Moreover, "Should any farmer, abandoning his fields, go into trade or wage labor, that person, needless to say, and all in his village shall be brought to judgment." This was reiterated in 1592: "[C]hange of residence . . . will not be permitted."[98]

Within six years, Hideyoshi's regime completed cadastral surveys of most of Japan's agricultural land. These aimed to register a single cultivator with "cultivating rights to every paddy and dry field." Taxes had to be collected "to avoid disturbance to the farmers. . . . Should there be an individual who makes an impossible demand of the farmers, that retainer shall be in offense." This alarmed some large landowners unwilling to concede tenants' rights, but many extensive holdings were also registered along with separate tax lists that recognized large landowners. "After the crops have been inspected, the lord should take two-thirds and the farmer one-third." Officials must "ensure that the fields do not become devastated." Hideyoshi wanted not a more equitable landownership or division of the harvest, but central hegemony and undisturbed cultivation. In return for acknowledgment of their regional domains, Hideyoshi's daimyo accepted national military obligations and nationwide separation of social classes in order "to make peasants the supporters of an urban military." The regime aimed to control agrarian communities by keeping farmers in their fields and removing soldiers into barracks towns.[99] In Sansom's words, this was to "establish the position of the actual cultivator as tenant and taxpayer, so that the ruler held in his hand the food supply of the nation." Now directly linked to the state, the peasant became "an independent unit, treated separately from his parents and other relatives."[100] Hideyoshi's regime left Japanese farmlands largely worked by owner-cultivators, with only the capital region, encompassing all four of the country's cities, more closely penetrated by commercial tenancy.[101]

Hideyoshi set out to subjugate the towns as well. The urban growth resulting from the removal of soldiers from the countryside was partly unintended, and the small merchant class remained relatively marginal and easily monitored. Reversing an earlier regional trend, Hideyoshi assessed national land taxes in kind. There was no national currency and no powerful commercial elite that required respect—or elimination. Commoner organizations in the capital had declined in activity since the later civil war period.[102] Towns could be subjected to close control, massive internal relocation, and neighborhood demolitions. In 1582–92, Hideyoshi moved most of Kyoto's 150–200 downtown temples to the city fringes. The Jesuit Luis Frois considered this "a deed completely without precedent in the capital. . . . He has caused all the Buddhist priests to move from their temples. . . . The suffering of the believers as well as the priests is great." In 1591, officials had commoners' homes cleared from nine blocks of another Kyoto neighborhood, and parts of two more, all rezoned for the military and nobility. A diarist described chaos as "the townspeople are scrambling to break down their homes." A week later: "I went out to view the transfer of the houses within Kyoto. The people throughout [the area] are miserable. It is as if the streets have been burned out." New roads "chopped up certain parts of the city." Two commercial sections remained untouched, and evidence is lacking of deliberate plans to punish townspeople.[103] But urban civilian populations were considered expendable, consistent with an ideology that favored farming.

Classical models also guided Hideyoshi as he reorganized agriculture and controlled urban life. Having personally risen "from peasant to lord of the realm," Hideyoshi not only found cultivation conducive to control and conquest but noted ancient precedent in his 1588 edict, stating that "the ruler Yao of China pacified the realm and [then] used precious swords and sharp blades as farming tools." Two years later, Hideyoshi visited the shrine of Japan's twelfth-century unifier Yoritomo, addressing the statue of the first shogun as follows: "You took all the power under Heaven. You and I only have been able to do this; but you were of high and illustrious descent, and not like me, sprung from peasants. But as for me, after conquering all the empire, I intend to conquer China. What do you think of that?" This "illustrious peasant ruler" would outdo an aristocrat. In the same year, Hideyoshi told Korean envoys: "I am the only remaining scion of a humble stock."[104]

In a different sense, Hideyoshi asserted that his pedigree was more exalted. Writing to the king of Korea in 1590, he claimed to have been conceived when the wheel of the sun entered his mother's womb in a dream.[105] Drawing upon indigenous Shintō thought, he considered himself the "Son of the Sun" (*hirin no ko*). And, with encouragement from Zen Buddhist advisers, he referred to Japan as "the country of the gods" (*shinkoku*), which had been transgressed by "false teachings from Christian countries." In 1591, Hideyoshi told the governor of Portuguese India that Japan's imperial deity (*kami*) was "the foundation of all sentient beings."[106] Historian Nam-lin Hur points out that for this Japan-centered worldview, Hideyoshi drew from a fifteenth-century Shintō thinker who had ranked indigenous Japanese religion above Confucianism and Buddhism, notably using an agrarian metaphor: "Our Japan begot seeds, China produced branches and leaves, and India opened flowers and fruits." Shintō, then, was "the roots of all teachings."[107] Its *Kojiki* creation myths told of legendary Empress Jingū's fourth-century victories in Korea. Hideyoshi also drew upon the advice of militaristic Zen Buddhist monks for his anti-Christian and foreign policies of "pacifying and protecting the nation" (*chingo kokka*).[108]

Hideyoshi's expansionist imperative, sprouting from such ancient antecedents, was fertilized by domestic agrarian and cultural visions. His final years promoted escalating violence within Japan as well as beyond. Abandoning his earlier pragmatism, Hideyoshi reverted to a brutality reminiscent of Nobunaga. As Sansom put it rather obliquely, he "was until his last years not addicted to slaughter for its own sake." Berry suggests Hideyoshi now occupied "a middle ground between madness and full self-possession." He exiled and condemned a close friend, the noted artist and aesthete Sen no Rikyu, in 1591. With 3,000 troops, Hideyoshi surrounded the house of this "master who codified the rubrics of the tea ceremony," forcing him to commit suicide.[109] Hideyoshi brandished his own aesthetic prowess in ostentatious displays of native Japanese symbolism derived from agriculture. In 1594 and 1598, he sponsored major elaborate rituals involving "lavish aristocratic cherry blossom viewings." Five thousand guests attended the first, complete with carnival masquerade and daimyos in fashionable Portuguese dress. Hideyoshi's preparations for the second, more formal occasion included renovations of the buildings and gardens of a prestigious temple to display his wealth and power.[110]

Hideyoshi envisaged conquest of Korea and China as further quests for homage and glory.[111] He sent missions to Korea's court in 1588–89 to denounce its lack of submissiveness. In 1590, he demanded that the king of the Ryukyu Islands pay tribute to Japan, not China. "Everything—excepting no foot or inch of land—has entered my grasp. Consequently, it is my basic desire to spread my administration to other regions." His enforcement of suzerainty over Ryukyu allowed Hideyoshi to gather forces and supplies there for his invasion of Korea.[112] But, Totman writes, his motives remained mysterious: "No one knows whether he was inspired by conquest legends of the *Kojiki,* the past exploits of Mongols, the example of globe-girdling Europeans, some inner messenger whom he alone could hear, or by a wish to exhaust daimyo armies in further warfare."[113]

Korean leaders could not fathom Hideyoshi and sent ambassadors to Japan in late 1590 to assess his intentions.[114] Treated rudely in his palace, they later complained that "his eyeballs send out fire" and that "*saké* of an inferior quality was handed around." Hideyoshi delayed them for months before replying to the Korean king that a soothsayer had foretold his power would "overspread the empire." According to the Korean account, he added: "I will assemble a mighty host, and, invading the country of the great Ming, I will fill with the hoar-frost from my sword the whole sky over the four hundred provinces.... I hope that Korea will be my vanguard. Let her not fail to do so." The Japanese version of Hideyoshi's reply to the Korean king quotes him as saying: "My object is to enter China, to spread the customs of our country to the four hundred and more provinces of that nation, and to establish there the government of our imperial city even unto all the ages.... My wish is nothing other than that my name be known throughout the three countries [of Japan, China, and India]."[115] A Japanese monk accompanied the envoys back to Korea carrying the message: "If Korea leaves us but a clear road to China, we will ask nothing else." The leader of the Korean delegation warned his king that Hideyoshi would launch an invasion. But Korea's king responded to the Japanese: "What talk is this of our joining you against China? From the earliest times we have followed law and right ... all lands are subject to China." He compared Japan's project to conquer China to "a bee trying to sting a tortoise through its armor."[116]

Two more Japanese diplomatic missions failed to secure Korea's submission. In mid-1591, Hideyoshi began preparations to invade. He informed the Portuguese viceroy of the Indies: "I have received an order from the imperial court instructing that the great generals [of Japan] exercise their authority to alien countries and regions." He added: "I intend to govern Ming China. For that, I will send out *sakura* or 'cherry' ships. Once they arrive in China, they will further advance to your land," that is, India.[117] Two months later, Hideyoshi warned the Spanish in Manila to "bear the banner of surrender and come to submit." Any delay caused by "creeping and crawling along" would make it "necessary promptly to attack" the Philippines. Hideyoshi wrote confidently to his mother in mid-1592: "I shall take China about the ninth month, and I shall receive [your gift of] formal clothing for the festival of the ninth month in the Chinese capital." He told his nephew and heir, Hidetsugu, that "Korea and China will be taken without trouble." Within two years, the Japanese emperor would transfer to China, he wrote. "We shall present the Emperor with ten provinces around the Ming capital." Then Hidetsugu, now Japan's imperial regent, would also become regent of China with 100 provinces there.[118] One of Hideyoshi's commanders, the Nichiren Buddhist daimyo Kato Kiyomasa, addressed his soldiers on the *Kojiki* legend of the Japanese Empress Jingū's fourth-century conquest of Korea.[119] According to a vassal of Kato, he would "capture the Korean king and revive the tribute."[120]

Korea certainly seemed an easier target than China. It lacked firearms, and only three of its towns were walled fortresses: Pusan, Tongnae, and Kimhae. But Korea was technologically advanced, with "a much higher degree of culture or cultivation" than Japan. The well-educated Korean elite had invented metal type printing as early as 1324 and produced high-quality pottery. But most of the population were rice farmers, or fishermen who made superb sailors.[121] Military artisanal capacity was high, but production levels were low. The Korean army would adopt the musket only after the landing of the Japanese forces, which were equipped with Western smoothbore models and hardened by decades of war.[122]

About 150,000 Japanese troops landed in Korea in May–June 1592, spearheaded by the Christian daimyo Konishi Yukinaga and his division of 18,000 coreligionists.[123] They soon found the walls of Korea's three southern fortresses "so low that defenders on the top were inundated by enemy shot and arrows and had to creep around on their knees to avoid being hit."[124]

The Japanese tried to wipe out the Korean forces, and massacres prolif-

erated. The Japanese took Pusan in a few hours on May 25. They took 8,000
heads, putting "every one who showed a sign of resistance to the edge of the
sword." Two days later, Konishi attacked Tongnae, defended by 20,000 Korean
troops. At a cost of 100 Japanese killed, he "filled the fosse with five thousand
dead." The next day a 20,800-strong division, commanded by Buddhist daimyo
Kato Kiyomasa, landed at Pusan. On May 31, Kato took Kong-ju [Kyŏngju?],
"putting three thousand Koreans to the sword." On the same day a third division of 12,000, under the Christian daimyo Kuroda, attacked Kimhae, "inflicting terrific damage on the enemy" and killing thousands more at Seishiu. Pushing north in early June, Konishi's forces killed another 3,000–8,000 Korean
troops in the Choryŏng pass.[125] A Korean officer remarked that in one week,
the Japanese "cut across a thousand *li*" of territory and advanced "straight to
the capital as if they were treading on no-man's land." The Korean king set
Seoul afire and fled north for P'yŏngyang. Konishi marched into the capital on
June 12.[126] Three Japanese divisions had killed 15,000–20,000 Korean soldiers
in three weeks.

Ancient precedents again provided a model. Jingū's fourth-century exploits
in Korea inspired one samurai to recall them in his diary. A Zen monk traveling with the troops added: "In the remote past Empress Jingū defeated the
'alien country,' and the latter asked for mercy. The empress accepted the surrender. On her way back she picked up a spear and carved on a rock in Ch'ungju:
'The King of Korea is a dog of Japan.' When I was in Ch'ungju, I recalled this
old story and indeed found the rock on which the empress had inscribed!"[127]

Japanese troops marched north toward the Chinese border, assembling an
advance force of 50,000 near P'yŏngyang by mid-July. While five other Japanese infantry divisions held the center and south of Korea, destroying undefended crops and homesteads, Hideyoshi planned to reinforce his northern
spearhead by dispatching four new divisions in several hundred ships sailing
directly from the Japanese port of Nagoya. But he had misjudged the Korean
navy, commanded by the brilliant admiral Yi Sunsin. Yi had designed heavily
armored "turtle ships," the first ironclad warships. These were speedy, maneu-
verable vessels whose rowers could about-face on their benches and suddenly
propel their craft into fast reverse, ramming surprised pursuers. In June 1592,
the Korean navy sank and burned 40 Japanese ships in two engagements. Yi
then destroyed a Japanese squadron carrying 700 soldiers and their crews, captured a supply convoy escorted by 26 warships, and sank several more Japanese
vessels. In a triumphant victory off Hansan Island in mid-July, Yi's navy sank
another 71 warships, after which "the very sea was red." He followed up the

same day with reinforcements, burning another 48 Japanese ships and driving the rest of Hideyoshi's armada back to Japan. This "Salamis of Korea," as it has been called, "signed the death-warrant of the invasion." In 10 more battles in December 1592 alone, Yi's navy sank over 400 Japanese warships.[128] Of all Japan's sea captains and sailors drafted that year, "the greater half of them died," Hideyoshi wrote early in 1593. He ordered Japan's home officials to press-gang "all the mariners" aged 15 to 60 who remained "on the seashores."[129]

The killing escalated as guerrilla resistance sprang up throughout occupied Korea. While their king fled P'yŏngyang for the Chinese border to request aid, 22,000 Korean peasants preferred to fight rather than starve after Japanese forces had pillaged their homes and rice fields. They joined surviving regular forces of 84,500 soldiers.[130] Forced to evacuate I-ch'i in the southern province of Chŏlla, the occupiers advanced to recapture the town. Soon "the ground was covered with one crimson matting of leaves," Japanese corpses piled in heaps as they fell. After their second attack, surviving Japanese took four days to burn their dead, then withdrew. In Seoul, the occupiers uncovered a plot to expel them from the capital, "and the townsmen who had been parties to it were roasted to death at slow fires." When 10,000 Japanese soldiers unsuccessfully attacked the Korean fortress of Chinju, nearly 5,000 of them fell. The occupation had almost collapsed.[131]

Japanese forces responded by turning their brutal war into a genocidal conflict. An advance contingent of 5,000 Chinese marched into P'yŏngyang, but the Japanese ambushed and killed 3,000 of them. The Chinese main force of 50,000 crossed the Yalu with cavalry and artillery in January 1593. Driving the Japanese southward from P'yŏngyang, they killed 2,300 of Konishi's troops.[132] The retreating Japanese then set Seoul afire. A Japanese diarist reported them "killing to a man all the Chinamen [Tōjin] that there were in the capital and burning all the houses outside the fortifications." A Korean source reports them massacring the city's Korean male population as well.[133] The Chinese attackers then lost nearly 10,000 troops outside Seoul. Konishi and Kato evacuated the capital in May. On their retreat south, they executed Hideyoshi's instructions to "render him an account of a Korean lord." This was the Korean commander of Chinju fortress, whose garrison had inflicted heavy casualties on Japanese attackers. After a second siege, Kato's troops stormed Chinju, massacring its garrison and all inhabitants. The Japanese killed over 60,000 Koreans and sent Hideyoshi the commander's head. Some 43,000 Japanese troops remained in Korea.[134]

The incoming Chinese commander found Korea's rural areas ravaged by the war and mass killing: "The country all about was lying fallow, and a great famine stared the Koreans in the face." He saw "a young child trying to suck milk from the breast of its dead mother" in a Seoul street. "Famishing men fought and killed each other, the victors eating the vanquished, sucking the marrow from the bones." A fever epidemic struck; "the dead bodies of its victims lay all along the road, the head of one being pillowed on the breast of another. The dead bodies in and immediately around Seoul were gathered and piled in a heap outside the Water Mouth Gate, and it is affirmed that the pile was ten feet higher than the wall."[135]

In truce talks, Ming and Japanese envoys agreed without Hideyoshi's assent that China would invest him as king of Japan, while Japan would evacuate Korea and never again invade. Hideyoshi remained to be persuaded, while at the urging of "hawkish" Zen advisers, he insisted on annexation of Korea's four southern provinces.[136] He also demanded tribute from Taiwan, quoting a soothsayer's prediction that "his authority shall emanate to the myriad peoples."[137] In April 1595, he displayed his continuing interest in Korea by visiting the shrine of its legendary conqueror, Empress Jingū.[138]

The escalating murder and megalomania abroad had grim domestic parallels. Brutality infected Hideyoshi's court. A Japanese account described the habits of his nephew and heir, the Regent Hidetsugu, grooming as regent of China. For musket practice, "having spied farmers in the fields, he would shoot them. Once, practicing archery . . . he summoned a passing traveler and slew him." The Jesuit Frois confirmed that "one of his chiefest delightes was to see poore men slaine and cruellie butchered: wherefor daily at an accustomes hour, for his pastime, and recreation, he played the parte of an executioner, in killinge, and murthering condemned persons . . . he tooke exceedinge delighte to cutt them in peices with suche dexteritie, as yf they had been but little birdes. Otherwise he would have them for a lyvelie marke to ayme at, either with darte or gunne: sometimes lyke unto a yonge Nero he opened and ripped upp woemen to see their entrails and place of conception." Hideyoshi himself turned on Hidetsugu in mid-1595, two years after the birth of a son and new heir. He ordered his nephew into exile and then commanded him to commit suicide, followed by his retainers and chief vassals. Frois reported that Hideyoshi had become so "transported with an unsatiable, and devilishe mynde of destroienge, and rootinge upp of all those that anie ways had belonged unto Hidetsugu that his butcherlie crueltei surpassed all the bowndes of Tirannie. for his purpose was to destroye the woemen, wyves and children of all those that he had alreadie murthered." Hideyoshi ordered 34 members of his nephew's family drawn through crowded streets in open carts to where Hidetsugu's head was displayed. Their painful cries could have "mooved not onlie men but stoanes into compassion and mercie. . . . When the cartes were come to the place of exequution, behold there a hangman." Hidetsugu's two sons and daughter, all under six years of age, "were first murthered, and then all the other Ladies in ranke one after an other were taken out of the carte, and . . . theire owne headdes were stricken of. All theire boddies by order from [Hideyoshi] were throwne into a pitte," over which a tomb and chapel were built proclaiming, "The Tombe of the Traitors." The mass murder ranged far beyond Hideyoshi's domestic sphere. When the Spanish galleon *San Felipe*, carrying silver from Acapulco to Manila, was wrecked off Shikoku in 1596, Hideyoshi had six Spanish Franciscans and 20 Japanese Christians crucified.[139]

A second war now loomed in Korea. Konishi's Japanese troops still occupied Pusan when a Chinese mission to invest Hideyoshi as king of Japan reached Osaka in 1596. Still unaware of their purpose, Hideyoshi refused to meet the Koreans accompanying them. China's language of investiture stated haughtily that "knowing the reverence due" the Middle Kingdom, Hideyoshi "may follow our ancient custom as respects dress" and in gratitude, "act worthily of your position as our minister." After the ceremony, the Chinese also requested that Japan dismantle all its forts in Korea and evacuate its garrisons. Hideyoshi exploded, threatening to kill the Chinese envoys. According to a Jesuit account, he "became inflamed. . . . So loudly did he vociferate and perspire that vapour exhaled from his head." He sent the Chinese ambassadors home, bearing gifts but no reply. "All his anger was turned against Korea. . . . He vowed that he would never make peace with that unhappy country."[140] He gave orders for a second invasion on March 19, 1597. Nine new divisions joined the garrisons holding out in southern Korea, totaling 141,500 Japanese troops.[141]

Hideyoshi gave his commander the genocidal directive, "Kill Koreans one by one, and empty the country."[142] Japanese soldiers were to be rewarded for each Korean put out of action. Heads of Korean commanders had to be supplied as proof, but the number of infantry a Japanese captured or killed could be documented by his presentation of their severed noses.[143] To the troops Hideyoshi issued more precise instructions: "A man has two ears but just one nose. By cutting a nose, you replace a head. When you capture one alive, first cut off his/her nose, then you are allowed to keep him/her as a prisoner."[144] The noses were to be sent pickled in barrels to Kyoto, where later in the year Hideyoshi built a misnamed "Ear-Mound" victory monument (*Mimizuka*).[145]

Hideyoshi specifically urged Japanese forces to "punish" Chŏlla province, "without leaving a thing behind."[146] Konishi's new Japanese fleet quickly captured or destroyed most of the Korean navy, and a Japanese garrison slaughtered 400 survivors reaching the shore. A shipment of the noses of the Korean dead reached Hideyoshi two months later.[147] Pushing inland, Konishi's forces attacked the Namwŏn fortress in Chŏlla province. Its Ming general fled when Konishi rejected his proposal for a ceasefire. More than 10,000 Koreans and Chinese fell into Japanese hands in the eighth month of 1597. A Japanese monk, serving as a physician with the invading forces, wrote in his diary: "Men and women in the fortress were all cut down without leaving anyone. There was no one saved. Those who had surrendered were also cut down. . . . At dawn I went outside the fortress. Dead people were scattered all over the road like sand." Hearing news of the victory, Hideyoshi wrote back to his field general: "I received your report that you had cut off 269 heads the other day. Today the same number of noses arrived. You worked your fingers to the bone. It is marvellous. I encourage you to keep doing a great job!"[148] Kato Kiyomasa, meanwhile, assigned his 10,000 troops a quota of three noses each.[149] They attacked Chinese forces in Chŏlla: "3,726 heads were taken, those of the officers and the noses of the private soldiers being pickled in salt and lime and forwarded to Hideyoshi."[150]

The Japanese ravaged Chŏlla's countryside around Namwŏn. A chronicler recorded: "[W]e gave chase and hunted them in the mountains and scoured the villages for the distance of one day's travel. When they were cornered we made a wholesale slaughter of them. During a period of ten days we seized 10,000 of the enemy, but we did not cut off their heads. We cut off their noses, which told us how many heads there were. By this time Yasuharu's total of heads was over 2,000."[151] A soldier wrote in his diary that "enemies were hiding under the floors and other places." The Japanese would assemble them at the eastern gates of their villages, where they begged for their lives. "We cut off all of them and killed all of them. This was for offering blood to our military god. For this sacrificial offering of blood, we cut off everyone and everything, regardless of women, men, dogs, and cats. Their number reached as many as 30,000." The Japanese soldiers offered this blood festival (*chi matsuri*) to Hachiman the Great Boddhisattva, an embryo Buddha reincarnating Emperor Ōjin, whom the divine Empress Jingū had carried in her womb during her ancient Korean conquests.[152]

Hideyoshi had a shipment of Korean noses buried at his Kyoto prayer temple in the ninth month of 1597. His leading Zen Buddhist monk performed a ritual, leaving an inscription: "Due to the distance, our warriors sent noses for the lord's inspection. Upon inspection, the lord did not bring up any feelings of revenge about the dead enemies. Instead, he deepened his mind of compassion."[153] Recording a different view, the Japanese Buddhist serving as a physician with the army described Korean fields and hillsides burning, soldiers running amok, parents murdered in front of crying children about to be enslaved. This monk concluded: "Hell cannot be in some other place apart from this."[154]

As in Japan, agriculture provided an ideological justification for the conquest of Korea. Hideyoshi explained to the Chinese in 1593: "[W]e sent many men and ordered [affairs] in order to achieve peace for the farmers and other peoples." While imposing the Japanese language and customs on Koreans, his commanders ordered a cadastral survey and a new distribution of land.[155] During their second invasion in 1597, Japanese generals issued manifestos ordering "all farmers to return to their homes and agricultural work or to be sought out and killed." Further, "all officials will be killed as a matter of course, along with their wives and children."[156]

After occupying most of the south, the Japanese fought to a standstill and retreated in the face of winter. The Korean navy recovered under Admiral Yi Sunsin and, with Chinese reinforcements, killed the Japanese admiral in a sea battle. In January 1598, 40,000 new Chinese troops marched through Seoul and besieged Kato's position in the south but were driven back by a Japanese relieving force of 50,000. More Chinese reinforcements arrived. Hideyoshi rejected Konishi's advice to pull back to Pusan. Some 60,000 Japanese troops held out in various garrisons. At Sunch'ŏn on October 30, 1598, they repulsed and pursued Chinese attackers, taking no fewer than 38,700 heads. Before burying the Chinese heads in a mound, the Japanese cut off the ears and noses and sent them pickled in barrels to Kyoto.[157] In just over a month, two field generals submitted 18,350 and 5,044 noses, respectively.[158]

Those buried in Hideyoshi's Mimizuka represented just a fraction of the estimated 100,000–200,000 noses cut from Korean victims and sent to Japan in 1597–98.[159] Many went to establish local "ear-mounds," which can still be found in northern Kyushu.[160] A Japanese general's war memoirs testified to the burial of 185,738 Korean and 29,014 Chinese "heads."[161] The Nabeshima clan alone delivered 29,251 Korean noses to Japan.[162] Japanese forces also seized over 100,000 Korean artisans and scholars and perhaps 50,000–60,000 women, and forcibly transported them to Japan or sold them as slaves abroad.[163]

After Konishi won more victories, the Chinese sued for peace. Then news arrived of Hideyoshi's death in the eighth month of 1598, at the age of 63. Konishi agreed to an armistice and began to withdraw from Korea. Admiral Yi Sunsin and his Chinese counterpart, pursuing the Japanese fleet, were killed in December, in the final engagement of the war.[164]

Korea lay in ruins, many of its people exterminated. As if bringing Hideyoshi's legacy home again, Japan now turned inward. In a civil war, his successor, Tokugawa Ieyasu, destroyed Konishi's army, with the help of another Christian daimyo and of Kato Kiyomasa.[165] The new Tokugawa shogunate launched discrimination against Christians in 1611 and "general persecution" in 1614. Two years later, the shogun ordered daimyo to intensify efforts to eradicate Christianity. Over 50 Christians were executed at Kyoto and Nagasaki in 1619, and 55 in 1622. A crackdown on external commerce accompanied this cultural repression. The Tokugawa issued five "closed-country directives" (*sakokurei*) in 1633–39. Japanese were forbidden on pain of death to travel abroad. The regime expelled all Portuguese in 1639, and the next year beheaded 61 members of a Portuguese embassy. In Kyushu in 1637, mostly Christian peasants launched the Shimabara revolt, which the government crushed at a cost of 10,000 troops and 20,000 peasants killed. According to historian Gavan McCormack, "the last stand" of a group of Christians at Hara castle ended in a slaughter by sword and fire in which the army took "around fifteen to sixteen thousand heads." A "nationwide inquisition" and purge of Japan's remaining Christians began in 1640. Some 600 executions in 1657–58 brought the toll to a total of 3,000 killed. By 1660, "there were practically no Christians left in Japan."[166]

Hideyoshi's genocidal invasions of Korea, inspired by expansionism and reinforced by cults of antiquity and agriculture, were followed by Tokugawa internal repression and trade restrictions that combined to destroy a large Japanese religious minority. The brutal militarization and unification of an agrarian empire seeking political domination and ethnic homogeneity had produced genocide abroad and violent cultural suppression at home.

CHAPTER 4

Genocidal Massacres in Early Modern Southeast Asia

C hristian, Muslim, and Buddhist forces in turn all perpetrated genocidal massacres in Southeast Asia between 1590 and 1800. The spread of
Christianity and Islam through the parts of the archipelago that now
comprise the Philippines and Indonesia occurred at roughly the same time as
ethnic consolidation of the mainland Buddhist kingdoms of Burma and Siam,
while largely Confucian Dai Viet remained politically divided until 1802. The
heterogeneous perpetrators of genocidal massacres occupied varying positions in the regional power structures. Newly arrived Iberian conquistadors,
like their predecessors in the Americas, employed massacre as a tactic to seize
power, but failed to conquer Buddhist Cambodia. Over the next two centuries,
budding indigenous empires in Java and Burma slaughtered newly defined
religious or ethnic opponents to extend or stabilize their control. In all these
cases, aggressive territorial expansion combined with cults of antiquity, and
with pastoral ideology or a cult of agriculture, to form an intellectual backdrop
to mass killing. In the mid-eighteenth century, threatened Mon and Khmer
polities in lower Burma and Cambodia directed genocidal massacres to reverse territorial losses or eliminate encroaching settlers competing for land
and other resources.

Conquistadors in Cambodia, 1585–99

A Portuguese caravel sank off Cambodia in 1560, near the mouth of the Mekong.
The poet Luis de Camões swam ashore, clutching the incomplete manuscript

of his future national epic, *Os Lusiadas*. He added a verse of lyrical gratitude to Cambodia and the Mekong for saving him from the storm that wrecked his ship.[1] Later Iberian adventurers in Cambodia would evince less sympathy for the country, but Camões's pastoral poem portraying continental conquests became a cultural backdrop to their depredations. Its Virgilian romance, however, was distinct from more utilitarian visions of the peasantry.

Os Lusiadas is a verse history of Portugal's feats of arms and discovery, with Vasco da Gama and the sea route to India as its central organizing theme. The epic links ancient times to modern, Rome to Portugal, West to East. Its title, meaning "The Sons of Lusus," was a "conscious classicism." As a young man, Camões's studies at the University of Coimbra had "filled his mind with the seductive visions of Pagan antiquity." As if by Hannibal's personal retribution, Camões then lost an eye fighting Moors in North Africa. His poem, published in Lisbon in 1572, began "Arms and the men," after the *Aeneid*'s opening, *arma virumque*. The literary scholar C. M. Bowra commented: "He addresses the King of Portugal as Virgil addresses Augustus." The goddess Venus protects da Gama in the Indian Ocean as she had Aeneas in the Mediterranean, giving him "all the regions of the East." Bacchus, by contrast, represents "the spirit of the East in its vanity, cunning, and disorder," opposing "the order and reason of the West."[2] *Os Lusiadas* has been called "the first epic poem which in its grandeur and its universality speaks for the modern world."[3] It updated Virgil's themes of love, pastoralism, war, and empire.

Virgil had pictured Aeneas's dead companion Pallas, on his grave of "country straw," lying "like a flower cut by the thumbnail of a young girl, a soft violet."[4] Camões used this same pastoral metaphor of death: "Like to a daisy-flow'r with colours fair, / By virgin's hand beheaded in the bud."[5] At sea on a Portuguese caravel, Virgilian pastoral became Iberian nautical, an idyllic ambience under sail: "The whisp'ring zephyr breath'd a gentle blast, / Which stealingly the spreading canvas fills."[6] The epic's sea gods live in an underwater palace, amid flowers, grass, and trees. On their return home from India, Venus treats the Portuguese explorers to the Island of Loves, a sylvan paradise with fruit, lush grass, tamed beasts, and frolicking nymphs.[7]

Camões's epic also vividly depicted wars of religion. As Moors are routed:

> Heads from the shoulders leap about the field;
> Arms, legs, without or sense or master, fly.
> Others, their panting entrails, wheel'd
> Earth in their bloodless cheek, death in their eye.[8]

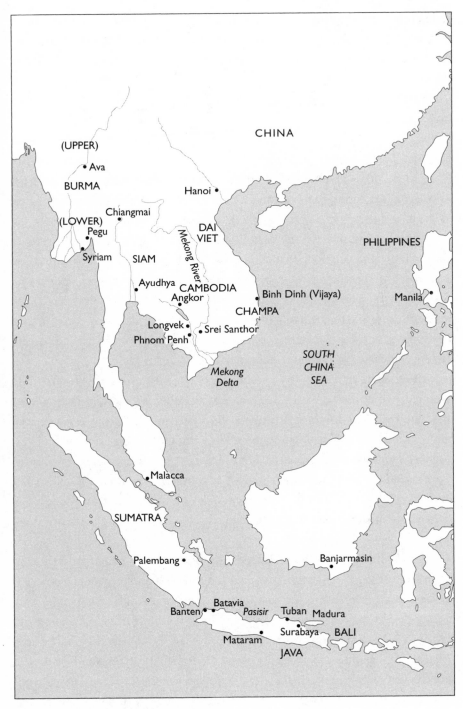

MAP 7. Early modern Southeast Asia

Camões advises the king of Portugal to reinvigorate the historic national spirit, just as Cato and Livy inspired English adventurers to a life of "resolution":

> Men have not now that life and general gust
> Which made them with a cheerful countenance
> Themselves into perpetual action thrust.
>
> On you with fixed eyes looks the cold Moor,
> In whom he reads his ruin prophesied.[9]

The poem ends with an appeal to the king to take the field in North Africa.[10] Glorifying his nation's achievements, Camões mapped Virgil's world on to the new globe.[11]

Camões died in 1580, the year that Philip II of Spain annexed Portugal, propelling conquistadors further across Southeast Asia. Cambodia, where Camões took part of his epic, now became one of their targets. Along with Siamese armies, Spanish and Portuguese crisscrossed the country in the late sixteenth century. In the name of its Christian conversion, they committed at least one genocidal massacre. Cambodia's internal divisions were also debilitating; civil wars "weakened the country for two centuries."[12]

The first Iberian to visit Cambodia was the missionary Gaspar da Cruz, who reached its then capital, Longvek, in 1556. He left after a year, disappointed that the country's 100,000 Theravada Buddhist monks "are worshipped for gods" and that "Christians cannot be made without the king's approval."[13] Portuguese Dominican missionaries arrived at Longvek in 1570 and Franciscans 15 years later. A 26-year-old Portuguese adventurer named Diogo Veloso also arrived in 1585, and spent the next decade in Cambodia. After surviving a Siamese siege of the capital in 1587, Veloso was adopted by King Sattha (r. 1576–94).[14]

Cambodia was one of mainland Southeast Asia's smaller powers, surrounded by the growing strength of Siam in the west and protected from Vietnamese encroachment in the east only by the rump realm of Champa, itself a long-term rival dismembered by Dai Viet a century earlier (see chapter 3). Ethnoreligious consolidation and royal power in Cambodia may have paralleled the unification processes that were transforming other Southeast Asian polities, and they might explain why missionaries made few voluntary converts to Christianity in Cambodia, but the country's small size and its frequent devastation by powerful neighbors also enabled other invaders to maximize their influence. One result was an attempted conquest of Cambodia by independent

Iberian adventurers, who staged a genocidal massacre of the entire Khmer court, reminiscent on a small scale of conquistador massacres in Caribbean and Mexican capitals.

Two Spaniards, Captain Gregorio de Vargas and the 21-year-old Blas Ruiz de Hernan Gonzalez, sailed from Canton to explore Cambodia in 1592. They may have contemplated its conquest and conversion to Christianity. When they docked en route in Champa, its king seized their junk and cargo. The two Castilians escaped and reached Cambodia in 1593, to find it threatened by another Siamese invasion. Seeing their chance, they advised King Sattha to send a request to Manila for Spanish assistance, in return for a promise to adopt Christianity, which the Castilians may have hoped would enable them to convert the whole country. The king agreed and gave his adopted Portuguese son, Veloso, a letter requesting support, written on gold leaf and dated July 20, 1593. As King Satthaʼs ambassador, Veloso left for the Philippines with Vargas, while Ruiz stayed on in Cambodia to fight for the king.[15] The Spanish governor-general in Manila replied favorably to the Cambodian request, but by the time Veloso arrived back in Cambodia in February 1594, the invading Siamese armies had occupied the country. King Sattha withdrew east across the Mekong to Srei Santhor and then, after a coup by Prince Ream, fled upriver to Laos. In late 1594, Ream retook the capital and then drove the Siamese forces out of Cambodia.[16] But meanwhile, having destroyed and pillaged Longvek, the retreating Siamese had arrested Veloso and deported him overland to their capital, Ayudhya, along with their Khmer prisoners and all the Portuguese missionaries in Cambodia. Ruiz and other Spaniards were put aboard a junk, but they commandeered it at sea, overpowering the Siamese guards, and sailed back to Manila in June 1594. Veloso followed a year later.[17]

Vargas, Veloso, and Ruiz all set out for Cambodia again in January 1596. They left Manila in a frigate and two junks, with 130 Spanish soldiers, this time accompanied by several friars and Filipino and Japanese Christians. Vargasʼs frigate was blown off course. Ruiz and Veloso arrived in Cambodia first, to learn of their friend King Satthaʼs exile in Laos. The new monarch, Ream I, wary of the Castilians, possibly planned to murder them.[18] Tensions rose. In April 1596, six Chinese junks arrived off Phnom Penh. For reasons that remain unclear, the Spaniards attacked and looted them and set fire to houses in the Chinese quarter, killing several hundred people.[19]

A month later, the Iberians turned their guns on King Ream Iʼs court. At the head of 40 heavily armed conquistadores, Ruiz and Veloso marched on the

Khmer capital, Srei Santhor.[20] A Dominican friar provided a contemporary account of what happened: "They crossed two rivers and having routed the guards who were on one of the rivers' bridges, arrived at the palace at two in the morning and attacked it as if they had been lions. They tore down walls, destroyed roofs, assaulted towers, broke doors open, killed men and proceeded thus until the sun's rays shone. The king attempted to flee with his wives. They shot him and ended his life. And they brought about a war in which the ground trampled by the Castilas shook, afraid of what was happening."[21] The Spaniards also killed king Ream I's son, burned the royal powder plant, and set fire to a temple containing jeweled Buddha images.[22]

The massacre ended at dawn, and "the damage became apparent." As told by the friar, it could have been a scene from the *Aeneid:* "The palaces destroyed, the earth strewn with corpses, the streets running with blood, the women wailing, some for their husbands, some for their sons, others for their brothers and so the city seemed like Rome burned, Troy annihilated, or Carthage destroyed." The friar, Gabriel de San Antonio, penned these passages for his book *Breve y verdadera relacion de los successos del reyno de Camboxa* (Brief and Truthful Account of the Events in the Kingdom of Cambodia).[23] The title of the book, published in 1604 to persuade the king of Spain to reconquer Cambodia, might have been intended as a rejoinder to Las Casas's indictment of Spanish cruelty in the New World.[24]

Veloso, Ruiz, and their 40 conquistadores retreated to Phnom Penh, harassed by 3,000 "Indians," as they called the Cambodians, who were "furious" at the news of the attack and their king's murder. San Antonio continues: "Arrows were falling thick and fast but the Castilas forced their way through. . . . They eventually crossed the river, still firing their arquebuses. . . . The Cambodians had a very courageous Indian as their leader; he wore a golden bracelet that looked like a coiled snake." Believing he was invulnerable, this Cambodian "rushed forward like a lion. The Castilas quickly disillusioned him because one of them ripped his middle open with a halberd." The victor was Ruiz: "[W]ith one blow he thrust the Indian through, shield and body." The other Cambodians fled. The Spanish returned to their boats, "sad for not having done more."[25]

The next morning, Vargas's frigate arrived in Phnom Penh. The commander found Veloso and Ruiz still covered with gunpowder.[26] Vargas disowned what the other Iberians had done, tried to make amends to the Cambodians and Chinese, and took his expedition back to Manila in July. A new king, Ream II, ascended the throne. But in late 1594, rebels sacked the capital and forced him to flee. War and "great anarchy" wracked the country.[27]

Veloso and Ruiz headed overland to Laos. Finding that Sattha had died there, they escorted his son to Cambodia and, with Lao help, placed him on the throne in return for personal fiefs south of the capital. The new king, Barom Reachea V, defeated and killed Ream II, but more rebellions plagued his reign. In 1597–98, Ruiz and Veloso's men executed five Khmer and Malay dignitaries in an unsuccessful attempt to impose order. Local Japanese assisted them. Lao troops numbering 6,000 also intervened against the rebels, but killed a Franciscan and several other Europeans before withdrawing.[28]

Ruiz and Veloso appealed for Spanish reinforcements. Ships delivered more friars and a few dozen soldiers.[29] Three additional warships set out from Manila in September 1598, with 200 soldiers, again accompanied by Japanese and Filipinos. But the two frigates were wrecked and sank en route. The third warship reached Cambodia in October with 25 Spanish soldiers and three Dominican friars. Military supplies and more Dominicans arrived from Hong Kong early the next year, along with a ship from Nagasaki captained by a Japanese-Portuguese mestizo and a Spaniard who had survived the wreck of the *San Felipe* off the island of Shikoku in 1596. The two ships anchored near the capital's Muslim quarter, and trouble broke out. In mid-1599, all sides appear to have turned on the conquistadores. Muslim Chams and Malays, now joined by Japanese, "with a few Cambodians," attacked the Spanish and Portuguese, burned their ships, and slaughtered nearly all of them, including Veloso and Ruiz. Of the entire expeditionary forces in Cambodia, only one friar, a soldier, and five Filipinos survived.[30]

The Chams and Malays then pursued and killed Barom Reachea V.[31] Cambodia briefly disintegrated into several territories. Even the rump principality of Champa seized part of the Mekong delta. Cambodia's royal chronicles record the feared "annihilation" of the country, "as if there were no sun to light the world."[32]

Royal Conquest and Religious Repression in Java

In contrast to the attempted Christian conversion of Cambodia, the Islamization of what is now the Indonesian world had progressed with a remarkable cultural syncretism. As Java became Islamic, it domesticated Islam. Muslim tombstones in east Java, possibly of aristocrats of the classical Majapahit em-

pire, combine Koranic texts, Old Javanese numerals, and Indian *Saka* dates
(1290, or 1368 C.E.). A fourteenth-century inscription from Malaya, recording
the introduction of Islamic law, refers to Allah by the Sanskrit title *dewata mu-
lia raya*. A fifteenth-century Malay-language inscription appears in both Arabic and Indic scripts.[33] Some Muslim kings in the Moluccas (the Spice Islands)
adopted the Islamic title *sultan,* while others retained the Indic *raja,* and Javanese Muslim monarchs titled themselves *ratu* or *susuhunan.* The Muslim holy
men who reputedly converted Java in the sixteenth century are known in local
tradition as the nine *walis* (saints in Arabic), but they all retain the Javanese
honorific title *sunan*—even those of non-Javanese origin.[34] And ironically, as
if to qualify their achievement in introducing Islam, they are also credited for
the centuries older *wayang,* the indigenous shadow theater that still portrays
Hindu epics in Java today. In the late sixteenth century, the ruler of Java's new
kingdom of Mataram sought help not only from the Muslim wali, Sunan Kali-
jaga, but also from the indigenous Javanese Goddess of the Southern Ocean.
On Java's north coast, in the town of Kudus, named for al-Quds (Arabic for
Jerusalem), a mosque built in 1549 and named after the al-Aqsa mosque in
Jerusalem was constructed with pre-Islamic design features such as Old Java-
nese split doorways. Historian Merle Ricklefs notes the "cultural assimilation at
work as Islam encountered the powerful high culture of Old Java," which made
Javanese Islam "rather different in style from that of Malaya or Sumatra."[35]

A Javanese ethnic identity slowly crystallized. Early Javanese Muslim texts
distinguished Islam (*agama Selam*) from "Javanese religion" (*gama Jawa*).
By the seventeenth century, Javanese texts began to mention "the people of
the island of Java" in quasi-ethnic terms, distinct even from the Sundanese-
speaking population of the western tip of the island. Islamization possibly reinforced an ethnic identity based on the Javanese language. Yet cultural categories remained fluid.[36] Ricklefs speculates that Java's invasion by foreign
forces in the seventeenth and eighteenth centuries may have further stimulated a Javanese ethnic identity, conceived in Islamic terms.

Cultural interaction had a commercial counterpart. As global maritime
trade expanded, Chinese merchants, Arabs, and other Muslim traders had
long established themselves in the port towns of Java's north coast, known as
the *pasisir.* This offered commercial opportunities to many Javanese peasants
there, who produced quantities of rice for export. In search of spices, the Dutch
East India Company (VOC) arrived in the Indonesian archipelago at the turn
of the seventeenth century. It set up headquarters at Batavia (now Jakarta), on

the northwest coast, and also sought pasisir rice, while slowly extending its dominion eastward.[37]

Meanwhile the rise of the new empire of Mataram, founded in central Java in the 1570s, brought escalating conflict, urban destruction, commercial strangulation, and religious repression. In 60 years of warfare, successive Javanese rulers tried furiously to control the new influence of merchants and Muslim religious leaders, and to reestablish the agrarian legacy of the classical empire of Majapahit. They repopulated the fertile rice lands of inland south-central Java, site of the first-millennium Buddhist and Hindu temples of Borobodur and Prambanan.[38] On its arrival the VOC found Mataram forcefully expanding through central and east Java.[39] In a series of campaigns, Susuhunan Agung (r. 1613–46), whom Ricklefs calls the "greatest of Java's warrior kings" of its "last great dynasty," brutally subjugated most of the Javanese-speaking heartland. Agung's forces also devastated the more cosmopolitan, flourishing trade-oriented pasisir cities and deported many people from conquered east Java to his inland capital.[40]

The death toll in these conquests was enormous, partly as a result of new military technology. By the 1620s Agung reportedly deployed at least 4,000 musketeers.[41] He laid waste to town after town, including, in 1619, Java's largest city, Tuban. A seventeenth-century Javanese chronicle records that "all was empty" in these towns. "The people of Pajang were defeated; they left their land. . . . The people of Tuban were defeated and left their land."[42] Crops failed, and Dutch sources reported that even by 1617 "a very large number of people have died of starvation." By 1624, so many men had been forcibly conscripted that "there was hardly anyone left" in Mataram "but His Majesty himself and some women." Agung's army, which lost 5,000 men in its conquest of the nearby island of Madura, killed the members of all but one of the Madurese princely families and took 100,000 prisoners back to Java. After a series of sieges and crop despoliations, the major coastal entrepôt of Surabaya fell in 1625, "not by assault but by starvation." The VOC reported that "not more than 500" people remained of Surabaya's population of 50,000–60,000, "the rest having died or gone away because of misery and famine." Dutch reports stated that "in many places" two-thirds of the inhabitants perished in epidemics in 1625–26. "Almost everywhere on Java the population was afflicted by death." In the town of Ceribon "more than two thousand people died during the east monsoon; in Kendal, Tegal, Japara and all the coastal towns of Java as far as Surabaya, as well as in various places in the interior, countless deaths occurred." Despite this heavy toll, the VOC reported in 1626 that Agung "forces great masses of the population from every quarter to settle in his vicinity and uses them for his extraordinarily great work projects." By the next year, Dutch reports commented that as a result of war and loss of life, "the part of Java subject to the [ruler of] Mataram is much depopulated, many good trading towns situated on the coast are deserted, agriculture is neglected, and a very large proportion of the people is reduced to penury."[43]

All this destruction in the Javanese heartland did not prevent Agung from attempting external expansion as well. He mounted two disastrous assaults on the VOC's Batavia headquarters in 1628–29.[44] Overseas interventions brought Javanese suzerainty in 1622 to part of Borneo, and three years later to the Sumatran kingdom of Jambi.[45] Agung mounted an expedition against Bali in 1632 and conquered Java's eastern salient by 1640.[46] The chronicle records "great commotion" as the conqueror extracted "all their labour . . . from the people of the east."[47]

Agung's victories ended a long struggle between Java's commercial seaports and its agrarian interior.[48] In establishing what the Dutch historian Bertrand Schrieke has called the paradigmatic "kingdom based on conquest," Mataram "destroyed the trade area completely." Agung told the Dutch: "I am not a trader," distinguishing himself from the ruler of Surabaya. He still sought commercial revenues but repressed all Javanese competition. After the VOC's conquest of Malacca in 1641, Agung imposed a state rice monopoly. He further asserted central control of agricultural areas by reining in their indigenous Javanese nobles, so that "the independent landed aristocracy was forced to become a court nobility."[49] Agung crushed rebellions in 1627 and 1630, including a revolt by Islamic religious teachers. He massacred the rebels and deported the local population from the Priangan region of west Java.[50]

Islamization proceeded under royal control. In 1633, Mataram abandoned the Javanese dating system for Islamic Era dates. Traditional Javanese theosophy, however, persisted in Agung's mystically philosophical writings and elsewhere. So did the aura of the "old imperial crown of Majapahit," from whose Hindu Javanese royal house Mataram claimed descent. The court accorded prominence to seers inherited from that tradition.[51]

In 1638 the ratu (king) of Banten in west Java became a sultan, the first Javanese monarch to adopt the Muslim title. Susuhunan Agung promptly sent a Mataram embassy to Mecca, gaining authorization to use an Arabic name along with the title "Sultan," which Agung adopted in 1641. However, Javanese chronicles record that it was the indigenous Goddess of the Southern Ocean who visited him in 1644 and prophesied his approaching death, which indeed occurred two years later. Agung's son, Amangkurat, took the throne—not as Sultan but, like his father earlier, as Susuhunan.[52] The chronicle records that he was "handsome and young" and that "buffalo and rhinoceros were set against spear-men" in games at the coronation celebrations in April 1646.[53] From Agung, the 27-year-old king inherited power over a Javanese population of around 3 million. While the father had been "brutal in the tradition which defined royal greatness" in precolonial Java, Ricklefs writes, the son proved simply "brutal without being successful or creative." Imposing what Javanese came to consider "the quintessential example of tyranny," Amangkurat dismembered the realm Agung had forged.[54]

Immediately on assuming the throne, Amangkurat I moved to intensify the royal stranglehold over any potential opposition. Agung had domesticated the indigenous regional nobles; by contrast, his son "did not rest until he had destroyed every one and all those associated with them." Amangkurat I "raged against princes, landed nobility, and officials alike."[55] The new king first organized the assassination of a court official named Wiraguna, with whose wife he had been involved as crown prince in 1637, having him killed along with others involved in the scandal.[56] According to a Javanese chronicle, Amangkurat I also ordered the execution of the courtier's entire family of 12.[57] The subsequent VOC ambassador at the court, Rijklof van Goens, reported the king's instruction that all those who "had brought charges against his father should with wife and children be exterminated as rebellious people."[58]

The nature of the new regime became clear as Amangkurat I's violence escalated and provoked opposition from his 19-year-old brother, Pangéran Alit. Seeing that "his best friends were all mostly lost," Alit now moved "to gather a new retinue." With "his remaining friends," Alit won support among Muslim leaders for an attack on the court.[59] Learning of his brother's plot against him, the king discussed its repression with his uncle, Sultan Agung's surviving brother, who, "aghast, requested his nephew not to make himself guilty of shedding his brother's blood." So Amangkurat I promised his uncle restraint, using words "held to be very holy among them." First, an investigation began. Alit had to provide "the names of his associates." When he refused, his followers were tortured. Some, whose children's lives were threatened, denounced Muslim leaders, but, van Goens reported, to "no avail: all except babes in arms were killed." The king had the severed heads of two of Alit's senior accomplices thrown at him, saying: "That is what they look like, those who would raise you to the kingship."[60]

The young Alit retaliated by attacking the court with 50 mounted men. According to van Goens, Alit "came in riding his horse (killing, with the help of his men, those who would prevent him from coming in on horseback). The King, seeing this, gave orders that his brother's companions should be killed at once, but that no one should be so bold as to shed royal blood." Having vowed restraint, Amangkurat I simply sacrificed many of his own men in order to justify eventually killing his brother, the prince, with impunity. Van Goens continues: "This happened so quickly, thanks to the great number of armed bodyguards, that they were all knocked off their horses in a short time. The desperate brother, who was seeking death, did his utmost to be killed under the heap of his aides, but was so avoided, that even his horse was not injured, although he stabbed more than twenty bodyguards to death before his feet with his long kris, from which the power of this tyrant's orders can be appreciated."[61]

Protected by many more bodyguards, Amangkurat I finally ordered Alit's horse killed, whereupon Alit stabbed a venerable courtier to death. The king lost patience, instructing his men: "I am guiltless of my brother's blood; do your duty." Alit stabbed another lord. Proclaiming his pristine innocence, the king finally "gave authorization for self-defence and soon the prince was pierced through." A chronicle reports that Amangkurat I "rejoiced in his heart" but feigned a display of grief, "made a bleeding gash in his upper left arm," had his head shaved, and "grieved a few days as a sign of mourning." As for Alit's followers, "[t]he Madurans were all killed as punishment."[62]

Amangkurat I spent the mourning period "racking his brains as to how he could take revenge on the popes," as van Goens termed the Islamic leaders and teachers (kiai) who had supported Alit. The king decided to compile a list of prominent religious leaders.[63] Promoting four trusted courtiers, Amangkurat I sent them across the countryside in all directions, with orders "to see to it that not a single person among all those who bore the title of pope within the entire jurisdiction of Mataram should elude him."[64] While the king secluded himself in the palace, relatives of the Islamic suspects were asked, "under pretext of a special request, about their names, their family, their actual residences, and so forth." The king planned, "when he judged appropriate, to strike them all dead with one blow." One day in 1648, the king had the Muslim leaders all assembled together at court. According to van Goens: "Everything relevant having been communicated to the King, who had the names of the guilty and of the innocent," Amangkurat I then instructed his followers that "each should secure his [men], without sparing man, woman or innocent children; giving them at the same time the indication that this must take place as soon as he had a cannon fire a shot from his court." He "armed himself on the day determined with good guardsmen, all divided under his faithful friends, and no sooner was the cannon shot fired but no fewer than 5 to 6,000 souls were horribly murdered within half an hour."[65]

In this way, 2,000 religious teachers and their wives, children, and followers perished in public.[66] But a Javanese chronicle reveals only that they "disappeared . . . upon the road" and adds: "The commotion of the people of Mataram was like the confusion of leaves blown in the wind; great and small were alarmed . . . the king constantly cherished a grim hatred."[67] Van Goens arrived in late 1649 to find the victims' remains still in public view.[68]

The day after the massacre, Amangkurat I appeared at court, looking "very wrathful and dismayed." He sat silent for an hour, "which increased the fear" and so "no one dared behold or look up." He blamed the Muslim leaders for his brother's death. A few survivors were presented to him, who confessed to plotting on Alit's behalf. "Flying into a passion the Sunan then had 7 or 8 lords whom he distrusted brought away and murdered. Their wives and children were also killed at once." He retired into the palace, van Goens reported later, "leaving behind all the old lords, who had been elevated in the time of his father, in great concern and distress."[69]

Throughout his long reign, Amangkurat I applied his new technique of "royal display and distance" in various ways. The Dutch historian H. J. de Graaf argues that for the next five years, he "showed a better side of his personality." According to historian Jean Taylor: "In his public appearances he was always surrounded by bodyguards. Twenty thousand men armed with pikes and some muskets formed a square around jousting and animal combat when the king attended; his inner bodyguard was female." All offenses required capital punishment: "[T]he accused were burned in oil or brought before the king, who personally stabbed them." Meanwhile, Amangkurat assembled a network of possibly 4,000 spies.[70]

Van Goens commented in 1648 on "this strange manner of their government . . . as the old are murdered in order to make room for the young."[71] The court purges continued. A Javanese chronicle describes the dignitary Kartatalis, "stabbed to death" in 1649, "doubling over upon his rattan mat." It names 11 others who later met similar fates, while lesser officials were "hacked to pieces."[72] Sons perished with fathers: "[R]eflective were those who saw."[73] As Ricklefs observes, "merely to be a person of distinction with a potential to gather a following was sufficiently dangerous." Amangkurat I killed the son of the surviving lord of Madura in 1656, along with his mother, two brothers, and three high officials.[74] Many of Agung's former associates also disappeared, "murdered upon the king's orders." In 1659, Amangkurat I killed his own father-in-law, the last prince of Surabaya, along with most of his family.[75] When the crown prince, Amangkurat's son by the Surabayan princess, apparently attempted a coup in 1661, the king had over 50 of his son's supporters murdered.[76] Three other sons soon threatened disloyalty.[77] Amangkurat dismissed the court's highest official in 1666 and had 15 royal servants beheaded.[78] The king's favorite paramour died the next year, possibly poisoned. When the crown prince had an affair with her intended replacement, Amangkurat I had her executed.[79] Schrieke writes: "One lord of the realm after another fell victim" as the king's violence cut down both the royal family and the aristocracy. His purges were partly political and partly produced by apparent insanity. But Schrieke, who suggests that the king "foresaw the impending dissolution of his empire and attempted to prevent it by carrying on a reign of terror," also sees ethnoreligious and economic divisions, which he refers to somewhat speculatively as "the reaction of the Arabistic Mohammedan coastal population . . . in the struggle against the Javanistic Islam of the agrarian Mataram."[80]

The economic stakes were high. From the commencement of his reign, Amangkurat I had determined to "to keep his land shut off" and to monopolize external trade. He wished to restrict the VOC to obtaining rice only from his royal treasury at Japara, not from the Javanese pasisir, where Batavia bought 10,000 tons of rice in 1648. A Dutch official reported that now "everyone . . . must ship their supply all to Japara" and "must collect his needs there, for people in any other places are not allowed to sell rice under pain of death."[81] Amangkurat I appointed superintendents in 1651 to control coastal ports and revenues, dominating and extorting Javanese, Chinese, and Dutch traders.[82] In the same year, he banned the construction of cargo ships in Java and ordered "that no one of his subjects may voyage out of the country, but [he] desires that everyone from elsewhere will come and seek his country, well knowing that same to be the chief chamber of supply for Batavia; and he thereby attracts everything imported by us to himself without anyone of his subjects being allowed to trade even a penny." The result was that "the moneys or whatever it may be are then delivered to the king's treasurers." In 1652 the king prohibited rice and timber exports; in 1655–57 and again in 1660–61, he ordered the complete closure of Java's ports.[83] The royal rice monopoly struck "a grievous blow at the last vestiges of private trade." Moreover, Amangkurat I attempted to further his independence from the VOC by encouraging the local cultivation of cotton. Schrieke concludes that "as a result of the diminished purchasing power of the people the attempt proved successful."[84] Similarly, Amangkurat I discouraged cultural exchange by introducing a tax on fees paid to traveling performers.[85]

By restoring economic primacy to Java's agrarian hinterland but impoverishing its population, Mataram managed to "to turn back the clock of history."[86] Thus, rice cultivation was an ideological project as well as an economic monopoly in an expanding territory. Amangkurat I sent settlers to establish new agricultural zones on Mataram's western Javanese frontier. Royal charters detail the dispatch of 1,100 people to clear jungle and build rice fields in the area of Krawang, 600 in another area, 200 in another. Their leaders were to collect the surplus paddy and deliver it to the capital. The lasting effect "was to plant Javanese speakers in Sundanese territory and Javanese Muslim culture in the [former] Hindu lands of Pajajaran. Sundanese tradition ascribes permanent rice fields to the Javanese."[87] The chronicle describes large-scale deportations, as Amangkurat moved workers to his agricultural enterprises. In 1649, "the Kalang people were ordered to move their homes across the river." Seven years later, the inhabitants of the city of Pasuruan "were transported to Mataram; thousands of couples were moved out, buffaloes, cows, and all the cattle were taken along."[88] At one point in 1661, Amangkurat I had 300,000 laborers, from the coast as well as the hinterland, working on irrigation projects.[89]

Along with efforts to dominate trade and develop agriculture, Amangkurat I pursued an expansionist territorial policy. In 1647, he attacked the Balinese in Java's eastern salient.[90] According to the chronicle, "The people of Bali were destroyed, driven away; on land none of them remained, and the warriors at sea were destroyed, disappeared, and fled."[91] Amangkurat I obliged the Sumatran ruler in Jambi to pay him homage in 1651, and he later complained that kingdoms on Borneo had failed to do so. He summoned "forty thousand ships—ten from each place," to attack Banten in 1656. He referred to himself in 1667 as the "Susuhunan Ratu of Mataram, whom God blesses in all his works" and "to whom all the kings of the Javanese and Malay lands pay homage." The next year the VOC learned that the Susuhunan "intended a war against the people of Borneo, and with this view, had given order for great numbers of vessels to be made ready." By 1673, Amangkurat I called himself "the master of all Java" and the "lord of thirty-three islands."[92]

However, opposition was by now "deeply rooted among the surviving dignitaries" of Mataram.[93] His sons fell out over a woman in 1672. The crown prince killed 33 members of his brother's entourage, and Amangkurat detained 4,000 of their followers to stop the fighting.[94] Purges continued as Amangkurat executed the governor of Japara in 1672, then dismissed his successor three years later.[95] Revolt flared anew as the people of "the ruined port-towns" and their non-Javanese allies, led by the grandson of the last lord of Madura, rose up against "the agrarian interior."[96] From 1674, poor crops and Amangkurat's monopoly forced even the VOC to import rice from Siam. Yet, as starvation spread along with rebellion, in early 1677 the king turned and sought aid from the VOC.[97]

This alliance with the Christians united his Muslim opponents. By mid-year the VOC were his last allies.[98] According to the Mataram chronicle *Babad Tanah Jawi,* as rebels approached the capital, Amangkurat I fled in despair. He refused to fight "because he realized that it was the will of Allah that this was to be the end of Mataram."[99] Nevertheless, Amangkurat ordered his son to make common cause with the VOC and exact vengeance on the east Javanese population (*bang wetan*), whom he called the major enemy. The king died in a small village by the roadside. VOC troops attended his funeral on July 13, 1677.[100]

The sons of Amangkurat I fought each another and the rebels. The VOC reported "famine, sickness, death, and people fleeing" and in the capital, "so many deaths" that "people fled away to the western regions."[101] As the chronicle put it, "the violence in men was in movement." Amangkurat I's bloodthirsty massacres and all Mataram's military might had failed to unify Java's interior and coastal constituencies. The kingdom collapsed into a half century of recurrent wars of succession, leaving "unknown numbers dead" and heralding a new era of Dutch dominance and the division of Java.[102]

Ethnoreligious Massacres in Early Modern Burma

Ethnoreligious differentiation developed slowly in vast, polyethnic Burma. Its three major groups spoke different languages but all practiced Theravada Buddhism and wet rice cultivation. Alliances formed, ruptured, and reformed between Burma's two main regions linked by the Irrawaddy River: the northern, upland interior, inhabited largely by Burmans and Shans, and the southern, lowland, coastal and delta regions, home of Mons, Burmans, and others.

The Burmese language, Victor Lieberman points out, was first written only in the eleventh century and became dominant at court in the twelfth. The first extant Burmese-language reference to "Burmans," and the first to Upper Burma as "the land of the Burmans," date to 1190 and 1235, respectively. Beginning in the 1360s, two decades of Shan raids on the northern Burman heartland then faded into wars that instead pitted the predominantly Burman and Shan north against the mostly Mon, multiethnic south. These conflicts of 1385–1425, according to Lieberman, "sometimes exhibited an ethnic element," yet the divisions were also regional, mixing members of different ethnic groups on each side while distinguishing the north, "the land of the Burmans," from the southern "land of the Mons."[103]

These blurred ethnic visions focused only very gradually. First, as elsewhere, rising religious impositions sharpened the perspective. In the late fifteenth century, the Mon king of Lower Burma ordered 16,000 Theravada Buddhist monks reordained, in order to "purify" the region, an order without ethnic implications.[104] The expanding southern dynasty of Toungoo, which had begun as a center of Burman refugees from Shan raids in the north, established a cosmopolitan court at the Mon port city of Pegu in 1539. Its most famous king claimed to be a Buddhist *cakkavatti,* or "World Ruler," whose loyal followers a Mon general described as "[a]ll [of us], his chosen men, in fact, whether Shans, Mons, or Burmans."[105]

Yet, contradictorily, ethnic distinction and religious purification also often buttressed one another. The first Burmese-language chronicles appeared in Upper Burma from the fifteenth century. The most prominent, dated c. 1520, celebrated not just an ethnolinguistic group but "our country of Burma," putatively visited by the Buddha in antiquity. One sixteenth-century chronicle sniffed that the south had "as many Mons as there are hairs on a bullock, but we Burmans are as few as the horns." In the north, moreover, Shan raids on Upper Burma resumed in the 1520s, culminating in a period of Shan domination of the multiethnic northern court of Ava.[106] A Burmese inscription charged: "The heretic Shans pulverized, ground to pieces, and utterly destroyed the Burma country." The Shan ruler of Ava massacred 360 leading monks in 1539, destroying monasteries and Buddhist texts. Shan courtiers "humiliated their Burman colleagues, taunting them and knocking off their distinctive headgear, until the exasperated Burmans massacred every Shan they could lay hold of." The Burman courtiers, however, then offered the crown to another Shan prince. Burman children sang: "Shans shall plough the fields, carry rations for us, while we Burmans fly overhead," and others called the Shans "wild and uncivilized."

Yet even as Toungoo's polyethnic southern forces marched north from Pegu, a mixed Shan and Burman army defended Ava until its fall to Pegu in 1555.[107]

Burman-Mon tensions emerged in the 1590s. The tables turned, and the Mon capital Pegu fell in 1598. Burma's new Restored Toungoo dynasty established an expanded empire, forcibly resettled conquered ethnic populations in irrigated rice-growing areas of its Burman-dominated northern hinterland, and removed the capital upriver to Ava again. Only then did ethnicity, along with regionalism, begin to entail a political loyalty.[108] Burman-Mon competition for land and resources on the southern frontier led rival groups to seize on ethnic markers as symbols of difference in the interest of more effective group mobilization. Mons and even Burmans from the south now lost influence in the northern capital; "the number of southern families who obtained appointments at the royal court declined steadily until by the early eighteenth century few, if any, could be found in leading positions at Ava."[109] From 1635, Burmans gained total control of the court and began to associate Burman ethnicity with religious orthodoxy, even against fellow Theravada Buddhist Shans and Mons, whose distinct languages and hairstyles they now highlighted as alien, creating a "fusion of religion and ethnicity." With Burman southward migratory settlement and intensifying warfare, religious universalism and imperial polyethnicity increasingly coexisted with the new ethnic chauvinism that was accompanied by the popularization of Burmese vernacular literature, including a new origin myth for the Burman people.[110]

As Burman farmers expanded south into the Irrawaddy delta and Ava replaced local Mon officials with Burman appointees, Mon revolts of the 1660s reinforced ethnic stereotypes. Seventeenth-century Dutch observers wrote that the Mons of Pegu "at present are tormented above all others" and predicted they "would in all probability put to death the Burmans." Burman encroachments continued, and by the mid-eighteenth century Mons composed only 60 percent of the delta's population.[111] They had to compete not only with Burman settlers but also with Karens arriving from the eastern hills, where the secession of the Shan kingdom of Chiengmai in the 1730s prefigured the disintegration of Ava's empire. Assaults from Manipur in the west and a bloody domestic purge of top Ava palace officials in 1735 intensified the crisis.[112]

The Mons of the south increasingly saw themselves as a people subjected to alien rule, resentful of Burman outsiders who monopolized government appointments and competed with them for trade and land. Mons rebelled twice in 1740. High taxation seems to have been the major grievance, but ethnic issues intruded. A Mon account put it: "The Mon people" first "conspired together and consulted a brahmin," saying: "We don't want to be subjects of the Burmese." The brahmin replied: "The astrological situation of the Burmese is very poor. But the heavenly signs shine brightly on the country of the Mons."[113] Ava briefly reestablished control, but in a second revolt in November 1740, Karens assassinated Ava's Burman appointee, acclaiming as king of Pegu one of their number, Smin Dhaw. Claiming to be the son of an Avan prince, Smin Dhaw quickly sent 10,000 Mon and Siamese troops to take the Ava-controlled port of Syriam. On December 4, 1740, Pegu's army entered the city "in tumult and violence," wrote the English East India Company's agent there. The victorious commander quickly issued "orders to be given to all strangers to keep at home and that they should not be molested."[114]

The Mon occupation of Syriam was bloody. A week or two later, Smin Dhaw wrote to the English representative to explain what his forces had done in the city. The new king of Pegu complained first of "the very great oppressions the poor Peguers formerly labour'd under by the Buramore [Burma] government and the massacre they intended on the casts of people called Siamers and Peguers." Smin Dhaw then explained that "having advice that the Burmar Prince of Syrian design'd to take and imprison all the Peguers, Siamers, Tavays and all strangers and resolved to burn them by treachery, I Samentho [Smin Dhaw] was obliged to send my soldiers to kill all the governing Burmars that were in Syrian; and as now the said governing Burmars are destroyed."[115] Corroboration of this reached British Madras the next month: "A ship from Pegu brought advice of a Revolution in that Countrey." After 80 years of Burman rule, the report said, "the Natives tired with Cruelty Rose upon 'em and killed 7 or 8,000 Burmars in Syrian only, wholly owing to a Struggle for Liberty." In the aftermath of this massacre, the British learned, "[t]he port of Syrian is Quiet."[116]

Smin Dhaw said he now hoped that "the strangers, Peguers, Siamers and Tavays will again be at peace," and he invited the British post at Syriam to protect "all the strangers, Christians, Moors, Mallabars and Chinese."[117] But war and ethnic conflict did not end there. The English agent claimed: "I saved the lives of above two thousand Burmars and have since been endeavouring by all means to regulate and moderate the Government." Meanwhile, Smin Dhaw's forces marched north against Prome. The Burmans there abandoned the city without resistance and "fled toward Ava to a man." Two months later, the British agent reported that the Burmans were "so infected with fear that they will not attempt a recovery by arms," and Smin Dhaw's victorious forces "will not rest" till they conquered Ava.[118] New fronts proliferated. In 1742–43, according to a Mon chronicle, Smin Dhaw "sent armies of 3,000 to attack Ava" and "700 to attack Toungoo, which surrendered without a fight," but then a force of 150 Karens "attacked Pegu at night. The Pegu forces killed all of them."[119]

Violence and ethnic confusion pervaded this imperial interregnum between the collapse of Burma's Toungoo dynasty and the rise of a successor. Smin Dhaw's successor, Banyà-dalá, was an ethnic Shan who vowed to restore the Mons' sixteenth-century Pegu kingdom of Bayin-naung.[120] He marched north and besieged and captured Ava in 1752, deporting 15,000 northern Burman courtiers and troops back to Pegu. Uncovering a plot among them two years later, Banyà-dalá massacred a thousand of these deportees, including the deposed Burmese monarch, in October 1754, provoking a successful Burman revolt in Prome. Meanwhile, some of the Mons defied ethnic loyalties by resisting the authority of Pegu, which conversely welcomed Burman allies but made them adopt Mon hairstyles and wear ear amulets of loyalty.[121]

Meanwhile, in the north, the all-conquering new Burman leader Alaung-hpaya (1714–60) gathered strength. The fall of Ava in 1752, he later recalled, had been followed by "destruction and disorder throughout the countryside, when mothers could not find their children, nor children their mothers, when the Mon rebels carried off people, selling and reselling them as slaves."[122] Alaung-hpaya mustered his forces by employing both universalist and ethnic appeals. He included Mon adherents in his army but at the same time, using the derogatory epithet for Mons, he warned Burmans in the southern enemy forces that "in planning to remain a subject of the Talaings [Mons], you are betraying both your lineage and your abilities." Appealing directly to these fellow ethnic Burmans in the Mon ranks, his own forces unfurled their distinctive Burman topknots in battle. Alaung-hpaya spared Burman prisoners of war, but he executed Mon captives. His more systematic ethnic discrimination was unprecedented in Burmese history, according to Lieberman. Even so, it was not completely successful; more than 5,000 Burman troops fought for the southern kingdom to the end. At any rate, Alaung-hpaya was determined to become the universal Buddhist monarch. He distributed a prophetic letter from Sakka, the king of the second Buddhist heaven, dated April 9, 1756: "He shall exalt the Faith . . . the Mons and Shans shall serve him, nor shall the Chinese, Siamese, or Indians escape his dominion."[123]

Alaung-hpaya intensified his campaign of ethnic chauvinism when his army attacked the Mon capital of Pegu in 1756.[124] According to a Mon account, written in Thai in the 1790s: "The Burmese laid siege to Pegu for one and a half years. The inhabitants were in a bad way. Some decided to join the Burmese side, and set fires in the city. Some lowered ropes to enable the Burmese to enter the city." Pegu fell on the morning of May 7, 1757. Alaung-hpaya's army razed the city and massacred the garrison, "with bodies piled so high in the gates that people within the city could not escape."[125]

The victors also slaughtered Mon civilians, especially the Buddhist monk-hood, many of whom had led the resistance.[126] A Burmese version of a Mon chronicle composed a decade later details what happened. "Alaungpaya took revenge on the Mons. . . . He flung most of them including over 3,000 monks [under] the elephants, killing them all. The Burmese officials used the monks' velvet robes for making cloaks for themselves. The cotton robes were used for making mattresses, rice bags, napkins and rugs. The monks' iron begging bowls were used as pots for cooking rice. . . . The surviving population was also badly treated. They suffered terribly at the hands of Burmese. The Burmese officials sold the Mon captives as cattle at different prices: 100 ticals of silver, 50 ticals, 25 ticals, 20 ticals and 15 ticals each. Thus the families were separated. The sons could not see their mothers, the mothers could not see their sons."[127]

"The monks helped the city to resist," Alaung-hpaya had reportedly complained.[128] The Thai-language Mon annals explained that Mon monks had allegedly made amulets "to protect the soldiers and to make them brave in war. Many people were therefore killed." Furious at the Mon monks, Alaung-hpaya "declared that they were not true *bhikkhus* [monks] and thus had his soldiers kill more than 1,000 of them. The *bhikkhus* fled in fright to the forests, to Chiang Mai, to Mûang Thai [the Thai kingdom] and to Tavoy."[129] The Mon monk who had composed the earlier chronicle explained his higher estimate of the toll: "At that time all the monks of the country who lived outside the city were gathered together in Pegu. There were over three thousand of them. The Burmese king having taken Pegu, put all the monks to death. Only the monks who lived right out east . . . went away on to the Siamese cities . . . to escape from death." Alaung-hpaya, according to this monk, "was of a very fierce and cruel disposition, and made no account at all of life. He put to death many monks," scattering their robes "all over land and water."[130]

Burma's north, writes the historian William Koenig, "had subdued the south for the last time."[131] The new Kòn-baung dynasty began. As much as Alaung-hpaya marshaled regionalism and ethnicity to subjugate other groups, he still "considered himself much grander than the leader of a particular ethnic community." He appointed loyal Mon officials and does not appear to have ordered them to adopt Burmese customs. However, he was unsatisfied with mere subjection. During his advance on the south Alaung-hpaya had already resettled large numbers of displaced Mons into the western delta. He now deported many more upriver to northern rice-growing areas near Ava and sponsored strategic settlements of Burmans in the south, adding to the flow of spontaneous migration that was swamping the Mons, who remained there as a "subject race."[132]

Alaung-hpaya planned further territorial expansion that may have reflected his visions of Embryo Buddhahood. Setting out to attack Siam, he told his son in 1759 that he planned to capture "Tavoy, Tenasserim, Ayudhya, Lamphun, and Chiengmai, and to instruct them in the Law. Then I shall tour the eastern Shan country and return to the capital." He proclaimed to the Siamese that he was an Embryo Buddha (*bodhisatta*) whose merit they should recognize. Alaung-hpaya claimed to be "touring the world with the sole objective of making more radiant the Buddha's religion." However, the siege of Ayudhya ended in retreat, as many of his troops died of disease. Alaung-hpaya himself succumbed on the return journey, in 1760.[133]

Alaung-hpaya and his sons, who maintained power in the new Kòn-baung dynasty, established a pervasive cult of antiquity while they ruled Burma almost uninterrupted from 1752 to 1819. Echoing Dai Viet's syncretism of indigenous and classical Chinese culture, Hideyoshi's combination of Shintō and Buddhism, and the eclectic Javanese domestication of Islam, the Kòn-baung dynasty fostered a complex cult of indigenous Burmese, Brahmanic, and Buddhist antiquity that persisted in Burma through the 1820s. Recalling Hideyoshi's claim to be the "Son of the Sun," Alaung-hpaya's early edicts portrayed him as descended from the "solar lineage" through the union of a Burmese serpent princess with the sun spirit, who had fathered the founding monarch of Burma's medieval empire of Pagan. Another common Southeast Asian Buddhist and putatively ancient model was the ideal "first king" (Maha Thamada), the earliest monarch-restorer and lawgiver in the Buddhist cycles of human deterioration and moral decline from initial perfection. Subjects of the kingdom were considered immoral, requiring regulation by such meritorious kings, and at the commencement of the world, the people had invited the first king to the throne. The role of a Maha Thamada monarch was to regulate human affairs, to "revile and degrade those who should be reviled and degraded and banish those who should be banished." Only an evil ruler "gives no consideration as to who should die and who should not, who should be mutilated and who should not." Alaung-hpaya's early biographer, comparing him to this mythical Buddhist founding monarch, claimed that he had acceded to the throne "as Maha Thamada had been invited."[134] Alaung-hpaya also portrayed himself as the Buddhist "superman," with the temporal attributes not only of Indic universal monarchs (*cakkavatti*) like Maha Thamada, but also of the special cakkavatti Sankha, herald of the emergent Buddha (*bodhisatta*) who ends the intervening cycle of progressive decline. This royal self-glorification surpassed the heretofore most extreme claims by an eleventh-century king of Pagan. Alaung-hpaya now imposed "the general use of capital punishment" for violations of Buddhist moral precepts.[135] His sons followed suit and went further, tracing their ancestry from the "pure" lineage of Buddhist kings, the "Sakyan race," and enshrining their claims in the compilation of the *New Pagan Chronicle.* The fourth son, Bo-daw-hpaya (r. 1782–1819), whose court produced this new compilation, outdid his father and brothers by telling monks he was the bodhisatta Metteyya, likening himself to the ancient Indian Buddhist emperor Asoka (c. 273–232 B.C.E.), and tracing his father Alaung-hpaya's lineage to a fabricated monarch of eleventh-century Pagan.[136]

Unprecedented territorial expansionism had necessitated this search for temporal legitimacy. The Kòn-baung dynasty reached its "high tide of empire" in the 1760s. Alaung-hpaya's first two sons had inherited their father's officer corps, steeled in the internecine wars of the previous decade. Their Burmese troops defeated three Chinese armies in the north in 1766–69, even while devastating Siam's capital, Ayudhya, in 1767. Lieberman puts the Siamese death toll at possibly hundreds of thousands. Burma launched further massive, costly, unsuccessful attacks on Siam in 1785–86.[137] According to a Thai account, "the sinful Burmese ravaged our villages and cities. . . . Our peaceful kingdom was abandoned and turned into forest. The Burmese showed no mercy to the Thai and felt no shame." In another series of campaigns, Burmese armies deported tens of thousands of Shans and other minorities to Upper Burma, and in 1784–85, 20,000 conquered Arakanese as well.[138]

The external aggression complemented an economic focus on domestic rice cultivation. The Kòn-baung state harbored an "innate distrust of foreigners." It sought little trade to diversify its agricultural economy, prohibiting even rice exports and maintaining a state monopoly on the surplus, recalling Java under Amangkurat I. From 1761 to 1794, Burma broke off contact with the

English East India Company and also with the French, but for a limited arms trade in 1770–84. The Ava court renewed its agricultural colonization policy in the south in 1790, granting land there to Burman settlers from the north and waiving taxes for the initial years of cultivation. The result of all these policies of militaristic expansion, ethnic violence and deportation, agricultural settlement, and royal opposition to competitive commercialization was disastrous. The population of over 2 million around 1760 fell by 17 percent in 1783–1802 alone, followed by further serious famine in the first decade of the nineteenth century.[139]

By then, the Burman court had brutally repressed six more Mon uprisings. This involved, in 1774, the execution of the last Mon king and his two surviving heirs. Though despite everything the Burman monarch would still marry a Mon princess, possibly 40,000 Mons fled to neighboring Siam. Burmans subjected the rest to mass deportations and cultural suppression.[140] A British visitor reported around 1790 that "by far the greater part of the Talain [Mons] had fled since the conquest of their country to Siam, and they continue to take every opportunity of making their escape."[141] Other Westerners reported that Mons adopted Burmese dress and language "in order to avoid extortion." One noted: "The Peguers no longer exist as a nation; they are nearly become extinct, or are incorporated with the Burman."[142]

Imperial, universal, and assimilationist thinking now proliferated in new historical works. Possibly the first Burmese-language chronicle to include the term *Burma* in its title appeared in 1798, and in the same decade a religious history fused Lower and Upper Burma's monastic lineages into a Buddhist pedigree supposedly even older than that of Sri Lanka.[143]

The Kòn-baung dynasty had emerged against a background of increasing warfare and ethnic polarization in Burma, including genocidal massacres by the threatened, briefly resurgent Mon kingdom. The subsequent early Kòn-baung orgy of violence and death betrayed some of the classic symptoms of other genocidal regimes: cults of antiquity, ethnic chauvinism, aspirations to universal rule, territorial expansionism, close control of commerce, and a preoccupation with land and agricultural settlement.

Ethnoreligious Violence in Cambodia, 1600–1800

Burman expansion at Mon expense paralleled that of Vietnamese into Cambodia and the two-way Siamese expansion into both Mon and Khmer lands.

Having razed the Cambodian capital, Longvek, in 1594, Siam intervened there again in 1601 and still occupied northern Khmer territory three years later. The Khmer king, Barom Reachea VII, reputedly told his court in 1617: "When the Thais [Siamese] have defeated and subjected the Lao and Mon countries, because of their resentment towards us, they will certainly raise troops to come and attack our country again. It is fruitful for us to contract an alliance with the Vietnamese kingdom.... If the Thais raise troops to come [to attack us], we will take the troops of the Vietnamese kingdom to help us make war, so that the Thais can no longer harm our country."[144]

Hoping to settle matters on the eastern front, Cambodia's crown prince married a Vietnamese princess.[145] But Siamese invasions from the west recommenced in 1621–23. Crossing into the frontier provinces, a Thai army found all the towns and villages empty. The Khmer king, Chey Chetta II, had ordered everyone into the forest. Similarly, in the 1630s, a Khmer army took the Siamese town Korat and deported its inhabitants into Cambodia. In that case, the king reprimanded his generals for not establishing an administration in Korat instead.[146]

As in the 1590s, when the Christian conquistadores had briefly benefited from Cambodia's subjection to Siamese invasion, now Islamic influence reached its zenith in Buddhist Cambodia, and violence escalated again. With help from local Malay Muslims, a young prince named Ponhea Chan seized the Cambodian throne in 1642, murdering the king as well as his own father. Chan married a Malay and took the name Ibrahim. He ordered his court: "You must all enter the religion of Allah. If anyone refuses to do so, he will have to leave the royal service."[147] Outside the royal palace on November 27, 1643, Cambodian soldiers murdered the ambassador of the Dutch East India Company, massacred 35 other VOC personnel, and seized two Dutch ships.[148] Ibrahim had launched what would become a 10-year war on VOC trading interests in Cambodia.

Batavia dispatched a flotilla of warships carrying 432 soldiers and marines. In naval battles on the Mekong in 1644, the Cambodians captured several warships and killed 156 Dutch troops. They drove back the VOC fleet at a cost of 1,000 Cambodian lives.[149] The Buddhist Khmer royal chronicle omits to mention this war, but it denounces the country's Muslim monarch, the only one in Cambodian history, for giving Islamic Cham and Malay mandarins "more power than the Khmer." Even Ibrahim's half brothers accused him of "discarding his faith." They feared that "the Khmer nation will disappear," and they invited the southern Vietnamese kingdom of Dang Trong to help overthrow Ibrahim.[150] The Nguyen forces from Dang Trong marched across Champa into Cambodia. They captured and deported Ibrahim, who later died in exile.[151] Cambodia thus regained its status as a Buddhist kingdom, as a result of the first Vietnamese military intervention there.[152] Over the next century, however, Dang Trong armies repeatedly intervened in Cambodia, mostly at the invitation of various claimants to the Khmer throne, now combating Thai-backed rivals.[153]

The Khmer chronicles record another rebellion in 1659. Its failure drove several thousand rebels to leave for Siam, accompanied by Cambodia's chief Buddhist abbot, who reputedly lamented: "The august kings and members of the royal family have sought only to kill one another in disputes over the throne, and that over several reigns. Now the people have fled and abandoned their villages and homes to go and live in foreign countries. It is without doubt sure that this country will know more wars." As if in gratuitous fulfillment of this prophecy, 3,000 "Chinese pirates" from a Taiwanese army descended on Cambodia by ship in 1667 and massacred possibly 1,000 Vietnamese residents of the country.[154] The Nguyen monarch held Cambodia responsible, and a state of hostilities persisted until 1672.

Like the conflicts between local Mons and Burman settlers in the Irrawaddy delta, colonization and competition for resources in the Mekong delta increasingly plagued relations between local Khmers and Vietnamese settlers, beginning around the turn of the eighteenth century. On Vietnam's central coast, Dang Trong seized the last port town of the principality of Champa in 1693. Known to Europeans as Cochinchina, Dang Trong continued to expand southward down the coastline. Within six years, 40,000 Vietnamese households had independently settled near the Mekong delta.[155] Upriver at Udong, the Cambodian court claimed the delta region, inhabited mostly by Khmers, who contested further Vietnamese encroachment. French missionaries there reported witnessing a genocidal Cambodian attack, led by a self-proclaimed Buddhist monk, on the Cochinchinese-controlled port of Hatien in 1731: "People say that the war originated because of a certain woman who claimed to be the daughter of their god sent to punish the excesses of the Cochinchinese against the Cambodians, magic is mixed up in it and a great deal of prestige. She raised a considerable army of Cambodians . . . thus armed and protected by several mandarins [they] marched against the Cochinchinese and made an enormous carnage of them[;] they counted more than ten thousand of them lost as they were not at all ready to oppose her." From there the genocidal massacres spread. "[T]hus they ravaged all the provinces of the south of Cochinchina, putting all to fire and blood, killed the great mandarin of the place called Say Gon [Saigon], and burned down the fine church of a Franciscan father." Yet, "They were not content with this. They killed all those [Cochinchinese] that they found in Cambodia, men, women and children."[156] Dang Trong armies responded with two unsuccessful attacks on Cambodia in 1731–32.[157] The Khmer court at Udong retained control of most of the Mekong delta.[158]

However, internecine strife plagued the Cambodian court. In 1737, a royal chronicle records, the Khmer king "did not trust his queen," nor three princes, "and tried to kill them. Their armies fought against each other."[159] A successor left a rare inscription in 1747 celebrating his victory over a rival princess. It claimed that the king's army, "blocking and searching every road," had tracked down the princess's supporters and then "drove out, pursued and scattered" them, "so that they became aware of the ruling monarch's power." Royal forces, the inscription went on, captured "many of the slaves and possessions" of the princess, presenting them to the king with all her "commanders, troops and goods."[160] Yet within months of the monarch's death, his son and successor was assassinated by a brother.[161] Then a former Khmer ruler (r. 1722–37) tried to regain the throne with the help of a Vietnamese invading force, but it was defeated after Siamese intervention in 1750, and once again a Khmer ex-monarch died in Cochinchina.

Having benefited from Siamese support, the new Khmer king, Ang Snguon (r. 1749–55), now presided over escalating violence. A French missionary in Cambodia reported that war "raged more than ever" there. In a letter dated April 8, 1751, M. Piguel informed his superior: "It is war inside [the country] every day; new princes appear who want the throne; now there are four of them." Ethnopolitical conflict with Dang Trong produced more genocidal massacres in 1750. "It is also war outside, against the Cochinchinese who are not far away. . . . There have been great cruelties on both sides. The Cambodians have massacred all the Cochinchinese that they could find in the country, including three mandarins; several Christians were caught up in this murder. . . . At first they took no prisoners, but killed all those they could find. Now they are sent as slaves to the king of Siam, to repay him for the help he has given to the king of Cambodia."[162]

A few months later another missionary, M. d'Azema, identified the author of this massacre. King Ang Snguon's Cambodia was "in a very sad state," d'Azema wrote. "[L]ast year the king had his son, who had been at the court of Cochinchina, killed on some suspicion of rebelling against him." It was the Khmer king himself, who, "some time later," at the end of July 1750, launched the attacks on every Vietnamese residing in Cambodian territory, including the Mekong delta; "he gave orders or permission to massacre all the Cochinchinese who could be found, and this order was executed very precisely and very cruelly; this massacre lasted a month and a half; only about twenty women and children were spared; no one knows the number of deaths, and it would be very difficult to find out, for the massacre was general from Cahon to Ha-tien, with the exception of a few who were able to escape through the forest or fled by sea to Ha-tien." Of Cambodia's "numerous" Vietnamese residents, d'Azema reported finding no survivors, "pagan or Christian."[163]

D'Azema was also able to observe Cambodian authorities' approval of these royally sponsored genocidal anti-Vietnamese massacres. In Phnom Penh, the missionary wrote, "the great mandarin of this place, who is the first after the king, and who governs everything," summoned him for an audience. From d'Azema, the Cambodian mandarin then learned of the Christian missionaries' expulsion from Cochinchina "on almost the same day" that the mass killing had begun in Cambodia. D'Azema reported: "He even told us that God was punishing the Cochinchinese for their iniquities, and especially for the impieties committed against our holy religion." Apparently at the same meeting with d'Azema, this Khmer mandarin offered to have a painting done of a European priest with "his foot on the throat" of a Vietnamese. The missionary declined this offer.[164] Later, d'Azema reported how the "pagans of the kingdom, king, princes, great and small," took the news of Cochinchina's mistreatment of missionaries and burning of churches as justification for their own massacres of the Cochinchinese. They "raised their hands to the sky saying that God is just, that he had used them [the Cambodians] to avenge us."[165]

Despite these series of genocidal massacres, the intensifying ethnic politics in mainland Southeast Asia still fell short of full polarization. Ethnic chauvinism had to contend with universalist Islamic and Buddhist aspirations, regional loyalties, personal patronage, and continuing dynastic claims over myriad subject peoples. Yet on specific occasions, local rulers did select members of an ethnic group for destruction. In the two cases of vigorous smaller kingdoms threatened by settlement or conquest, Pegu's monarch Smin Dhaw in 1740 and the Khmer king Ang Snguon in 1750 both ordered precisely targeted genocidal massacres. The larger, more confident polities also resorted to extermination. Amangkurat I's slaughter of Java's Islamic teachers in 1647, like Alaung-hpaya's ethnic massacres and destruction of Mon monkhood in Burma in 1752–60, occurred in contexts of territorial expansionism, agricultural settlement and conflict over resources, and cults of antiquity. These contexts for genocidal violence were recurring across the globe.

Part Two

SETTLER COLONIALISM

Introductory Note

The roots of race lie deep in the soil. One of the earliest epithets of ethnic discrimination connected culture directly to cultivation. The Latin *silva* (woods) came into English as "sylvan," especially in pastoral poetry. Yet it is also the root of the term *savage,* "salvage" in early modern English. Elizabethans also used the term *savagery* for unwelcome plants like hemlock that had to be uprooted by the plow. A later commentator even described the common people as "trashy weeds or nettles," suggesting that domestic inferiors could become as vulnerable as hostile indigenes to the charge of obstructing cultivation. The same term, then, denoted inimical groups *and* uninhabited land: "savages" implied forest-dwellers lacking agriculture, and a "sylvan" landscape required no people at all. Real problem and ideal solution rolled into one. Racial or ethnic prejudice, reinforced by charges of inability to cultivate, often revisited the idealized, empty, "virgin" land. Eighteenth-century English admiration for rural landscapes developed from European topographical painting in which "human figures were absent or unimportant."[1] Colonists applied the legal terms *vacuum domicilium* in North America and *terra nullius* in Australia, divesting indigenous inhabitants not only of land ownership, but sometimes even of their presence.[2]

The United States inherited its colonial intellectual history. After independence, Thomas Jefferson, heading a committee to investigate the future of America's "Western territory," recommended the creation of 14 new states, the first of which, "extending to the Lake of the Woods, shall be called Sylvania" (see map 15).[3] Writing in the *Freeman's Journal* in 1782, the American agrarianist

Philip Freneau first extolled the humbling of the eastern "savage tribes" and then went on to portray the west by almost ignoring its inhabitants: "[T]he trees of the forest are stately and tall, the meadows and pastures spacious, supporting vast herds of the native animals of the country, which own no master, nor expect their sustenance from the hands of men."[4] In much Western and U.S. literature, memoirs, and archives, purportedly real and ideal visions appear side by side, expressing both a prejudice against others and their romanticized disappearance. Contending images consistently recur together. The "savage" coexists with the Noble Savage. The sylvan merges with the pastoral and bucolic, imperceptibly bringing in both stock and keeper.

This idealized amalgam of agriculture and pastoralism has a material basis. Since ancient times, historian Brian Donohue writes, "European farming has been characterized by mixed husbandry, the marriage of herding and tillage." English farmers in particular adopted agricultural innovations in the sixteenth century that fostered further integration of pastoralism and cultivation. These advances, composing the "backbone of the agricultural revolution," first appeared in the 1560s, just as expansion into Ireland intensified.[5] One of England's key innovations was convertible husbandry, the alternation of crops and pasture by turning farmland over to selected grasses and back again, or "up corn down horn."[6] Well before the eighteenth century, England possessed "a higher ratio of domestic beasts per cultivated acre and per man than any other country, save the Netherlands." As Colin A. M. Duncan writes: "We now know that the tugging at grasses caused by nibbling sheep actually stimulates the release into the soil of chemicals beneficial to plant nutrition." It recycles "constantly regrowing grasses" and spurs "soil formation far in excess of natural rates."[7] Careful manuring of the soil further replenished it for cultivation and surplus crop production. In *An Inquiry into the Nature and Causes of the Wealth of Nations* (1776), Adam Smith wrote of the cultivator: "Not only his labouring servants, but his labouring cattle, are productive labourers." English farming had become equally agricultural and pastoral. Meadows and pasture provided fodder for stock, which deposited manure for cropland. Historian Steven Stoll writes that "the new husbandry eliminated the fallow and made every farm into a manure factory." Previously fallow land came under permanent intensive exploitation.[8]

Most important for indigenous peoples, the power of this "alliance between animals and grasses" also fueled territorial expansion. As Stoll writes: "[T]he complex consisting of wheat, barley, cattle and sheep moved along the boundaries of human settlement and European colonization."[9] A Connecticut farmer's diary for 1672 records the productive variety of this farming lifestyle. On July 20 that year, Thomas Minor wrote, "we reaped our rye. The 22nd we were cutting off oats, and fetching in the summer wheat and peas. Monday the 29th, we cut winter wheat." The next Saturday, Minor stored "all the English corn." Then, on September 2, "I fetched the calves from the farm. The 6th day, I made an end of sowing wheat." Then came the time to plant Indian corn and make apple cider. On November 6–7, "our sons killed their swine," and the next day, "the rams were brought from the island." On January 8, "I made an end of threshing of winter wheat and rye."[10]

Such a rich, intensive agrarian economy left little space for indigenous users of the land. Minor tells us almost nothing of his community's relations with the remnants of the local Pequot Indians, devastated in the war and genocide of 1637–38. He mentions only his visit to a neighbor's house "about his Indian Jean," and returning there six months later on "Indian business." We don't know what happened in July 1672 when "the committee met with squmacut people," an Indian group. It is easy enough to see how the survivors had become so marginalized in one generation. The extremely efficient, rapidly expanding English economy of multiple land uses simply spared few ecological niches for Indian subsistence. Donohue writes that in nearby Concord, Massachusetts, English yeoman colonists put "nearly every part of the landscape" to work, in "a mixed pasture and arable system designed to yield a comfortable subsistence directly from family land." The colonial settlement "was not simply filling out to its borders, it was filling in, too."[11]

In Thomas Jefferson's later conception, America west of the Ohio could even be divided into squares (called "hundreds"), with settlers assigned to occupy each. As political scientist James C. Scott has pointed out, these blocks of land, 10 miles square, were much more "legible" to an advancing state.[12] Laying down a new economy like tiles, the mathematical grid left no irregular spaces, smothering any chance for indigenous people to subsist on traditional land uses around settlers' holdings. The vision reflected not only a false notion that the land was previously empty, but an equal determination to fill it full. In 1803 Jefferson urged both "condensing instead of scattering our population" and "range after range, advancing compactly as we multiply."[13] Across the entire continent by 1862, "[e]very acre of our fertile soil," in the view of Abraham Lincoln's commissioner of agriculture, "only waits the contact of labor to yield its treasures; and every acre is opened to that fruitful contact by the Homestead Act." As historian David Nichols points out, "No Indian land was secure when 'every acre' was so coveted."[14]

Yet genocide and extermination require more than territorial expansion and ecological expulsion. Thomas Minor's diary entries for 1672 give no hint of the murderous hatred toward Indians that exploded nearby during King Philip's War just two years later. There is no reason to accuse Minor of any racism or violence. Singly or in combination, the idyllic images of pastoralism and the economics of expanding and intensive agriculture often accompany genocide but cannot fully explain it. Along with violent religious or racial prejudice, genocide usually requires territorial conquests, frequently based on classical models. Moreover, as chapter 9 shows for Africa, and historian Mark Levene has demonstrated for parts of Latin America, European states and settlers with agrarian traditions different from England's proved quite capable of developing their own genocidal colonial policies (see figs. 6–8).[15]

As the historian Howard R. Lamar has remarked about the American West and Bain Attwood has pointed out in *Telling the Truth about Aboriginal History*, assembling and verifying the historical sources on frontier conflicts is frequently difficult.[16] Disparate events occur far from public view or record. Surviving indigenous voices are few. Many sources are secondhand, many eyewitnesses silent. Some perpetrators of frontier violence may boastfully exaggerate the numbers of their victims; others deny, dissemble, or minimize their crimes. Most difficult to argue, however, is that perpetrators both exaggerated their killings and were deterred by legal jeopardy or social disfavor. In all too many cases, several sources corroborate one another, concur on significant details, or suggest a series of similar genocidal incidents. These rarely typify a whole frontier or implicate an entire society, yet scholars have shown that they occur frequently enough to require serious attention to the phenomena of colonial genocide and extermination.[17] The next five chapters reveal the relevance of settler preoccupations with antiquity and agriculture, as well as territorial expansion and racial division.

CHAPTER 5

The English Conquest of Ireland, 1565–1603

When England followed Spain and began to embark on imperial conquests, it, too, studied Roman models. During the Renaissance the continuing recovery, translation, and dissemination of classical texts influenced Catholic and Protestant alike. Fifteenth-century Spain's familiarity with Aristotle, Caesar, and Livy was complemented in the sixteenth century by the addition of Virgil and Polybius to the English canon. Like the Spanish before them, English expansionists linked classical accounts of the triumphs of Rome and the disappearance of Carthage to reemerging agrarian preconceptions of rural morality and fruitful land use. In England the ideology of cultivation became even more prevalent. As historian Liana Vardi puts it, images of agricultural labor now "penetrated the learned sixteenth-century panorama," fortified with "classical virtue and Christian salvation."[1] Inhabitants failing properly to cultivate coveted land increasingly merited subjugation, deportation, and even destruction.

Along with intensifying religious and ethnic prejudices, the Roman military model combined with the new agrarian ideology to launch English colonizers on a voyage to empire, with Ireland as the first port of call. Resistance they faced there also provoked a pastoral romanticism that imagined the landscape without its inhabitants. Antiquity, conquest, agriculture, and genocidal massacre became inextricably intertwined. The Latin word *colonum* (farmer) spawned the English twin terms *colony* and *colonel*, while agricultural "plantation" became the word for settler colonizations that effectively left little subsistence for the original inhabitants.

The Anglicization of Antiquity

Geoffrey of Monmouth's twelfth-century *History of the Kings of Britain*, starting with the great-grandson of Aeneas, was first printed in 1508. William Camden's *Britannia* proposed in 1586 to "restore antiquity to Britain, and Britain to its antiquity." For his first play that same year, Christopher Marlowe remade Virgil's *Aeneid* into "a conflict of cultures and colonizing powers." In *Dido, Queen of Carthage*, written in Cambridge in 1585–86, Aeneas strides the stage as a new European hero. On his way to found a new Troy, and a new Trojan race from which the Elizabethan English would claim descent, he stops off in Carthage.[2] Jupiter demands that "in blood must his good fortune bud" after "managing those fierce barbarian minds." Dido soon laments that "all the world calls me a second Helen" and fears that "as fair Troy was, Carthage might be sack'd." A third of Marlowe's play comprises direct translation or paraphrase from the *Aeneid*.[3]

Englishmen were already becoming familiar with the story of Carthage and Rome, and many took its purported lessons to heart. Renaissance humanist Thomas Elyot's *The Book Named the Governor*, published in 1531, drew heavily on Livy's account of the Second Punic War.[4] Elyot lamented that England's "noblemen be not as excellent in learning as they were in old time among the Romans and Greeks." Reprinted sevenfold by 1580, *The Book* cultivated "the gentle wits of noblemen's children," like "a fine and precious herb" tended "in the most mellow and fertile earth" by "a wise and cunning gardener." Elyot recommended that English boys under the age of 14 study Homer and "specially Virgil," for "[w]hat ploughman knoweth so much of husbandry as there is expressed?" Good farming made good men and rivaled nobility of lineage or wealth. "Quintius having but thirty acres of land," Elyot pointed out, was chosen by the Romans for "the highest dignity," led them to victory—then "repaired again to his plough."[5]

For older pupils, Elyot recommended Caesar's works, not only as history lessons but also for "necessary instructions concerning the wars against Irishmen or Scots, who be of the same rudeness and wild disposition that the Swiss and Britons were in the time of Caesar. Semblable utility shall be found in the history of Titus Livius [Livy], in his third Decades [books 21–30], whence he writeth of the battles that the Romans had with Hannibal and the Carthaginians." As models of loyalty, Elyot praised Rome's ancient allies of the town of Saguntum, who, rather than surrender to Hannibal, burned their town and themselves "with their wives and children," recalling the fate of Dido and of Hasdrubal's family in 146 B.C.E. And Elyot modeled selflessness on the conqueror Scipio, who "when he had gotten and destroyed the great city of Carthage, he was not therefore the richer one halfpenny ... honour resteth not in riches." Elyot also praised the "most noble emperor Octavius Augustus," and dedicated his *Book Named the Governor* to Henry VIII. It was used to tutor young James VI of Scotland.[6]

A canon designed to produce strong English leaders hammered home ancient models of conquest and ideology that gave pride of place to the Roman victors over Carthage. The tutor of Henry VIII's son reported in 1544 that the seven-year-old prince was "now ready to begin Cato" along with "other wholesome and godly lessons."[7] A *Historye of the Two Most Noble Captaynes of the World, Annibal and Scipio,* published in London in 1548, praised Henry VIII for his "wise and woorthy conquest" of Ireland.[8] A European edition of Plutarch's *Lives,* including those of Cato, Hannibal, and Scipio, appeared in English in 1579, dedicated to Queen Elizabeth.[9] Polybius's writings on "The Roman Military System," noted by Machiavelli early in the sixteenth century, had also attracted wide interest. "Polybius was read and studied about 1600 as perhaps never before or after."[10]

As it edged closer to the brink of empire, England's emerging leadership turned increasingly to classical precedent. In London in 1568, Gabriel Harvey obtained a Latin copy of Livy's history and began annotating it. Harvey read Homer, Virgil, and Tacitus, but he rated Livy highest: "No historian is as appropriate to ... a politician." Livy's lesson was in conquest. Harvey, a member of the Elizabethan "war party," wrote: "Love is lewdness, when time biddeth hate. Peace is to be refused," he added, when "time forceth men to war." He urged Englishmen, "peace laid aside, to prepare for war."[11]

The first conquests were to be Irish. In 1570–71, Harvey and a half dozen Elizabethan gentlemen met frequently to discuss Roman military strategy. The venue was the home of Harvey's friend Sir Thomas Smith, the royal secretary and author of *De Republica Anglorum* (1565), and his son Thomas junior. After reading books 21–30 of Livy, Harvey recorded on his copy: "I ran over this decade on Hannibal in a week, no less speedily than eagerly, ... with Thomas Smith [junior]. . . . We were freer and sometimes sharper critics of the Carthaginians and the Romans than was fitting ... and we chose not always to agree with either Hannibal, or Marcellus, or Fabius Maximus; nor even with Scipio himself." The Smiths, father and son, explicitly used classical works as handbooks for what they hoped to accomplish in Ireland. They had already petitioned the court for authorization to colonize the Ards Peninsula in Ulster. While preparing for this, Thomas the elder read Livy and recommended his son read Cope's *Historye* of Hannibal and Scipio. Livy and Plutarch were among Smith senior's three favorite authors.[12] Applying the Roman model to his planned settlements in Ulster, Smith used the Latin term *colonia* to derive the title "colonel" for the settlers themselves. A new capital, Elizabetha, would be built first, a citadel as in "Rome, Carthage, Venice," becoming what Carthage's "Byrsa was to Dido."[13]

A key lesson from Rome's wars, inspired no doubt by Cato as well as Scipio, stressed decisive, ruthless initiative. The most "resolute man in England," Harvey wrote, was "altogether for Caesar, & Livy." Hannibal, "a terrible Youth," was a "ventrous and redouted Captain," who "matched & tamed" the Romans, yet "Scipio beat him." Significantly, the "young Scipio" possessed dual qualities: "sweetest courtesie, & terriblest valour." It was his iron resolve that decided the war's outcome. To Harvey, "Hannibal was beaten first in spirit; [and] was immediately beaten in the flesh as well. . . . The sole essential for a great man is to seize the instant with great possibilities forcefully, with shocking power, and to play the powerful leader, when it is important to do so, with terrifying power." Beyond this obsession with "power," history added moral lessons that recalled Cato's concern to toughen up the Romans. Harvey wrote: "Had Carthage not been Rome's bitter enemy, Rome would never have become the powerful mistress of the world. The harsher the ill fortune, the greater the favourable fortune in the end."[14]

A debate occurred at the Smith home, on the different strategies for fighting Hannibal that the Roman commanders Marcellus and Fabius ("the Delayer") had advocated, according to Livy. Harvey wrote: "Thomas Smith junior and Sir Humphrey Gilbert [declared] for Marcellus, Thomas Smith senior and Doctor Walter Haddon for Fabius. . . . At length the son and Sir Humphrey yielded to the distinguished secretary: perhaps Marcellus yielded to Fabius. Both of them worthy men, and judicious. Marcellus the more powerful; Fabius the more cunning . . . each as indispensable as the other. . . . There are times when I would rather be Marcellus, times when Fabius." This debate was not academic. Humphrey Gilbert had already participated in one attempt to colonize Ulster and had spent most of 1566–70 fighting in Ireland. Smith junior, impressed like Harvey by Hannibal's veteran pragmatism in defeat, would die there in 1573.[15] Gilbert wrote in admiration of ancient Rome's political and territorial supremacy, sharing Cato's preoccupation with domestic and cultural threats as well as foreign enemies: "Cato, by banishing Vice in Rome, did deserve more honnour then Scipio did by conquering the Carthagians."[16]

The members of this circle saw Ireland in the role of Cato's Carthage. England's governor, or lord deputy, of Ireland from 1566 to 1571, Sir Henry Sidney, who first sought private financing to "induce" colonies there (a translation of Caesar's *deducere coloniam*), and in 1566 had sent Gilbert back to London to make the case,[17] had his young son, Philip Sidney, educated in Cato's moral axioms (when he was 12 years old, Philip's first Cato textbook was lost; a replacement was bought) as well as in Virgil, Caesar, and Livy. In mid-1576 Philip joined his father, who was now back in Ireland, then returned to England that October.[18] For the next four months, Philip Sidney and the ubiquitous Gabriel Harvey read the first three books of Livy. Harvey described "scrutinizing them" and "applying a political analysis." He later wrote: "Two outstanding courtiers thanked me for this political and historical inquiry: Sir Edward Dyer and Sir Edward Denny." Without stating why, Harvey added: "But let the project itself—once fully tried—be my reward. All I want is a lively and effective political analysis of the chief histories: especially when Hannibal and Scipio, . . . Pompey and Caesar flourished."[19]

The Smiths and the Sidneys were part of that grander political "project" to bring Ireland under English control. Sir Edward Denny left for Ireland in August 1580 with Arthur Grey de Wilton, the new lord deputy, whose appointment had been promoted by Robert Dudley, Earl of Leicester. Harvey advised Denny to hone his needed military skills by studying history, "setting downe what you reed, as in descriptions of battaillons, camps and marches."[20] The poet Edmund Spenser, a member of Leicester's household and another close friend of Harvey from the 1570s, also left for Ireland to work with Grey.[21] Spenser had just written a Latin poem calling Harvey "the great Cato of our era" (*nostri Cato Maxime saecli*). Harvey wrote back that he hoped to "justify" Spenser's praise, being involved in "greate and serious affaires." He added that "your great Catoes, . . . and our little Catoes, . . . make such a buzzing, and ringing in my head." Harvey took Spenser's place as Leicester's secretary. From Dublin, Spenser wrote him a sonnet, praising him as a "looker-on" who did not seek "the favor of the great. . . . But freely doest."[22] Renaissance letters demanded resolute deeds.

Four years later, Harvey again reread Livy and Machiavelli's *Discourses on Livy* (1531), "with diligent and curious obseruations of the notable actions of the Romans, accomplished at home, & abrode . . . the imperiall ciuil lawe of the prudent, valorous, & reputed just Romans."[23] To Livy's extensive praise for Cato the Censor, Machiavelli had added his own endorsement of Cato's "good example."[24] Harvey also read Polybius on the Punic Wars, and recognized Livy's aphorisms "copied from Polybius." In 1590, Harvey once again reread Livy, through St. Augustine's *De Civitate Dei:* "[F]or observations on Livy I prefer Augustine to any other theologian." Augustine had read the now lost books of Livy and written what Harvey called an "extremely important chapter" on the duration of the Punic Wars. Augustine wrote that they "terminated in the utter destruction of Rome's rival."[25]

Harvey, the Smiths, and their associates, imbued with enthusiasm for Cato and Livy, stood at the center of a circle of emerging radicals in the Elizabethan order. As the historians Lisa Jardine and Anthony Grafton conclude, "Harvey read the Carthaginian and Roman past above all in terms of the English present. A rising member of the rising war party, he ached for action, like his patrons."[26] Nicholas Canny calls this group extreme or "advanced" Protestants, compared to whom Henry Sidney was a moderate. Another historian, Brendan Bradshaw, describes them as "a group of radical young courtiers and intellectuals, led by Sir Philip Sidney, with the Earl of Leicester in the role of godfather, who strove to combine the ideals of protestantism and neo-chivalry, and to put military arms at the service of social renewal, the protestant cause, and the greater glory of England."[27]

The conceits of this group of radical Protestants spearheaded a broader culture of classicism and conquest. Historian Ciaran Brady notes that the anonymous play *Octavia,* "written and performed within the Sidney circle" in the 1570s, portrayed Caesar as a victim of "the malice and ambition of false friends." Henry Sidney donned "the Caesarean toga" to write his memoirs in 1583.[28] That year an Oxford-educated Elizabethan Dubliner, Richard Stanyhurst, published a translation into "English heroicall verse" of the first four books of Virgil's *Aeneid.*[29] In 1585, Marlowe began writing his *Dido, Queen of Carthage.* According to Merritt Hughes, "all Europe, from Lisbon to London, was emulating Virgil's apprenticeship in the pastoral as a discipline for writing epic poetry." What Hughes calls the "vogue of the pastoral tempted young men to experiment with eclogues, and the fast developing self-consciousness of nations and of princes encouraged them to dream of writing epics." When Edmund Spenser published *The Faerie Queene* in 1590, "it was prefaced with a stanza which every reader recognized at once as a translation of the famous lines linking the *Eclogues* and the *Georgics* to the *Aeneid*."[30]

These classic texts circulated quickly through successive generations. At Cambridge in 1578, Queen Elizabeth's godson John Harington received a letter from Lord Burghley urging him to read Livy, Caesar, Cicero, Aristotle, and Plato. Years later, Harington also praised the *Aeneid* as "approved by all men." Children, he said, "wade in Vergill and yet strong men do swim in it." He translated book VI, recounting Aeneas's journey into the underworld, where he found Cato and the Scipios. Harington then presented Burghley's grandson with his commentary on book VI.[31]

Virgil inspired epic deeds, too. Harington visited Ireland in 1586 to consider participating in the Munster plantation and returned in 1599 at the head of a cavalry troop to "marche against the Iryshe Rebells." There Harington gained an appreciation "of the whole state of the countrie"—and a knighthood. When he presented the Earl of Tyrone with one of his books and was asked to read from it, Harington let the book fall open, imitating the ancient divination practice *sortes Virgilianae* (random selection of a line from Virgil).[32] Meanwhile, his godmother Queen Elizabeth was translating Virgil's *Ars Poetica* into English.[33] King James VI of Scotland, schooled in Elyot, quoted the *Aeneid* in letters to her on their respective suppression of Irish and Scots rebels.[34] After Elizabeth's death and James's coronation as king of England, Harington presented the new monarch with his own revised translation, commenting that "no poet . . . doth better than vergill" and that "this vj[th] booke of virgill may bee fyt for Prynce Henry to reede." Comparing Anchises' advice to his son Aeneas:

> But Rule of Realms ys Roman art and glory
> to geve the law to all, take laws of none.
> To poynt what peace what war shalbee alowd
> To spare the subiect, and subdue the prowd.

Harington suggested that James I, like Anchises "a learned King writing to his deerest sonne," should single out "this passage" to his. Harington tried unsuccessfully to persuade James to make him lord chancellor of Ireland, writing that his "breeding and course of lyfe" as well as his "very *genius* in a sort lead to that Cowntry."[35]

Thus it was to Virgil, bard of Rome's *imperium*, that Marlowe turned for inspiration for his first play, on Rome and Carthage, just as England was launching a "drive toward domination."[36] Increasing contact and conflict with the Irish in the sixteenth century hung a new historical canvas that simultaneously convinced the English of their superiority while recalling their own ancient subordination to Roman rule. Persistent pre-Christian traditions in Catholic Ireland and, Edmund Spenser wrote in *A View of the Present State of Ireland*, the many Irish words "derived from the Brittish or Welch tongue," all reminded the English of "our ancestors the ancient Britons," who were similarly "rude and dispersed" until conquered by the Roman general Agricola.[37] In 1572 Thomas Smith wrote that England, once "as uncivill as Ireland now is, was by colonies of the Romaines brought to understand their lawes and ordres." And since then England had "more streightly & truly kept the mowldes" than had any other nation, even outperforming the classical model. "Yes more then the Italians and Romaines them selves."[38]

If England was Rome's heir, Gaelic society and economy reminded Spenser of ancient "Scythian barbarisme" on the borders of the Roman Empire. The barbaric Irish, he said, were "vaine" to claim descent from the more Romanized Spanish. A succession of genocidal slaughters in Spain had made that impossible. First, according to Spenser, "the Carthaginians in all the long Punick Warres" over Spain "did ... root out all that were affected to the Romans." Then the invading Romans who "beate out Hannibal, did doubtlesse cut off all that favored the Carthaginians, so that ... there was scarce a native Spaniard left." Then barbarians invaded Spain, and "all the nations of Scythia ... drowned and washt away whatsoever reliques there was left of the land-bred people, yea, and of all the Romans too." It was only later that Scythians and other barbarians from Spain "planted" in the north and west of Ireland, Spenser wrote, along with Gauls and Britons in its south and east.[39]

Spenser even speculated that the Irish were worse than normal barbarians. They may also have descended from Rome's ancient enemy and victim of its greatest triumph. In an early draft of his treatise, Spenser added Carthaginians to the Irish mix: "[A]ll those families which you name are descended of the Africans." The name MacCarthy he traced to "a Carthaginian ... Carthaye being almost verie Carthage." Likewise, Hasdrubal's lieutenant Dursica he described as forebear of the O'Driscolls, and even "O'Sullivan" supposedly hailed from "the Levant," Dido's birthplace.[40] Spenser dropped this passage from his final draft. Perhaps the Carthaginians' increasingly better-known fate made it not only impossible but imprudent to link them to the Irish. The genocide of Carthage was buried as deep in Spenser's *View of the Present State of Ireland* as it had been concealed in Virgil's allegory. But suspicion lingered that the Irish were contemporary counterparts of the barbarians Rome had conquered and enslaved, with no more right to their lands than any surviving inhabitants of the scorched earth of Carthage.

Land and Ideology

The vast majority of sixteenth-century Gaelic Irish were peasants, who "cultivated quite extensively, although their arable land was not enclosed." They tended crops and herded cattle for their landowners. All defensible arable land was under cultivation, but much of the country was hilly and boggy, suitable only for cattle and sheep. Even in these pastoral areas, "people lived in settled communities," moving their stock for transhumance only in summer months, a practice that English observers wrongly saw as nomadism; "in the mountainous regions where the plough could not be used, oats was sown with the spade in ridges." This versatile subsistence economy exploited the ecological diversity of the landscape.[41]

Some of the English were well aware of Irish agriculture. Henry Sidney lamented that war devastation in Kilkenny and Munster in 1566 had interrupted the cultivation or "manurance of the earth" in those regions, which, he added, "I have known as well inhabited as many counties are in England."[42] The Earl of Essex reported in 1574 that the O'Neill country in Ulster was not uninhabited forest but open plain whose crops could "be spoiled with a fewe horsemen." The adjoining woods could shelter cattle for a few days, "but they muste retourne to their fedinge in the plaines, and their to Manner for Corne."[43] Archaeological work in Ulster reveals regional patterns of land use including cereals, pasture, and woodlands.[44]

However, English colonial planning largely ignored the existing cultivation in Ireland. This viewpoint was possible—indeed, attractive—to prospective settlers there, because English law was based on ownership of the soil that required no documentation. The first legal textbook in England, published in 1496, concerned land law (other legal fields lacked textbooks until the nineteenth century). Yet until 1677, the law required no documents of landownership or land transfers. Ownership could be claimed on the basis of an exchange of goods or money, cultivation of the land, or other "labor" performed on it such as construction of a house or fences.[45] Sir Thomas More's *Utopia* (1515), published in English in 1551, implied this in its blueprint for colonization: "They

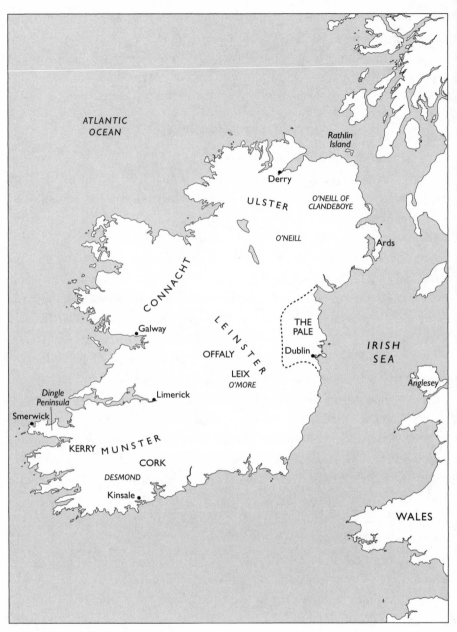

MAP 8. Sixteenth-century Ireland

consider it a most just cause for war when a people which does not use its soil but keeps it idle and waste nevertheless forbids the use and possession of it to others who by the rule of nature ought to be maintained by it."[46] Prospective farmers had a superior right to land over owners who failed to cultivate it. William Thomas argued in *The Pilgrim* (1552) that "the wild Irish, as unreasonable beasts, . . . could not be satisfied with the only fruit of the natural and unlaboured earth."[47] And under English law, they had no claim to it—that is, if they existed.

Colonial propagandists often described the land as not simply uncultivated but even uninhabited. One claimed in 1572 that the Ards region of Ulster lacked "only inhabitants, manurance, and pollicie . . . have I not set forth to you another Eutopia?" Henry Sidney advised colonists moving into Ulster in 1568 to bring seed and implements "as if they should imagine to find nothing here but earthe, and indeed little else shall they find saving only flesh, and some beasts for caring of the ground."[48] As early as the 1540s English rulers attempted to persuade Irish chiefs not only to discard their Gaelic titles and "bring up their children after the English manner, and the use of the English tongue," but also to cultivate their "lands as shall be meet for tillage, in manurance and tillage of husbandry."[49]

By 1575 Sidney had linked the supposed lack of cultivation to the Irish "race," stating that the land in Laois and Offaly "was spoiled and wasted, by the race and offspring of the old native inhabitors."[50] Before translating the *Aeneid*, Richard Stanyhurst wrote a hostile description of Gaelic Ireland in 1577. But by 1584, influenced now by the Counter-Reformation, he took pains to correct a prevalent notion that the subhuman Irish "wander scattered and dispersed through very dense woods."[51] Thirty years later, the English attorney general for Ireland still asserted that the Irish did not "plant any Gardens or Orchards, Inclose or improve their lands," with the result that "all the Irish Countries are found so wast and desolate at this day." Colonial visions of unfulfilled agricultural destiny died hard, even in the face of pragmatic military thinking that had to acknowledge the role of Irish farming: "[W]hen plough and breeding of cattle shall cease, then will the rebellion end."[52]

Overlooking Ireland's tillage agriculture, as Sepúlveda did when commenting on Mexico, colonial theorists explained its problems by reference to the collective ownership of the land, by the sept or clan, and its control by feudal lords. In 1565, Henry Sidney suggested dividing the Munster earldom of

Thomond "in to many men's hands [rather] than in one." The Privy Council agreed "that it is better for those counties of the wild Irish to be distributed into competent government of divers than to remain at the commandment of one or few." Apart from breaking the power of the Irish lords, Sidney hoped to "drive the now man of war to become the husband man." He planned to divide most of Ulster "among the various members of the O'Neill family," meanwhile keeping "secrete, even from some of [the Privy Council], the intention of habitation of ynglishe men in the north of yreland, untyll sotche tyme as Shane Onele [Shane O'Neill] shalbe subdued." That would involve dispossession and removal of many of Ulster's inhabitants, but not necessarily all.[53]

A member of the group of increasingly Catholic descendants of longtime Norman settlers, known in Ireland as the Old English, expressed a slightly different view. In his 1569 *Discors Touching Ireland,* the merchant Rowland White blamed Gaelic society's customary absence of inheritance by primogeniture for violent disputes and landowners' carelessness, though the purported effect was the same, "suffering their lands to become waste desolate and ruinous."[54] Colonists therefore planned to divide the supposedly uncultivated land not only among new English settlers but in some cases among Irish tenant smallholders. The colonial planners preserved Cato's original sense of colonum, meaning small farmer-settler. Over time, English land reform proposals continued to vary, from advocacy of the example and interests of individual rural "husbandmen" to a more controlled and militarized policy, later escalating in heightened violence to a racially based agrarian vision.

Rowland White set down his own vision for the land. He appealed to the crown in 1569 "to send over four thousand skillful plowmen" from England to rent "waste lands to inhabit and till." For "the outrooting of wickedness . . . plowmen (as good seeds) must be planted in place thereof . . . over growing the weeds of incivilitie." To White, the "good husbandry" of the Irish, even of the "skilfull amongst them," was "nothing comparable to those of England." The Irish, whom he considered "men reasonable," would appreciate both "the plentyfull placing of plowmen" and the benefits of English law, "giving all men property in profit as owners." They would even learn English "where so many Englishmen are spredde abroad thorough the land." White called for the overthrow of the Gaelic order and the adoption of English dress and hairstyle. But his English rural model for Ireland did not spring from racial prejudice or require military imposition. White ascribed "the manner of the man rather to his education than to his natural disposition" and advocated conversion of the

Irish to loyal subjection "rather by an amiable means of favorable reconcile-
ment than by any other force."[55] Others would soon add racism and violence
to this agrarian ideal.

Sidney's secretary Edmund Tremayne, writing in 1571, blamed Irish "absolute government" for "the distruction of all husbandrie." Lords rejected new
tenants from "our own nation," preferring Irish whom "they maie crush at their
pleasure" and "thrust out" at will. That offered no incentive for improvement
of the land. "And hereof cometh so badd husbandrie, as no man bettereth his
ground, maketh nor meddow, inclosure, nor orchard, nor buyldeth his house
or planteth any comaditie, because of his uncertentie to enjoye it." On the other
hand, Tremayne went on, "when Lawe shall take place, and those extreme ex-
torcions removed, Idleness wilbe banished which I meane these Idle Loyter-
ors that ar the caterpillars of the common welth, good husbandrie will go on-
werd, men wilbe driven to occupacons wherby more frutes shalbe taken of
the earth." In Tremayne's view, husbandry was also the basis of an agricultural
surplus, "the overplus that maie [be] spared," and thus, of trade: "what so ever
maie be gotten by arte and mens industries, maie be an increase to the use of
marchandice."[56]

An agricultural surplus was important to colonial planners. Most were bent
on profitable schemes that would enrich them personally or reduce costs to the
royal treasury as well as increase the security of English rule. Sidney aimed in
1570 "to fortifie, inhabit, and to mayntene tillage that within tyme may beare
the chardges."[57] White's call for measures to boost Irish manufacturing went
unheeded. Several colonial planners also talked of creating towns.[58] However,
Tremayne's description of "[c]ities and walled townes"—"the verie pillers of
the English state in this Land," as recent unrest had shown—made a military
point, not an ideological one. The garrison towns, "surest footing that we have,"
were themselves sited so "the housbond man maie attend his tillage." Tremayne
considered the existing towns to be far from "the right use of such commodities, as ther havens and fertile soiles doth offre them."[59] Cities should enhance
cultivation. The Earl of Essex required mills for wheat and malt in each of his
three planned fortified towns, with corn "sowed about the fortes." He predicted
his Ulster plan would support agriculture plus 100,000 cows and "an infinite
number of Sheepe, Swyne and Goates."[60]

The colonial vision was of communities of self-sufficient, loyal, English
farmers. For Ulster in 1567, Robert Cecil, later Lord Burghley, especially recommended recruiting "good husband men, plowe wryghtes, kart wryghtes

and smythes." Tremayne himself had first settled in Munster in 1570 for self-sufficiency, to "hold up" his family, "and in myne old daies to eat myne own bread in mye own house." Thomas Smith's plans for Ulster in 1570–71 involved a colony of "naturall Englishemen borne . . . at their own charges and perils." Essex repeated several years later that "Englishe tenntes are moste to be wished." Therefore, "if inhabitanntes come not oute of England," then he would simply settle his soldiers in Ulster. And "every one shall have certaine landes appointed him and the names of certaine yrrishe [Irish] tenanntes that shall live under him." The gentlemen planners of a new scheme for Munster in 1573, proposing to Burghley that this region "now possessed by disobedient people . . . shalbe inhabited by naturall Englishe men," required the right to "dispose by will or otherwyse any parte or parcel of the premisses to any sufficient Englishman that shall enhabit there."⁶¹

Some still contended that Irish people could contribute to this self-reliant agrarian vision. Tremayne took a view "somewhat contrary to the common opinion of our owne nation" when he wrote in 1571 that Irish "tennantes of this countrey birth will yield more gaine to the prince then Englishmen [of whom] none will come from home to inhabite here, but such as have no thing to begynne withal [and] will never do any good here." Two years later, the Munster planters, seeking title to all Irish-held lands there, informed Burghley that "the naturall inhabitants" may remain to farm the land but would necessitate a "sufficient noomber of Englishmen for the guarde and defence of suche as shall manure and inhabit the lands." When London favored a fully English colony, the organizers promised to find 3,000 Englishmen, half of them young laborers "brought upp as servants in husbandry" who would later be offered 60 acres each, plus 750 married men suitable for 360-acre "husbandry" holdings, and as many tradesmen who would receive pasture and garden land. Canny comments that this envisioned "a society modeled on that of England," with two laborers for every farmer and tradesman. But the planners also requested the right to rule by martial law, suggesting "that what they really wanted was freedom from the traditional restraints of English society."⁶²

Like other English colonialists who disdained pastoral economies, Sir Thomas Smith decried "the idle following of herds as the Tartarians, Arabians, and Irishmen do." Agriculture was central to his Ulster plantation: "Nothing doth more people the country with men, maketh men more civil nor bringeth more commodities to the sustenance of man than the plough." Each of his colony's soldiers would till 120 acres after two years or incur fines, thus "inhabiting the wastes of Ireland." His son Thomas junior would be "a maintainer of ploughs and tillage . . . come to enrich the country with corn." The gentleman colonist "shall have his ground ploughed and eared for him without his pains." Smith envisioned nucleated villages, partly communal in lifestyle even at the top of the social ladder: "as pleasant and profitable as any parte of Englande, especially when it shall be furnished with a companie of Gentleman and others that will liue friendly in fellowship together reioysing in the frute and commoditie of their former trauaile." As for their inferiors: "Your tenants, farmers, churls and labourers of the ground may still go abroad and live . . . dispersed, yet I would they should at the first be by parishes, . . . the more they resort together, and have common profit or peril, the more civil and obedient they be; else they will be and grow beastly and savage, which hath been hitherto one cause of the ruin of Ireland."[63]

Of the local population, Smith envisaged that the "degenerate" Old English could retain their lands. He even acknowledged that the "toylesome" Irish laborers worked with a "sweetness" that Smith feared would win them preference as farm workers and so "hinder the countrie much in the peopling of it with the English nation, makyng men negligent to provide English Farmours."[64] Smith promised the queen in 1570: "All Irishmen, especiallye native in that countrie which commonly be called churls, that will plow the grounde and beare no kind of weapon nor armoure, shallbe gently entertained, and for their plowinge and laboure shalbe well rewarded with great provision, that no injurie be offered to them."[65] When Smith suggested to Lord Deputy William Fitzwilliam in 1572 that English colonists "kepe" the Irish "in quiet, in order, in vertuous labor, and in justice," he added: "and to teache them our English lawes and civilitie, and leave robbing and stealing and killing one of the other." The Irish would then pay "a rent to norrrish therwith the garrisons and Colonies. They showld as fermers or copieholders have the use of the rest."[66] But they would still need instruction in "the English manner of ploughing and saving of the hay."[67] None of Smith's officials or soldiers would be allowed "to marry with the wild Irish."[68]

The Earl of Essex's vision for Ulster was more severe. He planned in 1574 to have the Irish of Clandeboye "dispersed into severall Lordshippes and well corrected, yf they breake lawes." He would tolerate no Irish or Scots soldiers, "neither kearne or Gallglace . . . with speare or Axe. I wish those to be converted to followe their labour in Husbandrie. And executed by martiall lawe, whensoever they be founde ydelle and weaponed."[69]

An extreme view of the proposed subjection of the Irish pastoral land-scape and population emerged in John Derricke's poem *The Image of Irelande*, written in 1577–78 and dedicated to Philip Sidney.[70] Historian Vincent Carey has summarized Derricke's imagined Ireland, a land of naked dancing sprites and wood nymphs who also spawned the malignant Irish *kern*, or foot soldier, what Derricke calls a "crooked generation" of "woodkern," with "glibbed heads" and "bloody hands." His poem portrays Henry Sidney "falling upon" these "noisome worms" like "pestiferous" vermin; he "doth neither pity them, nor yet his hand spare them." In the poem, this repression obliges the Irish rebel Rory Óg O'More to acknowledge that "the sept of my rebelling race, / Shall be extirped and abolished clean the land." The means of the O'Mores' annihilation are predictably agricultural: "A fearful scythe which doth prognosticate . . . That growth of things are at their ripened state, / Which must be cropped by scythe of dismal fate."[71]

Ethnic and annihilationist thinking gained ground as the colonization ex-panded and violence spread. English planning for the second Munster planta-tion began in 1580. The options discussed by the planners included "whether it should be totally inhabited with natural English men, or with a mixture of mere English and those of the English race born in the Pale, or whether part of the natural inhabitants, now rebels, might not either upon fines or rents reserved or both, be [allowed to] repossess their own." After the killing of the rebel Desmond in 1583, Lord Burghley commissioned Sir John Perrott to "re-people" the lands of Munster "with obedient people." Sir Francis Walsingham warned that "the natives of the country . . . will not manure them but in such idle manner as hath been used before." Ireland's treasurer, Sir Henry Wallop, agreed that the government should "repeople" Munster "with a better race and kind of people than the former were." Burghley, Walsingham, and other London officials now designed what historian Nicholas Canny calls "a rigidly structured hierarchical settlement" that would rely on leading veterans of the Munster wars, known as "servitors," and prestigious wealthy colonists from En-gland. The Munster plantation planners envisaged bringing over 11,400 "mere English persons without any intermixture of the mere Irish." The hierarchy would descend from 150 freeholders with 300-acre farms to as many "farmers" leasing 400 acres each to 1,100 copyholders on 100 acres each to 900 tenants and cottagers on smaller plots. As many as 62 "model villages" of at least 26 families would include "two gardeners, one wheelwright, one smith, one mason, one carpenter, one thatcher, one tyler, one tailor, one shoemaker, one butcher, one miller, a victualler, and the parish clerk." The settlers would also have to provide "warlike furniture of horsemen and footmen" for defense against "the savage or rebels." By 1587, when the poet Edmund Spenser arrived to join the Munster plantation, 160,000 acres had been surveyed, mostly in "perfect demonstration geometrical in sundry plots of all the particular parcels." Geoffrey Fenton proposed further plantations across Ireland, "after the line and square of Munster." Two years later, about 3,300 English settlers had arrived in Munster, and by 1598, around 4,000.[72]

Planters' projected roles for the Irish varied. Spenser thought they should be forced to farm. He dismissed "this keeping of cowes" as "a very idle" life, "a fit nurserie for a thief." "I doe not meane to allow any of those able bodies, which are able to use bodily labour, to follow a few cowes grazeing." Spenser advocated measures to "augment their trade of tillage and husbandrie" with laws requiring that "all the sonnes of husbandmen shall be trained up in their fathers trades," and that even owners of just 20 cattle "should keep a plough going." The more sympathetic Robert Payne considered the "better sort" of Irish to be "very civil and honestly given." Geoffrey Fenton urged English and Irish to "give good neighbourhood one to another" so that "both nations conform themselves to such conditions and tenures for their lands as her Majesty shall impose on them." Francis Bacon preferred "[p]lantation in a pure soil; that is where people are not displanted" in order to make room for others. "For else it is rather an Extirpation than a Plantation."[73]

However, most of the colonies allowed few native Irish. Planters trying to fulfill their contractual commitments "aimed to rid their properties of all Irish habitation." Jesse Smythes, a member of the Munster provincial council, rejected Irish tenants, of whom he said he "would rather set fire in the nest than such birds should roost in any land of his." Andrew Trollope considered the Irish "not thrifty, and civil and human creatures, but heathen or rather savage and brute beasts." Henry Billingsley expelled all Irish inhabitants from his Limerick property, settling 40 households "of English birth, freeholders, farmers, and copyholders." Sir Christopher Hatton, one of the planners of the Munster plantation, settled 30 English and 53 Old English, "Irish people descended of English race." Another community comprised 145 "persons of natural English birth." Edward Denny, who had read Livy with Gabriel Harvey in London, denied it was "politik that the inhabitants of this nation should be left wealthy, populous and weaponed till they were first brought to the knowledge of God, sovereignty of her Majesty, and to be answerable to the laws of the realm."

Denny thought all Irish lords disloyal and he opposed moderate measures to deal with the population: "[J]ustice without remedy must first tame and command them." Most of these English officials sought the proclamation of martial law.[74]

The vision of a controlled, militarized, ethnic English rural community initially included plans for English urban centers, yet increasingly targeted Irish towns as dominated by papists. The Munster colonial planners, or servitors, Canny writes, became "resentful and jealous of the towns." As the conquest proceeded, they accused the mostly Catholic Old English urban merchants of benefiting from the large wartime military expenditures, and even of selling "their merchandise to the rebels (underhand) at very excessive rates," making towns "the principal aiders, abettors, and upholders of this unnatural rebellion." The mercenary and publicist Barnaby Rich railed that the towns "did swarm with Jesuits, seminaries, and massing priests, yea and friars, that have recourse into Dublin itself."[75]

This religious prejudice did not imply an antiurbanism per se, but suspicion of cities had deep intellectual roots. In his *History of the World,* Sir Walter Ralegh argued that "the tyrannie of a Citie ouer her Subjects is worse, than the tyrannie of one man," and "the miseries, wherewith a tyrant lodeth his people, are not so heavie, as the burdens imposed by a cruell Citie." These included urban vice. "Was not Rome lasciuious, when Cato was faine to rise and leaue the Theater [before] . . . a shew of naked Courtisans, that were to be brought vpon the open stage?" Though Ralegh conceded that "[m]any Tyrants haue been changed into worthie Kings," and others' heirs had governed lawfully, he insisted that people living "under a tyrannicall Citie, haue no such hope." And "[i]f the subjects of Rome groned under such oppressions, what must we thinke of those, that were vassals vnto Carthage. . . . At Carthage all went quite contrarie."[76]

Rome's victory over Carthage was not the sole precedent for Elizabethan adventurers and colonists. A translation of a 1552 book by Hernán Cortés's secretary Gómara, *Istoria de la Conquista de Mexico,* appeared in London in 1578 under the title *The Pleasant Historie of the Conquest of the Weast India, now called new Spayne.*[77] The publication was a contribution to the imperial enterprise. Its choice was no doubt deliberate. Bartolomé de Las Casas had condemned Gómara as a writer who "was never in the Indies, and who wrote nothing but what Cortés himself told him to write, [and] fabricated many stories in Cortés' favour," while Bernal Díaz del Castillo denounced Gómara's narrative as "very contrary to what happened" and recounting "a great many other nonsensical things." Yet even in translation, Gómara's account of the Cholula massacre, for instance, informed English readers that on Cortés's signal, the Spaniards had "sette uppon the Townesmen, and within two houres slewe five thousand persons and more." Such violence opened the way to cultivation. The English version also reproduced Cortés's oration before his attack on Tlaxcala: "[I]f we shoulde leave this Lande, this Warre, . . . shall we then lyve at reste, loytring as ideil and loste folke: God forbidde, that ever oure nation shoulde have suche a name, havyng warres of honour. And whither (I pray) shall the Oxe goe where he shall not helpe to ploughe the grounde?"[78]

The agrarian vision was powerful. In Ireland, Treasurer Sir Henry Wallop claimed to have brought Wexford by 1590 "to better civility, inhabitation, and plough-going than heretofore in the memory of man."[79] Forest had to be cleared for farming. When war broke out again, Irish rebel leader Hugh O'Neill became "that tree which hath been the treasonable stock from which so many poisoned plants and grafts have been derived." Lord Mountjoy's lieutenant wrote: "The axe was now at the root of the tree." In 1598, colonists expelled from Munster by the rebellion urged genocide on the queen with typical agrarian metaphor: "Lett the feete of yore forces treade and trample downe these bryars that will not suffer yore plantes to prosper. . . . Lett them weare with theire heeles the very rootes out of the earth that they springe no more: soe shall you make Ireland a flourishing nursery for England."[80]

The Conquest

At the end of the fifteenth century most of Ireland was unconquered. Beyond the English Pale of territory surrounding Dublin, "independent and autonomous Irish jurisdictions covered much of the island."[81] But from 1494, Poynings' Law required English royal consent for Ireland's parliament to assemble or legislate. After almost annual Irish parliaments, the next four decades saw only eight.[82] In 1534 King Henry VIII imprisoned his Irish lord deputy, Fitzgerald, Earl of Kildare, and Fitzgerald's son rose in rebellion. Henry dispatched 2,300 troops, who took the rebel fortress of Maynooth in 1535, massacring the surrendered garrison and setting a brutal precedent.[83]

Henry made himself head of the (Anglican) Church of Ireland in 1536. Legislation the next year banned the Irish language. Yet the English Reformation and its legislative revolution also revived the Irish parliament, and dissent became "clearly discernible."[84] Henry's assumption in 1541 of the additional title king of Ireland was equally double-edged. It asserted English jurisdiction but also extended Henry's obligations to all his Irish subjects regardless of race. Much of the island retained de facto autonomy and, Canny notes, the Irish parliament of 1541–42 signaled an official though temporary halt to the attempted English conquest.[85]

A moderating influence on English policy was the European Renaissance humanist tradition of Erasmus, who had urged missionary rather than military action and "fatherly charity" even to non-Christian Turks, for "they also be men" and respond to "kindness." The English Reformation thinker Thomas Starkey believed human nature to be essentially good and the intellect its prime agent. In 1536, he criticized Henry VIII's government for its harsh actions against opponents and urged a policy based on persuasion. However, another early Reformation tendency, exemplified by Henry's chief minister, Thomas Cromwell, laid greater stress on obedience and coercive authority. In largely Catholic Ireland, greater difficulty faced religious reform. St. Leger, lord lieutenant from 1540–51, and the bishop of Meath preferred persuasion, according to Bradshaw, but Dublin's Archbishop Browne stressed control. The archbishop from 1567, Adam Loftus, agreed, seeking conformity however people felt "inwardly in their consciences."[86]

A more extreme form of the coercive policy won out. After Henry and his successors had delayed the next Irish parliament for 14 years, it was now required to herald new English policies of conquest and colonization. Parliament reconvened in 1557, amid building Irish resentment of the soldiers who had accompanied the arrival of the Earl of Sussex as lord deputy. Sussex had begun to drive the Irish population from the midlands counties of Laois and Offaly. In 1557, he proclaimed the O'More and O'Connor septs to be rebels and confiscated their lands.[87] In Ulster assisting Sussex in campaigns against local Scots, his brother-in-law, Sir Henry Sidney, wrote of camping with his forces on Rathlin Island "until we had spoiled the same of all mankind, corn, and cattle in it."[88]

Despite an expanding military presence and heightening repression, the Irish remained recalcitrant. English garrison levels, down to a few hundred troops in 1540, exceeded 1,500 men by the 1560s. Increasing use of scorched-earth policies only exacerbated "the failure of the state-sponsored religion to take root in any section of the indigenous population."[89] However, the major confrontation remained political. As repression and reform failed, Sussex cracked down on parliamentary dissent.

Successive monarchs explicitly authorized the resort to violence. The Catholic Queen Mary advised Sussex "to spare none others that hereafter shall contempn authority." At her accession in 1558, Queen Elizabeth also wanted Ireland "in perfect obedience," which she thought required "extending of force."[90] From 1558 to 1560, the crown issued martial law "commissions" to the sheriff of Kildare, Francis Cosby, and other officials to root out "traitors" in Laois and Offaly, with power to seize one-third of their possessions. Most new land grants there went to soldiers involved in the repression. A contemporary Gaelic account complained that the mere "spoken" allegation of an English officer "was a sufficient quarrel for the capten to rob, pray and kill the person ... and all his tenantes withowt other attoryte." The short-lived Irish parliament of 1560 was notable for the new seats taken up by New English colonizers to the detriment of local representatives.[91] For three years, martial law was rare.[92] But when Laois-Offaly's leading Irish land grantee rebelled, the garrison that tracked down and killed him in 1564 reported "a head-count of ninety O'Connors and thirty-five O'Mores."[93]

This repression was unsuccessful. By 1565, Canny points out, "it appeared that England would lose her last foothold in Ireland unless some drastic action was taken." English policy determined to take over the whole island.[94] Sussex's replacement as the new lord deputy, Sir Henry Sidney, arrived in Dublin in January 1566 to govern "thys unruly realm and people." Within two months, he asked Leicester for help, or "all wyll to wrak," pleading that no man ever "had so wayward a begynyng of a government." Irish raids riddled the Pale, carrying off "spoyles almost every day" and keeping "the people universally poore." Exemplifying the colonial dilemma, Sidney found the English soldiery disheveled, many "intollerable to the people," yet most "so alyed with the Irysh as I dare not trust them in any fort." In the south, "intestayne warres" had so ravaged Kilkenny and Munster that a man could ride "24 or 30 myles of lenghth and fynd no house left standyng." In the west, Thomond was possibly worse off, and in Connacht the Earl of Clanrickard, "almost the only loyall man of that province," was "so molested with hys one kynsmen and neygbourys," that he dared not leave his county "for fear of losyng yt."[95]

The first major threat was in the north. There, Shane O'Neill contested Elizabeth's claim to Ulster, insisting that its kings were his forebears: "Ulster was thearys and Ulster ys myne." O'Neill's greatest asset, Sidney now found, was "the hate" that the country harbored toward the Earl of Sussex. Shane could field "a thousand horsmen and 4000 footmen ... for he ys the only strong man of Ireland[.] hys cuntre was never so rich nor so inhabited[.] he armeth and weaponneyth all the peasants of hys cuntre the first that ever so dyd of an Irishman." If O'Neill wished, he could "burn and spoyle to Dublyn gates." Barbarian though he was, neither Attila the Hun "nor no Vandall nor Goth that ever was" deserved to be more feared "for over runyng any part of Chrystendom than thys man is for over runyng and spoyling of Ireland." Sidney warned Elizabeth that if she failed to "chastyze hym" in Ulster, O'Neill would "chase all hers out of Ireland." Urging decisive action, Sidney raised the ante. He appealed to the queen's honor, describing her as the flouted sovereign of Ulster, whose large population lived in ignorance "of the fear and law of god or obedyens to her maiestye," while "so mutch goodly land" of the queen's was being "extorted from her," and those who "should be her hyghnes free subietcys" had become O'Neill's "bond slaves." Sidney recommended that "her maiestye must put on a determynatiyon to chasten that canyball," which could not be done "without actuall war."[96] Fortunately for the English, local Scots murdered Shane O'Neill in 1567. From his own coterie, mostly extreme Protestants from England's West Country, Sidney appointed the adventurer Humphrey Gilbert as military governor of Ulster "to plant habitacion there of Ynglishe men." Sidney went on to spread martial law countrywide, issuing 89 individual martial law commissions by 1571.[97]

However, to the south, new rebellions erupted in 1568, led by James Fitzmaurice Fitzgerald of Desmond, and in 1569, led by the Butlers, brothers of the Earl of Ormond.[98] That year Sidney marched on Cork through the lands of a Fitzmaurice ally, ravaging, as he put it, "all his countrey burning all the corne that was gathered and spoiling the rest" and destroying "one of his Castells."[99] Sidney recalled in his memoirs that he had "left nothing alive in it."[100] At the time, he told the Privy Council that he had "the whole warde putt to the sword and throwen over the toppe of the Castell to the terror of all other wherein" and then "burnt and spoiled all his other houses." Later, "[i]n McDonoughs countrey we rased and burned all his houses, . . . spoiling their all that I colde."[101] Sidney recalled staying at Kilkenny up to "twenty days, holding in that time a royal session," which saw "executed above sixty persons . . . besides a great many hanged by martial law."[102]

Sidney met constitutional opposition, too, in the Irish parliament of 1569–71, which Canny ascribes in part to conquests that threatened landowners within and without the Pale.[103] Sidney's secretary Edmund Tremayne (who, like Gilbert, came from Devon) branded the Irish parliamentary opposition as "authors and maintenors of rebelles and Rebellion." In Bradshaw's account, as the number of parliamentary seats expanded, the Old English found support among new Gaelic members, successfully suspending Poynings' Law and blocking the use of Irish taxes to recruit, mostly from England, a standing army to be controlled by Sidney. But in his concluding address, the lord deputy reaffirmed his militaristic policy and his demand for a standing army. Sidney also attempted to divide his opponents along racial lines, reminding the Old English of "our ancestors" and describing the Irish as "a sort of barbarous people, odious to God and man, that lap your blood as greedily as ours."[104] With the violence of the conquest, race thinking was on the increase.

Another West Country man, John Hooker, an Exeter lawyer of "rude rusticity" and new member of the Irish parliament, was listening to Sidney's speech that day. Hooker had been hired by the West Country aristocrat and extreme Protestant Sir Peter Carew, who enjoyed government backing for extensive claims on Irish lands held by the Kavanaghs in Leinster, the MacCarthys in Cork, and others in the Pale. Carew also proposed "the suppressing and reforming of the loose, barbarous and most wicked life of that savage nation."[105] The Earl of Clancarr, Mac Carthy Mor, joined Fitzmaurice in revolt. The Earl of Ormond's brothers, Sidney reported, burned the town of Laughlin, slaughtering and drowning people amid "horrible rapes of yong maidens and wiefes before their parentes and husbandes faces." Later, asked "what the causes were that movid them to this Rebellion," the Butler brothers "alledged certen speaches uttered by the Lord deputie and certen claims made by Sir Peter Carew."[106] Bradshaw asserts that from this point "the conquest of Ireland is to be seen as part of a European movement of colonial expansion," with "a common frame of mind: aggressive, predatory, totalitarian, discriminatory."[107]

The group running England's Irish policy was indeed close knit, with regional and family connections that tempered without eliminating factional rivalries. Of the West Country group, Humphrey Gilbert was a half brother of Walter Ralegh, who was in turn a kinsman of Francis Drake. Both were close relatives of Peter Carew.[108] As head of government in Ireland, the Earl of Sussex, lord deputy in 1556–64, was succeeded by his brother-in-law Sir Henry Sidney (1566–71 and 1575–78), who in turn succeeded his second brother-in-law, William Fitzwilliam, who was lord deputy in 1571–75 and again in 1588–94. From London, a group led by Sidney's third brother-in-law, the Earl of Leicester Robert Dudley, rival of Sussex and employer of Spenser and Harvey, controlled most of the appointments to captaincies in Ireland from 1563 to 1599.[109] Leicester claimed to have observed by 1572 how to "reforme those dysordred people" of Ireland and "kepe those unconstant and rebellyous nacyons most under and in fear." He considered the Irish "most Insolent and most unthank-full, . . . a proude, dyssembling, and a mallycious people, always unfaythfull . . . [who] desarves contynewally ye rodd and syldome to be stroked on the hedd."[110]

As Irish resistance spread, English repression grew more barbaric and geno-cidal. During the five Irish uprisings from 1568 to 1576, English troop strength rose to 2,500 soldiers.[111] Colonel Humphrey Gilbert, military commander of Ulster, was transferred to Munster in 1569 to suppress the Fitzmaurice revolt under martial law.[112] Sidney assigned Gilbert 900 cavalry, 400 infantry, and a force of Irish foot soldiers.[113] Gilbert reported back: "I slew all those from time to time that did belong to, feed, accompany, or maintain any outlaws or trai-tors; and after my first summoning of any castle or fort, if they would not pres-ently yield it, I would not afterwards take it of their gift, but won it perforce, how many lives so ever it cost, putting man, woman and child of them to the sword."[114] Thomas Churchyard, who went to Munster with Gilbert, wrote that civilian noncombatants should be killed in order to starve the rebels of food, "so that the killying of theim by the sworde was the waie to kill the menne of warre by famine." To terrorize the "savage heathen," Gilbert ordered that "[t]he heddes of all those (of what sort soever thei were) which were killed in the daie, should be cutte off from their bodies and brought to the place where he incamped at night, and should there bee laide on the ground by eche side of the waie ledying into his owne tente so that none could come into his tente for any cause but commonly he muste passe through a lane of heddes." Sur-rendering Irish visitors then saw "the heddes of their dedde fathers, brothers, children, kinffolke, and freendes, lye on the grounde before their faces."[115]

Foreshadowing his reading on the Punic Wars, Gilbert believed that "no Conquered nacion will ever yelde willenglie their obedience for love but rather for feare." He dehumanized the Irish, saying "that he thought his Dogges eares to good, to heare the speeche of the greatest noble manne emongest them." Gilbert advised Sidney to use "absolute power" as necessary.[116] Sidney, for his part, informed London that Gilbert targeted "manne, woman and childe." Leading a small force to battle, Gilbert "brake so many of them, . . . [that] the name of an inglysh man is more terrible now to them, than the syght of an hundryth was before." Munster was now "in sutch quyet as it was never in memory of man . . . the iron ys now hot apt to receve what prynt should be stryken in yt."[117] Knighted by Sidney in January 1570, Gilbert returned to England, read Livy with Gabriel Harvey, and advocated replacing the rebellious Irish with English settlers.[118] Two years later, the queen commissioned Gilbert to prepare a report on military measures for Ireland.[119]

The English had proven to themselves that their colonial projects required displacement of large native populations. Neither religious reform nor pliant parliaments could assure the supremacy of the conquerors. It was necessary to terrorize and disperse or eliminate those whose lands they seized, and whom they increasingly portrayed as racially distinct. This in turn provoked more widespread resistance and necessitated escalating bloodshed.

Contributing further to the rationale for resolute repression was the cost of the English commitment. The queen was "parsimonious."[120] Most expenses had to be borne by those in Ireland. But these costs were difficult to impose. Sidney wrote from Dublin in February 1570: "I am hated of all here; of the nobility, for deposing their tyranny; of the merchant, who not receiving his money is become bankrupt; of the gentleman, who cannot get his rents through keeping of soldiers; the husbandmen cry out on me, and will do no work, for they are never paid for bearing the soldiers; the soldiers have twice refused to go to the field, when I punish one the rest are ready to mutiny."[121] Force was the sole resort. Sidney compared the Irish to horses that, if loosely reined, will run "with byt in the teeth."[122] In April 1570, a leading official in Connacht called for "fire and sword, the rod of God's vengeance" to subdue the Irish and "wake these cankered hearts and stubborn minds to yield for fear." The more widespread massacres that followed, according to historian Roy Foster, "were probably an innovation."[123]

The 1570s began with new English proposals that gradually revealed a new racialist thinking. Sidney's secretary Tremayne completed his *Notes and Propositions for the Reformation of Ireland* in June 1571. After his failed personal enterprise in Munster, Tremayne declared that "all thinges be amisse" in Ireland. He warned with ominous medical metaphor that "till the disseases be perfettclie founde, it is impossible to cure the body." Tremayne's diagnosis was that the Irish lords "have usurped the kings aucthoritie, taken his revenews," which "is the onlie cause of this generall rebellions." The disease had even infected "our own Englishmen where thei have been put in place to rule, framying their government after the irish." Military appointees also "smell of this rule." Within two generations, settlers "become as glad to be rid of us, as the naturall race of this Land." Anyone who "hath in this Land any inhabitance of their own" was thus unfit "to governe after english manner."[124]

Whether biological or environmental, the problem demanded a new ruling population. The safest cure was "to send good men, new and new, out of England, to rule." First, Tremayne urged appointment of bishops from England to the Irish dioceses and parliament. Second, since people born "of this countrey" were unqualified for office, he recommended appointing "to everie Bench one English iudge," with the lord chancellor "ever an Englishman, the Chief baron an Englishman, the chief remembrancer, the Master of the Rolles the sollic[it]er and Attorney to be English, the Surveyor of all other, most necessarie to be English or at least to have an English man ioyned with him." And third, the army must "take from the usurping lords their regall rule" and "reform the wickedness of these stubborn, rude and most barbarous people." Tremayne concluded: "Without the princes' sword ... no state can stand." As in the Pale, "the Armie must do it" in "all the realme."[125] Violence and ethnic prejudice were coming together.

Back in London, where he hosted readings of Livy at his home and plotted the perfection of the Roman imperial model, the royal secretary Thomas Smith was petitioning the queen.[126] He wanted "Arde and other landes" in Ulster, and he wanted to make them "civill and peopled with naturall Englishe men borne." His settlers needed "commodious" tracts totaling "1200 plowlands [144,000 Irish acres] or more, as they can with the sworde obtayne and get." Smith's group promised further "to suppresse and appease" any nearby Irish "that shall go about to mutine and rebel" and to pay Her Majesty for every acre "so soone as the lande be once woonne to be mere Englishe." Smith planned to ensure that "the inhabitantes retourne not to barbarousness nor be subtilye suppressed of the Irishe." Thus he insisted that every Englishman be forbidden to wear "any Irishe apparel upon paine of banishment with losse of his landes and fredome," and the Irish banned from wearing "Englishe apparel or weapon upon payne of deathe." Moreover, "no Irishman borne of Irish race and brought up Irishe shall purchace land, beare office, be chosen of any jurie, or admitted witness in any reall or personall action." To permanently assimilate the local Irish children, they were to be taught to speak English. The profits would come from English colonists paying rent to the Smiths, feudal tenants in chief who would remit about half this rent to the crown.[127] In November 1571, the Privy Council in London officially approved Smith's colonization of an area south of Belfast, namely "[a]ll possessions in Great Arde, Little Arde and Clandeboye" that Smith and his son "can obtain, possess or inhabit against the Irish."[128] An account of one conversation has Smith foreshadowing drastic population "reform" of Ireland: "I meane the whole countrey replenished with Englishe men."[129]

Thomas Smith Jr., fortified by Livy's accounts of Rome's defeat of Hannibal, led 100 men to Ulster in August 1572.[130] Sidney's successor as lord deputy, William Fitzwilliam, had warned in March that Smith's land grant could "bring the Irish into a knot," provoking a revolt by the local Clandeboye sept of O'Neills, who enjoyed English backing and also claimed the Ards.[131] Fitzwilliam cautioned again: "Thomas Smith is nowe at the length come to the Ardes . . . I wish his nombre suche as were hable to help, and not suche as shall neede helpe" nor "cawse that we shall neede other help." Learning that a force of 900 Scots had arrived to reinforce Shane O'Neill's successor, Turlough Luineach O'Neill, Fitzwilliam prepared "to brydle this rebellious people, whom nothing but feare and force can teach duetie and obedience." In short order, however, the Clandeboye sept leader, Sir Brian MacPhelim O'Neill, drove Smith's colonists off his land.[132]

Smith called for help. He wrote Fitzwilliam to urge the garrisoning of Ulster. "Colonies of English & warlike men plantid in the north" were necessary so that "Ireland shalbe civill." He urged that "those Scotte be chasid away" from Ulster "and those stowt rebelles dau[n]tid," but asserted that the English colonists "neither sought to expel, nor to destroy the yris race, but to kepe them in quiet, in order."[133] The difficulty became clear when an O'Neill ally's retainer murdered Thomas Smith Jr. in October 1573. The Smiths' scheme foundered.[134] Reading Ireland through Livy had proved more than a parlor game. Their colleague Humphrey Gilbert now declined to pursue his own proposal, which he had outlined the previous year in *The Discourse of Ireland*, for a "graunt of all suche land and Ilandes to be enhabited by my Company as shalbe wonne by them from the wylde Irishe and such licke rebelles there."[135]

Meanwhile, Leicester admonished Fitzwilliam to kill Irish leaders, subdue their "barbarous" people by force, and employ unrelenting repression. He urged support for the Earl of Essex to "overthrow the substance & pride of those Rebells." It was necessary to "first subdew the hedd and chef & the rest will fall lyke leaves of trees . . . force and the sword must kepe them under, for he wyll never obey law that doth not first fear and fele the sword." Leicester wanted the lord deputy of Ireland "not to spare the sword nor to ceasse contynewall following the marshall trade," rather than "rule by comon order and lawe, for lawe is lost uppon such till they first know obedyence & fear & that must be by marshall justyce."[136] He acknowledged that Ireland had "as well good subiectes as evell," but to him the evil ones, living "as wyld savage beasts," perhaps better represented "the thwart practyces of that lewd nacion."[137] Leicester told Fitz-william that the English and Irish were incompatible: "[Y]ou that be of ye mere Inglishe byrth shuld hold and concur to gether for ye are matcht" with the Irish, "a crafty and subtyll nacyn . . . ye cannot trust them to[o] lytle." Denounc-ing the "cankard harts & dysposytyon" of the Irish, their "Infidellyty and lewd-ness even universally," Leicester advised "severe ruling." He stressed that only "the severe prosecution" of the Irish in Ulster had "brought the hole province in best & spedyest order." Munster, too, had been "brought to great obedience" but would remain quiet only when it, like Ulster, "has ben planted [with our] people Immeddyatly." He warned that "a country" was "not wonne before it be planted to our obedyence." The Irish were "a wild barbarioius and treacherous people" while their country was "the devylls practysse . . . I fear yo shall hardely find an Irish man now to be trusted." Leicester advised Fitzwilliam to "use the benyfitt of any occasion" for success "by force or justyce," and "sewerly." He advised against lengthy dealings or "persuasion" with the Irish, especially with "any of their owen conntrey byrth. . . . They shuld fele the force of a gover-nor."[138]

Thus, the English set about winning Ireland by the severest example. Soon exception became the rule, and genocidal massacres targeted ever larger num-bers of Irish.

Gilbert's successor as president of Munster, John Perrott, reported in April 1573 that in two years he had "kylled and hanged" 800 "rebells and their ayders," in addition to those he killed in battle.[139] Gilbert's half brother, Walter Ralegh, had the captured rebel leader, James of Desmond, hanged, drawn, and quar-tered. His head was "set on the towne gates of the citie of Cork, and made the preie of the foules."[140] Official correspondence reports the frequency of this punishment: "some days two heads and some days four heads, and other some days ten heads."[141] John Hooker's *Irish Historie* records that "great companies" of rebels were slaughtered, "whose blouds the earth drank up." And their "car-cases the foules of the aire and the rauening beastes of the feeld did consume and deuoure." It was possible to traverse the southern half of Ireland "and not meet anie man, woman or child," nor "see anie beast, but the verie woolues, the foxes, and other like rauening beastes; manie of them laie dead being famished, and the residue gone elsewhere."[142]

Wholesale murder and ethnic displacement were not Queen Elizabeth's initial intention. She had directed that the Irish people be "well used." She told the Earl of Essex, setting out for Ulster in July 1573 with a grant to North Clandeboye, not to "seek too hastily to bring people that have been trained in another religion, from that which they have been brought up in."[143] She warned him not to harm anyone "that is knowne to be our good subject" and added that "the people of Ireland birthe ... may be contynewed in expectacion of favor, if they do lyve peasibly, as reason it is they shuld." Yet she added that local Scots, who were not English subjects, were a different matter: "[A] multitude of Scotte do remayne as ennemyes to us" in Ulster. Essex should "expel the said Scotte out of those countreys" and suppress "such of the Irish as will take part with the said Scotte, or otherwise will rebel against us, as of late they have notoriously."[144] However, in reply Essex promised only to "deal so with them as I found best" on arrival in Ireland, as "for the present I could not say what is best," though "I would not imbrue my hands with more blood than the necessity of the cause requireth."[145] Those involved in this new campaign included Sir Peter Carew and Sir Humphrey Gilbert.[146]

Famine became a military strategy. In May 1574, Edward Berkeley, an English official in Belfast, described the starvation resulting from the war "upon these wicked and faythles pepoll" in Ulster. The rebels had "no kynd of grayne nor hath sowne so much as too plowes will till. ... There releffe is all together mylke which is easely taken from them, all though we wollde not the next winter will. So of necessitye a nomber of them muste be famyshed." If Berkeley had second thoughts, they were eclipsed by racial and religious justifications for extermination. "How godly a dede it is to overthrowe so wicked a race the world may judge. For my parte I thinke ther canot be a greter Sacrifyce to god."[147]

Two months later, Elizabeth praised Essex for his "valiant and peaceful doings and travails in the province of Ulster." She was thankful that "you do rather allure and bring in that rude and barbarous nation to civility, and acknowledging of their duty to God and to us, by wisdom and discreet handling, than by force and shedding of blood; and yet, when necessity requireth, you are ready also to oppose yourself and your forces to them whom reason and duty cannot bridle."[148] The queen appointed Essex "governor of Ulster."[149]

Encouraged by the royal blessing, in October 1574 Essex drew up a plan for Ulster to ensure that "the Rebell shalbe utterlie extirped within two years." Even cattle herding would now be "answerable to the lawe at Dublin."[150] Of a force of 2,000 English soldiers in Ireland, stationing 1,300 in three new garrison towns in Ulster would open up lands that the crown could "recover and inhabite, with Englishe people." Turlough Luineach O'Neill's resistance, Essex confided to the Privy Council, left no option "but warre therby to expulse him, and utterlie to roote him out, or else so to weaken him by takinge awaie his dependanntes (for which the warre muste be the instrument)."[151]

What Essex meant by "rooting out" rebels and waging war to"take away" their dependents quickly became clear. The next month, his troops surprised and slaughtered several hundred Clandeboye O'Neills at a Belfast Christmas feast, dispatching their sept leader Brian MacPhelim O'Neill to his execution in Dublin.[152] According to Captain Thomas Lee, the English had promised protection to "three or four hundred of those country people . . . and brought them to a place of meeting, where . . . garrison soldiers . . . dishonourably put them all to the sword . . . with the consent and practice of the lord deputy," Fitzwilliam.[153] As the massacre proceeded, the Privy Council in London, unaware of it, sent Essex's plan back to him with "doubts to be resolved," asking whether he intended that those who "shall inhabit Clandeboy . . . shalbe Irisshe, or Englishe, or mixte of both . . . and what number shalbe planted in Clandeboy. . . . Besides Brian McPhelim and his sept"? And further, the council inquired whether "Sir Brian shall inhabit a parte of Clandeboy" and with how many Irish.[154] Essex's reply was nonchalant: "Touching Brian McPhelim and provision for him and his sept, a small proportion shall serve." He explained coyly that "your lordships have since . . . hearde of my procedinges with them," adding an unconvincing denial: "I never mente to unpeople the Cuntrie Clandyboy of their naturall inhabitanntes, but to have cherished them so farre fourthe as they would live quiet and deutifull. . . . I would have admitted all the natives their, to have dwelte in that circuite, but dispersed, and not in consort as nowe they doe." Having indeed largely "unpeopled" Clandeboye, Essex said he would allocate its remaining Irish inhabitants no more than "10,000 acres to them all."[155] By contrast, he proposed to give 10 English investors, or "Adventurers," 60,000 acres there.[156]

If total annihilation of the local Irish was not his goal, Essex did want them severely reduced in numbers and subjected to English domination. He stressed that his plan had precisely envisaged "the ordinarie soldiours" being able to master and "utterlie to unpeople or unweapon all the yrissherie" in Clandeboye, numbering (after the massacre) fewer than 10 horsemen and 400 "rascall" footmen. Indeed, Essex said, "I wish the inhabitanntes to be all Englishe, yf they might bee hadd." He then added, vacillating, "but the most profitable tenntes wilbe of the Irrishe and the more Irrishe the more profitable so as the

Englishe be hable to master them." In planning his settlement, Essex concluded: "My opinion therefore is, that it is not materiall of what nacon the people bee." But after his slaughter of the Clandeboye O'Neills, "ownce brought lowe the Irrishe shall not be suffered to growe in strengthe againe."[157] The few survivors presented no threat, but even in a labor shortage, must never be permitted to recover their numbers.

Essex's genocidal massacre of the O'Neill sept foreshadowed more aggressive action. He now requested frigates that Francis Drake had brought from the Indies.[158] And he petitioned the Privy Council in January 1575, stating that in previous English incursions into Ulster, "the Irishe have geven waie to their armies as the waves doe to a shippe: but the armies beinge retired in shorte time they did like the water close againe recovered strengthe and made head against the Englishe Pale." The time for accommodations was past. Essex objected to English monarchs giving the Irish "peaces, protections, pardons, captenries and all licencens libertie" instead of the "sworde for lawe justice and settled garrisons even in their bowels." He protested that England's wealth had long been a "nurse" to Ireland, which "hath suckt her drie." Essex therefore urged that "the presente opportunitie to expel the Scottes and reforme the Irishe be not loste."[159] The Earl of Leicester agreed, counseling escalation and advising that Essex "must bring fear and terror to his enemyes which is not heard of yet."[160]

The queen withdrew London's costly support for Essex's Ulster fortifications in May 1575, but he still pushed for a "show of war," as he put it, to gain a more favorable peace. "If I have tyme to terrifie the Rebells they will the rather seek peace wherby my conditions may be the better."[161] After parleying with Turlough Luineach O'Neill, Essex planned to attack the Scots in Ulster. "I will bend my companies against the Scotts in the Glens. It may be I shall banish them quicklie but if I so doe . . . they will presentlie retorne." He therefore suggested renting the Glens to a reduced force of "two hundreth Scotts and not above." And "since her Maiestie will not plant Englishe," Essex told her he preferred Scots in Ulster to the Irish: "[T]he Scott is the lesse ill of disposition, more inclinable to Civility, though more dangerous to the state if the numbers shold be great."[162]

Essex then set out to thin the Scots' numbers. In July 1575, his troops, led by John Norreys and Francis Drake, slaughtered all 600 Scots living on Rathlin Island, which was defended by a small Scottish force.[163] In a letter to the queen five days later, Essex detailed how the massacre was carried out. The initial English assault on the Scottish fort, for the loss of three soldiers, killed the defending Scots leader, while "the continual hurt that was done unto them" forced a Scottish constable to request a parley. Norreys agreed, "so as the constable would come himself in person out unto him without delay to make his demands. And yet not agreeing that he should safely return to the castle." The Scot asked for "their lives, their goods, and to be put into Scotland," but Norreys refused, offering to spare only the constable himself and his wife and child, with "the lives of all within to stand upon the courtesy of the soldiers." The constable, "knowing his estate and safety to be very doubtful, accepted this composition, and came out with all his company." The English soldiers, Essex told the queen, "being moved and much stirred with the loss of their fellows that were slain, and desirous of revenge, made request, or rather pressed, to have the killing of them, which they did all saving the persons to whom life was promised." A Scottish hostage in the fort was spared. "There were slain that came out of the castle of all sorts 200; and presently news is brought me out of Tyrone that they be occupied still in killing, and have slain that they have found hidden in caves and in the cliffs of the sea, to the number of 300 or 400 more."[164]

A bit sheepishly, Essex chalked this additional genocidal massacre up to his own foresight, resolution, and power. Caution had been unnecessary, he told the Privy Council: "Your lordships may therby see how all things doe fall owt, otherwise then was looked for (but no otherwaies than I assured my selfe of) by that experience I have gathered in this service against this people, by which you may perceave how easy a thing it is (if it had been well followed according to my plan) to have donne any thinge that was intended." He recommended rewards for those serving with him, singling out the large landholder, Sir Peter Carew.[165]

But Ireland, if not the Irish, killed Essex. He died of dysentery in Dublin, aged 36. His bloody record was not unique, Roy Foster comments, only more wanton.[166] In fewer than four years, his superior, Lord Deputy Fitzwilliam, had issued 67 martial law commissions. Sir Henry Sidney, returning to that office in 1575, followed up with 46 more over two years. This increasingly "privatized" the repression and plunder, empowering ever more English officials to "behave like *conquistadores*."[167]

Sidney faced a familiar threat in the midlands, where he had ended his first term as lord deputy by executing two O'More sept leaders. In 1572–73 Rory Óg O'More and 600 followers launched a serious rebellion in Laois and

Offaly, threatening the government-sponsored plantation, whose land was increasingly concentrated into the hands of proprietors dominating native Irish tenants. The family of Sidney's relative and subordinate Francis Cosby now owned 4,200 acres in Laois. His forces killed O'More sept leaders to the "terror" of others. But the protracted revolt decided the landowners on a policy of "the utter extirpation of all the landless septs in the plantation." Offaly planters recommended in 1576 that the clansmen be driven "to straight corners in the country and there cut short" in ambushes.[168] The next year Sidney reported the killing of Rory Óg O'More's wife and relatives and praised Cosby for "great diligence, pollecye and payne takinge" in eliminating "principal men" of the O'Mores and O'Connors. Sidney quickly granted Cosby a martial law commission empowering him to jail or execute "by martial law at his discretion" anyone aiding rebels. In September 1577, Sidney reported the killing of hundreds of Rory Óg O'More's followers. Two months later, he added that "some of his best and principall followers I dayle cut of . . . I meane, by the totall extirpacion of those rebells." And in February 1578: "I waste hym and Kyll of his men daylie."[169]

The climax came in March 1578. Cosby summoned several O'More clans to a parley at Mullaghmast. According to the Irish *Annals of the Four Masters*, as the O'Mores arrived at the meeting, "they were surrounded on every side by four lines of soldiers and cavalry who proceeded to shoot and slaughter them without mercy, so that not a single individual escaped." Two other Gaelic sources record the names of clan leaders killed, one perishing with 40 followers and the other with 74. The next month, Sidney reported to the queen "the execucion so blouddye, by cutting of his company from 500 to 50" in the extended campaign against the O'Mores.[170] After troops killed Rory Óg O'More in a skirmish three months later, his head was "set up upon the Castle of Dublin," Sidney wrote in his memoirs. "The slaughter was great on both sides . . . yet carried away he was."[171]

The president of Connacht, Nicholas Malby (1576–84), also pursued scorched-earth and terrorist tactics. Ciaran Brady writes that Malby "contemplated with equanimity the prospect of liquidating [the] entire kinship group" of the Earl of Clanrickarde. "In 1578 he secured O'Rourke's submission by besieging his chief castle and slaughtering all within, women and children without quarter." The English-Irish Earl of Ormond wrote to Burghley in 1581 denouncing Malby's administration as "Machevilles" who "can seek to cut a man's throat if they might." Sidney tried to appease Ormond with more violence: "In the wars with Rory Oge ... I hang[ed] a captain of Scots which served under Malby, and all his officers, and I think very near twenty of his men; and by Captain Furrs and his company many or more of them killed, and all for extortions done by him and his people upon the Earl of Ormond ... and yet he still complained he nor his could have no justice of me."[172]

In London in 1577, Sidney's son Philip wrote his *Discourse on Irish Affairs*, advising the queen not to outlay "excessive expenses to keep a realm, of which scarcely she hath the acknowledgment of sovereignty." The necessary funds should instead be raised from the Irish, "with force and gentleness" in the Pale, and then "in garrison upon the wild, and by such force bring them to pay the rents." Since at that point Spain and "all our feared neighbours have their hands full at home," Philip Sidney thought the time was right in Ireland for the English "to get by good means as much both rent and subjection as may be." He cited "the general nature of all countries not fully conquered" to reject the use of "gentle means" of achieving this. Like Leicester, he advocated "severe means." The Irish would forget "the fresh remembrance of their lost liberty" only when "they find the sweetness of due subjection." The people of Ireland "in no case are to be equalled" to the status of England. "For little is lenity to prevail in minds" like those of the Irish, whose "revengeful hate to all English" and "ignorant obstinacy in papistry" made them, Sidney thought, "in their souls detest the present government."[173]

Philip Sidney's views reflected growing official English sentiment in Ireland. The Irish were proving themselves to be a race apart, unreformable, even ungovernable, and not worth the effort. The sword was all they understood. Philip's father, Sir Henry, now claimed to have captured so many rebels that he could not list "the names of each particular varlet that hath died ... as well by ordinary course of the law, [and] martial law, as [by] flat fighting with them."[174] In 1577, Sir William Gerrard, lord chancellor of Ireland, regretted that the administration had not, 10 years earlier, "put on determynacon to subjecte the whole Irishrie to the sworde."[175] Yet he asked the next year: "[C]an the sword teach them to speake Englishe?" Barnaby Rich, a mercenary who fought in Ireland for much of the last quarter of the sixteenth century, sounded his *Allarme to England* in 1578. The Irish, he asserted, were unredeemable: "[T]here be a greater number that are not to be reformed but by most bitter and sharp punishment indeed."[176] Sir Thomas Cecil told the queen in 1580 of "the fear of conquest of late deeply grafted in the hearts of the wild Irish." Surveying "the slaughter of segments of the native Irish population" in 1560–80, historian

Nicholas Canny states that "at the least pretext—generally resistance to the English—they were dismissed as a 'wicked and faythles peopoll' and put to the sword."[177]

From 1565, nearly all England's lord deputies believed that religious conversion of the Irish could only follow their political obedience, not inspire it. Force was required because, as Canny points out, "every Irish overlord, whether Gaelic or Old English, held sway over people rather than territory"—feudal lords ruling "as little kings." But other officers of the crown in Ireland held that successful conformity first required persuasion. Instead of the sword, these men fostered direct evangelization and formal education, using the Irish vernacular. Robert Weston, lord chancellor of Ireland in 1567–73, considered fear of the sword effective "no longer than it hangeth over their heads," and he even contested the morality of conquest itself. Archbishop Lancaster of Armagh advised Francis Walsingham in 1580 that establishing a single school would be as effective "as a great number of marshall men." His successor actually warned Walsingham in 1585 that it "will be answered before the Highest . . . to shed their blood who for lack of teaching could never do better."[178]

The moderates were aware of the serious challenge facing Protestant religious reform of Ireland. Weston considered the Irish "all universally" to be "so blinded through corruption of nature, evil bringing up, continual acquaintance and customs of sin that they be void of all knowledge of God (like heathenish people), drowned in idolatry and infidelity with disobedience to God." Archbishop Long, for his part, termed the Irish "worse than horse and mule that have no understanding." But in a letter to Walsingham, using the prevalent agrarian metaphor, Long denounced those who allow "His garden to wax wild for lack of trimming, and then to pull up His plants that might fructify by the root." These men instead preferred education over violence because they considered the Irish afflicted by ignorance, not willfulness. But the dominant English officials held a more pessimistic and aggressive view of human nature.[179]

Genocide and Extermination

The occupation of Ireland gathered force along a genocidal path. By the 1580s, the English army there had tripled in size, to 8,000 men. During that decade alone, according to historian Richard Berleth, the Irish population would be "reduced by 30 percent, the land wasted, and the towns laid ruin. The indigenous culture was uprooted and destroyed." Massacres escalated. For instance, in 1580 the crown official in Wexford, Thomas Masterson, ambushed a sept of Kavanaghs, killing over 60. A second massacre of Kavanaghs took a similar toll several years later.[180]

Atrocities in Munster, where the 1579–83 Desmond rebellion won papal support, were even more widespread. English suppression, Thomas Church-yard wrote, involved "pitifull murther, for man, woman and child were put to the sworde."[181] Troops marched through Munster in March 1580 under three captains. One of them, Sir William Pelham, wrote: "We consumed with fire all inhabitations and executed the people wherever we found them." Another, the English-Irish Earl of Ormond, reported putting to the sword "forty-six leaders, 800 notorious traitors, and about 4,000 common people caught in cabin and field." The Irish *Annals of the Four Masters* recorded: "It was not wonderful that they should kill men fit for action, but they killed blind and feeble men, women, boys and girls, sick persons, idiots and old people."[182]

Edmund Spenser witnessed another massacre in Munster in 1580, his first year in Ireland.[183] He was serving as secretary to the new lord deputy, Arthur Grey de Wilton, whom the queen had instructed that July to "remove that false impression" in Irish minds that "we have a determination as it were to root them out."[184] However, Grey's friend and predecessor Henry Sidney, who compared him to Hannibal, counseled him to be ruthless.[185] In November 1580, after disarming 600 Spanish and papal troops who had landed then quickly surrendered at Smerwick on the remote Dingle peninsula, Grey and his captain Walter Ralegh slaughtered them all in cold blood.[186] Grey wrote crisply to Elizabeth: "I sent straight, certain gentlemen in, to see their weapons and armours laid down, and to guard the munition and victual left there for spoil. Then I put in certain bands, who straight fell to execution. There were 600 slain" (see fig. 4).[187]

Spenser, too, came down wholeheartedly on the side of extermination. Defending Grey in *A View of the Present State of Ireland* (1596), he wrote that the surrendering commander had "craved onely mercy, which it being not thought good to shew them, for daunger of them, if, being saved, they should afterwardes ioyne with the Irish; and also for terrour to the Irish." Therefore, Spenser concluded, "there was no other way but to make that short end of them as was made." He also described how Grey devastated Munster by economic warfare against this "most rich and plentifull countrey, full of corne and cattle." The English prevented its population from cultivating the land; "thus being kept from manurance, and their cattle from running abroad," the Irish starved. Between 20 and 70 people perished daily in January–March 1582, a toll of several thousand in the city of Cork alone. Spenser wrote: "Out of every corner of the woods and glynnes they came creeping forth upon their hands, for their legges could not beare them; they looked like anatomies of death, they spake like ghosts crying out of their graves; . . . that in a short space there were none almost left, and a most populous and plentifull countrey suddainely left voyde of man and beast."[188]

Killings continued unabated after the Smerwick massacre. In his two years in office, Grey later testified, "1,485" Irish leaders, gentlemen, and soldiers were "slayne," mostly under martial law, "not accounting those of meaner sort, nor yet executions by lawe and killing of churls, the accompt of which is besides number." He named the Kavanaghs and O'Mores among his victims.[189] Canny comments: "Never before had such destruction of property or such slaughter been witnessed in Ireland." Courtiers complained to the queen that Grey "was a bloodie man, and regarded not the life of her subjects no more than dogges, but had wasted and consumed all, so as now she had nothing almost left, but to raigne in their ashes." The queen then moved to prohibit "severity of punishing." Grey was recalled in August 1582 and a "general pardon" announced. Several hundred rebel leaders, gentry, and landowners had been killed in 1579–83 in Cork alone.[190] Burghley observed that Munster had been "dispeopled." A 1584 inquiry found "not one of thirty" inhabitants of Desmond's estates surviving and "those for the most part starvelings." One English settler there reported "great territories waste," and another found the inhabitants of his plantation "the poorest creatures . . . so lean for want of food as wonderful." In a nine-month rampage in Kilkenny in 1583–84, Francis Lovell, a client of Walsingham and former servant of Sidney, used a martial law commission to rob and kill almost 400 people, of whom perhaps half were later found to have been innocent.[191]

Grey's departure, followed by Malby's sudden death in Connacht in 1584 and the appointment of the now more conciliatory Sir John Perrott as lord deputy, led to a serious lull in the violence. As president of Munster from 1571 to 1573, Perrott had executed 800 "rebells and their ayders."[192] But now, he became the lord deputy most determined (if not the only one since 1555) to sponsor a "persuasive strategy" toward the Irish.[193] Perrott wrote in 1584 that presidents should not "make game" of the country. He berated the crown's justices, captains, and "all other officers" for "not kepinge the soldiours under marshall discipline but them selfes and their souldiers makinge as yt were a

praie of the poore, takinge from them what they like." These exactions, Perrott wrote, "hathe breed suche hatred in the hartes of the people againste the
Englishe government," which was "not the laste cause of the continewannce of
the warres." Yet Perrott insisted on selecting officials "who ought to have sufficient power, at the first to brede feare in suche disordered people. And if they
cannot with persuasion wyne them to obedience, then by force to bringe them
thereunto, confiscatinge their landes." Perrott requested 700 cavalry and 2,200
foot soldiers, first to attack the Scots of the isles, "and as neare as maie be, not
to leave any of the kinde of them," sparing only those who "will put in good
assurance and pledges not to send ayde to the Irisherie." He urged that Ireland's
"evill customes maie be altered unto better" and that its judges "and all other
officers shulde be Englishe men as neare as myght bee." In 1584–85, Perrott
issued 16 more martial law commissions, but the next year the queen ordered
him to curtail the practice. In 1587, Francis Lovell was charged and disgraced
for his slaughter in Kilkenny. Only five martial law commissions were issued in
Munster from 1587 to 1590.[194]

Yet the Gaelic areas were in constant unrest, and by now the Pale community was also estranged from Dublin and even "the great Anglo-Irish houses
had been fatally alienated." Legislation passed by the Irish parliament of 1585–
86 used the terms *English* and *Irish* to imply nationality rather than ethnicity.
Bradshaw comments: "The chasm between government and local community
had gaped wider so that the presence of Anglo-Irish within the government
now failed to bridge the gap. This was ominous." Opposition brought the parliament to a standstill. In his concluding address as Speaker, the English-Irish
moderate Justice Walsh defended constitutionalism. Because the queen was
"head of this body politic and in that respect allied to all," the crown's representatives in Ireland should "accept in the same sort of us, without any differences or distinctions of persons." Walsh aptly quoted Cato's favorite target, Scipio Africanus, who had defeated Hannibal but opposed destroying Carthage:
"Better to save one citizen than to overthrow a thousand enemies." Walsh was
addressing the last Irish parliament to meet for 27 years.[195]

Violence again escalated. Malby's successor in Connacht, Richard Bingham, who had served with Grey at Smerwick, was knighted by Perrott in
1584.[196] Two years later, Bingham surprised and slaughtered over 1,000 Scots
gallowglass and as many more of their unarmed camp followers, with "cold-
blooded thoroughness among men, women and children" that revived memo-

ries of both Smerwick and the Rathlin massacre of 1575. "I was never, since I was a man of war," one of Bingham's captains wrote, "so weary of killing men; for I protest to God, for as fast as I could I did but hough them and paunch them, sometimes on horseback, because they did run as we did break them, and sometimes on foot."[197] On another occasion, Bingham found the hideout of 30 "knaves" and slaughtered them, sending "a horse loade of heads" to his brother. In Mayo, Bingham's men arrested Owen O'Flaherty, stole 5,500 of his stock, then hanged 18 of his men without trial.[198] Perrott fell out with Bingham, as did others. His successor William Fitzwilliam, Archbishop Adam Loftus of Dublin, and Loftus's future successor all opposed Bingham's predations, and for their pains drew rebukes in 1588–89 from Francis Walsingham in London.[199] The Connacht provost marshal reported in 1590 that the victims of Bingham's military operations were "none but women, children and churles destroyed." Fitzwilliam overlooked these and other findings but did not renew Bingham's martial law commission.[200]

After two bloody decades of imperial adventures, some English officials began to fear the cost to their own principles of governance. In 1590, Mr. Justice Robert Gardener reported on the situation across Ireland, diagnosing "the diseases of that commonwealth." He focused on corruption and the abuse of martial law, including the "common allowance" given "for head silver to such as bring heads, never examining or knowing whose heads, whether of the best or worst so no safety for any man to travel; a strange course in a Christian Commonwealth." Archbishop Adam Loftus, by contrast, saw the violence as serving a religious purpose: "The sword alone without the word is not sufficient, but unless they be forced they will not once come to hear the word preached."[201] But in April 1591 a Wexford jury rejected the crown's case for martial law seizure of the property of five men hanged in Dublin, whom the jury found were not rebels at the time. By implication, historian David Edwards writes, "the state was guilty of murder." In October 1591, the queen finally abolished martial law.[202]

English colonial thinking had evolved significantly since the Irish-born Rowland White published his *Discors Touching Ireland* in 1569. White had eschewed racialism, focusing on Irish education and welfare, though accepting a need for harsh policing. Since then, historian Ciaran Brady writes, colonial publicists Edmund Spenser, William Herbert, Richard Beacon, and Anthony Trollope had all "paid exceptional but generally unacknowledged attention to

Machiavelli whose *Discourses on Livy* provided the most elaborate defence of the use of coercion and even tyranny."[203] Gradually, racialist thinking assumed prominence as well.

William Herbert's Latin text, written about 1588, on "the causes of the evil state of Ireland" emphasized its faulty political system, ignoring the supposed origins and nature of the population. Herbert proposed statecraft "remedies" that included the assassination of opposition leaders, but stopped short of Machiavellian political morality. He aimed to replicate England's civil polity by abolishing "Irish customs and public institutions" (but not the Irish language, which he fostered) and by sponsoring colonies and formal education, including universities. He advocated draconian repression only as a last resort.[204] In 1588, however, Herbert did argue for transplanting the Irish.[205] His later moderation in practice, and his attempts to woo Irish loyalties, may have been related to the greater difficulty of attracting and retaining English tenants on his barren Kerry estate. After settling in Munster in 1594, Herbert employed over 100 Irish tenants, and only 20 English. He favored a planter monopoly over the levers of power but was in constant dispute with his planter neighbor, the former London student of Livy, Edward Denny, who advocated extreme sanctions against the Irish.[206]

Richard Beacon, a crown legal officer in Munster, published his proposal in 1594. He advocated neither universities nor constitutional restraints but focused on a concept of "severe justice" that brought him to defend the violence of Richard Bingham in Connacht, comparing him to a Roman general taking necessary action against rebellious Gauls.[207] According to Bradshaw, Beacon thought in "apocalyptic and providential categories," including the rise and fall of nations and a transnational alliance of Protestants. Brady sees Beacon's proposals as a combination of stick and carrot.[208]

But a generation of violence had established its own radicalizing momentum. And a temporary lull in the terror may have afforded the terrorized space to regroup. The abolition of martial law in 1591 barely preceded "the conflagration of the 1590s." Donegal chieftain Hugh Roe O'Donnell, escaping after four years in an English prison, raised Ulster in rebellion in 1591. His father-in-law Hugh O'Neill became Earl of Tyrone in 1593 and joined the revolt the next year. Elizabeth proclaimed them both traitors. Untold numbers of noncombatants were to perish in the Nine Years' War from 1594 to 1603. England increased its garrison in Ireland to 21,000 men by the end of the decade. Now it reaped the whirlwind. The war cost London nearly £2 million, against its Irish revenues of

£30,000 per year. Incomplete battle casualty figures on both sides indicate at least 2,600 English dead and 6,000 Irish killed and wounded.[209]

The war prompted Edmund Spenser to distribute his extremist views in the form of a policy dialogue, *A View of the Present State of Ireland,* completed in 1596–97. Spenser, unlike his Munster neighbor Herbert, or even Richard Beacon, gave considerable attention to racial origins and typology of the Irish, whose barbarism made them unfit for English-style civil government. Ciaran Brady adds that neither Herbert nor Beacon "shared Spenser's pessimism as to the inefficacy of all existing laws; neither would have endorsed his insistence on the necessity of total and immediate war."[210] Spenser wrote that the Irish "all have their eares upright, wayting when the watch-word shall come, that they should all arise generally into rebellion, and cast away the English subjection." England, Spenser concluded, must reform Ireland "not by lawes and ordinances" but instead "by the sword." Using a typical metaphor of cultivation, he explained that "all these evils must first be cut away by a strong hand, before any good can bee planted, like as the corrupt braunches and unwholesome boughs are first to bee pruned, and the foule mosse cleansed and scraped away, before the tree can bring forth any good fruite." Spenser urged England to adopt "the most violent redresse that may be used for any evill." Surrender should be refused after the expiration of a 20-day grace period proclaimed "at the beginning of those warres," which would exclude "onely the very principalls and ringleaders" of the rebellion. "But afterwards I would have none received, but left to their fortune and miserable end." For such holdouts, "there is no hope of their amendment or recovery, and therefore needefull to be cut off." English law and religious proselytization would have to wait. Even after suppression of the rebels, "wee cannot now apply lawes fit to the people," so instead "wee will apply the people and fit them unto the lawes." The "bitternesse" of martial law would continue. And "if any reliques of the olde rebellion bee found by any, that either have not come in and submitted themselves to the law, or that having once come in, doe break forth againe, let them taste of the same cuppe in Gods name." These Irish, Spenser wrote, were "unfit to live in the commonwealth."[211]

The respite was over. Robert Devereux, second Earl of Essex, began in late 1595 to assume Burghley's dominant role in English security and Irish policy, which now reverted to pre-1586 practice. London abandoned "deluding parleys" and formally reintroduced martial law in late 1596. The crown issued 10 martial law commissions in March–October 1597, compared to one per year in

1594–96. Now the authorities regularly sent the heads of their victims to Dublin for public display at the gates. In 1597, Lord Deputy Thomas Burgh reported Dublin's air "thick corrupted" with "the heads daily brought in." In October of that year, the queen put Essex in command of her army in Ireland. In 1598 alone, the government issued 34 individual martial law commissions, and from March, all of them were of unlimited duration. One problem they addressed was Ireland's overcrowded jails, "now very much pestered with a great number of prisoners," mostly "poor men." Martial law commissioners now had to kill all prisoners awaiting trial, whether guilty or innocent. The disgraced mass murderer Richard Bingham obtained reappointment in 1598 as marshal of the Irish army, and his supporters from Connacht regained office. The Privy Council also appointed Edmund Spenser as sheriff of County Cork. It judged Spenser "fitt for that office" because he was "not unskillful or without experience in the service of the warrs." The next year, Spenser's patron Essex became lord deputy of Ireland.[212]

In October 1598, however, the rebels overran and swept away the Munster plantation. The Irish killed several hundred settlers and drove the rest, including Spenser, back to England. In two months of campaigning in 1599, Essex lost 5,000 men, mostly to disease. He in turn was now disgraced. But the English inflicted a crushing defeat on O'Neill and his Spanish allies at Kinsale in 1601, massacring other Irish garrisons in Munster "in the usual way."[213]

Now the English forces turned to extermination, clearing much of the country for renewed settlement. In Ulster, Essex's successor, Lord Mountjoy, adopted a scorched-earth policy. Historian John McGurk writes that "there are no figures for the various acts of devastation then carried out," but Foster adds that "the ensuing descriptions of starvation and cannibalism made unbearable reading even then. The strategy was spoliation." Mountjoy's commander Chichester described Irish as "beasts in the shape of men."[214] He marched north in November 1601, "sparing neither humans nor goods found on his path."[215] He reported: "We have burnt and destroyed along the Lough, . . . in which journeys we have killed above one hundred people of all sorts, besides such as were burnt, how many I know not. We spare none of what quality or sex soever, and it hath bred much terror in the people." In July the next year, Mountjoy wrote: "We do now continually hunt all their woods, spoil their corn, burn their houses, and kill so many churls [peasants], as it grieveth me to think that it is necessary to do this."[216] Later that month, he reported to the Privy

Council: "We can assure your lordships, that from O'Cane's country, where he now liveth, which is to the northward of his own country of Tirone, we have left none to give us opposition, nor of late have seen any but dead carcases, merely starved."[217] By September, he remarked on "the lamentable estate of that country, wherein we found every where men dead of famine, in so much that Ohagan protested unto us that between Tullogh Oge and Toome there lay unburied a thousand dead, and that since our first drawing this year to Black-water, there were above three thousand starved in Tyrone."[218]

Mountjoy's pursuit and extermination of the rebels continued in winter-time. "This brake their hearts; for the aire being sharpe, and they naked, and they being driven from their lodgings, into the Woods bare of leaves, they had no shelter for themselves. Besides that, their cattle (giving them no milke in the Winter), were also wasted by driving to and fro. And that they being thus troubled in the Seede time, could not sowe their ground. And as in Harvest time, both the Deputies forces, and the Garrisons, cut downe their Corne, be-fore it was ripe, so now in Winter time they carried away, or burnt, all the stores of victuals in secret places, whether the Rebels had conveied them." Mountjoy found "everywhere men dead of famine."[219] Meanwhile, George Carew, lord justice of Ireland, who had served with Sidney in the 1570s and risen to com-mand 3,000 troops as president of Munster by 1600, stormed Dunboy Castle in 1602. Spurning its offer to surrender on terms, Carew had the entire garrison executed.[220]

Mountjoy aimed to make Ireland a blank slate for England to write upon or, in another agricultural metaphor, a plantation free of "weeds." In February 1603, he regretted that he had not "sooner and more easily either have made this Country a rased table, wherin shee might have written her owne lawes, or have tied the ill disposed and rebellious hands, till I surely planted such a government as would have overgrown and killed any weeds, that should have risen under it."[221]

Elizabeth died in March 1603. Hugh O'Neill surrendered a few days later. He fled the country with several other Irish earls in 1607.[222] Five years later, the attorney general for Ireland, Sir John Davies, surveying English rule in "all the Records of this Kingdome," remarked that "the Irish generally, were held and reputed Aliens, or rather enemies to the Crowne," and that "they were so farre out of the protection of the Lawe, as it was often adjudged no fellony to kill a meere Irish-man in the time of peace." Nevertheless, Davies insisted, with yet another comparison to cultivation, just as "the Husbandman must first break the Land," until it is "thoroughly broken and manured," so also "a barbarous Country must first be broken by a warre."[223]

In one sense Mountjoy's "rased table" had been achieved. Canny suggests that by the early seventeenth century, Irish peasants were so "few in number in the aftermath of war (when the total population of the country might have been as low as 750,000)," while on the other hand "the influx of British proprietors" of Irish lands was so great, that surviving Irish tenants may even have found the imbalance "in their favour," as the English now lacked tenants to work their new property.[224]

Sir John Davies claimed in 1612 that King James I established a new policy of "mixt plantation" in Ireland. Now, "his Majesty did not utterly exclude the Natives out of this plantation, with a purpose to roote them out, as the Irish were excluded out of the first English colonies." Yet the cultivation fetish persisted. "Only, the Irish were in some places transplanted from the Woods & Mountaines, into the Plaines & open Countries, that being removed (like wild fruit trees) they might grow the milder, and beare the better & sweeter fruit." English control left the Irish nowhere to hide, with "notice taken of every person that is able to do either good or hurt. It is knowne, not only howe they live, and what they doe, but it is foreseen what they purpose or intend to do." The Irish, therefore, "conform themselves to the manner of England in all their behaviour." Davies envisaged that Ireland's "next generation will in tongue and heart, and every way else, become English so as there will bee no difference or distinction, but the Irish Sea betwixt us." Only three years earlier, Davies had described Ulster as "heretofore as unknown to the English here as the most inland part of Virginia."[225] A new world was being created—and another was emerging in its wake.

CHAPTER 6

Colonial North America,
1600–1776

E ngland's conquest of Ireland set a precedent for North America. As early as 1496, Henry VII had commissioned John Cabot to "conquer" heathen lands there for English "domination,"[1] but it was the veteran "Ireland hand," Humphrey Gilbert, who pioneered that expansion. Four years after completing *The Discourse of Ireland* in 1572, Gilbert wrote of a Spaniard who had come there from the West Indies telling him and Henry Sidney of a northwest Atlantic sea route to China navigated by "a Frier of Mexico."[2] In 1578, Queen Elizabeth authorized Gilbert to find "heathen and barbarous lands, countreys, or territories not actually possessed of any Christian prince or people," which Gilbert could "occupie and enjoy to him, his heirs and assigns for ever."[3] Gilbert "handed out paper grants of land-rights to anyone who could pay him," fitted out five ships, and sailed across the Atlantic in 1583. The expedition landed briefly in Newfoundland, which Gilbert promptly annexed. But disease and desertions defeated his effort to establish England's first American colony there. The next month, he went down with his ship in a storm near the Azores.[4]

More "Ireland hands" followed Gilbert to America. The next year, his half brother, Sir Walter Ralegh, took over Gilbert's patent from the queen. Concerning Indians, the advice from Richard Hakluyt, England's leading colonial publicist, was clear: "We will proceed with extremity." This meant to "conquer, fortify, and plant in soils, most sweet, most pleasant, most strong and most fertile, and in the end bring them all in subjection and to civility." Ralegh's kinsman Francis Drake, who had served under the first Earl of Essex in Ireland, now sailed off with 2,300 troops to harry the Spanish, sacking Cartagena, in modern-day Colombia, in 1586.[5] As general in charge of his own expedition, Ralegh appointed another kinsman, Richard Grenville, a Munster landlord who had advised Gilbert there in the 1560s. Ralph Lane, who had distinguished himself for "rapacity" in Ireland by demanding all of County Kerry, became the expedition's lieutenant.[6]

The failed settlement that Ralegh established at Roanoke in 1585–86, known as the "Lost Colony," depended for its short life on local Indian supplies of corn. Relations with the natives quickly deteriorated. When Indians stole a silver cup, Grenville sent a party to recover it. The frustrated English reported: "[W]e burnt, and spoyled their corne, and Towne." Yet the English could not support themselves, and Lane exhausted Indian forbearance by demanding daily supplies. Two weeks before he finally abandoned the colony, Ralph Lane attacked and killed Wingina, king of the Roanokes, and his advisers. Thomas Hariot wrote the next year that "in respect of troubling our inhabiting and planting," the Indians "are not to be feared," but he added ominously that "they shall have cause both to feare and love us."[7] Similar tension appeared in the title of Hariot's work, *Briefe and True Report of the New Found Land of Virginia,* recalling the title of Las Casas's exposé, and in Hariot's statement in the 1590 edition that "the Inhabitants of great Bretannie have bin in times past as sauvage as those of Virginia," recalling Spenser's view of the Irish as primitive Britons.[8]

After this first Virginia colony failed, Grenville died in a naval battle with a Spanish ship off the Azores in 1591. Lane returned to Ireland to become muster-master of the English forces there in 1592. During the Armada invasion of 1588, Walter Ralegh commanded a company in Munster. He participated in the second plantation there, receiving a grant of 12,000 acres and bringing in other Roanoke veterans, including John White.[9] But on his accession in 1603, prefiguring peace with the king of Spain, James I had Ralegh tried for sedition. Ralegh spent 13 years in the Tower of London, where he wrote his *History of the World,* reflecting on "what labour, practise, perill, bloudshed, and cruelty, the Kings and Princes of the world have undergone," leaving no trace of "Carthage, Rome and the rest," while "Caesar and Alexander, have un-made and slaine, each of them, more than a million men: but they made none, nor left none behind them."[10] Ralegh was executed in 1618.

If England looked to its Irish experience, some also regarded Spain's American conquests as a model, although yet others viewed them "as a negative paradigm." As broader European competition began for strategic advantage in North America, the English feared being shut out of the continent. In 1605, France established a base at Port Royal in Nova Scotia and founded Quebec in 1608. The next year, a Dutch expedition opened up trade in the Hudson valley. The English established a colony in Newfoundland in 1610 and forced the French to close Port Royal in 1613. According to historian Neal Salisbury, the French and Dutch worked more closely with the indigenous peoples they found, while the English regularly sought to secure their beachheads "by intimidating and coercing Indians."[11] There were exceptions to this rule, of course. France waged "a war of near extermination" against Fox Indians until their subjugation in 1731.[12]

Over these two centuries, English brutality also reached the level of genocide in several cases, though more often it did not. Some English colonists, like Roger Williams of Rhode Island, tried hard to treat Indians fairly; some Dutch commanders slaughtered them; and some Indians massacred colonists. Frontier atrocities were common on both sides as the English occupation expanded across North America. In that context, genocide sporadically erupted.

England established the second Virginia colony at Jamestown in 1607. Its supervisory Council of Virginia in London included Sir Ferdinando Gorges, sergeant major of the army in Ireland from 1599; the Earl of Southampton, who also served in Ireland in 1599–1600; Lord De La Warr, who fought there under the second Earl of Essex; and George Carew, formerly lord justice of Ireland, who had massacred the defeated defenders of Dunboy Castle in 1602. He was also a member of the private Virginia Company, which financed the Jamestown colony. Working with another Ireland hand, Lord Chichester, Carew planned the new government of Virginia.[13]

As veterans of Ireland set out to conquer North America, literary followers of Edmund Spenser captured the English imagination. Michael Drayton wrote the first successful odes in English, including the patriotic "Ballad of Agincourt" and "To the Virginian Voyage." He drew upon Hakluyt's *Principal Navigations* in 1606 to portray the new colony as "ours to hold, Virginia, Earth's onely Paradise. Where Nature hath in store / Fowle, Venison, and Fish / And the fruitfull'st Soyle /Without your Toyle, / Three Harvests more." Not all his verse was lyrical: "In kenning of the Shore . . . / Let Cannons roare, Frightning the wide Heaven." Drayton maintained a lifelong interest in the Virginia plantation. He begged his lady love to "Be more foolish then the Indians are / For Bells, for Knives, for Glasses, and such ware, / That sell their Pearle and Gold." In a 1621 elegy, "To Master George Sandys, Treasurer for the English Colony in

Virginia," Drayton asked his friend Sandys, translator of Ovid's pastoral *Meta-morphoses,* to describe Virginia to him "that I / May become learned in the soyle thereby." Indians were of less interest than their land: "But you may save your labour if you please, / To write to me ought of your Savages." Six years later, Drayton was lamenting the upending of British virtue by sin and "Bed-lam," in which men of Cato's hallowed quality went unappreciated: "That only he a Censor now is thought; And that base villaine . . . / Now like a God."[14]

Land and Ideology

On the basis of their land use, the indigenous populations of North America fell into several categories. Those living in what is now Canada, the high plains, and western mountains, were predominantly hunter-gatherers. In the more temperate and fertile lands in the east of what is now the United States, over 1 million Indians lived by cultivating corn and gardens of squash and beans; hunting and gathering supplemented these staple crops. In the northeast, hor-ticulture was left to women and produced small surpluses. In the southeast, "the men laboured in large communal fields" and produced big surpluses. The Cherokees, Choctaws, Chickasaws, and Creeks "had larger, more urbanized populations, with more elaborate ceremonies, and more impressive architec-ture, than the Northern horticulturists," including "large towns, with palisaded fort, council house, regular streets, and a central plaza."[15]

The first colonists were surprised to find these farming communities all along the eastern seaboard.[16] Writing home to Hakluyt in 1585, Ralph Lane rhapsodized about "the goodliest soil under the cope of heaven, so abound-inge with sweet trees" and luxuriant wheat; "and the Cane maketh very good and perfect suger." He added: "If Virginia had but Horses and Kine [cattle] in some reasonable proportion, I dare say myself being inhabited with English, no realme in Christendome were comparable to it."[17]

Yet, as in Ireland, the colonial project required visions not only of future agricultural potential but also of existing Indian failure to fulfill it. Gilbert had planned to enlist both Englishmen and Indians to "manure" (cultivate) the soil. The Indians could be taught "how the tenth part of their land may be so ma-nured and emploied, as it may yeeld more commodities to the necessary use of mans life, then the whole now dooth." Hakluyt believed that "every soyle of the world by arte may be made to yeelde things to feede and to clothe men."[18] Queen Elizabeth specifically awarded Gilbert "all the soyle of all such lands" he was to annex in her name. Lane found that Virginia produced wines, oils, flax, resins, and pitch, "but being Savages that possess the land, they know no use of the same." Adding that "the soil is of a huge unknowen greatnesse, and very wel peopled and towned, though savagelie," Lane made it clear that the horticulture and towns of the Indians failed to qualify. Should they not cooperate with the colonists and their superior cultivation, the violence that Gilbert, Grenville, Ralegh, Drake, and Lane had all used to kill and terrorize Irish "savage heathen" would serve as precedents.[19]

Many Europeans believed in their monopoly of the "arte" and "husbandrie" of agriculture and their corollary right to possess and cultivate the land. Neither the dependence of early colonists in Carolina and Virginia on Indian corn surpluses, nor their discoveries that the Algonquins were "ingenious" farmers, using "a graine of marveilous great increase," nor that 300 households of Kecoughtans had cleared nearly 3,000 acres "to receave Corne or make Vyneyards" shook the colonialists' vision of their own superior use of the land. As historian Karen Kupperman notes, English observers' accounts routinely revealed Indians living in "settled communities sustained by formal agriculture." Yet Captain John Smith in 1612 described Virginia "as Salvage as barbarous, as ill-peopled, as little planted, laboured and manured." Not even his discovery two years later that New England was "so planted with Gardens and Corne fields, and so well inhabited with goodly strong and well proportioned people" prevented him from anyway classifying that region as "not inhabited." A decade later, the Pilgrims' leader William Bradford came closer to the truth when he stated that "the Indians in those times did not have nearly so much corn as they have had since the English supplied them with hoes."[20] Ideology sadly exaggerated this real difference.

As conflict escalated, the English increasingly portrayed Indians as wastrels. Yet even as he urged conquest, the Virginia colonists' spokesman Edward Waterhouse conceded in passing that Indians farmed their land: "[W]e, who hitherto have had possession of no more ground than their waste, and our purchase . . . may now by right of Warre, and law of Nations, invade the country, and destroy them who sought to destroy us: whereby wee shall enjoy their cultivated places. . . . Now their cleared grounds in all their villages (which are situate in the fruitfullest places of the land) shall be inhabited by us." Samuel Purchas, however, justified conquest on opposite grounds, that God had meant the land to be farmed, not to remain a supposed "unmanned wild Countrey," over which Indians "range rather than inhabite."[21]

"Our land is full . . . their land is empty," wrote colonist Robert Cushman in 1622. "Their land is spacious and void, and they are few and do but run over the grass, as do also the foxes and the wild beasts. They are not industrious, neither have [they] art, science, skill or faculty to use either the land or the commodities of it; but all spoils, rots and is marred for want of manuring, gathering, ordering, etc . . . so it is lawful now to take a land which none useth and make use of it."[22] Governor John Winthrop of the Massachusetts Bay Colony drew upon the legal theory of *vacuum domicilium* to assert that the land was unoccupied because it had not been cultivated ("subdued") in a European manner, and therefore could legitimately be occupied for that superior purpose. Before departing England, Winthrop wrote: "As for the Natives in New England, they inclose noe Land, neither have any setled habytation, nor any tame Cattell to improve the Land by . . . soe as if we leave them sufficient for their use, we may lawfully take the rest." His discovery in 1633 that Narragansett land, for instance, was "full of Indians" failed to break the notion of vacuum domicilium. "Land was free to any who would possess it," wrote Winthrop.[23]

For their part, Indians both farmed the land and considered themselves its owners. In 1621, Squanto, "sent of God" to help the Plymouth Pilgrims, "showed them how to plant their corn," according to the Pilgrims' leader Bradford. William Wood wrote in 1634 that Massachusetts Indians had been "our first instructors for the planting of their Indian corn, by teaching us to cull out the finest seed, to observe the fittest season, to keep distance for holes, and fit measure for hills, to worm it and weed it, to prune it, and dress it." An indigenous concept of property also determined that when a Connecticut River Indian village sold a tract of land in 1636, it reserved its right to all "ground that is now planted"—and hunting, gathering, and fishing rights to the rest. (By contrast, three years later, after Dutch settlers there protested that Englishmen "were using our land" that the Dutch "had bought and paid for," the Puritan governor simply replied, "[T]he lands were lying idle.")[24] In the 1640s, the Narragansett chief Miantunnomoh complained: "Our fathers had plenty of deer and skins, our plains were full of deer, as also our woods, and of turkeys, and our coves full of fish and fowl. But these English having gotten our land, they with scythes cut down the grass, and with axes fell the trees; their cows and horses eat the grass, and their hogs spoil our clam banks, and we shall all be starved." In seventeenth-century Maryland, Indians protested that English settlers' cows were eating their corn crops, depriving them of their land: "Your hogs and

Cattle injure Us. We Can fly no farther[.] let us know wher to live & how to be secured for the future from the Hogs & Cattle."[25]

The facts mattered less to most English colonists than their own "art" in cultivation of the land. Some thought it "no Injury" to Indians, "we rather than they being the prime occupants, and they only Sojourners in the land."[26] Others thought they could inculcate the art of cultivation in the natives. The Massachusetts Bay General Court required every unmarried Indian adopting Christianity to "plante for himselfe."[27] Though some did, the prevalent cultivation fetish remained consistent with not just dispossession but displacement— and at times even genocide—of the country's previous occupants, whatever their form of land use.

Moreover, while England's own population almost doubled from 1550 to 1650, Indian communities suffered devastation from new diseases. Most diseases that Europeans had unwittingly brought to the New World in the sixteenth century quickly spread north on the mainland. By 1608, as many as 17 serious epidemics had reduced the Powhatans of the Virginia coast from perhaps 50,000 to no more than 14,000, of whom, John Smith wrote, "[t]he men be few."[28] This was just the start of a dramatic demographic decline. In his study *American Indian Holocaust and Survival,* the sociologist Russell Thornton calculated that in 1492, over 7 million people lived north of the Rio Grande, but by 1800 the number living within the boundaries of what is now the United States fell to about 600,000.[29]

Seventeenth-Century Virginia

War raged in Virginia from the first day of the second English colony in 1607. James I had instructed the colonists to "well entreate" the Indians, to whom the Virginia Company expected to offer "equal priviledges" and "faire and loving meanes." It, too, advised colonists "not to offend the naturalls."[30] Initially interested in trade and minerals, the company sent no farmers for the first year, exacerbating the settlement's severe food shortages. But from an outpost of discovery, the Virginia colony soon moved toward the Spanish model of direct appropriation of the indigenous Tsenacommacah territory and administration, and of its 28 tribes, ruled by the chieftain of the Powhatans.[31] As English agriculture also spread over Indian land, it brought the colony into increasing conflict.

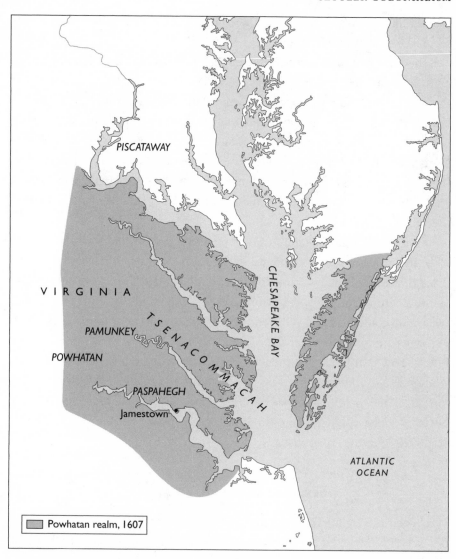

MAP 9. Early-seventeenth-century Virginia

Chesapeake Indians assaulted the initial British landing party, driving them back to their ships. Within a week, the settlers built a fort at Jamestown, but before they had unpacked their guns, 200 Powhatans attacked. Only fire from the ships prevented the Indians from destroying the fort. An uneasy truce, "punctuated by guerrilla raids on both sides" and by English acquisition of Indian corn, lasted several years. The company advised the colonists that if they could not take the chief Powhatan prisoner, "you must make him your tributary."

The first of three Anglo-Powhatan wars broke out in mid-1609. A winter of starvation reduced the besieged colony of 500 to fewer than 100 people in 1610.[32] Labor was now at a premium. The new governor De La Warr, knighted by Essex in Ireland, brought orders from the Virginia Company stating that the "enemy is the natives," who must be made to labor.[33] The English now planned "to make Tsenacommacah their own."[34]

When the Powhatans refused to turn over an English runaway, the governor sent forces upriver to "take Revendge" by attacking the chief town of the Paspahegh tribe. They killed 15 Indians, kidnapped their queen and her children, burned the houses, and destroyed the corn crops. In the boat on the return journey, the English raiders threw the children overboard and shot out "their Braynes in the water." Back in Jamestown, at the governor's pleasure, the English commander had the Paspahegh queen stabbed to death. From then on, David Stannard writes, "there would be no peace in Virginia."[35]

Two years later, Governor Dale continued to recapture and brutalize runaways who had gone to live with the Indians; he hanged, burned, staked, and shot them, hoping to instill labor discipline in others. Violence against Indians, too, was effective in deterring English servants from seeking "to live Idle" among them. In 1612, colonist William Strachey still insisted that the two communities could live together: "[N]oe Spanish Intention shalbe entertained by us neither, hereby to roote out the Naturalls as the Spaniards have done in Hispaniola and other parts." Strachey advocated attacking only Indian shamans, as agents of Satan. He urged that of the rulers, "their better sort shall by pattents and proclamations hold their landes as free burghers and Cittizens with the English and Subjectes to king James." Indian tribute would feed the English garrisons and sustain trade, "but the Naturalls being thus constrayned to paye duly this their Tribute will Clense double as much grownd as they doe." But the chief of the Paspaheghs told John Smith: "We perceive and well know you intend to destroy us, . . . and to enjoy our houses and plant our fields." When the first conflict ended in 1614, 500 people had perished on both sides. The colony's first commercial tobacco crop, that same year, also augured ill for the Indians.[36]

English policy evolved only slowly, through partial genocide to Indian slavery. The initial vision had aimed to "fit Virginia into Tsenacommacah," assuming direct control of its institutions and labor. By 1622, 48 English plantations spread over both the center and periphery of the Powhatan territory. Colonial promoter John Martin suggested twinning 32 English shires with the similar number of Powhatan domains, each sending 100 Englishmen to take over the 32 Indian "shires."[37]

Mutual slaughters in 1622 launched the decade-long second Anglo-Powhatan war. After Englishmen killed the Powhatan leader Nemattanew, Indians took up arms, and on March 22 they massacred 347 whites, over one-fifth of the colony's inhabitants. Retaliating with what historian Edmund Morgan calls a "policy of extermination," the English issued, according to James Axtell, "perhaps the first secular expression of genocidal intent." In response to the Virginia Company's initial advice to adhere to a code of justice, the colony's governor and council ruled that "wee hold nothinge injuste, that may tend to their ruine, (except breach of faith)."[38] In August 1622, the company recommended constructing "compact and orderly villages" on the model "of the Spaniards in the West Indies," and then on October 7, the Virginia Company decided on genocide: the Indians were to be rooted "out for being [any] longer a people on the face of the Earth." It called for "a perpetual war without peace or truce," advocating "burninge theire Townes, demolishing theire Temples . . . carying away theire Corne, and depriving them of whatsoever may yeeld them succor or relief."[39] Colonist and former company secretary Edward Waterhouse (whose uncle had been Essex's secretary when the latter slaughtered O'Neills in Ulster in 1574) insisted that "this massacre must rather be beneficiall to the plantation then impaire it, let all men take courage . . . in choosing the best Seats of the Country, which now by vanquishing of the Indians, is like to offer a more ample and fair choice of fruitfull habitations." Waterhouse urged "turning the laborious mattock into the victorious sword," directly linking conquest to cultivation.[40]

In January 1623, Governor Francis Wyat ("noble Wyat" in Drayton's elegy) reported to the Virginia Company that he had "anticipated your desires by setting uppon the Indians in all places," and that "we have slain divers, burnte theire townes, destroyed their wears and corne." Wyat expected to "geve them shortly a blow, That shall neere or altogether Ruinate them."[41] An Englishman posing as a "negotiator" poisoned 200 Indians in one incident, butchering another 50 later. The Virginia Council determined in 1623 that "we have slayne more of them this yeere, then hath been slayne before since the beginninge of ye colonie." In a two-day battle in July 1624, Axtell writes, sixty armed Englishmen "cut down eight hundred Pamunkeys on their home ground." The English, Morgan adds, had quickly extracted revenge for the 1622 massacre "many times over."[42]

John Smith now advocated the Spanish model for the treatment of Indians. In his *Generall Historie of Virginia* in 1624, he discussed "how to suppresss them" by simply alluding to "twenty examples of the Spaniards how they got the West-Indies."[43] In *A Plaine Pathway to Plantations,* Richard Eburne implied that Virginia had no room for Indians: "Imagine all that to be England where Englishmen . . . do dwell. (And it be the people that makes the land English, not the land the people.)" Thus conquest alone would not suffice to make the population English, which Indians could never be. They had to be replaced. Eburne recommended immigration so that "the bounds of this land of England" would "be speedily and wonderfully removed, enlarged, and extended."[44]

King James I ordered an investigation of the Virginia Company in 1623, leading to revocation of its charter the next year. Virginia now became a royal colony. Its population grew from 1,300 in 1625 to 8,000 in 1640. A decade of war with the Powhatans ended in 1632, but the colony's new goal of merely "defeating, rather than supplanting" Tsenacommacah failed to forestall further conflict. The third Anglo-Powhatan war broke out when Indians killed 500 settlers in another genocidal massacre in 1644. In two years Governor William Berkeley's forces pushed the Indians inland and arranged a peace treaty.[45] The colony's policy did not seek the Powhatans' total annihilation, but it required their full subjection and dispossession by force, with partial genocide, temporary segregation, and eventual slavery for survivors. Already the Powhatans were "soe rowted, slayne and dispersed, that they are no longer a nation." A 1669 census found surviving members of only 11 of the 28 Powhatan tribes existing in 1608.[46] In six decades, 17 tribes had disappeared.

Dispersal of the survivors completed the genocide on the Carthaginian model. Of other groups still unsubdued, Governor Berkeley wrote in 1666, "I think it is necessary to Destroy all these Northern Indians," and he suggested defraying the costs of the campaign by selling "the women and children" abroad as slaves.[47] The 725 Indian warriors remaining in Virginia three years later were "far too few in number to constitute a serious threat" to the 13,000 able-bodied English men, yet in 1676 the Susquehannahs, Doegs, and Piscattaways also came under genocidal attack. English militiamen murdered 30 Doeg and Susquehannah warriors, including six chiefs who came out to parley. Nathaniel Bacon, a colonial official who was about to lead "Bacon's Rebellion" against Berkeley, forced the issue by proclaiming war "against all Indians in generall." Morgan writes: "The friendly Occaneechees captured a number of Susquehannahs for him. After the prisoners had been killed, Bacon's men turned their guns on the Occaneechees and dispatched most of them too." Bacon soon turned his attention to "the peaceful Pamunkeys," whom his men tracked down in a swamp and captured with all their possessions.[48]

Governor Berkeley initially attempted to ride the rebel tiger without dishonoring his treaty with the Indians. But he, too, convinced that Indians "generally conspired against us in all the western parts of America," gave orders "to spare none that has the name of an Indian for they are now all our Enemies." The colonial assembly spelled out in 1676 that any Indians "who left their towns without English permission" were to be considered enemies, that troops would "have the benefit of all plunder either Indians or otherwise," and "that all Indians taken in warr be held and accounted slaves dureing life." After Bacon's death and the end of his rebellion, the assembly quickly ordered that soldiers who had captured Indians should "keepe all such Indian slaves or other Indian goods as they either have taken or hereafter shall take." By 1685, the Powhatans were said to be extinct. Two decades later, the other Virginia Indians were "almost gone," the survivors "vanishing." Many more, now brought from Carolina, had escaped annihilation only for slavery. Virginia legislation "lumped together" Indians and Negroes. From 1705, Virginia barred both from giving evidence in court.[49]

In the same year, Robert Beverley published his *History and Present State of Virginia,* whose title recalled Spenser's *View of the Present State of Ireland.* So did its language. Beverley described Virginia as an Arcadian idyll. The eyes of its inhabitants, he wrote, "are ravished with the Beauties of naked Nature. Their Ears are Serenaded with the perpetual murmur of Brooks. . . . Their Taste is regaled with the most delicious Fruits . . . the Plantations, Orchards and Gardens constantly afford 'em fragrant and delightful Walks." Even the remaining Indians were "happy . . . in their simple State of Nature," devoting "only a few Days in the Summer" to "the bare planting of a little Corn, and Melons." The Indians "claim no property in Lands. . . . Every one Hunts and Fishes. . . . Their labour in tending Corn, Pompions, Melons, &c. is not so great, that they need quarrel for room," though the English had "taken away great part of their Country." Yet Beverley also criticized the "Laziness" of the settlers and their failure to recreate his vision of English agriculture in a land still "over-run with Wood."[50]

Two decades later, Hugh Jones, an English visitor to Virginia, agreed that "the whole country is a perfect forest, except where the woods are cleared for plantations." The settlers maintained no urban centers: "[N]either the interests nor inclinations of the Virginians induce them to cohabit in towns." The rural hierarchy was headed by the "gentlemen's seats" with their "commodious" brick homes. Down the social ladder, Jones reported, "the common planters live in pretty timber houses," the overseers of slaves had wooden houses, and "[t]he Negros live in small cottages called quarters, in about six in a gang." The slaves "tend such land as the owner allots and orders, upon which they raise hogs and cattle, and plant Indian corn (or maize) and tobacco." While "some masters, careless of their own interest or reputation, are too cruel and negligent," the slaves, "increased by fresh supplies from Africa and the West India Islands, [are] kept under by severe discipline on occasion, and by good laws are prevented from running away. . . . Their work (or chimerical hard slavery) is not very laborious . . . to take care of the stock, and plant corn, tobacco, fruits, etc. which is not harder than thrashing, hedging, or ditching."[51]

This genteel, controlled, expanding rural idyll could also explode in genocidal rage. In 1711, the Virginia House of Burgesses, comprising two elected members from each county, dismissed Governor Spotswood's modest proposal to extend trade and education to the colony's Indian frontier. The house voted instead with a "violent disposition" for a war bill of £20,000, "for exterpating all Indians without distinction of Friends or Enemys."[52]

Early New England

The arrival of the English Pilgrims at Plymouth in 1621 launched the first European settlement in what became New England. The Puritan founder of this Massachusetts Bay Colony faulted earlier ventures for seeking "profitt and not the propagation of religion." The two would now "jump together." Yet, like many Virginia colonists, Winthrop had been ready to "settle me in Ireland, if it might be for [God's] glorye" and sent his son John Winthrop Jr. to Trinity College, Dublin, from 1622 to 1624.[53]

Puritans saw the Indians not as inferior but as "innately fair-skinned and wholly human," capable of eventual civilization if they rejected "the Devil's thrall." Yet ultimately, relations with Indians in New England proved "more extreme" than in Virginia. Even before the Pilgrims arrived, in 1614, an English crew had kidnapped 20 Wampanoag Indians from the Massachusetts area and transported them to England. One, Squanto, returned home with a second expedition five years later. In 1620, English sailors invited some Wampanoags aboard their ship and "shot them down without provocation."[54] Wampanoags

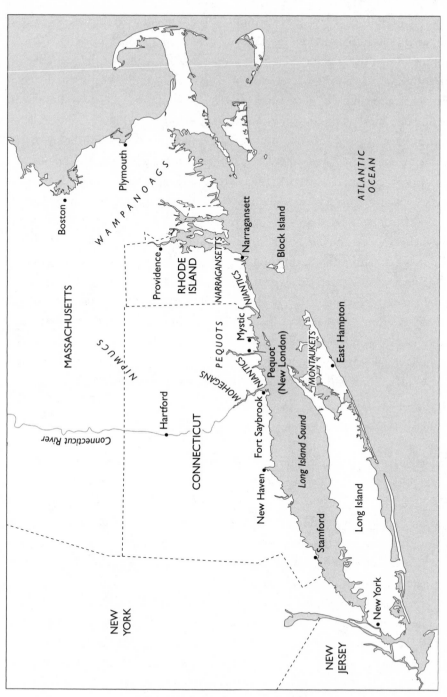

MAP 10. Seventeenth-century New England

then successfully attacked an English expedition, killing the captain and most of the crew. Meanwhile, "the plague" arrived in the area, wiping out in a matter of weeks up to three quarters of many Indian communities and making "a vast disaster zone" of southern New England. The "bones and skulls" awaiting the Pilgrims at Squanto's former home of Patuxet, "completely wiped out" by disease and now renamed Plymouth, "made such a spectacle" as to invoke "a new found Golgotha."[55]

Indians initially welcomed the Pilgrims and signed a treaty with them which provided that King James would "esteem" the Wampanoag leader as "friend and ally."[56] The Pilgrims, wrote their leader William Bradford, "began to plant their corn, in which service Squanto stood them in good stead, showing them how to plant it and cultivate it. He also told them that unless they got fish to manure this exhausted old soil, it would come to nothing." Squanto taught them how to trap fish for fertilizer. "They sowed some English seed, such as wheat and pease, but it came to no good."[57] Despite this cooperation, troops of the Plymouth settlement committed a massacre in 1623, when they surprised and "killed some few" Indians. On several occasions, when Indians stole English "trifles," Plymouth military commander Miles Standish "threatened to wipe out the entire band," until the Indian sachem (chief) had the goods returned and the culprits beaten.[58]

The Massachusett and Pawtucket communities welcomed the later settlement in Massachusetts Bay, whose members King Charles I charged in 1628 with the goal to "wynn and incite the natives . . . to the knowledge and obedience of the onlie true God." So many Indians took employment with settlers that the company asserted control over their labor and even banned settlers from constructing wigwams. From 1630 to 1633, 3,000 English settlers arrived, and another smallpox epidemic killed most local Indians. Governor Winthrop was exultant: "God hath hereby cleared our title to this place."[59]

Settlers from the two Massachusetts colonies soon moved west into the Connecticut River valley, where they competed with the Dutch and with one another. Massachusetts Bay established an English outpost at Fort Saybrook, at the river's mouth, while upstream at Hartford, the Connecticut General Court launched a second settlement. Both clashed with the local Pequot Indians, as did Narragansett Indians from the Rhode Island region and also the Dutch, who killed the Pequot grand sachem, Tatobem.[60] Other Indians, "not native Pequots" but known to them, killed an Englishman from Virginia and his crew of eight, and Niantic Indians on Block Island, affiliated with the Narragansetts, killed another.

The English blamed the Pequots. Massachusetts governor Henry Vane sent his deputy's son, John Winthrop Jr., to demand that they deliver the killers. Should they refuse, they were to be told that "we hold ourselves free from any peace or league with them as a people guilty of English blood." The Pequot sachem, Sassacus, denied responsibility, saying that Niantics had killed both the Englishmen. Winthrop had been instructed to return gifts that the Pequots had sent to Boston in 1634. Lion Gardener, commander at Fort Saybrook, vainly attempted to prevent Winthrop from delivering that provocative message. He urged Massachusetts to "desist from war a year or two, till we could be better provided for it." But, Gardener complained, "[t]he Pequit sachem was sent for, and the present returned, but full sore against my will."[61] Worse, in August 1636, Massachusetts Bay dispatched 90 troops, commanded by John Endecott and John Underhill, with orders from Winthrop "to putte to deathe the men of Block Island, but to spare the woemen & Children, & to bringe them awaye, & to take possession of the Iland." Most of the intended victims, unaligned Narragansetts, escaped. Underhill wrote: "[W]ee burnt and spoyled both houses and corne in great abundance."[62]

Returning to the mainland, the English then set out to attack the Pequots. Fort Saybrook's commander, Gardener, tried and failed to stop them, again warning that they were provoking the Indians, and complaining that the Massachusetts troops had "come hither to raise these wasps about my ears." Underhill later described how the Pequots had no inkling of the attack. They welcomed the approaching English ships, "running in multitudes along the water side, crying, What cheer, Englishmen, what cheer, what do you come for? They not thinking we intended war, went on cheerfully until they come to Pequeat river." The English kept their silence, as Underhill put it, to "have the more advantage of them." Eventually, the Pequots cried out, "What, Englishmen, what cheer, what cheer, are you hoggery, will you cram us? That is, are you angry, will you kill us, and do you come to fight?"[63]

As instructed, Endecott demanded that the Pequots produce the two Englishmen's killers, a large indemnity, and child hostages. After the Pequots fled, he wrote, "we spent the day burning and spoyling the Countrey." He later claimed to have killed two Indians.[64] But Gardener was dismissive: "The [Massachusetts] Bay-men killed not a man, save that one Kichomiquim, an Indian Sachem of the Bay, killed a Pequit; and thus began the war between the Indians

and us in these parts," in which "many honest men had their blood shed."[65]
Connecticut's Captain John Mason described Endecott's achievement as "only
one Indian slain and some Wigwams burnt. After which, the Pequots grew in-
raged against the English" and soon fell "violently upon them."[66]

Sassacus, the Pequot chief, attacked Fort Saybrook and "slew divers men."
Appealing for a truce, he asked Gardener, "Have you fought enough?" The
Pequots further "asked if we did use to kill women and children." Gardener
reported: "We said they should see thereafter." The Pequots then threatened to
kill "men, women and children." They tried to enlist the Narragansetts, telling
them that "the English were strangers, and were beginning to overspread their
country, and would deprive them of it in time if they were allowed thus to increase." But the Narragansetts sided with the English, and in April 1637, Massachusetts Bay declared war on the Pequots. Two weeks later, after Connecticut
settlers drove Indians from their homes, Pequot raiders killed nine settlers and
abducted two women. By the end of April, after more armed clashes, Pequots
had "[m]urdered about Thirty" English settlers in all, according to Mason.[67]
On May 1, the Connecticut General Court, eager to demonstrate its independence from Massachusetts Bay and possibly to seize Pequot land first, declared
an "offensive warr" against them.[68] From Boston on May 20, Winthrop requested Plymouth's aid against "the Pequots and all other Indians as a common
enemy."[69]

The 90 Connecticut soldiers who assembled in Hartford attended church
before setting off downriver. The minister urged them to "make their multitudes fall under your warlike weapons." Mason commanded three Connecticut
ships, reinforced by his Mohegan ally Uncas and 60 Indians in canoes. Mason
carried orders "limiting us to land our Men in Pequot River" to the east along
Long Island Sound. But after reaching Fort Saybrook, Mason decided instead
to sail further east, landing beyond both the Pequot River fort and the smaller
Pequot fort at Mystic. His new plan was to land in Narragansett, double back
overland, and storm Mystic from the rear. Mason reported that the "Hazard"
of so contravening or exceeding his orders, and "other" reasons that his report declined "to trouble you with," made him ask his chaplain to request "the
Lord, that Night, to direct how and in what manner we should demean ourselves in that Respect." In the morning the chaplain told Mason "he had done
as he had desired, and was fully satisfied to sail for Narragansett." But his deliberation over "several Reasons," beyond the decision to attack overland from
Narragansett, possibly involved the fact that, as Mason later wrote, "[w]e had

formerly concluded to destroy them by the Sword and save the Plunder."[70] Informed that most Pequot warriors were at the main fort on the Pequot River, Mason had decided to sail on and attack from the rear the Mystic fort containing mostly women and children. His fellow officer John Underhill later contrasted English tactics with those of the Pequots, whose wars were "more for pastime, then to conquer and subdue enemies."[71]

Five hundred Narragansetts joined the English, but most deserted on the march. Mason had the rest form an outer ring as his own men surrounded the Mystic fort, to let them "see whether English Men would now Fight or not." At dawn on May 26, 1637, Mason and Underhill led 77 troops against the Pequot fort. Climbing the northeast side of the hill, Mason "heard a Dog bark and an Indian crying Owanux! Owanux!" meaning "Englishmen! Englishmen!" He ordered all his forces to open fire, "the Indians being in a dead indeed their last Sleep." Once inside the fort, Mason penetrated a wigwam, then yelled: "We must Burn them." He grabbed "a Firebrand, and putting it into the Matts with which they were covered, set the Wigwams on Fire." The trapped Pequots, Mason wrote, "ran as Men most dreadfully Amazed. And indeed such a dreadful Terror did the Almighty let fall upon their Spirits, that they would fly from us and run into the very Flames, where many of them perished. And when the Fort was thoroughly Fired, Command was given, that all should fall off and surround the Fort." The fire raced through the village. Some Indians climbed to the top of the palisade, "others of them running into the very Flames; many of them gathering to windward, lay pelting at us with their arrows; and we repayed them with our small Shot: Others of the Stoutest issued forth, as we did guess, to the Number of Forty, who perished by the Sword."[72]

Meanwhile, Underhill had attacked the fort from the southwest. Some of his troops briefly stormed inside, but Underhill set fire to the southern end "with a train of powder," and they soon found that "the Smoak and Flames were so violent that they were constrained to desert the Fort."[73] Underhill wrote that the two fires "blazed most terribly, and burnt all in the space of half an hour."[74] As for the Indians, "[m]any courageous fellows were unwilling to come out, and fought most desperately through the palisadoes so as they were scorched and burnt with the very flame, and were deprived of their arms . . . the fire burnt their very bowstrings. . . . Many were burnt in the fort, both men, women and children. Others forced out, and came in troops to the Indians, twenty and thirty at a time, which our soldiers received and entertained with the point of the sword. Down fell men, women, and children."[75] Underhill added that "young soldiers that had never been in war" were shaken, "doleful was the bloody sight . . . to see so many souls lie gasping on the ground, so thick in some places, that you could hardly pass along."[76]

The Pequots, Mason wrote, were "utterly Destroyed, to the Number of six or seven Hundred" in just over one hour. "There were only seven taken captive, and about seven escaped." Mason was triumphant: "Thus was God seen in the Mount, . . . burning them up in the fire of his Wrath, and dunging the Ground with their Flesh: It was the Lord's Doings, and it is marvellous in our Eyes." God had "laughed his Enemies and the Enemies of his People to scorn, making them as a fiery Oven . . . filling the Place with dead Bodies!" Underhill wrote: "It is reported by themselves [the Indians], that there were about four hundred souls in this fort, and not above five of them escaped out of our hands."[77] Plymouth governor William Bradford, who did not participate in the assault, gave a similar estimate of "about 400 killed." Historian Alfred Cave considers Mason's figure of 600–700 dead "probably more accurate."[78] Underhill published a drawing of the fort under assault, showing 98 lodges (see fig. 5). Some were large; an average wigwam may have sheltered six or seven people. English losses were "two Slain outright, and about twenty Wounded" and 20 allied Indians wounded.[79]

All the Indian allies deserted except Uncas. They said the English fighting method "is too furious, and slays too many men." Underhill, too, wrestled with the implications of the massacre: "It may be demanded, Why should you be so furious? (as some have said). Should not Christians have more mercy and compassion?" He answered by appealing to ancient biblical precedent. "I would refer you to David's war. . . . Sometimes the Scripture declareth women and children must perish with their parents. . . . We had sufficient light from the Word of God for our proceedings." Bradford added: "It was a fearful fight to see them frying in the fire, with streams of blood quenching it; the smell was horrible, but the victory seemed a sweet sacrifice."[80]

Marching on to the Pequot River to meet their ships, the English clashed with 300 warriors from the main Pequot fort. According to Underhill, they "slew and wounded above a hundred Pequots, all fighting men." Others reached Mystic, "and beholding what was done, stamped and tore the Hair from their Heads." Enraged at the slaughter, the Pequots charged down the hill at the withdrawing English, who "faced about, giving Fire upon them: Some of them being Shot." Indians later told the English that one-third of these 300 Pequot warriors had been killed or wounded in these skirmishes. Then, as the English were sailing back east, Mason wrote, "we fell upon a People called the Nayan-ticks [Niantics], belonging to the Pequots, who fled to a Swamp for refuge."[81]

The English targeted any and all Pequots for destruction. Three days after the massacre, Wyandanch, a Montauk elder from Long Island, visited Fort Saybrook. According to Gardener, Wyandanch asked "if we were angry with all Indians. I answered No, but only with such as had killed Englishmen." Yet Gardener warned him: "[I]f you have Pequits with you . . . they might kill my men, . . . and so we might kill all you for the Pequits: but if you will kill all the Pequits that come to you, and send me their heads, then . . . you shall have trade with us." Gardener added, "If you have any Indians that have killed English, you must bring their heads also." Wyandanch later sent Gardener 12 Pequot heads, for which Gardener paid, "as I promised." Soon, he wrote, Wyandanch "had killed so many of the Pequits, and sent their heads to me" that surviving Pequots avoided Long Island. Wyandanch said he even feared that unless he traded with the English, they "will come and kill us all, as they did the Pequits."[82]

Not all English officials endorsed genocidal measures. Roger Williams named two Connecticut magistrates who were "almost averse" to killing women and children. The Narragansetts, too, Williams wrote, preferred "such Pequts as fall to them be not enslaved, like those which are taken in warr: but (as they say is their generall Custome) be used kindly, have howses and goods and fields given them." Williams agreed, saying that any Indians ready to surrender who knew that the English planned to mistreat them would only "turne wild Irish themselves."[83]

Yet English policy was to "utterly root them out." In June 1637, Massachusetts Bay, reasserting its control over Connecticut, sent 120 men to destroy the surviving Pequots as "enemies of God's people."[84] Two hundred voluntarily surrendered to the Narragansetts, who killed two of them. Massachusetts forces quickly seized the rest. William Hubbard described in his *Present State of New England,* an echo of Edmund Spenser's *View of the Present State of Ireland* published in 1677, how the adult males were sent to a classical hell: "The Men among them to the Number of thirty were turned presently into Charons Ferry-boat, under the Command of Skipper Gallop, who dispatched them a little without the harbour." The women and children "were disposed of" as slaves.[85]

With nowhere else to go, the surviving Pequots headed for Manhattan, slowed down "by reason of their Children, and want of Provision." English soldiers and ships pursuing them along the coast, Winthrop reported, "met here and there with some Pequots, whom they slew or took prisoners. They captured two sachems and beheaded them." Troops cornered 280 Pequots in a swamp west of New Haven on July 13. "We being loth to destroy Women and Children," as Mason put it, they captured 180 "old Men, Women and Children," whom "we divided, intending to keep them as Servants."[86] Winthrop specified later that some were sent to Connecticut settlers and "the rest to us" (in Massachusetts). Pequot boys went as slaves to the West Indies, "and the women and female children are distributed through the towns."[87] English policy was clear: the Pequot ethnic group had to disappear. The survivors were to be made unable to reproduce themselves as a community.

The troops advanced on the 80 Pequot holdouts near New Haven. Alden Vaughan writes: "When the soldiers entered the swamp that morning they found groups of Indians huddled close together on the ground awaiting their fate. They received it with dispatch: muskets packed with ten or twelve balls were fired at them from close range."[88] Sassacus and perhaps 40 Pequot warriors broke out of the English encirclement, heading west.[89] By July 28, Winthrop's captain reported, "we have killed 13 Sachems; but Sassacus and Mononotto are still living." Winthrop told Bradford: "In all, there have now been killed and taken prisoners about 700. The rest are scattered, and the Indians in all quarters are so terrified that they are afraid to give them sanctuary."[90] Sassacus, Mononotto, and their band reached the Hudson valley. There Mohawks killed both the Pequot sachems and 25 warriors, because, as Gardener put it, the Indians "all feared us." English traders obtained the scalps of Sassacus and six others and delivered them to Winthrop in Boston. Mason wrote: "The Pequots now became a Prey to all Indians. Happy were they that could bring in their Heads to the English: Of which there came almost daily to Winsor, or Hartford."[91]

Under the Treaty of Hartford of September 1638, the English exiled all Pequot survivors, dividing most among their Indian allies. As Mason recounted: "The Pequots were then bound by Covenant, That none should inhabit their native Country." The English transported 17 Pequot boys and women to slavery in the Caribbean. John Endecott personally requested from the governor a "girle and a boy if you thinke good."[92] Some 120 men were "given" to the Narragansetts, and the Mohegans received over 200 Pequot families.[93] The treaty specified that Indians may not shelter "any that may be Enemies to the English," but "shall as soon as they can either bring the chief Sachem of our late enemies the

Peaquots that had the chief hand in killing the English, to the said English, or take of their heads."[94]

The treaty stipulated that the vanquished "shall no more be called Pequots but Narragansetts and Mohegans." A witness to the war, Philip Vincent, wrote in 1638: "The Pequetans now seem nothing but a name."[95] Connecticut's General Assembly insisted even "that the name of the Pequots should become extinct; that the river that used to be called Pequot should be called the Thames, and the place called Pequot should no longer be so called, but its name changed to New London."[96] Mason's war veterans settled down in much of the Pequot country.[97] Roger Williams wrote that "not a Pequt is to be found," and "it is said ... they are gone farr and finally."[98]

Estimates of the Pequot population around 1637 concur at 3,000–4,000.[99] About 1,000–1,500 Pequots are thought to have been killed in the subsequent year of war. According to a 1643 Puritan account: "A very few of our men in a short time pursued through the wilderness, slew and took prisoners about 1,400 of them, even all they could find, to the great terror and amazement of all the Indians." Underhill wrote in 1638 that the English actually put to the sword "fifteen hundred souls." At Hartford after the war, Mason wrote, "The Pequots being demanded, how many of them were then living? [They] Answered, about One Hundred and Eighty, or two Hundred." This was probably a deliberate underestimate to conceal some survivors from the English. Yet fewer than 500 Pequot males had survived, and only 1,500–2,000 women and children. The death toll in 1637–38 probably exceeded 35 percent of the Pequot population.[100]

The genocidal phase of English policy lasted three years. The New Haven and Connecticut governments, calling a halt in 1640, "now declared their dislike of such as would have the Indians rooted out, as being of the cursed race of Ham."[101] Meanwhile, Mohegans and Narragansetts proved unable to absorb all their Pequot captives or insufficiently eager to erase their identity. Englishmen, too, had trouble keeping them "as Servants." Mason wrote that the 180 captives enslaved near New Haven "could not endure that Yoke; few of them continuing any considerable time with their masters." In 1646, John Winthrop Jr. settled "Pequot Plantations" (now New London), where he found 80 Pequot men and boys at Nameag. The next year, Mohegans raided this community and burned its wigwams. In 1650, Winthrop granted 350 western Pequots 500 acres of land at Noank (which the Connecticut General Court took back in 1714), and other Pequots further east received 500 acres. Both groups were now allowed to maintain their Pequot identity.[102] The English appointed two Pequot "governors" and granted the western Pequots another 2,000 acres. After settlers in Rhode Island drove the eastern Pequots into Connecticut in 1661, they received 280 acres there in 1685.[103] The elders told Daniel Gookin in 1674 that there were then 300 Pequot men in Connecticut. By the nineteenth century, fewer than 40 Pequots remained, and Connecticut allowed them to keep only 204 acres of land.[104]

The destruction of the Pequots had brought no end to conflict on Long Island Sound. In 1643, 400 Wiechqaesgeck Indians from the Hudson valley sought refuge from Mohawk attack outside New Amsterdam (New York). Leading Dutch colonists quickly petitioned Governor Willem Kieft to avenge Indian killings of traders, now that "God hath delivered them into our hands."[105] David Pieterszoon De Vries recounted: "The 24th of February, sitting at a table with the governor, he [the governor] began to state his intentions, that he had a mind to wipe the mouths of the Indians; . . . I answered him that there was no sufficient reason to undertake it. . . . But it appeared that my speaking was of no avail. He had, with his co-murderers, determined to commit the murder, deeming it a Roman deed."[106] Ancient models of conquest persisted as Kieft authorized the colonists "to attack a party of Indians lying behind Corlaer's plantation, and to act with them as they think proper." The settlers slaughtered 40 Wiechqaesgecks, and Dutch militia massacred another 80 at Pavonia. According to De Vries: "About midnight, I heard a great shrieking, and I ran to the ramparts of the fort, and looked over to Pavonia. Saw nothing but firing, and heard the shrieks of the Indians murdered in their sleep. When it was day the soldiers returned to the fort, having murdered or massacred eighty Indians, and considering they had done a deed of Roman valour, in murdering so many in their sleep."[107] De Vries described the scene: "Young children, some of them snatched from their mothers, were cut in pieces before the eyes of their parents; . . . other babes were bound on planks and then cut through, stabbed and miserably massacred, so that it would break a heart of stone." The Dutch threw others into the river, and when parents plunged in to save them, "the soldiers would not suffer them to come ashore but caused both old and young to be drowned." Surviving children and "old infirm persons . . . came out in the morning to beg for a piece of bread and for permission to warm themselves, but were all murdered in cold blood."[108] De Vries termed these massacres "a disgrace to our nation."[109] But "Kieft called it a truly Roman achievement."[110]

The new Dutch-Indian war spread east to the Connecticut River. The Dutch recruited Captain John Underhill, veteran of the Pequot genocide, and reported killing 120 Indians in a battle in February 1644. One night in March,

Underhill's 150 Dutch troops surrounded a fortified Indian village near Stamford. They poured withering fire into the village, shooting 180 Indians dead. As at Mystic, the attackers set fire to all the wigwams, incinerating everyone remaining inside, shooting or stabbing those who tried to flee the flames. The attackers killed 500 to 700 Indians; eight escaped.[111]

Diseases and genocidal massacres reduced the Indian population of southern New England from approximately 80,000 in the early seventeenth century to as few as 10,000 by 1674. The Puritans hoped to turn survivors into subjects, farmers, and Christians. In 1648, Massachusetts Bay outlawed both the purchase of Indian land and the provision of guns or ammunition to Indians. The law even admonished settlers to "keep their cattle from destroying the Indians corn, in any ground where they have the right to plant." Moreover, "for encouragement of the Indians toward the fencing in of their cornfields, such towns, farms, or persons, whose cattle may annoy them that way, shall direct, assist, and help them . . . and if any Indians refuse to fence their corn ground (being tendered help as aforesaid) . . . they shall keep off all cattle or lose one half of their damages." The next year, for similar reasons, settlers on Long Island began to oblige and assist Indians to fence their fields.[112]

A religious mission accompanied the agricultural one. The Massachusetts law of 1648 also stipulated that on pain of a £5 penalty, "no Indian shall at any time *powaw*, or perform outward worship to their false gods; or to the devil in any part of our Jurisdiction." In 1653, Narragansetts told Roger Williams that they feared to be "forced from their religion, and for not changing their religion, be invaded by war." The Wampanoag chief, Metacom ("King Philip"), reported that his people "had a great Fear to have any of their Indians should be called or forced to be Christian Indians." When the English took over the Dutch colonial territory in 1664, they banned powwows in New York and Long Island as well. But 10 years later, only 119 New England Indians had been baptized or were in full Christian communion.[113] In 1674, Boston's Joshua Moodey, preaching to the Artillery Election Company, urged New Englanders to "take, kill, burn, sink, destroy all sin and Corruption &C which are professed enemies to Christ Jesus, and not to pity or spare any of them."[114]

King Philip's War

After a series of reciprocal killings, Massachusetts and Plymouth declared war on Metacom and the Wampanoags in June 1675. Metacom's or "King Philip's"

War began. Connecticut and its Mohegan allies quickly joined in, but the largely Christian Nipmucs rose against the English. With Massachusetts and Connecticut the "most aggressively expansionist colonies in English America," this proved a many-sided New England civil war. Indians fought on both sides, while the Narragansetts, Niantics, and their English neighbors of Rhode Island all tried to stay out of the line of fire.[115] Massachusetts quickly resettled loyal Indians in selected locations and ruled that any Indians found "skulking" elsewhere could be killed on the spot.[116]

From the start of the war, the English showed little mercy to captives. In July 1675, a month after the fighting began, a group of Indians surrendered in return for their freedom from slavery. Plymouth's officer Benjamin Church complained bitterly that despite his own efforts, his superiors then ensured that "without any regard to the promises made," the Indians were "cary'd away to Plymouth, there sold, and transported out of the country." Hundreds of captured Wampanoags were sold into slavery in Bermuda.[117] Others were even less fortunate. A commander who captured an Indian woman in Hatfield in 1675 ordered her "to be torn in pieces by dogs."[118]

The Narragansetts of Rhode Island, whose numbers had already fallen in previous decades from 5,000 warriors to around 1,000, did not join Metacom's war against the English. At its outbreak, Roger Williams reported that the Narragansett sachems "professed to hold no agreement with Philip." In early July 1675, a Rhode Island magistrate confirmed to Connecticut troops that "the Indians have given no cause of Warre." But the Connecticut Council ordered that magistrate arrested for "delaying" its plans. Three weeks later, Connecticut governor John Winthrop Jr., conceded: "The Nahigansetts have hitherto continued in amity with the English. . . . I believe there is difficulty ynough with that one enemy [Metacom], and why to stir up another before an issue with the first." But the Connecticut Council had already falsely identified "a generall conspiracy of the heathen against the English," signifying that the Narragansetts were the colonists' next target. Considering themselves allies of the English, the Narragansetts turned over to them 100 Wampanoags, and the heads of seven of Metacom's warriors. Even Connecticut praised the Narragansett sachem Pessicus for his friendship and "actions against the enemy." But Massachusetts dispatched to Rhode Island a company of mercenary buccaneers licensed for "destroying the enemy" (implicitly including Narragansetts), with the right to keep any captives. Launching a war against "the only peaceful tribe in sight," they killed and captured 60 Narragansetts. A Rhode Island settler warned Winthrop: "I remember the time of the warres in Ireland (when I was young, in Queen Elizabeths days of famous memory) when much English blood was spilt by a people much like unto these" Indians. "And after these Irish were subdued by force, what treacherous and bloody massacres have they attempted is well knowne."[119]

Such peace counsel was rejected. On November 2, 1675, the Commissioners of the Puritan United Colonies proclaimed that the Narragansetts were "deeply accessory in the present bloody outrages." Six companies of foot and a cavalry troop from Massachusetts joined the forces of Governor Winslow of Plymouth, who became the commanding officer. They set out to stage a preventive attack on the Narragansetts. Some 300 Connecticut soldiers and 150 Mohegans and Pequots reinforced them on December 18. The next day, the English army surrounded the main Narragansett fort in the Great Swamp. It comprised 500–600 wigwams, housing 3,000 or 4,000 Indians, mostly women and children.[120]

Just as the Narragansetts and Mohegans had held back from the English massacre of Pequots at Mystic in 1637, the Mohegans and Pequots now allied with the English declined to participate in a new slaughter of Narragansetts. As the battle began, the latter parleyed with the Mohegans and Pequots, who "promised to shoot high, which they did," according to an English prisoner inside the fort. The English first attacked the entrance to the fort, losing six captains and "many of their men" shot dead. The soldiers broke through and fell upon the Indians, who "fought desperately and beat the English out of the fort." Again troops closed in on the palisade. They "ran on the very muscles of thyr guns, up to the Indeans port holes: & fired in at them, & leped over thyr brest workes, & run into thyr forte, & beat them out: & slew many of them." After a three-hour battle, "the English became masters of the place, and set fire to the wigwams."[121]

As at Mystic in 1637 and Stamford seven years later, the English fired the fort and killed Indians who fled their burning wigwams. One Englishman reported that his fellows "had now a Carnage rather than a Fight, for every one had their fill of Blood." Benjamin Tompson reflected: "Had we been cannibals here might we feast." He celebrated the attack with a poem: "Sundry the flames arrest and some the blade / By bullets heaps on heaps of Indians laid / ... Here might be heard an hideous Indian cry, / Of wounded ones who in the wigwams fry."[122] An Englishman whom the Narragansetts had held captive in the fort stated that the Indians later returned and counted 97 of their warriors killed and 48 wounded, "beside what slaughter was made in the houses and by the burning of the houses." Only five or six wigwams remained standing. Attackers led by Benjamin Church fired on a group of 60 to 70 Indian fighters, one of whom later told Church that the volley had "killed 14 dead on the spot and wounded a greater number," of whom many died of their injuries. Church reported: "Some of the enemy that were then in the fort have since informed us that nearly a third of the Indians belonging to all that Narragansett country were killed by the English and by the cold that night."[123] The English attack had killed between 300 and 1,000 women and children. It was "total war."[124]

The next month the Connecticut Council urged New York to send Mohawks against Philip to "utterly extirpate this bloody generation . . . to gratify the English." In the Connecticut valley of central Massachusetts, Indian attacks virtually ended in mid-March 1676, followed by two months of "relative peace." In May, new genocidal massacres began. English forces came across a group of Sokoki Indians on the Connecticut River, in a "considerable number, yet most of them old men and women."[125] At dawn, 150 Englishmen stormed the camp. According to an eyewitness, the soldiers "took most of the Indians fast asleep, and put their guns even into their Wigwams, whereupon the Indians that durst and were able did get out of their wigwams and did fight a little (in which fight one Englishman only was slain), others of the Indians did enter the River to swim over from the English, but many of them were shot dead in the waters." Others drowned. The English found "above two hundred" Indian corpses in or along the river. When more braves arrived, attacking across the river, they routed the English and killed 37 of them.[126]

At the end of May, Connecticut instructed a unit commanded by Major John Talcott to "kill and destroy them, according to the utmost power God shall give you."[127] Meanwhile, the Narragansetts sent an emissary to make peace with Massachusetts. On July 2, Talcott surrounded and attacked a group of 34 Narragansett men, including a former peace negotiator, and 137 women and children, all hiding in a Rhode Island swamp. Talcott reported that within three hours, his soldiers killed all the men and no fewer than 92 women and children. They "slew and tooke prisoner 171, of which 45 prisoners being women and children that the Indians saved alive, and the others slayne." Again, the clemency came not from the colonists but their Indian allies. The next day, Talcott attacked another Narragansett group at Warwick, killing 18 men and 22 women and children.[128]

Learning that Connecticut forces planned to ravage their crops "and perpetually to disrest them," a large group of Indian refugees left "to seeke another country" across the Hudson River. The Connecticut Council appealed unsuccessfully to New York's governor, Sir Edmund Andros, to dispatch Mohawks to attack them. Several weeks later, a second large group of refugees set out. Connecticut reiterated its "reasonable request" for "the utter extirpation of such as have imbrued their hands in the blood of many of his Majesties good subjects." Andros still demurred. Connecticut appealed directly to the Mohawks to deliver the refugees to Hartford as prisoners, but Andros intervened. Surviving Schagticoke Indians gratefully recalled that "wee were almost dead when wee left New England." Andros ruled that "whosoever doth or shall come in and submitt themselves and live quietly with our Indyans, shall be protected from any outrage or force and I shall not suffer them to be disturbed or harmed, but shall looke upon any violence offered that way, as done to my selfe."[129] This was not the Puritan policy.

During the week of July 11, 1676, for instance, Plymouth forces were pursuing and killing "dozens of Indians hiding in swamps." Plymouth allowed Benjamin Church's men to keep as their property "half the prisoners and arms" they took. In another swamp battle, Church captured or killed 173 more Indians. Some of the prisoners stated: "Sir, you have now made Philip ready to dye, for you have made him as poor, and miserable as he us'd to make the English; for you have now killed or taken all his Relations." Church sent most of the prisoners to Plymouth for trial, but they were sold as slaves. On August 12, 1676, one of his Indian allies shot and killed Metacom. Plymouth authorities had two other captured sachems beheaded, including one for whom Church had requested pardon. When other Indians surrendered in return for their freedom, the English "forgot their promises . . . and sold them, their wives and children with the rest."[130]

After the war's end, England's royal investigator Edmund Randolph reported more than "three thousand Indians, men, women and children, destroyed," in 14 months. English losses totaled 600 of a settler population of 52,000, but 30 percent of New England's 10,000 Indians had been killed.[131] Increase Mather wrote that so many Indians had perished "by the Sword and by Famine and by Sickness" that in the woods it was common "to find dead Indians up and down," with "none to bury them."[132]

The English enslaved very many survivors. One ship transported 70 Indian "heathen Malefactors men, women and Children" to Jamaica and slavery in September 1676. Hundreds more, including Metacom's son, went on sale in the Caribbean. A few were dispersed as far as Tangier in Africa. Historian James Drake writes that most colonists felt morally obliged "to avoid wholesale slaughter or enslavement of the Indian peoples" and often distinguished between categories of Indian enemies, but "the mass selling of enemy Indians into slavery" did occur and further drastically reduced Indian communities. The practice allowed the English, Drake writes, "both to dispense mercy and to reap a profit" as well as "carry out effectively genocidal policies while steadfastly believing to the end that they stood upon the moral high ground."[133] The combination of massacres, enslavement, and deportation almost destroyed entire societies.

Extermination and Genocidal Massacres in the Eighteenth Century

As English settlement moved west, so did the bloodiest Indian policies. The Boston synod criticized "many" Puritans in 1679 for "an insatiable desire after Land, and worldly Accommodations, so as to forsake Churches and Ordinances, and to live like Heathen, yea, only that so they might have Elbow-room enough in the world." The expanding New England frontier was sprouting "Nurseries of Ignorance." Ten years later, Cotton Mather sent Boston soldiers into battle with the cry: "Vengeance, Dear Country-men! Vengeance upon our Murderers. . . . Beat them small as the Dust before the Wind, and Cast them out, as the Dirt in the Streets. . . . Those Ravenous howling Wolves."[134] The English, historian James Axtell writes, rapidly spread "hard heelmarks where soft moccasins had always tread." The years 1689–1713 in turn brought "the heaviest Indian depredations" on New England's frontiers. From 1694, the General Court of Massachusetts offered troops and settlers a bounty for every hostile Indian, "great or small," dead or alive.[135] Five years later, Cotton Mather likened the Indians to ancient Scythians, as Spenser had the Irish a century earlier. Mather added that the devil had brought the Indians to America to hinder the spread of Christianity.[136]

Prefiguring the Virginia House vote of 1711 "for exterpating all Indians,"[137] Massachusetts began the new century by escalating its measures against them. In 1703, launching a series of proposals that recalled sixteenth-century Spanish practices and recurred through the eighteenth, the Reverend Solomon Stoddard of Northampton advised the Massachusetts governor to employ dogs, "trained up to hunt Indians as they do bears. . . . The dogs would do a great deal of execution upon the enemy." Dogs, he said, had helped Virginia prevail in its Indian wars. "If the Indians were as other people are and managed their war fairly after the manner of other nations, it might be looked upon as inhumane. . . . But they are to be looked upon as thieves and murderers; they do acts of hostility without proclaiming war. They don't appear openly in the field to bid us battle, [and] they use those cruelly that fall into their hands. They act like wolves and are to be dealt withall as wolves." The next year, the General Court of Massachusetts doubled the bounty it offered troops and settlers for killing hostile Indians. It now paid volunteers £100 for the scalps of "men or youths" over 11 years old who were considered "capable of bearing arms." Massachusetts also paid £10 for the scalps of women or boys aged 10 or 11, but offered no reward for killing children under 10, who were sold abroad as slaves.[138]

Many Indian children were born into slavery and then sold to new masters. New York colony passed a law in 1707 stipulating that "all and every Negro, Indian, Mulatto and Mestee Bastard child and children who are and shall be born of any Negro, Indian, Mulatto or Mestee shall follow ye state and condition of the mother and be esteemed reputed taken and adjudged a slave to all intents and purposes whatsoever." In 1712, a New York Indian girl was even sold in Madeira. The dispersal of Indian communities by enslavement reinforced the continuing impact of diseases on their populations. The number of Wampanoags on Martha's Vineyard, for instance, continued to fall precipitously, from 3,000 in 1642 to 800 in 1720 to only 313 in 1764. The Indian population of Block Island fell from over 1,200 in 1662 to just 51 people in 1774.[139]

Settlers on Long Island not only deprived the Montauketts of their lands but threatened them with disappearance as a community in other ways. Even as Massachusetts shipped Indian slaves to North Africa, defeated classical and biblical North African leaders came to serve as models for subjugated Long Island Indians. East Hampton colonists took over the last Montaukett land in 1687,[140] and a Long Island pastoralist contracted "Hannibal Indian" to herd his cattle. Hannibal undertook to "hunt the woods . . . search well all the Salt Marsh Meadows" and "find any cattle mired." Another Indian named "Pharaoh" appears in the record in 1698. Raising livestock as well as farming to survive, from 1700 the Montauketts could maintain their numbers only by attracting spouses from other Indian groups across the Sound. That was not long permitted. In 1719, East Hampton obliged Montaukett leaders, including Hannibal and three Indians all surnamed Pharaoh, to sign an agreement that Montauketts would not "take any strange Indians in[,] nor suffer any such to be on Muntoket to use or improve any part of said land directly or indirectly by taking of a squaw or squaws, if such Indians be not proper Muntokit Indians they shall not be allowed to use or improve any part of said land, they shall not enter to dwell on said Meantokit directly nor indirectly." Settlers considered the Montauketts' land too valuable for Indian farming. Prohibiting them from marrying other Indians or even accepting them on their land, the English condemned the Montaukett community to die out, and thus release its land for white use.[141]

The relentless English pressure on both the land and the Indians made them into serfs. Settlers had Hannibal sign another undertaking in 1747: "If any of the above said Natives shall hire out any land . . . the produce shall be taken from them." Later he had to warrant further that if any mixed-blood Indians "or Strangers or forren [foreign] Indians" ventured "to Come and live or improve on said land," then "the Trustees of East Hampton or the English Propriators have and shall have free and full Libertie and full power to prosecute all such offenders as Tresperserss and send them off of said Land."[142]

In his *Second Treatise of Government* (1690), John Locke had advanced the most concerted English-language argument for land ownership by cultivation. He wrote of the farmer that "whatsoever he tilled and reaped, laid up and made use of, before it spoiled, that was his peculiar right; whatsoever he enclosed, and could feed, and make use of, the cattle and product was also his." By contrast, those who failed to farm the land could not claim to own it. "But if either the grass of his inclosure rotted on the ground, or the fruit of his planting perished without gathering, and laying up, this part of the earth, notwithstanding his inclosure, was still to be looked on as a waste, and might be the possession of any other." Expansionist regimes or settler colonies, in this prevailing view, could therefore assume the right to occupy such land for cultivation. The vision of the superior claim of agriculture was one that Locke applied explicitly to Native American societies: "There cannot be a clearer demonstration of any thing, than several nations of the Americans are of this, who are rich in land . . . [and] a fruitful soil, apt to produce in abundance, . . . yet for want of improving it by labour, have not one hundredth part of the conveniences we enjoy."[143]

Locke's writings, which denied Indian agriculture, greatly influenced British colonists in America. An article in the *New York Weekly Post Boy* in 1746, for instance, took up some of Locke's themes for determining the possession of land. Its author argued for the "Rules of natural Justice," such as ownership by cultivation, rather than by law. Purchase of a title to land was thus no more necessary than "buying the Waters of the Rivers."[144] As the American frontier expanded during the eighteenth century, so did the influence of Locke's ideas, to the detriment of the rights of Indians and their visions of land use, provoking Indian resistance, reciprocal atrocities, and settler genocides.

Virginia's Executive Council began in 1745 to assign millions of acres of Indian lands west of the Appalachian Mountains to the land companies of Virginian gentlemen. Nine years later, Britain's Privy Council attempted to control the escalating land speculation by prohibiting individuals from taking more than 1,000 acres of Indian land each. Then, in a 1756 treaty, Britain reserved the area west of the Appalachians for Indians. It had just completed the deportation of French Acadians from Nova Scotia, which John Mack Faragher terms "the first episode of state-sponsored ethnic cleansing in North American history."[145] Yet a new war with France loomed, followed by further frontier conflict, an American settler revolt, and new genocidal massacres of Indians.

Britain's victory over France in the Seven Years' War (1756–63) and its American theater, known as the French and Indian War, opened up Indian country to "a flood of settlement" in the interior. In the late spring of 1763, the Ottawa chief Pontiac launched a new rebellion against British rule. His warriors massacred 56 soldiers at Lake Erie. In the Ohio valley, Shawnees and Wyandots joined up with Pontiac.[146]

The British reaction was fierce. The commander in chief of the British forces, General Jeffrey Amherst, ordered that any captured hostile Indians be "immediately put to death, their extirpation being the only security for our future safety, and their late treacherous proceedings deserving no better treatment from our hands." Amherst informed Colonel Henry Bouquet, a Philadelphia associate of Benjamin Franklin, that "he wanted to hear of no prisoners being taken" on Bouquet's march to relieve Fort Pitt in western Pennsylvania.[147]

Amherst's policy escalated to biological warfare after Bouquet passed on reports of battlefront losses. Amherst wrote back on July 7, 1763, urging: "Could it not be contrived to Send the Small Pox among those Dissafected Tribes of Indians? We must, on this occasion, Use Every Strategem in our power to Reduce them." Approaching Fort Pitt, Bouquet replied on July 13: "I will try to Inoculate the Indians by means of blankets." He added: "I wish we could make use of the Spaniard's method, and hunt them with English Dogs, Supported by Rangers, and some Light Horse, who would I think effectualy extirpate or remove that Vermine." Benjamin Franklin also supported using dogs against Indians, but now the army went much further.[148]

Pursuing his goal of "extirpation," Amherst reiterated to Bouquet on July 16: "You will Do well to try to Inoculate the Indians by means of Blanketts, as well as to try Every other method that can serve to extirpate this Execrable Race." Fort Pitt had anticipated these orders. Reporting on parleys with Delaware chiefs on June 24, a trader wrote: "[W]e gave them two Blankets and an Handkerchief out of the Small Pox Hospital. I hope it will have the desired effect." The military hospital records confirm that two blankets and handkerchiefs were "taken from people in the Hospital to Convey the Smallpox to the Indians." The fort commander paid for these items, which he certified "were had for the uses above mentioned." Historian Elizabeth Fenn has documented "the eruption of epidemic smallpox" among Delaware and Shawnee Indians nearby, about the time these blankets were distributed.[149]

The next month, after the murder of an English officer in Detroit, Amherst sent out a special unit with orders to treat the Senecas and Indians of the Great Lakes "not as a generous enemy, but as the vilest race of beings that ever infested the earth, and whose riddance from it must be esteemed a meritorious act, for the good of mankind. You will therefore take no prisoners, but put to death all that fall into your hands of the nations who have so unjustly and cruelly committed depradations." Amherst reiterated in a letter to another officer, also in August 1763: "Indeed their Total Extirpation is scarce sufficient Attonement for the Bloody and Inhuman deeds they have Committed." Later that month, the general added: "I shall only Say, that it Behoves the Whole Race of Indians to Beware ... of Carrying Matters much farther against the English, or Daring to form Conspiracys, as the Consequence will most certainly Occasion measures to be taken, that, in the End will put a most Effectual Stop to their very being."[150]

As war raged at the frontier, ethnic violence flowed back into the settled areas. Just four months later, on December 14, a mob gathered near the frontier region of Paxton. Benjamin Franklin later described them as "[f]ifty-seven men, from some of our Frontier Townships, ... all well mounted, and armed with Firelocks." The mob rode through the night and descended on a village of peaceable Indians at Conestogoe, in Lancaster County, Pennsylvania. They found six people at home, of whom Franklin wrote: "These poor defenceless creatures were immediately fired upon, stabbed, and hatcheted to Death! ... All of them were scalped and otherwise horribly mangled. Then their huts were set on Fire." The killers, known as the Paxton Boys, explained their genocidal intent against all Indians: "Whoever proclaimed war with part of a nation, and not with the whole?"[151]

Local British officials attempted to save the friendly Indians. They took the surviving 14 from Conestogoe into the Lancaster workhouse for protection. The governor of Pennsylvania, John Penn, issued a proclamation forbidding "all Persons whatsoever, to molest or injure any of the said Indians." But, Franklin went on, "those cruel Men again assembled themselves," surging into Lancaster on December 27, 1763. "Fifty of them, armed as before, dismounting," broke into the workhouse. One of the 14 Indians, Will Soc, stepped forward, saying: "I will meet them, for they are my Brothers." But the killers "shot him down at the Door, while the Word Brothers was between his Teeth." The defenseless Indians, Franklin protested, "all received the Hatchet! Men, Women and little Children were every one inhumanly murdered! in cold Blood!" A company of Royal Highlanders stationed in the town failed to intervene.[152]

Franklin recognized a genocidal massacre and condemned it outright.

> "If an *Indian* injures me," he asked, "does it follow that I may revenge that Injury on all *Indians*? It is well known, that Indians are of different Tribes, Nations and Languages, as well as the White People. In *Europe,* if the *French,* who are White People, should injure the *Dutch,* are they to revenge it on the *English,* because they too are White People? The only Crime of these poor Wretches seems to have been, that they had a reddish-brown Skin, and black Hair; and some People of that Sort, it seems, had murdered some of our Relations. If it be right to kill Men for such a Reason, then, should any Man, with a freckled Face and red Hair, kill a Wife or Child of mine, it would be right for me to revenge it, by killing all the freckled red-haired Men, Women and Children."

Franklin concluded that the Indians would have been safer far from Pennsylvania, if they had lived among "the ancient Heathens," the "cruel Turks," Moors, "Popish Spaniards," or "Negroes of Africa." And yet "our Frontier People call themselves Christians!" Their victims "would have been safe in any part of the known World, except in the Neighbourhood of the CHRISTIAN WHITE SAVAGES" of Paxton.[153]

By February 1764, the Paxton Boys led a swelling crowd of 250, heading for Philadelphia. Pennsylvania's surviving 140 Christian Indians were "still threatned to be murdered." Marched to New York under military protection, the Indians found themselves turned back, Franklin wrote, "disgracefully, on our Hands. O Pennsylvania!" He praised the British escort, and General Thomas Gage. He omitted to praise General Jeffrey Amherst, whose repeated orders to British troops only four months before had prefigured the genocidal thinking that Franklin so eloquently decried. Even General Gage, as commander in chief in North America, issued orders in September 1764 to Colonel Henry

Fig. 11 *Aboriginal Life in Australia.* From "The arrival of the First White Man" to "the revenge of the Whites, as they are hunted down and shot like dogs." Lithographs by Alfred Scott Broad (1854–1929), *The Pictorial Australian*, February 1886. National Library of Australia.

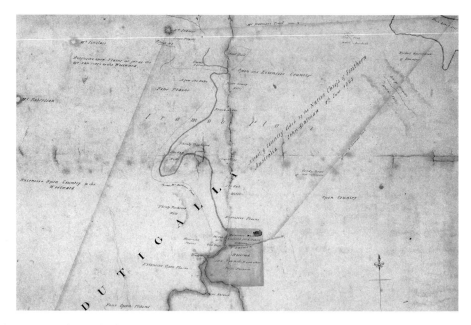

Fig. 12 Chart of John Batman's 1835 claim to the Melbourne area, which he called "Dutigalla—a tract of Country ceded by the Native Chiefs of Southern Australia to John Batman, 4th June 1835." State Library of Victoria. See p. 291.

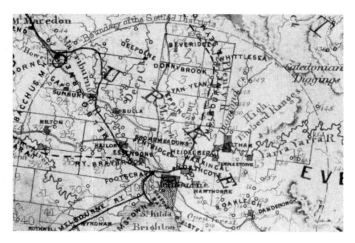

Fig. 13 The rapid intensive settlement by 1858, from Mt. Macedon to the "Caledonian Diggings," is shown in this detail of *The Squatting Map of Victoria (Port Phillip District, New South Wales) from the Colonial Government Surveys, Crown Lands Commissioners and Explorers Maps Private Surveys &c., Compiled and Published by Thomas Ham, Melbourne, 1858.* State Library of Victoria.

Fig. 14 Gippsland, Victoria, 1858, from the Acheron and Rubicon rivers to the McAr-
thur. Detail of Thomas Ham, *The Squatting Map of Victoria (Port Phillip District, New
South Wales) from the Colonial Government Surveys, Crown Lands Commissioners and
Explorers Maps Private Surveys &c.* State Library of Victoria. Until 1840 Gippsland had
been the home of the five clans of the Kurnai people. See also map 13.

The leopard with the harmless kid laid down
And not one savage beast was seen to frown

The wolf did with the lambkin dwell in peace
His grim carnivorous nature there did cease

The lion with the fatling on did move
A little child was leading them in love;

When the great PENN his famous treaty made
With indian chiefs beneath the Elm-tree's shade.

Fig. 15 *The Peaceable Kingdom,* by Edward Hicks (American, 1780–1849), 1826. Philadelphia Museum of Art, bequest of Charles C. Willis, 1956. Photo by Philadelphia Museum of Art.

Fig. 16 "He that by the plough would thrive—Himself must either hold or drive." Anonymous U.S. painting, c. 1820s. © Addison Gallery of American Art, Phillips Academy, Andover, Mass. Purchased as the gift of Mrs. Evelyn L. Roberts.

Fig. 17 The wagon train of Lieutenant Colonel George Armstrong Custer's Seventh Cavalry moves through Castle Creek Valley in the Black Hills of South Dakota, July 26, 1874 (see p. 360). Historian Brian W. Dippie terms this "Western exploration's most thrilling photograph," taken by William H. Illingworth, courtesy South Dakota State Historical Society/U.S. National Archives. Custer's adjutant and brother-in-law, Lieutenant James Calhoun, wrote in his diary on June 23: "The press has praised the Black Hill country to the skies. . . . We are informed in glowing terms 'that it is believed to be, a land of ambrosial luxury—flowing with milk and honey.'" Dippie, "Its Equal I Have Never Seen: Custer in the Black Hills—An Expedition to Paradise," *Columbia* (summer 2005): 18–27.

Fig. 18 The classical, the national, the indigenous, and the pastoral in Philadelphia's *Washington Monument*, unveiled 1897. "It was reported that the German sculptor Rudolph Siemering had originally designed the central figure as Frederick the Great. When he got the American commission, he used the same casting and simply changed the hat and the medals." From R. F. Brenner, *Philadelphia's Outdoor Art* (Philadelphia, 2002), 54. Photo by Ben Kiernan.

Fig. 19   French forces take Algiers, 1830. From Charles-André Julien, *Histoire de l'Algérie contemporaine* (Paris, 1964), 113. © Presses Universitaires de France, 1964.

Fig. 20   *The Caves of Dahara, 1845,* by T. Johannot. During the repression of the Dahra insurrection in 1845, General Pélissier used smoke to kill 500–1,000 Arabs, including women and children, in the Nekmaria caves. Drawing and caption from Charles-André Julien, *Histoire de l'Algérie contemporaine* (Paris, 1964), 353. © Presses Universitaires de France, 1964.

LA CRAPAUDINE.

Maintenant que j'ai appris à discipliner les hommes en Afrique, je pars en France faire l'application de mon Système sur ces bons Parisiens qui se disent en République.

Fig. 21 "Now that I have taught men discipline in Africa . . ." French general Louis-Eugène Cavaignac (1802–57) brings harsh repressive methods employed in North Africa back to France to suppress the 1848 Paris uprising. From Charles-André Julien, *Histoire de l'Algérie contemporaine* (Paris, 1964), 337. © Presses Universitaires de France, 1964.

Bouquet, whom Franklin advised and admired, to march against Indian towns to impose harsh peace terms, and should they fail to comply, Gage ordered Bouquet to attack and "extirpate the Shawnese and Delawares."[154]

After meeting leaders of the Paxton Boys, Governor Penn capitulated. He declined to charge them for their murders of the 20 Indians. Instead, at the Paxton Boys' request, Penn announced his new policy, "a bounty for any Indian scalps, male or female." Franklin was again outraged: "These things bring him and his government into sudden contempt."[155]

These massacres had occurred against the backdrop of three-cornered contention over frontier land claims. The previous year the British government had issued a royal proclamation prohibiting settlement west of the Appalachian Mountains and effectively ending the Virginian gentry's land speculations there. While Britain could not stop many individual farmers from squatting on Indian land, Virginia's land brokers were now unable to extract payment from them for it. They did not easily surrender one of their most lucrative sources of income, "the sale of Indian land to yeomen farmers." In 1767, the young George Washington, for instance, dismissed the 1763 proclamation as "a temporary expedient," and the next year he asked the Executive Council to honor land bounties promised to veterans during the French and Indian War. In 1768–69, the Loyal Company of Virginia, a land company of which Thomas Jefferson's father had been a member, had surveyors mark off land for hundreds of new homesteads in the Ohio and Tennessee valleys of what is now Kentucky. Jefferson asked the Loyal Company in February 1769 for 5,000 acres and requested two additional lots of 1,000 each from other land syndicates. But the British governor of Virginia nullified these surveys. Britain recognized Kentucky as belonging to the Cherokee and deprived Virginia land companies of over 10 million acres in requested grants. The Virginia House of Burgesses implored London to assign Kentucky to Virginia, but in vain. George Washington, who purchased thousands of acres in veterans' claims to bounty land, feared that individual pioneers would take up landholdings there and would circumvent land company claims to the territory by eventually acquiring titles "on the ground of pre-occupancy."[156]

An unstable coalition of trans-Appalachian Indian groups had shaped the British policy of restraint devised in fear of "a general Indian War." In the Ohio valley in 1773–74, without resorting to violence, Shawnees were able to stop Virginians surveying their hunting grounds. In April 1774, a Virginian official at Pittsburgh issued a veiled declaration of war. Virginians killed the family of a Mingo Indian, John Logan, who then began a series of retaliations. In October, 2,000 Virginian troops attacked Shawnee and Mingo towns. They drove the Shawnees across the Ohio, killing 200 in one battle. But in this 1774 engagement, the Shawnees inflicted heavy casualties on the 800-strong Virginian force: 81 killed and 140 wounded.[157] The war for their land had barely begun. Shawnees would soon face colonists freed from imperial restraint.

After American independence, George Washington's first secretary of war, Henry Knox, looked back on the colonial era in a report to the new president: "It is a melancholy reflection, that our modes of population have been even more destructive to the Indian natives than the conduct of the conquerors of Mexico and Peru. The evidence of this is the utter extirpation of nearly all the Indians in most populous parts of the Union."[158] One cause was imposition of imperial power; whether Britain's defeat resolved the problem for the future remained to be seen.

CHAPTER 7

Genocidal Violence in
Nineteenth-Century Australia

A s the navigator Captain James Cook sailed toward Australia's east coast
in 1770, the *Encyclopedia Britannica* was appearing in print. It defined
the word *Aborigines* as a term for "the original or first inhabitants of
any country, but particularly used to signify the ancient inhabitants of Latium,
... when Aeneas with his Trojans came into Italy." Aeneas's putative British descendants were about to found yet another Rome, assigning Australia's ancient
inhabitants a new role and a classical name.

Initially called "Indians," "blacks," or "Natives," they could also become "Aborigines" in part because of their nonagricultural economy. The first Englishman to encounter them, the buccaneer William Dampier, reached Australia's
northwest coast in 1688. Shocked that they lacked houses, sheep, poultry, and
"Fruits of the Earth," Dampier thought "they differ but little from Brutes." [1]
Across the continent in 1770, however, Cook found east coast Aborigines "far
happier" than "we Europeans," living "in the pure state of Nature" and possessing neither social hierarchy nor "Conveniences so much sought after in
Europe." Partly reflecting newer European ideas of nature, Cook saw a pastoral
idyll: "They live in a Tranquillity which is not disturb'd by the Inequality of Condition: The Earth and sea of their own accord furnishes them with all things
necessary for life." Yet he, too, noted that "they do not cultivate." [2] British views
of native Australians—as inferior, pristine, savage, or noble—were neither uniform nor impervious to observation and change. Yet one theme recurred: the
absence of agriculture.

At the onset of British colonization in 1788, the continent's Aboriginal people numbered about 500,000–750,000, by recent estimates. Just over a century later, fewer than 100,000 remained in 1901, the year of Australia's federation. Most Aborigines perished from new diseases like smallpox, measles, and tuberculosis, and whites probably killed about 20,000 or more. Blacks also killed possibly 2,500 whites, mostly in isolated attacks, but the killings of Aborigines by settlers and troops, though sporadic, involved much larger numbers.[3] Mass death from unwittingly introduced diseases is not genocide, yet the enormity of that loss cannot obscure the evidence of multiple deliberate killings and a series of genocidal massacres.

In the eastern Australian colonies, Aboriginal affairs remained a British imperial responsibility until 1856, yet London's policy was laissez-faire.[4] A pioneer of Aboriginal studies, Charles Rowley, attributed to the British "an innocence of the consequences, with an unacknowledged wish to be rid of the whole matter as cheaply and with as little fuss as possible." Aborigines were British subjects to be instructed and treated with "amity and kindness," but without rights to land, compensation, or representation. Their labor was devalued.[5] Making few specific provisions for Aboriginal lands, employment, or education, London usually left management of Aborigines to colonial authorities and settlers.

For example, the British government warned Cook in 1768 that "shedding the blood of those people is a crime of the highest nature" and two decades later instructed Arthur Phillip, first governor of the new prison settlement for convicts transported to New South Wales, to report "in what manner our intercourse with these people may be turned to advantage."[6] But the penal nature of colonial New South Wales and Van Diemen's Land (Tasmania)—their systemic cruelty and reserves of forced labor—fostered brutalization of both Aborigines and convicts. Half a century later, the more benign beginnings of the Western Australian settlement still saw Aborigines sentenced to seven years' detention for killing a pig or a ram, while colonial power declined to protect these British subjects from unofficial violence.[7] On grounds that non-Christians could not be sworn, New South Wales courts routinely rejected Aboriginal evidence until 1876.[8]

The extension of British law grew more difficult as the New South Wales (NSW) frontier receded over the western horizon. After the crossing of the Blue Mountains in 1813, a low-labor, land-hungry pastoral economy surged across the continent, escaping effective administration.[9] But even where the law was proximate and powerful, it usually failed to protect the crown's indigenous subjects from mass murder, punish the perpetrators, or deter future ones.

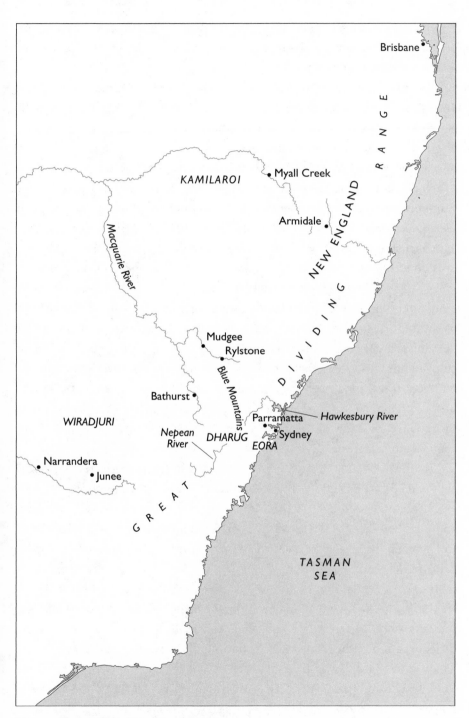

MAP 11. Early colonial New South Wales

Colonial priorities triumphed, and even enlightened attitudes produced no practical policies. Without being purposive or systematic, Britain's prejudices fostered systemic failures for Aborigines.

The result was genocidal for many Aboriginal groups, in part or in whole. The initial colonial experience that made such outcomes predictable, the policies that rarely emphasized their prevention, and the measures that denied Aborigines self-defense all indicate legal responsibility even on the part of passive officials. Massacres of Aborigines were usually the work of groups of settlers or colonial police, and less often of military units, sometimes in a part-time or volunteer capacity. But, as elsewhere, killings could occur with impunity in an ideological atmosphere that mixed expansionism, racism, and classical models with a fetish for cultivation and contempt for indigenous land use.

Ground-level conflict derived from differing ecological visions. Anthropologist A. P. Elkin, writing in 1951, analyzed Aborigines' vulnerability, as "a food-gathering people," to farming and pastoral interests whose "usurpation of hunting and food-gathering grounds" undermined their livelihood. First, "if the settlers are farmers, at once certain areas are put out of bounds." But "when cultivation is associated with grazing cattle and sheep . . . ever increasing in numbers, [they] require all the grass and must not be disturbed by the huntsmen's activities. So the native fauna must go, including the Aborigines, unless they change their way of living."[10] When this was impossible, war often led to genocidal massacres.

The British rarely pursued extermination, but frequently foresaw it. Officials and settlers brought to the colonies prevailing Lockean notions of property based on land usage. The Aborigines' perceived inability to value the land and mix their labor with the soil purportedly put them beyond civilization.[11] In Tasmania, historian Sharon Morgan writes, "[t]he two systems of land use— rural and nomadic—could not coexist. . . . The British were determined at all costs to have the land for their own exclusive use." The Scottish-born explorer and NSW surveyor-general Major Thomas Mitchell observed in 1848 that the intrusion of cattle, driving out the kangaroo, was "by itself sufficient to produce the extirpation of the native race, by limiting their means of existence."[12] The Chief Protector of Aborigines of the Port Phillip District, George Augustus Robinson, feared that "every acre of their native soil will shortly be so leased out and occupied as to leave them, in a legal view, no place for the sole of their feet."[13]

Just as English and American agriculture had long relied on pastoral inputs, in colonial Australia pastoralism also punctuated the ideology of settler cultivation. The Aborigines' lack of domesticable stock animals would have always made cultivation difficult. The British brought cattle and sheep and, like crops in rotation, relentless ideological pressure to farm alternated with the attractions of stock raising.

The British came to farm. Arthur Phillip brought to Sydney in 1788 the crown's instructions to assign 30-acre grants of land to convicts who completed their terms, so long as they cultivated it. In 1816, the editor of the *Hobart Town Gazette* looked to the day "when Agriculture shall be brought to a state of perfection" in Van Diemen's Land. "Agriculture has been the basis of Empires.— Rome derived all her greatness, all her grandeur, from her Agrarian Laws."[14] But the Aborigines, the explorer R. P. Lesson wrote when he crossed the Blue Mountains of NSW into the Bathurst Plains in 1824, were "true nomads, who have no fixed abode.... Hence comes that absence of art and the wretched state in which they stagnate."[15] Lesson echoed Hakluyt's sixteenth-century argument for cultivating "every soyle of the world by arte."[16] Pastoralists dismissed Aborigines with equal contempt. Explorer William Hovell complained in 1825 that Aborigines "fail to understand our method of stock raising and consider the animals are imported here for their own convenience," even though "every effort is made to convince them that their place is outside the fence."[17] A decade later, Lieutenant Governor George Arthur of Van Diemen's Land denied that "a migratory savage tribe, consisting of perhaps 30 to 40 individuals roaming over an almost unlimited extent of country could acquire such a property in the soil."[18]

Yet Aboriginal "fire-stick farming" had created the very grasslands that attracted English sheep graziers in Tasmania and elsewhere. Settlers rarely recognized that, as Don Watson puts it, Aborigines "farmed the land with fire." They used it to stimulate the growth of food plants, like daisy yams. Ashes fertilized them and even improved their taste.[19] This "regular, light, mosaic pattern of burning" also checked summer bushfires by depriving them of fuel.[20] The land commissioners of Van Diemen's Land reported in 1828 that for the new settler, "the Soil is in a great measure prepared for him, the grass feeds his Sheep and Cattle," while "he obtains the land free of all cost, and he generally finds as much clear as suffices for all the present purposes of agriculture."[21] An explorer of the island's north the previous year named indigenous pastureland there "the Surrey and Hampshire Hills." The destruction of the local Aborigines, however, also ended their land management. Then "scrub took over, gradually obliterating the open land so that sheep-grazing stopped around 1845, with considerable loss to the non-fire-stick farmers." Lieutenant Henry Bunbury found the European settlers unable to burn with "the same judgment and good effect" as Aborigines.[22] As in sixteenth-century Ireland and later in America, the cult of cultivation acknowledged no alternative land use.

A cult of antiquity buttressed this view. Just as the *Hobart Town Gazette* saw ancient Rome as Tasmania's model, early advocates of settlement in NSW like the Reverend John Dunmore Lang portrayed the Aborigines as Scythian barbarians, "part of that great family of nations which was known to the ancients" as "Sythians [sic]." Even in contesting the settlers' "damnable doctrine" that Aborigines were subhuman, Lang was recycling the sixteenth-century ethnomythology of Edmund Spenser in Ireland. As in 1596, Englishmen in 1824 still portrayed their colonies as being "in much the same social condition as Britain was when discovered by the Romans."[23]

After the British arrival in 1788, intermittent clashes slowly escalated to frontier warfare and some time later, sporadically, into genocidal massacres. No universal pattern prevailed. Diseases wiped out entire Aboriginal communities, sometimes even before physical contact with whites. Beyond their shared commitment to the deployment of force, British officials and settlers adopted varying approaches, as did diverse Aboriginal groups, who also ranged from conciliatory to aggressive, while some despairingly stopped rearing children or practiced infanticide. The key conflicts over land took different forms depending on the experience and interpretation of earlier or nearby events, local ecological and economic adaptation, and the mutual balance of military force at any time.

For example, as the early British settlement at Sydney was outnumbered, Governor Arthur Phillip tried to reach accommodation with local Aborigines.[24] However, in 1794, his successor expanded the colony and stretched its defenses by making 22 land grants to settlers on the Hawkesbury River, to the north. Four hundred whites, mostly convicts, confronted the Darug people, who gathered yams on the riverbanks. Settlers killed seven Darug and kidnapped children as unpaid laborers. In June 1795, Lieutenant Governor Paterson dispatched a detachment of the New South Wales Corps with orders to "kill any Darug they found and hang their bodies from gibbets." Troops killed eight in an ambush, and settlers killed five Darug in December. A sergeant stationed on the Hawkesbury in 1795–97 later recalled: "Parties of Soldiers were frequently sent out to kill the Natives."[25]

British officials made intermittent attempts to limit the killing. Governor George Hunter (1795–1801) urged self-defense but warned that wanton killing was murder. He had five farmers tried for murdering Aborigines in 1799, but on instructions from London, his successor, Philip King (1801–6), commuted their death sentences. The impunity set a pattern.[26] King ordered gatherings of Aborigines "driven back from the settlers' habitations by firing at them." Troops guarding wheat crops were to "fire on any native or natives they see. . . . Every means is to be used to drive them off." In 1802, settlers killed the Darug leader Pemulwuy and, three years later, another chief, Yaragowby, and seven followers. Twice forced to retreat, the Hawkesbury colonists remained vulnerable until a new outbreak of conflict ended in 1808–9. Darug population decline from fighting and disease left "no longer enough people to mount corn raids." Ninety troops of the NSW Corps' Veteran Company still occupied Darug areas in 1813.[27]

A new governor, Lachlan Macquarie (1812–21), tried to conciliate and Christianize as well as subjugate the Aborigines. He wrote to the secretary of state in London in 1814 recommending "the fostering Hand of Time, gentle means, and conciliatory manners to bring those poor unenlightened people into an important degree of civilization."[28] That December he invited all the colony's blacks to a "feast" in the Parramatta marketplace, where he suggested they abandon their "wandering predatory habits" to become "regular settlers."[29] He set up reserves for Aboriginal farmers and a school for children, the "Native Institution." In 1815, Macquarie granted land to the 16 remaining families of the Broken Bay "tribe," with huts, gardens, and farm tools. The next year, other Aborigines willing to take up cultivation were also promised land, seed, and implements. An annual officially sponsored feast at Parramatta regularly "attracted seven or eight tribes" from NSW coastal regions.[30] Aboriginal children from the Native Institution attended in 1816. "Several of the little ones read" to the crowd, the *Sydney Gazette* reported, and a proud parent exclaimed to Macquarie: "Governor that will make a good settler,—that's my Pickaninny [child]!"[31]

Macquarie's initiatives moderated but did not eliminate local violence over land and food. From May 1814, surviving Darug who had moved south from the Hawkesbury joined Darawal and Gandangara warriors in new raids on settlers' cornfields by the Nepean River. This provoked the government to "send out military aid to the settlers," the *Gazette* later recalled, "owing to which numbers of the natives had been killed." The 46th Regiment reinforced the NSW Corps'

Veteran Company in 1816. Near the Nepean that March, Aborigines surprised settlers on a punitive expedition, killing three. Macquarie ordered the army to "[s]trike them with Terror against Committing Similar Acts of Violence." Yet he carefully instructed officers to "[p]unish the guilty with as little injury as possible to the innocent Natives" and to "use every possible precaution to save the lives of Native Women and Children." Such orders, a military historian writes, proved "almost impossible to implement under frontier conditions." Captain Wallis, marching his troops by night into a cliff-top campsite, killed seven Aborigines, and seven more "met their fate by rushing in despair over the precipice."[32]

Official efforts to reduce violence focused on controlling Aborigines. A May 1816 government proclamation forbade any "black native, or body of black natives," from bringing weapons "within one mile of any town, village or farm." Aborigines in "unarmed parties exceeding six in number" who arrived at "any farm" must be asked to leave, and "if they persist in remaining . . . they are then to be driven away by force of arms by the settlers."[33] This was armed dispossession, not genocide, but worse lay ahead.

Genocidal Massacre on the Bathurst Plains

The British discovery of a new economic region in the interior, the resulting influx of settlers, and a new governor made the crucial difference to local Aborigines. When explorer William Lawson and two Sydney gentlemen crossed the Blue Mountains to the west in 1813, they discovered "a prodigious extent of fine level country" invaluable "to persons possessing large herds of cattle."[34] Another explorer, George Evans, found that "the inhabitants are numerous."[35] Of the estimated 3,000 Wiradjuri people, three clans totaling 500–600 lived here in mixed woodland and grassland. This would become the site of the town of Bathurst in the upper Macquarie River region.[36]

In the second half of 1814, a team led by Lieutenant William Cox built a road west across the Blue Mountains. A veteran of the repression that followed Ireland's 1798 rebellion, Cox had become paymaster of the NSW Corps, then a chief magistrate and owner of 1,600 hectares of land.[37] Cox wrote in his journal of descending the far slope to "very pretty forest ground" with grass "generally of a good quality—some silky; some hard, intermingled with rib grass, buttercup and thistle. Timber thin, and kangaroos—plenty." He then found "grass fit for cattle and sheep" and later, "the best and thickest on the ground that I have yet seen in this colony." Finally, Cox came across land that "resembled parks in England . . . I never saw finer grass, or more on the same quantity of land in a meadow in England than there was here, and just in a fit state for mowing. The whole of the line, about 20 miles due west, would make most excellent grazing farms, with the river in front." Hunting as they worked on the road, Cox's team ate "fresh kangaroo at least three times a week."[38] This country would be perfect for grazing, unless Aborigines ate the stock that deprived their game of the grass.

Yet Macquarie's policy promoted yeoman agriculture; the new lands had to attract farmers as well as graziers. The governor traveled Cox's road to the new district, which he named for the secretary of state for the colonies, the Earl of Bathurst. The official report of his journey and Macquarie himself, unlike Cox, noted both "the good pasture land and soil fit for cultivation." Moreover, "[t]he level and clean surface of these plains gives them at first view the appearance of lands under cultivation." Flax grew there, and the "fertile soil and rich pasturage" would long support "any increase of population and stock." Close to Bathurst were "50,000 acres of land clear of timber," half of it "excellent soil, well calculated for cultivation."[39]

However, cultivation demanded close settlement, and many farmers would come only if the region was peaceful. In six months of road building, Cox had reported seeing only "two parties of natives," up to six miles away, but Macquarie's expedition got closer and paid more attention. His aide-de-camp described the Wiradjuri as "a harmless and inoffensive race," and an explorer added, "I believe we are a great terror to them."[40] An officer reported: "Our people received strict instructions to use them kindly, to put no restraint on their movements but to let them go and come when they thought proper."[41]

Macquarie planned to make Bathurst a "township for the convenience of such settlers as may be indulged with grants of land."[42] He began to sow the seeds of pastoralism by founding the Government Stock Establishment there. But to promote agriculture as well as stock raising, his government carefully controlled both land settlement and labor in the new region.[43] Macquarie established a government farm station at Swallow Creek, 20 miles from Bathurst. His hopes to establish a cultivating peasantry included "emancipists," or ex-convicts.[44] In 1816, he reaffirmed the general practice of assigning a convict servant to each land grantee, even those with only 30 acres. As historian Sharon Morgan puts it, "Macquarie, recalling his Scottish youth, tended to favour the settlement of small farmers on the land—an early example in a succession of misguided leaders who envisaged an Australian yeomanry." His vision included the Aborigines, whom Macquarie hoped to persuade and assist to become farmers, too.[45] In December 1818, 300 Aborigines attended the Parramatta feast, including, for the first time, blacks from across the Blue Mountains, some from 100 miles away. They were dressed for the occasion; white feathers in their hair, animal teeth head-bracelets, and red and white face paint all made them seem "wild and outré."[46] Macquarie's dream of British villages in New South Wales may have dimmed a little that evening.

He pursued his plans for a mixed economy. The first land grant to a free settler in the Bathurst district went to grazier and road builder William Cox, whom the governor granted 800 hectares right across the Macquarie River from Bathurst.[47] The explorer William Lawson received 1,000 acres, but Macquarie equally encouraged smaller farms, making ten 50-acre grants.[48] Two years later, Cox was grazing 5,000 sheep on his Bathurst farm and conducting experiments with grasses. Macquarie tried to restrict the expansion of such large holdings and kept most of the region out of private hands, allowing only temporary access that required "few permanent stock-keeper's structures and few fences."[49] The governor informed London that he even planned to set aside 10,000 acres of newly discovered country for Aborigines.[50] By 1821, the Bathurst region's European population was still only 287, including convicts assigned to settlers. Just 2,520 acres had been alienated as private property.[51]

Macquarie's smallholder vision and restrictions on large runs interfered with the plans of his colonial rivals, the "Exclusionists," a group who envisioned a local landed gentry employing convict labor to herd their stock. The British government sided with the Exclusionists, replaced Macquarie in 1821, and ordered more land grants and sales. The new governor, Sir Thomas Brisbane, acknowledged the land hunger in 1823: "Not a Cow calves in the colony but her owner applies for an additional grant." He began to assign a convict servant for every 100 acres of land granted. By 1823, Brisbane had also abandoned Macquarie's three Aboriginal reserves near Sydney and two inland Aboriginal farms, and the next year he even discontinued the Native Institution for children.[52] Macquarie's departure, a triumph for large graziers, had ended the most systematic attempt to include Aborigines in rural development.

The cultivation ideal persisted amid the stock runs, in part to engage convicts in farm work. Brisbane promised London "constant endeavours" to deploy labor "to agricultural operations." By April 1823, he reported, 700 convicts were "cutting down trees and clearing the land . . . all over the country."[53] In the Bathurst Plains, Brisbane founded several Government Stock Stations.[54] Convinced of "the importance of Agricultural establishments" in preference to locating "the better sort of Convicts in towns," the governor supported a station at Emu Plains and in 1823 launched the Wellington Valley Agricultural Station, the first of a series of convict establishments planned to occupy "an immense space."[55] These state settlements would form a network of penal colonies on the lower Macquarie River, with up to 500 laborers serving as "Pioneers to the Free Settler." The station's commanding officer, Percy Simpson, received his pay on the basis of its wheat crop and the number of convicts it fed. They were soon cultivating 300 acres, with 70 men "ploughing and sowing, thrashing and grinding wheat." Relentless pressure to farm exacerbated the harsh convict regime. An ailing old man almost died after being "ordered to the fields." Colonial Secretary Goulburn instructed Simpson to ensure that during floggings, "the number from one to ten be deliberately counted between every stroke." A Wellington Valley prisoner termed the site a further "banishment in this land of exiles."[56]

The European population of the Bathurst region had suddenly tripled, reaching 1,267 in 1824. As much of the area was quickly taken up and surveyed, William Cox's son George set out with stock to establish his own run near Mudgee.[57] The 41,000 acres by now distributed to settlers supported 83,000 sheep and 15,000 cattle, with more to come as the Australian Agricultural Company received a British government grant of 1 million acres in 1824.[58] By the next year, the district was grazing 114,000 stock, with 91,000 acres of land alienated, a 36-fold increase in four years.[59] The rapid expansion and intensity of this occupation made conflict with Aborigines inevitable.

"The first serious trouble" had broken out in early 1822, on the property of William Cox, now one of "the largest holders of Sheep in the Colony."[60] Aborigines "drove away the stockmen, let the cattle out of the yard and started killing some sheep." In April, blacks killed one of William Lawson's convicts, whom he suspected of "provocation."[61] Lawson showed more understanding of Aborigines than Cox. Another settler concurred that the cause of Aboriginal unrest "very frequently was their ill-treatment by the whites."[62] Judge Barron Field of the NSW Supreme Court, visiting the region in October, added that the settlers' convicts "don't know how to treat" the "native Indians," whose "numbers are diminishing."[63] When Governor Brisbane established the Wellington Valley Agricultural Station in January 1823, his instructions were to begin "a friendly intercourse with the neighboring Blacks" and to "punish very severely any ill treatment of them."[64] Yet given the extensive new grazing of their lands, Aborigines were now more likely to clash with the widely dispersed stock keepers.

In September 1823, blacks killed a hut keeper northeast of Bathurst and later launched attacks to the west, "scattering the herds, spearing cattle and killing some of the stockmen." Lawson, as commandant of the new region, still felt that whites "in the first instance have been the aggressors." Aborigines claimed that "white men have driven away all the kangaroos and possums, and the black men must now have beef!"[65] After a raid on Judge John Wylde's station, Lawson sent soldiers and convicts to join Wylde's men in pursuit of "Jingler's tribe," but with orders to fire only in self-defense and "not to offer any violence to the native Women, or destroy them or their children." Wylde's employees killed an Aborigine in a skirmish, then had to flee the station. Attacks on Swallow Creek government farm also forced its evacuation in November.[66]

With conflict escalating, Lawson resigned as commandant. His replacement, Major James T. Morisset, brought different leadership to a dangerous situation. Wylde pressed him for a military operation and for a reward to be posted for the handing over of the Aboriginal chief, Windradyne, known as "Saturday," who had killed two bullocks. When soldiers accosted Windradyne, six men "had to break a musket over his body before he yielded," suffering broken ribs. After a month in irons, he "promised not to repeat the offence." However, raids on Wylde's cattle continued in January–February 1824, and the judge demanded further military action.[67]

A tragic misunderstanding over produce of the soil sparked open war. As Windradyne's band passed by a riverside market garden opposite Bathurst town, a farmer gave them potatoes. When the blacks returned next day and "began to help themselves," the farmer and his neighbors ran up shooting, killing several. Windradyne escaped.[68] In March, convicts from the Wellington Valley Agricultural Station were suspected to have murdered three Aborigines.[69] The atmosphere was hardening. The next month, Nelson Lawson, son of the ex-commandant, noted that the Aborigines were "very troublesome over the mountains," with "several of them shot." Two more, sent to the criminal court, were "likely to be hanged," he said, adding, ominously for Aborigines, "The sport is getting very scarce." In May, his brother William Jr. reported "several recently shot by soldiers" from Wylde's station.[70]

Windradyne's band hit back hard. One day in late May 1824, they killed seven stock keepers and shepherds in three attacks, "burning the huts and destroying the sheep and cattle." The *Sydney Gazette* reported on June 10 that "a party went out in quest of the natives, for the purpose of spreading destruction amongst their ranks." Five white servants shot dead an Aboriginal woman and two girls and were committed to trial for manslaughter. William Lawson Jr. wrote: "We have now commenced hostilities against them in consequence of their killing a great number of shepherds and stockmen, but afraid we shall never exterminate them, they have such an extensive mountainous country for them to flee from their pursuers." The white pursuers did capture "a horde of their women," whom they dispatched to Bathurst as hostages. Blacks killed six whites in June.[71]

Governor Brisbane struggled to control the violence. On June 18, he wrote to the secretary for the colonies for permission to raise a platoon of "Colonial Cavalry," not only for "keeping the Aborigines in check" but also "for the general Police of the Country," which he thought "most essential."[72] But as Bathurst magistrates, including Commandant Morisset, sentenced prisoners to 25 lashes for "groundless complaint," Brisbane awaited London's response, and the crisis exploded into wholesale killing.[73]

On July 22, 1824, the *Sydney Gazette,* whose editor was the government printer, took pains to deny the "distressing accounts from Bathurst within the last 3 or 4 weeks" of the killings of over 60 Aborigines. "From respectable authority we contradict these exaggerations, being informed that 8 or 9 of the natives only have been killed," and "about 5" Europeans.[74] However, reports from the field contradicted that authority, and the *Gazette* published two responses. One letter, dated July 29 and signed "Candid," reiterated that "it was reported very currently that sixty or seventy [Aborigines had] met with an untimely end." Candid suggested that "dispatches, which arrived at Headquarters" in June, had asserted that "parties of the blacks were found and fired upon," and others arriving in early July brought news of another clash in which five blacks were killed, and "three females . . . supposed to have been shot." Moreover, "in another instance, was not the resistance of the blacks so obstinate that, notwithstanding the fire of the English, the blacks were the masters of the field?" Another reader named "Honestus" wrote in on August 9: "About 20 Englishmen have already fallen miserably before those pitiless savages." The Aborigines, he added, "should be made to learn by terror. . . . We are now to oppose strength to strength" in order to end "the effusion of human blood."[75]

Conflict over land use had turned to genocidal massacre. Grazier William Cox, whose station had seen the first clash, now reportedly resorted to an agrarian metaphor to tell a Bathurst public meeting "that the best thing that could be done, would be to shoot all the blacks and manure the ground with their carcases." Cox or others "recommended likewise that the Women and Children should especially be shot as the most certain method of getting rid of the race."[76] The landowners' rage boiled over. Men of "position" declared "that the blackfellow was not a human being and that there was no more guilt in shooting him than in shooting a native dog."[77] Cox, Wylde, and six others signed a petition to urge "that such a large Military Force be sent out . . . as may at once overawe the natives and lead to the hope by taking prisoners, *or otherwise*, of bringing them at once to a state of due Subjection and Inoffensiveness."[78]

The Bathurst pastoralists took their protest to the capital. In late July, "a Meeting of the Magistrates and other Principal Inhabitants of the Colony" assembled at the Sydney Hotel. They urged the government to "prevent the future inconvenience of the settlers and their dependents, in the interior, from the incursions of the aboriginal tribes" and "to reward several praiseworthy individuals, who had stepped forward, . . . to preserve human life, and to save the stock of the country from total destruction." These praiseworthy "individuals" appeared to be the defendants on trial for manslaughter over the shooting of the three Aboriginal women. In court on August 6, the prosecutor argued that their killings of "women only" undercut the men's case of self-defense. But several leading colonists, including William Cox, gave evidence in praise of the five accused. Cox asserted that "the natives may now be called at war with the Europeans" and that "resistance is justifiable." A clergyman said he thought Macquarie's 1816 proclamation already allowed "that the settlers might kill the natives, although they themselves were not attacked." The jury acquitted all five defendants.[79]

Within a week Governor Brisbane declared martial law in the Bathurst region. His August 14 decree indemnified in advance any soldiers there who shot British subjects, including Aborigines.[80] Brisbane dispatched troops of the 40th Regiment to reinforce those stationed at Bathurst under the command of Major Morisset. In his new proclamation, the governor denounced the Aborigines for their "indiscriminate Attacks on the Stock Stations there, putting some of the Keepers to cruel deaths" and their plunder of stock. However, he also decried the "sanguinary Retaliation" by whites and "the slaughter of Black Women and Children" as well as that of "the lawless Objects of Terror" still threatening the Bathurst area. Brisbane directed that this "Mutual

Bloodshed may be stopped by the Use of Arms against the Natives beyond the ordinary Rule of Law in Time of Peace; and for this End, Resort to summary Justice has become necessary," but he authorized no such use of arms against settlers. Only Aborigines would feel the force of martial law in the field, though the governor ordered that "the helpless Women and Children are to be spared." Quickly, "the stock-owner magistrates crossed the mountains to organize and legitimize the 'summary justice,'" distributing guns to convict stockmen.[81]

The death toll rose under martial law. Brisbane wrote to Earl Bathurst that he was using the 75 troops now stationed in Bathurst to keep "these unfortunate people [Aborigines] in a constant state of alarm."[82] A Wesleyan missionary reported to his superiors on September 14: "From the most satisfactory sources I think that not fewer than a hundred blacks, men, women, and children, have been butchered." Four days later the "battle" of Bathurst is said to have begun.[83]

In the Mudgee area, the Aboriginal chief known as "Sunday" claimed prior ownership of all the land and complained of his dispossession: "Missa Cox only got it." At the end of September 1824, the *Sydney Gazette* reported two days of fighting in which three of William Cox's stockmen had killed 19 Aborigines, including 16 of them surprised unarmed while burying the first three, who had been attacked while driving off Cox's cattle near Mudgee the previous day. Military historian John Connor comments that "for a small group like the 'Mudgee tribe,' it was a high percentage casualty rate for a single action."[84]

By mid-October, the *Gazette* reported, "Bathurst with its surrounding vicinity is engaged in an exterminating war."[85] In a memorandum written 15 years later, George Bowman stated: "The Military did not attempt to take the Blacks and make Prisoners of them but shot all they fell in with."[86] In one reported incident, police trapped over 40 Aborigines in a swamp and killed them. The commanding officer collected "forty-five heads."[87] W. H. Suttor, whose father lived through the conflict and who eventually bought Cox's own farm, wrote later that "the blacks were shot down without any respect." Most fled "into the deep dells of the Capertee country and although some escaped, many were killed there." In Billiwillinga, Suttor wrote, soldiers feigning negotiations placed food "on the ground within musket range of the station buildings. The blacks were invited to come for it. Unsuspectingly they did come, principally women and children. As they gathered up the white man's presents they were shot down by a brutal volley, without regard to age or sex."[88] Local settler oral traditions tell of two massacres, each of possibly 30 or more Aborigines, at Clear Creek and Bell's Falls Gorge. Wiradjuri oral history also includes an account of the events at Bell's Falls Gorge.[89]

By November 1824, surviving Aborigines began to surrender. The full Wiradjuri death toll during that year is difficult to determine. Prior to the conflict, in 1815, the three Upper Macquarie clans were estimated to number 500–600, and a July 1824 Wiradjuri assembly near Bathurst, 600–700.[90] How many survived the bloodbath that followed is unclear. On December 11, Brisbane repealed martial law, offering Windradyne a pardon, and on December 28, Windradyne arrived in Parramatta with 140 members "of the Bathurst tribe." These joined 260 blacks from six or more other Aboriginal groups, mostly coastal tribes. The *Sydney Gazette* called the 400 Aborigines attending the Parramatta feast that year "by far the largest number ever known to have assembled on any similar occasion." Historian R. H. W. Reece wrote that "there is reason to believe that every Aborigine who was physically capable of making the journey would have been present."[91] If so, in six months, Wiradjuri numbers had fallen from 600–700 to as few as 140, plus the elderly, sick, and infants. A surviving population of around 400, including wounded, may be close to the truth. Specific reports of clashes and massacres in 1824 suggest a total toll of over 100 Wiradjuri killed and probably twice that number. One chronicler suggested "that between one quarter and a third of the Bathurst region Wiradjuri were killed," indicating a toll of 160–220. Citing another estimate of "over 100," a more recent study plausibly adds that the real toll "may have considerably exceeded this figure."[92]

Governor Brisbane himself had not set out to commit genocide, but he invoked a political and legal system that excluded and targeted Aborigines yet failed to protect them. He sought expansion while trying to restrain genocidal killings by local bands of settlers like Cox, but not to punish them, and in the end he attempted to cover up the massacres. On December 13, he congratulated Commandant Morisset for ensuring that "the Aboriginal Natives have learned to respect our powers without bloodshed," adding only: "It is impossible, perhaps, at all times, to prevent the infliction of injury upon them, by Individuals."[93] Brisbane even reiterated to Earl Bathurst that during martial law "not one outrage was committed, . . . neither was a life sacrificed, or even Blood spilt."[94]

However, Earl Bathurst refused Brisbane's request for authority to establish a colonial cavalry and he criticized Morisset. While Windradyne impressed the *Sydney Gazette* as "the most manly black native we have ever beheld," Bathurst recalled Brisbane and his assistant Major Goulburn, and relieved Morisset, who went on to command the new, harsher penal colony at Norfolk Island.[95] Renewed clashes between stockmen and Aborigines southwest of Bathurst in 1826 prefigured another Wiradjuri war on the Murrumbidgee River in the 1830s. Meanwhile, Windradyne died of an injury received in an intertribal clash. A local memorial recalled him as "first a terror but later a friend to the settlers." Wellington Valley Agricultural Station failed, closing in 1830.[96]

Four years later, Rev. J. D. Lang charged: "There is black blood at this moment on the hands of individuals of good repute in the colony."[97] An NSW official confirmed to the colonial secretary in 1836 that "a war of extermination ... took place here some years ago."[98] Grazier William Cox died the next year, leaving a reputation for humanitarianism. *The Memoirs of William Cox, J.P.,* a history compiled by his grandson, states that "the last" Bathurst Aborigine died about 1875, and that "the blacks really exterminated themselves."[99]

Tasmania: Agriculture and Genocide

William Cox's son James moved to Australia's second penal colony, Van Diemen's Land, with £400 in 1814 and became "one of the wealthiest men on the island," with over 12,000 acres. The colony's land commissioners reported in 1828: "He has fenced in Six thousand acres, fenced and laid down large Paddocks with artificial grasses, [and] has an excellent garden well stocked with fruit."[100] Unlike the Bathurst Plains, Tasmania's fertile soil and milder climate greatly favored not only sheep grazing but cultivation. British officials encouraged both by making large and small land grants. In the first two decades of Tasmania's colonization, authorities made 1,776 grants, totaling nearly 600,000 acres, to 1,500 Europeans.[101] Given the island's size and natural limits, the combination of intensive *and* extensive settlement threatened Aboriginal livelihoods even more than did pastoral expansion into the Bathurst region.

Before sighting any Aborigines, the colony's founder in 1803, Lieutenant John Bowen, doubted they would be "of any use to us." As earlier in NSW, the crown instructed his superior, Lieutenant-Governor David Collins, to treat the blacks with "amity and kindness." But this time London failed to commission a report on possibilities for beneficial contacts with them.[102] Until 1805, Collins delayed making a proclamation that Aborigines had the protection of English law.[103]

Meanwhile, troops shot at parties of blacks they encountered. On several occasions in 1803–4, surveyor Charles Grimes opened fire on large groups of

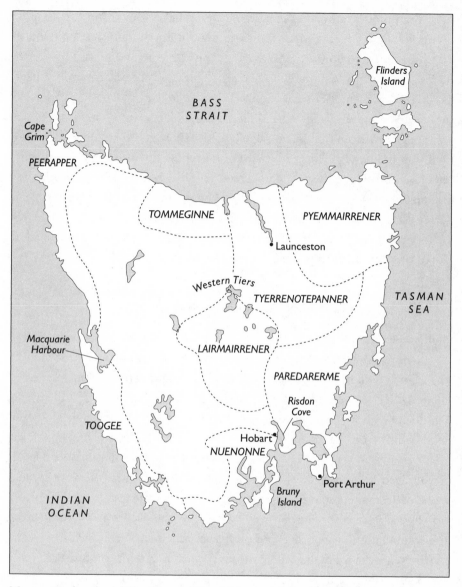

MAP 12. Early colonial Van Diemen's Land (Tasmania). Based on Australian Institute of
Aboriginal and Torres Strait Islander Studies, *Aboriginal Australia* (Canberra, 1996).

Aborigines on the banks of the Derwent River.[104] Then, near Risdon in May
1804, a hunting party of 300 Aborigines—men, women, children, and elders—
emerged from the trees in pursuit of kangaroos and wallabies. "They looked
at me with all their eyes," recalled Edward White, who testified under oath in
1830 that the blacks were not aggressive and had kept 200 yards distant from

the nearest farmstead. However, under the command of Surgeon-Magistrate Jacob Mountgarret and Lieutenant Moore, Royal Marines opened fire with muskets and cannon.[105] At least 3, possibly 40 Aborigines fell dead. White, whose sworn testimony under cross-examination provides the only disinterested eyewitness account, reported "a great many of the Natives slaughtered and wounded." The perpetrators left different accounts. Moore reported three shooting incidents that day: in one, an Aborigine was "killed on the spot" and another later "found Dead in the Valley;" troops also fired on groups of blacks in two further incidents, the second involving "a great party" of Aborigines. Three hours after the first shots, Moore added, Mountgarret told troops "to fire one of the Carronades to intimidate them," and "they dispersed." Moore, citing no death toll from this incident, reported merely that Mountgarret and his soldiers "followed them Some distance up the Valley" and "had reason to suppose more were wounded." Mountgarret himself reported finding a "fine native boy" whose "father and mother were both killed," and a third corpse, which he later dissected. According to White, Mountgarret sent "some of their bones" in casks to Sydney. Collins acknowledged only three dead, but a government inquiry in 1830 noted that the Aboriginal toll had "been estimated as high as 50." There is no reason to accept Moore's self-protective agnosticism on the cannonade's impact or dismiss White's direct testimony of "a great many . . . slaughtered."[106] By 1808, probably 100 more Aborigines and 20 Europeans had died in further clashes.[107] Two years later, the *Derwent Star* described the natives as "rendered desperate by the cruelties they have experienced from our people."[108]

By 1818, Tasmania's Aboriginal population had fallen by over half, from an estimated 4,000 or more to under 2,000.[109] The *Hobart Town Gazette* acknowledged the "great arrearage of justice which is due them. . . . The Aborigines demand our protection."[110] Despite government discouragement, "settlers would shoot on sight, . . . killing the men and taking the children from the women." The authorities asserted responsibility for such children.[111] A government order of March 1819 noted the "many former instances" of cruelties "repugnant to humanity" perpetrated against blacks and the more recent outrages of criminals "who sometimes wantonly fire at and kill the men, and at others pursue the women for the purpose of compelling them to abandon their children."[112] The *Gazette* denounced the shooting of an Aborigine by stockmen, and incidents in which black women were "deprived of their children" for provoking Aborigines to "rooted animosity" and the "savage murder" of a sealer.[113]

Yet the British authorities accelerated the colonization process, taking inadequate measures to prevent extermination of Aboriginal communities. From 1817 to 1824, the colony's white population increased sixfold, from 2,000 to 12,643. In particular, 3,400 new free settlers who arrived from 1820 to 1824 "changed the economic basis of the colony."[114]

The first 30 free settlers came to Van Diemen's Land in 1803–6, obtaining 100 acres of land and two convict laborers each. Officers also received land grants, and marines 80–130 acres, while British farmers transferred from Norfolk Island received 30–40 acres.[115] Farmers who lived on and cultivated their land would receive further grants.

As in NSW, much larger grants also established extensive pastoral holdings. Quick land dealers prospered, too. Grantees ignored regulations against resale within five years, and corruption allowed absentees to accumulate estates. Early grants included 2,000 acres for the Lieutenant Governor's wife and 600 for Jacob Mountgarret, commander at the Risdon Cove massacre, who bought up more land before being fired from the magistracy in 1814, when Governor Macquarie consigned him to "disgrace and infamy." Small grants continued, almost alternating with the large, yet some years saw few or none, as in the Bathurst Plains. Macquarie issued 356 grants in 1813, totaling 34,000 acres.[116] The next year saw only one large grant of 860 acres and one of 100. After James Cox moved to Tasmania, Macquarie granted 1,370 acres there to George Evans, also a reward for his exploration of the Bathurst Plains.[117] In 1818, the government made two grants of over 1,000 acres and two dozen under 100. The next year Lieutenant Governor Sorell received 3,000 acres, then 3,200 more. The dual pattern persisted even when the speed of occupation escalated. In 1820, 10,000 acres were distributed in 63 grants, mostly small ones to ex-convicts, but the next year, 47,000 acres went in only 116 grants. Then in 1823, 1,000 grantees received a vast total of 442,000 acres.[118]

This combination of very large grants and many small ones devastated the livelihood of Aborigines. Settlers quickly and thickly occupied almost all the island's productive land. Of the 600,000 acres assigned to 1,500 grantees by 1823, nearly 500,000 acres went to 1,143 people in 1821–23 alone. The area of occupation expanded exponentially even as smaller farmers proliferated on the frontier, where Aborigines confined to shrinking areas faced greater numbers of whites than ever. Families owning some land now accounted for most of Tasmania's 10,000 European settlers. Probably half of all the 1,776 grants went to ex-convicts. More than half the initial grants were under 100 acres, yet only one-third of supplemental grants went to such grantees. Most settlers had small farms, but most land went to large landowners, including 200 people awarded multiple grants.[119]

This pre-1823 acceleration of both small and large land grants, simultaneously fostering close settlement and rapid extension of the frontier, created a pattern so densely woven that it characterized individual farms. On the ideological level, the superiority of agriculture to Aboriginal land use legitimized the colonial occupation in the eyes of the colonists. On small farms themselves, the cultivators' self-sufficiency also bolstered pastoral expansion. One colonist wrote in the 1820s: "In the first place every settler depends as much as he can on the agricultural part of his farm, to pay his yearly expenses, and calculates his future riches in the accumulating number of his herd."[120] A new grantee put it this way: "After we have fenced the garden and the wheat, we shall begin to build substantially unless we should be so lucky as to take sheep or cattle for a third of their increase—a common mode of buying cattle in the colony."[121] Herds grew rapidly as did the need for land. Another resident marveled that it was "by no means uncommon to see a calf sucking a young heifer, at the moment the heifer herself is sucking her own mother." The land commissioners recorded their surprise when they "rode through a 60 acre farm to Mrs. McCarty on which she keeps 1200 sheep!!!"[122]

Despite a climate and soil suitable for agriculture, the fast-growing colony's worsening labor shortage promoted even faster pastoral expansion. Fewer of the depleting supply of convicts worked in agriculture than in NSW.[123] Pressure mounted for more land, and from 1823, large grants dominated. In the next eight years, the area granted expanded twentyfold. A grantee's capital now determined the grant's size; few were small. The government distributed 1 million acres of Tasmanian land from 1824 to 1831.[124] London investors formed the Van Diemen's Land Company in 1825 with a charter grant of 250,000 acres in northwest Tasmania.[125] The colony's European population of 7,400 in 1821 increased to 27,000 a decade later.[126]

In 1824, the new governor, George Arthur, identified the challenge he faced, that of fostering settler agriculture while coping with a runaway pastoral frontier. He complained that every settler was "much more disposed to extend his possessions than to improve them." Sheep, Arthur wrote, "multiply in a most remarkable degree in this country; but instead of the Agriculturists endeavouring to improve their land by the introduction of artificial grass, they alone seek to support them by extending their limits."[127]

Tasmania exported wheat to NSW by 1817 and already grazed more sheep. But the 1820s brought an extraordinary expansion of both farming and grazing. Tasmania's wheat, barley, and oats were all superior to those of NSW, and its 1822 wheat exports exceeded its five-year total for 1815–20. The island's 13,000 acres of wheat fields in 1821 increased to 30,000 by 1830. Van Diemen's Land remained the major colonial wheat producer until 1850, while its flocks multiplied from 128,000 to 682,000 sheep from 1818 to 1830. By 1829, the island was exporting more wool to Britain than NSW was. Its cattle herds tripled to over 100,000 from 1821 to 1829. This rapid joint expansion of both agriculture and pasture was characteristic of Tasmania, whose conditions were more conducive to cultivation than those of the mainland. The combined result, as Sharon Morgan points out, was that "while settlement was spreading, it was also becoming more dense, allowing less and less space for Aboriginal use of the land."[128]

Compared to the mainland, the island's small area was more quickly occupied by the lucrative, land-hungry pastoral industry. Tasmania's land commissioners reported in 1826 that settlers "generally observed" to them, "why should we buy land, when we can occupy as much as we please for nothing"? The commissioners predicted in 1828 that "in a short time" the land in the settled districts would run out.[129] Two years later, "not a single grant of fresh land" was possible in the entire area between Hobart and Launceston, and government land grants ended. New colonists now sought cheaper land in the other Australian colonies. Established entrepreneurial Tasmanian pastoralists also "felt that little further increase would be possible," and so by 1834 many of them commenced an "exodus" to the future colony of Victoria. By precisely the point when no more land was available on the island, no more Aborigines survived there, either.[130]

From the outset, an ideology of cultivation fueled the expansion of the frontier and intensification of agriculture. Landing at Risdon Cove in 1803, Bowen brought instructions to "proceed to the clearing of the ground on the public account for the cultivation of wheat and other plants" and to have settlers build American log fences.[131] Lieutenant Governor Collins illustrated the symbiosis of farming and stock raising with his goal to have the wheat fields "well Ploughed, and I hope to give it some Improvement by the Dung, which the Stock Yard will furnish." He established a government-run farm and lent ploughshares to settlers. A Norfolk Islander arriving in 1808 wrote: "I *never* in my life saw such charming Wheat." When the NSW Exclusionist John Oxley visited two years later, he remarked: "After the first Season, the Land becomes perfectly sweet, the Soil loose and easily ploughed with two Horses or Bullocks."[132]

Even as pastoralism overran the frontier, agricultural societies blossomed in Tasmania. Settlers founded the first colonial one in 1822, to honor "persons excelling in the different branches of agriculture." The more "practical" farmer George Hobler also tried to found a less exclusive body for "the agriculturalists of this country." In the 1829 season, Hobler set out to fell 1,000 native Mimosa trees, "the land they stand on to be broken up for corn." The *Tasmanian Almanack* claimed that plants could grow better there than "in any other part of the known world." Arriving from India, Augustus Prinsep found "[e]very kind of English fruit" on the trees "in luscious abundance." The land commissioners even located sons of the proprietor of England's *Farmer's Journal;* "they have some land in cultivation, and have some fencing done, and are very industrious."[133]

The ideological drive for agricultural improvement was constant. Every land grant came with a government order to clear and cultivate it, or face criticism. Officials and visitors from England kept denouncing settlers for their "slovenly mode of tillage," neglect of "manuring or fallowing," and lack of fencing.[134] The *Hobart Town Gazette* criticized those who "neglected to take advantage of the fine and seasonable weather" to raise crop production. English resident James Atkinson wrote in 1826 of his surprise that "the people, who, in the mother country, cultivate their lands with such persevering industry and intelligence, should here become so extremely slothful and negligent; yet such is the case—the state of agriculture being rude and miserable in the extreme." Linking cultivation to kinship, Atkinson wrote that a visitor to Tasmania "would scarcely be able to persuade himself that the inhabitants were derived from the same stock." Governor Arthur repeatedly complained that "too many land grants were left unimproved and cultivation requirements disregarded."[135]

All this carping underscored the official ideal of the yeoman farmer. The colony's land commissioner, who was close to Arthur, lauded independent cultivators from England, for whom migration meant "a delightful change to that class of People who are hard working, industrious Tenants at home, but who finding that all their labour and industry went to supply their Landlord, their Clergyman, and their Poor, have boldly ventured to come here." One yeoman had acquired "a Corn Mill in full work," while "the Wife and Daughters, milk the Cows, make Butter and Cheese, the sons Plough, drive, saw Timber for the Mill," and so become "more wealthy, comfortable and independent everyday." The commissioners also found the police superintendent's farm "most gratifying," with its "Hedge row of beautiful white Thorn, protected by an admirable Hurdle Fence. . . . The land itself is not of excellent quality, but the crops are superior from good culture. A large flock of highly improved Sheep . . . [and] a large well cropped Garden."[136]

The land commissioners themselves favored agriculture over pastoralism. "Nothing can equal the beauty of this part of the Country, one continued plain or downs without a Tree." They waxed lyrical on detecting "care and frugality" on a yeoman's farm: "Paddocks laid down with artificial grasses, . . . the Daughters milking night and morning, . . . Large fields of excellent Corn. The Stack yard full of grain, a nice Corn Mill at the Barn Door, supplying the whole district with flour. Health and contentment to be seen in the countenances of all." The point was simple: "These people had come out menials, they are now independent." To foster a civil society, the commissioners sternly took the side of the farmer, whom the regulations obligated to support convict "Ruffians" and to "cultivate, fence and improve for five Years," and who then had to compete with "the Owners of Stock Runs" possessing "immense Tracts." With much of its land still unimproved, the commissioners considered the island still "a Wilderness," while pastoralists, "the Men on these Runs, are demi Savages," and "Hordes of wild Cattle are destroying the Crops of the industrious Settlers." They scoffed that if "Wheat, the Staff of life, is the standard for Wages in other Countries, here, Rum is." So, "[i]f a Settler in the interior exclaims, How can the Government be so cruel as to compel me to cultivate when I have no market for my produce? Our answer is, fence your land, rouze yourself from your drunken Couch, send no more for Rum . . . cultivate at least as much as will supply your family."[137]

Nevertheless, the extraordinary expansion of the sheep industry impressed even the land commissioners who, after surveying perhaps half the island's farms, began to report more positively on its pastoral potential.[138] Yet official pressure to plant also paid off. From 1828 to 1830, Tasmania's cultivated area increased from 34,000 to 55,000 acres. Fields sown with English grasses covered 13,000 acres by 1835. Mills proliferated. The 1830 potato crop produced 5,900 tons "equal to the best" in England.[139] Agriculturalist Henry Widowson marveled in 1829 how not long before, "the plough might be said to be unknown in the island," whereas now "a pair of bullocks and a plough [are] within reach of the smallest land-holder."[140] Widowson's book, *Present State of Van Diemen's Land,* echoed both Edmund Spenser's *A View of the Present State of Ireland* (1596) and Thomas Jefferson's *Notes on the State of Virginia* (1782).

Colonists themselves recognized the link between agriculture and Aboriginal dispossession. In the view of the *Hobart Town Gazette,* "if any aggression was put upon the rights of these original natives, it was done at first in planting the British Standard, and in entering the first plough in the soil."[141] When officials acted to provide a single Aborigine with a farm, they did so only in return for his assistance against other blacks. In mid-1830, prominent settler John Batman recommended that "Black Bill," a "good farming man" who had been raised by "James Cox Esqr," son of William Cox of Bathurst, be assigned "a portion of land and some assistance from Government for six or twelve months, this, I think, would operate favourably upon his own people and might be the means of reconciling them." Governor Arthur agreed to grant Black Bill "One Hundred acres of Land, on the usual conditions, in consideration of his good conduct, whilst serving under Mr. Batman, in pursuit of the hostile tribes." These "conditions" required Black Bill to cultivate his land, but he died in December 1830 before he could take it up.[142] By then, settlers carried guns "between the handles of the plough."[143]

The Black War

Most Tasmanian Aborigines perished not from diseases but in armed conflicts. During the first 20 years of settlement, an annual average of fewer than two Aboriginal attacks on settlers were recorded. Historian N. J. B. Plomley concluded of these early Aboriginal raids that "many, if not all ... were reprisals for some sort of injury." However, after European pressure on the land escalated, attacks increased annually, from 11 Aboriginal attacks in 1824 to a height of 222 in 1830. From 1824, "the prime object" of the attacks on settlers "was to obtain the food and blankets in their dwellings." But Aborigines were now also "purposeful, being motivated by a need to drive the settlers from their territories in order to live their natural lives, as well as by the starvation which was the outcome of that territorial occupation." In what they called the Black War, whites devastated the Aborigines, whose numbers again plummeted, from about 1,500 in 1824 to only 350 in 1831.[144]

British legal discrimination denied the Aborigines protection. In 1825, London authorized the new governor of NSW, Ralph Darling, to repel Aboriginal "aggressions in the same manner as if they proceeded from subjects of any accredited state."[145] This also meant that in case of conflict, Aborigines now lacked the rights of British subjects. When blacks killed three white men on the Hunter River in NSW in 1826, settlers there petitioned Darling for troops or mounted police. He dispatched soldiers under Lieutenant Lowe. Darling's attorney general, Saxe Bannister, asked to see their "Instructions," and felt compelled to remind the governor that "indiscriminate slaughter of offenders, except in the heat of immediate pursuit or other similar circumstances, requires preliminary solemn acts," such as a declaration of martial law, and that "to order soldiers to punish any outrage in this way, is against the law." Darling dismissed Bannister's advocacy of the "cause of the natives." Lieutenant Lowe had an Aboriginal suspect tied to a stake and shot, and convict witnesses made possible his prosecution for manslaughter, but the court dismissed the case because convict testimony, like that of Aborigines, was not "entitled to credit." When Bannister successfully prosecuted three convicts for murdering an Aboriginal boy, Darling declined to carry out their sentences. Bannister complained: "The English rules of evidence, the absence of interpreters, and the ill-conduct of the people (both settlers and convicts, with special exceptions,) render it exceedingly difficult to cause the law to be put in force against murderers." Even "when conviction has been obtained, the government has sympathized too much with the oppressing class, and too little with the oppressed, to permit justice."[146] This also held true in Tasmania once conflict erupted there.

The Black War began in November 1823, when members of the Oyster Bay tribe killed two stock keepers on the east coast. In a nine-month period, Aborigines killed 13 more Europeans, seven in 1825, and 12 the next year.[147] In November 1826, Arthur exhorted magistrates to organize posses to hunt down blacks.[148] The editor of the *Colonial Times* thundered: "SELF DEFENCE IS THE FIRST LAW OF NATURE—THE GOVERNMENT MUST REMOVE THE NATIVES—IF NOT, THEY WILL BE HUNTED DOWN LIKE WILD BEASTS AND DESTROYED."[149] A week later, the paper reported "that the work of death has commenced among them, and that the Settlers and stock-keepers are determined to annihilate every black who may act hostile."[150]

Early the next year, according to the 1830 testimony of Gilbert Robertson, a landowner who had recently served as the Richmond district's chief constable, police there shot at and "killed 14 of the Natives, who had got upon a hill, and threw stones down upon them; the police expended all their ammunition, and being afraid to run away, at length charged with the bayonet, and the Natives fled."[151] Aborigines killed 30 Europeans during the year 1827.[152] Stockmen killed 10 Aborigines in a day, June 12, west of Launceston. After blacks murdered another stock keeper, the *Colonial Times* reported in July that soldiers of the 40th Regiment had tracked down an Aboriginal band. The paper went on: "The people over the second Western Tier have killed an immense quantity of the blacks this last week. . . . They were surrounded whilst sitting around their fires, when the soldiers and others fired at them when about thirty yards distant. They report there must be about 60 of them killed and wounded."[153]

As killings escalated, racial justifications did, too. Traveling unarmed in November 1827, the land commissioners reached a hut "five minutes after the Natives had robbed it" and were alarmed to be "living in a Tent, surrounded by a set of Wretches who value our lives as little as they do the Kangaroo's." The commissioners feared having their brains "beaten out with Waddies by such Ouran Outangs, disgrace would it be to the human race to call them Men." That month, Arthur deployed garrison troops to reinforce the civilian posses and police. He urged "the magistrates throughout the colony . . . to act themselves with vigor," so that "the black Natives may be driven from the settled districts. . . . Sufficient troops to give confidence to the inhabitants will be at the disposal of the civil power in every district." Reinforcements of the 40th Regiment and the NSW Royal Veteran Company arrived in the countryside.[154]

Blacks wounded an employee of the "practical agriculturalist," George Hobler, that December. He sent four armed men to track them, "get sight of their night fire and slaughter them as they lie around it." In his diary seven months later, Hobler wrote that "these savages murder about 20 settlers or servants every year." He complained that "Black Tom—a civilized native black," had been discharged from prison, though it was "well known he has aided in many murders." Writing in a stream of consciousness, Hobler added: "I suppose he must take some more lives before he loses his own, unless some stock keeper in self defence has the luck to shoot him . . . a few years ago they fled from a horse, now they way lay horsemen and spear them began sowing wheat . . ."[155] Here in Hobler's diary, blood and soil ran together in a single unpunctuated sentence.

The Van Diemen's Land Company obtained a charter from London in 1825, granting it 250,000 acres in the island's northwest. Its shepherds killed an Aborigine in November 1827, and early in 1828 a visitor, Rosalie Hare, reported "a great many Natives shot" by the company's employees. Hare, who stayed with the family of its administrator and magistrate, Edward Curr, wrote of "several accounts of natives having been shot by them, they wishing to extirpate them entirely, if possible." Curr led one raid on local Aborigines and himself reported in writing, "My whole and sole object was to kill them." Curr also expressed the "wish to have three of their heads to put on the ridge of the hut," offering his men rum for the heads.[156] In January 1828, according to Hare, a second company officer led employees on another raid, when they "surprised a party and killed 12." On February 10, employees massacred up to 30 more Aborigines at Cape Grim.[157] No legal action followed. Magistrate Curr wrote: "I had thought of investigating the case, but I saw first that there was a strong presumption that our men were right, second if wrong it was impossible to convict them, and thirdly that the mere enquiry would induce every man to leave Cape Grim." That could not be allowed to happen. Instead, from 1826 to 1834, the population of local Aborigines fell from over 300 to 100.[158]

Governor Arthur told his Executive Council on October 31, 1828, that a quick end to the war was needed to "save the Aboriginal race from being exterminated."[159] He declared martial law the next day and offered a bounty for each captured Aboriginal adult and child.[160] The *Hobart Town Courier* reported several weeks later that the 40th Regiment had "made an attack upon the Aborigines at the Great Lake at the source of the Macquarie River. Ten of the natives were killed on the spot."[161] Settler James George stated in his diary that the soldiers and others had "fired volley after volley in among the blackfellows, they reported killing some two score." In another incident, the *Courier* reported five more Aborigines shot.[162] Elsewhere, George Lloyd boasted of firing "7 double-barrelled guns, heavily charged with duckshot" making such a "wholesome impression upon the notoriously cruel Big River tribe that most of them" were "more or less severely wounded." Using a similar strategy of "creeping upon them and firing amongst them," Douglas Ibbens killed half the "eastern mob" of Aborigines. Gilbert Robertson told the 1830 Aborigines Committee inquiry that "great ravages were committed by a party of constables and some of the 40th Regiment ... that 70 of them were killed by that party ... firing all their ammunition upon them, and then dragging the women and children from the crevices in the rocks, and dashing out their brains." Robertson named three 40th Regiment participants as sources and invited the committee to question them, but it did not. Cassandra Pybus notes: "The final report of the Aborigines Committee ignored any evidence about organized violence toward Aborigines during Arthur's government."[163]

Colonists expanding or defending their landholdings became laws unto themselves. The administration could neither fully protect nor control them. In one incident involving an armed party led by pastoralist and entrepreneur John Batman, "three hundred buckshot were poured into an encampment at twenty yards distant."[164] This appears to describe an attack in September 1829, of which Batman reported: "The natives arose from the ground, and were in the act of running away into the thick scrub, when I ordered the men to fire upon them, which was done." He estimated they numbered 60 to 70 men, women, and children. Two seriously injured Aborigines whom Batman captured the next morning said that 12 black men and women were dead or dying from body wounds and that others had been "shot in the legs." Batman estimated that about 15 Aborigines had been killed or mortally wounded. The two prisoners were unable to march far, and Batman recorded: "After trying every means in my power, for some time, found I could not get them on I was obliged to shoot them." Two weeks later, Batman lied to police magistrate James Simpson, covering up these murders.[165] But Governor Arthur wrote on Batman's initial report: "shoots wounded Natives because they could not keep up."[166] The Quaker missionary James Backhouse, after visiting Batman three years later, reportedly stated that Batman had killed at least 30 Tasmanian Aborigines.[167] Batman's neighbor called him "a murderer of blacks." Arthur, who considered Batman sympathetic to blacks, acknowledged he "had much slaughter to account for," yet did not hold him to account.[168]

By February 1830, such chaos reigned that the editor of the *Tasmanian* added his voice to that of his counterpart at the *Colonial Times*, writing that "[e]xtermination seems to be the only remedy" for Aboriginal destruction.[169] Two months later, John Batman said he despaired of "these wretched race of People—I now think they are not to be reconciled by any means."[170] Murderous raids by surviving Aboriginal bands alternated with massacres and summary killings by armed settler posses and military units. The violence also implicated colonial officials. In late September 1830, the solicitor general of Tasmania, Alfred Stephen, addressed a public meeting in Hobart. He stressed that he was voicing his own views, not speaking as a government official. But because the Aborigines "have waged such a war upon the settlers, you are bound to put them down." Convicts were obliged to work in the most isolated frontier outposts, "where they are exposed to the hourly loss of their lives," Stephen said. The government, he added, must "protect this particular class of individuals, and if you cannot do so without extermination, then I say boldly and broadly exterminate! . . . capture them if you can, but if you cannot, destroy them."[171]

The colony's leading legal officer, speaking in a private capacity, had reinforced the voices of two leading newspapers. The rage for extermination that infected the elite also swept the settler community. Two weeks later, the Protector of Aborigines, George Augustus Robinson, wrote to his wife: "Nothing is heard of at Launceston but extirpating the original inhabitants."[172]

Governor Arthur, who resisted public calls for extermination, responded to the challenge with an extraordinary alternative: to round up and "remove" the Aborigines. In October 1830, Arthur assembled the "Black Line." A human chain of 1,000 armed convicts and 550 British soldiers, reinforced by police and armed settlers, stretched through the island. They set out in formation across the countryside, to sweep the Aborigines before them in an early case of what might be considered "ethnic cleansing." A senior government official wrote that "it has become apparent that unless means were devised for making them prisoners ... in some well adapted part of this country, or, otherwise ex- terminating the race, that the country must be abandoned." Historian Lyndall Ryan writes that of the 200 Aborigines in the settled districts in 1828, "fewer than fifty survived the settlers' guns to surrender." Another 250 were rounded up from remoter areas.[173]

The total Aboriginal death toll in the conflict was high. From primary sources, historian H. A. Willis has counted between 188 and 333 Aborigines killed by settlers or soldiers in individual incidents from 1803 to 1834. His tally omits the toll in other recorded incidents such as the raids of late June 1827, when a newspaper reported "about 60 of them killed and wounded." Lyndall Ryan has compiled a separate list totaling approximately 448 Aborigines killed in the Black War of 1823–31.[174]

Arthur lifted martial law in 1832. The government transferred all surviving Tasmanian Aborigines to Flinders Island. Within three years, only 100 survived. As Ryan writes, "Most had died in the various transit camps set up to process them upon capture."[175] After a year at Flinders Island, its commandant, W. J. Darling, ensign to the 63rd Regiment of Foot, looked back on the treatment of the Aborigines before their arrival. He denounced "the brutal treatment which it is beyond a doubt has been practiced upon them by *civilized savages,* shot down like dogs while sleeping round their fires, their women taken from them to gratify the lusts of white men, hunted and persecuted in all directions, and in fact looked upon as savage beasts of the forest, whom it was necessary to get rid of, no matter how."[176]

Aboriginal Protector Robinson gave the survivors new names. Parley, a young man of 29 from the west coast, became "Hannibal." Some received the names of other fallen classical heroes, such as Hector, Achilles, Leonidas, Cleopatra, or of Britain's more recently vanquished or despised opponents: Napoleon, Buonaparte, and Washington.[177] History thus prefigured the Aborigines' defeat. But cultivation could still uplift them. Robinson reported enthusiastically on joining the Aborigines to harvest Flinders Island's first corn crop: "What a gratifying sight ... I wished to have it cut with the sickle to instruct the natives, little thinking that they could reap it. The greater part of those natives never took a sickle into their hands before, yet was as expert as the rest. I was highly delighted with the scene."[178] In a public announcement to his people two years later, Walter George Arthur, a young Aborigine named for the governor, sounded less spirited: "I looked toward Mt. Franklin and I behold the men aploughing in a field. . . . You did know nothing at all about their ploughing the ground or any thing at all. Now you see there is none of the good people alive. No, they are dead and gone."[179]

Writing to London, Governor Arthur denied that his administration or the landowners bore responsibility for this catastrophe. He told the secretary of state for the colonies that Tasmania's Aborigines had "been reduced, I lament to say, almost to annihilation, by the animosity which always existed between the different tribes, and by the warfare so long waged, in detail, between them and the white settlers, or rather, I should say, the bushrangers and convict shepherds."[180] But the colonial state had presided over the toll. As Lyndall Ryan has pointed out, "No European was ever charged . . . for assaulting or killing an Aboriginal" in colonial Tasmania. Arthur later observed that "all aggression originated with the white inhabitants."[181] The ethnic cleansing policy he settled upon as a solution to the war and to save the Aborigines had perhaps hastened their demise, even as it made the state the lead actor in the tragedy.

On Flinders Island, Hannibal died in the mid-1840s, aged 39. His wife, Tinedeburric, had succumbed at 37, apparently childless. Only 57 Tasmanian Aborigines survived Hannibal, and the group dwindled to just 14 people in 1859, from an estimated population of 4,000 six decades earlier.[182] Walter George Arthur drowned in 1861, aged 41.

Some leading colonists saw the tragedy as justification for their actions. An official wrote in 1859 that "the race is fast falling away and its utter extinction will be hardly regretted."[183] That year the *Launceston Examiner* marveled "that such a revolution could have taken place in such a short period of time—the home of the blackman thus to be broken up—the waddy and the spear to give way that the Teutonic race may bring the plough and reaping machine into operation."[184] This account gave no inkling of settler violence; rather the Aboriginal home, waddy, and spear all "gave way." It failed to specify the fate of the people themselves, and the role of the settlers' stock in displacing the Aborigines' game. Myths of race and of cultivation had triumphed in tandem.

Land and Race, 1835–1900

The agrarian ideal still infused Aboriginal policy on the mainland. NSW governor Richard Bourke instructed the commandant of the new Port Phillip District in 1836 to conciliate local Aborigines "by kind treatment" and "endeavour to establish them in a village and to induce them to offer their labour in return for food and clothing." An immediate census was ordered to count "every person then residing in the District, specially noting those who have occupied any portion of the land by erecting a hut or grazing cattle or sheep."[185] Aborigines, however, were not counted.

Prevalent colonial thinking eulogized "hardy pioneers" of the "Anglo-Saxon race," yet some contested the view that blacks were incapable of settling on the land. In 1835, Judge W. W. Burton of the NSW Supreme Court hoped to rectify what he called the "great national injustice" that denied Aborigines "resting places upon their native soil." He urged Port Phillip authorities to "get these wanderers to settle" by "gathering their tribes 'into one' . . . [on] land reserved for black villages" and encouraging them to fish and work for "the security of civilized life." Following England's Irish model, the Presbyterian minister John Dunmore Lang also proposed to plant in NSW "a reputable tenantry" of Scots dispossessed by the Highland clearances. As Don Watson put it, "the minds of the pioneers were full of dreams of cow yards and cream cans and paddocks full of rustling maize."[186] The official cultivation ideal not only presumed to bring civilization to Aborigines but also appealed to the yearnings of landless Scots and English.

Occasionally the notion surfaced that Aborigines who failed to till the soil could legitimately be killed. Such thinking increasingly combined scientific determinism with concepts of race, property, and religion. Referring to the animal world, Charles Lyell wrote in *Principles of Geology* (1833): "[I]f we wield the sword of extermination as we advance, we have no reason to repine at the havoc committed . . . in thus obtaining possession of the earth by conquest." Rather, "[e]very species which has spread itself" had caused "the diminution, or the entire extirpation" of another. Like the lion in Africa, Lyell wrote, each had "slaughtered their thousands."[187] Taking up the analogy of wild beasts, the *Sydney Herald* claimed in 1838 that Aborigines had "bestowed no labour upon the land—their ownership, their right, was nothing more than that of the Emu or the Kangaroo." Only labor "upon the land" could give "a right of property to it." The editor asked, "[W]ho will assert that this great continent was ever intended by the Creator to remain an unproductive wilderness?" The British people had taken possession of it "under the Divine Authority, by which man was commanded to go forth and people, and *till* the land."[188] This same editorial opposed prosecuting the killers of 28 Aborigines in the Myall Creek massacre earlier that year. In 1842, the *Port Phillip Herald,* conceding that "the Aborigines may be the legitimate proprietors of the soil," still insisted that "it cannot be improper ... to reclaim their grounds from a useless waste to a state of fertility, giving employment to the idle, food to the hungry, and quick sure return to the adventurist capitalist."[189]

Established law legitimized colonial land-grabbing. Sir William Blackstone explained in 1844 in his *Commentaries on the Laws of England* that "[p]lantations or colonies" included distant countries where "lands are claimed by right of occupancy only, by finding them desert and uncultivated." A colonist in Queensland asserted a decade later that "this fine country never was intended only to be occupied by a nomad race who made no use of it," merely "going from place to place and living only on the wild animals and small roots of the earth and never in any way cultivating one single inch of ground."[190] This view prevailed, even though that very ground decisively favored pastoral over agricultural pursuits.

The dominant ideology also overruled dissident views, like those of explorers. An American, for instance, praised Aborigines in 1840: "I have sometimes doubted whether any different branch of the human family could have maintained its existence on the slender natural resources of interior Australia."[191] And Major Thomas Mitchell, having discovered lands "more extensive than Great Britain and equally rich in soil," explained in 1848 that "the native" seasonally fired grasslands and forests "in order that a young green crop might subsequently spring up, and so attract and enable him to kill or take the kangaroo with nets."[192] New shoots sprouting in the ashes not only attracted game but, Mitchell noted, created "the open forest in which the white men now find grass for their cattle, to the exclusion of the kangaroo." Later, with pastoral expansion and the end of what Aborigines called "care for the land," dense brush would replace these open woodlands in western Victoria, the Northern Territory, and the Australian Alps.[193]

The colonists brought a different farming culture. In 1844, Sydney's *Colonial Literary Journal* reprinted Edmund Spenser's poem "Trees" with a biographical sketch noting his "moral design" and genius. A local contributor to the same issue echoed a Spenserian argument about the Irish, stating that "the Aborigines have continued always at the same point in civilization, and have not been able to cultivate and enlarge those faculties which have been bestowed upon them." They were "purely the children of Nature," accounting for "the barbarism of a race which has had but scarcely any time to make improvements."[194] This colonist wrote under the pseudonym "Aeneas," recalling the classical origin of the term *Aborigines* and prefiguring by a decade the Australian-born poet Henry Kendall, whose Sydney was "this Troy," and Melbourne "a dream of Athens, or of Rome."[195]

"Aeneas" also fostered a new racial science in Australia. In 1844, he explained phrenology to colonial NSW readers, in 14 weekly articles in the *Colonial Literary Journal's* first months of publication. "The Irish character and formation of head," wrote Aeneas, resembled those of the French. "The violent extremes of character in the Irish are well known." Worse, "blinded and misguided by its priesthood and political agitators . . . the Irish nation . . . is now one of the least" of the nations.[196] As for Aborigines, their "great preponderancy of brain, . . . as in all savage nations, lies in the posterior parts of the head—the seat of the passions, and inferior sentiments; the moral and intellectual portions, with few exceptions, are very deficient."[197] Lack of "constructive ingenuity," Aeneas went on, explained "their inferiority as a people, and their degraded character (more so than is just)." Also the "inactivity and sluggishness, for which they are noted—being roused from their slothful torpor only by the trumpet-voice of passion, or the cravings of continued hunger."[198]

Nineteenth-century race thinking combined agrarian ideology with classical allusion. The modern Aeneas, aptly enough, noted the Aborigine's "love of roaming," admiring his ability to navigate "localities to which he is a partial and even entire stranger." Pastoral romanticism projected onto Aborigines even a Homeric imperative, "to chase the nimble-footed kangaroo over the flower-enamelled plains." Arcadian romps of "constant exercise," and "aversion to any fixed place of residence," propelled them on "periodical migrations." These "original natives of the soil" failed to settle even "where their wants were supplied." Lacking the sedentary longevity of European civilization, their "most energetic effort" resembled, ominously, "the short-lived, momentary flicker of an expiring taper."[199]

Classical pastoralism packed cultural power. A Scottish namesake, Aeneas Ranaldson McDonnell, 16th of Glengarry, landed on the Victorian coast in 1841 with a party of Highlanders. He then left, like his ancient antecedent, for greener pastures.[200] Other Scots kept coming, and Virgil, too, took root in NSW, in a climate favoring both cultivation and stock raising. A second Sydney contributor to the *Colonial Literary Journal* quoted Virgil: "I sang flocks, tillage, heroes." This writer praised the poet's "precepts on husbandry which even yet are applicable, not only to his own, but even to other climes, and perhaps have been followed too closely in some matters by European farmers."[201] For NSW readers he translated Virgil's instructions on planting vineyards and "useful hints to the agriculturalist." He recommended to "the practical farmer" Virgil's "judicious" advice: "Prudently praise large farms, but cultivate small ones."[202] The cult of the yeoman flourished even as shepherds, not cultivators, occupied the NSW countryside. Ironically, it was pastoralists who drove Aborigines from Arcadia. Epic yeomen displaced them only in literary pages.

These authors found justification in the American experience for eliminating Aborigines. Aeneas discussed the "craniological development" of the North American Indians, in whom he found "[d]estructiveness" to be "most eminent." He then added: "When the Spaniards discovered America, they found that portion of the West Indian Isles which lies in the Carribean sea, inhabited by a race of men called Charibs, one of the most ferocious and blood-thirsty nations that ever existed. In their sanguinary and destructive propensities, they only out-did the Spaniards themselves; and so brutish and untameable were their dispositions, that a war of extermination was the only method that could be adopted by their invaders."[203]

As Virgil had done, now "Aeneas" accepted the inevitable tragedy of genocide, though he did not advocate it. Unlike Spenser, he proposed "leniency" toward the indigenous people among whom he settled. He was "very far from feeling inclined to agree in toto" with those colonists who harbored "severe animadversions" toward Aborigines. Aeneas countered that, though mentally inferior, "the New Hollander is yet capable of improvement." So their self-proclaimed superiors should now "stretch their hand" to "the neglected Aborigines of the soil" and provide "enlightenment to their benighted and savage brethren." Aeneas condemned what he called the "indifference of the colonists to the weal of the Aborigines," to the "eternal disgrace of the Australian public."[204]

Yet even Aeneas ventured that "the most barbarous and uncivilized people ever known" could "far surpass" the Aborigines in ingenuity, and even he found Spain's earlier "war of extermination" to be "the only method that could be adopted."[205] Perhaps it was not surprising that other NSW settlers were using the term *extermination* specifically for Aborigines. Three years later, for example, author J. R. McCullough echoed geologist Charles Lyell on the inevitability of "extermination" when he compared Aborigines' fate to the "drainage of marshes" or "the disappearance of wild animals."[206]

In Australia, as earlier in America, models of ancient conquest and agrarian cultivation justified territorial expansion, racism, and, in some situations, extermination or genocidal acts. This ideological amalgam had a long heritage. It did not stem simply from colonial reality or frontier violence. As in Ireland and America, its power remained unchallenged by knowledge of the sophistication of indigenous land use, or in Australia, even by most settlers' own decided preference for pastoralism over agriculture. As late as the twentieth century, indigenous farmers who proved capable agricultural competitors were still driven off their farms to make way for white settlers.[207]

In the 1830s, the British government began assisting large-scale immigration to NSW, and the pastoral frontier pushed rapidly west. From 1837 to 1840, 25,000 new immigrants reached NSW; 62,000 followed in the next decade.[208] By 1852, Britain had also transported a total of 146,000 convicts to New South Wales and Tasmania.[209] The white population of all the Australian colonies now exceeded 400,000. By 1860, after a decade of gold rushes, it reached 1.1 million, while Aboriginal numbers are estimated to have fallen to 180,000 from a 1788 population of over 500,000.[210]

Population growth and agrarian ideology soon drove new colonial policies to "unlock the land" from extensive pastoral runs already occupied by "squatters." The idea was, as historian Richard Waterhouse puts it, to promote "small-scale agricultural production as morally virtuous and conducive to a stable and democratic society." A more successful program of "closer settlement" began in the 1880s, as the government bought up large properties for subdivision and sale to farmers. In the 1890s, the nationalist *Bulletin* magazine lauded these "selectors" as "the backbone of the nation, credited with turning waste country into farmland." The small cultivator represented the march of civilization, "the cultural superiority of a rural society characterized by a farming yeomanry." The ideology of "the Bush" as "a superior physical and moral environment" only intensified with the growth of the large Australian cities, especially Sydney and Melbourne, which the *Bulletin* derided for their "overcrowding, poverty, vice, disease and materialism."[211] What Waterhouse calls an Australian "consensus about the value and viability of a yeoman class" persisted long after 1900. Only then did the idealized vision of farming increasingly give way to seeing the land as "another business, nothing more."[212] Looking back in 1911 on the country's short history, historian James Collier propounded this view: "The only right is that of superiority of race ... the only real wrong on the part of the blacks is their all-round inferiority and their inability to till the ground or even make use of its natural pastures."[213]

Escalating Massacres in New South Wales, 1835–45

"The obliteration of the Tasmanians," Charles Rowley wrote, "appears spectacular partly because it is comparatively easy to think of them as a separate people. But whole populations on the mainland, of comparable size, were also disappearing."[214]

In cases of conflict, since 1825 Aborigines had lacked protections afforded British subjects, yet an opponent of that policy, Mr. Justice Burton of the NSW Supreme Court, ruled in 1836 that they were *not* "entitled to be recognized, as so many sovereign states, governed by laws of their own."[215] In this legal limbo, Aborigines enjoyed neither domestic protection nor alien sovereignty.

Conflicting messages came from London. The House of Commons Select Committee on Aborigines concluded in 1837 that "many deeds of murder and violence have undoubtedly been committed by the stock-keepers" and settlers. It also noted what Governor Arthur in Tasmania declined to acknowledge: "[M]any natives have perished by the various military parties sent against them." The committee concluded that "if we are ever to make atonement to the remnant of this people, it will require no slight attention, and no ordinary sacrifices on our part to compensate for the evil association which we have inflicted."[216] The secretary of state for the colonies now instructed NSW governor Bourke that "all natives must be considered as subjects of the Queen.... To regard them as aliens, with whom a war can exist, and against whom Her Majesty's troops may exercise belligerent rights, is to deny that protection to which they derive the highest possible claim."[217] The British government also appointed a chief protector and four assistant protectors of the Aborigines of NSW's newly settled Port Phillip District.[218]

Yet London often preferred to deny (rather than end) the colonial administration's role in the Aboriginal tragedy. Some in Britain blamed the "conflicts with the natives" merely on "aggression committed on the natives by the stockkeepers and inferior agents of the colonists"—ignoring aggression by the colonial state.[219] The record points to both. And when the state was not directly implicated in murders by settlers, it implicitly aided them by withholding both prosecution and preparedness to accept testimony from Aboriginal witnesses in court. Among the killers' many motives, officialdom rarely condoned settler racism, but it did reflect widespread sympathy for land hunger, desperate defense of stock, and the powerful agrarian imagination. A German settler in NSW, who claimed to have killed 30 Aborigines, told a missionary arriving in Sydney in 1837 that blacks were "less than human" and "fit only to be murdered and used as fertilizer."[220] Historian Robert Reece cites "the determined efforts of stockmen in northern NSW during the late 1830s to 'get rid' of all the Aborigines in their area." By November 1837, at least two major massacres had occurred there, the first of which may have taken up to 200 Aboriginal lives.[221]

Such colonists killed Aborigines in both quasi-governmental and private capacities. The year 1838 saw three more mass killings in north-central NSW. Troops acting as volunteer mounted police, under the command of Major James Nunn, massacred at least 60 Aborigines in late January. The killers were not tried.[222] Even government policy went unstated. Fearing "considerable sensation in the Colony," Governor George Gipps held back a previously prepared public statement that Aborigines "have an acknowledged right to the protection of the Government."[223] Six weeks later, whites conducted the "routine slaughter of 28 men, women and children" at Myall Creek station.[224] The station overseer explained that "success having attended the first two massacres, the murderers grew bold; and in order that their cattle might never more be 'rushed' it was resolved to exterminate the whole race of blacks in that quarter."[225] In a second mid-1838 incident in northern NSW, colonists massacred another 22 Aborigines.[226] Still Gipps withheld the official statement of his resolve to protect them.

Gipps had 12 men tried for the Myall Creek massacre; they were acquitted. A juror called blacks "a set of monkies and the earlier they are exterminated from the face of the earth the better." In a retrial, seven convict defendants were convicted and hanged in December 1838.[227] However, Assistant Protector of

Aborigines William Thomas noted that some settlers now became "more in-tent than ever on destroying the blacks" and put aside guns for a less detectable weapon. Thomas believed they now poisoned many Aborigines.[228]

If some settlers were bent on killing Aborigines in secret, the mounted police presented another problem for the authorities. As Gipps wrote in a con-fidential dispatch to London in April 1838, they were "all volunteers from regi-ments of the line ... and at liberty to resign their police duties, and return to their regiments when they please." Therefore, Gipps said, "much management is required" in order to prevent "any offence ... to the officers and men," which the NSW Executive Council feared might lead to "mischief" and mass resigna-tions.[229] A London official, by contrast, laconically deplored the "much blood-shed on either side," with consequences "alike clear and irremediable," and re-signedly doubted any possibility of discovering how "the extermination of the black race, can long be averted."[230]

Only in May 1839 did Gipps publish his declaration promising Aborigines equal protection. Then in August he issued another public notice prohibiting any supply of guns to Aborigines. A year later, after several attacks on whites in the new Port Phillip District to the south, Gipps introduced a new bill to out-law Aboriginal possession of firearms without a magistrate's permission. The NSW Executive Council passed the law, but a year later London disallowed it, on the grounds that "it would establish a wide and unfair distinction" between blacks and whites. In the interim the government disarmed those Aborigines who had guns.[231]

Most Aborigines never obtained firearms and remained vulnerable to slaughter by armed patrols. In 1841, after an initial clash causing "death on both sides," police came upon "great numbers" of Aborigines on the Orara River in northern NSW. A witness reported: "A cordon was formed, ... the camp was rushed and men, women and children were shot down indiscriminately. Some took to the river, and were shot as they swam." A second "river bank mas-sacre" quickly followed. In both cases, police had falsely blamed the Aborigines for crimes committed by whites. Now a wave of Aboriginal attacks struck the frontier and sparked white fears of a native "rising."[232]

Southwest of Bathurst, the second Wiradjuri war broke out. In 1832, Nar-rungdera clansmen had hospitably received settlers in their region, but a smallpox epidemic then killed half the clan, and by 1838, local whites "in their spare time went searching for Aborigines to shoot." An explorer arrived that December, after one such attack, to find "the Storekeepers were in the habit of occasionally making raids against them." As in Tasmania, Europeans assigned black leaders the names of Britain's vanquished enemies, such as "Boney," or classical leaders of the colonized, like "Brian Boru."[233]

The Narrungdera retaliated, killing a first white victim in January 1839. By mid-February, a traveler wrote of "regular guerrilla warfare." One settler sighted "150 armed Aborigines in solemn line." In the first half of the year, warriors killed or scattered 2,000 cattle and drove settlers from a 60-mile front on the Murrumbidgee River. The local commissioner of crown lands brought in mounted police, reporting the settlers to be "in a Great state of alarm." In his assessment, their establishment of stock stations on Aboriginal hunting grounds had provoked the conflict. Two years of a seemingly "perpetual state of warfare" ensued, with "death on either side being not uncommon." In May 1840, posses of settlers surrounded over 60 Wiradjuri men, women, and children on what is now called Murdering Island "and shot them down." According to local tradition, "only one man survived, by hiding in reeds." From Bathurst, where missionaries had taken over the failed Wellington Valley Agricultural Station, Rev. James Gunther reported in 1841 "that extermination by violence occurred more often than was commonly known." New killings were reported near Mudgee and Rylestone. In 1841, the second Wiradjuri war ended, like the first, "with the pastoralists in control."[234]

London refused to accord priority to preventing more violence. After Myall Creek, Gipps and the NSW Legislative Council tried to repeal the ban on Aboriginal court testimony. But London overruled the new law on the grounds that heathen testimony would flout "the principles of British Jurisprudence." When London changed its mind in 1843, it was the turn of the legislative council to reject the act. In Rowley's words, "when prosecution did occur, the penalty for homicide was inflicted almost exclusively on the Aboriginal offender."[235] A writer in the *New South Wales Magazine* in 1843 called for "rendering the current of events by which the grave is closing on our sable brethren, smooth and regular."[236] A British visitor wrote that whenever Aborigines "attempted resistance or retaliation, the fire-arms of the whites swept them off by hundreds."[237] A local historian estimated that in the period 1835–60, settlers killed possibly one-third of the approximately 3,000 Aborigines of the Three Rivers region of northern NSW.[238] Only in 1876 were Aborigines allowed to testify in NSW courts.[239]

Other racialist features of the colonial system also facilitated genocidal massacres. By 1856, Rowley writes, it was "standard procedure" to punish Aborigines collectively for crimes committed by members of their ethnic group. "It was usual to talk of guilty 'tribes' or 'mobs'; and the assumption of guilt by association led to massacres of whole groups in the isolation of the scrub." The Select Committee of the NSW Legislative Assembly on the Native Police Force accepted the "necessity of making war on" Aborigines, and significantly, Rowley noted, it showed "no consideration of the legal and other issues involved in the method of group punishments of British subjects."[240] In this way whites killed many Aborigines because of their membership of an ethnic or racial group.

Frontier Victoria, 1834–50

Settlers sailed in 1834 from Van Diemen's Land to NSW's Port Phillip District, later the colony of Victoria. The district's Aboriginal population in 1834 has been estimated at 5,000–10,000. Only 806 Aborigines survived in Victoria in 1886.[241] The colonist E. M. Curr estimated that 15 to 25 percent of the Aborigines, perhaps 2,000, had "died by the rifle."[242] Whites poisoned a much smaller number, mostly in 1839–49. Historian Richard Broome suggests a lower total of around 1,000 blacks killed by whites.[243]

For their part, Aborigines killed 59 Europeans in 40 attacks, all before 1850. Killings marked a minority of the 110 Aboriginal raids in that period. Most were thefts, provoked by hunger. In 1839, Moonin Moonin of the Ngurelban tribe complained that "Jumbuck and Bulgana" (sheep and cattle) were eating and destroying Aboriginal game pastures and staples like yams and *mirrn'yong* roots: "[T]oo many Jumbuck and Bulgana plenty eat it murnong—all gone murnong."[244] Four years later, an Aborigine named Yagan told Victoria's advocate general: "Why do you white people come in ships to our country and shoot down poor blackfellows who do not understand you—You listen to me! The wild blackfellows do not understand your laws, every living animal that roams the country, and every edible fruit that grows in the ground are common property.... For every black man you fellows shoot, I will kill a white man!"[245] Violence aside, historian Beverley Nance notes that introduced diseases alone "may have reduced the Aboriginal population by forty or fifty percent" before 1850.[246] By then, M. F. Christie writes, "Aboriginal resistance had been broken in almost all areas of Victoria."[247]

In contrast to the first decades of the NSW colony, mass killings of Aborigines began early in Victoria's settlement. Whalers, not settlers, may have

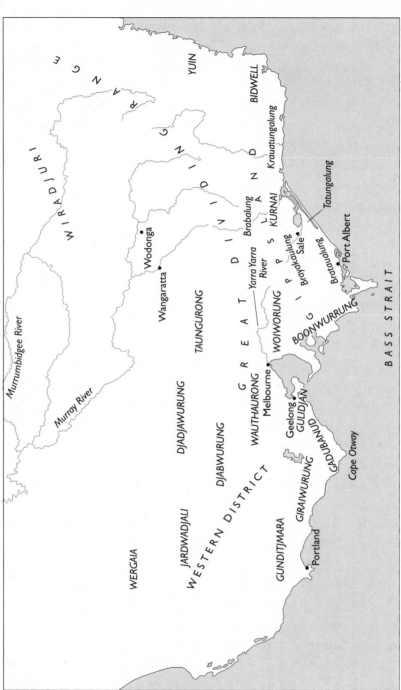

MAP 13. Port Phillip District (early colonial Victoria), with locations of major Aboriginal groups, including the five Kurnai clans. Based on Australian Institute of Aboriginal and Torres Strait Islander Studies, *Aboriginal Australia* (Canberra, 1996), and A. W. Howitt, *The Native Tribes of South-East Australia* (London, 1904; Canberra, 2001), 828–29. See also figs. 12–14.

perpetrated an initial massacre in 1833 or 1834, but the evidence is inconclusive. Possibly 30 Aborigines might have been killed in fighting over a beached whale near what became, in late 1834, the first settlement at Portland; of the local Kilcarer clan, two youths survived in 1841.[248] John Batman, whom Governor Arthur blamed for "much slaughter" in Tasmania, crossed Bass Strait to found a town at Melbourne in May 1835.[249] Along with other participants in the Van Diemen's Land catastrophe, Batman was followed to Victoria by George Augustus Robinson, who became the new Protector of Aborigines at Port Phillip in 1839, bringing with him 22 of the surviving Tasmanian Aborigines.

Batman's company drew up a treaty and tried to buy 600,000 acres of land from Melbourne Aborigines in exchange for tomahawks, mirrors, and other goods (see fig. 12). The company described its mission as "calculated to ensure the comfort and well-being of the natives." NSW governor Bourke proclaimed the area crown land, and London repudiated Batman's treaty on grounds that Aborigines had no legal authority to sell land. But Bourke advised recognizing the settlement and using official recognition to limit uncontrolled occupation from Tasmania and NSW. After a rival group of 200 settlers from Van Diemen's Land brought in 25,000 sheep, the government recognized the Port Phillip settlement in September 1836.[250] Meanwhile, Bourke promised in May that "all persons who may be guilty of any outrage against the Aboriginal natives" would be "brought to trial before the Supreme Court."[251] But in July a Sydney official warned the colonial secretary of a possible "war of extermination at Port Phillip."[252]

As violence flared, justice foundered. During 1836, whalers and sealers committed more "outrages" against black women and children, and Aborigines stealing flour murdered four Europeans.[253] One of the white victims, Charles Franks, had reportedly suffered "considerable loss" at Aboriginal hands in Tasmania and had maintained in Victoria "great aversion to the native blacks, and would not give them food."[254] A leading settler wrote after his murder: "Several parties are now out after the natives and I have no doubt many will be shot and a stop will be put to this system of killing for bread."[255] The next day, a posse of settlers, including John Batman's brother Henry, tracked down a group of 70–100 Aboriginal men, women, and children. A Tasmanian newspaper reported: "The avenging party fell upon the guilty tribe about daylight in the morning, having watched them the previous night, and putting into effect a preconcerted plan of attack, succeeded in annihilating them."[256] News of this "rencontre" also reached officials in Tasmania, who reported "upon respectable authority" to Sydney: "It is not stated however what resistance the natives made, but none of the opposing party were injured, although it is feared that there can be little or no doubt that ten of the tribe of Port Phillip natives were killed."[257] In Van Diemen's Land, Governor Arthur had questioned the leading Port Phillip settler, James Simpson, on a visit to Tasmania after the clash. Simpson, the same former police magistrate of Campbelltown to whom John Batman had lied to conceal his murder of two Tasmanian Aborigines in 1829, now reported back to Melbourne on an emerging cover-up of these recent shootings involving Batman's brother Henry. Simpson wrote that Arthur "was much pleased that I had expressed my opinions to the mode of retaliation on the Blks [blacks]: wished that I had acted with *more* determination in the matter—but altogether disagreed with me in the cautious course I adopted of not making myself acquainted with the extent of the punishment inflicted."[258] The figure of 10 killed could have been a discreet minimum.

Now a second Tasmanian newspaper claimed that only five Aborigines had been killed or seriously wounded.[259] A month later, in a carefully worded order, the colonial secretary one-sidedly prejudged both crime and guilt. He set up a two-part inquiry: first, "into all the circumstances attending the murder of Mr. Franks . . . by the natives," presenting it as a crime and Aboriginal guilt as a fact. Then, far more ambiguously but foreshadowing justification and exoneration of the settlers, another inquiry would follow into "the subsequent proceedings of the Europeans in retaliation of that outrage, ascertaining (if it be practicable) whether, as is alleged, any of the blacks were killed or wounded by those Europeans, or by the blacks of any other tribes."[260] The inquiry duly took depositions from members of the posse, including Henry Batman, who denied knowledge of any Aboriginal deaths. It found that "the account circulated in Sydney must have been very much exaggerated."[261] Henry Batman soon became Melbourne's chief constable.[262]

The legal system repeatedly failed to secure justice for Aborigines. In the same month, for instance, prosecutors charged a convict with the murder of an Aborigine and subpoenaed three whites as witnesses, including one suspected of having "given some encouragement to the prisoner to commit the murder." The witnesses sailed to Tasmania, none appeared at the trial, and the defendant was therefore acquitted. In 1837, the police magistrate at Geelong accepted the settler Charles Swanston's illegal attempt to prohibit "black or white men" from entering a huge area. After Aboriginal hunting threatened sheep there, the magistrate reported: "I saw some four natives that had been shot dead. I investigated the affray and gave much credit to the men for their good conduct."[263]

From 1837 to 1841, the white population of the Port Phillip District soared from 1,000 to 20,000. Aborigines protested that whites were taking over their land. A missionary reported of Port Phillip Aborigines in May 1839: "The Government is fast disposing of their lands . . . and no reserve whatever of land is made for the provision of the natives. . . . The result of which is that the natives who remain in the neighbourhood of the settled districts . . . after enduring incalculable deprivations, abuses, and miseries, will gradually pine—die away—and become extinct."[264] A group of Taoungurong (Goulburn) Aborigines heading for Melbourne complained that whites barring them from the town had failed to reciprocate Aboriginal openness: "Plenty White Man set down, Black Fellows no sulky, Plenty Black fellow set down & White man Sulky. No good that—Long time ago before White Man came Goldborn Black fellow sit down here." The next year, Melbourne Aborigines making for the town insisted that it was "no White Mans ground" but "Black Mans." Loddon or Jajowrong Aborigines likewise complained in 1840 of "the violent measures taken to exclude them from Melbourne" and of "the treatment they receive from many of the settlers." Four years later, one added: "[P]oor blackfellows White man take Blackfellows country and frighten him too." Despite their complaints, however, neither Melbourne nor Loddon Aborigines killed whites.[265]

Attributing four murders to the Taoungurong, Major Lettsom brought in military forces. On October 11, 1840, the soldiers raided and surrounded a camp of 400 Aborigines, mostly Taoungurong, but including some Yarra and Port Phillip blacks. They drove them all, including many women and children, on a forced march to Melbourne and shot two of the men. The assistant protector to the Loddon Aborigines, E. S. Parker, found "3 or 400 men women and children, incarcerated in the stockade yard." Jajowrong onlookers asked him, "Why had they been driven like sheep to that place? *Were they going to be shot?*—to be sent in a big ship to Sydney," and other questions. Several white "respectable inhabitants of the town" also took the side of the Aborigines, "who were receiving very cruel treatment from police and soldiery." The authorities seized all the captives' belongings, detained 31 Goulburn men, and subsequently convicted nine. The others were released, and 124 went to a reserve, "cow'd in spirits." One, Billy Hamilton, remarked: "Poor Blackfellow me now, no like long time ago before white Man come here, No Tomahawk, No Spear me now, Plenty hungry poor Blackfellows now."[266]

Exacerbated by killings, incarceration, the impact of diseases, and mistreatment of black women by white men, tension escalated within Aboriginal society. Rowley wrote that "revenge killings probably increased greatly with access to firearms." Aborigines often saw whites as "outside the inter-tribal feuding"; some attributed killings by whites to their manipulation by hostile tribes. In Aboriginal belief, deaths could not be accidental but resulted from the sorcery of other Aborigines and had to be avenged "as a necessary service to the dead." By 1850, Victorian Aborigines had killed 59 whites but possibly 200 other Aborigines, including perhaps 100 killed in an 1834 massacre.[267]

Many factors devastated Victoria's Aboriginal population. A missionary wrote from Geelong in 1840 that "the number of natives in this district is rapidly decreasing," by "at least ten percent" in a year. Some had died naturally, others from introduced venereal diseases, "and a few have died in war."[268] Venereal disease spread fast, reduced the birthrate, and raised infant mortality. Assistant Protector Parker reported just five syphilis cases among the 170 Loddon Aborigines in 1840, but 10 months later, it afflicted 90 percent of the women. Aboriginal infanticide also took a toll. The Geelong missionary knew of no more "than two children under 12 months of age in the three tribes . . . there have been births, but the children were half-caste and have therefore been destroyed."[269] Out of despair, some Aborigines also killed full-blooded children. In 1843, a headman named Billibellary reported that among the Yarra people, "the Black Lubras [women] say now no good Children, Blackfellow say No Country Now for them, very good we kill & no more come up Pickaniny." By 1844, Melbourne's assistant protector reported such infanticide "awfully on the increase." Parents saw no future for their children: "No good pickaninnys now no country."[270] Whites killed no Melbourne Aborigines, but their numbers fell by half from 1838 to 1850.[271]

Settler violence proliferated in parts of central, eastern, and western Victoria. Genocidal massacres resulted from the violent imposition of collective ethnic responsibility. As in NSW, an aboriginal protector in Port Phillip in 1840 reported that reprisals against blacks were "conducted on the principle that when an offence is committed by unknown individuals, the tribe to which they belong be made to suffer."[272] A Taoungurong tribesman lamented that year: "Blackfellow by and by all gone, plenty shoot'em white fellow long time, plenty plenty." In 1847, a settler near the Murray reported that "nearly all the tribes in this district are dead."[273] Six years later, a leading Wangaratta settler explained to Governor Latrobe: "People formed themselves into bands of alliance and allegiance to each other, and it was then the destruction of the natives really did take place."[274] Nance estimates that the Victorian Native Police alone, mostly under the command of Captain Henry Dana, killed 125 Aborigines from 1835 to 1850.[275]

Pastoral Visions and Violence in Gippsland

During the 1830s, the NSW Presbyterian minister J. D. Lang convinced 4,000 Highlanders to leave Scotland for Australia. Farquhar MacKenzie reached eastern Victoria in 1837, and found "the Australian savage" to be not only "the lowest in the scale of civilization" but also "the freest of mankind . . . not annoyed by failures in his crops or flocks and herds, [with] no rents to pay or fears of eviction."[276] Yet no pastoral romance could protect the Kurnai people of Gippsland. Diseases and a series of massacres followed by starvation reduced over 2,000 Kurnai to only 126 survivors by 1851.[277]

Jacky, an orphaned black from the Yarra mission, claimed that he had seen Captain Henry Dana's brother William, commander of the native police in eastern Victoria, and that William Dana had killed men, women, and children: "[D]own in Gippsland, shoot him black fellar plenty! . . . Captain Danna come down with him black police; they shoot him black fellar there, black lubra there, black picaninni there," Jacky gesticulated in different directions: "shoot him pla-a-anty!"[278] In Melbourne in mid-1845, Dana was convicted of unprovoked assault and fined £5—for a mounted attack on a squatter whom he lashed with a whip in the street. Dana then resumed command of the native police in Gippsland.[279]

Settlers' pastoral ambitions provoked massacres of Aborigines to stop them spearing stock. A leading perpetrator in Gippsland was the prominent Scottish cattle grazier Angus McMillan. He was the son of a Presbyterian lay missionary and gentleman farmer who had introduced improved sheep breeds to Skye, then joined a Protestant group that supervised farming on the Scottish Catholic island of Barra. Young Angus left Barra in 1837 and found the Reverend J. D. Lang in Glasgow, singing the praises of Scots Britons and urging listeners to make "the hills and vales of Australia resound with the wild note of the pibroch and the language of the ancient Gael." Along with many native Gaelic speakers, McMillan embarked, carrying a copy of Lang's *History of New South Wales*. Keeping a diary of "the long voyage of death," he wrote: "I have got my hand to the plough, I must not look back."[280] McMillan carried a letter of introduction to Captain Lachlan Macalister, son of a Skye landlord, who hired him as an overseer in NSW before both men crossed into eastern Victoria.[281]

Lang estimated the Aboriginal population of Gippsland, mostly members of the Kurnai, at 2,700 in 1835. Local historian Peter D. Gardner describes the five Kurnai groups as "completely isolated," surrounded by "rugged mountains to the north, east and west, and by the ocean to the south. They had little contact with neighbouring tribes."[282] Afraid of the sea, they called it "the back of the world" (nark-abun-dhu). Even other Aborigines knew little of the Kurnai, whom they called Warrigals, or "wild" blacks. Gippsland's crown land commissioner, C. J. Tyers, who arrived in 1844, wrote the next year: "Their isolated position is such that their fierce and predatory habits have received no check by the partial civilization of the tribes [of other regions], nor has anyone from those tribes been found . . . who could understand their language—From this circumstance the Chief Protector [George A. Robinson] on his visit to Gipps Land last year was unsuccessful in his attempts to communicate with them."[283] Though by 1840 one Aboriginal group near Melbourne could mimic a "perfect brogue," singing "Hura my boys, it's time for us to go bonny highland laddie," Tyers informed Melbourne as late as March 1846 that "we had no means of communicating with Gippsland blacks until now."[284]

Angus McMillan made two expeditions into east Gippsland in 1839 and set up a grazing run for Macalister. Moving west the next year, McMillan quickly clashed with Kurnai clans, pushing on to the Avon River in October 1840. In a "first attack" that month, Aborigines killed some of his cattle, provoking a pattern of violence. According to one account, McMillan assembled a party of eight men "to teach the blacks a lesson. There was a desperate fight but history is silent as to the casualties amongst the natives."[285] Silence enveloped the Aboriginal toll in later incidents, too.

McMillan established a new stock run of 16,000 acres, "Bushy Park." The Macalister family selected 60,000 acres nearby. According to McMillan's diary for 1840: "On the 22nd December the blacks attacked us." Five of his men opened fire before the Aboriginal leader could throw the first spear. "The blacks were in hundreds, but seeing their leader killed, they bolted in confusion."[286] A local historian wrote that Aborigines speared more cattle the next year, and McMillan retaliated with a "massacre" carried out "with the ruthlessness of settlers who have no public opinion to fear."[287] Another source says "a heavy toll, was, I believe, taken of the blacks." The year 1841 saw the Kurnai's first murder of a settler, one of McMillan's stockmen, and more retaliatory kill-ing.[288]

In early or mid-1843, Aboriginal Protector Robinson reported after touring Gippsland the next year, "some depraved white men had in a fit of drunken-ness, shot and killed some friendly natives."[289] Possibly in retaliation, Aborigi-nes murdered Lachlan Macalister's nephew Ronald that July. The *Port Phillip Herald* reported: "This makes five persons murdered within little more than twelve months."[290] Angus McMillan immediately organized a local "highland brigade," which set out on a punitive expedition. Trapping members of the Yau-ung group of the Brataualung clan around a waterhole at Warrigal Creek, the settlers killed possibly 50 or more people on the spot.[291] There is no contem-porary evidence for that figure, but in a book published 50 years later, George Dunderdale, Gippsland's former clerk of courts, explained the massacre: "It was of course, impossible to identify any blackfellow concerned in the outrage and therefore atonement must be made by the tribe." Those shot, he went on, were thrown into the waterhole, "to the number it was said of about sixty men, women and children; but this was probably an exaggeration."[292] Another local man, William Hoddinott, who was born on the run next to Warrigal Creek, knew two youths who escaped the massacre with wounds. He too wrote much later that the "highland brigade" had stormed the blacks' camp and "fired into them, killing a great number, some escaped into the scrub, others jumped into the waterhole, and as fast as they put their heads up for breath, they were shot until the water was red with blood." Settlers kept up the killing "as long as their ammunition lasted. . . . More than a hundred of the blacks were killed."[293]

The settler violence far exceeded the Aboriginal depredations before or afterward. When Crown Land Commissioner Tyers arrived in January the next year, he reported that Gippsland Aborigines had up to that point killed four white shepherds. Grazier Ronald Macalister was presumably a fifth victim; in May 1844, McMillan told Robinson that blacks had so far killed five whites in Gippsland. Two years later, Aborigines were spearing 150 cattle annually, ac-cording to Tyers.[294] But in a single hunt, whites slaughtered 940 kangaroos to protect their crops, grass, and cattle.[295]

Cattle losses provoked most of the white killings of the Kurnai. After blacks speared two cows, Tyers wrote, "Mr. McMillan and others pursued them and came up with them on the ranges. Blacks poised their spears—party fired—not known if any blacks were killed—number of natives said to be two hundred." Tyers mounted his own expedition against Kurnai in early 1844. Coming upon a group of Aborigines, his police disregarded orders "not to fire except in self-defence." Tyers reported: "[O]ne of the party fired and was followed by the whole." Again, he reported no casualties.[296] Clerk of Courts Dunderdale, who knew Tyers, described another incident in which native police accompanied Tyers to investigate cattle spearing. "The two black troopers discharged their carbines. The commissioner had seen nothing to shoot at, but his blacks soon showed him two of the natives a few yards in front, both mortally wounded. Mr Tyers sent a report of the affair to the Government, and that was the end of it."[297]

A letter Tyers wrote to Lachlan Macalister in late 1846 reinforces the conclusion that many Aborigines were killed for spearing cattle: "I am aware that you have been a great sufferer from their depredations but . . . the number of lives already sacrificed at the head of your run is sufficient proof that the wild blacks *do not* commit devastation with impunity. The severe lessons they have already been taught, having produced no good result, may almost lead to the inference that they will continue the practice of spearing cattle in spite of the consequences."[298]

Other Aborigines fell in battle against superior firepower. John Campbell, former storekeeper of the Gippsland Company, moved the company's brass cannon to his own station near Sale. When a group of Braiakaulung assembled nearby with spears and clubs, the Campbells fired it over their heads, as "they did not desire to kill if they could avoid it." They then "loaded the gun to the muzzle with nails, broken bottles and anything they could lay hands on and awaited the final charge of the enemy. As was expected the blacks in a large body and armed with their native weapons made a determined rush to force their way into the building . . . the gun was discharged right in amongst them . . . many of them were fatally wounded."[299]

In 1846, Henry Meyrick, a sheep farmer from Western Port, traveled overland to Gippsland, where he lived for a year before his death in 1847. Shocked by what he found, Meyrick wrote privately: "The blacks are very quiet here now, poor wretches. No wild beast of the forest was ever hunted down with such unsparing perseverance as they are." Settlers, he said, rode into Aborigines' camps and fired indiscriminately on them, "as is the custom whenever smoke is seen." Continued daily spearings of cattle, Meyrick thought, could justify shooting tribesmen, "but what they can urge in their excuse, who shoot the women and children, I cannot conceive," for indeed, "the men, women and children are shot whenever they can be met with." He added that "these things are kept very secret, as the penalty would certainly be hanging . . . if I could remedy these things, I would speak loudly though it cost me all I am worth in the world, but as I cannot, I will keep aloof and know nothing and say nothing." Meyrick concluded in 1846: "[I]t is impossible to say how many have been shot, but I am convinced that no less than four hundred and fifty have been murdered altogether."[300]

The full truth never emerged, and violence against Gippsland blacks continued. In late 1846 and 1847, Tyers later testified, "at least fifty were killed" during unsuccessful hunts for a supposedly captive "white woman."[301] A visitor reported in early 1847 that some settlers sought "nothing more or less than their extermination." Killings continued in smaller incidents.[302] According to the memoir of an east Gippsland pioneer: "The spearing of a cattle beast was taken by some settlers as a capital offence and on one well-known occasion when a beast was speared, the owner and a man went out to find the culprits, and finding two natives and their gins at a camp surprised and slaughtered the four. The owner afterwards said that he sank his tomahawk into the blackfellows back 'like into a fat pig.'" However, opinions had changed as more settlers arrived and blacks became fewer. "The majority of the early pioneers were noted for their humanity, and the above incident was looked upon by them as an act of ferocious brutality. There are no blacks living in eastern Victoria now."[303]

Looking back decades later, a local newspaper reported that "the wild blacks or warrigals as they were called, had been driven into the mountains where they were half starved and became walking skeletons."[304] The last of the Kurnai came out of the bush in 1854. Of more than 2,500 in the 1830s, Tyers counted 80 survivors in 1858 (see fig. 14).[305]

Victoria's Western District

Massacres and individual killings by settlers, along with other violence and hunger, took a deadly toll on the Aborigines of Victoria's Western District as well. During a six-month expedition through the district in 1841, accompanied by the Tasmanian Aborigine Pevay, Protector Robinson noted only one outbreak of venereal disease and a single case of pneumonia.[306] There were wider reasons for what he called "the decrease of the aboriginal population of the Western District . . . since its occupation by Europeans." Already by 1841, "[m]any tribes from various causes have become extinct." At Kilambete, for instance, "[t]he original occupants of the locality with one solitary exception are defunct." Robinson reported that the 300 Wodouros were declining, the people of the Mallone locality "becoming extinct," the Omebegorrrege of the Merri "now defunct," the Colorer Conedeets "greatly reduced," the Tapoc Conedeets "a mere remnant," and the Darkogang "nearly extinct." Only two Eurite men survived, and two Kilcarer.[307]

Settlers could kill Aborigines with impunity. Traversing the Wannon region in June 1841, Robinson met the remnants of the Darkogang people. When he asked where their country was, "they beat the ground and vociferated, 'Deen! Deen!' (here! here!), and then, in a dejected tone, bewailed the loss of their country." Robinson reported: "Disease and natural decay, feuds, snakes and white men have reduced their numbers. Passed the spot where a dire conflict between the Messrs. Whyte (settlers) and the aboriginal natives happened, on which occasion 17 of the latter were slain." The protector added: "I could but deplore the absence (in so short a time) of the original inhabitants. Sheep and cattle were there, but the natives and their favorite emus were gone; no numerous fires, as recorded by Sir Thomas Mitchell, were to be seen, not a solitary smoke was visible." Seven years later, a visitor to the Wannon found its remaining Aborigines "inert," some "almost dying with hunger."[308]

The Whyte brothers and their employees had massacred members of the Konongwootong tribe in March 1840. The brothers admitted killing 20–30 blacks, while an employee testified in a deposition "that between thirty and forty men, exclusive of women and children were shot dead, only one escaping out of the whole tribe." But the crown solicitor declined to order a trial, perversely disallowing these self-incriminating depositions on the grounds that they came from potential defendants, not impartial witnesses. In a further raid against Aborigines the next month, the Whytes again admitted "some of the natives must have been killed." Again, no trial resulted.[309] A participant in one of these massacres later published a newspaper account with extensive details, claiming, "I was one of them, shot sixty-nine in one afternoon."[310]

Robinson gathered reports of more killing in the Western District. Passing near Lake Terang, he wrote in 1841: "The Colijans and Jarcoorts have been greatly reduced.... This rapid decrease is attributable to several causes: disease and natural decay, unnatural causes, attacks from hostile tribes, and European assassination. Whole sections have been annihilated by contending tribes, and some, it is affirmed, by Europeans. A section of the Jarcoorts . . . have been totally destroyed by the latter." Only 58 survived. Escapees told Robinson that a Mr. Frederick Taylor "was prominent in the dire proceedings."[311]

The survivors' testimony was correct. Frederick Taylor had arrived in the Western District after working from 1837 for Charles Swanston, helping him exclude blacks from their hunting grounds south of Geelong. After Taylor became manager of the Glenormiston run, 35 to 40 blacks were shot dead there in early 1839. Taylor then left the area, fearing both revenge and prosecution.[312] His overseer asserted that now there were "only two men left alive of the tribe." A witness, Wangegamon, recalled the slaughter: "Mr. Taylor was on horseback, they came up in an extended line and immediately fired upon the natives, I ran to the other side of the river and lay down behind a tree among the grass, they killed more than thirty men women and children, my lubra and child were among the dead, the white people threw them into the water and soon left the place, the water was much stained with blood." Two other witnesses confirmed this statement. But the superintendent of the Port Phillip District, C. J. Latrobe, ruled merely that the charges against Taylor "ended in satisfactory disproval."[313] Meanwhile, Taylor was found running sheep on a Scottish farmer's property in Gippsland; in 1847, over the protests of Land Commissioner Tyers, Taylor occupied a run with 11,000 sheep and 1,000 cattle.[314]

The new settler on Taylor's former Glenormiston run, Niel Black, wrote in his journal at the end of 1839: "A few days since I found a Grave into which about 20 [Aborigines] must have been thrown. A Settler taking up a new country is obliged to act towards them in this manner or abandon it."[315] Black reiterated that an attempt to settle in an outlying area required "the conscience of the party" to be "sufficiently seared to enable him to, without remorse, slaughter natives right and left." Settlers, he wrote, "universally" considered this necessary: "Two thirds of them does not care a single straw about taking the life of natives provided they are not taken up by the Protectors." Black added: "I could not stand the thought of murdering them, and to tell the truth I believe it is impossible to take up a new run without doing so, at least the chances are 50 to 1." His station's former overseer told Black that "35–40 natives have been dispatched on this establishment," so that now "[t]he poor creatures are terror stricken and will be easily managed."[316] This area's history, a local newspaper editor later wrote, involved "such a long record" of "cold-blooded murder on the part of the 'superior race' that it dare not be, and therefore never will be, written."[317]

Devastated Western District Aborigines grew disconsolate. In July 1841, Robinson reported on five days of meetings with another 20 tribal groups: "The natives . . . complained much of ill usage since their [whites'] occupancy of their country. . . . They denied having taken sheep." Robinson tried to record the Aborigines' case in their own words: "It was hungry blackfellow who took sheep. Long time ago, they had plenty of kangaroo, parum-pun, tuerercorn (roots eaten by the natives); and [back] then they were not hungry and did not take sheep. [But now] Kangaroo all gone, jumbuc (sheep) eat the roots." The Aborigines appeared mystified by white animosity: "No hungry; what for sulky; shoot too much blackfellow; no sulky blackfellow no spear white fellow take it kangaroo. What for no put white fellow gaol?"[318]

As white impunity persisted, exterminations continued through the 1840s. An 1844 report from the district stated that the 500 Gunditjmara had been reduced to 200: "There could be no reasonable doubt but that during these two years at least two hundred of these blacks have been shot, or otherwise deprived of life in various encounters with the white settlers."[319] In 1846, a search party "massacred . . . all but one of the Cape Otway Aborigines," the Kolakngat people.[320]

Statistical evidence of Aboriginal deaths in large-scale killings, compared to the numbers felled in ones and twos, suggests a partial pattern involving groups of perpetrators, in local conspiracies to murder Aborigines. Historian Jan Critchett at first estimated that whites killed 300–350 Aborigines in the Western District from 1834 to 1848. At least two early massacres there took a total of about 80 lives by April 1840.[321] Critchett also documented nine additional mass killings of six or more Aborigines, which took another 75 lives.[322] Of her initial total of 300–350 dead, then, nearly half (about 155 people) died in killings of six or more victims. However, after further study, Critchett added: "The number of Aborigines killed in conflict with Europeans was, I now believe, far larger than my previous estimate." For the period 1803–59, Ian Clark has exhaustively detailed the evidence on a total of "approximately 107 separate massacres and killings" carried out at 93 locations in the Western District. At 53 of these sites, whites killed "one or two" Aborigines, 73 in all. Some 65 more died in another 17 homicide incidents, each involving the killing of *three to five* Aborigines. Yet most significantly, at as many as 21 locations, six or more blacks were killed, in major incidents that inflicted a toll of around 350 dead in western Victoria alone.[323] Along with hunger, illness, and falling reproductive rates, European violence played a key role in the destruction of most of the indigenous Victorians. The pattern appears to have been threefold. Some settlers eschewed the violence. The frequency of smaller incidents indicates fairly widespread but not universal involvement in localized killings of Aborigines.

Yet the greater death toll from mass killings suggests that on occasion specific perpetrators acted in concert to kill numerous Aborigines. Rather than "rare and isolated," frontier massacres may still be underestimated.[324] Historian Tom Griffiths writes that a man descended from settlers and Aborigines "told me he had once destroyed a station's records 'to protect people from an explosive political situation' and 'in the hope that it might clear the air for a fairer future.' He described where and how he set the evidence of massacre to flame."[325]

Killings by whites, Aboriginal intertribal violence and infanticide, and introduced diseases all spared fewer than 2,000 of possibly 10,000 Aborigines in Victoria between 1834 and 1857. A witness questioned in 1858 by the Select Committee on Aborigines of the colony's legislative council stated: "[I]nferior races should pass away before the superior races . . . since we have occupied the country, the aborigines must cease to occupy it."[326] The committee indeed concluded: "Victoria is now occupied by a superior race" (see fig. 13).[327]

Genocide in the Outback, 1850–1900

Queensland formed the northern reaches of the expanding NSW colony. Here British justice reached the frontier even more rarely than in Port Phillip. Settlers poisoned 50 Aborigines to death in the Brisbane valley in 1842, a crime that was "merely the biggest of many such attempts" whose perpetrators went unpunished.[328] In an exception, a British soldier served a six-month sentence in 1850 for wounding an Aborigine in a military assault.[329] Sadly, the rise of representative government in the colonies in the 1850s did not improve the plight of Aborigines in Queensland.

Crucial factors included the region's size and its suitability for extensive grazing rather than close agricultural settlement. "With the beginning of pastoral occupation around 1840," writes Queensland historian Raymond Evans, "the frontier did not merely spread; it galloped." One pioneer wrote that the first settlers' inroads were "marked with blood, the forests were ruthlessly seized, and the native tenants hunted down like their native dogs."[330] By 1859, when Queensland separated from NSW, the new colony already boasted "thirteen hundred squatting stations" and millions of sheep. Its first governor estimated in 1862 that "the tide of colonization" was extending the colony's boundaries to the north and west at a rate of 200 miles each year. This roaring expansion produced a crescendo of genocidal killings that exceeded all previous Australian catastrophes. What the governor termed a "steady, silent flow" of pas-

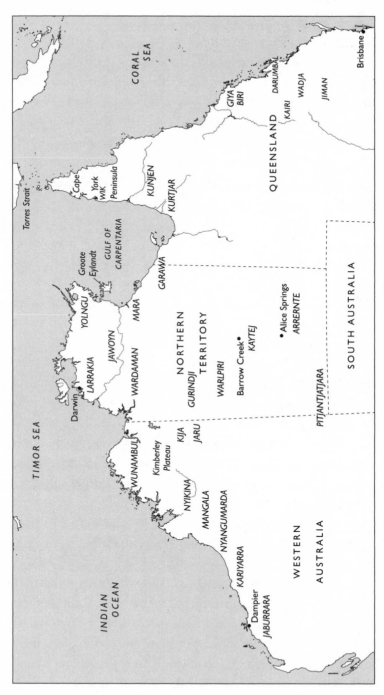

MAP 14. Colonial Queensland, northern and western Australia, with approximate locations of selected Aboriginal groups. Based on Australian Institute of Aboriginal and Torres Strait Islander Studies, *Aboriginal Australia* (Canberra, 1996).

toral settlement included a series of large-scale massacres of Aboriginal communities between 1850 and 1883, a period during which no Queensland court returned a single conviction of any settler for a crime committed against an Aborigine.[331] Aborigines were permitted to testify in the colony's courts only from 1884.[332]

Violent Aboriginal resistance to the rapid settler occupation of the interior also sparked a vicious frontier war that contributed to the genocidal outcomes. Beginning in late 1855, when members of the Darumbal tribe killed six station workers in central Queensland, various Aborigines there massacred five more groups of settlers in six years, mostly including women and totaling about 40 victims in all. Settlers and native police retaliated by murdering, in a six-year period, as many as 300–500 Aborigines from four tribes—the Darumbal, Jiman, Wadja, and Kaira.[333] The future journalist George Lang, son of Sydney's Rev. J. D. Lang, arrived in the area in late 1857, soon after members of the Jiman had killed 11 members and employees of the Frazer family. He wrote his uncle from there a few months later: "I learned from various sources that a party of twelve—squatters and their confidential overseers—went out mounted and armed to the teeth and scoured the country for blacks, away from the scrubs of the murder of the Frazers altogether, and shot upwards of eighty men, women and children. Not content with scouring the scrubs and forest country they were bold enough to ride up to the Head Stations and shoot down the tame blacks whom they found camping there. Ten men were shot in this way at Ross's head station on the Upper Burnet. Several at Prior's station and at Hays and Lambs several more. The party in scouring the bush perceived an old blind blackfellow upon whom they immediately fired sending a ball through his back." In addition, Lang wrote, "[t]he Native Police say they have shot over seventy blacks." His total of about 150 killed is corroborated by other sources. Later visitors, too, reported that "great destruction must have taken place among the tribe," and that many Jiman who had survived these attacks were still wounded or permanently crippled. In the twentieth century no surviving Jiman could be found.[334]

For many settlers these conflicts concerned land as much as they did Aboriginal atrocities. In November 1857, the editor of the *North Australian* newspaper urged effective retaliation for the Frazer murders, in order that an excellent grazing region need not "be vacated and left to the original inhabitants who have no right to occupy the soil."[335] The next year, the *Moreton Bay Courier* newspaper called on settlers to choose "an exterminating warfare against them, or to abandon our outstations." Yet some considered the Queensland Native Police force "disgraceful." A Rockhampton citizen complained that the town had witnessed both "the bloodiest of murders committed upon the innocent natives" and "the greatest solicitude upon the part of those who saw the deeds that they should not be talked about."[336]

The violence did attract official attention. The Select Committee on Aborigines of the Queensland Legislative Assembly held hearings on Aboriginal policy in 1861, condemning "the indiscriminate slaughter which appears on more than one occasion to have taken place." Routine police orders were to "disperse any large assemblage of blacks," which meant "firing at them," an officer told the committee. The police officer was asked: "Do you not think there is any other way of dealing with them, except by shooting them?" He replied: "No, I don't think they can understand anything else except shooting them," later adding: "I know so little of the blacks. They run before me—I never see them." Because he was "valuable and zealous," however, the committee recommended that this officer be reprimanded rather than dismissed. Other Queensland officials openly advocated killing Aborigines. Attorney general Radcliffe Pring agreed in July 1861 that "dispersing" blacks meant "nothing but firing into them" to inflict retribution "when it was deserved." Future premier Arthur Macalister stated that "[i]f extermination were desired—and that appeared to be all that could be done," then the task required the native police. The governor's private physician and proprietor of the *Queensland Guardian,* Dr. William Hobbs, editorialized that "no white man who shot an Aborigine, in self-defense or in sport should be exposed to trial or sentence."[337] None was.

Violence predictably escalated. The last and largest of the six massacres of whites occurred in October 1861, when members of the Kairi or Wadja tribe killed 19 members of a party of 22 settlers at Nagoa, in central Queensland.[338] Late the next month, according to a December newspaper report, "the Native Police overtook the tribe of natives who committed the late outrage at Nagoa, and succeeded in driving them into a place from whence escape was impossible. They then shot down sixty or seventy, and then only ceased firing upon them when their ammunition was expended." The editor of the *Sydney Morning Herald* and leading colonial historian Rev. John West accused the Queensland government of "wholesale destruction," "horrible massacres" including "butchery of those seventy people," and complicity in "annihilation of the race."[339]

In July 1865, this time acting without apparent provocation, a native police squad attacked a Darumbal ceremonial gathering near Rockhampton, shooting 18 Aborigines and burning their corpses. Several years later, after blacks speared and mutilated a shepherd, an army of 100 settlers accompanied by native police rounded up another Darumbal group of men, women, and children who had been hiding in hill caves near the Nogoa River. The attackers flushed them out and, according to an eyewitness, "[a]n estimated three hundred Aboriginals were shot or drowned in the lake." This massacre reduced the Darumbal to remnants, like the Jiman, Wadja, and Kairi.[340]

The editor of the Clermont newspaper, the *Peak Downs Telegram,* again recognized that the conflict stemmed from a contest for the land when he asserted in 1866 that "a war of extermination is the only policy to pursue, the alternative being an abandonment of the country which no sane man will advocate for an instant." Two years later, a press report from Burketown on the Gulf of Carpentaria asserted: "Everybody in the district is delighted with the wholesale slaughter dealt out by the native police," commanded by Sub-Inspector D. W. Uhr, and they thanked him for "ridding the district of fifty-nine (59) myalls" in reprisal for a killing of a settler and several horses.[341] In 1873, a posse of officials and miners shot possibly 80 Aborigines on the Palmer River.[342]

Genocidal intent surfaced in multiple assertions by proponents, provoking public denunciations by critics. Historian Henry Reynolds has shown that Queensland officials often condoned mass killings, and that local newspapers covered government involvement in them. Rev. Tennyson Woods reported in 1874 that a senior official had told him that despite sympathy for blacks, the colony "could not get on until they were exterminated." The editor of the *Brisbane Courier* accused native police officers in 1876 of perpetrating "a war of extermination" with "unnatural ferocity." The next year, the *Cooktown Courier* explained what "we Queenslanders do": "When we come into a new district, we bring with us the Native Police" and "set" them on the Aborigines, "massacring them indiscriminately." In 1880, the *Queenslander* accused the native police of "a fitful war of extermination waged upon the blacks," who were "shot like wild dogs at sight." A native police officer told the *Sydney Morning Herald:* "Not one of them would ever be brought in alive, so that there was nothing for it but to take their lives." Members of Queensland's parliament agreed that the term "dispersal" meant "wholesale massacre." One stated that "the sole function of the native police" was to "shoot them down whenever they could get at them."

The minister responsible for the native police in 1879–81 later wrote privately of "the unfortunate blacks" that "wherever they are seen by the Native Police, the rule has been to shoot them." A former premier of Queensland argued in 1880 that the Aborigines of Queensland's interior had now been "pretty well shot down and got rid of." Having seen none on the Warrego, he was told they had "all been shot down by the police" there, and he believed the "same thing" was now "going on in the west of Rockhampton." Yet a future premier conceded that "blacks had suffered great injustice" but had often "got only what they thoroughly deserved."[343]

From 1824 to 1908, Reynolds has estimated, approximately 8,000–10,000 Aborigines were killed in Queensland. In 1896, a royal commission began to investigate. In his *Report on the Aborigines of North Queensland*, Commissioner Archibald Meston decried the "shame to our common humanity." Aborigines in the far northern Cape York peninsula survived "like hunted wild beasts, having lived for years in a state of absolute terror" of white predators.[344] The next year, Queensland passed what Colin Tatz has called the world's first statute to protect a human species from elimination.[345] The view of a squatter exemplified the challenge of social Darwinism: "For untold centuries the aborigines have had the use of this country, but in the march of time they, like the extinct fossil, must make way ... the sooner they are taught that a superior race has come among them, and made to feel its power the better for them. ... Survival of the fittest is nature's law."[346]

In the newer frontiers of Australia's west and north, the pattern of violence recurred, even though Aboriginal affairs remained a British imperial responsibility in Western Australia until 1898. There, troopers killed 25 or more Aborigines at the "Battle of Pinjarra" in 1834.[347] Seven years later, the explorer George Grey recommended the cultivation of "cotton, sugar, indigo, and rice" in the Kimberley region of the northwest.[348] Killings of local Aborigines began when settlers and miners arrived decades later. An explorer in 1884 wrote of shooting an "old man" who had waved a boomerang at him from a distance. On another occasion, "when Aborigines killed some miners, other diggers responded by driving a group of Aborigines up a gully and slaughtering them with repeating rifles."[349] In a further clash in 1893, police killed 23 natives for the loss of a constable. From December 1894 to March 1895, three police teams killed or wounded 49 Aborigines.[350] Four months later, Western Australia's undersecretary informed the colony's premier, Sir John Forrest: "There can be no doubt from these frequent [police] reports that a war of extermination in effect is being waged against these unfortunate blacks in the Kimberley district and that the owners and managers of stations are tacitly, if not deliberately encouraging such a state of things . . . then the police are called in to kill and slay. How often do we read that the Police 'fell in' or 'came up' with a party of natives and there follows a record of slain, or the statement 'they were taught a severe lesson.'" The next year, police killed nine more Aborigines in another clash.[351]

Aborigines in the Northern Territory were also victims of mass murder. Historian Tony Roberts has compiled evidence of 53 "massacres" and other "multiple killings of Aboriginals" in the Gulf Country alone from 1872 to 1916. In central Australia, too, patrols killed no fewer than 650 Aboriginal men between 1860 and 1895. Reynolds estimates that in all of tropical Australia, including north Queensland, Europeans killed "as many as 10,000 blacks" in skirmishes from 1861 to 1930.[352]

After 1800, a new colonial economy rapidly enveloped the entire Australian continent. The first colonies of convicts and yeoman farmers were left in the dust of an advancing frontier and accelerating pastoral occupation. The initial intensive agricultural settlements set a pattern of close occupation of the land that jeopardized Aboriginal survival there, and was then compounded by the extensive expansion of grazing runs. The continuing pressure of agrarian ideology even when actual settlement patterns were pastoral took on new virulence with the spread of scientific racism, which justified mass murder of indigenous communities to safeguard investments in animal stock.

CHAPTER 8

Genocide in the United States

merica's Declaration of Independence in 1776 ushered in a new era for colonists and Native Americans alike. Yet the new nation maintained its colonial heritage of territorial expansion, frontier warfare, agrarian ideology, and fascination with ancient models of conquest. The last decades of British rule had bequeathed a lethal legacy to the infant Republic. Building on that, Americans perpetrated their own genocidal massacres during the war of independence, when they fought Indians as well as the British, and later while expanding across the continent throughout the nineteenth century.

U.S. policies toward Indians did not mandate genocide, but it was practiced when considered necessary. Its frequency increased with the spread and intensity of war, expansion, and agrarianism. In the initial opening up of the western frontier, and later in Texas, California, and the Great Plains, genocides resulted from a ruthless policy of conquest in which Indian land was the prize and Indians the obstacle. Repeatedly, American tactics included threatening genocide, offering bounties for Indian scalps, and exacting massively disproportionate revenge for Indian atrocities. Seizure of Indian lands often meant massacring their inhabitants, and settlers' extensive and later intensive cultivation of these lands rarely allowed Indian survivors a subsistence, provoking bitter resistance, sometimes to the end, resulting in genocide. As in the colonial era, writes military historian John Grenier, Americans "chose the most effective means of subjugating the Indians they faced. They sent groups of men, sometimes a dozen, sometimes hundreds, to attack Indian villages and homes, kill Indian women and children, and raze Indian fields."[1] These Americans knew what their actions would bring. Even survivors were unable to feed themselves, and often perished.

Land and Race in the Revolution and Early Republic

Many eighteenth-century Americans read the work of international law theorist Emerich de Vattel, whose themes echoed those of John Locke. In *The Law of Nations* (1758), Vattel described Spain's conquests of Mexico and Peru as "notorious usurpation" of "civilised empires" of settled peoples. By contrast, he argued, North America's colonization "might have been entirely lawful," because the Indians inhabiting "those vast tracts of land rather roamed over them than inhabited them."[2] For Vattel, as for Locke, cultivation meant civilization. Vattel recognized neither in indigenous North America. He added, significantly, that "nations are justified in uniting together as a body with the object of punishing, and even exterminating, such savage peoples."[3]

At least from a distance, Americans were just as inclined to see those savages as noble people, in classical, agrarian, and pastoral terms. Thomas Jefferson echoed Edmund Spenser's view of the Irish two centuries before, in his *View of the State of Ireland* (see p. 176). Jefferson's *Notes on the State of Virginia* (1781–83) compared Indians "in their present state with the Europeans North of the Alps, when the Roman arms and arts first crossed those mountains." His comparison to the Gauls was favorable, and he strongly defended Indians from the Comte de Buffon's charge that they exhibited "no activity of mind." He found "the Indian then to be in body and mind equal to the whiteman." By contrast, Jefferson thought, "the black man, in his present state, might not be so," and he even quoted Cato in the original Latin to show that ancient Romans had treated slaves worse than did contemporary Virginian slaveholders.[4]

The more romantic New York–born American poet and patriot Philip Freneau, writing in the Philadelphia *Freeman's Journal* in 1782, quoted Nature herself, describing the Indians as "a few tribes of wandering Tartars." These, he added, were "literally the children of nature, wild as the winds and waves, and free as the animals that wander in the woody or the wat[e]ry waste." European poets who had dreamed of "their fabulous Arcadias" were unaware, Freneau wrote, "that the happy scenes, the innocent people and pastoral ages they sung of" existed in America. Once Europeans discovered it, "they of course conceived they had the right to extirpate the innocent natives, or drive them from the sea coasts to the interior." Freneau contested that right: "The most specious

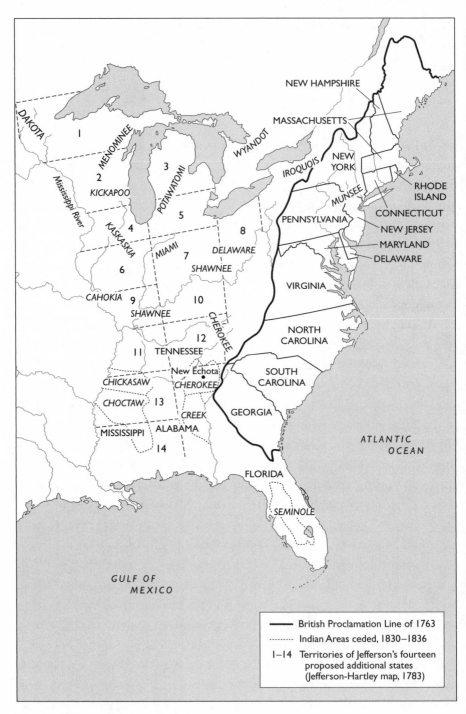

MAP 15. U.S. expansion, 1776–1840

pretext for this procedure seems to have been, that the aborigines of America did not exert themselves sufficiently to cultivate and improve the lands nature had so liberally bestowed on them."[5] Unlike Vattel, Freneau denounced "these casuists" who justified robbing noble savages of their forested Arcadia. (See also fig. 15.)

Yet this sylvan canopy shielded an agrarian, racist understory. Freneau concurred that the settlers had "humbled the savage tribes, and by the force of industry rendered a large proportion of this new country rich and flourishing." He asserted that the soil of the American interior, too, "has no less impatiently expected the operations of the industrious plough." As for "the natives of the polar regions" of America, they "bear so little resemblance in the features of the mind to what the civilized world calls a man, that they scarcely deserve the name." In some circles, at least, historian Alden Vaughan wrote, by the time of the American Revolution the Indian had become, like the Negro, "an object of Anglo-American racism."[6]

To justify its territorial expansion, the fledgling United States took up Locke's argument for ownership by simple cultivation. A few months after Freneau's article appeared, the *Freeman's Journal* published three reflections signed "Caractacus" that all argued for Virginia's claim on the trans-Appalachian region. Caractacus believed that "[w]hen a family, nation or people emigrate to any part of the globe, they have a right, *jure divino*, to cultivate so much of the unoccupied soil as is necessary to support them." However, the additional right of property in those lands could come "by compact alone." Caractacus observed that "all lands, especially on this side of Ohio, were taken from the savages by force of arms last war, and at the expense of both blood and treasure." Because Britain, whose king acted as "lord of the soil," had "paid no regard to Indian deeds, neither ought America."[7] Otherwise, Caractacus feared, "the whole wilderness will be lost to the United States." The United States, he argued, had now succeeded the British monarch "as lord of the soil." Caractacus wrote that in contrast, Indians had lacked legal ownership: "[N]ations not formed into political bodies, have no more property in the soil around them, than they have in the circumambient air." Therefore, "the Indians in America, who were not formed into bodies politic, who ranged over but did not cultivate the soil, which is the only test of occupancy, never had a right to the lands."[8]

As new Americans theorized their relations with the Indians, their classical allusions extended well beyond Jefferson's comparison with ancient Gauls. The week before Freneau's article appeared, the *Freeman's Journal* published two anonymous contributions, side by side, signed respectively by "Cato" and "Censor." Just as their Roman namesake had harried the Scipios with corruption allegations, the Philadelphia Censor railed against "frivolous disputes" and denounced seekers of "individual gain" who had cost the state "a considerable sum." Significantly, this Censor urged official sponsorship of a yeoman soldiery, by preferential sales of land to officers and troops in lieu of back pay, thus forming "a useful body of settlers after the war."[9] Race, antiquity, and agriculture provided a powerful combination to urge Americans westward.

Nothing less than empire was at stake. In 1781, Jefferson told a visiting Kaskaskia chief from the Illinois: "The Americans alone have a right to maintain justice in all the lands on this side of the Mississippi." Like Caractacus, Jefferson explained to the chief that America had won these lands from the English, who had taken them from the French.[10] If Jefferson became obsessed with territorial expansion, others looked to American domination by a different route, that of continental commerce. Already in 1775 Lewis Evans foresaw "all the Wealth and Power that will naturally arise from the Culture of so great an extent of good Land." In 1782, Thomas Hutchins, "Geographer of the United States," predicted a world-historical empire. Its people, "so far from being in the least danger from the attacks of any other quarter of the globe, will have it in their power to engross the whole commerce of it." In a 1771 poem, "The Rising Glory of America," Philip Freneau imagined the future American West as "empires . . . kingdoms, pow'rs and states where now are seen / But dreary wastes and awful solitude."[11] As empire vanquished solitude, agriculture erased anonymity. Freneau wrote in 1782 that the West remained "inhabited by savage nations as yet almost unknown, and without a name." But Hutchins quickly foresaw that North America "will hereafter be trod by the first people the world ever knew."[12] It was clear who those people would be. The *Town and Country Almanac* in 1792 addressed "the Yeoman of the United States," or "Ye honest Sons of the earth," as "the basis of the Western Empire!"[13]

This empire would be agricultural. The West's "savage groves," Freneau wrote, potentially contained the "many fertile countries" of a future North American continental colossus. He predicted: "Agriculture, the basis of a nation's greatness will here probably be raised to its pinnacle of perfection."[14] At first, American leaders considered even Indian cultivation a key to both U.S. expansion and Indian survival. In Jefferson's view, Indian adoption of agriculture would ensure American territorial acquisition. As president, he told Andrew Jackson in 1803 that U.S. Indian policy had two main objects: preserving peace and "obtaining lands." To achieve the latter goal, the main method would be "leading the Indians to agriculture." Jefferson added: "When they shall cultivate small spots of earth, and see how useless their extensive forests are, they will sell, from time to time, to help out their personal labor in stocking their farms."[15] Conversely, agriculture alone could save the Indians, wrote General James Wilkinson, commander in chief of the U.S. Army: "[I]f this People are not brought to depend for subsistence on their fields instead of their forests, and to realize Ideas of distinct property, it will be found impossible to correct their present habits, and the seeds of their extinction, already sown, must be matured."[16]

Agriculture itself had sown some of those seeds. In the year America declared independence, Adam Smith wrote: "No equal capital puts into motion a greater quantity of productive labour than does that of the farmer. Not only his labouring servants, but his labouring cattle, are productive labourers. In agriculture, too, nature labours along with man; and though her labour costs no expense, its produce has its value, as well as that of the most expensive workman." Smith estimated "the work of nature" to contribute "frequently more than a third of the whole produce" of farming, an added value inaccessible to "manufactures."[17] This had become especially true of English agriculture since the late fifteenth century, with the alternation of crops and pasture, known as convertible husbandry.[18] Recognition of its remarkable productivity naturally spread to America. In 1816, Jefferson took up Adam Smith's view of the unique benefits of agriculture: "[T]o the labor of the husbandman a vast addition is made by the spontaneous energies of the earth ... for one grain of wheat committed to the earth, she renders twenty, thirty, and even fifty fold, whereas to the labor of the manufacturer nothing is added."[19] The perceived power and virtue of America's agriculture fueled the nation's political self-assurance.

Poetic idealization followed. Timothy Dwight extolled "the scene, where happiness expands, in living green! Through the whole realm, behold convenient farms / Fed by small herds, and gay with cultur'd charms." The *Massachusetts Magazine* added: "But peace and pleasure, smiling, bless the soil, / And he who sows enjoys the product of his toil."[20] (See also fig. 16.)

In his 1782 *Letters from an American Farmer*, the French settler St. John de Crèvecoeur famously asked: "What is an American?" His answer was an agrarian myth: "[W]e are all tillers of the earth, from Nova Scotia to West Florida. We are a people of cultivators." Every American "works for himself" in "the most perfect society now existing in the world," according to Crève-

coeur. "Precious soil," he added, "feeds, it clothes us," even providing, in precise
Virgilian pastoral, "the very honey of our bees."[21] George Logan's 1791 *Letters,
Addressed to the Yeomanry of the United States,* "by a Farmer," not only lauded
"an independent yeomanry" but also decried urban vices. Government, Logan
wrote, must "support each individual citizen in the right of soil."[22] For his part,
Freneau insisted in 1799 that "our AMERICAN FARMERS are VIRTUOUS. . . . To
them we look—they are our bulwark, the guardians of our rights, the supporters of our dignity, and the pillars of our CONSTITUTION."[23]

George Washington placed agriculture "amongst the most favourite
amusements of my life," ran a "model farm," and consulted British agriculturalist Arthur Young on its management.[24] He informed Young in 1791 that in
America, "much ground has been scratched over and none cultivated or improved as it ought to have been."[25] Benjamin Franklin, too, considered agriculture "the most honorable of all employments, being the most independent"
and "[t]he great Business of the Continent." Ever the urbanite himself, even
Franklin reckoned: "For one Artisan, or Merchant, I suppose we have at least
100 Farmers, by far the greatest part Cultivators of their own fertile Lands."
America was based on "industrious frugal Farmers, inhabiting the interior."[26]

Jefferson popularized the concept that honest yeomen would preserve the
infant democracy. In 1776, he had drafted a constitution for Virginia giving
every adult 50 acres of land. In *Notes on the State of Virginia,* he added that
historically, farmers had proved uniquely proper: "Corruption of morals in the
mass of cultivators is a phenomenon of which no age nor nation has furnished
an example." Jefferson instead considered corruption "the mark" of those "not
looking up to heaven, to their own soil and industry," for subsistence. Not husbandmen but "the other classes" accounted for a state's "unsound" parts.[27] "The
small landholders are the most precious part of a state."[28]

None of this agrarianism suggests that Washington, Franklin, or Jefferson
had genocidal inclinations. Just as Hesiod had once idealized the farmer but
objected to violence, America's founders idealized the farmer as the pillar of
democracy. Their agrarian ideology spurned both cities and hunters, yet was
not necessarily violent or racist. Franklin had denounced "Christian White
Savages" who massacred friendly Indians (see p. 246).[29]

Agrarian ideology served to reinforce genocidal thinking when it was
accompanied by expansionism and racism. And agrarianism was a key fix-
ture of the firmament at the birth of the United States. As Henry Nash Smith
wrote, the "yeoman" was an ideal model in late eighteenth-century America,

with agriculture widely considered "the only source of real wealth." Even those American leaders favoring commerce and manufacturing acknowledged that agriculture had "more consequence."[30] This national obsession with the land implicitly left no place for its Indian inhabitants even if they farmed it.

Eastern intellectuals and gentlemen agriculturalists who favored intensive cultivation over what they considered the extensive, wasteful practices of frontier yeomen still saw the latter as a necessary stage in the historic improvement of the land from wilderness and Indian neglect. Eventually the superior settler would arrive "to convert every spot of ground, over which he is able to draw water, into meadow."[31] In 1818, the Society of Virginia for Promoting Agriculture acknowledged the importance to frontier expansion of the initial land-degrading extensive farming methods: "Taking possession of an immense wilderness, covered with thick forest, our ancestors were compelled to employ immense labour in clearing it.... Continual cultivation was produced by necessity, and [soil] exhaustion the unavoidable consequence. New lands invited and rewarded the labourer; and cutting down and wearing out, became habitual."[32] Agricultural ideology was supreme even though its strongest advocates were often disappointed. Had frontier farming followed their strictures for intensive agriculture, the occupation of further Indian lands would have slowed. But the combined pressure of extensive settlement on the ground, backed by an agrarian state ideology, still devastated Indian inhabitants.

The dominant American view was that men had a natural right to land. If society did not allocate it to them, Jefferson wrote in 1774, each individual "may appropriate to himself such lands as he finds vacant, and occupancy will give him title."[33] Men could acquire land by cultivation, status from its ownership, and happiness from laboring amid nature. Americans considered the idealized freehold husbandman, cultivator, or "yeoman" uniquely prominent in their political life and the proper beneficiary of their government. Indeed, 90 percent of Americans were engaged in agriculture. Henry Nash Smith adds that the nineteenth-century vision of continental expansion by migration and agriculture "more nearly corresponds to the actual course of events" than America's parallel maritime, mercantile strategy.[34]

The agrarianism of Jefferson and others conditioned their views of Indians, whom their policies seriously impacted.[35] Jefferson regarded Indian lands in the interior as wide open for white pioneers. In *Notes on the State of Virginia,* he wrote: "[W]e have an immensity of land courting the industry of the husbandman. Is it best then that all our citizens should be employed in its improvement?" His reply was resounding: "Those who labor in the earth are the chosen people of God."[36] (See also fig. 10.)

Jefferson advised against manufacturing and dismissed cities as a "canker" fostering "degenerate" ideas. "While we have land to labor, then, let us never wish to see our citizens occupied at a workbench. . . . [L]et our workshops remain in Europe. It is better to carry provisions and materials to workmen there, than bring them to the provisions and materials [i.e., to America], and with them their manners and principles." Urban ideological contamination threatened America. "The mobs of great cities add just so much to the support of pure government, as sores do to the strength of the human body."[37] We glimpse here the biological metaphor on its political march to the twentieth century. Jefferson reiterated in 1787: "I think our governments will remain virtuous for many centuries; as long as they are chiefly agricultural. . . . When they get piled upon one another in large cities, as in Europe, they will become corrupt."[38]

American government could remain "chiefly agricultural" only at the expense of Native Americans and only "as long as there shall be vacant lands in any part of America."[39] Vacant or not, this "immensity of unimproved lands, courting the hand of husbandry,"[40] beckoned new farmers from Europe. Thus the Declaration of Independence had chided George III for "obstructing the Laws for the Naturalization of Foreigners; refusing to pass others to encourage their migration hither, and raising the conditions of new Appropriations of Lands."[41] Jeffersonian democracy, based on territorial expansion and European immigration, also required that Indians give up their lifestyle, their lands, or their lives—without the vote.

War, Expansion, and Genocidal Massacres

Some emerging American leaders maintained colonial and even genocidal views toward Indians, at least in wartime. North Carolina's delegation to the U.S. Continental Congress proclaimed that "the duties of a Christian" included such determined action against the Cherokee Indians as "to extinguish the very race of them and scarce to leave enough of their existence to be a vestige in proof that the Cherokee nation once was."[42] In 1776, the delegates advocated reprisal against Indian attacks "to carry fire and Sword into the very bowels of their country." William Henry Drayton of South Carolina urged "that the [Cherokee] nation be extirpated, and the lands become the property of the public. For my part, I shall never give my voice for a peace with the Cherokee Nation upon any other terms than their removal beyond the mountains." Drayton told soldiers: "Cut up every Indian cornfield, and burn every Indian town." South Carolina offered £75 for male Indian scalps. General Griffith Rutherford of North Carolina destroyed 36 Cherokee towns in 1776 alone. Three years later, forces commanded by Evan Shelby attacked another Cherokee community, "burning 11 towns," according to Jefferson.[43]

The Declaration of Independence, adopted in July 1776, accused the British monarch of encouraging "the merciless Indian Savages, whose known rule of warfare is an undistinguished destruction of all ages, sexes, and conditions." Yet, according to historian Colin G. Calloway, "Most of the Indians who eventually sided with Britain did so after American acts of treachery, inability to provide trade, and continued pressure on their lands convinced them they had no choice."[44] William Nester adds: "Of the Indians killed during American campaigns into the wilderness, most were women, old men and children." The frontier war for U.S. independence, he asserts, was "at once genocidal and decisive," against Indians and British respectively.[45]

Genocide was contingent on conflict. As war policy, Jefferson urged the deportation or even extermination of some hostile Indian groups. American settler encroachments provoked serious Cherokee attacks even as he drafted the Declaration of Independence.[46] The next month, Jefferson advised his boyhood friend John Page, president of the Council of Virginia:

> I am sorry to hear that the Indians have commenced war, but greatly pleased you have been so decisive on that head. Nothing will reduce those wretches so soon as pushing the war into the heart of their country. But I would not stop there. I would never cease pursuing them while one of them remained on this side the Mississippi. So unprovoked an attack and so treacherous a one should never be forgiven while one of them remains near enough to do us injury. The Congress having had reason to suspect the Six nations intended war, instructed their commissioners to declare to them peremptorily that if they chose to go to war with us, they should be at liberty to remove their families out of our settlements, but to remember that they should not only never more return to their dwellings on any terms but that we would never cease pursuing them with war while one remained on the face of the earth.[47]

Eight days later, Jefferson repeated the latter phrase as he further explained the burden on Indians: "[W]e knew the Senecas meditated war. We directed a declaration to be made to the six nations in general that if they did not take the most decisive measures for the preservation of neutrality we would never cease waging war with them while one was to be found on the face of the earth." Though the Senecas "immediately changed their conduct," Cherokee raids continued. Jefferson now urged that Congress carry out its threat of deportation: "I hope the Cherokees will now be driven beyond the Missisipi [*sic*] and that this in future will be declared to the Indians the invariable consequence of their beginning a war. Our contest with Britain is too serious and too great to permit any possibility of avocation from the Indians. This then is the season for driving them off, and our Southern colonies are happily rid of any other enemy and may exert their whole force in that quarter."[48] Jefferson thus employed what we might call "ethnic cleansing" as a wartime defensive weapon and a means of seizing new land. As an alternative, he repeatedly countenanced genocide as a last resort. Jefferson did not advocate extermination of Indians because they were Indians.

Other American leaders did that. Most stopped short of genocide, but they often allowed troops a license to commit murder on an ethnic basis. A month after the Declaration of Independence, Jefferson described even friendly Indians as "a useless, expensive, ungovernable ally."[49] American forces often acted as if they agreed. In November 1777, U.S. captain Matthew Arbuckle arrested the neutral Shawnee chief Cornstalk and his son, who had visited his fort under a flag of truce. Arbuckle asserted that "the Shawanese are all our enemies." A few days later, American militiamen stormed their cabin and slaughtered the detained chief, his son, and two other Shawnees, propelling most of their tribe into war with the United States. The murderers were tried but acquitted when the witnesses refused to testify against them, a reticence common enough in frontier wars.[50]

U.S. leaders occasionally resorted to the threat of genocide if other tactics failed. Jefferson dispatched the Virginian general George Rogers Clark, an old friend and associate, on a new campaign against "some Indian Tribes to the westward of the Missisipi." In January 1778, Jefferson and George Mason promised 300 acres of western land to each of Clark's volunteers, assuring him of "the Justice & Generosity" of the Virginia Assembly. According to military historian John Grenier, Clark knew that the American "reputation as warriors who without hesitation killed women and children preceded them."[51] Clark left Williamsburg on January 18 and, he wrote later, raised a "little Army" with the aim of "puting an end to the Indian War on our fronteers." By July, Clark had discovered the weakness of U.S. Indian policy. As he later reported to Mason on the Ohio Indians: "[I] always thought we took the wrong method of treating with Indians, and strove as soon as possible to make myself acquainted with the French and Spanish mode which must be prefferable to ours, otherwise they could not possibly have such great influence among them." Thus, Clark first negotiated with various Indian groups. In the town of Cohos, however, "a party of Puans [Winnebago] and others endeavored to force by the Guards into my Lodgings and Bear me off; but was happily Detected and made Prisoners." Clark then "summoned the different Nations to a grand Council," and threatened them with genocide, telling them "if they did not want their own Women and Children massacred, they must leave off killing ours and only fight Men under Arms ... but they could blame no Person but themselves when their Nation should be given with the English to the Dogs to eat." However, Clark informed Mason, "Peace was what I wanted with them if I got it on my own terms," and after five weeks at Cohos, he reported, "I had settled a peace with ten or twelve different Nations."[52]

Congress, by contrast, soon hardened its Indian policy, which passed down the line. Late in 1778, Clark stated that "the Absolute orders of Congress to the Army now in Indian Country is to Shew no mercy to those that have been at war against the States." He added that "to excel them in barbarity was and is the only way to make war upon Indians." In a lightning attack into the Illinois country, Clark surrounded the British lieutenant governor Hamilton in the St. Vincents fort in January 1779. Later that year, Clark wrote to inform George Mason how he had pressured Hamilton to surrender: "I told him (which was really the truth) that I wanted a sufficient excuse to put all the Indians and partisans to death, as the greatest part of those Villians was then with him."[53] Clark explained in his memoir why he wanted "to put them to Death or other ways treat them." He wrote: "I thought proper that the Cries of the Widows and Fatherless on the Frontiers that they had occationed now Required their Blood from my Hands."[54]

The violence escalated when Clark's forces captured several Indian warriors returning to the British fort. He wrote Mason that this presented "a fair opportunity" to show the Indians that the British governor Hamilton could not protect them. So, Clark went on, while the British watched from the fort, he "Ordered the Prisoners to be Tomahawked in front of the Garrisson." Hamilton observed the murders and reported that one Indian was "tomahawked either by Clarke or one of his Officers, the other three foreseeing their fate, began to sing their Death song, and were butchered in succession." A young Ottawa chief, "having received the fatal stroke of a Tomahawk in the head, took it out and gave it again into the hands of his executioner." Clark had the corpses "flung into the River."[55] Hamilton surrendered and later quoted Clark as saying "that he expected shortly to see the whole race of Indians extirpated, that for his part he would never spare man, woman or child of them on whom he could lay his hands."[56]

Meanwhile, Clark informed Mason: "And calling together the Neighbouring Nations, the Peankeshaws, Kickapoes, & others . . . [I] told them that we were so far from having any desire on their Lands . . . we claimed no Land in their Country." In June 1779, in the name of "all the Great Chiefs and Warriers of the Ouabash in open Council," the Peankeshaw grand chief Francis made peace with Clark. Moreover, expressing an Indian conception of genocide, Francis accused the English of inciting the crime by "encouraging all People to raise the Tommahawk Against the Big Knives [Americans], saying that they were a bad people, Rebellious, and ought to be put from under Sun and their names to be no more." Clark accepted the chief's offer of lands at the Ohio falls.[57]

The selective threat of genocide again proved useful in renewed American attacks on the Shawnees. Clark had "hopes of giving the Shawneess a Drubing," which would require Indian allies. Having neutralized the Peankeshaws and Ouabash, he now wrote to "the different Tribes near the Lakes that was at war with us." He warned them that "no peace for the future will be granted to those that do not lay down their Arms immediately . . . this is the last Speech you may ever expect from the Big knives, the next thing will be the Tomahawk. And You may expect in four Moons to see Your Women and Children given to the Dogs to eat, while those Nations that have kept their words with me will Flourish and grow like the Willow Trees on the River Banks."[58]

Along with territorial expansion, the allure of the pastoral was an ever more powerful attraction to the Americans. On November 19, 1779, Clark lyrically described the Illinois country as "more Beautiful than any Idea I could have formed of a country almost in a state of Nature. . . . On the River You'll find the finest Lands the Sun ever shone on; in the high Country You will find a Variety of poor and Rich Lands with large Meadows extending beyond the reach of your Eyes Varigated with groves of Trees appearing like Islands in the Seas covered with Buffaloes and other Game; in many Places with a good Glass You may see all those that is on their feet in half a Million of Acres; so level is the Country which some future day will excel in Cattle."[59] That did not bode well for the Indians.

Six weeks later, Jefferson ordered that the Ohio Shawnees and three other Indian groups must be either exterminated or driven from their land.[60] In a letter to Clark on January 1, 1780, Jefferson wrote: "I think the most important object which can be proposed with such a force is the extermination of those hostile tribes. . . . The Shawanese, Mingos, Munsies and Wiandots can never be relied on as friends, and therefore the object of the war should be their total extinction, or their removal beyond the [Great] lakes or the Illinois river and peace." Thinking better of it, however, Jefferson crossed out that passage in his letter. He went on instead to suggest that Rogers march "against those tribes of Indians between the Ohio and Illinois rivers who have harassed us with eternal hostilities, and whom experience has shewn to be incapable of reconciliation." He added that "the Shawanese, Mingoes, Munsies, and the nearer Wiandots are troublesome thorns in our sides. However we must leave it to yourself to decide on the object of the campaign. If against these Indians, the end proposed should be their extermination, or their removal beyond the lakes or Illinois river. The same world will scarcely do for them and us."[61] Reconsidering the goal of "their total extinction," Jefferson thus left it to Clark to choose either "extermination" or "removal" of the four Indian groups. Of these, the Shawnees had numbered about 1,800 people in the 1760s, the Mingoes about 2,500. The Munsees were a subgroup of the 3,500 Delawares who also inhabited the upper Ohio valley. American troops invaded Shawnee territory eight times from 1774 to 1794, as 80,000 settlers "poured into Shawnee hunting territories." In the decade from 1779, the Shawnees had to relocate and rebuild their capital four times.[62]

At the end of January 1780, Jefferson again recommended that Clark take further action against the Shawnees. "We would have you cultivate peace and cordial friendship with the several tribes of Indians (the Shawanese excepted). Endeavour that those who are in friendship with us live in peace also with one another. Against those who are our enemies let loose the friendly tribes. The Kikapous should be encouraged against the hostile tribes of Chickasaws and Choctaws and the others against the Shawenese. With the latter be cautious of the terms of peace you admit. An evacuation of their Country and removal utterly out of interference with us would be the most satisfactory. Ammunition should be furnished gratis to those warriors who go actually on expeditions against the hostile Tribes."[63] Three months later, Jefferson instructed Clark: "Nothing is more desirable than the total suppression of Savage Insolence and Cruelties."[64] In May 1780, the U.S. commander at Fort Pitt, Daniel Brodhead,

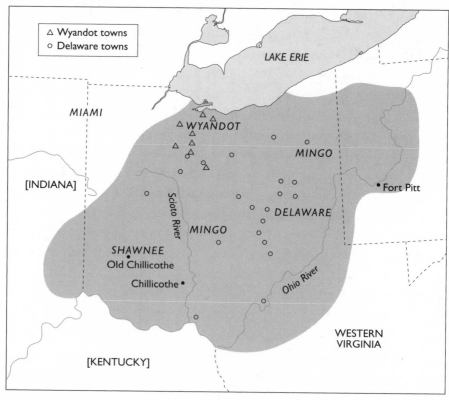

MAP 16. Indian habitations in the Ohio Country, 1753–86

also urged Clark to "make an attack upon the Shawnese and their allies," adding: "I am persuaded that they are the most hostile of any Savage Tribe and could they receive a severe chastisement it would probably put an end to the Indian war."[65] At the end of the year, Washington ordered Brodhead to cooperate with Clark.[66]

This campaign against the Shawnees launched a new phase of U.S. expansion. Two years earlier, Jefferson had informed Clark of the importance of "establishing our northwestern boundary."[67] In December 1780, he specified instead that his basic goal was to "add to the Empire of liberty an extensive and fertile country."[68] Jefferson's instructions to Clark included the seizure of Detroit from the British and "acquiring possession of Lake Erie." The U.S. southern commander Nathaniel Greene protested, saying that such expansionism jeopardized the country's survival: "History affords no instance of a nation being so engaged in conquest abroad as Virginia is at a time when all her powers were necessary to secure herself from ruin at home."[69]

When Clark again raided Shawnee territory in 1782, Daniel Boone, who accompanied him, reported that Clark's forces burned five villages "and spread desolation through their country." The Shawnees fought on until 1786, when they complained, as Clark put it, that "we were putting them to live on ponds, and leaving them no land to raise corn on."[70] Clark informed them: "The destruction of your women and children or their happiness depends on your present choice." The Shawnees replied: "This is not the way to make a good or lasting Peace." To avoid the continuing threats of genocide, they had to sign a treaty ceding their eastern lands.[71]

Yet the treaty gave the Shawnees no peace, as settlers pushed west in another "campaign into the towns" of the Shawnees, including the Maquachakes, whose chief, Moluntha, had signed the treaty. Eight hundred Kentucky militia led by Benjamin Logan burned both Maquachake towns. In the second town, the Shawnees made no resistance but "rose their Yankee colours" to receive the American troops. Colonel Hugh McGary murdered Chief Moluntha with an ax. Court-martialed for this, McGary received a one-year suspension. Logan's forces destroyed seven other Shawnee towns and killed nine other chiefs. Major Ebenezer Denny wrote: "Logan found none but old men, women and children in the towns; they made no resistance, the men were literally murdered." Surviving Shawnees fought, fled, splintered, and dispersed.[72]

As governor of Virginia, Jefferson launched new attacks on the Cherokees in 1780–81. Arthur Campbell's forces destroyed over 1,000 houses of the Overhill Cherokees in 1780. He reported to Jefferson that they devastated the 11 main towns and killed 29 men. The next year, John Sevier "burned fifteen Middle Cherokee towns." In 1782, Sevier's son took part in another campaign against Lower Cherokees, reporting: "We destroyed their towns, stock, corn, & everything they had."[73]

In 1779, Washington had also decided "to carry the war into the Heart of the Country of the six nations" of the Iroquois northwest, "to ruin their crops now in the ground and prevent them planting." That fall, General John Sullivan burned down 40 Iroquois towns and destroyed 160,000 bushels of corn. An Onondaga chief complained that American forces attacking his town had "put to death all the Women and Children, excepting some of the Young Women, whom they carried away for the use of their soldiers and were afterwards put to death in a more shameful manner."[74]

During the Revolution, Pennsylvania paid $1,000 each for both male and female Indian scalps. In 1781, fearing Indian attack, the American commander

Brodhead recruited 150 Pennsylvania militiamen "who considered killing Indians the same as hunting wild animals." They marched on the Delaware capital at Coshocton, capturing 15 warriors, whom the Americans bound and then executed with tomahawks. One militia unit turned its sights on Delawares who had become Moravian Christians, but Brodhead intervened to stop the attack.[75] Then, in February 1782, frontier Indians killed a white man, a woman, and a child. Colonel James Marshall, the military commander in Washington County of western Pennsylvania, ordered Lieutenant Colonel David Williamson and 160 militiamen to raid the Moravian Delaware community at Gnadenhutten. On March 8, as the 90 unarmed Indian captives prayed for their lives, the American militiamen beat them all to death and scalped them (see fig. 9). The victims included 61 women and children. An observer stated that "they killed rather deliberately the Innocent with the guilty and it is likely the majority was the former." Williamson subsequently obtained promotion, and never stood trial for his crime of murdering Indians because of their race.[76]

After the 1781 victory over the British and formal independence two years later, America's peacetime Indian policy began to take shape. The Cherokees signed a peace treaty with the new state in 1785. In its treaty with the Creeks five years later, the United States promised them "implements of husbandry" so that they would "become herdsmen and cultivators instead of remaining in a state of hunters."[77]

Yet the continuing movement of settlers to Indian land, and Indian harassment, provoked more wars. An American major stationed on the Ohio River in 1788 watched as "181 boats, 406 souls, 1,558 horses," and 92 wagons went past his post in six weeks, demonstrating "the amazing increase flowing into the western world from the old Atlantic states."[78] The U.S. secretary of war, Henry Knox, complained two years later of Indian depredations that "annoyed the boats in descending the Ohio," indeed, worrying "all men whose views or interests are westward." The attackers were "the remnants of the Shawanese, and the banditti from several tribes associated with them," at most "two hundred fighting men." Knox ordered 400 troops and militia to "extirpate, utterly, if possible, the said banditti," but he insisted that "the friendly, or even neutral tribes, be uninjured."[79] In 1794, Knox reiterated to Washington his concern about frontier conflict: "It would afford a conscious pleasure, could the assertion be made on our parts, that we have considered the murder of Indians, the same as the murders of whites, and have punished them accordingly. This however, is not the case." Knox could cite "multitudes" of examples of white impunity "in almost every part of the country, from its first settlement to the present time."[80]

For his part, Jefferson wrote of war with Indians in 1791: "I hope we shall give them a thorough drubbing this summer, and then change our tomahawk into a golden chain of friendship."[81] In his view, surviving Indians could become American farmers or emigrate across the Mississippi. By 1794, some of the Cherokees had moved as far as Texas. Jefferson's agrarian philosophy directed that the first priority went to forestalling white emigration across the Mississippi "until we have filled up all the vacant country on this side." In his vision of intensive settlement, little or no land in the East would remain for Indians. The West could meanwhile be reserved for them, at least for 50 years.[82]

The year after Jefferson became president in 1801, the U.S. government promised the state of Georgia that it would purchase all Indian territory there, assign it to the state, and remove the Cherokees from it. With his acquisition of the Louisiana Purchase in 1803, Jefferson formally proposed their deportation, instituting the U.S. policy of voluntary or forced removal.[83] Noting that America's incorporation of Louisiana "more than doubled the area of the United States," he urged the policy of "tempting all our Indians on the East side of the Mississippi to remove to the West."[84]

Over time, Jefferson's projects for Indians ranged widely, from peaceable assimilation with white American farmers to what we would now call ethnic "cleansing" of the Indians, first in wartime, then in peace, and extending to extermination if he deemed it necessary. In his mind, all these options involved the disappearance of Indian communities. Jefferson told Governor William H. Harrison in February 1803 that his policy was to "finally consolidate our whole country to one nation only." This, he directed, Harrison must keep secret, as it was "improper to be understood by the Indians." Jefferson recommended that they "should see only the present age of their history." The future that he envisaged, without distinct Indian nations, would alarm them. Jefferson predicted that "our settlements will gradually circumscribe and approach the Indians, and they will in time either incorporate with us as citizens of the United States, or remove beyond the Mississippi." Jefferson's obsession remained the expansion to the Mississippi of intensive American farming. To achieve that, Indian removal was as convenient as genocide. He told Harrison: "The Cahokias extinct, we are entitled to their country by our paramount sovereignty. The Piorias, we understand, have all been driven off from their country." The

Kaskaskias, "being reduced to a few families, I presume we may purchase their whole country."[85]

Even as peaceable acquisition and assimilation proceeded, Jefferson continued to see ethnic cleansing and even genocide as legitimate U.S. responses to war and opportunity. He told Harrison: "Should any tribe be foolhardy enough to take up the hatchet at any time, the seizing [of] the whole country of that tribe, and driving them across the Mississippi, as the only condition of peace, would be an example to others, and a furtherance of our final consolidation." Four years later, in 1807, Jefferson instructed his secretary of war that the United States preferred peace, but "if ever we are constrained to lift the hatchet against any tribe, we will never lay it down till that tribe is exterminated, or is driven beyond the Mississippi." He added, "In war, they will kill some of us; we shall destroy all of them." America might even strike preemptively: "[I]t will be a subject of consideration whether, on satisfactory evidence that any tribe means to strike us, we shall not anticipate by giving them the first blow. . . . It will make a powerful impression on the Indians, if those who spur them to war, see them destroyed without yielding them any aid."[86]

As hostility with Britain rose again in 1808, Jefferson again threatened Indians with deportation, or worse, should they side with the British: "No nation rejecting our friendship, and commencing wanton and unprovoked war against us, shall ever after remain within our reach." The next year he warned chiefs of the Shawnees, Wyandots, and others not to join forces with Britain: "[T]he tribe which shall begin an unprovoked war against us, we will extirpate from the earth, or drive to such a distance as that they shall never again be able to strike us." While the United States wanted friendship, Jefferson advised the Indians to "look in the faces of your wives and children and ask, 'shall we expose these our own flesh and blood to perish from want in a distant country and have our race and name extinguished from the face of the earth?'"[87]

When attempting to assimilate Indians as U.S. citizens, Jefferson stressed to them the importance of cultivation. He told Indians that "temperance, peace and agriculture will raise you up," and that the United States sought "to encourage and aid you in the culture of the earth."[88] In a letter to John Adams on the eve of the War of 1812, Jefferson praised the Cherokees as "far advanced in civilization. They have good Cabins, inclosed fields, large herds of cattle and hogs." One Cherokee branch, Jefferson wrote, was even "now instituting a regular representative government." Such progress was proof against "English seductions" of Indians. On the other hand, Indian failure to adopt agriculture drew Jefferson's hostility, even if it also served his hopes for further U.S. expansion. "But the backward [Indians] will yield, and be thrown further back. They will relapse into barbarism and misery, lose numbers by war and want, and we shall be obliged to drive them, with the beasts of the forest into the Stony mountains. They will be conquered however in Canada. The possession of that country secures our women and children forever from the tomahawk and scalping knife."[89]

Following the outbreak of the War of 1812, once again Jefferson accepted the purpose and precedent of genocide. He wrote to the German scholar Alexander von Humboldt:

> You know, my friend, the benevolent plan we were pursuing here for the happiness of the Aboriginal inhabitants in our vicinities. We spared nothing to keep them at peace with one another, to teach them agriculture and to encourage industry by establishing among them separate property. . . . On the commencement of our present war, we pressed on them the observance of peace but the unprincipled policy of England has defeated all our labors for the salvation of these unfortunate people. They have seduced the greater part of the tribes, within our neighborhood, to take up the hatchet against us, and the cruel massacres they have committed on the women and children of our frontiers taken by surprise, will oblige us now to pursue them to extermination, or drive them to new seats beyond our reach.

He concluded by acknowledging U.S. involvement in a continuing global narrative of genocide: "The confirmed brutalization, if not extermination of this race in our America is therefore to form an added chapter in the English history of the same colored man in Asia, and of the brethren of their own colour in Ireland and wherever else Anglo-mercantile cupidity can find a two-penny interest in deluging the earth with blood."[90]

After the War of 1812, Indian agriculture and Jefferson's recognition of it were denied and forgotten. An 1823 judgment of the U.S. Supreme Court citing "the original fundamental principle, that discovery gave exclusive title to those who made it," excluded Indians, whose "power to dispose of the soil at their own will" was thereby "denied."[91] Chief Justice John Marshall ignored Jefferson's view of Cherokee agriculture when he said: "The tribes of Indians inhabiting this country were fierce savages . . . whose subsistence was drawn chiefly from the forest." So the Europeans' discoveries, Marshall added, had given them "an exclusive right to extinguish the Indian title of occupancy." The Court added: "We will not enter into the controversy, whether agriculturists, merchants, and manufacturers, have a right on abstract principle, to expel hunters from the territory they possess, or to contract their limits."[92] The controversy, then, had been settled by *faits accomplis,* which the Court determined not to question.

Even Lewis Cass, an early U.S. authority on Indians, disregarded their farming. He wrote in 1830 that they merely "traversed" but did not occupy the land. As secretary of war from 1831 to 1836 under Andrew Jackson, Cass was to supervise the expulsion of Indians from the southeastern states to Oklahoma.[93]

Ethnic Cleansing: The Trail of Tears

In the War of 1812, Andrew Jackson defeated both the British at New Orleans and the Creeks in Alabama. In his 1814 campaign against the Creek Red Sticks, Jackson organized devastating "envelopment" of Creek towns, a tactic designed by his nephew-in-law, John Coffee. Their forces regularly attacked undefended villages "occupied only by women, children, and old men while the warriors were in the field. Soldiers killed indiscriminately."[94] They killed 3,000 Creeks, "approximately 15 percent of the entire Nation," including 850 warriors who fell at the battle of Horse Shoe Bend in 1814.[95]

After the battle, Jackson proclaimed to his troops: "The fiends of the Tallapoosa will no longer murder our women and children. . . . They have disappeared from the face of the Earth. In their places a new generation will arise who know their duties better. The weapons of warfare will be exchanged for the duties of husbandry; and the wilderness which now withers in sterility and seems to mourn the desolation which overspreads it, will blossom as the rose, and become the nursery of the arts. . . . How lamentable it is that the path to peace should lead through blood, and over the carcases of the slain!! But it is in the dispensation of that providence, which inflicts partial evil to produce general good."[96] Neither agriculture nor peace nor "general good" would protect the Creeks or other southern Indians. Jackson's prediction of "a new generation" meant one of different stock from "the slain." That was a metaphor for extinction he would use again.

The 1814 Treaty of Fort Jackson divested the vanquished Creeks of 23 million acres. Over the next six years, as U.S. treaty commissioner to the southern Indians, Jackson persuaded the other tribes "by fair means or foul, to sell to the United States a major portion of their lands in the southeast," including land in an area where he now had a new financial interest. In 1816, Jackson secured for his nephew Coffee an appointment to head the government surveys of the Indian lands in Alabama. They both became shareholders in Coffee's land speculation company. In 1818, Jackson was the sole bidder for land in an area of Alabama alleged to have been fraudulently acquired from Cherokees, in a treaty the Senate would not ratify. He and Coffee paid the official price, one-eighth of local market value. Jackson later bought another 2,700 acres of former Indian land in Mississippi.[97]

Jackson's Indian removals and land schemes occupied the public ground between personal intimacy and grand policy. He had adopted a Creek boy orphaned by his troops, only to see him die of tuberculosis at 16. By 1820, Jackson had secured for the United States 50 million acres, about half the territory southern Indians had held in 1812. He set about "cleansing" the region of Indians. In 1816, some Cherokees emigrated to the Arkansas River, and in 1817–18, Jackson removed 6,000 poverty-stricken Cherokees from Georgia. Several hundred led by Duwali and others settled in Mexican east Texas.[98]

However, in 1817 the 15,000 Cherokees remaining in the southeastern United States established their own bicameral legislature and an executive, judiciary, and army. The legislature outlawed further land sales to the United States and in 1827 adopted a written constitution and bill of rights modeled on that of the United States, declaring the Cherokee nation "sovereign and independent." They set up five schools, while the 30,000 Choctaws and Chickasaws in Mississippi and Alabama ran 13 more. In 1821, Sequoyah invented the Cherokee writing syllabary, into which parts of the Bible were translated, and in 1828 the bilingual weekly *Cherokee Phoenix* began publication. Cherokee farmers raised large herds of cattle, horses, sheep, goats, and pigs; grew corn, wheat, oats, potatoes, tobacco, and indigo; and exported cotton to New Orleans. According to Anthony F. C. Wallace, whites in Georgia came to fear that the Indian, "if left in place to govern himself in his own territory would beat the white man at his own game—raising cotton—and prevent forever the further acquisition of Indian land. . . . It was not the 'savagery' of the Indians that land-hungry whites dreaded; it was their 'civilization.'"[99] Yet U.S. federal courts denied Indians, until 1847, equal recognition as witnesses competent to testify.[100]

The pressure rose. As nominee of the Democratic Party, Jackson won the 1828 presidential election. Georgia quickly passed legislation applying the state's legal and police powers to the Cherokee territory. In his inaugural address in March 1829, Jackson called for a federal Indian Removal Act. He told Choctaws that the United States "would be obliged to sustain the States in the exercise of their right."[101] In the congressional debate that followed, one speaker remarked, "What is history but the obituary of nations?"[102]

In May 1830, Congress passed the removal bill, which Jackson signed into law. The removal was to be voluntary, yet most Indians would leave only under threat and harassment. Jackson fired the superintendent of the Indian Office, who had favored voluntary removal but opposed harassment, and sacked half of his experienced field staff. The federal government began withholding its payments of existing agreed annuities for acquired Indian land until the Indians had migrated west. The state governments of the South abolished tribal governments and laws, banned tribal assemblies, imposed taxes and other obligations on Indians, denied them the right to vote or testify in court, encouraged white land-grabs, and sold off Indian lands. Wallace writes: "Thousands of intruders swarmed over the Indian country in a frenzied quest for land and gold, destroying Indian farms and crops." Missionaries attempting to defend Indian interests were arrested and jailed, but two appealed their convictions. The Supreme Court found, in their favor, that Georgia had no right to override U.S. authority over Indians and could not legally assert sovereignty over the Cherokees. But in a second case, the Supreme Court found against the Cherokees on the technicality that, as a "domestic dependent nation," the Indians lacked the legal standing to bring a suit before it. Their "guardian," the United States, refused to intervene to protect its "ward" nation.[103]

In his second annual message to Congress, Jackson stated that "the fate of the aborigines of this country" had moved humanity to tears and to "devising means to avert it, but its progress has never for a moment been arrested, and one by one have many powerful tribes disappeared from the earth. To follow to the tomb the last of his race and tread on the graves of extinct nations excite melancholy reflections. But true philanthropy reconciles the mind to these vicissitudes as it does to the extinction of one generation to make room for another."[104] He saw such extinction as both inevitable and providential.

The president's nephew-in-law Coffee bribed Choctaw chiefs into signing a removal treaty in 1830. They gave up 11 million acres in return for 15 million acres in Oklahoma. The Choctaw nation numbered around 25,000 people. Of the first 1,000 to set out in 1830, only 500 survived the winter trek. From 1831 to 1833, 9,000 more reached Oklahoma. Hundreds died en route, and 4,000 perished from cholera on arrival. About one-fifth of the Choctaws had died in four years. After five years of white encroachment, the 6,000 Chickasaws were transported to Oklahoma in 1837–38, with much less loss of life. The 23,000

Creeks still in Alabama voted to stay and respect state law, but they, too, were ejected. After a band of Indians held up a stagecoach in 1836, Jackson's administration launched the Second Creek War. U.S. forces captured and manacled 800 warriors and marched them west with their families. Of 3,000 Creeks who set out, 700 died on the trail. A U.S. officer reported that the 2,300 survivors were in "total destitution." Another 18,000 followed, and in all, thousands of Creeks perished during these removal operations from 1832 to 1838.[105]

The 16,000 "Eastern Cherokees" remaining in Georgia, Alabama, Tennessee, and North Carolina were led by John Ross (1790–1866), son of a Scottish Loyalist and a woman of one-quarter Cherokee descent. Educated at a white academy, Ross had served with Jackson in the First Creek War. He married a Cherokee and ran a 300-acre plantation in Georgia, with 20 slaves and a mansion worth $20,000. Ross, the principal chief, and the majority of the Cherokee council opposed removal. But Major John Ridge, speaker of the council, who had also served with Jackson and owned his own plantation, slaves, and investments, was more inclined to favor removal as necessary for Cherokee survival.[106]

Asking for $20 million, Ross turned down Jackson's offer of $3 million for all Cherokee lands in Georgia and Alabama. According to Wallace, "what white Georgia feared most was the rise of men like John Ross." In 1832, Georgia's state government proclaimed itself owner of the Cherokee lands and sold them off. Yet over the next two years, federal efforts to promote mass emigration convinced only 1,000 Cherokees to leave.[107] Meanwhile, in Washington, D.C., the Tennessee congressman Davy Crockett had protested against the bill for Cherokee removal: "None of my colleagues agree with my sentiments. But if I should be . . . the only man in the United States who disapproved of it, I would still vote against it. . . . A treaty is the highest Law of the Land, but there are those who do not find it so. They want to juggle with the rights of the Indians and fritter them away. It's all wrong. It's not justice! . . . These Indians are the remnants of a once powerful race and they must be fairly treated."[108]

Federal politicians twice convinced lesser Cherokee leaders to sign removal treaties, but the Cherokee council repudiated each one. Georgia militia then arrested John Ross and a white journalist and closed down the *Cherokee Phoenix* by force. Federal and state officials summoned the Cherokee nation to a meeting, which the majority antiremoval faction boycotted. Some 300–500 Indians attended, led by Major Ridge, and signed the Treaty of New Echota in December 1835. This small minority of the Cherokee nation agreed to abandon all Cherokee lands east of the Mississippi and move within two years to an 8-million-acre allotment in Oklahoma. General Ellis Wool, in charge of supervising the removal, joined others in denouncing the treaty as fraudulent. Jackson reprimanded him as "disrespectful," prohibited the Cherokee council from further discussing the treaty, and sent in federal troops. Three hundred Cherokees who had signed the treaty left quickly for Oklahoma, followed by another 900 the next year.[109]

In 1836, the new U.S. president, Martin Van Buren, declared: "No State can achieve proper culture, civilization, and progress . . . as long as Indians are permitted to remain." The Senate ignored a protest petition from 15,665 Cherokees. Only 250 showed up for deportation on the deadline of May 23, 1838, and 17,000 stayed home. Seven thousand U.S. regular troops and militia struck quickly. According to James Mooney, who interviewed participants: "Squads of troops were sent to search out with rifle and bayonet every small cabin hidden away in the coves or by the sides of mountain streams, to seize and bring in as prisoners all the occupants."[110] Three thousand people died in this roundup and in the camps to which they were confined awaiting deportation. One thousand more, including Ross's wife, Quatie, died en route to Oklahoma. Another 1,000 fled into the hills of North Carolina, eluding capture. Between one-fifth and one-quarter of the Eastern Cherokee population perished in 1838–39 alone.[111]

Extermination in Texas

While the American pioneer settler Stephen F. Austin was visiting Texas for the first time in 1821, Mexico gained its independence from Spain. The Mexican province of Texas was home to about 3,500 whites and 20,000 Indians.[112] Austin had an amicable first meeting with the Cocos group of Karankawa Indians near the mouth of the Colorado River. He wrote in his journal of the two sides "parting apparently good friends," but he immediately added an ominous accusation: "These Indians and the Karanquas may be called universal enemies to man—they killed of all nations that came into their power, and frequently feast on the bodies of their victims—the [approach of] an American population will be the signal of their extermination for there will be no way of subduing them but for extermination."[113]

The ancestors of the Karankawas had resisted French, Spanish, and Comanche Indian intrusions on their land. When Thomas Jefferson asserted a claim

MAP 17. Indian habitations in Mexican Texas and the Republic, 1820–46

on the area in 1804, asking the German explorer Alexander von Humboldt whether "white, red, or black people" lived there, Humboldt informed him that the coastline of the thinly populated east Texas savanna was "lined with little islands inhabited by independent Indians."[114] From 1821, Austin's new settlers quickly clashed with the Karankawas, who included 200 to 300 warriors.[115]

War with the American settlers also reflected competing visions of land use in Texas that would shape its subsequent history. Karankawas hunted in the lush open prairie grasslands extending on both sides of the Colorado River.[116] Just before his first meeting with Karankawas, Austin had found this land to be "all first rate," mostly "rich Prairie" that "lays beautifully."[117] As he established his young colony, its members took up coastal commerce and inland agriculture. A settler from Missouri, Horatio Chriesman, reached the mouth of the Colorado River in 1822. Like other settlers, Chriesman approached cultivation in earnest. "We had," he later recalled, "about eight acres of corn which if not worked immediately was certain to be lost. I could not stop the plough to hunt. I took no sustenance save a few stinted drinks of buttermilk until after I finished ploughing."[118] Another settler recalled Austin trying to "induce" the Tonkawa Indians "to cultivate the soil." Austin gave the Tonkawa chief, Carita, farming implements and seed corn, but Carita replied that "the Great Spirit had told the Tonkewas not to raise corn but hunt" and to "look to their white friends." At this, Austin retorted sharply "that *he* was inspired to say that the Tonkewas would starve if they did not go to work."[119]

Fighting flared as more settlers arrived. John Henry Moore, born in 1800 in Rome, Tennessee, is said to have run away to Texas, when he had had enough of college Latin, to become a farmer and stock raiser.[120] After Karankawas killed two settlers in 1823, Moore joined a posse of young whites in a retaliatory raid on a Karankawa camp, where they killed and scalped 19 Indians.[121] Only two Karankawas escaped. One of the attackers explained their success "in killing so many Indians, without any of us getting wounded. We can only account for it, from the fact of the Indians being so greatly alarmed, that they did not even attempt to fire upon us."[122] Moore confirmed the massacre: "The fight was an entire surprise. We all felt it was an act of justice and self-preservation. We were too weak to furnish food for Carankawaes, and had to be let alone to get bread for ourselves." Recalling that "twenty-three were left dead" on the prairie, Moore described the Karankawas as "large, sluggish Indians, who fed mostly on fish and alligators, and occasionally, by way of feast, on human flesh." He added that "frequent" Indian attacks provoked the whites "to their chastisement with alacrity."[123] A visitor to Austin's colony remarked that "an unceremonious fashion which prevailed, of shooting down red men wherever they were found, was the order of the day."[124]

After Austin led a 90-man expedition against the Karankawas in 1824, his company commander, Captain Horatio Chriesman, continued their pursuit, killing 23. Other settlers ambushed Karankawas disembarking from a canoe, and shot nine dead.[125] In 1825, the American colonists entered a second war, against Comanches at San Antonio. Austin also received orders from Mexico's military commandant "to gather the largest force possible" and march against the Tahuiases and "to attack the Wacos without delay and destroy their villages." However, the arrival of a Comanche force obliged Austin to defer this attack and to propose a pact with the Wacos.[126] As fighting continued against the Karankawas, Austin issued a genocidal command: "I have been compelled in view of the security of our people, to give positive orders to the Lieutenant of Militia in that section, to pursue and kill all those Indians wherever they are found, with the exception of Prudencia's party, provided said Prudencia remains west of Buffalo Bayou, because it would be impossible to make a distinction between his people and the others, if they continue mixed together in our vicinity."[127]

Austin explained that the "Wacos, Tawanakys, Comanches, Cherokees and all the Indians to the east of us . . . are very much dissatisfied that their country has been given to the American Empresarios to be settled." Aware of the implications of his role, Austin speculated to fellow colonists: "If we destroy the Waco Villages will not the other tribes consider it as a warning of the fate that must in the end befall them if the American settlements progress? and is there no danger that they may become alarmed and unite to cut us off in our infancy?" Austin also knew the American historical precedents. "The history of the first settlements in the U. States, presents numerous and horrible examples of such combinations, which in most instances might have been avoided by a greater degree of prudence and forbearance on the part of the settlers."[128]

Austin apparently decided on forbearance toward the Wacos but not toward the Karankawas. A week later, he seems to have ignored settlers who petitioned him to "treat with" the Karankawas.[129] Early in 1826, following the murder of two settler families, a party of Austin's colonists massacred a large community of Karankawas on the Colorado River.[130] Captain Buckner led a charge of 60 men: "The Indians had their squaws and papooses with them, and some of them were killed by the promiscuous firing that ensued. The fire of the Texans was so rapid and deadly that many of the Indians endeavored to escape it by plunging into the river, but even after they had succeeded in reaching the opposite shore many were shot and fell back in the stream. An eye-witness of the scene says that the river was literally red with blood. Between forty and fifty of this band of savages were killed." According to a local history: "All but five or six Indian warriors were killed. These escaped in their canoes. The settlers followed and overtook them at a point six miles above and completely exterminated them."[131] Other posses "murdered and broke up small bands of Karankawas" until the survivors sued for peace and agreed to withdraw to the west in 1827. Now even Prudencia's friendly band fled. Killings of remnants in attacks on Karankawa camps continued through 1832 and 1833.[132]

Agriculture forged ahead as the Indians retreated. Guests at an 1832 ceremonial dinner toasted "[t]he farmers of Texas" and its first settlers, who "have expelled the savage, subdued and planted the forest." Austin's colonists enslaved 35 Karankawas who tried to return, and a woman settler wrote that "these fierce children of the woods once roamed, free as the lion of the desert" but had now become "the hewers of wood and drawers of water to their invaders." Another early settler wrote of the 1820s that "in the first settleing of Texas, the old settlers told us they were quite a large tribe of Indians, and knowing that they were always at war with the other tribes and whites, they were reduced to a very small band when I first knew them." By 1836, the estimated 200–250 Karankawas remaining on Austin's grant included only 25–30 braves. Settlers simply brushed off their offer to fight in the war of independence against Mexico.[133]

Yet eastern Indians were heading for Texas. Its borders remained porous, and Mexican control incomplete. The first Cherokee community to reach Texas crossed its northern border, the Red River, in 1820. Two years later, the governor of Texas, pending approval from Mexico City, authorized the Cherokees to "cultivate their lands and sow their crops, in free and peaceful possession" and added, "[T]hey shall be considered Hispano-Americans." They dispatched to Mexico City a delegation of six leaders, including the future principal chief of the Texas Cherokees, Duwali, also known as Colonel Bowl. On arrival in Mexico City in 1823, the Cherokee delegates requested land in Texas "to setel a Poor orfan tribe of Red Peopel," stating they had been "much persecuted" in the United States and were "afraid to return" there.[134] The new Mexican government sent the Cherokee delegates back to what it called "their country" in Texas. It ordered that pending a final decision, "the families already settled, should be well treated." Thus the Cherokees launched a 10-year partially successful legal campaign for title to the Texas lands they were farming. In 1833, Duwali formally petitioned the Texas state authorities for ownership, stating that the Cherokees, "after the government had promised to give them said tract of land, they settled in it, and from that time forward have cultivated it." The 800 Texas Cherokees, Duwali's petition said, lived "chiefly by tilling the soil" and by raising their 3,000 cattle and 500 horses.[135] They were not the only deportees from the United States who hoped to find shelter in Texas. Under an 1835 treaty with the United States, the Caddo Indians of Louisiana also had to give up their land there, move outside U.S. boundaries, and never return.[136] Almost immediately, however, both Indian groups confronted what U.S. Cherokee chief John Ross called "a new republic, made up of many of the old foes of the Indians—Texas."[137]

The young Texas republic won its independence from Mexico in 1836. Davy Crockett had fallen at the battle of the Alamo, and Stephen F. Austin died of illness that same year. New settler occupation of Indian land brought more conflict, but the Texas republic's first president, Sam Houston, an adoptive Cherokee who shared Crockett's respect for Indians, pursued reconciliation.[138] In return for their neutrality against Mexico, Houston signed a treaty with the Cherokees giving them land in northeast Texas, a treaty the new Texas Senate declared null and void within months.[139] By September 1838, using an approach that historian W. E. S. Dickerson calls "largely successful," Houston also reached five agreements with seven other Indian groups.[140] Even after Comanches reportedly killed "about 40 whites" on the San Antonio River in July, Houston informed the Cherokee chief Duwali: "I have given an order that no families, or children of Indians shall be disturbed."[141] Houston reiterated his order a week later: "The Troops . . . will treat the Indians, and their property, as its guardians; preventing all injury."[142]

However, Houston's vice president and successor, Mirabeau Buonaparte Lamar, abandoned this reconciliation policy when he commenced his own three-year term as president of Texas in December 1838. From his early adulthood in Georgia, Lamar had been a proponent of Indian removal, Negro slavery, and states' rights.[143] As president of Texas, he would become best known for founding its capital, naming it for Austin, and establishing the Texas education system. However, Lamar also brought to Texas and to its presidency other predilections more common among perpetrators of ethnic warfare. These included strong views on agriculture, classical antiquity, and empire. In his early travels from Georgia, Lamar had professed something of a distaste for cities, finding Mobile "a dirty little town" and recoiling at "the extreme filthiness" of New Orleans. These views changed as he saw Mobile grow into "a populous city, reared up as if by magic, like one in a fairy land, with beauty unrivaled." But Lamar's first visit to Texas in 1835 persuaded him that here was "the land of promise and fruition." He quickly petitioned the government "for my league of land as a citizen of Texas." The next year, he hoped to secure that land "when the war is over." When he became president, Lamar aimed to develop the new country as "a great agricultural community with an open commerce with all the world."[144]

Raised in the early nineteenth century on his family's prosperous Georgia plantation, the young Mirabeau, with his father and older brother Lucius Quintus Cincinnatus, had supervised the slaves who did most of the necessary farm work. His classical education included works on Roman history. As a pupil he pondered problems like "Was Brutus Justifiable in Assassinating Caesar?" and "Were the Europeans Justifiable in Conquering and Taking Possession of America in the Manner They Did?"[145] In a school performance before an audience of Georgia farmers, Lamar played Brutus in Shakespeare's *Julius Caesar*. A classmate recalled: "Every one felt that the lofty patriotism and heroic virtues of the old Roman would find a fit representative in Lamar. I remember, in our rehearsals, how completely his identity would be lost in that of Brutus. He seemed to enter into all the feelings and the motives which prompted the great soul of the Roman to slay his friend for his country's good."[146]

Lamar vented his classical learning a quarter of a century later, when he fought with the victorious Texan independence forces at the battle of San Jacinto. Having distinguished himself in the defeat of Mexican general Santa Anna, Lamar recommended hanging the captured dictator as "the Nero of the present day." Houston opted instead to release Santa Anna, giving him a horse to ride out of Texas forever.[147] After his own inauguration as president of the republic in 1838, Lamar returned to the theme of antiquity when he told Congress: "Our young Republic has been formed by a Spartan spirit. Let it progress and ripen into Roman firmness, and Athenian gracefulness and wisdom."[148] Just as Rome had been besieged by barbarians, Lamar saw Indian tribes intruding on Texas with "Vandalic ferocity."[149]

In his inaugural presidential address, Lamar imagined Texas as both agrarian and expansionist. He envisaged "her vast extent of territory, stretching from the Sabine to the Pacific, and away to the Southwest as far as the obstinacy of the enemy may render it necessary for the sword to make the boundary; embracing the most delightful climate and the richest soil in the world, and behold it all in the state of high cultivation."[150] Two weeks later, Lamar outlined his plan to "lay the foundations of a great empire." This involved both territorial expansion and farm cultivation. He had already proposed building a line of "block and trading houses to the Pacific shore." Now he told Texans that their new country was "the youngest among the family of nations.... Providence has placed her before you a perfect blank.... As yet her prairies are unploughed; her forests are unfelled."[151] Aided by "a knowledge of the past," white yeoman farmers were to fill this "blank." "Cultivation is as necessary to the supply of rich intellectual and moral fruits, as are the labors of the husbandman to bring forth the valuable productions of the earth."[152] Lamar envisaged a Texan economy "devoted to agriculture and commerce," manufacturing only "a few articles of primary necessity," with "the great mass of her population" tilling "her generous and untiring soil."[153] In his first year in office, Lamar approved a homestead law providing 640 acres to every family of settlers arriving before 1840 and 50 acres for every citizen, plus "all implements of husbandry" and "five milch cows, one yoke of work oxen, or one horse."[154]

Lamar's vision of occupying an empty land ignored its Indian inhabitants, including the 600–800 Texas Cherokees who already practiced shifting cultivation on riverbanks and lived in townships.[155] Yet their presence required a policy. Texas military officers like General Thomas Jefferson Rusk, who had chafed under Houston's restraints, now offered encouragement for Lamar's aggressiveness toward Indians. Rusk enjoyed considerable support in the Texan army.[156] Born in South Carolina, where leading pro-slavery advocate John C. Calhoun had helped him start a law career, Rusk had moved to Texas and become a leading signatory of its Declaration of Independence. He became major general of the republic's militia in 1838, and in the month after Lamar's election, attacked the Kickapoo Indians, destroying their main village. Fighting alongside Rusk was Colonel Hugh McLeod, a West Point graduate and lieutenant in the Third U.S. Infantry, who had become adjutant general of the Army of the Republic of Texas.[157] Describing their October 16 attack on the Kickapoos, McLeod wrote president-elect Lamar: "[T]he grass was full of trails of blood— we have since heard they lost about 30."[158]

The Texan attack provoked a new Indian atrocity. Writing to Cherokee chief Duwali on October 20, Rusk raged at the Kickapoos, who had "a day or two past murdered two families of women and children[—]for this they deserve death and will assuredly meet it[;] they cannot live in peace in this Country ... blood shall pay for the blood which has been shed."[159] The author of a report on the October 18 murders promised Lamar that, given command of "one thousand mounted men" for a year, "I will put to silence every hostile tribe of Indians in Texas."[160]

Thus the Texan officers began urging "extermination" of Indians on Lamar before he took office. At Rusk's request, Colonel McLeod wrote Lamar on October 25 to present Rusk's view: "The time he says has arrived for a general, prompt and vigorous campaign against the Indians," whose frontier atrocities required a genocidal response. "It may do for those at a safe distance who have no interest at stake, to prate the sickly sentiments of a mistaken humanity, but the man whose cabin is in ashes, whose family are wanderers and himself hunted down like a wild beast, *must* answer blow by blow, and take blood for blood—that time has come, and General Rusk proposes to concentrate the effective force of the Ea[stern] Section of the Country, upon the Indi[an] territory, and *exterminate the race*." Only the "unequivocally friendly" Indians would be spared: "the Shawnees, Delawares, Cherokees, Kickapoos and Choctaws." Targets for extermination appeared to include the Comanches and the Caddoes. McLeod was confident of Lamar's support: "I think you will approve the plan."[161]

Four weeks later, McLeod reported that Brigadier General Dyer had ordered troops "to destroy a band of Caddoes (60 men)" near the U.S.–Texas border, and if necessary "to follow them across the line and exterminate them." Rusk's troops crossed into the United States, disarming the Caddoes, who had quickly surrendered. McLeod now wrote Lamar, "[T]hese are not *all* the Caddoes," for many more "are among the wild Indians of Texas." McLeod and Dyer's 4th Brigade converged on them, too. McLeod urged Lamar: "Let us drive these wild Indians off, and establish a line of block houses, and we have done all we can *now*—If the U States *will not remove their own Indians,* to wit, Cherokees, Shawnees, Delawares, Kickapoos Choctaws, Alabamas, and Coshattes, to say nothing of these Caddoes who they have literally ordered and driven into our territory—I say if the U.S. is faithless enough to refuse to remove them[,] We must await a more auspicious moment than the present, to exterminate them."[162]

President Lamar took office on December 10, 1838. His first statement to Congress combined a warning to the Indians with a proposal for their agricultural settlement. "As long as we continue to exhibit our mercy without shewing our strength," Lamar said, "so long will the Indian continue to bloody the edge of the tomahawk." Recalling the imagery of Edmund Spenser and John Derricke in sixteenth-century Ireland, Lamar asserted that when war proves unavoidable, it must be "pursued as will best secure a speedy and lasting peace. If that better mode consists in severity to the enemy, then severity to him, becomes clemency to all." Lamar concluded: "If the wild cannibals of the woods will not desist from their massacres; if they will continue to war upon us with the ferocity of Tigers and Hyenas, it is time we should retaliate their warfare, not in the murder of their women and children, but in the prosecution of an exterminating war upon their warriors, which will admit of no compromise and have no termination except in their total extinction or total expulsion."[163]

Lamar quickly proposed "a line of military posts" to subject "all intercourse" with the Indians "to the control of the Government." He recommended they become farmers, with each Indian family "permitted to enjoy such improvements as they occupy, together with a suitable portion of land." However, any Indians refusing to accept "our laws in all criminal matters" or in "matters of contract to the authorized agents of the Government," Lamar warned, "should be viewed as enemies, and treated accordingly."[164] Lamar announced his intention to remove all but native Indians from Texas, repudiating the Cherokee Treaty of 1836. For the next three years, his administration would expend over half its budget on Indian affairs, in what one officer called "a war of extermination."[165]

In the first weeks of Lamar's administration, Rusk and others became more impatient as hostilities quickly escalated. Some estimates of the two-year toll of Indian depredations soared to "four hundred scalps." Rusk wrote Lamar in January: "I fear if a decisive blow is not struck against the Indians before spring we shall be much troubled with them." McLeod reported completing a forced march "unparalleled, since De Soto's." His troops had "destroyed the Caddo villages," whose inhabitants had fled. McLeod found this "the finest portion of Texas," a pastoral idyll. "The Ukraine cannot excel these prairies in the beauty and fleetness of its *wild* horses." He added with a classical flourish: "I've been riding so long, that I have almost become a Centaur."[166]

An ugly public mood pressed the new administration for a sweeping policy to end Indian atrocities. A soldier asked the president in February to "visit them with the same kind of warfare that they give us, we should spare neither age sect nor condition for they do not." A friend of Lamar's proposed a final solution: "Is it better for our citizens to be daily murdered, or for us to declare a war of extermination against them. I shall never fight freely and willingly but under a declaration of extermination. Our country can never prosper till the red skins are disposed of."[167]

At Lamar's instigation, the Texas Congress authorized Captain John Henry Moore, veteran of the 1823 massacre of 19 Karankawas and now an officer in the Texas independence forces, to raise three companies of Volunteers to fight prairie Indians.[168] On January 26, 1839, Moore's Volunteers marched up the Colorado River "against the Comanche."[169] As they advanced, Lamar's war secretary informed the government's Indian agent that it was pursuing "grave deliberation" on Cherokee land claims while targeting the Comanche: "The atrocious conduct of the Indians of the Prairies, precludes the idea of any adjustment with them until ample satisfaction shall have been obtained for the destruction of our slaughtered citizens."[170]

In the darkness before dawn the next morning, Captain Moore's three companies of 63 whites and 16 Lipan Indians crept toward a Comanche village beside a small stream in the valley of the San Saba River. One of Moore's men, Noah Smithwick, later recalled that "the sleeping Indians" were "not dreaming of an attack." However, as Moore reported, "opposite the centre of the Town we were discovered by the enemy at which moment I ordered a charge which was promptly obeyed and carried to near the centre of the village, the men throwing open the doors of the wigwams or pulling them down and slaughtering the enemy in their beds." Moore reported that his men had "about 3 shots each," which they "discharged with great accuracy at only a few feet distance, and in many instances by placing the muzzle against the object." Smithwick recalled: "[W]e made a rush for it, pouring a volley right into the lodges. Taken completely by surprise the savages bounded from their lodges and scattered like partridges. Our men rushed in among the lodges. The women and children screaming, dogs barking, men yelling and shooting, in a moment transformed the peaceful scene."[171]

Surviving Comanches regrouped in their defense. As smoke filled the air, the Indians charged and the whites beat them back at close range. Then over 300 Comanches surrounded the Texans, according to Moore, "and immediately opened a fire upon us which was soon silenced." The Comanches produced a white flag that Sam Houston had given them. The fight was over. The Texans had lost one man, while Moore reported a "very considerable" Comanche toll: "[T]heir loss must have been very great. In supposing their loss to have been 30 or 40 Killed and 50 or 60 wounded I make an estimate much below what I believe to be correct."[172] Yet in the view of the Texas government, this toll apparently fell short of "ample satisfaction." Addressing the people of Texas two weeks later, Lamar asserted that "savages are waging upon our exposed and defenceless inhabitants, an unprovoked and cruel warfare, massacring the women and children." He requisitioned six more companies of Volunteers to defend "a bleeding people."[173]

Lamar's administration now launched a new war on the Texas Cherokees, just two months after the United States had completed the deportation of the Eastern Cherokees to neighboring Oklahoma. In May 1839, Texas rangers intercepted a Mexican agent carrying letters addressed to Chief Duwali. Without further evidence of collaboration, Lamar ordered a military post established in the Cherokee territory. Duwali threatened to respond with force, telling Rusk that the troops' approach "has alarmed our women and children very much."[174] However, on May 26, Lamar warned Duwali that "the Cherokees will never be permitted to establish a permanent and independent jurisdiction" in Texas. They must now "return to their own tribes beyond the Red River."[175] Lamar added: "Whether it be done by friendly negociation or by violence of war, must depend on the Cherokee." Should the Indians "put in jeopardy the lives and property of our citizens, . . . the inevitable consequence will be a prompt and sanguinary war, which can terminate only in their destruction or expulsion."[176]

The next month, the president issued a more urgent ultimatum, backed by a still more explicit threat of genocide. As Rusk and three companies of troops marched on their villages in June, Lamar ordered "the immediate removal of the Cherokee Indians and the ultimate removal of all other emigrant tribes." He authorized that compensation be paid for their possessions, one-quarter in cash, totaling up to $25,000. But unless the Indians "at once" agreed to leave, Lamar concluded, "nothing short of the entire destruction of all they possess and the extermination of their tribe will appease the indignation of the white people against them."[177]

In the days of negotiations that followed, Texan threats continued. "If you remain in friendship with the wild Indians and Mexicans we will be forced to kill your people in defense of our frontier," Rusk told Duwali. "You are between two fires and if you remain you will be destroyed." After the Cherokees and their Shawnee allies finally agreed to depart, Rusk reiterated his warning: "Had we gone to war, women and children would have suffered." However, the Indians refused an additional Texan demand that they disarm before departure. Duwali said his young men "were frightened and did not want to give up their gunlocks. They believed the Texans would kill them as soon as they were unarmed." Therefore, no agreement was signed before the Indians began their retreat.[178]

Rusk and McLeod pursued them, reinforced by two regiments of regulars and the Texas vice president and secretary of war. When they caught up with the Indians on July 15–16, 1839, three regiments of 500–900 well-armed Texan troops engaged 500–800 Cherokee, Shawnee, and Delaware warriors. The at-

tackers lost seven dead and killed about 120 Indians. At the end of the day, Chief
Duwali, aged 83, remained on the field mounted on his sorrel horse, wearing
a large black three-cornered military hat, a bright silk vest, and "a handsome
sword and sash which had been given him by President Sam Houston . . . a
magnificent picture of barbaric manhood."[179] Texans shot Duwali's horse out
from under him. Rising to walk away, he took a bullet in the back, then sat up
again. Captain Robert Smith ran up and shot Duwali in the head at close range.
That night, the chief's son and successor, John Bowles, crept back onto the
battlefield and retrieved Duwali's hat.[180] Rusk noted "from the trails of blood"
that the other Cherokee survivors "must have suffered severely." As they fled
Texas, "their dead bodies were found scattered along the trail for miles."[181]

Troops continued the pursuit until July 24, burning several Indian villages and hundreds of acres of corn. Hunters shot Cherokees crossing the
Red River into U.S. Indian Territory. In December, the Texan army confronted
John Bowles, wearing his father's black hat, leading remnants of the tribe into
Mexico. "Many, including John Bowles," fell in a fierce firefight, and 27 women
and children, including Bowles's family, were captured. McLeod sent Duwali's
hat to ex-president Sam Houston, who retorted that Duwali had been "a better
man than his murderers" and insisted that the Cherokees "had never drawn
one drop of white man's blood."[182] Yet, looking back a year later, Lamar asserted instead that "the Cherokees were our natural enemies."[183] Rusk and
McLeod drove the survivors into Arkansas by the end of 1839. Of about 800
Texas Cherokees, perhaps one-quarter were dead. Few ever returned. A decade
later, different reports put Cherokee numbers in Texas at 100 or 25, "only five of
whom were warriors."[184]

The Cherokees and their Shawnee allies had fought their last battles
together. Lamar signed a treaty with the Shawnees in August 1839, promising
them compensation in return for their leaving the republic also. However, as in
the case of the Cherokees, the Texas Senate declined to ratify the treaty. Lamar
moved the republic's capital to Austin, on the Indian frontier. He then spent
$2.5 million in 1840 on a new campaign against the Comanches.[185]

The war began in response to an Indian gesture of peace and an offer to
return white captives. Hugh McLeod, promoted by Lamar to inspector general
of the army, became one of the republic's two key negotiators with the Comanches. In January 1840, a Penateka Comanche delegation visited San Antonio
to solicit a peace on behalf of the Comanche general council. The Texas secretary of war ordered: "Should the Comanche come in without bringing with

them the Prisoners, as it is understood they have agreed to do, you will detain them."[186] Seven weeks later, 33 chiefs and warriors and 32 other Comanches came to a parley at the Council House at San Antonio. McLeod described this party of "sixty-five—men, women and children" in a report to Lamar the next day, in which he acknowledged "your orders," in case the need arose, to "take hostages for the safe return of our own people."[187]

The Comanches had brought several Mexican and white hostages. However, McLeod and his fellow Texan commissioners demanded release of 15 other hostages, rejecting Chief Muk-wuh-rah's explanation that those were in the hands of Comanche bands independent of the Penateka. As Texan troops moved up and occupied the Council House, the commissioners informed the chiefs "that they were *our* prisoners," as McLeod reported to Lamar. The chiefs tried to force their way out, calling for aid from the warriors outside. A fight broke out. Texan troops killed all 30 chiefs and warriors and five Comanche women and children, capturing 27 more. Among the Indian men, McLeod wrote, "[t]he loss of the enemy was total." They had killed six Texans and a Mexican.[188]

Historian David La Vere writes that this Texan action "set off the wars of the Southern Plains, which lasted until 1875." Comanches, Kiowas, and Wichitas "became implacable foes of Texas and distinguished between Americans, whom they liked, and Texans, whom they hated." Comanches launched attacks deep into the republic.[189] Waves of mounted braves stole 1,500 horses and killed 22 whites and slaves in August 1840.[190] However, at the battle of Plum Creek, Texan forces killed as many as 80 Comanches for the loss of one trooper. The *Texas Sentinel* reported: "The Comanches, within the last four months, have lost one-fourth of their whole number. They must be getting very tired of such a war."[191]

Lamar now appointed John Henry Moore, promoted to colonel since his slaughter of Comanches the previous year, to command a new punitive expedition deeper into Comancheria. Some 90 Texans and 12 Lipan scouts set off up the Colorado River in September 1840. They located a Penateka camp of 60 lodges by a small river. Moore quietly deployed a detachment of sharpshooters across the stream. At first light, the mounted Texans attacked into and around the tipis, shooting dead 50 surprised Comanches of all ages, male and female. Survivors fled into the river. In minutes, Texan riflemen firing at close range from both banks killed another 80. Moore reported back to Austin in early November: "The bodies of men, women, and children were to be seen on every hand wounded, dying, and dead." That day the Texans had killed 130 Comanches for the loss of a single attacker.[192]

Continuing destruction of Indian communities enabled Texas to expand its territory. After a murderous Texan attack on a Karankawa camp in 1840, the survivors "disappeared suddenly and silently and drifted toward Mexico."[193] That June, Lamar proclaimed that "our settlements have spread out over a wider surface." The Indians "have been duly chastised, and driven back into deeper wilds," while in their "familiar haunts," the president added, "adventurous pioneers are still stretching their fields, and planting the standards of Civilization."[194]

Lamar pursued territorial expansionism in another theater as well. Shortly before his 1838 inauguration, he had received a letter from an "old acquaintance," Thomas Bradford of Alabama. Bradford urged Lamar to embark on "the conquest of the whole of Mexico" and to lead "an expedition to extend your republic to the pacific." Tensions with Mexico and its proxy "hordes of Indians," Bradford believed, justified such "aggressive measures," which would also deliver "liberty to a large portion of the human race" and plant the Texas flag "immovably on the walls of the city of Mexico." Bradford claimed he had "consulted, financially, with some of the heaviest capitalists in the United States.— *The money can be had*—Now is the time."[195] Lamar shared the view that Texas should remain independent and expand to the Pacific. When he failed to obtain Mexican recognition of Texas, he forged an alliance with the rebel regime in Yucatán and leased the Texas navy to it.[196] Rusk and McLeod also believed in aggressive Texan expansion.[197]

Lamar wrote to the people of Santa Fe on April 14, 1840, proposing that New Mexico join the Republic of Texas. Failing to get Texas congressional approval for such expansion, Lamar followed this up with an expedition to Santa Fe. In 1841, he called for volunteers and dispatched what became a disastrous venture, with a military component commanded by McLeod. Mexican forces captured the entire convoy.[198]

The Texas Indian wars continued until Sam Houston's return as president in late 1841.[199] Houston quickly reversed Lamar's "principle of exterminating the hostile Indians and removing the friendly ones."[200] Cherokees, Delawares, Chickasaws, Caddoes, Tawakonis, Kichais, Biloxis, and Wacos all signed a treaty of friendship with the Texas republic in September 1843. A second treaty a year later included Shawnees, Lipans, Anadarkos, and Comanches.[201]

Warfare resumed after the U.S. annexation of Texas in 1846. Within three years, the *Corpus Christi Star* newspaper proclaimed: "There is but one remedy for these things—war, an exterminating Indian war."[202] U.S. major general Persifor F. Smith instructed his officers in 1850: "All predatory Indians, no matter where discovered, will be pursued, attacked, and put to death. It is not advisable to take prisoners." In 1852, U.S. cavalry attacked a camp of sleeping Lipans and "fired indiscriminately into the lodges," killing 25 Indians, while settlers massacred yet another band of Karankawas in a surprise attack.[203] The survivors fled. With several braves, the last Karankawa chief, Hozzie Mercer, visited the daughter of an early settler who had once brought the Indians food and maintained a pact with them. On learning that her father had died, "[h]e sighed and said the best friend to poor Indian was gone. Then he returned to his canoes and proceeded down the river, and that was the last she saw of old Hozzie Mercer."[204] After a surviving band of 40 Karankawas were expelled from Mexico in the 1850s and returned to Texas, ranchers "killed every one of them." A man known as "Indian Tom," abandoned as a boy in 1843, may have been the last Karankawa. During the Civil War, according to a white acquaintance, he joined the Confederate army "and gave his life for the people who had exterminated his forefathers." Another account has it that Indian Tom, captured by federal forces, defied orders to work, whereupon an officer "ran a sword through him."[205]

The Indians' killers prospered. Thomas Jefferson Rusk headed the bar of the Republic of Texas before returning as major general of the militia in 1843, then resigned when Sam Houston overruled his plans to attack Mexico. After annexation, Rusk won election to the U.S. Senate, which in 1857 voted him its president pro tem. Hugh McLeod married Lamar's cousin, maintained his violent opposition to Houston, and was a Confederate lieutenant during the Civil War until his death in 1862. At age 61, Colonel John H. Moore joined the Texas cavalry, served on a committee to help finance the Confederate war effort, and "lost most of his property, much of which was slaves, but he recovered financially before his death."[206]

Genocide in California

The extermination of Indians in Texas occurred in a changing intellectual climate regarding race. The founder of U.S. anthropology, Samuel Morton, argued that what he considered to be the great races—Africans, Asians, Europeans, and Indians—were actually separate species of different origins, a theory known as polygenesis. In 1839, Morton published *Crania Americana; or, A Comparative View of the Skulls of Various Aboriginal Nations of North and South America.*

Morton incorporated a hierarchy of land use into the new racial science when he asserted in 1842 that "that soil which now rejoices the hearts of millions of freemen, would be yet overrun by lawless tribes of contending barbarians" but for the Europeans' "mental superiority." The next year, pro-slavery advocate Josiah Nott coined the use of the term *hybrid* for humans in his article, "The Mulatto a Hybrid—Probably Extermination of the Two Races If the Whites and Blacks Are Allowed to Intermarry."[207]

This sharpening of perceived divisions between the races, historian Elliott West points out, came just as the United States was about to expand its territory by two-thirds. Its 1845–48 acquisitions, which included California, Texas, and Oregon, also doubled the number of languages spoken within the United States. Ethnic issues suddenly assumed new prominence as the country gained startling geographic reach, triggering what West calls "an American racial crisis." The dramatic challenge of the possible expansion of Negro slavery from the South compounded that of incorporating the Hispanic, Chinese, and especially Native American populations living in the West. The U.S.–Mexican War that began in 1846 opened the way not only to the Civil War but also to what West terms the "[w]ar against Indian America," conducted in a new climate of scientific racism.[208]

The new racism met an old system in California, where Spanish and Mexican rule had depended on Indian forced labor. During the first three years of Franciscan missions there (1769–72), possibly one-quarter of the Indians under their control died, and malaria killed another 20,000 in 1833. The estimated precontact Indian population declined by half to around 150,000 in 1848.[209]

U.S. rule of California began in 1845. Settlers and miners poured in after the discovery of gold in 1848, numbering 92,000 by 1851 and 380,000 by 1860. California became a state in 1850. For the next two years, federal commissioners negotiated 18 treaties with 139 California Indian groups, who ceded most of their territory in exchange for assigning one-fourteenth of the state to reservations. Yet the U.S. Senate refused to ratify any of these agreements, making Indians "trespassers on the public domain," denied citizenship and banned from marrying Anglo-Americans and from testifying in court.[210] In December 1850, the San Francisco newspaper *Alta California* pronounced racial destruction of the Indians "unavoidable," for they would vanish "like a dissipating mist before the morning sun from the presence of the Saxon."[211]

State extermination policies became explicit a month later. The first U.S.

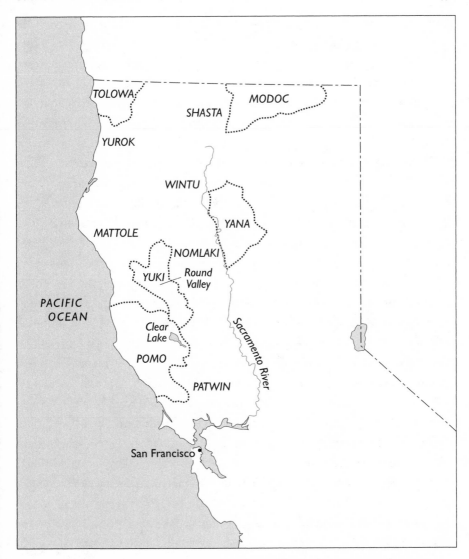

MAP 18. Selected Indian habitations in northern California under U.S. rule, 1845–75

governor of California, Peter Burnett, told the state legislature in January 1851 that the white man "cannot sit up all night to watch his property; ... after being robbed a few times he becomes desperate, and resolves upon a war of extermination." Burnett predicted that "[a] war of extermination will continue to be waged between the races until the Indian race becomes extinct."[212] His successor, Governor John McDougal, repeated the same month through a representative that unless Indians surrendered their lands, California would "make war upon" them, "which must of necessity be one of extermination of many of the tribes."[213] Another San Francisco newspaper editorialized in 1856: "Extermination is the quickest and cheapest remedy, and effectually prevents all other difficulties when an outbreak [of Indian violence] occurs."[214]

Enslavement of Indians was one route to extermination. In its first session in 1850, the California legislature legalized the forced indenture of Indian children. A white master merely needed a justice of the peace to certify that he had not obtained the child by force. In 1854, the California superintendent of Indian Affairs reported that slavers often murdered Indian parents while abducting the children, then marketed them with impunity as "orphans." Six years later, the legislature extended the period of legal forced indentures and expanded the law to cover adult Indians. From 1850 to 1863, "an estimated 10,000 California Indians, many of them children, were sold or indentured."[215] *Alta California* reported in 1854: "Nearly all the children belonging to some of the Indian tribes in the northern part of the state have been stolen." California's superintendent of Indian Affairs, Thomas Henley, reported to his Washington superior in 1856 that "in some instances entire tribes were taken en mass."[216] The demographer Sherburne F. Cook estimated that 3,000–4,000 California Indian children were enslaved from 1852 to 1867.[217] By 1860, California's indigenous population had fallen from over 100,000 to only 32,000.[218]

Direct killings also exacted much of the toll, in what historian H. H. Bancroft called "a hundred or two" wars of "brutal butchering." U.S. Army troops committed the first two massacres. In early 1846, a unit led by Captain John C. Frémont and Kit Carson attacked what was probably a gathering of Yana on the Sacramento River, killing between 120 and 200 Indians. Three years later, federal troops perpetrated another mass killing, of 135–250 Pomo Indians in the Clear Lake area. A California newspaper reported a decade later: "The Clear Lake Tribe has dwindled from 10,000 in 1849 to a mere remnant of about 500 in all."[219]

Local militia and volunteers, not U.S. regular forces, did most of the killing after 1849. The U.S. Congress, however, rewarded all forms of military service with land grants through the Bounty Land Law. This March 1855 legislation guaranteed 160 acres of land to all former U.S. officers and private soldiers "in any of the wars in which this country has been engaged," and to "each of the survivors of the militia, or volunteers, or State troops of any State or Territory," who had been paid by the United States and served 14 days or participated in a battle, and also to wagon masters and teamsters who had served under "competent authority in time of war," or to their heirs if they had died.[220]

By 1868, the 2,000–3,000 Yana had suffered "a series of massacres," and "were virtually exterminated." Only 100 remained alive.[221] But the most systematic Californian genocide reduced the estimated 12,000 Yuki to only 600, in the decade 1854–64. Historian Benjamin Madley has documented the Yukis' destruction in their lush Round Valley homeland. A state Indian agent reported in June 1856: "I have visited many valleys in all parts of the country, but have never [seen] anything that will compare to this." He described "grasses in the valley ... up even with our horses' backs" and concluded that the valley was "green all year round," its soil "well adapted to raising vegetables of all kinds and grain." The superintendent of Indian Affairs visited Round Valley the next month, judging it "the best grazing country in the state." A settler later recalled that "in 1856 the first expedition by the whites against the Indians was made ... there were so many of these expeditions ... we would kill on average fifty or sixty Indians on a trip ... frequently we would have to turn out two or three times a week."[222] By April 1857, the *Petaluma Journal* was reporting "wholesale killing" in response to Indian attacks on settlers' stock: "[W]ithin the past three weeks, from 300 to 400 bucks, squaws, and children have been killed by the whites."[223] The first Yuki killing of a settler occurred that September, with two whites reported murdered. U.S. Army major Edward Johnson, who commanded the local garrison, stated in 1859: "The whites have waged a relentless war of extermination against the Yukas, making no distinction between the innocent and the guilty. They have ruthlessly massacred men, women and children.... Some six hundred have been killed in the last year."[224] The *Sacramento Union* newspaper wrote: "The aborigines are melting away as the snows of the mountains in June.... They are doomed to steady extirpation."[225]

In 1859, the white bounty hunter H. L. Hall led a massacre of 240 men, women, and children after accusing an Indian of killing a horse. Stating that "a nit would make a louse," Hall rejected volunteers who were unwilling to kill Indian children and women. Hall testified that in one incident: "I think all the squaws were killed because they refused to go further. We took one boy into the valley, and the infants were put out of their misery, and a girl ten years of age was killed for stubbornness." Army lieutenant Edward Dillon accused "[t]he monster Hall," aided by locals, of having "well nigh depopulated a country, which but a short time since swarmed with Indians."[226] A settler testified to an investigation by the state legislature that these killings of Yuki were continuing in 1860.[227] That year, California's superintendent of Indian Affairs, Mr. McDuffie, reported that "the killing of Indians is a daily occurrence." His successor, Superintendent George Hanson, confirmed the next year that the Indians "are now being hunted down like wild beasts and killed," and in December 1862, he reported that settlers had recently "massacred . . . 108 Indians."[228]

Other native Californians suffered similar massacres. Militiamen attacked the annual ritual gatherings of the Tolowa people, killing "several hundred people" in 1853, piling up "seven layers of bodies in the dance house when they burned it" the next year, and killing 70 Indians in a battle at the mouth of the Smith River in 1855. From 1859 to 1861, local newspapers advertised bounties for Indian scalps; after one massacre, "enormous claims were presented to the Legislature." In 1860, Major G. J. Raines reported that Volunteers had raided "the home of a band of friendly Indians," the Wiyots on Indian Island, "murdering all the women and children" and leaving the tribe "practically destroyed." The *San Francisco Bulletin* commented in June 1860: "Even the record of Spanish butcheries in Mexico and Peru has nothing so diabolical."[229]

J. Ross Browne, appointed in 1857 by the U.S. government to investigate, wrote a decade later: "The federal government, as is usual in cases where the lives of valuable voters are at stake, was forced to interfere. Troops were sent out to aid the settlers in slaughtering the Indians. By means of mounted howitzers, muskets, Minie rifles, dragoon pistols, and sabers, a good many were cut to pieces. But on the whole, the general policy of the government was pacific. It was not designed to kill any more Indians than might be necessary to secure the adhesion of the honest yeomanry of the state."[230]

The agrarian ideal was compelling. Addressing the San Joaquin Valley Agricultural Society in 1862, Thomas Starr King praised grain crops that "average double those of the Eastern States" and fruit trees "ripening all around . . . in surpassing luxuriance," excelling "anything known in the most favored districts of the Rhine lands, France or Italy." California, King said, "is really the field of two immense "horns of plenty," "crammed with all the riches of granaries and orchards."[231] The new state's promoters aggressively presented it to eastern audiences and potential settlers as an agrarian "cornucopia of the world" and nursery of independent rural virtue. By the late nineteenth century, when portrayals of California turned to extol its burgeoning urban and industrial activity, most of its Indians had perished. Survivors numbered only 15,000 in 1900.[232]

Genocidal Massacres on the Great Plains

"The pale-faced people are numerous and prosperous because they cultivate the earth," U.S. president Abraham Lincoln told a group of Indian leaders in 1863. Unlike Indians, he went on, whites "produce bread, and depend upon the products of the earth rather than wild game for a subsistence." The fetish of cultivation was about to gain new ground. Ranking members of the Lincoln administration recommended allocating Indians individual farms that would "lead them to depend upon the cultivation of the soil for subsistence" and to acquire "the simple arts of husbandry and pastoral life." [233]

Lincoln, however, never made the point asserted by the prominent American journalist Horace Greeley, dismissing the Indians of the Great Plains: "These people must die out—there is no help for them. God has given this earth to those who will subdue and cultivate it, and it is vain to struggle against his righteous decree." [234] In a further explicit link between agriculture and genocide, it was also said that Indians were being "improved off the face of the earth." [235] Lincoln's agriculture commissioner, Isaac Newton, asserted that "when tillage begins, barbarism ends." To Newton, this meant the "sturdy independence" of yeoman freeholders. "Whatever improves the condition and character of the farmer feeds the life springs of National Character, wealth, and power." Cities fostered corruption; the United States "must always remain an agricultural nation." To encourage westward migration, the Homestead Act of 1862 provided 160 acres of surveyed public land to any adult U.S. citizen who was a household head in return for a small fee. "Every acre of our fertile soil," in Newton's view, "only waits the contact of labor to yield its treasures; and every acre is opened to that fruitful contact by the Homestead Act." As historian David Nichols notes, this implicitly threatened "every acre" of Indian land. [236]

Newton not only saw agriculture as "the great and essential art of life" but, reminiscent of Mirabeau Buonaparte Lamar in Texas, he also blamed the downfall of the Roman Empire on the demise of its small farmers: "[L]abor became disrespectable, the soil a monopoly, and the masses of the people reckless, unpatriotic and degraded." Rome had neglected both "the division and cultivation of the soil." Newton did not compare American Indians to the ancient barbarian hordes who had brought down imperial Rome, but many of his contemporaries did. [237]

Race science reinforced both agrarian myth and classical lesson. Louis Agassiz, one of America's most famous scientists, an opponent of Darwin and proponent of polygenesis, wrote to the U.S. secretary of war in 1865, requesting "the bodies of some Indians. . . . All that would be necessary would be to forward the body express in a box . . . one or two handsome fellows entire and the heads of two or three." The Army Medical Museum began asking field officers to collect "adult crania," and by the 1890s, in what the historian Elliott West has called "three decades of publicly funded skull-duggery," the army had dispatched 2,000 Indian crania to Washington.[238]

As the Civil War raged from 1861 to 1865, eastern colonists continued to flood west. Some encroached on Sioux lands in Minnesota, where Indians faced starvation. Sioux youths killed five settlers in 1862, igniting an Indian revolt. Whites feared a wider uprising, though as Secretary Caleb Smith informed President Lincoln the next year, he lacked "evidence of a pre-meditated design" by Indians.[239] Lincoln had established a new Department of the Northwest under General John Pope, who arrived in September 1862 and told Colonel Henry Sibley: "It is my purpose utterly to exterminate the Sioux." Sibley aimed to "sweep them with the besom of death" and soon condemned 303 Sioux prisoners. Lincoln reduced the list to 38 men, all hanged that December. Minnesota's *Daily Republican* announced the next year: "The State reward for dead Indians has been increased to $200 for every red-skin sent to Purgatory. This sum is more than the dead bodies of all the Indians east of the Red River are worth." Meanwhile, in New Mexico, General James Carleton ordered Kit Carson to fight the Apaches, adding, "all Indian men of that tribe are to be killed whenever and wherever you may find them."[240] Union militiamen of the California Volunteers, under the command of Colonel Patrick E. Connor, perpetrated a massacre on the Great Plains, by the Bear River in southern Idaho. Attacking a camp of 450 Northwestern Shoshoni on January 29, 1863, the Volunteers killed about 280 Indians, including 90 women and children.[241]

The year 1864 was an election year in the Colorado territory, where whites were settling on Cheyenne and Arapaho land. The *Rocky Mountain News* sought settler support for the Colorado governor's proposals for the territory's statehood. The paper proclaimed in March 1863 that Indians "ought to be wiped from the face of the earth," one of 10 occasions that year on which it urged extermination of Indians. After two soldiers fell in a clash, 25 Indians died in reprisal. The military commander predicted: "[N]ow is but the commencement of war with this tribe, which must result in exterminating them."[242] A Methodist Episcopal church elder, Colonel John Chivington of the 1st Colorado Cavalry, campaigned for Congress on his policy to "kill and scalp all, little and big."[243] On May 31, 1864, Chivington ordered Major Edward Wynkoop, commander of Fort Lyon: "The Cheyennes will have to be soundly whipped before they will be quiet. If any of them are caught in your vicinity kill them, as that is the only way."[244] Echoing an English officer in seventeenth-century Ireland, and more recently H. L. Hall in California, Chivington often stated his view that "Nits make lice."[245]

After unidentified Indians massacred a settler family in early June 1864, the *Rocky Mountain News* called for "extermination against the red devils."[246] Colorado governor John Evans proclaimed on August 11 that "most of the Indian tribes of the plains are at war and hostile" and that "all citizens of Colorado" would be armed and paid to "kill and destroy, as enemies of the country, wherever they may be found, all such hostile Indians." The *News* urged troops to "go for them, their lodges, squaws and all."[247] General Samuel Curtis instructed Chivington and the militia: "I want no peace until the Indians suffer more." Major Wynkoop reported to Chivington: "My intention is to kill all Indians I may come across until I receive orders to the contrary from headquarters."[248]

Leading 700 soldiers, Chivington rode into Sand Creek village on the morning of November 29, 1864. He had ordered his troops to take no prisoners. His guide later reported that nearly all the 600 Indians there were women and children. Only 35 were braves, along with a smaller number of old men. Chivington knew the Indians had turned in their weapons at Fort Lyon, and most Cheyenne men were out hunting. Chief Black Kettle held up a white flag and a U.S. flag. Yet Chivington gave the order: "the troops opened fire on this mass of men, women and children, all began to scatter and run."[249] That day the troops slaughtered from 100 to 500 unarmed women and children, scalping nearly all. Ashbury Bird of the 1st Colorado Cavalry said he counted 350 bodies and estimated "between 400 and 500 Indians killed." That evening Chivington reported killing four chiefs "and between 400 and 500 other Indians." He boasted of having destroyed "one of the most powerful villages in the Cheyenne nation." In Denver, a visiting senator was shocked at the exterminationist atmosphere among the whites. Chivington lost his election for Congress but never faced prosecution.[250]

Black Kettle miraculously escaped the massacre. He led survivors south, holding to a policy of peace. In December, however, other Cheyenne warriors joined forces with Sioux and Arapaho and later destroyed a U.S. Army wagon train. The army dispatched General Patrick E. Connor, promoted after his California Volunteers had perpetrated the Bear River massacre, with over 3,000 troops and orders to reject "overtures of peace or submission" and to "kill every male Indian over twelve years of age."[251]

Two years later, the stakes again escalated. On September 10, 1868, General Philip H. Sheridan wrote to the governor of Kansas, Samuel Crawford, that his goal was "to make war on the families and stock of these Indians" in order to draw their warriors within reach.[252] Crawford proclaimed the need to "either exterminate the tribes or confine them upon reservations." The U.S. government's peace commission, meeting in Chicago in October, adopted a decision proposed by General Sanford, that for support and protection, Indians should "locate permanently on their agricultural reservations" or face military force if they refused removal.[253]

On November 27, 1868, 700 men of the 7th Regiment of U.S. Cavalry, commanded by Lieutenant Colonel George Armstrong Custer, launched a surprise attack on Black Kettle's Cheyenne village on the Washita River in Oklahoma. The village's 51 lodges housed the survivors of the 1864 Sand Creek massacre. They did not consider themselves at war, but their attackers had orders to kill everyone they came upon. Black Kettle was a first victim. Two of Custer's scouts estimated from 40 to 75 women and children killed.[254] By 1870, the Cheyenne and Arapaho were confined to reservations.

But the Lakota Sioux, led by Red Cloud, had opened another front. In one battle in December 1866, they killed 80 U.S. soldiers, including their commander, Captain William J. Fetterman, who had asserted: "With eighty men I could ride through the Sioux nation."[255] The disaster provoked General William Sherman to urge General Grant: "We must act with vindictive earnestness against the Sioux, even to their extermination, men, women and children. Nothing else will reach the root of this case." The term *extermination* became "one of the most frequently used words in Sherman's vocabulary."[256] Nevertheless, in 1868, he signed the Treaty of Laramie giving the Sioux "absolute and undisturbed use and occupation" of the Black Hills of South Dakota.[257]

U.S. forces frequently employed the genocidal massacre as a war tactic, even against unarmed noncombatants, women, and children. In northern Montana on January 23, 1870, 200 troops commanded by Major Eugene Baker of the 2nd U.S. Cavalry surrounded a camp of Piegans led by Chief Heavy Runner, on the Marias River. Corporal Dan Starr later recalled that Baker (echoing Hall in California and Chivington in Colorado) "announced as a motto, 'Nits make lice.' This was the customary way of indicating that children were not to be spared."[258] Good Bear Woman, aged 29, said she "saw the soldiers come over the hill" and surround the camp, and then "noticed Chief Heavy Runner, the leader of the camp, come out of his lodge and go to meet the commanding officer. He handed him some papers, which the commanding officer read, then he tore them up and threw them away. As Heavy Runner turned about face, soldiers fired upon him and killed him."[259] Two witnesses in the U.S. forces, Joe Kipp, a part-Indian scout, and Horace Clarke, concurred that Heavy Runner had offered no resistance.[260] Clarke said the Piegan warriors were absent: "The young men were on a hunt." The U.S. soldiers "charged into the village, shooting left and right, and cutting down any within reach ... slaughtering by wholesale men, women and children." Only one Indian fired back, a single shot, which killed a soldier.[261] According to Major Baker, "We killed one hundred and seventy-three Indians," and he later reported that these included "fifty-three women and children." Yet U.S. Indian agent Lieutenant William Pease and General Alfred Sully, Bureau of Indian Affairs superintendent for Montana, reported that over 150 elderly Indians, women, and children were killed (and only 15 men of fighting age). Joe Kipp added that, besides Heavy Runner, those killed were "such Indians as could not hunt, being the old men, women and children." Kipp said he counted 217 bodies.[262] Captain Lewis Thompson of the 2nd Cavalry recalled: "Only a few escaped. The woods and streams were full of the dead." He considered this noncombatant toll "not an unusual result when towns are destroyed, yet sad enough." The operation's results, Thompson wrote later, included "perfect quietness."[263]

Leading U.S. military commanders took a similar view. Later in 1870, referring to the Civil War but also after years of fighting Indians, General Philip Sheridan stated that the "proper strategy" in wartime includes "causing the inhabitants so much suffering that they must long for peace, and force their Government to demand it. The people must be left nothing but their eyes to weep with over the war." Congress decided in 1871 to make no further treaties with Indians.[264] Two years later General Sherman ordered Brigadier General E. R. Canby to fight the Modoc Indians in such a way "that no other reservation for them will be necessary except graves among their chosen Lava Beds."[265] After warriors killed Canby during peace talks the next month, Sherman wrote of genocide as a means to achieve total military subjugation: "All the Modocs are involved. ... Therefore, the order to attack is against the whole, and if all be swept from the face of the earth, they themselves have invited it. The place is like a fortress, and during an assault, the soldier cannot pause to distinguish between male and female, or even discriminate as to age; as long as resistance is made, death must be meted out, but the moment all resistance ceases, the firing will stop."[266]

Two years later, Sheridan informed Sherman that the Sioux in Dakota "would never make war on our settlements as long as we could threaten their families and villages" in the Black Hills. So in 1874, he authorized General George A. Custer to reconnoiter that region where, the 1868 treaty had stipulated, "no white person shall be permitted."[267]

Custer's expedition to the Black Hills unveiled a new pastoral romance. What historian Brian Dippie terms an "Arcadian fantasy" flourished as Custer's 600 cavalry rode through the Indian lands in July 1874.[268] There, the *New York Tribune* reported, they found an "Eden in the sky without the forbidden fruit," which Custer named Floral Valley.[269] His dispatch portrayed an idyllic scene: "Every step of our march that day was amidst flowers of the most exquisite colors and perfume. So luxuriant in growth were they that men plucked them without dismounting from the saddle.... It was a strange sight to glance back at the advancing columns of cavalry, and behold the men with beautiful bouquets in their hands, while the headgear of their horses was decorated with wreaths of flowers fit to crown a queen of May."[270] Custer's brother-in-law, Lieutenant James Calhoun, wrote in his diary: "Here nature spreads herself open." He added a few days later that "though the woodnymph with her many fabled fairies has not been found here in her sylvan glory," pine, spruce, and oak had duly "taken her place" (see fig. 17).[271]

Both men mixed agrarian with pastoral themes. Calhoun thought it "a great pity that this rich country should remain in a wild state, uncultivated and uninhabited by civilized men.... In this wild region man will ultimately be seen in the full enjoyment of true pleasure, in the possession of happiness obtained by honest labor." Raised on a farm, Custer was more prosaic: "The soil is that of a rich garden, and composed of a dark mold of exceedingly fine grain. ... I know of no portion of our country where nature has done so much to prepare homes for husbandmen.... The open and timbered spaces are so divided that a partly prepared farm of almost any dimensions, from an acre upward, can be found here." The *New York World* proclaimed: "The Garden of America Discovered." This region was "An Agricultural and Pastoral Paradise."[272]

One of the expedition's major effects would be the seizure and cultivation of that paradise. William E. Curtis, a reporter for the *Chicago Inter-Ocean*, interviewed a Sergeant Becker of the expedition's Engineer Corps, one of "a great many Germans in the army," who made "excellent soldiers." Curtis reported that Becker had taken "a wonderful fancy" to the Black Hills. The German drew a map for future gold prospectors, "staked out 160 acres which he says he will pre-empt," and "laid out the limits of a lager-beer garden." The region's fertility and "healthful fragrance," Curtis wrote, matched those of "any locality on Uncle Sam's farm." Because the Indian "will never make any use of the rich soil that has been waiting centuries to be utilized," Curtis denied that it would "be robbing him to deprive him of it."[273] Reporter N. H. Knappen of the *Bismarck Tribune* added: "[N]ow all that remains to be done, is for Congress to open this beautiful land for settlement, and protect those who go there, from its present worthless inhabitants—the Indians."[274]

America's urbanization had heightened the rural romance. "The daily occupation of city life," Curtis mused on the march, whether in "the factory, the counting house, or the wareroom," had left urban dwellers with "no wish for anything beyond—no men enjoy life more, and few fear death as much." A strange contrast had emerged: "[Y]our city man hates dying above all things; your frontiersman will look death in the face as calmly as he sits by his camp fire." One breath of rural life in that "pure and beautiful world," this Chicago reporter added, was "worth whole gallons of city air." Urban living, artificial and "factitious," simply "shut out nature" from men's hearts as they "become attached to the world."[275] This was the rural ideal, antimaterialist, warlike, and rampant.

Accompanying the agrarianism were models from antiquity and violent racism. The *New York Tribune* reporter wondered, "[D]id Caesar have such a wagon train?" As soldiers pitched camp, he reported, they asked their commander, " 'How many miles to-day?' just as Xenophon was asked." The *Chicago Inter-Ocean*'s headline dubbed the expedition "Custer's *Anabasis*."[276] As the expedition set out, the reporter for the *St. Paul Daily Press* expressed confidence that "we can handle all of the Indians" in the Black Hills region.[277] Custer insisted that the Indians "will be the party to fire the first shot," but Lieutenant Calhoun found the troops "exceedingly anxious to give the Indians a free taste of lead."[278] Though the Sioux kept their distance for the expedition's duration, a trooper added racialism to the ideological mix when he recalled its peaceful progress with the adage that "the only good Indian" is a dead one. "The only good Indian found upon the trip . . . was in a Tree lashed upon a Frame Work of Willows. . . . The Body was that of a young Brave."[279] For his part, Lieutenant Calhoun predicted that "the hives of industry will take the place of dirty wigwams. Civilization will ere long reign supreme and throw heathen barbarism into oblivion. . . . Christian temples will elevate their lofty spires upward towards the azure sky while places of heathen mythology will sink to rise no more."[280]

Defending the Black Hills in 1876, Lakota warriors killed Custer and 225 of his soldiers at the Little Big Horn. The *San Francisco Chronicle* now urged "no treating or temporizing with the red brutes," whose "fiendish atrocities" made them "worse than wild beasts." As agrarian civilization advanced, the *American Settler* pronounced in 1881, "[T]he uncultivated must give place to the cultivated."[281] Five years later, in his book *Massacres of the Mountains,* the American historian Jacob P. Dunn considered "two reasons given for killing women and children." First, frontiersmen believed "that the only way to make Indians sign a treaty which they will keep is, when at war with them, to kill them at every opportunity. . . . There is not a bit of doubt that killing women and children has a very dampening effect on the ardor of the Indian." The second reason was vengeance, Dunn wrote: "There is a certain amount of justice in the theory of meting to a man in his own measure." More powerful, however, was precedent. As secretary of the Indiana Historical Society, Dunn objected to criticisms of western frontier massacres leveled by Americans from "the East," where "the names of the Pequods and the Conestoga Indians exist in your books." Nor did Dunn accept censure from "you of the Mississippi Valley," whom he described as stained by "the blood of Logan's family and the Moravian Indians," or from "you of the South, while a Cherokee or a Seminole remains to tell the wrongs of his fathers."[282] Genocide, then, justified its own repetition.

In 1891, the editor of South Dakota's *Aberdeen Saturday Pioneer,* L. Frank Baum, called for "the total annihilation of the few remaining Indians." Baum, author of the children's classic *The Wizard of Oz,* said it would be "better that they should die than live the miserable wretches that they are."[283] Eight days later, 400 Sioux men, women, and children reached Wounded Knee, escorted by Custer's former unit, the 7th Cavalry. The troops disarmed the Sioux the next day, and during a search for remaining weapons, a shot rang out, killing a soldier. Both sides opened fire. Troops with breech-loading Hotchkiss guns massacred nearly 300 Indians, including 170–200 women and children. Miles from the scene, a witness reported, "we found them scattered along as they had been relentlessly hunted down and slaughtered while fleeing for their lives." Now Baum recommended that "we had better, in order to protect our civilization, follow it up . . . and wipe these untamed and untamable creatures from the face of the earth." American Horse, a friendly Indian who had witnessed the massacre, judged "civilization" differently: "Of course it would have been all right if only the men were killed; we would feel almost grateful for it. But the fact of the killing of the women, and more especially the killing of the young boys and girls . . . is the saddest part."[284]

Sociologist Russell Thornton has estimated the Indian population of the area now within the United States at about 600,000 in 1800. By the 1890s, only 250,000 Indians survived.[285] Theodore Roosevelt stated: "I don't go so far as to think that the only good Indians are dead Indians, but I believe nine out of ten are, and I shouldn't like to inquire too closely into the case of the tenth." Echoing Andrew Jackson in 1830, Roosevelt said the fate of Native Americans "was as ultimately beneficial as it was inevitable."[286] By 1914, the U.S. Bureau of Indian Affairs commissioner, Cato Sells, advocated the eventual "disintegration of the Indian reservations," integration of Indians in white schools, and the "elimination of the Indian as a distinct problem for the Federal or the State governments."[287]

CHAPTER 9

Settler Genocides in Africa, 1830–1910

The French Conquest of Algeria, 1830–1875

I n a remarkable echo from antiquity, the French political thinker Alexis de Tocqueville might have been mistaken for Cato the Censor when he wrote in 1833 that "the poor and honest population of our countryside" made the best overseas colonists (see p. 54). "The peasant," Tocqueville acknowledged, was hard to persuade to emigrate. "But it is only with men of that sort that the core of a good colony can be formed."[1]

Cato's echo resounded from North Africa to North America and back. France had launched its invasion of Algeria in 1830 (see fig. 19). After Tocqueville made his famous journey through the United States the next year, he began to study Algerian history. His *Democracy in America* appeared in 1835, and he wrote his "First Letter on Algeria" in 1837. According to historian Jennifer Pitts, Tocqueville "considered America a model for French Algeria." As he wrote home in 1841, several weeks into his first visit to Algeria: "I thought I was in America."[2] In his view, "The Spaniards were unable to exterminate the Indian race by those unparalleled atrocities . . . but the Americans of the United States have accomplished this . . . without shedding blood."[3] Tocqueville ignored the bloodshed of the previous half century, but he was writing, of course, before the worst slaughter of Indians in Texas, California, and the Great Plains.

In Algeria, colonization and genocidal massacres proceeded in tandem. From 1830 to 1847, its European settler population quadrupled to 104,000. Of the native Algerian population of approximately 3 million in 1830, about

500,000 to 1 million people perished in the first three decades of French conquest.[4] The invading army of a French ally, the bey of Tunis, massacred eight Algerian tribes near Mostaganem in 1831, but the French army conducted even more murderous warfare. Its destruction of the El Oufia tribe in 1832 included killing over 500 men, women, and children in a single night. A French civil official reported several large tribes "almost annihilated" in the west of Algeria. In reprisals for an ally's assassination in 1839, colonial forces reported beheading the inhabitants of Ouled Aziz, without disclosing the number of victims.[5] French governors-general conceded that their military operations were "bloody," especially from 1839 to 1845. Colonial troops under Colonel Pélissier, attacking followers of the rebel Bu Maza, trapped "the entire tribe" of Ouled Rhia in a cave at Dahra in 1845. They lit fires at the entrance, by one account "smoking 500 men, women and children to death." Another source recalled "700 bodies found the next morning in the cave" (see fig. 20).[6]

While approving Algeria's conquest and colonization, Alexis de Tocqueville recommended moderation in the methods used. He opposed both critics of the enterprise and the extreme measures that French forces employed. It is useful to compare Tocqueville's thinking with that of proponents of earlier brutal conquests and to assess how such a project attracted his support even as it exacted such a disastrous human toll.

To Tocqueville, Algeria offered an agrarian opportunity that would strengthen the French nation and character. Agrarianism and suspicion of cities pervaded French society in the 1830s. A member of the Chamber of Deputies lamented that "the barbarians who now threaten society are not in the Caucasus, nor in the steppes of the [Russian] Tartary; they are in the suburbs of our manufacturing cities."[7] Tocqueville, too, considered the French an essentially rural, self-sufficient people. In an 1833 essay on colonization, he described France as a "continental" power to which "commerce is but an appendage." In contrast to "navigating or commercial peoples," he wrote, "the sea has never excited" Frenchmen; only those with "mediocre talents" or "declining fortunes" went into maritime enterprises. A Frenchman, in Tocqueville's view, "loves the domestic hearth, he rejoices at the sight of his native parish." However, once uprooted and transplanted "under another sky," he abandons civilization and "becomes a passionate lover of the savage life. He prefers savannahs to city streets, hunting to farming."[8] Agrarian at home, the Frenchman went pastoral abroad.

Four years later, Tocqueville described the same dichotomy among the

MAP 19. The French conquest of Algeria, 1830–75

newly colonized peoples of Algeria. There, however, he related it to a pristine human antiquity and to the Arabs' subsequent decline from a romanticized agricultural self-sufficiency. By contrast, the Kabyles, or Berbers, he wrote, "are always sedentary; they cultivate the soil," yet they also lived independently, "as in the first age of the world." Indeed, Tocqueville remarked, "[i]f Rousseau had known about the Kabyles, sir, he would not have uttered such nonsense about the Caribs and other Indians of America; he would have sought his models in the Atlas [mountains]," of North Africa. There, the Kabyles lived "almost as free as the isolated individual who enjoys his savage independence in the heart of the woods" (see fig. 23). They practiced "complete . . . equality."[9]

The Arabs, however, Tocqueville considered to be merely "half-savage." Any progress from a primeval egalitarian independence had produced only a decline that somehow remained immutable, leaving Arabs with aristocracies but little agriculture. Preferring adventure to city life and hard work, they "sleep under the stars, their sabers in their fists" and "would sooner flee into the desert than vegetate under a master." Only the Turks had brought to Algeria a semblance of public administration. Arabs were "always more willing to feel than to think." Like other "Orientals," Tocqueville concluded, their culture was "hardly" subject to change.[10] Far from the common human origins exemplified by the Kabyles, Arabs seemed a different "race."

For Frenchmen like Tocqueville, the Arabs scratched a distinct ideological itch. Yet his exotic description of them was also instrumental, betraying much less of the romance he reserved for the Kabyles. It was Arabs' supposed neglect of Algeria's lands that justified the French conquest to Tocqueville, who took a similar view to those of settlers in Australia and North America. As they were nomadic herdsmen, and only "alternately" sedentary agriculturalists, most of the Arabs' land "always remains uncultivated and the rest is cultivated with little art."[11] Arabs holding "the entire extent" of Algeria had "never cultivated more than a very small part. So the Arab population is quite sparse; it occupies much more terrain than it can possibly cultivate every year." Thus, he thought, "a foreign population can easily establish itself next to them without causing them to suffer."[12]

In his second letter on Algeria, also written in 1837, Tocqueville turned his attention to the French conquest and its excesses. "You can hardly imagine the profound ignorance in France just seven years ago about everything concerning Algeria. We had no idea either of the different races that inhabited it or of their customs; we did not know a word of the languages these people speak." Worse, on seizing Algiers in 1830, "we hastened to gather up every single Turk" and deported "the lot." Then, Tocqueville wrote, the French proceeded "to tear up or burn all written documents, administrative records, and papers" and "even destroyed a large number of streets in Algiers so as to rebuild them according to our own method, and we gave French names to all those we consented to leave alone." Having destroyed its predecessor "root and branch," the new administration owned nothing, or "believed itself reduced to seizing at random whatever it needed, with no regard for law and rights." Algeria "fell into appalling anarchy. . . . Even the shadow of justice disappeared, and everyone resorted to force." Instead of these "mistakes," Tocqueville suggested, "we simply should have put ourselves in the place of the defeated" and "bent to their ways," employing the Turks and learning "the Arabs' language, prejudices, and ways," so as to earn their respect before trying, eventually, "to make French the country around us."[13]

Having criticized these extreme methods of the colonial conquest, Tocqueville recommended that from 1837 onward, the French should "first carefully distinguish the two large races." Unsurprisingly, he believed that "the soul of the Kabyles is open to us." With their "love of material pleasures," these independent farmers were "more positive, less devout," and should be subdued "by our arts and not by our arms," given the "attraction that draws savages toward civilized man." By contrast, he went on, "the Arabs are not solidly attached to the land," and they "value immaterial pleasures." Against them, political measures were needed, for Tocqueville considered that "our immense military superiority is almost useless." To keep the peace with the Arabs, France should divide and rule, "not letting them establish a single ruler" or become "united against us." Moreover, the French themselves must "give up this taste for uniformity that torments us" and take another lesson from the Roman Empire, pluralism: "[T]he barbarian was subjected to barbarian laws, and the Romans followed Roman laws." Finally, he wrote, "fusion will come" later, when "two peoples of different civilizations can manage to refound themselves as . . . a single people from the two races."[14]

In adopting this "immense goal" of cultural amalgamation, Tocqueville no longer saw Arab society as static. Though he felt that their past failure to cultivate much land had certainly justified and still facilitated European settlement, he now found "a great number" of Arabs already "devoting themselves seriously to agriculture." The Arabs were "thus not naturally and necessarily shepherds." Some could "be intermixed" with French farmers. Tocqueville's model for the future was a militarized harmony of assimilation: "Arabs and French, living in the same guardhouse and sharing the same hardships."[15] It was as if Thomas Jefferson had landed on the Barbary Coast.

Two months later, the French launched their final assault on the city of Constantine.[16] Troops numbering 20,000 bombarded and attacked the town of 30,000, leaving corpses of the inhabitants strewn "everywhere on the ground where they fell defending their hearths step by step." In one house, a military medical officer reported, "The threshold, the courtyard, the stairs, the apartments, all these places were covered with bodies so close together that it was difficult to take a step without treading on them. And what to say of this trail of bodies on the tortuous contour of the precipice where the unfortunate women had tumbled with their children on being seized with fright at our entry into the town. It was horrible to see."[17] Yet, according to historian Charles-André Julien, "the most murderous period" of the war was still three years away.[18]

Tocqueville arrived on his first visit to Algeria in May 1841. Sixty thousand French troops were deployed there, and fighting was in full swing.[19] On May 1, an expeditionary force trapped a rebellious tribe in the mountains. Fleeing survivors left the terrain "covered with corpses," according to a military correspondent: "The tribe of the Ouled Sultan was completely destroyed and dispersed."[20] Tocqueville arrived in Algiers on May 7 and spent a month in the colony. He found much of urban Algiers "in a state of destruction and reconstruction. On all sides, one sees nothing but recent ruins, buildings going up. . . . It is Cincinnati transported onto the soil of Africa." Yet traveling 10 miles from the city meant "being beheaded."[21] Arab resistance was strong, especially the forces of "Abd-el-Kader's government, far more powerful and centralized than that of the Turks." The French general de Lamoricière, whom Tocqueville had known for 13 years and who had served in Algeria since 1830, told him that the Arab resistance leader was collecting "three million in taxes from the province of Oran alone." However, Lamoricière's forces were driving the Arabs off: "[W]e have harassed them so well that not a single one is left within 15 to 20 leagues of Oran."[22]

Militarization escalated. Algeria's new governor-general, Marshal Thomas-Robert Bugeaud (1840–47), a former landowning agriculturalist in France, pursued the strategy of the "soldier ploughman" (*soldat laboureur*).[23] He saw Algeria's future as "[m]ilitary colonization" and announced: "The civilian population has nothing to recommend it."[24] The director of public instruction in Algiers told Tocqueville that the army "can do anything it likes in an instant by using violence." Five days later, the French commander at Philippeville said of the Arabs: "Nothing but force and terror, Gentlemen, succeeds with these people." This colonel added that he had just launched a *razzia,* a punitive attack on a tribe, for having "allowed men to cross its territory on their way to rob and kill us." He reported: "[A]fter having killed five or six men, I spared the animals." In another recent incident, interrogating a murder suspect, "I had his head cut off. You can see his head on the Constantine gates." The militarism repelled some colonial officials. The attorney general thought the French should leave Algeria "as quickly as possible." Indeed, the "monstrosities" of the judiciary system "astonished us," Tocqueville wrote.[25] The bishop of Algiers told him of meeting with Abd-el-Kader's lieutenant, who had "revealed his exhaustion with the war, his terror of the way the French carried it out, his deep sense of the miseries that it led the Arabs to suffer."[26] However, a French doctor predicted: "Without violating the laws of morality we will be able to fight our African enemies with powder and iron in combination with famine, . . . without spilling blood, each year we will be able to decimate them by attacking their food supplies."[27] The military officer Montagnac was more direct, warning all his troops "that if they happened to bring me an Arab alive, they would receive a volley of blows with the flat of a sword."[28]

Tocqueville heard French commanders arguing that "to subjugate the Arabs, we should fight them with the utmost violence and in the Turkish manner, by killing everything we meet." He was distressed by "officers who took it to the point of bitterly regretting that we have started to take prisoners in some places, and many assured me that they encouraged their soldiers to spare no one." This exasperated Tocqueville. "For my part, I returned from Africa with the distressing notion that we are now fighting far more barbarously than the Arabs themselves. For the present, it is on their side that one meets with civilization." Yet, as he put it, "[t]he Arab element is becoming more and more isolated, and little by little it is dissolving. The Muslim population always seems to be shrinking."[29] Tocqueville, shocked at "this flood of violence and injustices," reached a devastating conclusion: "*[N]one of our colonies* has ever at *any* time been treated like Algiers. . . . Algiers is singularly bad, even within our detestable system of colonization."[30] (See also fig. 21.)

Yet even this extreme violence did not deter Tocqueville from pursuing imperial priorities. Five months later, he opened his famous "Essay on Algeria" by stating: "I do not think France can think seriously of leaving Algeria. In the eyes of the world, such an abandonment would be the clear indication of our decline." Moreover, France could dominate the Mediterranean with Algerian ports, starting with the one "opposite Carthage."[31] French policy should seek "partial colonization and total domination" of Algeria, he wrote. Tocqueville considered that France's war of conquest demanded certain "unfortunate necessities," for instance, "that we burn harvests, that we empty silos, and finally that we seize unarmed men, women and children," measures obligatory for "any people that wants to wage war on the Arabs." War had trumped his earlier hopes for racial assimilation. In Europe itself, Tocqueville noted, "we wage war on governments and not on peoples," while "the civilian populations do not escape upon conquest," making victory possible "without attacking the governed." By contrast, he wrote, victory in Algeria required the targeting of civilians. "We shall never destroy Abd-el-Kader's power unless we make the position of the tribes who support him so intolerable that they abandon him."

Therefore, Tocqueville recommended, "all means of desolating these tribes must be employed. I make an exception only of those condemned by humanity and by the law of nations. . . . I believe that the right of war authorizes us to ravage the country and that we must do it, either by destroying harvests during the harvest season, or year-round by making those rapid incursions called razzias, whose purpose is to seize men or herds" (see fig. 22). He thus stopped short of advocating extermination, though he acknowledged that the razzias often targeted unresisting civilians when he wrote that "these murderous voyages . . . seem to me to be indispensable sometimes." France must also mount occasional large expeditions, Tocqueville went on, "[t]o destroy everything that resembles a permanent aggregation of population or, in other words, a town." He concluded: "I think it is of the greatest importance not to let any town remain or rise in Abd-el-Kader's domain."[32]

While Tocqueville wished to "prevent the Arabs from founding towns," he romanticized an agricultural future while looking askance at even the French-controlled cities.[33] "Old Algiers seemed an immense fox burrow," he wrote after an evening visit to the Casbah: "narrow, dark, smoky. The population, at this hour, seems idle and dissolute." Earlier that day, by contrast, he had waxed lyrical in rural Algiers: "Delicious country. . . . Prodigious vegetation. . . . A promised land, if one didn't have to farm with gun in hand."[34] To Tocqueville, the conquest demanded agricultural colonization, but prudence suggested care in choosing where to begin establishing the farming settlements. "Nothing irritates and alarms the natives more than the introduction of European farmers; good sense indicates that we must not start in the province in which the most violent and hostile sentiments against us already exist." The Arabs must not be able to "see us take and cultivate their lands." For, he added, "the moment the ploughman appears behind the soldier," or "the day a European plow touches the soil," is a point at which the conflict "is no longer between governments, but between races."[35] The advancing combination of "ploughman" and "soldier" spelled death or flight for many Arabs. As the colony's official newspaper put it in 1840, "[I]t is necessary that as the army pushes back the Arabs, the colonists cover the soil that the enemy abandons, and fill the void that the war has made."[36]

Proponents of civilian and military cultivation differed over how to fill that void. In Tocqueville's view, settlers were the key to the colony's future but they had been subordinated to General Bugeaud's demand that civilians "remain under military rule."[37] Tocqueville thought Bugeaud personified "this imbecile sentiment" existing "at all levels" of the soldiery, who could not own land and harbored "furious jealousy" toward French civilians supposedly prospering from the sacrifices of troops in battle. Settlers whom Tocqueville met agreed that yeoman farmers should pioneer agricultural colonization. One "*very well-informed* colonist" told him: "Some day we'll be able to plant wheat, but only if it is farmed by small landowners who work the land themselves. The same is true of cotton . . . on condition that the cotton is grown on small plots that the farmer and his family can oversee. To farm cotton in large quantities is inevitably to ruin oneself."[38] Most sympathetic to this view was the man Tocqueville considered "very reasonable" and "our best choice," his longtime acquaintance, General Lamoricière. "He is the only officer I have met who was really favorable to colonization and to the colonists." Tocqueville recommended "placing Lamoricière in command," despite one of his worst vices, as Tocqueville described it: "an extreme disdain for human life."[39]

Bugeaud, however, stayed on as governor-general for another six years. One of his officers, writing in 1841 at the same time as Tocqueville, reported that Bugeaud "upgraded to the level of combat a miserable razzia in which his native cavalry cut the throats of several dozen defenseless women and old people."[40] Another officer, Montagnac, under Lamoricière's command, described a razzia in 1842: "[T]he inhabitants, woken by the approach of the soldiers, come out pell-mell with their flocks, their women and their children; all of them are fleeing in all directions; rifle shots come from all sides on these miserable people surprised and defenseless; men, women, children are pursued and soon rounded up by a few soldiers who lead them off." The troops pillaged the camp, burning everything left. Montagnac praised Lamoricière's "new system of war," which destroyed the "means of existence" of the Arabs, seizing all they had: "women, children, flocks, booty, etc." He described women and children surrendering: "They are killed, their throats cut; the cries of the terrified, the dying, mix with the noise of the animals lowing."[41] That year Bugeaud urged French forces to "destroy the villages, cut down the fruit trees, burn or uproot the harvests, empty the silos, scour the ravines, the rocks, and the grottoes to seize the women, the children, the elderly, the flocks, and the furniture. Only in this way can one make these proud mountain people bend."[42]

The correspondence of another French officer, Saint-Arnaud, revealed that the 1842–43 campaigns involved little fighting but systematic devastation and burning of "all the villages." In April 1842, for instance, he wrote: "The country of Beni Menasser is superb. . . . We have burnt everything, destroyed everything. Oh! war! How many women and children, taking refuge in the snows of

the Atlas, died there of cold and misery." In February 1843: "The fires still burning in the mountains indicated the march of the column. . . . Piles of corpses
pressed one against the other, frozen to death during the night. They were
the unfortunate population of the Beni-Naâsseur, whose villages I was burning."[43]

Passions rose as the killing escalated. Another officer complained in 1845
of the "terrible and barbarous" razzia and "the profound demoralization that it
casts into the heart of the soldier who cuts throats, steals, and rapes."[44] In the
French Chamber of Deputies that same year, Marshal Soult attacked the action
of Colonel Pélissier, whose troops had set fires at the mouth of the Dahra cave,
asphyxiating over 500 members of the Ouled Rhia tribe. Governor-General
Bugeaud dispatched a strongly worded defense of Pélissier, stating that the
colonel had acted on Bugeaud's own orders.[45] In another French parliamentary
debate in June 1846, Tocqueville's friend Francisque de Corcelle denounced an
article published the previous month in a French newspaper in Algiers entitled
"What Are the Signs That Show That a Human Race Is Destined for Destruction by a Providential Decree?" Corcelle quoted the article as asserting that in
the past, Mexicans, Caribbeans, and "redskins" (*peaux rouges*) had all had to
"disappear before superior races." According to Corcelle, its author compared
"the Arabs of Algeria and Morocco" to "redskins" and added: "The extinction
of this guilty race . . . is a harmony."[46] Tocqueville himself told the parliament
the next day that although "keeping Africa under our laws, with the aid of the
indigenous populations, is a chimera," he opposed their expulsion. "Above all,
I do not want to exterminate them, as has been, if not proposed, then at least
suggested or insinuated several times, and as those African newspapers that
were mentioned yesterday have demanded in the name of philanthropy."[47]

Abd-el-Kader's surrender in 1847 took the conquest into a new phase.[48]
General de Lamoricière, whom Tocqueville had known since 1828 and had
recommended for command in 1841, now became France's minister of war.[49]
In September 1848, a French captain reported the burning of an Arab village,
where his soldiers "did not shrink at the murder of the elderly people, the
women, and the children. What was most hideous was that the women were
killed after being raped. It is true to say that the general appeared thoroughly
disgusted during this scene of desolation. The Arabs do not defend themselves
at all."[50] The next month, Lamoricière told families of French colonists departing for Algeria: "It falls to civilizing and intelligent labor to finish what force
has begun. Gunpowder and bayonets have done what that they could in Alge-

ria, it is now up to the hoe and to the plough to complete their task . . . remember that these plains which you are going to fertilize with your sweat have long been watered with the blood of your brothers in the army, who have shed it for you."[51] The plow closely followed the sword (see figs. 25 and 26).

From the outset, the historian Kamel Kateb writes, the contest over land fostered among settlers and "a not insignificant part of the French administration of Algeria" a desire either to "exterminate the indigenous population" or to drive it out of the cultivable coastal strip. However, this sentiment also met opposition among the French population and armed forces. One reason was its unfeasibility. A Frenchman wrote in 1863: "Concerning the Arab element, many questions are asked, including what system should be pursued to achieve domination, whether extermination, enslavement, expulsion, [or] assimilation. Extermination, enslavement, such was the system Spain pursued in America." However, "it was understood that there were immense differences. The Arabs are too brave, too vigorous, too unafraid of our army."[52] There is no extant primary evidence of French plans for their extermination, but debate continued. In the same year, Napoléon III took it upon himself to write to the Algerian newspaper *Le moniteur* that "to drive the whole Arab population into the desert and to inflict on it the plight of the North American Indians [is] something impossible and inhumane."[53] Yet after the repression of the Kabyle insurrection of 1871, a Colonel Philibert charged that similar notions continued to circulate among officialdom in Algeria: "The goal is to destroy them, to exterminate them, to hunt them down. . . . In leading circles, unfortunately, such things are said and even written" (see fig. 24).[54]

By 1875, the French conquest was complete. The war had killed approximately 825,000 indigenous Algerians since 1830. A long shadow of genocidal hatred persisted, provoking a French author to protest in 1882 that in Algeria, "we hear it repeated every day that we must expel the native and if necessary destroy him."[55] As a French statistical journal urged five years later, "the system of extermination must give way to a policy of penetration."[56]

German Views of Indigenous Peoples

In the late nineteenth century, as German settlers and armies occupied southwest Africa and encountered its native inhabitants, they brought with them their impressions of how European powers and the United States had previously dealt with indigenous peoples. They also carried their own cultural his-

Fig. 22 *A Razzia,* by D.-A.-M. Raffet. From Charles Nodier, *Portes-de-Fer* (Paris, 1849), 102, reproduced in Charles-André Julien, *Histoire de l'Algérie contemporaine* (Paris, 1964), 336. © Presses Universitaires de France, 1964.

Fig. 23 *Kabyle Shepherd* (or *Shepherd: High Plateau of Kabylia*), after 1861, by Eugène Fromentin-Dupreux, 1820–76. Philadelphia Museum of Art, bequest of Miss William Adger, 1933. Photo by Graydon Wood. See p. 366.

Fig. 24   General Lallemand captures and burns the Kabyle village of Tizi-Ouzou, May 11, 1871. From a photograph by M. Portier, *L'illustration,* August 5, 1871, 81, reproduced in Charles-André Julien, *Histoire de l'Algérie contemporaine* (Paris, 1964), 481, 627. © Presses Universitaires de France, 1964.

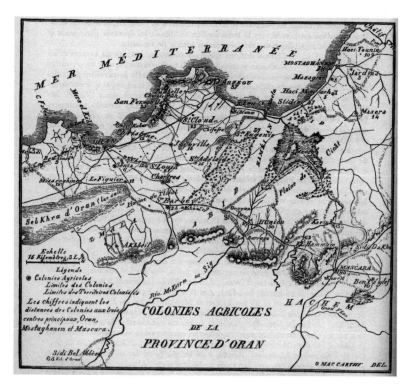

Fig. 25 French map of agricultural colonization of Oran province, Algeria. "Colonies agricoles de la province d'Oran, 1848." From Charles-André Julien, *Histoire de l'Algérie contemporaine* (Paris, 1964), 366. © Presses Universitaires de France, 1964.

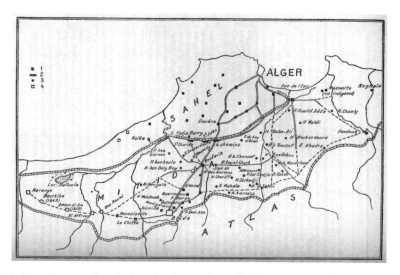

Fig. 26 French map of agricultural colonization of Algiers province. "La colonization de la Mitidja (1840–1849)." From Charles-André Julien, *Histoire de l'Algérie contemporaine* (Paris, 1964), 368. © Presses Universitaires de France, 1964.

Fig. 27 Heinrich Himmler, 1935, photographed near his home at Gmund am Tegern-see in Bavaria. Courtesy of U.S. Holocaust Memorial Museum, Photo Archives, #60440.

Fig. 28 Adolf Hitler (right) and Hermann Göring (left) at Hitler's mountain home,
"Haus Wachenfeld," in the Bavarian Alps. Photo from Ignatius Phayre, "Hitler's Mountain Home," *Homes and Gardens,* November 1938, 193. Phayre described this "sunny
sub-alpine home, hundreds of miles from Berlin's uproar, and set amid an unsophisti-
cated peasantry of carvers and hunters." Of the "Squire of Wachenfeld," Phayre wrote:
"It is over twelve years since Herr Hitler fixed on the site of his one and only home. . . .
Here, in the early days, Hitler's widowed sister, Frau Angela Raubal, kept house for him
on a 'peasant' scale. . . . [Sometimes], when State affairs are over, the Squire himself,
attended by some of his guests, will stroll through the woods into hamlets above and
below. There rustics sit at cottage doors carving trinkets and toys in wood, ivory and
bone. . . . Frauen Goebbels and Göring, in dainty Bavarian dress, arrange dances and
folk songs."

Fig. 29 Open mass grave with thousands of Jews, Proskuriv, 1941 or 1942. Muzeum Wojska Polskiego. U.S. Holocaust Memorial Museum, Photo Archives, #17881.

Fig. 30 "The Collective Farm System Has Come to an End! . . . 'Every Hard-Working Peasant Will Get Land of His Own!'" Nazi propaganda poster, Ukraine, February 1942. Courtesy Naukovo-dovidkova biblioteka tsentral'nykh derzhavnykh arkhiviv Ukraïny, 271sp., reproduced in Karel C. Berkhoff, *Harvest of Despair: Life and Death in Ukraine under Nazi Rule* (Cambridge, Mass., 2004), 121.

tory reflecting more distant, conflicting understandings of both African and Native American peoples. In a pertinent case as early as 1723, the German enlightenment philosopher Christian Wolff had delivered a speech in defense of the "heathen but virtuous Hottentots" of southwest Africa, to which the University of Halle responded by banning him from teaching its students.[57] By the end of the eighteenth century, many Germans expressed a range of notions about both Africans and American Indians, similar to the variety of views then circulating elsewhere in Europe. While Immanuel Kant wrote that Indians were "incapable of producing any kind of culture" and ranked "deeply below even the Negro," Johann Gottfried Herder countered that "[t]he Negro, the American, the Mongol" all possessed "gifts, skills, pre-formed talents" that Europeans lacked. "The *Cherokee* and *Huswana*," in Herder's view, were "as much letters in the great alphabet of our kind as is the best-educated English- or Frenchman." Moreover, Herder went on, "the Negro has the same right to think of the white man as an aberration, as the white man has to see him as a beast, a black animal; and so does the American."[58]

Germans heard American views as well. Writing to the Prussian scientist Alexander von Humboldt in 1813, Thomas Jefferson argued that Britain's recent incitement of its Indian allies to commit atrocities against Americans "will oblige us now to pursue them to extermination, or drive them to new seats beyond our reach." The United States, Jefferson wrote, "may pursue at our leisure whatever plan we find necessary" for its self-defense, and America's "confirmed brutalization, if not extermination of this race" would only add another chapter to England's history of "deluging the earth with blood."[59] Humboldt, who had just sent Jefferson his book on Mexico that expressed a hope for further Spanish efforts on behalf of its Indians "to protect this unfortunate race," is unlikely to have sympathized with U.S. brutalization or extermination of Native Americans.[60] Indeed, German literature increasingly displayed sympathy for the doomed "noble savage." The popular writer Friedrich Gerstäcker, who lived in the United States from 1837 to 1843, expressed a "strong desire to learn something about the natives of this land." He concluded that they were experiencing a long-term decline, since "before the early generations of Indians there [had] lived a stronger, more civilized race in North America." On his return to Germany, Gerstäcker described Indians as "courageously romantic." These "sons of the forest," he wrote in 1844, now "corrupted by the mean and low speculations of the 'pale faces,'" were sadly and inexorably "vanishing."[61]

German empathy for genocidal violence emerged slowly, in the wake of nineteenth-century nationalism. In 1841, the leading scholar of ancient Germanic language and literature, August Heinrich Hoffmann von Fallersleben (1799–1874), composed his patriotic poem "Deutschland Über Alles," which was eventually to become the country's national anthem. Two years later, Hoffmann listened to the recently returned German traveler Gustav Dresel tell of his experiences in the Republic of Texas from 1838 to 1840. He urged Dresel to write them down and, by 1846, Hoffmann wrote in his autobiography, "Gustav was diligently working on his Texan diary and during the evening hours read to us bit by bit what he had finished."[62] Dresel wrote with sympathy of the young republic and its settlers, and he encouraged German emigrants to join them in taking up the land there: "It is a fine and noble task to guide the sixty to seventy thousand people who leave Germany every year, to concentrate them as much as possible, to preserve thereby the German element." Dresel added, "In the West of the United States there are splendid tracts of land eminently suitable for the German farmer," and he predicted the establishment of "whole communities" with "land in all the Western states." In particular, he thought that Texas possessed a unique "productive power of the soil" and that its settlers required "the moral force to conquer an independent position among independent people." For the Indians of Texas, Dresel expressed a "melancholy" romanticism and further predicted: "Their ultimate fate is complete extinction." The 1840 Texan massacre of 35 Comanches (see p. 347), he described as a tragedy, but one lacking injustice: "The delegates of the Texas government insisted on their just claim. The dispute ended in violence and finished with a frightful fight. . . . None of the Indians surrendered; they all died a hero's death." In what Dresel called "the glorious battle" of Plum Creek, another "two hundred redskins lost their lives."[63]

According to Hoffmann, as Dresel was completing his manuscript, he "gave me the finished pages for revision." Hoffman wrote a preface for it and prepared the book's text for the printer. Dresel's work inspired Hoffman to write his *Texanische Lieder* (Texan Songs) and a poem he called "Yankee Doodle."[64] Having started off as a liberal nationalist, Hoffmann ended his career in 1874 celebrating a Germany united under Prussian leadership, which adopted his poem "Deutschland Über Alles" as the German national anthem.

German expansionists increasingly seized upon U.S. wars with Native Americans as precedents or justification for colonial war and, eventually, genocidal tactics. The U.S. general Philip H. Sheridan met the Prussian statesman and future German chancellor Otto von Bismarck in September 1870, two years after enunciating his goal to "make war on the families and stock of these Indians."[65] It was Bismarck whom Sheridan now advised that "proper strategy" in wartime "consists in the first place in inflicting as telling blows as possible upon the enemy's army, and then causing the inhabitants so much suffering that they must long for peace, and force their Government to demand it. The people must be left nothing but their eyes to weep with over the war."[66] Published in 1898 in the diary of Bismarck's confidant Moritz Busch, this statement referred to the Civil War, but some German national thinkers tarred the United States with the brush of Indian savagery. Friedrich Nietzsche wrote of "an Indian-like savageness, which is inherent in the Indian blood, in the way Americans covet Gold: and their breathless work pace—the actual vice of the New World— already starts to drive old Europe wild through infection."[67] Germans likely noted other colonial cases, too. The Prussian Order of Merit went in 1874 to British historian Thomas Carlyle after completion of his multivolume study *Frederick the Great.* In his earlier book *Chartism* (1839), published in German translation in 1895, Carlyle had written that the Irish must "be improved a little, or exterminated," and in 1848, during Ireland's Great Famine, he had reiterated that "if no beneficent hand will chain [the Irishman] into wholesome slavery, and, with whip on back . . . get some work out of him—Nature herself . . . has no resource but to exterminate him."[68]

Such views slowly gained ground in Germany. The famous German novelist Karl May, author of numerous books set in the American West that featured sympathetic depictions of doomed Indians, wrote in 1892: "[I]t is a cruel law that the weak has to make room for the stronger. However, as this law permeates the whole creation and is valid in all of this earth's nature, we have to assume that this cruelty is either only cruel at first glance, or is capable of Christian mitigation, as the eternal truth that has given this law is eternal love at the same time." The historian Jens-Uwe Guettel points out that May's view of Indians' tragic but inevitable extinction simultaneously "blamed and exculpated white Americans and Europeans."[69]

German Settler Colonialism

After the close call of the 1848 revolution, German conservatives like the young Prussian diplomat Otto von Bismarck took to lauding the peasantry as a "loyal" class. Outspokenly antirevolutionary in 1848, Bismarck was a successful landowner "with conventional prejudices about the superiority of rural life," even though Prussia was the most industrialized German region, with 15,000 steam engines in 1865.[70] Appointed prime minister of Prussia in 1862, Bismarck fought three successful wars against Denmark, Austria, and France that led to the creation in 1871 of a German empire under Prussian leadership.

A new political coalition emerged in the Germany of the 1880s and 1890s that united what historian Woodruff Smith calls "disparate strands of romantic agrarianism into a functional aggregate ideology widely employed in conservative politics." Germany's rapid industrialization since the 1850s had made the small farmer "a symbol of pre-industrial society, of all that was threatened by modernity." At the same time, agrarianists and the newly proliferating proponents of *völkisch* ideology agreed "that the true embodiment of the *Volk* was the peasantry."[71] Land and race were linked.

Settler colonialism brought them even closer. The German geographer Friedrich Ratzel (1844–1904) traveled through North America in 1873–75, and over the next two decades, while a professor at the Royal Polytechnic in Munich, he published substantial books on the United States. No agrarian romantic, Ratzel praised America's cities as the peak of its culture, yet he also "registered well on things that grew, wild or cultivated, and on the small farmers and stockraisers."[72] In another work, *Anthropogeographie* (1891), Ratzel argued that "contact with culture" had caused the "dying out" of races and "the decline of peoples of inferior cultures." He cited both American Indians and Aboriginal Australians as examples of "inferior" peoples destroyed by superior Europeans.[73] Prior to the arrival of Europeans, in Ratzel's view, America, Australia, and southern Africa were "the least stimulated areas of the earth." He explained their fate in metaphors of cultivation and neglect of the land: "Before the Europeans and Arabs had cultivated large states in America, Australia and inner Africa by conquest and colonization, these vast areas were not politically utilized. The political value of their land lay fallow. Politics as well as agriculture led to a gradual knowledge of the powers that lie dormant in the earth." He added that states themselves were intimately connected with agriculture, which intertwined its land and people. "These live on its soil, draw their sustenance from it, and are otherwise attached to it by spiritual relationships. Together with this piece of earth they form the state." A nation, Ratzel wrote, is inseparable from the land it occupies. "Just as an individual struggles with virgin land until he has forced it into cultivable fields, so too does a nation struggle with its land making it, through blood and sweat, increasingly its own." In the more primitive state, he argued, its people "settle less densely and are more scattered; their cultivation is poorer and is readily moved from one field to another." Moreover, the territorial "enlargement" of states operated "continuously" in a related pattern: "[T]he growth of the state over the surface of the earth can be compared to the downward growth which leads to an attachment to the soil. It is more than a metaphor when one speaks of a people as taking root."[74]

Ratzel's classical models also demonstrated his theme of proliferating agriculture. "The great success of Rome lay in the cross-fertilization of a robust peasantry and a more mobile, worldly element.... Caesar's greatness lay in the fact that he gave to the more stable body a definite secure boundary as well as spatial expansion." To this Roman precedent, however, Ratzel appears to have added native German mythology. The role he assigned to a "mobile, worldly element" apparently reflected conventional contemporary visions of the ancient Germans as wandering pastoralists who had invigorated the Roman Empire. In his view, "the formation of states pushes forward from seas and steppes (regions of movement) into forest and arable lands (regions of persistence)." By contrast, the hunters of Native America had possessed neither herds of stock nor "forward" movement. To its detriment, "pre-Columbian America was without pastoral peoples" and thus lacked the benefit of "continuous political ferment." Primitive states "never advanced without foreign influence" and those that did progress (like the Germans) left "wander sagas" and "sagas of origin." As in other contexts, the pastoral romance reinforced the cult of cultivation. Ratzel considered these classical developments to exemplify key features of the growth of states, which included "territorial annexation and amalgamation." This trend was trans-Atlantic. "The marches of eastwardly expanding Germany which, as they were conquered piece by piece, were fortified and colonized, are repeated along the growing edges of America in the west."[75]

By 1892, Ratzel had singled out the country's new colony of Southwest Africa as a promising overseas destination for German settlers. Five years later, he linked racial conflict, agriculture, and territorial expansion by coining the important new German term *Lebensraum* (living space). As Benjamin Madley summarized this view, "[O]nly a *Volk* with a strong agricultural base could flourish." By 1901, when Ratzel published an article elaborating his theory, "*Der Lebensraum*," Southwest Africa was already "Germany's most populous settler colony."[76]

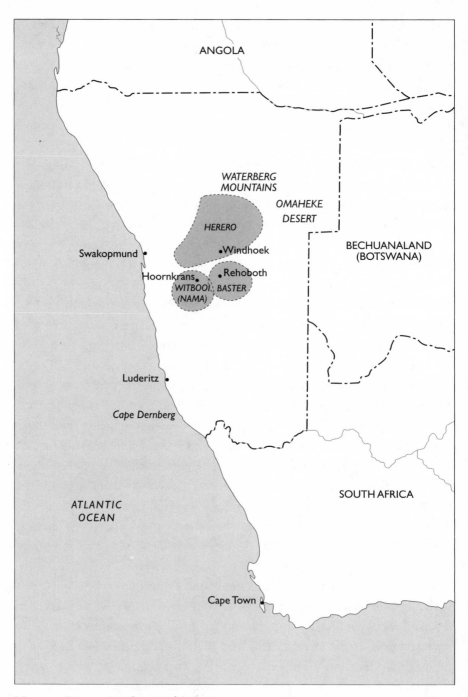

ANGOLA

WATERBERG
MOUNTAINS
OMAHEKE
DESERT

HERERO

Swakopmund •
•Windhoek

BECHUANALAND
(BOTSWANA)

Hoornkrans•
•Rehoboth
WITBOOI
(NAMA)
BASTER

Luderitz •

Cape Dernberg

ATLANTIC
OCEAN

SOUTH AFRICA

Cape Town

MAP 20. German Southwest Africa, 1887–1910

Conquest and Genocide in Southwest Africa

German conquest of the territory had begun in 1885 with the arrival of imperial commissioner Dr. Heinrich Göring, the father of the future Nazi leader Hermann Göring. The land the Germans most coveted in Southwest Africa belonged to two indigenous peoples, the Herero and the Nama. The Herero, a 75,000-strong group of cattle herders, occupied the center of the new colonial territory. To the south, the Nama, a linguistic group of Khoi-San or Bushmen (Hottentot) communities, numbered possibly 20,000. A third ethnic group of 30,000 Damara were partly employed and enslaved by Herero and Nama.[77]

Early Herero resistance to German settlement forced imperial commissioner Göring to briefly abandon his colony in 1888. The commander of the German reinforcements, Curt von François, concluded: "Nothing but relentless severity will lead to success." He and Göring set about enforcing African subjection. In 1893, von François staged a surprise attack by 200 German troops on the Nama town of Hornkranz, whose chief, Hendrik Witbooi, had refused to recognize German authority. The German commander ordered his men to "destroy the tribe of the Witboois." The ninety victims included 78 women and children. After 18 months of resistance, Witbooi submitted to the Germans in September 1894.[78] The colonial governor, Theodor Leutwein, predicted that "15 years from now, there will not be much left for the natives." That secret had to be kept: "If they learn about this now, revolution is inevitable."[79]

Two years later, Nama rebels again briefly took up arms, as did some of the Herero. But their major leaders, Hendrik Witbooi and the Herero chief, Samuel Maharero, now supported the Germans, who repressed the rebels and executed their ringleaders. Then, in turn, a typhus outbreak, a locust plague, and drought killed 10,000 Herero, and a rinderpest epidemic wiped out 80 percent of their cattle herds.[80] Meanwhile, the Colonial Office subsidized German settlers who were planning to set up small farms. As the German writer Clara Brockmann later put it: "every man who applied was sold land; often he was from the city and had no experience with agriculture."[81] Governor Leutwein told a local German newspaper in late 1903 that "the final result of our Colonial Policy" would be "that the Natives will be reduced to poverty."[82] In the previous three years, white settlers had already taken over nearly one-quarter of Hereroland, and the Germans planned a railway line cutting through it. Now Samuel Maharero decided to fight back. He wrote to Witbooi: "Let us die fighting rather than die as a result of maltreatment." To the leader of another community, Maharero suggested: "[O]ur weak nations all over Africa should stand up against the Germans, let them rather finish us off and let them live alone in our country."[83] But the Herero had to fight alone.

The war began in mid-January 1904, when Herero started attacking white farms. As they slaughtered German settlers and traders, the Herero fighters largely respected their chief Maharero's orders to spare women, children, other Africans, and non-German whites. All but 10 of their first 150 victims were German men.[84] After some hard-fought, indecisive conventional battles, the 3,000-strong Herero units won two victories in March and April 1904. But reinforcements poured in from abroad, bringing German strength to 2,500, and more were on the way.[85]

German officials opted for ruthlessness without restraint. The Colonial Society stated that "Europeans can assert themselves only by maintaining the supremacy of their race at all costs." In May, General Lothar von Trotha was appointed commander of the German forces. He told Governor Leutwein that Kaiser Wilhelm II wanted victory: "His Majesty simply said that he expected me to crush the rebellion by all means." It is not clear that these means specifically included genocide. Historian Isabel V. Hull comments: "The phrase 'by all means' was a standard expression routinely used in connection with colonial revolts." The director of the Colonial Office told the Reichstag that "Germany's honor demands the repression of the uprising by all means." At any rate, from the start, genocidal actions were not to be ruled out if necessary to achieve these goals. Indeed, as the Colonial Society put it, "the swifter and harsher the reprisals taken . . . the better the chances of restoring authority."[86]

Lothar von Trotha's four decades of previous military experience included colonial suppression in German East Africa and fighting the Boxer Rebellion in China. Even before his arrival in Southwest Africa in June 1904, von Trotha quickly vetoed Leutwein's planned proclamation offering amnesty to all innocent Herero. He told a Berlin newspaper that "no war may be conducted humanely against nonhumans." Von Trotha later proclaimed: "It was and is my policy to use force with terrorism and even brutality. I shall annihilate the revolting tribes with rivers of blood and rivers of gold. Only after a complete uprooting will something emerge." He deployed a force of 5,000 men to surround the Waterberg Mountains, where the Herero nation of 60,000 people and their herds had gathered.[87]

Among the advice that Kaiser Wilhelm II received on the Herero campaign was an ominous letter suggesting that German troops "thoroughly poison their water holes."[88] It is unknown whether such counsel reached von Trotha. As he moved his forces into position, he may have deliberately left the Herero one possible escape route—southeast into the Omaheke Desert. The general staff in Berlin had favored that outcome, "because the enemy would then seal his own fate, being doomed to die of thirst in the arid sandveld."[89]

The German troops commenced their attack on August 11, 1904. They soon began "indiscriminate killing of the wounded, male prisoners, women and children." Herero casualties quickly reached 5,000 killed and 20,000 wounded since January. German units seized the water holes, forcing the surviving 50,000 Herero to head into the Omaheke Desert. The pursuing German troops massacred almost everyone they found, including women and children, and poisoned the water holes in the desert. Von Trotha's orders expressly permitted the shooting of "all armed men who were captured." By the end of September, the Germans had "effectively destroyed most of the Herero people."[90] Troops reached the colony's last known water hole on September 29, and the next day von Trotha ended their pursuit of the Herero.

Then, on October 2, the general issued an "Extermination Order" (*Vernichtungsbefehl*). He proclaimed: "The Herero people must leave this land. If it does not, I will force it to do so by using the great gun [artillery]. Within the German border every male Herero, armed or unarmed, with or without cattle, will be shot to death. I shall no longer receive women or children, but will drive them back to their people or have them shot at. These are my words to the Herero people." To his soldiers, von Trotha spelled out that "this proclamation will result in taking no more male prisoners, but will not degenerate into atrocities against women and children. The latter will run away if one shoots at them a couple of times." However, on October 4, von Trotha wrote to the chief of the general staff: "I believe that the nation must be destroyed as such. . . . I think it better that the nation perish rather than infect our troops."[91]

Governor Leutwein favored negotiations and complained that von Trotha had refused them "without consulting me." The governor asked Berlin for "clarification: how far does my authority extend?" When the German Foreign Office replied that von Trotha had sole authority to deal with the natives, Leutwein resigned, and in November 1904 von Trotha became the governor of Southwest Africa for the next 12 months.[92] "Fourteen hundred heads are in our hands," announced the director of the Colonial Department of the Foreign Office, praising von Trotha in January 1905.[93]

Only 1,000 Herero, including Samuel Maharero, successfully crossed the desert and reached British Bechuanaland (now Botswana) alive. Fewer than 2,000 others escaped north to Ovamboland or south to Namaland. At least 30,000 had perished in a matter of weeks, mostly in the desert. The official German military history noted "the shocking fate that the mass of the people had met in the desert" and concluded: "The punishment had come to an end. The Herero had ceased to be an independent tribe." German forces rounded up the remaining 17,000 Herero for work as slave laborers.[94]

Meanwhile, the Nama saw the writing on the wall. Like Maharero, their chief, Hendrik Witbooi, had long cooperated with the colonial authorities. The previous year, Witbooi had resisted Maharero's appeal to "die fighting." But now, Nama scouts in the German forces were deserting with confirmation of the brutal annihilation of the Herero and complaints of their own maltreatment. The pattern of continual German encroachment on Nama lands was also clear. In fact, Governor Leutwein had recently informed Berlin of his plan to "disarm the south" after defeating the Herero. Leutwein recommended "destruction of the tribal organizations" and the institution of "pass laws." Witbooi declared war just two days after von Trotha's "Extermination Order" against the Herero. Most of the Nama tribes responded, and Witbooi raised an army of 2,000. But by then the German forces numbered 15,000 and had already broken the Herero resistance. The Nama also confronted the ingrained contempt of settlers. According to the German land commissioner Dr. Paul Rohrbach: "From the point of view of the economy of the country, the Hottentots are generally regarded, in the wider sense, as useless, and in this respect, providing no justification for the preservation of this race." That "prevailing view," Rohrbach wrote, "led to their losses being regarded with indifference, if not with satisfaction."[95]

Fighting a guerrilla war in mountainous terrain far from German railway lines, the Nama stretched colonial power to the limit. In over 200 clashes in the first year, Nama fighters inflicted as many German casualties as the Herero had—and more than they suffered themselves. The Germans considered one Nama leader, Jacob Morenga, "an outstanding soldier." Like Maharero, Morenga enforced a ban on harming noncombatants and favored taking and releasing prisoners. When Hendrik Witbooi was fatally wounded in October 1905, Morenga and other Nama commanders fought on. The next month, the German government replaced von Trotha and he returned to Berlin.[96]

Settlers called explicitly for genocide of the Nama. The editor of the leading German newspaper in Southwest Africa said: "The Herero should not be destroyed—the Witboois [Nama], yes—the reason being that the Herero are needed as laborers, and the Witboois are an insignificant tribe."[97] In December 1906, a Social Democrat in the German parliament blamed the partial annihilation of the Nama on agricultural interests: "The Farmer lobby . . . is hoping, wishing and working towards a continuation of the war, so that land will be taken from the 'natives.' It is irresponsible of the Government to toe this line and to follow this unbelievable land policy, which necessarily will lead partly to the annihilation and partly to the enslavement of these [Herero and Nama] peoples." This speaker accused "exploitation-crazed farmers" of aiming to "annihilate and partly render 'natives' landless."[98] The troops of von Trotha's successor tracked down the Nama resistance leader Jacob Morenga and killed him in September 1907. The next year, they bought off the last Nama commander in his Bechuanaland exile.[99]

Meanwhile, the surviving Herero had been deported as slave laborers to coastal towns like Swakopmund, where they "died like flies." In an article in the *Swakopmunder Zeiting,* von Trotha wrote that "the destruction of all rebellious Native tribes is the aim of our efforts." In 1904–5, mortality in Swakopmund doubled to 355 deaths in a native population of 1,217, then 325 more died in April–May 1905 alone. The next month, the chief medical officer at Swakopmund reported that the town contained "over 1,000 Herero prisoners, men, women and children. Most of those who arrived here are literally skin and bone." A missionary requested that "only work fit Hereros be sent to Swakopmund, because they died there." However, according to the base commandant: "There is a great demand for Native labour. . . . It is difficult to send back the weak Hereros interned in Swakopmund as suggested . . . because there are no replacements for them."[100]

Of the 17,000 Herero survivors rounded up after the 1904 war and sent to slave labor camps, 6,000 perished by 1907. A German sweep through Hereroland in September 1905 killed another 1,000 Herero and captured 260. The kaiser's expropriation order of December 1905 authorized the seizure of the "entire moveable and fixed property of the tribe." In April 1907, German commander Ludwig von Estorff informed Berlin of his horror at conditions in the camps: "For such hangmen's services I can neither detail my officers, nor can I accept responsibility." Official German statistics reported the deaths of 45 percent of the survivors laboring in internment. The work camps were then closed, and "the surviving Hereros were divided into small groups and shipped off to work on the farms and ranches of the German settlers . . . dispersed on hundreds of ranches and farms spread over thousands of square miles." By 1911, the total Herero population numbered only 15,130.[101] Probably 60,000, or 80 percent of the Herero nation, had died since January 1904.[102] The survivors lost their property, sustenance, and community.

In May 1907, most of the Nama territory became colonial government property too. Four months later, 1,800 Nama men, women, and children were deported to Shark Island; 1,032 of them had died there by April 1908. Of a population of perhaps 20,000 in 1904, only 9,800 Nama survived in 1911. Of the 30,000 ethnic Damara innocent bystanders, 10,000 perished in the wars from 1904 to 1907.[103] Historian Krista O'Donnell writes that the survivors of all three of the colony's indigenous groups quickly became enmeshed in a labor regime of native ordinances that instituted "total passport control, limited mobility, compulsory labor contracts, and the confiscation of all land and livestock." Men now made up only 30 percent of the indigenous population.[104]

The destruction of the Herero proved to be the opening genocide of the twentieth century. Among the three main Southwest African ethnic groups, totaling 125,000 people before 1904, German repression took approximately 80,000 lives in three years, at a cost of 676 German dead, 907 wounded, and 97 missing.[105] The toll exacted by Europe's leading military power highlights the contrast between the German policy toward civilians and that of their Herero and Nama opponents, who made concerted efforts to spare women and children. As historians Jon Bridgman and Leslie Worley point out, "representatives of the German government" set out "to destroy a whole people with the knowledge and the tacit approval of the Kaiser and the General Staff."[106]

All these events provoked some Germans only to look back for colonial precedents that might justify them. In his 1906 book on the ongoing war in Southwest Africa, Captain Maximilian Bayer of the German *Schutztruppe* forces asserted that "only the strong have a right to continue to exist" and that "the weak and purposeless will perish in favor of the strong. This process is played out in a variety of ways, like, for example, the end of the Indian Americans because they were without purpose in the continued development of the world." Similarly, he went on, "the day will come when the Hottentot [Nama] will perish, not any loss for humanity because they are after all only born thieves and robbers, nothing more."[107] In the same year, the *Prussian Yearbook* published an article entitled "A Colonization Method Now Forgotten," which offered a vivid, seven-page description of early colonial New South Wales without once mentioning the Australian Aborigines. Juxtaposing the role and corruption of convict labor with the British colony's subsequent "progress," the German author concluded: "[E]ven a method of colonizing that brought about such grotesque conditions—and that today would surely give rise to the most merciless criticism in all quarters—does not keep a colony from prospering."[108]

If some Germans searched for models, others deplored the genocide. While Conservative Party spokesmen insisted that "the white race" had to "consider itself everywhere to be the master race" and described the Herero as "bloodthirsty beasts in the form of humans," by contrast the Social Democratic parliamentarian August Bebel called the suppression of the Herero "not just barbaric, but bestial." Bebel accepted neither racial hierarchy nor racial purity, and he even ridiculed German fears of "mixed races."[109] In fact, Germany's general election of 1907 became known as the "Hottentot Election" for its heated political debate over the ongoing suppression of the Nama people. In an electoral campaign "Guide to Colonial Policy" published that year, Berlin's Action Committee for Colonial Policy complained strongly of "the endless criticisms of our colonies voiced by the Social Democrats." These unfair criticisms, the committee asserted, "portray the violence done to the colored races as outrageous, as totally without precedent or exemplar."[110]

Precedents did exist, the committee retorted, in America. "That is why we must remember that in 1643 Virginia's parliament issued a resolution to end striving for peace with the Indians and to exterminate them all by force." As a result, English settlers had "bathed in the blood of the redskins and wrested huge tracts of land from the luckless tribes." Later in the seventeenth century, the committee went on, Virginian colonists "incurred a new horrendous war with the Indians, unleashed in the wake of the underhanded murder of six Indian chiefs" (see p. 223). America thus furnished a precedent for German colonial brutality, just as Britain's convict colony of New South Wales had. "Such slaughter, robberies and dissoluteness, much as they are to be condemned, no more reduced the uses of the colony for the home country than they ruled out the introduction of civilization."[111]

Past genocides provided both precedent and excuse for current ones, while the historical record resounded against recent proponents of self-determination as new, convenient converts. As the United States entered World War I a decade later, a cartoon in a German satirical magazine pictured President Woodrow Wilson telling two Indians, described as the "last Mohicans": "You cowards! If you had not allowed us to wipe you out, you could now fight for America's freedom!"[112]

In the lead-up to the 1907 German elections, the government's colonial director, Bernhard Dernburg, also drew upon English colonial precedent in America to justify the German genocide in Africa. In a speech in Berlin in January 1907, Dernburg asserted that "in earlier times" English traders had sold alcohol and guns to natives and thus "brought about conditions in which large masses of people were destroyed." Dernburg went on: "Of course there can be no question that in the process of civilization some native tribes, just like some animals, must be destroyed if they are not to degenerate and become encumbrances on the state." For Germany, at least, this was no great challenge. "In our German colonies we are happily not too heavily burdened by these elements. But the history of colonization in the United States—surely the greatest effort at colonizing the world has ever seen—had as its first act the almost total annihilation of the original inhabitants." Subsequent human progress, however, had supposedly allowed Germany to avoid this genocidal model in its own colonies. Instead, he claimed, "we are able to proceed with methods of preservation."[113] It was apparently not Germany's fault that the prisoners on Shark Island had "died off" (eingehen), as Dernburg told the Reichstag.[114]

Asserting Germany's superiority over the United States in the "preservation" of its colonial subjects, Dernburg not only made propaganda use of the American precedent but explicitly denied his government's genocide of the Herero and Nama, even as he blamed its continuing victims. Most of Southwest Africa was pastureland, he said. "It is quite desolate at the present time, but not, as one might assume, essentially as a consequence of German occupation and the ensuing war, but the result of tens of years of feuds between the resident Hottentots and Bantu tribes in which the predatory and powerful Hottentots oppressed the Herero, who were weaker and, because of their large herds, were settled."[115] The genocide of the Herero pastoralists thus became a crime of savages in the face of European civilization.

What was actually "preserved," however, was not the Herero people but the bucolic romance of their German destroyers. Dernburg lamented, for example, that "our painters have so far refrained from taking their inspiration from the rewarding blue sky of Southwest Africa." Yet the landscape of the colony boasted "a generous nature, a grandiose animal and plant world," which he saw as "the gift of wild beauty." It was to be regretted, he concluded, that colonization had "a tendency to a certain level of destruction and repression," as it made "corrections in the vision of God's open nature." Art must compensate for this, Dernburg concluded. It should promote "all that is noble and beautiful in a free, unspoiled world."[116] After four years in "our new Germany on African soil," bereft now of much of its native population, the writer Clara Brockmann returned home in 1910 full of praise "for Southwest Africa, *for the land of purity, peace, and strength.*"[117]

Brockmann was not the only woman activist to apply the rhetoric of national pride and purity abroad. German newspapers praised her books *The German Woman in Southwest Africa* (1910) and *Letters from a German Girl in Southwest* (1912), and colonial promoters recommended them to new settlers. She pointed out, for instance, that the colonial hierarchy gave German servant girls, "having the same race" as the male colonists, a rise in station, "above the native servants." Immigrant women could contribute to this promising environment in Southwest Africa, free of the social ills and political rancor accompanying Germany's industrialization at home. Brockmann's forceful racism identified a role for women colonists not only in reducing frontier racial miscegenation, by introducing "German family life" and bearing the male settlers pure German children, but also in establishing the ideal German family farm: "[A] profitable farming operation . . . cannot reach full flourishing development without the cooperation of the housewife." Praising German women in Southwest Africa, from servants to independent farmers, Brockmann enlisted the German female immigrant as "a fighter for Germany's greatness." A male Conservative Party parliamentarian agreed, telling the Reichstag, only partly in jest, that the German woman "is the best export item we could possibly have."[118]

Against this backdrop of genocide and colonial fantasy, German settlers imagined themselves in danger from the few remaining survivors, or perhaps their ghosts. Southwest Africa's indigenous men and women continued to suffer egregious violence even after the commencement of German official attempts to establish a legal regime. For example, the settler Elisabeth Ohlsen was tried in 1911 for murdering her Bergdamara farmhand with a club, crushing his skull as he lay prostrate. A German surgeon testified to her paranoia about native violence, quoting her as having asserted that "[a]ll natives, even those in Windhoek, were trying to kill them," while the local farmers' association refuted her claims and condemned such mistreatment of workers. Ohlsen was nevertheless acquitted on the grounds of self-defense. The next year, settler Ludwig Cramer faced trial for torturing about 10 native workers, killing several, including two women. He feared that fugitive Herero fighters, led by a man named Katoakonda, inhabited the bush around his farm and that his workers were helping them steal his cattle. After Cramer had beaten a servant maid, she told her mistress, "Look, Missis, before all the land and animals belonged [to] the Herero. Ka'konda was a great Captain then, but today he is nothing and must work. Do you think this pleases him?" Cramer subsequently tortured Katoakonda's pregnant wife, Konturu, until she collapsed from his beatings, "then had her supported while he continued the blows." He shackled and trod on Konturu, causing her to miscarry. Yet many German settlers supported Cramer. One raged against "the useless native women." Another complained that "these beings are allowed to attack their white mistresses" and are then "at worst locked up. . . . Here these females have the best lives . . . why does such an animal not receive her equal share of 15 or 25 strokes like a man?"[119]

Back in Berlin, during a Reichstag debate on the outlawing of interracial marriages, Colonial Director Wilhelm Solf denounced Abraham Lincoln's emancipation of American slaves as a "warning Menetekel for all colonizing nations." Should German colonies follow suit, he feared, "white girls might return with Hereros, Hottentots, and Bastards as husbands." Solf insisted on the importance of race, "for with respect to the colored man even the proletarian is master." Another speaker stated: "The native who is supposed to learn from the white man must see him as a being who stands far and powerfully above him." Yet another argued that "certain racial mixtures are harmful to the national and racial interest." In this 1912 debate, according to historian Helmut Smith, "no one in the Reichstag raised a voice, as Bebel had done in 1906, to ridicule talk about the allegedly deleterious consequences of racial mixing." Here was, Smith writes, a new element in German conservatism, "an ideologically driven, future-oriented racism," which was accompanied by "the increasing willingness to accept brutality in the service of an idea and the increasing blindness to the violence done, not to nations or classes, but to humans."[120] Those making the decisions simply did not consider their victims fully human.

Part Three

TWENTIETH-CENTURY GENOCIDES

Introductory Note

Colonial genocides of premodern and early modern times were mostly products of expanding empires and their settlements. By contrast, genocidal massacres perpetrated by contracting, threatened polities, like those of the Mon kingdom in Burma in 1740 and the Khmer kingdom of Cambodia in 1750 (chapter 4), were comparatively rare. By the early twentieth century, however, European regimes or their independent successors abroad had colonized not only those two Southeast Asian kingdoms but most of the rest of the globe as well. During the nineteenth century, as we saw in chapters 7 and 8, colonial and settler states had conquered two continents almost entirely: North America and Australia. European powers carved up most of Africa after 1870. By 1910, the world had become smaller, the great powers greater, and contests for territory more closely fought. A new phenomenon emerged: genocides perpetrated by national chauvinist dictatorships that had seized control of tottering, shrinking, or new empires, aiming to reverse real or perceived territorial losses or conquer new regions from established powers.

To the problems confronting these and other genocidal regimes, the twentieth century, and in particular the outbreak of World War I in 1914, offered new technological, political, or organizational solutions. Innovations such as large-scale industrial production of armaments, including heavy weaponry and new vectors of mass destruction, instantaneous radio and telegraph communications, widespread civilian enlistment into military organizations, and rapid mass transportation by land and sea all facilitated projects as ambitious and extensive as genocide. The advent of "total war" and totalitarianism now offered prospective genocidists not only cover and ideological rationales for their crimes but unprecedented efficiency and tempting feasibility. Moreover, as before—and perhaps to an even greater extent—rapid modernization also provoked neotraditional ideological reactions that reinforced genocidal impulses. As the world became more modern, the resort to ancient models and precedents intensified. And as it became more urban and industrialized, both the significance and the idealization of agriculture became more urgent.

The greater population pressure on the land also increased the numbers of potential victims. The estimated worldwide population, which doubled to nearly 1,000 million in the three centuries from 1500 to 1800, had then multiplied exponentially in the nineteenth century alone, to a global figure of around 1,750 million people by 1910.[1] The world's considerably larger populations and labor forces made land much scarcer, leaving human resources in relatively reduced demand. For expansionist regimes, then, mass killing now presented potentially much greater benefits and much less risk in terms of labor shortages. And for a new series of totalitarian party-states propounding "scientific" race or class ideologies, entire groups of specific people became inimical or expendable. The Communist giants, Stalin's USSR and Mao's China, pursued mass killing of domestic political enemies and social "classes." They were somewhat less preoccupied with racial categories or territorial expansionism, and not at all with historical antiquity, while Stalin, at least, harbored no hint of agrarian idealism either. Despite these important exceptions, the major themes of previous eras persisted in many other cases during a new, even more extensive, century of genocide.

CHAPTER 10

The Armenian Genocide

National Chauvinism in the Waning Ottoman Empire

Serving as military attaché at the Ottoman embassy in Berlin during 1909, the rising Young Turk leader Enver Pasha was well placed to learn from the German military in the wake of its destruction of a recalcitrant ethnic group, the Herero of Southwest Africa. As an infantry officer from 1899 to 1902, when he graduated second in his class at the Istanbul War College, Enver had greatly impressed his German instructor, General von Ditfurth, who proposed several years later that Enver be assigned a post in the Royal Prussian Army's command headquarters.[1] Enver's role as a leader of the successful 1908 mutiny against the Ottoman sultan did not dispel German leaders' trust in him; indeed, it proved well founded when he later staffed the Ottoman armed forces with German commanders. And finally, after the fall of the Young Turk regime in late 1918, it was a German gunboat that sped Enver, his colleague Talât Pasha, and five other top-level Young Turk officials to safety across the Black Sea.[2] With Talât, Enver slipped back into Berlin and spent the years 1919–20 there.

Before World War I, the Ottoman Empire had become known as "the sick man of Europe." Its military defeats and territorial losses convinced the Young Turks that severe action was needed to save it. In 1915, during his regime's genocide of the Ottoman Armenian minority, Talât told the U.S. ambassador: "Turkey had lost province after province . . . the Turkish Empire had dwindled almost to the vanishing point. If what was left of Turkey was to survive, . . . [Talât said] he must get rid of these alien peoples."[3] The empire's prewar geographic diminution, as Turkish racial chauvinists in the heartland were increasingly joined by ethnic compatriots exiled from lost territories, literally brought home a sense of its embattlement that later fueled the Armenian genocide. Turks fleeing abandoned outposts of the empire concentrated in Anatolia, and some assumed leading roles in the emerging Young Turk movement and subsequently in the genocide. The movement's thinking exhibited features resembling that of earlier genocide perpetrators, including preoccupations with ethnicity, external territories, and land and its cultivation, as well as backward-looking visions of preserving or restoring ancient glories.

Historical Background to the Armenian Genocide

In the fourth century c.e., the mountain monarchy of Armenia, occupying much of eastern Anatolia, was arguably the first nation to adopt Christianity. Muslim armies overran the last Armenian kingdom of Cilicia in 1375. Turks incorporated most of the Armenian lands in the sixteenth century, as the Ottoman Empire reached its height, conquering Egypt, Syria, and Iraq. But successive Turkish defeats, including that at Vienna in 1683, finally halted Ottoman expansion. Now, fear of decline preoccupied Ottoman strategists. As early as 1625, for instance, courtiers warned that if European traders gained access to the Yemeni coastal trade, "before very long, the Europeans will rule over the lands of Islam." After humiliating treaties with Western powers in 1699 and 1718, Ottoman statesmen, historian Bernard Lewis writes, "discussed with brutal frankness the decrepit state of the Empire and the abject performance of its armies."[4]

First Persia occupied the eastern part of historic Armenia, then Russia annexed it. Russia also won the right to intervene in the Ottoman Empire to protect the rest of the Armenians and other Christians remaining within it. In 1821, the outbreak of the Greek revolution and war of independence heralded a century of further Ottoman imperial retrenchments.[5] Although an adviser warned the sultan, "[L]et us not cede an inch of our territory," Greece became independent in 1828. Five years later, Russia gained "a privileged right of protectorship over Turkey," which ended only after Ottoman reforms of 1839 and 1856 had conceded "the principle of equality of non-Muslims." The sultan now had to demonstrate "generous intentions towards the Christian populations of his Empire."[6]

Ottoman society was traditionally divided into ethnoreligious communities known as *millets*—Muslim, Jewish, Greek Orthodox, and Armenian. As the historian Richard Hovannisian describes it, "The millet system allowed the

Armenians to retain their cultural-religious identity in a plural society, but it rendered them powerless politically and militarily." Until 1876, the Ottoman sultanate, known as the Sublime Porte, barely implemented the externally imposed reforms to protect Christians. But their formal acceptance had established a link between imperial retreat and rights for internal Christian minorities. When communal violence erupted in Lebanon and Syria in 1860, with Muslims and Druzes massacring 40,000 Maronite Christians, the Porte reacted quickly by executing 167 culprits in Damascus. Yet this failed to stop a 6,000-strong French expeditionary force landing in Beirut and imposing an agreement on "protecting the Christians." An 1874 Ottoman financial collapse was followed by uprisings in Bosnia and Herzegovina and other revolts by Bulgarians, Serbs, and Montenegrins. Turkish forces slaughtered as many as 15,000 Bulgarian civilians in May 1876.[7]

At that point, the Ottoman Empire still dominated the Balkans and arguably even remained the largest European power on the African continent.[8] Then the "Scramble for Africa," in which the other metropolitan empires colonized the continent by 1900, coincided with a new rash of disastrous Ottoman losses both there and in Europe: the Russo-Turkish war of 1877–78, the Anglo-French displacement of Turkish overlordship in Egypt in 1879, and the 1896 Cretan insurrection and Greco-Turkish war leading to the Turkish evacuation of Crete in 1898. Now, as historian James Reid puts it, "the collapse of the Ottoman Empire deprived the ruling elite of any security it once had and created a condition of paranoia."[9] It was then that the first major Ottoman massacres of Armenians occurred, in Turkish Anatolia in 1894–1896.

As the empire shrank and increasingly surrendered its diversity, the Ottoman ethnic balance became more unstable. Approximately 2.5 million Armenians composed 6.5 percent of the empire's 38.5 million people in 1876. Ottoman Turks numbered 13.5 million, or 35 percent.[10] There were two major concentrations of Armenians. In the western cities of Constantinople (Istanbul) and Smyrna (Izmir), non-Muslim Armenians, along with Greeks and Jews, totaled 56 percent and 62 percent of these urban populations.[11] But in six provinces of eastern Anatolia, the majority of the Armenians composed "an unarmed, settled, Christian population living among armed, often nomadic Muslims." Armenians coexisted uneasily with Kurdish Muslim tribal groups, whose rulers had long tried to remain autonomous of the empire and to dominate and tax Armenians independently, despite occasional collaborations such as a joint Kurdish-Armenian rebellion at Zeitun, near Van, in 1862.[12]

As the Ottoman territorial collapse accelerated, the plight of the Armenians reached crisis point. First, the "bloody Sultan," Abdul Hamit II (r. 1876–1909), ended the period of Ottoman reform by abrogating the liberal constitution in 1878.[13] Second, formal autocracy did not prevent the intrusion of direct European financial supervision of the empire from 1881; within 15 years, France alone owned 70 percent of Ottoman securities assets.[14] Third, having quickly suppressed another major Kurdish uprising in 1878, Sultan Abdul Hamit decided to turn and support Muslim Kurds against their Armenian subjects and tenants in eastern Anatolia. From 1891 to 1899, the Ottomans organized Kurdish militia there into official irregular armed units known as Hamidiye.[15] Fourth, in the twin contexts of imperial repression and external intervention, both Turkish and Armenian nationalists began organizing. As the empire turned to France for military technology and instruction, Ottoman students encountered the ideas of the French Revolution as well. Their first opposition grouping, formed in Paris in 1889, launched a journal there called *La Jeune Turquie*, a precursor of the Young Turk movement. Western influence also nourished the emergence of Armenian revolutionary nationalist and socialist groups, including the Hnchak and Dashnak parties.[16]

In 1894, three Armenian highland villages at Sassoun near Lake Van refused to pay the double taxation demanded by central government representatives and local Kurdish chieftains. The villagers protested that they "certainly would prefer serving the Turks," but that they "couldn't serve two masters at the same time."[17] The Armenian Hnchak Party's attempt to organize a revolt produced "some isolated acts of brigandage," and the local Ottoman governor incited Kurdish pastoralists to attack Armenians. According to the British vice-consul, C. M. Hallward, who investigated in the area some weeks later: "There was no insurrection . . . the villagers simply took up arms to defend themselves against the Kurds." When four Hamidiye cavalry regiments failed to subdue the Armenians, the sultan ordered 12 army battalions into action with artillery batteries. Massacres of "enormous dimensions" ensued "without distinction of age or sex . . . of old people, the sick and the children." Troops and militia burned groups of villagers alive and bayoneted others; 60 women were raped and murdered in a church. Vahakn Dadrian calls this campaign "the first instance of organized mass murder of Armenians in modern Ottoman history," at least in peacetime. Vice-consul Hallward reported that "a large majority of the population of some twenty-five villages perished, and some of the villages were unusually large"; he estimated the death toll at 8,000. The

Ottoman Fourth Army Corps lost 150 men "fighting in disguise in company with Kurds."[18]

In June the next year, local revolutionaries in Macedonia began a terror campaign against Ottoman occupation there. They enlisted the aid of Armenian explosives experts, "a master bomb maker" from Constantinople, and two Armenians from the Caucasus who were "excellent pyrotechnicians." The first secretary of Sultan Abdul Hamit II later revealed that the sultan, incensed by such Armenian revolutionary activity, "decided to pursue a policy of terror and severity against the Armenians.... [He] elected the method of dealing them an economic blow [and] to inflict upon them a decisive strike to settle scores."[19]

The Hnchak Party organized a 4,000-strong Armenian demonstration in Constantinople in September 1895. However, the police, acting on "secret orders emanating from the Palace," equipped Muslim mobs with "secret weapons, especially thick cudgels." Attackers murdered hundreds of the Armenian marchers. The next three months saw 41 massacres of Armenian communities in eastern Anatolia. In the hill town of Zeitun, whose population were nearly all Armenians, their fierce resistance killed as many as 5,000–10,000 Turkish troops in three months, but such success was exceptional. The killings were usually one-sided, as in December 1895, when Turks burned to death 2,500 Armenian women and children in Urfa cathedral. In June 1896, 500–700 Armenians in Van held off Turkish attacks before being massacred, while outside the town, they could not save 350 Armenian hamlets and villages, which were all reportedly destroyed. Two months later, after Armenian Dashnak Party members seized the Imperial Ottoman Bank to protest the slaughter and to demand international intervention, another 5,000 Armenians were killed in Constantinople.[20]

Armenian scholar Vahakn Dadrian writes that in these massacres, with several exceptions, most of the victims were men in urban centers, killed quickly near their homes or places of work in short local campaigns of several days' duration. He analyzes the main purpose as "large-scale economic, cultural, and psychological destruction through selective massacres." Ronald Suny sees the "pattern of massacre as a means of maintaining the decaying status quo, as the preferred alternative to reform." A Russian diplomat reported in 1901 that Armenian survivors in Sassoun subsisted in "almost feudal dependence" on local Kurds: "[E]ach Armenian is assigned to some Kurd and is obligated to labor for him; Kurds sell their serfs when they need money; if a Kurd kills a serf, the lord takes revenge by killing a serf belonging to the murderer."[21]

Some sources estimate the toll of the 1894–96 killings at 80,000–100,000 Armenians dead by December 1895 and possibly as many more by late the next year.[22] The attackers devastated 2,500 towns and villages and 645 churches and monasteries. The survivors in over 550 villages were forcibly converted to Islam—at least 75,000 Armenians in four provinces—though some eventually reverted to Christianity. One provincial governor wrote to Sultan Abdul Hamit: "50,000 Armenians fled across the border, 30,000 are still hiding in the woods, 45,000 have converted to Islam and 10,000 probably died. Thanks to Your Majesty's wise measures the Muslims are now everywhere in the majority." The sultan declared in 1897 that "the Armenian question" was now "closed."[23] Unfortunately, it wasn't.

Young Turks and Armenians

The emerging opposition to the sultan's regime included nationalists, Islamists, and liberals. The many Muslim emigrants and refugees from the Russian occupation of the Crimea and Caucasus, Bernard Lewis explains, "found a ready opening" in Turkey. Some of the founding members of the Young Turks were Tatars from Russian-occupied territories. For instance, the teacher and editor Murad Bey (1853–1912), educated in the Caucasus, was "the idol of the intellectual classes" in Turkey and later became a pan-Islamist.[24] Other early associates of the Young Turks included Ottoman liberals and, after the 1894–96 massacres, the Armenian Hnchak and Dashnak parties as well. In Paris the first congress of Ottoman liberals, writes the historian Hovannisian, assembled "Turkish, Armenian, Arab, Greek, Kurdish, Albanian, Circassian, and Jewish intellectuals," all of whom "joined in demands for equal rights." A second congress in 1907 called for the overthrow of the sultan and for representative government. But a fierce new Turkish nationalism was already in the air. The Young Turks themselves split in 1902 over the liberals' advocacy of European intervention in support of the Armenians. The nationalist group, led by the French-educated Ahmed Riza, opposed the sultan's regime but also rejected any infringement of the independence of the empire.[25] This tendency eventually dominated the Young Turk movement through its Committee of Union and Progress (CUP; Ittihad in Turkish), though Riza himself later broke with it.

Some even began to embrace Turkish nationality as a racial formation. Yusuf Akçura, a Russian Tatar educated in France, rejected pan-Islamism as well as pan-Ottomanism, preferring "a Turkish national policy based on the Turkish race," including its members in Russia and elsewhere.[26] Akçura asserted in 1904 that "the Turks within the Ottoman realms would unify quite tightly with both religious and racial bonds—more tightly than with just religious ones." He conceded that "[t]he great majority of those Turks whose union is possible are Muslim" and that "Islam could be an important element in the formation of a great Turkish nationality." Yet, he went on, "the general trend of our era involves races," and so for Islam to "perform this service in the unification of Turks it must change in a manner that accepts the emergence of nations within it.... Therefore, it is only through the union of religions with race, and through religions as buttressing and even serving ethnic groups, that they can preserve their political and societal importance." Akçura rejected multinational Ottomanism and argued that even pan-Islamism would only "split into Turkish and non-Turkish components." Looking to "a world of Turkish-ness," Akçura praised "the brotherhood born of race."[27]

The Young Turks' new racial thinking quickly turned against Armenians. By 1906–7, rising Young Turk leaders Drs. Mehmed Nazim and Behaeddin Shakir described the Armenians as enemies of Turkish and Caucasian Muslims "to be dealt with."[28] These two physician-politicians called Armenians "tubercular microbes" that were contaminating the state.[29] Ethnic Turks from beyond the Ottoman state, conversely, received special favor. When Yusuf Akçura became founding editor of the journal *Turk yurdu* (Turkish Homeland) in 1912, he was one of three Russian Turks on its editorial board of six. An associated club espoused the advancement of the Turks as "the foremost of the peoples of Islam."[30]

The intellectual heritage of the Young Turks was also partly international. Author Konstanty Polklozic-Borzecki, for instance, had left Poland after the unsuccessful 1848 revolution, assuming the Turkish name Mustafa Celaleddin Pasha. Like other Polish and Hungarian exiles who were often "more Turkish than the Turks," Borzecki cherished a lifelong "vigorous Russophobia" from his early experiences.[31] According to Bernard Lewis, he brought with him "the romantic nationalism of central Europe" and played some role in the introduction of new ideas into Ottoman Turkey. Borzecki's historical work, *Les Turcs anciens et modernes,* published in Istanbul in 1869, claimed that the Turks belonged to a "Turanian" subsection of the Aryan race, and it outlined European Turcological theories, emphasizing "the great role of the Turkish peoples in human history." He even suggested that the Turkish language might be the father of all European tongues.[32]

Along with new racial theories, the Young Turks favored territorial expansion. Prior to World War I they dreamed of a "pan-Turanian" empire of all Turkic-speaking peoples. They initially chose to name their country "Turkestan," a name with irredentist Central Asian connotations. Yusuf Akçura questioned in 1904 whether "the true power of the Ottoman state" lay in simply "preserving its current geographical shape." He instead called for "the unification of the Turks—who share language, race, customs, and even for the most part, religion, and who are spread throughout the majority of Asia and Eastern Europe." This meant "the Turks' formation of a vast political nationality . . . from the peoples of the great race," encompassing Central Asian Turks and Mongols "from Peking to Montenegro."[33]

Another member of the board of *Turk yurdu* was Ziya Gökalp, a leading theoretician of the "pan-Turanian" movement, which sought the political unification of all Turkic-speaking lands, including Russian-ruled Turkmenistan and China's Sinkiang province. Gökalp, an eastern Anatolian Kurd who became a leading member of the CUP Central Committee in 1911, described himself in verse as "a soldier" for the nation. "I obey without question. . . . With closed eyes." In an anti-Russian poem in 1914, he predicted: "Turkey shall be enlarged and become Turan."[34] Like Yusuf Akçura, Ziya Gökalp also adopted racial theories. He found "Greeks, Armenians, and Jews" to be "a foreign body in the national Turkish state." To his expansionism and "mystical vision of blood and race," Gökalp added a cult of Turkic antiquity. To him, Turkey's national revival meant reestablishment of the medieval golden age of pre-Islamic Turkic military leaders, like Genghis Khan and Tamerlane. Turkish armies pushing eastward would supposedly find their own origins in "a Shangri-La-like area in the steppes of Central Asia."[35]

The territorial expansionism projected by the Young Turks of course had to contend not only with shrinking imperial Ottoman borders but also with other ethnic groups occupying the eastern lands they coveted. Most notably, Armenian peasants inhabited large areas of eastern Anatolia and Russian Armenia that straddled the route to "Turkestan."

The racialist, expansionist trends in Turkish nationalism probably fostered the increasing importance of Young Turk military officers, some of them Prussian-trained, in the revolutionary movement's path to power before World War I. Underground CUP cells appeared among serving field officers in 1906. Two years later, Enver Pasha came under the sultan's suspicion and fled into the hills with another officer and 200 troops. Rebellion spread, mutinies broke out, and in July 1908, the sultan was forced to restore the 1876 constitution.[36]

The Young Turks came to power at the head of the CUP. The next month, the CUP's Shakir and Talât reacted angrily to Armenian hopes for self-rule, ending CUP negotiations with the Hnchak Party.[37] Still hopeful of some reforms, however, the Armenian Dashnak Party maintained its alliance with the CUP for four more years, to no avail.

Ottoman territorial collapse accelerated with the Austrian annexation of Bosnia and Herzegovina in 1908, the declaration of Bulgarian independence in 1909, revolts in Albania in 1910–12, the Italian seizure of Tripoli in 1911–12, and the Balkan Wars of 1912–13. By the outbreak of World War I, "only the Armenians and Arabs" remained subject nationalities of the empire.[38] As non-Muslims, the Armenian community was most vulnerable to the outraged Turkish response. "The Balkan dogs are trampling on Islam," went a Turkish nationalist slogan, while a pro-CUP newspaper threatened ominously that "it will be impossible to spare eastern Turkey," Anatolian home of most Armenians. The region meant even more to Turks, a CUP leader said: "Anatolia is the well spring of every fibre of our life. It is our heart, head, and the air we breathe."[39]

The successive external defeats and territorial losses meant that the percentage of Armenians as part of the rump Ottoman Empire actually rose. The 1905–6 Ottoman census had counted the total population of the empire at around 21 million. Of these, 15.5 million, or 74 percent, were Muslims, including Armenian forced converts; 1,031,708 were Armenian Orthodox (5 percent); 2.8 million of Greek Orthodox faith (14 percent); 191,000 other Christians (including many Armenians); and 253,000 Jews.[40] At the outbreak of World War I, following the loss of the mostly Orthodox Balkan provinces in 1913, the 1.5 million or more Armenian Christians now made up as much as 6 percent of the rump empire, which comprised little more than Anatolia, plus the Arab countries, which were about to secede. In Anatolia itself, then, Muslim Turks and Kurds made up 83 percent of the population in 1912 and non-Muslims 17 percent, including Armenians at 7–8 percent.[41] Ottoman territorial retreat, Balkan secession, and Muslim immigration had all focused the ethnic conflict on Anatolia. Despite the 1894–96 massacres and many forced conversions to Islam, Armenians now made up a greater proportion than they had of the much larger old empire. Yet these Armenians who had survived the 1890s massacres suddenly faced a "growing insistence on the Turkishness of what remained," even as their homelands in eastern Anatolia lay directly in the path to the new Central Asian targets of CUP territorial expansion.[42]

In early 1909, Enver Pasha took up his post in Berlin as military attaché at the Ottoman embassy. In Turkey in March and April, a coalition of Ottoman monarchists, Islamic fundamentalists, and liberals attempted to seize power from the CUP, forcing Enver briefly to return home to help suppress them. The Ottoman Third Army marched in from Saloniki and restored order in Istanbul, but across the Anatolian peninsula in Adana, insurgents remaining at large attacked the prosperous local Armenian community, which had largely survived the massacres of 1894–96 and was still associated with the CUP regime. Armenians repulsed the initial insurgent attacks on their areas, the British consul arranged a truce, and the Armenians agreed to disarm. New Turkish military units arrived in Adana after the suppression of the coup attempt in Istanbul, and for reasons that remain murky, these troops joined in cooperation with local officials to murder 25,000 Armenians in what Dadrian calls "one of the most gruesome and savage bloodbaths ever recorded." It briefly provoked a horrified reaction. In the Ottoman Chamber of Deputies, the empire's grand vizier denounced "the reactionary, criminal scoundrels who were bent on massacring and plundering the Armenians through a surprise attack." Some 124 Turks and seven Armenians were hanged.[43] Sultan Abdul Hamit II fell from office. In a speech over the mass grave of the victims, Enver Pasha even proclaimed that Muslims and Christians "lying side by side" were "henceforward fellow-patriots who would know no distinction of race or creed."[44]

Despite official expressions of horror, the catastrophe proved only the start of a new slaughter of Armenians. The Young Turk movement became radicalized and set out to erase both traditional and liberal visions of Ottomanism, with their greater tolerance for distinctions of race and creed, now privileging both Turks and Islam instead. The CUP soon banned national minority associations and clubs and imposed a policy of language Turkification.[45] Then, on August 6, 1910, during further upheavals in Macedonia and Albania, a secret top-level CUP conclave assembled in Saloniki. Dr. Nazim, who had described the Armenians as archenemies three years before, served as vice president at this meeting. Despite Enver's recent public speech, CUP leader Talât announced that equality between Muslims and infidels was "unrealizable." He added: "There can therefore be no question of equality until we have succeeded in our task of Ottomanizing the Empire," which was feasible because "[t]he army is solidly ranged in our support . . . we remain all-powerful."[46]

Discarding the imperial framework of autonomous millets, the CUP now advocated "the complete Ottomanization of all Turkish subjects," by coercion if necessary. The British ambassador recognized this forceful policy break on the part of the Young Turks: "[T]o them 'Ottoman' evidently means 'Turk' and their present policy of 'Ottomanization' is one of pounding the non-Turkish elements in a Turkish mortar." The head of the CUP's parliamentary branch advised relying "solely on military might" in dealing with the minorities. Other party branches debated the methods: "deportation," "uprooting," and even "extermination of all Christians hostile to young Turkey." The CUP decision, according to a contemporary Turkish sociologist, was "to assimilate them through coercive methods if necessary." The British Foreign Office further predicted that "the Young Turks will endeavour to extend the 'levelling' system to the Kurds and the Arabs." Dr. Nazim, elected head of the Saloniki branch of the CUP, favored "severe repression." But Talât recommended stealth also: "We need to tranquillise our neighbors," he said, while state officials in the provinces "ought to remain in ignorance" of the undisclosed CUP plans. This concern persisted as the genocide subsequently unfolded. Talât said: "Let the Armenians wait, opportunities will certainly come our way too. Turkey belongs only to the Turks."[47]

The Young Turks' increasing territorial ambitions, racial hatred, militarism, and reliance on Turkish peasant troops extended to a related disdain for supposedly nonfarming peoples. England's Edmund Spenser had as early as 1598 grouped the Armenians with the Irish as people who lived "by keeping of cattle," which he said made them "very barbarous and uncivill."[48] To the preference for rural cultivator over pastoralist, the Young Turks added their own suspicions of urban dwellers, especially those of non-Muslim faiths. Enver Pasha would later claim that his Young Turk army had drawn "all its strength from the rural class," adding that "all who seek to enrich those who do not work should be destroyed."[49] Before World War I, the word *Turk* itself, meaning "Muslim" in the West, had a connotation in Turkey of "rural" or "mountain people." By contrast, as we have seen, the Ottoman cities of Istanbul and Izmir comprised non-Turkish majorities of Armenians, Greeks, and Jews.[50]

The leading Young Turk ideologue, Yusuf Akçura, considered the peasantry to be "the basic matter of the Turkish nation" and the group requiring the greatest assistance, a view he combined with his ethnic-based Turkism and his pan-Turkist territorial irredentism.[51] The Young Turk leader Talât Pasha was founding honorary president of the farmers' association in 1914–16.[52] According to Feroz Ahmad, "[I]n their first flush of glory and while they were at their most radical," the Young Turk leaders proposed "measures intended to lighten the burden of the peasant," including land distribution, low-interest loans, tithe reductions, agricultural schools, and a cadastral system, and they "promised to encourage the development of agriculture in every way possible." It was considered "vital to save the peasant from the feudal lords." Stressing "the importance of the small farmer," Young Turk intellectuals also urged co-operativization.[53]

However, the political leadership quickly encountered the stranglehold of the local elites in rural areas: the top 5 percent of landowners owned 65 percent of the land. The Young Turks then "took the path of least resistance," accom-modating landlord power in the interest of their priority goal, "salvation of the empire," and pursuing only modest reforms to modernize and commercialize agriculture. They still promoted "ambitious irrigation projects," including cre-ation of "another Egypt" in Cilicia, and they even envisaged eventual "nation-alization of agriculture and the joint cultivation of the soil." Dr. Nazim boasted in 1917 that "our peasants, who made fortunes through the unwarranted rise in food prices, can pay three liras for a pair of stockings for their daughters." In fact, under the Young Turks, most peasants suffered from increased forced labor and land expropriations, but the regime's ideological claim to foster the peasantry and cultivation is clear.[54]

This radical wing of the Young Turks grabbed power in 1913. With 200 fol-lowers, Talât and Enver marched into the Sublime Porte on January 26, killed the Ottoman war minister, and subsequently took over the government. The assassination of the grand vizier five months later completed the Young Turks' coup. Enver became war minister, Talât minister of the Interior, and Jemal Pasha minister of the navy.[55] This triumvirate ruled the Ottoman Empire for the next six years. The new Association for the Promotion of Turkish Strength set about training youth "to enable the nation to become again a warrior na-tion" and prevent "the decay of the Turkish race." Under the new regime Ar-menians experienced escalating attention—for instance, in a letter written in November 1913: "You Armenians . . . you accursed ones have brought many perils on the head of our esteemed government [and] paved the way for for-eign assault. . . . Turkish youth . . . shall not delay the execution of their assigned duties." That same month another threatening letter reached the Armenian press: "The Turkish sword to date has cut down millions of *gâvurs* [infidels], nor has it lost its intention to cut down millions more hereafter." The Turks, this letter went on, displaying biological hatred, would "clean up the Armenian *gâvurs* who have become tubercular microbes for us."[56]

Meanwhile, the CUP Central Committee and the Interior Ministry created a clandestine internal "Special Organization."[57] Its wartime head, Eshref Kush-cubashi, later described it as "a secret outfit" that became "the fundamental edifice for ensuring the internal and external security of the Ottoman State.... For this purpose it cultivated its own cadres, uniforms, treasury, and ciphers, becoming a state within a state." The three main goals of this Special Organization (SO) were "unifying Turkey, Islamic Union, and Pan-Turkism."[58] Kushcubashi added that the object of its attention was those areas of the empire where "non-Turkish and non-Muslim races and nationalities," whose loyalty was "suspect," formed a majority. The SO included the CUP leaders Talât, Dr. Nazim, Ziya Gökalp, and Dr. Shakir.[59] Its tasks expressed the major concern of the Young Turks: the country's decline from the glory of a distant past. In Kushcubashi's words, this demanded reduction of "the damages of past legacies which the Ottoman state had been carrying on its shoulders as the burden and bequest of the centuries."[60]

Any reversal of Ottoman imperial decline through new territorial expansion required military reorganization, in which Enver and his German connections now played a key role. After crushing the 1909 rebellion, Enver had returned to his Berlin post until September of that year, then revisited Germany in 1910 and 1913, and, in secret, again the following spring. The kaiser personally received him with obvious favor. Early in 1914, Enver dismissed 1,100 Ottoman military officers, including a number of generals, and replaced them with younger CUP loyalists. Within two months, German military commanders arrived in Turkey. One became the commander of the First Ottoman Army Corps and inspector general of the army, another German officer became Enver's chief of staff, and a third took up the command of the Ottoman navy. The uniform of the Ottoman forces became "German field gray."[61]

The expansionist project could now begin. From August 14, 1914, the CUP foreign minister pressed Germany for a promise of postwar assistance to annex the eastern Aegean islands and also to make, on Turkey's behalf, "a small correction of her eastern border which shall place Turkey into direct contact with the Moslems of Russia," at the obvious expense of Russian Armenia. The Ottoman Empire entered World War I on Germany's side in November 1914. Declaring war, the CUP regime announced its territorial ambition in its projected "destruction of our Muscovite enemy, in order to obtain thereby a natural frontier to our Empire, which should include and unite all branches of our race." Enver quickly invaded the Caucasus, but met humiliating defeat at Russian hands in December 1914–January 1915.[62]

Genocide

Planning for genocide at home accompanied this territorial expansion abroad. Also in December 1914 or January 1915, Talât, Nazim, and Shakir presided over a secret high-level CUP conference.[63] Ahmed Essad, head of the Ottoman Interior Ministry's Department II, Intelligence, who acted as the conference secretary, later provided the victorious British forces with a document discussed at the conference. This "strictly confidential" ten-point document, subsequently translated verbatim by the British High Commission in Constantinople, began with an instruction: "[C]lose all Armenian Societies, and arrest all who worked against the Government at any time among them and send them into the provinces such as Bagdad or Mosul, and wipe them out either on the road or there." The document's third point began by calling on officials to "[e]xcite Moslem opinion" and ended, "[P]rovoke organized massacres as the Russians did at Baku." Its fifth point also targeted Armenians: "Apply measures to exterminate all males under 50, priests and teachers, leave girls and children to be Islamized." The eighth point was: "Kill off in an appropriate manner all Armenians in the Army—this to be left to the military to do."[64] As Peter Balakian has written in *The Burning Tigris,* "by February 25, 1915, all the Armenian men in the Ottoman army were officially disarmed and thrown into labor battalions," from which most of them, numbering in the tens of thousands, were soon withdrawn to secluded areas and massacred. Meanwhile, again in late 1914 and early 1915, Dr. Shakir visited Erzurum and arranged for the CUP's Special Organization to operate autonomously in eastern Anatolia and to take control of the killing squads that were to strike the Armenians there.[65]

The genocidal scheme was apparently launched in late February 1915. Shakir returned briefly to Istanbul from Erzurum, according to one of his CUP assistants there, with a plan to attack the Armenian "internal enemy ... which was threatening the rear of the Turkish army." According to an Armenian source connected to the Young Turks' German allies, 75 top-ranking CUP members, including Shakir, Nazim, and Talât, assembled at Enver's initiative on February 26 in order to discuss "a very urgent matter." The CUP participants concluded in agreement, "[I]t's about time."[66] The authorities released large numbers of criminals from Turkish jails and recruited them into the killing squads that Nazim and the SO formed into a 12,000-strong force, which a then CUP member would later call an "army of murderers." The Ottoman statesman Resid Akif Pasha subsequently asserted in the Senate that in his office of president of the Council of State, he had been privy to secret documents revealing that the Ministry of Interior's deportation orders for Armenians were synchronized with informal CUP instructions to the SO to launch "the great massacres" of deportees on the march.[67]

Soon, writes historian Richard Hovannisian, "The whole of Asia Minor was put in motion." The first deportation of Armenians took place on April 8, 1915, emptying the hill town of Zeitun.[68] Across the country, in a single night two weeks later, scores of Constantinople's Armenian leaders and intellectuals were rounded up, deported, and killed. Then, in May, Talât ordered massive deportations across Anatolia. From June to September that year, the CUP forcibly drove the Armenian populations out of Cilicia, and then from the east and southeast of Anatolia.[69]

These deportations mostly meant death. In the province of Ankara, for instance, where only 88 of the 1,800 Armenians who lived in the town of Yozgad escaped roundup and removal, a local county police chief reported by cipher, on July 17, 1915, that the county's Armenians had been "deported, that is destroyed." Five days later, the county military governor informed the Fifth Army's deputy commander that the deportees had been "sent on to their destination," which provoked an inquiring response, asking what this "destination" was. The governor confirmed that "they were killed." Another official reported by cipher telegram on September 11 that 61,000 Armenians had been deported from Ankara province, whose prewar Armenian population was 63,605.[70]

What we know of the killing process is illuminated by the dissension it caused. The CUP discharged the Ankara province governor, Mazhar, for his refusal to carry out the orders to massacre the deportees. For similar reasons the governor of Aleppo province, Celal, also lost his post, and two lower-ranking governors were reportedly murdered. Celal later wrote that in response to his "request for funds to resettle the surviving deportees Talât sent instead a Director of Deportations," whose arrival introduced "the most barbaric methods," including "the actual extermination of the deportees." Another staff member of the Interior Ministry revealed that Minister Talât's representative had informed him of "personally receiving Talât's orders of extermination."[71]

The most extensive massacres occurred in eastern Anatolia. In Trabzond province on the Black Sea, the government newspaper *Trabzonda meshveret* warned Armenians in mid-June 1915 not to resist or try to escape deportation, or they would "be sent before the Court Martial for execution." The newspaper promised "safe conduct" to compliant Armenians during their deportation,

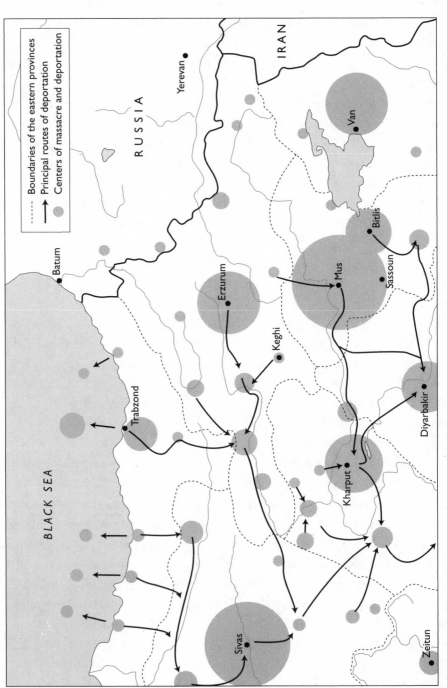

MAP 21. The Armenian genocide, 1915–18. Based on a map compiled by the Armenian National Institute.

which it said would last "until the conclusion of the war as they would be sent away to inhabit and settle down in places prepared for them in the interior provinces."[72] That was deception. Just a week later, on June 21, Dr. Shakir sent a cipher telegram to the CUP secretary of Harput province insisting on implementation of the real CUP policy: "Are the Armenians who are being deported from your area, being liquidated? Are the harmful people who you say are being banished and dispersed, being destroyed, or are they being merely removed and sent away?"[73]

One of Shakir's leading collaborators was General Mahmud Kâmil, commander in chief of the Third Ottoman Army, whose zone comprised the six eastern provinces of Anatolia where most Armenians lived. Talât, Shakir, Nazim, and Ziya Gökalp had urged Enver to appoint Kâmil to this post, which he had done in February 1915. Kâmil then signed and dispatched a telegram threatening that "[a]ny Muslim who protects an Armenian will be hanged in front of his house, which will also be burned down. If the culprit is an official he will be dismissed and court-martialled."[74] Lieutenant Colonel Stange, a German officer who witnessed mass murders in the eastern provinces, reported to Germany's Foreign Office in August 1915 that General Kâmil "ruthlessly and constantly pushed for the expediting of the deportations . . . despite the fact that he must have known of the massacre of the Armenians who were dispatched with the previous convoys."[75] In this way, the CUP organized and oversaw the murder of well over half a million people during 1915 alone.[76]

CUP and SO leaders were relentless. The Ottoman governors of two of the eastern provinces, Erzurum and Trabzond, both attempted to exempt the ill, children, and single women from deportation. The local CUP committees overruled both men. On July 28, 1915, Germany's vice-consul in Erzurum predicted to his government that the cruelty of the CUP's measures would mean "the certain death" of the deportees. "These Committee men," he added, "are bluntly admitting that the purpose of their actions is the total obliteration (*die gänzliche Austrottung*) of the Armenians. As an authoritative person word for word declared, 'We will have in Turkey no more Armenians after the war.'"[77] The governor-general of Erzurum province, Münir, sent a cipher telegram, uncovered after the war, stating that "the convoys consisting of Erzurum's wealthy Armenians, who were being deported by way of Keghi, have been set upon and annihilated by Behaeddin Shakir's killer bands."[78]

In Trabzond, too, the U.S. consul Oscar Heizer reported that Nail Bey, the province CUP secretary, insisted on the deportation of the Armenians' children rather than allowing them to be cared for as orphans. "Nearly 3,000 children were installed in empty houses, of which there were many.... This plan did not suit Nail Bey, and in about ten days he advertised that any Mahommedan, who wanted to take girls or boys, could apply to these homes and a great many children were taken. He himself chose ten of the best-looking girls and kept them in a house for his own pleasure, and the amusement of his friends. Many of the children were loaded into boats and taken out to sea and thrown overboard. I myself saw where 16 bodies were washed ashore."[79]

In the immediate aftermath of the massive 1915 deportations, the Ottoman Senate debated the legality of a CUP "Temporary Law" to expropriate the property of the Armenian deportees. This only exacerbated the internal dissension within the Turkish state. The former founding leader of the Young Turks, Senator Ahmed Riza, rose in protest to stop the law's promulgation. He told the Senate on September 21, 1915, that "nobody has the right and authority to seize one's goods and property." Two months later, Riza again complained that "this law was put into effect temporarily and currently it is being applied. By the time this law reaches us for consideration, there will be neither goods nor property left [to worry about]. What are we going to consider then?" He criticized as illegal both the dispossession of the Armenians and the "Temporary Law" used for that purpose. "It is a fact that the Armenians, the owners of these goods and possessions, did not voluntarily abandon them; they were forced to abandon their domiciles and were coerced into deportation. The government through its officials is having their properties sold." Riza concluded with a denunciation that put himself in the Armenians' place: "Grab my arm, eject me from my village, then sell my goods and properties. Such a thing can never be lawful. Neither the conscience of the Ottomans, nor the law can allow it." As the plunder proceeded, unable to convince his fellow senators, Riza warned bravely that "the enforcement of this law will mean breach of trust and tyranny."[80]

Yet the deportations and killings raged on. In mid-1916, the German ambassador to Istanbul, Wolff Metternich, reported confidentially on the basis of his top-level CUP contacts: "The Committee demands the extirpation of the last remnants of the Armenians, and the government must yield.... That authority of the Committee reaches into all the provinces.... Turkification means license to expel, to kill or destroy everything that is not Turkish."[81] During that summer of 1916, Turkish forces massacred another 200,000 Armenian survivors in the Mesopotamian desert.[82] The German vice-consul at Erzurum reported that Enver's uncle, General Halil (Kut) Pasha, had ordered "the massacre" of his Armenian battalions, and a Turkish officer in Halil's First Expeditionary Force later testified that "Halil had the entire Armenian population (men, women and children) in the areas of Bitlis, Mus, and Beyazit also massacred without pity. My company received a similar order. Many of the victims were buried alive in especially prepared ditches." After the war, Halil himself wrote in his memoirs of having killed "300,000 Armenians," adding that "it can be more or less. I didn't count." He further asserted: "I have endeavoured to wipe out the Armenian nation to the last individual."[83]

A well-placed inside source successfully exposed much of this at the time. General Mehmet Vehip took over the command of the Ottoman Third Army from Mahmud Kâmil in early 1916. He soon received a request from the military authorities running the Baghdad Railway Construction Project for the transfer there of 2,000 of the surviving Armenian labor battalion soldiers. After General Vehip sent the Armenians off in June 1916, he learned that they were ambushed and massacred en route. Outraged, General Vehip court-martialed the commander in charge of the victims' transfer and subsequently reported to the Turkish troops: "[H]aving established through a trial the fact of the murder of the labor battalion contingent which I had ordered transferred to the command of the IVth Army, the gendarmery commander of Sarkisla, Captain Nuri Efendi, has been executed by hanging." At his trial, Nuri also implicated the governor-general of Sivas province, Ahmet Muammer, as having ordered the massacre. Talât then saved Muammer from court-martial only by transferring him out of General Vehip's jurisdiction.[84] Vehip even tried to arrest Dr. Shakir, who he said later had "procured and engaged in the command zone of the IIIrd Army the butchers of human beings . . . he organized gallowsbirds as well as gendarmes and policemen with blood on their hands and blood in their eyes." Vehip protested to the German military plenipotentiary in Turkey about "the campaign of exterminating the Armenians." In a 1918 written deposition for the Turkish military tribunal, Vehip further described Shakir: "Travelling with a special automobile, he stopped by at all major centers where he orally transmitted his instructions." Vehip concluded: "The massacre and annihilation of the Armenians and the looting and plunder of their properties were the result of the decisions of the Central Committee of Ittihad [CUP]. . . . The victims involved human multitudes, which lent themselves to being easily rounded up, were defenceless, and which were set upon. The atrocities were carried out under a program that was determined upon and represented a definite case of premeditation."[85]

Again Senator Ahmed Riza contested the mistreatment of Armenians. He opposed a 1916 law allowing the CUP's SO to recruit convicts. Another speaker in the Senate added that "criminal cohorts never deserve the honor" of serving in the army. However, the deputy director of the Department of the Army, Lieutenant Colonel Behiç Bey, countered that "in some provinces the engagement of these convicts proved useful. The majority of these criminals was not made part of the military but was placed under the command of the Special Organization in which outfit their involvement proved profitable." Riza retorted: "We know about the nature of that organization; we shall call it to account later on."[86]

The Young Turks stuck to their expansionist goals. Enver's early 1915 military defeat in the Caucasus had merely forced a postponement. Dr. Shakir told the acting American consul at Erzurum in February 1916: "It is imperative that from Istanbul to India and China there be only one unitary Muslim population. . . . This vast project will be accomplished through the scientific genius and organizational talent of the Germans and the valiant arm of the Turks." The 1917–18 collapse of the opposing tsarist armies in the Caucasus created a new military opportunity for the revival of pan-Turanianism. Young Turk armies again pushed into Russian Armenia, where 300,000 survivors of the 1915 genocide had taken refuge, and the invaders now extended the genocide of Ottoman Armenians "to the Russian Armenians." In the words of the allied German military attaché von Lossow, this CUP campaign involved "the total extermination of the Armenians in Transcaucasia also." He added that "Talât's government party wants to destroy all Armenians, not only in Turkey, but also outside Turkey."[87]

Final military defeat and the conclusion of World War I brought down the Young Turks' regime in October 1918. The Turkish domestic opposition now moved to end the regime's crimes and hold its leaders accountable. The president of the Ottoman Senate, Ahmed Riza, expressed the hope that Sultan Vahdeddin "will not allow that the orphans and widows of those Armenians who were savagely killed off, those Arabs who were hanged and exiled, be overwhelmed by miseries on this earth. There shall be no more people weeping and moaning in places of exile."[88] In March 1919, the sultan described the CUP's measures against Armenians as "crimes against the laws of humanity and state."

A special Turkish military tribunal indicted the Young Turk leaders in April 1919 for crimes of "deportation and massacre" (*tehcir ve taktil*).[89]

The special military tribunal also indicted Trabzond province's governor-general, Cemal Azmi, and its CUP secretary, Nail Bey, for the "deportation and massacre" of Armenians.[90] This court-martial's May 1919 verdict stated

> Ostensibly engaged in carrying out the deportations, [the defendants] in reality [proceeded] to organize the massacre and annihilation [*taktil ve ifna*] of the Armenians. [They] engaged some mean and villainous people, repeat criminals, and consorting gendarmes, supposedly for the purpose of escorting the deportee convoys. However, after reaching some distance away from the city, at a spot concealed from the public eye as much as possible, the men were separated from the women in the convoy of the Armenians, who were deprived of the means of protection. The brigands, employed by the above mentioned persons, first robbed [the deportees] of their goods and possessions and then [proceeded to] kill and destroy [the men].... Under the pretext of transporting them by the sea route to another place, the male and female infants were taken in split groups on board of barges and caiques to the high seas and, hidden from sight, were thrown overboard to be drowned and destroyed.

For these "premeditated" crimes, Cemal Azmi and Nail Bey received death sentences.[91]

Then, on July 5, 1919, the military tribunal convicted the CUP leadership, Talât, Enver, Cemal, and Dr. Nazim in absentia. They, too, were found guilty of the crime of "massacre" (*taktil*), an Ottoman Turkish term that a leading Turkish political scientist has translated by the modern term for "genocide" (*soykirim*). These CUP defendants, who had fled to Germany the previous year, were condemned to death. The next year, Dr. Behaeddin Shakir received the same sentence in his trial. Many others were tried in two dozen other tribunal proceedings in 1919–20.[92]

As for the human toll in the genocide, the CUP minister of Marine, Jemal, himself estimated 600,000 dead, and a postwar Interior minister, also named Jemal, gave a figure of 800,000, which other Turkish sources accepted.[93] Using different demographic data, other analyses suggest figures of up to about 1.2 million dead. The 1919 Turkish court-martial concluded that the CUP massacres of Armenians had the characteristics of a "final solution" (*hall ve fasl*).[94]

CHAPTER 11

Blut und Boden

Germany and Nazi Genocide

D uring the extermination of the Nama people in Southwest Africa in 1907, Germany's colonial director, Bernhard Dernburg, told a Berlin audience that "some native tribes, just like some animals, must be de- stroyed." Linking racial supremacy with family landownership, Dernburg went on to assert that Southwest Africa and other German agricultural settlements abroad helped to counter "the splintering of our estates in Germany" by pro- viding possibilities for the emigration of farmers' younger sons. He reported that "the pick of the second sons of better-off farmers" were either already en route or now "ready to emigrate to Southwest Africa, and to our other colo- nies, there to start over, so as to avoid breaking the family homestead apart."[1] This concern to maintain the integrity of the traditional German farm over the interests of its individual family members would later become a major feature of Nazi agricultural policy, once again linked to German expansion and geno- cide, in this case the most extensive mass murder in history, the Holocaust of European Jews.

In his book *Modernity and the Holocaust,* sociologist Zygmunt Bauman argued that the Nazi genocide of nearly 6 million Jews from 1941 to 1945 was an industrial, bureaucratic, totalitarian enterprise that could hardly have been conceived and accomplished before the twentieth century.[2] The Holocaust certainly fit this description of modernity even better than did the Armenian genocide. Yet the Nazi obsession with supposed *traditional* values and with classical and medieval German models also outdid the Young Turk hope of reviving the Turkish peasantry or reconquering long-lost "Turan." Especially in cases of genocide, it is difficult to prise modernity apart from tradition. As elsewhere, German modernity both provoked and encompassed reaction against change, and it coexisted with more authentic traditional visions. These included not only preoccupations with antiquity and agriculture but also a tradition of antisemitism, including the centuries-old prohibition on landowner-ship that had long restricted most Jews to nonagricultural and urban occu-pations. While Nazi antisemitism was a virulent independent factor, related visions resembling those of other genocidal regimes reinforced it. This chapter first details these more common ideological factors before turning specifically to Nazi racism and hatred of the Jews and to the catastrophic impact upon them of all these idealist notions, utopian or dystopian. Combining aggressive territorial expansionism with mass murder by means of both advanced tech-nology and face-to-face killing, Nazi "scientific" racial extermination specifi-cally targeted Jews at the same time as it purported to reclaim a once pristine, lost agrarian Germandom, and it was also inspired or justified by putative an-cient models of race, war, and conquest.

Antiquity and the Holocaust

Nazis often claimed to follow venerable military precedents as they pursued their war goals. In keeping with ideas dating from the Reformation, they found classical inspiration in the ancient army of Arminius ("Hermann"), who de-stroyed three Roman legions commanded by Varus in the Teutoburg forest in the year 9 c.e. While calling Arminius "the first architect of our liberty," Adolf Hitler ruled it impossible "to fight a battle in a forest."[3] He chose a more aggressive, medieval model. Charlemagne's putative federation of "the quar-relsome and bellicose Germans" moved Hitler to call him "one of the greatest men in world history."[4] In *Mein Kampf* in 1924, Hitler urged that "the new Reich must again set itself on the march along the road of the Teutonic knights of old, to obtain by the German sword sod for the German plow and daily bread for the nation. . . . We take up where we broke off six hundred years ago."[5] After those early eastern conquests, as the Nazi peasant leader Richard Walther Darré pointed out in 1930, medieval Germans had taken one-third of the conquered territory from the "subjugated population" and put it to use "for the Teutonic conquerors' own resettlements."[6]

Nazis lamented the reversal of this medieval Germanic expansion. As with the Young Turks, German perceptions of geographic diminution of the historic heartland formed the ideological backdrop to aggressive war accompanied by genocide. Medieval Germany had dominated central Europe, but its territory had since shrunk. Though modern Germany was not the direct heir to the Holy Roman Empire, the relatively recent unification of the German Reich in 1871 only heightened the contemporary nationalist sense of territorial losses, suddenly repeated in World War I.[7] To Darré, the post-1918 peace represented a humiliating conquest of Germany, one that "almost two millennia ago" the Roman general Varus had "failed to accomplish" against the opposition of "the Germanic people."[8]

From its inauguration in 1933, the Third Reich aimed to recover this lost ground by means of what Hitler had called "the new Germanic march."[9] The territorial recovery would be historical, even hereditary. After his appointment as the first Nazi agriculture minister, Darré announced at the celebration of the 1934 anniversary of a medieval peasant rebellion: "First there was the German peasantry in Germany before what is today served up as German history. . . . Everywhere one will find primordial peasant customs that reach far back into the past."[10] In his 1930 book, *Neuadel aus Blut und Boden* (New Nobility from Blood and Soil), Darré praised "the original Teutonic form of integrating nobility among the people on the basis of *internal* values," particularly racialist and agrarian ones. He claimed that this ancient agrarian world of Julius Caesar's opponents, "Ariovistus and the Suebi" and the Goths, had been based on the integrity of the German clan, household, and family farm plot. Darré lamented that subsequently, during the Middle Ages, "the spreading feudal system destroyed the old universal freedom of the Teutonic peasant and led to a Christian manorial nobility." This he said had produced the "quite un-Germanic form" of an elevated nobility. Darré now called upon "we Germans" to return to their heritage, "an authentic nobility in the old Teutonic sense." According to him, modernity merely corroborated tradition: "[T]he morality of our Germanic forbears . . . was based on the recognized hereditary inequality of mankind, and today's science is returning to this insight." Darré asserted that according to medieval Teutonic common law, the German nobleman "derives his origins from a divine ancestor, whose blood (as it were: germ mass!) [*sic*] had to be passed on with the greatest possible purity from his progeny to future generations." Indeed, Darré speculated, "the Teutonic nobility in some tribes achieved a completely thoroughbred state, where absolutely no foreign blood was allowed."[11] Darré thus claimed the blessing of ancient Teutonic custom and law for new Nazi racialist policies.

Along with their own contemporary policies, the Nazis drew upon three putatively ancient models for their state. The first was what historian Walter Goffart calls "the deeply entrenched myth of a prehistoric and early Germany." The Roman historian Tacitus's *Germania* and other classical sources described the region now called Germany as occupied by a multiplicity of ethnic groups, lacking any unity or center and extending deep into what is now eastern Europe and even southern Russia. According to Goffart, then, "There was no Germanic world before the Carolingian age. . . . If Europe has had a supreme invented tradition, that of the [collective] Germans before Germany is it."[12]

This myth has a long history. In the seventh century, Goffart writes, the Frankish kingdom "acquired a pedigree" when a chronicler described the first Franks as, "like the descendants of Aeneas, refugees from the fall of Troy." The Carolingian era also introduced the term *thiudiscus,* or *gens theodisca,* meaning the people speaking the vernacular. This became the word *Deutsche,* or Germans, not the same as the ancient *Germanen.* Two centuries later, another medieval author claimed that the Saxons were descended from Macedonian soldiers of Alexander's armies.[13]

The myth intensified with modernity. Just as the Renaissance rediscovery of works by Livy and Polybius spurred English pursuit of imperial Roman models, the identification in 1451 of a copy of Tacitus's Latin text *Germania* ushered in a new myth of an ancient Germany, complete with circumstantial descriptions of the lives, morals, and customs of peoples deemed to be of the same stock. From the eve of the Reformation, then, the modern Germans (*Deutsche*) traced their ancestry to the Germani; the term *German* first appeared in English in 1530. The work of Tacitus, it has been said, became for Germans "the Magna Carta of their national self-confidence, and "the main 'fragment of reality' around which the megalomaniac delirium of the Germans organized itself in modern times."[14] Goffart comments that "[t]he faith in Germanic continuity has prevailed for many centuries, damaging everything it has touched."[15] In the first decade of the twentieth century, the philologist Gustav Kossinna, professor of prehistory at the University of Berlin, even extended the genealogy of the *Urgermanen* (original Germans) as far back as the second millennium B.C.E. and attributed to them a "first" migration (*Völkerwanderung*) that supposedly traversed Europe. The Nazis later endorsed Kossinna's temporal and territorial expansions of the German world along with his racist and chauvinist perspectives.[16]

Second, like Elizabethan Englishmen in Ireland and others since, Nazis saw antecedents for themselves in ancient Rome. In *Mein Kampf*, Hitler wrote that Roman history as he saw it "remains the best mentor, not only for today, but probably for all time." War and conquest were its models. Hitler implicitly endorsed the ideological views of Cato the Censor when he asserted that "through the cares of the Punic Wars the Roman state began to dedicate itself to a higher culture." By contrast, Hitler argued that Carthage, like others who "lay down their arms without compelling reasons," had deservedly "lost its character." According to Hitler, Germany had misguidedly accepted the 1918 armistice and was now threatened with the same fate. "The fall of Carthage is the most horrible picture of such a slow execution of a people through its own deserts," he wrote. As for the subsequent decline of Rome itself, Hitler later insisted, predictably, that "[t]he Jew can take credit for having corrupted the Graeco-Roman world."[17]

Other Nazi leaders took the Roman parallel further. In 1930 Richard Walther Darré even claimed a common origin: "The patrician families of Old Rome were Indo-Germanic," derived from "the same racial substratum," and thus "we cannot find any differences between the Old Roman and Germanic concept of the relation of the idea of family to the soil." Later, however, Roman domestic policy had supposedly abandoned this pristine path for commercial corruption: "[W]ith the defeat of Carthage, Rome won control of the economic point of intersection of Mediterranean commerce," and so "monetary thinking set in." By the time of Caesar, Darré went on, Roman law "had little in common with the old patrician law," while "the Germanic people clashed with Caesar's Roman realm." Since then, "a constant battle has been waged between the Germanic and Late Roman concepts of the state."[18]

Sparta was a third ancient model for the Nazis. In his secret *Second Book*, dictated in 1928, Hitler recommended that a state should "limit the number allowed to live" and added: "The Spartans were once capable of such a wise measure.... The subjugation of 350,000 Helots by 6,000 Spartans was only possible because of the racial superiority of the Spartans. This, however, was the result of systematic racial preservation, so we see in the Spartan state the first racialist state."[19]

As the Nazis rose to power, other like-minded Germans were looking to classical models to link to Germany's supposed ancient heritage. The social anthropologist H. F. K. Günther, who joined the Nazi party in 1932, had strongly influenced Nazi thought with his book *The Ethnology of the German People* (1928).[20] The next year, Günther published *The Racial History of the Greek and*

Roman Peoples, in which he praised classical Sparta's military discipline as a putatively "Nordic" feature and explained its decline as a result of Spartan "de-nordicization" and later racial contamination.[21] Also in 1929, Darré published *The Peasantry as the Life Spring of the Nordic Race,* in which he argued that classical Sparta had declined due in part to "biological causes." In contrast to ancient Germany's "old Nordic" inheritance laws that maintained a family's communal connections to its land, Sparta had imprudently allowed the division of land among heirs, Darré wrote, thus facilitating concentration of land-ownership and giving rise to both absenteeism and the distribution of land to racial inferiors.[22] Here Sparta in its decline had set a further precedent, fore-shadowing the decline of modern Germany. Darré's lament at the dilution of traditional Teutonic aristocratic families echoed after his political career ended in 1942, when Hitler remarked: "In Britain they have the sound law that only the eldest son of a peer can inherit the title; in our country we have nobles by the score, who cannot make a living and will not die."[23] The lingering impact of German partible inheritance obstructed the restoration of a pristine past.

At least in its ancient heyday, Sparta was the Nazis' classical state of choice. In 1928, Hitler rated it more highly than even the ancient Germans.[24] Darré's 1940 work *On the Vital Principle of Two Political Philosophies (Confucius and Lycurgus)* focused closely on the ancient Spartan lawgiver.[25] After invading the Soviet Union, Hitler seemed to imagine its citizens as Helots when he revisited the Spartan model of military power and territorial expansion: "In Sparta six thousand Greeks ruled three hundred and forty-five thousand helots. They came as conquerors, and they took everything."[26] This vision percolated down through the ranks. Three months later, a Nazi officer serving as department head in the Reichskommissariat for the Consolidation of German National Characteristics specified that "the Germans would have to assume the position of the Spartiates, while . . . Letts, Estonians, etc., were in the position of the Perioikoi and the Russians were the Helots" (*Heloten*).[27]

Nazi historical thinking also incorporated the Roman-barbarian divide, assigning virtues to both sides. After conversations with Hitler, the governor-general of Nazi-occupied Poland, Hans Frank, told members of his General Government in December 1941 that after "the regermanization of the eastern territories of the Reich," Poland would become "the next to be totally German-ized." Frank added that "the Führer has given me authority to initiate prepa-rations" to rename regions for ancient groups in order to restore Germanic dignity. Thus, he said, "the Goths' Gau will be set up further east," and the rump

General Government of Poland could then "become the Vandals' Gau. It is well known that the Vandals are the Germanic tribe who have been slandered the most. Their homes were here: here they began the first Germanic culture."[28] In May 1942, Hitler spoke of building walls at the limit of Germany's new eastern settlements to divide Europe from Asia "as in Roman times."[29]

More modern precursors like Native Americans also stood in for barbarians in the Nazi mind. Hitler told Frank in 1940 that before Germanization of Poland, "all the representatives of the Polish intelligentsia must be murdered," and he decreed: "The General Government is a Polish reservation, a great Polish labor camp."[30] Two years later, praising "the Goths" of the Crimea, Hitler added: "The struggle we are waging there against the Partisans resembles very much the struggle in North America against the Red Indians. Victory will go to the strong." Time would consolidate that victory; after all, he asserted, "[w]hen we eat wheat from Canada, we don't think about the despoiled Indians." Just as on the Rhine in ancient times, where "the Germanic conquerors had driven the aboriginals into the mountainy bush in order to settle in their place on the fertile lands," now in the Ukraine, Hitler remarked in late 1941, "it was we who drove the aboriginals into the Pripet marshes." In the future, he said, "[w]e'll supply the Ukrainians with scarves, glass beads and everything that colonial peoples like." A year later, Hitler offered an earlier example of colonial violence against Native Americans, suggesting they had set a precedent for their own destruction by the conquistadors, whose violence in turn prefigured Germany's contemporary aggression and slaughter: "[I]t was not Cortez who brought cruelty to the Mexicans—it was there before he arrived. The Mexicans, indeed, indulged in extensive human sacrifice, and when the spirit moved them, would sacrifice as many as twenty thousand human beings at a time! In comparison, Cortez was a moderate man."[31] By this perverse logic, claiming Cortés as a "moderate" justified Nazi genocide.

Idealization of Cultivation

"I've just learnt," Hitler remarked in August 1941, "that the feeding of the Roman armies was almost entirely based on cereals." Now that vast new lands were coming under German occupation, he said, "[t]he Ukraine, and then the Volga basin, will one day be the granaries of Europe." These regions merited such responsibility only with German agricultural settlement. "The German peasant is moved by a liking for progress . . . every inch of ground is zealously exploited." By contrast, Hitler claimed, "[t]he Slavs are a mass of born slaves," Communist commissars were "entirely ignorant" of farming, and "[t]he Ukrainian peasant has no notion of duty." But in Germany, gushed the Nazi dictator, "all winter long we could keep our cities supplied with vegetables and fresh fruit. Nothing is lovelier than horticulture." Germans were simply more advanced because of their imagined history: "Our ancestors were all peasants. There were no hunters amongst them" (see fig. 28).[32]

A few months later Hitler returned to the pastoral and agrarian romance of ancient Greece, calling it "a marvellous garden, in which oak forests alternated with orchards."[33] It was a persistent theme. He had written in *Mein Kampf*: "What has been profitably Germanized in history is the soil which our ancestors acquired by the sword and settled with German peasants." According to Darré, medieval Teutonic law also supported the Nazi preoccupation with peasant and blood. However, "[a]t the Representative Assembly at Oldesloe in the year 1392, free peasants appeared for the last time as equals together with nobles and clergy on Twelfth Night, on which occasion there was discussion of blood vengeance. This was the last assembly at which peasants appeared!" They had later "disappeared into the mists of serfdom." Although "quite a few German nobles . . . were mindful of their traditional obligation to act so as to maintain farming," these had proved too few. Germany now needed a "new aristocracy from blood and soil."[34]

Hitler declared the farmer "the most important participant" in the Nazi revolution.[35] He lamented in *Mein Kampf* that Germany's leaders in World War I had "renounced the acquisition of new soil." Instead they had fostered "an industrialization as boundless as it was harmful," causing "the weakening of the peasant class." Hitler considered "a healthy peasant class as a foundation for a whole nation.... A solid stock of small and middle peasants has been at all times the best protection against social evils."[36] Linking blood and soil, Hitler went on: "*The foreign policy of the folkish state must safeguard the existence on this planet of the race embodied in the state, by creating a healthy, viable, natural relation between the nation's population and growth on the one hand and the quantity and quality of the soil on the other hand. As a healthy relation we may regard only that condition which assures the sustenance of a people on its own soil.*" In his view, Germany must "shift to the soil policy of the future."[37] Moreover, "[a] glance at population statistics shows us that the future of the nation," Hitler said in 1933, "depends exclusively on the conservation of the peasant."[38]

The roots of National Socialism were of course neither ancient nor medieval but sprouted from the newer *Volkisch* tradition deriving from late-eighteenth-century romanticism.[39] Since then, two seemingly contradictory features of the German demographic landscape had reinforced modern thinking about the importance of agriculture. First, the new strength and proliferation of the small German farmer was an unfolding political fact. From 1882 to 1907, the total area of German farmland in the hands of smallholders owning 2–20 hectares had steadily increased as large estates progressively broke up.[40] Second, a romantic reaction in favor of the countryside was a product of Germany's simultaneous extremely rapid urbanization. Berlin's population, for instance, had increased from 350,000 to 1.7 million between 1860 and 1896, and that of the Greater Berlin metropolitan area reached 3.7 million in 1910. The German capital was the West's most crowded urban agglomeration. Historian Kevin Repp writes that "the average population density in Berlin exceeded that of any other city in the Western world in 1900."[41] With this relatively sudden and extreme urbanization clear in the consciousness of many of their audience, the Nazis' romanticization of the soil was almost commonplace. The Wilhelmine social reformer Adolf Damaschke had written: "[Y]es, the land has a mystical power! Today this mystique is revealed to our people! Only for the land called Germany can we demand sacrifices from our people, sacrifices unheard of in history since Germans were destined to live upon this piece of the earth. Not money, not any goods or values that can be shoved back and forth—only the 'mystique of the land' speaks: I am the Fatherland, I am the holy!"[42] Like others, Damaschke also urged "the rooting of the nation in the soil through the labour of the individual and the whole on common ground," and he considered a healthy rural population to be "a fountain of youth for the nation." Damaschke headed the League of German Land Reformers, which termed the land "the foundation of national being," from 1898 until his death in 1935.[43]

Yet Nazism was not an inevitable outgrowth of this common German thinking about land, nor was it the country's sole reaction to the swelling urbanization. For instance, Damaschke chose a quite different path from the Nazis, who shunned him late in his life. Mysticism about land might have spurred him to oppose what he considered "excessive migration to industrial areas," but it did not prevent him concentrating his reformist energies in the cities, in particular on resolving their pressing housing shortages. Damaschke's goal of "many German children in air and light and sunshine, German children healthy in body and soul," was more concrete than ideological, moderate rather than extremist.[44]

The political culture that Adolf Damaschke shared with the early Nazis did not prevent him parting with them on other important issues as well. Like the Nazis, for instance, Damaschke looked to medieval Germany for inspiration. As he put it: "The land rights of the middle ages sought to secure free access to nature for all, and thus the possibility of earning a living through free labour." He praised the medieval eastern settlements as "the greatest social deed of the German people of the middle ages," which had laid "the foundations for German greatness." Yet he also lauded medieval cites, especially for their lack of land speculation: "[E]ven in the largest cities of the middle ages, there simply were no mass apartment buildings at all." Here again, Damaschke's more modernizing, reforming focus is apparent. Medieval Germanic law "is not dead," he approvingly quoted a colleague as stating in 1912. "It lives and is rich enough in creative energy to bring forth new forms in which the entire content of modern existence can be secured." Nationalist though not chauvinist, Damaschke advocated German colonialism and yet took his social reforms to colonial territories. He also believed in "an organic rootedness of German nationality in German soil," as well as "German ascendance," and he may well have been personally antisemitic. But Damaschke strongly opposed antisemitic political parties, earning the dislike of the early Nazis, a different plant flourishing in the same soil.[45]

Richard Walther Darré encapsulated that difference. In the late 1920s, he took up government contracts in the field of animal breeding. Darré forged a reputation with his publications on selective breeding, "which became the basis of his subsequent racist anthropological theoretisation." In 1930, the year he joined the Nazi Party, Darré published *Neuadel aus Blut und Boden,* in which he argued for an "incipient new German nobility," which "must once again become a vital source of thoroughbred leadership talent. It must have at its command mechanisms that retain time-tested blood in the hereditary line, [and] reject deficient blood." Such mechanisms, he thought, were available from early German history and the role it assigned the free peasant farmer. In ancient times, Darré claimed, "the word 'peasant' was an honorific and expressed the concept of personal freedom." The "transmission of blood was symbolically linked to the—eternally lit—fire on the hearth," based on "a specifically defined landed property." Here was the Nazi variant of the yeoman model: "[T]he soil belonging to such a Germanic peasant was only as extensive as needed to nourish the family." Household and clan units, not communal groups, controlled the land, belying "all interpretations eager to pretend that the Teutonic people practiced communism of the soil." Rather, Darré argued that, along with monogamy, "the soil was merely a necessary *link* in the homogeneity of the clan" in its "purity—that is, breeding." The soil linked land and *Volk*. To "the Teutonic person," it would have been "inconceivable . . . to make the agriculturally useful soil independent of the concept of family." In this way, "the Teutonic people not only preserved proven leadership blood but also perpetuated it and thus deliberately bred."[46]

Similarly, in ancient Rome, according to Darré, "the line of succession formed a tree, as it were, rooted in the soil." By this he meant that "the soil belonging to a generation was assigned undivided to the heir, so that the eternally burning hearth fire, monogamy, and the indivisible landed property formed and remain a thoroughly living unit." The Nazi concept of agriculture thus drew upon the imagined genetic purity of the family farm: "*the responsibility to serve the soil, taking into account the family and its preservation.*"[47]

Communism and capitalism were both alien to this Nazi view of race, soil, family, and history. As Darré saw things, Communist concepts of collective property in land, for instance, "developed from the grazing habits of the nomads," not from agriculturalists. At the other extreme, capitalism, and "a right of private property that placed the individual in the foreground," was equally objectionable to Darré: "A selfish sense of ownership of the soil is totally foreign to both the Old Roman and the Germanic legal sense," because of its "separation of the individual from the idea of generations." Thus, in Darré's view, Germany's nineteenth-century economic development came "at the price of German morality and civilization" by potentially "destroying the Indo-Germanic idea of family."[48]

Following their seizure of power in 1933, the Nazis announced that "under Adolf Hitler we want to build up Germany as his peasant militia." All this gave Darré new hope. As minister of agriculture, he announced the next year: "Neither princes, nor the Church, nor the cities have created the German man. Rather, the German man emerged from the German peasantry. . . . [The] German peasantry, with an unparalleled tenacity, knew how to preserve its unique character and its customs against every attempt to wipe them out. . . . One can say that the blood of a people digs its roots deep into the homeland earth through its peasant landholdings, from which it continuously receives that life-endowing strength which constitutes its special character."[49]

Darré moved the annual Peasants Assembly to the new location of Goslar, a town, as he put it, "in the heart of the original German peasant land" and "the core of the old German Reich of the Saxon emperors . . . in the vicinity of the cradle of the peasant duke, Henry the Lion." Darré had meanwhile helped convince the Nazis' future deputy leader, Heinrich Himmler, of "the need for a new racial-German aristocracy," according to historian Richard Breitman.[50] In Munich in the 1920s, Himmler had studied agriculture intensely for several years as "an impassioned agriculturalist," according to Rudolf Höss, the man he later placed in command at Auschwitz.[51] By 1930, Himmler headed the Bavarian branch of the Artamanen, a sect advocating return to a Teutonic rural lifestyle. Höss, who had fought in the German army in Turkey during the Armenian genocide and was also a member of the Artamanen, later recalled: "It was the objective of the Artaman society to induce and aid ideal healthy young Germans of every party and ideology who, because of widespread unemployment, were without proper occupation, to return to the countryside and to settle there once again." Himmler's ideal was thus "the primeval German peasant warrior and farmer."[52] The editor of the SS newspaper *Das Schwarze Korps*, Gunter d'Alquen, later described Himmler as "a theoretical agriculturalist with an academic education" that influenced "his character formation and its consequences," including "[m]any of the practices he enlarged on subsequently with regard to breeding, selection, and perhaps even what he understood by extermination of vermin." The German biologist Paul Brohmer wrote in this period that "biological laws operative in animals and plants also apply to man. . . . Thus, the teaching of animal breeding and plant cultivation can effectively prepare the way for conceptions of racial biology."[53] Breitman adds that Himmler also "thought he could apply the principles and methods of agriculture to human society" and that "Darré, like Himmler, had studied agronomy and the two men knew all about the breeding of livestock." Himmler, "architect" of the Holocaust, appointed Darré the founding head of the SS Race and Settlement Office; "until they quarreled in the late 1930s the two men both tried to turn the SS into their new stock" (see fig. 27).[54]

Imposing the Nazi ideal of rural life on Germany demanded, among other things, the enforcement of peasant economic self-sufficiency and restrictions on personal and commercial rights. Hitler's Nazi Party, or NSDAP, adopted a new "Agrarian Program" in 1930, and on coming to power three years later, his regime passed both the Reich Agriculture Law and the Reich Hereditary Farm Law. The Nazi publication *Reich Agriculture* announced in 1934: "National Socialism starts out from the fundamental understanding that soil is not a commodity but the living space (*Lebensraum*) of the people (*Volk*). That is why ownership of land obligates the owner to work for the people. Further, land is the life basis of the people."[55] The book's Nazi authors, Hermann Rieschle and Wilhelm Saure, identified rural indebtedness as "the ultimate cause of all the misery that besets agriculture and the farming community." Debt dispatched the German farmer, "banished from house to house." He was deprived of his plot, these writers believed, by "the Roman-Judaic land law" that gave his creditors a legal title to it and thus prevented the farmer from preserving "his ancestors' heritage." Therefore, the Reich Hereditary Farm Law of September 29, 1933, both prohibited partible inheritance and barred owner-farmers from contracting debts or mortgages against their land. Rieschle and Saure wrote: "In this way every new indebtedness on rural soil is blocked . . . in the course of several decades rural soil in Germany will be practically unencumbered and protected." Moreover, now "the unwholesome compulsion on the farmer to bring as high as possible a part of his produce to market is relieved, making possible a gradual shift to self-sufficiency." The long-term result for the peasant sector would be "the self-balanced family enterprise," restricting the dominance of trade and the market only to agricultural enterprises not covered by the Reich Hereditary Farm Law. Most important was the overall benefit to Germany—that now "the hereditary farm cannot be lost to the family."[56] Linking blood and soil, article 15 of the Hereditary Farm Law stipulated that "only men of German or related blood can become farmers (*Bauern*)."[57] The model of German yeomanry explicitly excluded Jews.

Nazism combined antisemitism with the view that, as Himmler put it, "[t]he yeoman of his own acre is the backbone of the German people's strength and character."[58] When Poland fell in 1939, Himmler toured the conquered land with his amanuensis Hanns Johst, who wrote: "And so we stood there like prehistoric farmers and laughed. . . . All of this was now once more German soil! Here the German plough will soon change the picture. Here trees and bushes will soon be planted. Hedges will grow, and weasel and hedgehog, buzzard and hawk will prevent the destruction of half the harvest by mice and other vermin."[59] Nazi-sponsored resettlement researchers praised the "pure, healthy peasants" in Poland's ethnic German villages, with their "healthy colonial peasant strengths," and they urged the settlement of SS veterans in the east to foster a "warrior-nobility" (*Kriegeradel*) there, "in the original biological sense of the word 'noble.'"[60]

Many Nazis shared this sense of "the superior virtue of rural life."[61] Martin Bormann, head of the Nazi party chancellery and an old friend and assistant of Himmler, was another "passionate agriculturalist."[62] *Blut und Boden* (Blood and Soil) became the title of a film made for use in Nazi Party meetings, subtitled "Foundation of the New Reich." Historian David Welch asserts that "the peasant provides the constant culture hero for National Socialism."[63] Goebbels commissioned at least seven feature films on the topic of "blood and soil." This ideological theme persisted despite the partial isolation of Darré's circle within the Nazi Party after 1936. Instead of closer attention to rural affairs, German armament and Nazi war plans required increased industrial production and urban growth—as well as rural recruits. Unlike Darré, perhaps, Hitler "had a use for the peasantry, rather than any particular sympathy," in the words of the historian J. E. Farquharson. An official guide to German citizenship described the independent peasant holding in less than romantic terms, as "a form of life which the state gives to a *Bauer* and his kin. The *Bauer* has to carry out the work allotted to him by the state."[64]

Meanwhile, a dark, primeval, pastoral cult rivaled and reinforced that of agriculture. Another semidocumentary, "The Eternal Forest" (*Ewiger Wald*), expressed "anti-intellectual sentiments" and "idolatry" of the woods: "Our ancestors were a forest people. . . . No people can live without forest, and people who are guilty of deforesting will sink into oblivion. . . . However, Germany in its new awakening has returned to the woods." *Ewiger Wald* depicts "a pure German race, in which the peasant represents the primordial image of the Volk—a Master Race whose roots lie in the sacred soil fertilized for centuries by the richness of their blood."[65]

Yet the Nazis believed that only advanced industrial killing could give Germany back this primeval past. Himmler projected Auschwitz itself as "*the* agricultural research station for the eastern territories." He instructed Höss in 1940: "All essential agricultural research must be carried out there. Huge laboratories and plant nurseries were to be set out. All kinds of stockbreeding was to be pursued there." Early the next year, Höss wrote, Himmler visited Auschwitz with plans for "the prisoner-of-war camp for 100,000 prisoners." But he added: "In addition there will be the agricultural research station and farms!" In mid-1942, Himmler observed "the whole process of destruction of a transport of Jews" and ordered: "The gypsies are to be destroyed. The Jews who are unfit to work are to be destroyed. . . . Armaments factories will also be built. . . . The agricultural experiments will be intensively pursued, for the results are urgently needed."[66] Hitler had insisted in 1941 on the creation of "a Garden of Eden in the newly occupied eastern territories."[67] "The German colonist ought to live on handsome, spacious farms," he added, surrounding cities with a wide "belt of handsome villages connected by the best roads."[68]

The vision of a rural idyll in the newly conquered east created a dilemma for German policymakers. If its existing populations remained there, they, not the Germans, would become the main beneficiaries of an agrarian Eden. Nazis therefore generated plans for massive deportations of the native inhabitants but also expressed concern over Germany's own industrialization, which had deprived it of its rural past and supposedly even caused its birthrate to fall. The desk officer for racial matters in the Reich Ministry for the Eastern Territories warned solemnly in 1942: "[W]e should not pursue further the thought of concentrating industry within the Reich and agriculture in the foreign-ethnic territories. Putting this thought into practice could mean the biological death of Germany. . . . To give the eastern nations, especially the Russians and Ukrainians, a chance at a purely agrarian life would practically be the same thing as the suicide of the German people if they themselves in the last resort are cut off from that same life through Germany's own continuous industrialization."[69]

As in the case of the Young Turks, once the Nazis were in power, their peasant policy and their cult of antiquity both came up against "the requirements of a powerful war economy, necessarily based on industry." Yet as Barrington Moore wrote of the agrarian policy, "a few starts were made here and there."[70] One of them was Auschwitz.

Cities and Jews

The Nazi ideological aversion to cities sprang from this same faith in rural virtues. If the purebred ancestors of the Germans were "all peasants," they included neither city dwellers nor Jews, whom Nazis considered the archetypal urbanites. Here Hitler's analysis of ancient Europe concurred with that of Darré: "The Germanic people made their settlements outside the cities, . . . and lived on the land, following their laws." Cities, Darré wrote, were "in themselves very un-Germanic organizations."[71]

The strong connection between rural and racial thinking had obvious ramifications for Jews, prominent as they were in early-twentieth-century German urban and intellectual life. Worse, Nazis explained that because of low birthrates in urban areas, "[t]he big city is the death of the nation." Berlin was an "asphalt desert."[72] Modern Germany was purportedly plagued by "the deracinated mode of thinking of urbanites." Darré complained: "Today's city dweller has so far lost all understanding of the basic principles of agriculture." Urbanites ignored "the natural necessity of a healthy agricultural life." Even in rural areas, Darré lamented that under "the influence of 'modern' trends" and "apparent progress," an emerging "money economy that is entirely independent of the soil" was only exacerbating "one of the most terrible imaginable breakdowns in the sphere of national characteristics." As a result, "our people has fallen ill in its economic thinking" and "turned away from the Germanic-Teutonic concepts of property." For "agriculture and therefore our people," in Darré's view, abandonment of those older ideas was "calamitous." Germans had "lost their connection to the soil" and, contrary to its organic function, "*the soil has been deprived of its moral responsibility.*" Stressing "the *moral* obligations the owner of the land had to meet," Darré took the racialist, idealist view, rejecting materialism and urging that "the moral obligations of the blood idea [*sic*] actually must precede the farmer's economic obligations." Thus, "the final decision had to be made in the area of the blood questions."[73] As in other genocidal ideologies, an "idea" of race trumped material reality.

In the Nazi vision, Jews were not "rooted in the soil" as were "real nations" such as Germans and Poles.[74] Historian Jeffrey Richards writes: "The Jew was characterized as materialist and thus the enemy of Volkist spiritualism, as a rootless wanderer and therefore the opposite of Volkist rootedness, and as the epitome of finance, industry and the town and thus alien to the agrarian peasant ideal of the Volk."[75] Hitler proclaimed that "a nation can exist without cities, but ... a nation cannot exist without farmers."[76] In *Mein Kampf,* he urged that "[i]ndustry and commerce recede from their unhealthy leading position" and "cease to be the basis of the nation's subsistence and become a mere instrument to that end."[77] He explained that modern industrial cities were "abscesses on the body of the people (*Volkskörper*)—places where all evils, vices, and sicknesses appear to unite. They are above all hotbeds of blood-mixing and bastardization."[78] In 1942, Hitler reiterated that the peasantry "is the solid backbone of the nation, for husbandry is the most chancy occupation on earth. ... Work on the land is a schooling which teaches energy, self-confidence, and a readiness to make swift decisions; the town-dweller, on the contrary, must have everything exactly mapped out for him." Himmler agreed: "Cowards are born in towns. Heroes in the country."[79]

Finally, Nazi antiurban and antisemitic preoccupations also reinforced the recurring sylvan fantasy of a shadowy, eternal German past where trees ruled invisible people. And that notion, of a spiritual forest empty even of farmers, in turn made it possible to imagine large areas depopulated and returned to their pristine state.

Territorial Expansionism

Out of the forests first came warriors—even before farmers. Hitler wrote in *Mein Kampf* that "the first plowshare in its day bore the name of 'sword.'" Like the followers of ancient Arminius, warriors were more mobile. Sacred German soil, in the Nazi view, had no specific boundaries. Hitler proclaimed that "for Germany ... the only possibility of carrying out a healthy territorial policy lay in the acquisition of new land in Europe itself ... it could be obtained by and large only at the expense of Russia."[80] In 1928, he added: "We calculate our own sacrifices, weigh the extent of the possible success and will stride forward to the attack, regardless of whether it will come to a halt ten or a thousand kilometers behind the present lines. For wherever our success ends, it will always be only the point of departure for a new struggle."[81] Indeed, after his invasion of Poland, Hitler reportedly stated that even "the Jewish question was really a space question" since he still "had not even sufficient space for his own people." As he put it in 1941: "What India was for England, the territories of Russia will be for us."[82] The next year, Hitler planned to send "soldier-peasants" (*Wehrbauern*) to the eastern settlements.[83] In 1943, Himmler told SS leaders: "If the SS together with the farmers, and we together with our friend Backe [Darré's successor as agriculture minister], then run the colony in the east on a grand scale, without any restraint, without any question of tradition, but with nerve and revolutionary impetus, we shall in twenty years push the national boundary 500 kilometres eastwards.... We shall charge ahead and push our way forward little by little to the Urals ... or in a hundred years beyond the Urals."[84]

The Nazis strained to outdo even their medieval Teutonic forebears, after whose conquests, Darré had sniffed in 1930, "only one-third" of the conquered territory was confiscated for German settlements. Darré has been called "the main theoretician of eastward continental expansion and agricultural settlement" as well as the author of the Nazi doctrine of Blut und Boden.[85] Despite his declining influence after 1936, Darré's views were widely shared. As early as 1919, at the age of 19, Himmler had written in his diary: "I work for my ideal of German womanhood with whom, some day, I will live my life in the east and fight my battles as a German far from beautiful Germany."[86] According to

Rudolf Höss, in 1930 Himmler again "spoke of the forcible conquest of large sections of the East."[87] Reinhard Heydrich talked of German *Wehrbauern* reclaiming land there for agriculture and holding back "the storm-flood of Asia."[88]

The Third Reich would recover the territories lost not only by the First but by the Second Reich as well. Hitler projected himself as the ruler of a country unjustly compressed as a result of World War I. Peace presented no alternative to reconquest. He wrote in 1924: "Germany will either be a world power or there will be no Germany."[89] In an extraordinary speech in August 1939, he described Germany and Poland each "with rifles cocked": "We are faced with the harsh alternative of striking now or of *certain annihilation* sooner or later." "I have taken risks," he went on, "in occupying the Rhineland when the generals wanted me to pull back, in taking Austria, the Sudetenland, and the rest of Czechoslovakia."[90] Thus, even as he recited his list of territorial gains, Hitler was still proclaiming the threat of Germany's "certain annihilation." This was much less plausible than the Ottoman fears of imperial diminution. Striking is Hitler's tactical assumption that German *territorial* stability was unachievable. Failure to expand meant annihilation. Then, actual expansion was denied or dismissed as insufficient to deter enemies.

A month after launching his invasion of the Soviet Union in June 1941, Hitler held a conference in his headquarters at which he revealed secret plans for permanent annexation of many of the conquered regions: "[W]e must know clearly that we shall never leave those countries." On this occasion, the Führer specified the following conquests: "The Crimea has to be evacuated by all foreigners and to be settled by Germans only" and, along with "a considerable hinterland ... should become Reich territory," the hinterland being "as large as possible"; second, "the Volga Colony too will have to become Reich territory"; third, "the entire Baltic country will have to be incorporated into Germany"; and finally, "the Kola Peninsula will be taken by Germany."[91]

Territorial expansion especially attracted extremists from the German periphery. Like the Young Turks, Nazi leaders hailed disproportionately from previously "lost" territories beyond the supposedly shrinking prewar homeland. *Volksdeutsch* from Austria and the German communities in central Europe were strongly represented in the Nazi leadership, including Hitler, Rosenberg, and Kaltenbrunner.[92] With their peripheral perspective of German life in other countries, these men likely heightened the metropolitan sense of ethnic and territorial threat. To take another example, the bureaucratic orga-

MAP 22. Nazi-occupied Europe, 1939–45. Based on Wendy Lower, *Nazi Empire Building and Holocaust in Ukraine* (Chapel Hill, 2005), 4–5. Copyright © 2005 by the University of North Carolina Press. Used by permission.

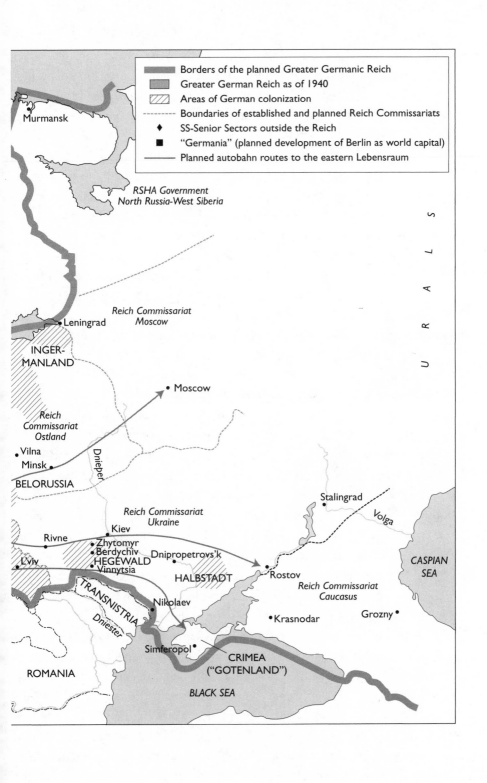

Borders of the planned Greater Germanic Reich
Greater German Reich as of 1940
Areas of German colonization
Boundaries of established and planned Reich Commissariats
SS-Senior Sectors outside the Reich
"Germania" (planned development of Berlin as world capital)
Planned autobahn routes to the eastern Lebensraum

Murmansk

RSHA Government
North Russia-West Siberia

Leningrad

INGER-
MANLAND

Reich Commissariat
Moscow

U R A L S

Moscow

Reich
Commissariat
Ostland

Vilna
Minsk

BELORUSSIA

Dnieper

Reich Commissariat
Ukraine

Stalingrad

Volga

Rivne
Zhytomyr
Berdychiv   Dnipropetrovs'k
Lviv   HEGEWALD
Vinnytsia
Kiev

HALBSTADT

Rostov

CASPIAN
SEA

Reich Commissariat
Caucasus

Krasnodar   Grozny

TRANSNISTRIA

Nikolaev

Dniester

Simferopol

CRIMEA
("GOTENLAND")

ROMANIA

BLACK SEA

nizer of the Final Solution, Adolf Eichmann, born in Germany in 1906, grew up in Austria from the age of eight and lived there until 1933. Eichmann first joined the Austrian National Socialist Party in 1932, and then, in Germany under Kaltenbrunner's influence, enlisted in an Austrian-exile unit of the SS, outlawed in Austria at the time.[93]

Conversely, like the Armenians in the case of the Ottoman Empire, the Jews, Poles, and Russians came to be seen as obstructive occupants of the eastern territories where the Nazis planned to settle Aryan farmers who would cultivate it properly. Touring Poland with Himmler in 1939, his amanuensis Johst dismissed it as "not a state-building nation. . . . A country which has so little feeling for systematic settlement, that is not even up to dealing with the style of a village, . . . is a colonial country!" Auschwitz commandant Rudolf Höss recalled: "Himmler considered his true life's work to be the spread of the continued existence of the German people, secured by a superior peasantry on a healthy economic basis and provided with a sufficient amount of land. All his plans for settlements, even long before the assumption of power, were directed to this objective. He never made a secret of the fact that this could be accomplished only if land was seized by force in the East."[94]

Domestic Nazi peasant policy appears to have fueled this expansionism, sometimes inadvertently. According to a 1942 report prepared by the desk officer for racial matters in the Reich Ministry for the Eastern Territories, the Nazis' 1933 Reich Hereditary Farm Law had had an unintended effect: "[T]he tendency of the law to give almost everything to one child and practically nothing to the other children has led the German farmer to restrict himself to one child," stoking the great Nazi fear of a low German birthrate. The report continued: "In 1933 the lawmaker was not in a position to grant the farmer's other children an appropriate compensation. But once we have a large German settlement area in the East, we will be in a position here too to effectively intervene and to fight against the tendency to limit the family to one child." In this view, Germany's population growth would resume only if territorial expansion offered its farmers the prospect of new land for their younger sons.[95]

Looking east, the Nazis considered both Slavs, occupying this coveted farmland, and urbanized Jews to be in conflict with the destiny of the German peasantry, though of course in different ways. The new land had to be ethnically purified of both groups. Himmler stated: "One only possesses a land when even the last inhabitant of this territory belongs to one's own people."[96] In 1942, the Nazi planner Heinrich Wiepking-Jürgensmann asserted that "the spirit and energies of the human races are distinguished from each other in the landscape with the sharpness of a knife." He claimed that Poles preferred to live in "a sterile wasteland ... concealed by vapours and gases, permeated by nauseating waterways, so that one believes oneself in a grey and eerie landscape of the underworld, not in a place of earthly human habitation."[97]

The Jews' presence in a region the Nazis wanted, and their failure to cultivate it at all, doubly determined their fate. Historian Christopher Browning has pointed out that the Nazi "achievement of *Lebensraum* through the invasion of Russia and the Final Solution to the Jewish Question through systematic mass murder were intimately connected."[98] Hitler initially envisaged "three belts of population—German, Polish and Jewish—from west to east." Pragmatic considerations gave first priority to deporting rural Poles to make way for German settlers before expelling or exterminating Jews.[99] By late 1943, however, Himmler was telling SS leaders that "the most copious breeding should be from this racial elite of the German people. In twenty to thirty years we must really be able to provide the whole of Europe with its ruling class." He repeated that "the whole of Europe" would be "controlled, ordered and led by us, for the Germanic people." The Nazi official Konrad Meyer went further: "It is not enough to settle our race in those areas and eliminate people of an alien race. Rather, these spaces have to take on a character that corresponds to the nature of our being."[100]

Race and Space[101]

Virulent racial hatred exerted an independent force on Nazi policy. As early as 1922, Hitler was very clear about his plans for the Jews: "Once I really am in power, my first and foremost task will be the annihilation of the Jews. . . . I will have gallows built in rows . . . until the last Jew in Munich has been exterminated. Other cities will follow suit, precisely in this fashion, until all Germany has been completely cleansed of Jews." Two years later, he wrote in *Mein Kampf* that during the Great War, if "twelve or fifteen thousand of these Hebrew corrupters of the people had been held under poison gas, as happened to hundreds of thousands of our very best German workers in the field, the sacrifice of millions at the front would not have been in vain."[102]

Yet, upon taking power in Germany in 1933, the Nazi leader was prepared to wait until a new war offered the opportunity and the cover needed to plan and implement such destruction. Analyzing the "pathological hatred for the Jews" at the heart of Hitler's worldview, the historian Gerald Fleming distinguished two elements: "the one a traditionally inspired and instinctively affirmed anti-semitism that due to its racialist/biological component took a particularly rigid form; and the other *a flexible, goal-oriented* antisemitism that was prag-matically superimposed on the first."[103] For instance, Hitler's new regime at first moved cautiously to eliminate Jews from Germany, balancing pragmatic goals with racial and rural ideology. The Reich Interior Ministry and the Ge-stapo initially encouraged Jews to leave for Palestine, which required prepara-tory training of Jewish youth in farming techniques. Despite Nazi views of the "well-known reluctance of the Jews to engage in manual labor, especially in agriculture," by March 1934, Zionist organizations were training nearly 2,400 Jews in agricultural retraining camps in Germany. The Reich Ministry of Agri-culture and the Reich Employment Office both protested. Herbert Backe, state secretary of agriculture under Walther Darré, feared that even if Jews were segregated in their rural camps, they would soon be "visiting neighboring vil-lages," engaging in relations with German farmers, and even participating in "mixed dancing." Backe opposed any "relocation of Jews to the countryside" as "undesirable," because they would "always find a way of establishing the desired connection with the agricultural population." However, the Interior Ministry countered that it was "to be welcomed when the Jews in Germany ... seek agri-cultural training." The Gestapo also reiterated its policy of "no opposition to the retraining of unemployed Jews in agriculture" on the grounds that it would "facilitate the emigration of the trainees from Germany." Indeed, the desired "much greater emigration of Jews" was "possible only when the emigrants have been trained in agriculture." Jews were even able to undertake such training on "Aryan" farms, until 1938, when the Nazis set out to remove Jews totally from Germany's economy and escalated the level of violence against them with the *Kristallnacht* pogrom.[104]

After Hitler went to war in 1939 and continued to intensify his expansion-ist and anti-Jewish policies, other ethnic and population groups also became important Nazi targets. The 5–6 million Jewish victims were the largest single group to be exterminated, along with many other "non-Aryans." The Nazis murdered millions of Poles and Russians and up to half a million Gypsies. In-cluding these campaigns of mass murder and war-related deaths from combat, destruction, and famine, the total number of victims of Hitler's wars of aggres-sion has been estimated at 40–45 million.[105]

Fig. 31   Himmler inspecting cotton fields in Ukraine, fall 1942. U.S. Holocaust Memorial Museum, Photo Archives, #60407, courtesy of James Blevins, and Wendy Lower, *Nazi Empire-Building and the Holocaust in Ukraine* (Chapel Hill, 2005),175.

Fig. 32 Nazi portrait of German farmer in Ukraine, 1943. From *Volk und Rasse,*
February 1943. See p. 451.

Deutſcher Bauer aus Der Ukraine

Nach Zeichnung von ᛋᛋ-Bildberichter Walter Stengl

Fig. 33 Nazi portrait of German farmer in Ukraine, 1943. From *Volk und Rasse*,
February 1943.

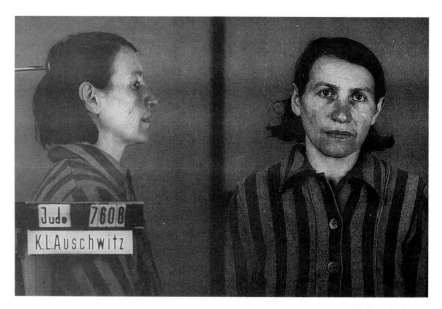

Fig. 34 Auschwitz prisoner, photographed with her head held in a bracket. From *Sterbebücher von Auschwitz* (Munich, 1995), 1:28. Courtesy of Prof. Dr. h.c. Hartmut Lehmann, Max-Planck-Institute für Geschichte, Göttingen.

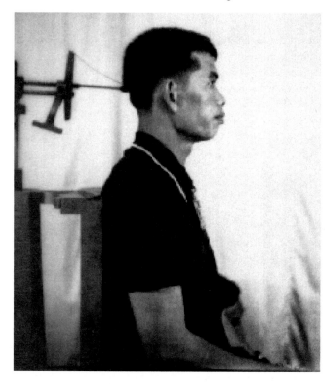

Fig. 35 Prisoner of the Khmer Rouge, no. 04070, photographed with his head held in a bracket. S-21, Tuol Sleng Museum of Genocide, Phnom Penh, Ministry of Culture, Royal Government of Cambodia.

— PRODUIRE, pour que tous les Français aient du pain.
— AIDER les familles moins favorisées.
— SUIVRE ET FAIRE SUIVRE LES MOTS D'ORDRE DU MARÉCHAL ET DE SON MINISTRE DE L'AGRICULTURE.

PAYSANS, MES AMIS, JE VOUS FAIS CONFIANCE ET JE COMPTE SUR VOTRE DÉVOUEMENT POUR M'AIDER A RELEVER LA FRANCE

Maréchal Pétain.

Fig. 36 "And now for agricultural production to meet the country's needs." Vichy French propaganda leaflet, signed by Marshal Philippe Pétain. From Christian Faure, *Le Projet culturel de Vichy: Folklore et révolution nationale 1940–1944* (CNRS Editions/ Presses Universitaires de Lyon, 1989), 109.

Fig. 37 Vietnamese cartoon depiction of Pol Pot's Khmer Rouge regime piling up skulls and burning books. The ancient Chinese Emperor Ch'in Shih Huang Ti says: "You're doing a very good job of following my example!" From *Van Hoa Nghe Thuat*, no. 9 (Hanoi, 1978), courtesy of David G. Marr. Drawing by Nguyen Nghiem.

Fig. 38   *El nuevo campesino* (The New Peasant), undated (1970s?), cover of Guatemalan government pamphlet. Courtesy Greg Grandin, from the personal papers of Eduardo Taracena, provided to Grandin by Taracena's nephew. See p. 583.

Fig. 39 "Work is the best way to fight communism." From *El nuevo campesino* (The New Peasant), undated pamphlet. Courtesy Greg Grandin, from Eduardo Taracena's personal papers.

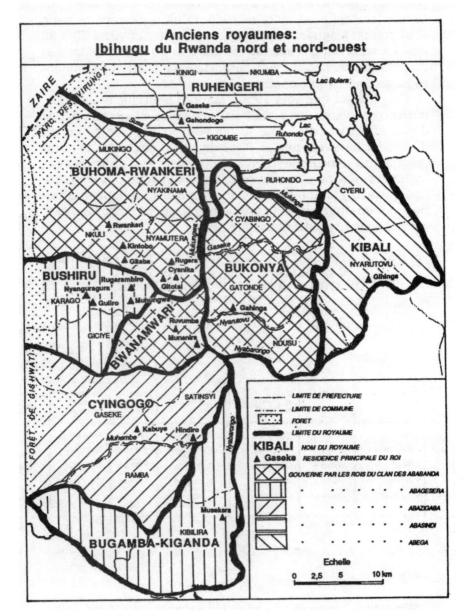

Fig. 40 Rwandan genocide perpetrator Ferdinand Nahimana's map of "Former kingdoms of north and northwest Rwanda." From Nahimana, *Le Rwanda: Emergence d'un
état* (Paris, 1993), 150. Courtesy Editions L'Harmattan. See p. 560.

The Nazi vision and practice of unrelenting war threatened Germans, too, of course, since Hitler had no plans for peace for them. He had prophesied in a 1929 speech in the Hofbräuhaus: "The earth is a plaything (*Spielball*) and we National Socialists will never refrain from using our people in the game pursued by the powers of this world. Till the end of all days we want to see the German people keep fighting in the midst of this competition."[106] Besides slaughtering Jews and Gypsies, Hitler targeted German homosexuals, Communists, liberals, trade unionists, and other oppositionists. In the Nazis' purge of German culture, they burned books and paintings, abolished literary and film criticism, and banned modern music. The day after Kristallnacht, Hitler even speculated that he "might one day exterminate the intellectual classes in Germany if they no longer proved to be of use."[107] His announced intention to "preserve the race even if necessary at the expense of the individual" did not privilege all members of the preferred race; on the contrary, it subjected many of them to measures to "protect" it. These measures included the "mercy killing" of mentally handicapped Germans. As in the case of other races, the Nazis used agricultural metaphors for this slaughter and repression. The commentary to the 1937 film *Opfer der Vergangenheit* (Victims of the Past) proclaimed: "To prevent the growth of weeds is to promote the healthy plants that will be of some value."[108] Himmler also used an agricultural metaphor in ordering that homosexuals be eliminated "root and branch."[109]

These violent campaigns, domestic and "foreign," against both Germans and aliens, were linked in other ways, too. On the day his armies invaded Poland, Hitler also authorized that every "incurably sick" German be "granted a merciful death."[110] Noting that Nazi "eugenics" eliminated over 70,000 Germans with hereditary illnesses, historian George L. Mosse pointed out the close link, spanning the ethnic divide, between the destruction of Germans and Jews: "Putting euthanasia into practice meant that the Nazis took the idea of 'unworthy' life seriously, and a life so defined was characterized by lack of productivity and degenerate outward appearance," while similarly, "ideas of unproductivity and physical appearance were both constantly applied to Jews."[111] Richard Evans adds that more than racism was involved: "It was not these people's racial identity that marked them out for elimination, but their supposed biological inferiority, irrespective of race." By the same token, Gypsies, though defined in 1935 as "alien to the German species," were in the early years of the war "not persecuted on 'racial' grounds, but on the basis of an 'asocial and criminal past' and a security threat." Some of the more assimilated, known as Sinti, "even served in the armed forces until the order came in 1942 that all Gypsies must be sent to Auschwitz."[112]

Social and racial prejudices swirled and mingled. "One can see how confused Nazi racism was," Yehuda Bauer comments, "when Jewish grandparents were defined by religion rather than so-called racial criteria."[113] Thus, the November 14, 1935, "Nuremberg law" defined a "mixed-blood" Jew (*Mischlinge*) as "anyone who is descended from one or two grandparents who are fully Jewish as regards race. . . . A grandparent is deemed fully Jewish without further ado, if he has belonged to the Jewish religious community." Raul Hilberg adds that "a person was to be considered Jewish if he had three or four Jewish grandparents. . . . If an individual had two Jewish grandparents, he would be classified as Jewish only if he himself belonged to the Jewish religion [or] was married to a Jewish person. The critical factor in every case was in the first instance the religion of the grandparents."[114]

Yet biological metaphors dominated Nazi discourse. The Law for the Protection of German Blood and German Honor, passed on September 15, 1935, asserted that "the purity of German blood is a prerequisite for the continued existence of the German people."[115] Slavs were "subhumans"—*untermenschen*.[116] Jews were "vermin" and "lice."[117] In 1939–40, Hitler and other leading Nazis coined the term *ethnic cleansing* (*völkische Flurbereinigung*).[118] They "cleaned" occupied areas of Jews and were obsessed with the concept of racial "purity."

Hitler announced his priorities on January 30, 1939: "Today I will once more be a prophet: if the international Jewish financiers in and outside Europe should succeed in plunging the nations once more into a world war, then the result will not be the Bolshevizing of the earth, and thus the victory of Jewry, but the annihilation of the Jewish race in Europe!"[119] Germany invaded Poland seven months later, on September 1, 1939. The Nazi leadership seemed to anticipate that the troops might have inhibitions about mass murder. Initial orders instructed German forces to kill Jewish men, Communists, and members of the Polish resistance, but as the soldiers and police became inured to murder of civilians, later orders included the killing of women and children.[120] Even so, as early as November 1939, the German army commander of the Ober-Obst military region, Colonel General Blaskowitz, was complaining in writing about the SS terror tactics in Poland. According to Hitler's adjutant, who read the memorandum, Blaskowitz expressed "very great concern about illegal shootings, arrests and confiscations [and] worries about the discipline of the troops who witness these things with their own eyes." He had protested "without success" to local Nazi Gestapo and SD police officers, who he said responded by referring to their "instructions from the SS leadership." Blaskowitz requested that his superiors "reestablish conditions of legality, above all that executions should only be carried out after due process of law." Having read this memorandum, Hitler commented revealingly that "one can't fight a war with Salvation Army methods." He suggested Blaskowitz "be relieved of his command since he is unsuitable."[121] The Nazi regime annexed four western Polish regions to Germany and established a "General Government" to rule the remainder of occupied Poland.[122]

As in the Ottoman regime during World War I, dissension spread with the slaughter. On February 2, 1940, Blaskowitz received a message from Infantry General Ulex, German commander in chief of the southern section of the front. Ulex wrote: "The acts of violence by the police forces, which have increased recently, demonstrate a quite incredible lack of human and moral feeling, so that it can be called sheer brutalization. . . . It seems as if the superiors privately approve of this activity." Ulex even urged "the recall and disbanding at a stroke of all the police units, including all their superior officers and all those leaders in the departments of the 'General Government' who have witnessed these acts of violence for months."[123] Four days later, Blaskowitz wrote a new memorandum for the visiting army commander in chief: "It is misguided to slaughter tens of thousands of Jews and Poles as is happening at present; . . . what the foreign radio stations have broadcast so far is only a tiny fraction of what has happened." The general added: "The acts of violence against the Jews which occur in full view of the public inspire among the religious Poles not only deep disgust but also great pity for the Jewish population, to which up to now the Poles were more or less hostile. In a very short time we shall reach the point at which our arch-enemies in the eastern sphere—the Pole and the Jew, who in addition will receive the particular support of the Catholic Church— will, in their hatred against their tormenters, combine against Germany right along the line." As Hitler had urged, this firm opposition to the atrocities would cost Blaskowitz his command.[124] Meanwhile, on July 22, 1940, the 18th Army Command ordered all soldiers and officers to "refrain from any criticism of the struggle being waged with the population in the General Government, for example the treatment of the Polish minorities, the Jews, and Church matters. The achievement of a final solution of this ethnic struggle, which has been raging for centuries along our eastern frontier, requires particularly tough measures."[125] Yet Hans Frank, head of the General Government, also saw the difficulties of eliminating Polish resistance there: "This task cannot be fulfilled through a gigantic extermination programme in which people are, so to speak, mowed down. We cannot after all kill 14,000,000 Poles."[126]

Polish territory became a German colony. A former German colonial official in Cameroon, Viktor Böttcher, took over the Poznan district of Poland, now annexed to the "Old Reich." In May 1940, he even professed outrage at the defeated Polish state for its alleged "brutal suppression of its minorities." Böttcher listed among his pressing tasks "the reparation of the injustice done to the ethnic Germans and the creation of a flowering, thickly settled cultural area that furnishes the Old Reich with the greatest possible quantity of food-stuffs." He demanded that "certain races must be kept away from the German people" and that "a line must be drawn between Germans and Poles." German schools proliferated, and youth camps inculcated "the national value of a healthy agricultural population."[127] As the Nazis sorted Poland's population according to their racial hierarchy, the Reich governor of West Prussia announced in December that "the germanization action will initially have to be confined to agricultural and factory workers, artisans, and small peasants. One will be able to assume the presence of German blood in a family on the basis of typically German abilities and gifts (e.g. technical skills, a sense of how to look after household and farm appliances properly)."[128] In the Lublin district, an SS brigadier general added that besides "racial" features and surnames, "often the layout of the house, the construction of the farm buildings . . . points to German influence and a German ancestry."[129]

Agricultural and racial policies remained closely intertwined, despite changes of personnel. Richard Walther Darré, who had been losing influence since 1936, had by now fallen out with Himmler, and the rising star Herbert Backe, the Reich state secretary of agriculture, would in 1942 replace Darré as agriculture minister.[130] In April 1940, Backe drew up a racial hierarchy for the General Government, with Jews at the bottom of the ladder: "I am not interested in the Jews. Whether or not they get any fodder to eat (*füttern*) is the last thing I am concerned about. I am only interested in the Poles in so far as I see in them a reservoir of labour. . . . We are not talking of rations for Poles but only of the possibilities of feeding them." As for the Ukrainians, Backe went on, "we must treat [them] fairly well, . . . we will guarantee their food supplies to a certain extent. . . . Then come the Germans, to start with the category of ethnic

MAP 23. Poland under Nazi occupation. Based on Leni Yahil, *The Holocaust* (New York, 1990), and Norman Davies, *God's Playground: A History of Poland,* vol. 2, *1795 to the Present* (Oxford, 1981).

Germans." The final and top category, "the Wehrmacht and the civil servants," would receive the best treatment. "The majority of the Polish people will still be treated significantly better than the Jews. We have no interest in the Jews," he repeated.[131] This purported "lack of interest" in fact expressed a bias against sparing Jews. They could be killed at will, or worse. The perpetrators of this genocide displayed no lack of a conscious desire to achieve it.

Murder reached a new peak after the June 1941 Nazi invasion of the Soviet Union, where Hitler had called for "a war of extermination." Einsatzgruppen units quickly began to round up and slaughter hundreds of thousands of Jews in captured Soviet territories.[132] For example, the Einsatzgruppe A commander, responsible for the Baltic states, reported in October that "the cleansing operation of the Security police had the goal of the most comprehensive elimination possible of the Jews. Extensive executions were thus carried out by special units in the cities and the plains." The commander in Latvia concurred in a January 1942 report: "The aim of the Einsatzkommando 2 from the beginning was a radical solution of the Jewish problem through the execution of all Jews." By October, he reported, German units and Latvian auxiliaries had murdered "about 30,000" Latvian Jews, and then "on 9 November 1941 11,034 Jews in Dünaberg and, at the beginning of December 1941, 27,800 Jews in Riga were executed." From Ukraine, the Einsatzgruppe C reported in November that "up to now around 75,000 Jews have been liquidated."[133]

German forces also slaughtered Soviet commissars and soldiers en masse. Hitler and his circle resolved at a meeting in mid-July 1941 that "this giant area would have to be pacified as quickly as possible; the best solution was to shoot anybody who looked sideways." In September, Hitler likened "the brutes who populate our Russian p.o.w. camps" to "subhuman creatures" who could be treated with "extreme harshness." By February 1942, 2 million Russian prisoners of war had perished or were murdered at German hands. Hitler proclaimed on October 10, 1941: "The law of existence prescribes uninterrupted killing, so that the better may live."[134]

In July 1941, SS Sturmbannführer Höppner reported from Poznan to Adolf Eichmann of Himmler's Reich Security Main Office presenting a proposal "to sterilize all those Jewesses who are still fertile so that the Jewish problem would be finally solved with the present generation." Höppner also asked "whether the most humane solution might not be to finish off those Jews who are incapable of work with some quick-acting preparation."[135] In October 1941, Hitler resolved that "[t]he Jewish question takes priority over all other matters."[136] One of the organizers of the industrial mass murder of Jews was Dr. Erhard Wetzel, a lawyer who had worked in the Race and Settlement Main Office and was now desk officer for racial matters in the Reich Ministry for the Eastern Territories. That October, Wetzel began to collaborate with Viktor Brack of the NSDAP chancellery, preparing what he termed "accommodations as well as gassing apparatus necessary for the solution of the Jewish question" in the east. On October 25, Wetzel assured the Reich commissar for the Eastern Territories that "there need to be no concerns if those Jews who are not capable of working are removed with Brack's methods."[137]

The Nazis planned the destruction of the Jewish people as the first major phase of an apocalyptic project of ethnic engineering of the conquered eastern territories. By late 1941, Himmler's Central Office for Reich Security (RSHA) was also drawing up a comprehensive plan for the future of these territories, known as "General Plan East." In November, Wetzel learned that the plan included provision for the resettlement of no fewer than "31 million foreign ethnic individuals" over the next three decades. By then only "14 million foreign ethnics were to remain in the area," along with 8 million German residents and new settlers. Wetzel later calculated, however, that "the Plan is based on wrong population figures," since the "foreign ethnic population" of the territories was 51 million, not 45 million as the plan stated. "Only if we assume that the roughly 5 to 6 million Jews who live in this area were eliminated before the evacuation can we arrive at the figure of 45 million." Thus, Wetzel concluded that the resettlement of the Jews mentioned in the plan "becomes unnecessary with the solution of the Jewish question." All he could imagine might be needed then was "possible transport of those Jews that might remain after this war into compulsory labor camps in the northern Russian or Siberian territory."[138]

Meanwhile, in Poland, Hans Frank urged in December 1941 that the Jews "will have to be finished off." "We must exterminate the Jews wherever we find them, and wherever it is at all possible to do so." In the General Government, he added, "We cannot shoot these 3.5 million Jews, we cannot poison them, but we must be able to intervene in a way which somehow achieves a successful extermination."[139] By now the Nazis had launched their *Endlosung,* or "the final solution of the Jewish question," which they then discussed at the Wannsee conference, convened near Berlin on January 20, 1942. Its declared aim was "to cleanse German living space of Jews in a legal manner."[140] Ten days later, Hitler echoed his January 1939 "prophecy" when he told a crowd at Berlin's Sports

Palace, "[T]he result of this war will be the complete annihilation of the Jews" (see fig. 29).[141]

Two weeks after that, Goebbels wrote in his diary: "The Fuhrer once more expressed his determination to clean up the Jews in Europe pitilessly. . . . Their destruction will now go hand in hand with the destruction of our enemies. We must hasten this process with cold ruthlessness." On March 6, 1942, Erhard Wetzel represented the Reich Ministry for the Eastern Territories at a conference held at Himmler's Reich Central Security Office, on "The Final Solution to the Jewish Question." Goebbels noted on March 27: "The Jews in the General Government are now being evacuated eastward. The procedure is a pretty barbaric one and not to be described here more definitely. Not much will remain of the Jews. On the whole it can be said that about 60 percent of them will have to be liquidated whereas only 40 percent can be used for forced labour."[142] In an April 1942 memorandum, Wetzel claimed that in addition, "we have expelled about 500,000 Jews from Reich territory," but he also acknowledged what was happening to them when he specified that "one cannot solve the Polish problem by liquidating the Poles in the same way as the Jews."[143]

"I was unsure what exactly was going on around me," recalled Roma Nutkiewicz of events in Warsaw in mid-1942, when she was the 15-year-old daughter of a Jewish family, "but my father concluded that the Germans intended to murder all of us." Nazis were "blockading buildings, taking all the residents out, shooting some, beating up others, expelling the rest, and closing another block to Jewish residents." On the morning of July 22, "the rumor of the coming deportation spread throughout the ghetto." The next day, "[w]hat we saw froze the blood in our veins. German soldiers, with assistance from the ghetto police, grabbed people off the street and loaded them on to waiting trucks. The first victims were the homeless poor." Finally, on August 10, "[b]efore we left, we were treated to a full-scale traditional pogrom. German, Lithuanian, and Ukrainian soldiers, intoxicated with hate and sadism, went on a spontaneous violent rampage of killing, burning, and looting."[144]

To the east, in their first "sweep" of the occupied Soviet territories, from June 1941 to April 1942, Einsatzgruppen, Gestapo, and other German units had already massacred over 700,000 Jews. A special report to Hitler, signed by Himmler, on the months August–November 1942 alone, lists under "Jews executed" the figure of 363,211. The killing continued to escalate, and the second "sweep" of Soviet Jews is estimated to have murdered 1.5 million more in 1942–43.[145]

On October 5, 1942, Hermann Graebe, manager of a German construction company, visited the site near Dubno in occupied Ukraine where the SS were in the process of murdering the town's 5,000 Jews. Graebe witnessed mass shooting of people wearing "yellow patches on the front and back of their clothing so that they were identifiable as Jews." He recounted:

The people who had got off the lorries—men, women, and children of all ages— had to undress on the orders of an SS man who was carrying a riding or dog whip in his hand. They had to place their clothing on separate piles, for shoes, clothing and underwear. I saw a pile of shoes containing approximately 800– 1,000 pairs, and great heaps of underwear and clothing.

Without weeping or crying out these people undressed and stood together in family groups, embracing each other and saying good-bye while waiting for a sign from another SS man who stood on the edge of the ditch and also had a whip. . . . I walked round the mound and stood in front of the huge grave. The bodies were lying so tightly packed together that only their heads showed, from almost all of which blood ran down over their shoulders. Some were still moving. Others raised their hands and turned their heads to show that they were still alive. The ditch was already three quarters full. I estimate that it already held about a thousand bodies. I turned my eyes towards the man doing the shooting. He was an SS man; he sat, legs swinging, on the edge of the ditch. He had an automatic rifle resting on his knees and was smoking a cigarette. The people, completely naked, climbed down steps which had been cut into the clay wall of the ditch, stumbled over the heads of those lying there and stopped at the spot indicated by the SS man. They lay down on top of the dead or wounded; some stroked those still living and spoke quietly to them. Then I heard a series of rifle shots. I looked into the ditch and saw the bodies contorting or, the heads already inert, sinking on the corpses beneath. Blood flowed from the nape of their necks. I was surprised not to be ordered away, but I noticed three postmen in uniform standing nearby. Then the next batch came up, climbed down into the ditch, laid themselves next to the previous victims and were shot.[146]

The General Plan East, according to Wetzel's April 1942 commentary on it, proposed far-reaching ethnic transformation of the conquered territories by various means, from "eradication" of "the Jewish half-breeds" to "relocation of the racially undesirable foreign ethnics to western Siberia" to "breaking up the ground of the Russian people." Finally, Wetzel proposed "a deliberately negative population policy." In sum, he calculated that anticipated population increases meant that "46 to 51 million individuals would accordingly have to be relocated."[147] Wetzel reported that according to the plan, "80–85 per cent of the Poles . . . or 16–20.4 million Poles will be deported." He suggested that "several million of those Poles who are the most dangerous for us" should be sent to South America, especially Brazil, in exchange for repatriation of South

America's ethnic Germans. However, the "overwhelming number of racially undesirable Poles," including farmers, "must be considered for resettlement in the East" in order to "spread them out" across Siberia. According to the plan, these Polish deportees would be accompanied by 65 percent of the western Ukrainians. Additionally, "75 percent" of the White Russians "will be moved" and half of the Czechs, or "about 3.5 million." As for the Russians, who, Wetzel wrote, "for all practical purposes are not mentioned in the General Plan," he proposed that the Nazis "remove these clans that are racially related to us.... It is a matter of a few million."[148]

According to Wetzel, "the principal task" remained, namely, "to further weaken the Russian character." His report noted a number of possible measures to achieve this. He cited the recent research of Prof. Dr. Wolfgang Abel, commissioned by the Wehrmacht high command, which had concluded that "the Russians contain far stronger Nordic racial traits than had been supposed until now." Worse, "the Russian nation is biologically far stronger than the German people," indicating "a particular danger the Russians pose for the future of our people." Wetzel specified "the biological danger represented by the enormous fertility of these primitive people" and reported: "Abel saw only the following solutions: Either the extermination of the Russian people, or, on the other hand, the Germanization of the Nordically determined parts of the Russian people." Wetzel considered Abel's proposal for "liquidating the Russian ethnic character" to be "not feasible." He instead proposed, first, "breaking up" Russia into separate territories: Siberia, and central, east, and north Russia, with "no central authority in Moscow," even in a Moscow under German rule. In line with the plan's proposed deportation of 31 million people to the east, Wetzel recommended weakening Russia by "pumping non-Russian elements into that region," for example, "moving the White Ruthenians to the Ural region or the northern Caucasus regions that might in part be included in the European settlement reservations" and sending into Siberia "Walloon engineers," Czech farmers, workers, and technicians, "Hungarian industrial purchasing agents, and the like," thereby "making a resurgence of the Russian people impossible."[149]

Second, Wetzel proposed measures to achieve "the racial exhaustion of the Russian ethnic character," such as removing its talented "Nordic clans" and Germanizing them. This would also help Germany, he argued. Even if German birthrates rose with increased agricultural settlements, Wetzel warned that "we will always be forced—if only for the healthy instinct to want to remain a world power—to supply our national body with the Nordic racial elements of other peoples." Thus Germany "must also fall back on Nordic clans of the eastern peoples," such as "the more or less Nordic looking types" of Russian POWs "descended from the still healthy Russian agricultural population." Just as "the Bolsheviks base their entire force on this peasantry," Wetzel thought the Nazis should make use of them, too (see fig. 30).

Third, Wetzel argued for "the destruction of a people's biological strength." In the interests of "weakening the Russian national body," Germany should encourage Russians to employ contraceptives, abortion, and sterilization and to raise small families. Moreover, it should allow more Russian children to die. "Infant mortality must not be combated. Nor can there be any education of mothers concerning infant care and childhood diseases." Russian medical training should be minimal, with no support provided for orphanages.

Finally, the plan also envisaged "the return" of all the long-standing ethnic German communities of Ukraine, Crimea, and elsewhere in the USSR to designated eastern "settlement regions" reserved for Germans. Wetzel feared, however, that it would be difficult to convince people to leave Germany for these regions: "[T]he idea of resettling in the East is not popular with the large mass of the Germans." He recommended supplementing Germany's Reich Hereditary Farm Law by offering to "descendants of the testator who are not the principal heir" some land in the east, "free of charge and in more than sufficient size." Such land would be awarded only to "farmers' sons who are free of hereditary diseases."[150] Blood and soil continued hand in hand. Heinrich Himmler provisionally approved the General Plan East in June 1942. He further demanded a more specific "Overall Settlement Plan" and escalated the program to include "the total Germanization of Estonia and Latvia," along with Poland, "in no more than twenty years" and the "total resettlement" of Lithuania's population (see fig. 31).[151]

Sixteen-year-old Roma Nutkiewicz of Warsaw, separated from her parents and young brother the previous year as the Nazis emptied the Warsaw ghetto, arrived on May 3, 1943, in an overcrowded train wagon at the Majdanek extermination camp. She did not yet know that her father, mother, and brother had already met their deaths there:

> Someone opened the sliding doors from outside, and for a second the sudden light blinded me. The Germans, however, did not allow us any time to collect ourselves. Immediate yells in German echoed: "Schnell! Schnell! Runter!" [Quick! Quick! Down!] We jumped down from the train. Left behind were some corpses, but none of us turned back to see who had died during the journey....
> At the moment of disembarking, the women and men were separated. Uncle

Abraham turned to check on us, and a German soldier pushed him roughly. He fell to the ground, and the German began to beat him mercilessly. Abraham bled from wounds all over his body. Much as we wanted to help, we were too afraid to approach him. He managed to get up and run with the other men in the direction of the men's camp. It was the last time I saw my uncle.

The women were chased into the women's camp, where we went through our first selection. My aunt and I passed the first selection and were sent to the right. We were led into a hall and told to take off all our clothes except our shoes. We stood in line for the shower. On both sides German soldiers patrolled, looking for more candidates for extermination. It was a horrible sight: young soldiers smacked naked women around, forcing them to run to their deaths; the women, shamed by their nudity, rather than protest or resist, devoted all their energies to trying to cover as much of their private parts as they could with their arms. My aunt suddenly pushed into my hand my uncle's big gold watch and told me to put it in my shoe. She was barely done speaking when a German soldier grabbed her by the hair and pulled her outside the line to send her to the gas chamber. Before I could comprehend what had happened, she was gone.[152]

At the very height of this slaughter, Nazi ideologues remained preoccupied not only with war and genocide but also with racial theorizing, antiquity, and agrarianism. The February 1943 issue of *Volk und Rasse* (People and Race), a Munich journal edited by SS Standartenführer B. K. Schultz of Himmler's Central Office of Race and Resettlements, combined a detailed report on "Two Racial-Science Studies in the General Government" with two articles on the other major Nazi ideological themes. First, Heinrich Gottong investigated "the confusing variety of the racial nature of the population" in Poland. He asserted that Poles had long subjected local ethnic Germans to "the processes of selection, which occurred in the aftermath of the military and political encounters between the individual ethnic and power groups and which were intended to destroy the leading strata," a fate that "in its most extreme form" Poles had supposedly imposed on local Germans. However, after studying small sample groups of Polish and German men, measuring and extensively tabulating numerous physical traits such as "eye color, head index, face index, and overall height," Gottong reported: "What is remarkable are the long, widely extending shape of the back of the head among the largest part of the German group. But since a considerable width of the head is observed the index seems disproportionately high." Gottong thought his calculations could point to a welcome "predominance of the Dalo-Nordic race." He deduced that the German population in Poland had satisfactorily "held on to its culture, and its national consciousness was able to effectively withstand the danger of absorbing foreign blood and race elements." Indeed, such positive "selection," the article concluded, "could come about only on the basis of the Dalo-Nordic race."[153]

The other two articles in that same issue of *Volk und Rasse* pursued the complementary Nazi preoccupations with history, expansion, and agriculture. In "Romans and Germans," H. Rübel explained that "the ancient Germans were farmers who lived on the products of their fields and their barns" until the legions marched in, "crushed the seedlings, ravaged the fields, and had the harvest burned." This partial conquest had introduced into Germany the "races of the Roman racial chaos," the empire's mixture of "all the peoples of the Mediterranean," which soon "fused together on German soil, giving birth to a racial broth." Germany then might have gone the way of France, which was later "totally Romanized and the Nordic race within its borders became entirely extinct or was exterminated." However, the German warrior chief Arminius, resisting "the lure of a foreign culture and decadent civilization," had heroically challenged the Romans "in open battle, man to man, and destroyed their entire army."[154]

Having been "freed once and for all of the danger of Romanization," Germany was eventually in a position to pursue its own expansion. In "German Farmers in the Ukraine," published in the same 1943 issue of *Volk und Rasse*, the author, Otto Kolar, romanticized about "one of the most emotional moments for a German soldier." On a recent visit to a Ukrainian village, he had found "Germans whose ancestors left their homeland about two hundred years ago" to embark on "a truly enormous colonial achievement." By 1914, these Germans numbered 524,000 and "were already tilling an area of 5,350,000 hectares!" Even after two centuries, including "systematic extermination" under Soviet rule, these farmers "were able to keep their blood pure to this day," preserving German culture and language in "a brilliant cultural performance" based on a mere "fairytale memory of home." The Nazi visitor came upon "an old farmer" who was "leaning against the doorframe of the small, clean farmhouse—I thought myself transported back into a German landscape! I saw this image—I saw Germany before my eyes! . . . His shining eyes filled with tears—which seemed to say to me, It is good that you have come—at long last!" (see figs. 32–33).[155] In this ideological context of territorial expansion based on claims of ethnic antiquity and agricultural superiority, attributing extermination to ancient and modern enemies could justify genocide now. The Nazis' industrialized murder of Jews in the USSR and Eastern Europe continued to the bitter end.

A small group of a dozen former German settlers in East Africa, coming in search of "their own, newer acres in the enlarged Germany," took up farming in the annexed Polish territory of the Warthegau. In September 1943, a German newspaper in Lodz hailed the newcomers as "precious German blood from far outside the gates of the German Reich," people who had found "the extended land of the future of German settlement." The newspaper reported that one of these settlers, Heinz Grosse, a man "of farming blood and trained as a farmer" who "wanted to be a free man on free soil," had spent 12 years as a coffee planter in Africa before taking up a 2,000-acre property in the Warthegau. Grosse had arrived there to discover "all the inadequacies of the Polish period," including "the famished soil" and an "immediate need for farm improvements," since "almost all the barns and stables lacked light and air." Grosse then set about "thoroughly cleansing the fields" and updated their cultivation with new crops. He built a large cowshed and for the pigs, "new, brightly lit, and warm sties." According to the newspaper, "The farmstead has an inviting appearance between the white birches and green fir trees." The author wrote that the trunks of the birch trees "gleam in the sun" on this large property, "handsomely situated" and "ornamented with a green frame, with its own forest." Here in this sylvan Eden, Grosse had ordered the planting of 250,000 trees. Tired of single-crop agriculture, he "no longer felt any longing for the tropics." Rather, the paper concluded: "Here, in the reconstruction of the East . . . the farmer could engage in real versatility, he could still perform truly pioneer work in every area."[156] This was a new, empty land of opportunity.

The next month, speaking to SS leaders on October 4, 1943, Heinrich Himmler, architect of the Holocaust, secretly confirmed to them what he termed "the extermination of the Jewish people. It's one of those things which are easy to talk about. 'The Jewish people will be exterminated,' says every party comrade, 'It's clear, it's in our programme.' . . . We had the moral right, we had the duty to our people, to destroy this people which wanted to destroy us." Two days later, Himmler continued, as recorded on tape: "I do not consider myself justified in eradicating the men—so to speak killing or ordering them killed—and allowing the avengers in the shape of the children to grow up for our sons and grandsons. The difficult decision had to be taken, to cause this *Volk* [people] to disappear from the earth."[157] Himmler now extended this murderous Nazi policy toward Jews by applying some of the same language to Russians: "What happens to a Russian or a Czech does not interest me in the slightest. . . . Whether 10,000 Russian females fall down from exhaustion while digging an anti-tank ditch interests me only in so far as the anti-tank ditch for Germany is finished. . . . I wish the SS to adopt this attitude to the problem of all foreign, non-Germanic peoples, especially Russians."[158] Approximately 3.3 million Russian prisoners of war died or were killed in German hands during World War II. The total death toll of Soviet citizens in the Nazi war of aggression is estimated at around 27 million.[159]

The mass murder of Jews also accelerated as the war ground on. In July 1943, 16-year-old Roma Nutkiewicz left the Majdanek extermination camp on another German train transport, to spend the next 19 months in the Auschwitz-Birkenau complex. That October, Heinz Schulz, the commander of the crematorium there, assigned Nutkiewicz and nine other girls to work in the "Canada" labor camp commando along with Polish, Slovakian, and Greek Jewish women. She later recalled: "Every morning three hundred inmates of commando Canada marched in rows of five out of Birkenau's Lager B to the music of a band. Just before we reached the gate, on our right, we passed the children's block. We saw their frightened, sad faces glued to the shack's windows. We knew what lay ahead for them. Indeed, keeping them alive for a few days was the height of cruelty. Rather than letting the kids die in their parents' arms, the Germans made them go through the pain of separation, see their parents disgraced or killed, experience a few days of brutality, humiliation, and starvation, and then end up nevertheless in the gas chamber and crematorium." Every day, Nutkiewicz wrote, supervisors reminded the laborers "that we would end up as the same white smoke we saw puffing out of the crematorium's chimneys. One of the German officers said, in a rather empathetic tone, that he hoped they would have enough gas to kill us when it was our turn to die, because otherwise they would have to just daze us and then take us to the crematorium and burn us alive." Eight of the other nine girls in her unit perished in the gas chambers or from illness.[160]

The slaughter of Hungarian Jews took place in the final year of the war. Nazi forces killed as many as half a million people following the direct German takeover of Hungary in March 1944.[161] Auschwitz commandant Rudolf Höss testified two years later: "The largest number of people gassed and cremated within twenty-four hours was somewhat over 9,000. This figure was achieved in the summer of 1944 during the action in Hungary." Only at the end of November, as Soviet forces closed in on Auschwitz and the looming German defeat sparked secret negotiations between the Nazis and the Allies, did Himmler order an end to the gassings at Auschwitz-Birkenau and destruction of the machinery there, after it had killed 1 million of the approximately 5.3 million Jewish victims of the Nazi Holocaust.[162]

History's most extreme case of genocide is clearly unique in several ways. A state-sponsored attempt at total extermination by industrialized murder of unarmed millions has no parallel before or since. The wholesale destruction of the Jews, and the invasions of most of Europe and the USSR that made it possible, required an advanced economy and a heavily armed modern state. Yet the Nazi killing machine also had a more antiquated power source. It was operated by interlocking ideological levers that celebrated race, territory, cultivation, and history.

CHAPTER 12

Rice, Race, and Empire

Japan and East Asia

A victory for the Nazi regime in World War II is unlikely to have ended its race wars. Germany's distant search for "Nordic clans" even among "eastern peoples" stemmed from the perception of an eventual threat posed by its Axis ally, Imperial Japan. In 1942, the Nazi official Erhard Wetzel predicted that the "self-determination of the numerically strong Asian people after this war" would then confront Germany with Japanese power. "A Greater Asia and an independent India are formations that dispose over hundreds of millions of inhabitants. A German world power with 80 or 85 million Germans by contrast is numerically too weak." Ensuring Nazi Germany's supremacy in Europe, Wetzel wrote, required restricting Russian families to one or two children, but this only created a new dilemma: "How far we thus weaken the white race in view of the dangers from Asia."[1] Himmler warned the next year that "battles of destiny against Asia" will "certainly break out again."[2] The contenders were well matched. In Asia from 1931 to 1945, Japanese militaristic expansion caused up to 20 million civilian deaths.[3]

The first signs of this eventual catastrophe may have been an outbreak of terrorism that struck Japan in 1859–60. In five surprise attacks, independent samurai bands killed four European sailors, the secretary to the American legation, and one of the Japanese shogun's top ministers. Then one night in 1861, 14 samurai brandishing long swords stormed the British legation. Before they were driven off, the attackers killed two guards, wounding 10 others and two English officials. The legation "looked as if it had been sacked after a serious conflict," with "furniture and bedding all hacked, books even cut through

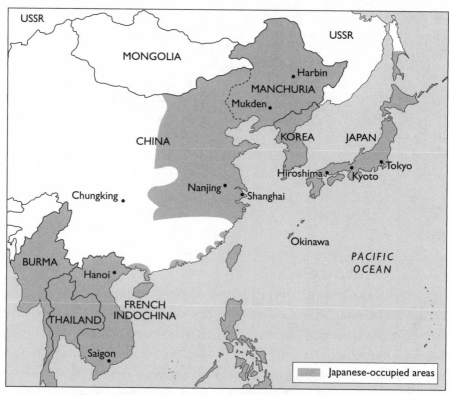

MAP 24. Japan and East Asia, 1931–45

by the sabers." The assailants, pursued by the shogun's troops, all committed suicide or were killed. The next year, another warrior mounted a second assault on the legation, killing two British soldiers before committing suicide. A few months later, a procession of 300 Japanese came upon four English civilians, including a woman. A single samurai suddenly stripped to the waist, drew his sword, and charged, hacking at the English. One man, "nearly cut to pieces, fell from his horse," dead. In 1864, a samurai band slashed two English officers to death. The wave of terrorism by these "men of spirit" (*shishi*), aiming to "revere the emperor and expel the barbarians" (*sonno jōi*), subsided only in 1868, when a new Meiji regime, itself determined to "overthrow the shogunate system and to expel barbarians," seized power and ended the entire Tokugawa era (1600–1868).[4]

The architects of the Meiji reform program called it a "Restoration" of the "ancient imperial system" (*kodai ōchō*), based now on the emperor instead of the shogun. But this was no xenophobic return to a past indigenous model. The

Meiji oligarchs quickly created a polity unprecedented in Japan, based on German advice and a Prussian model, with an important exception. They carefully drew upon early Japanese history to present the new imperial system, in the words of Emiko Ohnuki-Tierney, "as if it had existed since ancient times."[5]

Against an early-nineteenth-century backdrop of anti-Chinese nativist feeling in Japan and European encroachments in East Asia, the shogun's treaties with five Western nations in 1858 had shocked future reformers and samurai terrorists alike. They saw this as "a humiliating assault upon Japan's sovereignty and national power." Ten years later, the Meiji reformers set out with a remedy, to industrialize and militarize Japan.[6] They would achieve this in part by establishing a new proto-totalitarian imperial authority, modernizing the military and abolishing the age-old samurai caste in 1874, even as they reached further back into the country's past to highlight the appearance of "restoration." For that purpose they emphasized the ancient figure of the emperor and the importance of agriculture, which both became key ideological features of Japan's new expanding imperial, militarist political system. Over time, traditional agrarian ideology intensified in reaction to industrialization, yet it also merged with military expansionism and eventually recast a role for new samurai.

At first, however, modernization and westernization advanced to the distinct martial drumbeats of a new past and an alien nativism. In their first decree, the Meiji officials proposed to return to the "events of antiquity."[7] In 1869, they inaugurated the Yasukuni shrine to "Call Back the Souls" of those who had fallen in the war to oust the shogunate the year before. Excluding the country's existing religious leadership from the ceremony, the army appointed a new "Military High Priest," who stressed loyalty to the emperor. Universal conscription began two years later. The Japanese military gradually achieved dominance by deploying its own new, unique constitutional access to the emperor as its commander in chief.[8]

Emperor, Antiquity, and Agriculture

The new Meiji Constitution of 1889 promoted the emperor from one of many deities in the Japanese pantheon to a new divine status as Almighty God. It created a novel obligation of loyalty to the emperor. Along with his new sacredness, inviolability, and command of the armed forces, the Manual of the Imperial Household, promulgated with the constitution, spelled out his "infi-

nite" antiquity: "The emperor belongs to one line for eternity." Ohnuki-Tierney
notes that this "assigned primordiality also to Japan and all Japanese," who were
now considered "one family" with the emperor. The Meiji reintroduction of archaic terminology, retrieved from ancient documents, such as "Manifest Deity"
(dating from 720 C.E.), reinforced this new cult of antiquity. The ambiguous
traditional religious concept of a "human-deity" (*hitogami*) acquired stark
new meaning: "the emperor as God in human form." The new constitution and
other Meiji documents employed these archaic terms, which also appeared in
new school textbooks and songs. Japanese schoolchildren now had to memo-
rize the names of all past emperors, beginning with Japan's legendary founder,
whose dispatch by the Sun Goddess and subsequent imperial accession were
set at 2,600 years ago and were reenacted annually from 1872.[9]

The German adviser Lorenz von Stein, finding Japan lacking an institution
like Christianity, suggested introducing a "substitute" for religion. Creating
a new state Shintoism, the imperial household took control of 170,000 local
shrines. In 1870, as the Rising Sun emblem became the national flag, an imperial edict banned "foreign religions," which had "plagued" Japan since medieval times, targeting Buddhism, Confucianism, and Christianity, persecution
of which began again in 1891. By 1906, the new state religious monopoly officially recognized only one shrine in each Japanese village. Overriding widespread progressive opposition, the policy succeeded in implanting its new concept of antiquity even in the minds of critics, who accepted the authenticity of
this proclaimed heritage. A liberal historian, for instance, opposed Shintoism
as being old-fashioned, rather than innovative in form, while the influential
Christian Ebina Danjō (1856–1937) denounced it as "primitive" and "chau-
vinistic."[10]

The Meiji regime glorified agriculture along with antiquity. A division of
"lower-class warriors, farmers," merchants, and outcastes had played a key role
in the 1868 victory over the shogunate. Now, extending his traditional role as
guarantor of the rice crop, the emperor made semiannual imperial tours in
which he "watched peasants in the field in order to demonstrate his appreciation of their toils." Meiji officials deliberately resurrected ancient terms and
titles for the emperor, used by peasant border guards in eighth-century poetry.
The indigenous preimperial title *kimi* became the first word of the new Japanese national anthem. Meiji officials also coined terms for their soldiers and
the imperial army by adopting ancient vocabulary from these poems.[11]

Meiji agrarian ideology grew on traditional ground, more solid than the claims made for Japanese antiquity. "Agriculture is the root, manufacture and commerce are the branches," wrote an eighteenth-century sage.[12] The pre-1868 legal hierarchy had placed farmers above both manufacturers and merchants, just below the samurai warrior caste. Japanese already ascribed to their non-agricultural minorities, the Ainu and outcastes, "innate" qualities approaching a "beastly nature," consigning them to "abominable" occupations like butchering, and even excluding them from history. Some Japanese considered native rice varieties superior to Chinese ones, as a sign of the superiority of Japan's people. Rice had long become the symbol of Japanese identity; even the cherry blossom embodied the Deity of Rice Paddies, who represented the ancestors. One eighteenth-century emperor ate only rice, refusing even other grains. The imperial household prohibited consumption of meat, which came to be associated with Westerners. Even after the Meiji lifted the ban on meat, some continued to claim that rice agriculture demonstrated Japanese superiority, while others mocked the adoption of a more Western diet. Meat did become popular but was renamed; horse meat acquired an association with rice by being called "cherry blossoms."[13]

The continued hegemony of agriculture was not at all surprising. Before 1868, the urban industrial sector was small. In the capital, workers were outnumbered by samurai, who composed nearly half of the city's 1 million inhabitants.[14] In 1903, 79 percent of Japanese still lived in communities of fewer than 10,000 people.[15] However, as industry and commerce expanded, the ideological identification of the small farmer with Japanese tradition heightened the sense of threat to the countryside. A leading Meiji conservative warned in 1884 against neglect of rural areas: "Agriculture is the foundation of the family and the foundation of the country."[16] Denouncing the speed of industrialization, agronomist Yokoi Tokiyoshi coined the Japanese term "agrarianism" (*nōhonshugi*) in an 1897 essay of that title. He feared that "the pitiful farmers will gradually be oppressed by the urban rich." Yokoi added: "The vitality of a country . . . is particularly well developed among farm families," who also provided the best military recruits, he argued in a vein familiar elsewhere.[17] It took a dissident writer to lament that "poets and novelists . . . tend to treat the city as a sink of iniquity and exalt the hamlet as paradise incarnate." Agrarianism spread with urbanization.[18] The 1890s term "mainstay owner-farmers" (*chūken jisakunō*) enshrined an emerging cult of the supposedly threatened yeoman cultivator.[19] Farming remained "the economic cornerstone of the nation," and rural landlordism spread slowly. While the 1898 civil code favored landlords over tenants, and the government attempted to increase the size of farm units, most remained small-scale. Diverse opposition blocked official plans to develop large farms.[20]

A second large-scale Meiji agricultural program enjoyed more success, in combination with a new expansionism: ethnic Japanese settlement of the northern island of Hokkaido. This began early, with the creation of the Hokkaido Colonization Board in 1869. Massive Japanese farmer-settler immigration quickly dispossessed the island's ethnic Ainu people, who were also devastated by disease and poverty. The Ainu population fell from a 95 percent majority in Hokkaido in 1873 to only 22 percent of the island's inhabitants in 1897. By the time of Japan's military victories over China in 1894–95 and then Russia in 1904–5, the Hokkaido program had set a precedent for further expansion into Korea and China.[21] The cult of antiquity played a continuing role. "Asia is one," wrote a Japanese historian in *The Ideals of the East* (1902), and Japan "is the museum of Asiatic civilization."[22]

Military aggression abroad went hand in hand with domestic and agricultural expansion. As early as 1874, Japan sent troops to Taiwan, imposing colonial rule there in 1895.[23] After an 1876 landing in Korea, Japanese forces put down the Tonghak peasant rebellion there in 1894, at a cost of 50,000 lives, including mass killings ordered by Imperial Army Headquarters in Hiroshima. In the same year, Japan's agriculture minister urged the dispatch of farmers overseas to relieve pressure on the land at home.[24]

Tokyo adopted a policy of "reentry into Asia." In 1909, the foreign minister proposed sending 1 million Japanese settlers to Manchuria. After Japan's annexation of Korea the next year, a Japanese intellectual gushed, "[N]ow Korea has room for ten million immigrants and Formosa two million." Over the next two decades half a million Japanese settled in Korea, and over 10,000 became landlords there.[25] The Japanese rulers put down the Mansei rebellion in 1919, killing nearly 8,000 Koreans and jailing 50,000.[26] One expansionist, who assumed Japan's sole right to move into "vacant" lands, selectively complained of *Chinese* who "ignore" others' prior claims to ownership of Korean land. He asserted indignantly that "Chinese have moved into the wastelands of Korea and are farming them without permission. When we voice protests against it, they think that there is nothing wrong with entering empty lands and farming them, and they believe that absolute rights belong to the users of the land."[27] The implication was that Japan alone could assume such rights.

Idealizing the Peasantry

As capitalist land concentration progressed in Japan, the number of independent Japanese peasant farmers declined. The state began trying to bolster small
agricultural landowners as the backbone of both traditional rural society and
the army. Historian Thomas Havens writes that the "anxiety about the fate of
village Japan" soon spread far beyond state circles. Together, both rapid industrial development and the reaction against it only strengthened an emerging
totalitarian militarism. In an 1899 English-language work, a Japanese official
launched a new concept, the "warrior's way," or *bushidō*, with the statement:
"Chivalry (*bushidō*) is a flower no less indigenous to the soil of Japan than its
emblem, the cherry blossom."[28] An official of the Imperial Agricultural Association deplored the loss of "self-rule" on the part of "the dignified, self-
respecting villages which form the foundation of our Japanese empire."[29] In
1900, an influential Meiji figure urged that "men of rank and wealth spend a
part of the year in the country" and that they should "cultivate pastoral tastes
as in England." A few years later, another agrarianist, describing farmers as "the
mother of a rich nation and a strong army," held up the model of George Washington's return to his farm after victory, like Cincinnatus of ancient Rome.[30]
The major magazine of the now proliferating rural "virtue" societies lauded
Theodore Roosevelt as an "agricultural reformer," along with the Tokugawa
agricultural moralist, Ninomiya Sontoku. Monthly rural meetings discussed
Sontoku's teachings and "methods of cultivation." In Japanese elementary
school textbooks from 1910 to 1945, the two models most often cited were Sontoku and the Meiji emperor.[31]

Thus the intellectual foundations for war and genocide slowly crystallized.
As in Germany, agrarianists increasingly targeted urban society. Yokoi Tokiyoshi wrote: "Cities are extremely weak in their ability to produce their own
population." The towns, he added, "depend on the country," without which
"cities would be bound to collapse."[32] In a major essay published in 1904 entitled "Respecting Japanese Agriculture," another prominent agronomist,
Kawakami Hajime, opposed Japan's burgeoning urbanization, urging farmers
not "to abandon their precious occupations or leave the priceless fields of their
ancestors." He asserted that "most people who argue in favour of emphasizing
agriculture do so because of its relationship with the military, public order, or
hygiene" rather than for economic reasons. To this Kawakami added the tra-

ditional Confucian physiocratic argument: "[C]ommerce . . . is the branch and agriculture the root." In his view, "the existence of rural people is the foundation of a nation's wealth and strength," and he blamed "our continued suffering" on the decreasing number of farmers. Though a pacifist at the time, Kawakami shared the view that "agriculture is the wellspring of a strong army. . . . Because brute force is necessary, we must also preserve agriculture."[33]

Agrarian thinking proved highly compatible with both imperial nationalism and the official cult of antiquity. Kawakami's later career as a famous Marxist only underlines the extensive appeal of agrarianism after 1900. From pacifists to authoritarian militarists, from romantics glorifying the premodern village to officials who saw agriculture protecting the nation while industry developed it, from those who idealized local autonomy or communalism to others who called for modern producers' cooperatives—Japan, as Havens puts it, became "rife with farm thinkers." Prominent novelists lamented "the decline of the village spirit." One even pioneered utopian "new villages" where Japanese could "fulfill our destinies without need of money."[34] Yokota Hideo, a leading conservative journalist at the *Yomiuri shinbun,* wrote in 1914: "[T]he brilliance of our national essence, which all lands should envy, is that it is maintained by the farmers. . . . The most important thing our farm villages produce are the silent apostles of nationalism. . . . Our two-thousand-year-long history is the history of one great family, with the imperial throne at the center. Thus the farmers are truly the creators of this brilliant history." Japan, Yokota later wrote, "is uniquely classless in all the world, an ideal country unique in all history."[35] He added in a 1917 *Yomiuri* article: "[T]he land is the thing closest to nature. The land is the most powerful thing . . . the source of all life."[36]

However, by then the Japanese state was no longer actively encouraging village self-sufficiency. After about 1905, officials adopted a laissez-faire approach, while new politicians replaced the old Meiji oligarchs, and Japan's annexations of Korea and Taiwan opened the country to increasing rice imports and competition for Japanese farmers. As Carol Gluck writes, the countryside seemed "besieged." The *Tokyo asahi* newspaper pronounced in 1911: "The spiritual blow caused by the destruction of the owner-farmers who constitute the middle class is so profound it is frightening."[37] By 1914, capitalism and class polarization were threatening Yokota Hideo's vision: "Ever since the impoverishment of the self-cultivating farmer class, the owner-farmers have fallen." As a result, "the farmer's life today" had become that of "an animal, not a man." Yokota restated his ideal in stressing the danger to it: "Who can speak of the natural harmony of the farm villages? Who says that the villages are gardens of flowers?" Instead, a future loomed of "large landlords with agricultural laborers clustered around them like ants."[38]

Even worse from this viewpoint, from 1900 to 1917, the Japanese factory workforce almost tripled, to 1 million industrial laborers. Working-class consciousness rose. By 1910, the government saw a "contagious epidemic" of socialist "infection," which had to be "eradicated" at its "roots." Commentators described cities as a "destructive force in society" and denounced them as the "Rome" that would bring Japan's own imperial decline.[39] For Yokota, writing in 1914, the prospect of socialism heralded "a fearful national crisis."[40] The League of Nations' postwar rejection of Japan's request for a founding statement on "racial equality" only stoked Japanese national feeling, yet insufficiently for nationalists like Yokota, who apparently saw it as simply vindicating his lament for the "demise of patriotism."[41]

The economic threat escalated after World War I. The wartime sixfold increase in manufacturing output was followed by both industrial retrenchment and low farm prices, with agricultural recession and crises lasting into the mid-1930s. Rural society seemed more threatened than ever. The Japan Landlords' Association, founded in 1925, immediately declared: "Agriculture is the foundation of the state," but "the farm villages have at last lapsed into an economic and spiritual crisis."[42] Worse lay ahead. The price of rice fell 44 percent from 1926 to 1931. Silk prices dropped by two-thirds. From a 308-yen annual surplus in 1925, the average farm household registered a 77-yen deficit by 1930. The next year's farm prices fell to only 40 percent of the 1920 level, and average rural debt rose to 830 yen per household. This was a dramatic blow to a country with one of the highest proportions of employment in agriculture (lower only than British India and Finland). Farming and fishing, which had accounted for 55 percent of Japan's workers in 1920, employed only 44 percent in 1940, despite the industrial depression that in 1932 forced many urban workers back to the land.[43]

The deteriorating climate slowly forced the state to take increasing measures to protect farmers and foster owner-cultivation. Japan became a democracy, and tenants obtained the vote in 1925. The next year, the government passed modest regulations to help some establish themselves as owner-farmers. The regulations had little effect, but small-scale cultivators still represented about one-quarter of Japan's farm households; the average farm size was just above one hectare, and one-third of all cultivators worked farms less than half that size. The continuing economic threat made the ideological climate increasingly receptive to a new hybrid of agrarian and nationalist thinking, and these political strands began to merge.[44]

Tenancy disputes soared. From only 256 in 1918, the number rose tenfold to nearly 2,500 in 1930.[45] Violence peaked in 1930, with reports of 175 violent incidents and 1,000 arrests. Even the large landlord-oriented Imperial Agricultural Association felt the influence of owner-cultivator agrarianism as well as nationalism. Its secretary wrote in 1929: "Agriculture in our country has the family system as its base. . . . Family-managed farming, i.e. the small-farm system, promotes and nurtures the broad spirit of protecting the *kokutai* [national essence]." Landlords and tenants, he claimed, "have been chased into the same net" and were "wrenched just as much" by industrial and commercial capitalism. Rural-urban lines of conflict were drawn.[46]

Romantic agrarian theories of scholars like Gondō Seikyō (1868–1937) fueled the new aggressive nationalism. Seikyō's father, a masterless samurai (*ronin*), had first pursued the family tradition by studying history, then took up European medicine, befriended the future Meiji agriculture minister, and pioneered scientific farming once the new regime let samurai choose their occupations. His son Gondō grew up on the family farm and studied the Confucian classics. The combination of agriculture, tradition, and nationalism eventually led to expansionist thinking. From age 18, Gondō spent several years in China and Korea, then left his pregnant wife to spend six years in a Nagasaki temple. In 1902, he joined the staff of the new Amur River Society, an anti-Russian lobby group that advocated Japan's continental Asian interests. The Ministry of War and military officers began turning to Gondō for advice and lectures on China, and he became founding editor of the society's journal *East Asia Monthly*. Revisiting Korea in 1906, he advocated its amalgamation into a unified Japanese-Korean empire, with local "self-rule" on the traditional farm village model.[47]

After Japan's annexation of Korea in 1910, Gondō turned to stock breeding and lecturing on early history. Sensationally, he followed up his 1920 work *Basic Principles of Imperial People's Self-Rule* by publishing a purported seventh-century Japanese manuscript, *The Book of Nan'en*. Now considered a premodern forgery, the manuscript describes an idyllic early Japanese rural society and its mythical expansion into Korea. Gondō drew heavily from this text in his major works, including *People's Guide to Self-Rule* (1927). His Self-Rule Study Society became well known. Gondō lectured on Japanese history at a prestigious academy and often addressed audiences concerned about rural relief.[48] His history combined antiquity, race, and a fetish for agriculture. In Gondō's view, ancient Asian societies were based on peasant agriculture, in contrast to classical Western states, which he claimed had emerged from pastoral societies. In another series of works on ancient Japan published in the aftermath of World War I, the Kyoto philosopher Watsuji Tetsuro glorified the original creative spirit of Yamato—a classical name for the Japanese people based on the state's putative divine founding at Yamato in 660 B.C.E. He saw parallels between Japan and ancient Greece, which he said was destroyed by Roman "materialism," with America now following in Rome's footsteps.[49]

The post–World War I agrarian crisis thus coincided with a new wave of intense nationalism based on claims of the unique ethnic spirit of the Japanese people. Rural, racial, antiquarian, and idealist strands of thought intertwined in powerful new ways, attracting widespread appeal by "yoking farm and nation" to sentiments of ethnic roots. This combination was a recipe for political violence. In his 1922 work "Revolutionary Europe and Renascent Asia," the scholar Ōkawa Shūmei rejected the notion of "the white man's burden" as an insult to the "yellow races." Praising the "Japanese spirit" and denouncing modernity as both a "prison" and a "hospital," Shūmei went on to urge "cleansing" by terror. Violence had already burst onto the political scene. Radical restorationists assassinated the Japanese prime minister in 1921, launching a series of terrorist incidents that would claim the lives of two more prime ministers in the 1930s. The radicals explicitly invoked Japan's sixteenth-century unification (see chapter 3), identifying it as a precedent in which the "lower overthrew the upper."[50] When a virulent "agricultural fascism" appeared in Japan in 1927, it, too, quickly linked up with intellectuals. In the 1930s the "Japan Romantic School" launched its journal with what it called a "farewell to realism" and the aim "to wage war" against literary modernism and naturalism.[51]

Agrarianism and Violence

The emerging coalition also drew upon a dashing militaristic tradition, now imbued with new energy. An officer at the Army Staff College later recalled practicing his horsemanship one afternoon in the 1920s. "I saw a young captain mount his steed and, lashing his whip, take off for the riding grounds at nearly full gallop. Normally a rider starts out at a walk and gradually works up to a trot and then a canter . . . I was astounded at the unconventional approach of

that dauntless officer." The horseman was Captain Chō Isamu, launching his
20-year military career of aggression and terror.[52]

Militarism gradually acquired a new insurgent intellectual foundation that
paraded as Japanese tradition. Gondō Seikyō taught from 1927 to 1930 at a private school devoted to the study of East Asian sages and "the spirit of the Japanese people." Aiming "to cite the past in order to awaken the present," Gondō
praised seventh-century Japanese laws that "protected farm production as an
occupation." In contrast, he criticized the Tokugawa era for its "devious merchants" and the Meiji regime for introducing "a strange doctrine of emperor
loyalty" and even "imported" institutions such as "Prussian style nationalism"
and "a European style private property system" that "cut the people off from
the land." That had permitted concentration of landownership, Gondō wrote,
which undermined "our ancient customs," swallowed up small farms, and left
"hardly any surplus timberlands or swamplands." He lamented: "[T]he entire
country has been standardized." Gondō taught that Japan's history, by contrast,
revealed "no concept whatever of state; since antiquity the national essence
of our country has been the system of people's self-rule based on farmers."
His thinking nevertheless assumed imperial expansion: "If the whole world
became a part of the Japanese empire, the concept of the Japanese state would
become unnecessary." Gondō's pupils included military instigators of future
terrorist violence along with "generals, admirals and government officials" who
occasionally attended his talks.[53]

Another prominent agrarianist who lectured to the radical military officers was Tachibana Kōzaburō, also a son of a prosperous former samurai. In
1915, Tachibana formed Kyōdai Mura (Fraternal Village), a small-farm community based on labor "in the warmth of nature and the good earth." His
"utopia," aimed at integrating "earth and devotion," made him famous. In 1929,
Tachibana founded the Aikyōkai, or Community Loving Society, to "rescue the
devastated farm villages." Its founding declaration read: "Back to the Land! . . .
The season for us to rise and risk our fate fighting for the fatherland has come.
. . . For the earth of Japan! Advance! To the farmers' era!"[54]

A crop of new institutions sprang up as agrarianists and militarists slowly
formed an intellectual and activist coalition. A month after launching the
Aikyōkai, Tachibana began to receive visits from a radical priest, Inoue Nisshō,
who founded the Ketsumeidan (Blood Brotherhood). Also in 1929, the future
wartime prime minister, Tōjō Hideki, and other middle-ranking military officers concerned over the new democracy and its reduced role for the armed

forces in politics, formed the Issekikai (One Evening Society) to push for radical reforms. The next year, ultraright military officers formed the Sakurakai (Cherry Blossom Society) to "wash out the bowels of the completely decadent politicians."[55] The Sakurakai's founder, Lieutenant Colonel Hashimoto Kingorō, had served in a diplomatic post in Turkey and was an admirer of the postgenocidal nationalist reforms of Kemal Ataturk.[56] Hashimoto argued that "the pressures of surplus population" now gave Japan just three options: "emigration, advance into world markets, and expansion of territory." Foreign anti-Japanese measures blocked the first two "doors" and left Japan only the third option. Hashimoto was a native of Fukuoka, like his Sakurakai colleague Chō Isamu, the dashing horseman who had so impressed a junior officer.[57]

In his 1930 book *Nōmindō* (The Way of the Farmer), an official of the Imperial Agricultural Association wrote: "There is no great difference between the way of the farmer and the way of the warrior. He who holds a sword is a warrior and he who holds a plough or a hoe is a farmer." In 1931, Tachibana Kōzaburō's new book blamed what he called "financial power" for "the ripening of the national state based on the modern townsman." Mankind had "turned its back on the earth," he claimed, and capitalism "crushes agriculture." Again, supposed origins were determinative: Western societies were urban in origin, Asian civilization was agrarian.[58] "Ever since the beginning," Tachibana protested, "the farmers have been destined to an essential historical position. . . . Without them there is nothing." Only concepts of race and nation, he thought, could combine rural with urban through "the capacity of farmers and city residents to act as a national people" and thus extend communalism to the cities.[59]

Militarists and agrarians alike moved into action. A concatenation of events, only partially coordinated, created conditions for a new 14-year war against China that would cost the lives of 390,000 Japanese soldiers and, historian John Dower estimates, "approximately ten million Chinese war dead."[60] The first moves were domestic. In March 1931, Hashimoto Kingorō of the Cherry Blossom Society and other extremist army officers hatched an abortive plot for a coup in Tokyo. The next month, Tachibana founded the new Community Loving Academy, designed to educate "proper Japanese workers of the earth," along with a youth group whose members he intended "to sacrifice themselves" for the movement based on their "love for the soil." From August, young military officers also regularly attended the academy's lectures.[61]

War was fast approaching. In September 1931, with the backing of some officers in Tokyo, Japan's Kwantung army, stationed on China's South Manchurian Railroad, staged the "Manchurian Incident" that launched Japanese military aggression against China. In Tokyo the next month, Hashimoto and other radical officers in the Cherry Blossom Society hatched a second plot to massacre Japan's prime minister and cabinet and "prevent the government from squandering the fruits of our victory in Manchuria." A ringleader of the conspiracy, the young Major Chō Isamu, swore to go ahead "even if it means that we shall have to threaten the Emperor with a sword." Military superiors suppressed the Tokyo plot but did not punish its leaders. The Tokyo Military Police commander entertained Chō Isamu for a week with "sake and women."[62] The army command quickly transferred Chō to a Kwantung army post in China, where he then helped organize the military occupation of Manchuria.[63] The General Staff disregarded the attempts of successive Japanese prime ministers to limit the Kwantung army's advances there. After clashes with Chinese troops, the army sent planes to bomb China's most densely populated city, Shanghai. While the war slowly expanded, Chō spent two years on an exchange program in the United States.[64]

Japanese intellectual support for the war also crystallized quickly. In November 1931, Tachibana helped launch the Japan Village Rule League, pledged "to overthrow materialistic civilization" and to "establish agrarian culture." Its precepts seemed compatible with those of the ultranationalist journal *Cogito,* inaugurated the next year as the leading outlet of Japan's romantic movement, which its anti-Communist leader described as "the bridge in the night to a new dawn."[65] "The time has come," Tachibana pronounced in a series of lectures to young naval air officers in January 1932, for "the defeat of the materialistic civilization." He urged them "to sweep the earth clean of capitalist domination."[66] New Japanese military expansion would win agrarianist aid.

In his lectures to the officers, Tachibana explained his trajectory from historical interpretation to armed action. First, "Without the land, there are no people in Japan." A new land policy had to be modeled on the "ancient East Asian land system." Social dissension should be rare, he said, because "Japan has a cohesion unparalleled in the rest of the world, centering on the majestic, eternal imperial line." However, in the modern era, Tachibana stated, money had enabled people to "buy and sell things," with the result that "[f]inally they even sell the nation." He sweepingly denounced "all who belong in the leadership stratum" because they "continually dare to act traitorously." Tachibana darkly informed the future terrorists that traitors had few rights: "[H]e who does not love the country is not human." He found it necessary to "remove the existing leadership." On the road to patriotic reform, "we must cut down with a single stroke, in their very shoes, all who betray this path, no matter what important positions they may occupy." Japan needed "an emergency government" made up of "talented men from every quarter."[67]

In this cause, Tachibana told his audience, "you soldiers" could find no better collaborators than "we farmers." In history, only "the unity of agriculture and the military" had allowed Japan to "be herself." Now that eternal essence would "cause the world revolution to open fire." In 1932, eliding agrarianism, race, and expansion, Tachibana was already dreaming aloud of "the historic greater Japan," which could not only "pulverize American power" but also "sweep away" China's government, "liberate India," make Russia cater to its farmers, and "rouse the Germans." A big Japanese army, he said, based on "the soldier-farmer," would act as "a central pillar of world peace."[68]

Gondō Seikyō also enjoyed the height of his influence in 1931 and early 1932. Becoming known as a theoretician of terror, he, too, attracted many of the radical military and naval figures, who came to hear lectures in his house as they planned insurrection. The Blood Brotherhood leader, Inoue Nisshō, described Gondō as an "interesting old man," rather inflexible, "a rare sort of man these days." A thin, frail 63-year-old "with a very prominent nose," Gondō weighed only 90 pounds.[69] But he did not shrink from violence. In early 1932, he lent the conspirators a vacant house for meetings near his home. There, on January 31, Gondō showed them how to kill with a knife. He told the prospective assassins: "[T]he dagger should be held on the hip ready for use with the left hand. Ordinarily people do not do this ... and hence end up letting their victims escape." In separate attacks in February and March, extremist young officers who were members of the Blood Brotherhood murdered two of Japan's financial leaders. Following the first assassination, police interrogated Gondō but pressed no charges. He then sheltered one of the conspirators of the second murder.[70]

Tachibana probably also attended key preparatory meetings for the insurrection but initially remained inactive.[71] After the assassinations, he agreed to join military officers in a coup attempt. Gondō attended planning meetings, too. On May 15, 1932, the military insurrectionists and 11 of Tachibana's Death-Defying Farmers' Band (Nōmin Kesshitai) assassinated Prime Minister Inukai Tsuyoshi. Five days later, Tachibana's followers distributed his January lectures in mimeographed form. With Gondō's help, Tachibana escaped to Manchuria but was later apprehended.[72] In the trial that followed, judges permitted Tachibana and the assassins to make public declarations from the courtroom, where they often lamented the "plight of the peasants," winning considerable sympathy.[73]

Agrarianism and Expansion

The 1932 Tokyo military insurrections effectively ended political party rule in Japan. They entrenched the power not only of the armed forces but increasingly, of radical expansionists.[74] Pressure was already building. In May, the month of the coup attempt, the academic journal *Shakai seisaku jihō* published a special issue, "Manchurian Migration," including one article by a member of the House of Peers raising the possibility of sending "a trillion" Japanese emigrants there. Other articles blamed overpopulation for making Japan "putrid, like stagnant water" and urging emigration to "purify" it; another was entitled "A Practical Proposal on Emigrating Farm Labor to Manchuria." The year 1932 saw the publication of 107 new scholarly articles on Japanese resettlement in Manchuria. Two months before the May coup, the Finance Ministry had blocked proposals for mass colonization, but in June it relented and released a research budget for the policy. A pilot emigration plan won cabinet approval in August. That same month, the Kwantung army in Manchuria established the new puppet state of Manchukuo, and Tokyo began funding the annual emigration there of 500–1,000 Japanese households. After the League of Nations condemned Japan's military incursions, Tokyo walked out of the organization in March 1933. The Kwantung army continued its advance across North China and into Inner Mongolia.[75]

After the 1932 coup, Admiral Saitō Makoto became prime minister, but right-wing nationalists considered him too moderate and forced him to resign in 1934. He was succeeded by the more pliable Admiral Okada Keisuke.[76] In a 1933 report, the Home Office Police Bureau reflected this increasing radical influence when it asserted that "truly sincere nationalist movements" sought "to diffuse the spiritual essence of our Empire throughout the world." However, the bureau complained that the political pressure kept mounting: "Since about 1931, the situation has changed. We have seen the rapid emergence of the so-called modern nationalist movements." These seek "a radical social revolution, while accompanying this trend there has been a rapid increase in the circulation of inflammatory literature of an extreme kind."[77] In June 1934, the army published a pamphlet also advocating "the world-wide spread of the imperial influence."[78] The link to agrarian ideology was clear when the Ministry of War followed up in October with a plan for "the rebirth of farm, mountain and fishing villages."[79]

The Tokyo regime was already taking some action to support independent peasant farmers while pursuing its war against China. A leading nationalist called Japan's villages "the army's electoral constituency."[80] While most officials had always acknowledged that the nation needed (in Havens's words) "happy, healthy farmers," the depression demanded new approaches. The vice minister of agriculture who took office in 1931, Ishiguro Tadaatsu, was an agrarianist who had opposed the 1926 owner-cultivator land-purchase regulations because they insufficiently favored small farmers. The appointment of this determined ideologue for the yeoman cause brought new dynamism to official rural policy. With Ishiguro's support, the 1932 "farm rescue Diet" legislated new public works in 12,000 Japanese villages. Some 5,000 villages received credit and other assistance. Overall funding was tight, however, and the voice of ideology spoke louder. The Saitō cabinet urged farmers "to sober up and take pains to cut away the causes of their troubles" by themselves utilizing "their spirit of mutual aid with their neighbours, a good custom which has been in existence in the villages for a long time." A top Agriculture Ministry official told farmers that "economic rehabilitation begins with spiritual rehabilitation ... we uplift our families by farming, and we rebuild our villages by farming." The state established a Conscientious Farmers' Association to publicize the thinking of "farm moralists" who recommended traditional rural virtues of "diligence" and "yielding to others."[81]

The actual results were mixed. Just as Young Turk agrarian reform plans had languished in the face of landlord power during World War I, farm-debt adjustment legislation in Japan in 1933, aiming to encourage the "spirit of old farmers," did not deliver small cultivators much debt relief.[82] The secretary of the pro-landlord Imperial Agricultural Association wrote that not so much aid was really necessary, because already "the farm villages possess the essentials for their own rebirth: land, water, fresh air, and sunlight." He said they simply needed to be left to their own devices, free of taxes, interest, markets, ideologies, and "cities, and the like, but probably the source of it all is the pressure of capitalism." He added: "When the sun comes up, we cultivate. ... If we merely observe the laws of agriculture and work hard at operating our farms, we will have stability of livelihood." None of this provided great assistance to small farmers. Annual tenancy disputes continued to increase, from 2,500 in 1930 to 6,800 in 1936.[83]

Irrespective of peasant material interests, the intellectual outcome of the political pressure to adopt a pro-peasant posture was clear. Agriculture and ethnicity became ideologically inseparable. The Kyoto philosopher Watsuji Tetsuro's influential 1935 work, *Climate and Culture,* characterized Asian societies by their supposedly distinctive, irregular, "monsoonal" farming conditions. These fostered a luxuriant agriculture dominated by a violent, unpredictable, teeming nature, where "death stands . . . by the side of man." Japan's own climate, Watsuji wrote, was so severe as to demand the rigorous communal discipline of its people. By contrast, Europe's temperate "meadow climate," Watsuji argued, was more consistent, lenient, "logical and rational." It required less intensive farm labor and was more conducive to pastoralism. Worse, Mediterranean conditions also fostered urban growth and industrialism. After a visit to Europe, Watsuji compared the city tram to a "wild boar" trampling on crops in the fields and disturbing the traditional order.[84]

In another book, published in 1935 while he remained in detention for his role in the 1932 coup, Tachibana Kōzaburō also focused his ire on cities. Tokyo, London, and New York, he wrote, "did not sprout from the land. These world cities exist for themselves. . . . Today they have come to swell up fat by regarding the national land and farm villages as sacrifices on behalf of their own existence. The world's great cities have turned into parasites which will not stop until they destroy the farm villages of the world."[85] Tachibana urged: "We must sweep clean the dominance of modern Western materialistic civilization." Humanity had to blunt what he called the urban "burgher spirit" and should revert "to the unique origin and foundation of human existence which has long been discarded: the land." This meant a combination of rice and race: "[T]he sole foundation which should be cultivated is agriculture. Japan's destiny is the capacity for united action of the Japanese race that is unparalleled in the world. . . . First we must mark out a spiritual transformation and return to our true nature."[86]

A month after the May 1932 coup, Gondō Seikyō advocated "governing through nature." The "utmost happiness," he reiterated, came "from laboring to grow agricultural products." From 1934 until he was near death in 1937, Gondō published a new journal for Japanese farm leaders. He also supported the country's military expansion into Manchuria as a means to open up a new location for Japanese farmers to exercise self-rule.[87] Gondō's last book, published a year before Japan's wider invasion of China in 1937, described "the basis of politics" in both countries as similar. It was society itself—in Japanese *shashoku,* derived from the Chinese *she-chi,* meaning the gods of earth and grain. Gondō took a Chinese term from the *Shu ching* (Book of History) for rites propitiating these gods and applied it to Japan's ancient Shinto agricultural deities. For him this cult of cultivation defined the Japanese nation: "Eight kinds of heavenly sins—obstructions to agriculture—were recognized throughout the country." Citing a putative third-century Japanese emperor's view that "agriculture is the foundation of the world," Gondō added, "If there is no land, there is no place for men to live; if there is no millet [*shoku*], there is nothing for the people to eat."[88]

Gondō even opposed mechanization, which he said enabled a few capitalists to control "most of the goods of the *shashoku.*"[89] He now added that "the expansion of cities" had "upset" the urban-rural balance. Worse, "most of the cities are currently in a state of twilight, where wickedness and confusion abound." These "enormous" cities, which "consume great amounts," threatened the future. Gondō called them "mere organs for the ruling class."[90] In such a vision, the capital city of the Chinese enemy, Nanjing, could only be yet more inimical, and require more hostile attention.

Another prominent Japanese agrarianist, who enjoyed state sponsorship, focused specifically on settling Japanese farmers in China. Born in the capital in 1884, Katō Kanji had studied farm administration at Tokyo Imperial University and found many of his neighbors to be "urban trash who ought not to be sent out from the farm villages." Katō's farm education programs won strong Agriculture Ministry support from 1926, and from the mid-1930s he benefited from the patronage of the vice minister, Ishiguro Tadaatsu.[91] Like other agrarianists, Katō elided Japanese agriculture, antiquity, ethnicity, and empire. He published his major work in 1934, stating that "'to live' is to understand agriculture" and praising "the great life force known as the Japanese empire." He identified "the spirit of Japanism" with "respect for the emperor" and aimed "to put the spirit of the Japanese empire into the hearts of the farmers." Katō saw Japan's farm villages as the optimal site for emulation of the ancients by "cultivating and training the ideal faith of the Yamato race." He, too, dismissed agricultural machinery in favor of what he called "single hoe-ism," or manual labor.[92]

Katō acknowledged no geographical limits to either Japanese agriculture or his Shinto faith. He urged the government to "assemble the sons of the farm villages, have worthy persons train them as settlers, and send them abroad." In the same year, the Agriculture Ministry began a new program to "enrich the farmers' spirits" and funded the first of a series of new training centers, run by Katō. The Ministry of War funded the program too, and Katō's centers became seedbeds for emigrant farmers transplanting to Manchuria, where he opposed any employment of local Chinese or Manchus. Like other Japanese agrarianists who asked "what sort of person is best for colonization in Manchuria and Mongolia," Katō's model was the farmer-soldier: "[N]ot only should he be thoroughly devoted to agriculture but he must also be ready to draw his gun. . . . Small arms and machine guns will suffice."[93] In February 1936, he added: "Nothing is more important than hardening the spirit of Japan, the spirit of Yamato . . . the true farmers living in this faith will for the first time be able to become imperial farmers . . . [and] must for a time spring up, lay aside their sickles, and take up swords. The unity of agriculture and the military is a natural thing."[94]

The Japanese empire had reached a turning point. Members of the army's ultranationalist "Imperial Way" (Kōdō-ha) faction emphasized the Japanese soldier's "spiritual power" and the Yamato spirit. The equally expansionist but more pragmatic "Control" (Tōsei-ha) faction instead emphasized central command, careful planning, and resource mobilization. In mid-1935, recalling the samurai terrorists of the 1860s, a Kōdō-ha officer walked into the office of the Tōsei-ha leader, the chief of military affairs Nagata Tetsuzan, and cut him down with his sword. Meanwhile, Cherry Blossom Society leaders Hashimoto and Chō organized new meetings of young insurrectionist officers. In another assault in February 1936, radical military terrorists assassinated former prime minister Saitō and two serving ministers, narrowly failing to kill Prime Minister Okada.[95] An imprisoned army conspirator explained, in agrarian terms: "The lower classes of the nation—the most healthy core of the nation's citizens—remain an unploughed field. It is necessary to arouse them."[96]

As in the early 1930s, these attacks again turned up the ideological heat. The political pressure became intense. In August 1936, the cabinet approved the 20-year "Millions to Manchuria" plan to resettle one-fifth of Japan's farmers, 1 million households, promising each family 20 hectares of Manchurian farmland. A government pamphlet explained that China's "illiterate" inhabitants needed "a superior race well-trained in agricultural techniques to guide these backward Chinese farmers in the field." After November 1936, Japan's national education system specifically endorsed agrarianism (*nōhonshugi*) in its ethics textbooks as part of official civic ideology.[97]

Militarist expansion and racist agrarianism were marching almost in step. The 1936 coup proved a long-term political victory for the Kōdō-ha army faction and its idealist vision of "spiritual power." The murders soon led to the ascendancy of Prince Konoe Fumimaro, who was close to the Kōdō-ha faction and became prime minister in June 1937. The Imperial Way had prevailed. In 1937, the Thought Bureau of Japan's Education Ministry published *Cardinal Principles of the National Polity*. This required school text, of which 2 million copies were printed, asserted that an "original" trait of the Japanese people made them superior to other Asians and "intrinsically quite different" from Westerners in "our national character," language, and customs. "Our nation has, since its founding, developed on the basis of a pure, unclouded, and contrite heart." The text added: "Our country is a divine country governed by an Emperor who is a deity incarnate," its people descended from the Sun Goddess, "kinsmen" long united by "one blood and mind," in all of whom "the imperial blood may be said to run."[98] Racist and idealist thinking trumped the material world. As a contemporary Japanese Sinologist noted, "When we studied Chinese history and geography we never studied the fact that there were humans there."[99]

Conquest and Cultivation in China

The Japanese army launched its new, all-out war against China in July 1937. Forces associated with Lieutenant Colonel Chō Isamu, a leader of the Cherry Blossom Society and of its 1931 Tokyo coup plot, provoked a clash on Beijing's Marco Polo Bridge. Soon after, the Konoe government gave the army permission to attack the Chinese capital, Nanjing, leading to a major episode of mass killing there.[100]

The Japanese 10th Army began its attack on the city on November 5, 1937, when Lieutenant Colonel Chō was an army intelligence officer serving as an information staff officer with Japan's Shanghai Expeditionary Force. Later that month, the Japanese army took Shanghai, and Chō transferred to the army general headquarters for the China Area, joining the inner circle of commander in chief, General Matsui Iwane. Soon afterward, on the banks of the Yangtze River in Nanjing, Chō ordered Japanese troops to direct machine-gun fire at a large crowd of fleeing Chinese, which included some soldiers as well as women and children. When the troops hesitated, according to a Japanese account, "Chō lost his temper, roared 'This is how you kill people,' drew his sword, and killed some of the soldiers with blows through the shoulder. Shocked, the other soldiers opened fire, and that's how the slaughter took place."[101]

Japanese forces entered Nanjing on December 12, and the next day the city fell. Five days later, a Japanese 6th Division officer telephoned Japan's China Area army headquarters: "Excellency, we have 12,000 or 13,000 Chinese penned up here. What do we do with them?" Chō Isamu replied: "Yatte Shimae. Katazukerunoda" (Be done with it. I'll clean it up.)[102] It was a deliberate—and fateful—order. Chō later explained his approach: "In the hell of the battlefield it is a virtue for a man to become a beast. In a dog-eat-dog war between poor countries, manners, morals, decency and humanitarian concerns lose their importance. . . . Pillage leads to violence and rape comes with that." Yet his commander in chief, General Matsui Iwane, had ordered that no prisoners were to be executed.[103] Though surviving documents are scarce, historians believe that Chō Isamu issued a separate order in Matsui's name to kill all Chinese prisoners.[104] At any rate, it is clear that on-the-spot orders from Chō and other officers ensured that Japanese forces killed up to 100,000 Chinese prisoners of war and as many civilians during the two months following Nanjing's fall. On December 15, Western reporters watched Japanese troops kill 1,000 Chinese men, shooting them in small groups.[105] In these weeks, soldiers also raped approximately 20,000 Chinese women.[106]

Fifty miles upriver from Nanjing, Chō's Cherry Blossom Society colleague Colonel Hashimoto Kingorō commanded the Japanese garrison at Wuhu. Here, on December 12, as the troops entered Nanjing, Japanese warplanes, their pilots acting on orders, sank the American gunboat *Panay*, killing two people and wounding many. Implicated in this attack, Hashimoto received a promotion to general on his return to Tokyo.[107] In 1938, the army also promoted Lieutenant Colonel Chō to full colonel.[108] Thus, the two leading founders of the Cherry Blossom Society participated in the 1937 massacre in the Nanjing area, and both received promotions afterward.

Nanjing now became part of the new Japanese empire in China. Public and private investment in Manchuria alone rose from 161 million yen in 1931 to 1,076 million in 1939.[109] Near the Manchurian city of Harbin, in a secret laboratory known as Unit 731, Japanese army surgeon Ishii Shiro and staff officer Prince Takeda had been developing biological weapons. These were now ready for testing, and a subunit, the TAMA Detachment, was established in Nanjing in 1939.[110] Meanwhile, Japanese leaders openly discussed an "ultimate war" and the "war to end wars."[111]

Even as Japan's brutal aggression extended across China, and its investment in military technology and Manchurian heavy industry soared, domestic policy attention quickly focused once again on the Japanese peasantry, which still accounted for most of the country's population and 46 percent of the army's enlisted men. New measures taken in 1937 linked rural policy directly to the expanded war. First, Tokyo's Agriculture Ministry approved a plan to subsidize mass emigration to Manchukuo, with "the overall goal of exporting nearly one-third of the domestic farm population" from Japan. Within five years, 57,000 Japanese farm families emigrated to Manchuria. For those who remained in Japan, rural life quickly improved as wartime inflation relieved debt. Also in 1937, the government passed new regulations aiming to support yeomen owner-cultivators (*jisakunō*) and to create as many as 1 million new small independent farmers in Japan. The next year brought additional measures to improve tenancy conditions.[112] In 1937, the Agriculture Ministry also surveyed owner-cultivator households in 1,000 Japanese villages in order to determine the "standard optimum holding" for the independent family farm, free of long-term debt. This farm size was fixed at four acres. To provide that size holding for all rural households, the ministry calculated that the bottom 31 percent of Japan's rural population, those families owning less land or none, should move to Manchuria. The rest would then become "middle-sized farmers" (*chūnō*).[113]

The yeoman ideal itself migrated to Manchuria with the poorer Japanese peasants. According to a 1938 Agriculture Ministry publication on the settlements there: "The purpose of the village colonization plan is to turn all the farmers in the village into *chūnō* through the planned limitation of farm households." Planners considered the chūnō, besides being the official "ideal" or "model," as "representative," or "someone any ordinary person could identify with." The goal was "a group of solid, middle-sized farmers working together," lifting rural productivity by use of livestock, machinery, and "joint management of lands."[114] Japanese emigration researchers also sought to measure the "appropriate scale standard farm household" that could operate under the official model, that is, within "the limits set by labor power of the household." The prevailing agrarian ideology further defined the "stable farm household" as a self-sufficient grain-cultivating family unit, drawing no income from "entertainment, sericulture, lumbering, fishing, or tenancy fees." The Colonial Ministry's "Proposed Standards for the Management of Collective Farm Immigrants in North Manchuria" described the settlers as jisakunō (yeoman farmers). It promised each immigrant 49 acres of land, 10 sheep, a cow, horse, and sow, a plow, three sheds, a wagon, and farm tools. The plan envisaged all these settlers alike, as self-sufficient owner-farmers, engaged in mixed cropping, animal husbandry, and mutual cooperation. The Colonial Ministry's model even set them annual yields for each crop and breeding targets for livestock. The Japanese farmers, who supposedly brought to China "superior agricultural technology," actually received little machinery, just many admonitions on self-help.[115] Their role was as much ideological as developmental.

Tokyo's ministers of colonization combined this voluntarist sloganeering with kindred agrarian, militarist, expansionist, racial appeals. One minister, addressing "soldiers of the hoe" in 1939, urged them, "Go and colonize the continent! For the development of the Yamato race, to build the new order in Asia!" Later that year, another minister of colonization praised in similar vein the "pioneers who battled with the soil of North Manchuria" for their contribution, which he called "[t]he Strength of One Hoe," to "the holy endeavor of the race." A song of the official settler Youth Brigade went: "We are Japan's advance guard onto the soil. . . . We come gripping hoes / So we will open the land." A colonization manual heralded the "new continental Japan." By April 1941, Japanese owned 20 million hectares of Manchuria (having paid for only 11 million), including 3.5 million of the 15 million hectares already under cultivation there. They uprooted Chinese and Korean peasants from a quarter of the region's farmland, in part by forced sales and evictions, allegedly after "systematically misclassifying cultivated fields as uncultivated." Even so, Japanese settlers farmed only 200,000 hectares of this previously cultivated 3.5 million hectares. Again, the project was more about territorial ambition and ideal roles than practical agriculture. Around four-fifths of the settlers were poor or landless Japanese peasants, and the authorities sent half to colonies along the Soviet border and 40 percent to pacify areas of local Chinese resistance.[116]

With difficulty, racial and kinship hierarchy now replaced earlier expressions of cultural superiority. Tokyo's foreign minister Matsuoka Yōsuke asserted in 1938 that "the mission of the Yamato race is to prevent the human race from becoming devilish." The next year, a colonial promoter revealed the inherent ideological challenge when he impossibly called Manchuria a "brother country to which Japan had given birth." Another wrote: "Japan is the stem family and Manchuria is the branch family." The Yamato people were, alternately, the heart, pivot, axis, or "head" of "the five races" of Asia. The Japanese "frontier spirit" brimmed with "the blood of youth," while reports returned to Japan that "the Manchurians are a very dirty race" and the Chinese too had "dirty racial habits."[117]

By contrast, the prevailing pastoral imagery of Japanese settlers was idyllic, fecund, almost Virgilian. A 1939 photograph of a shepherdess and family at home with their sheep, entitled "The Joy of Breeding," bore the caption: "Looking out onto a spectacular view, the young mother, the continental dog, and the plump and healthy second generation born in Manchuria play happily together on the second story of the shepherd's house." A drawing entitled "The Joy of the Harvest" portrayed "immigrant soldiers of the hoe at the close of day busy harvesting. The glow of the sunset is reflected in the face of the young father. The Manchurian Japanese baby suckles at the ample breast of his mother."[118]

In reality, most new Japanese settlers failed to cultivate their land themselves, become self-sufficient, engage in mixed farming, or cooperate with one another. In 1939, an official "Basic Outline of Manchurian Settlement Policy" had to reiterate these four original goals. The ideals required force, in the absence of much economic attraction to peasants. Thus by 1941, Japanese laws tied the settlers to their new land and obliged them to farm it collectively without resort to the market.[119] Agriculture vice minister Ishiguro explained the new official favor directed toward small-producer self-sufficiency by emphasizing that "the essence of agriculture is noncommercial." Thus, "manufacturing and selling things in order to buy other things . . . is not the essence of farmers' livelihood." Once more, peasants were supposed to serve agriculture, not vice versa. Farming remained an ideological project as much as an economic practice. Promoted to minister of agriculture in November 1940, Ishiguro again stressed the need to "battle the emphasis on free enterprise capital," a resistance he claimed to have waged for three decades as an agriculture official. Reiterating the nonmaterial nature of the agrarianist project, Ishiguro again linked farming with idealist visions of race and antiquity when he asserted that the phrase "agriculture is the foundation of the nation" had become "the racial faith of the Yamato people."[120]

Now Japan was girding for world conflict. Its army crossed into Soviet-controlled Mongolia in 1939 and secretly fought a major conventional border war against Soviet forces. In the heat of battle the dashing Chō Isamu allegedly "astonished Soviet officers by lying down to take a nap on the borderline." The Japanese lost that war, but when their army marched unopposed into French

Indochina in 1941, General Chō was there too. Staying at Saigon's Majestic Hotel, he took a junior officer to see the movie *Waves of the Danube* and to his "favorite haunt," a riverside sukiyaki restaurant. There the two men "drank till we were thoroughly besotted." At a soirée with French officials, Chō "showed up in a *Kamishimo* gown and astonished everyone by reciting a classical *joruri* narrative." Similarly, Chō "would instruct his officers by singing to them in the old-fashioned *naniwabushi* style," while at drinking parties he even punched high-ranking superiors. Confident aggression was the order of the day. Promoted to major general in October 1941, Chō became assistant chief of staff of Japan's Southern army.[121]

Expansion, racism, and cults of violence and agriculture all combined to explosive effect. In August 1940, Foreign Minister Matsuoka Yōsuke unveiled Japan's Greater East Asia Co-Prosperity Sphere, announcing that "the mission of Japan is to proclaim and demonstrate the *kōdō* (Imperial Way) throughout the world." Tokyo signed the Tripartite Pact with Germany and Italy in September, and Japanese emperor Hirohito urged all "races to assume their proper place in the world." Two months later, the 1932 coup leaders Tachibana Kōzaburō and the radical priest Inoue Nisshō walked out of jail in a general amnesty. As a leading industrialist ominously termed the Japanese "the sole superior race in the world," a popular song from the fighting forces in China portrayed rivers and mountains "stained with the red blood of loyalty." Reality was no constraint on ideological ambition or military power. The report of a Japanese research team, "Investigation of the Resistance Capacity of the Chinese," commissioned by the South Manchurian Railway and presented to the Kwantung army in 1940, concluded that a self-sufficient Chinese rural economy sustained the stiff local resistance confronting the Japanese military force, which was therefore unlikely to subdue China. Officers at the general staff headquarters in Tokyo received these conclusions in silence, until an impetuous young officer asked: "So, then, what sites would it be best for us to bomb? I'd like to know the key points."[122] The dilemma only provoked more violence. A member of a Japanese secret service organization deployed at this time by the North China Area army and Imperial Headquarters recalled one of its pacification slogans, *Mekkyo Wahei,* or "Return to peace by killing off the communists."[123]

War, resistance, and repression led to genocide. For instance, from 1940 to 1944, a range of sources reported Japanese use of biological warfare (BW) in various parts of eastern China. A Japanese prisoner of war told his American captors that in 1942, advancing Japanese troops themselves suffered massive

casualties when they overran a Chinese zone just after their own planes had
delivered a BW bombardment there, and that in Nanjing he later saw TAMA's
records stating that at least 1,700 Japanese troops had died of cholera. During
and after the war, the Chinese Nationalists and Communists, and the Soviet
Union, all made allegations of hundreds of deaths in various BW attacks. Six
Japanese veterans of Unit 731 largely corroborated the story. Its two clandestine Japanese units in Harbin and Nanjing had grown into large bureaucratic
institutions by 1945. Both performed medical experiments on living prisoners
of war, mostly Chinese and some whom the Japanese called "half-breeds," as
well as Soviet and a few American prisoners. These BW experiments are believed to have killed 3,000 prisoners. Actual BW deployments across China
took far more lives. Unit 731's production capacity allegedly reached eight tons
of bacteria per month.[124] According to a recent series of regional estimates,
the Chinese death toll from Japan's biological warfare alone was as many as
580,000.[125]

Extermination by conventional weapons was even more extensive. From
1940 in particular, Japanese military policy in China became one of "Nanjing
writ large," to use Gavan McCormack's term. Unable to quell resistance in rural
North and Central China, Japanese counterinsurgency evolved into a series
of operations to "absolutely extinguish, pacify and punish." Troops forced the
Chinese peasants into patrolled camps and turned the countryside into free-
fire or "unpopulated zones" (*mujin chiku*) for unchecked implementation of
the slogan "three alls" (*sankō sakusen*): "kill all, burn all, loot all." The result by
1945, McCormack writes, was a North China littered with countless burned
villages, "people reducing kilns" (*renjinro*), and mass graves called "ten thousand people pits" (*bajinkō*).[126]

Territorial, racial, and agrarian expansion went together. By 1941, Katō
Kanji's agricultural centers were training "continental soldiers of the Yamato
race acting under a vast ideal," with encouragement from Prime Minister
Konoe. In January 1941, the government announced its goals of increasing the
Japanese population from 70 to 100 million by 1960, reducing urbanization
by building more rural factories and schools, and maintaining 40 percent of
the Japanese in the agricultural sector. Japanese now referred to themselves
as the world's "leading race" (*shidō minzoku*). On August 3, 1941, the leading
Tokyo newspaper *Asahi* declared, under the headline "'Japanese Purity' Finally
Proven," that scientists had "proved that the 'purity of blood' of the Yamato
race is unsurpassed in the world."[127] The Kyoto school of philosophers notably

termed the interaction of "blood" and "soil" the key to history. "Only as the folk experience war do they become aware of the state." Awareness itself was an ideal. The world was now "the moral training ground of the state."[128]

War and Race

The Imperial Japanese forces launched a new Pacific War with their attack on Pearl Harbor on December 7, 1941. The next day, Tokyo adopted an "Outline of Information and Propaganda Policies for the War between Japan and the Anglo-American Powers." Through what it now called "total war," Japan sought a "new world order" that would "enable all nations and races to assume their proper place." In January 1942, a prominent Tokyo magazine featured an article entitled "Establishing a Japanese Racial Worldview," describing Japan's people as "the most superior race in the world." The article summed up the symbolism of official ideology by stating that "the purity associated with Shinto" was "tinged with the pinkness of blood." Here beauty and delicacy became metaphors for violence, leading eventually to the equation of life with sacrificial death. "It is this very warmth of life which has made the cherry blossom the symbol of the Yamato spirit." The next month, the Imperial Rule Association took the antiquity and superiority myths much further when it published the book *The Great Shinto Purification Ritual and the Divine Mission of Japan*. It asserted that Japan was the "parent land" of an ancient "world-wide family system," and that even the early Sumerian civilization owed its name and culture to Japan's August Sovereign, *Sumera Mikoto*. This fantasy supposedly indicated the need for other nations to take their "due places" in a new "fundamental vertical order."[129]

Meanwhile, the Population and Race Section of the Research Bureau of Tokyo's Ministry of Health and Welfare was preparing a secret study entitled *An Investigation of Global Policy with the Yamato Race as Nucleus*. Completed on July 1, 1943, this six-volume, 3,000-page report, of which only 100 copies were printed, described the Japanese as "the leading race," which would remain so "forever," assigning other races to their "proper place." The report frequently deployed the terms *blood and soil* and *living space*, revealing official links with Nazi racism as well as an approach—more cultural than biological—that stressed Japanese and Asian shared consciousness of a "collective racialism."[130] In the cause of this ideology, Tokyo imposed its state Shinto religion, the Japanese language, and Japanese names on all Koreans. Japan asserted its cultural superiority by punishing the speaking of Korean and mobilizing tens of thousands of Korean "comfort women" for sexual services to Japanese troops.[131]

While Japan would thus "assimilate other races into Nipponism," the report also noted that its control of its Greater East Asia Co-Prosperity Sphere required that "the blood of the Yamato race" had to be "planted in the soil" of the other Asian countries, and yet remain pure. The report projected that 12 million Japanese would be settled abroad, mostly as farmers, within seven years. Their agriculture was to be a central pillar of the emerging empire. The report predicted that by 1950 as many as 2.5 million Japanese would be farming the land in Manchukuo and 1.35 million in Korea, with another 2 million Japanese farmers in China and Southeast Asia and 2 million more cultivating land in Australia and New Zealand. In order to maintain "the southern areas as a supplier of raw materials," the Japanese navy was already discouraging "the fostering of manufacturing industries in occupied areas." Tokyo's policy toward the commercially oriented overseas Chinese of Southeast Asia was to "gradually expel them." At war's end, the 2 million Koreans working in Japan would be sent home as well. Resident Japanese populations of Korea and Taiwan would be increased to 10 percent of these territories' inhabitants. In this way, territorial and agricultural expansion would follow the Nazi model of lebensraum and secure "the living space of the Yamato race," while the settlers sent abroad must be sure to "remain aware of the superiority of the Japanese people." Then, the report asserted, "our country will hold the key to the very existence of all the races of East Asia."[132]

By the time this official document was printed, Japanese forces were already on the defensive. Yet official rhetoric was escalating. In May 1943, at Attu in the Aleutian Islands, 2,500 stranded Japanese troops fought fanatically to the death, heavily outnumbered by Americans. The imperial government celebrated their heroism with an allusion from a sixth-century Chinese chronicle, *gyokusai,* or "jewel smashed," signifying the preciousness of self-sacrifice in refusal to compromise. Idealist themes combining purity with violence recurred the next year in the song "Companion Cherry Blossoms," which ran, "Flowered in the garden of the same military school / Just as the blossoms calmly scatter / We too are ready to fall for our country." Prominent author Tokutomi Iichirō wrote that "the Greater East Asia War is a purifying exorcism, a cleansing ablution." Iichirō's book *Citizen's Reader for Certain Victory* portrayed Japan in 1944 as "the model, the pattern, the standard" for "the two billion people of the world," against the Americans, the Jews, and their "evil and ugly plutocracy."

War meant beauty and purity. One Japanese magazine declared in October 1944 that "the more of them that are sent to hell, the cleaner the world will be." Another dismissed Americans as akin to an ancient indigenous tribe subdued by Japanese in the first millennium: "Our ancestors called them Ebisu or savages long ago," worth only as much "as a foreign ear of corn . . . Americans are devils in human skin." The magazine added: "Beat and kill these animals that have lost their human nature! . . . the blood of the Divine Country's three thousand years cannot allow these beasts to run rampant."[133]

As Japan faced tightening military encirclement, it mobilized the ultimate metaphor of Japanese purity and identity for mass violence. In late 1944, Tokyo created the Special Attack Forces (Tokkōtai), or kamikaze suicide units. These were an invention of Vice Admiral Ōnishi Takijirō, who wrote: "The purity of youth will usher in the Divine Wind." Young suicide pilots formed only the front ranks of a potentially genocidal civilian war strategy. By December, the government and media were broadcasting the slogan ichioku tokkō to portray Japan's entire population of "one hundred million" (ichioku) as members of a mass suicidal unit who were to sacrifice themselves against American landing forces. By March 1945, the cabinet's Total War Research Bureau was lauding Japan's "unique racial power," and the next month saw the appearance of an auto-genocidal slogan, ichioku gyokusai: "the shattering of the hundred million like a beautiful jewel."[134] The regime was prepared if necessary to send 100 million Japanese to their deaths. In July, Rear Admiral Kurihara Etsuzo proclaimed: "When every Japanese subject is made fully aware of the fact that to die for the Emperor is to live, then will the Japanese people bring tremendous power into play." A Mainichi newspaper editorial explained: "Ours is a race which is possible only in relation to the structure on which its State rests. The day when the 3,000 year history of our country, a history of a state of oneness between the Sovereign and the people, ends, is the day when our race goes out of existence."[135]

Okinawa was the initial test of this strategy of mass death in war. Having been promoted once more, General Chō Isamu served as chief of staff of the 32nd Japanese Army at the final battle there. He successfully demanded that Tokyo deploy five divisions there and boasted of how he had threatened his superiors with the prospect of their ritual suicide: "If Okinawa should fall because you didn't take my recommendation, the section heads of the General Staff Office will have to commit seppuku." American forces landed on Okinawa in the early spring of 1945, and Chō's rash counterattacks failed to expel them.

He joked to his commander, Colonel Hiromichi Yahara: "Hey, Yahara, when will it be okay for me to commit *hara-kiri*? Is this a good time?" The U.S. troops slowly overran the Japanese positions on Okinawa in three months of fierce fighting that left 12,000 Americans and 65,000 Japanese troops dead, along with 40,000 Okinawan conscripts. The Japanese forces also coerced no fewer than 100,000 Okinawan civilians, one-third of the island's civilian population, into a series of mass suicides. From his headquarters in a cave, Chō's superior officer General Ushijima issued his orders to Japanese soldiers to "fight to the end." General Chō then dipped a brush in red ink and added a line to the dispatch: "Do not suffer the shame of being taken prisoner. You will live for eternity." On June 17, Chō and Ushijima read the U.S. surrender demand. They "both laughed and declared that, as SAMURAI, it would not be consonant with their honor to entertain such a proposal."[136]

As his own end came, Chō retained the romantic notions that for him had justified so much murder. He reminded Yahara of "the beautiful movie" *Waves of the Danube:* "I remember the scenery and music from that film we saw in Saigon . . . at the theater across from the Majestic Hotel." He added: "You and I always behaved properly. We shared much pain together." At a final ceremonial banquet in the cave, Chō's secretary addressed him with the secret farewell greeting of *yakuza* gangsters. In a whisper, Chō asked Yahara for a promise to "never utter a word" about Chō's failed battle plans. At 4:00 the next morning, June 23, 1945, Chō Isamu and General Ushijima assumed a ritual posture. Yahara wrote that Chō was "very intoxicated" after drinking King of Kings whisky. He offered Yahara a piece of pineapple on the end of his sword and told Ushijima: "Excellency, you will go to paradise. I to hell." Both generals stabbed themselves in the naked abdomen with traditional hara-kiri daggers. A master swordsman swiftly beheaded them.[137]

The genocidal samurai romance was over. Chō's last note was addressed to the founder of the Cherry Blossom Society, Hashimoto Kingorō. Implying that their idealist fantasy had ended in ruin, Chō's letter stated: "Before material supremacy one can do nothing. With my own words I assume responsibility for the defeat."[138] Ever the romantic, Chō accepted no responsibility at all for the millions of victims of the vicious ideal of Japanese purity and aggression.

CHAPTER 13

Soviet Terror and Agriculture

The historian of the Soviet Union Robert Conquest has likened rural Ukraine in the early 1930s to "one vast Belsen." However, the historian of Germany Charles Maier distinguishes Stalinist mass murder from the Nazi death camps: "No Soviet citizen had to expect that deportation or death must be so inevitable by virtue of ethnic origins." Richard Evans agrees: "[T]he arbitrariness of Stalinist terror contrasted with the absolute predictability of Nazi terror," he writes. "There was no Soviet Treblinka, built to murder people on their arrival."[1] Yet even without gas chambers, Stalinist mass shootings and Gulag camps took life on a massive scale. In total, Stalin's terror and his forced agricultural collectivization in the 1930s killed possibly as many people as Hitler did, excluding war casualties. Andrea Graziosi writes that "the scale and the concentration of hunger-related deaths in Ukraine, and the policies then adopted by the regime, make the 1932–33 famine a phenomenon which, at least in Europe, can be compared only to later Nazi crimes."[2]

Ideological and political parallels in the Nazi and Soviet systems have long been a focus of the theory of totalitarianism: the personal dictatorship, the party-state, and their relentless "mobilization" and purging of populations in new campaigns. Nor can the millions of victims of the Third Reich and the Great Terror be neatly categorized into racial and class enemies, respectively. Just as Hitler murdered German oppositionists as well as Jews, Stalin engaged in wholesale killing of Soviet ethnic as well as political groups.

Another historical similarity between Germany and Russia is the continuing importance of the traditional autonomous rural community, or the peasant "estate." [3] In rural Russia, a distinct peasant sector persisted from prerevolutionary times well into the 1920s and the early Stalin era. As historian Stephen Wheatcroft has pointed out, that was less true of faster developing agricultural areas like Ukraine and North Caucasus.[4] On the other hand, Germany was much more industrialized, yet Hitler's regime proclaimed itself to be based on the German peasantry and the preservation of the peasant estate, while by contrast the Bolsheviks, and Stalin in particular, made no secret of their general subordination of agricultural to more "advanced" urban interests. In practice, as we have seen, the Nazis also mustered and relied upon German industrial power, while many Bolsheviks did attempt to foster rural development. Yet the ideological distinctions remain as clear as the political commonalities.

Soviet revolutionaries had to confront their country's vast peasant hinterland. Both the Russian village and its superior level of rural administration, the *volost,* were institutional products of the 1861 peasant reform, which had freed the traditional agrarian commune (*mir*) from outside forces like landowners and the state.[5] This naturally strengthened the peasant estate; otherwise, Russian rural life changed little. Peasants maintained their traditional combination of extensive agriculture and animal husbandry. The mir routinely organized village farmland into "three fields," each divided into strips worked by the individual peasant households, with one in three fields left entirely fallow each year. Early Soviet agricultural experts denounced the backwardness of what they called this "uncultured three-field system with its 'wild' fallow, cattle grazing on fields, and unvarying grain crops." Without great success, the experts urged more intensive land use and the rotation of different crops. In 1919–21, these Russian specialists also deplored the lack of agronomic expertise in the Soviet countryside. They instead praised the U.S. model for its "strictly scientific research of vital phenomena," by means of which, they wrote, "the Washington Department of Agriculture recreated the methods of farming and enriched the country." Endorsing a technological vision of the future of Soviet agriculture, Lenin claimed in 1919 that 100,000 tractors would turn the peasants into Communists.[6]

The materialist, internationalist early Soviet views of progress and development contrasted with what Bolsheviks considered the "voluntarist" and racialist Nazi notions of Germany's ancient heritage and unique rural tradition. Nazi rural specialists indeed idealized the racially superior, family-oriented individual German farmer and dismissed the communal mir as a precursor to Bolshevist collectivism. Richard Walther Darré, for instance, wrote in 1935:

"This Russian *mir,* which already very closely approaches communist thought processes though it never entirely touches them, is quite substantially the reason why the Russian peasantry did not unswervingly oppose the Communist dictatorship, as our farmers showed no hesitation in opposing Communism in the years following 1918. The basic difference between the Russian *mir* and the Indo-Germanic/Germanic attachment to the soil lies in the fact that the former took into account only the totality of the community and the latter is subordinate to the concept of family as such."[7] By contrast, the early Soviet agricultural specialists did not forcefully distinguish between cultural traditions, nor did they regard them as timeless. They even argued that similar patterns of communal land use had characterized traditional Germany as well as Russia. The Bolsheviks' distinction was between backwardness and progress. As one put it in 1921, "Russian peasants farm so primitively . . . compared to profitable agriculture abroad." They now "must come to understand . . . new scientific methods of working the soil."[8] Lenin, too, lamented that the mir "confines the peasants, as in a ghetto, in petty mediaeval associations of a fiscal, tax-extorting character."[9] Eventually, however, Stalinism came to reject both the traditional Russian agrarian commune and the self-sufficient yeoman cultivator. It would instead imprison the Soviet peasantry in a Communist-constructed "ghetto." Soviet economic models, even for agriculture, were essentially urban. In the *Communist Manifesto,* for instance, Marx and Engels had derided "the idiocy of rural life."[10]

The Bolsheviks' political models from history were neither racial nor territorial. They occasionally drew instead on chilling early modern precedents. In a letter to Molotov dated March 19, 1922, Lenin called Niccolò Machiavelli "a wise writer on problems of state." Without mentioning his name or citing his other writings, Lenin quoted Machiavelli's recommendation that any "cruel actions" that were needed "to achieve a certain political objective" must be carried out energetically and rapidly, "because the popular masses will not tolerate a long period in which cruel actions are undertaken." Therefore, Lenin went on, "we must now at this moment undertake a decisive and merciless battle with the Black Hundred clergy and suppress their opposition with so much cruelty that they will not forget it for several decades. . . . The greater the number of representatives of the reactionary clergy and the reactionary bourgeoisie which we succeed in shooting for this reason, the better."[11] After Lenin's death in 1924, Stalin sought models of a more indigenous, nationalist kind. With few qualms about "a long period" of cruelty, he praised the ruthless modernizing tsar who in 1721 became Russia's first emperor: "When Peter the Great, conducting business with the more advanced countries of the West, feverishly built mills and factories to supply the army and strengthen the defences of the country, it was a special sort of effort to leap clear of the confines of backwardness."[12] At another point Stalin put it differently: "Ivan the Terrible and Peter the Great didn't cut off enough heads."[13]

In contrast to Nazi myths of antiquity and romanticization of the peasantry, the Soviet Communists adopted myths of modernization and industrial romanticism that also proved disastrous. Conquest terms this "little more than a transfer of hopes and illusions from an imaginary peasant to an almost equally imaginary proletarian."[14] No idealization of rural tradition played any part in the thinking behind the mass killings of the Lenin and Stalin regimes, nor in the millions of deaths in the catastrophic Soviet famines of 1921–22 and 1931–33. In this sense and few others, Stalin's mass crimes (and to a lesser extent Mao's, described in chapter 14) are different from the other cases examined in this book. The major Communist dystopias of the twentieth century sprang from a materialist ideology and lacked important idealist features of other genocidal regimes. In the USSR and China, class-based and political purges inflicted massive death tolls, and the Communists' different ideological and physical struggles *against* the peasantry eventually assumed some ethnic features as well.

Bolsheviks and Peasants

Historian James Heinzen calls the Russian Revolution "the largest peasant revolution in history." In 1917 and 1918, the peasantry seized control of nearly all land owned by the state, the royal family, rural gentry, the church, and private firms.[15] Tillers gained tenure, though still regulated by the local agrarian commune, in a combination legalized by the new Bolshevik regime when it nationalized land. The redistributions of larger productive farms leveled out landholdings and reduced the quantity of surplus production for the market. A more subsistence-oriented middle peasantry proliferated in the countryside and the communes. Robert Conquest argues that the kulak, or exploitative rich farmer, "had disappeared by 1918."[16] However, Lenin's claim that "in October 1917 we grasped power together with the whole of the peasantry," if partially true, ignored their looming differences.[17] Initially, the Bolsheviks did hope for what Zinoviev called "the transformation of old Russia into the commune state," based on the commune as maintained by the land legislation of 1917–18. Yet the Bolsheviks were "a party of the cities." Their August 1917 party statute "did not contain a single article about organization in the countryside. The pre-revolutionary Bolshevik Party included fewer than 500 peasants and only four rural cells.[18] After the revolution, Maxim Gorky even hoped that the "stupid, turgid people in the Russian villages will die out," in favor of "a new race" that would be "literate, rational, energetic."[19] Gorky complained of "the deadweight of illiterate village life which stifles the town" and even of "the animal-like individualism of the peasantry."[20]

The new Soviet regime quickly became preoccupied with both urban industrialization and winning the civil war, which erupted in May 1918. The Bolsheviks held on to power in the cities but faced major challenges in parts of the countryside, to which they responded with ferocity. Seeking "the monopoly of food," a Bolshevik decree of May 9 declared "a merciless war on the kulaks" for grain.[21] Violence escalated on all sides. An early 1919 central Communist Party document noted the need "to neutralize the Cossackry through the merciless extirpation of its *elite*," and a commander recommended the "percentage shooting of adult males."[22] In July 1919, I. I. Rejngold, a Bolshevik leader in the Don region, urged "a policy of indiscriminate mass extermination." Sokolnikov's Communist army shot 8,000 people there in several weeks. Meanwhile, anti-Communist Ukrainian peasant insurgents slaughtered over 50,000 Jews, and Denikin's White troops carried out more massacres. In late 1920, the Bolshevik commander Evdokimov received the Order of the Red Banner for executing 12,000 Whites in several days.[23]

The economic challenge was dire. Wartime compulsory government grain requisitions from the peasantry had fallen from 8.3 million tons in 1916–17 under the Imperial and Provisional governments to only 1.2 million tons under the Bolsheviks in 1917–18. If this lifted a burden from the countryside, famine and disease spread in urban areas, where mortality almost tripled.[24] Dwarfing the civil war's 800,000 military casualties, as many as 8 million civilians perished from urban famine and rural violence from 1918 to 1920.[25] Deaths and dispersal reduced the urban population by one-fifth. Petrograd's 1916 population of 2.41 million fell to as low as 0.74 million by 1920. Despite lower rural productivity, Bolshevik grain requisitions rose again, to 1.8 million tons in 1918–19 and up to 6 million in 1920–21, as the regime forcibly seized peasant produce to feed the cities and the army. A Bolshevik dissident termed this "the dictatorship of food supply over agriculture."[26] As Yuzuru Taniuchi put it, the party's early notion of a commune state in the countryside now "died hard" under the harsh confiscations of War Communism in 1918–20, betraying a bitter urban-rural conflict.[27]

Contradictions plagued the party too. While espousing rule by terror in other fields, Lenin called in December 1918 for an end to the use of force to impose agricultural collectivization. A new Bolshevik policy of conciliating the middle peasant (*seredniaki*) emerged in mid-1919, though the party had declared in February that "[a]ll forms of individual land tenure should be regarded as transitory and dying away." Then, in 1920, the deputy people's commissar of food supply, V. V. Osinskii, proposed a plan for state regulation of agriculture, involving "militarization" and "compulsory regulation of agricultural production as a whole," that he hoped would "develop into state organization of production." The All-Russian Congress of Soviets approved the plan in December 1920.[28] Over the next two years, a second, rural famine killed more than 3 million people. The wartime devastation and demand for horses, which reduced both the cultivated area and the number of draft animals by 30 percent, along with a poor 1920 harvest and the 1921 drought, were all major causes of this catastrophe, but Lenin acknowledged as early as March 1921 that Bolshevik policies had contributed to it. Karl Radek declared them "the price of victory over the imperialists and White Guards."[29] That same month, the regime suppressed with great bloodshed an uprising by Kronstadt sailors calling for democracy, egalitarianism, and an end to the economic severity of War Communism. The rebels claimed: "In return for almost totally requisitioned grain, and confiscated cows and horses, they [peasants] got Cheka raids and firing squads."[30]

The Communists finally concluded that they had to choose either "to start an open war against the mass of the peasantry" or to make economic concessions to them in the form of "an agreement with the countryside."[31] Lenin admitted in March 1921: "We must not try to hide anything, but must say openly that the peasants are dissatisfied. . . . We must reckon with this and reexamine our policy." Yet his approach to the peasantry barely disguised his contempt. He urged the People's Commissariat of Agriculture to select three "old, Russian, land working peasant men . . . (it would be very good if they were both non-party and Christian)" and assign to them a nonvoting "consulting voice." Token peasants embodied the Bolshevik urban myth. Independent peasants could not progress. Agriculture expert M. E. Shefler put the commissariat's view: "It is absolutely impossible to imagine [peasant agriculture] spontaneously making advances." The Russian village, he said, was "extremely backward, dark, deprived of adequate knowledge, [and] not accustomed to producing in a cultured way.... Just look at Siberia where huge expanses of land are either empty or irrationally sown.... Or look at the state of animal husbandry, so backward and disgusting. Powerful state intervention is needed to drain swamps, combat abandoned land [and] restore territory afflicted by drought."[32]

Moscow's relaxation of the pressure during the period of the New Economic Policy (NEP, 1921–29) did make major concessions to what it called the "toiling peasantry" and attempted to reconstitute the urban-rural relationship.[33] Lenin introduced NEP as the party's deliberate retreat to the economy's "commanding heights" (heavy industry, foreign trade, and banking), which he said should be pursued "seriously and for a long time." The NEP overruled but did not silence the objections of those Bolsheviks who feared that "the little peasant [*muzhichek*] will get stronger [and] will try to get the soviets in his hands."[34] The Russian "Law on Toilers' Land Use" of 1922 banned the sale of land and employment of nonfamily labor, but permitted peasants to choose individual, communal, or collective farming. A leading commissariat official acknowledged that the law "allows the individualization of farming to a large degree" but also claimed that it focused on "raising the productivity of 97 percent of agriculture.... To work toward this goal is communist (although by appearances it does not seem to be communist)."[35] The Commissariat of Agriculture abandoned any plans for widespread collective farms and began to develop into a 70,000-strong state agency mandated to modernize the countryside. Moscow abolished its Food Supply Commissariat, and in 1924 it adopted a new policy of "face to the countryside." By then the regime had organized the rural population of nearly 100 million people into 120,000 rural soviets.[36]

The Communists' ideological mistrust of the peasantry persisted, but so did their NEP policies. Trotsky saw the peasantry as "the protoplasm" out of which "new classes" continued to emerge, and Lenin warned that it was "engendering capitalism." Zinoviev admitted in 1925 that "we hardly know the countryside." Kalinin complained that the state was going as far as leaving villages alone. Moscow even had to acknowledge the traditional village gathering (*shkod*), the assembly that ran the commune (mir), as the local unit of Soviet state authority.[37] Communes accounted for 95 percent of sown land in Russia in 1927. A year later, state and collective farms still occupied only 2.7 percent.[38]

Tension was inherent in this standoff. In the face of a powerful state, peasant society remained strong. Four hundred thousand agrarian communes effectively rivaled the soviets for power in the rural areas.[39] Authorities in the Stalingrad region complained in 1926 that "the supreme authority in the village is not the rural soviet, but the [village] gathering," which governed the mir and played a "decisive" role. "The significance of the rural soviet is nil and their authority has collapsed."[40] The central party newspaper *Izvestiya* acknowledged in 1927 that "the basic and decisive stage in the local and economic life of the countryside is not the rural soviet, but still the gathering."[41] The next year, Communist analysts complained again that the village gathering remained "the primary link of peasant self-government." Thus, they said, "our agrarian commune which was retaining the antique-looking form of management, the customs, the tradition, and so on continued to be almost untouched by the October Revolution."[42]

As many as 393,000 seasonal workers, half of those in the Soviet countryside, worked for the communes in 1922. Two years later, the communes were employing 450,000 shepherds. For these and other village and agricultural tasks, the communes successfully taxed the peasantry as much as 10 percent of the total revenues of all local administration budgets, raising an estimated 100 million roubles in 1927. The commune could even keep its accounts secret from the soviet.[43] The peasant sector remained a virtually autonomous estate. "Until recently," a Communist journal complained in 1928, the rural commune "was divorced from the whole of Soviet society. In the commune its own special activities were opposed to the soviet's activities. . . . Kulaks [rich peasants] have the right to vote and high authority" in the commune, even though "they are excluded from the soviet."[44] By contrast, barely 2,300 of the rural soviets possessed independent budgets. Communes alone could raise funds from the peasantry without fierce resistance. The soviets remained dependent on peasant organizations "in every aspect of village administration." This meant that they relied especially on "the wealthy strong part of the peasants," who dominated the communes.[45]

The Russian Commissariat of Agriculture adopted a gradualist approach to agricultural development. Commissar Smirnov wrote in 1927 that the first goal was "to transform our agrarian country into an industrial-agrarian country." This required "introducing agricultural machines [and] making agriculture more intensive." Commissariat policy did not advocate collectivization but a "fundamental reconstruction of the commune along more efficient and productive lines," which it claimed would "use territory rationally." Its goal for the commune was "improved, multifield crop rotation, with strips that are few, wide, and well-suited for working the land [and for] correctly organized pasturing of cattle." One deputy commissar called for "better forms of land use . . . fruitful animal husbandry and more lucrative crops," along with better access to machinery, fertilizer, and improved seeds. Another defended the commissariat for its "feeling of realism, an understanding of peasant life." Robert Conquest writes that by early 1927, the Soviet peasantry "had good reason to look forward to a tolerable future."[46]

However, the Bolshevik majority still gave priority to both industrialization and class struggle. Many Communists deplored the influence of the "kulaks" and middle peasants running the communes over the landless or seasonal laborers they hired. Worse, laborers who were not members of the commune were at their mercy, and poor peasants paid a disproportionate share of commune taxes. Frustratingly for Communists, however, these same poorer commune members considered better-off fellow villagers as neighbors, not class enemies.[47] The Soviet newspaper *Izvestiya* complained that the commune structure favored a sense of "equalization" rather than class struggle.[48] Urban-based Communist campaigns to mobilize poor peasants against the rich usually fell on deaf ears. Attempts to organize peasant women and youth also met hostility from peasants who saw these initiatives as urban interference in the traditional rural order. Peasants also complained about Communist neglect of rural areas, the use of rural taxes for urban projects, the continuing lower educational opportunities and standards in rural areas, the building of hospitals for townspeople but not for peasants, and the higher pay for urban over rural soviet employees.[49]

All that is unsurprising. As Heinzen has pointed out: "Over 90 percent of Communist Party members lived in cities, yet 85 percent of the population resided in the countryside." Most Bolsheviks were ill equipped to tackle what Taniuchi calls the "peasant sense of group identity as opposed to townsmen." Whatever Marxist class category individual peasants belonged to, most of them found urban-rural conflict more threatening than class domination in the countryside. The town-country divide thus gave the Bolsheviks only two options. In the mid-1920s, rather than hostility, the party adopted compromise with the countryside as a whole. But, as Heinzen writes, "the state presence was nowhere strong in rural Russia." Communist successes came mostly in the cities, and the urban-rural gap only widened.[50]

The party's urban bias and its quest for control prefigured an eventual showdown in the form of a Soviet political offensive against the countryside and its dominant institution, the commune. But after Lenin's death in January 1924, Stalin's independent role became a major exacerbating factor. In his search for total power over the party, Stalin did not shrink from playing the peasant card against those Bolsheviks among his rivals who were most susceptible to the charge of neglecting rural interests. For instance, initially, in May 1924, Stalin had asserted traditional Bolshevik faith in urban industrialization and reiterated Lenin's doubt that a single country, "least of all an agrarian country like Russia," could achieve socialism without aid from "developed countries." Then in December Stalin reversed himself, denouncing rivals like Trotsky who he now claimed "underestimated the peasantry." Stalin suggested that Russia could indeed develop unaided, asserting that its history had made Russian peasants unique: "Traditionally, the Soviet peasants have always valued" the workers as their political ally, he claimed, and "cannot but be exceptionally well-disposed towards economic collaboration with the proletariat." However, Stalin's appreciation of peasant qualities went little beyond an assertion that they would welcome urban leadership. He concluded that "the village follows, and must follow, the town." Moreover, in early 1926 Stalin turned the same accusation against Zinoviev and Kamenev, his former allies against Trotsky, now citing *their* supposed "lack of faith" in the party's ability to lead the peasantry. Thus, to defeat the more orthodox Marxist, urban, worker-oriented Left, Stalin temporarily pursued the more pro-peasant policies of the party's Right, headed by Bukharin, Rykov, and Tomsky. He even announced: "It is not the function of the peasantry to serve as a subject for exploitation or as a colony for the proletariat."[51]

This rare series of exchanges saw Stalin actually claim to defend the peasantry against purported detractors and to justify his policies in the interests of the peasantry. He did not pit peasants directly against workers, praising them rather as loyal to workers. Stalin's tactics differed from those of genocidists who romanticized the rural and denigrated urban dwellers. Yet at this crucial turning point as he rose to dominance, even Stalin resorted to a cynical, idiosyncratic if still ideological form of peasant jingoism to force his policies through.

The power struggle intensified. Outmaneuvered, in April 1926 Zinoviev and Kamenev joined forces with Trotsky in a new, combined Left Opposition, saying: "Stalin is not interested in ideas. It is power alone which attracts him. He is cunning and cruel."[52] He was also quick, and ready to consolidate his power in the party and over the country. It was also in April 1926 that Stalin ended the NEP's initial focus on resolving agricultural problems and called for new attention to industry, which required resources from the countryside. Agriculture produced nearly half the national income, as Heinzen notes, and industry less than one-quarter. The demands on agriculture for industrialization—"food and raw materials for the cities, for the army, and to export"—only expanded the city-country divide.[53] The state now demanded more grain but offered lower prices for it. Peasants began to use their grain to fatten livestock, for which market prices still applied.[54] The result threatened not only urban grain supplies but also future agricultural capacity, as draft animals were slaughtered and sold in 1928–30.

New political conflicts paralleled the economic contest in the rural areas. While the Soviet regime increased its pressure on richer cultivators to surrender more of their produce, it also had real difficulty identifying them or its own putative poor peasant allies. Party organizations, finding no clear class division in villages, chose political loyalty rather than economic criteria to select those allies who were now to be classified as "poor peasants." The category of class enemies also broadened. Targeting the more prosperous top of the rural hierarchy, Stalin's supporters pushed down the list and increasingly used the term *kulak-zachitochnyi,* blurring the distinction between allegedly exploitative kulaks at the top and the independent upper-middle peasants.[55] In January 1927, Molotov, head of the Party Committee on Work in the Village, urged disfranchisement of the kulaks, who he said represented only 3–4 percent of the Soviet population. However, an official report later in the year found "massive" disfranchisement even of middle peasants. At the December 1927 15th Party Congress, which adopted a policy of moderate collectivization, Molotov and others attacked the commune as the "last hideout" of kulak interests.[56] Stalin and Molotov spoke of "liquidation" of the kulaks. The congress urged the soviets to assert control of the communes, and banned the disfranchised rural groups from participating in the village gathering. It further determined that poor peasants were the party's main rural base of support.[57] That, too, left the other peasants vulnerable. In February 1928, Stalin's ally Mikoyan announced that it was now middle peasants who were supposedly hoarding the bulk of the grain, unwilling to sell it for lack of consumer products to buy. Stalin admitted in April that his actions against kulaks were also deliberately targeting "the upper wealthy strata of the middle peasants."[58] This sounded more like an assault on the peasantry itself. Three months later, Stalin announced to a secret party plenum that the peasants would be required to pay a "tribute" to meet the needs of industrialization.[59]

Naturally, peasants saw this as an attack on their villages. As it moved to take control of the countryside, the Soviet state found them, in Taniuchi's words, "integrated as a whole by communal ties." The peasantry itself now came "face to face with the regime and the Party." And with the cities. Stalin's rapid industrialization measures had meanwhile boosted the urban labor force, contributing to a new food crisis in the cities and the introduction of rationing there from 1928. According to the official plan for 1928–32, the urban population would further increase from 26 to 32 million, and in fact by 1932 as many as 38 million city dwellers were receiving food rations. Rural produce had to support them all. Stalin's determination "to industrialise this peasant country at breakneck speed" was leading to catastrophe.[60]

Stalinism and Peasants

Stalin and Molotov's dominant faction routed Trotsky's Left Opposition in November 1927. Stalin now quickly wheeled to attack the Right, the faction that had most fostered the NEP and agricultural growth. At the 15th Party Congress the next month, Molotov even tarred as Trotskyists those he labeled the "agrarian professors" of Russia's Agriculture Commissariat, while from the Left, Zinoviev targeted them as the "kulak party" in the commissariat. However, the Left did not advocate forced collectivization. To isolate the Right, Stalin now adopted some of Trotsky's critiques but went much further, advancing collectivization by force. Suddenly the Commissariat of Agriculture found itself, as Heinzen puts it, "under ferocious attack for having advocated policies that the party leadership had endorsed for years."[61]

In a series of "wholesale firings" in February–March 1928, Stalin's Central Committee sacked agriculture commissar Smirnov, his deputies, and other specialists. By May, the OGPU, or Soviet security police, predecessor of the NKVD and KGB, had identified 75 suspects in the commissariat. Smirnov's successor, Nikolai Kubiak, had close ties to the OGPU and signaled the regime's thinking when he wrote on March 2 that "the peasantry's mood is extremely bad and already is taking an outspoken, petty-bourgeois, counterrevolutionary form." However, even Kubiak derided as dangerously irresponsible the new official target to increase agricultural yields by 30–35 percent in five years. From the Politburo, rightists Bukharin and Rykov opposed the return to civil war–style grain requisitioning, while a wave of state terror swept through villages. Bukharin confided to Kamenev that Stalin considered himself "the only man who could make the peasants swallow the extraordinary measures" (*ja odin ix smogu provesti*).[62] "He will have to drown the risings in blood," Bukharin added, calling Stalin "this Genghis Khan who will destroy us all."[63]

As the purges spread from Moscow, ethnic and class prejudices surfaced together. In March 1928, Stalin launched a show trial of a group known as the Shakhty engineers, mostly German citizens and former tsarist specialists.[64] Instructions went out in May ordering the Ukrainian GPU branch to crack down on hostile members of the urban intelligentsia while stepping up repression of Ukrainian kulaks in rural areas. In mid-year, the Soviet OGPU started examining the cases of 9,000 engineers and other professionals. A massive purge of the entire Soviet state apparatus began when widespread "investigations" of Agriculture officials commenced in November 1928. Party inspectors now sought "detailed, concrete examples of alien elements in the apparatus." Such "alien" elements supposedly collaborated with "Right deviationists" thought likely to retard industrialization. The official purge of the Commissariat of Agriculture began in January 1929. After Stalin's rout of the Communist Party's moderate faction the next month, purges of the rest of the state apparatus began in April. Stalin had Bukharin expelled from the Politburo in November 1929 (followed by Rykov and Tomskii in 1930), and in December Kubiak's brief tenure as commissar of agriculture also ended.[65]

A 1929 Central report identified the Agriculture Commissariat's agencies as dangerous precisely because they "come into direct contact with the broad mass of peasants" while they allegedly remained "choked with employees" of tsarist background. In fact by then, Heinzen writes, the commissariat had been "vanquished and rendered impotent." The victors, however, were not the peasants. From 1929 a new contract system forced the mir to deliver their produce to the state according to specific grain requisition quotas.[66] As state investment in industry doubled from 1927 to 1930, grain collections doubled from 11 to 22 million tons.[67] The state, which took 15 percent of the 1928 crop, would collect as much as 27 percent in 1930. To ensure this, at the end of 1929 Stalin launched what many consider "a full-blown attack on the peasantry." He revealed to a December meeting of agricultural scholars his goal of "liquidation of the kulaks as a class."[68] What Stalin proclaimed to be an offensive against "kulaks," followed by his imposition of agricultural collectivization and new grain requisitions, was actually far broader, and it exposed the increasingly vulnerable Soviet peasantry as a whole to a catastrophic famine in which millions died.

The new Stalinist repression escalated through several phases. "Dekulakization" came first. The population of the USSR in 1929 was around 155 million. The authorities targeted 5 million people, members of up to 1 million "kulak" families, and the OGPU began deporting them from their villages in November.[69] The "Category I" targets supposedly included 60,000 "particularly vicious" or supposedly counterrevolutionary kulak men.[70] However, by October 1930, as many as 284,000 people had been arrested in this category, though the OGPU classified less than half of them as kulaks. They probably accounted for most of the 20,000 recorded extrajudicial executions in the USSR in 1930. Deportees in "Category II" included 120,000 kulak families described as "showing less active opposition, but nevertheless arch-exploiters with an innate [*sic*] tendency to destabilize the regime." The third category included 400,000 kulak families "loyal to the regime," who were also to be deported, to sites within their own districts.[71] During 1930–31, perhaps 200,000 families sold their possessions and left their villages to evade these deportations; as many as 381,000 families, or 1.8 million people, were dispatched to distant regions. By 1932, a total of 1.3 million deported peasants were living in OGPU-controlled "Special Settlements." Another 260,000 arrived in 1933. By then, the regime had deported 2.2 million peasants to distant exile, plus about the same number to areas within their districts and another 120,000 to Gulag prison camps. Probably more than 100,000 of the deportees died in 1930–31 alone. Nearly 250,000 perished in 1932–33, and another 400,000 escaped from the Special Settlements.[72] By 1936, up to 600,000 people had simply "vanished."[73] The OGPU concluded from the chaos that its own dekulakization brigades, ironically, had been infiltrated by "a socially alien and often criminal element" that had plundered other peasants. From 1932 to 1940, a total of no fewer than 390,000 peasants are recorded to have perished in places of "kulak" resettlement.[74]

The next phase involved forced collectivization of those farmers remaining in their villages. This meant "moving 25 million individual peasant economies" into 250,000 collective farms. From 1928, the proportion of peasants living in collectives rose from only 3 percent to 60 percent (representing 14.5 million of 23 million families) by March 1930.[75] Peasant resistance to this collectivization was widespread. The OGPU claimed that rural religious adherence played a "colossal role" in inspiring the 1,300 cases of peasant unrest it recorded in 1929.

However, the next year the figure rose tenfold to 14,000 peasant disturbances, of which only 1,500 involved protesters who opposed the regime's closing of churches. Rather, fully 7,400 of these 1930 disturbances were directed against collectivization, including 141 outright peasant revolts from February to April alone. The year 1930 also saw 1,200 murders in separate acts of "terrorism." The authorities themselves killed hundreds if not thousands of peasants in their repression of these disturbances. In March 1930, Stalin denounced the so-called excesses of his collectivization campaign. Some 9 million peasant families in turn left the collectives by September, but 5 million remained, and the pressure increased again in 1932, with the numbers of collectivized families tripling to 15 million in mid-year and reaching 22.5 million (85 percent) in mid-1933.[76]

Meanwhile, a series of famines struck the USSR. The causes were complex, climatic, and regional, but in large part Stalinist central policy was also to blame. Enforced collectivization of their possessions had spurred peasants to sell or consume their livestock on an unprecedented scale. The number of oxen and work horses plummeted from 30 million in 1928 to only 19 million in 1932. As the collective farms were supposed to supply tractors, the budgets for draft animal fodder fell by more than half, but tractors had added only 4 million horsepower.[77] From a peak in 1930, harvests fell drastically.

The famines began with a poor 1931 grain crop in Kazakhstan, compounded by official pressures to sedentarize its nomadic populations as well as devastating reductions in local livestock over the previous two years. Reports of famine deaths commenced in early 1932, and 50,000 Kazakh refugees fled into the Central Volga. Stalin received a letter in August stating that over 10,000 Kazakhs had died of famine. By mid-1933, the rural population of Kazakhstan fell from 5.9 to only 2.5 million. The death toll there is estimated at approximately 1.4 million; many more fled as refugees to other republics and even to China. Apart from Russian residents of the republic affected by the famine, ethnic Kazakhs throughout the USSR suffered a statistical population loss of 1.1 million from 1927 to 1937, to which must be added those who were born and died within that decade.[78]

The worst was still to come. In the rest of the Soviet Union in 1932–33, registered deaths alone exceeded by 2.9 million the average number for 1926 and 1927, and the OGPU recorded another 300,000 excess deaths in its camps for deportees. Many more deaths went unregistered. Worst hit now were the major grain-growing areas of Ukraine and Russia. In one district of Ukraine, more than 3,000 people had died by March 1933, only 742 of whose deaths had been registered. The number of unregistered deaths is debated by scholars, within the range of 1.1 to 3.9 million. Excess deaths in the USSR during the famine years of 1931–33 thus totaled between 5.7 and 8.5 million.[79]

Responsibility for most of these deaths in rural areas clearly lies with Stalin's regime, the restrictions it imposed on private gardening plots and its determination to collect grain for the cities and for export.[80] Due to very fine weather, the 1930 USSR grain crop of 77 million tons had compared well with a 72-million-ton average for 1928–29. But as noted, collectivization also increased state procurements from 15 percent to as much as 27 percent from 1928 to 1930, and Soviet grain exports soared from 0.3 to 4.8 million tons. A combination of bad weather and worse policy explains the poor harvests from 1931 to 1935. Each of these, according to a table published by historian Moshe Lewin, fell below 70 million tons, and declined annually from 1932. Even so, annual state grain procurements from 1930 to 1935 ranged from 19 to 28 million tons, compared to only 11–17 million in 1928–29. At the end of 1930, 2 million tons of unshipped grain rotted at railway stations.[81] Despite the drought-afflicted poor 1931 harvest of 69 million tons, procurements again increased to 33 percent (23 million tons), and grain exports also rose to 5.2 million tons. As the height of the famine approached in 1932, owing this time to wet weather, the harvest rose only slightly, to 69.8 million tons. Finally, now the state did reduce grain exports sharply, to 1.7 million tons, and procurements slightly, to 27 percent, but 19 million tons of grain procurements remained a high level of imposition on the peasantry. As in 1931, Stalin and the Politburo had again overestimated the harvest. Moreover, after the smaller 1933 harvest of 68 million tons, Moscow's procurements rose again to 34 percent, or 23 million tons of grain, of which 1.68 million was exported. The harvest fell slightly again in 1934, but procurements rose once more to 38 percent, though exports dropped further to 0.77 million tons. In short, the state's enforced seizure of 42 million tons of grain from rural areas in the two famine years of 1932 and 1933, of which the USSR did export 3.4 million tons, caused most of the 5–8 million deaths.[82]

The regime made some attempts at mitigation. The 1.6 million tons of grain exported in the agricultural year 1932–33 was far below the 8 million tons proposed in the five-year plan. Some grain exports even in famine conditions might be justified by the geographic or transportation difficulties facing internal distribution, assuming cash food purchases to be more cost-efficient. And the USSR's annual January–June preharvest grain exports fell continuously, from 1.4 million tons in 1930 to 0.2 million in the first half of 1933, the period of greatest mortality. However, the 1932 reductions in state procurements and exports proved hopelessly inadequate. So did the regime's attempts to deliver food relief. In a series of decisions in 1932–33, the Politburo reversed its policy to reserve grain relief for the cities. In March 1932, it "substantially reduced" the food rations for 20 million city dwellers, and over the next few months the urban death rate doubled in the main famine regions. Between August 1932 and January 1933, the Politburo reluctantly reduced grain collection plans by 4 million tons, and the state failed to collect a planned 1 million more. In 1932–33, it released 2–3.5 million tons of grain collections for rural consumption as food, seed, and fodder, of which 330,000 tons were for food. Another half a million tons were allocated for reserve stocks. Economic historians Davies and Wheatcroft report "extensive food assistance supplied to hungry children."[83] Yet all this was obviously far worse than inadequate. The USSR's 1932 mortality rates of 30 per 1,000 more than doubled, to 70 per 1,000 in 1933.[84] Whatever their goals, most state agencies, even including the repressive apparatus, were largely overwhelmed by the scale of the famine tragedy.

Yet Stalin's determination to extract grain from the peasantry was clear. At a Politburo meeting in November 1932, he partly blamed procurement difficulties on collective farmers opposed to Soviet power, and he called on Communists to retaliate with "a knockout blow" that would "answer this blow by some collective farmers and collective farms."[85] At the height of the famine in March 1933, Politburo member Kosior informed the Soviet leader: "The unsatisfactory preparation for sowing in the worst affected regions shows that the hunger has not yet taught many collective farmers good sense." In May, Stalin again blamed the peasants for it, derisively calling them "esteemed grain growers." He accused them of "sabotage," which he acknowledged was "quiet and outwardly harmless (without bloodshed)," yet he still called it a "war" against his regime. That month, a high Soviet official revealed the seriousness of the calamity when he claimed: "In most villages, the 'conspiracy of silence' has been broken. People once more speak in the meetings even though, for the moment, they do so in order to ask for bread, or to promise that, if they will be fed, they will work properly." A speaker at a June regional party meeting confirmed this interpretation: "The grain procurements are that part of our work by which we . . . put the peasant in the channel of proletarian discipline." During the year 1933, the regime deported another 268,000 peasants and urbanites.[86] In January 1934, Stalin announced: "The policy of industrializing the country [and] eliminating the kulaks . . . has triumphed."[87] He explained the next year that in order to develop the country from "some islands of industry which were lost in a sea of tiny peasant farms," it had been "necessary to make sacrifices and carry out the strictest economies. It was necessary to economise also on food . . . in order to accumulate the necessary resources for the creation of industry."[88] In 1935, state procurements rose to a record 28.3 million tons, which Stalin's colleague Lazar Kaganovich privately hailed as "an absolutely fantastic, stunning victory, a victory of Stalinism."[89]

The Ethnic Element in Stalin's Terror

The millions of Russian famine victims were outnumbered by Kazakhs and Ukrainians. At first the Ukrainian Soviet Republic, composing 20 percent of the population of the USSR, does not appear to have been disproportionately targeted. Since 1923, Moscow's policy of "Ukrainization" of institutions both there and among the 8 million Ukrainians in the Russian Soviet Republic had made considerable advances, including the creation of dozens of Ukrainian-language universities.[90] Ukrainians then suffered bitterly from dekulakization, but not more than other Soviet nationalities. Of 381,000 kulak families deported in 1930–31, 64,000 (17 percent) were from Ukraine. In April 1932, the Soviet Politburo planned to deport 38,000 more families, including 6,000 from Ukraine (16 percent). As the famine set in, Ukrainians received small amounts of food relief, though probably even more inadequate than that accorded to Russians. The state distributed grain reserves in Ukraine after floods there in 1931, and the next year 35,000 tons of wheat marked for export was diverted to feed southern Ukrainian cities or villages.[91] For the year 1932–33, the Politburo set aside 330,000 tons for food relief, including 194,000 tons for Ukraine. However, in the catastrophic first quarter of 1933, only 280,000 tons of grain stocks were reserved for the whole of Ukraine, barely more than the 251,000 tons for the much smaller though predominantly urban population of Moscow and its region.[92]

The famine death toll shows that Ukrainians did suffer disproportionately. Excluding Kazakhstan's 1.4 million victims, the 2.93 million excess deaths registered in the USSR in 1932 and 1933 included 1.54 million from Ukraine, more than half of the victims. In addition, many of the 310,000 deaths registered in Russia's North Caucasus were from the Ukrainian minority there. Probably more than half of the 1.1 to 3.9 million unregistered dead were also Ukrainians.[93] If the total Soviet famine death toll fell in the range of 5 to 8 mil-

MAP 25. Ethnic republics and ethnic cleansing in Stalin's USSR. Based on Terry Martin, *Affirmative Action Empire*, map 3.

lion, it included between 2.3 and 6 million Ukrainians.[94] The famine ravaged all the Soviet grain-growing regions, but Ukraine, the largest, most of all. The authors of a 2002 demographic study calculated a death toll of 2.6 million people in Ukraine alone.[95] In other Soviet republics, perhaps half a million Ukrainian deportees and local Ukrainians also perished from the famine.

Ethnic discrimination exacerbated the regime's criminal neglect. From 1928, as historian Terry Martin points out, "the extreme centralization and statism of the revolution from above pushed the Bolsheviks towards a greater reliance on the one nationality most closely identified with the Soviet state: the Russians." As early as March 1928, Lazar Kaganovich perceived that some Ukrainians were already seeing it this way: "[T]he grain requisition campaign has led to an increase in chauvinism . . . there are conversations that Moscow is taking our bread, sugar," especially complaints from "kulaks." That May, Moscow ordered a new round of national repression and investigations in Ukraine, including preparations for a major purge trial of 45 Ukrainian intellectuals that was to commence two years later. It was at this point, in November 1928, that Stalin held up the expansionist Russian emperor Peter the Great as a historical model.[96] In March 1930, the Politburo ordered what historian Timothy Snyder calls "perhaps the first purely ethnic deportation in Soviet history," of over 10,000 families, "in the first line those of Polish nationality," who were expelled from border areas near Poland.[97]

Russian nationalism, Martin adds, became more evident in Stalin's discourse. The dictator emphasized in December 1930, for instance, that "the Soviet working class, and above all, the *Russian* working class [Stalin's emphasis]," who were "its acknowledged leaders," had demonstrated "a more revolutionary and activist politics than any other proletariat of the world could dream of." Stalin's national sentiment fully gushed two months later when he portrayed Russia as a routine victim of history: "But we don't want to be beaten. . . . The history of old Russia consisted, among other things, in continual beatings due to backwardness. The Mongol Khans beat Russia. The Turkish nobles . . . The Swedish feudals . . . The Polish-Lithuanian lords . . . The Anglo-French capitalists . . . The Japanese barons beat Russia. Everyone beat Russia, due to her backwardness. . . . We are 50–100 years behind the leading countries. We have to cover this distance in ten years. Either we do it, or they crush us."[98] Stalin's posture of claiming simply legitimate defense against perennial ethnic injustice ominously resembled the thinking of the Young Turks and even the Nazis, even though the latter routinely concocted alleged foreign threats. If Stalin's statement reflected real fear in late 1930 of future German aggression, he apparently didn't mention it at this point, two years before the Nazis took power.

Instead, as the famine loomed, Stalin's nationalism increasingly targeted Ukrainians. In early June 1932, he wrote to Kaganovich and Molotov: "Pay serious attention to Ukraine." He warned that even its Communist Party leaders Chubar and Kosior were "completely ruining Ukraine." By this, Stalin did not mean they were starving it but the opposite; they were refusing to collect Ukraine's full grain target, which Stalin considered Moscow's property. He denounced Chubar two weeks later for attempting on Ukraine's behalf "to get yet again millions of kilograms of grain from Moscow. . . . I think we've given more to Ukraine than we should have. Giving more grain is pointless." On June 18, Stalin denounced the "several tens of thousands" of Ukrainians who, he complained, "have already fled across the entire European regions of the USSR and are demoralizing our collective farms with their complaints and whimpering."[99] He allowed some reduction in planned requisitions from Ukraine, but they remained high.

Within two months, Stalin concluded that agents of Poland's leader, Marshal Józef Piłsudski, had promoted what Stalin saw as an upsurge in Ukrainian nationalism, "within (and without)" the Communist Party of Ukraine. On August 11, resolving to remove Chubar from office, Stalin dispatched Kaganovich to run Ukraine: "The *chief thing* now is Ukraine. Things in Ukraine are terrible. It's *terrible* in the Party . . . we may lose Ukraine . . . Piłsudski is not daydreaming. . . . The worst thing is that the Ukrainians simply *do not* see this danger." Ignoring the threat to Ukrainians' survival posed by Moscow's grain requisitions, Stalin saw only a threat to Moscow from Polish spies. Now, as he put it, "the fight with counter-revolution in such a large and unique republic as Ukraine" required "quickly transforming Ukraine into a true fortress of the USSR, a truly model republic. We won't spare money on this task." The Ukrainian Terror had begun. The republic's GPU arrested 16,000 people in six weeks, from November 1 to December 15, 1932.[100]

As he created this nightmare, Stalin was not dreaming, any more than Piłsudski. Snyder's examination of Poland's intelligence reports of this era led him to conclude that the late 1920s were "the golden age of Polish intelligence and counter-intelligence in Soviet Ukraine." For a few weeks in the spring of 1930, Ukraine appears to have been vulnerable. Polish reports reveal a sizable infiltration by Warsaw's agents, who included many Ukrainians and Russians. By early 1932, Poland had spy missions even in various GPU branches as well as "on the Dniester fleet, and in the Kiev and Kharkiv garrisons." But the danger receded when Warsaw signed a nonaggression pact with the USSR in July 1932. Stalin, who knew the previous month that Ukraine was devastated by "impoverishment and famine," responded not by relaxing the pressure on it but by forging full steam ahead. In August he and Kaganovich agreed to blame the famine on "Piłsudski's work" and on the Ukrainians themselves, of whom Kaganovich wrote dismissively to Stalin: "The theory that we Ukrainians are innocent victims creates solidarity and a rotten cover-up for one another."[101]

With the starvation approaching its height and Poland no longer any threat, Stalin drove home his advantage. On December 14, 1932, the Soviet Politburo reversed nine years of "Ukrainization," namely the development of Ukrainian-language schools and other institutions in Ukraine and Russia's North Caucasus region. Moscow now proclaimed that what it called "the lightheaded, non-Bolshevik 'Ukrainization' of almost half the North Caucasus districts did not serve the cultural interests of the population." The Politburo defined its "most evil enemies" as "the saboteurs of grain requisitions with Party tickets in their pocket," who were allegedly active along with kulaks and Ukrainian nationalists in Ukraine and North Caucasus. On January 22, 1933, Stalin and Molotov sent out a circular telegram cynically warning that "a massive outflow of peasants 'for bread' has begun" from Ukraine and the North Caucasus. They added that "like the outflow from Ukraine last year, [this] was organized by the enemies of Soviet power." The two Soviet leaders ordered the North Caucasus "not to allow a massive outflow of peasants" or any similar "entry into the North Caucasus from Ukraine," and Ukraine was likewise instructed to prevent "a massive outflow of peasants from Ukraine into other regions." At one point Stalin and Molotov even attempted to deny that the refugees were peasants, when they ordered Russian regional leaders "to immediately arrest all 'peasants' of Ukraine and North Caucasus who have broken through into the north."[102] Moscow also launched "mass operations" against Ukrainian so-called Galician émigrés, urban intelligentsia, rural teachers, and agronomists as well as Polish and German intellectuals. By March 1933, Ukrainian jails and concentration camps held 90,000 people, and those of the North Caucasus 75,000.[103] A year later, Ukrainians comprised 19 percent of all Gulag inmates.[104] This proportion was just below the percentage of the USSR's population who lived in Ukraine. Unlike the famine, the escalating political repression of Ukrainians did not single them out on an ethnic basis. The targets also included Poles and other nationalities.

Yet that was only the beginning. The 1933 Nazi takeover in Germany provoked no immediate intensification of Soviet action against ethnic Germans, but the reduced Soviet repression of 1934–35 was followed by a series of brutal political and ethnic purges and "national operations." Terry Martin writes that from 1935 to 1938, nine of the USSR's other nationalities—Poles, Germans, Finns, Estonians, Latvians, Koreans, Chinese, Kurds, and Iranians—"were all subjected to ethnic cleansing." Stalin had these ethnic groups forcibly deported from their territories. Then, in 1937, mass shootings of members of national groups began, after a purge of Red Army officers commenced in May. On July 2, the Politburo secretly instructed the regions to provide estimates of how many "kulaks" and "criminals" each region's authorities wished to be "administratively arrested and executed" or exiled. At a subsequent Politburo meeting on July 20, Stalin dashed off a short note: "ALL Germans working on our military, semi-military and chemical factories, on electric stations and building sites, in ALL regions are ALL to be arrested." The NKVD quickly launched its "German operation" under order no. 00439 of July 25, 1937. By November 1938, the NKVD had rounded up 57,000 people in this "German operation," of whom 41,898 were sentenced to be shot. Some 34,000 more Soviet Germans were sentenced in other repressive campaigns in 1937–38.[105]

Ethnic and political repression now combined in a geometric acceleration of this new outbreak of mass murder. Official statistics reveal the sudden surge in state-sponsored killings. Annual recorded extrajudicial executions in the USSR had exceeded 20,000 in 1930 but had then fallen steadily to 1,118 in 1936.[106] Now the count skyrocketed to no fewer than 353,000 executions in the year 1937 alone.[107] Forty thousand members of the Soviet elite itself were shot in 1937–38. And immediately after order no. 00439 came no. 00447, or the "kulak eradication program." For over a year from its signing on July 30, 1937, this order determined "the punishment of former kulaks, criminals, and other anti-Soviet elements," of whom 320,000 were sentenced to be shot. For every region, the NKVD established initial quotas for those to be executed and for those to be imprisoned for 8–10 years. The quota for the Moscow region was 5,000 people to be shot and 30,000 incarcerated; for Leningrad, 4,000 and 10,000, respectively. Ukraine's quota was set at 8,000 to be shot and 20,800 incarcerated. Regions to which many kulaks and others had been exiled also received high quotas: western Siberia, southern Urals, and the Azov-Black Sea territory. In all, under order no. 00447, Moscow ordered 75,950 people shot and 269,100 incarcerated. During 1937–38, however, these quotas were actually overfulfilled by factors of two and four. On January 31, 1938, for instance, the Politburo approved an increase of 57,200 to the quotas, including 48,000 more executions. The next day it resolved "to reduce the inmate population of the Far Eastern camps" and ordered the execution of "an additional twelve thousand prisoners." On February 17, 30,000 people were added to the Ukrainian quotas. From 1937 to 1938, the proportion of those arrested who were to be shot increased from one-quarter to one-half. The other half comprised 330,000 people. With such large numbers incarcerated under order no. 00447 alone, the population of the Soviet prison camps increased by 700,000 in 1938. The overcrowding tripled their mortality rates from diseases and other causes of death.[108]

Two weeks after Stalin launched the roundup of Germans, the Politburo turned its attention to Poles, initiating the second and largest "national operation" with order no. 00485, dated August 11, 1937. The authorities sentenced 140,000 people for alleged membership of "the Polish Military Organization and its networks," of whom 70 percent were Poles and Soviet citizens of Polish origin. Some 80 percent, 111,091 people, were sentenced to death. In 1937–38, 120,000 Poles and Polish Soviet citizens, 18 percent of all those living in the USSR, were arrested and sentenced. Beginning in September 1937, seven more campaigns followed, targeting Finns, Estonians, Rumanians, Bulgarians, Greeks, Chinese, and alleged Japanese spies. In the course of all the "national operations," a total of 336,000 people were sentenced, of whom 247,157 were shot. The proportion of executions (74 percent) was even higher than for the antikulak operation (49 percent). The number of Ukrainians in the Soviet Gulag rose steadily from 1937 to 1940, but the proportion of Ukrainian inmates fell as Russians, Germans, and Poles were incarcerated in disproportionate numbers.[109]

Given his political targets in the party and the Soviet elite, Stalin's ethnic preoccupations emerged in a piecemeal process.[110] According to historian Nicolas Werth, "until May 1938, the NKVD leadership did not seem concerned by the ethnic origin of those arrested," and it began systematically recording data on their ethnic origin only in September. Werth writes that "Soviet citizens of Polish origin paid the heaviest toll of all ethnic minorities." Soviet Germans made up 69 percent of those sentenced under the "German operation," with 34,000 more sentenced in other campaigns in 1937–38. However, the total of 72,000 Germans sentenced represented only 6 percent of the Soviet German population of 1.2 million, and few of the victims were from the Autonomous Republic of the Volga Germans. Though the death toll of these national operations was enormous, the proportion of Poles sentenced (18 percent) was the highest among the ethnic groups. Werth concludes that "ethnicity as such was not the prime criterion" but rather any possible connection with enemy states, like Germany, Poland, and Japan.[111]

Unlike the Nazi genocides and the 1932–33 Soviet famine, Stalin's political and ethnic mass killings appear to have overwhelmingly targeted adult males, with family members, especially spouses, frequently sent to the Gulag, where many perished. From 1934 to 1940, women made up 6–8 percent of the Gulag population and children under 19 about 1 percent.[112] Among those executed, the proportions of women and children are likely to have been smaller again. The Soviet regime set large quotas for mass arrests and executions, and its mass killing was more arbitrary than that of the Nazis. Yet it was also more clearly directed at adult men as potential political opponents. Though most victims were quite innocent of the charges laid against them, the Soviet authorities usually made a thin pretence at legality by keeping individual records of the "investigation" of those they executed, whereas the Nazis murdered entire families and communities, leaving no record even of their names.

The Soviet victims of Stalin's repression in the 1930s may have numbered as many as 2 million. After a total of 40,137 recorded extrajudicial executions in the years 1930–36, Stalin's Great Terror took at least 681,692 more lives in 1937–38 alone. The mass killings of 1930–38 composed 90 percent of the USSR's total of 799,455 documented extrajudicial executions between 1921 and 1953.[113] To these must be added the deaths of possibly 1 million exiled peasants, inmates of the Gulag camps, prisons, and labor colonies, and other categories of victims who died as a direct result of execution, exile, or imprisonment, not counting the millions of famine victims.[114]

This vast slaughter could only have been engineered from the top of the regime. However, in ending the mass operations on November 17, 1938, Stalin's Politburo secretly and disingenuously blamed "enemies of the people who had wormed their way into the NKVD," supposedly in order to "evade the party's control." NKVD chief Yezhov resigned for "health reasons."[115] Stalin stayed in power, and over 2 million inmates remained in prisons, labor camps, and labor colonies.[116] In 1939, political sentencing fell to one-tenth of the 1938 level, but another 87,000 Soviet prisoners died in jail by 1951. Severe repression continued, especially following the Nazi invasion of the USSR in June 1941, until after Stalin's death in 1953. By that time, 1,054,000 people had died in the Gulag since 1934. Another 64,000 extrajudicial executions took place from 1939 to 1953, including 23,000 in 1942 alone and many thousands more after victory in 1945.[117] After reductions during the war, from 1948 to 1953 the Soviet labor camp population exceeded even the 1938 level.[118] Stalin launched a new pogrom against Jews just before his death.[119] However, the era that he had inaugurated with forced collectivization in 1930 and brought to a close eight years later, as suddenly as it began, was by far the bloodiest of Soviet or even Russian history.

Stalin helped Lenin create a repressive, one-party, multinational state that turned to foster both industrial and agricultural recovery in the 1920s. After he inherited this Soviet political system, however, Stalin gradually employed escalating waves of purges of oppositionists, mass starvation of peasants, and partial ethnic exterminations to create a Moscow-dominated industrialized economy in the 1930s. Reversing Lenin's late pragmatism, Stalin turned a ruthless, but increasingly factionalized, veteran Communist Party into a terrorized instrument of his own personal dictatorship. He destroyed millions of lives at the expense of what in the 1920s had been relatively promising agricultural progress and of Soviet security in the face of Nazi invasion in the 1940s. Most of the dead fell victim to Stalin's top-down totalitarian control, his flawed conviction of a superior method of land use, and ethnic animus that swept up national groups in the repression of political opposition. To previous genocide perpetrators' preoccupations with territorial expansion, pastoralism or intense cultivation, and racial or religious extermination, Stalin had added the forced collectivization of agriculture and the mass murder of officials of his own regime and of members of ethnic minorities supposedly linked to neighboring powers.

CHAPTER 14

Maoism in China

A Rural Model of Revolutionary Violence

I n his lectures to Japanese terrorists as they prepared for their bloody 1932 coup attempt, the agrarian nationalist Tachibana Kōzaburō pointed out the need for Japan somehow to "make Russia realize her mistakes and force her to carry out a revolution based on the 85 percent of her population who are farmers." He accused Stalin's USSR of "sacrificing the farmers" in order to develop "American-style heavy industry." By contrast, Tachibana went on, "the present Chinese communist army" had won victories over "the Chinese military clique" precisely because "it is a farmers' army." [1]

As elsewhere, the Bolshevik Revolution weighed heavily on the early history of the Chinese Communist Party (CCP), founded in 1920. [2] Like their mentors in Russia, China's revolutionaries sought a sharp break with their country's past. Rather than cultivate its antiquity, they assaulted traditional Chinese political institutions, religion, and culture, seeking all-out modernization. However, as Tachibana recognized, the CCP's peasant strategy also marked an important difference between the Soviet and Chinese Communist movements.

At first, the difference was the reverse of the one Tachibana noted in 1932. The early Bolshevik hope of a rural "commune state" quickly failed in Russia, and under Stalin the USSR abandoned it as domestic policy, but it continued to influence the policy of the Communist International (Comintern) toward struggles against imperial powers in colonial and semicolonial regions. Initially, even Bukharin had shared the vision of "the cities of the world inundated in a rising sea of village protest." [3] Moscow still saw the peasantry of the underdeveloped countries as "the central problem in our whole policy." [4] In the early

1920s, the Comintern even called for establishment of "the dictatorship of the poor peasantry" in nations like China.[5] There, Moscow urged "total war against landlords" and a "communist movement in the villages." In an ironic contrast, the early CCP leadership initially opposed this, still preferring an orthodox Marxist working-class strategy, and it warned in 1920 that China must "not adopt the Bolshevik methods blindly."[6]

At that time, however, China was even less economically developed than Russia. Chinese workers were far fewer than their Russian counterparts, and their dominance seemed as distant as an industrialized Chinese future. China's peasants were much more economically deprived, but more important, they were much more numerous and composed the only possible successful revolutionary force. So in the long run, agrarianism influenced Chinese Communism more than its Soviet predecessor and model. Unlike most Bolsheviks in the USSR (especially under Stalin), Chinese Communists accorded a progressive role in their revolution to the peasantry itself, not just formally but sometimes actually unleashing peasant power.

As early as the mid-1920s, the CCP entered a distinct phase of peasant Communism, even as Stalin forcefully rejected such a strategy for the USSR. This began in south China, with an outburst of violence that reciprocated and accelerated the brutality of nineteenth- and twentieth-century Chinese political struggles. Ideologically, the peasant focus of the early CCP persisted in the party's subsequent history and laid much of the groundwork for later policies once Mao Zedong assumed the party's leadership in 1935. After that, agrarian preoccupations became combined and intertwined with Maoist centralization of party power, especially in the rural areas affected by the CCP's land reform campaigns and its adoption of policies of heightened class struggle in 1947–48. After the party's defeat of the ruling Chinese Nationalist Party (Kuomintang, or KMT) in 1949 and the establishment of Mao's national CCP regime in Beijing, these features of centralization and agrarian ideology reappeared in turn in two socially disastrous domestic campaigns: the "Great Leap Forward" of 1958–60 and the "Great Proletarian Cultural Revolution" of 1966–76. With their huge death tolls, both proved to be massive indictments of Mao's rule, yet in divergent ways each campaign revealed the continuing influence of both Soviet and early CCP ideological precedents, as well as more traditional, non-Communist contexts for genocide such as territorial expansion. The Great Leap, for instance, which coincided with the military incorporation and intensification of Chinese control of the territory of Tibet, was the larger calamity in absolute numbers and involved a more Stalinist focus on crash industrialization, yet with much less ruthless violence in China proper. The Cultural Revolution was more purposefully destructive, partly resembling a Stalinist purge of the party but with greater mass involvement and taking comparatively fewer lives. It departed from Stalinism by returning to a more agrarian ideological preoccupation, yet, in some ethnic minority areas like Tibet, this also took on a cultural xenophobia, relatively new to the CCP but perhaps echoing Stalin's view of Ukraine. With the key exception of Tibet (which might be considered a case of CCP "internal expansion"), these two Chinese domestic disasters, unlike most other cases examined in this book, occurred in the absence of significant racialist animus or driving territorial ambition. The combined weight of peasant Communism, forced industrialization, and Stalinist centralization was itself sufficient to wreak unprecedented human destruction in the world's most populous country.

Peasant Communism

"Look at his white hands and face," the peasants said: "There is no mistake. He is a counter-revolutionary landlord's son and a class enemy."

I liked his face, which was open and innocent, and said I thought there was no crime on it. . . . P'eng P'ai smiled and took me by the hand.

"You are just as young and innocent as he," he said. "Class justice is not personal but a necessary measure of civil war. We must kill more, not less, in case of doubt. . . . The peasants are a hundred times less cruel than the landlords, and they have killed very, very few in comparison. The peasants know what is necessary for self-defence; if they do not destroy their class enemies they will lose morale and have doubt of the success of the revolution. This is their duty and yours."[7]

The speaker of these words, a member of the CCP Central Committee, was no peasant himself. "My people," Peng Pai later wrote, were "big landowners." His 30 relatives each had "fifty peasants as slaves."[8] The family owned 100 shops in the town of Haifeng, in Kwangtung province of south China.[9] Peng Pai came from a wealthier background than his junior comrade Mao Zedong, whose father was a rich peasant. Yet their careers were related. Historian Roy Hofheinz has described Peng Pai as "the father of Chinese rural communism" and "the first full practitioner of people's war in the Maoist sense."[10] In 1926, Mao said of Peng's achievements, "No other model is possible."[11] Forty years later, in a surer sign of his debt to Peng, Mao attempted to conceal it during the

Cultural Revolution, which suppressed memory of Peng Pai from the historical record.[12]

Peng Pai's contribution to Chinese peasant communism began early in his career. As a young man he traveled to Japan, and began studying politics and economics at Waseda University in 1919. Like many of China's youth in the aftermath of World War I, nationalism propelled Peng into radical political action. With other Chinese students in Tokyo, he took part in the nationalist May Fourth Movement. He then became involved in a Japanese university Socialist group specifically devoted to resolving "agrarian problems" and to forming agricultural cooperatives and peasant unions. Along with nationalism, agrarianism was reaching its height in Japan, and Peng was "deeply influenced by this trend," according to Shinkichi Eto's study of his career. Robert Marks, another historian who also emphasizes Peng's populist bent, points out that he later displayed admiration for the Russian anarchist Prince Kropotkin as well as for Karl Marx. In a third major study of Peng, Fernando Galbiati concurs and adds that while he was in Japan, Peng's free-ranging eclecticism even drew him briefly to Christianity.[13]

On his way home after graduation in 1921, Peng Pai met the leading Chinese Marxist Chen Duxiu and joined his Socialist Youth Corps. Peng wrote an appeal, "To My Countrymen," attacking the system of private property and calling openly for "a social revolution to destroy the law, the government and the state." At first, however, Peng Pai "hoped that social revolution could be brought about through education," and he formed an Association for Studying Socialism.[14]

Peng developed his violent bent slowly. Kwangtung's progressive-nationalist warlord, Chen Jiongming, who had supported Peng's studies in Japan, now put him in charge of education in his home county of Haifeng, but Peng became disillusioned with priming students "on what 'Confucius said . . .' and on how the osprey honked." He later denounced some schools as "simply prisons to put a stop to peasants' complaints of cold and hunger." He created new schools and revised the curriculum. Chen fired him in 1922 for organizing a May Day parade involving his students and "many boys and girls of wealthy families" sporting a banner saying "Bolshevisation." Peng published his analysis "that the agent of social revolution was China's peasantry, and it was the task of intellectuals to help organize them."[15] He then left teaching to plunge into the peasant movement.

With tenacity and genuine assistance from peasants, Peng recruited tens of thousands of supporters.[16] He set up the Provincial Peasant Union of Kwang-tung. Its 13 leaders included six intellectuals, and its cadres included "many students and teachers of high social prestige locally," mostly "from the upper or middle classes." They gave the movement some insurance against repression. As Eto points out, "[I]t would have been difficult to arrest the foreign-educated P'eng P'ai, who was the son of a major landlord." In his home counties east of Canton City, Haifeng and Lufeng (together known as Hai-lu-feng), the peasant movement grew peacefully in 1923. Peng used nonviolent, piecemeal methods, emphasizing moderate reform and amelioration of peasant living conditions. He backed this up with "strong-arm tactics" to flex collective muscle against those alleged to be extortionists.[17]

That Peng Pai's coalition consisted of farmers and students partly explains his success in building a local movement from the ground up, but Kwangtung's extreme social problems and the polarization of class relations in the province also played their part. Most peasants there did not own their land. Unlike in most of China, the rate of tenancy among peasants in early-twentieth-century Kwangtung averaged around 50 percent. Two-fifths of the first 12,000 members of Peng's peasant union were landless tenants; as many were partial tenants and hired laborers. According to the historian Galbiati: "The gap between rich and poor was widening, and peasants had no means of redress or even of being heard. . . . Tenants had to endure terrible exploitation. To pay the high rents, they incurred further debts, pawned tools and clothing, and subsisted on inadequate food." Some even had to sell their families; others were tortured by landlords. In Peng's youth, starvation often followed harvest failures or other disasters. Visible on the roads were "small groups of people leaning on sticks. They are pale and skeletal and now and then some fall, never to stand again."[18]

Social divisions could be bitter, too. In Haifeng, according to Galbiati, traditional clan battles "could embroil up to 120 villages for months or years." Hearts extracted from the bodies of captured enemies might even be "sliced up and served with garlic for condiment." On the other hand, clan loyalties could also strengthen peasant communal solidarity. One local community of "10,000 people all with the same surname" was considered "a kind of communist village—the clan owning all the fields, which were divided equally."[19]

A turning point came in August 1923, when local gentry assembled 300 vigilantes and stormed Peng's peasant association headquarters. They kidnapped

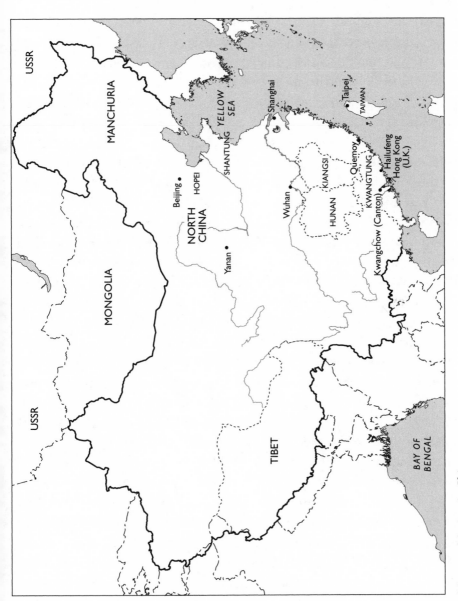

MAP 26. Maoism in China

and beat up 25 of its leaders. Even by this stage, no one had yet been killed on either side. However, the attack forced the closure of the association's premises, and peasants found themselves forcibly banned from organizing, at a time of "the worst famine in living memory." In Peng Pai's continuing pursuit of class conflict, his heretofore characteristic "disdain for armed defence" now ended. He joined the CCP in late 1923 and went underground in March 1924. Peng also broke irrevocably with his former patron Chen Jiongming, reflecting bitterly: "I saw them all, the gentry, the landlords, the capitalists, the officials, the compradores, the whole lot of them. A bunch of round-faced, fat-bellied monsters crawling around Ch'en like flies. I boiled with anger, and hated the fact that I was unable with one sweep of a machine gun to mow them all down."[20]

The early CCP leaders, however, still gave priority to the urban working class over the peasantry and precedence to a broader "National Revolution" over Communism. The CCP general secretary Chen Duxiu criticized the strategy of "a communist movement in the villages" as being "somewhat romantic," insisting that "a communist movement needs the factory workers as their main force." The peasant's "conception of private ownership," he said, meant that "at the present time, only the national movement is suitable for the villages . . . only the national movement can overthrow the warlords and open the way for a communist movement." Though considering a peasant movement important, Chen Duxiu denied that it could be class-based and doubted that "the peasants will immediately commence a communist-style socialist revolutionary movement." He favored one that encouraged their nationalism instead.[21]

For his part, the young Mao Zedong still shared that gradualist view of rural revolution but was already moving toward a more radical reliance upon the peasantry rather than the working class. At the CCP's Third Congress in July 1923, Mao stated first that China must wait: "National revolution in China must be after the world revolution." Socialist revolution in the industrial sector was even further off. At that stage, he thought only rapid capitalist development could make the "Chinese proletariat increase a great quantity." Failing such an unlikely possibility, in his view, the CCP should rely upon neither capitalists nor workers but on peasants. Unlike Chen Duxiu, Mao argued that peasants were the Chinese Communists' key constituency, not only numerous but oppressed: "No bourgeois revolution is possible in China. . . . All anti-foreign movements [were] carried on by those who have empty stomach but not Bourgeoisie." In his vision, the revolutionary task thus fell to the petty bourgeoisie, including the peasantry. The Kuomintang, Mao went on, "is dominated by Petit

Bourgeois," which "for the present time" could play the leading role. He concluded: "That is why we should join Kuomintang. . . . Peasants and small merchants are good material for Kuomintang."[22]

The CCP adopted the strategy of "national revolution" but moved only very slowly toward a peasant policy. Supported by the Comintern, the CCP formed a United Front with the KMT against China's warlord armies. Peng Pai accepted appointment as secretary of the new KMT Peasants' Department in 1924. There, with little Communist Party encouragement at a time when the CCP itself still lacked its own Peasant Department, Peng Pai organized the Peasant Movement Training Institute. Also involved was Mao Zedong. Like Peng Pai, Mao joined the KMT in 1924 and was elected an alternate member of its Central Executive Committee. According to his biographer Stuart Schram, Mao "threw himself into his task of organizing cooperation with the Kuomintang so enthusiastically that he was soon looked upon with suspicion in his own party." Only after returning home to Hunan in 1925 for a rest from these pressures did Mao make his "discovery of the revolutionary force among the peasantry."[23] Like Peng, he had found more initial interest in peasant movements in the Kuomintang than in the CCP.

Peng Pai, while secretary of a special CCP branch in Haifeng, sponsored radical local rural reforms that went far beyond existing party policy in 1925. He pushed through a 25 percent rent reduction and organized a peasant self-defense corps. Then, in the midst of a local anti-Communist revolt, the warlord Chen Jiongming and others helped landlords and police to retake control of Hai-lu-feng. Using the slogan "It is better to kill a thousand than to let one Communist escape," they murdered 70 peasant organization leaders and members, and over 200 more throughout the two counties.[24]

These massacres were a watershed. After the CCP's then ally, KMT leader Chiang Kai-shek, had routed the attackers, Peng Pai returned to Haifeng and to the fray with a bloodthirsty address that he delivered to local peasant delegates on October 25, 1925: "We have to shift from sorrow to power. We are mad for merciless extermination of the enemy: we thirst for the last drop of the enemy's blood as compensation for our martyred comrades. . . . 'Benevolence' to the enemy is cruelty to the revolutionary side. From now on we must go forward following the tracks of the martyrs' blood, and must exterminate our enemy to the last."[25]

According to a later CCP account, the local Communists now "executed a great many illegal landlords, local rascals and oppressive gentry. Every Party member performed some executions." They raided and burned down "reaction-ary hamlets." The peasant movement was already growing fast in many parts of China, but its violence in Hai-lu-feng was greater than elsewhere and so were peasant casualties. Peng, a member of both the CCP and the KMT's Provincial Executive Committee, enforced security of tenancy and rent reductions of 64 percent in Hai-lu-feng. By comparison, in Canton itself the two parties' United Front government could proclaim no rent reductions at all.[26] In 1926, the KMT officially proclaimed a policy of rent reduction, which the CCP, still lagging on the peasant issue, had yet to adopt. At this point, however, it began to respond. Mao was then in Canton, working in the KMT's Peasant Movement Training Institute. In September 1926, Schram writes, "Mao took the whole student body of the Peasant Movement Training Institute on a two-week visit to Haifeng, where they were given lectures by Peng Pai and shown an agrarian revolution in action."[27] Mao gave unqualified praise to Peng's achievements: "Hai-feng ... historically has been crowded by a complex group of local bullies, bad gen-try, grasping officials, and corrupt bureaucrats. [Since Peng Pai began working there] it has been the object of envy by all the other counties in the province.... This is the only form for the Chinese revolution to take; there is no other. Every place in all of China must become like Hai-[feng] and Lu-[feng] counties; then the national revolution will be successful."[28] Interestingly, Peng Pai and now Mao were much closer than was the CCP leadership to what had been the early Comintern view of China. Readily accepting "Bukharin's dream," Peng proclaimed that "the revolution has left the cities and has entered the country-side."[29]

Mao's famous analysis of March 1927, his *Report on an Investigation of the Peasant Movement in Hunan,* shared and partly vindicated Peng Pai's faith in a peasant revolution. Mao proclaimed that "a revolution is not a dinner party. ... To put it bluntly, it is necessary to create terror for a while in every rural area.... Proper limits have to be exceeded in order to right a wrong."[30] More violent vindication suddenly arrived, in the form of a brutal betrayal by some-one who had until now been an ally. That April, Chiang Kai-shek's KMT forces fell murderously on the Communists in Canton, destroying the United Front and Communist organizations there. Peng's aggressive approach immediately won further favor in the CCP, which elected him the next month to its Cen-tral Executive Committee, at the Fifth Party Congress in Wuhan. With Mao and others, Peng proposed the radical confiscation of "all landed property." The CCP leaders still rejected this, preferring to limit confiscations to "all the landed property of the large landowners." However, the party finally set up a National Peasant Union, headed by Mao with Peng Pai on its provisional executive committee. In August 1927, Mao called for "the immediate formation of soviets, the abandonment of the Kuomintang, and the confiscation of all land without exception."[31]

Two weeks after Chiang's coup in Canton, the Communists in Haifeng responded by arresting all local officials and killing most of them along with other "anti-revolutionaries." The KMT army then attacked and seized the town, reinstating landlord power. Peng Pai complained later that the revolutionaries had simply failed to kill enough people while they had the chance. While the CCP leadership wavered in Wuhan, its Hai-lu-feng branch proclaimed: "Whenever the officials of the reactionary military, administrative and tax organisations, tax collectors, informers, spies, soldiers, and cooks and servants of the reactionary associations are found, they should be executed."[32]

Violent revolution spread. In the countryside of Hai-lu-feng, the local party's program of "land to the tillers" encouraged peasants not only to withhold rent but also to kill landlords. In September 1927, the Communists regained Haifeng from the KMT and established a "Workers-Peasants' Dictatorship," with what they called the "sole task" of "the extermination of anti-revolutionaries."[33] A November "Resolution on Killing All Reactionaries" stated: "[A]ll persons aiding the enemy and all reactionaries, such as corrupt officials, greedy bureaucrats, bully landowners, evil gentry, spies, propagandists, policemen, Peace Preservation corpsmen, messengers and tax collectors for the enemy, and all those who work in their offices must be seized and executed."[34] Haifeng fell again, but the Communists regained it on November 1. Now a soviet government was formally inaugurated. An inside party source, stating that "[t]he people were free to execute traitors," revealed a chilling slogan: "We often warned, 'Don't let one slip away from the net, even if some be killed on false charge.' ... Some of the peasants of Lu-feng, seeing the extremes of our levies, executions, and burnings, and our recommendations to them for violence, have said, 'If you go to extremes the peasant union will fail.'"[35]

Peng Pai reportedly recalled that "we constantly warned party officers and comrades at all levels that we would rather kill in error than allow anyone to escape our net." A Communist source specified the number of victims: no fewer than 1,822 "landlords and evil gentry."[36] Every parcel of land was confiscated, including those of small landowners, and redistributed among all. The Revolutionary Government resolved "to exterminate all the landowners." Captured enemy soldiers were publicly executed and "Western-trained doctors" vilified.[37] At first, the party had to offer executioners bonuses of silver for each killing. But Eto writes that "the peasants were led in ruthless retaliation, and once the peasants were aroused, the Party did not control their violence."[38]

That violence was astonishing. Three thousand members of the Lin lineage of landlords were "virtually exterminated" in five months in mid-1927. Late that year, soviet forces wiped out a "very large Catholic village," murdering several thousand people; they massacred the inhabitants of three other villages and "systematically destroyed" two hamlets.[39] The Communists had proved at least as bloody as the traditional violent clan warfare and the brutality of their contemporary political enemies. What is striking is the brutalization of Peng Pai's movement since its initial "disdain for armed defence" up to 1923 or even as late as 1925.

Peng could still count on his ability to arouse peasant fervor. Hofheinz describes him as "magnetic . . . ever the raconteur," even "a snappy dresser" who went about unarmed. Significantly, he envisaged creating a system not of shared poverty but of plenty, "rural reform and improvement even at the height of brutality." In a speech on November 18, 1927, Peng is reported to have proclaimed that "in Haifeng the killing had begun. Now the home county was Red and peasants would no longer have to scrimp to pay their year-end debts. The peasant would pay rent only to himself; the gentry and landowning bully would get the beatings. And perhaps, he rhapsodized, the year after next they could buy large machines from outside countries to till the land. And the year after that perhaps every village would have electric lights, running water, leisure places, schools, and libraries."[40]

Peng brought his party's leaders along with him. In November 1927, disillusioned with the failure of its moderate rural strategy and of its pursuit of the disastrous KMT alliance, the CCP leadership swung its policy to the extreme left, adopting the policies of the Hai-lu-feng party organization. That year it was Peng Pai who founded the CCP's journal Red Flag, and in July 1928 he joined the Politburo as head of the CCP's Peasant Department.[41] By then, however, the Hai-lu-feng Soviet had already collapsed. In February–March 1928, anti-Communist forces invaded the area again, killing several thousand people and inflicting 1,000 casualties on the peasant army. Peng Pai fled. In August 1929, a former Hai-lu-feng comrade betrayed him to the KMT. After he attempted escape, his Kuomintang jailers sentenced Peng to execution.[42] At the hearing, he reportedly gave the court "a full declaration of his work" and said: "We in

Hai-Lu-feng killed a lot of KMT counterrevolutionaries like you. There is no need to question me further: just take me out to be shot."[43]

Peng Pai's career demonstrated a distinctive combination of awesome violence with the cultivation and manipulation of a mass movement promising economic development.[44] Unlike many later Communist leaders, Peng worked happily and deliberately in full public view. Deviousness was not his drawback. His straightforward brutality seemed directed toward meeting peasant demands for land as much as ideological goals. Extreme as he was, Peng made no attempt to collectivize peasant land, establish communal mess halls, or otherwise undermine peasant family life (despite some feminist influences and the "radical bloodthirstiness" of local women's units.) Trained abroad and ready, unlike his CCP superiors, to "adopt the Bolshevik methods," Peng was an internationalist who also appeared devoid of racial or xenophobic preoccupations. In contrast to Stalin's and Mao's subsequent comprehensive repression of their own Communist parties, few internecine purges struck Peng's Hai-lu-feng CCP branch. Hofheinz also points to the absence of "the mass-line techniques of rule" that Mao and Liu Shaoqi were later to develop at Yanan: "no real cooperatives,... no army-run farms,... no rectification campaigns, no arguments about the proper style of leadership."[45] Although an eclectic freethinker, Peng did not try to abolish religion, either; he recalled in his memoirs early peasant collaborators who had "solemnly" warned him against that: "When you're making propaganda in the villages, leave the subject of their gods and saints alone." Peng reported: "I made no objection."[46]

The most striking features of Peng Pai's Hai-lu-feng Soviet include its single-minded rural preoccupation and its conception of peasants as proletarians; the ruthless and radical class exterminations; the total land confiscations; the rapid drive toward Communism; the scant pretence at separation of party and state. Much of this later came to be identified with Maoism. Even "that eternal badge of the higher political cadre, the fountain pen," first appeared in Hai-lu-feng.[47] Decades afterward, it became the emblem of rank in the CCP and finally among Cambodia's Khmer Rouge.

The class conflict that traditionally divided Hai-lu-feng and Peng's radical initiatives there both set the scene for Mao Zedong's successful rural strategy for the Chinese Revolution. Yet the CCP's military disasters of 1927 shocked Mao. By the time the CCP swung left that November, CCP colleagues reportedly accused him of "hesitation to exterminate the anti-revolutionaries" and "failure to press the agrarian revolution." Mao was dismissed from his party

posts. According to Eto, he "turned away from simple terrorism and endeavoured to preserve his military force. He tried to broaden the base of his support as much as possible."[48]

Nevertheless, the later Maoist suppression of the historical record about
Peng Pai, from 1965 to 1978, suggests that Mao owed Peng a real debt that he
preferred not to acknowledge.[49] As early as 1936, Mao belittled Peng by blaming his "policy of putschism" for the short life of the Hai-lu-feng Soviet. In its
place as China's "first soviet government," Mao falsely claimed the honor for
his own forces and the "Jiangxi Soviet" on the Hunan province border in 1931–
34.[50] There, he added, in an attempt to emphasize innovation on his own part,
"we promoted a democratic programme, with a moderate policy" which, Mao
carefully observed, earned the "recrimination" of unnamed "*putschists* in the
party, who were demanding a terrorist policy of raiding, and burning and killing of landlords." They apparently criticized Mao for pursuing a "rich-peasant
line."[51]

Yet the United Front policy that eventually made Mao famous neither
quickly nor entirely overshadowed the class struggle. In June 1933, for instance, he attacked "the landlords' and rich peasants' open counterrevolutionary struggle," which had enabled them to "snatch the fruits of the land
revolution." Hofheinz writes: "In South Kiangsi province, where Mao built his
Central Soviet Republic, a primitive economy and savage suppression tactics
drove him to adopt harsh confiscation and political terror tactics." Historian
Suzanne Pepper adds that through most of the 1930s the CCP's policies of
"general redistribution of landlord land" to peasants again produced "leftist
errors" in which "the landlords were left with no means of support, while the
rich peasants were allotted only the poorest land."[52] Later CCP measures to
slow such generation of domestic enemies were still barely apparent in 1936.

The Peng Pai strategy of reliance on the peasantry had now become Mao's
hallmark. Historians concur on this while debating the balance of rural power.
Hofheinz lists the key characteristics of the peasant movement as Maoism's
major inheritance: the rural strategy, "mass work [and] faith in crowds," the use
of force through mobilizing an "armed local population," and the party's "total
autonomy" in relation to foreign Communists and domestic allies, including
the peasantry, with the Communist Party serving as "a device to impose solutions on and extract power from the countryside."[53]

Questioning a "top-down" interpretation, however, Galbiati sees the Hai-
lu-feng Soviet as "a traditional peasant revolt in a modern setting." Peng Pai,

aiming "to enable the peasants to stand on their own feet," came to champion "peasant interests as Communist goals." The CCP, Galbiati continues, saw little choice; "otherwise, the peasants would not have rallied to it." Indeed, the CCP occasionally became "submerged in a total rural takeover" in which traditional peasant vengeance and violence "often went beyond or against Party directives." For his part, Marks adds that Haifeng peasants demanded land, in the face of which insufficiently radical party policies "led to a growing split between the CCP cadre and the peasants." Hofheinz writes that in November 1927, "even in the heat of civil war the strength of small-holder opinion could not be resisted."[54]

As in Bolshevik Russia in the 1920s, the vast peasantry and the organized party were well matched. South China's especially polarized landholding pattern had allowed Peng Pai to forge an extraordinary coalition. As the Communist revolution slowly spread to other parts of China, however, it met greater peasant resistance. Throughout the country in the 1930s, almost half the peasantry were smallholders who owned enough land to support their families. Only 30 percent were full tenants.[55] Confrontation loomed as long as the party saw the peasantry as the foundation of a radical Communist revolution. According to Hofheinz, "From 1928 to 1949 the Chinese Communist movement shaped every decision in order to avoid the pitfalls while preserving the vision of the peasant movement period."[56] This moderation of tactics, including the United Front, meant no strategic departure. Mao's tactical innovation complemented Peng Pai's strategic rural legacy. Mao saw the latter as central, and eventually had to obliterate Peng's memory to claim the peasant strategy as his own.

The Land Reform Campaigns, 1947–52

In the period of the Long March, as the KMT drove the CCP from most of south China in the mid-1930s, the main theater of Communist activity shifted to the north. Agrarian relations there were quite unlike those of the south. The prevailing pattern of agriculture in the north of China was not large landlordism and tenancy but "small-scale owner farming." The richest 10 percent of landholders owned 40 percent of the land there, but as many as 50 percent were small owners, and only 20 percent were landless. Yet poverty was still widespread. In the North China provinces of Hopei and Shantung in the 1930s, respectively 40 percent and 25 percent of farming families failed to cover their expenses, and 43 percent and 28 percent were in debt.[57] As historian Edwin Moise writes: "The poor of China needed every scrap of wealth they could obtain. Death by starvation was at least a distant possibility for a large fraction of the peasantry. In the rural areas of northern China, famine probably claimed something like 8 percent of every generation." And the poor "could reasonably expect that their children would be even poorer."[58]

Economic deprivation amid relative equality of landownership in North China meant that CCP land redistributions could not directly resolve the poverty of an already landowning smallholder peasantry. Moreover, as Mao admitted in 1934, land reform had often temporarily lowered agricultural output.[59] And from 1931 the expanding Japanese invasion of China also had to be confronted. So in 1936–37, the CCP formed a second United Front with the KMT to oppose Japan, and it restricted its rural program to rent reduction instead of the confiscation and redistribution of landlords' land. In 1942, the Party Central Committee reaffirmed this moderate policy of "reduc[ing] feudal exploitation, not eliminating it." By the time of the Japanese surrender in September 1945, Moise writes that in the zones it controlled, "the CCP had made about half the population middle peasants," and middle peasants made up one-third of its People's Liberation Army. In October, the CCP's Zhou Enlai asserted that reductions in land rents and interest rates were the chief party goals, and that land redistribution and nationalization should be indefinitely postponed.[60]

Yet the very next month, Mao revealed that China's victory over the Japanese now enabled the CCP to move against domestic enemies: "Rent reduction must be the result of mass struggle ... excesses can hardly be avoided ... [and] can be corrected afterwards." Worse, a new outbreak of all-out civil war with the KMT began in July 1946. Within two years, in the final throes of that struggle, the CCP launched what historians have called a new "radical agrarian policy and harsh Party rectification," and it also echoed Stalin by conducting "a rather paranoid purge of its own organizations."[61]

The new land policy radicalization began in Manchuria, occupied by Japan from 1931 to 1945, where the agrarian pattern was much more polarized than in North China. In northern Manchuria in particular, the top 14 percent of landholders owned as much as 88 percent of the land, and 63 percent of households were landless. The central Manchuria figures were slightly less extreme, resembling more the polarized inequality of land ownership in south China. At the end of World War II, the CCP quickly seized much of Manchuria from the Japanese, and in April 1946 it ordered confiscation and redistribution of the lands owned by the Japanese and their clients there. A CCP directive noted the next month that "the masses have obtained land directly from the land-lords. . . . In the face of the broad mass movement, the local Party commit-tees . . . must support all the equitable demands and rightful actions of the peasants, and approve land [ownership] which has already been obtained or is being obtained by the peasants." According to the CCP's Liu Shaoqi, the di-rective ordered cadres "to leave the rich peasants' land and property basically untouched."[62]

In part, local pressures drove the CCP to revert to Peng Pai's peasant policy. Historian Tanaka Kyoko suggests that "the Party decided to follow the peas-ants' radicalism." In these new frontline areas, the CCP still considered unity with powerful landlords particularly necessary, and so it would have preferred to exercise caution, but it was faced with "spontaneous radicalization of the mass movement." In mid-1946, Mao maintained a moderate posture, propos-ing "first extending rent and interest reduction to the whole country and then taking proper measures for the gradual achievement of 'land to the tiller.' " But by late 1946, Tanaka says, "the CCP came to realize that . . . the peasants would not be active in supporting the Party unless land reform was thoroughly im-plemented."[63]

As in the 1920s, then, "small-holder opinion" greatly influenced the CCP, distancing the Chinese Communist Party from Stalin's policies. In December 1947, Mao insisted on "firm unity with the middle peasants," stating that "it is necessary to listen to the opinions of the middle peasants and make conces-sions to them if they object." He said that CCP members (unlike Soviet officials in the 1930s) must "avoid the mistake of classifying middle peasants as rich peasants." The party's campaign slogan was *fanshen*, literally "to turn the body over," which Moise translates in economic terms as "acquiring enough wealth to become an independent farmer." During this period, he writes, the CCP gave poor-peasant leagues and peasant associations "tremendous power." A re-gional CCP "Letter to the Peasants" denounced "alien class elements, oppor-tunists, traitors and puppet personnel, who have infiltrated the Party" and its organs, adding, "however you want to punish them, you can." The CCP news-paper *Renmin ribao* announced in newly liberated areas: "For the masses to take action themselves, even if they become disorderly, is better than for us to lead them." A Peasants' Association committee even announced: "We must place the Communist Party under our supervision.... We loudly cry, 'All power to the peasant representative assemblies!'"[64]

However, the party's extension of its new land reform from Manchuria to North China, where landlordism was much less prevalent, revealed that the CCP had more at stake. Tanaka explains that party strategy, as earlier at Yanan, was to achieve "mass mobilization" in the changed climate from an anti-Japanese war to a Chinese civil war. This was a political, not an economic, goal. Suzanne Pepper adds that the party's aim was to overturn "the existing rural elite": "Whether or not it was dominated by landlords in any given village was not the issue."[65] Party policy now threatened a confrontation with the North China peasantry, for which the CCP remained ill prepared. The mutual mass slaughter of Kwangtung in the 1920s did not recur, but the party's object of "eliminating the landlord class as a whole" was extremely radical. In one case, "the peasants even killed four of the most hated 'despots.'" The CCP also extended redistribution to property other than land.[66] This appears to confirm that the party sought dominance by displacement or destruction of the rural elite, whatever its source of power—and whatever the impact on the peasantry.

On the other hand, the owner-farmer ideal also remained pervasive in the party. Mao claimed in February 1947 that already in two-thirds of the liberated areas, "the land problem has been solved." His definition remained moderate: "[T]he policy of land to the tillers has been carried out; this is a great victory." Mao did add that "we must check carefully and must 'even up' to ensure that the peasants with little or no land obtain some land and the local gentry and local tyrants are punished." This radicalization that Mao envisaged still aimed at equalizing private land ownership (plus unspecified "punishment")—not yet communalization or formation of cooperatives. The CCP's September 1947 National Land Conference adopted the policy of "equal per capita distribution of land," and its Outline Land Law, aiming at "land to the tiller," declared that "all the village people shall obtain land equally."[67]

Even where the yeoman ideal was impractical, the party pursued it in the face of reality, and with deleterious consequences. The Central Committee and Mao vastly exaggerated when they proclaimed that landlords and rich peasants owned three-quarters of China's land. The goal of the CCP's 1946–47 land reform, in Tanaka's words, was "to make every peasant a middle peasant," possessing enough to support their families. Yet, especially in North China, with its much less pronounced concentration of landholdings, any equalization of holdings unavoidably meant confiscating some land from middle peasants and instead making "every peasant a poor peasant." By late 1947, Mao himself was calling for moderation of the land reform, and in April 1948 the CCP retreated from its radical agrarian policy. Mao had aimed to win over the middle peasants of North China, but he had found the ideal of equal distribution of land to be incompatible with their interests.[68]

The tension between party and peasants rose, and even wracked the CCP itself. By April 1947, Mao's leading colleague, Liu Shaoqi, came to believe that landlords and rich peasants had infiltrated the local CCP organizations and had usurped control of the liberated villages. Liu proposed creating poor peasant leagues to share power with the party's Peasant Associations for the implementation of land reform and subjecting village cadres to free criticism by the villagers. The next month, Mao took "the crucial decision to reveal the hitherto secret Party membership in order to have all Party members in the villages examined by the masses." This harsh party "rectification" campaign may have set an early precedent for the Cultural Revolution. Mao later claimed that in 1947–48, CCP cadres had been guilty of "tailism" and of "following whatever poor peasants said." He was scapegoating. Mao's ambitions for total party control more than matched local peasant power. As in Russia in the 1920s, peasant and party interests both held strong and were in sufficient balance to set the stage for an epic confrontation like that in Stalin's USSR in the 1930s. The CCP's pronounced softening of its policy in 1948–50 only postponed a confrontation with the peasantry.[69]

The CCP's rural priority after victory in 1949 was extermination of landlords. During 1950–52, Moise writes, "the CCP was quite open on the subject of killings. It was perfectly willing to say, with large headlines in *Nanfang ribao,* that people were being shot. It even published statistics, and the totals were quite large." Mao later gave a confidential figure of 800,000 people executed by the government's security forces up to 1954. Moise suggests that the total death toll in the CCP's land reforms and campaigns of repression probably exceeded 1 million.[70]

The Great Leap Forward

China's 1958–61 famine, caused by Mao's Great Leap Forward, was "the most murderous in human history."[71] Census data shows that the country's 1957 mortality rate of 1.08 percent rose in three years to 2.54 percent. In 1960 alone, China's total population fell by 4.5 percent. From 1958 to 1961, at least 13 million people and probably close to 30 million people starved to death.[72] The toll far exceeded even that of Stalin's famine of 1932–33. However, the apparent ethnic or expansionist character of this catastrophe was limited to Tibet. In China proper, the victims were disproportionately Han Chinese rather than ethnic minorities.

Nor did any urgent external threat provoke the policies causing the disaster. Like the CCP's military suppression of Tibet in 1959, the epochal Sino-Soviet split emerged during the Great Leap Forward, but only in its latter stages. Stalin had died in 1953, but Mao still saw China's alliance with the USSR as "the rising East wind" as late as 1959.[73] Relations ruptured only with Yugoslavia during the Leap. If the Great Leap was a defensive program to achieve self-reliance, nothing required risking such a crash economic program.

In his seminal study of the Great Leap, Roderick MacFarquhar noted the close relations between the Soviet and Chinese Communist giants after 1949. These included joint stock companies, joint management of a Chinese railway, the stationing of Soviet troops in the jointly used Port Arthur military base, and the banning of third-country nationals from such areas. In the second half of 1958, the Soviets pushed their luck, requesting a naval radio station. When Mao refused, Khrushchev arrived in China to ask for a full naval base. "Mao reacted violently," according to MacFarquhar. He publicly praised a Soviet-trained Chinese military writer whose recent work "sniped at foreign advisers . . . [and] subscribed to the Maoist doctrine that it is men and not weapons that are decisive in war."[74]

Such antimaterialist voluntarism, along with Mao's peasant revolutionary strategy, composed his signature contribution to third world guerrilla warfare. The 1958 outburst may have signaled the seriousness of a looming dispute with the Soviets. Yet, MacFarquhar noted, Mao's major grievance at that point was Soviet "excessive caution" with the United States: "China's strategy was economic competition, to increase its strength through economic development, in order to impress the Americans, the Japanese, and Tito. . . . Mao decided that it was essential to go it alone to prove to Khrushchev that his critique of 'appeasement' was correct by showing that the Americans would back down if confronted."[75]

If expansionism was not a feature of Mao's posture, militarism certainly was. Mao notoriously asserted, in relation to a nuclear war, "that even if half the population of the world were wiped out this would not be a total disaster." This was also the period of his pamphlet "Imperialists and All Reactionaries Are Paper Tigers." In August 1958, within weeks of meeting Khrushchev but without consulting him, Mao ordered "a massive artillery barrage" of the KMT-held island of Quemoy to force the Nationalists to withdraw. In a month, "tens of millions of Chinese" were enlisted in the militia. The Great Leap Forward also began in August 1958. In the major conflict with the United States, China demanded a role as an equal partner with the Soviet Union. When Khrushchev postulated that all Communist nations would make the transition to Communism "more or less simultaneously," the Chinese welcomed this Soviet concession of priority. Nevertheless, the split continued to widen.[76] Parity was not one of Mao's goals.

Mao's emerging break with the USSR after Stalin's death did highlight the similarities between the Communist dictators. Two major features of the Great Leap Forward were its crash collectivization program and its voluntarist concept of an ideological "Communist wind" that would flatten material obstacles. Both recall Stalin's USSR of the 1930s. So does a third feature of the Leap, crash industrialization: the attempt, in an overwhelmingly agricultural country, "to leap forward simultaneously in industry and agriculture."[77] Consistent with this, a fourth major feature of Mao's Leap was massive urbanization.

Yet there were important differences. Just as China was materially less developed than Russia, its "Communist wind" was more voluntaristic, backed by greater idealism but fewer economic resources. The horrendous human cost of the Great Leap Forward owed more to ignorant, arrogant planning and criminally negligent economic mismanagement than to the callous destruction of peasant communities characteristic of the 1932–33 Soviet famine and the targeted mass shootings of the Great Terror. The CCP's repression of Tibet echoed Stalin's violent purges of diverse ethnic communities, but his personal contempt for the peasantry had no Chinese parallel.

Mao first sponsored a "little" Leap Forward in 1956, which he abandoned under pressure from more orthodox comrades. His renewed "Great Leap" originally referred to the massive 1957–58 drive to mobilize labor for water conservancy in the countryside. After the CCP's enlarged Politburo conference decided in August 1958 to establish People's Communes throughout China, the term "Great Leap Forward" applied to them.[78]

These communes combined agriculture and industry. They could consist of 2,000 to 10,000 households. The *People's Daily* claimed in 1958 that commune members "are guaranteed meals, clothes, housing, schooling, medical attention, burial, haircuts, theatrical entertainment, money for heating in winter and money for weddings." More radical change remained a distant goal. In a March 1958 speech, Mao claimed: "The family, which emerged in the last period of primitive communism, will in future be abolished. . . . Under the present system of distribution of 'to each according to his work,' the family is still of use. . . . After maybe a few thousand years, or at the very least several hundred years, the family will disappear."[79]

Communal eating halls, the *People's Daily* recognized, already involved "the change of the habits, in existence for thousands of years, of all the peasants." So did boarding nurseries and primary schools. In MacFarquhar's words, "Parents had to give up their bourgeois emotional attachments, stop worrying about their children and concentrate on work." Grandparents also became redundant, as "happiness homes for the aged" were established. The result in one area was that without children, grandparents, or family mealtimes, home life was completely redefined: "Each family was to have a one- or two-room flat, but without a kitchen."[80]

Economic scarcity and a modicum of CCP pragmatism tempered this ideological ambition. According to MacFarquhar, "[O]ver the whole country, the average amount distributed as free supply accounted for only 20–30 per cent of the total income of commune members." The maximum was 40 percent.[81] Wages and markets continued to play a necessary role. A popular ditty parodied the austere collectivized lifestyle:

> At the sound of the cease-work bell,
> We enter the mess hall to eat.
> Taking one mouthful of rice,
> We find sand between our teeth;
> Helping ourselves to the vegetable,
> We find grass stalks in it.
> We lay down the chopsticks,
> And go to work again.[82]

The CCP theoretical journal *Red Flag,* founded by Peng Pai in 1927, was relaunched during the Leap in 1958. *Red Flag* quickly defined "communist labour" as "voluntary labour, without set quotas, done without expectation of remuneration." Yet this never became generalized. Even the radical Zhang Chunqiao (later one of the "Gang of Four") concentrated his attacks not on wages but on piece rates, which the Great Leap abolished. An extreme proposal for "the ending of commodity production and the abolition of currency" foundered. The Leap's massive labor mobilization actually injected an extra 4 billion yuan in wages and subsidies into the market economy.[83]

The Leap thus began as a materialist attempt to create "an era of plenty." Agricultural development was under the direction of T'an Chen-lin, a CCP Politburo member and former printing worker. T'an's aim was prosperity, what MacFarquhar calls a "communist cornucopia," or "'goulash communism' with a vengeance": "After all, what does communism mean? First, taking good food, . . . a meat diet . . . delicacies . . . to each according to his needs. . . . Second, clothing . . . of various designs and styles, not a mass of black garments . . . overcoats lined with fox furs. . . . Third, housing . . . up to the standard of modern cities. . . . All live in high buildings. Needless to say, there are electric light, telephone, piped water, receiving sets and TV. . . . Fourth, communications . . . all travellers and commuters use transport. . . . Fifth, higher education for everyone and education is popularized."[84] This recalls Peng Pai's original vision of rural material prosperity more than his terror campaigns or Stalin's collectivization famine. However, in Mao's case, ideology intervened. The hybrid effect of "grafting" the ideology of the communes "on to what started as a supercharged production drive" now brought into play a new "ideological fervour and asceticism" that contradicted the more materialist initial goal of "an era of plenty."[85] The collectivization drive became known in China by early 1959 as a "Communist wind," a derogatory term in CCP usage for a campaign blowing too far left. Mao had put it this way in March 1958: "If something can't be done, then don't force it. Just now there's a puff of wind, a ten degrees typhoon. Don't obstruct it publicly. Get a clear picture of it in internal discussions. Compress the air a bit. Eliminate false reports and exaggerations. . . . It is not good if some targets are too high." Such moderate advice to top officials became rare at the height of the Leap, and anyway at ground level a "ten degrees typhoon" seems magnified a hundredfold. As one peasant told CCP army chief Peng Dehuai seven months later, "Apart from when the centre sends down a high-ranking cadre, who can stand up against this wind?"[86]

A moderate Communist, Peng Dehuai heard of peasants' cooking pots being confiscated and melted down—to help reach the steel target! He complained of a policy "fever in the brain," and spoke of the party "beating a gong with a cucumber." By early 1959, Mao himself was leading the campaign against the Communist wind, blaming local officials for overzealousness: "The cadres gave them only sweet potato gruel to eat and their faces were unsmiling." They "extorted things from production brigades and teams ... they were resolutely corrected and persuaded ... that egalitarianism was no good."[87] However, when Peng Dehuai confronted Mao publicly in September 1959, he proved unrepentant and reacted instead with new insistence on pushing forward: "It is only a partial failure. We have paid a price, blown some 'communist wind,' and enabled the people of the entire nation to learn a lesson.... Collective mess halls have deep economic roots. They should not nor can they be blown away by a gust of wind." Heels dug in. Voluntarism prevailed. Liu Shaoqi now talked of a "boat sailing against the current which must forge ahead or be driven back." Mao urged: "Hard, bitter struggle, expanding production, the future prospects of communism—these are what have to be emphasized, not individual material interest. The goal to lead people toward is not 'one spouse, one country house, one auto-mobile, one piano, one television.' This is the road of serving the self, not the society."[88]

Gone with the wind was the goal of material plenty, the "goulash communism" of T'an Chen-lin. As ideology reigned, famine and disaster set in. According to another Politburo member, Mao discovered too late "that we could not have a 'gust of communist wind,' but should operate on a system of three-level ownership [private, communal, and state]. If we had done that, things would have been different."[89]

Like the heady Stalinists after the Soviet bumper crop of 1930, the CCP Politburo decided to establish communes in August 1958, having been assured of "a summer harvest 69 per cent up on 1957." The Politburo also doubled the nation's 1958 grain target and raised the steel production target to exactly double the 1957 output. This was "the turning point in the leap." A "key element" was the policy of bringing industry to the countryside. By mid-September 1958, 20 million people were engaged in producing iron and steel, with native-style furnaces accounting for 14 percent of the steel output, 49 percent by October. Agriculture was neglected. As MacFarquhar put it, China achieved its 10.7-million-ton steel target in mid-December: "But in the fields, bumper harvests of grain, cotton and other crops awaited collection. A massive tragedy was in the making."[90]

The industrial workforce had increased from 9 million in 1957 to over 25 million in 1958, and 10 billion workdays, "about one-third of the time normally devoted to the production of grain, were lost to agriculture" in the first year of the Leap. Industrial output increased by 66 percent, but the chairman of the State Planning Commission wondered "how much has been lost after all?"[91]

Waste in the countryside was enormous, and peasants ate their reserves. Local officials allowed communal mess halls to serve extravagant rations, while providing exaggerated production reports. The state fell for its own propaganda targets. It believed the 1958 crop to be even better than it was, and forged ahead with the development of industry.

The process continued unabated until 1960. The agricultural labor force fell by 40 million. Compounding the CCP's ironclad industrial ambitions, disastrous climatic conditions in 1959 and 1960 brought crop failures and the world's greatest-ever famine. Too late to prevent the tragedy, Mao abandoned the industrialization priority in favor of "[t]aking agriculture as the basis."[92]

When the *People's Daily* referred to "the rivalry between the cities and the countryside for labour power,"[93] it was not cheering for the countryside. A major thrust of the Great Leap was "a colossal shift of labour . . . from countryside to town and city," a "haemorrhage of peasants to the cities." China's urban population grew from 99 million in 1957 to 130 million in 1961. The urban labor force tripled, from 9 million in 1957 to nearly 29 million in 1959, as did the number of workers in heavy industry, from 5 million in 1957 to 16 million in 1960. The new urbanites needed 6 million tons of additional grain from the countryside—adding 20 to 30 percent to the necessary state procurements, which reached their peak in the famine year of 1959–60.[94]

As the Leap advanced, its urban focus accentuated. Some 1958 experiments with urban communes were revived in 1959–60. Backyard steel furnaces were replaced with plans to modernize and upgrade the urban steel industry. As MacFarquhar puts it: "The essential feature of the revived leap was the change of commitment from 'native'-type industry to modern industry. . . . Critical . . . was the assistance of bourgeois industrialists and technicians. They had to be calmed and enlisted." President Liu Shaoqi conceded that the state should "satisfy the industrial and commercial circles with material benefits."[95]

The transfer of resources from countryside to town and from agriculture to industry led to an urban food supply crisis by early 1959 and contributed to the massive underproduction of food in rural areas in 1959–60. Grain rations fell from 203 kilograms per head in 1957 to 164 kilograms in 1960. After the famine struck, the result was a belated but extraordinarily excessive correction. "We must disperse the residents of the big cities to the rural areas," said Mao in 1960. CCP economic planner Chen Yun concurred: "If we don't send urban people to the countryside, we will again draw on peasants' rations." The party closed down 100,000 urban enterprises and by 1961, moved 10 million people from urban to rural areas, and another 10 million by 1965.[96] Confirming that 20 million people had been sent back to the countryside, Mao reportedly exclaimed: "We have twenty million people at our beck and call. What political party other than the ruling Chinese Communist Party could have done it?"[97]

The Cultural Revolution

In September 1965, when Mao's associate Lin Biao launched his dramatic international clarion call "Long Live the Victory of People's War," like Peng Pai in the 1920s, he borrowed almost verbatim from Bukharin's early concept of a sea of villages enveloping the cities of the world.[98] Its domestic counterpart, however, was the largely urban phenomenon known as the Great Proletarian Cultural Revolution, which broke out a few months later. President Liu Shaoqi quickly became one of its targets. Estimates of the number of victims of Mao's Cultural Revolution in the decade from 1966 to 1976 range widely, from 250,000 to as many as 7–8 million people killed or driven to suicide. One commonly accepted estimate suggests a toll of 400,000; another, over a million.[99]

Apart from the quartet of homegrown radical leaders later known as the Gang of Four, China's rising stars now included an alternate member of the CCP Politburo, Kang Sheng, who had once worked as a Comintern official and had lived in Moscow at the height of Stalin's purges, from 1932 to 1937, before joining Mao in Yanan. Kang Sheng has been called "a truly faithful follower of Mao." He was promoted in 1966 to the CCP Politburo Standing Committee, whose other members by 1969 included only Mao, Lin Biao, Zhou Enlai, and Chen Boda.[100]

As Mao's influence peaked, the search for enemies accelerated. The process of the purge often proved more important than the identity of its object. In 1967, the CCP newspaper *Kuangming Daily* recalled an earlier cartoon in which "a smoker is smouldering with anger because he could not light his cigarette after finishing a box of matches." The paper now described this scene as "an outburst of wrath of counter-revolutionary sentiments." Even enemy expressions of remorse were suspect, if not intolerable. Chekiang Radio railed in outrage against a political target who had made "two statements of repentance in succession." The radio denounced such repentance as "extremely frantic counter-attacks."[101]

The Cultural Revolution has inspired varying scholarly analyses, notably of its emphasis on reform of the individual. A "worker-PLA group," for instance, "resolved to lead the broad masses of teachers and students" to "explode a revolution deep in their souls, and fiercely seize power from 'self-interest' in their minds," while a Cultural Revolution poem promised: "[T]he cancer of 'self' we'll incise." There was nothing cultural about this, in the view of Sinologist Simon Leys: "The tabula rasa that the 'Cultural Revolution' established in all areas of culture, intelligence, and learning was meant as a radical measure to protect the power of an incompetent and half-literate ruling class."[102] Indeed, it slowly ground to a halt only after Lin Biao, Chen Boda, and Kang Sheng all mysteriously disappeared in 1971–72. Mao's own death in 1976 set the scene for China's slow emergence back onto the world stage and into a new phase of economic development and more restrained political violence.

A leading scholar of the Cultural Revolution, Lynn T. White III, has termed it "China's holocaust." Comparing human tolls, he writes that in the European Holocaust the murderous Nazi bureaucracy ensured that more people died than did in China, yet "[m]ore people suffered in the Cultural Revolution" because it swept up a "gigantic urban population." The two phenomena are further comparable, White continues, because Mao's notionally class-oriented campaign for pride in the proletarian "family" in fact "created something like racial prejudice" or even "a moral equivalent of tribal divisions," in which "official sponsorship of the proletariat as the salt of the earth led to rationalized injustice for others." However, White also notes important differences from the Nazi case. In terms of ethnic divisions, in China "the violence confused identities and cultures far more than it clarified them." And Hitler's personal role in the Holocaust "contrasts with Mao's more indirect involvement in the less-organized murders and suicides of the Cultural Revolution."[103] White sees the Cultural Revolution as far less controlled, less bureaucratic or top-down.

Despite the massive tragedies that Mao's dictatorship imposed on China, he also differed from his unacknowledged early model, Peng Pai. Mao was in some ways considerably more devious as well as more moderate. When Peng Pai stated, "We must kill more, not less, in case of doubt" and "Don't let one slip away from the net, even if some be killed on false charge," Peng blatantly fostered the excessive violence that resulted from needlessly exaggerating conflict. Mao enunciated a different, more supple approach that emphasized a combination of coalition building and political manipulation. He distinguished first between what he called "antagonistic contradictions" and nonantagonistic ones, or, as he called the latter, "contradictions among the people," and, in a

more philosophical context, between "principal" and "secondary" contradictions. Mao also chose to warn against "[t]hose with a 'Left' way of thinking
[who] magnify contradictions between ourselves and the enemy to such an extent that they take certain contradictions among the people for contradictions
with the enemy, and regard as counter-revolutionaries persons who are not
really counter-revolutionaries."[104] These formulae again distanced Mao from
Stalin's policies. Yet Mao pursued ruthless violence when it came to his personal power and ideological ambition, and on other occasions he often simply
disregarded his own cautions, causing the deaths of millions of Chinese.

CHAPTER 15

From the Mekong to the Nile

Genocide in Cambodia and Rwanda

T he successive tragedies of Cambodia and Rwanda in the late twentieth century revealed many of the underlying social and ideological patterns of genocide, despite important differences that might otherwise preclude parallels. These two tropical countries are overwhelmingly agricultural, and before each suffered genocide, they shared similar demographics. Of Cambodia's 1975 population of approximately 8 million, an ethnic Khmer majority made up over 80 percent. In 1994, an ethnic Hutu majority accounted for 85 percent of the 7 million Rwandans.[1] The two perpetrator regimes, the Khmer Rouge and Hutu Power, shared preoccupations with racism, antiquity, and agriculture, and they even harbored significant territorial ambitions, all of which echoed major obsessions of previous genocidal regimes.

Yet the two catastrophes were politically and culturally as unrelated as they were geographically distant and dissimilar. Rwanda, "the Land of a Thousand Hills" (*La Terre des Mille Collines*), scarcely resembles the vast alluvial plain of predominantly lowland Cambodia. Much smaller, Rwanda has richer soil but far less available land than Cambodia. Rwanda is approximately 80 percent Christian, Cambodia 80 percent Buddhist. Significantly, most victims of the Pol Pot regime in Cambodia came from its ethnic Khmer majority, while most targets of the Rwandan genocide were minority Tutsi. There is no evidence that the perpetrators, who inhabited opposite ends of the political spectrum, ever paid any attention to one another. Their lack of political contact and compatibility, however, only underlines the deeper commonalities of contemporary genocide.

Cambodia

The Nazi invasion of France in 1940, and the advent of the pro-German Vichy regime of Marshal Philippe Pétain, brought the French colonies of Indochina under the rule of xenophobic European nationalism. The new French governor-general, the Pétainist rear admiral Jean Decoux, arrived in Indochina in mid-1940. Imperial Japanese military forces, uneasy allies of Vichy, also moved into the region over the next year.

Cambodia, Vietnam, and Laos had endured violent French conquest and colonial domination since the late nineteenth century.[2] Now they faced a more unstable, more ideological regime that officially combined colonialism with patriotism and accorded tradition a novel role. As historian Eric Jennings writes, the conservative "National Revolution" of Vichy France emphasized "authenticity, simplicity, hierarchy, and the return to tradition," to the soil and the homeland, *le terroir et la terre*. This was a revolution "tailored for Basques, Bretons and Burgundians rather than for Vietnamese, Laotians and Cambodians."[3] Its imposition in Indochina was forceful. Historian Penny Edwards writes that "Decoux's achievements in Cambodia included the abolition of all elected bodies, the violent dispersal of peaceful protests, the internment of Cambodian activists and a crackdown on press freedom."[4] In 1942, for instance, the French authorities suppressed the first independent Khmer-language newspaper, *Nagaravatta*.

Along with authentic local nationalism, Admiral Decoux also had to contend with the occupation forces of Japan, a formidable regional power that appealed to neighboring colonized peoples with the slogan "Asia for the Asians." In this strange strategic and ideological theater, the new Vichy policy based on what Jennings calls "French *völkisch* essentialism" produced not only antisemitic laws in Indochina but also a "nativist turn" that saw the colonial power marshaling neo-orientalist symbols to foster more controlled local nationalisms, in part by glorifying "distant Indochinese pasts." The French thus tried to assign their subjects "imaginary, idealized, hierarchical, and wishfully oligarchic" histories parallel to the Vichy portrayal of the French past. Tradition would create new nations, *petites patries*, under French rule.[5]

Decoux wished Cambodia would develop "a sincere national spirit." He ordered local administrators to maintain Khmer "ancestral customs, moral values, and traditional hierarchies," and he urged Cambodian youth groups to excavate their roots by participating in archaeological work at the ancient

temples of Angkor. The new approved Cambodian national anthem proclaimed: "The temples are asleep in the forest, Reminding us of the greatness
of Great Angkor, As the rock of the Khmer race is eternal." Therefore, while
Decoux's wartime colonial policy strained to foster competing new loyalties
to both France and its Indochina federation, it also deliberately stimulated
local racialist and cultural particularism, lending intellectual support even to
possible expansionist Khmer visions of a "greater Cambodia." Especially after
Thailand seized Cambodia's northwest provinces from French control in 1941,
Decoux encouraged Khmer irredentism along with national revivalism.[6]

The Vichy regime's prescriptions of *petite* patriotism, traditional hierarchy,
ethnic origins, and "natural" rural elites all merged with its ideology of the
land. In France, Jennings writes, Vichy had "pilfered selectively from fascist
doctrines" like the cult of the soil (see fig. 36). Indochina, too, proved fertile
ground for "the folkloric, essentialist, ruralist and traditionalist stock themes
of Vichy's cultural agenda." Now French and Vietnamese anti-Communists, for
instance, "interwove the image of the unspoiled paddy field with Pétain's cult of
the earth—'the soil that never lies.'" A 1942 Indochina government publication
celebrating "peasant thought" of both France and Vietnam elicited praise from
the colonial journal *L'action* for "the wonderful peasant race embodied by the
Annamite farmer." Indochinese youth groups fostered by Decoux's "recultura-
tion" policy were soon reported "trudging through the mud, surrounded by
vermin in remote villages; . . . among the peasants of the delta, among the
lumberjacks in the forests. Everywhere they ask questions, they investigate,
they improve their understanding of the country."[7]

Significantly, French colonial notions of the importance of the soil extended
well beyond Vichy ideology. The distinguished savant and colonial official Paul
Mus, who joined the Free French in 1943 and later supported Vietnamese independence, had perceived beneath the various indigenous cultures of Indochina
what he called an underlying "cadastral religion" involving "the divinization of
the energies of the soil" through the medium of the ancient kin of its inhabitants. Mus wrote: "[What] better intermediaries could there be to define the
union of the group and its soil than the ancestors of the group, buried in the
soil and thus restored to it?" He suggested that in ritual terms, these indigenous
"dead chiefs" had been "the land itself made man." Mus thus saw a cultural link
between the lands and peoples of Indochina, between *l'habitat et l'habitant.*[8]

However, Decoux's wartime administration went far further. Echoing fascist thinking, it considered Cambodian youths "indolent" and sought to make

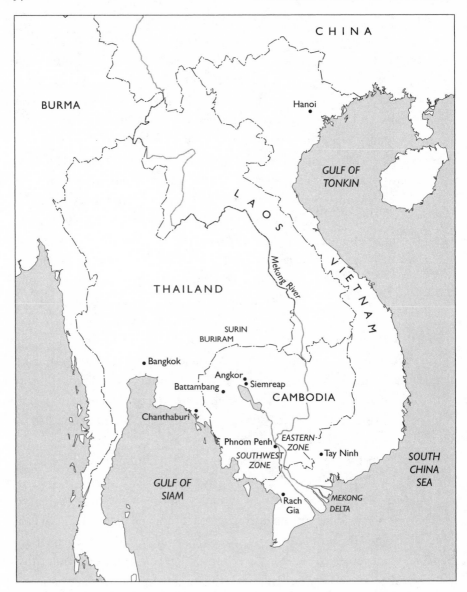

MAP 27. Cambodia and its neighbors, 1975–79

them "virile." Directly importing Vichy's metropolitan model, the French administration successfully sponsored a large Cambodian youth group, Yuvan.
All this, however, only seemed to produce more ethnonational than colonial
loyalty. Vichy's troubled attempt to imbue Cambodia with a controlled patriotism probably peaked in Phnom Penh on October 23, 1944, birthday of the
young Khmer king, Norodom Sihanouk. Fifteen thousand Cambodian youths

paraded before Decoux for over an hour, after "this mass of youth had fervently sung the *Marseillaise* and the Cambodian national anthem." Here optimistic officials saw proof that Vichy-sponsored youth groups had "thoroughly conquered the Khmer population."[9]

This was the prevailing intellectual atmosphere in which Pol Pot grew up. Born in 1925, the young man then known as Saloth Sar spent most of his childhood in Phnom Penh's royal palace compound and then, from 1942 to 1946, at the Collège Norodom Sihanouk, whose pupils heard each morning the Pétainist anthem, "Maréchal, nous voilà!" Khieu Samphan, then a fellow student a year behind Sar, would become head of state in his Khmer Rouge regime in 1976.[10] Sar's future wife, Khieu Ponnary, as Penny Edwards writes, "made front-page news" in 1942 when she passed the baccalaureate, the first Khmer woman to do so, inspiring "a lengthy article which cited Marshal Pétain's exhortation to national rebirth."[11] A decade later, on her return from studies in France, Ponnary became founding editor of *Neary*, the first Cambodian women's magazine, whose pages included translations of French farm fables such as "The Ploughman and His Children."[12] Meanwhile, in 1949, Saloth Sar set out for France himself, equipped with a French government scholarship and a limited worldview that emphasized racial difference. According to his traveling companion, fellow student Mey Mann, when they passed through Saigon, a bustling urban center with a predominantly Chinese market quarter, the two Khmer youths felt quite out of place, like "dark monkeys from the mountains."[13]

The pervasive French conception of Cambodia influenced even the anticolonial nationalism of its new generation. Saloth Sar's first mentor in Paris, fellow Khmer student Keng Vannsak, considered that Buddhism and Hinduism from India had contaminated what he surmised to be the ancient Khmer "original Culture." In 1952, Pol Pot chose his first pseudonym, "the Original Khmer," for an article he published in a Paris student magazine edited by Vannsak.[14] As Vannsak later explained in print, Buddhist Cambodia needed to reexcavate its bedrock, the "Khmer Cultural Base," with "its autochthonous, indigenous, specific, non-Indian structure," which had been entombed for centuries "under the great shroud of Indianism," by which he meant Hindu-Buddhist thought: "Brahmaism, Vishnuism, Saivism, Buddhism, Monarchy of the 'God-Kings' and the 'Buddha-Kings.'" The contemporary result in Cambodia, Vannsak maintained, was not the real "Khmer Culture" but what he dismissed as an "Indo-Cambodian bastardy" plagued by "Indianizing and Sinicizing Myths."[15] Vannsak spent a lifetime researching Khmer literature for that underlying culture.

Though Keng Vannsak never became a Communist, Saloth Sar did join the French Communist Party along with a dozen other Khmer students in Paris, including Khieu Samphan slightly later.[16] At the University of Paris, Samphan wrote a 1959 dissertation arguing that Cambodia should adopt economic autarchy, in part because during Vichy rule, Cambodia's wartime isolation had supposedly fostered autonomous development of its economy. As he put it, "the only periods of serious industrialization in underdeveloped countries arose during periods of world war, a time when forced autarky reduced foreign competition and cut off foreign capital. The period of isolation was very brief in Cambodia, as the country was quickly absorbed into the Japanese imperial orbit. Imports were not greatly reduced by the war. In spite of this, some productive enterprises were able to emerge," especially handicraft industries. Without crediting Vichy policy, Samphan preferred an example "even more striking," the kindred regime in Peronist Argentina, where "the authorities did not stand aside as victims of the situation, but actively sought to exploit it" and adopted policies whereby "industrial production increased by 80 percent between 1938 and 1951," while in postwar Cambodia, under resumed foreign competition, "[n]ational crafts are fading away and dying."[17]

Meanwhile, back in Cambodia, a more grassroots, rural-based Khmer Communist movement had emerged within the domestic nationalist struggle for independence from French colonialism. Its founding leaders were Khmer Buddhist monks, and the rank and file, mostly peasants, received training from Vietnamese revolutionaries committed to a worldwide, Communist-led anticolonial struggle headed by the USSR. French intelligence reported in 1952 that Cambodian rebel activity even included "several autarchic agricultural enterprises, like *kolkhozes*."[18] Their model was Soviet, not the undeveloped Vichy-era autarchy of Khieu Samphan's dissertation.

By contrast, the former Vichy ideology of hierarchy and soil, or "work, family and homeland," continued to greatly influence the Khmer elite it had fostered, which included the young Sar and Samphan, who returned from Paris in 1953 and 1959, respectively. For instance, the "king's representative," Nhek Tioulong, proclaimed in 1951 that all Cambodians must "Work" according to their station in life: "Officials, be loyal and faithful servants of the State and of the People. Farmers, be good farmers; artisans, try to be good artisans."[19]

Most important, that traditional view of the utility and virtue of farmers and rural life proved surprisingly receptive to the Maoism that was about to engulf first China and then Cambodia, after its independence from France in 1954. A decade later, for example, in July–August 1965, a delegation of the king-dom's Royal Khmer Socialist Youth visited China just prior to the outbreak of the Cultural Revolution. The Cambodians cabled a message home from Beijing, praising Mao's attempt to "create a type of new man in China" and to "suppress the superiority of intellectual labour over manual labour." Prince Sihanouk, who had abdicated his throne in 1955 to play a direct and dominant political role, immediately responded that Cambodia should take up "this example." He added, significantly: "We have until now followed too slavishly the paths traced by Western civilization, and that has caused us certain social problems, that of unemployed intellectuals, that of pure intellectuals who are much less compe-tent citizens than the new men who are being formed in China." The prince urged "thoroughgoing reform." Ten days later, he announced the establish-ment of a Royal Khmer Socialist Youth cooperative, which he called a "mixed (Khmer-Chinese) enterprise for agriculture and pastoral activity." [20]

Sihanouk remained unaware that three years earlier, Saloth Sar had quietly taken over Cambodia's Communist underground, then known as the Workers' Party of Kampuchea, after the mysterious death in 1962 of its founder, the former monk Tou Samouth. Sar was even now secretly visiting Mao's China and was still there in September 1965 when Sihanouk conducted a state visit. On his clandestine return to rural Cambodia in 1966, Saloth Sar discarded his party's fraternal ties to the Workers' Party of Vietnam by giving it a new name, the Communist Party of Kampuchea (CPK), that laid claim to a higher ideological status, equivalent to that of the Chinese Communist Party. In the same year, Sar established the CPK journal *Tung krahom* (Red Flag), which he named after the Chinese Communist magazine started by Peng Pai in 1927 and relaunched during the Great Leap Forward in 1958. [21]

As much as Saloth Sar, Khieu Samphan, and their younger generation of mostly elite, French-trained Communists scorned the previously Vichy-sponsored Khmer monarchy and mandarinate, they also rejected the pro-Vietnamese Communism of their own veteran revolutionary predecessors. And just as fiercely as they opposed the traditional Khmer hierarchy, they maintained an ideological fervor for rural life that Maoist egalitarianism and the Cultural Revolution only reinforced. The new, largely French-educated elite who now led the CPK even adopted an anti-intellectual, antiurban policy. In May 1968, the Sihanouk regime denounced rebel "Khmers Rouges" in the jungles of northeast Cambodia, where Saloth Sar had secretly taken over the northeast zone CPK branch, for "inciting people to boycott schools and hospitals and leave the towns."[22] At a mass meeting that Khieu Samphan organized in February 1970, rebels said of Sihanouk, "Let him break the soil like us for once," and they insisted that "no distinctions" be made "between Khmers."[23]

This new egalitarianism, then, was both racial and rural. Khieu Samphan had left Phnom Penh three years earlier to join the CPK insurgency, on the advice of Saloth Sar. In his memoirs, Samphan recalled his first meeting with the CPK guerrilla commander, Mok, in the Cambodian jungle in 1967. He described the experience in terms that suggest he was mesmerized by a rural romance. In a peasant hut that evening, Samphan wrote, he found Mok dressed "like all the peasants" in black shorts and unbuttoned short-sleeved shirt. "The diffuse glow of the lamp nevertheless revealed to us the deep and piercing eyes which stood out on his bearded face. . . . He asked affably about our trip and recommended that we never leave the house." The daring Mok himself "moved about freely, . . . sometimes bare-chested, revealing his hairy chest and arms. . . . In fact, in the face of his activity, I became well aware of my limits. And more deeply, I felt pride to see this man I considered a peasant become one of the important leaders of a national resistance movement."[24]

The new CPK's radical rural departure from its more orthodox proletarian Communist roots is evident in documents it published in 1971, as it began to expand throughout the countryside after the Vietnam War engulfed Cambodia, following General Lon Nol's overthrow of Sihanouk's neutral regime the previous year. The party divided Khmer society into five *vanna* (classes): feudal, capitalist, petty bourgeois, peasant, and worker. In theory the working class was "the leader" of the party's "worker-peasant alliance," but in practice the CPK assigned workers no political role. As these documents stated, "In the countryside it is fixed to make the three lower layers of peasants the base [of the revolution]. In the towns it is fixed to make the whole petty bourgeoisie the base." Workers, whom the CPK divided into the "pure" and the suspect "partly pure" working class, were not the party's practical constituency. After the CPK won its 1975 victory and forcibly emptied Cambodia's cities, another party document explicitly acknowledged this: "Concretely, we did not rely on the forces of the workers. The workers were the overt vanguard, but in concrete fact they did not become the vanguard. In concrete fact there were only the peasants."[25]

Despite its rejection of traditional authority, the CPK's victorious new regime, which took the name Democratic Kampuchea (DK), became ever more hierarchical and totalitarian. The party's claim to be leading a "worker-peasant" revolution meant merely that Cambodians were to become an unpaid rural plantation workforce, tending vast fields of irrigated rice land. In September 1975, a few months after the CPK deported the urban population into the countryside, party documents opined somewhat confusingly that because the deportees, "our new peasants," had no means of production, "so they are workers." As for the longtime rural inhabitants, "We can't push forward modern agriculture by remaining peasants." Here and elsewhere, the CPK made occasional, often symbolic gestures to Stalinist industrialization or Maoist orthodoxy, but its dominant vision remained overwhelmingly rural, and its propaganda was peasant-oriented. As DK head of state Khieu Samphan claimed in 1977: "In many places, water is flowing freely, and with water the scenery is fresh, the plants are fresh, life is fresh and people are smiling. . . . The poor and lower middle peasants are content. So are the middle peasants."[26] A few months later, Pol Pot added: "People from the former poor and lower middle peasant classes are overwhelmingly content . . . because now they can eat all year round and become middle peasants."[27] That seemed to be the party's vision of the future, not the emancipation of the working class. A CPK journal went far beyond even Maoism when it announced that the countryside itself, not the urban proletariat, composed the vanguard of the revolution: "We have evacuated the people from the cities which is our class struggle." These unorthodox Communists wrote laconically of the proletariat: "There is a worker class which has some kind of stand. We have not focused on it yet."[28] Time had transcended the historical proletariat: "We do not use old workers. . . . We do not want to tangle ourselves with old things."[29] In crushing their enemies, Khmer Rouge cadres regularly resorted to agricultural metaphors such as "pull up the grass, dig up the roots" and proclaimed that the bodies of city people and other victims would be used for "fertiliser." In the Cambodian countryside from 1975 to 1979, the CPK's extreme revolution caused the deaths of approximately 1.7 million people from overwork, diseases, starvation and, in probably 500,000 cases, outright murder of political and ethnic "enemies."[30]

The CPK targeted a range of political and "class" groups. Especially at first, these were the remnants of the defeated Lon Nol regime (1970–75), long accused of opposition to peasant interests, but the victims increasingly included any suspected opponents or rivals at all, including large sections of the CPK's own rank and file and many peasants associated with them. Several Khmer

Rouge songs struck bitter notes of political extermination. "The Red Flag," for instance, which began "Glittering red blood blankets the earth—blood given up to liberate the people," concluded: "Don't spare a single reactionary imperialist: drive them from Kampuchea." Even a song entitled "The Beauty of Kampuchea," celebrating the "Khmer children" serving in the army, ended with: "[T]hey chase the Lon Nol bandits, with swords and knives hacking at them, killing them, until the Lon Nol bandits are destroyed." Another song, "Rainfall in Pisakh," concluded: "Intertwined as one, our anger shoots out at the imperialists—the Americans, and their reactionary lackeys, killing them until they disappear."[31] Upgrading a traditional term for routing enemies, *kchat kchay* (scattering), DK adopted a more final goal, "scatter them to the last" (*kchat kchay os roling*).[32]

Like many agrarianists in other countries, or even Prince Sihanouk, who nodded in the same direction with less ideological obsession, the CPK's cult of the peasant might have been relatively harmless but for its additional racialist and historical preoccupations. These lay behind Saloth Sar's early adoption—in Paris in 1952—of the pseudonym "Original Khmer." They derived not only from the dominant Vichy ideology of his youth but also from the worldview of the traditional Khmer elite, among whom he spent his adolescence in the royal palace compound.

Cambodian leaders had occasionally perpetrated genocidal massacres before. As early as 1750, Western missionaries reported that by order of the Khmer king, "[t]he Cambodians have massacred all the Cochinchinese [Vietnamese] whom they could find in the country." For six weeks, "this order was executed very precisely and very cruelly," and no survivors were found (see pp. 159–60).[33] Resisting Vietnamese military occupation in the 1830s, a Cambodian rebel leader proclaimed: "We are happy killing Vietnamese. We no longer fear them; in all our battles, we are mindful of the three jewels [of Buddhist teaching]."[34] In April 1970, the French ambassador to Phnom Penh warned that new massacres of thousands of ethnic Vietnamese by the pro-American forces of Lon Nol's Khmer Republic could become "a real genocide." The Quai D'Orsay's Judicial Affairs Division concurred, stating that "the acts currently being perpetrated in Cambodia could come within the scope of the UN Convention against Genocide."[35] From the banks of the Mekong River, horrified reporters watched as hundreds of corpses of the murdered Vietnamese civilians floated downstream into South Vietnam. As many as 310,000 more ethnic Vietnamese fled across the border in 1970. Just five years later, the victorious CPK expelled another 150,000 Vietnamese residents. Then, in 1977–78, it successfully organized the hunting down and wholesale murder of the last 10,000–20,000 ethnic Vietnamese remaining in Cambodia.[36]

Pol Pot enjoined the CPK in 1978 to "firmly stir up national hatred and class hatred for the aggressive Vietnamese enemy, in order to turn this hatred into a material hatred." In his view, an idea became concrete by bloodshed. Pol Pot also planned for his DK forces to attack into Vietnamese territory and "kill the enemy at will, and the contemptible Vietnamese (*a-yuon*) will surely shriek like monkeys screeching all over the forest." In a role reversal of his youthful experience in Saigon in 1949, now it was Vietnamese who would feel like "monkeys." Pol Pot predicted that nothing but "piles of the enemy's bones" would be left, "thrown over our land."[37]

The DK regime thus perpetrated genocide against Cambodia's ethnic Vietnamese population. It also targeted several other ethnoreligious groups in Cambodia. It systematically and forcibly dispersed minority communities, forbade the use of minority and foreign languages, repressed Buddhism, Christianity, and Islam, and directed a fierce extermination campaign against the ethnic Cham Muslim minority, one-third of whom, over 90,000 people, perished in the four years from 1975 to 1979.[38]

Reflecting its indigenous racist and Vichyite antecedents as well as its Stalinist and Maoist models, the virulence of the CPK's revolution came from its combination of racial and political extermination and also from its vague ideal of the peasantry, a fungible social body that it winnowed to exclude many real farmers and expanded to include the CPK leaders who were mostly from elite backgrounds. In terms of absolute numbers, then, most of the regime's victims were members of political and social sectors of Cambodia's ethnic Khmer majority; half of the 1.7 million who perished were Khmer peasants. Yet the CPK also targeted ethnic minorities disproportionately. Most of the minority groups, especially the Vietnamese and Cham, suffered death rates far above their proportion of the population.

The CPK deployed the discourse of racism against all its enemies. Soon, even most of the Khmer victims were accused of having "Khmer bodies with Vietnamese minds." While making no claims of genetic racism or "scientific" precision, the CPK leadership employed biological metaphors that suggested the threat of contamination. It referred to enemies as "diseased elements," "microbes," "pests buried within," and traitors "boring in," just as Nazis had talked of Jews as "vermin" and "lice."[39] Pol Pot considered the CPK's revolution the only "clean" one in history, just as the Nazis had "cleaned" areas of Jews; and his regime, equally obsessed with "purity," launched its most extensive massacres of Cambodians, in the Eastern Zone in May 1978, with a call to "purify ... the masses of the people."[40] The resulting bloodbath killed over 100,000, possibly as many as 250,000 eastern Khmers, as the CPK internalized its own threat of racial destruction.[41] "We resolved the Eastern Zone cleanly (sa'at)," Pol Pot pointed out triumphantly in July 1978, and listed its five regions: "Region 24, clean. Region 23 clean, like the whole nation. Regions 20–21–22 are being cleaned." Now, he said, "The Party is clean. The soldiers are clean. Cleanliness is the foundation."[42]

As this fetish for purity suggests, despite the CPK's Marxist-Leninist heritage, its ideology was antimaterialist, again resembling racialist thinking elsewhere. The party's leaders also rejected pragmatic progressive reform of the country's economic capacity in favor of a utopian consciousness demanding total transformation that more orthodox Marxists would term philosophical "idealism." The CPK described the year 1977, for instance, as "a period of a little prosperity," only to highlight the risk of materialist seduction, that "we could be taken to pieces by grain, bullets, and various other material things."[43] The CPK's truncated version of Stalin's *Dialectical and Historical Materialism*, which acknowledged no debt to his text, simply deleted its extensive historical and materialist sections, leaving an ideological rump that Marxists might term "dialectical voluntarism." Totally omitted were those parts of the Soviet text discussing the material nature of the world, the primacy of matter, objective truth, modes of production, productive forces, and relations of production. Through these deletions, the 1976 CPK version transformed what for Stalin had been merely an opening discussion on the "dialectical method," including the notion that all phenomena are interrelated, into what the CPK termed the central "essence" of dialectical materialism and a rationale for witch hunts and repression. Thus, when a problem arises, "[l]ook for a person who has something to do with this matter." The CPK made a continuing habit of "losing" the materialism from its Marxist mindset. As late as 2004, Khieu Samphan's memoir translated the Khmer term *sompeareaniyum paticce:samuppad* (dialectical materialism) as simply "la dialectique."[44]

The CPK's idealism extended to the incorporation of an indigenous model from Khmer antiquity. Its English-language guide to Cambodia's ancient Angkor temples was probably the closest thing to a politically neutral document that the DK regime produced. These spectacular stone monuments needed little boosting for the few diplomats and party guests whom the CPK admitted into the country or allowed to visit the historic site. The 22-page typescript, based in part on previous French-language tourist guides, begins in stilted English: "Angkor Wat had been built between 1113 and 1152 in the reign of the King Suryavarman II. It was a funerary temple dedicated to the God Vishnu of which Suryavarman is believed to incarnate after his death." The guidebook drew visitors' attention to one scene carved in stone on the walls depicting "the struggle of innumerable demons against Vishnu," in which "he makes a frightful massacre of them."[45]

Not all Cambodia's enemies were supernatural. Others were historical and perennial. The neighboring temple of Angkor Thom, the DK guidebook went on, was built "after the invasion of Cham troops in 1177, who had completely destroyed the capital and taken away greatest part of the country's richess [*sic*]. ... There was nothing left around Angkor after the passing of the Chams."[46] A later glossy DK publication featured a photograph of relief carvings at Angkor Thom, depicting naval battles with Chams, captioned: "Struggle of the people of Kampuchea against foreign invasion." This booklet added: "The marvellous monuments of Angkor [are] considered by the whole Humanity as one of the master-pieces of the brilliant civilization and the creative spirit of the working people of Kampuchea."[47] As Pol Pot put it in 1977, "If our people can make Angkor, we can make anything." DK officials described Cambodian history as "essentially endogenous."[48] The regime's most concrete model thus came from Khmer antiquity. The national anthem of the new state assigned its founding victory "greater significance than the Angkor period" (*mian ney thom theng leu samay angkor*).[49] Stalinism and Maoism offered the CPK the political means to achieve this ideal.

The pure Khmer tradition of the past had to be restored. As Pol Pot put it in 1978, "[L]oose morals make the good and clean social environment in every unit become bad. ... We must resist this situation because it affects tradition (our society used to be good and clean)."[50]

We have seen in earlier chapters how most genocidal regimes of whatever ideology proclaim a need to "purify" not only a race but a territory. Conquest and genocide have often gone hand in hand. Just as the Young Turks and Nazis tried to expand Turkey and Germany into contiguous hinterlands ("Turkestan" and Lebensraum), the Communist DK regime was militaristic and expansionist, too. Neither extreme of the political spectrum has proven immune to these features of genocidal practice. The CPK's irredentist vision of reconquering

Kampuchea Krom, or "Lower Cambodia," the traditional Khmer term for the Mekong delta of southern Vietnam, meant mobilizing primordial racial rights and connections to the land. Idealization of the ethnic Khmer peasantry as the true "national" class, the ethnic soil from which the revolutionary state grew, was also consistent with territorial irredentism.

For the Young Turks, centuries of Ottoman geographic diminution, and for the Nazis, Germany's post–World War I territorial losses, provided the backdrop in each case to aggressive expansionism accompanied by genocide. For its part, Pol Pot's regime saw Cambodia's post-Angkorean territorial decline as a millennial theme, uninterrupted by several twentieth-century enlargements of its borders.[51] The timeless CPK view of the past simply stressed "2,000 years of exploitation" under its predecessors, "royal and feudal authorities" who sold off the national soil to foreigners.[52]

Again resembling the Young Turks and Nazis, the CPK leaders hailed disproportionately from such "lost territories." Two of the top three Khmer Rouge officials of the party "Center" fit this category. Pol Pot's deputy, Nuon Chea, grew up in the northwest border province of Battambang, which Thailand occupied from 1794 to 1907 and again in 1941–46. The CPK's no. 3, Ieng Sary, was a Khmer Krom (Lower Cambodian) born in Vietnam's Mekong delta. A third member of the CPK's Standing Committee, its defense and security chief, Son Sen, who had studied in Paris with Saloth Sar and Ieng Sary and became DK's deputy prime minister in 1975, was also a Khmer Krom.[53] These three leaders likely reinforced Pol Pot's own racialist obsessions with Vietnam, heightening the CPK Center's sense of a territorial threat facing Cambodia and its need to retaliate to recoup historical losses. In his major public speech in 1977, for instance, Pol Pot urged his people to "prevent the constant loss of Cambodia's territory."[54] This mindset of millennial territorial diminution moved DK to pursue both a Spartan-style "tempering" (*lot dam*) of the country's population to become hardened purveyors of violence and the reconquest from Vietnam of long-lost territory in "Kampuchea Krom."[55] The cost in Cambodian lives is unknown, but according to Hanoi's statistics, DK troops killed approximately 30,000 Vietnamese civilians and soldiers in the two years of Cambodian cross-border raids that began in early 1977.[56]

The DK regime launched attacks in 1977–78 against not only Vietnam but also Cambodia's other neighbors: Laos and Thailand. There, too, DK's leadership harbored irredentist ambitions on ancient Khmer-speaking regions that once formed part of the extensive Angkor empire. For instance, according to the Lao ambassador to DK (a former monk who had studied Buddhism in

Cambodia in the 1950s), the Pol Pot regime claimed "all territory in Laos where there are stone inscriptions with *Khom* [old Khmer] script." In Thailand, DK irredentism centered on the largely Khmer-speaking Thai provinces of Surin, Buriram, and Prachinburi, territories lost to Cambodia since the sixteenth century. A series of DK military attacks on Laos and Thailand commenced at the end of 1976 and in January 1977.[57]

DK's attacks on Vietnam began soon afterward, in March–April 1977. Perhaps for racial reasons, and possibly in line with Chinese pressure on DK to make an alliance with Thailand, Vietnamese territory became the focus of Phnom Penh's most extensive military ambitions. On its eastern sea border with Vietnam, during 1977 DK unilaterally declared a new expanded frontier claim (to which Hanoi objected). Internal CPK documents also reveal a demand for territorial "changes" on land "at some points in the present border line." In speeches in various parts of Cambodia throughout 1977–78, numerous senior CPK officials went further and publicly announced their ambition to "retake Kampuchea Krom," the entire Mekong delta.[58]

The DK regime severed diplomatic relations with Hanoi on December 31, 1977. Four days later, Pol Pot secretly ordered more incursions into Vietnamese territory: "[G]o in and wage guerrilla war to tie up the enemy by the throat, shoulders and ribs on both sides, his waist, his thighs, his knees, his calves, his ankles, in order to prevent his head turning anywhere and to increase the possibility of our large or medium-sized forces smashing and breaking his head."[59] A CPK security report of March 1978 claimed that most of the Khmer population of Kampuchea Krom were supposedly "seeking to join with the Kampuchean army in order to kill all the Vietnamese [*komtech yuon aoy os*]."[60]

DK even publicly proclaimed this policy of killing "all the Vietnamese." Pol Pot had told a large meeting in eastern Cambodia in January 1978: "Each Cambodian is to kill 30 Vietnamese."[61] This produced a clear, public, official statement of genocidal intent. On May 10, 1978, the DK radio station formally exhorted its listeners to kill 30 Vietnamese for every fallen Cambodian, and so eventually to exterminate the entire Vietnamese people in their own country. In that way, this Radio Phnom Penh broadcast explained, Cambodia's 8 million people would sacrifice "only 2 million troops to crush the 50 million Vietnamese, and we would still have 6 million people left."[62] Genocide went together with territorial expansion.

In a secret speech in July 1978, Pol Pot again stated: "[W]e have to go into their territory. Since January 1978, we have stayed east of the [Vietnamese border line], five kilometers from the border, carrying out nonstop guerrilla activities. All the way to the southwest the guerrilla activities are similar: we target (*tamrong*) [the Vietnamese towns] Loc Ninh and Roung Damrei [Tay Ninh] (Kompong Rokar, Thnaot, Kompong Rotes) in Svay Rieng, Prey Veng, but the important place is the southwest, from the Mekong River to the Bassac River we go straight over (*kat tamrong*); we control from Taing Chou to Chau Doc (Moat Chhrouk) and attack nearly all the way to Kramuon Sar [Rach Gia]; we control a large area of territory."[63]

The DK regime, then, not only threw Cambodia's population into a Maoist perpetual revolution based on forced rural labor but also marched it into a millennial ethnic and territorial war against Vietnam. Pol Pot exhibited an inbred, elite detachment about sacrificing his people in an expansionist race war. As he proclaimed in 1978, Cambodians dying over a long period did not deter him: "We are not worried that the source of our army would become exhausted, for the people of the lower classes are very numerous."[64] The CPK's conception of its cannon fodder as a vast renewable resource may have encouraged its genocidal tactics. However, they failed to save DK from rapid defeat by the Vietnamese army in January 1979.

In 1992, the ousted DK head of state, Khieu Samphan, returned to Cambodia's political scene under the auspices of the United Nations. He demanded that U.N. officials expel ethnic Vietnamese civilians who had fled Cambodia before or during the genocide of 1975–79 but had since come back. To back up his demand, Samphan raised the specter of a recurrence of the 1970 genocidal massacres, when the Mekong River became choked with the corpses of Vietnamese residents, floating south downstream into Vietnam. Now, two decades later, Samphan threatened the "nightmare" of a repetition of that slaughter: "If the Cambodian people cannot see a peaceful resolution to the problem, they will seek other means. So [the] nightmare might become a reality."[65] He proved as good as his word. In December 1992, the bodies of Vietnamese fishermen were found floating in the Mekong, as the Khmer Rouge began a new series of genocidal massacres.[66] Only Pol Pot's death in 1997, and the surrender of Khieu Samphan and Nuon Chea the next year, ended the Khmer Rouge threat to Cambodia's people.

Rwanda

Within months of Khieu Samphan's threat, it found an echo across the Indian Ocean in Rwanda. A Hutu ethnic ideologue named Léon Mugesera threatened to deal in very similar terms with his own country's Tutsi minority. In a November 1992 radio broadcast, Mugesera proposed sending Tutsi "back" to Ethiopia by killing them and casting their bodies into Rwanda's north-flowing Nile tributary, the Nyabarongo River. He announced: "I inform you that your home is Ethiopia, that we will send you there via Nyabarongo so that you can arrive there fast."[67] Arguing that Tutsi traitors deserved the death penalty, Mugesera chillingly echoed Khieu Samphan's threat to resort to "other means." If Rwanda's judicial system "no longer serves the people," Mugesera said, "we other members of the population . . . must do it ourselves and exterminate this scum."[68] His appeal prefigured the 1994 Rwandan genocide, just as Samphan's threat recalled the Cambodia of the 1970s and augured a new outbreak of ethnic slaughter.

Rwanda's tragic twentieth-century history began after Imperial Germany colonized the Tutsi kingdom located in the center of the country in 1898. Rwanda became part of Germany's East African dominions. The next step came in 1910, following the genocidal German suppression of the Herero and Nama in Southwest Africa (see chapter 9). Germany's colonial military force, the Schutztruppe, invaded the autonomous Hutu kingdoms of northern Rwanda, crushing resistance there with the aid of Tutsi royal forces and southern Hutu. This began a colonial conquest that intensified differences and exacerbated conflicts between Hutu and Tutsi, leaving many Hutu, especially in Rwanda's north, with bitter memories of Tutsi rule, and in some cases, animosity against the Hutu from the more integrated south. The process continued after Belgium took over Germany's central African colonies of Rwanda and Burundi in 1916. Belgian forces pursued the conquest, incorporating the northern Hutu principalities into the colonized Tutsi kingdom of central Rwanda, and Belgian rulers solidified the previously fluid differences between their Hutu and Tutsi subjects by issuing them all with official identity cards that clearly stated their ethnic affiliation.

Belgium's two colonies in the Great Lakes region of Africa eventually gained their independence just a few years after the French departure from Cambodia and Vietnam in 1954. Rwanda and Burundi, small, densely populated neighboring countries, each comprised a Hutu majority and a Tutsi minority along with a smaller group of Twa, often called "pygmies." Some 14 percent of Rwandans were Tutsi, and 1 percent Twa. All three groups speak the same language, Kinyarwanda. In addition, nearly all Hutu and Tutsi are Christians (a few Tutsi are Muslims), and significant intermarriage also linked them,

MAP 28. Rwanda and its neighbors, 1994

especially in Rwanda's mixed southern region. However, a Hutu sense of historical injustice, compounded by Belgian colonial favoritism toward elite Tutsi, widened the ethnic divisions.

The two new African states took divergent paths. When Burundi became independent of Belgium, a Tutsi-dominated minority assumed power. However, in Rwanda, a Hutu revolution broke out in 1959 after a late reversal of colonial policy that now gave the Hutu majority Belgian assistance. The revolution abolished the country's Tutsi monarchy and drove tens of thousands of Tutsi out of Rwanda, allowing Hutu farmers to occupy their lands. A subsequent United Nations special commission of inquiry into this violence found that it had been propelled by a Hutu racism that resembled "Nazism against the Tutsi minorities."[69] The country's first president, Grégoire Kayibanda (1962–73), a Hutu from the south, declared independence in 1962. The next year, further violent outbreaks killed several thousand more Tutsi. Three decades later, a leader of the 1994 genocide would claim these events as a precedent, even quoting (without proof) President Kayibanda as having threatened Tutsi in 1963 with "the total and sudden end of the Tutsi race."[70] Local persecution of Tutsi and regional ethnic violence again escalated in 1972, after Burundi's Tutsi-dominated military regime massacred perhaps 200,000 Hutu there, provoking as many more to flee north for safety in Hutu-dominated Rwanda.[71] The 1972 mass murder of Hutu in Burundi forebode, as if in a magnifying mirror, the 1994 genocide of Tutsi in Rwanda.

In a 1973 coup d'état, Rwanda's military commander Juvénal Habyarimana overthrew the Kayibanda regime. Rwanda had reached a crossroads. The new regime initially appeared somewhat torn between maintaining or muting ethnic tension. Thus, Habyarimana asserted later, he had been "obliged to take action" not only because "certain groups around the President started to defect from the road that was taken by the 1959 Revolution" but also because "towards 1973 one has raised the ethnic problem again." Habyarimana was at first more concerned with reversing the balance of power among Hutu alone, replacing hitherto dominant southerners with his fellow northerners. Since the south was more ethnically integrated and northerners less accommodating, this boded ill for Tutsi, too. However, the new president quickly proclaimed a policy of ethnic reconciliation and even an attachment to "the principle of the equality of all the ethnic groups in our country," even though by this he appears to have meant, at least in part, a quota system to reverse a supposed continuing Hutu subordination to Tutsi.[72] Habyarimana called himself a "pure-blooded"

Hutu ("un Muhutu pur sang"), and he allowed a purist, anti-Tutsi faction of northern Hutu led by his wife and in-laws, a group known as *akazu* or "the little house," to assume prominence in his regime's inner councils. From 1975, the president's Mouvement révolutionnaire national pour le développement (MRND) became the country's sole legal political party. Even so, until 1990 at least, as Belgian scholar Philip Verwimp points out, Tutsi in Rwanda still fared much better than Hutu did in Burundi: "[N]o Tutsi was killed for political or ethnic reasons, Tutsi were represented at the National University, they were allowed to go into business and some Tutsi became wealthy businessmen."[73]

A turning point came in 1990, when armed Tutsi refugees made an attempt to reoccupy the country. That October, the Uganda-based, predominantly Tutsi Rwandan Patriotic Front (RPF) launched a military incursion across the northern border. The Tutsi exiles' campaign to return to their homeland by force quickly provoked a Hutu reaction of escalating virulence. For instance, the next month *Kangura* magazine proclaimed: "The Hutu are until now proud of being Hutu; in fact, they are willing to fight against anyone who would take their identity from them." The Habyarimana regime's radicals, including its akazu faction, increasingly organized themselves as "Hutu Power" chauvinists and launched new massacres of Tutsi civilians. Yet the RPF was soon winning the political war. By 1992, the "pride" was noticeably on its side. *Kangura*'s appeals to Hutu sounded more desperate: "Find out again your ethnicity because the Tutsi have taught you not to recognize it. You belong to an important ethnicity of Bantu group. . . . Know that a proud and bloodthirsty minority mixed with you in order to dilute you, divide you, dominate you and massacre you. . . . The nation is artificial but ethnicity is eternal." The magazine also betrayed its fear that RPF propaganda could undercut ethnic division by successfully asserting that Hutu and Tutsi were all Rwandans (Banyarwanda): "[T]he Tutsi have fabricated a tribe which does not exist anywhere: the Banyarwanda tribe." *Kangura* even tried to deny that Rwandans shared a common language: "[W]hen the Tutsi nomads noticed that they had lost their language like other nomads, they have tried in vain to convince the world that Kinyarwanda language existed. It must be known that only Kihutu exists as a language of Hutu."[74]

Kangura adopted a biological metaphor for its racism against Tutsi and the RPF, whose troops the magazine called "cockroaches" (*inyenzi*). In its March 1993 issue, an article entitled "A Cockroach Cannot Give Birth to a Butterfly" proclaimed: "A cockroach gives birth to another cockroach. . . . The history of

Rwanda shows us clearly that a Tutsi stays always exactly the same, that he has never changed. The malice, the evil are just as we knew them in the history of our country."[75]

President Habyarimana died in a still unexplained plane crash on April 6, 1994. The northern-dominated, chauvinist *akazu* and "Hutu Power" elements of his regime immediately seized control of the country and briefly ruled Rwanda until July 1994, when the insurgent RPF army drove them from power. This genocidal Hutu Power regime, prefigured by *Kangura's* pronouncements, resembled perpetrators of other genocides in its dehumanization of "racial" targets. Perhaps continuing to compensate for the lack of ethnocultural distinctions between Hutu and Tutsi, the propaganda of Hutu Power focused on past injustices and, especially, fear of future contamination. It described the Tutsi population as "cockroaches" whose presence necessitated a "big clean-up."[76] It even advocated a "final solution to the ethnic problem."[77] At the height of the slaughter in mid-May 1994, the Hutu Power private radio station, Radio télévision libre des milles collines (RTLM), called for continuing efforts to "exterminate the Tutsi from the globe" and "make them disappear once and for all."[78]

Hutu Power's language of purity, contamination, and solution recalls CPK statements about ethnic Vietnamese and other enemies. In Cambodia most of the victims were majority Khmer; in Rwanda, majority Hutu moderate politicians were only the first to be killed. The short-lived Hutu Power regime then quickly killed thousands more Hutu, especially intellectuals, and others in the more pluralist south of the country, accusing them of lacking zeal for its larger campaign to exterminate the Tutsi.[79] The number of Hutu victims of the 1994 genocide is estimated in the thousands, perhaps up to one-tenth of the total toll of half a million to 1 million people murdered in just three to four months. In the case of the Hutu of Rwanda, as with the Khmer majority under DK and even Germans under Nazism, the subjection of individuals to the overweening interest of their "race" only made them more vulnerable to violence purportedly "protecting" them from racial contamination.

"Before the arrival of the Tutsis," wrote a leading perpetrator of the Rwandan genocide, Théoneste Bagosora, in 1995, Rwanda had been a peaceful Hutu realm. In ancient times, he asserted, "the Hutus of the great Bantu family and the Twa or pygmies of the smaller ethnic group were living harmoniously since as early as the 9th century." Then, in the sixteenth century, intruding on this arcadia came a race of northern interlopers, whom Bagosora called "these

Nilotic Hamitic Tutsis from Abyssinia."[80] Such spurious historical interpretation was nothing new. It derived from a theory of colonial anthropology, long known as the "Hamitic Hypothesis" for the distinction it drew between Hutu and Tutsi on the basis of separate Hamitic and Bantu "races," and suppositions of their different historical origins.[81]

The colonial scholarship had since spawned an indigenous school. Precolonial Tutsi domination and Hutu resistance to it (rather than to Belgian rule) now became a theme of official Rwandan historiography. The major Hutu chauvinist historian was Ferdinand Nahimana, whom the International Criminal Tribunal for Rwanda convicted of genocide in 2003, along with the editor of *Kangura* magazine. Nahimana had begun his historical research in November 1978 in the northwest of Rwanda, home of President Habyarimana and his wife, Agathe Kanziga, a princess of the defunct northwestern Hutu court of Bushiru. Publishing his initial findings the next year, Nahimana wrote that long before "the expansion and installation of Tutsi power" throughout Rwanda, the Hutu population "had organized itself little by little into important family groups, then into States." He claimed to have uncovered new evidence of the long history of these "little States." On the basis of 19 oral accounts he elicited from "direct descendants of the last Hutu princes who reigned over these independent territories," Nahimana presented in 1981 what he called "a more complete list" of as many as nine northern Rwandan Hutu monarchies. For each, he offered "a chronological list" of petty kings, including the name of the last ruler of each kingdom. From there, Nahimana projected all the Hutu realms back into history, adding a generation of 33 years for each reign. He concluded that they had all first "emerged in the course of the sixteenth century (6 monarchies) and the seventeenth century (3 monarchies)." The first king of Bushiru, for instance, supposedly ruled from 1600 to 1633. Nahimana calculated that Buhoma, a kingdom for which his sources had named 12 monarchs, was "the most ancient" such Hutu court, its founding ruler having "reigned between 1499 and 1532." Nahimana added with more emphasis and accuracy that some of these "little States" had survived into the 1920s as "independent Hutu principalities, which had resisted and still resisted the expansion and installation of the Tutsi monarchy." In the case of the kingdom of Buhoma, he asserted that only after a long history of "429 years (1499–1928)" did the kingdom fall to "Tutsi occupation" on the death of its last monarch. Even then, only Belgian "intervention" had made this possible. Nahimana showed that Bushiru, too, came under permanent central authority as late as 1930 (see fig. 40).[82]

These northwest principalities thus became models of Hutu antiquity and resistance to the central Tutsi court, which was ruled by its Nyiginya dynasty. Nahimana went on to present, in a 1986 doctoral dissertation at the University of Paris, a history of the Hutu north and northwest regions of Rwanda, their relations with the Nyiginya dynasty and the Belgians in what he called the dominant "colonio-nyiginya power," showing how the latter eventually integrated those regional courts and thus how "Rwanda became a unified state."[83] Nahimana saw it as an oppressive Tutsi state, and he located the antecedents of what he approvingly called "the great Rwandan revolution of 1959–1962" in Hutu resistance to these and other early-twentieth-century developments. In another book, *Le blanc est arrivé, le roi est parti* (The White Man Has Come, the King Has Gone), Nahimana described the conversion of Rwandans to Catholicism as another joint Belgian-Tutsi imposition on the Hutu: "From the years 1917–1918, the great Tutsi, adjusting to the prevailing conditions, joined with the missionaries and formed with them a 'national coalition' which forced the peasantry, still attached to its religious customs, to convert to Catholicism."[84]

A northerner himself, Nahimana focused on the regional resistance to Tutsi in Rwanda's north. In a third book, published in 1993, he traced Tutsi attempts at "infiltration" of the region as far back as the sixteenth century. Describing the fate of the Hutu kingdom from whose court President Habyarimana's wife was descended, he added: "Bushiru is one of the peripheral regions especially known for having held out for a long time against the invaders coming from modern central Rwanda. Its last leader, Nyamakwa, is famous for his resistance to the installation of the representatives of colonial and nyiginya power." For instance, Nahimana wrote of great violence around 1920: "A Belgian military agent named Bidoul was sent to 'pacify' Bushiru with a platoon of riflemen and a cannon. He met the Abashiru warriors on the Birembo hill. The battle immediately began. It was very murderous; all the Abashiru who had risen up to fight fell, riddled with cartridges. Shocked by the murderous rapidity of the assailants' fire, the inhabitants of Bushiru scattered without really knowing where they must hide. Bidoul and his troops set about massacring everyone they met." Despite the catastrophic killing and devastation, the Hutu prince Nyamakwa "escaped and took refuge in the forest of Gishwati with a good part of the population." He retained power in Bushiru until 1925, before Belgium replaced him with a Tutsi chief. Nahimana concluded from this that "the emergence of the kingdom of Rwanda as a unified state was therefore the fruit of wars of conquest," which the local Hutu populations experienced as "a veritable calamity." Finally, in a contemporary note aimed at the Tutsi-led RPF "aggressors" who had recently attacked into Rwanda in 1990, Nahimana pointed out "what an error it is to claim that before 1900 or 1959, the country was a paradise" under a "strong and peaceful" Tutsi monarch."[85]

This historiography celebrating Hutu resistance to Tutsi intrusion enabled it to become an ideological theme of the 1994 genocide of the Tutsi, perpetrated in the name of repelling the RPF incursion. For a historian, Ferdinand Nahimana acquired unusual influence in Habyarimana's Rwanda. In 1990, he became director of the national Office of Information. Two years later, Rwanda's army chief proposed to Habyarimana that Nahimana be officially commissioned to prepare lessons on "civic and psychological preparation" for soldiers in Rwanda's military forces, including a syllabus for each army battalion that outlined history classes critical of the Tutsi monarchy, defunct since 1959.[86] Then, in 1993, Nahimana became founding director of the new private radio station RTLM, owned by akazu leaders and other northwesterners close to Habyarimana's regime. In one of its first radio programs, RTLM's editor in chief interviewed Nahimana, starting off with an assertion: "There is no difference between the RPF and the Inyenzi [cockroaches, i.e., Tutsi]. Perhaps as a historian you could explain the relationship between the RPF and the *Inyenzi* to our listeners?" In his response Nahimana agreed and added that the Inyenzi were "those who fled after the Rwandan revolution in 1959 [because] they refused to adhere to a democracy."[87]

The historical revenge of Hutu Power was bloody. Two days before the 1994 genocide began, Colonel Théoneste Bagosora told U.N. officers that the "ethnic divide" in Rwanda was "ancestral." A month later, as the regime's slaughter of unarmed Tutsi civilians reached a peak, its ambassador to the U.N. explained away the massacres as a two-sided "inter-ethnic war of unbelievable cruelty" that had emerged from the "age-old history of the nation," based on hatreds "forged over four centuries of cruel and ruthless domination of the Hutu majority by the haughty and domineering Tutsi minority."[88] Among the possibly 1 million victims of Hutu Power was 80-year-old Rosalie Gicanda, widow of Rwanda's last Tutsi monarch, who had died in 1959. On April 20, 1994, Lieutenant Pierre Bizimana and his unit burst into the former queen's Butare home, where she and her mother lived as devout Catholics with a group of women and girls. The soldiers took Gicanda and six others away in the back of a pickup truck, shot them behind the national museum, and returned two days later to kill her centenarian mother.[89]

Hutu Power ideology combined its conceptions of history and race with novel notions about agriculture and territory. For instance, Nahimana had concluded from his 1978 research in northwest Rwanda that the term *umuhinza,* applied to local Hutu rulers brought under the Tutsi monarchy in the early twentieth century, came from a word that denoted both "agricultural prosperity" and "territorial security." Once colonial rule had deprived them of political authority, these northwest Hutu princes retained local ritual prestige through their title umuhinza, which meant, in part, "the farmer par excellence governing a people of cultivators," or "President of Crops."[90]

From independence in 1962, Rwanda's successive Hutu-dominated regimes saw Tutsi, by contrast, as either urban dwellers or cattle-raising pastoralists, not hardy peasant cultivators like the Hutu. The first president, Grégoire Kayibanda, proclaiming a "social revolution," insisted that "the Tutsi must also cultivate."[91] As Philip Verwimp has shown, the protogenocidal regime of the second president, Juvénal Habyarimana (1973–94), went much further in its preoccupation with peasant themes. The romanticization of agriculture, as under racist regimes elsewhere, was a stepping-stone on a more general idealist pathway. Habyarimana appeared to consider Kayibanda's ideology too materialistic. He first distinguished his regime from that of his predecessor by proclaiming a "moral revolution," rather than a "social" one. Consistent with this idealist emphasis, Habyarimana's initial justification for his 1973 coup d'état was "to ban once and for all, the spirit of intrigue and the feudal mentality" and "to give back to labor and individual yield its real value," on the grounds that "the one who refuses to work is harmful to society."[92]

Here Habyarimana meant *agricultural* labor. In 1974, he revived the colonial practice of forced rural labor, or *umuganda,* stating: "First the population must get down to work—the Government and myself want to emphasize the value of work on the land. Thus we shall devote each Saturday to tilling the soil with hoes in our hands."[93] He declared 1980 to be "the year of the protection of the soil," and in an interview that year he proclaimed what he called "the primacy of the interests of the rural collectivity over individual interests." Habyarimana stated that his own parents "were cultivators, simple peasants," and that it was "in the countryside, on the hills, in life with the land, that they have influenced me the most." Three years later he asserted, "Our food strategy gives absolute priority to our peasants," and in 1984, he added that "the government always takes care of the peasant families," who were "the essential productive forces of our country."[94] Habyarimana's agrarian rhetoric escalated over time. In 1987, he praised Rwanda's peasants for "their total devotion to the work, every day" and for "their fabulous capacity to adapt, their pragmatism, their genius, their profound knowledge of our eco-systems." Habyarimana even declared that from then on, all Rwandans would be termed "peasants" (*Umuturage*). The year 1988 became the year of "protection of the peasant revenue." As he put it, "It is the Rwandan peasant that makes Rwanda live."[95]

Much of this thinking is familiar from earlier genocides, including that in Communist Cambodia. The ideological leveling, placing the entire Rwandan population into a single social category, and the compulsory enlistment of every citizen, "including babies and old people," in the one legal political party (Habyarimana's MRND) also resembled CPK rule and its extension to the whole Cambodian citizenry of harsh disciplinary measures formerly restricted to party members.[96] The Rwanda regime's economic focus on "food self-reliance" also echoed the DK goal of "self-reliance" based on agricultural production. When Habyarimana stated in 1987, "Auto-development is not a slogan for us, it is not an effort to theorize," but rather it "is our conviction that progress needs to come from our own forces," he again sounded much like Pol Pot and Khieu Samphan.[97]

Another echo of the Khmer Rouge in Rwanda was umuganda, or unpaid collective rural labor, a policy Habyarimana had inaugurated by "cultivating a plot of land together with his close friends." He announced in 1986: "A country is constructed by hands, not by words! Rwanda will be constructed by the sweat on our face and not by useless speculations!"[98] Two years later, his historian Nahimana rhapsodized about "the spectacular engagement of the Rwandan intellectuals who, trained for office work and therefore for the deft handling of language, pen and paper, have taken up the hoe, the pruning knife, or any other manual tool and have joined with the peasant masses to move earth with their hands and to live the effective reality of manual labor. . . . Thus, in participating in *Umuganda,* the intellectuals have collaborated with President Juvénal Habyarimana; together, they have restored value to the hoe, to manual labor, and they have especially revived the confidence of the Rwandan peasant in its daily action to make the soil yield the food which everyone greatly needs."[99]

Verwimp considers that Physiocratic economic theories coming via Belgium or France had probably influenced Habyarimana's regime, too, and he adds that literature about Nazism was found at his home after his death. There is no such evidence of Cambodian or other Communist influence in Rwanda, despite its close relations with China, which supplied the agricultural tools, including a million machetes, that many of the Hutu killers wielded against their victims in 1994. Yet Habyarimana shared key ideological preoccupations with the Khmer Rouge. For instance, Verwimp writes, the Rwandan leader "considered cities a place of immorality, theft and prostitution," and his judgment was that "Rwanda is a peasant economy and should remain one."[100] Nonagricultural activity, urban or pastoral, incurred official disfavor. In 1987, on the twenty-fifth anniversary of Rwandan independence, Habyarimana's officially commissioned celebration volume asserted, "Man is a distinguished product of his soil," and "the Rwandan detests not only the cities, he does not even like the villages." Rwanda alone "is his vast village." The volume's author added that the 1959 "peasant revolution" had overthrown "the pastoral feudalism" of the Tutsi monarchy, thus ending "centuries" of struggle when "the hoe and the cow fought over the grass," with the final supremacy of Hutu farmers handing "the hoe its revenge."[101]

As in Cambodia and elsewhere, the trumpeting of peasant supremacy reflected reality less than it did official ideology. It faced challenge from the mid-1980s, according to historians David Newbury and Catharine Newbury: "Rwandan academics and intellectuals began to write openly about the difficult conditions faced by rural cultivators, the exploitative practices of merchants," and the excesses of government "moniteurs agricoles." Jean Rumiya, a historian at the National University of Rwanda, explicitly lamented the failure of the yeoman model: "The prototype of the wealthy man is no longer the well-off peasant, respected by his peers, or the government official who returns to his hill, but the city dweller, preferably in Kigali, whose living standard attains an international level in the areas of leisure, transport, or lodging. This paradise has a strong attraction for youth."[102] In this critical view, rather than returning to his plow, Rwanda's figurative Cincinnatus had been contaminated by urban corruption and cosmopolitanism. Thus the escalating pressure of peasant poverty only accentuated the ideological attraction of the yeoman model.

The regime responded in kind to the rural crisis, producing more agrarian propaganda, and also deflecting the critique onto the supposedly urban Tutsi. For instance, Nahimana, already a rising star as the Habyarimana regime's major interpreter of the Rwandan past, was equally intent on assuming the voice of its Hutu peasantry. As director of Rwanda's Office of Information from 1990, Nahimana urged that "the rural populations [must] have their own means of information," allowing, he said, "at last, 'rural truth' to come out."[103]

State-sponsored genocidal massacres of Tutsi began in 1990–91, and agrarian propaganda played a key role. In a series of further slaughters in 1992, writes Gérard Prunier, "[t]here was a 'rural' banalisation of crime. Killings were *umuganda,* collective work, chopping up men was 'bush clearing' and slaughtering women and children was 'pulling out the roots of the bad weeds.' The vocabulary of 'peasant-centered agricultural development' came into play, with a horrible double meaning." In northwest Rwanda in 1992–93, Hutu power holders turned their region's independent history against the Tutsi and pursued them with violence described in the vocabulary of farm labor. According to the historian Alison Des Forges, "[O]fficials warned that killers were lurking in the nearby Gishwati forest," a historic site of Hutu resistance, "and they organized the population to 'clear the brush.' The brush' referred to Tutsi who were thought to provide cover to the RPF."[104]

The refusal of violent Hutu chauvinism to consider Tutsi as farmers also fit their supposed origin as intruders. RTLM proclaimed in a December 1993 broadcast: "Tutsi are nomads and invaders who came to Rwanda in search of pasture." On January 6, 1994, an RTLM announcer mocked Tutsi for their supposed traditional dependence on cow's milk instead of grain: "[M]ost of the [Tutsi] people were drinking milk[;] some drank milk because they simply had some nostalgy [*sic*] of it.... There should have been a shortage of milk in dairies. Someone wrote to me: 'Please, help! They are taking all the milk out of the dairy!'" RTLM's editor in chief announced the next year, just three weeks before the genocide began in April 1994: "We have a radio here, even a peasant who wants to say something can come, and we will give him the floor. Then, other peasants will be able to hear what peasants think."[105] The radio station combined this agrarian theme with both violence and racism of its own. One listener who subsequently became a killer recalled hearing broadcasts of statements such as: "[W]hile a Hutu is cultivating, he has a gun" and "You should have them [guns] with you when you are cultivating. When the enemy comes up, you shoot at each other. When he retreats, then you take up your hoe and cultivate!" Radio RTLM's racism against Tutsi was expressed in slogans like "clear the bushes" or "separate the grass from the millet" and "pull out the poison ivy together with its roots."[106] Another listener stated: "RTLM talked about Hutu as cultivators, the children of cultivators (*Benesebahinzi*)," and it said that "everyone should join in the violence against the enemy." This was considered "a matter of peasant culture," another recalled hearing: "They said to peasants (*abaturage*): 'go to cultivate.'" Perhaps even venting an ideological preference for individual yeoman farming, the radio's propagandists, according to this listener, held each armed peasant responsible for a single plot of land. "They said that a person with a gun should cultivate one ridge."[107]

Written documents reflecting government orders, as well as the more official broadcaster, Radio Rwanda, used similar language when urging people to hunt down Tutsi during the April–July 1994 genocide. Radio Rwanda instructed citizens on April 12, for instance: "They must close ranks, remember how to use their usual tools [i.e., weapons] and defend themselves ... do communal work [*umuganda*] to clear the brush, to search houses, beginning with those that are abandoned, to search the marshes of the area to be sure that no *inyenzi* have slipped in ... so they should cut this brush."[108]

Meanwhile, RTLM combined agrarian metaphor with racial vilification. It rebroadcast the same statement several times: "The *inyenzi* have always been Tutsi. We will exterminate them. One can identify them because they are of one race. You can identify them by their height and their small nose. When you see that small nose, break it."[109] The prefect of Kigali, Tharcisse Renzaho, putting this perspective in another guise, later portrayed the 1994 killings as the result of provocation, from ethnic Tutsi attacks on an agrarian Hutu paradise. Thus he blamed the supposedly "interethnic" massacres on the RPF opposition, "the Monoethnic Tutsi Army," which had disrupted "the sweet years of the Second Republic, when milk and honey flowed in plenty."[110] Verwimp remarks that the genocide "was indeed a 'final solution,' to get rid of the Tutsis once and for all," and also "to establish a pure peasant society."[111]

For years, the Hutu Power worldview also focused on territorial issues. Its forms of expansionism were both internal and aimed beyond Rwanda's borders. The akazu faction that ran the genocidal regime of 1994 was a secret, clanlike network of extremist Hutu officials from the country's northwest, mostly from the Bushiru region incorporated into the Rwandan kingdom in the 1920s.[112] According to Gérard Prunier, the 1973 coup by Juvénal Habyarimana not only brought to power a Bushiru princess (his wife, Agathe Kanziga) but also ushered in a wave of "northern revenge" by "marginalised, fiercely Hutu, anti-royalist Rwanda" over the more liberal and tolerant Hutu communities of southern Rwanda once represented by the Kayibanda regime. Then, after Habyarimana's death on April 6, 1994, these akazu chauvinists immediately turned to conduct the genocide of Tutsi. Prunier describes them as " 'the real northwesterners,' the representatives of the 'small Rwanda' which had conquered the big one."[113] Their campaign against the Tutsi and the relatively pluralist southern Hutu suggests that the akazu aimed to extend throughout Rwanda the ethnic Hutu purity of the defunct northwest kingdom of Bushiru.

Their internal expansionism transformed a jealously guarded regional identity into a racialized form of domestic irredentism.

Hutu Power's ethnoterritorial ambitions were also external. In his first academic publication in 1979, the Hutu Power historian Ferdinand Nahimana had pointed out that the expanding "Tutsi kingdom of Rwanda had broadly extended its influence" through a zone comprising Rwanda, eastern Congo, and southern Uganda. Yet he also asserted that "this influence did not always signify political and administrative submission" of the local polities to Tutsi power. Rather, he insisted, like the Hutu kingdoms of northwest Rwanda, "these territories beyond modern Rwanda never ceased to be ruled by their own authorities. That is to say that the Tutsi royal court of Rwanda did not replace the local royal court." A non-Tutsi court would send tribute as demanded, but would do so only until "it felt able to stand up to an eventual attack from the monarch." Such territories, Nahimana suggested in conclusion, shared with Rwanda's Hutu northwest a tradition of resistance to Tutsi rule.[114] The historical potential therefore existed for a contemporary anti-Tutsi alliance transcending Rwanda's frontiers.

Nahimana's historical celebration of local Hutu resistance to the Tutsi kingdom did not prevent him complaining in 1987 that Belgian and British colonial regimes had also "murdered and mutilated" this same kingdom of Rwanda, having "amputated" it before World War I by detaching Kinyarwanda-speaking districts from it to enlarge their colonies in Congo and Uganda.[115] Almost as these early writings of Nahimana prefigured, by the time of the fall of Hutu Power in July 1994, traditional Hutu claims to the northwest extended beyond the rest of Rwanda and now spread outside its borders as well. The MRND's youth wing, known as Interahamwe, took its genocidal violence into neighboring countries and attacked local Tutsi populations there. They "not only continued to kill Tutsis in Rwanda but also targeted Banyarwanda Tutsis living in Eastern Congo." These Hutu militias ranged across the Kivu provinces of Congo, massacred the local Tutsi cattle herders known as Banyamulenge, and also penetrated Congo's Masisi plateau in an attempt "to gain support amongst the Banyamasisi Hutu and to eliminate the Banyamasisi Tutsi."[116] Prunier explains that in this way the Interahamwe could also "carve out for themselves a kind of 'Hutuland' which could be either a base for the reconquest of Rwanda or, if that failed, a new Rwanda outside the old one." Meanwhile, Hutu forces from Rwanda joined those in Burundi, too, and "increasingly operated together against the common ethnic enemy," the Tutsi.[117]

Conclusion

The historian Alison Des Forges has described a mimeographed anonymous document found in Rwanda's Butare prefecture after the genocide, entitled "Note relative à la Propagande d'Expansion et de Recrutement." This document, which describes propaganda techniques used by the genocidists, also includes a detailed analysis of Roger Mucchielli's book *Psychologie de la publicité et de la propaganda,* published in Paris in 1970. The Rwandan document recommends a propaganda tactic that it calls "Accusation in the mirror," explaining that "the party which is using terror will accuse the enemy of using terror."[118] RTLM employed this tactic when it broadcast the claim, late in the genocide, that "the objective of the Tutsis is obviously to exterminate the Hutu, the majority mass."[119] The Khmer Rouge used this technique, too. For instance, in October 1978, after the DK regime had killed all 10,000 or more Vietnamese remaining in Cambodia and had publicly called for the extermination of "the 50 million Vietnamese" in Vietnam, DK radio asserted that Hanoi was exterminating its Khmer Krom minority, of whom the Vietnamese government "kills all the male babies at birth."[120] Perpetrator regimes appear to sense that if genocide can ever be justified, it is only as a defense against genocide. Yet the "Accusation in a mirror" technique has the additional advantage of disarming and dividing opponents by conjuring up another genocidal enemy.

The parallels between the Cambodia and Rwanda genocides go beyond such propaganda tactics or the choice of river routes to dispatch murdered ethnic enemies "back" to their supposed homelands. Just as the postgenocidal Hutu Power attacks on Tutsi in Congo and Burundi recalled those of the Khmer Rouge against Cambodia's neighbors two decades earlier, so also the catastrophes in Cambodia and Rwanda span the spectrum of twentieth-century ideologies of mass murder. From opposite horizons of the political imagination, the utopian Communism of the Khmer Rouge and the reactionary violence of Hutu Power converged to epitomize a hundred years of genocide. In many ways the Khmer Rouge replicated Stalin and Mao, while Hutu Power echoed Enver Pasha and Adolf Hitler. Yet they also shared virulent racism, a bitter sense of lost ethnic dominance, inchoate cults of agriculture, and ambitions of territorial expansion. And in those additional yet equally crucial ideological features, the two killer regimes resembled not only one another but also a succession of pre-1900 genocidal actors. Whether such themes will retain their power in the twenty-first century remains to be determined.

Epilogue

Racial and Religious Slaughter from Bangladesh to Baghdad

After the conquest of continents in the nineteenth century, the frontier ran out in the twentieth. As colonialism reached its peak, globalization set in, and by the end of the century, it had reached the last uncontacted indigenous groups in the Australian desert and Amazon rainforest. From the early 1900s, as agricultural settlement and local resistance continued in remote regions, new technology and communications made possible more centralized administration of giant totalitarian regimes and imperial powers. But as the century progressed, power, technology, and communications also linked diverse populations around the world and disseminated developments in more global patterns. These included postwar decolonization, the emergence of multiple new states, and a global arms trade—but also global patterns of genocide, whose major ideological themes persisted despite the end of the pastoral frontier and of centuries of settler-indigenous conflicts over land. In the last third of the twentieth century, the world became more urbanized than ever before. Yet the frequency of genocide accelerated. Several patterns are clear despite varying cultural and geographic contexts. Disparate outbreaks of genocide remained similar enough to demonstrate some long-term continuities in perpetrator preoccupations.

The ideological and racialist catastrophes in Cambodia and Rwanda punctuated two more transnational waves of genocide that crashed on widely separated shores in the late twentieth century. In the first wave, in the period 1965–83, three of the globe's most brutal *military* dictatorships—in Indonesia, Pakistan, and Guatemala—set out to annihilate large opposition movements by the mass slaughter not only of political opponents but also of ethnic, national, or racial communities. All three regimes enjoyed U.S. and other international support.[1] None of the perpetrators of their crimes against humanity ever faced trial, and many held positions of power for decades afterward.

Most important for the future was the Pakistani army leadership, which was responsible for possibly the most extensive of these genocides—in what became Bangladesh—yet subsequently retained office in Pakistan with impunity. Under various military dictatorships run by its successors, that country also hosted the incubation of another wave of genocidal movements, this one firmly based not on concentrated state terror but on a more dispersed religious *fundamentalist* terrorism. In Pakistan and its northern neighbor Afghanistan, a range of Islamist groups sprang up in reaction to the 1979 Soviet invasion and brutal occupation of Afghanistan, and, in the 1990s, in opposition to the dictator Saddam Hussein in Iraq, the U.S. military presence in Saudi Arabia, violent Russian repression in Chechnya, and the Serb genocide of Muslims in Bosnia.

These flourishing fundamentalist movements, and the Islamist schools (*madrasah*) based in Pakistan that have supported them, offered fertile soil for the growth of international terrorist groups like Al-Qaeda. Between long stays in the Afghan-Pakistan border region, Al-Qaeda's extremist Saudi leader, Osama bin Laden, also spent five years in Sudan, whose ruling Islamist dictatorship gave equal prominence to Arab ethnic dominance over local African groups. During the 1980s and 1990s, that regime perpetrated genocide in southern Sudan, killing and starving to death up to 2 million local Christians and animists. Then, from 2003, in the opening genocide of the twenty-first century, Khartoum moved to support Arab Janjaweed militias in Sudan's western region of Darfur in their slaughter of African Islamic coreligionists there. That same year, the chaos in Iraq following the U.S. invasion handed an Al-Qaeda offshoot the opportunity to recruit a genocidal insurgent faction there. In different cultural contexts, in greater or lesser degrees, all these perpetrators—military, civilian, racist or religious—took up key ideological concerns that had characterized previous genocidal regimes.

Bangladesh

Pakistan's Islamic military regime murdered probably 300,000 and possibly 1 million fellow Muslims in Bangladesh in 1971. This crime sprouted not from religious fanaticism but from a militaristic opposition to democracy in an ideological soil fertilized by racism, expansionist domination, and resentment of urban populations. The extraordinary violence and exemplary impunity of its perpetrators also scattered the seeds of a new crop of catastrophes.

Britain's 1947 partition of India assigned most of its predominantly Muslim regions to the new state of Pakistan, which itself came into being geographically and ethnically divided. West Pakistan, the larger territory containing the new capital, soon dominated distant East Bengal, also largely Muslim and, now as East Pakistan, home to 54 percent of the new state's population. West Pakistan's military-dominated Islamic elite comprised mostly ethnic Punjabis and Pathans, who considered East Pakistan's Bengali Muslims to be insufficiently martial, insufficiently Islamic, and overly influenced by India's Hindu culture and by the local Bengali Hindus, who composed 13 percent of East Pakistan's population and numbered 10 million by 1971. Unlike the democracy that quickly flourished in India, the new Pakistani regime became a military dictatorship. It repeatedly intervened in East Bengal to frustrate the popular will. It dismissed an elected government there in 1954 and prevented the holding of elections four years later. Finally, in 1971, the army even blocked Pakistan's newly elected national parliament from convening.[2]

From the beginning, West Pakistani regimes set out to "cleanse" East Bengal's language and culture of Hindu influences, and in the 1960s, Pakistan even imposed a state ban on the broadcast of songs written by the Nobel Prize–winning Bengali cultural icon, the Hindu writer Rabindra Nath Tagore. Despite the common Islamic faith, a sense of racial and historical superiority reinforced a West Pakistani cultural prejudice that increasingly stressed East Bengali ethnic difference. Pakistan's military dictator, Ayub Khan, stated in 1967 that East Bengalis "probably belong to the very original Indian races." Even now, he argued, they remained "under considerable Hindu cultural and linguistic influence" and demonstrated "all the inhibitions of downtrodden races," including those that Ayub Khan called Bengali "popular complexes" and a "defensive aggressiveness" that he considered a natural outcome of their "historical background."

Even in West Pakistan, military rule proved unstable. Popular demonstrations there overthrew Ayub Khan's regime in 1969, leading to the country's first ever national elections the next year. In an upset, East Pakistan's pro-independence Awami League won a national majority. Quickly, Pakistan's army chief, General Yahya Khan, intervened to both arrest the democracy and suppress this threat at its source: the people of East Bengal. On February 22,

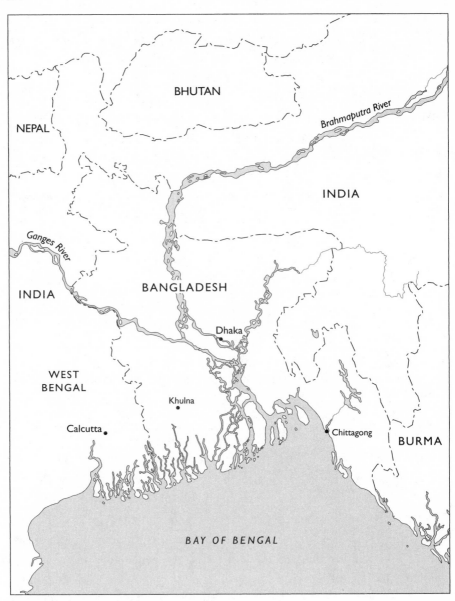

MAP 29. Genocide in Bangladesh, 1971

1971, Yahya Khan reportedly told a group of generals, "Kill three million of them, and the rest will eat out of our hands." Yahya appointed a new governor-general of East Pakistan, General Tikka Khan, who announced soon after his arrival there that he would implement a "Final Solution." He even reportedly threatened to kill 4 million people in 48 hours.[3]

The killing began on March 25, 1971, when Tikka Khan mounted Operation Searchlight, a "massive armed strike against the population of Dhaka," the capital city of East Bengal. With thousands of new West Pakistani reinforcements, the army started by targeting East Pakistani intellectuals and students, Bengali Hindus, and those whom historian Rounaq Jahan calls "the urban *lumpenproletariat*." According to Pakistani lieutenant general Kamal Matinuddin, the commanding officer of the attack on Dhaka University, Brigadier Jehanzeb Arbab, later admitted "over-reaction and over-kill by the troops under his command." On March 28, Archer Blood, the U.S. consul general in Dhaka, sent a cable to Washington headed "Selective Genocide." He reported that the "authorities have a list of Awami League supporters whom they are systematically eliminating by seeking them out in their homes and shooting them down," and that with army support, "non-Bengali Muslims are systematically attacking poor people's quarters and murdering Bengalis and Hindus." On April 1, the chief secretary of the government of East Pakistan told officers of the U.S. Agency for International Development that "the Hindu community in East Pakistan had always conspired against Pakistan." Jahan sees a broader pattern: "The army's campaign against the cities and towns not only led to massive civilian casualties" but also drove possibly 30 million people out of the cities into the countryside, while another 10 million East Bengalis fled to India. Pakistan's Lieutenant General A. A. K. Niazi, who arrived in April as commander of the Eastern Command, condemned Operation Searchlight "as a violation of the mission and equivalent to the Jallianwalabagh massacre in the Punjab by the British in 1919." According to the writer Sarmila Bose, General Niazi complained that the operation had provoked "widespread mutiny among Bengali officers and men" and made "virtually the entire population hostile." Yet the massacres continued. When asked the reason for the extent of the killing, General Tikka Khan reportedly replied: "I am not concerned with the people. I am concerned with the land." On May 14, Consul General Blood dispatched a cable to Washington entitled "Slaughter of Hindus." He detailed "a common pattern of Army operations whereby troops entered a village, enquired where the Hindus lived, and then killed the male Hindus." Blood estimated a death toll of "thousands" in the seven weeks since March 25. On May 19, he informed Washington that "a young West Pak officer (helicopter pilot)" had admitted that the army was killing Hindu men. "He justified this on the basis Hindus were enemies and that East Pakistan had to be 'cleansed.' He said he was engaged in a jihad, holy war." Blood later wrote that "on more than one occasion Pakistani soldiers boasted to me that they had come to East Pakistan 'to kill Hindus.'"[4]

As Pakistani forces tried to reimpose control, murderous violence continued for most of 1971. Troops raped Bengali women and girls, while "cities and towns became bereft of young males." Only near that year's end did an Indian invasion in support of the East Bengali resistance finally stop the slaughter. Even as India's troops drew closer, just a week before they forced the Pakistani army in East Bengal to surrender, "the Pakistani government engaged in its most brutal and premeditated genocidal campaign." Soldiers burned villages and slaughtered their inhabitants and again targeted urban areas; apparently working from a list of names held by the military governor, they set out "to kill the most respected and influential intellectuals in each city and town." The final toll, variously estimated from 300,000 to well over 1 million, included disproportionate numbers of local Hindus and city dwellers, though most victims were Muslim Bengali villagers. In support of the Pakistani army, some Islamic fundamentalist groups such as Jaamat-e-Islami also played a role in the killing.[5] The U.S. consul general, whose government had supplied Pakistan with $3.8 million in military equipment after the killing began in March, later wrote that although "the term 'genocide' was not appropriate to characterize all killings of Muslim Bengalis," he thought it did apply "fully to the naked, calculated, and widespread selection of Hindus for special treatment."[6]

Bangladesh had paid an enormous price for its emergence as a new independent state. In Pakistan, by contrast, the perpetrators of the mass murders went unpunished. Indeed, the armed forces and allied Islamic groups continued to dominate Pakistani governments for decades to come, legitimizing new bouts of political and religious slaughter, when Islamist madrasah in Pakistan took up the training of terrorist recruits from across the globe.[7] In 2006, Al-Qaeda's deputy leader denied the 1971 genocide but asserted its significance when he claimed that Pakistan was the victim: "Pakistani memory has yet to forget the catastrophe caused by the civil war in East Pakistan," while America, he added, "doesn't forgive" Pakistan for hosting "the largest Islamic schools with wide influence among the Muslims of South and Central Asia."[8]

Indonesia and East Timor

A second serious outbreak of mass killing began just a few years later, and lasted until the final months of the twentieth century. In 1999, a U.N. intervention put a stop to Indonesia's 25-year annexation of East Timor, an occupation that had also exhibited many of the elements of earlier genocides. As in the case of West Pakistan's armed forces, it was precisely the common genocidal trait of territorial expansion that also took the Indonesian military across a further boundary, that between political killing and national extermination.

Independence from Holland in 1949 made Indonesia the world's largest Muslim country, but its official multicultural ideology precluded the option of an Islamic state like that in Pakistan. After seizing power in a 1965 military coup in Jakarta, General Suharto launched an army-sponsored massacre of the very large but mostly unarmed Communist opposition, the Partai Kommunis Indonesia (PKI). The PKI was the world's biggest nonruling Communist party, and Suharto later described its destruction as a struggle against political contamination: "I had to organize pursuit, cleansing, and crushing." He ordered an "absolutely essential cleaning out" of the PKI and its sympathizers from public life and government. The Australian embassy in Jakarta reported in late October 1965 that "on all sides and in all areas, 'cleansing,' 'purging' . . . proceeds apace."[9] As his paratroops moved into Central Java, Suharto's fellow officer General Nasution reportedly said, "All of their followers and sympathizers should be eliminated" and ordered the Communist Party's extinction "down to its very roots." Jakarta's police information chief told the U.S. ambassador in mid-November that with the "blessing" of the army, "50 to 100 PKI members are being killed every night in East and Central Java by civilian anticommunist groups." The Australian embassy estimated on December 23 "about 1,500 assassinations per day since September 30th." By February 1966, two confidential Western agencies agreed on "a total of about 400,000 killed," and the deputy U.S. ambassador thought that the full toll could be much higher.[10]

In some ways these mass killings of a political opposition movement prefigured the genocide in Bangladesh five years later. Most victims were Javanese peasants, usually nominal Muslims, who had supported the PKI or were suspected of doing so. As in Bangladesh, the army ran the campaign while fervent Muslim groups did much of the killing, which was regionally concentrated in Java and Bali, where the PKI had won many votes in elections during the 1950s.[11] Paratroop commander Sarwo Edhie reportedly conceded that in Java, "we had to egg the people on to kill Communists." Historian Geoffrey Robinson states that in Bali, the army's intervention ensured that "only PKI forces were killed and that they were killed systematically." Yet in parts of Sumatra and Sulawesi, according to a contemporary Canadian embassy report, "where

there are rabid Muslim religious groups all PKI members have been beheaded."
The U.S. ambassador concurred that in north Sumatra, "Muslim fervor" in
Aceh "has apparently put all but [a] few PKI out of action" and "placed their
heads on stakes along [the] road." In Medan, two officials of the Muslim youth
group Pemuda Pancasila separately told U.S. representatives that "their organization intends [to] kill every PKI member they can catch." In a few months,
the army and allied Muslim groups slaughtered over half a million suspected
Communists.[12] The U.S. Central Intelligence Agency described the killing as
"one of the worst mass murders of the twentieth century, along with the Soviet
purges of the 1930s, the Nazi mass murders during the Second World War, and
the Maoist bloodbath of the early 1950s."[13]

A decade later, the armed forces of Suharto's Indonesia launched a new
military campaign beyond their country's borders. Unlike members of the PKI,
the victims now were of another nationality and religion, inhabitants of the
small neighboring Portuguese colony of East Timor, who were mostly Catholics or animists. Jakarta sought to destroy the territory's leftist independence
movement, Fretilin, which had won local elections in the Timorese villages
in 1975, defeated an opposition coup in the capital, Dili, and taken power in
the territory.[14] In December 1975, invading Indonesian forces seized Dili in
a bloody assault. Yet in the countryside, Fretilin waged continuing resistance,
controlling much of the half-island's mountainous hinterland.[15]

The Suharto regime's anti-Communist political motives remained similar
to those that had driven its extermination of the PKI, but it could not destroy
Fretilin, which it termed "gangs of security disruptors" (known by the Indonesian acronym GPK).[16] Despite its massive losses, Fretilin's extensive influence in East Timor enabled it to keep harassing the occupying forces from
guerrilla bases in the populous hill country. Jakarta's effort to wipe out this
resistance embroiled the Indonesian army in a genocidal counterinsurgency,
in which it deployed mass killing and starvation as weapons of subjugation.
A U.N.-sponsored Truth Commission concluded in 2005 that these policies
amounted to "extermination as a crime against humanity committed against
the East Timorese population."[17] Of the 1975 population of 628,000, possibly
150,000 people disappeared in the next four years.[18]

The Truth Commission reported that Jakarta's extermination campaign included policies that caused at least 84,000 deaths under state-imposed famine
conditions and over 12,000 murders of political opponents. Also among the

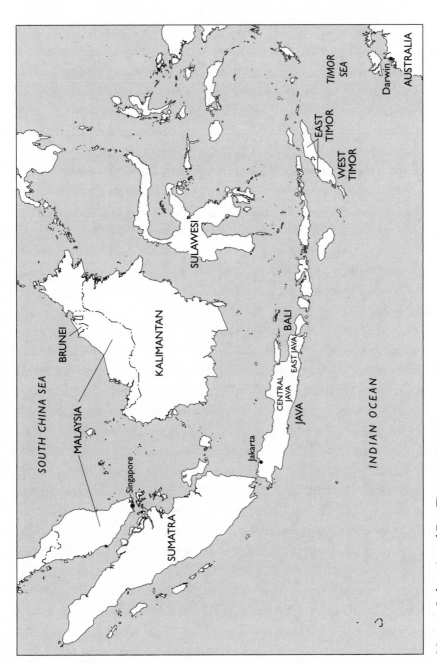

MAP 30. Indonesia and East Timor, 1965–99

first victims were members of Timor's 20,000-strong ethnic Chinese minority, whom Indonesian forces singled out for "selective killings" (in contrast to 1965–66). On the first day of the East Timor invasion, Indonesian troops murdered 500 Chinese in Dili. Later, "[i]n Maubara and Liquica, on the northwest coast, the entire Chinese population was killed," and soon surviving Chinese in the territory numbered only "a few thousand."[19] The more extensive form of extermination, a man-made famine, ravaged East Timor in 1979–80, after Indonesian aerial bombardment of upland villages and cultivated gardens forced many Timorese to surrender in the lowlands, where food was scarce. Indonesia counted the territory's population at only 522,000 in mid-1979.[20]

Although the local ethnic Chinese had kept their distance from Fretilin, the military's new racism against them was a small part of a broader political "cleansing" of East Timor. While insisting that "God is on our side," Indonesian intelligence and military commanders in Dili acknowledged in confidential documents in 1982 that "despite the heavy pressure and the disadvantageous conditions under which they operate, the GPK [Fretilin] has nevertheless been able to hold out in the bush," and can still deploy "a very sizeable concentration of forces in one place." After seven years of occupation, these documents added, Fretilin "support networks" still existed "in all settlements, the villages as well as the towns." Thus, "threats and disturbances are likely to occur in the towns as well as in the resettlement areas." The chief of Indonesian intelligence for the province, Williem da Costa, and its military commander, A. Sahala Rajagukguk, respectively described their goals as "to obliterate the classic GPK areas" and "to crush the GPK remnants to their roots and to prevent their reemergence," so that the conquered territory would, in Rajagukguk's words, "eventually be completely clean of the influence and presence of the guerrillas." In 1984, a major new military campaign even attempted what one Indonesian commander called the obliteration of Fretilin "to the fourth generation."[21]

To their preoccupations with political bloodlines and cleansing, Indonesian-appointed officials added an attempt to reorganize rural cultivation. Traditional Timorese swidden agriculture on dispersed hill fields eluded Indonesian control, and each village required closer supervision. Military commander Rajagukguk ordered local officials to "suspect everyone in the community," aiming to uncover and block "every attempt by inhabitants or the GPK to set up gardens to provide logistical support for the GPK." For his part, intelligence chief da Costa ordered officials to "[r]e-arrange the location" of Timorese farm plots, allowing the population to tend "no gardens or fields" far from villages, stipulating that "[n]o garden or field of anyone in the village should be isolated," that all plots must "be close to each other," and that "[w]hen people go to their gardens or fields, ... they should go and return together." [22] The overriding motive for such measures was military, but the result resembled the ideological inspiration of the close-knit, communal Javanese village.

Beginning in 1980, Jakarta also established new "transmigration" villages in East Timor into which it moved 500 families of Javanese and Balinese peasants with surer loyalties. As Indonesia considered the territory agriculturally backward, the first group of 50 Balinese transmigrants were given the task to "train East Timorese farmers in the skills of irrigated farming," despite a long tradition of irrigation agriculture in the very area of their settlement. By 1984, Jakarta had settled about 5,000 Balinese "model farmers" across the territory. Here, too, glorification of an imagined superior cultivation trumped Timorese reality. An eyewitness reports that after an Indonesian unit had massacred 400 Timorese civilians near Lacluta in 1981, a soldier justified the killing with a remark considered "part of the wisdom of Java. He said: 'When you clean your field, don't you kill all the snakes, the small and large alike?'" [23]

Indonesian forces again targeted Timorese kinship networks in early 1999, in the leadup to a long-awaited U.N.-sponsored referendum on the territory's independence. Army and militia commanders threatened to "liquidate . . . all the pro-independence people, parents, sons, daughters, and grandchildren." [24] Jakarta's governor of the territory also ordered that "priests and nuns should be killed." [25] The military commander in Dili warned: "[I]f the pro-independents do win . . . all will be destroyed. It will be worse than 23 years ago." [26] Indonesian troops were ready. A May 1999 army document ordered that "massacres should be carried out from village to village after the announcement of the ballot if the pro-independence supporters win." The East Timorese independence movement "should be eliminated from its leadership down to its roots" and hundreds of thousands of the territory's inhabitants were to be deported. [27]

The new wave of mass killing and deportations began immediately after the U.N.'s announcement of the result of the August 30, 1999, ballot, revealing that 79 percent of Timorese had voted for independence. Indonesian-trained militias murdered about 1,500 people in a few weeks. The massacres and forced population movements halted only when U.N. peacekeeping troops arrived and Indonesian forces withdrew from the territory. A U.N.-established court later convicted one of the perpetrators of "a crime against humanity in the form of genocide." [28]

The tragedy of East Timor once again demonstrated the virulent mix of violence with ethnic or religious prejudice, territorial expansionism, and the idealization of cultivation.

Guatemala

Across the Pacific, as extermination progressed in East Timor, a third U.S.-backed military dictatorship was committing genocide.[29] Guatemala's U.N.-sponsored truth commission, the Commission for Historical Clarification (CEH), reported its findings in 1999. It concluded that from 1962 to 1996, the country's anti-Communist armed forces, while combating leftist opponents, had conducted a "criminal counterinsurgency," perpetrated 626 individual massacres, and killed over 200,000 people, "the vast majority" of whom were Guatemalan civilians, one-quarter of them women. However, "in ethnic terms, the vast majority were Mayans," members of 23 indigenous Indian groups who constituted 60 percent of Guatemala's population of 10 million. During an intense genocidal period in 1981–83, "when more than half the massacres and scorched earth operations occurred," the Guatemalan armed forces under Ladino (non-Indian) command specifically targeted five Maya groups inhabiting the highlands. The army's goal was to wipe out leftist guerrillas who recruited among these groups. Yet the CEH found that the military regime's anti-Indian racism, "expressed repeatedly by the State as a doctrine of superiority," also helped to explain the indiscriminate army brutality "against hundreds of Mayan communities in the west and northwest of the country."[30]

Along with the violent racism, territorial irredentism added to the ideological backdrop of this tragedy, as in other cases of genocide. Guatemala officially claimed territory in neighboring Belize, and its maps depicted that country as Guatemala's twenty-third department. On more than one occasion in the 1970s, its armed forces threatened to invade Belize. The Guatemalan government maintained its territorial claim as the genocide began under General Lucas Garcia in 1981. His successor, General Efraín Rios Montt, who seized power in a coup in March 1982 and escalated the killing, temporarily reduced the size of the irredentist claim across the border, yet still pursued expansion. As president at the height of the massacres of Mayans, Rios Montt declared in January 1983 that "previously Guatemala claimed all the territory of Belize, but now the Guatemalan position has changed: we want the district of Toledo to form part of our territory." That district still accounted for 21 percent of the

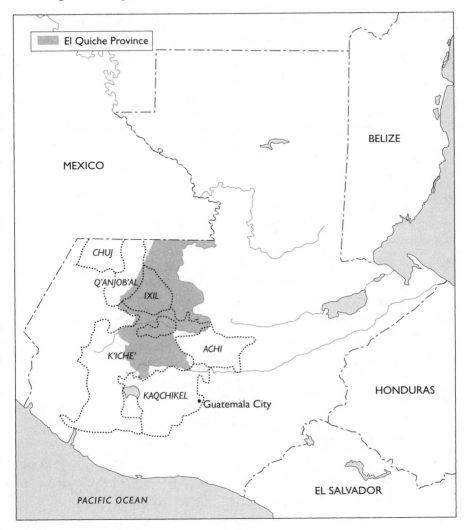

MAP 31. Guatemala, 1954–96

total area of Belize. After another coup, the new government announced in August 1983 that once again "Guatemala will now claim all Belize."[31]

Other familiar features reinforced the dominant ideology behind the domestic slaughter of Guatemalans. Faith in rural virtue bolstered what the CEH called a "fundamentalist anti-communism." The cover of the Guatemalan anti-Communist pamphlet *El nuevo campesino* (The New Farmer) featured a drawing of a peasant and a plow. Inside are sketches of farmers in their fields, wielding agricultural tools and bags of well-earned cash (see figs. 38–39). Under a portrait of a peasant harvesting his crop with a machete is the caption: "Communism finds an infertile field where there are people who like to work."[32] As in similar cases, the ideological significance of the image lay beyond its reality. While Rios Montt declared, "We have no scorched-earth policy. We have a policy of scorched communists," his army routinely destroyed dissident villages and forced surviving starving peasants to relocate in a counter-guerrilla strategy the military called "Beans and Bullets." A Guatemalan army officer alternatively summarized the policy as "If you are with us, we'll feed you, if not, we'll kill you."[33] The CEH reported: "Aggression was directed against elements of profound symbolic significance for the Mayan culture, as in the case of the destruction of corn."[34]

Manipulation of historical symbols played a role, too. The Spanish colonial genocide of Guatemalan Indians in the sixteenth century (see pp. 93–95) still resonated in the twentieth. Indigenous identity in Quetzaltenango, for instance, continued to stress settler/native, Ladino/Mayan distinctions. Many Mayans cherished the memory of the indigenous Quiché prince Tecún Umán, who resisted the conquistador Pedro de Alvarado and fell in battle in 1524. A local Mayan, when asked in 1997 "What is the difference between Indians and Ladinos?" replied: "We have the blood of Tecún, they [the Ladinos] have the blood of Pedro de Alvarado."[35] During the genocide, one Indian shaman even announced that Tecún had returned to earth at the head of a guerrilla army "to bring justice to Guatemala."[36] Ladino perpetrators themselves took up the theme of Guatemalan antiquity, even deploying the memory of this previous genocide victim against his contemporary descendants threatened with the same fate. In the 1960s, according to historian Greg Grandin, the Guatemalan government and army "appropriated and militarized" a cult of Tecún Umán that Ladino intellectuals in the highlands had developed in the early twentieth century. The CEH truth commission report also noted that the government's counterinsurgency campaigns made frequent use of "Mayan names and symbols for task forces and other military structures." For instance, the Iximché Task Force, which operated from April to December 1982, took its name from the Cakchiquel capital, razed by Alvarado in 1526, that became the first Spanish settlement in Guatemala. Historian Jennifer Schirmer confirms that the government's National Committee for Reconstruction "appropriated the Quiché Indian hero Tecún Umán" in the pages of the official *Cultural Magazine of the Army*. She adds that the National Committee even adopted "*Popol Vuh* (the major religious text of the Quichés when fighting the Spaniards in the sixteenth century) as its own philosophy."[37]

The regime believed that ethnic and political divisions substantially coincided. According to a 1972 government intelligence manual: "The enemy has the same sociological traits as the inhabitants of our highlands." Though Mayans constituted 60 percent of the country's population, they made up as much as 83 percent of the military's victims (17 percent were Ladino).[38] The CEH concluded that "the violence was fundamentally directed by the State against the excluded, the poor, and above all, the Mayan people" and that "the identification of Mayan communities with the insurgency was intentionally exaggerated by the State." State "terror and persecution" obliged many Mayans "to conceal their ethnic identity, manifested externally in their language and dress," while even "concealment of their rituals became progressively more widespread."[39] Along with this racial and cultural targeting, the military and police also resorted to biological metaphors of contamination for their campaigns of political repression, some of which they termed "cleansing operations" (*operaciones de limpieza*).[40]

Iraq

Genocide erupted next in Iraq. After Saddam Hussein seized power in a 1979 coup within the fascist Baath regime in Baghdad, he launched a series of political mass murders that eventually spread to the killing of possibly 100,000 members of Iraq's rebellious Kurdish minority, for which he was charged with genocide after his ouster in 2003.[41] His 2006 hanging aborted that case.

Saddam had cut his political teeth on rural reform. After playing a leading role in the 1968 Baath Party takeover, he served first as Iraq's vice president and in the early 1970s controlled "one small department called the Peasants Department," according to a former official in his government. Then, "In no time at all, Saddam was head of security, he was head of the Peasants Department, he was head of relations with the Kurds, he was head of the committee that controlled the oil."[42] Partly at Saddam's initiative, the Baath Party pushed through agrarian reform. Its legislation broke up large landholdings, dividing them among peasants, and "created a large number of small holdings." Rural living standards increased, causing foreign observers to speculate on "the rise of middle-level peasants." Agriculture still employed half the labor force in 1976, when the Baath government began a 10-year campaign that doubled rural expenditures and injected over U.S.$4 billion into agricultural development. Yields rose, but the area of cultivation declined. Urbanization increased, as did food imports. Despite the expansion of industry and of the oil sector that financed it, agriculture continued to employ 30 percent of Iraq's labor force in

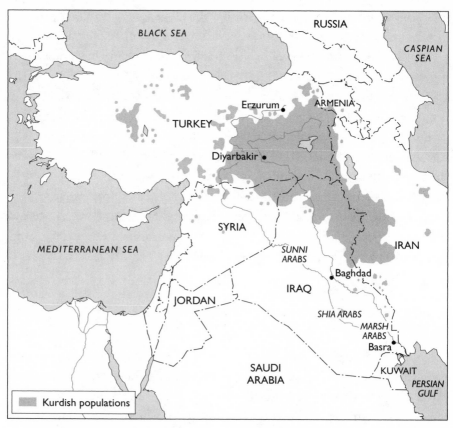

MAP 32. Iraq under Saddam Hussein and U.S. occupation, 1979–2007

1986, yet provided only 7.5 percent of GDP. The Baath Party only intensified its attention to rural issues. In the 1970s, according to a U.S. government study, "the party seemed to have few roots in the countryside, but after the ascent of Saddam Husayn to the presidency in 1979 a determined effort was made to build bridges between the party cadre in the capital and the provinces." Nearly all the new second-rank officials promoted at a 1982 Baath congress had "distinguished themselves by mobilizing party support in the provinces."[43]

During his first decade as president, Saddam also demonstrated his preoccupations with territorial expansion and with models from Iraq's long history. His armed forces invaded two of Iraq's neighbors. Saddam attacked Iranian territory in 1980, provoking a bloody conflict that ended in stalemate in 1988. Two years later, he invaded and annexed Kuwait, making it Iraq's nineteenth province, until the United States expelled Saddam's occupying forces the next year. A year after taking power, Saddam had told his official biographer that he modeled himself on the ancient Babylonian ruler who had conquered Jerusalem in 586 B.C.E. "Nebuchadnezzar stirs in me everything relating to pre-Islamic ancient history. And what is important to me about Nebuchadnezzar is the link between the Arabs' abilities and the liberation of Palestine," Saddam said. "That is why whenever I remember Nebuchadnezzar I like to remind the Arabs, Iraqis in particular, of their historical responsibilities." A decade later, an Iraqi Arts Festival was entitled "From Nebuchadnezzar to Saddam Hussein," and the dictator stood for a photograph in a replica of Nebuchadnezzar's war chariot. Under Saddam, according to historians, Baath Party ideology "increasingly embraced the ancient history of Iraq, to the extent that provinces were renamed with ancient or medieval names; thus al-Hilla province became Babil province (Arabic for Babylon). Nebuchadnezzar II was even proclaimed an enemy of Zionism because of his attack on Jerusalem in 587 B.C.E." A later conqueror of Jerusalem, the medieval Muslim commander Saladin, who defeated the Crusaders, was another model for Saddam. In 1987, the Iraqi regime convened a conference, entitled "The Battle of Liberation, from Saladin to Saddam Hussein," held in Tikrit, birthplace of both men. An Iraqi children's book published that year, *The Hero Saladin,* featured a cover picture of Saddam, described as "the noble and heroic Arab fighter Saladin II Saddam Hussein."[44]

The historical Saladin was an ethnic Kurd, not an Arab. Within a year, his fellow Kurds became Saddam's next victims. The Kurdish minority of 3 million people composed one-fifth of Iraq's population, concentrated in the north. While "a number of large and powerful Kurdish tribes" supported the central government, other Kurds provided most of the membership of the opposition Iraqi Communist Party. More important, 30 years of secessionist Kurdish rebellions had enjoyed intermittent Iranian support, and by early 1988 the rebels controlled "most of the northern areas of Iraq."[45] Saddam's brutal "Anfal" counterinsurgency campaign attempted to reconquer the region, using poison gas and massive conventional forces, and depopulating entire areas. The Kurdish victims numbered at least 50,000, possibly as many as 180,000.

Bosnia

The political and ethnic catastrophes in Cambodia and Rwanda, and the crimes of dictatorships in Bangladesh, Indonesia, Guatemala, and Iraq, all exemplify in varying degrees the widespread late-twentieth-century deployment of ideo-

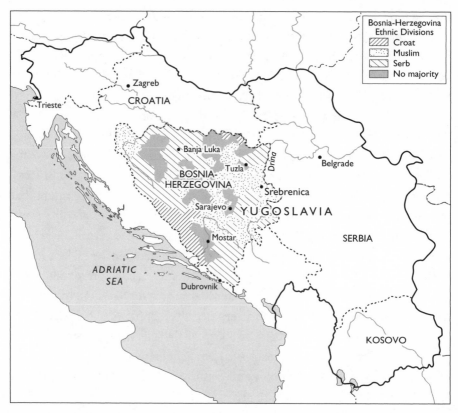

MAP 33. Yugoslavia, 1919–96

logical and racial "cleansing" to combat supposed political or biological contamination. Such propaganda could coexist with the contradictory assertion
of genetic difference. Perpetrators were preoccupied with their own ethnic
group's susceptibility to threats even when they proclaimed it to be superior.
As historian Norman Cigar comments, "This dualistic self-view of superiority
and accompanying vulnerability bordering on paranoia can be a particularly
explosive mix."[46] In the early 1990s, that combination fueled the genocide in
Bosnia, where perhaps 200,000 local Muslims perished at the hands of Bosnian Serb forces.

The scene was set by an earlier genocide in Yugoslavia. Under Nazi occupation during World War II, German units and the Croatian puppet Ustashe
regime killed approximately 65,000 of Yugoslavia's 75,000 Jews, and half a
million Serbs. This catastrophe exacerbated the Serb chauvinism that surfaced
as early as 1941, when Chetnik leaders first called for a "Homogeneous Serbia." The postwar ethnic integration fostered by Josip Broz Tito's Communist

regime incurred chauvinist wrath as well. In a 1987 article entitled "The Semi-Arabs against the Europeans," a Serbian intellectual described Yugoslavia's Muslims as members of an inferior, non-European, "semi-Arab subculture" that reflected their "desert ancestors" and other elements of purported "genetic predetermination," including even a "special gene of the Ottoman soldiery." A Serb nationalist leader declared in 1991 that "within this Yugoslav area, biologically we [Serbs] are the strongest nation and have the strongest historic roots." Yet such strength was somehow inadequate to ensure immunity from an insidious minority. Bosnian Serbs depicted Islam as a "malignant disease" threatening to "infect" Europe.[47]

The domestic appeal of Serb racism was spotty, and ironically, it even derived much of its force from frustration at that fact. Chauvinists were outraged at fellow Serbs' participation in the multicultural pluralism of Communist Yugoslavia. The high level of ethnoreligious intermarriage in Bosnia-Herzegovina reached 40 percent in that republic's industrial towns: in 1981, 15 percent of the children of Bosnia-Herzegovina came from ethnically mixed marriages, and half the republic's population had interethnic relatives. Other Serbs viewed this as contamination of their nation. In poetry he wrote in 1993–94, Serb military commander Bozidar Vucurevic described the largely Muslim town of Trebinje as "urban pestilence" and the Croatian city Dubrovnik as "Serbia's spleen" and "the mausoleum of red blood cells."[48] As elsewhere, such virulent racism inflicted casualties on both sides of supposed ethnic divides. The feared contamination could just as easily leap religious barriers, too. Genocidists justified their actions as preventative attacks on "infected" members of both groups. In Bosnia in 1991–95, Serb perpetrators considered fellow Orthodox, but politically dissident, Serbs to be a special threat and treated them with the same brutality as their much more numerous Muslim victims.[49] Comparable racism in Guatemala and Rwanda moved other Christians to commit genocide against coreligionists and moved Muslims to do likewise in Bangladesh and more recently in Darfur.

Territorial Expansionism

Bosnian Serb forces showed yet again the power of territorial aggression to promote ethnic mass murder. Calling for a "Greater Serbia" in 1941, Chetnik leaders had recommended "cleansing the lands of all non-Serb elements." The 1986 intellectuals' cultural manifesto known as the "Serbian Memorandum," which laid much of the ideological basis for the genocide in Bosnia, included an appeal for "the complete national and cultural integrity of the Serbian people, . . . no matter in which republic or province they might find themselves living."[50] Five years later, Slobodan Milosevic, the Serbian leader of post-Tito Yugoslavia, warned that "it is always the powerful who dictate what the borders will be, never the weak. Thus, we must be powerful." Serbia's new borders would incorporate not only Montenegro and Bosnia but parts of Croatia, too. Another Yugoslav official, Mihailj Kertes, predicted "a great Serbian state from Montenegro to the left bank of the Neretva with Dubrovnik as the capital."[51]

Territorial expansion went hand in hand with ethnic aggression. Just as Hitler in 1939 had threatened the Jews with annihilation if war broke out, Bosnian Serb leader Radovan Karadzic asserted in 1991 that Bosnia's Muslim community would "disappear from the face of the Earth" if it decided to "opt for war" by choosing an independent Bosnia-Herzegovina. He added later that "Muslims are the most threatened, . . . not only in the physical sense . . . rather, this is also the beginning of the end of their existence as a nation." Karadzic further stated in 1992: "The time has come for the Serbian people to organize itself as a totality, without regard to the administrative [existing] borders." The next year, the speaker of the Bosnian Serb parliament proclaimed the need "to grasp our ethnic space," while Belgrade's army chief of staff pursued the Nazi precedent even more explicitly when he referred to "our *lebensraum* in Bosnia."[52] A Serb nationalist leader added: "Our ideal, brothers, which we will attain, is to lead our motherland of Serbia, Montenegro, Macedonia, all of Bosnia-Herzegovina, . . . and [in Croatia] all of the Serbian Krajina under the roof of a single state." Bozidar Vucurevic, who became the Serb governor of Herzegovina, promised to "correct the injustice with regard to the borders which Josip Broz [Tito] drew with his dirty finger. He gave Serbian lands cheaply to the Croatians and Muslims." Vucurevic thought it would be "pure Serbian masochism to keep Broz's borders." The Italian border was another target, in the words of the top Bosnian Serb military commander Ratko Mladic, who was indicted for genocide in 1995: "Trieste is an old Serbian city, too, and will be ours in the end. The Serbian army will finish this war, just like the previous two, on the Trieste-Vienna line."[53] Genocide and expansionism still marched in step.

Like the perpetrators in Cambodia and Rwanda, Serb nationalists employed the common propaganda technique of "Accusation in a mirror." The Serbian Memorandum had paved the way in 1986 by denouncing Muslim Albanians, with great hyperbole, for "[t]he physical, political, legal and cultural genocide perpetrated against the Serbian population of Kosovo."[54] Then, during his 1992–93 operations against Bosnian Muslims, Serb general Mladic repeated that it was Serbs who were threatened with extinction, and that German and Croatian as well as Muslim goals all included "the complete annihilation of the Serbian people." Mladic complained: "We Serbs always wait until it reaches our throats. Only then do we retaliate." His response, then, posed as mere self-defense: "I have not conquered anything in this war. I only liberated that which was always Serbian, although I am far from liberating all that is really Serbian."[55]

Restoring Lost History

Speaking at the 600th anniversary of the 1389 Serbian defeat at the hands of Ottoman armies in the battle of Kosovo, Serbia's leader Slobodan Milosevic proclaimed, "Six centuries later, again we are in battles and quarrels. They are not armed battles, though such things should not be excluded yet." The Bosnian Serb general Ratko Mladic also yearned for a long-lost era of ethnic Serbian grandeur. Serbs had once been a populous nation: "In the thirteenth century, we were more numerous than the Germans. Now, there are just over twelve million of us, while they have grown to one hundred fifty million." Serbia's minister of culture added in 1992: "Serbs are one of the five imperial peoples. It is an ancient people and one of the most Christian ones."[56]

The authors of the 1986 Serbian Memorandum explained their country's alleged decline by complaining that for the previous 50 years "the Serbian nation was incapable of deriving support from its own history." Under "the shadow cast by the Serbian socialist and labor movement," the memorandum went on, "[m]any aspects of this history itself were even brought into question." Its authors declared that Communist Yugoslavia had paid inadequate attention to Serbia's nineteenth-century "democratic bourgeois tradition" and to "the contribution made by Serbian bourgeois society to law, culture, and statesmanship." The memorandum blamed "Austrian Marxists, confirmed opponents of movements of national liberation," for a Yugoslav Communist nationalities policy that continued to obstruct Serbian efforts at "preserving or reviving historical self-confidence." By 1986, according to the memorandum's authors, this had resulted in "the cultural achievements of the Serbian people" being officially "ignored" or allowed to "retrogress." Even their language was "being displaced and the Cyrillic script is gradually being lost." The memorandum alleged that "[n]o other literary and artistic heritage is so disordered, ravaged and confused as the Serbian heritage." The contemporary crisis of Yugoslav Communism had "destroyed the old system of values."[57]

Idealization of Rural Life

Serbia's eroding traditions were largely rural, and its nationalism had long possessed a distinct antiurban element. Serb perpetrators of the Bosnian genocide saw their Muslim victims as city dwellers, contrasted to Serb peasants. Following the Ottoman conquest, Muslims constituted 27 percent of the Balkan population by 1600. The Orthodox Serb majority lived mostly in villages, under Turkish rule from the towns. A mid-nineteenth-century writer commented that Serbia, Montenegro, Herzegovina, and Bosnia were all so rural that "one cannot imagine that other people exist except for peasants and farm-hands" and that "in Serbia they are the most prevalent" of all. Serbs, he continued, did not consider townspeople as being "among the Serbian people, and even scorn them." In contrast to Turks and Greeks, another Serb wrote, "our people seem to have the least propensity to found cities and towns." In the kingdom of Serbia in the nineteenth century, urban dwellers constituted only 16 percent of the population, to the satisfaction of a third Serbian writer: "The rural population is protected against the bias and abnormality of the town culture that mechanizes life." Even so, a fourth commentator worried that "with the genesis of the towns and the growth of the intelligentsia the creative genius of the village and the peasant is slowly disappearing." In fact, rural ways persisted even in Serbia's capital, Belgrade. As late as 1938, another writer asserted, the typical "mental alignment of the Belgrader" included "respect for one's ancestors and the ideas of the old Serbian state, integrity contained in folk poems and other oral traditions preserved in the family and the rural household." Yet again, nationalists were unsatisfied. In 1932, another Serbian writer lamented the lack of agrarian influence in the capital when he dismissed it in antiurban terms: "Belgrade was semi-provincial, demimondaine, primitive, immoral, secretive, brutal, inconsiderate, intimate, hypermodern and anarchistic. Raging and wretched at the same time."[58]

The city of Belgrade incurred the wrath of the most recent wave of Serbian nationalists, too. In 1992, one declared: "Belgrade is the Serbian Hong Kong. It is not part of the Serbdom, it has betrayed the Serbdom." Sonja Karadzic, daughter of Radovan Karadzic, proclaimed herself "very disappointed" with Belgrade and its "liberalism." Her father added in 1993: "We from Durmitor Mountain are a free people, we have very often felt that towns are like prisons." Pastoral solitude was a familiar if ironic ideal for ideologues of ethnic community. The next year, Karadzic's minister of information in the Bosnian Serb state, Republika Sprska, expressed his ultranationalist preference for untamed wilderness over fellow Serb multitudes: "[H]ere in the forest, I can scream to my heart's content. I can be completely free, while those in the middle of Belgrade cannot." Another Serb nationalist stated: "The lurching city of Belgrade, with its intellectual circles that only care about ingratiating themselves to the West, has ceased to be the capital of its own volition. It is no longer the capital in spirit." In this view, the authentic Serb nation was rural, though in this case perhaps more militaristic and ideological than agricultural: "Real Serbian national feelings are being tempered and hardened across the Drina River."[59]

Triangulating their pro-rural, antiurban, and racist instincts, Serb nationalist forces in the 1990s treated the towns of targeted ethnic groups with especial viciousness. Radovan Karadzic saw the Bosnian capital Sarajevo as the neck of a snake: "If we did not hold Sarajevo, there would be no state.... Never hold a snake by the tail, but by the neck." He set out "to kill the city in it." One Serbian writer called Sarajevo an "unnatural creation," and another confessed to "Neronian" joy as the city burned under Serb bombardment. The Serb commander in chief Bozidar Vucurevic, who expelled all Muslims from Trebinje and then destroyed the town's mosque, also dismissed coastal Dubrovnik as "neither a Serbian nor a Croatian town but a Latin town built on Serbian rocks. Life within it was always whorish and there was never room for an honest Serb. Zero elevation produced a zero category of people." Another Serb called Dubrovnik "a prostituted city of hotel keepers visited by American grandmothers, British queers, stupid Frenchmen and German typists."[60] Racial and rural prejudice intertwined.

Parts of the 1986 Serbian Memorandum prefigured the ethnic and territorial notions behind the genocide in Bosnia and helped legitimize it. Karadzic stated in a 1990 interview with the Belgrade daily *Nin:* "We are now openly saying what could not even be whispered before: the Serbs in Bosnia and Herzegovina are pinning all their hopes on their mother country, Serbia, and will never allow a state border to separate them from Serbia."[61]

Predominantly Muslim towns obstructed this vision. In 1992, therefore, General Ratko Mladic signed a directive ordering the "ethnic cleansing" of the urban enclaves of Srebrenica, Zepa, and Gorazde. After several years of brutal attacks on Muslim communities elsewhere in Bosnia, which killed tens of thousands, Radovan Karadzic gave the following order to his forces in March 1995: "By planned and well-thought-out combat operations, create an unbearable situation of total insecurity with no hope of further survival or life for the inhabitants of Srebrenica and Zepa." Mladic gave the Muslims of Srebrenica the choice to either "survive or disappear." His forces overran the city, separated men from women, and murdered at least 7,000 Muslim men in July 1995 alone. In a series of cases in The Hague from 2001 to 2005, the International Criminal Tribunal for the Former Yugoslavia convicted the Bosnian Serb officers Radislav Krstic, commander of the Drina Corps, and Vidoje Blagojevic, a colonel who commanded the Bratunac Brigade, of aiding and abetting the genocide at Srebrenica.[62] The tribunal also indicted Karadzic and Mladic, but in 2007 both remained at large.[63]

Genocide in the Twenty-first Century

A year after publication of the Serbian Memorandum, in October 1987, a group from the Darfur region of western Sudan, calling itself the Committee of the Arab Gathering, sent a similar letter of ethnic complaint to the Sudanese prime minister in Khartoum. The country's Arab Islamist regime was already involved in a long war of conquest against black Christian and animist communities of southern Sudan. This document proved to be an early warning of another genocide, in Darfur, to be launched there by local Arab militias 16 years later. Purporting to represent the views of 27 Arab tribes from the Darfur region, the 1987 letter overlooked the fact that Darfur ("land of the Fur," one of its main African tribes) had been incorporated into Sudan as late as 1916. Instead, the document began with local Arab claims to historical longevity, authenticity, and superiority: "The Sudanese ethnic group currently known as the Arab tribes of Darfur entered Sudan in the 15th century." The authors asserted that these Arabs were "the makers of civilization" of the Darfur region, "whether in government, religion or language." They even claimed to represent a regional majority, with Arabs supposedly making up "more than 70% of the total population of Darfur" and occupying 80 percent of the area of South Darfur and 50 percent of North Darfur.[64]

In fact, Arabs composed only 2.5 million of Darfur's 6.5 million people, a proportion the Arab Gathering implicitly acknowledged in claiming that educated Arabs represented only "40% of all educated Darfurians." The region's 4 million non-Arab Africans lived on much less than half the land, and as the Arab Gathering further pointed out, "The Arabs are over represented in the army." Yet that was not enough. The Gathering's statement asserted that "we Arabs feel that we are deprived of true representation in the leadership of Dar-

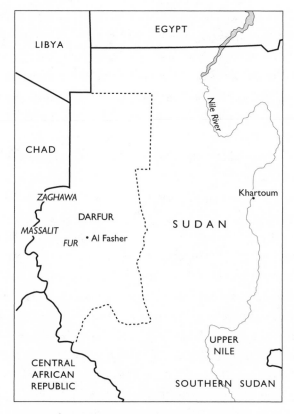

MAP 34. Sudan, Darfur, and Chad

fur," having purportedly become "a majority without weight." It insisted that "the administration of each region should be placed in the hands of the sons of that region," and that Arabs should hold "50% of all government constitutional posts." The statement concluded with an implied threat, using language ominously resembling that of Khieu Samphan and Léon Mugesera: "[S]hould the Arabs not be allowed their fair share in government, we are afraid that things may get out of the hands of wise people." Such a development would allow "the ignorant people and mob" to cause "a catastrophe with dire consequence."[65] What this meant was revealed the next year, in a tape-recorded meeting where the future commander of Darfur's Arab Janjaweed militia, Musa Hilal, was overheard thanking Arab militia from neighboring Chad for "providing his tribe in Sudan with the necessary weapons and ammunition to exterminate the African tribes in Darfur."[66]

That threatened catastrophe in Darfur proved to be the opening genocide of the twenty-first century. In 2003, with the support of Khartoum, Janjaweed militias launched a murderous racialist land-grab, in just four years killing and starving to death over 300,000 members of Darfur's African agricultural tribes, the Fur, Massalit, and Zaghawa. The Janjaweed perpetrators are mostly fast-moving, camel-herding pastoralists, an exception to the pattern of agrarian influence on genocidists. They propound no ideology of cultivation, and their victims are the farmers; the killers have emptied the land, not settled it. Nor have Janjaweed attacked the Fur, Massalit, and Zaghawa residents of Darfur's towns. Yet these perpetrators do possess, along with their own racism and historical mythology, a familiar interest in territorial expansion across international frontiers. At the end of 2005, Sudanese army and Janjaweed forces attacked from Darfur into neighboring Chad, raiding and emptying 60 Chadian villages.[67] Two months later, reporter Nicholas D. Kristof wrote: "After killing several hundred thousand people in its own Darfur region, Sudan's government is now sending its brutal janjaweed militias to kill the same tribes here in Chad."[68] In an attack on April 12–13, 2006, Janjaweed units, "moving further and further into Chad," shot or hacked to death 118 villagers. New waves of attacks on a dozen villages in October and November killed 200 eastern Chadians and drove out 3,000 more. Some of the victims identified their attackers as Janjaweed in Sudanese military uniforms, while others recognized local Arab residents. Kristof reported from Chad on November 21, 2006: "The genocide that started in Darfur in 2003 is now threatening to topple the governments of Chad and the Central African Republic."[69]

Al-Qaeda

At another distant frontier of the Muslim world, a different group of Arab extremists had organized along religious rather than ethnic lines. Just before the 1979 Soviet invasion of Afghanistan, the Pakistani government and its military Inter-Services Intelligence agency (ISI) began to heavily back the Afghan opposition forces, known as *mujahedeen,* as did the United States, which in the years 1979–89 supplied the ISI with approximately $3 billion for distribution to them.[70] Across the border in Afghanistan, the mujahedeen were joined by a force of Arabs fighting an anti-Soviet jihad, or Muslim holy war, led by the Saudi heir Osama bin Laden and his new organization Al-Qaeda (the base), formed in 1988.

Soviet troops withdrew from Afghanistan in 1988 after a decade-long occupation, and some of the Communist-led Afghan soldiers began to defect to the Islamic opposition. In early 1989, 400 Afghan Communist troops came out of the southern city of Jalalabad to surrender near the Pakistani border. To the horror of the Afghan mujahedeen, who had promised quarter to their countrymen, a group of Arab jihadis massacred 60 of the Afghan defectors— literally cut them to pieces, packed their remains into fruit cases, and sent them by truck back into Jalalabad with a message to its Communist garrison, "This is what awaits the *moulheds* [unbelievers]!" The garrison commander radioed his mujahedeen counterparts that his troops would now "fight to the end, preferring to die in combat rather than be cut into pieces by the Arabs."[71] The Afghan Communists held out for three more years, until their destruction brought more widespread slaughter and a new civil war, from which the Islamist Taliban movement, Al-Qaeda's eventual Afghan ally, emerged victorious only in 1996.

Osama bin Laden returned home to Saudi Arabia in 1990. He quickly clashed with the Saudi regime over its hosting of the U.S. forces arriving to confront Saddam Hussein's Iraqi army, which had just invaded Kuwait. The Al-Qaeda leader then abandoned his native country and spent the next four years in Sudan, under the protection of the Islamist regime still pursuing genocide against the non-Muslim Africans in southern Sudan. Al-Qaeda also tried to gain a foothold among Bosnian Muslims fighting Serb aggression, but failed. The underground leader of the Islamic Jihad movement in neighboring Egypt, Ayman al-Zawahiri, joined bin Laden in his exile in Khartoum.[72] After the Taliban's victory brought Afghanistan under Islamist fundamentalist rule in 1996, Al-Qaeda relocated its headquarters back there.

Al-Qaeda was already recruiting in neighboring Pakistan, where the radical Islamist party Jaamat-e-Islami, whose members had participated in the genocide in Bangladesh in 1971, led an Islamist alliance that increased its parliamentary representation from two seats in 1993 to 60 in 2002. A Pakistani recruit for Al-Qaeda's new and increasingly brutal global jihad swore an oath in 1995 to "slaughter infidels my entire life."[73] Three years later, bin Laden issued a potentially genocidal fatwa from Afghanistan: "The ruling to kill the Americans and their allies—civilians and military—is an individual duty for every Muslim who can do it in any country."[74] Al-Qaeda operatives killed over 220 people in car bombings that struck the U.S. embassies in Kenya and Tanzania in 1998. The next month, an Al-Qaeda official in Afghanistan drafted a confidential questionnaire about the tactics of jihad under Islamic sharia law, seeking guidance from other jihadis for what he called a "lawful study that I am doing on the killing of civilians." His first question was: "Since you are the representative of the Islamic Jihad group, what is your lawful stand on the killing of civilians, specifically when women and children are included? And please explain the legitimate law concerning those who are deliberately killed."[75]

Conjuring up moral support, Al-Qaeda decided, as had the anti-Islamic Serb leader Radovan Karadzic, to "attack the head of the snake." To Al-Qaeda this meant the United States, a serpent carrying Egypt and other secular Muslim regimes in its tail.[76] Justifying mass murder continued to preoccupy Al-Qaeda's operatives even after its attacks on the United States took the lives of over 2,700 people on September 11, 2001. One of the organizers of those attacks, Ramzi bin al-Shibh, subsequently composed a tract entitled "The Truth about the New Crusade: A Ruling on the Killing of Women and Children of the Non-Believers." He went so far as to argue for killing up to "four million" American civilians: "Some might say that it is the innocent, the elderly, the women, and the children who are victims, so how can these operations be legitimate according to *sharia*? And we say that the sanctity of women, children, and the elderly is not absolute. There are special cases." They were numerous. In bin al-Shibh's interpretation, "God said to assault whoever assaults you, in a like manner." Therefore, he concluded, "In killing Americans who are ordinarily off limits, Muslims should not exceed [killing] four million non-combatants, or render more than ten million of them homeless." This would be, bin al-Shibh asserted, "no more than reciprocal."[77] Meanwhile, two months after September 11, the Al-Qaeda leader Osama bin Laden proclaimed publicly: "Yes, we kill their innocents and this is legal religiously and logically.... What we are practicing is good terror. We will not stop killing them and whoever supports them." He then added, "Killing Jews is top priority," revealing bin Laden's campaign to be genocidal under a strict legal interpretation of the 1948 Genocide Convention's prohibition of mass murder of an ethnic group. In 2003, another radical Saudi dissident produced "A Treatise on the Laws of the Use of Weapons of Mass Destruction against the Unbelievers," in which he stated that "use is permissible, even if you kill them without exception," up to as many as "nearly ten million."[78]

Al-Qaeda combined ethnoreligious violence with territorial expansionist ambitions that resemble those of other genocidal movements. For instance, bin Laden's deputy Ayman al-Zawahiri explained in 2005 that driving the U.S. occupying forces from Iraq should lead to a "second stage: Establish an Islamic authority or emirate, then develop it and support it until it achieves the level of a caliphate—over as much territory as you can to spread its power." Then a third stage would follow: "Extend the jihad to the secular countries neighbouring Iraq"; and a fourth, "the clash with Israel." It was "extremely important," Zawa-hiri explained, "that the mujahedeen must not have their mission end with the expulsion of the Americans from Iraq, and then lay down their weapons, and silence the fighting zeal."[79] Al-Qaeda's ambitions for its projected caliphate extended not just to the United States, Europe, and Africa but also to the Muslim communities of Southeast Asia, including southern Thailand and the southern Philippines, and even to recovery of the new "lost territory" of East Timor.[80]

Bin Laden's preoccupation with "the defense of the Prophet's tradition," namely restoring and even rivaling the purity of early Islam, likewise echoed the cults of antiquity of other genocidists.[81] According to a visitor to Al-Qaeda's Afghan encampment in 1996, "Some of bin Laden's followers had taken on the names of military commanders from early Islamic conquests, and I felt as though I had stepped back into the past."[82] In bin Laden's videotaped discussion with a Saudi sheikh in November 2001, the two men appealed to seventh-century Islamic precedent for their cause: "I remember, the words of Al-Rabbani, he said they made a coalition against us in the winter with the infidels like the Turks, and others, and some other Arabs. And they surrounded us like . . . in the days of the prophet Muhammad. Exactly like what's happening right now. . . . And the day will come when the symbols of Islam will rise up and it will be similar to the early days . . . like the old days, such as [under the Prophet's Companions] Abu Bakr and Othman and Ali and others. In these days, in our times, . . . the greatest jihad in the history of Islam."[83] Later medieval history maintained its salience, too. Bin Laden claimed in 2002 that "Cheney and Powell" had already "reaped more murder and destruction in Baghdad than Hulagu the Tatar," the grandson of Genghis Khan who sacked Baghdad in 1258.[84]

Al-Qaeda operatives now active in various countries also took up this notion of an ancient, epic struggle. In a telephone conversation taped by Italian police, Rabei Osman Sayed Ahmed, the Egyptian who claimed to have masterminded the 2004 terrorist attacks on Madrid commuter trains, seemed to be "in a trance" as he imagined striking right to Europe's classical capital, telling another potential suicide bomber: "Rome, if God wishes we are entering, even entering Rome, . . . we are opening Rome . . . if God wishes, Rome is opening. It will be."[85]

Al-Qaeda continued to stress its model of Islamic antiquity after the U.S. ground invasion of Iraq in 2003, when bin Laden moved to support an Iraqi Islamic insurgent group there. The next year this group, under its Jordanian leader Abu Musab al-Zarqawi, who had also fought the Soviets in Afghanistan, adopted the name "Al-Qaeda in Mesopotamia." From the Afghan-Pakistan border, Al-Qaeda leaders strove to maintain contact with Zarqawi and to communicate their viewpoint to him, until his death in Iraq in 2006. For instance, in mid-2005 Al-Qaeda's no. 2, Zawahiri, wrote to Zarqawi, praising what he called "your historic battle against the greatest of criminals and apostates in the heart of the Islamic world, the field where epic and major battles in the history of Islam were fought." Zawahiri pointed out that "the victory of Islam will never take place until a Muslim state is established in the manner of the Prophet in the heart of the Islamic world." That now required, he told Zarqawi, a return to "the pure way of the Prophet" by the establishment of "a caliphate along the lines of the Prophet's." Within Islam, significantly, the new caliphate emerging in Iraq would need to fight the Shi'a heresy just as its predecessor had in the days of the Prophet, when the inimical "function" of Shi'ism had supposedly been "to accuse the companions of Muhammad of heresy in a campaign against Islam." For such historical reasons, then, Shi'a Muslims could never be trusted: "Their prior history in cooperating with the enemies of Islam is consistent with their current reality of connivance with the Crusaders."[86]

Along with their ethnoreligious hatred, territorial expansionism, and politicized cult of Islamic antiquity, some Al-Qaeda leaders even further resembled their genocidal antecedents when they were living in Sudan in 1992–96. In *The Looming Tower: Al-Qaeda and the Road to 9/11,* Lawrence Wright details how in Sudan, Al-Qaeda became "largely an agricultural organization." Bin Laden bred Arabian horses, developed what a local associate considered a "romantic attachment to native stock," and bought three large tracts of fertile Sudanese farmland, one totaling a million acres. He became "perhaps the largest landowner in the country," and his agricultural company "enjoyed a near monopoly on Sudan's major farm exports." He "declared that Sudan could feed the entire world if it was properly managed," and at one point, Wright states, bin Laden even "said he resolved to quit al-Qaeda altogether and become a farmer."

Subsequently, the Al-Qaeda leaders still occasionally described their activities in muted agrarianist terms. For instance, bin Laden and Zawahiri stated in their 1998 fatwa: "The Arabian Peninsula has never—since God made it flat, created its desert, and encircled it with seas—been stormed by any forces like the crusader armies now spreading in it like locusts, consuming its riches and destroying its plantations."[87] In the months before September 11, 2001, Zawahiri also used metaphors of cultivation to describe the Al-Qaeda mission now again based in Afghanistan. As he fostered the merger of his original organization, the Egyptian-based group Islamic Jihad, with Al-Qaeda's Afghan headquarters, Zawahiri employed a postmodern mixture of agrarian vocabulary and commercial code to urge his followers to transfer their "farms" (probably cells) from "the village" (Egypt) to Afghanistan, which he depicted as a superior base for their "trade," jihad. He wrote: "As you know the situation below in the village has become bad for traders [jihadis]. . . . We are also dispersed over various cities. However God had mercy on us when the Omar Brothers Company [Afghanistan's Taliban regime] here opened the market for traders." Zawahiri reported that the Taliban had also offered to "[e]ncourage commercial activities in the village." Thus, he continued in his tradecraft code, "Colleagues here believe that this is an excellent opportunity to encourage sales in general, and in the village in particular."[88]

Some members of Egypt's Islamic Jihad, however, opposed Zawahiri's relocation to Afghanistan as fruitless. Again using agrarianist language, one of them protested to Zawahiri, saying that the Islamist struggle in Egypt desperately demanded their group's greatest attention: "Count the number of laborers in your farms," he said of their depleted forces in Egypt, and "then see if anyone has stayed." He added that, of "the many projects where you enthusiastically participated," only a few "greenhouses" had enjoyed "limited success." Moving Islamic Jihad's base to Afghanistan, this dissident wrote, was just "throwing good seeds onto barren land." Worse, he added, "the time and place are not suitable for this type of agriculture. Cotton may not be planted in Siberia, just as apples cannot be planted in hot areas. I'm sure you are aware that wheat is planted in winter and cotton in summer. After all our efforts we haven't seen any crops in winter or summer. This type of agriculture is ridiculous." And, in a classic combination of agrarianism and antiquity, the writer then recommended that Zawahiri "[a]sk those with experience in agriculture and history."[89] At any rate, recruitment and war took priority. A 2002 Al-Qaeda appeal ended with an extract from the Koran that promised its followers the religious reward of a familiar pastoral paradise: "Allah, take the lives and property of the believers, so that the Garden of Eden will be for them . . . they will fight for Allah, they will kill and be killed."[90]

Several years later in Iraq, Abu Musab al-Zarqawi unveiled his new, even more extreme version of Al-Qaeda's approach. It, too, had ominous precedents that crossed cultural boundaries. Echoing both Karadzic and bin Laden, Zarqawi announced that Iraq's Shi'a Muslim majority population were "the lurking snake," also calling them "the crafty and malicious scorpion." But he drew upon longer traditions when he added that the Shi'a "are where the disease lies" and called them anti-Muslim "friends of the Jews, Franks [Christians] and polytheists." Using language redolent of Hitler's about Jews, Zarqawi also called the Shi'a "the rat of the dike," adding that the early modern "Shi'a Safavid state," which ruled Iran from 1502 to 1736, had been, like Czechoslovakia was to the Nazis, "a dagger that stabbed Islam and its people in the back."[91]

Zarqawi's assignment of historical blame went as far back as the Mongol invasions of the thirteenth century. He approvingly quoted the early-fourteenth-century sheikh al-Islam Ibn Taymiyya's denunciation of the Shi'a: they were "one of the greatest reasons for the eruption of Genghis Khan, the king of the infidels, into the lands of Islam, for the arrival of Hulagu in the country of Iraq." In that early era, he claimed, the Shi'a sect had not only "pillaged the troops of the Muslims when they passed among them going to Egypt the first time," but also, perhaps even more seriously, the Shi'a had supplied "help for the Tartars and Franks" in their war "against the Muslims." Confronting the contemporary Shi'a threat, according to Zarqawi, required mass murder: "[T]he tree of triumph and empowerment cannot grow tall and lofty without blood . . . the perfume of fragrant blood spilled on behalf of God." Therefore, Zarqawi concluded, "Let blood be spilled," for he insisted that "God's religion is more precious than anything and has priority over lives, wealth and children."[92]

In this cause, violence against civilians was not merely necessary but a recommended tactic to promote the desired goal of protracted holy war. Zarqawi aimed "to drag the Shi'a into the battle because this is the only way to prolong the fighting between us and the infidels." For him, a major problem was reluctance on both sides, not just among the Shi'a. Zarqawi even had to force his chosen constituency in Iraq, its Sunni Muslims, into the war: "Our fighting against the Shi'a is the way to drag the [Islamic] nation into the battle." Thus, Zarqawi went on, "the only solution is for us to strike the religious, military, and other cadres among the Shi'a with blow after blow until they bend to the Sunnis. Someone may say that, in this matter, we are being hasty and rash and leading the [Islamic] nation into a battle for which it is not ready, [a battle] that will be revolting and in which blood will be spilled. This is exactly what we want, since right and wrong no longer have any place in our current situation. The Shi'a have destroyed all those balances. God's religion is more precious than lives and souls." Therefore, Zarqawi concluded, "If we are able to strike them with one painful blow after another until they enter the battle, we will be able to [re]shuffle the cards." Then, the Americans "will enter a second battle with the Shi'a. This is what we want."[93]

Al-Qaeda's global goal was proliferating warfare, which would be conducive to genocide of infidels. A month after the September 11 attacks on the United States, which were apparently planned as a provocation to war, bin Laden predicted to his host, Taliban leader Mullah Omar, that America's anticipated retaliatory invasion of Afghanistan would help end the world hegemony of the United States. The war would impose on the United States "great long-term economic burdens, leading to further economic collapse, which will force America, God willing, to resort to the former Soviet Union's only option: withdrawal from Afghanistan, disintegration, and contraction."[94] A month later, a sympathetic visiting Saudi sheikh told bin Laden that "this is what everyone is hoping for. Thank Allah America came out of its caves. We hit her the first hit and the next one will hit her with the hands of the believers."[95] After the U.S. invasion of Iraq, bin Laden gloated that now "the third world war has begun in Iraq."[96]

Meanwhile, like other genocidal movements before it, Al-Qaeda's pronouncements in Iraq also took on a muted antiurban theme. In this case, military necessity was a major factor. The country's towns and topography had proved difficult for rural guerrilla warfare. "What prevents us from [calling] a general alert," Zarqawi complained in 2004, "is that the country has no mountains in which we can take refuge and no forests in whose thickets we can hide." He quoted with approval the genocidal death wish of Imam al-Nawawi (1232–77): "[I]f the city and the desert fought each other until all without exception perished unless they professed belief in the oneness of God, this would be good."[97] A triumphant agrarian note sounded only two months later: "God honored us and so we harvested their heads."[98] By May 2005, Zarqawi was urging his forces to "concentrate our suicide operations, to shake up the presence of the enemy in these cities and compel him to get out of the cities and go to places in which the enemy can be sniped."[99]

This tactical search for a rural guerrilla front does not necessarily convey ideological contempt for towns. Yet if Al-Qaeda manages to seize significant territories, it is likely to display greater cruelty toward their urban populations, which would prove difficult to control and too independent to be tolerated. An emerging territorial caliphate might also value the utility of a productive peasantry and, like other genocidal regimes, demonstrate an ideological preoccupation with the virtues of cultivation, though typically showing no leniency to actual cultivators.

In the course of military campaigns, Zarqawi stated in 2005, "Killing Muslims who are acting as a shield is not the most preferable option, but is necessary if you must kill them to get at the enemy." Thus, he put it, "killing Muslims . . . is defending ourselves." Preserving Muslim lives was a secondary matter, like the soul. For Zarqawi, "restoring the religion is more important than restoring the soul."[100] His "religion," it seems, was killing.

By mid-2005, Zarqawi's insurgent violence against large crowds of Shi'a civilians had escalated so dramatically that Iraq's leading Shi'a cleric was moved to publicly denounce this "mass extermination" of his community, protesting that Iraq was heading toward "genocide."[101] Even more telling was an extraordinary rebuke that resounded from the Afghan-Pakistan border. Al-Qaeda's deputy leader, Ayman al-Zawahiri, wrote to Zarqawi in Iraq: "[W]hy were there attacks on ordinary Shia? . . . And can the *mujahedeen* kill all of the Shia in Iraq? Has any Islamic state in history ever tried that? And why kill ordinary Shia considering that they are forgiven because of their ignorance?"[102] Astonishingly, Zarqawi's bloody campaign against the Shi'a of Iraq had succeeded in making the top Al-Qaeda leaders sound moderate by comparison. Genocide was plumbing new depths. Zarqawi continued to target the Shi'a, his language now less sanguinary but still demanding purity and order. He instructed his followers to "reduce the attacks on Sunni areas" but to work harder at "cleansing them, calmly, of spies and Shias" and to "move the battle to the Shia depths."[103]

Meanwhile, Osama bin Laden returned his gaze to his former ally Sudan, which he claimed needed help "to defend Islam, its land and its people" against a "Zionist-crusaders war," by which he meant any defense of Darfur's African Muslims against Khartoum's genocide. "I call on mujahedeen, especially in Sudan and the Arab peninsula, to prepare for a long war against the crusader plunderers."[104]

Conclusion

The modern era and modern genocide both began with a revival of interest in the ancient world. Genocide also combined virulent forms of religious sectarianism with territorial expansionism and emergent agrarian and racist thinking. Even at the dawn of the twenty-first century, a postmodern commercial-terrorist "nonstate actor" like Al-Qaeda still sees itself as refighting ancient battles in a contemporary setting to establish an ethnically pure, agrarian utopia on the graves of those they consider their traditional victims—Crusaders, Franks, Muslims, and Jews.

This book has explored four telltale characteristics of genocide that recurred regularly from the fifteenth century to the twenty-first: the preoccupation of perpetrators with race, antiquity, agriculture, and expansion. The early modern rediscovery of Rome's destruction of Carthage, for instance, provoked repeated sixteenth-century comparisons with the indigenous victims of contemporary cases. In colonial Ireland and Mexico, commentators even speculated that the hapless indigenes were descended from the dispersed Carthaginian survivors. British policy in the Scottish Highlands in 1692 was to inflict the fate of Carthage on the Macdonald clan.[105] Hitler considered Roman history "the best mentor" and Carthage the most appropriate example of a victim, "the most horrible picture of such a slow execution of a people through its own deserts."[106]

The much earlier metaphor of the Garden of Eden, whether as pristine ethnic preserve, uninhabited pastoral idyll, or superior agricultural economy, also attracted a succession of commentators, from seventeenth-century Spanish colonizers of the New World to their English contemporaries to the Nazis in the twentieth century and Al-Qaeda in the twenty-first.[107] With catastrophic irony, the myth of an untouched empty land usually played a key role in spurring the displacement and destruction of its actual inhabitants. So did the settler fetish for cultivation of that land and the predisposition of intensive agriculturalists to leave little or none of it unoccupied to allow for hunter-gatherer or pastoralist subsistence. Throughout the early modern and modern eras, agricultural metaphors have easily expressed mass murder of target groups. A Spanish settler in sixteenth-century Mexico talked of using Indian blood to irrigate his fields, and a seventeenth-century English officer talked of "dunging the Ground with their Flesh" (see pp. 100, 231), while British and German settlers in Australia threatened to use the bodies of Aborigines for fertilizer (see pp. 262, 286). The Khmer Rouge administered that very fate to Cambodian city dwellers.

Even as urbanization spread over the globe in the twentieth century, a violent form of agrarianism still flourished through its final decades. From Eastern Europe to Southeast Asia, from Central America and Central Africa, genocidal regimes across the political spectrum that massacred ethnic enemies also sponsored agriculturalists and settlers, whom they called "model farmers" in a variety of vocabularies. The Nazis used this term (*vorbildliche Bauern*) in 1943 to praise German settlers in the southern Russian steppe and even promoted Germans from East Africa as superior farmers in a "model district" (*Muster-bezirk*) annexed from Poland. In 1976, the Khmer Rouge transplanted "model peasants" (*kasekor kumruu*) from Cambodia's Southwest Zone to its less loyal, underpopulated Northwest. Four years later, the Indonesian military regime began sending model farmers (*petani teladan*) from Bali to occupied East Timor, and from 1983 the Guatemalan genocidal dictatorship set up "model villages" (*aldeas modelo*) for approved surviving cultivators. For its own model peasants, Rwanda's Habyarimana regime used the term "advancing farmers" (*abahinzi ba kijyambere*).[108]

Finally, fetishes of purity and contamination have strengthened the racism and violence that promote genocide. Many perpetrators used biological metaphors to justify genocidal massacre. In 1580, the brutal English commander in Ireland, Lord Arthur Grey de Wilton, whom we met on page 204, informed Queen Elizabeth that he had been dutifully "strict in dealing with religion," for Catholicism was a disease, "a Canker never receiving Cure without corrosive medicines."[109] In 1641, another English commander, Sir Charles Coote, justified his order to kill not only Irish men and women but also children "more than a span long," with the metaphor, "Kill the nits and you will have no lice."[110] On January 9, 1642, as allied Scottish troops massacred up to 3,000 Irish Catholic civilians, including children, they shouted. "Nits make Lice."[111] In the nineteenth century, this slogan reemerged in both the Australian outback and the American West, as a common call to massacre Indians and Aborigines: "Nits grow into lice."[112] The Nazis, too, likened Jews to "lice," while Al-Qaeda called the Shi'a community the locus "where the disease lies." The cure and prevention of the crime of genocide must lie, at least in part, in the diagnosis of its recurring causes and symptoms.

Notes

Introduction

1. Manuel de Nóbrega, quoted in Anthony Pagden, *The Fall of Natural Man: The American Indian and the Origins of Comparative Ethnology* (Cambridge, 1982), 83.

2. *New York Times*, Nov. 9, 2004, F2; I. Tattersall and J. H. Schwartz, *Extinct Humans* (Boulder, 2000), 221; Slavomil Vencl, "Interprétation des blessures causées par les armes au Mésolithique," *L'anthropologie* 95:1 (1991): 219–28, at 219; L. H. Keeley, *War before Civilization: The Myth of the Peaceful Savage* (New York, 1996), 38.

3. Keeley, *War before Civilization*, 38, 69; Vencl, "Interprétation des blessures," 223.

4. G. Bucellati, "Amorites," and Jo Ann Hackett, "Canaanites," in *Oxford Encyclopedia of Archaeology in the Near East* (New York, 1997), 1:110, 412.

5. Paul Freedman, *Images of the Medieval Peasant* (Stanford, 1999), 91.

6. John Roberts, ed., *The Oxford Dictionary of the Classical World* (Oxford, 2005), 389–90.

7. Freedman, *Images of the Medieval Peasant*, 93–94.

8. Nicholas Robins, "Genocide and the Great Rebellion of 1780–82 in Peru and Upper Peru," *Journal of Genocide Research* 7:3 (2005): 351–75; Philippe R. Girard, "Caribbean Genocide: Racial War in Haiti, 1802–04," *Patterns of Prejudice* 39:2 (2005): 138–61; rGyal-dbang lnga-pa, *Rgya-Bod-Hor-Sog-gi . . .* (Xining, 1993), 225, quoted in Elliot Sperling, "'Orientalism' and Aspects of Violence in the Tibetan Tradition," in Thierry Dodin and Heinz Räther, eds., *Imagining Tibet: Perceptions, Projections, and Fantasies* (Boston, 2001), 317–18.

9. Keith Thomas, *Man and the Natural World: Changing Attitudes in England 1500–1800* (Oxford, 1983), 278, 274.

10. Watkin Tench, *1788,* ed. Tim Flannery (Melbourne, 1996), 118-19; John Connor, *The Australian Frontier Wars, 1788–1838* (Sydney, 2002), 28; George Henry Haydon, *Five Years' Experience in Australia Felix* (London, 1846), ch. 6, in G. Mackaness, *George Augustus Robinson's Journey into South-Eastern Australia, 1844* (Sydney, 1941), 62–64, 13.

11. Greg Grandin, *The Last Colonial Massacre: Latin America in the Cold War* (Chicago, 2004).

12. Andrew Mack et al., eds. *The Human Security Report 2005* (Oxford, 2005): www.human securityreport.info (accessed Mar. 7, 2005).

13. John Alcock, *Mons Perfeccionis* (Westmestre, 1497); Bartolomé de Las Casas, *The Devastation of the Indies: A Brief Account* [1552] (Baltimore, 1992), 70; Colin Tatz, *With Intent to Destroy: Reflecting on Genocide* (London, 2003), 186n1; Sean O'Faolain, *The Great O'Neill* (New York, 1942), 101.

14. Raphael Lemkin, *Axis Rule in Occupied Europe* (Washington, November 1944). James

Fussell notes that the preface, with its use of the term *genocide,* is dated October 1943 (personal communication). Ann Curthoys, "Raphael Lemkin's Tasmania: An Introduction," *Patterns of Prejudice* 39:2 (2005): 162–96; John Docker, "Are Settler-Colonies Inherently Genocidal? Re-Reading Lemkin," in A. Dirk Moses, ed., *Empire, Colony, Genocide: Studies in Global Destruction* (New York, 2007).

15. "Convention on the Prevention and Punishment of the Crime of Genocide," in Robert Gellately and Ben Kiernan, eds., *The Specter of Genocide: Mass Murder in Historical Perspective* (New York, 2003), 381-84; *Bringing Them Home: Report of the National Inquiry into the Separation of Aboriginal and Torres Strait Islander Children from Their Families* (Sydney, 1997), 275; R. Manne, *In Denial: The Stolen Generations and the Right, Quarterly Essay* 1 (2001): 64–65 (citing Australian Archives, ACT A659/1 40/1/408), 38–40; David L. Nersessian, "The Contours of Genocidal Intent: Troubling Jurisprudence from the International Criminal Tribunals," *Texas International Law Journal* 37 (Spring 2002): 231-98, at 235–36.

16. Nersessian, "Contours," 236–37, 275–76; on emerging jurisprudence, see William A. Schabas, "Was Genocide Committed in Bosnia and Herzegovina?" *Fordham International Law Journal* 25 (2001–2): 23–53.

17. Nersessian, "Contours," 251–52.

18. Lawrence LeBlanc, *The United States and the Genocide Convention* (Durham, 1991).

19. Nersessian, "Contours," 258; Adam Jones, ed., *Gendercide and Genocide* (Nashville, 2004).

20. Leo Kuper, *Genocide: Its Political Use in the Twentieth Century* (New Haven, 1981), 59ff.; Frank Chalk and Kurt Jonassohn, *The History and Sociology of Genocide* (New Haven, 1990), 26.

21. Flavius Josephus, *Jewish Antiquities* 2.487–498: www.livius.org/jo-jz/julius/pogrom.html (accessed Oct. 14, 2005).

22. "Clan MacDonald v Clan MacLeod (1375–1602)": www.freefirezone.net/showthread .php?p=138044; Tam Anderson, "Scottish Battles and Conflicts": http://members.aol.com/_ht_a/ skyelander/sbattles.html (both accessed Aug. 18, 2005).

23. Human Rights Watch, *"We Have No Orders to Save You": State Participation and Complicity in Communal Violence in Gujarat* (2002), v. 14, 3(C): http://hrw.org/reports/2002/india (accessed Sept. 5, 2005); "Treat Communal Violence as Genocide," *Hindu,* Dec. 25, 2005.

24. Chérif Bassiouni, "Crimes against Humanity," *Crimes of War Project:* www.crimesofwar .org/thebook/crimes-against-humanity.html (accessed Sept. 23, 2006).

25. *Oxford Latin Dictionary* (Oxford, 1968); *Old French-English Dictionary* (Cambridge, 2000); *Middle English Dictionary* (Ann Arbor, 1954); C. T. Lewis and C. Short, *A Latin Dictionary* (Oxford, 1962); J. F. Niermeyer and C. Van De Kieft, *Mediae Latinitatis Lexicon Minus* (Leiden, 2002); R. E. Latham, *Revised Medieval Latin Word-List from British and Irish Sources* (London, 1965); John Hobbes, *Leviathan* II.xxiv.128; *Oxford English Dictionary Online* (Oxford, 2000); *Encyclopaedia Britannica* (Edinburgh, 1771); Alan Atkinson, *The Europeans in Australia,* vol. 2 (Melbourne, 2004), 157–58.

26. Rome Statute of the International Criminal Court (1998): www.un.org/icc, article 7, 1-2; Bassiouni, "Crimes against Humanity."

27. C. Rowley and Henry Reynolds, "Aborigines since 1788," in *Australian Encyclopedia* (Sydney, 1988), 280; Grant Foreman, *The Five Civilized Tribes* (Norman, 1934), 413; Robert F. Heizer and Allan J. Almquist, *The Other Californians* (Berkeley, 1971), 46–48, 61. California Indians won the right to sit on juries in 1879.

28. *Draft Code of Crimes against the Peace and Security of Mankind, . . . Adopted by the International Law Commission,* 48th sess., U.N. doc. A/51/10 (1996), art. 17 cmt. 5, in Nersessian, "Contours," 264 (emphasis added); *Prosecutor v. Jelisic,* appeal judgment, July 5, 2001, 46: www.un.org/ icty/jelisic/appeal/judgement (accessed Oct. 25, 2004).

29. *Prosecutor v. D. Tadic,* opinion and judgment, May 7, 1997: www.un.org/icty/tadic/trialc2/ judgement (accessed Mar. 14, 2005), quoted in Nina Silove, "Genocide in East Timor," in Colin Tatz et al., eds., *Genocide Perspectives II: Essays on Holocaust and Genocide* (Sydney, 2003), 231; article 30 (b) of the Rome Statute of the International Criminal Court; Nersessian, "Contours," 262–68; Morten Bergsmo, "Intent," in Dinah L. Shelton, ed., *Encyclopedia of Genocide and Crimes against Humanity* (New York, 2005), 2:530.

30. William A. Schabas, *Genocide in International Law: The Crime of Crimes* (Cambridge, 2000), 245; Nersessian, "Contours," 267; cf. Schabas, *Genocide in International Law,* 245–56; 248–54 *Prosecutor v. Akayesu* (case no. ICTR-96-4-T), judgment, Sept. 2, 1998, para. 498, quoted in Cécile Aptel, "The Intent to Commit Genocide in the Case Law of the International Criminal Tribunal for Rwanda," *Criminal Law Forum* 13 (2002): 277; *Prosecutor v. Jelisic,* appeal judgment, July 5, 2001, para. 49, quoted in Cécile Tournaye, "Genocidal Intent before the ICTY," *International Comparative Law Quarterly* 52 (April 2003): 452.

31. *Draft Code of Crimes Against the Peace and Security,* art. 17, cmt. 5. Nersessian adds: "The Draft Code was held to be good authority on genocide by both international criminal tribunals" ("Contours," n28).

32. Schabas, *Genocide in International Law,* 214, 217ff., 222–24; *Prosecutor v. Jelisic,* appeal judgment, July 5, 2001, para. 47: www.un.org/icty/jelisic/appeal/judgement (accessed Oct. 25, 2004).

33. Ibid., para. 48.

34. Pioneers in genocide studies include sociologists Vahakn Dadrian, Helen Fein, Irving Louis Horowitz, Kurt Jonassohn, Leo Kuper, and Eric Markusen; political scientists Daniel Chirot, Barbara Harff, Raul Hilberg, Robert Melson, Roger Smith, and Colin Tatz; psychologist Israel Charny; lawyers Chérif Bassiouni, William A. Schabas, and Gregory H. Stanton; and historians Yehuda Bauer, Frank Chalk, Richard Hovannisian, and Henry Huttenbach.

35. Lawrence Weschler, *A Miracle, a Universe: Settling Accounts with Torturers* (New York, 1990); in 1996 Yale's Cambodian Genocide Program uncovered the archives of the Khmer Rouge secret police: www.yale.edu/cgp/resources.html; John Dinges, *The Condor Years: How Pinochet and His Allies Brought Terrorism to Three Continents* (New York, 2004); "Hidden Files Force Brazil to Face Its Past," *New York Times,* Jan. 31, 2005, A6, and "A Visit to Guatemala's Past," Sept. 12, 2005.

36. Thomas, *Man and the Natural World,* 251; Woodruff D. Smith, *The Ideological Origins of Nazi Imperialism* (New York, 1986), 87–88.

37. Ramsay MacMullen, *Feelings in History* (Claremont, Calif., 2003), ii, 54, 84, 86.

38. Smith, introduction to *Ideological Origins.*

39. Virgil, *Eclogues,* tr. J. Michie (London, 2000), 1,xv; *The Georgics of Virgil,* tr. C. Day Lewis (London, 1940), I.1–2, p. 15 (Gilbert Highet).

40. Hesiod, *Theogony, Works and Days,* tr. M. L. West (Oxford, 1988), 16; Thomas, *Man and the Natural World,* 250; Walter Ralegh, undated, in Felix Pryor, *Elizabeth I: Her Life in Letters* (Berkeley, 2003), 135.

41. Raymond Williams, *The Country and the City* (New York, 1973), 22; Richard Hofstadter, *The Age of Reform: From Bryan to F.D.R.* (New York, 1956), 24–25; Smith, *Ideological Origins,* 85–86.

42. Victor Lieberman, personal communication, Aug. 2005; Stephen Vlastos, ed., *Mirror of Modernity: Invented Traditions of Modern Japan* (Berkeley, 1998), 2 (emphasis in original).

43. Tetsuo Najita and H. D. Harootunian, "Japanese Revolt against the West," in Peter Duus, ed., *The Cambridge History of Japan,* vol. 6, *The Twentieth Century* (Cambridge, 1991), 764.

44. Adolf Hitler, *Hitler's Second Book,* ed. Gerhard Weinberg (New York, 2003), xxi, 21; Horace Walpole wrote in 1763, "The Romans were triflers [in comparison] to us" (Gregory E. Dowd, *War under Heaven* [Baltimore, 2002], vii).

45. Francesco Petrarch, *The Secret,* ed. Carol E. Quillen (Boston, 2003), 1; Niccolò Machiavelli, *The History of Florence* [1525] (New York, 1970), vii, 56.

46. Cherie K. Woodworth, "The Tsar's Descent from Caesar: Clans, Genealogy, Mythmaking, and Statehood in Medieval Russia, 1400–1550" (Ph.D. diss., Yale University, 2001); Freedman, *Images of the Medieval Peasant,* 107.

47. Thomas, *Man and the Natural World,* 255–56; Robert Gellately, "The Third Reich, the Holocaust, and Visions of Serial Genocide," in Gellately and Ben Kiernan, eds., *The Specter of Genocide: Mass Murder in Historical Perspective* (New York, 2003), 262.

48. Author's interviews with Keng Vannsak, Montmorency, 1979–80; "Khmaer da'em" [Saloth Sar], "Monarchie ou Democratie?" *Khemara Nisit* (Paris) 14 (Aug. 1952); Vannsak, "Tragédie d'un peuple, mort d'une culture," *Connaissance du Cambodge,* 2 (Mar. 1977): 1–2; Vannsak and J. Delvert, *Recherche du fonds culturel khmer* (Paris, 1971); Vannsak, "Bôn' Phka . . . : Un exemple de dékhmer-

isation," *Préserver la culture kmère* 11–12 (Mar.–Apr. 1978): 34–40: Najita and Harootunian, "Japanese Revolt against the West," 712, 745, 755.

49. Liana Vardi, "Imagining the Harvest in Early Modern Europe," *American Historical Review* 101:5 (1996): 1357–97; Thomas, *Man and the Natural World,* 243; Deane Neubauer, Globalization Research Network, "Mixed Blessings of the Megacities," *YaleGlobal,* Sept. 24, 2004: http://yaleglobal.yale.edu/display.article?id=4573 (accessed Nov. 12, 2004).

50. Hofstadter, *The Age of Reform,* 23. For a different view of a later period, see Lawrence Goodwin, *The Populist Moment* (New York, 1978).

51. Vardi, "Imagining the Harvest," 1357; Freedman, *Images of the Medieval Peasant,* 17, 12, 213; Vardi, "Imagining the Harvest," 1357–58, 1364, 1373.

52. Thomas, *Man and the Natural World,* 246; Smith, *Ideological Origins,* 87.

53. Thomas, *Man and the Natural World,* 254–59.

54. Ibid., 258–60, 262–63.

55. Vardi, "Imagining the Harvest," 1357.

56. Neubauer, "Mixed Blessings"; Shelley, "On Love," in Thomas, *Man and The Natural World,* 252.

57. Edmund Morgan, *American Slavery, American Freedom* (New York, 1975), 54–55; William Cronon, *Changes in the Land: Indians, Colonists, and the Ecology of New England* (New York, 1983), 41ff., 48–53.

58. Anthony F. C. Wallace, *The Long, Bitter Trail: Andrew Jackson and the Indians* (New York, 1993); Heather Goodall, *Invasion to Embassy: Land in Aboriginal Politics in New South Wales, 1770–1972* (Sydney, 1996), chs. 6–11, e.g., pp. 136–44.

59. Benjamin Madley, "From Africa to Auschwitz: How German South West Africa Incubated Ideas and Methods Adopted and Developed by the Nazis in Eastern Europe," *European History Quarterly* 35:3 (2005): 451–52. The 1931 footage is included in the 2004 BBC documentary *Genocide in the Second Reich.*

60. Henry Friedlander, *The Origins of Nazi Genocide: From Euthanasia to the Final Solution* (Chapel Hill, 1995), 11–13, 19; Madley, "From Africa to Auschwitz."

61. Vahakn N. Dadrian, *German Responsibility in the Armenian Genocide: A Review of the Historical Evidence of German Complicity* (Watertown, 1996); Dadrian, *The History of the Armenian Genocide: Ethnic Conflict from the Balkans to Anatolia to the Caucasus* (Providence, 1997), 410–12, 402–10; Dadrian, *German Responsibility,* 202.

62. "Abbreviated Lesson on the History of the Kampuchean Revolutionary Movement" [1977], in C. Boua, D. P. Chandler, and B. Kiernan, eds., *Pol Pot Plans the Future: Confidential Leadership Documents from Democratic Kampuchea, 1976–1977* (New Haven, 1988), 218.

63. N. J. B. Plomley, *Jorgen Jorgenson and the Aborigines of Van Diemen's Land* (Hobart, 1991), 49; Henry Melville, *The History of Van Diemen's Land from the Year 1824 to 1835* [1835] (Sydney, 1965); George Augustus Robinson, diary entry dated Sept. 22, 1838, in N. J. B. Plomley, ed., *Weep in Silence: A History of the Flinders Island Aboriginal Settlement* (Hobart, 1987), 589.

64. Daniel Chirot and Clark McCauley, *Why Not Kill Them All? The Logic and Prevention of Mass Murder* (Princeton, 2006), 17; Benjamin Valentino, *Final Solutions: Mass Killing and Genocide in the 20th Century* (Ithaca, 2004), 243.

65. Cormac Ó Gráda, *Black '47 and Beyond: The Great Irish Famine* (Princeton, 1999); Colm Tóibín and Diarmaid Ferriter, *The Irish Famine: A Documentary* (New York, 2001); Mohammad Gholi Majd, *The Great Famine and Genocide in Persia, 1917–1919* (Lanham, 2003).

Chapter 1. Classical Genocide and Early Modern Memory

1. Hesiod, *Theogony, Works and Days,* tr. M. L. West (Oxford, 1988), 29.

2. Hesiod, *Works and Days,* 41, 44, 52, 37, 53, 50–51, 43, 54; *Theogony,* 20–21; *Works and Days,* 39, 48.

3. Hesiod, *Works and Days,* 46, 48; *Theogony,* 28; *Works and Days,* 44, 55, 51, 55–57, 38, 43–44.

4. David Stannard, *American Holocaust: The Conquest of the New World* (New York, 1992), 165–66.

5. Glenn W. Most, "Hesiod's Myth of the Five (or Three or Four) Races," *Proceedings of the*

Cambridge Philological Society 43 (1997): 104–27; West, introduction to Hesiod, *Theogony, Works and Days,* xiv; *Works and Days,* 40–42, 52.

6. Hesiod, *Works and Days,* 43–44, 41; W. Forrest, *A History of Sparta, 950–192 B.C.* (New York, 1968), 38.

7. Forrest, *History of Sparta;* Michael Whitby, ed., *Sparta* (New York, 2002), 98, 158.

8. Whitby, *Sparta,* 191, 194.

9. Paul Cartledge, *Spartan Reflections* (Berkeley, 2001), 89; Cartledge, "Early Lakedaimon: The Making of a Conquest-State," in J. M. Sanders, ed., *Philolakon* (London, 1992), 49–55; G. E. M. de Ste. Croix, *The Origins of the Peloponnesian War* (London, 1972), 94–95.

10. Cartledge, *Sparta and Lakonia: A Regional History, 1300 to 362 B.C.,* 2nd ed. (London, 2002), 89, 97, 152, 103, 255; Cartledge, *Spartan Reflections,* 148.

11. N. Luraghi and S. Alcock, eds., *Helots and Their Masters in Laconia and Messenia* (Cambridge, 2003), 52.

12. Cartledge, *Sparta and Lakonia,* 141–42, 83, 118. Sparta may have at first planned to make the Tegeans Helots. Donald Kagan notes that on taking the city, it did not annex Tegea (*The Outbreak of the Peloponnesian War* [Ithaca, 1969], 10). Ste. Croix, *Origins,* 93.

13. Kagan, *Outbreak,* 12; Cartledge, *Sparta and Lakonia,* 118–20; also Ste. Croix, *Origins,* 94.

14. Thucydides, *History of the Peloponnesian War,* I.101, V.14; Ste. Croix, *Origins,* 89.

15. Cartledge, *Sparta and Lakonia,* 141–42, 152; Cartledge, *Spartan Reflections,* 148.

16. Thucydides, *History of the Peloponnesian War,* I.128; Cartledge, *Sparta and Lakonia,* 187–88 and 186–87, suggesting that the Helot revolt probably lasted four or six years rather than ten.

17. Thucydides, *Peloponnesian War,* I.102 (emphasis added), 103; Cartledge, *Sparta and Lakonia,* 187–88.

18. Thucydides, *Peloponnesian War,* II.67.3, III.68.2, V.83; see Cartledge, *Spartan Reflections,* 130.

19. Cartledge, *Spartan Reflections,* 89.

20. Ste. Croix, *Origins,* 90, 92; Cartledge, *Spartan Reflections,* 24, and *Sparta and Lakonia,* 140, 187–88.

21. Cartledge, *Spartan Reflections,* 88–89; Thucydides, *Peloponnesian War,* IV.80.

22. Cartledge, *Sparta and Lakonia,* 153–59, 84.

23. Kagan, *Outbreak,* 26–27; Oxford Classical Dictionary online, "Sparta," 2; Cartledge, *Spartan Reflections,* 24, 89; Cartledge, *Sparta and Lakonia,* 134.

24. Thucydides, *Peloponnesian War,* I.10.2; Oxford Classical Dictionary online, "Sparta," 2; Cartledge, *Sparta and Lakonia,* 157, 134, 148–49; Niccolò Machiavelli, *Discourses on Livy,* ed. and tr. Julia Conaway Bondanella and Peter Bondanella (New York, 1997), 387.

25. Oxford Classical Dictionary online, "Sparta," 2.

26. Cartledge, *Sparta and Lakonia,* 154, 134 (citing Thucydides, *Peloponnesian War,* I.6.4); Cartledge, *Spartan Reflections,* 117.

27. Whitby, *Sparta,* 98; Cartledge, *Spartan Reflections,* 123, 113.

28. Aristotle, *Politics,* 1251b–1252b, 1256a,b, 1258a,b, quoted in Anthony Pagden, *The Fall of Natural Man* (Cambridge, 1982), 91.

29. Aristotle, *Oeconomica,* tr. C. Cyril Amstrong, Loeb ed. (1997), I.II, 1343a–b.

30. Victor Davis Hanson, *The Other Greeks: The Family Farm and the Agrarian Roots of Western Civilization* (Berkeley, 1999), 212ff., 216–17; Frank Chalk and Kurt Jonassohn, *History and Sociology of Genocide* (New Haven, 1989), 65–73.

31. M. Dubuisson, "Delenda Est Carthago," *Studia Phoenicia* 10 (1989): 279–87; F. Limonier, "Rome et la destruction de Carthage," *Revue des études anciennes* 101:3–4 (1999): 405–11; W. Huss, *Geschichte der Karthager* (Munich, 1985), 436–57; E. Maroti, "On the Causes of Carthage's Destruction," *Oikumene* 4 (1983): 223–31.

32. Plutarch, *The Lives of Aristeides and Cato,* tr. D. Sansone (Warminster, 1989), 159; Serge Lancel, *Carthage* (Oxford, 1995), 410; E. Badian, *Foreign Clientelae (264–70 B.C.)* (Oxford, 2000), 130–33; M. Gelzer, "Nasica's Opposition to the Destruction of Carthage," *Philologus* 86 (1930–31): 261–99.

33. Polybius, 36.2.1; W. V. Harris, "Rome and Carthage," *Cambridge Ancient History,* vol. 8, *Rome and the Mediterranean to 133 B.C.,* 2nd ed. (Cambridge, 1989), 148–49, 152.

34. Maroti, "Carthage's Destruction," 228, citing *Rhet. ad Herenn.*, IV.14, 20; Polybius, 18.3.59.

35. U. Vogel-Weidemann, "Carthago Delenda Est," *Acta Classica* 32 (1989): 80; Huss, *Geschichte*, 441–42.

36. Harris, "Rome and Carthage," 160. "Such a diktat [to abandon their city] was the equivalent of a death sentence [to Carthage] . . . the destruction of its temples and cemeteries, the deportation of its cults, were a more surely mortal blow than displacing the population" (Lancel, *Carthage*, 413). See Badian, *Foreign Clientelae*, 138.

37. Appian, *Roman History*, 8.126; Polybius, 38.8.10.12, 38.1.1.6, adding that the Carthaginians were "for the future insensible of their sufferings."

38. Appian, *Roman History*, 8.19.128–31.

39. Ibid., 8.19.131; Polybius, 38.20–21.

40. Strabo put Carthage's population c. 149 at 700,000 (17.3.15). B. H. Warmington suggests 200,000, though "in the early third century . . . it would be surprising if it did not approach 400,000" (*Carthage* [London, 1980], 124–27). Appian said the population rose "greatly" after 201 (8.10.69), as archaeology "fully confirmed" (Vogel-Weidemann, "Carthago Delenda Est," 79–95, 86–87). In the siege "large sectors of the rural population took refuge within the city walls" (Huss, *Geschichte*, 452). A. E. Astin, *Scipio Aemilianus* (Oxford, 1967), 36, 53, 280–81; Yann Le Bohec, *Histoire militaire des guerres puniques* (Monaco, 1995), 311, estimates over 55,000 survivors; Huss, *Geschichte*, 455–56n133.

41. Appian, *Roman History*, 8.20.135. Tunis, Hermaea, Neapolis, and Aspis "were demolished" (Strabo, 17.3.16), Bizerta was destroyed, and seven towns spared (Le Bohec, *Histoire militaire*, 314).

42. The Athenian conquerors of Melos in 416 "put to death all the grown men" (Thucydides, *Peloponnesian War*, V.115).

43. Astin, *Scipio Aemilianus*, 51, 53; Appian, *Roman History*, 8.12.83–85, 89.

44. Harris, "Rome and Carthage," 154, 161 ("submission and disarmament were not enough").

45. A friend of Scipio Africanus urged a Senate debate on Carthaginian policy in 201 "not to exterminate whole races, but to bring them into a better state of mind" (Appian, *Roman History*, 8.9.58). Fifty years later, Polybius wrote that Romans' "disputes with each other about the effect on foreign opinion very nearly made them desist from going to war" on Carthage (36.1.2.4). He recounted Greek views on Rome's destruction of the city (36.2.9); "it is not easy to find a subject more renowned" (36.1.1). Astin, *Scipio Aemilianus*, 52–53, 276–80; Gelzer, "Nasica's Opposition," 261–99; Plutarch, *Lives of Aristeides and Cato*, 157.

46. A. E. Astin, *Cato the Censor* (Oxford, 1978), 127–28; Badian, *Foreign Clientelae*, 125.

47. B. Dexter Hoyos, "Cato's Punic Perfidies," *Ancient History Bulletin* 1:5 (1987): 120.

48. Harris, "Rome and Carthage," 155, 160, 153. Strabo specified that Carthaginian war preparations followed Rome's final ultimatum (17.3.15); for other views, see Ben Kiernan, "The First Genocide: Carthage, 146 BC," *Diogenes* 203 (2004): 27–39, 37n118. The Senate's order to the Carthaginians "to abandon their city and move inland was the best method to incite this humiliated people, . . . exasperated with Rome and ready to do anything to retrieve its lost homeland" (Limonier, "Rome et la destruction de Carthage," 407). Vogel-Weidemann suggests Rome's "vindictiveness may have been rather a matter of cold policy, namely, to do away once and for all with centers of traditional anti-Roman leadership and, possibly, to set an example" ("Carthago Delenda Est," 88), citing W. V. Harris, *War and Imperialism in Republican Rome* (New York, 1979), 234–40, and Diodorus to the effect that from 168 B.C., "at any price whatsoever," Rome "sought to secure her predominance by fear and intimidation and by destroying the most eminent cities" (83, 85–86).

49. *Cornelius Nepos: A Selection, Including the Lives of Cato and Atticus*, tr. N. Horsfall (Oxford, 1989), 35, 37–38 (Pliny, *NH*, 8.11); Plutarch, *Lives*, 173.

50. Livy, *Rome and the Mediterranean*, tr. H. Bettenson (Harmondsworth, 1976), 34.4., 144.

51. Vogel-Weidemann, "Carthago Delenda Est," 92n73, citing Cato's speech *De bello Carthaginiensi*, in H. Malcovati, *Oratorum Romanorum Fragmenta* 3 (1967), fr. 195.

52. *Cato and Varro on Agriculture*, tr. W. D. Hooper and H. B. Ash (Cambridge, Mass., 1993), x.

53. Livy, *Rome and the Mediterranean*, 155–58; *Cornelius Nepos*, 5; Plutarch, *Lives*, 113–17; R. C.

Knapp, "Cato in Spain, 195/194 B.C.," in C. Deroux, ed., *Studies in Latin Literature and Roman History* (Brussels, 1980), 2:44–45.

54. Maroti, "Carthage's Destruction," 226; Astin, *Cato*, 126–27; Plutarch, *Lives*, 157–59.

55. "The way in which Cato propagated his Italian chauvinism appealed to them" (F. J. Meijer, "Cato's African Figs," *Mnemosyne* 37:1–2 [1984]: 122–23); Marcus Cato, *De Agri Cultura*, 8.1, and Marcus Terentius Varro, *De Re Rustica*, I.41, in *Cato and Varro on Agriculture*, 21, 273.

56. Maroti, "Carthage's Destruction," 228; Cicero, *On the Good Life*, tr. Michael Grant (London, 1971), 171.

57. Cato, *De Agri Cultura*, in *Cato and Varro on Agriculture*, 3.

58. Polybius, *The Rise of the Roman Empire*, tr. Ian Scott-Kilvert (London, 1979), 529.

59. *Cato and Varro on Agriculture*, ix; Plutarch, *Lives*, 95, 143–47.

60. Appian, *Roman History*, 8.12.86–89; Harris, "Rome and Carthage," 156.

61. Livy, *Rome and the Mediterranean*, 141–47; see also Nels W. Forde, *Cato the Censor* (New York, 1975), 101–4.

62. Plutarch, *Lives*, 143, 153, 115, 133.

63. Ramsay MacMullen, "Hellenizing the Romans (2nd Century B.C.)," *Historia* 44 (1991): 429–30, 434.

64. *Cornelius Nepos*, 5–6; *Cato and Varro on Agriculture*, x–xi; Livy, *Rome and the Mediterranean*, 144; Plutarch, *Lives*, 101; MacMullen, "Hellenizing," 427–28, 433. On Roman nobles' openness to Greek culture, see MacMullen, "Hellenizing," 426; J. Briscoe, "Cato the Elder," in S. Hornblower and A. Spawforth, eds., *Oxford Companion to Classical Civilization* (Oxford, 1998), 146.

65. *Cornelius Nepos*, 6, and commentary, 57; see also *Cato and Varro on Agriculture*, xii.

66. Frank M. Snowden Jr., *Blacks in Antiquity* (Cambridge, Mass., 1970); Susanna Morton Braund, "Roman Assimilations of the Other: *Humanitas* at Rome," *Acta Classica* 40 (1997): 15–32.

67. *Cornelius Nepos*, 5, 36n47; Astin, *Cato*, 171, quoting Cato's *Ad Filium* from Pliny, *NH*, 29.13–14.

68. "[A] trove of Greek philosophical treatises which turned up in 181 had been barely looked at before being destroyed by senatorial order—it was feared that their teachings would arouse doubts about religion." In 173, Rome expelled the teachers of Epicurean philosophy (MacMullen, "Hellenizing," 435). On Cato's "paranoia about Greek physicians" and view of "alien statuary as a profanation," 436nn62, 63.

69. Plutarch, *Lives*, 147–49.

70. MacMullen, "Hellenizing," 432n41; Plutarch, *Lives*, 129.

71. Plutarch, *Lives*, 159–61; V. Krings, "La destruction de Carthage," *Studia Phoenicia* 10: 335.

72. Dubuisson, "'Delenda Est Carthago,'" 285.

73. Julius Caesar, *De Bello Gallico*, 4.4–18, tr. Anne Wiseman and Peter Wiseman, "The Usipetes and the Tencteri" and "The First Germanic Expedition": www.livius.org/caa-can/caesar/caesar_t20.html, www.livius.org/caa-can/caesar/caesar_t27.html (accessed Oct. 18, 2005).

74. Caesar, *De Bello Gallico* 6.34.1–35.1, tr. Anne Wiseman and Peter Wiseman, "Ambiorix": www.livius.org/am-ao/ambiorix/ambiorix.html#cont (accessed Oct. 19, 2005).

75. Tacitus, *Annales*, 12.39, tr. http://classics.mit.edu/Tacitus/annals.8.xii.html (accessed Oct. 18, 2005); Peter Salway, *A History of Roman Britain* (Oxford, 1993), 79.

76. Jasper Griffin, *Virgil* (New York, 1986), 27, 36ff.

77. Virgil, *Georgics* 2, tr. *Internet Classics Archive*: http://classics.mit.edu/Virgil/georgics.html (accessed Oct. 30, 2006).

78. Virgil, *Georgics* 3, quoted in Griffin, *Virgil*, 52.

79. Ellen Oliensis, "Sons and Lovers: Sexuality and Gender in Virgil's Poetry," in Charles Martindale, ed., *The Cambridge Companion to Virgil* (Cambridge, 1997), 297–99.

80. Griffin, *Virgil*, 84, 62; Virgil, *The Aeneid: A New Prose Translation*, tr. David West (London, 1991), 212.

81. Griffin, *Virgil*, 63–64, 54.

82. Virgil, *The Aeneid*, 3–4.

83. Ibid., 41, 45, 47.

84. Ibid., 18.

85. Ibid., 19–23.

86. Ibid., 24–27, 57, 37, 53.

87. Ibid. See Philip R. Hardie, Virgil's "Aeneid": Cosmos and Imperium (Oxford: 1986), 282–84.

88. Virgil, The Aeneid, 95, 100–1, 147, 159.

89. West, introduction to The Aeneid, ix; W. Y. Sellar, Virgil (Oxford, 1897), 59, 68.

90. Livy, Rome and the Mediterranean, 430 (XXXIX.40).

91. Ibid., 596 (XLIV.44), introduction to ibid., 20.

92. Polybius, Histories, vol. VI, books XXXVI.1–9, 16, XXXVIII.7–8, including the fragment reproduced in Plutarch's Apophthegmata, 19–22, 200, and book XXXIX.8.

93. N. G. Wilson, From Byzantium to Italy: Greek Studies in the Renaissance (London, 1972), 2.

94. Scott-Kilvert, introduction to Polybius, The Rise of the Roman Empire, 35–36; Niccolò Machiavelli, Discourses on Livy (New York, 1997), 362n23; A. Momigliano, "Polybius' Reappearance in Western Europe," in Essays in Ancient and Modern Historiography (Middletown, 1977), 86, 88–90; Strabo's Geography, books III, VIII, and Appian's Libyca, 69, Roman History, VIII.20.135, also mention the destruction of Carthage.

95. Appian, Roman History, I.ix; Aubrey Diller, The Textual Tradition of Strabo's Geography (Amsterdam, 1975), 97, 102, 126, 132–34. A Greek manuscript copy of Strabo reached England between 1575 and 1639. The Greek text was first published in Venice in 1516 (118, 160).

96. Livy, Rome and the Mediterranean, 596 (XLIV.44), introduction to ibid., 20. Marcia Colish adds that a ninth-century manuscript of Silius Italicus's first-century epic Punica came to light in 1416, to be first printed a century later (personal communication, Sept. 27, 2004).

97. J. L. Nelson, "Go Away and Learn," London Review of Books, Apr. 15, 2004, 23–25.

98. Ibid.

99. James H. McGregor, The Shades of Aeneas: The Imitation of Vergil and the History of Paganism in Boccaccio's Filostrato, Filocolo, and Teseida (Athens, Ga., 1991), 3–4, 7. See also Craig Kallendorf, Virgil and the Myth of Venice (Oxford, 1999).

100. R. Howard Bloch, "Eneas Before the Walls of Carthage: The Beginnings of the City and Romance in the Suburbs," French Literary Studies 29 (2002): 2.

101. Robert Bartlett, The Making of Europe: Conquest, Colonization, and Cultural Change, 950–1350 (Princeton, 1993), 236.

102. Stannard, American Holocaust, 175–78.

103. Quoted in R. R. Davies, Domination and Conquest: The Experience of Ireland, Scotland and Wales, 1100–1300 (Cambridge, 1992), 26–27.

104. Brut Y Tywysogyon; or, The Chronicle of the Princes, Peniarth Ms. 20 version, tr. Thomas Jones (Cardiff, 1952), 19, 27–28, 31, 37; Brut Y Tywysogyon, Red Book of Hergest version (Cardiff, 1955), 39.

105. See David Nirenberg, Communities of Violence: Persecution of Minorities in the Middle Ages (Princeton, 1996).

106. Paul Freedman, Images of the Medieval Peasant (Stanford, 1999), 88.

107. Pagden, Fall of Natural Man, 24; Wilson, From Byzantium to Italy, 1.

108. Aristotle, Oeconomica, 324; Aristotle, Politics, 1330a.

109. Aristotle, Politics, 1251b–1252b.

110. Ibid., 1253b–1255b, 1330a.

111. Pagden, Fall of Natural Man, 20–23.

112. Ibid., 63, 41.

113. Bartlett, Making of Europe, 236–39; Francis Jennings, The Invasion of America (New York, 1975), 7.

114. Eric D. Weitz, A Century of Genocide: Utopias of Race and Nation (Princeton, 2003), 17n.

115. Bartlett, Making of Europe, 238–40.

116. E. J. Hobsbawm, Nations and Nationalism since 1780 (Cambridge, 1990), 15–17.

117. Pagden, Fall of Natural Man, 38–39, 63–65.

118. Colin Burrow, "Chapmaniac," London Review of Books, June 27, 2002, 21.

119. Geoffrey of Monmouth, The History of the Kings of Britain [c. 1136] (London, 1966), 53.

120. Sir Walter Ralegh, *The History of the World in Five Books* (London, 1614). In the 1820 Edinburgh edition, chapters on the first two Punic Wars run to 444 pages. For quotations from the *Aeneid*, see Walter Ralegh, *The History of the World*, ed. C. A. Patrides (London, 1971), 78, 79, 95, 139.

121. Ibid., 49–50, 390; Rome "swallowed" Carthage (79).

122. John Prebble, *Glencoe: The Story of the Massacre* (London, 1968), 153, 177–84, 202–3, 214–19, 230–31.

123. Bartlett, *Making of Europe*, 240–41; Jennings, *Invasion*, 4.

124. Lewis Hanke, *Aristotle and the American Indians* (Bloomington, 1959), 154–55.

125. Lisa Jardine, *Worldly Goods: A New History of the Renaissance* (New York, 1996), 86–88.

126. Bartlett, *Making of Europe*, 241–42; Weitz, *Century of Genocide*, 17n.

127. Jorge Cañizares Esguerra, "New World, New Stars: Patriotic Astrology and the Invention of Indian and Creole Bodies in Colonial Spanish America, 1600–1650," *American Historical Review* 104:1 (1999): 33–34, 38, 53; 35, 60–63, 58.

128. Cartago was the capital of Costa Rica until its destruction by an earthquake in 1823.

129. William H. Prescott, *History of the Conquest of Mexico and History of the Conquest of Peru* (New York, n.d.), 675; Marie Tanner, *The Last Descendant of Aeneas: The Hapsburgs and the Mythic Image of the Emperor* (New Haven, 1993), 59–60; Henry Kamen, *Empire: How Spain Became a World Power* (New York, 2003), 76.

130. Fernand Braudel, *The Mediterranean and the Mediterranean World in the Age of Philip II* (London, 2000), 2:43, citing Biblioteca Nazionale, Florence, Capponi Codice V, f° 343v°-44.

Chapter 2. The Spanish Conquest of the New World, 1492–1600

1. Beatriz Pastor Bodmer, *The Armature of Conquest: Spanish Accounts of the Discovery of America, 1492–1589* (Stanford, 1992), 12; Kirkpatrick Sale, *The Conquest of Paradise* (New York, 1990), 15n.

2. Inge Clendinnen, "'Fierce and Unnatural Cruelty': Cortés and the Conquest of Mexico," *Representations* 33 (1991): 99n81; J. H. Elliott, "The Mental World of Hernán Cortés," *Transactions of the Royal Historical Society*, fifth series 17 (London, 1967): 41–58, at 42; William H. Prescott, *History of the Conquest of Mexico and History of the Conquest of Peru* (New York, n.d.), 157.

3. Bernal Díaz del Castillo, quoted in Prescott, *Conquest of Mexico*, 686; also 128–29.

4. Elliott, "Mental World," 43–45, citing, inter alia, works of Viktor Frankl.

5. A. Pagden, in Hernán Cortés, *Letters from Mexico* (New Haven, 1986), xliii.

6. Livy, *Rome and the Mediterranean*, tr. H. Bettenson (London, 1976), 596 (XLIV.44), Introduction, 20; Livy, *The War with Hannibal*, tr. A. de Sélincourt (London, 1972), 9–10.

7. Prescott, *Conquest of Mexico*, 682–83.

8. Bernal Díaz del Castillo, *The Discovery and Conquest of Mexico, 1517–1521*, tr. A. Maudsley (New York, 1956), 110; Cortés, quoted in Elliott, "Mental World," 45.

9. Bernal Díaz, quoted in Pagden, introduction to Cortés, *Letters from Mexico*, lxi; see also Francisco López de Gómara, *Istoria de la Conquista de Mexico* [1552], in L. B. Simpson, tr. and ed., *Cortés: The Life of the Conqueror by His Secretary* (Berkeley, 1964), 199.

10. Bernardino de Sahagún, *Historia general de las cosas de Nueva Espana*, prologue to book 1, quoted in Tzvetan Todorov, *The Conquest of America* (Norman, 1999), 231.

11. Pagden, introduction to Cortés, *Letters from Mexico*, lvii.

12. Ibid., lxvii–lxviii; Cortés to Charles V, May 15, 1522, in *Letters from Mexico*, 160.

13. Pagden, introduction to Cortés, *Letters from Mexico*, liv.

14. Pagden, *The Fall of Natural Man: The American Indian and the Origins of Comparative Ethnology* (Cambridge, 1982), 133.

15. Ibid., 11, 24–25, 37, 58; Lewis Hanke, *All Mankind Is One* (De Kalb, 1974), 41.

16. Juan Ginés de Sepúlveda, "*Democrates Alter*; or, On the Just Causes for War against the Indians" [1544], in *Introduction to Contemporary Civilization in the West*, 2nd ed. (New York, 1954), 1:496; Pagden, *Fall of Natural Man*, 130, 81–82.

17. Sepúlveda, "*Democrates Alter*," 496–97; Lewis Hanke, *Aristotle and the American Indians* (Bloomington, 1959), 46–47.

18. Pagden, *Fall of Natural Man,* 117, 25.

19. M. Marty, foreword and "Summary of Sepúlveda's Position," in Bartolomé de Las Casas, *In Defense of the Indians* [1550], tr. Stafford Poole (DeKalb, 1992), xiv, 12–13.

20. Juan Ginés de Sepúlveda, *Demócrates segundo o de las justas causas de la guerra contra los indios* [1547] (Madrid, 1951), 101, quoted in Hanke, *Aristotle and the American Indians,* 69.

21. Sepúlveda, "*Democrates Alter,*" 493–94.

22. Sepúlveda, *Democrates Alter, sive de justas belli causi apud Indios* ("On the Just Causes of War on the Indians"): www.elcamino.cc.ca.us/Faculty/jsuarez/1Cour/H10A/WpTolSepuld.htm (English translation, accessed June 19, 2004).

23. Pagden, *Fall of Natural Man,* 40; Hanke, *Aristotle and the American Indians,* 16.

24. Bartolomé de Las Casas, *History of the Indies,* tr. Andreé Collard (New York, 1971), 112 [book 2, ch. 13]; Pagden, *Fall of Natural Man,* 77.

25. Hanke, *Aristotle and the American Indians,* 139n35.

26. Aristotle, *Politics,* 1252b 5ff., 1255a 29ff., quoted in Pagden, *Fall of Natural Man,* 47; also 41, 96; Aristotle, *Politics,* 1330a.

27. Aristotle, *Politics,* 1252b; see also Pagden, *Fall of Natural Man,* 69.

28. Pagden, *Fall of Natural Man,* 71; Hernán Cortés to Charles V, Oct. 30, 1520, in *Letters from Mexico,* 101–8.

29. Gregorio García [1606] and Bernardo de Lizana [1633], cited in Jorge Cañizares Esguerra, "New World, New Stars: Patriotic Astrology and the Invention of Indian and Creole Bodies in Colonial Spanish America, 1600–1650," *American Historical Review* 104:1 (1999): 47, 49.

30. Neil L. Whitehead, "The Crises and Transformations of Invaded Societies: The Caribbean (1492–1580)," in Frank Solomon and Stuart B. Schwartz, eds., *The Cambridge History of the Native Peoples of the Americas,* vol. 3, *South America,* part 1, 868; Pastor, *Armature,* 53, 285n12.

31. Bartolomé de Las Casas, *Brevissima relacion de la destruycion de las Yndias* [1552], tr. Herma Briffault as *The Devastation of the Indies: A Brief Account* (Baltimore, 1992), 29. Sherburne F. Cook and Woodrow Borah, *Essays in Population History: Mexico and the Caribbean* (Berkeley, 1971), 1:376–410, suggest a figure as high as eight million.

32. Las Casas, *History of the Indies,* 126 [book 2, ch. 18], citing Diego de Deza, archbishop of Seville.

33. Irving Rouse, *The Tainos: Rise and Decline of the People Who Greeted Columbus* (New Haven, 1992), 155.

34. Pastor, *Armature,* 53, 285n12. Las Casas called Oviedo an author of "vain lies" and an "empty trifler" who "fabricated his history." Pagden, *Fall of Natural Man,* 137, and "*Ius et Factum:* Text and Experience in the Writings of Bartolomé de Las Casas," in Margarita Zamora, tr., and Stephen Greenblatt, ed., *New World Encounters* (Berkeley, 1993), 92.

35. Las Casas, *Devastation,* 27, 30–33.

36. Columbus, Oct. 12 and 14, 1492, quoted in Pastor, *Armature,* 41–44; Sale, *Conquest,* 97, 112.

37. Columbus, "Letter to the Sovereigns of 4 March 1493 Announcing the Discovery," in Zamora and Greenblatt, *New World Encounters,* 4–5, 8.

38. Ibid., 6, 8.

39. Sale, *Conquest,* 122; Las Casas, *Devastation,* 37–38; Columbus, "Letter to the Sovereigns of 4 March 1493," 4, 6, 11n17, 3, 6–7.

40. Columbus, "Letter to the Sovereigns of 4 March 1493," 5.

41. Bishop of Santa Marta, quoted by Pedro Mexía de Ovando in the late sixteenth century. Pagden, *Fall of Natural Man,* 23, 237.

42. Pagden, *Fall of Natural Man,* 68, 72, 90.

43. See the 1533 description of the Mexicans by Jacobo de Testera, in Pagden, *Fall of Natural Man,* 75.

44. Lewis Hanke, *The Spanish Struggle for Justice in the Conquest of America* (Boston, 1965), ch. 5.

45. Las Casas, *Historia de las Indias,* I:13, quoted in Pagden, "*Ius et Factum,*" 92.

46. Las Casas, *In Defense of the Indians,* 32, 31.

47. Pagden, *Fall of Natural Man,* 51–52, 55. In 1541, João de Castro espoused a similar view to that of Palacios Rubios (Pagden, *Fall of Natural Man,* 214n72).

48. Sepúlveda, *"Democrates Alter,"* 497.

49. Rouse, *Tainos,* 147–51.

50. Whitehead, "Invaded Societies," 871.

51. Las Casas, *Devastation,* 35–37.

52. Las Casas, quoted in Whitehead, "Invaded Societies," 871–72.

53. Las Casas, *Devastation,* 37–38; Columbus, "Letter to the Sovereigns of 4 March 1493," 6, 11n17.

54. Rolena Adorno, *The Intellectual Life of Bartolomé de Las Casas* (New Orleans, 1992), 2.

55. Bill M. Donovan, introduction to Las Casas, *Devastation,* 3; Felix Jay, *Three Dominican Pioneers in the New World* (Lewiston, 2002), 2.

56. Queen Isabella, quoted in Pagden, introduction to Cortés, *Letters from Mexico,* lxviii.

57. Rouse, *Tainos,* 154; Las Casas, *Devastation,* 39–40; Las Casas, *History of the Indies,* book 2, 99.

58. Whitehead, "Invaded Societies," 867–68.

59. Pagden, *Fall of Natural Man,* 29; Las Casas, *Devastation,* 42, 40.

60. Las Casas, *Historia de las Indias* [1559], excerpt tr. in Jay, *Three Dominican Pioneers,* 15.

61. Las Casas, *Devastation,* 3; Adorno, *Intellectual Life,* 3; Jay, *Three Dominican Pioneers,* 2.

62. Las Casas, *Historia de las Indias,* in Jay, *Three Dominican Pioneers,* 16.

63. Las Casas, *Devastation,* 43.

64. Henry Kamen, *Empire: How Spain Became a World Power* (New York, 2003), 85–86.

65. Balboa to the king, Jan. 20, 1513, quoted in Angel de Altolaguirre, *Vasco Núñez de Balboa* (Madrid, 1914), 22; see R. Konetzke, "La esclavitud de los indios como elemento en la estructuración social de Hispanoamérica," in *Estudios de historia social de España* (Madrid, 1949), 1:446.

66. J. G. Varner and J. J. Varner, *Dogs of the Conquest* (Norman, 1983), 39–41; Peter Martyr, *De Orbe Novo,* III, 1, quoted in Todorov, *The Conquest of America,* 141: "Six hundred, including the cacique, were thus slain like brute beasts. . . . Vasco ordered forty of them to be torn to pieces by dogs."

67. Kamen, *Empire,* 86–87.

68. Las Casas, *Historia de las Indias,* in Jay, *Three Dominican Pioneers,* 25.

69. Las Casas, "Entre los remedios," 7, quoted in Tzvetan Todorov, *La conquête de l'Amérique: La question de l'autre* (Paris, 1982), 182.

70. Adorno, *Intellectual Life,* 3; Jay, *Three Dominican Pioneers,* 2, 11–12n10, 12.

71. Las Casas, *Historia de las Indias,* book 3, 182, in Jay, *Three Dominican Pioneers,* 16.

72. Las Casas, *Historia de las Indias,* in Jay, *Three Dominican Pioneers,* 17.

73. Jay, *Three Dominican Pioneers,* 3, 4, 13, 17.

74. Las Casas, *Historia de las Indias,* quoted in Jay, *Three Dominican Pioneers,* 10.

75. Montesinos, quoted in Las Casas, *Historia de las Indias,* in Jay, *Three Dominican Pioneers,* 18.

76. Las Casas, *Historia de las Indias,* in Jay, *Three Dominican Pioneers,* 19–23.

77. Ibid., 24–29.

78. Ibid., 30–31; Pagden, *Fall of Natural Man,* 47–49.

79. Memorandum, in Las Casas, *Historia de las Indias,* in Jay, *Three Dominican Pioneers,* 36–37.

80. Jay, *Three Dominican Pioneers,* 4; quoted in Pagden, *Fall of Natural Man,* 34–35.

81. Las Casas, *Historia de las Indias,* in Jay, *Three Dominican Pioneers,* 37.

82. Donovan, introduction to Las Casas, *Devastation,* 4; Las Casas, *Devastation,* 43–47.

83. Las Casas, *History of the Indies,* book 2, 110; Pagden, *Fall of Natural Man,* 35.

84. Las Casas, *History of the Indies,* book 3, 208; Donovan, introduction to Las Casas, *Devastation,* 3–4; Las Casas, *Historia de las Indias,* quoted in Pagden, *"Ius et Factum,"* 90.

85. Donovan, introduction to Las Casas, *Devastation,* 4–5.

86. Quoted in Hanke, *Spanish Struggle,* 31–33.

87. Whitehead, "Invaded Societies," 868; Las Casas, *Historia de las Indias,* in Jay, *Three Dominican Pioneers,* 37.

88. Pastor, *Armature,* 53; Rouse, *Tainos,* 158.

89. Las Casas, *Devastation,* 41–42.

90. Pagden, introduction to Cortés, *Letters from Mexico,* xlii–xlvi.

91. Pagden, 471n60, and introduction to Cortés, *Letters from Mexico,* 1.

92. Inga Clendinnen, *Aztecs: An Interpretation* (Cambridge, 1991), 91; Hugh Thomas, *Conquest: Montezuma, Cortés, and the Fall of Old Mexico* (New York, 1995), 25.

93. Florentine Codex (in Nahuatl), translated excerpt in Stuart B. Schwartz, ed., *Victors and Vanquished: Spanish and Nahua Views of the Conquest of Mexico* (New York, 2000), 91–92.

94. Ibid., 97.

95. Gilbert M. Joseph and Timothy J. Henderson, eds., *The Mexico Reader* (Durham, 2002), 122; Mark Cocker, *Rivers of Blood, Rivers of Gold: Europe's Conquest of Indigenous Peoples* (New York, 1998), 111; David E. Stannard, *American Holocaust: The Conquest of the New World* (New York, 1992), 267. For higher figures and a critique of them, see Cook and Borah, *Essays in Population History,* and David Henige, *Numbers from Nowhere: The American Indian Contact Population Debate* (Norman, 1998).

96. Pagden, introduction to Cortés, *Letters from Mexico,* 1; Florentine Codex, in Schwartz, *Victors and Vanquished,* 120.

97. Díaz, *Discovery and Conquest,* 131.

98. Cortés to Charles V, Oct. 30, 1520, in *Letters from Mexico,* 59; cf. Díaz, *Discovery and Conquest,* 123.

99. Cortés to Charles V, Oct. 30, 1520, in *Letters from Mexico,* 59–60, 62.

100. Díaz, *Discovery and Conquest,* 132, 135; Prescott, *Conquest of Mexico,* 242.

101. Cortés to Charles V, Oct. 30, 1520, in *Letters from Mexico,* 72.

102. Ibid., 73.

103. Florentine Codex (in Nahuatl), translated excerpt in Schwartz, *Victors and Vanquished,* 121.

104. Cortés to Charles V, Oct. 30, 1520, in *Letters from Mexico,* 73; Díaz, *Discovery and Conquest,* 178–79.

105. Andrés de Tapia, "Relation of Some Things That Happened to the Very Illustrious Don Hernando Cortés," excerpt in Schwartz, *Victors and Vanquished,* 118; Díaz, *Discovery and Conquest,* 179.

106. Excerpt from the Florentine Codex, in Schwartz, *Victors and Vanquished,* 121.

107. Tapia, "Relation of Some Things," 118; Cortés to Charles V, Oct. 30, 1520, in *Letters from Mexico,* 73.

108. Díaz, *Discovery and Conquest,* 179; Cortés to Charles V, Oct. 30, 1520, in *Letters from Mexico,* 74.

109. Tapia, "Relation of Some Things," 118; also Díaz, *Discovery and Conquest,* 179.

110. Cortés to Charles V, Oct. 30, 1520, *Letters from Mexico,* 73–74.

111. Tapia, "Relation of Some Things," 119; Gómara, *Cortés,* 129.

112. Prescott, *Conquest of Mexico,* 274; Pagden, in Cortés, *Letters from Mexico,* 465–66; see also Thomas, *Conquest,* 261–64.

113. Excerpt from the Florentine Codex, in Schwartz, *Victors and Vanquished,* 121.

114. Díaz, *Discovery and Conquest,* 181; Cortés to Charles V, Oct. 30, 1520, in *Letters from Mexico,* 75–76.

115. Clendinnen, *Aztecs,* 270.

116. Pagden, in Cortés, *Letters from Mexico,* 475–76.

117. Cortés to Charles V, May 25, 1522, in *Letters from Mexico,* 174–75.

118. Clendinnen, *Aztecs,* 116, 271.

119. Ibid., 272–73.

120. Gómara, *Cortés,* 325–26; Cortés, Oct. 15, 1524, in *Letters from Mexico,* 336.

121. Ibid., 318–19.

122. Cortés to Charles V, Oct. 30, 1520, in *Letters from Mexico,* 93–94.

123. Cortés to Charles V, May 15, 1522, in *Letters from Mexico,* 204.

124. Message included in ibid., 205–6.

125. Pagden notes Cortés's "constant plea for seeds to be sent from Spain" (*Letters from Mexico,* 511–12n69).

126. Arthur S. Aiton, "The Secret Visita against Viceroy Mendoza," in *New Spain and the Anglo-American West* (Los Angeles, 1932), 1:12nn26, 27.

127. Cortés to Charles V, Oct. 15, 1524, in *Letters from Mexico,* 321–22.

128. Ibid., 336; Pagden, in *Letters from Mexico*, lix–lx.

129. Las Casas, *Devastation*, 68–74.

130. Cortés, Oct. 15, 1524, in *Letters from Mexico*, 316–17.

131. Las Casas, *Devastation*, 70.

132. *The Annals of the Cakchiquels*, tr. Adrián Recinos and Delia Goetz (Norman, 1953), 119–20.

133. Pedro de Alvarado, *Cartas de Relación a Hernán Cortés* [1524], first relación, quoted in *Annals of the Cakchiquels*, 120n228.

134. *Annals of the Cakchiquels*, 120–26.

135. Cortés, *Letters from Mexico*, 429–30.

136. *Annals of the Cakchiquels*, 127–30.

137. Pagden, *Fall of Natural Man*, 34.

138. *Annals of the Cakchiquels*, 130–31.

139. Ibid., 131–34.

140. Las Casas, *Devastation*, 72.

141. Las Casas, *History of the Indies*, 126–28, 161–72 [book 2, chs. 19, 57ff]; the decree is excerpted in Whitehead, "Invaded Societies," 867–68.

142. Las Casas, *History of the Indies*, 162 [book 2, ch. 57], quoting Cristóbal de la Tovilla, *La Barbarica*.

143. Ibid., 163 [book 2, ch. 57], 165–66 [book 2, ch. 58].

144. Fray Tomás de Toro, Cartagena, May 31, 1535, quoted in J. Friede and B. Keen, eds., *Bartolomé de Las Casas in History* (DeKalb, 1971), 491.

145. Gómara, *Cortés*, 405–6.

146. Aiton, "The Secret Visita against Viceroy Mendoza," 20; Hanke, *Spanish Struggle*, 89.

147. Aiton, "The Secret Visita against Viceroy Mendoza," 10–16; quoted in Hanke, *Spanish Struggle*, 13.

148. Donovan, introduction to Las Casas, *Devastation*, 6; Pagden, *Fall of Natural Man*, 66.

149. Friede and Keen, *Bartolomé de Las Casas in History*, 493.

150. Adorno, *Intellectual Life*, 10; Donovan, introduction to Las Casas, *Devastation*, 7.

151. See Friede and Keen, *Bartolomé de Las Casas in History*, 489–504; Hanke, *Spanish Struggle*, 89–91; Todorov, *La conquête de l'Amérique*, 177–82.

152. Toribio de Motolinía, *Motolinía's History of the Indians of New Spain*, tr. Francis B. Steck (Washington, 1951), first treatise, ch. 3, 101.

153. Gerónimo de Mendieta, *Historia Eclesiástica Indiana*, book 4, ch. 1, quoted in Jay, *Three Dominican Pioneers*, 7; Sale, *Conquest*, 159–61. See also Gerónimo de Mendieta, *Historia Eclesiástica Indiana: A Franciscan's View of the Spanish Conquest of Mexico*, tr. Felix Jay (Lewiston, 1997).

154. Pagden, *Fall of Natural Man*, 108; Hanke, *Spanish Struggle*, 100–1; Pagden, *Fall of Natural Man*, 114, 117.

155. Sepúlveda, *Democrates Alter*: www.elcamino.cc.ca.us/Faculty/jsuarez/1Cour/H10A/Wp TolSepuld.htm (accessed June 19, 2004); Sepúlveda, "*Democrates Alter*," 496.

156. For different views: R. Quirk, "Some Notes on a Controversial Controversy: Juan Ginés de Sepúlveda and Natural Servitude," *Hispanic American Historical Review* 34:3 (1954): 357–64; Pagden, *Fall of Natural Man*, ch. 5.

157. Quirk, "Some Notes on a Controversial Controversy," 359.

158. Aristotle, *Politics*, 1330a: "Those who are to cultivate the soil should best of all, if the ideal system is to be stated, be slaves . . . but as a second best they should be alien serfs." Aristotle recommended that "all slaves should have their freedom set before them as a reward."

159. Sepúlveda, *Democrates secundus sive de justis causis belli apud Indios* [1544], in Pagden, *Fall of Natural Man*, 116–17.

160. Sepúlveda, *Democrates Alter*: www.elcamino.cc.ca.us/Faculty/jsuarez/1Cour/H10A/Wp TolSepuld.htm (accessed June 19, 2004).

161. Sepúlveda, "*Democrates Alter*," 496; *Democrates Alter*: www.elcamino.cc.ca.us/Faculty/ jsuarez/1Cour/H10A/WpTolSepuld.htm (accessed June 19, 2004).

162. Pagden, *Fall of Natural Man*, 110, 119, 108; Donovan, introduction to Las Casas, *Devastation*, 9.

163. Pagden, *Fall of Natural Man*, 35, 207n47.

164. Luis Sánchez, "Memorial to President Espinosa, 1566," in Charles Gibson, ed., *The Black Legend: Anti-Spanish Attitudes in the Old World and the New* (New York, 1971), 90–93.

165. Pagden, *Fall of Natural Man,* 84.

166. Alonso de Zorita, *oidor* (judge) of the royal *audiencia* of New Spain, 1554–64, quoted in Friede and Keen, *Bartolomé de Las Casas in History,* 494.

167. Todorov, *La conquête de l'Amérique,* 181.

168. Sale, *Conquest,* 159–61; Todorov, *La conquête de l'Amérique,* 170–71.

Chapter 3. Guns and Genocide in East Asia, 1400–1600

1. Victor Lieberman, *Strange Parallels: Southeast Asia in Global Context, c. 800–1830,* vol. 1, *Integration on the Mainland* (New York, 2003), 42–43, 135.

2. Sun Laichen, "Ming–Southeast Asian Overland Interactions, 1368–1644" (Ph.D. diss., University of Michigan, 2000), 11–12.

3. Beatriz Pastor Bodmer, *The Armature of Conquest: Spanish Accounts of the Discovery of America, 1492–1589* (Stanford, 1992), 29; Kirkpatrick Sale, *The Conquest of Paradise* (New York, 1990), 380–81n2.

4. Sun, "Ming–Southeast Asian," 70–71.

5. John K. Whitmore, "The Two Great Campaigns of the Hong-duc Era (1460–97) in Dai Viet," *Southeast Asia Research* 12:1 (2004): 120.

6. O. W. Wolters, *History, Culture, and Region in Southeast Asian Perspectives,* rev. ed. (Ithaca, 1999), 52.

7. Lieberman, *Strange Parallels,* 1:368, 360–61, 371.

8. Ibid., 1:368–69; Sun, "Ming–Southeast Asian," 71.

9. *Le Dai-Viet et ses voisins, d'après le Dai-Viet Su Ky Toan Thu,* tr. Bui Quang Trung and Nguyen Huong (Paris, 1990), 52; Lieberman, *Strange Parallels,* 1:370.

10. *Le Dai-Viet et ses voisins,* 54–57; Whitmore, "Two Great Campaigns," 120–21.

11. J. K. Whitmore, "Chu Van An and the Rise of 'Antiquity' in Fourteenth-Century Dai Viet," *Vietnam Review* 1 (1996): 50–61; Francesco Petrarch, *The Secret,* ed. Carol E. Quillen (Boston, 2003), 1–4.

12. Whitmore, "Chu Van An," 52–57.

13. O. W. Wolters, "Chu Van An: An Exemplary Retirement," *Vietnam Review* 1 (1996): 62.

14. John K. Whitmore, *Vietnam, Ho Quy Ly, and the Ming (1371–1421)* (New Haven, 1985), 6.

15. Whitmore, "Chu Van An," 51, 56–57; *Le Dai-Viet et ses voisins,* 52; Wolters, *History, Culture,* 52–53.

16. Nguyen The Anh, "The Vietnamization of the Cham Deity Po Nagar," in K. Taylor and J. Whitmore, eds., *Essays into Vietnamese Pasts* (Ithaca, 1995).

17. Whitmore, *Vietnam,* 32.

18. Sun, "Ming–Southeast Asian," 5–7n15, 55–58; cf. Geoffrey Parker, "The Gunpowder Revolution," in Parker, ed., *The Cambridge History of Warfare* (New York, 2005), 105.

19. John K. Whitmore, "The Last Great King of Classical Southeast Asia: 'Che Bong Nga' and Fourteenth Century Champa" (paper presented at the Asia Research Institute, Singapore, 2004).

20. Whitmore, *Vietnam,* 40, 58, 76, 24ff., 33ff., 76, 39–43, 58, 49–50.

21. Ibid., 68, 45, 53–54, 61, 71–75; Sun, "Ming–Southeast Asian," 72, 68–69.

22. Whitmore, *Vietnam,* 43; Lieberman, *Strange Parallels,* 1:379–80.

23. Sun, "Ming–Southeast Asian," 60–64.

24. Ibid., 65–68, 279.

25. A. B. Woodside, *Vietnam and the Chinese Model* (Cambridge, Mass., 1971), 21.

26. Whitmore, *Vietnam,* 65, 67; John K. Whitmore, "Colliding Peoples: Tai/Viet Interactions in the 14th and 15th Centuries," ms. p. 7, quoted in Lieberman, *Strange Parallels,* 1:379n111.

27. Whitmore, "Two Great Campaigns," 122–23; Lieberman, *Strange Parallels,* 1:384.

28. Sun, "Ming–Southeast Asian," 273–74; Woodside, *Vietnam and the Chinese Model,* 20.

29. Whitmore, "Two Great Campaigns," 123.

30. Georges Maspéro, *Le royaume du Champa* (Paris, 1928), 237.

31. Sun, "Ming–Southeast Asian," 260, 72.

32. Geoff Wade, tr., "The Ming shi Account of Champa" (working paper no. 3, Asia Research Institute, National University of Singapore, June 2003), 11–12.

33. Whitmore, "Two Great Campaigns," 123–25; Sun, "Ming–Southeast Asian," 67.

34. Whitmore, "Two Great Campaigns," 125, 129; Wade, "Ming shi Account of Champa," 12.

35. Sun, "Ming–Southeast Asian," 279.

36. Maspéro, *Royaume du Champa*, 237; Whitmore, "Two Great Campaigns," 128, 126.

37. Sun, "Ming–Southeast Asian," 277, 262, 279; Whitmore, "Two Great Campaigns," 125, 128–29.

38. Maspéro, *Royaume du Champa*, 237–38.

39. Wade, "Ming shi Account of Champa," 12–13.

40. Maspéro, *Royaume du Champa*, 238–39 n6.

41. Le Thanh Khoi, *Histoire du Vietnam des origines à 1858* (Paris, 1981), 239.

42. *Le Dai-Viet et ses voisins*, 90; John K. Whitmore, "New View," ms. p. 70, quoted in Lieberman, *Strange Parallels*, 1:379n111.

43. Whitmore, "Two Great Campaigns," 130.

44. Wade, "Ming shi Account of Champa," 14–15.

45. Sun, "Ming–Southeast Asian," 261; Whitmore, "Two Great Campaigns,"133.

46. Whitmore, "Two Great Campaigns," 132–33; Sun, "Ming–Southeast Asian," 265.

47. Sun, "Ming–Southeast Asian," 262–63, 266; Whitmore, "Two Great Campaigns," 133.

48. *Dai-Viet Su Ky Toan Thu*, 2:835, in Sun, "Ming–Southeast Asian," 266–67.

49. John K. Whitmore, "*Chung-hsing* and *Cheng-t'ung* in Texts of and on Sixteenth Century Viet Nam," in Taylor and Whitmore, *Essays into Vietnamese Pasts*, 118.

50. Nguyen The Anh, "The Vietnamization of the Cham Deity Po Nagar," in Taylor and Whitmore, *Essays into Vietnamese Pasts*,

51. *Le Dai-Viet et ses voisins*, 90; William Duiker, *Historical Dictionary of Vietnam* (Lanham, 1998), 132.

52. Whitmore, "*Chung-hsing* and *Cheng-t'ung* in Texts of and on Sixteenth Century Viet Nam," 120.

53. *Le Dai-Viet et ses voisins*, 90–91; Nguyen The Anh, "Vietnamization of the Cham Deity."

54. Maspéro, *Royaume du Champa*, 240; Wade, "Ming shi Account of Champa," 13–14.

55. Li Tana, *Nguyen Cochinchina: Southern Vietnam in the Seventeenth and Eighteenth Centuries* (Ithaca, 1998), 32; Lieberman, *Strange Parallels*, 1:415.

56. Choi Byung Wook, *Southern Vietnam under the Reign of Minh Mang (1820–1841): Central Policies and Local Response* (Ithaca, 2004), 165.

57. Li Tana, *Nguyen Cochinchina*, 32; Lieberman, *Strange Parallels*, 1:411.

58. D. G. E. Hall, *A History of Southeast Asia* (London, 1985), 462. The wars of 1771–1802 sparked another Cham exodus. Jean Delvert, *Le paysan cambodgien* (Paris, 1960), 22; Po Dharma, "A propos de l'exil d'un roi cam au Cambodge," *BEFEO* 62 (1983): 253–66.

59. Lieberman, *Strange Parallels*, 1:412. Some 60,000 Chams lived in Vietnam in 1970, 250,000 in Cambodia (G. Moussay, "Coup d'oeil sur les Cam aujourd'hui," *Bulletin de la société des études indochinoises de Saigon* 46 [1971]: 10).

60. George Sansom, *A History of Japan, 1134–1615* (Stanford, 1961), 263–64.

61. Mary Elizabeth Berry, *The Culture of Civil War in Kyoto* (Berkeley, 1994), 2; Mary Elizabeth Berry, *Hideyoshi* (Cambridge, Mass., 1982), 26–34.

62. James Murdoch, *A History of Japan* (London, 1925), 2:165, 167.

63. Sansom, *History of Japan*, 264–65; Otis Cary, *A History of Christianity in Japan* (New York, 1909; repr. 1970), 78–81.

64. Murdoch, *History of Japan*, 2:312; Berry, *Culture of Civil War*, 1–54; Berry, *Hideyoshi*, 50.

65. Conrad Totman, *Early Modern Japan* (Berkeley, 1993), 40.

66. Sansom, *History of Japan*, 352, 263–64.

67. Berry, *Hideyoshi*, 100, 209.

68. Ibid., 35–39.

69. Cary, *Christianity in Japan*, 74; Murdoch, *History of Japan*, 2:152–53; Berry, *Hideyoshi*, 12–13, 19–20, 39.

70. Berry, *Hideyoshi*, 41, 44–46.

71. Murdoch, *History of Japan,* 2:155, 163–64.

72. Cary, *Christianity in Japan,* 82; Berry, *Hideyoshi,* 46, 86; Murdoch, *History of Japan,* 2:164–65; Totman, *Early Modern Japan,* 43.

73. Jeroen Lamers, *Japonius Tyrannus: The Japanese Warlord Oda Nobunaga Reconsidered* (Leiden, 2000), 76–77.

74. Berry, *Hideyoshi,* 47.

75. Murdoch, *History of Japan,* 2:155–56; Totman, *Early Modern Japan,* 42.

76. Berry, *Hideyoshi,* 47–48, 52–53; Totman, *Early Modern Japan,* 43–44.

77. Berry, *Hideyoshi,* 63–64, 70.

78. Murdoch, *History of Japan,* 2:167n8, 319.

79. Ibid., 2:165–66; Berry, *Hideyoshi,* 63–64, 76, cf. 64–65.

80. Berry, *Hideyoshi,* 56–57, 59.

81. In 1579 a Jesuit official welcomed Nobunaga's persecution of Buddhists: "Thus in future we shall have fewer enemies." The 1582 Jesuit report added: "This man seems to have been chosen by God to open and prepare the way for our holy faith." Murdoch, *History of Japan,* 2:167; Cary, *Christianity in Japan,* 83.

82. Berry, *Hideyoshi,* 41, 61–62, 65, 67, 80, 66–71.

83. Ibid., 75, 77–78.

84. Ibid., 79–80; Cary, *Christianity in Japan,* 100.

85. Berry, *Hideyoshi,* 80, 86.

86. Ibid., 83–93.

87. Ibid., 91–92; Totman, *Early Modern Japan,* 47.

88. Cary, *Christianity in Japan,* 98–99; Berry, *Hideyoshi,* 92–93.

89. Nam-lin Hur, "The Country of the Gods and Hideyoshi: Warfare and Ideology in Premodern East Asia" (paper presented to the 2004 Meeting of the Association for Asian Studies, San Diego), and "Zen Monks and the Diplomacy of Foreign Conquest in Late Sixteenth-Century Japan" (paper presented at the 2003 AAR Annual Meeting, Atlanta). I am grateful to Prof. Hur for permission to quote from these papers.

90. Murdoch, *History of Japan,* 2:305; Berry, *Hideyoshi,* 91, 207.

91. Berry, *Hideyoshi,* 94–96; Murdoch, *History of Japan,* 2:303.

92. Emiko Ohnuki-Tierney, *Kamikaze, Cherry Blossoms, and Nationalisms: The Militarization of Aesthetics in Japanese History* (Chicago, 2002), 27–28, 12, 73, 86.

93. Ibid., 79, 88, 27–31, 36, 53, 56–57, 86, 65.

94. Berry, *Hideyoshi,* 53.

95. Sansom, *History of Japan,* 331.

96. Ibid., 331–32.

97. Berry, *Hideyoshi,* 102–3.

98. Sansom, *History of Japan,* 332; Berry, *Hideyoshi,* 106, 110.

99. Berry, *Hideyoshi,* 112, 118–19, 145, 120–21, 124, 107, 110.

100. Sansom, *History of Japan,* 333.

101. Thomas C. Smith, *The Agrarian Origins of Modern Japan* (Stanford, 1959), 3–5.

102. Berry, *Hideyoshi,* 107–8, 115; Berry, *Culture of Civil War,* 224.

103. Berry, *Hideyoshi,* 107, 200–201.

104. Berry, *Hideyoshi,* 103, 107; Murdoch, *History of Japan,* 2:305–6, 313, 309.

105. Jurgis Elisonas, "The Inseparable Trinity: Japan's Relations with China and Korea," in *Cambridge History of Japan,* vol. 4, *Early Modern Japan* (Cambridge, 1991), 265.

106. Hur, "The Country of the Gods and Hideyoshi" and "Zen Monks."

107. Yoshida Kanetomo (1435–1511), quoted in Hur, "The Country of the Gods and Hideyoshi."

108. Hur, "Zen Monks."

109. Sansom, *History of Japan,* 371; Berry, *Hideyoshi,* 223–24.

110. Ohnuki-Tierney, *Kamikaze, Cherry Blossoms, and Nationalisms,* 34.

111. Berry, *Hideyoshi,* 208, 216.

112. Murdoch, *History of Japan,* 2:311; Berry, *Hideyoshi,* 212.

113. Totman, *Early Modern Japan,* 47–48.

114. James B. Palais, *Confucian Statecraft and Korean Institutions: Yu Hyongwon and the Late Choson Dynasty* (Seattle, 1996), 77.

115. Murdoch, *History of Japan,* 2:307–10; Berry, *Hideyoshi,* 208.

116. Palais, *Confucian Statecraft and Korean Institutions,* 77; Murdoch, *History of Japan,* 2:310–11.

117. Quoted in Hur, "The Country of the Gods and Hideyoshi"; Berry, *Hideyoshi,* 208, 212.

118. Berry, *Hideyoshi,* 209, 211.

119. Yuki Tanaka, personal communication, Mar. 22, 2004, information from Prof. Manji Kitajima; Stefan Tanaka, *Japan's Orient: Rendering Pasts into History* (Berkeley, 1993), 74.

120. Hur, "The Country of the Gods and Hideyoshi," quoting from *Kiyomasa koma jin oboegaki.*

121. Palais, *Confucian Statecraft and Korean Institutions,* 76; Murdoch, *History of Japan,* 2:312–14.

122. Palais, *Confucian Statecraft and Korean Institutions,* 84–85; Berry, *Hideyoshi,* 100.

123. Murdoch, *History of Japan,* 2:317–20, 330–31; Berry, *Hideyoshi,* 209.

124. Palais, *Confucian Statecraft and Korean Institutions,* 91.

125. Sansom, *History of Japan,* 354; Murdoch, *History of Japan,* 2:321, 323–55.

126. Palais, *Confucian Statecraft and Korean Institutions,* 87; Murdoch, *History of Japan,* 2:324.

127. Hur, "The Country of the Gods and Hideyoshi," quoting from the unprinted document *Shukuro kō.*

128. Murdoch, *History of Japan,* 2:334–38; Palais, *Confucian Statecraft and Korean Institutions,* 82.

129. Elisonas, "The Inseparable Trinity," 264–65.

130. Murdoch, *History of Japan,* 2:338; Palais, *Confucian Statecraft and Korean Institutions,* 82.

131. Murdoch, *History of Japan,* 2:339–40, 342.

132. Ibid., 2:343.

133. Elisonas, "The Inseparable Trinity," 280.

134. Palais, *Confucian Statecraft and Korean Institutions,* 83; Murdoch, History of Japan, 2:340, 346–48.

135. Quoted in Murdoch, *History of Japan,* 2:346.

136. Hur, "Zen Monks."

137. Murdoch, *History of Japan,* 2:349; Berry, *Hideyoshi,* 212.

138. Yuki Tanaka, personal communication, Mar. 22, 2004, information from Prof. Manji Kitajima.

139. Berry, *Hideyoshi,* 221, 219, 225.

140. Murdoch, *History of Japan,* 2:351–54; Hur, "Zen Monks."

141. Murdoch, *History of Japan,* 2:355.

142. Manji Kitajima, *Toyotomi Hideyoshi no Chōsen shinryaku* (Tokyo, 1995), 196; translation by Hur in "Zen Monks," 9.

143. Kum Pyong-dong, *Mimizuka: Hideyoshi no hanakiri mimikiri o megutte,* rev. ed. (Tokyo, 1994), 41. Also Kim Hong-kyu, ed., *Hideyoshi, Mimizuka, yonhyakunen* (Tokyo, 1998), 66, 74, and Kim Pong-Hyun, *Hideyoshi no Chōsen shinryaku to gihei tōsō* (Tokyo, 1995), 378, both cited in Gavan McCormack, "Reflections on Modern Japanese History in the Context of the Concept of Genocide," in Robert Gellately and Ben Kiernan, eds., *The Specter of Genocide: Mass Murder in Historical Perspective* (New York, 2003), 276.

144. Manji Kitajima, *Toyotomi Hideyoshi,* 196, translated by Hur in "Zen Monks," 9.

145. Murdoch, *History of Japan,* 2:357–58; Kum Pyong-dong, *Mimizuka,* ch. 3.

146. Kum Pyong-dong, *Mimizuka,* 38. The classical Japanese reads literally: "Punish straightforwardly the Red Country without leaving a thing behind." Hideyoshi divided his war map of Korea into regions, assigning the color red to Chŏlla province, blue to Ch'ungch'ŏng. Thanks to Simon Kim for the translation.

147. Murdoch, *History of Japan,* 2:356; Berry, *Hideyoshi,* 233.

148. Manji Kitajima, *Toyotomi Hideyoshi,* 195, quotations translated by Hur in "Zen Monks."

149. Kum Pyong-dong, *Mimizuka,* 57–59; Manji Kitajima, *Toyotomi Hideyoshi,* 448, in Hur, "Zen Monks."

150. Murdoch, *History of Japan,* 2:356.

151. *Wakizaka ki* chronicle, quoted in Stephen Turnbull, *Samurai Invasion: Japan's Korean War, 1592–1598* (London, 2002), 197.

152. Hur, "The Country of the Gods and Hideyoshi."

153. Quoted in Hur, "Zen Monks."

154. Elisonas, "The Inseparable Trinity," 292–93.

155. Berry, *Hideyoshi,* 214, 282; Sansom, *History of Japan,* 355.

156. Elisonas, "The Inseparable Trinity," 290–91.

157. Murdoch, *History of Japan,* 2:356–58.

158. Manji Kitajima, *Toyotomi Hideyoshi,* 448, in Hur, "Zen Monks."

159. Kim Hong-kyu, *Hideyoshi, Mimizuka, yonhyakunen,* 74, and Kim Pong-Hyun, *Hideyoshi no Chōsen shinryaku to gihei tōsō,* 378, cited in McCormack, "Reflections," 276.

160. Yuki Tanaka, personal communication, Mar. 22, 2004.

161. Okawachi Hidemoto, *Chōsen monogatari* (Tale of Korea), cited in Kum Pyong-dong, *Mimizuka,* 62

162. Kim Hong-kyu, *Hideyoshi, Mimizuka, yonhyakunen,* 74, and Kim Pong-Hyun, *Hideyoshi no Chōsen shinryaku to gihei tōsō,* 378, cited in McCormack, "Reflections," 276.

163. Kim Hong-kyu, *Hideyoshi, Mimizuka, yonhyakunen,* 127, and Kim Pong-Hyun, *Hideyoshi no Chōsen shinryaku to gihei tōsō,* 382–89, cited in McCormack, "Reflections," 276.

164. Berry, *Hideyoshi,* 235; Murdoch, *History of Japan,* 2:359.

165. "Christianity and the Daimyo," in *Cambridge History of Japan,* 4:365; Cary, *Christianity in Japan,* 138.

166. "Christianity and the Daimyo," 368–72; George Sansom, *A History of Japan, 1615–1867* (Stanford, 1963), 39–41, 37; Gavan McCormack, personal communication.

Chapter 4. Genocidal Massacres in Early Modern Southeast Asia

1. B. P. Groslier, *Angkor et le Cambodge au XVIème siècle d'après les sources portugaises et espagnoles* (Paris, 1958), 145–46; *Os Lusiadas,* X, 127–30.

2. *Os Lusiadas,* X, 138, 1–2; C. M. Bowra, "Camões and the Epic of Portugal," in *From Virgil to Milton* (London, 1945), 87–90, 97–98, 101, 103, 111–14, 125.

3. Bowra, "Camões and the Epic of Portugal," 86.

4. Virgil, *The Aeneid: A New Prose Translation,* tr. David West (London, 1991), 274.

5. *Os Lusiadas,* III, 134, 1–8; Bowra, "Camões and the Epic of Portugal," 107.

6. *Os Lusiadas,* I, 19, 1–4; Bowra, "Camões and the Epic of Portugal," 96.

7. Bowra, "Camões and the Epic of Portugal," 126–29.

8. *Os Lusiadas,* III, 52, 1–4; Bowra, "Camões and the Epic of Portugal," 95.

9. *Os Lusiadas,* X, 146, 1–4 and I, 16, 1–4; Bowra, "Camões and the Epic of Portugal," 131–32.

10. Bowra, "Camões and the Epic of Portugal," 133.

11. Richard Helgerson, "Camões, Hakluyt, and the Voyages of Two Nations," in Nicholas B. Dirks, ed., *Colonialism and Culture* (Ann Arbor, 1992), 28.

12. Khin Sok, *Le Cambodge entre le Siam et le Vietnam (de 1775 à 1860)* (Paris, 1991), 37.

13. David P. Chandler, *A History of Cambodia* (Boulder, 1983), 81–82.

14. L. P. Briggs, "Spanish Intervention in Cambodia 1593–1603," *T'oung-Pao* 39 (1949): 134, 136, 147–48; Chandler, *A History of Cambodia,* 83.

15. Briggs, "Spanish Intervention," 132–37, 148.

16. Mak Phoeun, *Histoire du Cambodge de la fin du XVIe siècle au début du XVIIIe* (Paris, 1995), 47; Briggs, "Spanish Intervention," 149–50.

17. Mak Phoeun, *Histoire du Cambodge,* 61; Briggs, "Spanish Intervention," 150–51.

18. Briggs, "Spanish Intervention," 152–53; Mak Phoeun, *Histoire du Cambodge,* 69–70.

19. Groslier, *Angkor et le Cambodge,* 41; Mak Phoeun, *Histoire du Cambodge,* 68–70.

20. Briggs, "Spanish Intervention," 153.

21. Gabriel de San Antonio, *Breve y verdadera relacion de los successos del reyno de Camboxa* (S. Pablo de Valladolid, Pedro Lasso, 1604), 19–20, repr. in A. Cabaton, tr., *Brève et véridique relation des évenements du Cambodge* (Paris, Ernest Leroux, 1914), 20. Thanks to Paul Freedman for his translation from the original Spanish. A translation from French is Gabriel Quiroga de San Antonio, *A Brief and Truthful Relation of Events in the Kingdom of Cambodia* (Bangkok, 1998), 21.

22. Mak Phoeun, *Histoire du Cambodge*, 70.

23. San Antonio, *Breve y verdadera relacion de los successos del reyno de Camboxa*, 19–20; San Antonio, *Brief and Truthful Relation*, 21–23.

24. Bartholomé de Las Casas, *Brevissima relacion de la destruycion de las Indias* (Seville, 1552).

25. San Antonio, *Brief and Truthful Relation*, 23; Briggs, "Spanish Intervention," 138.

26. Groslier, *Angkor et le Cambodge*, 42.

27. Mak Phoeun, *Histoire du Cambodge*, 78.

28. Groslier, *Angkor et le Cambodge*, 44; Mak Phoeun, *Histoire du Cambodge*, 80, 84–86; Briggs, "Spanish Intervention," 154–56.

29. Groslier, *Angkor et le Cambodge*, 45.

30. Briggs, "Spanish Intervention," 153–57; San Antonio, *Brief and Truthful Relation*, 39.

31. Mak Phoeun, *Histoire du Cambodge*, 91.

32. *Chroniques royales du Cambodge (de 1594 à 1677),* tr. with an introduction by Mak Phoeun (Paris, 1981), 82, 75–80 (on the territorial dismemberment).

33. M. C. Ricklefs, *A History of Modern Indonesia since c. 1300* (Stanford, 1993), 4–6.

34. Ibid., 8, 10.

35. Ibid., 53, 41, 38, 7.

36. M. C. Ricklefs, *War, Culture, and Economy in Java, 1677–1726: Asian and European Imperialism in the Early Kartasura Period* (Sydney, 1993), 11–12, 22.

37. Ibid., 3, 5.

38. Ibid., 30; Ricklefs, *Modern Indonesia since c. 1300,* 40.

39. Ricklefs, *Modern Indonesia since c. 1300,* 41.

40. B. Schrieke, *Indonesian Sociological Studies,* vol. 2, *Ruler and Realm in Early Java* (The Hague, 1957), 146–47; Ricklefs, *Modern Indonesia since c. 1300,* 42–44.

41. Michael Charney, *Southeast Asian Warfare, 1300–1900* (Leiden, 2004), 67.

42. *Babad ing Sangkala* [Chronicle of the Chronograms], in M. C. Ricklefs, *Modern Javanese Historical Tradition: A Study of an Original Kartasura Chronicle and Related Materials* (London, 1978), 33.

43. Schrieke, *Indonesian Sociological Studies,* 2:146–49, 218; Ricklefs, *Modern Indonesia since c. 1300,* 43–44.

44. Ricklefs, *Modern Indonesia since c. 1300,* 45; Schrieke, *Indonesian Sociological Studies,* 2:126.

45. Schrieke, *Indonesian Sociological Studies,* 2:222–24, 226.

46. Ibid., 2:150; Ricklefs, *Modern Indonesia since c. 1300,* 47.

47. *Babad ing Sangkala,* in Ricklefs, *Modern Javanese Historical Tradition,* 41.

48. Schrieke, *Indonesian Sociological Studies,* vol. 1 (The Hague, 1955), "Central Java, 1500–1625," 80–82.

49. Ibid., 184, 267n567, 266n558, 75, 184.

50. Ricklefs, *Modern Indonesia since c. 1300,* 46; Schrieke, *Indonesian Sociological Studies,* 2:218, 150.

51. Schrieke, *Indonesian Sociological Studies,* 1:77.

52. Ricklefs, *Modern Indonesia since c. 1300,* 47.

53. *Babad ing Sangkala,* in Ricklefs, *Modern Javanese Historical Tradition,* 47.

54. Ricklefs, *War, Culture, and Economy in Java,* 5, 11, 30.

55. Schrieke, *Indonesian Sociological Studies,* 1:184; 2:219.

56. M. C. Ricklefs, *A History of Modern Indonesia since c. 1200,* 3rd ed. (Stanford, 2001), 92.

57. H. J. de Graaf, *De Regering van Sunan Mangku-Rat I Tegal-Wangi, Vorst van Mataram, 1646–1677,* 2 vols. (The Hague, 1961), 1:27. Translation by Philippe Hunt.

58. Ibid., 1:23.

59. Ibid., 1:24; Ricklefs, *History of Modern Indonesia since c. 1200*, 92.

60. de Graaf, *De Regering van Sunan Mangku-Rat I*, 1:24, 28.

61. *De Vijf Gezantschapsreizen van Rijklof van Goens naar het hof van Mataram, 1648–1654*, uitgegeven door Dr. H.J. de Graaf (The Hague, 1956), 247–48. Translation by Philippe Hunt.

62. de Graaf, *De Regering van Sunan Mangku-Rat I*, 25, 29, 32.

63. Ibid., 32; Ricklefs, *Modern Indonesia since c. 1300*, 69–70.

64. *De Vijf Gezantschapsreizen van Rijklof van Goens*, 249.

65. Ibid., 249–50; de Graaf, *De Regering van Sunan Mangku-Rat I*, 32–34; M. C. Ricklefs, *Jogjakarta under Sultan Mangkubumi, 1749–1792* (London, 1974), 18.

66. Ricklefs, *Modern Indonesia since c. 1300*, 69–70; Schrieke, *Indonesian Sociological Studies*, 1:77; Jean Gelman Taylor, *Indonesia: Peoples and Histories* (New Haven, 2003), 164.

67. *Babad ing Sangkala*, in Ricklefs, *Modern Javanese Historical Tradition*, 53.

68. *De Vijf Gezantschapsreizen van Rijklof van Goens*, 254; Ricklefs, *Modern Javanese Historical Tradition*, 176.

69. de Graaf, *De Regering van Sunan Mangku-Rat I*, 33–34.

70. Ibid., 34; Taylor, *Indonesia*, 160–61, 163.

71. de Graaf, *De Regering van Sunan Mangku-Rat I*, 34.

72. *Babad ing Sangkala*, in Ricklefs, *Modern Javanese Historical Tradition*, 55, 69, 71, 73, 79, 81, 83.

73. Ibid., 71, 81.

74. Ricklefs, *War, Culture, and Economy in Java*, 31.

75. Ricklefs, *Modern Indonesia since c. 1300*, 70; Ricklefs, *War, Culture, and Economy in Java*, 32; H. J. de Graaf, *Islamic States in Java, 1500–1700* (The Hague, 1976), 54, 66.

76. Ricklefs, *War, Culture, and Economy in Java*, 31–32; Ricklefs, *Modern Indonesia since c. 1300*, 72; Ricklefs, *Modern Javanese Historical Tradition*, 177.

77. Schrieke, *Indonesian Sociological Studies*, 2:17.

78. Ricklefs, *Modern Javanese Historical Tradition*, 179.

79. de Graaf, *Islamic States in Java*, 66.

80. Schrieke, *Indonesian Sociological Studies*, 1:76, 78, 201–2.

81. Ibid., 75; Ricklefs, *War, Culture, and Economy in Java*, 5.

82. de Graaf, *Islamic States in Java*, 58–59.

83. Ibid., 59–61; Ricklefs, *Modern Indonesia since c. 1300*, 71; Taylor, *Indonesia*, 164.

84. Schrieke, *Indonesian Sociological Studies*, 1:75–76.

85. Anthony Reid, *Southeast Asia in the Age of Commerce*, vol. 1, *The Lands Below the Winds* (New Haven, 1988), 202.

86. Schrieke, *Indonesian Sociological Studies*, 1:267n567.

87. Taylor, *Indonesia*, 164.

88. *Babad ing Sangkala*, in Ricklefs, *Modern Javanese Historical Tradition*, 55, 67.

89. Ricklefs, *Modern Javanese Historical Tradition*, 178.

90. Ibid., 175.

91. *Babad ing Sangkala*, in Ricklefs, *Modern Javanese Historical Tradition*, 51.

92. Schrieke, *Indonesian Sociological Studies*, 2:222–24, 140.

93. Ricklefs, *War, Culture, and Economy in Java*, 31.

94. Ricklefs, *Modern Javanese Historical Tradition*, 181.

95. de Graaf, *Islamic States in Java*, 62.

96. Schrieke, *Indonesian Sociological Studies*, 1:61; Ricklefs, *War, Culture, and Economy in Java*, 31.

97. Ricklefs, *War, Culture, and Economy in Java*, 32–34.

98. Ibid., 34–41.

99. Schrieke, *Indonesian Sociological Studies*, 2:92.

100. Ricklefs, *War, Culture, and Economy in Java*, 42; de Graaf, *Islamic States in Java*, 74.

101. Schrieke, *Indonesian Sociological Studies*, 2:274, 142, 144.

102. *Babad ing Sangkala*, in Ricklefs, *Modern Javanese Historical Tradition*, 93; Ricklefs, *War, Culture, and Economy in Java*, 42–43; Schrieke, *Indonesian Sociological Studies*, 2:150–52, 219, 274–75.

103. Victor Lieberman, *Strange Parallels: Southeast Asia in Global Context, c. 800–1830,* vol. 1, *Integration on the Mainland* (New York, 2003), 114–15, 118, 132, 135, 139; William J. Koenig, *The Burmese Polity, 1752–1819* (Ann Arbor, 1990), 60.

104. Lieberman, *Strange Parallels,* 1:138.

105. Victor Lieberman, *Burmese Administrative Cycles* (Princeton, 1984), 29; Lieberman, *Strange Parallels,* 1:154.

106. Lieberman, *Strange Parallels,* 1:134, 132, 198; Arthur Phayre, *History of Burma* (London, 1883, repr. Bangkok), 86–88; Lieberman, *Burmese Administrative Cycles,* 25, 30.

107. Lieberman, *Strange Parallels,* 1:132–35, 139–40; Lieberman, *Burmese Administrative Cycles,* 30.

108. Koenig, *Burmese Polity,* xiii, 6–7; Lieberman, *Strange Parallels,* 1:135.

109. Victor Lieberman, personal communication; Lieberman, "Ethnic Politics in Eighteenth-Century Burma," *Modern Asian Studies* 12:3 (1978): 463.

110. Lieberman, *Strange Parallels,* 1:198–201, 136–37.

111. Lieberman, "Ethnic Politics," 463, 465; Lieberman, *Strange Parallels,* 1:203, 199, 204.

112. Koenig, *Burmese Polity,* 9–11; Lieberman, *Burmese Administrative Cycles,* 189.

113. Koenig, *Burmese Polity,* 12; Lieberman, "Ethnic Politics," 464.

114. Jonathan Smart (Syriam) to Fort St. George (Madras), Mar. 17, 1740/41, India Office Records, London, in *Records of Fort St. George: Letters to Fort St. George, 1681/82–1744/45,* 29 vols. (Madras, 1916–33), vol. 26, *1741,* 36. Victor Lieberman kindly provided a copy of this letter.

115. Smart to Fort St. George, Dec. 23, 1740, and "Translate of the Letter from King Sementho [Smin Dhaw] to Mr. Smart," delivered Dec. 21, in *Records of Fort St. George,* 26:8–9. Lieberman kindly provided copies; see his "Ethnic Politics," 463–64.

116. "Fort St. George General dated 31th Janry 1740," in India Office Records, Abstract of Letters Received from "Coast" and "Bay," 1734–44, in Correspondence with India (Examiner's Office), E/4/4, p. 332.

117. "Letter from King Sementho to Mr. Smart," 9.

118. Smart to Fort St. George, Mar. 17, 1740/41.35–36.

119. *Phongsawadan mòn phama* [Annal of the Mon of Burma], in *Prachum phongsawadan phak thi 1* [History Series, Part 1] (Bangkok, 1963), 2:71–73. Kennon Breazeale very kindly sent me a copy of his translation of this Thai-language document compiled c. 1793, updated c. 1826, and first published in 1869–70.

120. Phayre, *History of Burma,* 145.

121. Koenig, *Burmese Polity,* 12–13, suggests "perhaps twenty thousand" deportees; Lieberman, *Burmese Administrative Cycles,* 230; Lieberman, "Ethnic Politics," 466–68, 472–73; Lieberman, *Strange Parallels,* 1:204, 412.

122. Lieberman, *Burmese Administrative Cycles,* 230–31.

123. Lieberman, "Ethnic Politics," 464n22, 473, 479; Lieberman, *Burmese Administrative Cycles,* 236–37, 249, 244.

124. Koenig, *Burmese Polity,* 13, cites Alaung-hpaya's "open appeals to Burman ethnic chauvinism."

125. *Phongsawadan mòn phama,* 112; Lieberman, *Burmese Administrative Cycles,* 248.

126. Lieberman, "Ethnic Politics," 473, 476–77; Lieberman, *Strange Parallels,* 1:184, 199–200; Phayre, *History of Burma,* 166.

127. BL OR 3464, British Library, MS Orient. 3464, pp. 148–50. This is a Burmese translation of a Mon history of Pegu by the monk of Athwa, probably composed in the late 1760s, according to Victor Lieberman, who kindly supplied a copy. Translation from the Burmese by U Khin Maung Gyi.

128. Quoted in Emmanuel Guillon, *The Mons: A Civilization of Southeast Asia,* tr. James V. di Crocco (Bangkok, 1999), 203.

129. *Phongsawadan mòn phama,* 114–15.

130. *Slapat Rajawan Datow Smin Ron* [A History of Kings], by the Mon "monk of Athwa," tr. R. Halliday, *Journal of the Burma Research Society* 13 (1923): 64–65.

131. Koenig, *Burmese Polity,* 13.

132. Lieberman, *Burmese Administrative Cycles,* 249; Koenig, *Burmese Polity,* 13, 31–32, 54, 32.

133. Lieberman, *Burmese Administrative Cycles*, 265, 268–69; Alaung-hpaya's name means "Embryo Buddha" (Phayre, *History of Burma*, 149).

134. Koenig, *Burmese Polity*, 86, 65–71.

135. Ibid., 71–79, 87–88, 76, 80, 270n48.

136. Ibid., 86, 78, 83, 88.

137. Lieberman, *Strange Parallels*, 1:327; Koenig, *Burmese Polity*, 30, 16–21.

138. Thai account dating from 1793, in Lieberman, *Strange Parallels*, 1:327; Koenig, *Burmese Polity*, 31.

139. Koenig, *Burmese Polity*, 24–26, 57, 32, 58–59.

140. Ibid., 32; Lieberman, "Ethnic Politics," 480; Lieberman, *Strange Parallels*, 1:205, 330.

141. Francis Buchanan, quoted in Koenig, *Burmese Polity*, 61.

142. Lieberman, *Strange Parallels*, 1:205–6. Siam's rulers, too, were "cruel towards the subdued enemy or to those who are rejected by the king." A sixteenth-century Portuguese reported that the customs of Siam's commoners "and almost the language, are like those of Pegu"; by the 1680s a Frenchman noted "they have merged so completely with the Siamese that it is quite difficult to tell them apart." Siamese humiliation of Lao princes provoked a Lao uprising in 1826–27, with rebels selecting ethnic Thais for execution (1:324–28). Lieberman, "Ethnic Politics" (472–79), qualifies "the trend towards ethnic polarization."

143. Lieberman, *Strange Parallels*, 1:198–99.

144. *Chroniques royales*, 94, 106, 120.

145. Michael Vickery, review of Mak Phoeun, *Histoire du Cambodge*, in *Bulletin de l'Ecole Française d'Extrême-Orient (BEFEO)* 83 (1996): 407.

146. *Chroniques royales*, 132–34, 165–66, 321.

147. Ibid., 180, 334–36, 185–90, 342.

148. Mak Phoeun, *Histoire du Cambodge*, 273.

149. W. J. M. Buch, "La compagnie des Indes Néerlandaises et l'Indochine," *BEFEO* (1937): 219–21; Mak Phoeun, *Histoire du Cambodge*, 273–76.

150. *Chroniques royales*, 191, 359, 354, 195, 368–70.

151. Vickery, review of Mak Phoeun, *Histoire du Cambodge*, 415, 409.

152. Ibid., 409; Mak Phoeun, *Histoire du Cambodge*, 294ff.

153. Mak Phoeun, *Histoire du Cambodge*, lists the first five Vietnamese military interventions: 1658–59, 1673–79, 1682–88, 1688–90, 1699–1700. Lieberman, *Strange Parallels*, 1:411, says there were 13 by 1772.

154. *Chroniques royales*, 370; Mak Phoeun, *Histoire du Cambodge*, 323–26.

155. Choi Byung Wook, *Southern Vietnam under the Reign of Minh Mang (1820–1841): Central Policies and Local Response* (Ithaca, 2004), 165.

156. Pierre du Puy du Fayet, Jean de Antoine de la Court, and Charles Gouge, to the Directors, Missions Etrangères de Paris [136], July 26, 1732, 739:925–30. Translation by Nola Cooke, who very kindly supplied her detailed notes from the Missions Etrangères de Paris archives, Paris. See also Lieberman, *Strange Parallels*, 1:412.

157. Khin Sok, *Le Cambodge entre le Siam et le Vietnam*, 36.

158. Mak Phoeun, "La frontière entre le Cambodge et le Viêtnam du XVIIe siècle à l'instauration du protectorat français présentée à travers les chroniques royales khmères," in Pierre-Bernard Laffont, ed., *Les frontières du Vietnam* (Paris, 1989), 139–40.

159. Yumio Sakurai and Takako Kitagawa, "Ha Tien or Banteay Meas in the Time of the Fall of Ayutthaya," in Kennon Breazeale, ed., *From Japan to Arabia: Ayutthaya's Maritime Relations with Asia* (Bangkok, 1999), 160.

160. *Silacarik Nagar Vatt ning Pateanukram* [Inscriptions Modernes d'Angkor], 2nd ed. (Phnom Penh, 1958), no. 39, N.41 (B), 114. See the different translation by D. P. Chandler, "An Eighteenth Century Inscription from Angkor Wat," *Journal of the Siam Society* 59:2 (1971): 158.

161. Khin Sok, *Le Cambodge entre le Siam et le Vietnam*, 36–37.

162. M. Piguel to Mgr. Lefebvre, Apr. 8, 1751, in Adrien Launay, *Histoire de la mission de Cochinchine, 1658–1823: Documents historiques*, vol. 2, *1728–1771* (Paris, 1924), 368.

163. M. d'Azema to M. de Noëlène, undated, quoted in M. J-B. Maigrot to Mgr. de Martiliat,

Sept. 16, 1751, and d'Azema to Directeurs du Séminaire des M.-E., Cambodia, June 20, 1757, in Launay, *Histoire de la mission de Cochinchine,* 2:366, 370; Khin Sok, *Le Cambodge,* 37.

164. D'Azema to De Noëlène, undated, and Piguel à Lefebvre, Apr. 8, 1751, in Launay, *Histoire de la mission de Cochinchine,* 365–66, 368.

165. D'Azema to Directeurs du Séminaire des M.-E., June 20, 1757, in Launay, *Histoire de la mission de Cochinchine,* 370–71.

Part 2. Introductory Note

1. Francis Jennings, *The Invasion of America: Indians, Colonialism, and the Cant of Conquest* (New York, 1976), 74; Keith Thomas, *Man and the Natural World: Changing Attitudes in England, 1500-1800* (Oxford, 1983), 270, 265.

2. William Cronon, *Changes in the Land: Indians, Colonists and the Ecology of New England* (New York, 1983), 56-57; Henry Reynolds, *The Law of the Land* (Melbourne, 1992), 12-14, 27-29.

3. "Report on Government for Western Territory," Mar. 1, 1784, in P. L. Ford, ed., *The Writings of Thomas Jefferson,* 3:407–10. Jefferson's map is in Hildegard Johnson, *Order upon the Land: The U.S. Rectangular Land Survey and the Upper Mississippi Country* (New York, 1976), 41. See also Map 15 in this book.

4. Philip Freneau, "The Pilgrim, No. VIII," *Freeman's Journal; or, The North American Intelligencer* (Philadelphia), Jan. 9, 1782, 1.

5. Brian Donohue, *The Great Meadow: Farmers and the Land in Colonial Concord* (New Haven, 2004), 55, 70; Steven Stoll, *Larding the Lean Earth: Soil and Society in Nineteenth-Century America* (New York, 2002), 55–56.

6. Colin A. M. Duncan, "Adam Smith's Labouring Cattle: The Role of Nature in History and Political Economy" (paper prepared for the Yale Agrarian Studies Seminar, Nov. 7, 2003), 9.

7. Thomas, *Man and the Natural World,* 26; Duncan, "Adam Smith's Labouring Cattle," 9–10.

8. Adam Smith, *An Inquiry into the Nature and Causes of the Wealth of Nations* (London, 1776), quoted in Duncan, "Adam Smith's Labouring Cattle," 7; Stoll, *Larding the Lean Earth,* 56; Donohue, *Great Meadow,* 55, 166.

9. Stoll, *Larding the Lean Earth,* 56–57.

10. "The Diary of Thomas Minor, Stonington, Connecticut: Excerpt" [1672], in John Demos, *Remarkable Providences: Readings on Early American History* (Boston, 1991), 125–27.

11. Ibid., 124-26; Donohue, *Great Meadow,* 192–94, 152, 154.

12. James C. Scott, *Seeing Like a State: How Certain Schemes to Improve the Human Condition Have Failed* (New Haven, 1998), 50–51.

13. Jefferson to Horatio Gates, July 11, 1803, in A. A. Lipscomb and A. E. Bergh, eds., *The Writings of Thomas Jefferson* (Washington, 1904), 10:402; Jefferson to Breckinridge, Aug. 12, 1803, quoted in David Day, *Conquest: A New History of the Modern World* (Sydney, 2005), 276.

14. David A. Nichols, *Lincoln and the Indians: Civil War Policy and Politics* (Urbana, 2000), 185.

15. Mark Levene, *Genocide in the Age of the Nation State,* vol. 2, *The Rise of the West and the Coming of Genocide* (London, 2005), 96–97. For cases from Southeast Asia, see Ben Kiernan, "Colonialism and Genocide in Nineteenth-Century Cambodia," in A. Dirk Moses, ed., *Empire, Colony, Genocide* (New York, 2007).

16. Howard R. Lamar, personal communication; see his *New Encyclopedia of the American West* (New Haven, 1998); Bain Attwood, *Telling the Truth about Aboriginal History* (Sydney, 2005).

17. Patrick Wolfe, *Settler Colonialism and the Transformation of Anthropology: The Politics and Poetics of an Ethnographic Event* (London, 1999); Alison Palmer, *Colonial Genocide* (Adelaide, 2000); Tony Barta, "Relations of Genocide: Land and Lives in the Colonization of Australia," in Isidor Wallimann and Michael N. Dobkowski, eds., *Genocide and the Modern Age: Etiology and Case Studies of Mass Death* (Westport, 1987), 237–51; A. Dirk Moses, "Antipodean Genocide? The Origins of the Genocidal Moment in the Colonization of Australia," *Journal of Genocide Research* 2:1 (2000): 89–106.

Chapter 5. The English Conquest of Ireland, 1565–1603

1. Liana Vardi, "Imagining the Harvest in Early Modern Europe," *American Historical Review* 101:5 (1996): 1364.

2. William Camden, *Britannia* (London, 1586), A2; Emily Bartels, *Spectacles of Strangeness: Imperialism, Alienation, and Marlowe* (Philadelphia, 1993), 29.

3. Christopher Marlowe, *The Complete Plays,* ed. J. B. Steane (London, 1969), 585; act I, scene 1, 86, 92; act 5, scene 1, 144–47.

4. Thomas Elyot, *The Book Named the Governor* [1531] (London, 1962), 38, 63, 84, 173–74, 184–88.

5. Ibid., 40, vi, 15, 30–32, 105.

6. Ibid., 38, 84, 63, 101, 203–4, 80.

7. Richard Cox, in Lisa Jardine, *Worldly Goods: A New History of the Renaissance* (New York, 1996), 261.

8. Lisa Jardine and Anthony Grafton, "'Studied for Action': How Gabriel Harvey Read His Livy," *Past and Present* 129 (Nov. 1990): 57.

9. Plutarch, *The Lives of the Noble Grecians and Romans,* tr. Thomas North (London, 1579), including "The Lives of Annibal and Scipio African" (from the 1559 European edition); *Plutarch's Lives of the Noble Grecians and Romans, Englished by Sir Thomas North* (London, 1895–96), 1:3–5; also Elizabeth Story Donno, "Old Mouse-Eaten Records: History in Sidney's Apology," *Studies in Philology* 72:3 (1975): 275, 291.

10. Arnaldo Momigliano, "Polybius' Reappearance in Western Europe," in *Essays in Ancient and Modern Historiography* (Middletown, 1977), ch. 6, 88, 91, 93–94; Polybius 6.19–42.

11. Jardine and Grafton, "'Studied for Action,'" 36n16, 76, 69, 59, 70, 61.

12. Ibid., 40–42, 54, 57–58; D. B. Quinn, "Sir Thomas Smith (1513–1577) and the Beginnings of English Colonial Theory," *Proceedings of the American Philosophical Society* 89 (1945): 545.

13. Quinn, "Sir Thomas Smith," 546–47; Nicholas Canny, *Making Ireland British, 1580–1650* (Oxford, 2001), 121–22.

14. Harvey, quoted in Jardine and Grafton, "'Studied,'" 54, 58, 70–72, 62.

15. Jardine and Grafton, "'Studied for Action,'" 40–42, 58; Nicholas P. Canny, *The Elizabethan Conquest of Ireland: A Pattern Established, 1565–1576* (Sussex, 1976), 88; Canny, "The Ideology of English Colonization: From Ireland to America," *William and Mary Quarterly* 30 (1973): 577.

16. Sir Humphrey Gilbert, *Queene Elizabethes Achademy* [c. 1570] (London, 1869), 11. Rory Rapple dates this composition to 1570 (personal communication, Sept. 11, 2004).

17. Quinn, "Sir Thomas Smith," 544, 546.

18. Alan Stewart, *Philip Sidney: A Double Life* (New York, 2000), 45, 157–64.

19. Jardine and Grafton, "'Studied for Action,'" 36–38.

20. Canny, *Making Ireland British,* 4; Jardine and Grafton, "'Studied for Action,'" 39.

21. Lisa Jardine, "Encountering Ireland: Gabriel Harvey, Edmund Spenser, and English Colonial Ventures," in Brendan Bradshaw et al., eds., *Representing Ireland: Literature and the Origins of Conflict, 1534–1660* (Cambridge, 1993), 65.

22. Edwin Greenlaw et al., eds., *The Works of Edmund Spenser: A Variorum Edition,* vol. 10, *The Prose Works* (Baltimore, 1949), 10, 442; Jardine and Grafton, "'Studied for Action,'" 36, 49, 74.

23. Jardine and Grafton, "'Studied for Action,'" 42–43.

24. Livy, *Rome and the Mediterranean,* tr. H. Bettenson (London, 1976), e.g., 430 (XXXIX.40); Niccolò Machiavelli, *Discourses on Livy* (Oxford, 1997), 249 (book III, ch. 1).

25. Jardine and Grafton, "'Studied for Action,'" 43–45, 53; Augustine, *De Civitate Dei,* book 3, ch. 21.

26. Jardine and Grafton, "'Studied for Action,'" 72.

27. Canny, *Making Ireland British,* 64, 119; Canny, "Ideology of English Colonization," 585; Brendan Bradshaw, "Robe and Sword in the Conquest of Ireland," in Claire Cross et al., eds., *Law and Government under the Tudors* (Cambridge, 1988), 162.

28. Ciaran Brady, introduction to Henry Sidney, *A Viceroy's Vindication? Sir Henry Sidney's Memoir of Service in Ireland,* ed. Ciaran Brady (Cork, 2002), 9.

29. *The First Foure Bookes of Virgil's Aeneis,* tr. Richard Stanyhurst (London, 1583).

30. Merritt Y. Hughes, *Virgil and Spenser* (New York, 1969), 318–19.

31. Jason Scott-Warren, *Sir John Harington and the Book as Gift* (Oxford, 2001), 19, 218, 214–15.

32. Ibid., 20, 185, 223, 179.

33. Alison Weir, *The Life of Elizabeth I* (New York, 1998), 440.

34. James to Elizabeth, Apr. 13 and June 5, 1594, quoting *Aeneid* VII, in Leah S. Marcus et al., eds., *Elizabeth I: Collected Works* (Chicago, 2000), 376–77, 380–81.

35. Scott-Warren, *Sir John Harington,* 214–17, 20, 223–24.

36. Bartels, *Spectacles of Strangeness,* xiv.

37. Canny, "Ideology of English Colonization," 583, 586–90; Edmund Spenser, *A View of the State of Ireland,* ed. Andrew Hadfield and Willy Maley (Oxford, 1997), 112n.

38. Thomas Smith to William Fitzwilliam, Nov. 8, 1572, Bodleian Library, Oxford, Carte MSS. 57, no. 227, p. 436r.

39. Spenser, *View of the State of Ireland,* 44–47, 61–66, 49–52.

40. Greenlaw et al., *Works of Edmund Spenser,* 10:92n.

41. Canny, *Elizabethan Conquest,* 10, 14–15; Hiram Morgan, "The Colonial Venture of Sir Thomas Smith in Ulster, 1571–1575," *Historical Journal* 28:2 (1985): 268.

42. Lord Deputy Sydney to the Earl of Leicester, Mar. 1, 1566. Public Record Office (PRO), SP 63/16, no. 35, p. 3.

43. "The annsweare of the Earle of Essex to the doubtes, conceaved uppon his Platt for the reformation of Ulster," British Library, Add 48015, fols. 323r–332v, p. 2.

44. V. A. Hall and L. Bunting, "Tephra-Dated Pollen Studies of Medieval Landscapes in the North of Ireland," in P. J. Duffy, et al., eds., *Gaelic Ireland: Land, Lordship, and Settlement, c. 1250–c. 1650* (Dublin, 2001), 219–21.

45. Patricia Seed, *American Pentimento: The Invention of Indians and the Pursuit of Riches* (Minneapolis, 2001), 12–14.

46. Thomas More, *Utopia,* in Edmund Morgan, *American Slavery, American Freedom* (New York, 1975), 23.

47. William Thomas, *The Pilgrim: A Dialogue on the Life and Actions of Henry VIII* [1552], quoted in Howard M. Jones, *O Strange New World: American Culture, the Formative Years* (New York, 1964), 169.

48. "A Letter sent by T. B. Gentleman . . . of the peopling and inhabiting the Cuntrie called the Ardes," quoted in Jones, *O Strange New World,* 176; Canny, *Elizabethan Conquest,* 74.

49. Agreement between the government and MacGilpatrick [1543], quoted in James Muldoon, "The Indian as Irishman," *Essex Institute Historical Collections* 111 (1975): 274.

50. Sidney to the Lords of the Council, 1575, quoted in Jones, *O Strange New World,* 168.

51. R. F. Foster, *Modern Ireland, 1600–1972* (London, 1988), 32–33.

52. Sir John Davies, *A Discoverie of the True Causes Why Ireland was never entirely Subdued, nor brought under Obedience of the Crowne of England, Untill the Beginning of His Maiesties happie Raigne* (London, 1612; London, 1747), 171–72; Foster, *Modern Ireland,* 33–34.

53. Canny, *Elizabethan Conquest,* 23–24, 50, 51, 69.

54. Rowland White, "Discors Touching Ireland" [c. 1569], *Irish Historical Studies* 20:80 (1977): 454.

55. Ibid., 456–58, 449.

56. Edmund Tremayne, *Notes and Propositions for the Reformation of Ireland,* June 1571. PRO, SP 63/32, no. 66, 12pp., at 4, 9.

57. Canny, *Elizabethan Conquest,* 77.

58. White, "Discors Touching Ireland," 455; Canny, *Elizabethan Conquest,* 68, 75, 82.

59. Tremayne, *Notes and Propositions,* 5, 11–12.

60. "The annsweare of the Earl of Essex to the doubtes," pp. 10–11, 15.

61. Canny, *Elizabethan Conquest,* 75, 78, 85, 82; "The annsweare of the Earl of Essex to the doubtes," fols. 323r–332v, p. 16.

62. Tremayne, *Notes and Propositions,* 11; Canny, *Elizabethan Conquest,* 82–83.

63. Morgan, "Colonial Venture," 268–78; Quinn, "Sir Thomas Smith," 553n53.

64. Morgan, "Colonial Venture," 273; Quinn, "Sir Thomas Smith," 553.

65. "The Petition of Thomas Smythe and His Associates [c. 1570]," in C. L. Kingsford, ed., *Report on the Manuscripts of Lord de L'Isle and Dudley Preserved at Penhurst Place* (London, 1934), 1:15.

66. Smith to Fitzwilliam, Nov. 8, 1572, no. 236, p. 436r.

67. Quinn, "Sir Thomas Smith," 552.

68. Morgan, "Colonial Venture," 275; Canny, *Making Ireland British,* 121.

69. "The annsweare of the Earle of Essex to the doubtes," pp. 5, 17.

70. John Derricke, *The Image of Irelande* (London, 1581).

71. Vincent P. Carey, "John Derricke's *Image of Irelande,* Sir Henry Sidney, and the massacre at Mullaghmast, 1578," *Irish Historical Studies* 31:123 (1999): 312–17.

72. Canny, *Making Ireland British,* 125–31, 107–9, 138, 162, 146.

73. Spenser, *View of the State of Ireland,* 149–50; Canny, *Making Ireland British,* 132–34, 136.

74. Canny, *Making Ireland British,* 154, 143, 147–49, 158, 161.

75. Ibid., 170–71.

76. Sir Walter Ralegh, *The History of the World,* ed. C. A. Patrides (London, 1971), 353–56.

77. Francisco López de Gómara, *The Conquest of the Weast India* (London, 1578; New York, 1940); Gómara, *Cortés: The Life of the Conqueror by His Secretary,* tr. and ed. L. B. Simpson (Berkeley, 1964), xv.

78. Gómara, *Cortés,* xvi, xxi; Gómara, *Conquest of the Weast India,* 157, 134.

79. Canny, *Making Ireland British,* 111.

80. Robert Lacey, *Robert, Earl of Essex: An Elizabethan Icarus* (London, 1971), 232; Cyril Falls, *Elizabeth's Irish Wars* (London, 1950), 328; Marcus Tanner, *Ireland's Holy Wars* (New Haven, 2001), 30.

81. Sean Duffy, *Ireland in the Middle Ages* (Dublin, 1997), 181; Canny, "Ideology of English Colonization," 575.

82. Brendan Bradshaw, "The Beginnings of Modern Ireland," in Brian Farrell, ed., *The Irish Parliamentary Tradition* (Dublin, 1973), 69–71.

83. Steven G. Ellis, *Tudor Ireland: Crown, Community, and the Conflict of Cultures, 1470–1603* (London, 1985), 127; Grenfell Morton, *Elizabethan Ireland* (London, 1971), 16. Irish wars, "up to then, though they had been frequent, had not been bloody" (G. A. Hayes-McCoy, "The Tudor Conquest, 1534–1603," in T. W. Moody and F. X. Martin, *The Course of Irish History* [Cork, 1967], 175). Most male members of the Fitzgerald family were executed, and the crown confiscated their lands. Nicholas Canny, "Early Modern Ireland, c. 1500–1700," in R. F. Foster, ed., *The Oxford History of Ireland* (Oxford, 1989), 103–4.

84. T. C. Barnard, *Cromwellian Ireland: English Government and Reform in Ireland, 1649–1660* (Oxford, 2000), 173; Bradshaw, "Beginnings," 72–74; Brendan Bradshaw, "Sword, Word, and Strategy in the Reformation of Ireland," *Historical Journal* 21:3 (1978): 479.

85. Nicholas Canny, "Revising the Revisionist," *Irish Historical Studies* 30:118 (1996): 252; Bradshaw, "Beginnings," 76–78, 87.

86. Bradshaw, "Sword, Word, and Strategy," 500, 495–96, 500, 479, 481.

87. Bradshaw, "Beginnings," 78–79; Carey, "John Derricke's *Image of Irelande,*" 307.

88. Henry Sidney, quoted in Stewart, *Philip Sidney,* 19.

89. Foster, *Modern Ireland,* 34; Ciaran Brady, *The Chief Governors: The Rise and Fall of Reform Government in Tudor Ireland, 1536–1588* (Cambridge, 1994), 228; Canny, "Early Modern Ireland," 103–9; Bradshaw, "Sword, Word, and Strategy," 475.

90. Bradshaw, "Beginnings," 72, 79; Canny, *Elizabethan Conquest,* 38.

91. Carey, "John Derricke's *Image of Ireland,*" 307–8; Bradshaw, "Beginnings," 80–81.

92. David Edwards, "Ideology and Experience: Spenser's View and Martial Law in Ireland," in Hiram Morgan, ed., *Political Ideology in Ireland, 1541–1641* (Dublin, 1999), 132.

93. Carey, "John Derricke's *Image of Ireland,*" 308.

94. Canny, *Elizabethan Conquest,* 41; Canny, "Ideology of English Colonization," 576.

95. Sydney to Leicester, Mar. 1, 1566, pp. 1–3.

96. Ibid., pp. 8–10, 14, 16.

97. Canny, *Elizabethan Conquest,* 60, 72, 123; Edwards, "Ideology and Experience," 132.

98. Canny, *Elizabethan Conquest,* 142.

99. Lord Deputy Sydney and Council to the Privy Council, Oct. 26, 1569. PRO, SP 63/29, no. 70, p. 2.

100. Sidney, *A Viceroy's Vindication?* 70; Willy Maley, "Apology for Sidney: Making Virtue of a Viceroy," *Sidney Journal* 20:1 (2002): 105.

101. Sydney and Council to the Privy Council, Oct. 26, 1569, pp. 2–4.

102. Sidney, *A Viceroy's Vindication?* 76.

103. Canny, *Elizabethan Conquest,* 140–41.

104. Tremayne, *Notes and Propositions,* 8; Bradshaw, "Beginnings," 82–83.

105. Bradshaw, "Beginnings," 83, 85; Canny, *Elizabethan Conquest,* 123; Canny, "Ideology of English Colonization," 588.

106. Canny, *Elizabethan Conquest,* 142; Sydney and Council to the Privy Council, Oct. 26, 1569, pp. 2, 5, 8. See also Sean O'Faolain, *The Great O'Neill* (New York, 1942), 78.

107. Bradshaw, "Beginnings," 83.

108. Raleigh Trevelyan, *Sir Walter Raleigh* (New York, 2004), 1, 3–4, 33. Ralegh also employed John Hooker to research his genealogy (95).

109. Canny, "Revising the Revisionist," 244–45; Canny, *Making Ireland British,* 75–76.

110. Robert Leicester, 5 Dec. [1572?], Bodleian Library, Oxford, Carte MSS., 56, no. 39, p. 103r.

111. Canny, *Elizabethan Conquest,* 142; Canny, *Making Ireland British,* 66.

112. Canny, *Elizabethan Conquest,* 60, 101; Ciaran Brady, "Faction and the Origins of the Desmond Rebellion of 1579," *Irish Historical Studies* 22:88 (1981): 295.

113. Sydney and Council to the Privy Council, Oct. 26, 1569, p. 5.

114. Gilbert to Sidney, quoted in O'Faolain, *Great O'Neill,* 76. David B. Quinn wrote that Gilbert's "method of waging war was to devastate the country, killing every living creature encountered." Introduction to *The Voyages and Colonising Enterprises of Sir Humphrey Gilbert* (London, 1940), 1:17.

115. Thomas Churchyard, *A Generall Rehearsal of Warres and joyned to the same some tragedies and epitaphs* (London, 1579), quoted in Canny, "Ideology of English Colonization," 582, and Patricia Palmer, *Language and Conquest in Early Modern Ireland* (Cambridge, 2001), 124.

116. Quinn, introduction to *Voyages and Colonising Enterprises of Sir Humphrey Gilbert,* 1:17.

117. Lord Deputy Sydney to Cecill, Jan. 4, 1570, PRO, SP 63/30, no. 2, pp. 1–3.

118. Morgan, *American Slavery,* 20.

119. "A discourse for the reformacion particularly of Munster in Irlande," Quinn, introduction to *Voyages and Colonising Enterprises of Sir Humphrey Gilbert,* 1:18.

120. Canny, *Making Ireland British,* 64.

121. Sir Henry Sydney to Sir William Cecil, Feb. 24, 1569[-70], in Kingsford, *Report on the Manuscripts of Lord de L'Isle and Dudley,* 1:12.

122. Sydney to Cecill, Jan. 4, 1570, p. 3.

123. Brendan Bradshaw, "The Elizabethans and the Irish," *Studies* (Spring 1977): 47; Foster, *Modern Ireland,* 34.

124. Tremayne, *Notes and Propositions,* 1, 3, 4, 11–12.

125. Ibid., 12, 6–7, 9–10.

126. Ellis, *Tudor Ireland,* 266.

127. "The Petition of Thomas Smythe and His Associates [c. 1570]," 1:12–15; Quinn, "Sir Thomas Smith," 556–57.

128. Morgan, "Colonial Venture," 263.

129. Jardine, "Encountering Ireland," 67.

130. Jardine and Grafton, " 'Studied for Action,' "; Canny, *Elizabethan Conquest,* 87–88.

131. Falls, *Elizabeth's Irish Wars,* 113; Morgan, "Colonial Venture," 262, 265, 271.

132. Lord Deputy Fitzwilliam to Queen Elizabeth, 25 Sept. 1572, PRO, SP 63/37, no. 59, p. 2; Morgan, "Colonial Venture," 263; Ellis, *Tudor Ireland,* 267.

133. Smith to Fitzwilliam, Nov. 8, 1572, no. 236, pp. 435–36.

134. Morgan, "Colonial Venture," 272.

135. Humphrey Gilbert, "The Discourse of Ireland" [1572], in Quinn, ed., *Voyages and Colonising Enterprises of Sir Humphrey Gilbert,* 1:128.

136. Robert Leicester, 26 Oct. [1572?], Bodleian, Carte MSS., 56, no. 97, pp. 220r, 220v, 221r.

137. Ibid., pp. 220v, 221v.

138. Robert Dudley, Earl of Leicester, to Fitzwilliam, Aug. 24, 1572, Bodleian Carte MSS., 57, no. 227, pp. 414–16.

139. Canny, *Elizabethan Conquest,* 102–3.

140. John Hooker, *The Irish Historie . . . unto 1587,* 433, quoted in Palmer, *Language and Conquest,* 124.

141. *Calendar of State Papers, Ireland,* 1574–85, p. xciv, in Palmer, *Language and Conquest,* 123.

142. Hooker, *The Irish Historie . . . unto 1587,* 459–60, quoted in Palmer, *Language and Conquest,* 124.

143. Essex to the queen, July 20, 1573, no. III, in Walter B. Devereux, *Lives and Letters of the Devereux, Earls of Essex in the Reigns of Elizabeth, James I, and Charles I, 1540–1646* (London, 1853), 32; Morgan, "Colonial Venture," 263.

144. Queen to William Fitzwilliam, July 17, 1573, Bodleian Library, Oxford, Carte MSS. 56, no. 260, pp. 565v, 566r, 565r.

145. Essex to the queen, July 20, 1573, 32.

146. Canny, "Ideology of English Colonization," 578.

147. Edward Berkeley to Burghley, May 14, 1574, PRO, SP 63/46, no. 15.

148. Queen to Essex, July 13, 1574, no. XII, in Devereux, *Lives and Letters of the Devereux,* 73–74.

149. Morgan, "Colonial Venture," 267.

150. Essex to Council, Oct. 12, 1574. British Library, Add 48015, fol. 313v.

151. Earl of Essex to Council, Oct. 8, 1574, British Library, Add 48015, fols. 314r–318r., pp. 1, 4–5.

152. Carey, "John Derricke's *Image of Irelande,*" 323–24; Ellis, *Tudor Ireland,* 267; Canny, "Ideology of English Colonization," 581.

153. Thomas Lee, *A Brief declaration to the government of Ireland* [1594], in *Desid. Cur. Hib.,* ii, 91, quoted in Carey, "John Derricke's *Image of Irelande,*" 323.

154. "Doubtes to be resolved by the Earle of Essex," undated, British Library, Add 48015, fols. 314/320.

155. "The annsweare of the Earle of Essex to the doubtes," pp. 4–5.

156. "The meanes howe my Lord of Essex . . . ," undated, British Library, Add 48015, fols. 337r–337v, p. 1.

157. "The annsweare of the Earle of Essex to the doubtes, "pp. 4, 6.

158. Ibid., p. 11.

159. "The Erle of Essex letter to my Lordes of the Counsell," Jan. 12, 1574[5], British Library, Add 48015, fols. 321r.–321v., pp. 1–2.

160. Leicester to Ashton, May 1575, PRO, SP 63/51/48, quoted in Canny, *Elizabethan Conquest,* 234–35.

161. "Instructions Given by Walter Devereux, earl of Essex, to Mr. Ashton Dispatched towards Queen Elizabeth and the Privy Council," June 1, 1575, PRO, SP 63/52, no. 5; fols. 14r–16r; Ellis, *Tudor Ireland,* 268.

162. "Instructions Given by Walter Devereux, earl of Essex, to Mr. Ashton," pp. 4–5.

163. Steven G. Ellis, *Ireland in the Age of the Tudors, 1447–1603* (London, 1998), 303; Canny, "Ideology of English Colonization," 580; Falls, *Elizabeth's Irish Wars,* 116.

164. Essex to the queen, from Newry, July 31, 1575, no. XXII, in Devereux, *Lives and Letters of the Devereux,* 113–17.

165. Walter Devereux, Earl of Essex, to the Privy Council, July 31, 1575, PRO, SP 63/52, no. 78.

166. Falls, *Elizabeth's Irish Wars,* 118–22, 116; Foster, *Modern Ireland,* 34.

167. Edwards, "Ideology and Experience," 133–34.

168. Brady, *Chief Governors,* 260–63; Carey, "John Derricke's *Image of Ireland,*" 310–12, 320.

169. Carey, "John Derricke's *Image of Ireland,*" 311, 317, 319–20.

170. Ibid., 318–21, quoting *Annals of the Four Masters,* the *Annals of Loch Ce,* and Thady Dowling's *Annales Hiberniae;* see also "Account of the massacre at Mullaghmast," Royal Irish Academy, MS 12.0.12, quoted in Brady, *Chief Governors,* 263–64.

171. Sidney, *A Viceroy's Vindication?* 101; Maley, "Apology for Sidney," 104.

172. Brady, *Chief Governors,* 283; Canny, *Making Ireland British,* 94; Sidney, *A Viceroy's Vindication?* 109.

173. Philip Sidney, "Discourse on Irish Affairs," in K. Duncan-Jones et al., eds., *Miscellaneous Prose of Sir Philip Sidney* (Oxford, 1973), 8–12.

174. Edwards, "Ideology and Experience," 134.

175. Gerrard to Walsingham, Feb. 8, 1577, PRO, SP 63/57/18, quoted in Canny, *Elizabethan Conquest,* 135.

176. "Lord Chancellor Gerrard's Notes of His Report on Ireland," *Analecta Hibernica* 2 (1931): 93–291, quoted in Palmer, *Language and Conquest,* 122–23; Bradshaw, "Sword, Word, and Strategy," 483.

177. Canny, *Making Ireland British,* 124; Canny, *Elizabethan Conquest,* 160.

178. Bradshaw, "Sword, Word, and Strategy," 479, 481, 484–88; Canny, *Elizabethan Conquest,* 3, 23.

179. Bradshaw, "Sword, Word, and Strategy," 489–90; Bradshaw, "The Elizabethans and the Irish," 49.

180. Canny, *Making Ireland British,* 66; Richard Berleth, *The Twilight Lords: Elizabeth I and the Plunder of Ireland* (Lanham, 2002), 31; Brady, *Chief Governors,* 276.

181. Churchyard, *A Generall Rehearsal of Warres,* quoted in Palmer, *Language and Conquest,* 123.

182. Ormonde and Pelham, in O'Faolain, *The Great O'Neill,* 101–2; Falls, *Elizabeth's Irish Wars,* 132–33.

183. Raymond Jenkins, "Spenser at Smerwick," *Times Literary Supplement,* May 11, 1933, 331.

184. Canny, *Making Ireland British,* 118–19.

185. Alexander C. Judson, *The Life of Edmund Spenser* (Baltimore, 1945) (vol. 11 of Greenlaw, *The Works of Edmund Spenser*), 84; Edwards, "Ideology and Experience," 134.

186. Hadfield and Maley, introduction to Spenser, *View of the State of Ireland,,* xiii; Falls, *Elizabeth's Irish Wars,* 144; Ellis, *Tudor Ireland,* 281–82; Ellis, *Ireland in the Age of the Tudors,* 316; Alfred O'Rahilly, *The Massacre at Smerwick (1580)* (Cork, 1938).

187. Grey to Elizabeth, Nov. 12, 1580, in A. Hatfield and J. McVeach, eds., *Strangers to that Land: British Perceptions of Ireland from the Reformation to the Famine* (Gerrards Cross, 1994), 102–4.

188. Spenser, *View of the State of Ireland,* 105, 101–2; Ellis, *Ireland in the Age of the Tudors,* 317; Canny, *Making Ireland British,* 71–72.

189. Edwards, "Ideology and Experience," 135; Ellis, *Ireland in the Age of the Tudors,* 317.

190. Canny, "Early Modern Ireland," 110; Spenser, *View of the State of Ireland,* 103; Edwards, "Ideology and Experience," 136.

191. Canny, *Making Ireland British,* 128, 133, 150; Edwards, "Ideology and Experience," 141–42.

192. Canny, *Making Ireland British,* 92; Canny, *Elizabethan Conquest,* 101–3; Canny, "Revising the Revisionist," 250.

193. Bradshaw, "Sword, Word, and Strategy," 484.

194. Sir John Perrott, "The cause why Irelande hathe continued so long disordere, and a meane to reforme the same," 1584, British Library, Add. Mss. 48015, fols. 291r–293r, pp. 1–3; Edwards, "Ideology and Experience," 137–39, 142.

195. Brady, *Chief Governors,* 207–9; Bradshaw, "Beginnings," 84–86; F. E. Adcock, "'Delenda Est Carthago,'" *Cambridge Historical Journal* 8:3 (1946): 117–28.

196. Edwards, "Ideology and Experience," 138.

197. Falls, *Elizabeth's Irish Wars,* 160–61, put the toll at 1,400 Scots fighters and "nearly as many more camp-followers, women and children"; Berleth, *Twilight Lords,* 209–10, says 1,000.

198. Palmer, *Language and Conquest,* 78, 124; Edwards, "Ideology and Experience," 141.

199. Bradshaw, "Sword, Word, and Strategy," 483–84; Edwards, "Ideology and Experience," 138.

200. Canny, *Making Ireland British,* 95; Edwards, "Ideology and Experience," 141.

201. Canny, *Making Ireland British,* 91; Bradshaw, "Sword, Word, and Strategy," 481.

202. Edwards, "Ideology and Experience," 142.

203. White, "Discors Touching Ireland," 460–63; Brady, *Chief Governors,* 297.

204. Ciaran Brady, "Spenser's Irish Crisis: Humanism and Experience in the 1590s," *Past and Present* 111 (1986): 24; Bradshaw, "Robe and Sword," 142–48, 150, 153; Canny, *Making Ireland British,* 123. In many ways, Herbert's treatise was a later, less moderate version of White's *Discors Touching Ireland,* 460–63.

205. Brady, "Spenser's Irish Crisis," 24; cf. Bradshaw, "Robe and Sword," 152.

206. Canny, *Making Ireland British,* 153–54, 142, 150, 157–58.

207. Bradshaw, "Robe and Sword," 152–53; Nicholas Canny, "Edmund Spenser and the Development of an Anglo-Irish Identity," *Yearbook of English Studies,* I, *Colonial and Imperial Themes,* vol. 13, 1983, 1–19, at 8.

208. Bradshaw, "Robe and Sword," 154; Brady, "Spenser's Irish Crisis," 24.

209. Canny, *Making Ireland British,* 74; Lacey, *Robert, Earl of Essex,* 224; John McGurk, *The Elizabethan Conquest of Ireland: The 1590s Crisis* (Manchester, 1997), 264, 244–45; Spenser, *View of the State of Ireland,* 94n.

210. Hadfield and Maley, introduction to Spenser, *A View of the Present State of Ireland,* xi; Brady, "Spenser's Irish Crisis," 26n33, 24–25.

211. Spenser, *View of the State of Ireland,* 92–93, 99–101, 135, 152.

212. Edwards, "Ideology and Experience," 150–55; McGurk, *Elizabethan Conquest,* 250.

213. Falls, *Elizabeth's Irish Wars,* 322–23; Morton, *Elizabethan Ireland,* 129–30.

214. Foster, *Modern Ireland,* 34–35; McGurk, *Elizabethan Conquest,* 243; Falls, *Elizabeth's Irish Wars,* 335; Morton, *Elizabethan Ireland,* 134–36; Canny, *Making Ireland British,* 167.

215. Morton, *Elizabethan Ireland,* 91; Falls, *Elizabeth's Irish Wars,* 326.

216. Mountjoy to Carew, July 2, 1602, *Calendar of Carew mss, 1601–3,* 263–64, quoted in Vincent P. Carey, " 'What Pen Can Paint or Tears Atone?': Mountjoy's Scorched Earth Campaign" [1602–3], in Hiram Morgan, ed., *The Battle of Kinsale* (Wordwell, 2004), 210–11.

217. Mountjoy and Council to Privy Council, July 29, 1602, *Calendar of Carew mss, 1601–3,* 282–84, in Carey, " 'What Pen?' " 211.

218. Fynes Moryson, *An itinerary containing his ten yeeres travell through the twelve dominions of Germany, Bohmerland, Scotland and Ireland* (Glasgow, 1907), 3:260, in Carey, " 'What Pen?' " 212.

219. Morton, *Elizabethan Ireland,* 135; Ellis, *Tudor Ireland,* 311.

220. Jones, *O Strange New World,* 173–74; Ronald Dale Karr, " 'Why Should You Be So Furious?' The Violence of the Pequot War," *Journal of American History* 85:3 (1998): 887; Canny, *Making Ireland British,* 163, 166.

221. Foster, *Modern Ireland,* 34–35, Mountjoy to Privy Council, Feb. 25, 1603; Moryson, *An itinerary,* 3:277, quoted in Carey, " 'What Pen?' " 213.

222. Canny, *Making Ireland British,* 184.

223. Davies, *Discoverie of the True Causes,* 102, 8–9.

224. Nicholas Canny, *Kingdom and Colony: Ireland in the Atlantic World, 1560–1800* (Baltimore, 1988), 44.

225. Davies, *Discoverie of the True Causes,* 278, 268–69; Canny, *Elizabethan Conquest,* 1.

Chapter 6. Colonial North America, 1600–1776

1. Francis Jennings, *The Invasion of America: Indians, Colonialism, and the Cant of Conquest* (New York, 1975), 5.

2. Humphrey Gilbert, "A Discourse of a Discoverie for New Passage to Cataia" [April 1576], in David B. Quinn, ed., *The Voyages and Colonising Enterprises of Sir Humphrey Gilbert* (London, 1940), 1:154–55.

3. Ivor Noel Hume, *The Virginia Adventure* (Charlottesville, 1994), 21.

4. David B. Quinn, ed., *The Roanoke Voyages, 1584–1590* (New York, 1991), 2:497; Hume, *Virginia Adventure,* 21–23.

5. Hume, *Virginia Adventure,* 23, 28; Raleigh Trevelyan, *Sir Walter Raleigh* (New York, 2004), 1; Hume, *Virginia Adventure,* 45; Edmund Morgan, *American Slavery, American Freedom* (New York, 1975), 35.

6. David B. Quinn, "Ireland and Sixteenth Century European Expansion," *Historical Studies*

1 (1958): 32n17; Morgan, *American Slavery,* 32; Nicholas P. Canny, *The Elizabethan Conquest of Ireland: A Pattern Established, 1565–1576* (Sussex, 1976), 101; Trevelyan, *Sir Walter Raleigh,* 1, 7; Canny, *Making Ireland British, 1580–1650* (Oxford, 2001), 83, 110.

    7. Morgan, *American Slavery,* 36, 38–39, 41–42, 37.

    8. Alden Vaughan, *Roots of American Racism: Essays on the Colonial Experience* (New York, 1995), 45.

    9. Hume, *Virginia Adventure,* 29; Howard M. Jones, *O Strange New World: American Culture, the Formative Years* (New York, 1964), 174; Canny, *Making Ireland British,* 84–85, 144, 157.

    10. Sir Walter Ralegh, *The History of the World in Five Books* (London, 1614); abridged in Ralegh, *The History of the World,* ed. C. A. Patrides (London, 1971), 9–12, 49–50, 364.

    11. Vaughan, *Roots,* 44; Neal Salisbury, "Native People and European Settlers in Eastern North America, 1600–1783," in B. Trigger and W. Washburn, eds., *Cambridge History of the Native Peoples of the Americas,* vol. 1, *North America* (New York, 1996–99), 401–2, 433.

    12. Mason Wade, "French Indian Policies," in Wilcomb E. Washburn, ed., *History of Indian-White Relations,* vol. 4 of *Handbook of North American Indians* (Washington, 1988), 26.

    13. Neal Salisbury, *Manitou and Providence: Indians, Europeans, and the Making of New England, 1500–1643* (New York, 1982), 91–92, 95; Jennings, *Invasion,* 107; Jones, *O Strange New World,* 173–74, adds Carleill. Popham, a Munster planter, also turned to New England (Salisbury, *Manitou,* 92, 96); Canny, *Making Ireland British,* 58, 163, 166, 206–7, 213, 426; Ronald Dale Karr, "'Why Should You Be So Furious?' The Violence of the Pequot War," *Journal of American History* 85:3 (1998): 887. Cf. Vaughan, *Roots,* 40–44.

    14. W. B. Hunter Jr., ed., *The English Spenserians* (Salt Lake City, 1977), 1–2, 198–99, 223–25, 244–49.

    15. Anthony F. C. Wallace, *The Long, Bitter Trail: Andrew Jackson and the Indians* (New York, 1993), 16, 18–19, 44.

    16. Ralph Lane wrote back to Sir Francis Walsingham in 1585 that Virginian produce was "of pryce in Christendom," or at least "to the smelle pleasing." Morgan, *American Slavery,* 36.

    17. Lane to Richard Hakluyt, Sept. 3, 1585, in D. B. Quinn and A. Quinn, eds., *The First Colonists: Documents on the Planting of the First English Settlements in North America, 1584–1590* (Raleigh, 1982), 22.

    18. Another early sponsor of English settlement said: "God did create lande, to the end that it sholde by Culture and husbandrie, yeeld things necessary for mans lyfe." Morgan, *American Slavery,* 22–24.

    19. Patricia Seed, *American Pentimento: The Invention of Indians and the Pursuit of Riches* (Minneapolis, 2001), 13; Lane to Hakluyt, Sept. 3, 1585, in *The First Colonists,* 22; James Q. Wilson, *The Earth Shall Weep: A History of Native America* (New York 1998), 64.

    20. April Lee Hatfield, "Spanish Colonization Literature, Powhatan Geographies, and English Perceptions of Tsenacommacah/Virginia," *Journal of Southern History* 69:2 (2003): 272; Wilson, *The Earth,* 49, 73; Karen O. Kupperman, *Indians and English: Facing Off in Early America* (Ithaca, 2000), 143, cf. 155; William Bradford, *Bradford's History of the Plymouth Settlement, 1608–1650* (New York, 1920), 86, 110.

    21. Edward Waterhouse, *A Declaration of the State of the Colony and Affaires in Virginia,* quoted in Paul R. Bartrop, "The Powhatans of Virginia and the English Invasion of America," in Colin Tatz, ed., *Genocide Perspectives* (Sydney, 1997), 1:81; Wilson, *The Earth,* 71.

    22. Robert Cushman, "Reasons and Considerations touching the lawfulness of removing out of England and into the parts of America" [1622], in John Demos, *Remarkable Providences: Readings in Early American History* (Boston, 1991), 6–7; *Mourt's Relation, or a Journal of the Plantation of Plymouth* (London, 1622), quoted in David E. Stannard, *American Holocaust: The Conquest of the New World* (New York, 1992), 235.

    23. Stannard, *American Holocaust,* 235–36; Jennings, *Invasion,* 135–38, 28; Seed, *American Pentimento,* 14.

    24. *Bradford's History,* 80; William Wood, *New England's Prospect* (London, 1634; Amherst, 1977), 89; Wilson, *The Earth,* 84–85; Seed, *American Pentimento,* 17.

    25. Lion Gardener's narrative, in *History of the Pequot War: The Contemporary Accounts of*

Mason, Underhill, Vincent, and Gardener, Massachusetts Historical Society, 3, Mass. Hist. Coll., 3 (1833; repr. 1980): 142; Colin G. Calloway, *The American Revolution in Indian Country: Crisis and Diversity in Native American Communities* (New York, 1995), 4.

26. A 1636 English view quoted in Kirkpatrick Sale, *The Conquest of Paradise* (New York, 1990), 286.

27. Quoted in James Muldoon, "The Indian as Irishman," *Essex Institute Historical Collections* 111 (1975): 282.

28. Wilson, *The Earth,* 62; Sale, *Conquest,* 305–6; Bartrop, "Powhatans," 68, cites estimates of 12,000–14,000.

29. Russell Thornton, *American Indian Holocaust and Survival: A Population History since 1492* (Norman, 1987), 36, 133; Wilson, *The Earth,* 20, cites estimates for the 1492 population ranging from 2 to 18 million.

30. Morgan, *American Slavery,* 46–47; David Price, *Love and Hate in Jamestown* (New York, 2003), quoted in Caleb Crain, "He That Will Not Worke Shall Not Eate," *New York Times Book Review,* Oct. 19, 2003, 13.

31. Hatfield, "Spanish Colonization Literature," 257, 265–66, 271.

32. Frederic W. Gleach, *Powhatan's World and Colonial Virginia* (Lincoln, 1997), 129; Bartrop, "Powhatans," 72–73; Morgan, *American Slavery,* 71–73; Hatfield, "Spanish Colonization Literature," 266.

33. Jones, *O Strange New World,* 174; Sale, *Conquest,* 278.

34. Hatfield, "Spanish Colonization Literature," 271.

35. Morgan, *American Slavery,* 73–74; Stannard, *American Holocaust,* 106.

36. Morgan, *American Slavery,* 74, 78, 130; Hatfield, "Spanish Colonization Literature," 259, 270, 273; Wilson, *The Earth,* 69; Bartrop, "Powhatans," 74.

37. Hatfield, "Spanish Colonization Literature," 276–79.

38. Bartrop, "Powhatans," 77; James Axtell, *The European and the Indian: Essays in the Ethnohistory of Colonial North America* (New York, 1981), 313; Morgan, *American Slavery,* 130, 99–100.

39. Hatfield, "Spanish Colonization Literature," 280; Wilson, *The Earth,* 71; Bartrop, "Powhatans," 82, 67.

40. Waterhouse, *A Declaration of the State of the Colony,* quoted in Bartrop, "Powhatans," 81–82, and Gleach, *Powhatan's World,* 159; Canny, *Elizabethan Conquest,* 161.

41. Bartrop, "Powhatans," 82–83; see Michael Drayton's elegy "To Master George Sandys," uncle of Wyat's wife, in Hunter, *The English Spenserians,* 248.

42. James Axtell, *After Columbus: Essays in the Ethnohistory of Colonial North America* (New York, 1988), 218–19; Morgan, *American Slavery,* 100; Bartrop, "Powhatans," 84; Stannard, *American Holocaust,* 107.

43. Hatfield, "Spanish Colonization Literature," 270.

44. Richard Eburne, *A Plaine Pathway to Plantations* [1624], quoted in Gleach, *Powhatan's World,* 123.

45. Morgan, *American Slavery,* 136, 149, 328, 231; Hatfield, "Spanish Colonization Literature," 281; Bartrop, "Powhatans," 83–88.

46. Bartrop, "Powhatans," argues that they "were victims of destruction on a genocidal scale, but they were not victims of genocide" (98, 92, 94).

47. Berkeley, quoted in Morgan, *American Slavery,* 233, and Henry Wiencek, *An Imperfect God: George Washington, His Slaves, and the Creation of America* (New York, 2003), 42.

48. Morgan, *American Slavery,* 250–55, 259, 266, 268.

49. Ibid., 260, 264, 329–30; Sale, *Conquest,* 294; Rhys Isaac, *The Transformation of Virginia, 1740–1790* (Chapel Hill, 1999), 12, 14; Bartrop, "Powhatans," 96.

50. Robert Beverley, *History and Present State of Virginia* (London, 1705), quoted in Isaac, *Transformation of Virginia,* 13–15, 19.

51. Rev. Hugh Jones, *The Present State of Virginia* [1724], quoted in Isaac, *Transformation of Virginia,* 15–16, and excerpts in Demos, *Remarkable Providences,* 300–1.

52. *The Official Letters of Alexander Spotswood,* ed. R. A. Brock, *Collections of the Virginia Historical Society,* n.s., 1 (1882): 134, quoted in Axtell, *The European and the Indian,* 314; Isaac, *Transformation of Virginia,* 111; Morgan, *American Slavery,* 359–60.

53. John Winthrop, quoted in James Muldoon, "The Indian as Irishman," 279–80; Wilson, *The Earth,* 78.

54. Vaughan, *Roots,* 197; Wilson, *The Earth,* 71; Salisbury, *Manitou,* 108.

55. *Bradford's History,* 86; Wilson, *The Earth,* 72–77.

56. Treaty of Mar. 22, 1621, in Alden Vaughan, *New England Frontier: Puritans and Indians 1620–1675,* 3rd ed. (Norman, 1995), 339; Wilson, *The Earth,* 80–85.

57. *Bradford's History,* 84–85. See also James Axtell, "The Scholastic Philosophy of the Wilderness," *William and Mary Quarterly,* 3rd ser., 29:3 (1972): 337.

58. Jennings, *Invasion,* 186–87, citing George F. Willison, *Saints and Strangers* (New York, 1945), ch. 15; *Bradford's History,* 112–13; Salisbury, *Manitou,* 123.

59. Axtell, "The Scholastic Philosophy of the Wilderness," 339–40; Wilson, *The Earth,* 83–86.

60. Jennings, *Invasion,* 189.

61. Lion Gardener's narrative, in *History of the Pequot War,* 114, 123–24; Alfred A. Cave, *The Pequot War* (Amherst, 1996), 58–59; John A. Strong, *The Algonquian Peoples of Long Island from Earliest Times to 1700* (Interlaken, 1997), 155.

62. Karr, " 'Why Should You Be So Furious?' " 899–900; Cave, *Pequot War,* 109; Jennings, *Invasion,* 209–10.

63. Gardener's narrative, in *History of the Pequot War,* 126; Underhill's narrative, in Jennings, *Invasion,* 211.

64. Vaughan, *Roots,* 186; Karr, " 'Why Should You Be So Furious?' " 899–902.

65. Gardener's narrative, in *History of the Pequot War,* 127–28, 139.

66. Maj. John Mason, *A Brief History of the Pequot War* (Boston, 1736), 18; cf. Steven T. Katz, "The Pequot War Reconsidered," *New England Quarterly* 64 (1991): 212. Cave writes: "Pequot acts of war followed, rather than preceded, English aggression" (*Pequot War,* 119). Vaughan sees responsibility on both sides: "But most of all, the Bay colony's gross escalation of violence and of excessive demands for prisoners and reparations made all-out war unavoidable" (*Roots,* 194). Jill Lepore notes "the contrived basis for the Pequot War" (*The Name of War* [New York, 1999], 258n15).

67. Mason, *Brief History,* 18–19; Gardener, in *History of the Pequot War,* 132; *Bradford's History,* 286; Vaughan, *Roots,* 182; Salisbury, *Manitou,* 219; Cave, *Pequot War,* 133; Wilson, *The Earth,* 87–89.

68. Jennings, *Invasion,* 217; Mason, *Brief History,* 19, calls it "an offensive and defensive War."

69. Winthrop to Bradford, May 20, 1637, in *Bradford's History,* 284. Cave, *Pequot War,* 138–39, terms this a "repeated warning."

70. Cave, *Pequot War,* 137; Mason, *Brief History,* 20–22, 28. See Jennings, *Invasion,* 220.

71. Jennings, *Invasion,* 222; for a different view, see Cave, *Pequot War,* 209–10; Sale, *Conquest,* 319.

72. Mason, *Brief History,* 25–27, 35, 27–29; Jennings, *Invasion,* 222–23; Wilson, *The Earth,* 90; Cave, *Pequot War,* 210.

73. Mason, *Brief History,* 30.

74. Underhill, quoted in Laurence M. Hauptman, "The Pequot War and Its Legacies," in Hauptman and James D. Wherry, eds., *The Pequots in Southern New England: The Fall and Rise of an American Indian Nation* (Norman, 1990), 73.

75. Underhill, quoted in Jennings, *Invasion,* 223, and in Cave, *Pequot War,* 150.

76. Cave, *Pequot War,* 151–52.

77. Mason, *Brief History,* 35, 30–31; Underhill's narrative, quoted in Jennings, *Invasion,* 223.

78. Cave, *Pequot War,* 151; *Bradford's History,* 287. Winthrop, also absent, tallied the dead at 150 "fighting men, and about one hundred and fifty old men, women and children" (Jennings, *Invasion,* 222n57). Gardener, not present either, wrote that Mason's forces had "slain three hundred, burnt their fort, and taken many prisoners" (*History of the Pequot War,* 137). Over 500 dependents for 150 Pequot warriors seems a reasonable ratio. Dependents of the 450 or more warriors at both forts would normally have exceeded 2,000, including some in the other fort. Mason estimated "the Enemy from the other Fort: Three Hundred or more" warriors (*Brief History,* 31). Vaughan put the toll at perhaps 500 "Pequot men, women, and children" (*Roots,* 178).

79. John Underhill, *Newes from America* (London, 1638), in Jennings, *Invasion,* 224. The sketch shows 55 English soldiers firing guns, 20 Pequots with bows and arrows and none with fire-

arms, and in the outer encirclement, 55 Indian allies of the English drawing bows and arrows (see fig. 5). In the first wigwam Mason entered, "he was beset with many Indians.... At length William Heydon espying the Breach in the Wigwam, supposing some English might be there, entered; but in his Entrance fell over a dead Indian; but speedily recovering himself, the Indians some fled, others crept under their Beds." Mason, *Brief History*, 28, 31; Jennings, *Invasion*, 225.

80. Mason, *Brief History*, 31; Cave, *Pequot War*, 152–53; Jennings, *Invasion*, 223; *Bradford's History*, 287–88.

81. Mason, *Brief History*, 31, 32, 34; Cave, *Pequot War*, 154–55, 157.

82. Gardener's narrative, in *History of the Pequot War*, 137–38, 141. Writing in 1660, Gardener lamented that Wyandanch, "your trusty friend, is . . . persecuted to this day with fire and sword" (147).

83. Jennings, *Invasion*, 226n65, 225–26.

84. Philip Vincent, "A True Relation of the Late Battell Fought in New England" [1638], quoted in Adam J. Hirsh, "The Collision of Military Cultures in Seventeenth Century New England," *Journal of American History* 74:4 (1988): 1198; Wilson, *The Earth*, 92; Cave, *Pequot War*, 158.

85. Hubbard, *Narrative* (1677), 127, quoted in Jennings, *Invasion*, 226; Vaughan, *New England Frontier*, 148, says 22 of 24 braves were executed.

86. Mason, *Brief History*, 36, 37–39; Winthrop to Bradford, July 28, 1637, in *Bradford's History*, 289.

87. Winthrop to Bradford, July 28, 1637, 290.

88. Vaughan sources this massacre account to Hubbard (1677), who cites "some that are yet living and worthy of credit" (*New England Frontier*, 149, 375n56). See Jennings, *Invasion*, 144n55, and Winthrop to Bradford, July 28, 1637, 289–90. Mason describes several fights and "Tumult growing to a very great Heighth," but adds: "We afterwards searched the Swamp, and found but few Slain" (*Brief History*, 39).

89. Mason, *Brief History*, 39, says 60–70 escaped; Vaughan, *New England Frontier*, 149, says 20–30; Winthrop, in *Bradford's History*, 290, says "not twenty escaped"; Cave, *Pequot War*, 161, says Sassacus and 41 others reached the Hudson valley.

90. Winthrop to Bradford, July 28, 1637, 290–91.

91. Gardener, in *History of the Pequot War*, 138; Cave, *Pequot War*, 161; Mason, *Brief History*, 39–40.

92. Cave, *Pequot War*, 162; "nor should any of them be called Pequots any more, but Moheags and Narragansetts forever." Mason, *Brief History*, 40; Jennings, *Invasion*, 226; Stannard, *American Holocaust*, 115.

93. Kevin McBride, "The Historical Archaeology of the Mashantucket Pequots, 1637–1900," in Hauptman and Wherry, *The Pequots*, 104–5; Jennings, *Invasion*, 226.

94. Treaty of Hartford, Sept. 21, 1638, in Vaughan, *New England Frontier*, 341.

95. Vaughan, *New England Frontier*, 341; Hirsh, "Collision of Military Cultures," 1198.

96. William T. Williams, letters dated July 19 and 23, 1832, in *History of the Pequot War*, 120.

97. Vaughan, *New England Frontier*, 152. When some Pequots resettled "at Pawcatuck, a Place in Pequot Country, contrary to their late Covenant," Connecticut authorities sent Mason with 40 men "to supplant them, by burning their Wigwams and bringing away their corn," which he did. Mason concluded that "the Lord was pleased to . . . give us their Land for an Inheritance" (*Brief History*, 40–44).

98. Roger Williams, quoted in Hirsh, "Collision of Military Cultures," 1198.

99. Karr, " 'Why Should You Be So Furious?' " 894; McBride, "Historical Archaeology," 105. Before the English arrival, elderly Indians told the supervisor of Massachusetts' mission reservations in 1674, the Pequots could "raise four thousand men, fit for war." A 1633–34 smallpox epidemic killed up to three quarters of the tribe. Jennings, *Invasion*, 26; Vaughan, *Roots*, 187; Karr, " 'Why Should You Be So Furious?' " 895n53.

100. McBride, "Historical Archaeology," 105; Hauptman, "The Pequot War and Its Legacies," 76; Underhill, quoted in Cave, *Pequot War*, 169; Mason, *Brief History*, 40.

101. Quoted in Axtell, *The European and the Indian*, 313.

102. Mason, *Brief History*, 39; McBride, "Historical Archaeology," 105; John A. Strong, *The*

Montaukett Indians of Eastern Long Island (Syracuse, 2001), 13; McBride, "Historical Archaeology," 105–6.

103. Jack Campisi, "The Emergence of the Mashantucket Pequot Tribe, 1637–1975," in Hauptman and Wherry, *The Pequots*, 118–19. The 1672 diary of Stonington farmer Thomas Minor reveals little of the nearby Pequots beyond his visit to "Mr. Stanton's house about his Indian Jean," and his return months later on "Indian business." We don't know why "the committee met with squmacut people" in July 1672. "Diary of Thomas Minor" [1672], in Demos, *Remarkable Providences*, 124–26.

104. Jennings, *Invasion*, 26; McBride, "Historical Archaeology," 107; Campisi, "Mashantucket," 124–25.

105. David Pieterszoon De Vries, *Short Historical and Journal Notes of Several Voyages . . .* [1655], tr. H. C. Murphy, in *New-York Historical Society Collections*, 2nd ser., 3 (1857): 114; Strong, *The Algonquian Peoples of Long Island*, 176–77.

106. De Vries, *Short Historical and Journal Notes*, 114–15.

107. John Fiske, *The Dutch and Quaker Colonies in America* (Boston, 1899), 1:184–85; De Vries, *Short Historical and Journal Notes*, quoted in Jennings, *Invasion*, 164–65.

108. David Pieterszoon De Vries, quoted in Strong, *The Algonquian Peoples of Long Island*, 177–78.

109. De Vries, *Short Historical and Journal Notes*, 114; Strong, *The Algonquian Peoples of Long Island*, 178.

110. Fiske, *The Dutch and Quaker Colonies*, 1:184–85; Chandler Whipple, *The Indian and the White Man in Connecticut* (Stockbridge, 1972), 74, dates this to 1634.

111. Fiske, *The Dutch and Quaker Colonies*, 1:187–88; Strong, *The Algonquian Peoples of Long Island*, 183–84; Whipple, *The Indian and the White Man*, 74; Stannard, *American Holocaust*, 115, quoting Richard Drinnon, *Facing West: The Metaphysics of Indian Hating and Empire Building* (Minneapolis, 1980), 46–47.

112. Jennings, *Invasion*, 29 (1674 research of Daniel Gookin); second code of laws of Massachusetts Bay Colony, 1648, in Vaughan, *New England Frontier*, 344; Strong, *Montaukett Indians*, 20, 23, 34, 36, 45.

113. Second code of laws of Massachusetts Bay Colony, 1648, in Vaughan, *New England Frontier*, 345; Jennings, *Invasion*, 277; Wilson, *The Earth*, 95; Strong, *Montaukett Indians*, 33; Wilson, *The Earth*, 95.

114. Joshua Moodey, quoted in Jill Lepore, *Name of War*, 121.

115. Jennings, *Invasion*, 299, 302ff., 308–9, 326, 299; James D. Drake, *King Philip's War: Civil War in New England, 1675–1676* (Amherst, 1999), 109, 155.

116. Order of a Boston council, Aug. 30, 1675, quoted in Muldoon, "The Indian as Irishman," 286.

117. Axtell, "The Scholastic Philosophy of the Wilderness," 349; Wilson, *The Earth*, 97.

118. Increase Mather, quoted in Axtell, "Scholastic Philosophy of the Wilderness," 344.

119. Jennings, *Invasion*, 26, 302–5, 307–8, 310–11, 312 (quoting Samuel Gorton to Winthrop, Sept. 11, 1675).

120. *Letters of Roger Williams, 1632–1682, Publications of the Narragansett Club* (Providence), 1st ser., 6 (1874): 380–81n1, quoting Holmes, *Annals*, 1:575–76; Lepore, *Name of War*, 88.

121. *Letters of Roger Williams*, 381, 380n1; Lepore, *Name of War*, 88.

122. *News from New-England*, and Benjamin Tompson, *New England's Crisis* (Boston, 1676), 223–24, both quoted in Lepore, *Name of War*, 281n75, 89.

123. *Letters of Roger Williams*, 381; Jennings, *Invasion*, 312n43; Col. Benjamin Church, *Diary of King Philip's War 1675–1676* (Boston, 1716; Chester, 1975), 101–2.

124. Drake, *King Philip's War*, 119; Jennings, *Invasion*, 312; *Letters of Roger Williams*, 380n1; Lepore, *Name of War*, 281n74.

125. Jennings, *Invasion*, 313, 319; Drake, *King Philip's War*, 151.

126. *A True Account of the Most Considerable Occurrences that have Hapned in the Warre Between the English and the Indians in New England* (London, 1676), 3–4, quoted in Stannard, *American Holocaust*, 116; see also Drake, *King Philip's War*, 151; Jennings, *Invasion*, 319.

127. Connecticut's instructions to Talcott, May 24, 1676, quoted in Jennings, *Invasion*, 319.

128. Talcott to Connecticut Council, July 4, 1676, in Jennings, *Invasion,* 319–20; Drake, *King Philip's War,* 155.

129. Jennings, *Invasion,* 322–23. In 1737, Connecticut established a reservation for over 300 Schagticokes. "U.S. Agency Recognizes a Fourth Tribe in Connecticut," *New York Times,* Jan. 30, 2004, B1, B5.

130. Drake, *King Philip's War,* 156–57, 138, 161–62; Axtell, "Scholastic Philosophy of the Wilderness," 350.

131. Jennings, *Invasion,* 324n38; he gives a 1674 population range of 8,600–10,750 (29).

132. Quoted in Stannard, *American Holocaust,* 117.

133. Drake, *King Philip's War,* 158, 136–39, 160; Lepore, *Name of War,* 163, 168, 170; see also Strong, *The Algonquian Peoples of Long Island,* 279–82.

134. Quoted in Axtell, "Scholastic Philosophy of the Wilderness," 358, 348–49.

135. Ibid., 340, 361, 344.

136. Muldoon, "The Indian as Irishman," 288.

137. *The Official Letters of Alexander Spotswood,* 134, quoted in Axtell, *The European and the Indian,* 314; Isaac, *Transformation of Virginia,* 111; Morgan, *American Slavery,* 359–60.

138. Rev. Solomon Stoddard to Gov. Joseph Dudley, Northampton, Oct. 22, 1703, in Demos, *Remarkable Providences,* 372–74; Axtell, "Scholastic Philosophy of the Wilderness," 344–45, 351.

139. Strong, *The Algonquian Peoples of Long Island,* 281; Jennings, *Invasion,* 26–27.

140. Strong, *Montaukett Indians,* 33, 38–41, 56–61; Montauketts claimed they had not received the payment for this land even after 1700. Strong, *Algonquian Peoples of Long Island,* 260–61.

141. Philip Rabito-Wyppensenwah, "The Hannibals: A Montaukett Family," in Gaynell Stone, ed., *The History and Archaeology of the Montauk* (Stony Brook, 1993), 355, 349; Strong, *Montaukett Indians,* 46, 60; Strong, *Algonquian Peoples of Long Island,* 260–61.

142. Rabito-Wyppensenwah, "The Hannibals," 349–50.

143. John Locke, "Of Property," in *Second Treatise of Government* [1690], ch. V.

144. *New York Weekly Post Boy,* June 7, 1746, quoted in Chester E. Eisinger, "The Freehold Concept in Eighteenth-Century American Letters," *William and Mary Quarterly* 4 (Jan. 1947): 47.

145. Woody Holton, "The Ohio Indians and the Coming of the American Revolution in Virginia," *Journal of Southern History* 60:3 (1994): 456, 458; John Mack Faragher, *A Great and Noble Scheme: The Tragic Story of the Expulsion of the French Acadians from their American Homeland* (New York, 2005), 473.

146. Colin G. Calloway, *The American Revolution in Indian Country* (New York, 1995), 39; Howard H. Peckham, *Pontiac and the Indian Uprising* (Princeton, 1947), 171–74; B. M. Pritzker, *A Native American Encyclopedia* (New York, 2000), 470, 478.

147. Gen. Jeffrey Amherst, quoted in Peckham, *Pontiac,* 226, citing Amherst Papers, PRO, WO34, LIV, 171; Edmund S. Morgan, *Benjamin Franklin* (New Haven, 2002), 131.

148. Elizabeth A. Fenn, "Biological Warfare in Eighteenth Century North America," *Journal of American History* 86:4 (2000): 1555–56, 1574–75; Morgan, *Benjamin Franklin,* 131.

149. Fenn, "Biological Warfare," 1554–58; Calloway, *American Revolution in Indian Country,* 5n13.

150. Amherst, quoted in Peckham, *Pontiac,* 227; letters of Aug. 7 and 27, 1763, in Fenn, "Biological Warfare," 1574.

151. Benjamin Franklin, *A Narrative of the Late Massacres, in Lancaster County, of a Number of Indians, Friends of This Province . . .* (Philadelphia, 1764), in Wilcomb E. Washburn, ed., *The Indian and the White Man* (New York, 1964), 246–48; Walter Isaacson, *Benjamin Franklin* (New York, 2003), 211.

152. Franklin, *A Narrative of the Late Massacres,* 249–50; Gregory Evans Dowd, *War under Heaven: Pontiac, the Indian Nations, and the British Empire* (Baltimore, 2002), 193.

153. Franklin, *A Narrative of the Late Massacres,* 253–56.

154. Isaacson, *Benjamin Franklin,* 212; Franklin, *A Narrative of the Late Massacres,* 254–58; Gage to Bouquet, Sept. 2, 1764, quoted in Dowd, *War under Heaven,* 162–63; Morgan, *Benjamin Franklin,* 131.

155. Isaacson, *Benjamin Franklin,* 213.

156. Holton, "Ohio Indians," 453–55, 478, 475, 458, 461, 467–70, 476 (Washington to Dunmore, June 15, 1772).

157. Ibid., 462–67, 473–74; Richard White, *The Middle Ground: Indians, Empires, and Republics in the Great Lakes Region, 1650–1815* (New York, 1991), 357–58; Anthony F. C. Wallace, *Jefferson and the Indians: The Tragic Fate of the First Americans* (Cambridge, 1999), 53.

158. Knox to Washington, Dec. 29, 1794, *American State Papers, 7, Indian Affairs* 1:543–44.

Chapter 7. Genocidal Violence in Nineteenth-Century Australia

1. D. J. Mulvaney, "The Australian Aborigines, 1606–1929," *Historical Studies* 8 (1958): 135; M. F. Christie, *Aborigines in Colonial Victoria, 1835–86* (Sydney, 1979), 35. See also W. S. Ransom, ed., *The Australian National Dictionary* (Melbourne, 1988), 1–3.

2. *The Journals of Captain Cook*, vol. 1, quoted in D. J. Mulvaney and Peter White, eds., *Australians to 1788* (Sydney, 1987), 343, and Mulvaney, "Australian Aborigines, 1606–1929," 137.

3. P. White and D. J. Mulvaney, *Sydney Morning Herald*, Feb. 25, 1987. Radcliff-Brown's 1930 estimate of 300,000 Aborigines in 1788 is widely rejected. Noel Butlin, *Our Original Aggression: Aboriginal Populations of Southeastern Australia, 1788–1850* (Sydney, 1983), estimates 1 million; Colin Tatz, "probably 500,000" (*Encyclopedia of Genocide*, ed. I. W. Charny [Oxford, 1999], 111); Robert Murray cites "half a million to one million" ("Seven Myths about Australia," *Quadrant* 286 [1992]: 40–41); cf. W. D. Borrie, "Population," in *Australian Encyclopedia* (Sydney, 1988), 2352–53. Using different methods, Henry Reynolds, *The Other Side of the Frontier: Aboriginal Resistance to the European Invasion of Australia* (Ringwood, 1982), 122–23, 200, and Richard Broome, "The Struggle for Australia: Aboriginal-European Warfare," in M. McKernan et al., eds., *Australia: Two Centuries of War and Peace* (Sydney, 1988), 116–20, both estimate 20,000 or more Aborigines killed. Murray notes "the shooting of 20,000 Aborigines—or even twice that number, as is possible" ("Seven Myths," 40–41). In possibly the largest massacres of whites, Aborigines killed 12 in South Australia in 1840 and 19 in Queensland in 1861 (Reynolds, *Other Side*, 121, 79–81).

4. C. D. Rowley and H. Reynolds, "Aborigines since 1788," in *Australian Encyclopedia*, 280; Rowley, *The Destruction of Aboriginal Society* (Ringwood, 1972), 54.

5. Rowley, *Destruction*, 53, 29, 34, 44, 46, noting a frontier premise that "non-Aboriginal land claims override Aboriginal rights to life" (154); A. McGrath et al., "Aboriginal Workers," *Labour History* 69 (1995).

6. Mulvaney, "Australian Aborigines, 1606–1929," 136; Lyndall Ryan, *The Aboriginal Tasmanians* (St. Lucia, 1981), 75.

7. R. H. W. Reece, " 'Laws of the White People:' The Frontier of Authority in Perth in 1838," *Push from the Bush* 17 (1984): 27n37; Rowley, *Destruction*, 30.

8. Rowley and Reynolds, "Aborigines since 1788," 280; R. Hughes, *The Fatal Shore* (New York, 1988), 275; c.f. J. B. Hirst, *Convict Society and Its Enemies* (Sydney, 1983).

9. Rowley, *Destruction*, 35.

10. A. P. Elkin, "Reaction and Interaction: A Food Gathering People and European Settlement in Australia," *American Anthropologist* 53 (1951): 166.

11. I am grateful to Colin Tatz for discussions on this point.

12. Sharon Morgan, *Land Settlement in Early Tasmania: Creating an Antipodean England* (Cambridge, 1992), 3; John Mulvaney and Johan Kamminga, *Prehistory of Australia* (Sydney, 1999), 62.

13. Heather Goodall, *Invasion to Embassy: Land in Aboriginal Politics in New South Wales, 1770–1972* (Sydney, 1996), 48; Rowley, *Destruction*, 44.

14. Morgan, *Land Settlement*, 7, 76, quoting *Hobart Town Gazette*, June 29, 1816, 2.

15. R. P. Lesson, "Journal across the Blue Mountains in 1824," quoted in Michael Pearson, "Bathurst Plains and Beyond: Colonisation and Aboriginal Resistance," *Aboriginal History* 8:1 (1984): 63–64.

16. Hakluyt, quoted in Edmund Morgan, *American Slavery, American Freedom* (New York, 1975), 22.

17. W. H. Hovell, "Diary of My Travels within the Colony of New South Wales" [1825], quoted

in Richard Waterhouse, "Rural Culture and Australian History: Myths and Realities," *Arts* 24 (2002): 96.

18. Quoted in Rob Watts, "Making Numbers Count: The Birth of the Census and Racial Government in Victoria, 1835–40," *Australian Historical Studies* 121 (April 2003): 33.

19. Don Watson, *Caledonia Australis: Scottish Highlanders on the Frontier of Australia* (Sydney, 1997), 94; Shayne Breen, *Contested Places: Tasmania's Northern Districts from Ancient Times to 1900* (Hobart, 2001), 21–22; Mulvaney and Kamminga, *Prehistory of Australia,* 60.

20. Josephine Flood, *Archaeology of the Dreamtime: The Story of Prehistoric Australia and Its People* (New Haven, 1990), 168.

21. A. McKay, ed., *Journals of the Land Commissioners for Van Diemen's Land, 1826–28* (Hobart, 1962), 86.

22. Flood, *Archaeology of the Dreamtime,* 223–24; Rhys Jones, "Fire Stick Farming," *Australian Natural History* 16 (1969): 224–28; Mulvaney and Kamminga, *Prehistory of Australia,* 60.

23. Watson, *Caledonia Australis,* 119, 123, quoting *Quarterly Review,* April 1824, 57–58.

24. John Connor, *The Australian Frontier Wars, 1788–1838* (Sydney, 2002); Inge Clendinnen, *Dancing with Strangers* (Melbourne, 2003).

25. Hughes, *Fatal Shore,* 275; Connor, *Australian Frontier Wars,* 36–41, 43.

26. R. H. W. Reece, *Aborigines and Colonists: Aborigines and Colonial Society in New South Wales in the 1830s and 1840s* (Sydney, 1974), 105–6; Rowley, *Destruction,* 28n6.

27. Reece, *Aborigines and Colonists,* 107; Connor, *Australian Frontier Wars,* 39–40, 43–46, 47–48.

28. Macquarie to secretary of state, *Historical Records of Australia,* ser. 1, 8, 368, quoted in Mulvaney, "Australian Aborigines, 1606–1929," 142.

29. Macquarie, quoted in R. H. W. Reece, "Feasts and Blankets: The History of Some Early Attempts to Establish Relations with the Aborigines of New South Wales, 1814–1816," *Archaeology and Physical Anthropology in Oceania* 2:3 (1967): 191.

30. Reece, "Feasts," 191–94; Reece, *Aborigines and Colonists,* 5, 17; Pearson, "Bathurst Plains," 71.

31. *Sydney Gazette,* Jan. 4, 1817, quoted in Reece, "Feasts," 193.

32. Connor, *Australian Frontier Wars,* 46–52; *Sydney Gazette,* Aug. 12, 1824, quoting government printer Robert Howe, transcription in T. Salisbury and P. J. Gresser, *Windradyne of the Wiradjuri: Martial Law at Bathurst in 1824* (Sydney, 1971), 48–49.

33. *Sydney Gazette,* Aug.12, 1824, transcription in Salisbury and Gresser, *Windradyne,* 48–49.

34. *Sydney Gazette,* May 22 and June 16, 1813, and W. C. Wentworth, *Journal of an Expedition across the Blue Mountains,* quoted in Richard Waterhouse, "Australian Legends: Representations of the Bush, 1813–1913," *Australian Historical Studies* 115 (2000): 203.

35. George Evans, Mar. 10, 1814, quoted in Salisbury and Gresser, *Windradyne,* 12.

36. Peter Read, *A Hundred Years War: The Wiradjuri People and the State* (Canberra, 1988), 3; Pearson, "Bathurst Plains," 68–69.

37. *Memoirs of William Cox, J.P., Lieutenant and Paymaster of N.S.W. Corps* (Sydney, 1901), 17, 108; "Cox, William (1764–1837)," in *Australian Encyclopedia,* 848–49.

38. *Memoirs of William Cox,* 73, 77, 81, 90–91, 97, 100, 75–78, 99.

39. Macquarie to Cox, June 10, 1817, in *Memoirs of William Cox,* 111–17.

40. *Memoirs of William Cox,* 72; Salisbury and Gresser, *Windradyne,* 13, 15.

41. H. C. Antill, "Journal of an Excursion over the Blue Mountains," in Pearson, "Bathurst Plains," 63.

42. Salisbury and Gresser, *Windradyne,* 13.

43. Pearson, "Bathurst Plains," 69.

44. Read, *A Hundred Years War,* 18; Salisbury and Gresser, *Windradyne,* 15, 17.

45. Morgan, *Land Settlement,* 9–10; Pearson, "Bathurst Plains," 71.

46. *Sydney Gazette,* Jan. 2, 1819, quoted in Reece, "Feasts," 194.

47. "Cox, William (1764–1837)," 848–49.

48. Waterhouse, "Australian Legends," 203; Salisbury and Gresser, *Windradyne,* 15.

49. "Cox, William (1764–1837)," 848–49; Pearson, "Bathurst Plains," 69.

50. Macquarie to Bathurst, Feb. 24, 1820, cited in Reece, *Aborigines and Colonists*, 110.

51. Salisbury and Gresser, *Windradyne*, 15, 17; Pearson, "Bathurst Plains," 71.

52. Salisbury and Gresser, *Windradyne*, 16–17; Morgan, *Land Settlement*, 8–9; Reece, "Feasts," 194.

53. Brisbane to Bathurst, Apr. 28, 1823, *Historical Records of Australia*, ser. 1, 11 (1917): 79.

54. Read, *A Hundred Years War*, 12; Pearson, "Bathurst Plains," 69.

55. Brisbane to Bathurst, Apr. 28, 1823, 79–80.

56. David A. Roberts, "'A Sort of Inland Norfolk Island'? Isolation, Coercion, and Resistance on the Wellington Valley Convict Station, 1823–26," *Journal of Australian Colonial History* 2:1 (2000): 55, 57, 58, 60–62, 64–66.

57. Pearson, "Bathurst Plains," 71; *Memoirs of William Cox*, 128.

58. Salisbury and Gresser, *Windradyne*, 17–18, 27, quoting letter to *Sydney Gazette*, Aug. 12, 1824.

59. Connor, *Australian Frontier Wars*, 55; Pearson, "Bathurst Plains," 71.

60. J. P. M. Long, *Bathurst, 1813 to 1840*, quoted in Salisbury and Gresser, *Windradyne*, 19; L. E. Threlkeld, *Australian Reminiscences and Papers*, Australian Institute of Aboriginal Studies, 40 (Canberra, 1974), 49.

61. Pearson, "Bathurst Plains," 72; Salisbury and Gresser, *Windradyne*, 19.

62. Salisbury and Gresser, *Windradyne*, 22.

63. Barron Field, *Journal of an Excursion across the Blue Mountains of New South Wales, October 1822*, quoted in Salisbury and Gresser, *Windradyne*, 19, and in Pearson, "Bathurst Plains," 65.

64. Read, *A Hundred Years War*, 12; Pearson, "Bathurst Plains," 69.

65. Salisbury and Gresser, *Windradyne*, 20, 35, quoting *Sydney Gazette*, Jan. 8, 1824.

66. Read, *A Hundred Years War*, 8; Pearson, "Bathurst Plains," 73.

67. Pearson, "Bathurst Plains," 74; Salisbury and Gresser, *Windradyne*, 20–21, quoting *Sydney Gazette*, Jan. 8, 1824.

68. Salisbury and Gresser, *Windradyne*, 22.

69. David A. Roberts, "The Bells Falls Massacre and Oral Tradition," in Bain Attwood and S. G. Foster, eds., *Frontier Conflict: The Australian Experience* (Canberra, 2003), 157.

70. Pearson, "Bathurst Plains," 74.

71. Salisbury and Gresser, *Windradyne*, 22–26; quoted in Pearson, "Bathurst Plains," 74.

72. Salisbury and Gresser, *Windradyne*, 30; Pearson, "Bathurst Plains," 75.

73. Roberts, "'A Sort of Inland Norfolk Island'?" 67.

74. *Sydney Gazette*, July 22, 1824, quoted in Salisbury and Gresser, *Windradyne*, 26.

75. *Sydney Gazette*, Aug. 12, 1824, quoted in Salisbury and Gresser, *Windradyne*, 26–27. Roberts says "Candid" was an educated convict, William Watt. "'A Sort of Inland Norfolk Island'?" 64n49.

76. Threlkeld, *Australian Reminiscences and Papers*, 49.

77. Lt. Richard Sadleir, R.N., *The Aborigines of Australia* (Sydney 1883), 48, dates this at 1826, but Reece, *Aborigines and Colonists*, 111, says this "was evidently the same meeting" addressed by Cox in 1824.

78. Petition dated July 16, 1824, quoted in Pearson, "Bathurst Plains," 75 (emphasis added).

79. *Sydney Gazette*, July 29, 1824, quoted in Salisbury and Gresser, *Windradyne*, 27–28. The *Gazette*'s report of the testimony of Hassall and Cox is reproduced at 49–50.

80. R. H. W. Reece, "The Aborigines in Australian Historiography," in John A. Moses, ed., *Historical Disciplines and Culture in Australasia* (St. Lucia, 1979), 258; Alan Atkinson, *The Europeans in Australia* (Melbourne, 2004), 2:155.

81. Brisbane's proclamation, dated Aug. 14, 1824, in Salisbury and Gresser, *Windradyne*, 53–54; Roberts, "The Bells Falls Massacre," 151.

82. Brisbane to Bathurst, quoted in Salisbury and Gresser, *Windradyne*, 31. Rowley, *Destruction*, 29–30, says Brisbane's reports "discreetly veiled" the results of the "demonstration of force," whose "death toll was not tallied." See also Hughes, *Fatal Shore*, 276.

83. W. Walker, "To the General Secretaries of the Wesleyan Missions," from the Native Settlement, Sept. 14, 1824, *Bonwick Transcripts*, vol. 5, 1433, Mitchell Library, Sydney, quoted in Salisbury

and Gresser, *Windradyne*, 32–33; "Windradyne," in *The Encyclopedia of Aboriginal Australia*, gen. ed. David Horton, Australian Institute of Aboriginal and Torres Strait Islander Studies, Canberra (CD-ROM, n.d).

84. *Memoirs of William Cox*, 130; *Sydney Gazette*, Sept. 30, 1824, quoted in Salisbury and Gresser, *Windradyne*, 33; Pearson, "Bathurst Plains," 76; Connor, *Australian Frontier Wars*, 61.

85. *Sydney Gazette*, Oct. 14, 1824, quoted in Salisbury and Gresser, *Windradyne*, 33.

86. George Bowman to Robert Scott, Jan. 5, 1839, miscellaneous papers of Judge W. W. Burton, no. 102, Archives Office of New South Wales, quoted in Reece, *Aborigines and Colonists*, 161.

87. *Monitor*, July 7, 1826, quoted in Roberts, "The Bells Falls Massacre," 157n5; Threlkeld, *Australian Reminiscences and Papers*, 49, 74n43.

88. Salisbury and Gresser, *Windradyne*, 31 (quoting W. H. Suttor, *Australian Stories Retold* [Bathurst, 1887], 45), 22–23. Suttor bought Cox's former property from his son Alfred. *Memoirs of William Cox*, 131, 138.

89. Roberts, "The Bells Falls Massacre," 150–57, esp. 156.

90. Pearson, "Bathurst Plains," 68–69; Salisbury and Gresser, *Windradyne*, 27, *Sydney Gazette*, Aug, 12, 1824.

91. *Sydney Gazette*, Dec. 30, 1824 (excerpt in Salisbury and Gresser, *Windradyne*, 36–37), describing Windradyne's group as a "reinforcement." Reece, "Feasts," 195, names five of six or seven other tribes represented at this Dec. 1824 feast. He notes that the Parramatta feast usually "attracted seven or eight tribes" from coastal regions (*Aborigines and Colonists*, 17).

92. Read, *A Hundred Years War*, 10; Pearson, "Bathurst Plains," 77. Pearson puts the European death toll at 22. Reece suggests possibly 100 killed (*Aborigines and Colonists*, 111; see also 161).

93. Brisbane to Morisset, Dec. 13, 1824, quoted in B. W. Champion, "James T. Morisset of the 48th Regiment," *Royal Australian Historical Society Journal*, 20:4 (1934): 215.

94. Brisbane to Bathurst, Dec. 31, 1824, quoted in Champion, "James T. Morisset," 215, and Roberts, "The Bells Falls Massacre," 152.

95. Salisbury and Gresser, *Windradyne*, 36, quoting *Sydney Gazette*, Dec. 30, 1824; Roberts, " 'A Sort of Inland Norfolk Island'?" 54; Champion, "James T. Morisset," 213, 225.

96. Reece, "Feasts," 195; Bill Gammage, "The Wiradjuri War, 1838–40," *Push from the Bush* 16 (Oct. 1983): 3–17; Read, *A Hundred Years War*, 11–12, dating Windradyne's death to 1827; Salisbury and Gresser, *Windradyne*, 42–43, indicate 1829 or 1835.

97. J. D. Lang, *An Historical and Statistical Account of New South Wales*, 2 vols. (London, 1834), 1:38, quoted in Reece, "Aborigines in Australian Historiography," 259.

98. George Mackillop to colonial secretary, July 28, 1836, in *Historical Records of Victoria*, Foundation Series, vol. 2A, *The Aborigines of Port Philip, 1835–1839* (Melbourne, 1982), 40.

99. "Cox, William (1764–1837)," 848–49; *Memoirs of William Cox*, 131.

100. McKay, *Journals of the Land Commissioners*, 54, 73; *Memoirs of William Cox*, 20, 138.

101. Morgan, *Land Settlement*, 22, 25, 166–69.

102. Ibid., 144; Ryan, *Aboriginal Tasmanians*, 75.

103. Lloyd Robson, *A History of Tasmania*, vol. 1, *Van Diemen's Land from the Earliest Times to 1855* (Melbourne, 1983), 46; Ryan, *Aboriginal Tasmanians*, 76.

104. Morgan, *Land Settlement*, 144–45.

105. Robson, *History of Tasmania*, 1:4–6; c.f. Mark Cocker, *Rivers of Blood, Rivers of Gold: Europe's Conquest of Indigenous Peoples* (New York, 1998), 124–25.

106. Philip Tardif, "Risdon Cove," in Robert Manne, ed., *Whitewash: On Keith Windschuttle's Fabrication of Aboriginal History* (Melbourne, 2003), 218–24, includes the text of White's eyewitness account (see also 40–42). Keith Windschuttle tries to deny this evidence of the massacre in *The Fabrication of Aboriginal History*, vol. 1, *Van Diemen's Land, 1803–47* (Sydney, 2002), 16–26. Ryan, *Aboriginal Tasmanians*, 75; Rowley, *Destruction*, 45.

107. Ryan, *Aboriginal Tasmanians*, 77; Morgan, *Land Settlement*, 145, 153–55.

108. *Derwent Star*, Jan. 29, 1810, quoted in Morgan, *Land Settlement*, 155. Settlers also participated in intertribal killings. A chief named Lamanbunganah, at war with his brother, told Capt. James Kelly in 1816 that his brother had allied with "five or six white men, well armed," who "intended to come and attack his (Laman's) tribe and kill them all." *The Log of the Circumnavigation of Van Diemen's Land by Captain James Kelly, 1814–1815*, quoted in Morgan, *Land Settlement*, 158–59.

109. Ryan, *Aboriginal Tasmanians,* 79. Listing the precontact population estimates, Tim Murray and Christine Williamson note that "the only scientifically rigorous attempt" suggests more than 3,000–5,000. Manne, *Whitewash,* 314–15. See also Breen, *Contested Places,* 18.

110. *Hobart Town Gazette,* Apr. 25, 1818, quoted in Morgan, *Land Settlement,* 146.

111. Rowley, *Destruction,* 44, 120. Settlers would often "chase the mother through the bush until she had to leave her children, and then make a selection" of child labor.

112. Quoted in James Boyce, "Fantasy Island," in Manne, *Whitewash,* 38.

113. *Hobart Town Gazette,* Nov. 28, 1818, Mar. 20, 1819, quoted in Morgan, *Land Settlement,* 146.

114. Clive Turnbull, *Black War: The Extermination of the Tasmanian Aborigines* (Melbourne, 1948), 60; Ryan, *Aboriginal Tasmanians,* 83.

115. Morgan, *Land Settlement,* 6–10, 15.

116. Breen, *Contested Places,* 34–38; Morgan, *Land Settlement,* 7–8, 10, 13, 16. On Mountgarret, see Manne, *Whitewash,* 219, and McKay, *Journals of the Land Commissioners,* 76.

117. Pearson, "Bathurst Plains," 63; Morgan, *Land Settlement,* 16.

118. Morgan, *Land Settlement,* 16, 9, 166–67, 19.

119. Ibid., 19, 22, 25, 166–69, 19, 31.

120. Peter Harrison's journal, quoted in ibid., 70.

121. William Parramore, quoted by E. M. Cooper, *The Story of the Parramore Family: Early Settlers in Van Diemen's Land—1823* (Yankalilla, S.A., 1953), in Morgan, *Land Settlement,* 53.

122. Quoted in Morgan, *Land Settlement,* 67, 60.

123. Ibid., 134–35.

124. Boyce, "Fantasy Island," 54, 56. From 1824 to 1831 alone, the government granted or sold 1.5 million acres, quadrupling in just seven years the total land area granted from 1803 to 1823. Morgan, *Land Settlement,* 22.

125. Robson, *History of Tasmania,* 1:187–90; Alan Atkinson says London promised the Company 500,000 acres. "Free Settlers before 1851," in James Jupp, ed., *The Australian People* (Sydney, 1988), 39.

126. Boyce, "Fantasy Island," 56.

127. Arthur to Horton, Oct. 26, 1824, quoted in Morgan, *Land Settlement,* 23.

128. Morgan, *Land Settlement,* 59, 76, 80, 83, 65, 67, 165.

129. Ibid., 150, 154–55, 164; McKay, *Journals of the Land Commissioners,* 24, 87.

130. Morgan, *Land Settlement,* 22–23, 59 (see also 51, 118), 163.

131. Morgan writes: "In island colonies such as Van Diemen's Land . . . there was so much less space to push the aborigines into. Thus matters came to a head with alarming speed" (*Land Settlement,* 163).

132. Ibid., 82, 89, 80, 81.

133. Ibid., 78–82, 124, 92, 97; McKay, *Journals of the Land Commissioners,* 23.

134. Morgan, *Land Settlement,* 112, 154, 69, 75, 142.

135. *Hobart Town Gazette,* July 20, Sept. 21, 1816, and James Atkinson, *An Account of the State of Agriculture and Grazing in New South Wales* (London, 1826), quoted in Morgan, *Land Settlement,* 78; McKay, *Journals of the Land Commissioners,* vi.

136. McKay, *Journals of the Land Commissioners,* xxiv–xxv, 22, 38.

137. Ibid., 39, 91–92, 25, 28, 57, 24, 38, 62, 85.

138. Around March 1827, the *Journals of the Land Commissioners* begin to replace common descriptions like "only fit for Sheep" (e.g., pp. 5, 8) with others such as "excellent Sheep walk" (e.g., 63, 81). The main author himself left an estate of 65,000 acres (xxi, xxv).

139. Morgan, *Land Settlement,* 82, 87–88.

140. Henry Widowson, *Present State of Van Diemen's Land; comprising of its agricultural capabilities, with observations on the present state of farming* (London, 1829), quoted in Morgan, *Land Settlement,* 79.

141. *Hobart Town Gazette,* Nov. 18, 1826, 2, quoted in Morgan, *Land Settlement,* 150.

142. Morgan, *Land Settlement,* 159–60, 196; cf. 99.

143. Louisa Meredith, *My Home in Tasmania,* quoted by Boyce, "Fantasy Island," 62.

144. N. J. B. Plomley, *The Aboriginal/Settler Clash in Van Diemen's Land, 1803–31* (Launceston,

1992), 14, 22–23; Henry Reynolds, *An Indelible Stain? The Question of Genocide in Australia's History* (Melbourne, 2001), 71.

145. Bathurst to Darling, July 14, 1825, quoted in Reece, *Aborigines and Colonists*, 113, and Reece, "Aborigines in Australian Historiography," 258.

146. Reece, *Aborigines and Colonists*, 110n, 112–16.

147. Ryan, *Aboriginal Tasmanians*, 87–88, 90. Tatz writes that in 1824 "settlers were authorized to shoot Aborigines" (*Genocide in Australia*, 15); Plomley, *The Aboriginal/Settler Clash*, 59–60.

148. Government notice, Nov. 29, 1826, in Turnbull, *Black War*, 73–75; Rowley, *Destruction*, 46; Ryan, *Aboriginal Tasmanians*, 90.

149. *Colonial Times*, Dec. 1, 1826, quoted in Reynolds, *An Indelible Stain?* 53.

150. *Colonial Times*, Dec. 8, 1826, quoted in N. J. B. Plomley, ed., *Weep in Silence: A History of the Flinders Island Aboriginal Settlement* (Hobart, 1991), 8.

151. Lyndall Ryan, "Who Is the Fabricator?" in Manne, *Whitewash*, 244–45. See also 268–71.

152. Ryan, *The Aboriginal Tasmanians*, 92.

153. Breen, *Contested Places*, 25–28; *Colonial Times*, July 6, 1827; Ryan, "Who Is the Fabricator?" 242.

154. McKay, *Journals of the Land Commissioners*, 67; Government notice and garrison orders, Nov. 29, 1827, quoted in Rowley, *Destruction*, 46; documents in Turnbull, *Black War*, 78–80.

155. Hobler's diary, Dec. 15, 1827 and July 29, 1828, in Morgan, *Land Settlement*, 148–49.

156. Robson, *History of Tasmania*, 1:187–90; Ryan, *Aboriginal Tasmanians*, 135–37; Boyce, "Fantasy Island" and Ian McFarlane, "Cape Grim," both in Manne, *Whitewash*, 17–78, 277–98, at 26, 281, 285, 295, 284; on Curr, see also McKay, *Journals of the Land Commissioners*, 11.

157. McFarlane, "Cape Grim," 281–82; Geoff Lennox, "The Van Diemen's Land Company and the Tasmanian Aborigines," *Tasmanian Historical Research Association* 37:4 (1990): 170–74.

158. Curr, Oct. 7, 1830, in Lennox, "Van Diemen's Land Company," 171; McFarlane, "Cape Grim," 294.

159. Executive council minutes, Oct. 31, 1828, quoted in Henry Reynolds, "Genocide in Tasmania?" in A. Dirk Moses, ed., *Genocide and Settler Society: Frontier Violence and Stolen Indigenous Children in Australian History* (New York, 2004), 144. See also Breen, *Contested Places*, 30–31, and Benjamin Madley, "From Terror to Genocide: Britain's Tasmanian Penal Colony and Australia's History Wars," *Journal of British Studies*, forthcoming 2008.

160. Ryan, *Aboriginal Tasmanians*, 101, 106, 109; Tatz, *Genocide in Australia*, 15

161. *Hobart Town Courier*, Dec. 9, 13, 1828, quoted by Ryan, "Who Is the Fabricator?" 246–47. A correspondent at Great Swan Port added in the *Launceston Advertiser*: "Parties are continually out in quest . . . Mr. David Ryner shot a black man near Mr. Lyne's on Monday last. Nine were killed and 3 taken, near St Paul's River and about the same time ten were shot and two were taken, near the Eastern Marshes" (Feb. 9, 1829, quoted by Ryan, "Who Is the Fabricator?" 247). There was a military station at St. Paul's River. McKay, *Journals of the Land Commissioners*, 90.

162. Cassandra Pybus, "Robinson and Robertson," in Manne, *Whitewash*, 273, 275n24.

163. Boyce, "Fantasy Island," 33; Pybus, "Robinson and Robertson," 272–73.

164. Christie, *Aborigines*, cites this and other evidence that "Batman himself had been responsible for shooting fifteen Aborigines" (27–28).

165. Manne, *Whitewash*, 30–32. Batman's account is quoted there at length, and partially in Windschuttle, *The Fabrication of Aboriginal History*, 1:156–57. None of the 14–15 blacks Batman acknowledged killing or fatally wounding in this incident is listed in Windschuttle's table 10, "Aborigines Killed by Whites, Van Diemen's Land, 1803–1834," 387–97. "Going Down in History," *Age*, Sept. 6, 2003.

166. Alastair H. Campbell, *John Batman and the Aborigines* (Melbourne, 1988), 32.

167. James Backhouse, *A Narrative of a Visit to the Australian Colonies* (London, 1843), 147, cited in Christie, *Aborigines*, 28.

168. Morgan, *Land Settlement*, 48; Manne, *Whitewash*, 30–32.

169. *Tasmanian*, Feb. 26, 1830, and *Colonial Times*, Dec. 1, 1826, quoted in Reynolds, *An Indelible Stain?* 53.

170. Batman to Anstey, Apr. 15, 1830, quoted in Campbell, *John Batman*, 39.

171. *Colonial Times*, Sept. 24, 1830, quoted in Reynolds, *An Indelible Stain?* 55–56.

172. Oct. 10, 1830, in N. J. B. Plomley, *Friendly Mission: The Tasmanian Journals and Papers of George Augustus Robinson, 1829–1834* (Hobart, 1966), 435; cf. 432–33.

173. Boyce, "Fantasy Island," 56–57, G. T. W. B. Boyes, Oct. 31, 1830; Ryan, *Aboriginal Tasmanians*, 113, 183.

174. H. A. Willis, "A Tally of Those Killed during the Fighting between Aborigines and Settlers in Van Diemen's Land 1803–34," 2002: www.historians.org.au/forumsupport/Casualties-VDL.PDF (accessed Mar. 26, 2006); *Colonial Times*, July 6, 1827; Ryan, "Who Is the Fabricator?" 242, and "List of Multiple Killings of Aborigines in Tasmania: 1804–1835" (forthcoming).

175. Henry Reynolds, *Fate of a Free People: A Radical Re-examination of the Tasmanian Wars* (Melbourne, 1995); Ryan, *Aboriginal Tasmanians*, 183.

176. W. J. Darling to colonial secretary, Feb. 20, 1833, in Plomley, *Weep in Silence*, 998.

177. Reynolds, *Fate of a Free People*, 166; Ryan, *Aboriginal Tasmanians*, 184, app. 3.

178. Robinson, diary entry, Dec. 10, 1835, in Plomley, *Weep in Silence*, 317.

179. *Flinders Island Weekly Chronicle*, Oct. 16, 1837, in Plomley, *Weep in Silence*, 1010.

180. George Arthur to T. Spring Rice, Jan. 27, 1835, in *Historical Records of Victoria*, 2A:6.

181. Ryan, *Aboriginal Tasmanians*, 88, 94; Anna Haebich, *Broken Circles: Fragmenting Indigenous Families, 1800–2000* (Fremantle, 2000), 82–84; Boyce, "Fantasy Island," 36–37; Plomley, *Weep in Silence*, 998.

182. Rowley, *Destruction*, 51–52; Ryan, *Aboriginal Tasmanians*, app. 3, 200, 209.

183. H. M. Hull, *Royal Kalendar, and Guide to Tasmania for 1859* (Hobart, 1859), quoted in Ryan, *Aboriginal Tasmanians*, 212.

184. *Launceston Examiner*, Apr. 16, 1859, quoted in Breen, *Contested Places*.

185. Quoted in Watts, "Making Numbers Count," 35, 39; A. G. L. Shaw, *A History of the Port Phillip District: Victoria before Separation* (Melbourne, 1996), 67–68.

186. Waterhouse, "Rural Culture," 89; Mr. Justice Burton to Sir Richard Bourke, Nov. 22, 1835, in *Historical Records of Victoria*, 2A:154–56; Watson, *Caledonia Australis*, xv, 80.

187. Lyell, *Principles of Geology* (1830–33), 2:156, quoted in Keith Thomas, *Man and the Natural World: Changing Attitudes in England, 1500–1800* (Oxford, 1983), 242.

188. *Sydney Herald*, Nov. 7, 1838, quoted in Rowley, *Destruction*, 37.

189. *Port Phillip Herald*, Feb. 4, 1842, quoted in Christie, *Aborigines*, 39.

190. Sir W. Blackstone, *Commentaries on the Laws of England* (London, 1844), 1:107, quoted in Christie, *Aborigines*, 37; John Watts, *Personal Reminiscences of Life in South Australia and Queensland, 1840–1868*, quoted in Waterhouse, "Rural Culture," 97.

191. Charles Pickering, *The Races of Man* (London, 1841), quoted in Watson, *Caledonia Australis*, 129.

192. Watson, *Caledonia Australis*, 109; Mulvaney and Kamminga, *Prehistory of Australia*, 62.

193. Mulvaney and Kamminga, *Prehistory of Australia*, 59–62.

194. Edmund Spenser, "Trees Characterised," and "Biography: Spenser," *Colonial Literary Journal* (Sydney), Sept. 5, 1844, 170, 162–63; "Aeneas," "Phrenology No. VII," *Colonial Literary Journal*, Aug. 29, 1844, 156, and "Phrenology No. VIII," Sept. 5, 1844, 172–73.

195. T. T. Reed, ed., *The Poetical Works of Henry Kendall* (Adelaide 1966), 198, 378, quoted in J. B. Hirst, "The Pioneer Legend," *Historical Studies* 18 (Oct. 1978): 319.

196. Aeneas, "Phrenology No. IV," *Colonial Literary Journal*, Aug. 8, 1844, 107.

197. Aeneas, "Phrenology No. VIII," 172–73; Reece, *Aborigines and Colonists*, 88–90.

198. Aeneas, "Phrenology No. VII," 156; Aeneas, "Phrenology No. VIII," 172.

199. Aeneas, "Phrenology No. VIII," 172–73; Aeneas, "Phrenology No. VII," 156.

200. Watson, *Caledonia Australis*, 174–75.

201. T.L.D [T.L. Dodd?], "Virgil on the Vine, No. 1," *Colonial Literary Journal*, Aug. 8, 1844, 108; T.L.D., "Virgil on the Vine, No. II," Aug. 22, 1844, 140–41.

202. T.L.D, "Virgil on the Vine, No. II," 140–41.

203. Aeneas, "Phrenology, No. VI," *Colonial Literary Journal*, Aug. 22, 1844, 139.

204. Aeneas, "Phrenology No. VII," 156; Aeneas, "Phrenology No. VIII," 173.

205. Aeneas, "Phrenology No. VIII," 172; Aeneas, "Phrenology, No. VI," 139.

206. J. R. McCullough, *A Dictionary: Geographical, Statistical, and Historical* (London, 1847), 2:230, quoted in Mulvaney, "Australian Aborigines, 1606–1929," 145.

207. Goodall, *Invasion to Embassy*, ch. 11.

208. Atkinson, "Free Settlers before 1851," 40–42; Gammage, "The Wiradjuri War, 1838–40," 3–17, 4.

209. S. Nicholas and P. R. Shergold, "British and Irish Convicts," in Jupp, *Australian People*, 23, 25.

210. Borrie, "Population," 2349, 2352; White and Mulvaney, *Sydney Morning Herald*, Feb. 25, 1987. Australia counted 31,000 Aborigines in 1911 (Tatz, *Genocide in Australia*, 9) and in 1921, 62,000 (Rowley, *Destruction*, 382). Borrie says a more accurate figure is 70,000, falling to 67,000 in 1933 before rising to 70,000 in 1947 ("Population," 2352–53).

211. Waterhouse, "Rural Culture," 83–102. See also Richard Waterhouse, *Vision Splendid: A Social and Cultural History of Rural Australia* (North Fremantle, 2005).

212. *Bulletin*, Mar. 8, 1890, quoted in Waterhouse, "Rural Culture," 84, 85–89.

213. James Collier, *The Pastoral Age in Australasia* (London, 1911), 129–30, quoted in Reece, "Aborigines in Australian Historiography," 260.

214. Rowley, *Destruction*, 43.

215. Reece, *Aborigines and Colonists*, 119.

216. *Historical Records of Victoria*, 2A:62.

217. Lord Glenelg to Sir Richard Bourke, July 26, 1837, in ibid., 2A:69.

218. Campbell, *John Batman*, 212.

219. James Stephen to A. Y. Spearman, Aug. 30, 1837, in *Historical Records of Victoria*, 2A:28.

220. *Die Biene auf dem Missionfelde* 2 (1839): 14, quoted in Raymond Evans and Bill Thorpe, "Indigenocide and the Massacre of Aboriginal History," *Overland* 163 (Winter 2001): 29.

221. Reece, "Aborigines in Australian Historiography," 261; Reece, *Aborigines and Colonists*, 42–47; Geoffrey Blomfield, *Baal Belbora: The End of the Dancing* (Sydney, 1981), 119–22; Atkinson, *Europeans in Australia*, 2:158.

222. *Historical Records of Victoria*, 2A:342; Reece, *Aborigines and Colonists*, 32–34; Roger Milliss, *Waterloo Creek: The Australia Day Massacre of 1838, George Gipps, and the British Conquest of New South Wales* (Sydney, 1994); Lyndall Ryan, "Waterloo Creek: Northern New South Wales 1838," in Attwood and Foster, *Frontier Conflict*, 33–43; Rowley, *Destruction*, 37–38.

223. *Historical Records of Victoria*, 2A:346–49.

224. Rowley and Reynolds, "Aborigines since 1788," 277.

225. *Monitor*, Dec. 14, 1838, quoted in Reece, *Aborigines and Colonists*, 42–43.

226. Rowley, *Destruction*, 151; Reece, *Aborigines and Colonists*, 40n.

227. Christie, *Aborigines*, 45; *Historical Records of Victoria*, 2A:343–44.

228. William Thomas, journal entry for Apr. 1, 1839, quoted in Christie, *Aborigines*, 46. For further evidence of poisonings of Aborigines in this period, see Gammage, "The Wiradjuri War, 1838–40," 14; Waterhouse, "Rural Culture," 96n40.

229. Sir George Gipps to Lord Glenelg, Apr. 27, 1838, in *Historical Records of Victoria*, 2A:349.

230. James Stephen to Sir George Grey, Nov. 1, 1838, in ibid., 2A:346.

231. *Historical Records of Victoria*, 2A:344; Milliss, *Waterloo Creek*, 699–701.

232. Rowley, *Destruction*, 112–14; Blomfield, *Baal Belbora*, 81; Reece, "Aborigines in Australian Historiography," 258.

233. Gammage, "The Wiradjuri War, 1838–40," 5–8, 15.

234. Ibid., 7–12; Read, *A Hundred Years War*, 13, 17–21, 24; Pearson, "Bathurst Plains," 78.

235. Reece, *Aborigines and Colonists*, 179–81; Rowley, *Destruction*, 128, 153.

236. Quoted by A. P. Elkin, "Reaction and Interaction," *American Anthropologist* 53 (1951): 181.

237. J. C. Byrne, *Twelve Years' Wanderings in the British Colonies from 1835 to 1847*, vol. 1 (London, 1848), quoted in Waterhouse, "Australian Legends," 209.

238. Blomfield, *Baal Belbora*, xvi, 138, and (for specific incidents) 32ff., 37, 46–47, 81, 90, 115, 119, 121.

239. Rowley and Reynolds, "Aborigines since 1788," 280, 284.

240. Rowley, *Destruction*, 39, 41–43; see also 161.

241. Christie, *Aborigines*, 7, 206–7; Beverley Nance, "The Level of Violence: Europeans and Aborigines in Port Phillip, 1835–1850," *Historical Studies* (Oct. 1981): 533; Richard Broome, *Aboriginal Victorians: A History since 1800* (Sydney, 2005), 54.

242. E. M. Curr, *The Australian Race* (Melbourne, 1886–87), 1:209, in Christie, *Aborigines*, 78.

243. Christie, *Aborigines*, 46–47; George Augustus Robinson, "The Aboriginal Protectorate of Port Phillip: Report of an Expedition to the Aboriginal Tribes of the Western Interior, by the Chief Protector" [1841], ed. A. S. Kenyon, *Victorian Historical Magazine* (Mar. 1928): 144; Broome, *Aboriginal Victorians*, 80–81.

244. Nance, "Level of Violence," 539–42; James Dredge, Dec. 6, 1839, quoted in Christie, *Aborigines*, 41.

245. Brough Smith, *Aborigines of Victoria*, 2:228, quoted in Fr. Duncan McNab, "Note on the Condition of the Aborigines of Queensland," London, Oct. 24, 1879, in R. Evans et al., *Exclusion, Exploitation, and Extermination: Race Relations in Colonial Queensland* (Sydney, 1975), doc. C, 380–81.

246. Nance, "Level of Violence," 539.

247. Christie, *Aborigines*, 68; on Aboriginal resistance before 1850, see 53–80.

248. Jan Critchett, "Encounters in the Western District," in Attwood and Foster, *Frontier Conflict*, 57; Ian D. Clark, *Scars in the Landscape: A Register of Massacre Sites in Western Victoria, 1803–1859* (Canberra, 1995), 17–22; Clark and Edward J. Ryan, *The "Convincing Ground" Massacre Site, Portland Bay: An Ethnohistorical Assessment Prepared for Aboriginal Affairs Victoria*, School of Business, University of Ballarat, May 6, 2005, esp. 3–9; Robinson, "Aboriginal Protectorate," 150.

249. Manne, *Whitewash*, 30–32.

250. Christie, *Aborigines*, 25–29.

251. Bourke's proclamation of May 3, 1836, in Campbell, *John Batman*, 166; Max Waugh, *Forgotten Hero: Richard Bourke, Irish-born Governor of New South Wales, 1831–1837* (Melbourne, 2005), 110–12, 133ff.

252. George Mackillop to colonial secretary, July 28, 1836, in *Historical Records of Victoria*, 2A:40–41.

253. *Historical Records of Victoria*, 2A:36–37, 52, 54.

254. Morgan, *Land Settlement*, 156; *Historical Records of Victoria*, 2A:43–44.

255. Gellibrand to Swanston, July 14, 1836, quoted in Campbell, *John Batman*, 170.

256. *Colonial Times*, Aug. 7, 1836, quoted in Campbell, *John Batman*, 171.

257. John Montagu to colonial secretary, Aug. 18, 1836, in *Historical Records of Victoria*, 2A:41–42.

258. Simpson to Wedge, Aug. 19, 1836, quoted in Campbell, *John Batman*, 172 (emphasis in original).

259. *True Colonist*, Aug. 7, 1836, cited in Campbell, *John Batman*, 171.

260. Colonial secretary to William Lonsdale, Sept. 13, 1836, in *Historical Records of Victoria*, 2A:42–43.

261. William Lonsdale to colonial secretary, Nov. 7, 1836, in *Historical Records of Victoria*, 2A:50. The testimony of Henry Batman, who claimed that he "took care to fire quite out of their reach," is on pp. 46–48. See also Campbell, *John Batman*, 172.

262. Campbell, *John Batman*, 200.

263. William Lonsdale to attorney general, Nov. 25, 1836, and Jan. 29, 1837, in *Historical Records of Victoria*, 2A:60–61, 37; Campbell, *John Batman*, 204.

264. Christie, *Aborigines*, 25–29; Rev. J. R. Orton to Wesleyan Missionary Society, May 13, 1839, in *Historical Records of Victoria*, 2A:120.

265. Quoted in Nance, "Level of Violence," 542–45.

266. Ibid., 547–48.

267. Rowley, *Destruction*, 59; Nance, "Level of Violence," 533–38.

268. Rev. B. Hurst to C. J. La Trobe, May 7, 1840, in *Historical Records of Victoria*, 2A:150.

269. Christie, *Aborigines*, 43; Hurst to La Trobe, May 7, 1840, 2A:150.

270. Nance, "Level of Violence," 549; Rowley, *Destruction*, 60.

271. Nance, "Level of Violence," 533, 542–43. John Montagu to colonial secretary, Aug. 18, 1836, described a "rencontre" with armed settlers in which "ten of the tribe of Port Phillip natives were killed." *Historical Records of Victoria*, 2A:41–42. It is not clear if this group were "Melbourne Aborigines."

272. Parker to Robinson, Oct. 5, 1840, quoted in Christie, *Aborigines*, 43.

273. Quoted in Christie, *Aborigines*, 24; Rowley, *Destruction*, 57.

274. George Faithfull to Latrobe, Sept. 8, 1853, quoted in Connor, *Australian Frontier Wars*, 120–21.

275. Nance, "Level of Violence," 540, 552.

276. Watson, *Caledonia Australis*, 88.

277. P. D. Gardner, *Gippsland Massacres: The Destruction of the Kurnai Tribes, 1800–1860* (Ensay, 2001); Gardner, *Our Founding Murdering Father: Angus McMillan and the Kurnai Tribe of Gippsland, 1839–1865* (Ensay, 1990); Watson, *Caledonia Australis*, 210–41.

278. L. A. Edgar, *Among the Black Boys* (London, 1865), 74–75, quoted in Gardner, *Our Founding Murdering Father*, 52; Marie H. Fels, *Good Men and True: The Aboriginal Police of the Port Phillip District, 1837–1853* (Melbourne, 1988), 184–85; Nance, "Level of Violence," 552.

279. Phillip Pepper and Tess Araugo, *The Kurnai of Gippsland* (Melbourne, 1985), 42.

280. Watson, *Caledonia Australis*, 80–81, 56, 105, 108–9, 111–12, 114, 116, 118.

281. Ibid., 81–82, 138–39; Gardner, *Our Founding Murdering Father*, 42.

282. Gardner, *Gippsland Massacres*, 23–24, 14; Gardner, *Our Founding Murdering Father*, ix.

283. Pepper and Araugo, *The Kurnai*, 21; Gardner, *Our Founding Murdering Father*, 34–35.

284. Broome, *Aboriginal Victorians*, 24; Tyers to Latrobe, Mar. 30, 1846, quoted in Pepper and Araugo, *The Kurnai*, 47.

285. Gardner, *Our Founding Murdering Father*, 17; Gardner, *Gippsland Massacres*, 13, 42, 46.

286. Gardner, *Gippsland Massacres*, 42, 54, and, quoting McMillan, 45.

287. John Wilson, Avon Shire historian, quoted in ibid., 46.

288. Gardner, *Gippsland Massacres*, 14, 44–52, 103–5; Gardner, *Our Founding Murdering Father*, 37–39.

289. Quoted in Gardner, *Gippsland Massacres*, 54.

290. *Port Phillip Herald*, July 29, 1843, quoted in Gardner, *Our Founding Murdering Father*, 40.

291. Gardner, *Gippsland Massacres*, 53–66, 86–88, 105; Pepper and Araugo, *The Kurnai*, 18.

292. George Dunderdale, *The Book of the Bush* (London, 1898), quoted in Gardner, *Gippsland Massacres*, 53–54; Pepper and Araugo, *The Kurnai*, 43, 24.

293. William Hoddinott ("Gippslander"), *Gap* magazine, 1925, and *Bairnsdale Advertiser*, May 21, 1940, quoted in Gardner, *Gippsland Massacres*, 53, 63–64, and *Our Founding Murdering Father*, 39, 41.

294. Pepper and Araugo, *The Kurnai*, 25; Tyers, in Gardner, *Our Founding Murdering Father*, 33, 35 and *Gippsland Massacres*, 14, 56.

295. Pepper and Araugo, *The Kurnai*, 40.

296. C. J. Tyers quoted in ibid., 33–34.

297. Dunderdale, *The Book of the Bush*, 266, in Pepper and Araugo, *The Kurnai*, 43; Fels, *Good Men*, 194.

298. Tyers to Macalister, Nov. 26, 1846, quoted in Fels, *Good Men*, 194.

299. Pepper and Araugo, *The Kurnai*, 41–42, quoting press accounts and a subsequent police record of "the reported killing of some blacks."

300. H. H. Meyrick Papers, and F. J. Meyrick, *Life in the Bush*, quoted in Pepper and Araugo, *The Kurnai*, 58–59; Gardner, *Gippsland Massacres*, 69.

301. Tyers, 1859, quoted in Julie Carr, *The Captive White Woman of Gipps Land: In Pursuit of the Legend* (Melbourne, 2001), 52; see also Fels, *Good Men*, 177–94; Gardner, *Gippsland Massacres*, 68–75, 108–11; Pepper and Araugo, *The Kurnai*, 51–57.

302. *Port Phillip Herald*, Jan. 21, 1847, quoted in Reynolds, *An Indelible Stain?* 94; Gardner, *Gippsland Massacres*, 76–85, 88, 106–7.

303. Quoted in Gardner, *Gippsland Massacres*, 106.

304. *Maffra Spectator*, June 11, 1896, quoted in Gardner, *Our Founding Murdering Father*, 30.

305. Gardner, *Our Founding Murdering Father*, 35; Pepper and Araugo, *The Kurnai*, 112.

306. Robinson, "Aboriginal Protectorate," 143, 153.

307. Ibid., 143, 146–50, 152, 166.

308. Ibid., 152; Philip Chauncy, quoted in Jan Critchett, *A Distant Field of Murder: Western District Frontiers, 1834–1848* (Melbourne, 1990), 174.

309. Quoted in Christie, *Aborigines,* 44–45; Clark, *Scars in the Landscape,* 145–52.

310. "Shooting Blackfellows," *Gippsland Guardian,* July 6, 1860, reprinted from *Ararat Advertiser* and in Gardner, *Gippsland Massacres,* 95–96.

311. Robinson, "Aboriginal Protectorate," 144.

312. Campbell, *John Batman,* 202–3; Clark, *Scars in the Landscape,* 105–18; Christie, *Aborigines,* 40–41.

313. Critchett, *Distant Field of Murder,* 128–29; quoted in Clark, *Scars in the Landscape,* 116–17.

314. Pepper and Araugo, *The Kurnai,* 37–38, 46.

315. Quoted in Critchett, "Encounters in the Western District," 58.

316. Quoted in Christie, *Aborigines,* 40, and in Clark, *Scars in the Landscape,* 111.

317. The editor of the *Hampden Guardian,* Sept. 12, 1876, quoted in Critchett, "Encounters in the Western District," 58.

318. Robinson, "Aboriginal Protectorate," 159.

319. W. Westgarth, *Report on the Condition, Capabilities, and Prospects of the Australian Aborigines* (Melbourne, 1846), 8n., quoted in Christie, *Aborigines,* 78–79.

320. *Port Phillip Gazette,* Aug. 29 and Sept. 2, 1846, cited in Nance, "Level of Violence," 552; for different accounts, see Clark, *Scars in the Landscape,* 121–23, citing *Argus,* Sept. 1, 1846; Christie, *Aborigines,* 43. The massacre may have been wrongly attributed to native police officer H. W. Smythe and 10 armed blacks under his command; see Fels, *Good Men,* 280n64.

321. Critchett, *Distant Field of Murder,* app. 3, 130–31, 78. Citing this book, Keith Windschuttle falsely asserts that Critchett "counts a total of 200 Aborigines killed by whites" (*Quadrant,* Nov. 2000, 21); Critchett, "Encounters in the Western District," 57.

322. The individual tolls were 10, 8, 7, 9, 9, 8–20, "9 or 10," 6, and 9; Critchett, *Distant Field of Murder,* 130–31. Citing this book, Windschuttle incorrectly states that "only three events ... involved mass killings" of Aborigines in western Victoria from 1834 to 1848, though he terms the Aboriginal killing of six shepherds a "mass killing of Europeans" (*Quadrant,* Nov. 2000, 21).

323. Critchett, "Encounters in the Western District," 58, 57; Clark, *Scars in the Landscape,* 9, passim.

324. "Most killings of Aborigines occurred not in large numbers but in ones and twos ... there were some massacres, but they were rare and isolated," "unusual events" with "their own specific causes." Keith Windschuttle, "Aboriginal Deaths: Why the Guesswork Is Not Educated," *Age,* 20 Sept. 2000. See also notes 321–22 above.

325. Tom Griffiths, "The Frontier Fallen," *Eureka Street* 13:1 (2003): 27.

326. Christie, *Aborigines,* 207; Report of the Select Committee on Aborigines, *V. & P. Leg. Counc. Vic. 1858/59,* quoted in Mulvaney, "Australian Aborigines, 1606–1929," 144–45.

327. Report of the Select Committee on Aborigines, *V. & P. Leg. Counc. Vic. 1858/59,* D.8, iv, quoted in Gardner, *Gippsland Massacres,* 36.

328. Reynolds, *Other Side,* 84; Reece, *Aborigines and Colonists,* 49; Rowley, *Destruction,* 157; Waterhouse, "Rural Culture," 96, documents four other poisonings; Patrick Collins, *Goodbye, Bussamarai: The Mandandanji Land War, Southern Queensland, 1842–1852* (St. Lucia, 2002), 18–22.

329. Raymond Evans, "'Plenty Shoot 'Em:' The Destruction of Aboriginal Societies along the Queensland Frontier," in Moses, *Genocide and Settler Society,* 168; Collins, *Goodbye, Bussamarai,* 20.

330. Evans, "'Plenty Shoot 'Em,'" 163; C. P. Hodgson, *Reminiscences of Australia* (London, 1846), 223, quoted in Reynolds, *An Indelible Stain?* 100–1.

331. Evans, "'Plenty Shoot 'Em,'" 163, 168.

332. Rowley and Reynolds, "Aborigines since 1788," 280, 284.

333. Evans, "'Plenty Shoot 'Em,'" 155–56; Reynolds, *An Indelible Stain?* 124.

334. G. D. Lang to his uncle, Maryborough Wide Bay, Mar. 31, 1858, text reprinted in Evans et al., *Exclusion, Exploitation, and Extermination,* 375–76; Reynolds, *An Indelible Stain?* 124–26.

335. *North Australian,* Nov. 17, 1857, quoted in Reynolds, *An Indelible Stain?* 122–23.

336. *Moreton Bay Courier,* May 8, 1858, and *Brisbane Courier,* Apr. 2, 1861, in Reynolds, *An Indelible Stain?* 115.

337. Rowley, *Destruction,* 161–63; *Queensland Guardian,* July 27, 1861, quoted in Reynolds, *An Indelible Stain?* 103–4; W. Hobbs, *Queensland Guardian,* Feb. 14–21, 1861, in Evans, "'Plenty Shoot 'Em,'" 164.

338. Evans, "'Plenty Shoot 'Em,'" 155 (Kairi); Reynolds, *An Indelible Stain?* 122 (Wadja).

339. *Rockhampton Bulletin,* report reprinted in *Queensland Times,* Dec. 13, 1861, and John West, *Sydney Morning Herald,* Dec. 12, 1861, both quoted in Reynolds, *An Indelible Stain?* 126–28.

340. Evans, "'Plenty Shoot 'Em,'" 156.

341. *Peak Downs Telegram,* reprinted in the *Queenslander,* Mar. 31, 1866, quoted in Henry Reynolds, *Why Weren't We Told? A Personal Search for the Truth about Our History* (Melbourne, 1999), 119, and Reynolds, *An Indelible Stain?* 115; *Port Denison Times,* July 4, 1868, and *Queenslander,* June 13, 1868, quoted in Evans, "'Plenty Shoot 'Em,'" 165–66.

342. John Pilger, *A Secret Country* (London, 1992), 53, citing N. S. Kirkman, "The Palmer River Goldfields, 1873–1883," B.A. honors thesis, James Cook University of North Queensland, 1981.

343. Reynolds, *An Indelible Stain?* 113, 105–10.

344. Reynolds, *Other Side,* 122; Tatz, *Genocide in Australia,* 13, 15–16, citing Archibald Meston, "Report on the Aborigines of North Queensland," *Queensland Votes and Proceedings* 4:85 (1896).

345. *Aboriginals Protection and Restriction of the Sale of Opium Act, 1897;* Tatz, *Genocide in Australia,* 16; Tony Roberts, *Frontier Justice: A History of the Gulf Country to 1900* (St. Lucia, 2005), 255–56.

346. Thomas Major, *Letters from a Squatter's Notebook* (London, 1900), 165, quoted in Waterhouse, "Rural Culture," 95–96.

347. Rowley, *Destruction,* 67; Neville Green, "Windschuttle's Debut," in Manne, *Whitewash,* 187–98. Keith Windschuttle wrote that diaries of members of Stirling's 1834 expedition say "they killed only a proportion" of the 70–80 Aborigines ("Myths of Frontier Massacres," *Quadrant,* Oct. 2000, 18); Tatz, *Genocide in Australia,* 16, writes of "hundreds of massacres" in the west over the next century.

348. Lesley Head, "The Northern Myth Revisited? Aborigines, Environment, and Agriculture in the Ord River Irrigation Scheme," *Australian Geographer* 30:2 (1999): 151.

349. J. H. Ricketson, *Journal of a Voyage to Cambridge Gulf, the Northwest of Western Australia* and *A Ride through the Northern Territory of South Australia, 1884–85,* cited in Waterhouse, "Rural Culture," 94, 96.

350. *Nor-West Times* and *West Australian,* Sept. 30 and Sept. 28, 1893, in Andrew Gill, "Aborigines, Settlers, and Police in the Kimberleys, 1887–1905," *Studies in Western Australian History* 1 (1977): 17n168, 18.

351. Octavious Burt to Forrest, July 17, 1895, quoted in Gill, "Aborigines, Settlers, and Police," 17, and Chris Cunneen, *Conflict, Politics, and Crime: Aboriginal Communities and the Police* (Sydney, 2001), 50. See also Neville Green, *The Forrest River Massacres* (Fremantle, 1995); Green, "The Evidence for the Forrest River Massacre," *Quadrant* 397, 398 (2003), 39–43; cf. Rod Moran, *Massacre Myth* (Bassendean, 1999).

352. Roberts, *Frontier Justice,* 139–42; R. Kimber, "Genocide or Not? The Situation in Central Australia, 1860–1895," in Colin Tatz, ed., *Genocide Perspectives* (Sydney, 1997), 1:33–65; D. J. Mulvaney, "Barrow Creek, Northern Australia, 1874," in Attwood and Foster, *Frontier Conflict,* 44–51; Rowley, *Destruction,* 267, 288–89; John Cribbin, *The Killing Times: The Coniston Massacre, 1928* (Sydney, 1984); Reynolds, *Other Side,* 200–1.

Chapter 8. Genocide in the United States

1. John Grenier, *The First Way of War: American War Making on the Frontier* (New York, 2005), 12.

2. Quoted in Anthony F. C. Wallace, *The Long, Bitter Trail: Andrew Jackson and the Indians* (New York, 1993), 38; James Q. Wilson, *The Earth Shall Weep* (New York, 1998), 48–49.

3. Vattel, *Law of Nations,* 246, quoted in Elizabeth A. Fenn, "Biological Warfare in Eighteenth Century North America," *Journal of American History* 86:4 (2000): 1574.

4. Thomas Jefferson, *Notes on the State of Virginia,* ed. William Peden (Chapel Hill, 1982), 63, 58ff., 141; Jefferson to Chastellux, June 7, 1785, in Julian P. Boyd, ed., *The Papers of Thomas Jefferson* (Princeton, 1950–), 8:186.

5. Philip Freneau, "The Pilgrim, No. VIII," *Freeman's Journal; or, The North American Intelligencer* (Philadelphia), Jan. 9, 1782, 1.

6. Ibid.; Alden Vaughan, *Roots of American Racism* (New York, 1995), 198.

7. *Freeman's Journal,* May 22, 1782, 1; April 24, 1782, 2.

8. Ibid., May 8, 1782; May 22, 1782, 1.

9. Ibid., Jan. 2, 1782, 2; June 20, 1781, 2; Feb. 20, 1782, 2.

10. Jefferson to Jean Baptiste Ducoigne, 1 June 1781, in Boyd, *Papers of Thomas Jefferson,* 6:62.

11. Henry Nash Smith, *Virgin Land: The American West as Symbol and Myth* (Cambridge, 1970), 124, 9.

12. Freneau, "The Pilgrim, No. VIII," 1; Smith, *Virgin Land,* 9.

13. "To the Yeoman of the United States," Poulson's *Town and Country Almanac* (1792), quoted in Chester E. Eisinger, "The Freehold Concept in Eighteenth-Century American Letters," *William and Mary Quarterly,* 3rd ser., 4 (Jan. 1947): 56.

14. Freneau, "The Pilgrim, No. VIII," 1.

15. Jefferson to Jackson, Feb. 16, 1803, in A. A. Lipscomb and A. E. Bergh, eds., *The Writings of Thomas Jefferson* (Washington, 1904), 10:357–58.

16. Gen. James Wilkinson (1797), quoted in Anthony F. C. Wallace, *Jefferson and the Indians: The Tragic Fate of the First Americans* (Cambridge, 1999), 276, 156.

17. Adam Smith, *An Inquiry into the Nature and Causes of the Wealth of Nations* (London, 1776), quoted by Colin A. M. Duncan, "Adam Smith's Labouring Cattle: The Role of Nature in History and Political Economy" (paper prepared for the Yale Agrarian Studies Seminar, Nov. 7, 2003), 7.

18. Duncan, "Adam Smith's Labouring Cattle," 9–10.

19. Jefferson to Benjamin Austin, Jan. 9, 1816, in A. Whitney Griswold, "The Agrarian Democracy of Thomas Jefferson," *American Political Science Review* 40:4 (1946): 670. In 1837, the *Cultivator*'s editor praised the new husbandry system, which "regards the soil as a gift of the beneficent Creator . . . like our free institutions." Steven Stoll, *Larding the Lean Earth* (New York, 2002), 90.

20. Timothy Dwight, quoted in Eisinger, "Freehold Concept," 51.

21. St. John de Crèvecoeur, *Letters from an American Farmer* (London, 1782), quoted in Smith, *Virgin Land,* 127–28; Crèvecoeur, quoted in Eisinger, "Freehold Concept," 49.

22. George Logan, *Letters, Addressed to the Yeomanry of the United States* (Philadelphia, 1791), quoted in Smith, *Virgin Land,* 277n11; Logan, quoted in Eisinger, "Freehold Concept," 47–48.

23. Philip Freneau, *Letters on Various and Important Subjects* (Philadelphia, 1799), 18, quoted in Eisinger, "Freehold Concept," 58.

24. Griswold, "Agrarian Democracy," 659.

25. Washington to Arthur Young, Dec. 5, 1791, quoted in Stoll, *Larding the Lean Earth,* 34–35.

26. Franklin, quoted in Eisinger, "Freehold Concept," 49, and in Smith, *Virgin Land,* 125.

27. Griswold, "Agrarian Democracy," 660; Smith, *Virgin Land,* 128; Jefferson, *State of Virginia,* 164–65.

28. Jefferson to Madison, Oct. 28, 1785, in Griswold, "Agrarian Democracy," 661; Smith, *Virgin Land,* 128.

29. Quoted in Edmund S. Morgan, *Benjamin Franklin* (New Haven, 2002), 131.

30. Smith, *Virgin Land,* 126; Eisinger, "Freehold Concept," 55–58.

31. Benjamin Rush, 1806, quoted in Stoll, *Larding the Lean Earth,* 85–88.

32. *Memoirs of the Society of Virginia for Promoting Agriculture* (Richmond, 1818), iii, in Stoll, *Larding the Lean Earth,* 44–45. In the North, too, a visitor wrote the next year: "It is the custom with farmers to sow or cultivate a much greater quantity of land than they can properly manage" (36).

33. Thomas Jefferson, *Summary View of the Rights of British America* (Williamsburg, 1774), 21, quoted in Anthony Marc Lewis, "Jefferson and Virginia's Pioneers, 1774–1781," *Mississippi Valley Historical Review* 34 (1948): 553.

34. Farmers "as a class came to be associated with the idea of a democratic state," while farming became "tinged with glory" (Eisinger, "Freehold Concept," 44–48); Smith, *Virgin Land,* 126, 12.

35. Unlike Physiocrats, who favoured large estates, Jefferson spoke for the economic interests and virtues of small farmers and settlers. Griswold, "Agrarian Democracy," 667; Eisinger, "Freehold Concept," 59.

36. Jefferson, *State of Virginia,* quoted in Griswold, "Agrarian Democracy," 667. In 1785, Jefferson added that in "my own theory, . . . all our citizens would be husbandmen" (669).

37. Ibid., 668.

38. Jefferson to James Madison, Dec. 20, 1787, quoted in Griswold, "Agrarian Democracy," 668.

39. Ibid.

40. Jefferson to Benjamin Austin, Jan. 9, 1816, quoted in Griswold, "Agrarian Democracy," 670.

41. Quoted in Edmund Morgan, *The Birth of the Republic, 1763–89* (Chicago, 1977), 160–61.

42. Quoted in Thomas Hatley, *The Dividing Paths: Cherokees and South Carolinians through the Era of Revolution* (New York, 1993), 193.

43. Colin G. Calloway, *The American Revolution in Indian Country* (New York, 1995), 197, 48–49, 55, 49.

44. Morgan, *Birth of the Republic,* 160–61; Calloway, *American Revolution,* 31.

45. William R. Nester, *The Frontier War for American Independence* (Mechanicsburg, 2004), 1, 3.

46. John K. Mahon, "Indian–United States Military Situation, 1775–1848," in Wilcomb E. Washburn, ed., *History of Indian-White Relations,* vol. 4 of *Handbook of North American Indians* (Washington, 1988), 144.

47. Jefferson to John Page, Aug. 5, 1776, in Boyd, *Papers of Thomas Jefferson,* 1:485–87; Lewis, "Jefferson and Virginia's Pioneers," 568–69.

48. Jefferson to Pendleton, Aug. 13, 1776, in Boyd, *Papers of Thomas Jefferson,* 1:494.

49. Jefferson to Page, Aug. 20, 1776, in Boyd, *Papers of Thomas Jefferson,* 1:500.

50. Calloway, *American Revolution,* 39, 162–68; Wallace, *Jefferson and the Indians,* 62.

51. Jefferson, Mason, and Wythe to Clark, Jan. 3, 1778, quoted in Lewis, "Jefferson and Virginia's Pioneers," 570–75; Grenier, *The First Way of War,* 156.

52. George Rogers Clark to George Mason, Nov. 19, 1779, *Illinois Historical Collections* (Illinois State Historical Library), 8, 116, 123–29.

53. George Rogers Clark, Nov. 1778, quoted in Calloway, *American Revolution,* 48; Wallace, *Jefferson and the Indians,* 6, 62–64; Clark to Mason, Nov. 19, 1779, 144.

54. Clark's account quoted in Richard White, *The Middle Ground: Indians, Empires, and Republics in the Great Lakes Region, 1650–1815* (New York, 1991), 376–77.

55. Clark to Mason, Nov. 19, 1779, 144. In his later account, Clark reported that his force had "killed three on the spot and brought 4 in," whom Clark then had "Tomahawked by the Soldiers and flung into the River." White, *Middle Ground,* 376–77.

56. Wallace, *Jefferson and the Indians,* 65, 59, 67; White, *Middle Ground,* 375–78.

57. Clark to Mason, Nov. 19, 1779, 146–47, 152–53.

58. Ibid., 151, 153, 148–49.

59. Ibid., 154.

60. Wallace, *Jefferson and the Indians,* 65; Calloway, *American Revolution,* 53, 172.

61. Jefferson to Clark, Jan. 1, 1780, in Boyd, *Papers of Thomas Jefferson,* 3:258–59, and n1 (deletion).

62. Woody Holton, "The Ohio Indians and the Coming of the American Revolution in Virginia," *Journal of Southern History* 60:3 (1994): 461; Calloway, *American Revolution,* 55, 174; R. Douglas Hurt, *The Ohio Frontier: Crucible of the Old Northwest, 1720–1830* (Bloomington, 1996), 20.

63. Jefferson to Clark, Jan. 29, 1780, in Boyd, *Papers of Thomas Jefferson,* 3:276; Clark's copy is reprinted in J. A. James, ed., *George Rogers Clark Papers, 1771–1781* (Springfield, 1912), 390.

64. Jefferson to Clark, Apr. 19, 1780, in Boyd, *Papers of Thomas Jefferson,* 3:356. See also Lewis, "Jefferson and Virginia's Pioneers," 577–78.

65. Brodhead to Clark, May 20, 1780, in James, *George Rogers Clark Papers,* 419–20.

66. Washington to Jefferson, Dec. 28, 1780, in Lewis, "Jefferson and Virginia's Pioneers," 586n78.

67. In Jan. 1778, Jefferson instructed Clark that his upcoming expedition, "if successful," would help "in establishing our northwestern boundary." Lewis, "Jefferson and Virginia's Pioneers," 576.

68. Jefferson to Clark, Dec. 25, 1780, quoted in Holton, "The Ohio Indians," 477.

69. Jefferson to Clark, Sept. 26 and Dec. 15, 1780, quoted in Lewis, "Jefferson and Virginia's Pioneers," 585; Greene, quoted in Wallace, *Jefferson and the Indians,* 71.

70. Calloway, *American Revolution,* 54, 175.

71. Mahon, "Indian–United States Military Situation," 149; Calloway, *American Revolution,* 175.

72. Calloway, *American Revolution,* 176–81.

73. Wallace, *Jefferson and the Indians,* 58, 64–65, 60; Calloway, *American Revolution,* 50.

74. Calloway, *American Revolution,* 51, 53.

75. Calloway, *American Revolution,* 49; C .A. Weslager, *The Delaware Indians: A History* (New Brunswick, 1972), 314–15.

76. Bernard W. Sheehan, *Seeds of Extinction: Jeffersonian Philanthropy and the American Indian* (New York, 1973), 187; Weslager, *The Delaware Indians,* 315–17.

77. Quoted in Francis Paul Prucha, *The Great Father: The United States Government and the American Indians* (Lincoln, 1984), 1:56.

78. Quoted in ibid., 1:62.

79. Knox to Gen. Harmar, June 7, 1790, *American State Papers, 7, Indian Affairs* 1:97–98.

80. Knox to Washington, Dec. 29, 1794, *American State Papers, 7, Indian Affairs* 1:543–44.

81. Wallace, *Jefferson and the Indians,* 60; Jefferson to Charles Carroll, Apr. 15, 1791, quoted in Wallace, *Jefferson and the Indians,* 172; Ronald Takaki, *Iron Cages: Race and Culture in 19th-Century America* (New York, 1990), 56.

82. Wallace, *Long Bitter Trail,* 88; Jefferson, Nov. 1, 1803, quoted in Smith, *Virgin Land,* 15, 126.

83. Wallace, *Long, Bitter Trail,* 88, 8; Wallace, *Jefferson and the Indians,* 275.

84. Jefferson to Gen. Horatio Gates, July 11, 1803, in A. A. Lipscomb and A. E. Bergh, eds., *The Writings of Thomas Jefferson* (Washington, 1904), 10:402–3. Jefferson bore partial responsibility for "the tragedy which he so elegantly mourned: the dispossession and decimation of the First Americans" (Wallace, *Jefferson and the Indians,* viii). Jefferson's hope for removal of "all our Indians" was one he had committed to paper as early as 1776, when he urged retaliation for Indian attacks "while one of them remained on this side the Misisippi" (Jefferson to John Page, Aug. 5, 1776, 485–86).

85. Jefferson to Gov. W. H. Harrison, Washington, Feb. 27, 1803, in Lipscomb and Bergh, *Writings of Thomas Jefferson,* 10:371–73.

86. Ibid., 371; Jefferson to Dearborn, Aug. 28, 1807, in Lipscomb and Bergh, *Writings of Thomas Jefferson,* 11:345–46; Richard Drinnon, *Facing West: The Metaphysics of Indian-Hating and Empire-Building* (Minneapolis, 1980), 96.

87. Jefferson to the Chiefs of the Ottawas, Chippewas, Powtewatamies, Wyandots, and Senecas of Sandusky, Apr. 22, 1808; and Jefferson to the Chiefs of the Wyandots, Ottawas, Chippewas, Powtewatamies, and Shawanese, Jan. 10, 1809, in Lipscomb and Bergh, *Writings of Thomas Jefferson,* 16:431–32, 463–64.

88. Jefferson to the Miamis, Powtewatamies, Delawares, and Chippewas, Dec. 21, 1808; and Jefferson, Jan. 10, 1809, in Lipscomb and Bergh, *Writings of Thomas Jefferson,* 16:439, 462.

89. Jefferson to John Adams, June 11, 1812, reprinted in Washburn, *The Indian and the White Man,* doc. 25, pp. 94–95.

90. Jefferson to Alexander von Humboldt, Dec. 6, 1813, text in Helmut de Terra, "Alexander von Humboldt's Correspondence with Jefferson, Madison, and Gallatin," *Proceedings of the American Philosophical Society* 103:6 (1959): 792–93. Jens-Uwe Guettel drew this to my attention. See Mary Young, "Indian Policy in the Age of Jefferson," *Journal of the Early Republic* 20 (2000): 298.

91. 21 U.S. (8 Wheat.) 543, 5 L. Ed. 681 (U.S. Sup. Ct. 1823), cited in *Indian Tribes as Sovereign Governments* (Oakland, 1998), 103. Margaret Moody drew this to my attention.

92. Quoted in Wallace, *Long, Bitter Trail,* 116, and Francis Jennings, *The Invasion of America: Indians, Colonialism, and the Cant of Conquest* (New York, 1975), 60.

93. Lewis Cass, "Removal of the Indians," *North American Review* 30 (1830): 77, quoted in Jennings, *Invasion,* 81; Wallace, *Long, Bitter Trail,* 41–48.

94. Wallace, *Long, Bitter Trail,* 63, 51, 57.

95. Robert Remini, *Andrew Jackson and His Indian Wars* (New York, 2001), 79–80.

96. Jackson, Proclamation, Apr. 2, 1814, quoted in Takaki, *Iron Cages,* 102–3.

97. Wallace, *Long, Bitter Trail,* 50–52, 4–5, 63. The First Seminole War broke out in 1817 amid tensions over border raids by Seminoles from Spanish Florida and their sheltering of escaped slaves from Georgia and Alabama. Jackson predicted that land values in Florida would soon rise. A business associate of Jackson and another nephew bought up thousands of acres in Pensacola just before Jackson invaded Florida. He captured Pensacola, Spain sold Florida to the United States, and Jackson briefly became governor. In 1823, the Seminoles ceded their lands in return for a central Florida reservation, surveyed by Jackson's nephew and business partner, John Coffee. Wallace, *Long, Bitter Trail,* 53–54, 95.

98. Ibid., 88, 53; Russell Thornton, *The Cherokees: A Population History* (Lincoln, 1990), 83.

99. Wallace, *Long, Bitter Trail,* 59–64, 10–11.

100. Grant Foreman, *The Five Civilized Tribes* (Norman, 1934), 413: "It was only as late as 1847 that Indians were made competent witnesses in the white man's court." *Report of Commissioner of Indian Affairs* (1855).

101. Wallace, *Long, Bitter Trail,* 88, 64, 5, 74.

102. *Register of Debates in Congress,* 21st Cong., 1st sess., 1829–30, 1103 (thanks to Jamey Carson).

103. Wallace, *Long, Bitter Trail,* 70–76.

104. Jackson, second annual message to Congress, Dec. 6, 1830, quoted in Takaki, *Iron Cages,* 103.

105. Wallace, *Long, Bitter Trail,* 77–83, 64, 83–88; Wilson, *The Earth,* 166.

106. Wallace, *Long, Bitter Trail,* 9–10, 89–91.

107. Ibid., 89.

108. Davy Crockett, speech to the House of Representatives, 1833, quoted in *Indian Historian* 1 (Summer 1968): inside cover.

109. Wallace, *Long, Bitter Trail,* 90–92; Stannard, *American Holocaust,* 122.

110. Wilson, *The Earth,* 163; Wallace, *Long, Bitter Trail,* 93; Stannard, *American Holocaust,* 123.

111. Theda Perdue and M. D. Green, *The Cherokee Removal: A Brief History with Documents* (New York, 2005), 167–68; Wallace, *Long, Bitter Trail,* 10, 94; Thornton, *The Cherokees,* 73–76, 88–89.

112. "Journal of Stephen F. Austin on His First Trip to Texas, 1821," entry for Aug. 12, *Quarterly of the Texas State Historical Association* 7 (July 1903–Apr. 1904): 296; W. E. S. Dickerson, "Indian Relations," *Handbook of Texas Online:* www.tsha.utexas.edu/handbook/online (accessed Feb. 6, 2005).

113. "Journal of Stephen F. Austin," entry for Sept. 17, 1821, 304–5; Kelly F. Himmel, *The Conquest of the Karankawas and the Tonkawas, 1821–1859* (1999), 46. On cannibalism, see 21–22, and John Columbus Marr, "The History of Matagorda County, Texas" (master's thesis, University of Texas, Austin, 1928): "Probably the Karankawas were not really cannibals" (33–34).

114. Humboldt to Jefferson, undated, translation in "Jefferson Seeks Humboldt's Help and Asserts U.S. Claims beyond Louisiana," and "Humboldt Supplies Precise Details and Evaluation of Areas as Far as the Rio Grande," n3: www.ku.edu/~maxkade/humboldt/subwashington.htm (accessed Oct. 16, 2005). In 1821, the Gulf pirate Jean Lafitte and 200 buccaneers armed with cannons attacked and killed 30 of the 300 Karankawas living on Galveston Island, and drove away all survivors. David La Vere, *The Texas Indians* (College Station, 2004), 178; Himmel, *Conquest,* 18.

115. "Recollections of Judge Thomas M. Duke," in "Reminiscences of Early Texans," *Quarterly of the Texas State Historical Association* 6 (July 1902–April 1903): 247–48, 250.

116. Marr, "History of Matagorda County," 2–4; Himmel, *Conquest,* 18, 14.

117. "Journal of Stephen F. Austin," entry for Sept. 16, 1821, 299–300, 303–4.

118. "Recollections of Capt. Horatio Chriesman," in "Reminiscences of Early Texans," *Quarterly of the Texas State Historical Association* 6 (July 1902–April 1903): 236–37.

119. "Recollections of Judge Thomas M. Duke," 252.

120. "Moore, John Henry (1800–1880)," *Handbook of Texas Online* (accessed May 23, 2005).

121. "Reminiscences of Capt. Jesse Burnam" (including John H. Moore's account), *Quarterly of the Texas State Historical Association* 5 (July 1901–April 1902): 15–16; Himmel, *Conquest,* 48–49.

122. W. B. Dewees, letter from Colorado River, Aug. 29, 1823, in Dewees, *Letters from an Early Settler of Texas* (Waco, 1968), 39–40.

123. John H. Moore's account, excerpted in "Reminiscences of Capt. Jesse Burnam," 16; Burnam recalled: "We killed fourteen and wounded seven" (15); Himmel, *Conquest,* estimates 19 Indians killed (49).

124. Anon., *A Visit to Texas* (New York, 1834), 240, quoted in Himmel, *Conquest,* 45.

125. Carol A. Lipscomb, "Karankawa Indians," *Handbook of Texas Online* (accessed May 28, 2005); "Reminiscences of Early Texans," 238–39; Marr, "History of Matagorda County," 31; "Reminiscences of Capt. Jesse Burnam," 18. For another 1824 incident of unprovoked settler violence against Karankawas, see "Reminiscences of Early Texans," 250.

126. Austin to Mateo Ahumada, Sept. 10, 1825, in Eugene C. Barker, ed., *The Austin Papers* (Washington, 1924), vol. 2, part 2, 1197–98, and Austin, "Referendum on Indian Relations," Sept. 28, 1825, 1208–11.

127. Austin to Ahumada, Sept. 10, 1825, 1198; Lipscomb, "Karankawa."

128. Austin, Sept. 28, 1825, in Barker, *The Austin Papers,* vol. 2, part 2, 1211.

129. The contrasting approaches to different Indian groups became clear the next year. A 100-strong party of Austin's colonists practiced new restraint when they attacked a village of Wacos and Tawakonis in 1826. One attacker recalled: "We now received orders to ride in quickly and fire. We obeyed, but only succeeded in killing one man." They pursued the Indian braves: "As our frontiers are ever exposed to the fury of the Indians, we determined to set them an example of not injuring the women or children." Himmel, *Conquest,* 52–53, 43–44. Austin also attempted to enlist the Cherokees, promising them "if you turn out in this expedition and destroy the Towakany villages . . . it will be the means of securing you land in the country for as many of your nation as wish to remove here." Austin to "Richard Fields and other Chiefs and Warriors of the Cherokee Nation," Apr. 24, 1826, quoted in E. W. Winkler, "The Cherokee Indians in Texas," *Quarterly of the Texas State Historical Association* 7 (Oct. 1903): 127–28.

130. La Vere, *The Texas Indians,* 179; Himmel, *Conquest,* 50–51.

131. J. W. Wilbarger, *Indian Depredations in Texas* (Austin, 1889; Austin, 1967), 210; "Recollections of Judge Thomas M. Duke," 250, estimates that Buckner's attackers killed "about thirty" Indians; Marr, "History of Matagorda County," 35–36.

132. Twenty settlers stormed a Karankawa camp in a dawn attack in 1832, "killed four or five, and dispersed the remainder"(Himmel, *Conquest,* 50–51, 53); Marr, "History of Matagorda County," 42. When other settlers attacked a second camp the next year, "a pretty severe fight ensued in which several of the Carancahuas were killed and wounded," which was said to have taught them "a good lesson." Wilbarger, *Indian Depredations in Texas,* 214, quoted in Himmel, *Conquest,* 54.

133. Marr, "History of Matagorda County," 76–78; Himmel, *Conquest,* 54; A. B. Giles, Trespalacios, Sept. 27, 1882, text in Marr, "History of Matagorda County," 37–38; 42–43.

134. A. Hotchkiss to M. B. Lamar, Houston, Dec. 5, 1838, in C. A. Gulick, ed., *The Papers of Mirabeau Buonaparte Lamar* (Austin, 1922), 2:310–11; F. Durcy to Francois Grapp, Nov. 10, 1825, in Barker, *The Austin Papers,* vol. 2, part 2, 1231; Winkler, "Cherokee Indians in Texas," 96, 103, 133.

135. Winkler, "Cherokee Indians in Texas," 105–6, 147, 150, 153–56, 163, 158–59.

136. Dickerson, "Indian Relations."

137. John Ross, "Letter in Answer to Inquiries from a Friend," July 2, 1836, in Perdue and Green, *Cherokee Removal,* 157.

138. Washburn, *History of Indian-White Relations,* 652.

139. "Cherokee War," *Handbook of Texas Online* (accessed Feb. 6, 2005).

140. Dickerson, "Indian Relations."

141. W. Roberts to M. B. Lamar, Aransas, July 12, 1838, and S. Houston to [Chief] Col. Bowl [Duwali], Nacogdoches, Aug. 12, 1838, in Gulick, *Papers of Mirabeau Buonaparte Lamar,* 2:183, 201.

142. S. Houston, general order, Aug. 18, 1838, in Gulick, *Papers of Mirabeau Buonaparte Lamar,* 2:206.

143. J. C. Ramsay Jr., *Thunder beyond the Brazos: Mirabeau B. Lamar* (Austin, 1985), 14–16, 143–44, 21.

144. Ibid., 26, 24, 29, 31, cf. 45; 143.

145. Herbert Pickens Gambrell, *Mirabeau Buonaparte Lamar: Troubadour and Crusader* (Dallas, 1934), 19; Ramsay, *Thunder,* 213n5, 9, 11, 13; Gulick, *Papers of Mirabeau Buonaparte Lamar,* 1:29–30.

146. Gambrell, *Mirabeau Buonaparte Lamar,* 19–21.

147. Ramsay, *Thunder,* 37–39.

148. Lamar, "Message to Both Houses," Dec. 21, 1838, in Gulick, *Papers of Mirabeau Buonaparte Lamar,* 2:349.

149. Lamar to citizens of Galveston, June 2, 1840, in Gulick, *Papers of Mirabeau Buonaparte Lamar,* 3:402.

150. Lamar, inaugural address, Dec. 10, 1838, in Gulick, *Papers of Mirabeau Buonaparte Lamar,* 2:320.

151. Lamar, "Message to Both Houses," Dec. 21, 1838, 368; Gambrell, *Mirabeau Buonaparte Lamar,* 240–41, 245.

152. Lamar, "Message to Both Houses," Dec. 21, 1838, 348.

153. Ibid., 364, 365, 368.

154. Gambrell, *Mirabeau Buonaparte Lamar,* 243–44.

155. Diana Everitt, *The Texas Cherokees: A People between Two Fires* (Norman, 1990), 110; Thornton, *The Cherokees,* 84.

156. Lamar had risen to army commander in chief in 1836 but immediately forfeited his appointment to Rusk, who trounced him with over 1,500 votes to 179 in a poll of the troops, only to lose to Lamar in the vice presidential race. T. J. Rusk to M. B. Lamar, Aug. 24, and H. McLeod to Lamar, Aug. 26, 1838, in Gulick, *Papers of Mirabeau Buonaparte Lamar,* 2:209–10; Ramsay, *Thunder,* 43–47.

157. "Rusk, Thomas Jefferson (1803–1857)," "McLeod, Hugh (1814–1862)," and "Cherokee War," *Handbook of Texas Online* (accessed Feb. 6, 2005).

158. H. McLeod to M. B. Lamar, Oct. 22, 1838, in Gulick, *Papers of Mirabeau Buonaparte Lamar,* 2:266.

159. T. J. Rusk to Col. Bowl [Duwali], Oct. 20, 1838, in Gulick, *Papers of Mirabeau Buonaparte Lamar,* 2:255.

160. D. H. Campbell, Houston, Oct. 22, 1838, in Gulick, *Papers of Mirabeau Buonaparte Lamar,* 2:264.

161. Col. Hugh McLeod to Vice President M. B. Lamar, Nacogdoches, Oct. 25, 1838, in Gulick, *Papers of Mirabeau Buonaparte Lamar,* 2:270–71 (emphasis in original).

162. McLeod to Lamar, Port Caddo, Nov. 21 and Dec. 1, 1838, in Gulick, *Papers of Mirabeau Buonaparte Lamar,* 2:298–99, 308–9.

163. Lamar, "Message to Both Houses," Dec. 21, 1838, 352–53.

164. Ibid., 354; Gambrell, *Mirabeau Buonaparte Lamar,* 238–39.

165. Dickerson, "Indian Relations"; Lamar, "Message to Both Houses," Dec. 21, 1838, 353. A commissioned officer in the army of the republic in 1840–45 who became an Indian agent for the government of Texas and then the United States, wrote: "From 1838 to 1842 the Republic of Texas attempted to carry on a war of extermination against our border Indians." Robert S. Neighbors (1815–1859), Jan. 8, 1855, in K. F. Neighbours, *Indian Exodus: Texas Indian Affairs, 1835–1859* (Olney, 1973), 20. Historian Francis Paul Prucha writes that Lamar "sought the expulsion or extermination of the Indians. The result was almost continual warfare." "United States Indian Policies, 1815–1860," in Washburn, *History of Indian-White Relations,* 48.

166. F. Huston to Lamar, Houston, Dec. 31, 1838; Rusk to Lamar, Red River Country, Jan. 9, 1839; McLeod to Lamar, Red River, Jan. 9, 1839; McLeod to Lamar, Nacogdoches, Jan. 18, 1839, in Gulick, *Papers of Mirabeau Buonaparte Lamar,* 2:377, 405, 406, 423.

167. William T. Saddler to Lamar, Feb. 22, 1839, and Joseph R. Jenkins to Lamar, Mar. 5, 1839, in Gulick, *Papers of Mirabeau Buonaparte Lamar,* 2:464–65, 484–85.

168. Neighbours, *Indian Exodus,* 10; Himmel, *Conquest,* 48–49; "Moore, John Henry (1800–1880)."

169. Report of Capt. J. H. Moore to Albert Sidney Johnston, LaGrange, Mar. 10, 1839, in *Texas Indian Papers* (Austin, 1959), 1:57.

170. A. S. Johnston to Martin Lacy, Houston, Feb. 14, 1839, in *Texas Indian Papers*, 1:55–56.

171. Moore to Johnston, Mar. 10, 1839, 57–59; Himmel, *Conquest*, 83.

172. Moore to Johnston, Mar. 10, 1839, 58–59.

173. Lamar, president's address, Feb. 28, 1839, in Gulick, *Papers of Mirabeau Buonaparte Lamar*, 2:474–75.

174. Everitt, *Texas Cherokees*, 103.

175. Mary Whatley Clarke, *Thomas J. Rusk: Soldier, Statesman, Jurist* (Austin, 1971), 125.

176. M. B. Lamar to Chief Bowles [Duwali], May 26, 1839, in *Texas Indian Papers*, 1:61–66; see also the excerpts in Everitt, *Texas Cherokees*, 103–4, and www.texasindians.com/cherokee.htm (accessed May 6, 2005)

177. Lamar, from Houston, June 27, 1839, excerpted in Clarke, *Thomas J. Rusk*, 127.

178. Mary Whatley Clarke, *Chief Bowles and the Texas Cherokees* (Norman, 1971), 101–2; Clarke, *Thomas J. Rusk*, 131.

179. Clarke, *Chief Bowles*, 108, 111, 113; Clarke, *Thomas J. Rusk*, 128–33; Hampson Gary, "Neches," *Handbook of Texas Online* (accessed Feb. 6, 2005); Everitt, *Texas Cherokees*, 108.

180. Clarke, *Thomas J. Rusk*, 133–34; Clarke, *Chief Bowles*, 113.

181. Everitt, *Texas Cherokees*, 108; Clarke, *Thomas J. Rusk*, 134–36.

182. Clarke, *Chief Bowles*, 111–117; "Cherokee War."

183. Lamar to citizens of Galveston, June 2, 1840, 402.

184. In 1840, with U.S. help, the Cherokees in Indian Territory secured the release of their people still held prisoner in Texas. Lamar permitted "the wives and some of the children of Chief Bowles," en route from Mexico to the United States, to transit through Texas with an escort. Other Cherokees took refugee in a Kickapoo village. Clarke, *Chief Bowles*, 114; Thornton, *The Cherokees*, 84, 86–87.

185. Dickerson, "Indian Relations"; Herbert Gambrell, "Lamar, Mirabeau Buonaparte (1798–1859)," *Handbook of Texas Online* (accessed Feb. 21, 2004).

186. "McLeod, Hugh (1814–1862)"; A. Sidney Johnston to W. S. Fisher, Austin, Jan. 30, 1840, *Texas Indian Papers*, 1:105–6.

187. "Letter from Col. Hugh McLeod, Communicating the Defeat of the Comanches at San Antonio, March 20, 1840," doc. F, appendix to the *Journal* of the Fifth Legislature of the Republic of Texas, 136, Beinecke Library, Yale University.

188. "Council House Fight," *Handbook of Texas Online* (accessed Feb. 6, 2005); "Letter from Col. Hugh McLeod," 137–38.

189. La Vere, *Texas Indians*, 188; "Council House Fight"; Gary Clayton Anderson, *The Conquest of Texas: Ethnic Cleansing in the Promised Land, 1820–1875* (Norman, 2005).

190. Craig H. Roell, "Linville Raid of 1840," *Handbook of Texas Online* (accessed Feb. 6, 2005).

191. *Texas Sentinel* (Austin), Aug. 15, 1840.

192. J. H. Moore, report to Austin dated early Nov. 1840, quoted in T. R. Fehrenbach, *Comanches: The Destruction of a People* (New York, 1974), 348 (La Vere says Moore "reported that his troops killed 125 men, women and children," *Texas Indians*, 185); Texas State Library and Archives Commission, "Indian Relations in Texas—The Comanche War": www.tsl.state.tx.us/exhibits/indian (accessed May 6, 2005).

193. Lipscomb, "Karankawa"; Marr, "History of Matagorda County," 45.

194. Lamar to citizens of Galveston, June 2, 1840, 403.

195. T. Bradford to Lamar, Montgomery, Nov. 15, 1838, in Gulick, *Papers of Mirabeau Buonaparte Lamar*, 2:292–93.

196. "Lamar, Mirabeau Buonaparte (1798–1859)."

197. "Rusk, Thomas Jefferson (1803–1857)"; "McLeod, Hugh (1814–1862)."

198. "Texan Santa Fe Expedition," *Handbook of Texas Online* (accessed Feb. 6, 2005); "McLeod, Hugh (1814–1862)."

199. Prucha, "United States Indian Policies," in Washburn, *History of Indian-White Relations*, 48.

200. Dickerson, "Indian Relations."

201. Everitt, *Texas Cherokees,* 115.

202. *Corpus Christi Star,* June 2, 1849, quoted in Himmel, *Conquest,* 108.

203. Himmel, *Conquest,* 98–101; Anderson, *The Conquest of Texas,* 254, 262.

204. Giles, Trespalacios, Sept. 27, 1882, 38.

205. Lipscomb, "Karankawa"; Marr, "History of Matagorda County," 46–48; Himmel, *Conquest,* 100–105.

206. "Rusk, Thomas Jefferson (1803–1857)"; "McLeod, Hugh (1814–1862)"; "Moore, John Henry (1800–1880)."

207. Elliott West, "Reconstructing Race," *Western Historical Quarterly* (Spring 2003): 16, 11; Wallace, *Long, Bitter Trail,* 112–13.

208. West, "Reconstructing Race," 8, 24.

209. Albert L. Hurtado, *Indian Survival on the California Frontier* (New Haven, 1988), 46, 1, 198; Wilson cites a toll of 70,000 from a malaria epidemic in 1838. The population of coastal California Indians fell from perhaps 70,000 to as few as 15,000. Wilson, *The Earth,* 439, 214, 224–26; Stannard, *American Holocaust,* 142.

210. B. D. Wilson, *The Indians of Southern California in 1852,* ed. J. W. Caughey (Lincoln, 1995), xxxiii; R. F. Heizer and A. J. Almquist, *The Other Californians: Prejudice and Discrimination under Spain, Mexico, and the United States to 1920* (Berkeley, 1977), 76–79; J. J. Rawls, *Indians of California: The Changing Image* (Norman, 1984); Wilson, *The Earth,* 228, 237–38; Stannard, *American Holocaust,* 143.

211. *Alta California* (San Francisco), Dec. 5, 1850, quoted in Benjamin Madley, "California's Yuki Indians and the American Genocide Debate" (forthcoming).

212. Gov. Peter Burnett, "Message to the California State Legislature," Jan. 7, 1851, *California State Senate Journal* (1851): 15, quoted in Hurtado, *Indian Survival,* 134–35.

213. Col. J. Neely Johnson, representing Gov. John McDougal, Jan. 25, 1851, *California State Senate Journal* (1851): 677, quoted in Hurtado, *Indian Survival,* 136; Stannard, *American Holocaust,* 144–45.

214. *San Francisco Bulletin,* Sept. 1, 1856, quoted in Madley, "California's Yuki."

215. Stannard, *American Holocaust,* 143–44; Wilson, *The Earth,* 228.

216. Quoted in William B. Seacrest, *When the Great Spirit Died: The Destruction of the California Indians, 1850–1860* (Sanger, 2003), 257, and Robert Heizer, *The Destruction of California Indians* (Santa Barbara, 1974), 233; Madley, "California's Yuki."

217. Sherburne F. Cook, *The Conflict between the California Indian and White Civilization* (Berkeley, 1976), 61; Castillo suggests "well over 4,000" Indian children were enslaved. *Handbook of North American Indians* III (Washington, D.C., 1978), 109. Ben Madley kindly provided these references.

218. Hurtado, *Indian Survival,* 169, 194; Wilson, *The Earth,* 228; Stannard, *American Holocaust,* 142, 145.

219. Russell Thornton, *American Indian Holocaust and Survival: A Population History since 1492* (Norman, 1987), 110; David Roberts, *A Newer World: Kit Carson, John C. Frémont, and the Claiming of the American West* (New York, 2001), 149–57; Robert F. Heizer, ed., *Collected Documents on the Causes and Events in the Bloody Island Massacre of 1850* (Berkeley, 1973), 10-15; Heizer, *Destruction,* 39, 243–45; Wilson, *The Earth,* 229–30; Hurtado, *Indian Survival,* 104–6.

220. *Crescent City Herald,* May 2, 1855, 1. Thanks to Ben Madley for this citation.

221. Thornton, *American Indian Holocaust and Survival,* 109–11; Wilson, *The Earth,* 230–31.

222. Benjamin Madley, "California's Yuki"; Madley, "Patterns of Frontier Genocide, 1803–1910: The Aboriginal Tasmanians, the Yuki of California, and the Herero of Namibia," *Journal of Genocide Research* 6:2 (2004): 167–92.

223. *Petaluma Journal,* Apr. 15, 1857, quoted in Madley, "California's Yuki."

224. Geiger to Henley, Sept. 24, 1857; Maj. Edward Johnson, May 1, 1859; and settler Dryden Laycock, 1860 testimony; all quoted in Madley, "California's Yuki."

225. *Sacramento Union,* Aug. 22, 1859, quoted in Madley, "California's Yuki."

226. Madley, "California's Yuki"; Heizer, *Destruction,* 296.

227. Geiger to Henley, Sept. 24, 1857; Maj. Edward Johnson, May 1, 1859; and settler Dryden Laycock, 1860 testimony.

228. Madley, "California's Yuki."

229. Stannard, *American Holocaust*, 313n123; Wilson, *The Earth*, 231–33; Thornton, *American Indian Holocaust and Survival*, 108.

230. J. Ross Browne, *Crusoe's Island* (New York, 1867), 285–92, excerpted in Heizer and Almquist, *The Other Californians*, 86–87.

231. Excerpt in Claire Perry, *Pacific Arcadia: Images of California 1600–1915* (New York, 1999), 61.

232. Perry, *Pacific Arcadia*, 62–66, 164–65; Wilson, *The Earth*, 237, cites a figure of 31,000 in 1870; Stannard, *American Holocaust*, 145–46.

233. David A. Nichols, *Lincoln and the Indians: Civil War Policy and Politics* (Urbana, 2000), 186–87, 183–84.

234. Horace Greeley in 1859, quoted in Jackson Lears, "How a War Became a Crusade," *New York Times*, March 11, 2003, A25.

235. D. W. Mitchell, *Ten Years in the United States* (London, 1862), 62.

236. Nichols, *Lincoln and the Indians*, 184–86.

237. Ibid., 184–85.

238. West, "Reconstructing Race," 19.

239. Caleb Smith to Abraham Lincoln, Feb. 12, 1863, quoted in Nichols, *Lincoln and the Indians*, 76–79.

240. Pope to Sibley, Sept. 17, and Sibley to Ramsay, Aug. 25, 1862, in Nichols, *Lincoln and the Indians*, 87–88, and 94, 98, 112, 117; *Daily Republican* (Winona), Sept. 24, 1863, copy supplied by Chris Mato Nunpa; James Carleton to Kit Carson, Oct. 12, 1862, in Nichols, *Lincoln and the Indians*, 165.

241. Kass Fleisher, *The Bear River Massacre and the Making of History* (Albany, 2004), xi, 41–42, 61–63.

242. Stannard, *American Holocaust*, 129–30.

243. Stan Hoig, *The Sand Creek Massacre* (Norman, 1961), 19; Stannard, *American Holocaust*, 131.

244. Col. Chivington to Maj. Wynkoop, May 31, 1864, quoted in Hoig, *Sand Creek*, 83.

245. D. Svaldi, *Sand Creek and the Rhetoric of Extermination: A Case Study in Indian-White Relations* (New York, 1989), 291, quoted in Stannard, *American Holocaust*, 131, 313n123.

246. Hoig, *Sand Creek*, 58–59; Stannard, *American Holocaust*, 130.

247. Gov. Evans, Aug. 11, 1864, in Hoig, *Sand Creek*, 68–69; Stannard, *American Holocaust*, 130.

248. Curtis to Chivington, Sept. 28, 1864, in Nichols, *Lincoln and the Indians*, 170; Hoig, *Sand Creek*, 90.

249. Hoig, *Sand Creek*, 155–56, 167, 192; Stannard, *American Holocaust*, 130–32, 313n125.

250. Hoig, *Sand Creek*, 184 (other estimates, 177–92), 154; Stannard, *American Holocaust*, 133–34.

251. Hoig, *Sand Creek*, 174; Fleisher, *The Bear River Massacre*, 41, 65; Wilson, *The Earth*, 275.

252. Sheridan to Gov. Crawford, quoted in Stan Hoig, *The Battle of the Washita* (Lincoln, 1976), 69.

253. Gov. Samuel Crawford, proclamation of Oct. 10, 1868, in Hoig, *Battle of the Washita*, 100–101; 185.

254. Hoig, *Battle of the Washita*, 125, xiii, 130, 189, 200–01.

255. Dee Brown, *The Fetterman Massacre* (Lincoln, 1962), 150.

256. Sherman, Dec. 1866, quoted in Ralph K. Andrist, *The Long Death: The Last Days of the Plains Indian* (New York, 1964), 124; J. P. Dunn, *Massacres of the Mountains: A History of the Indian Wars of the Far West, 1815–1875* (New York, 1886), 382; Wilson, *The Earth*, 276–79.

257. Herbert Krause and Gary Olson, eds., *Prelude to Glory* (Sioux Falls, 1974), 153; Brian Dippie (lecture, Yale University, Nov. 5, 2004).

258. Corp. Dan Starr, quoted in Thomas B. Marquis, *Custer, Cavalry, and Crows* (Bellvue, 1975), 31–34, excerpted in Stan Gibson and Jack Hayne, *Witnesses to Carnage: The 1870 Marias Massacre in Montana*: www.dickshovel.com/parts2.html (accessed Oct. 9, 2001).

259. Good Bear Woman (Mrs. No Chief), quoted in Gibson and Hayne, *Witnesses*, 13.

260. Joe Kipp and Horace Clarke, quoted in Gibson and Hayne, *Witnesses*, 11, 9.

261. Clarke and Kipp, quoted in Gibson and Hayne, *Witnesses*, 9–11.

262. Gibson and Hayne, *Witnesses,* 2, 3, 11. For Piegan survivor accounts, 11–19. Dunn, *Massacres of the Mountains,* suggests the toll was about 60 warriors "and 113 women and children" (451).

263. Capt. Lewis Thompson, 2nd U.S. Cavalry, quoted in Gibson and Hayne, *Witnesses,* 5.

264. Sheridan, Sept. 8, 1870, in Moritz Busch, *Bismarck: Some Secret Page of His History* (New York, 1898), 1:128, quoted in Jay Winter, "Total War and the Armenian Genocide," in Robert Gellately and Ben Kiernan, eds., *The Specter of Genocide: Mass Murder in Historical Perspective* (New York, 2003), 208–9; Wilson, *The Earth,* 279.

265. Sherman to Canby, Mar. 12, 1873, quoted in Dee Brown, *Bury My Heart at Wounded Knee* (New York, 1972), 230. Ben Madley drew my attention to this citation.

266. Sherman, letter to a friend in Washington, D.C., Apr. 17, 1873, in Peter Cozzens, ed., *Eyewitnesses to the Indian Wars, 1865–1890,* vol. 5, *The Army and the Indian* (Mechanicsburg, 2005), 113.

267. Sheridan to Sherman, Mar. 25, 1875, in Peter Cozzens, ed., *Eyewitnesses to the Indian Wars, 1865–1890,* vol. 4, *The Long War for the Northern Plains* (Mechanicsburg, 2004), 189; Krause and Olson, *Prelude to Glory,* 4, 153–54.

268. Brian W. Dippie, "Its Equal I Have Never Seen: Custer Explores the Black Hills in 1874," in *Columbia* (Washington State Historical Society) (Summer 2005): 18–27.

269. *New York Tribune,* Aug. 17, 1874, reprinted in Krause and Olson, *Prelude to Glory,* 210, 212.

270. G. A. Custer to assistant adjutant general, Dept. of Dakota, Aug. 3, 1874, in Krause and Olson, *Prelude to Glory,* 171.

271. Calhoun, July 20 and 30, 1874, in L. A. Frost, ed., *With Custer in '74: James Calhoun's Diary of the Black Hills* Expedition (Provo, 1979), 40, 58.

272. Calhoun, July 20, 1874, 40; Custer to assistant adjutant general, Dept. of Dakota, Aug. 3, 1874, 174–75; *New York World,* Aug. 16, 22, 1874, in Krause and Olson, *Prelude to Glory,* 163, 179.

273. *Chicago Inter-Ocean,* Aug. 27 and Sept. 5, 1874, in Krause and Olson, *Prelude to Glory,* 126, 136.

274. N. H. Knappen, "Black Hills," *Bismarck Tribune,* Sept. 2, 1874, in Krause and Olson, *Prelude to Glory,* 29.

275. *Chicago Inter-Ocean,* Aug. 27, 1874, in Krause and Olson, *Prelude to Glory,* 125.

276. "A New Gold Country," *New York Tribune,* Aug. 29, 1874, and *Chicago Inter-Ocean,* Sept. 8, 1874, in Krause and Olson, *Prelude to Glory,* 222–23, 139.

277. "Custer's Expedition," *St. Paul Daily Press,* July 28, 1874, in Krause and Olson, *Prelude to Glory,* 82.

278. Custer, July 15, 1874, and Calhoun, July 18, 1874, in Frost, *With Custer in '74,* 35, 39.

279. Fred Snow, "Snow's Reminiscence" [1893], reprinted in Krause and Olson, *Prelude to Glory,* 270, 28.

280. Calhoun, July 20, 1874, in Frost, *With Custer in '74,* 40.

281. Ray Allen Billington, *Land of Savagery, Land of Promise: The European Image of the American Frontier* (New York, 1981), 132, 138, quoting *American Settler,* June 11, 1881.

282. Dunn, *Massacres of the Mountains,* 366–67, 382.

283. *Aberdeen Saturday Pioneer,* Dec. 20, 1891, quoted in Stannard, *American Holocaust,* 126.

284. Jeffrey Ostler, *The Plains Sioux and U.S. Colonialism from Lewis and Clark to Wounded Knee* (New York, 2004), 338–45; Andrist, *Long Death,* 350–52; Wilson, *The Earth,* 284–85.

285. Thornton, *American Indian Holocaust and Survival,* 133; Stannard, *American Holocaust,* 146.

286. Stannard, *American Holocaust,* 245, citing T. G. Dyer, *Theodore Roosevelt and the Idea of Race* [1980].

287. Quoted in Robert Bensen, ed., *Children of the Dragonfly* (Tucson, 2001), 9.

Chapter 9. Settler Genocides in Africa, 1830–1910

1. Alexis de Tocqueville, "Some Ideas about What Prevents the French from Having Good Colonies," in *Alexis de Tocqueville: Writings on Empire and Slavery,* ed. Jennifer Pitts (Baltimore, 2001), 2.

2. Pitts, *Tocqueville*, xii, xiv, xx–xxi.

3. Alexis de Tocqueville, *Democracy in America* [1835] (New York, 1990), 1:355.

4. Pitts, *Tocqueville*, 250n3, 232n60; Kamel Kateb, *Européens, "Indigènes" et Juifs en Algérie (1830–1962): Représentations et réalités des populations* (Paris, 2001), 47; Pierre Montagnon, *Histoire de l'Algérie* (Paris, 1998), 169–70; Montagnon, *La conquête de l'Algérie* (Paris, 1986), 414, quoted in Olivier Le Cour Grandmaison, "Liberty, Equality, and Colony," *Monde diplomatique* (June 2001): 12–13, citing Denise Bouche, *Histoire de la colonisation française* (Paris, 1998), 2:23.

5. Kateb, *Européens, "Indigènes,"* 41–42.

6. *La dépêche algérienne, Les nouvelles* (noting "the 700 bodies"), and *Echos des nouvelles*, all dated June 20, 1903, clippings in Papiers Louis Rinn, Archives du Gouvernement Général de l'Algérie, series 10 (Papiers personnels), 3X/1 (thanks to George R. Trumbull IV for copies); Pitts, *Tocqueville*, 250n5; Kateb, *Européens, "Indigènes,"* 41.

7. John Merriman, *A History of Modern Europe*, vol. 2, *From the French Revolution to the Present* (New York, 1996), 693.

8. Tocqueville, "What Prevents the French from Having Good Colonies," 1–2.

9. Alexis de Tocqueville, "First Letter on Algeria (23 June 1837)," in Pitts, *Tocqueville*, 6–8.

10. Ibid., 9–13.

11. Ibid., 7–8.

12. Alexis de Tocqueville, "Second Letter on Algeria (22 August 1837)," in Pitts, *Tocqueville*, 24.

13. Ibid., 15–17, 19.

14. Ibid., 19–25.

15. Ibid., 24–26.

16. Charles-André Julien, *Histoire de l'Algérie contemporaine: La conquête et les débuts de la colonization (1827–1871)* (Paris, 1964), 141–42.

17. *Rapports sur les expéditions de Constantine, 1836–37*, quoted in Kateb, *Européens, "Indigènes,"* 42.

18. Julien, *Histoire de l'Algérie contemporaine*, 314.

19. Alexis de Tocqueville, "Essay on Algeria (October 1841)," in Pitts, *Tocqueville*, 76.

20. Letters of M. Daguan, May 24, 1841, quoted in Kateb, *Européens, "Indigènes,"* 41.

21. Tocqueville's diary entries, Algiers, May 7–8, 1841, in Pitts, *Tocqueville*, 36–37.

22. Pitts, *Tocqueville*, 238–39 (nn6, 10), 39–40 (Tocqueville's diary, May 1841).

23. Kateb, *Européens, "Indigènes,"* 3.

24. Tocqueville's diary, June 1841, in Pitts, *Tocqueville*, 58, xxxvi–xxxvii, 245n19.

25. Tocqueville's diary, May 24 and 30, 1841, in Pitts, *Tocqueville*, 44, 56, 47, 50.

26. Tocqueville's diary, May 23, 1841, in Pitts, *Tocqueville*, 43.

27. M. Bodichon, *Revue d'Orient* (July 1841): 40, quoted in Kateb, *Européens, "Indigènes,"* 40.

28. Julien, *Histoire de l'Algérie contemporaine*, 316.

29. Tocqueville, "Essay on Algeria (October 1841)," 70, 111.

30. Tocqueville's diary, May 30 and 24, 1841, 57, 48 (emphasis in original).

31. Tocqueville, "Essay on Algeria (October 1841)," 59–60.

32. Ibid., 66, 70–73.

33. Ibid., 72.

34. Tocqueville's diary, May 8, 1841, in Pitts, *Tocqueville*, 37.

35. Tocqueville, "Essay on Algeria (October 1841)," 82–83.

36. *Le moniteur algérien*, Nov. 24, 1840, quoted in Kateb, *Européens, "Indigènes,"* 4.

37. Tocqueville's diary, June 1841, 58.

38. Tocqueville's diary, May 30 and 23, 1841, 57, 42.

39. "Essay on Algeria (October 1841)," 74, 80; for details, see Julien, *Histoire de l'Algérie contemporaine*, 316.

40. Changarnier to Castellane, Alger, Oct. 18, quoted in Julien, *Histoire de l'Algérie contemporaine*, 319.

41. Montagnac, letters from Mascara, Dec. 19, 1841–Feb. 2, 1842, and Mar. 31, 1842, quoted in Julien, *Histoire de l'Algérie contemporaine*, 317–19.

42. Maréchal Bugeaud, "De la stratégie . . ." [1842], quoted in Kateb, *Européens, "Indigènes,"* 40.

43. Saint-Arnaud, Apr. 7, 1842, and Feb. 8, 1843; for more details, see Julien, *Histoire de l'Algérie contemporaine*, 319.

44. Canrobert to Castellane, Ténès, July 18, 1845, quoted in Julien, *Histoire de l'Algérie contemporaine*, 319–20.

45. *La dépêche algérienne*, June 20, 1903, 3X/1.

46. Corcelle, June 8, 1846, in Pitts, *Tocqueville*, 249n6, quoting an unidentified Algerian newspaper dated May 2, 1846.

47. Tocqueville, June 9, 1846, intervention reprinted in Pitts, *Tocqueville*, 118.

48. Pitts, *Tocqueville*, xxxvi.

49. Ibid., 80n, 238–39nn6, 10; 244–45nn13, 16.

50. Capitaine Lafaye, Sept. 23, 1848, quoted in Julien, *Histoire de l'Algérie contemporaine*, 320.

51. Gen. de Lamoricière, Oct. 8, 1848, speech reproduced in part in "Histoire de la semaine," *L'illustration*, Oct. 14, 1848, 98. Jennifer Sessions kindly provided this citation.

52. G. Mouillié, *Essai de topographie médicale*, Feb. 6, 1863, quoted in Kateb, *Européens, "Indigènes,"* 5.

53. Napoléon III, letter, *Le moniteur*, Feb. 6, 1863, quoted in Kateb, *Européens, "Indigènes,"* 5, 6.

54. Ch. Philibert, *Expédition dans les Béni-Menaceur en 1871* (Paris 1873), quoted in Kateb, *Européens, "Indigènes,"* 4.

55. Kateb, *Européens, "Indigènes,"* 47, 49, 6, quoting M. Wahl, *L'Algérie* (Paris, 1882).

56. E. Mignot, "La France dans l'AFN," *Journal de la Société de Statistique de Paris* (1887), quoted in Kateb, *Européens, "Indigènes,"* 6.

57. Jens-Uwe Guettel, "Indianthusiasm, Ethnocentrism, Racism: Germans and Indians, 1790–2005," International Security Studies paper, Yale University, 2007, 6n13, citing Albert R. Schmitt, *Herder und Amerika* (The Hague, 1967), 9–11, 109.

58. Immanuel Kant, "Über den Gebrauch teleologischer Prinzipien in der Philosophie," *Der Teutsche Merkur* 1 (1788): 121, and Johann Gottfried Herder, *Briefe zu Beförderung der Humanität* (Riga, 1793–97), 2; both quoted in Guettel, "Indianthusiasm," 8–9.

59. Jefferson to Alexander von Humboldt, Dec. 6, 1813, in Helmut de Terra, "Alexander von Humboldt's Correspondence with Jefferson, Madison, and Gallatin," *Proceedings of the American Philosophical Society*, Dec. 15, 1959, 792–93. Jens-Uwe Guettel kindly drew this to my attention.

60. Alexander von Humboldt, *Political Essay on the Kingdom of New Spain*, tr. John Black (London, 1811), 1:134–217: www.fordham.edu/halsall/mod/1800humboldtmexico.html (accessed Oct. 15, 2005).

61. Friedrich Gerstäcker, *Streif- und Jagdzüge durch die Vereinigten Staaten von Nord-Amerika* (Dresden, 1844), 83; Guettel, "Indianthusiasm," 13–17.

62. Gustav Dresel, *Tagebuch von Gustav Dresel über seinen Aufenthalt in Texas, 1837–41*, in *Deutsch-amerikanische Geschichtsblätter* (Chicago, 1922), 20–21:338–476, preliminary note. Thanks to Jens-Uwe Guettel for this reference and translation.

63. Gustav Dresel, *Gustav Dresel's Houston Journey: Adventures in North America and Texas* (Austin, 1954), 123–24, 34, 109–10, xx.

64. Dresel, *Tagebuch von Gustav Dresel über seinen Aufenthalt in Texas, 1837–41*, preliminary note; Dresel, *Gustav Dresel's Houston Journey*, xx, 149n67.

65. Sheridan to Gov. Crawford, quoted in Stan Hoig, *The Battle of the Washita* (Lincoln, 1976), 69.

66. Moritz Busch, *Bismarck: Some Secret Page of His History* (New York, 1898), 1:128, quoted in Jay Winter, "Total War and the Armenian Genocide," in Robert Gellately and Ben Kiernan, eds., *The Specter of Genocide: Mass Murder in Historical Perspective* (New York, 2003), 208–9.

67. Friedrich Nietzsche, *Die fröhliche Wissenschaft* (Stuttgart, 2000), 216, in Guettel, "Indianthusiasm," 18.

68. Thomas Carlyle, *Chartism* (1839), ch. 4, in *Works*, 29:139; Paul Henkel, ed., *Socialpolitische Schriften von Thomas Carlyle* (Göttingen, 1895), 1–101; Carlyle, "The Repeal of the Union," *Examiner*, Apr. 29, 1848; and James A. Davies, "The Effects of Context: Carlyle and the *Examiner* in 1848," *Yearbook of English Studies* 16 (1986): 58–59, quoted in Claude Rawson, *God, Gulliver, and Genocide: Barbarism and the European Imagination, 1492–1945* (Oxford, 2001), 234.

69. Karl May, *Winnetou I* (1892; Bamberg, 1950), 5–6; Guettel, "Indianthusiasm," 19–20; Guettel, "Reading America, Studying Empire," Yale Ph.D. diss., 2007, 257.

70. David Blackbourne, *Fontana History of Germany, 1780–1918* (Oxford, 2003), 231, 253, 250.

71. Woodruff D. Smith, *The Ideological Origins of Nazi Imperialism* (New York, 1986), 26, 85–88.

72. Friedrich Ratzel, *Die Vereinigten Staaten von Nord-Amerika* (Munich, 1878–93); C. O. Sauer, "The Formative Years of Ratzel in the United States," *Annals of the Association of American Geographers* 61:2 (1971): 246–47, 249–50.

73. Benjamin Madley, "From Africa to Auschwitz: How German South West Africa Incubated Ideas and Methods Adopted and Developed by the Nazis in Eastern Europe," *European History Quarterly* 35:3 (2005): 432–33.

74. Friedrich Ratzel, "The Laws of the Spatial Growth of States" [1896], in Roger E. Kasperson and Julian V. Minghi, eds, *The Structure of Political Geography* (Chicago, 1969), 26, 20, 18, 22–23; Casper Erichsen, "Dark Conquests: Extermination and Colonial Conquest in German Southwest Africa, 1904–08," Genocide Studies Seminar paper, Yale University, Oct. 6, 2005, 6–7.

75. Ratzel, "The Laws of the Spatial Growth of States," 26–27, 23–24.

76. Madley, "From Africa to Auschwitz," 432–33.

77. Jon Bridgman and Leslie J. Worley, "Genocide of the Hereros," in S. Totten, W .S. Parsons, and I. W. Charny, eds., *Century of Genocide: Critical Essays and Eyewitness Accounts* (New York, 1995), 6; Jan-Bart Gewald, *Herero Heroes: A Social-Political History of the Herero of Namibia, 1890–1923* (Oxford, 1999); Mark Cocker, *Rivers of Blood, Rivers of Gold: Europe's Conquest of Indigenous Peoples* (New York, 1998), 287, 290, 345.

78. Cocker, *Rivers*, 3, 4, 297–99.

79. Horst Dreschler, *Let Us Die Fighting*, 43, 83, quoted in Cocker, *Rivers*, 295–96, 303.

80. Cocker, *Rivers*, 307–8, 310–12.

81. Lora Wildenthal, " 'She Is the Victor': Bourgeois Women, Nationalist Identities, and the Ideal of the Independent Woman Farmer in German Southwest Africa," in Geoff Eley, ed., *Society, Culture, and the State in Germany, 1870–1930* (Ann Arbor, 1996), 388–89.

82. Leutwein, letter to the editor of *Deutsch Südwestafrikanische Zeitung*, Nov. 5, 1903, quoted in I. Goldblatt, *History of South West Africa* (Cape Town, 1971), 147.

83. Bridgman and Worley, "Genocide," 8; Cocker, *Rivers*, 311–12, 314, 319.

84. J. M. Bridgman, *The Revolt of the Herero* (Berkeley, 1981), 74; Cocker, *Rivers*, 314, 320.

85. Cocker, *Rivers*, 320–24.

86. Quoted in Madley, "From Africa to Auschwitz," 442; Isabel V. Hull, "Military Culture and the Production of 'Final Solutions' in the Colonies: The Example of Wilhelminian Germany," in Gellately and Kiernan, *Specter of Genocide*, 145–46.

87. *Berliner Lokalanzeiger*, Aug. 2, 1904, in Hull, "Military Culture," 154; Cocker, *Rivers*, 328–30.

88. Cocker, *Rivers*, 327; Madley, "Africa to Auschwitz," 442, cites a 1906 German General Staff history.

89. Bridgman and Worley, "Genocide," 16.

90. Hull, "Military Culture," 154–55; Bridgman and Worley, "Genocide," 21–22; Cocker, *Rivers*, 331–32.

91. Hull, "Military Culture," 155–56.

92. Bridgman and Worley, "Genocide," 19; Hull, "Military Culture," 146.

93. Helmut Walser Smith, "The Talk of Genocide, the Rhetoric of Miscegnation: Notes on Debates in the German Reichstag concerning Southwest Africa, 1904–14," in Sara Friedrichsmayer et al., eds., *The Imperialist Imagination: German Colonialism and Its Legacy* (Ann Arbor, 1998), 113.

94. Bridgman and Worley, "Genocide," 22; Cocker, *Rivers*, 343; Hull, "Military Culture," 151.

95. Goldblatt, *History of South West Africa*, 142, 147–48; Cocker, *Rivers*, 334, 336.

96. Cocker, *Rivers*, 336–41; Hull, "Military Culture," 146.

97. *Deutsch Südwestafrikanische Zeitung*, Dec. 14, 1904, quoted in Goldblatt, *History of South West Africa*, 147; Erichsen, "Dark Conquests," 38.

98. Lebedour, Reichstag, Sitzung 140, Dec. 13, 1906, 4367, quoted in Erichsen, "Dark Conquests," 39–40.

99. Cocker, *Rivers,* 336–41.

100. Goldblatt, *History of South West Africa,* 145–47.

101. Bridgman and Worley, "Genocide," 22–23; Hull, "Military Culture," 144, 160; Cocker, *Rivers,* 343, 345.

102. Smith, "The Talk of Genocide," 110.

103. Madley, "From Africa to Auschwitz"; Cocker, *Rivers of Blood,* 344–45, 290.

104. Krista O'Donnell, "Poisonous Women: Sexual Danger, Illicit Violence, and Domestic Work in German Southern Africa, 1904–1915," *Journal of Women's History* 11:3 (1999): 38.

105. Smith, "The Talk of Genocide," 110; Hull gives a total of 1,500 German dead, "half of them from illness." "Military Culture," 144.

106. Goldblatt, *History of South West Africa,* 142–44; Bridgman and Worley, "Genocide," 4.

107. Maximilian Bayer, *Der Krieg in Südwestafrika und Seine Bedeutung für die Entwicklung der Kolonie* (Leipzig, 1906), 9; quoted in Erichsen, "Dark Conquests," 8.

108. Dr. C. H. P. Inhulfen, "Eine in Vergessenheit geratene Kolonisationsmethode" (A Colonization Method Now Forgotten), *Preussische Jahrbücher* (Berlin) 126 (Oct.–Dec. 1906): 282–88.

109. Smith, "The Talk of Genocide," 116, 111–12, 118.

110. Kolonialpolitisches Aktionskomite, ed., *Kolonialpolitischer Führer* (Berlin, 1907), 42–43. I am grateful to Erik Grimmer-Solem for a copy of this booklet, and to Ruth Hein for the translation.

111. Ibid., 43.

112. *Simplicissimus,* May 1, 1917. Thanks to Jens-Uwe Guettel for drawing this to my attention.

113. Bernhard Dernburg, in Schmoller, Dernburg, Delbrück, et al., "Dissolution of the Reichstag and Colonial Policy," Jan. 8, 1907, *Kolonialpolitisches Aktionskomite,* ed. (Berlin, 1907), 8. Erik Grimmer-Solem kindly provided a copy of this booklet; the translation is by Ruth Hein.

114. Smith, "The Talk of Genocide," 113.

115. Dernburg, "Dissolution of the Reichstag," 12–13.

116. Ibid., 10–11.

117. Wildenthal, " 'She Is the Victor,' " 374, 378 (emphasis in original).

118. Ibid., 376, 378, 381, 392, 386.

119. O'Donnell, "Poisonous Women," 45, 31–36, 48–49.

120. Smith, "The Talk of Genocide," 116–18, 121, 123.

Part 3. Introductory Note

1. "Historical Estimates of World Population": www.census.gov/ipc/www/worldhis.html (accessed May 29, 2006).

Chapter 10. The Armenian Genocide

1. Major von Stempel, German military attaché, Constantinople to Berlin, *Militärbericht Nr. 147,* den. 28 Februar 09, J. no. 3, 09, German Foreign Ministry Archives, Türkei 159, no. 3, 2/28/09; copy kindly supplied by Vahakn N. Dadrian, tr. Ruth Hein.

2. Vahakn Dadrian, *German Responsibility in the Armenian Genocide* (Watertown, 1997), 171–72, 209.

3. Ibid., 258n2.

4. M. Chahin, *The Kingdom of Armenia* (London, 1987), 288–292; Richard G. Hovannisian, ed., *The Armenian People from Ancient to Modern Times* (New York, 1997), 1:chs. 4, 11; 2:ch. 1; Hovannisian, "Etiology and Sequelae of the Armenian Genocide," in George J. Andreopoulos, ed., *Genocide: Conceptual and Historical Dimensions* (Philadelphia, 1994), 117; Bernard Lewis, *The Emergence of Modern Turkey,* 2nd ed. (Oxford, 1968), 25–38, 332.

5. James J. Reid, "Philosophy of State-Subject Relations, Ottoman Concepts of Tyranny, and the Demonization of Subjects: Conservative Ottomanism as a Source of Genocidal Behaviour, 1821–1918," in L. Chorbajian and G. Shirinian, eds., *Studies in Comparative Genocide* (London, 1999), 65.

6. Vahakn N. Dadrian, *The History of the Armenian Genocide: Ethnic Conflict from the Bal-*

kans to Anatolia to the Caucasus, 2nd rev. ed. (Providence, 1997), 8–24; Lewis, *Emergence of Modern Turkey,* 325.

7. Hovannisian, "Etiology and Sequelae of the Armenian Genocide," 118; Dadrian, *History,* 23–24, 27–30.

8. Mark Cocker, *Rivers of Blood, Rivers of Gold: Europe's Conquest of Indigenous Peoples* (New York, 1998), 284.

9. Reid, "Philosophy of State-Subject Relations," 75–78.

10. Robert Melson, *Revolution and Genocide: On the Origins of the Armenian Genocide and the Holocaust* (Chicago, 1992), 47, citing figures from Roderic Davison.

11. Dadrian, *History,* 152; Ronald Suny, "Ideology or Social Ecology: Rethinking the Armenian Genocide" (paper presented to conference on State-Organized Terror, Michigan State University, Nov. 1988), 24.

12. Suny, "Ideology," 13, 18–19; Dadrian, *History,* 131.

13. Suny, "Ideology," 9, 16.

14. Richard G. Hovannisian, in Frank Chalk and Kurt Jonassohn, eds., *The History and Sociology of Genocide: Analyses and Case Studies* (New Haven, 1990), 252; Dadrian, *History,* 76.

15. Suny, "Ideology," 18–19, 9, 20.

16. Lewis, *Emergence of Modern Turkey,* 56, 196–97; Richard G. Hovannisian, in Chalk and Jonassohn, *History and Sociology of Genocide,* 255; see also Melson, *Revolution and Genocide,* 50–51.

17. Dadrian, *History,* 114.

18. Ibid., 114–118; Melson, *Revolution and Genocide,* 45.

19. Dadrian, *History,* 50–51, 161.

20. Melson, *Revolution and Genocide,* 46–49; Dadrian, *History,* 119–21, 127–31, 151, 131–38, 155; Dadrian, *Warrant for Genocide: Key Elements of Turko-Armenian Conflict* (New Brunswick, 1999), 75–83, 85.

21. Dadrian, *Warrant for Genocide,* 85; Suny, "Ideology," 20, 22; Tumanskii, Russian vice-consul at Van, in M. S. Lazarev, *Kurdskii vopros (1891–1917)* (Moscow, 1972), 40, quoted in Suny, "Ideology," 19.

22. Hovannisian, "Etiology and Sequelae of the Armenian Genocide," 120; Melson, *Revolution and Genocide,* 47; Dadrian, *History,* 155, 175.

23. Dadrian, *History,* 156–57, 163; Dadrian, *Warrant for Genocide,* 142.

24. Lewis, *Emergence of Modern Turkey,* 193, 215.

25. Hovannisian, in Chalk and Jonassohn, *History and Sociology of Genocide,* 257; Lewis, *Emergence of Modern Turkey,* 201–3.

26. Lewis, *Emergence of Modern Turkey,* 326–27.

27. Yusuf Akçura, *Uç tarz-i siyaset* [Three Kinds of Politics] (Istanbul, 1911). Barak Salmoni kindly provided a copy of his English translation and preface.

28. Dadrian, *Warrant for Genocide,* 94.

29. Vahakn Dadrian, "The Determinants of the Armenian Genocide" (working paper GS 02, Genocide Studies Program, Yale Center for International and Area Studies, New Haven, 1998), 15; Peter Balakian, *The Burning Tigris: The Armenian Genocide and America's Response* (New York, 2003), 164.

30. Lewis, *Emergence of Modern Turkey,* 350.

31. Roderic H. Davison, *Reform in the Ottoman Empire, 1856–1876* (Princeton, 1963), 76, 231.

32. Lewis, *Emergence of Modern Turkey,* 345–46; Davison, *Reform in the Ottoman Empire,* 231–2.

33. Akçura, *Uç tarz-i siyaset.*

34. Balakian, *Burning Tigris,* 163, 165; Lewis, *Emergence of Modern Turkey,* 351.

35. Balakian, *Burning Tigris,* 164–66.

36. Lewis, *Emergence of Modern Turkey,* 207–9.

37. Dadrian, *Warrant for Genocide,* 94.

38. Feroz Ahmad, *The Young Turks* (Oxford, 1969), 154, quoted in Dadrian, *History,* 192.

39. Balakian, *Burning Tigris,* 161–62.

40. Soner Cagaptay writes: "In 1905–6, there were 15,508,703 Muslims (who spoke mainly Turkish and Arabic, but also Kurdish, Bosnian, Albanian, Greek, Bulgarian, etc. . . .); 2,823,063 Greek Orthodox (mainly Greek and also Arabic, Albanian, Bulgarian and Turkish speaking Orthodox Christians); 1,031,708 Armenian Orthodox, that is Gregorian Armenians (a classification excluding the numerically smaller Catholics and Protestant Armenians); and 253,475 Jews in the Empire. (There were also 139,285 Catholics, and 52,485 Protestants in the same year of whom a good number were Armenians.) The total population of the Empire in 1905–6 was 20,884, 630" (personal communication).

41. Suny, "Ideology," 23.

42. Lewis, *Emergence of Modern Turkey*, 349.

43. Dadrian, *History*, 179–83.

44. Lewis, *Emergence of Modern Turkey*, 217.

45. Ibid., 217–19.

46. Dadrian, *History*, 179–80; Dadrian, *Warrant for Genocide*, 94, 96.

47. Dadrian, *History*, 179–80, 184nn5, 7; Dadrian, *Warrant for Genocide*, 96, 98; Balakian, *Burning Tigris*, 172.

48. Edmund Spenser, *A View of the State of Ireland*, ed. Andrew Hadfield and Willy Maley (Oxford, 1997), 150.

49. Gregor Alexinsky, "Bolshevism and the Turks," *Quarterly Review* 239 (1923): 185–86.

50. Suny, "Ideology," 24.

51. *Turk yurdu* 12:1333 (1917): 3521, in Feroz Ahmad, "The Agrarian Policy of the Young Turks, 1908–1918," in *Economie et societés dans l'empire Ottoman*, Colloques internationaux 601 (Paris 1983), 287–88; Akçura, *Uç tarz-i siyaset*.

52. Ahmad, "The Agrarian Policy of the Young Turks," 284n34.

53. Ibid., 276, 278, 286.

54. Ibid., 279, 282–83, 286–87.

55. Balakian, *Burning Tigris*, 159.

56. Dadrian, *History*, 196; Balakian, *Burning Tigris*, 163, 173.

57. Dadrian, *History*, 197.

58. Cemal Kutay, *Birinci dünya harbinde Teshkilât-i Mahsusa* [The Special Organization during World War I] (Istanbul, 1962), 36, excerpt and translation in Vahakn Dadrian, *Documentation of the Armenian Genocide in Turkish Sources* (New York, 1991), 126–27.

59. Dadrian, *History*, 197; Dadrian, "Determinants," 15–16; Balakian, *Burning Tigris*, 181–82, 179.

60. Kutay, *Birinci dünya harbinde Teshkilât-i Mahsusa*, 18, in Dadrian, *Documentation of the Armenian Genocide in Turkish Sources*, 126.

61. Vahakn Dadrian, personal communication, Sept. 5, 2005; Balakian, *Burning Tigris*, 167–68.

62. Balakian, *Burning Tigris*, 171, 178.

63. Vahakn Dadrian, "The Secret Young Turk Ittihadist Conference and the Decision for the World War I Genocide of the Armenians," *Journal of Political and Military Sociology* 22:1 (1994; repr. 1995): 163–91.

64. Ibid., 164; Balakian, *Burning Tigris*, 189–90.

65. Balakian, *Burning Tigris*, 178, 182, 179.

66. Dadrian, *History*, 219, 226–27.

67. R. Hrair Dekmejian, "Determinants of Genocide: Armenians and Jews as Case Studies," in Richard G. Hovannisian, ed., *The Armenian Genocide in Perspective* (New Brunswick, 1986), 85–96, at 93; Dadrian, "Determinants," 16–17.

68. Richard G. Hovannisian, "The Historical Dimensions of the Armenian Question, 1878–1923," in Hovannisian, *The Armenian Genocide in Perspective*, 29; Balakian, *Burning Tigris*, 179.

69. Hovannisian, "Historical Dimensions of the Armenian Question," 29; Balakian, *Burning Tigris*, 179.

70. Vahakn N. Dadrian, "The Armenian Genocide in Official Turkish Records," special issue, *Journal of Political and Military Sociology* 22:1 (1994; repr. 1995): 128, 131; Dadrian, *Documentation of the Armenian Genocide in Turkish Sources*, 103, 136.

71. Dadrian, *Documentation of the Armenian Genocide in Turkish Sources,* 103–4, 123, 136.

72. *Trabzonda meshveret,* June 14/27, 1915, quoted in Dadrian, "The Armenian Genocide in Official Turkish Records," 37.

73. Text and translation in Dadrian, "The Armenian Genocide in Official Turkish Records," 65–66.

74. Text and translation in ibid., 62–63.

75. German Foreign Ministry Archives, report dated Aug, 23, 1915, quoted in Dadrian, "Determinants," 12.

76. Balakian, *Burning Tigris,* 179.

77. Dadrian, "Determinants," 10–12.

78. Text and translation in Dadrian, "The Armenian Genocide in Official Turkish Records," 68–69.

79. Report of Apr. 11, 1919, quoted in Dadrian, "The Armenian Genocide in Official Turkish Records," 36–37.

80. Transcripts of the Ottoman Senate, 3rd election period, 1st sess., vol. 1, 26th sitting, Sept. 28, 1915, and 2nd sess., vol. 1, 10th sitting, Nov. 30, 1915, both excerpted and translated in Dadrian, "The Armenian Genocide in Official Turkish Records," 46–50.

81. German Foreign Ministry Archives, report dated June 30, 1916, in Dadrian, "Determinants," 13–14.

82. Balakian, *Burning Tigris,* 179–80.

83. Dadrian, "The Armenian Genocide: An Interpretation," in Jay Winter, ed., *America and the Armenian Genocide of 1915* (Cambridge, 2003), 64–65.

84. Dadrian, "Determinants," 8–9.

85. Excerpt and translation in Dadrian, "The Armenian Genocide in Official Turkish Records," 58–61; Dadrian, "Determinants," 7–10.

86. Transcripts of the Ottoman Senate, 3rd election period, 3rd sess., vol. 1, 15th sitting, Dec. 12, 1916, quoted in Dadrian, "The Armenian Genocide in Official Turkish Records," 53–55.

87. Dadrian, *History,* 204, 349.

88. Transcripts of the Senate, 3rd election period, 5th sess., vol. 1, 2nd sitting, Oct. 19, 21, 1918, excerpt and translation in Dadrian, "The Armenian Genocide in Official Turkish Records," 90–92.

89. Dadrian, "The Armenian Genocide in Official Turkish Records," 82, 35.

90. Ibid., 35.

91. *Takvimi vekâyi,* Aug. 6, 1919, excerpt and translation of May 22, 1919 verdict in Dadrian, "The Armenian Genocide in Official Turkish Records," 44–45; Dadrian, "The Armenian Genocide," 89–90.

92. Dadrian, "The Armenian Genocide in Official Turkish Records," 87–89, 31, 68–69, 106, 127.

93. Dadrian, *Documentation of the Armenian Genocide in Turkish Sources,* 93; Dadrian, "The Armenian Genocide in Official Turkish Records," 11, 24n61.

94. Winter, introduction to *America and the Armenian Genocide,* 1, 19; *Takvimi vekâyi* 3540, 8, quoted in Dadrian, "Determinants," 7–8.

Chapter 11. *Blut und Boden*

1. Bernhard Dernburg, in Schmoller, Dernburg, Delbrück, et al., "Dissolution of the Reichstag and Colonial Policy," Jan. 8, 1907, in *Kolonialpolitisches Aktionskomite,* ed. (Berlin, 1907), 8, 15. Erik Grimmer-Solem kindly provided a copy of this booklet; the translation is by Ruth Hein.

2. Zygmunt Bauman, *Modernity and the Holocaust* (Ithaca, 1989). Other interpretations are discussed in Omer Bartov, *Germany's War and the Holocaust: Disputed Histories* (Ithaca, 2003).

3. Adolf Hitler, Oct. 21 and Aug. 8–11, 1941, in *Hitler's Table Talk, 1941–44: His Private Conversations,* tr. N. Cameron and R. H. Stevens (London, 1973), 78, 25; Derek Williams, *Romans and Barbarians* (New York, 1998), ch. 2.

4. Feb. 4, 1942, in *Hitler's Table Talk,* 289.

5. Adolf Hitler, *Mein Kampf,* tr. Ralph Manheim (New York, 1999), 140, 654; Debórah Dwork and Robert Jan van Pelt, *Auschwitz: 1270 to the Present* (New York, 1996), 82.

6. Richard Walther Darré, *Neuadel aus Blut und Boden* (Munich, 1935; Munich 1941), 43 (tr. Ruth Hein). The book was first published in 1930. See Gustavo Corni, "Richard Walther Darré: The Blood and Soil Ideologue," in R. Smelser and R. Zitelmann, eds., *The Nazi Elite* (New York, 1993), 19.

7. Ben Kiernan, "Myth, Nationalism, and Genocide," *Journal of Genocide Research* 3:2 (2001): 190.

8. Darré, *Neuadel aus Blut und Boden,* 74.

9. Hitler, *Mein Kampf,* 140.

10. Darré, quoted in David Welch, *Propaganda in the German Cinema* (Oxford, 1983), 101–2.

11. Darré, *Neuadel aus Blut und Boden,* 39, 43, 47, 39–40 (parenthesis in original), 46.

12. Walter Goffart, "An Entrenched Myth of Origins: The Germans before Germany," in *Barbarian Tides: The Migration Age and the Later Roman Empire* (Philadelphia, 2006), 40, 55, 43.

13. Fredegar, *Chronicon* 2.4–6, 8, 3. 2, and Widukind, *Res gestae Saxonicae* 1.2, both quoted in Goffart, "Entrenched Myth," 42, 45–46.

14. Demandt, *Der Fall Roms,* 104–5, and Leon Poliakov, *The Aryan Myth* (New York, 1974), 80, both quoted in Goffart, "Entrenched Myth," 43, 48, 281.

15. Goffart, "Entrenched Myth," 52.

16. Hans Reinerth, "Die Urgermanen," in *Vorgeschichte der deutschen Stämme: Germanische Tat und Kultur auf deutschen Boden* (Leipzig, 1940), and Hermann Aubin, "Zur Frage der historischen Kontinuität im Allgemeinen," *Historische Zeitschrift* 168 (1943), both cited in Goffart, "Entrenched Myth," 42, 278.

17. Hitler, *Mein Kampf,* 423, 612, 668; Nov. 5, 1941, in *Hitler's Table Talk,* 118.

18. Darré, *Neuadel aus Blut und Boden,* 61–62, 65, 61.

19. Adolf Hitler, *Hitler's Second Book,* ed. Gerhard Weinberg (New York, 2003), xxi, 21.

20. Klaus Vondung, introduction to in Eric Voegelin, *Race and State* (Baton Rouge, 1997), xv-xvi. Günther's *Rassenkunde des deutschen Volkes* went through 15 printings by 1930 (p. 86); Henry Friedlander, *The Origins of Nazi Genocide: From Euthanasia to the Final Solution* (Chapel Hill, 1995), 12–13.

21. H. F. K. Günther, *Rassengeschichte des Hellenischen und des Römischen Volkes* (1929); see Elizabeth Rawson, *The Spartan Tradition in European Thought* (Oxford, 1991), 337.

22. Richard Walther Darré, *Das Bauerntum als Lebensquell der Nordischen Rasse* (Munich, 1929; Munich, 1938); Rawson, *Spartan Tradition,* 340.

23. Aug. 6, 1942, in *Hitler's Table Talk,* 618–19.

24. Hitler's *Second Book,* 21; Rawson, *Spartan Tradition,* 342–43.

25. Richard Walther Darré, *Vom Lebensgesetz zweier Staatsgedanken (Konfuzius und Lykurgos)* (Goslar, 1940).

26. Nov. 5, 1941, in *Hitler's Table Talk,* 116.

27. SS-Hauptsturmführer Schubert, Feb. 4, 1942, according to Dr. Erhard Wetzel's Mar. 11, 1942 report on *Der Generalplan Ost,* in *Vierteljahrshefte für Zeitgeschichte* 6 (1958): 296. See also excerpts of Wetzel's Apr. 27, 1942 memorandum (297ff.), in J. Noakes and G. Pridham, eds., *Nazism, 1919–1945,* vol. 3, *Foreign Policy, War, and Racial Extermination* (Exeter, 1997), 977–79, 987.

28. Hans Frank, Dec. 16, 1941, doc. 683 in Noakes and Pridham, *Nazism, 1919–1945,* 3:966.

29. *Tagebücher von Goebbels,* May 24, 1942, cited in Robert Gellately, "The Third Reich, the Holocaust, and Visions of Serial Genocide," in Gellately and Ben Kiernan, eds., *The Specter of Genocide: Mass Murder in Historical Perspective* (New York, 2003), 262.

30. Hitler to Hans Frank, Oct. 2, 1940, in Noakes and Pridham, *Nazism, 1919–1945,* 3:988.

31. Hitler, Aug. 8, 1942, Oct. 17, Nov. 5, Sept. 17, 1941, Aug. 22, 1942, in *Hitler's Table Talk,* 621, 69, 115–16, 34, 655.

32. Aug. 8–10 and 19, Sept. 17, Nov. 5, 1941, in *Hitler's Table Talk,* 26, 28, 33, 26, 116.

33. Feb. 4, 1942, in *Hitler's Table Talk,* 289.

34. Hitler, *Mein Kampf,* 390; Darré, *Neuadel aus Blut und Boden,* 42, 74–75.

35. Welch, *Propaganda,* 96–97, 102.

36. Hitler, *Mein Kampf,* 233–34, 138. See also Barrington Moore Jr., *Social Origins of Dictatorship and Democracy* (Harmondsworth, 1973), 450.

37. Hitler, *Mein Kampf,* 642–43 (emphasis in original), 654.

38. J. E. Farquharson, *The Plough and the Swastika: The NSDAP and Agriculture in Germany, 1928–1945* (London, 1976), 216.

39. Welch, introduction to *Propaganda*.

40. Robert Conquest, *The Harvest of Sorrow: Soviet Collectivization and the Terror-Famine* (Oxford, 1986), 21–22.

41. Kevin Repp, introduction to "Berlin Moderns: Art, Politics, and Commercial Culture in Fin-de-Siècle Berlin." I am grateful to Repp for allowing me to read and quote from this book manuscript and for his helpful comments on this chapter.

42. Quoted in Kevin Repp, *Reformers, Critics, and the Paths of German Modernity: Anti-Politics and the Search for Alternatives, 1890–1914* (Cambridge, Mass., 2000), 68.

43. Ibid., 84, 102, 80–81.

44. Ibid., 68, 82, 84–86, 81.

45. Ibid., 84–85, 87–88, 102, 83, 81, 89–90, 95.

46. Corni, "Richard Walther Darré," 19–20; Darré, *Neuadel aus Blut und Boden*, 40–43, 45, 47.

47. Darré, *Neuadel aus Blut und Boden*, 65, 62–63 (emphasis in original).

48. Ibid., 64, 66, 63n1.

49. Farquharson, *The Plough and the Swastika*, 203; Welch, *Propaganda*, 101–2.

50. Farquharson, *The Plough and the Swastika*, 204; Richard Breitman, *The Architect of Genocide: Himmler and the Final Solution* (New York, 1991), 34.

51. In 1934, Höss had "wanted to settle on the land," but Himmler recruited him to the active SS and had him posted initially to Dachau. Rudolf Höss, *Commandant of Auschwitz*, tr. C. Fitzgibbon (New York, 1960), 227; Dwork and van Pelt, *Auschwitz*, 189–90, 207.

52. Rudolf Höss Aufzeichnungen, Institut für Zeitgeschichte, Munich, F 13/5, 279/283; Vahakn N. Dadrian, *German Responsibility in the Armenian Genocide* (Cambridge, Mass., 1996), 202; Breitman, *Architect*, 35.

53. Gunther d'Alquen Unterredung, Institut für Zeitgeschichte, Munich, ZS 2, Mar. 13–14, 1951, 95; Paul Brohmer, *Biologieunterricht und völkische Erziehung* (Frankfurt, 1933), 72; Welch, *Propaganda*, 122.

54. Breitman, *Architect*, 12–13, 34–35.

55. Dr. Hermann Reischle and Dr. Wilhelm Saure, *Aufgaben und Aufbau des Reichsnährstandes* (Berlin, 1934; reprinted as *Der Reichsnährstand: Aufbau, Aufgaben und Bedeutung*, 3rd ed. [Berlin, 1940]). Tr. Ruth Hein.

56. Rieschle and Saure, *Der Reichsnährstand*, 15–17; Farquharson, *The Plough and the Swastika*, 110–11.

57. Dr. Erhard Wetzel, Berlin, Apr. 27, 1942, "Stellungnahme und Gedanken zum Generalplan Ost des Reichsführers SS" [Commentary and Considerations on the General Plan East of the Reich Leader SS], *Vierteljahrshefte für Zeitgeschichte* 6 (1958): 320; see also Farquharson, *The Plough and the Swastika*, 110.

58. Heinrich Himmler, quoted in BBC documentary series *The Nazis,* part 1, "Helped into Power" (1997).

59. Michael Burleigh, *The Third Reich: A New History* (New York, 2000), 447–48.

60. Walter Kuhn, Sept. 5 and 29, 1939, and Otto Reche, May 15, 1940, quoted in Michael Burleigh, *Germany Turns Eastwards: A Study of "Ostforschung" in the Third Reich* (Cambridge, 1988), 175–77.

61. David Schoenbaum, *Hitler's Social Revolution* (London, 1967), 161, quoted in Welch, *Propaganda*, 96.

62. Höss Aufzeichnungen, F 13/5, 286. See also Jochen von Lang, "Martin Bormann: Hitler's Secretary," in Smelser and Zitelmann, *The Nazi Elite*, 8, 12.

63. Welch, *Propaganda*, 97, 101, 103.

64. Farquharson, *The Plough and the Swastika*, 259, 3, 119; Avraham Barkai, *Nazi Economics: Ideology, Theory, and Policy* (New Haven, 1990), 155–56.

65. Welch, *Propaganda*, 108.

66. Höss, *Commandant of Auschwitz*, 230, 232, 234, 238.

67. Nuremberg doc. L-221, minutes of a meeting dated July 16, 1941, in *Trial of the Major War*

Criminals Before the International Military Tribunal, Nuremberg, 14 November 1945–1 October 1946 (Nuremberg, 1949), 38:88, translation in Office of U.S. Chief of Counsel for Prosecution of Axis Criminality, *Nazi Conspiracy and Aggression,* vol. 7 (Washington, 1946).

68. Hitler, Aug. 8–9, 1941, in *Hitler's Table Talk,* 24.

69. Wetzel, "Stellungnahme und Gedanken zum Generalplan Ost," 303.

70. Moore, *Social Origins of Dictatorship and Democracy,* 450.

71. Nov. 5, 1941, in *Hitler's Table Talk,* 116; Darré, *Neuadel aus Blut und Boden,* 67.

72. Farquharson, *The Plough and the Swastika,* 220, 204.

73. Darré, *Neuadel aus Blut und Boden,* 60–61, 74 (emphasis in original).

74. Apr. 22, 1938 conference resolution, quoted in Burleigh, *Germany Turns Eastwards,* 162.

75. Jeffrey Richards, *Visions of Yesterday* (London, 1973), 288.

76. Woodruff D. Smith, *The Ideological Origins of Nazi Imperialism* (New York, 1986), 242.

77. Hitler, *Mein Kampf,* 138. See also Moore, *Social Origins of Dictatorship and Democracy,* 450.

78. *Hitler's Second Book,* 27; quoted in Henry Turner, *Reappraisals of Fascism* (New York, 1975), 136.

79. Aug. 6, 1942, in *Hitler's Table Talk,* 619; Himmler, quoted in "Helped into Power."

80. Hitler, *Mein Kampf,* 139–140, 654; Welch, *Propaganda,* 97.

81. Hitler, quoted in Christian Leitz, *Nazi Foreign Policy, 1933–1941: The Road to Global War* (London, 2004), 5.

82. Hitler, Mar. 12, 1940, quoted in Christopher R. Browning, *The Path to Genocide* (Cambridge, 1992), 15–16; Aug. 8, Sept. 17, 1941, in *Hitler's Table Talk,* 24, 33.

83. *Tagebücher von Goebbels,* May 24, 1942, quoted in Gellately, "The Third Reich, the Holocaust, and Visions of Serial Genocide," 262.

84. Heinrich Himmler, Oct. 4, 1943, doc. 642 in Noakes and Pridham, *Nazism, 1919–1945,* 3:920–21.

85. Darré, *Neuadel aus Blut und Boden,* 43; Smith, *Ideological Origins of Nazi Imperialism,* 243.

86. Quoted in Peter Padfield, *Himmler* (London, 1990), 13.

87. Höss Aufzeichnungen, F 13/5, 279/283. Himmler returned to this theme nine years later in a speech to SS leaders a month after the invasion of Poland, where ethnic German warrior-settlers would hold off "Slavdom." Burleigh, *Third Reich,* 446–47. N. Goodrick-Clarke, *The Occult Roots of Nazism* (New York, 1992), ch. 14.

88. Heydrich, quoted in Neil Ascherson, "Imagined Soil," *London Review of Books,* Apr. 6, 2006, 12.

89. Hitler, *Mein Kampf,* quoted in Leitz, *Nazi Foreign Policy,* 143.

90. Anthony Read and David Fisher, *The Deadly Embrace: Hitler, Stalin, and the Nazi-Soviet Pact, 1939–1941* (New York, 1988), 241–42 (emphasis added).

91. Nuremberg doc. L-221, minutes of meeting dated July 16, 1941, 87–90.

92. R. Hrair Dekmejian, "Determinants of Genocide: Armenians and Jews as Case Studies," in Richard G. Hovannisian, ed., *The Armenian Genocide in Perspective* (New Brunswick, 1986), 92–93.

93. Leni Yahil, *The Holocaust: The Fate of European Jewry* (Oxford, 1990), 104–5.

94. Burleigh, *Third Reich,* 447; Höss Aufzeichnungen, F 13/5, 295.

95. Wetzel, "Stellungnahme und Gedanken zum Generalplan Ost," 319–20.

96. Himmler, quoted in "Evil Rising," *New York Times Book Review,* Mar. 14, 2004, 13.

97. Quoted in Ascherson, "Imagined Soil," 12.

98. Christopher R. Browning, *The Path to Genocide: Essays on Launching the Final Solution* (New York, 1992), 26. See also Burleigh, *Germany Turns Eastwards;* Klaus Hildebrand, *The Foreign Policy of the Third Reich* (Berkeley, 1973).

99. Browning, *The Path to Genocide,* 8–9, 12–13, 22.

100. Himmler to SS leaders, Posen, Oct. 4, 1943, in Noakes and Pridham, *Nazism, 1919–1945,* 3:920–21; Meyer, quoted in Ascherson, "Imagined Soil," 12.

101. This couplet was coined by Eberhard Jäckel and Gerhard Weinberg; see Leitz, *Nazi Foreign Policy,* 3.

102. Maj. Joseph Hell, "Aufzeichnung," 1922, Institut für Zeitgeschichte, ZS 640, p. 5; quoted in Gerald Fleming, *Hitler and the Final Solution* (Berkeley, 1984), 17; Hitler, *Mein Kampf,* ch. 15, 679.

103. Fleming, *Hitler and the Final Solution,* 69, 29 (emphasis added). Saul Friedlander, in the introduction to Fleming's book, adds that antisemitism "gives Nazism its *sui generis* character . . . the Jewish problem was at the center, the very essence" (xxxii).

104. Francis R. Nicosia, "Jewish Farmers in Hitler's Germany: Zionist Occupational Retraining and Nazi 'Jewish Policy,' " *Holocaust and Genocide Studies* 19:3 (2005): 376, 368, 374–75, 380–82.

105. Leitz, *Nazi Foreign Policy,* 3; Gabrielle Tyrnauer, " 'Mastering the Past': Germans and Gypsies," in Frank Chalk and Kurt Jonassohn, eds., *The History and Sociology of Genocide: Analyses and Case Studies* (New Haven, 1990), 366–77.

106. Hitler, Feb. 24, 1929, from Jochen Thies, *Architekt der Weltherrschaft: Die "Endziele" Hitlers* (Dusseldorf, 1976), 53, quoted in Leitz, *Nazi Foreign Policy,* 141.

107. Richards, *Visions of Yesterday,* 292; Richard Evans, *In Hitler's Shadow* (New York, 1989), 81.

108. Farquharson, *The Plough and the Swastika,* 110; Richards, *Visions of Yesterday,* 289; Welch, *Propaganda,* 123.

109. Quoted in Peter Tatchell, "Survivors of a Forgotten Holocaust," *London Independent,* June 12, 2001.

110. M. Domarus, ed., *Hitler: Reden und Proklamation, 1932–1945* (Munich, 1965), quoted in Welch, *Propaganda,* 123; Robert Gellately, *Backing Hitler: Consent and Coercion in Nazi Germany* (New York, 2001).

111. George L. Mosse, *Towards the Final Solution: A History of European Racism* (Madison, 1987), 215–20, excerpt repr. in Chalk and Jonassohn, *History and Sociology of Genocide,* 356. See also Friedlander, *Origins of Nazi Genocide;* Gellately, *Backing Hitler.*

112. Evans, *In Hitler's Shadow,* 79; Tyrnauer, " 'Mastering the Past,' " 368, 376, 377.

113. Yehuda Bauer, excerpted in Chalk and Jonassohn, *History and Sociology of Genocide,* 345.

114. Raul Hilberg, "Anatomy of the Holocaust," in Chalk and Jonassohn, *History and Sociology of Genocide,* 360–61.

115. Quoted by Bauer in Chalk and Jonassohn, *History and Sociology of Genocide,* 348.

116. See, e.g., Hélène Carrère D'Encausse, *Stalin: Order through Terror* (New York, 1981), 91.

117. Fleming, *Hitler and the Final Solution,* xxxv, quoting Ernst Nolte.

118. Gellately, "The Third Reich, the Holocaust, and Visions of Serial Genocide," 247; Burleigh, *Germany Turns Eastwards,* 116, 272. Following suit in 1941, Serb chauvinists proposed "cleansing the lands of all non-Serb elements." Norman Cigar, *Genocide in Bosnia* (College Station, 1995), 18.

119. Hitler, Reichstag speech of Jan. 30, 1939, quoted in Leitz, *Nazi Foreign Policy,* 5.

120. Gellately, *Backing Hitler;* Christopher R. Browning, *Ordinary Men: Reserve Police Battalion 101 and the Final Solution in Poland* (New York, 1992).

121. Hitler's adjutant Maj. Engel, Nov. 18, 1939, doc. 656 in Noakes and Pridham, *Nazism, 1919–1945,* 3:940–41.

122. Browning, *Ordinary Men,* 39.

123. Gen. of the Infantry Ulex, "To the C.-in-C. East," Spala, Feb. 2, 1940, transcribed in memo of Col. Gen. Blaskowitz, Feb. 6, 1940, doc. 655 in Noakes and Pridham, *Nazism, 1919–1945,* 3:939.

124. Col. Gen. Blaskowitz, Feb. 6, 938–39.

125. Gen. von Küchler, commander 18th Army, July 22, 1940, doc. 657 in Noakes and Pridham, *Nazism, 1919–1945,* 3:941.

126. Hans Frank, Mar. 2, 1940, doc. 680 in Noakes and Pridham, *Nazism, 1919–1945,* 3:962.

127. Viktor Böttcher, "Brücke aus dem Altreich nach dem Osten," *Litzmannstädter Zeitung* (Lodz), May 30, 1940. Copy kindly provided by Wendy Lower.

128. Forster, Dec, 14, 1940, doc. 662 in Noakes and Pridham, *Nazism, 1919–1945,* 3:948.

129. Public notice signed by SS Brig. Gen. Odilo Globocnik, Lublin, May 22, 1941, reprinted in Mechtild Roessler, Sabine Scheiermacher et al., eds., *Der Generalplan Ost: Hauptlinien der nationalsozialistischen Planungs und Vernichtungspolitik* (Berlin, 1993). Thanks to Wendy Lower for this citation.

130. Corni, "Richard Walther Darré," 18; Noakes and Pridham, *Nazism, 1919–1945,* 3:920, give the date as May 23, 1942.

131. Herbert Backe, Apr. 23, 1940, doc. 702 in Noakes and Pridham, *Nazism, 1919–1945,* 3:989–90.

132. Hitler to his military leaders, Mar. 30, 1941 (diary of Gen. Halder), in Noakes and Pridham, *Nazism, 1919–1945,* 3:1086; Friedlander, introduction to Fleming, *Hitler and the Final Solution,* xxii. Christopher R. Browning, *The Origins of the Final Solution* (Lincoln, 2004).

133. Reports of Einsatzgruppe A (Oct. 15, 1941), Dr. Rudolf Lange (Jan. 1942), and Einsatzgruppe C (Nov. 3, 1941), all excerpted in Noakes and Pridham, *Nazism, 1919–1945,* 3:1092–95.

134. Nuremberg doc. L-221, minutes of meeting dated July 16, 1941, 92; Sept. 14, 1941, in *Hitler's Table Talk,* 30; Noakes and Pridham, *Nazism, 1919–1945,* 3:915n27.

135. Höppner to Eichmann, July 16, 1941, in Noakes and Pridham, *Nazism, 1919–1945,* 3:1103.

136. Hitler, quoted in Fleming, *Hitler and the Final Solution,* 27, 31.

137. Noakes and Pridham, *Nazism, 1919–1945,* 3:977; Nuremberg doc. NO-365, NO-996–997, quoted in *Vierteljahrshefte für Zeitgeschichte* 6 (1958): 305n21.

138. Wetzel, 27 "Stellungnahme und Gedanken zum Generalplan Ost," 297–300, 305.

139. Hans Frank, report to a meeting of senior officials of the General Government, Dec. 16, 1941, in Noakes and Pridham, *Nazism, 1919–1945,* 3:1126–27, and Office of U.S. Chief of Counsel for Prosecution of Axis Criminality, *Nazi Conspiracy and Aggression* (Washington, 1946), 2:634: http://fcit.coedu.usf.edu/holocaust/resource/document/DocJewQn.htm (accessed Apr. 4, 2004).

140. "Wannsee Protocol, January 20, 1942" translation: www.yale.edu/lawweb/avalon/imt/wannsee.htm (accessed Mar. 22, 2004).

141. Hitler, Jan. 30, 1942, text of speech as monitored by Foreign Broadcast Monitoring Service, Federal Communications Commission, quoted in Martin Gilbert, *The Holocaust* (New York, 1985), 285: http://fcit.coedu.usf.edu/holocaust/resource/document/DocJewQn.htm (accessed Apr. 4, 2004). See also Browning, *Origins of the Final Solution.*

142. Entries for Feb. 14 and Mar. 27, 1942, in *The Goebbels Diaries 1942–1943,* tr. L. P. Lochner (New York, 1948), 86, 147–48: http://fcit.coedu.usf.edu/holocaust/resource/document/DocJewQn.htm (acc. Apr. 4, 2004); Wetzel, "Stellungnahme und Gedanken zum Generalplan Ost," 305n21.

143. Wetzel, "Stellungnahme und Gedanken zum Generalplan Ost," 312; doc. 690 in Noakes and Pridham, *Nazism, 1919–1945,* 3:979.

144. Roma Nutkiewicz Ben-Atar and Doron S. Ben-Atar, *What Time and Sadness Spared: Mother and Son Confront the Holocaust* (Charlottesville, 2006), 63–65, 70.

145. Report no. 51, quoted in Fleming, *Hitler and the Final Solution,* 129; Noakes and Pridham, *Nazism, 1919–1945,* 3:1102.

146. Hermann Graebe, testimony to the Nuremberg Tribunal, Nov. 10, 1945, in Noakes and Pridham, *Nazism, 1919–1945,* 3:1100–1.

147. Wetzel, "Stellungnahme und Gedanken zum Generalplan Ost," 317, 301, 314, 301.

148. Wetzel's Apr. 27, 1942, memorandum, excerpt in Noakes and Pridham, *Nazism, 1919–1945,* 3:978; full text, "Stellungnahme und Gedanken zum Generalplan Ost," 308–12, 319, 316.

149. This and the following two paragraphs draw upon Wetzel, "Stellungnahme und Gedanken zum Generalplan Ost," 309–18.

150. Ibid., 322, 319–20.

151. Himmler, June 12, 1942 (doc. NO-2255), in *Vierteljahrshefte für Zeitgeschichte* 6 (1958): 325.

152. Nutkiewicz Ben-Atar and Ben-Atar, *What Time and Sadness Spared,* 99–100.

153. Heinrich Gottong, "Zwei Rassenkundliche Untersuchungen im Generalgouvernement," *Volk und Rasse* 2 (Feb. 1943): 21, 29.

154. H. Rübel, "Römer und Germanen," *Volk und Rasse* 2 (Feb. 1943): 32–36.

155. Otto Kolar, "Deutsche Bauern in der Ukraine," *Volk und Rasse* 2 (Feb. 1943): 29–32; for an illustration, see www.calvin.edu/academic/cas/gpa/volkrass.htm (acc. Jan. 14, 2006).

156. "Auch Ostafrikaner wurden im Warthegau angesiedelt," *Litzmannstädter Zeitung,* Sept. 26, 1943.

157. Heinrich Himmler, Oct. 4, 1943, doc. 908 in Noakes and Pridham, *Nazism, 1919–1945,* 3:1199–1200; and Oct. 6, 1943, quoted in Padfield, *Himmler,* 468–69.

158. Himmler, Oct. 4, 1943, doc. 642 in Noakes and Pridham, *Nazism, 1919–1945*, 3:919–20.

159. Noakes and Pridham, *Nazism, 1919–1945*, 3:1180–81, 915; Catherine Merridale, *Night of Stone: Death and Memory in Twentieth-Century Russia* (New York, 2000), 215.

160. Nutkiewicz Ben-Atar and Ben-Atar, *What Time and Sadness Spared*, 105–6, 111–17, 130.

161. Yahil, *The Holocaust*, 506–19.

162. Noakes and Pridham, *Nazism, 1919–1945*, 3: 1180–81; Fleming, *Hitler and the Final Solution*, 168; Robert Gellately, introduction to Leon Goldensohn, *The Nuremberg Interviews* (New York, 2004), xxvi.

Chapter 12. Rice, Race, and Empire

1. Dr. Erhard Wetzel, April 27, 1942, "Stellungnahme und Gedanken zum Generalplan Ost des Reichsführers SS," *Vierteljahrshefte für Zeitgeschichte* 6 (1958): 315–16, 318.

2. Himmler's speech to SS leaders in Posen, Oct. 4, 1943, in. J. Noakes and G. Pridham, eds., *Nazism, 1919–1945*, vol. 3, *Foreign Policy, War, and Racial Extermination* (Exeter, 1997), 921.

3. Werner Gruhl, "The Great Asian-Pacific Crescent of Pain: Japan's War from Manchuria to Hiroshima, 1931 to 1945," in Peter Li, ed., *Japanese War Crimes* (New Brunswick, 2003), 243, 250.

4. Michael R. Auslin, "Terrorism and Treaty Port Relations: Western Images of the Samurai during Bakumatsu and Early Meiji Japan," in J. Hanes and H. Yamaji, eds., *Images and Identity: Rethinking Japanese Cultural History* (Kobe, 2004), 147–70; Emiko Ohnuki-Tierney, *Kamikaze, Cherry Blossoms, and Nationalisms: The Militarization of Aesthetics in Japanese History* (Chicago, 2002), 61.

5. Ohnuki-Tierney, *Kamikaze, Cherry Blossoms*, 86, 70–72, 77, 79, 97.

6. Thomas Havens, *Farm and Nation in Modern Japan: Agrarian Nationalism, 1870–1940* (Princeton, 1974), 183; Ohnuki-Tierney, *Kamikaze, Cherry Blossoms*, 67, 61, 70.

7. Tetsuo Najita and H. D. Harootunian, "Japanese Revolt against the West: Political and Cultural Criticism in the Twentieth Century," in Peter Duus, ed., *The Cambridge History of Japan*, vol. 6, *The Twentieth Century* (Cambridge, 1991), 716, 712.

8. Ohnuki-Tierney, *Kamikaze, Cherry Blossoms*, 82–85, 13, 95–96.

9. Ibid., 86, 12, 100, 78, 72–74, 76–77, 85.

10. Ibid., 70, 88, 68, 90, 91–94.

11. Ibid., 80, 12, 79, 74–76.

12. Ogyu Sorai (1666–1728), quoted in Stephen Vlastos, "Agrarianism without Tradition: The Radical Critique of Prewar Japanese Modernity," in Vlastos, ed., *Mirror of Modernity: Invented Traditions of Modern Japan* (Berkeley, 1998), 80–81.

13. Ohnuki-Tierney, *Kamikaze, Cherry Blossoms*, 66, 80–81, 56, 65, 342, 64, 27–31, 87, 64, 66.

14. Auslin, "Terrorism and Treaty Port Relations," 153.

15. R. P. Dore and Tsutomu Ōuchi, "Rural Origins of Japanese Fascism," in James W. Morley, ed., *Dilemmas of Growth in Prewar Japan* (Princeton, 1971), 209.

16. Shinagawa Yajirō, quoted in Vlastos, "Agrarianism without Tradition," 81–82.

17. Yokoi Tokiyoshi, *Nōhonshugi*, quoted in Vlastos, "Agrarianism without Tradition," 82–83.

18. Kōda Rohan (1899), quoted in Carol Gluck, *Japan's Modern Myths: Ideology in the Late Meiji Period* (Princeton, 1985), 185–86.

19. Hirata Tōsuke, quoted in Gluck, *Japan's Modern Myths*, 188.

20. Havens, *Farm and Nation*, 127, 139–40, 144.

21. Louise Young, *Japan's Total Empire: Manchuria and the Culture of Wartime Imperialism* (Berkeley, 1998), 311–12. See also Brett Walker, *Conquest of Ainu Land: Ecology and Culture in Japanese Expansion, 1590–1800* (Berkeley, 2001).

22. Okakura Tenshin, *The Ideals of the East* [1902], quoted in Najita and Harootunian, "Japanese Revolt," 715.

23. Young, *Japan's Total Empire*, 23, 27.

24. Gavan McCormack, "Reflections on Modern Japanese History in the Context of the Concept of Genocide," in Robert Gellately and Ben Kiernan, eds., *The Specter of Genocide: Mass Murder in Historical Perspective* (New York, 2003), 278; Young, *Japan's Total Empire*, 23; Havens, *Farm and Nation*, 276.

25. Quoted in Najita and Harootunian, "Japanese Revolt," 714; Young, *Japan's Total Empire*, 311–14, 316.

26. Tessa Morris-Suzuki, *Shōwa: An Inside History of Hirohito's Japan* (Sydney, 1984), 45.

27. Katō Kanji, *Nihon nōson kyōiku* [Japanese Farm Education] (Tokyo, 1934), 210–11, quoted in Havens, *Farm and Nation*, 290.

28. Havens, *Farm and Nation*, 47, 110, 114, 118, 150; Ohnuki-Tierney, *Kamikaze, Cherry Blossoms*, 61, 13.

29. Yamazaki Nobukichi, *Nōson jichi no kenkyū* [Studies on Farm Village Self-Rule] [1908], quoted in Havens, *Farm and Nation*, 161.

30. Tokutomi Sohō and Yamazaki Enkichi, quoted in Gluck, *Japan's Modern Myths*, 178–80.

31. Gluck, *Japan's Modern Myths*, 190–91.

32. Quoted in ibid., 180.

33. Kawakami Hajime (1879–1946), "Nihon sonnōron" [Respecting Japanese Agriculture], *Kyoyūken bunko* [June 1904], quoted in Havens, *Farm and Nation*, 115–19.

34. Havens, *Farm and Nation*, 112–14, 117, 119.

35. Yokota Hideo (1889–1926), *Nōson kyūsairon* [On Rescuing the Farm Villages] (Tokyo 1914), 32–33, and *Nōson kaikakusaku* [Rural Reform Policy] (Tokyo, 1916), both quoted in Havens, *Farm and Nation*, 123.

36. Yokota Hideo, *Yomiuri shinbun* [Aug. 2, 1917], quoted in Havens, *Farm and Nation*, 125.

37. Havens, *Farm and Nation*, 150, 163, 122, 136; Gluck, *Japan's Modern Myths*, 180, 188.

38. Yokota Hideo, *Nōson kakumeiron* [On Rural Revolution] (Tokyo, 1914), 35, 44, quoted in Havens, *Farm and Nation*, 123–27.

39. Gluck, *Japan's Modern Myths*, 175–76, 178.

40. Yokota Hideo, *Nōson kyūsairon*, quoted in Havens, *Farm and Nation*, 128.

41. John W. Dower, *War without Mercy: Race and Power in the Pacific War* (New York, 1986), 204; Yokota Hideo, *Nōson kakumeiron*, quoted in Havens, *Farm and Nation*, 128.

42. Dai Nihon Jinushi Kyōkai, "Sengen" [Declaration] [Oct. 1925], in Havens, *Farm and Nation*, 154.

43. Dore and Ōuchi, "Rural Origins of Japanese Fascism," 190; Havens, *Farm and Nation*, 134–38, 152.

44. Havens, *Farm and Nation*, 140–41, 145–47.

45. Young, *Japan's Total Empire*, 324.

46. Dore and Ōuchi, "Rural Origins of Japanese Fascism," 186; Havens, *Farm and Nation*, 155–56.

47. Havens, *Farm and Nation*, 164–68, 180.

48. Ibid., 170–77.

49. Najita and Harootunian, "Japanese Revolt," 723, 744–45.

50. Havens, *Farm and Nation*, 188–89; Najita and Harootunian, "Japanese Revolt," 730–33, 713.

51. Ohnuki-Tierney, *Kamikaze, Cherry Blossoms*, 97; Najita and Harootunian, "Japanese Revolt," 754–55.

52. Col. Hiromichi Yahara, *The Battle for Okinawa* (New York, 1995), 17.

53. Havens, *Farm and Nation*, 177, 194, 199, 202–10.

54. Ibid., 234–38, 243.

55. Ibid., 243, 298; Mikiso Hane, *Japan: A Short History* (Oxford, 2000), 142.

56. Ben-Ami Shillony, *Revolt in Japan: The Young Officers and the February 26, 1936 Incident* (Princeton, 1973), 26; Anon., "Ex-General Hashimoto," 9-pp. typescript dated Feb. 22, 1948, Yale Divinity School Library, New Haven, 3–4.

57. Hashimoto Kingorō, *Addresses to Young Men*, quoted in Iris Chang, *The Rape of Nanking* (New York, 1997), 26; Ohnuki-Tierney, *Kamikaze, Cherry Blossoms*, 97; Shillony, *Revolt in Japan*, 37.

58. Yamazaki Nobukichi, *Nōmindō* [1930], and Tachibana Kōzaburō, *Nōsongaku* [Farm Village Studies] [1931], 169, quoted in Havens, *Farm and Nation*, 161, 256; Najita and Harootunian, "Japanese Revolt," 727.

59. Tachibana Kōzaburō, *Nōsongaku*, 297–98, 177, quoted in Havens, *Farm and Nation*, 249, 267.

60. Young, *Japan's Total War*, 429; Dower, *War without Mercy*, 296; McCormack, "Reflections on Modern Japanese History," 265–86.

61. Hane, *Japan*, 144; Shillony, *Revolt in Japan*, 180; Havens, *Farm and Nation*, 239, 243.

62. Shillony, *Revolt in Japan*, 27–28, 106; Hane, *Japan*, 144.

63. Frank B. Gibney, "Two Views of Battle," introduction to Yahara, *Battle for Okinawa*, xvii.

64. Hane, *Japan*, 144–46; Yahara, *Battle for Okinawa*, 230.

65. Havens, *Farm and Nation*, 240–41; Ohnuki-Tierney, *Kamikaze, Cherry Blossoms*, 5.

66. Tachibana Kōzaburō, *Nihon aikoku kakushin hongi* [Basic Principles of Japanese Patriotic Reform], mimeographed Jan. 1932 lectures, quoted in Havens, *Farm and Nation*, 255.

67. Tachibana Kōzaburō, *Nihon aikoku kakushin hongi*, in Havens, *Farm and Nation*, 252, 259–60, 264, 268, 271.

68. Ibid., 269–72.

69. Havens, *Farm and Nation*, 177–79, 163, 178.

70. Ikafube Takahiko, quoting Gondō, in Havens, *Farm and Nation*, 299, also 163, 179.

71. Havens, *Farm and Nation*, 243.

72. Hane, *Japan*, 141; Havens, *Farm and Nation*, 163, 239, 243, 305, 248, 303.

73. Dore and Ōuchi, "Rural Origins of Japanese Fascism," 196, 205; Havens, *Farm and Nation*, 246–47.

74. Dore and Ōuchi, "Rural Origins of Japanese Fascism," 196.

75. Young, *Japan's Total Empire*, 311, 327, 321; Hane, *Japan*, 146–47.

76. Hane, *Japan*, 147.

77. Quoted in Dore and Ōuchi, "Rural Origins of Japanese Fascism," 207.

78. *Shisōsen* [The Ideological Struggle], published by the Japanese army on July 25, 1934, quoted in Dore and Ōuchi, "Rural Origins of Japanese Fascism," 200–1.

79. Quoted in Havens, *Farm and Nation*, 308.

80. Quoted in Dore and Ōuchi, "Rural Origins of Japanese Fascism," 197; Hane, *Japan*, 91.

81. Havens, *Farm and Nation*, 162, 148–50.

82. Ibid., 152.

83. Okada On, *Nōson kōsei no genri to keikaku* [Basic Principles and Plans for Farm Village Rebirth] (Tokyo, 1933), 80–81, 179, quoted in Havens, *Farm and Nation*, 157–58; Young, *Japan's Total Empire*, 325.

84. Najita and Harootunian, "Japanese Revolt," 746–49.

85. Tachibana Kōzaburō, *Kōdō kokka nōhon kenkokuron* [Theory of Building an Imperial State on Agriculture] (Tokyo, 1935), 9, quoted in Havens, *Farm and Nation*, 256, 248.

86. Tachibana Kōzaburō, *Kōdō kokka nōhon kenkokuron*, 187, 192–93, 35, 208, quoted in Havens, *Farm and Nation*, 249–51.

87. Havens, *Farm and Nation*, 195–96, 180, 170.

88. Gondō Seikyō, *Jichi minseiri* [Principles of People's Self-Rule] (Tokyo, 1936), 248–49, quoted in Havens, *Farm and Nation*, 195, 201.

89. Havens, *Farm and Nation*, 216.

90. Gondō, *Jichi minseiri*, 261–62; Havens, *Farm and Nation*, 220–21.

91. Havens, *Farm and Nation*, 278–79, 282, 286–87.

92. Katō Kanji, *Nihon nōson kyōiku* [Japanese Farm Education] (Tokyo, 1934), 4, 103–4, 166–67, quoted in Havens, *Farm and Nation*, 279, 281, 285–86, also 283–84; Young, *Japan's Total Empire*, 366.

93. Havens, *Farm and Nation*, 286–87, 290, 310, 290–91, quoting Katō, *Nihon nōson kyōiku*, 199, 214.

94. Katō Kanji, "Kōkoku nōmin no jikaku to shimei" [Consciousness and Destiny of Imperial Farmers], *Iyasaka* 161 (Feb. 1936), quoted in Havens, *Farm and Nation*, 292.

95. Hane, *Japan*, 147–48, 141, 149; Yahara, *Battle for Okinawa*, 17.

96. Yasuda Yu, *Gokuchu shuki* [Notes in Prison], quoted in Dore and Ōuchi, "Rural Origins of Japanese Fascism," 196.

97. Young, *Japan's Total Empire*, 307, 321, 371; Havens, *Farm and Nation*, 287, 11.

98. Hane, *Japan*, 147–52; Dower, *War without Mercy*, 221–22, 228.

99. Takeuchi Yoshimi, quoted in Najita and Harootunian, "Japanese Revolt," 770.

100. Gibney, "Two Views of Battle," xvii; Hane, *Japan*, 154–55.

101. Honda Katsuichi, *The Nanjing Massacre: A Japanese Journalist Confronts Japan's National Shame* (Armonk, 1999), 7, xv, xviii, 169.

102. Frank Gibney, introduction to Honda, *Nanjing Massacre*, vii; military historian Hata Iku-hiko translated what is apparently this same order as "Just kill them." Beatrice S. Bartlett, introduction to *American Missionary Eyewitnesses to the Nanking Massacre, 1937–38*, Yale Divinity School Library Occasional Publication, no. 9 (New Haven, 1997), xiv, quoting Hata Ikuhiko, *Nankin jiken* (Tokyo, 1986), 143.

103. Timothy Brook, ed., *Documents on the Rape of Nanking* (Ann Arbor, 1999), 66, 163, 248–49; Gibney, introduction to Honda, *Nanjing Massacre*, vii, xv.

104. Daqing Yang, "The Challenges of the Nanjing Massacre," in Joshua A. Fogel, ed., *The Nanking Massacre in History and Historiography* (Berkeley, 2000), 141.

105. McCormack, "Reflections on Modern Japanese History," 272; Chang, *Rape of Nanking*, 145.

106. Bartlett, introduction to *American Missionary Eyewitnesses to the Nanking Massacre*, v.

107. Chang, *Rape of Nanking*, 107; Anon., "Ex-General Hashimoto," 7; Yahara, *Battle for Okinawa*, 17n.

108. Honda, *Nanjing Massacre*, 169.

109. Young, *Japan's Total War*, 428.

110. John W. Powell, "Japan's Germ Warfare: The U.S. Cover-up of a War Crime," *Bulletin of Concerned Asian Scholars* 12:4 (1980): 3–5, 15 n3; Yuki Tanaka, *Hidden Horrors: Japanese War Crimes in World War II* (Boulder, 1996), 135–39.

111. Najita and Harootunian, "Japanese Revolt," 721, 733–34.

112. Young, *Japan's Total Empire*, 328; Havens, *Farm and Nation*, 152, 148–49, 292–93, 310.

113. Young, *Japan's Total Empire*, 335, 337.

114. Sugino Tadao, *Seishōnen ni uttau* and *Bunson keikaku no jissei mondai*, no. 1, 5–7 and no. 4, 1–18, of *Bunson keikaku sosho* (Nōson kōsei kyōkai, 1938), quoted in Young, *Japan's Total Empire*, 338–39.

115. Young, *Japan's Total Empire*, 340–45.

116. Ibid., 364, 367–68, 402–3, 400, 404, 406.

117. Dower, *War without Mercy*, 244; Young, *Japan's Total Empire*, 366–67, 370, 372.

118. Young, *Japan's Total Empire*, 369.

119. Ibid., 347–49.

120. Ishiguro Tadaatsu, "Nōmin dōjōchō ni atau," *Mura* [Village] (Aug. 1938), and speech in Uchihara, Nov. 1940, quoted in Havens, *Farm and Nation*, 151, 153.

121. Yahara, *Battle for Okinawa*, 16–18, 230.

122. Dower, *War without Mercy*, 280–81, 214, 217; Havens, *Farm and Nation*, 243, 247; Young, *Japan's Total Empire*, 281.

123. "Prisoner of War Interrogation Report" [Shimada Akira], Headquarters 10th Army, July 24, 1945, in Yahara, *Battle for Okinawa*, 235.

124. Powell, "Japan's Germ Warfare," 3–7.

125. Daniel Barenblatt, *A Plague upon Humanity: The Secret Genocide of Axis Japan's Germ Warfare Operation* (New York, 2004), 173–75. See also Sheldon H. Harris, *Factories of Death: Japanese Biological Warfare, 1932–1945, and the American Cover-up* (New York, 2002).

126. McCormack, "Reflections on Modern Japanese History," 273–74.

127. Havens, *Farm and Nation*, 290; Dower, *War without Mercy*, 271, 203, 269.

128. Najita and Harootunian, "Japanese Revolt," 742.

129. Dower, *War without Mercy*, 205, 211–12 (quoting *Bungei Shunjū*, Jan. 1942), 225–26.

130. Ibid., 262–68, 276–77.

131. McCormack, "Reflections on Modern Japanese History," 278; Yayori Matsui, "Women's International War Crimes Tribunal on Japan's Military Sexual Slavery," in Li, *Japanese War Crimes*, ch. 15; Tanaka, *Hidden Horrors*, ch. 3.

132. Dower, *War without Mercy*, 284, 274–75, 287, 288, 285, 289, 277, 290.

133. Ibid., 231–32, 214, 223–25, 247–48 (*Manga* and *Manga Nippon*, both Oct. 1944).

134. Ibid., 216, 232–33.

135. *Nippon Times*, July 3 and 7, 1945, quoted in David C. Earhart, "All Ready to Die: Kamikaze-fication and Japan's Wartime Ideology," *Critical Asian Studies* 37:4 (2005): 569–70, 591–92.

136. Earhart, "All Ready to Die," 574, 594, 585–86; Yahara, *Battle for Okinawa,* 222, 15, 42, 134, 156, 231.

137. Yahara, *Battle for Okinawa,* 153–56, 168.

138. "Prisoner of War Interrogation Report," 232.

Chapter 13. Soviet Terror and Agriculture

1. Robert Conquest, *The Harvest of Sorrow: Soviet Collectivization and the Terror-Famine* (Oxford, 1986), 3; Charles S. Maier, *The Unmasterable Past: History, Holocaust, and German National Identity* (Cambridge, Mass., 1988), 76; Richard J. Evans, *In Hitler's Shadow* (New York, 1989), 88.

2. Stephen G. Wheatcroft, "The Scale and Nature of German and Soviet Repression and Mass Killings, 1930–45," *Europe-Asia Studies* 48:8 (1996); Andrea Graziosi, *The Great Soviet Peasant War: Bolsheviks and Peasants, 1917–1933* (Cambridge, Mass., 1996), 65.

3. Sheila Fitzpatrick, *Stalin's Peasants: Resistance and Survival in the Russian Village after Collectivization* (New York, 1994), 19ff.; Robert Koehl, "Feudal Aspects of National Socialism," in Henry A. Turner Jr., ed., *Nazism and the Third Reich* (New York, 1972), 156–57.

4. Stephen G. Wheatcroft, "Crises and Peasantry," in E. Kingston-Mann and T. Mixter, eds., *Peasant Economy, Culture, and Politics of European Russia, 1800–1921* (Princeton, 1991), 136–38.

5. Yuzuru Taniuchi, *The Village Gathering in Russia in the Mid-1920s* (Birmingham, 1968), 8–10.

6. James W. Heinzen, *Inventing a Soviet Countryside: State Power and the Transformation of Rural Russia, 1917–1929* (Pittsburgh, 2004), 64, 15, 42; Conquest, *Harvest of Sorrow,* 49.

7. Richard Walther Darré, *Neuadel aus Blut und Boden* (Munich, 1941), 63 (tr. Ruth Hein).

8. Heinzen, *Inventing,* 64, 60 (quoting A. Mitrofanov).

9. Lenin, quoted in Conquest, *Harvest of Sorrow,* 22.

10. Karl Marx and Friedrich Engels, *The Communist Manifesto.*

11. Lenin to Molotov, Mar, 19, 1922, published in *Izvestiya Tsk,* no. 4 (1990): 190–95, quoted in R. W. Davies, *Soviet History in the Yeltsin Period* (London, 1997), 12.

12. Stalin's speech to an enlarged Central Committee plenum, Nov. 1928, quoted in Robert C. Tucker, *Stalin in Power: The Revolution from Above, 1928–1941* (New York, 1990), 64.

13. Quoted in Anton Antonov-Ovseyenko, *The Time of Stalin* (New York, 1981), 212.

14. Conquest, *Harvest of Sorrow,* 20.

15. Heinzen, *Inventing,* 1, 5, 24–25.

16. Graziosi, *Soviet Peasant War,* 11–12; Heinzen, *Inventing,* 23, 25; Conquest, *Harvest of Sorrow,* 43, 5.

17. Lenin at the 1919 Eighth Party Congress, *Sochineniya,* 4-oe izd., t. 29, 180, quoted in Taniuchi, *Village Gathering,* 11, 44.

18. Taniuchi, *Village Gathering,* 14 (quoting Zinoviev in 1920), 11, 20; Conquest, *Harvest of Sorrow,* 46.

19. Maxim Gorky, *O russkom krestyanstve* (Berlin, 1922), 43–44, quoted in Conquest, *Harvest of Sorrow,* 20.

20. Maxim Gorky, "*Lénine*" et "*Le paysan russe*" [1922] (Paris, 1925), 140–41, and *Russki Sovremennik* [1924], both quoted in Moshe Lewin, *Russian Peasants and Soviet Power* (New York, 1975), 22.

21. Conquest, *Harvest of Sorrow,* 46.

22. Graziosi, *Soviet Peasant War,* 48 (citing Peter Holquist, *A Russian Vendée,* 432–37), 26.

23. I. I. Rejngol'd, July 6, 1919, quoted in Graziosi, *Soviet Peasant War,* 20–21; 24, 31.

24. R. W. Davies and Stephen G. Wheatcroft, *The Years of Hunger: Soviet Agriculture, 1931–33* (London, 2003), 403–4.

25. Graziosi, *Soviet Peasant War,* 32n64; Davies and Wheatcroft, *Years of Hunger,* 403–4; Conquest, *Harvest of Sorrow,* 53–54.

26. Davies and Wheatcroft, *Years of Hunger,* 404; Heinzen, *Inventing,* 44, 24–25, 33–36.

27. Taniuchi, *Village Gathering,* 1, 16, 18.

28. Heinzen, *Inventing,* 25, 38–40.

29. Davies and Wheatcroft, *Years of Hunger,* 404–5; Graziosi, *Soviet Peasant War,* 33; Heinzen,

Inventing, 52–53; Conquest states: "The great famine of 1921 was not due to any conscious decision that the peasant should starve" (*Harvest of Sorrow,* 55).

30. Conquest, *Harvest of Sorrow,* 53.

31. *Kommunisticeskaja partija Ukrainy v rezoljucijax* [1921], in Graziosi, *Soviet Peasant War,* 37.

32. Heinzen, *Inventing,* 51, 75–76, 59 (quoting M. E. Shefler, Oct. 1921).

33. Fitzpatrick, *Stalin's Peasants,* 24.

34. www.soviethistory.org/index.php?action=L2&SubjectID=1921nep&Year=1921; Heinzen, *Inventing,* 61.

35. Pavel Mesiatsev, 1922, quoted in Heinzen, *Inventing,* 72.

36. Heinzen, *Inventing,* 1–3, 55; Taniuchi, *Village Gathering,* 3, 1, 6.

37. Quoted in Lewin, *Russian Peasants and Soviet Power,* 41, and Taniuchi, *Village Gathering,* 45; 34, 73.

38. Heinzen, *Inventing,* 3, 191.

39. Graziosi, *Soviet Peasant War,* 47; Taniuchi, *Village Gathering,* 12.

40. *Sovetskoe stroitel'stvo,* no. 5 (1926): 44, quoted in Taniuchi, *Village Gathering,* 38–39.

41. *Izvestiya TsK VKP (b),* no. 29 (1927): 3–5, quoted in Taniuchi, *Village Gathering,* 77–78.

42. *Vlast' sovetov,* no. 18 (1928): 21, and no. 21 (1928): 28, quoted in Taniuchi, *Village Gathering,* 39, 49.

43. Taniuchi, *Village Gathering,* 50, 65, 63.

44. *Vlast' sovetov,* no. 22 (1928): 11, quoted in Taniuchi, *Village Gathering,* 32–33.

45. Taniuchi, *Village Gathering,* 35–37.

46. Heinzen, *Inventing,* 187–91; Conquest, *Harvest of Sorrow,* 13.

47. Taniuchi, *Village Gathering,* 52, 61, 67.

48. *Izvestiya TsK VKP (b),* no. 29 (1927): 3–5, quoted in Taniuchi, *Village Gathering,* 78.

49. Taniuchi, *Village Gathering,* 52, 77, 51–52.

50. Heinzen, *Inventing,* 4, 199; Taniuchi, *Village Gathering,* 52, 77.

51. Lewin, *Russian Peasants and Soviet Power,* 160–64.

52. Ibid., 166.

53. Taniuchi, *Village Gathering,* 61, 74; Heinzen, *Inventing,* 4.

54. Moshe Lewin, *The Making of the Soviet System* (New York, 1985), 144.

55. Taniuchi, *Village Gathering,* 76; Heinzen, *Inventing,* 187.

56. *Bednota,* Feb. 5, 1927, and *Vlast' sovetov,* no. 1, 9, (1927): 22, quoted in Taniuchi, *Village Gathering,* 47; Heinzen, *Inventing,* 192; Taniuchi, *Village Gathering,* 78.

57. Lewin, *Making of the Soviet System,* 96; Taniuchi, *Village Gathering,* 61, 79.

58. Mikoyan, in *Pravda,* Feb. 10, 1928, in Lewin, *Making of the Soviet System,* 97; Taniuchi, *Village Gathering,* 48.

59. Stalin, speech to the July 1928 plenum, quoted in Fitzpatrick, *Stalin's Peasants,* 99.

60. Taniuchi, *Village Gathering,* 80; Davies and Wheatcroft, *Years of Hunger,* 406, 433–34, 441.

61. Heinzen, *Inventing,* 186, 192–93; Lewin, *Russian Peasants and Soviet Power,* 147–59.

62. Heinzen, *Inventing,* 195–96, 198, 194; Graziosi, *Soviet Peasant War,* 55n.

63. Bukharin to Kamenev, *Sotsialisticheskii vestnik* 9 (1929): 10, quoted in Lewin, *Making of the Soviet System,* 99; Lewin, *Russian Peasants and Soviet Power,* 166.

64. Heinzen, *Inventing,* 197.

65. Terry Martin, *Affirmative Action Empire: Nations and Nationalism in the Soviet Union, 1923–1939* (Ithaca, 2001), 250; Heinzen, *Inventing,* 197–98, 200, 202, 275n48.

66. Heinzen, *Inventing,* 199, 1–2; Fitzpatrick, *Stalin's Peasants,* 39.

67. Davies and Wheatcroft, *Years of Hunger,* 434; Graziosi, *Soviet Peasant War,* 60; Lewin, *Making of the Soviet System,* 166.

68. Graziosi, *Soviet Peasant War,* 58–60, 71; Graeme Gill, *Stalinism* (Atlantic Highlands, 1990), 16; Heinzen, *Inventing,* 8; Fitzpatrick, *Stalin's Peasants,* 48, 54.

69. Graziosi, *Soviet Peasant War,* 64, 47.

70. Nicolas Werth, "The Mechanism of a Mass Crime: The Great Terror in the Soviet Union, 1937–1938," in Robert Gellately and Ben Kiernan, eds., *The Specter of Genocide: Mass Murder in Historical Perspective* (New York, 2003), 226.

71. Davies and Wheatcroft, *Years of Hunger,* xv; Werth, "Mechanism of a Mass Crime," 217n9, 226.

72. J. Arch Getty, Gábor T. Rittersporn, and Viktor N. Zemskov, "Victims of the Soviet Penal System in the Pre-war Years: A First Approach on the Basis of Archival Evidence," *American Historical Review* 98:4 (1993): 1024; Graziosi, *Soviet Peasant War,* 47, 50–51, 56.

73. Werth, "Mechanism of a Mass Crime," 228–29.

74. Graziosi, *Soviet Peasant War,* 48–49; Getty, Rittersporn, and Zemskov, "Victims of the Soviet Penal System," 1024.

75. Davies and Wheatcroft, *Years of Hunger,* 435; Heinzen, *Inventing,* 191; Graziosi, *Soviet Peasant War,* 52, 55.

76. Graziosi, *Soviet Peasant War,* 47, 52–55; S. G. Wheatcroft, personal communication, June 2004.

77. Davies and Wheatcroft, *Years of Hunger,* 438.

78. Ibid., 408–9, 412, 415, 409.

79. Ibid., 412–13, 415. Wheatcroft and Davies prefer a 1930–33 toll estimate of 5.7 million over another of 8.5 million; more precise 1931–33 famine toll estimates should exclude possibly 50,000 executions in 1930–31. OGPU data put this latter figure at 31,000. Michael Ellman, "The Role of Leadership Perceptions and of Intent in the Soviet Famine of 1931–1934," *Europe-Asia Studies* 57:6 (2005): 827.

80. See also Ellman, "The Role of Leadership," 829.

81. Lewin, *Making of the Soviet System,* 166; Graziosi, *Soviet Peasant War,* 60, 57. For different annual harvest figures and calculations, see Davies and Wheatcroft, *Years of Hunger,* 448–49, and their *Economic Transformation of the Soviet Union, 1913–1945* (Cambridge, 1996), 286–88.

82. Lewin, *Making of the Soviet System,* 166; Graziosi, *Soviet Peasant War,* 60; Davies and Wheatcroft, *Years of Hunger,* 435, 439.

83. Davies and Wheatcroft, *Years of Hunger,* 433, 407, 433 (3.5 million tons), 440 (2 million tons), 418.

84. A. Blum, *Naître, vivre et mourir en URSS, 1917–1991* (Paris, 1994), 99, cited in Graziosi, *Soviet Peasant War,* 64.

85. Stalin, Nov. 27, 1932, quoted in Ellman, "The Role of Leadership," 830–31.

86. Kosior to Stalin, Mar. 15, 1933, and Stalin to Sholokhov, May 6, 1933, quoted in Ellman, "The Role of Leadership," 830, 824; 823, 831; Graziosi, *Soviet Peasant War,* 59, 68–69.

87. Stalin to the 17th Party Congress, Jan. 28, 1934, in J. Arch Getty and Oleg V. Naumov, *The Road to Terror: Stalin and the Self-Destruction of the Bolsheviks, 1932–1939* (New Haven, 1999), 130.

88. Stalin, May 4, 1935, quoted in Ellman, "The Role of Leadership," 832.

89. Lewin, *Making of the Soviet System,* 166; Graziosi, *Soviet Peasant War,* 69.

90. Conquest, *Harvest of Sorrow,* 13, 30–31, 62; Martin, *Affirmative Action Empire,* 75ff., 91, 100, 116, 290.

91. Martin, *Affirmative Action Empire,* 293; Graziosi, *Soviet Peasant War,* 50, 67.

92. Davies and Wheatcroft, *Years of Hunger,* 440; Graziosi, *Soviet Peasant War,* 63.

93. Davies and Wheatcroft, *Years of Hunger,* 415–16; Martin, *Affirmative Action Empire,* 291.

94. Conquest, *Harvest of Sorrow,* 303–6; Davies and Wheatcroft, *Years of Hunger,* 415.

95. J. Vallin, F. Mesle, S. Adamets, and S. Pyrozhkov, "A New Estimate of Ukrainian Population Losses during the Crises of the 1930s and 1940s," *Population Studies* 56:3 (2002): 252.

96. Martin, *Affirmative Action Empire,* 270–71, 293, 250; Tucker, *Stalin in Power,* 64.

97. Timothy Snyder, *Sketches from a Secret War: A Polish Artist's Mission to Liberate Soviet Ukraine* (New Haven, 2005), 102.

98. Martin, *Affirmative Action Empire,* 270–72.

99. Stalin's letters to Kaganovich, June 2 and 15, 1932, quoted in Martin, *Affirmative Action Empire,* 296–98; Stalin's letter of June 18, 1932, quoted in Terry Martin, "The 1932–33 Ukrainian Terror: New Documentation on Surveillance and the Thought Process of Stalin," in W. W. Isajiw, ed., *Society in Transition: Social Change in Ukraine in Western Perspectives* (Toronto, 2003).

100. Stalin's letter of Aug. 11, 1932, quoted in Martin, *Affirmative Action Empire,* 297–98, 302.

101. Snyder, *Sketches from a Secret War,* 86, 89, 101–2, 105–6 (quoting Stalin to Kaganovich, June 18, and Kaganovich to Stalin, Aug. 16, 1932).

102. Martin, *Affirmative Action Empire,* 302–3, 306–7.

103. Martin, "The 1932–33 Ukrainian Terror," 2; Martin, *Affirmative Action Empire,* 306.

104. Getty, Rittersporn, and Zemskov, "Victims of the Soviet Penal System," 1028n45.

105. Martin, *Affirmative Action Empire,* 311; Werth, "Mechanism of a Mass Crime," 222–23, 231–32, 237.

106. Stephen G. Wheatcroft, "Towards Explaining the Changing Levels of Stalinist Repression in the 1930s: Mass Killings," in Wheatcroft, ed., *Challenging Traditional Views of Russian History* (London, 2002), 125, table 6.4.

107. Getty, Rittersporn, and Zemskov, "Victims of the Soviet Penal System," 1023; Werth, "Mechanism of a Mass Crime," 217.

108. Werth, "Mechanism of a Mass Crime," 223, 219, 223–25, 229, 225, 230–31.

109. Snyder, *Sketches from a Secret War,* ch. 6; Werth, "Mechanism of a Mass Crime," 232, 236–37, 232–33; Getty, Rittersporn, and Zemskov, "Victims of the Soviet Penal System," 1028.

110. Getty, Rittersporn, and Zemskov, "Victims of the Soviet Penal System," 1029, 1043.

111. Werth, "Mechanism of a Mass Crime," 236–37.

112. Getty, Rittersporn, and Zemskov, "Victims of the Soviet Penal System," 1025, table 2.

113. Wheatcroft, "Changing Levels of Stalinist Repression," table 4; Werth, "Mechanism of a Mass Crime," 217, 223n32; Getty, Rittersporn, and Zemskov, "Victims of the Soviet Penal System," 1022, table 1.

114. Getty and Naumov, "Numbers of Victims of the Terror," in *The Road to Terror,* 591–92.

115. Werth, "Mechanism of a Mass Crime," 237–38.

116. Getty, Rittersporn, and Zemskov, "Victims of the Soviet Penal System," 1023.

117. Wheatcroft, "Changing Levels of Stalinist Repression," table 5; Getty, Rittersporn, and Zemskov, "Victims of the Soviet Penal System," 1023–24; Werth, "Mechanism of a Mass Crime," 217.

118. Getty, Rittersporn, and Zemskov, "Victims of the Soviet Penal System," 1039–40.

119. Joshua Rubinstein and Vladimir P. Naumov, eds., *Stalin's Secret Pogrom: The Postwar Inquisition of the Jewish Anti-Fascist Committee* (New Haven, 2001).

Chapter 14. Maoism in China

1. Tachibana Kōzaburō, *Nihon aikoku kakushin hongi* [Basic Principles of Japanese Patriotic Reform], Jan. 1932 lectures, quoted in Thomas Havens, *Farm and Nation in Modern Japan: Agrarian Nationalism, 1870–1940* (Princeton, 1974), 265, 270–72.

2. Jung Chang and Jon Halliday, *Mao: The Unknown Story* (New York, 2005), 19.

3. Roy Hofheinz Jr., *The Broken Wave: The Chinese Communist Peasant Movement, 1922–1928* (Cambridge, Mass., 1977), 300.

4. Stuart Schram, *Mao Tse-tung* (Harmondsworth, 1968), 79.

5. Jonathan D. Spence, *To Change China: Western Advisers in China, 1620–1960* (Harmondsworth, 1980), 185.

6. "Remember the Third Anniversary of the Russian Communist Government," *Communist* (Shanghai, 1920), quoted in Adrian Chan, "The Communist Peasant Policies during the Canton Government: Marxist, Russian, or Chinese?" (paper presented to the Second National Conference of the Asian Studies Association of Australia, University of New South Wales, May 14–19, 1978), 8.

7. Shinkichi Eto, "Hai-lu-feng—The First Chinese Soviet Government," parts 1 and 2, *China Quarterly* 8 (Oct.–Dec. 1961): 161–83, and 9 (Jan.–Mar. 1962): 149–81; part 2 at 161, 175.

8. Peng Pai, "Memoirs of a Chinese Communist," *Living Age* 344:4399 (1933): 118: "My father received about a thousand sacks of rice a year as payment for rent … the tenants with their families numbered five hundred" (118); Eto, "Hai-lu-feng," 1:167.

9. Robert B. Marks, *Rural Revolution in South China: Peasants and the Making of History in Haifeng County, 1570–1930* (Madison, 1984), 155.

10. Hofheinz, *Broken Wave,* 246, preface, and 234.

11. Mao Zedong, "The National Revolution and the Peasant Movement" [Sept. 1926], cited in Angus W. McDonald Jr., *The Urban Origins of Rural Revolution: Elite and Masses in Hunan Province, China, 1911–1927* (Berkeley, 1978), 261–62.

12. Fernando Galbiati, *P'eng P'ai and the Hai-lu-feng Soviet* (Stanford, 1985), 368–73.

13. Hofheinz, *Broken Wave,* 143; Eto, "Hai-lu-feng," 1:167–68; Marks, *Rural Revolution,* 159–61, 166; Galbiati, *P'eng P'ai,* 56–58.

14. Galbiati, *P'eng P'ai,* 68; Eto, "Hai-lu-feng," 1:168; Hofheinz, *Broken Wave,* 144.

15. Hofheinz, *Broken Wave,* 142ff. (168–78 for detailed discussion), 145; Galbiati, *P'eng P'ai,* 32; Eto, "Hai-lu-feng," 1:169; Marks, *Rural Revolution,* 169, 173.

16. See Marks, *Rural Revolution,* 183; Peng's exaggerations in "Memoirs," 123.

17. Eto, "Hai-lu-feng," 1:172; Hofheinz, *Broken Wave,* 152–56 (for population figures, see Galbiati, *P'eng P'ai,* 12), 151.

18. Hofheinz, *Broken Wave,* 180 (see also Marks, *Rural Revolution,* 209 and 183, table 4); Marks, *Rural Revolution,* 183; Galbiati, *P'eng P'ai,* 51–53.

19. Galbiati, *P'eng P'ai,* 17, 20, 23, 362.

20. Hofheinz, *Broken Wave,* 168, 301, 172; Marks, *Rural Revolution,* 190; Galbiati, *P'eng P'ai,* 151.

21. Chen Duxiu, in the official CCP weekly *Hsiang Tao,* Aug. 1, 1923, quoted in Chan, "Communist Peasant Policies during the Canton Government," 13–14.

22. "Mou" [Mao Zedong], remarks at Third CCP Congress, 1923, handwritten notes by Comintern agent H. Sneevliet, Sneevliet archive doc. 275, Internationaal Instituut voor Sociale Geschiedenis, Amsterdam.

23. Eto, "Hai-lu-feng," 1:177–82; Schram, *Mao Tse-tung,* 76, 78, 81.

24. Eto, "Hai-lu-feng," 2:152–55; Marks, *Rural Revolution,* 206.

25. Eto, "Hai-lu-feng," 2:156.

26. Hofheinz, *Broken Wave,* 338; Eto, "Hai-lu-feng," 2:156–59.

27. Suzanne Pepper, *Civil War in China: The Political Struggle, 1945–1949* (Berkeley, 1978), 230; Schram, *Mao Tse-tung,* 92.

28. McDonald, *The Urban Origins of Rural Revolution,* 262.

29. Marks, *Rural Revolution,* 222.

30. Mao Zedong, *Report on an Investigation of the Peasant Movement in Hunan* (Peking, 1965), 11–12.

31. Eto, "Hai-lu-feng," 2:161–62; Schram, *Mao Tse-tung,* 125.

32. Hofheinz, *Broken Wave,* 238; Eto, "Hai-lu-feng," 2:165–67.

33. Eto, "Hai-lu-feng," 2:168–69.

34. Hofheinz, *Broken Wave,* 255: "Devastation had become, in fact, the main goal of social policy. Suppression of the counter-revolution was the euphemism for widespread executions, many carried out without orders."

35. Ibid., 245–49; Eto, "Hai-lu-feng," 2:169.

36. Hofheinz, *Broken Wave,* 336n10, 255, 337.

37. Eto, "Hai-lu-feng," 2:169–71, 175; Hofheinz, *Broken Wave,* 152. Hofheinz notes that the peasant movement took "an anti-foreign turn in 1925," yet "it was only in mid-December 1927, after the crushing of the Canton uprising, that acts of violence against foreigners and Christians began to be reported." Further: "The Haifeng government handled its only contact with the Western world with great circumspection" (264, 280).

38. Eto, "Hai-lu-feng," 2:171–72, 174–75.

39. Hofheinz, *Broken Wave,* 272, 267, 274, 275.

40. Ibid., 188, 203, 218, 224, 252–53. By contrast, Mao "was never inclined to a lyrical praise of rural electrification."

41. Eto, "Hai-lu-feng," 2:169, 176–77; Galbiati, *P'eng P'ai,* 359; Hofheinz, *Broken Wave,* 246, preface, 234.

42. Eto, "Hai-lu-feng," 2:178–80.

43. Zhou Enlai, "P'eng, Yang, Yen, Hsing na ssu t'ung-chih pei ti-jen pu-sha ching-huo" [The Events of the Detention and Killing by the Enemy of the Four Comrades P'eng, Yang, Yen, and Hsing], *Hung-ch'i jih-pao,* Aug. 30, 1930, and *P'eng-P'ai yen-chiu shih-liao* [Historical Materials for the Study of P'eng P'ai] (1981), 330, quoted in Galbiati, *P'eng P'ai,* 2.

44. Hofheinz, *Broken Wave,* 159. Peng Pai may be compared with Pol Pot in background, education, and political formation, though not in style or policy. See also Roger Normand, "At the Khmer Rouge School: The Teachings of Chairman Pot," *Nation,* Aug. 27, 1990, 198–202, esp. 200.

45. Marks, *Rural Revolution*, 211; Hofheinz, *Broken Wave*, 283, 258–59, 266 ("Widows and other bereaved enemy women may be married off to someone else at the discretion of the district government" [255]), 280.

46. Peng, "Memoirs," 122. Pol Pot, for instance, never imitated the free style of Peng Pai's account.

47. Marks, *Rural Revolution*, 167; Hofheinz, *Broken Wave*, 270.

48. Eto, "Hai-lu-feng," 2:176–77; Schram, *Mao Tse-tung*, 125; Eto, "Hai-lu-feng," 2:180–81.

49. Galbiati, *P'eng P'ai*, 368–73. Peng's son, deputy magistrate of Haifeng, and four relatives died in the Cultural Revolution, which assaulted Peng's name. Some 104 cadres were slain and 1,680 people dismissed for loyalty to Peng, who was rehabilitated in 1978, after Mao died.

50. Galbiati, *P'eng P'ai*, 365–67. On 366 he notes: "The Hai-lu-feng Soviet was beyond all arguing the first Communist government on Chinese soil." Hofheinz, too, dates the foundation of the Hai-lu-feng Soviet, "the first Chinese soviet government," at Nov. 1, 1927 (*Broken Wave*, 249), while Mao dates his candidate for the honor only "November 1927." See Edgar Snow, *Red Star over China* (Harmondsworth, 1973), 194.

51. Snow, *Red Star*, 194–95, emphasis added; Edwin E. Moise, *Land Reform in China and North Vietnam: Consolidating the Revolution at the Village Level* (Chapel Hill, 1983), 34.

52. Moise, *Land Reform in China*, 35; Hofheinz, *Broken Wave*, 297; Pepper, *Civil War in China*, 288–89.

53. Hofheinz, *Broken Wave*, 300–3. He sees "the real demands of the peasantry" as "peace, protection, and relief" (293).

54. Galbiati, *P'eng P'ai*, 361–65; Marks, *Rural Revolution*, xv, xvi, 211; Hofheinz, *Broken Wave*, 254.

55. In the whole of China in the 1930s, 30 percent of the farmers were tenants, 24 percent were partial tenants, and 46 percent owned at least enough to support themselves. Pepper, *Civil War in China*, 233.

56. Hofheinz, *Broken Wave*, 297.

57. Tanaka Kyoko, "Mao and Liu in the 1947 Land Reform: Allies or Disputants?" *China Quarterly* 75 (Sept. 1978): 590–91; Pepper, *Civil War in China*, 240.

58. Moise, *Land Reform in China*, 31–32.

59. Pepper, *Civil War in China*, 310.

60. Tanaka Kyoko, "The Civil War and Radicalization of Chinese Communist Agrarian Policy, 1945–1947," *Papers on Far Eastern History* 8 (Sept. 1973): 50, 89; Moise, *Land Reform in China*, 67; Pepper, *Civil War in China*, 246; Moise, *Land Reform in China*, 39–40.

61. Tanaka, "The Civil War," 74; Tanaka, "Mao and Liu," 566; Moise, *Land Reform in China*, 43.

62. Tanaka, "The Civil War," 80, 89, 80, 84–85; Moise, *Land Reform in China*, 47, 57.

63. Tanaka, "The Civil War," 85, 70–71, 97.

64. Moise, *Land Reform in China*, 64–66, 49, 59, 63–64, 54.

65. Tanaka, "The Civil War," 49, 77; Pepper, *Civil War in China*, 329.

66. Tanaka, "The Civil War," 74, 105–6.

67. Tanaka, "Mao and Liu," 576–78; Moise, *Land Reform in China*, 65.

68. Moise, *Land Reform in China*, 71; Tanaka, "Mao and Liu," 577–78, 590, 573, 592–93, 583–84.

69. Tanaka, "Mao and Liu," 576–78; Moise, *Land Reform in China*, 75ff, 80.

70. Moise, *Land Reform in China*, 111, 141–42, chs. 5–7. In 1949, the CCP had ordered former KMT members "to register with a promise of pardon in return for spontaneous self-declaration," but "large numbers . . . perished during the campaigns in 1950–51." *China News Analysis*, Nov. 26, 1954, 5, cited in E. Wirth Marvick, ed., *Psychopolitical Analysis: Selected Writings of Nathan Leites* (New York, 1977), 237.

71. Edward Friedman, "Maoism and the Liberation of the Poor," *World Politics* 39:3 (1987): 410.

72. Roderick MacFarquhar, *The Origins of the Cultural Revolution*, vol. 2, *The Great Leap Forward, 1958–1960* (New York, 1983), 330; Edward Friedman, "After Mao: Maoism and Post-Mao China," *Telos* 65 (Fall 1985): 26, citing Basil Ashton et al., "Famine in China, 1958–1961," *Population*

and Development Review (1985); Chang and Halliday, *Mao,* 438, suggest a toll of nearly 38 million.

73. MacFarquhar, *The Great Leap Forward,* 135. See also Lorenz Luthi, *The Sino-Soviet Split* (Princeton, 2007).

74. MacFarquhar, *The Great Leap Forward,* 349, 93–96, 64, 66.

75. Ibid., 91, 96–97.

76. Ibid., 97–101, 133; Lorenz M. Lüthi, "The Sino-Soviet Split, 1956–1966" (Ph.D. diss., Yale University, 2003).

77. MacFarquhar, *The Great Leap Forward,* 119.

78. Ibid., 30–32; he notes that the other "most significant product of the great leap" was the backyard steel furnaces.

79. Ibid., 303; Stuart Schram, ed., *Mao Tse-tung Unrehearsed: Talks and Letters, 1956–1971* (Harmondsworth, 1974), 115.

80. MacFarquhar, *The Great Leap Forward,* 103–6.

81. Ibid., 303.

82. Ibid., 370, quoting a Chinese newspaper cited by Chandrasekhar, *Communist China Today,* 56.

83. Ibid., 106–8, 130–31, 115, citing Peng Dehuai.

84. Ibid., 82–85. See the full quotation from T'an Chen-lin on p. 84.

85. Ibid., 85.

86. Quoted in ibid., 43, 195.

87. Ibid., 196–97, 203; Schram, *Mao Tse-tung Unrehearsed,* 134.

88. MacFarquhar, *The Great Leap Forward,* 219, 221, 247, 294, 297.

89. Ibid., 304, quoting T'ao Chu in late 1961.

90. Ibid., 82, 85, 298, 114–16.

91. Ibid., 119, 121.

92. Ibid., 328, 171. Mao proposed this slogan only in 1959; it was first used in 1960, when it was described as "conspicuously" new (301).

93. *People's Daily,* May 16, 1958, article by Shansi province secretary, T'ao Lu-chia, quoted in MacFarquhar, *The Great Leap Forward,* 119.

94. MacFarquhar, *The Great Leap Forward,* 328, 317, 299; Thomas P. Bernstein, "Stalinism, Famine, and Chinese Peasants," *Theory and Society* 13:3 (1984): 351, 369.

95. MacFarquhar, *The Great Leap Forward,* 312–13.

96. Ibid., 138, 329–30; Friedman, "After Mao," 36, quoting *Mao Zedong sixiang wansui* (1967), 226–27 (reprinted in Japan and Hong Kong); Bernstein, "Stalinism," 352.

97. MacFarquhar, *The Great Leap Forward,* 335.

98. Hofheinz, *Broken Wave,* 300.

99. *Agence-France Presse,* report dated Feb. 3, 1979; Roderick MacFarquhar and Michael Schoenhals, *Mao's Last Revolution* (Cambridge, Mass., 2006).

100. Jean Daubier, *A History of the Chinese Cultural Revolution* (New York, 1974), 76, 37, 259.

101. *Kuangming Daily* and Chekiang Radio, quoted in *Union Research Service,* Mar. 21, 1967, 353, and Aug. 22, 1967, 212, cited in Marvick, *Psychopolitical Analysis,* 225–26.

102. Simon Leys, *The Burning Forest* (New York, 1986), 165–66; *Chinese Literature* (June 1969): 62, in Marvick, *Psychopolitical Analysis,* 220.

103. Lynn T. White III, *Policies of Chaos: The Organizational Causes of Violence in China's Cultural Revolution* (Princeton, 1989), 330, 326.

104. Mao Tse-tung, *Four Essays on Philosophy* (Peking, 1968), "On Contradiction" and "On the Correct Handling of Contradictions among the People," 96.

Chapter 15. From the Mekong to the Nile

1. René Lemarchand, "The Rwanda Genocide," in Samuel Totten, W. S. Parsons, and I. W. Charny, eds., *Century of Genocide: Critical Essays and Eyewitness Accounts,* 2nd ed. (New York, 2004), 395–412. For other comparisons, see Susan E. Cook, ed., *Genocide in Cambodia and Rwanda: New Perspectives* (New Brunswick, 2005).

2. Ben Kiernan, "Serial Colonialism and Genocide in Nineteenth-Century Cambodia," in A. Dirk Moses, ed., *Empire, Colony, Genocide* (New York, 2007).

3. Eric Jennings, "Conservative Confluences, 'Nativist' Synergy: Reinscribing Vichy's National Revolution in Indochina, 1940–1945," *French Historical Studies* 27: 3 (2004): 635, 604; Jennings, "L'Indochine de l'Amiral Decoux," in E. Jennings and J. Cantier, *L'Empire colonial sous Vichy* (Paris, 2004).

4. Penny Edwards, "'Propagender:' Marianne, Joan of Arc, and the Export of French Gender Ideology to Colonial Cambodia (1863–1954)," in Tony Chafer and Amanda Sackur, eds., *Promoting the Colonial Idea* (London, 2002), 124; Edwards, *Cambodge: The Cultivation of a Nation, 1860–1945* (Honolulu, 2007).

5. Ann Raffin, *Youth Mobilization in Vichy Indochina and Its Legacies, 1940–1970* (Lanham, 2005), 63–67; Jennings, "Conservative Confluences," 603–4, 624; Jennings, "L'Indochine," 31–32.

6. Raffin, *Youth Mobilization*, 149; Jennings, "Conservative Confluences," 614–15, 620; Jennings, "L'Indochine," 45, 49.

7. Jennings, "Conservative Confluences," 605–6, 627–28, 609–11, 632; Jennings, "L'Indochine," 43.

8. Susan Bayly, "French Anthropology and the Durkheimians in Colonial Indochina," *Modern Asian Studies* 34:3 (2000): 602ff., 608–10.

9. Raffin, *Youth Mobilization*, 122–33; Jennings, "L'Indochine," 43, 45; Jennings, "Conservative Confluences," 615.

10. Jennings, "L'Indochine," 46n.; David P. Chandler, *Brother Number One: A Political Biography of Pol Pot* (Boulder, 1992), 18–19.

11. Edwards, "'Propagender'" 126.

12. *Le Cambodge*, Aug. 2 and 3, 1951, 4; Sept. 18, 1951, 4; Ben Kiernan, *How Pol Pot Came to Power: Colonialism, Nationalism, and Communism in Cambodia, 1930–1975*, 2nd ed. (New Haven, 2004), 120.

13. Toni Stadler, personal communication, 1991, quoting Mey Mann's 1989–90 reminiscences; Ben Kiernan, *The Pol Pot Regime: Race, Power, and Genocide in Cambodia under the Khmer Rouge, 1975–1979*, 2nd ed. (New Haven, 2002), 10.

14. "Khmaer Da'em" [Saloth Sar], *Khemara Nisit* 14 (Aug. 1952).

15. Keng Vannsak, "Tragédie d'un peuple, mort d'une culture," *Connaissance du Cambodge* 2 (Mar. 1977): 1–2; Vannsak and J. Delvert, *Recherche du fonds culturel khmer* (Paris, 1971); Vannsak, "Bon' Phka . . . Un Exemple de dékhmerisation," *Préserver la culture kmère* 11–12 (Mar.–Apr. 1978): 34–40.

16. Kiernan, *How Pol Pot Came to Power*, 118–22, 172.

17. Khieu Samphan, *Cambodia's Economy and Industrial Development* (Ithaca, 1979), 36, 76–77.

18. *Etude sur les mouvements rebelles au Cambodge, 1942–52*, Archives d'Outre-Mer, Aix-en-Provence, Cambodge 7F 29 (7), 87.

19. Raffin, *Youth Mobilization*, 64; *Le Cambodge*, Jan. 10, 1951, 2.

20. Kiernan, *How Pol Pot Came to Power*, 219.

21. Roy Hofheinz Jr., *The Broken Wave: The Chinese Communist Peasant Movement, 1922–1928* (Cambridge, Mass., 1977), 246; Roderick MacFarquhar, *The Origins of the Cultural Revolution*, vol. 2, *The Great Leap Forward, 1958–1960* (New York, 1983), 73.

22. BBC *Summary of World Broadcasts*, FE/2784/A3/2.

23. Kiernan, *How Pol Pot Came to Power*, 287–88.

24. Khieu Samphan, *Prowatttisat kampuchea thmey thmey nih ning koul chomhor rebos khnyom cia bontor bontoap* [Cambodia's Recent History and My Successive Standpoints] (Phnom Penh, 2004), 27, 35.

25. *Rien saut daoy songkep nu prowatt chollana padevatt Kampuchea kraom kar duk noam rebos Paks Kommunis Kampuchea* [Abbreviated Lesson on the History of the Kampuchean Revolutionary Movement Led by the Communist Party of Kampuchea] [1977?], in D. P. Chandler, B. Kiernan, and C. Boua, eds., *Pol Pot Plans the Future: Confidential Leadership Documents from Democratic Kampuchea, 1976–1977* (New Haven, 1988), 219.

26. Kiernan, *Pol Pot Regime,* 165, 204 (quoting Khieu Samphan, Apr. 15, 1977).

27. Pol Pot, speech of Sept. 27, 1977, U.S. CIA, *Foreign Broadcast Information Service,* Sept. 29, 1977, H4.

28. *Tung padevat,* special issue (Sept.-Oct. 1976): 40, 52; Kiernan, "Kampuchea and Stalinism," in Colin Mackerras and Nick Knight, eds., *Marxism in Asia* (London, 1985, 232–50).

29. Democratic Kampuchea, "Kumrung pankar buon chhnam khosang sangkumniyum krup phnaek rebos pak, 1977–80" [The Party's Four-Year Plan to Build Socialism in All Fields, 1977–80], July–Aug. 1976, 52.

30. Kiernan, *Pol Pot Regime,* 458.

31. B. Kiernan and C. Boua, *Peasants and Politics in Kampuchea, 1942–1981* (London, 1982), 326–28.

32. *Silacarik nagar vatt ning pateanukram* (Phnom Penh, 1958), 114; Chandler, Kiernan, and Boua, *Pol Pot Plans the Future,* 170.

33. Adrien Launay, *Histoire de la mission de Cochinchine, 1658–1823: Documents historiques,* vol. 2, *1728–1771* (Paris, 1924), 368, 366, 370.

34. David P. Chandler, *A History of Cambodia* (Boulder, 1983), 131; Kiernan, "Serial Colonialism and Genocide in Nineteenth-Century Cambodia."

35. Quoted in Philip Short, *Pol Pot: The History of a Nightmare* (London, 2004), 545.

36. Nayan Chanda, *Brother Enemy* (New York, 1986), 16, 86–87; Kiernan, *Pol Pot Regime,* 55–58, 107–9, 296–98, 423–25; Alexander Laban Hinton, *Why Did They Kill? Cambodia in the Shadow of Genocide* (Berkeley, 2005), 154, 219; Timothy Carney, in Karl Jackson, ed., *Cambodia 1975–1978* (Princeton, 1989), 83n3; Michael Vickery, *Cambodia, 1975–1982* (Boston, 1984), 136.

37. "Sekkedei nae noam rebos 870" [Guidance from 870 (Pol Pot)], Jan. 3, 1978, 6, 12, 15–16.

38. United Nations, AS, General Assembly, Security Council, A/53/850, S/1999/231, Mar. 16, 1999, Annex, *Report of the Group of Experts for Cambodia Established Pursuant to General Assembly Resolution 52/135;* Ben Kiernan, "The Ethnic Element in the Cambodian Genocide," in Daniel Chirot and Martin E. P. Seligman, eds., *Ethnopolitical Warfare: Causes, Consequences, and Possible Solutions* (Washington, 2001), 83–91; Kiernan, *Pol Pot Regime,* 251–88, 427–31.

39. Hinton, *Why Did They Kill?* 155; D. P. Chandler, "A Revolution in Full Spate," in D. Ablin and M. Hood, eds., *The Cambodian Agony* (Armonk, 1987), 129; *Ieng Sary's Regime: A Diary of the Khmer Rouge Foreign Ministry, 1976–79,* tr. Phat Kosal and Ben Kiernan (New Haven, 1998), 30: www.yale.edu/cgp; Gerald Fleming, *Hitler and the Final Solution* (Berkeley, 1984), xxxv, quoting Ernst Nolte. Perceptions of Nazi–Khmer Rouge parallels may be found in Hinton, *Why Did They Kill?* 212–13, 282–85; Bettina Arnold, "Justifying Genocide," in Alexander Laban Hinton, ed., *Annihilating Difference* (Berkeley, 2002), 109–10; René Pierre Costa, *Le Cambodge: La decomposition! Des analogies entre Pol Pot et . . . Hitler* (Paris, 2002).

40. Pol Pot, July 22, 1975, in "Pol Pot and the Kampuchean Communist Movement," in Kiernan and Boua, *Peasants and Politics in Kampuchea,* 233; BBC, *Summary of World Broadcasts,* FE/5813/A3/4, May 15, 1978, Phnom Penh Radio, May 10, 1978. In its Sept.–Oct. 1976 issue, the CPK monthly *Tung padevat* noted the need for a cooperative to be "purified."

41. Ben Kiernan, *Cambodia: Eastern Zone Massacres* (New York, 1986).

42. Pol Pot, "Toussena: Sopheapkar padevatt kampuchea baccabon" [Observations of the Situation of the Kampuchean Revolution Today], July 13 (?), 1978, 13, 8, 16; original held in Santebal archive, Documentation Center of Cambodia, doc. D02180, 17 bbk; microfilm copy at Yale's Sterling Library.

43. *Rien saut daoy songkep nu prowatt chollana padevatt Kampuchea kraom kar duk noam rebos Paks Kommunis Kampuchea,* 221.

44. Ben Kiernan, "Kampuchea and Stalinism," in C. Mackerras and N. Knight, eds., *Marxism in Asia* (London, 1985), 235–41; Khieu Samphan, *Prowatttisat kampuchea thmey thmey nih ning koul chomhor rebos khnyom cia bontor bontoap* (Phnom Penh, 2004), 75; cf. the French edition, *L'histoire récente du Cambodge et mes prises de position* (Paris, 2004), 81.

45. Democratic Kampuchea, *Angkor,* 1976 typescript, Wason Collection, Cornell University, 1, 9.

46. Ibid., 11.

47. *Democratic Kampuchea Is Moving Forward* (Phnom Penh, 1977), 6.

48. Quoted in D. P. Chandler, "Seeing Red: Perceptions of Cambodian History in Democratic Kampuchea," in Chandler and Ben Kiernan, *Revolution and Its Aftermath in Kampuchea* (New Haven, 1983), 35.

49. *Democratic Kampuchea Is Moving Forward*, 2.

50. Pol Pot, "Toussena," 16.

51. Ben Kiernan, "Myth, Nationalism, and Genocide," *Journal of Genocide Research*, 3:2 (2001): 187–206; Anthony Barnett, "Cambodia Will Never Disappear," *New Left Review* 180 (1990): 101–25.

52. Kiernan, *Pol Pot Regime*, 360.

53. Kiernan, "Myth, Nationalism, and Genocide."

54. Pol Pot, speech of Sept. 27, 1977.

55. Kiernan, *Pol Pot Regime*, 103–5, 357–69, 425–27.

56. *Far Eastern Economic Review*, July 14, 1988, 14: "Gen. Le Kha Phieu told journalists that 55,000 people had died since a border war erupted between Cambodia and Vietnam in 1977. He said 30,000 people died, presumably including soldiers and civilians, during the Khmer Rouge border attacks prior to Vietnam's invasion at the end of 1978. Another 25,000 soldiers had died since the occupation began, he said."

57. Kiernan, *Pol Pot Regime*, 357–69, esp. 366–69.

58. Ibid., 102–25, 357–66, 386–90.

59. "Sekkedei nae noam rebos 870," 4–8.

60. Chan [Mam Nay], "Ompi sopheakpar niw srok Phnom 7 (Svay Tong) Kampuchea Krom" [On the Situation in the Seven Mountains (Svay Tong) District of Kampuchea Krom], S-21, Mar. 19, 1978, 5. For further analysis and a full translation of this document, see Kanika Mak, "Genocide and Irredentism under Democratic Kampuchea" (working paper no. 23, Genocide Studies Program, Yale Center for International and Area Studies, New Haven, 2004).

61. Author's interviews with Heng Samrin, Phnom Penh, Dec. 2, 1991, and Dec. 7, 1992.

62. BBC, *Summary of World Broadcasts*, FE/5813/A3/2, May 15, 1978, Phnom Penh Radio, May 10, 1978.

63. Pol Pot, "Toussena," 8.

64. Pol Pot, Phnom Penh, Jan. 17, 1978, *Speech Commemorating the 10th Anniversary of the Founding of the Revolutionary Army of Kampuchea,* French version published by the Comité des Patriotes du Kampuchéa Démocratique en France (Paris, 1978), 5.

65. *Indochina Digest,* Aug. 21, 1992. The quotation appeared in the *Far Eastern Economic Review.*

66. "Khmer Rouge Deny Knowledge of Bridge Demolition," Reuters, Phnom Penh, Oct. 15, 1992; *Indochina Digest,* Dec. 24, 1992; "UN Says the Khmer Rouge Killed 12 Ethnic Vietnamese," *New York Times,* Dec. 30, 1992; *Indochina Digest,* Jan. 8, 1993; Justin Jordens, in S. Heder and J. Ledgerwood, eds., *Propaganda, Politics, and Violence in Cambodia* (New York), 1996.

67. Léon Mugesera, Radio télévision libre des mille collines (RTLM), Nov. 22, 1992, quoted in Charles Mironko, "Social and Political Mechanisms of Mass Murder: An Analysis of Perpetrators in the Rwandan Genocide" (Ph.D. diss., Yale University, 2004), 143.

68. Mugesera, RTLM, Nov. 22, 1992, in Alison Des Forges, *"Leave None to Tell the Story": Genocide in Rwanda* (New York, 1999), 84–86. Des Forges kindly provided a court-accredited French translation of the Kinyarwanda original: "Au cas ou donc la justice n'est plus au service du peuple, comme cela est écrit dans notre constitution que nous avons votée nous-mêmes, c'est dire qu'a ce moment, nous autres composantes de la population au service de laquelle elle devrait se mettre, nous devons le faire nous-mêmes en exterminant cette canaille."

69. Linda Melvern, *Conspiracy to Murder: The Rwandan Genocide* (London, 2004), 7.

70. "Message du Président Kayibanda Grégoire aux Rwandais émigrés ou réfugiés à l'étranger le 11 Mars 1963," quoted in Col. BMS Théoneste Bagosora, *L'assassinat du Président Habyarimana; ou, L'ultime operation du Tutsi pour sa reconquête du pouvoir par la force au Rwanda* [Yaoundé, Oct. 30, 1995], 16, document from Linda Melvern archive, University of Aberystwyth, Wales (Melvern kindly supplied a copy); Des Forges, *"Leave None,"* 105–6.

71. René Lemarchand, "The Burundi Genocide," in Totten, Parsons, and Charny, *Century of*

Genocide, 321–37; Noam Chomsky and E. S. Herman, *The Political Economy of Human Rights* (Boston, 1979), 1:106–9.

72. Habyarimana interview, July 12, 1980, excerpt in Philip Verwimp, "Development Ideology, the Peasantry, and Genocide: Rwanda Represented in Habyarimana's Speeches" (working paper 13, Genocide Studies Program, Yale Center for International and Area Studies, New Haven, 1999), 30; Mahmood Mamdani, *When Victims Become Killers: Colonialism, Nativism, and the Genocide in Rwanda* (Princeton, 2001), 138–42.

73. Quoted in Omer Marchal, *Au Rwanda: La vie quotidienne au pays du Nil rouge* (Brussels, 1987), 92; Philip Verwimp, "Development and Genocide in Rwanda: A Political Economy Analysis of Peasants and Power under the Habyarimana Regime" (Ph.D. diss., Catholic University of Leuven, 2003), 15.

74. J.-P. Chrétien, *Les médias du génocide* (Paris, 1995), 96, 110–11. Translations by Charles Mironko.

75. Des Forges, *"Leave None,"* 73.

76. Gérard Prunier, *The Rwanda Crisis: History of a Genocide* (New York, 1997), 54, 171, 188, 200; Des Forges, *"Leave None,"* 51, 249–51, 405–6. See also Scott Strauss, "Organic Purity and the Role of Anthropology in Cambodia and Rwanda," *Patterns of Prejudice* 35:2 (2001): 47–62.

77. Prunier, *Rwanda Crisis,* 200–1, 221–22.

78. Des Forges, *"Leave None,"* 412.

79. Prunier, *Rwanda Crisis,* 231, 249–50; Des Forges, *"Leave None,"* 19, 475, 555; Lemarchand, "The Rwanda Genocide," 402–3; Melvern, *Conspiracy to Murder,* 170, 192.

80. Bagosora, *L'assassinat du Président Habyarimana,* 14.

81. For discussion of Rwandan precolonial and colonial historiography, see Mironko, "Social and Political Mechanisms," chs. 2, 3.

82. Ferdinand Nahimana, "Les principautés Hutu du Rwanda septentrional," in *La civilisation ancienne des peuples des grands lacs* (Paris and Bujumbura, 1981), 125, 119, 115–16, 128–31, 134.

83. Ferdinand Nahimana, *Le Rwanda: Emergence d'un état* (Paris, 1993), 5, 15.

84. Ferdinand Nahimana, *Le blanc est arrivé, le roi est parti: Une facette de l'histoire du Rwanda contemporain* (Kigali, 1987), 180, 151.

85. Nahimana, *Le Rwanda,* 245, 130, 295–97, 317–18, 315.

86. Melvern, *Conspiracy to Murder,* 41.

87. Gaspard Gahigi, interview with Ferdinand Nahimana, RTLM, June 1993, quoted in International Monitor Institute (IMI), "Kantano Habimana and Humor as a Weapon": www.imisite.org/rwanda.php#3 (accessed Jan. 13, 2006).

88. Melvern, *Conspiracy to Murder,* 126, 235.

89. Des Forges, *"Leave None,"* 470–71. In 1998, a Rwandan court convicted Bizimana of genocide.

90. Nahimana, "Principautés Hutu du Rwanda septentrional," 123–24.

91. Philip Verwimp, "Development Ideology," 15.

92. Habyarimana speech of Oct. 14, 1973, quoted in ibid., 14.

93. *Le Monde,* Mar. 31, 1974; Mamdani, *When Victims Become Killers,* 146.

94. Verwimp, "Development and Genocide in Rwanda," 14, 30 (Habyarimana interview, July 12, 1980); Habyarimana speeches of July 5, 1983 and July 5, 1984, in Verwimp, "Development Ideology," 14ff.

95. Verwimp, "Development and Genocide in Rwanda," 18, 13–14, 9.

96. Peter Uvin, *Aiding Violence: The Development Enterprise in Rwanda* (London, 1998), 24; Prunier, *Rwanda Crisis,* 76; Kiernan, *How Pol Pot Came to Power,* xix.

97. Verwimp, "Development and Genocide in Rwanda," 16–17; Samphan, *Cambodia's Economy and Industrial Development.*

98. Verwimp, "Development and Genocide in Rwanda," 21.

99. Ferdinand Nahimana, *Conscience chez-nous, confiance en nous: Notre culture et la base de notre développement harmonieux* (Ruhengeri, 1988), 58.

100. Verwimp, "Development and Genocide in Rwanda," 12; Verwimp, "Development Ideology," 18–21.

101. Marchal, *Au Rwanda,* 44, 24, 18. Philip Verwimp drew this volume to my attention.

102. David Newbury and Catharine Newbury, "Bringing the Peasants Back In: Agrarian Themes in the Construction and Corrosion of Statist Historiography in Rwanda," *American Historical Review* 105:3 (2000): 872–73.

103. Mironko, "Social and Political Mechanisms," 148–49, citing Chrétien, *Les médias du génocide*, 64.

104. Prunier, *Rwanda Crisis*, 139–42; Des Forges, *"Leave None,"* 89.

105. Des Forges, *"Leave None,"* 68–69; RTLM, Dec. 2, 1993, and Mar. 19, 1994, quoted in Mironko, "Social and Political Mechanisms," 153, 151; Jan. 6, 1994, quoted in IMI, "Kantano Habimana": www.imisite.org/rwanda.php#3 (accessed Jan. 13, 2006).

106. Confessed perpetrator, Gisenyi prison, Sept. 25, 2000, quoted in Mironko, "Social and Political Mechanisms," 170, and further excerpts of the interview that Mironko kindly provided to the author.

107. Quoted in Mironko, "Social and Political Mechanisms," 172; his interview in Gisenyi prison (Sept. 25?), 2000, transcript supplied by Charles Mironko.

108. Prefect Renzaho, Radio Rwanda, Apr. 12, 1994, in Des Forges, *"Leave None,"* 249; see also 549, 552.

109. Melvern, *Conspiracy to Murder*, 206–7.

110. Tharcisse Renzaho, *Guerre civile et les massacres inter-ethniques d'avril 94*, undated typescript, 14; original in Linda Melvern archive of *Conspiracy to Murder*, copy kindly supplied by Melvern, 2005.

111. Verwimp, "Development Ideology," 45. See also Philip Verwimp, "A Quantitative Analysis of Genocide in Kibuye Prefecture, Rwanda" (discussion paper series DPS 01.10, Center for Economic Studies, Catholic University of Leuven, May 2001).

112. Des Forges, *"Leave None,"* 44; Prunier, *Rwanda Crisis*, 19, 86.

113. Prunier, *Rwanda Crisis*, 86, 124, 222, 167–68.

114. Nahimana, "Principautés Hutu du Rwanda septentrional," 135.

115. Nahimana, *Le blanc est arrivé*, 113.

116. Lt. Col. Rick Orth, "Rwanda's Hutu Extremist Genocidal Insurgency: An Eyewitness Perspective" (unpublished MS, 2000), 15, also citing Jeff Drumtra, "Where the Ethnic Cleansing Goes Unchecked," *Washington Post*, weekly ed., July 22–28, 1996, 22.

117. Prunier, *Rwanda Crisis*, 381, 378–79.

118. Des Forges, *"Leave None,"* 65–66. For discussion of Stalin's use of such techniques, see Michael Ellman, "The Role of Leadership Perceptions and of Intent in the Soviet Famine of 1931–1934," *Europe-Asia Studies* 57:6 (2005): 824–27.

119. RTLM, June 22, 1994, in IMI, "Kantano Habimana": www.imisite.org/rwanda.php#3 (acc. Jan. 13, 2006).

120. Kiernan, *Pol Pot Regime*, 300n168, 386n1.

Epilogue

1. Documentation of U.S. support for Suharto's 1965–66 killings in Indonesia: *Washington Post*, May 21, 1990, A5, *Columbia Journalism Review* 29 (1990): 9–14; for Indonesia's takeover of East Timor, Ford-Kissinger-Suharto transcript, Dec. 6, 1975, 8ff., National Security Archive, George Washington University: www.gwu.edu/~nsarchiv/NSAEBB/NSAEBB62/doc4.pdf (accessed Oct. 30, 2006); and for Pakistan during the 1971 genocide: Hassan Abbas, *Pakistan's Drift into Extremism* (Armonk, 2005), 63–65. U.S. president Reagan called Guatemala's genocidal dictator Efraín Rios Montt "a man of great personal integrity," "totally dedicated to democracy" but "getting a bum rap." Weekly Compilation of Presidential Statements, Dec. 13, 1982, quoted in Jennifer Schirmer, *The Guatemalan Military Project: A Violence Called Democracy* (Philadelphia, 1998), 33. On U.S. support for Cambodia's Khmer Rouge regime, see Henry Kissinger's statement to the Thai foreign minister, Nov. 26, 1975, 8 ("You should also tell the Cambodians that we will be friends with them. They are murderous thugs, but we won't let that stand in our way"): www.gwu.edu/~nsarchiv/NSAEBB/NSAEBB193/HAK-11-26-75.pdf (accessed Oct. 30, 2006); and for Saddam's Iraq in the 1980s, Michael Dobbs, "U.S. Had Key Role in Iraq Buildup," *Washington Post*, Dec. 30, 2002, A01; Joyce Battle, ed., *Shaking Hands with Saddam Hussein: The U.S. Tilts towards*

Iraq, 1980–1984 (Washington, 2003): www.gwu.edu/~nsarchiv/NSAEBB/NSAEBB82 (accessed Oct. 30, 2006).

2. Archer K. Blood, *The Cruel Birth of Bangladesh: Memoirs of an American Diplomat* (Dhaka, 2002), 216–22. This and subsequent paragraphs also draw on Rounaq Jahan, "Genocide in Bangladesh," in S. Totten, W. S. Parsons, and I. W. Charny, eds., *Century of Genocide: Critical Essays and Eyewitness Accounts,* 2nd ed. (New York, 2004), 297–98. See also Subrata Roy Chowdhury, *The Genesis of Bangladesh: A Study in International Legal Norms and Permissive Conscience* (New York, 1972), esp. 95–122, 142–48.

3. Robert P. Payne, *Massacre* (New York, 1973), 50; quoted in Adam Jones, "Genocide in Bangladesh, 1971": www.gendercide.org/case_bangladesh.html (accessed Oct. 30, 2006); Jahan, "Genocide in Bangladesh," 299, 303.

4. Jahan, "Genocide in Bangladesh," 298, 300–1; Blood, *Cruel Birth of Bangladesh,* 213–19, 303; Payne, *Massacre,* 46; Sarmila Bose, "Anatomy of Violence: Analysis of Civil War in East Pakistan in 1971," *Economic and Political Weekly,* Oct. 8, 2005.

5. Jahan, "Genocide in Bangladesh," 298–303.

6. Blood, *Cruel Birth of Bangladesh,* 216–17, also quoted in Bose, "Anatomy of Violence"; Payne, *Massacre,* 102, quoted in Jones, "Genocide in Bangladesh"; Anwar Iqbal, "Sheikh Mujib Wanted a Confederation: US Papers," *Dawn,* July 7, 2005.

7. Eddie Chua, "JI School Grooming More Terrorists," *Asia News Net,* Feb. 2, 2006; Carlotta Gall, "Afghan Tactics, Tied to Taliban, Point to Pakistan," *New York Times,* Feb. 15, 2006, A1, 12. See also *New York Times,* Jan. 21, Feb. 19 and 28, 2007.

8. Ayman al-Zawahiri, Apr. 2006, excerpt in *Asia Times,* May 5, 2006: www.truthout.org/docs_2006/050506G.shtml (accessed Oct. 30, 2006).

9. Benedict Anderson, "Petrus Dadi Ratu," *Indonesia* 70 (Oct. 2000): 1–7; R. E. Elson, *Suharto: A Political Biography* (Cambridge, 2001), 125; David Jenkins, "The Silent Watchers," *Sydney Morning Herald,* July 12, 1999.

10. Suharto's formal order was signed on Nov. 15, 1965. Arnold C. Brackman, *The Communist Collapse in Indonesia* (Singapore, 1969), 118–19; Robert Cribb, ed., *The Indonesian Killings, 1965–1966: Studies from Java and Bali* (Clayton, 1990); Marian Wilkinson, "Hidden Holocaust," *Sydney Morning Herald,* July 10, 1999; Jenkins, "Silent Watchers"; Cribb, "Genocide in Indonesia, 1965–66," *Journal of Genocide Research* 3:2 (2001): 219–39.

11. Charles Coppel, *Indonesian Chinese in Crisis* (Kuala Lumpur, 1983), 58–61, puts the number of Chinese killed in 1965–66 at 2,000, "disproportionately low" given their percentage of the population; Andi Achdian, "The Pemuda Violence and 1965 Massacres in Indonesia" (forthcoming Ph.D. diss., University of Nottingham); Wilkinson, "Hidden Holocaust"; Jenkins, "Silent Watchers"; Iwan Gardono Sujatmiko, "The Destruction of the Indonesian Communist Party (PKI)," (Ph.D. diss., Harvard University, 1992); Herbert Feith, *The Indonesian Elections of 1955* (Ithaca, 1957).

12. John Hughes, *The End of Sukarno* (London, 1968), 181; Geoffrey Robinson, *The Dark Side of Paradise* (Ithaca, 1995), 295–97; Wilkinson, "Hidden Holocaust"; Jenkins, "Silent Watchers."

13. CIA, Directorate of Intelligence, *Intelligence Report: Indonesia—1965* (Washington, 1968), 71n, quoted in Cribb, *The Indonesian Killings,* 5.

14. James Dunn, *Timor: A People Betrayed* (Milton, 1983), 100.

15. For a map of the areas still reportedly occupied by Fretilin in Aug. 1976, see Carmel Budiardjo and Liem Soei Liong, *The War against East Timor* (London, 1984), 23.

16. Ibid., 82.

17. Sian Powell, "UN Verdict on East Timor," *Australian,* Jan. 19, 2006.

18. On Nov. 12, 1979, Indonesia's foreign minister, Mochtar Kusumaatmadja, gave a figure of 120,000 Timorese dead from 1975 to Nov. 1979 (John Taylor, *East Timor: The Price of Freedom* [London, 1999], 203).

19. Final Report of the Commission for Reception, Truth and Reconciliation in East Timor (CAVR), 2005: www.ictj.org/cavr.report.asp (acc. Feb. 6, 2006); Powell, "UN Verdict on East Timor"; Taylor, *East Timor,* 68–70, 164, 207 (citing *Far Eastern Economic Review,* Sept. 8, 1985).

20. Taylor, *East Timor,* 89–90, 98; Budiardjo and Liong, *War against East Timor,* 212–13.

21. Indonesian documents translated in Budiardjo and Liong, *War against East Timor,* 241–42, 182, 215, 222, 227, 194–96, 216, 184, 242, 193, 228; Taylor, *East Timor,* 151.

22. Budiardjo and Liong, *War against East Timor*, 212, 214, 218–19, 229, 205, 219–20.

23. Taylor, *East Timor*, 124–25, 102; Gabriel Defert, *Timor-Est: Le génocide oublié* (Paris, 1992), 182.

24. Andrew Fowler, "The Ties That Bind," Australian Broadcasting Corporation, Feb. 14, 2000, quoted in Noam Chomsky, *A New Generation Draws the Line: East Timor, Kosovo, and the Standards of the West* (London, 2000), 72; for further details, see Annemarie Evans, "Revealed: The Plot to Crush Timor," *South China Morning Post*, Sept. 16, 1999.

25. Evans, "Revealed."

26. Brian Toohey, "Dangers of Timorese Whispers Capital Idea," *Australian Financial Review*, Aug. 14, 1999; John Aglionby et al., "Revealed: Army's Plot," *Observer*, Sept. 12, 1999; and other sources quoted in Chomsky, *A New Generation Draws the Line*, 72–76.

27. Chomsky, *A New Generation Draws the Line*, 74.

28. James Dunn, "Crimes against Humanity in East Timor, January to October 1999: Their Nature and Causes," Feb. 14, 2001, republished in Hamish McDonald et al., *Masters of Terror: Indonesia's Military and Violence in East Timor in 1999* (Canberra, 2002), 60–98; CAVR Final Report, annexe 1, "East Timor 1999," by Geoffrey Robinson; Court of Appeal, Dili, Armando Dos Santos judgment, July 15, 2003, 16ff., 24.

29. Schirmer, *Guatemalan Military Project*, 33; Greg Grandin, *The Last Colonial Massacre: Latin America in the Cold War* (Chicago, 2004).

30. Commission on Historical Clarification (CEH), *Guatemala: Memory of Silence*, 1999; English translation: http://shr.aas.org/guatemala/ceh/report/english/conc1.html (accessed Dec. 3, 2002); Greg Grandin, "History, Motive, Law, Intent: Combining Historical and Legal Methods in Understanding Guatemala's 1981–1983 Genocide," in Robert Gellately and Ben Kiernan, eds., *The Specter of Genocide: Mass Murder in Historical Perspective* (New York, 2003), 339.

31. Janine Sylvestre, *The Cost of Conflict: The Anglo-Belize/Guatemala Territorial Issue* (1995), chs. 8, 10: www.belizenet.com/bzeguat.html (accessed Feb. 10–11, 2006), quoting Rios Montt, Jan. 13, 1983, and Foreign Minister Fernando Andrade Diaz Duncan, Aug. 24, 1983; Greg Grandin, personal communications, Feb. 10–11, 2006.

32. *El nuevo campesino*, undated (1970s?), 9 pp., a pamphlet in the personal papers of the late Eduardo Taracena, whose nephew supplied it to the historian Greg Grandin. Grandin describes Taracena as "one of the young anti-communist students who helped spearhead the overthrow of Arbenz" in 1954 and remained "active in Guatemalan far-right politics through the 1960s and 1970s" (personal communication).

33. Benjamin A. Valentino, *Final Solutions: Mass Killing and Genocide in the Twentieth Century* (Ithaca, 2004), 214–15; Schirmer, *Guatemalan Military Project*, 35.

34. CEH, *Guatemala: Memory of Silence*, para 62: http://shr.aas.org/guatemala/ceh/report/english/conc1.html (accessed Dec. 3, 2002), 13.

35. Ibid.; Schirmer, *Guatemalan Military Project*, xiv, 114–15; Greg Grandin, *The Blood of Guatemala: A History of Race and Nation* (Durham, 2000), 284.

36. Robert M. Carmack, ed., *Harvest of Violence: The Maya Indians and the Guatemalan Crisis* (Norman, 1988), 69, 165.

37. Grandin, *Blood of Guatemala*, 289; *Guatemala: Memory of Silence*, para 62, Eng. trans., 13; Schirmer, *Guatemalan Military Project*, xiv, 114–15.

38. CEH, *Guatemala: Memory of Silence*, 3:322; Grandin, "History, Motive, Law, Intent," 349, 339; CEH, *Guatemala: Memory of Silence*, 1.

39. CEH, *Guatemala: Memory of Silence*.

40. Schirmer, *Guatemalan Military Project*, 70, 199.

41. Benjamin R. Foster, Karen Polinger Foster, and Patty Gerstenblith, *Iraq Beyond the Headlines: History, Archaeology, and War* (Singapore, 2005), 202–3; "Hussein Charged with Genocide in 50,000 Deaths," *New York Times*, Apr. 5, 2006, A1.

42. "Secrets of His Life and Leadership: An Interview with Said K. Aburish," PBS Frontline, "The Survival of Saddam," Jan. 25, 2000: www.pbs.org/wgbh/pages/frontline/shows/saddam/interviews/aburish.html (accessed June 3, 2006).

43. U.S. Department of the Army/Library of Congress, *Iraq: A Country Study* (Washington,

1988?): http://countrystudies.us/iraq/41.htm, http://countrystudies.us/iraq/57.htm (accessed June 3, 2006); Maj. Larry D. Huffman, USMC, "Underlying Causes for the Iraqi Debacle": www.global security.org/military/library/report/1991/HLD.htm (accessed June 3, 2006).

44. Eric H. Cline, "Does Saddam Think He's a Modern-Day Saladin?" *History News Network,* Mar. 10, 2003: hnn.us/articles/1305.html (accessed June 2, 2006); Foster, Foster, and Gerstenblith, *Iraq Beyond the Headlines,* 205–6.

45. U.S. Department of the Army/Library of Congress, *Iraq: A Country Study,* http://countrystudies.us/iraq/32.htm (accessed June 3, 2006).

46. Norman Cigar, *Genocide in Bosnia: The Policy of "Ethnic Cleansing"* (College Station, 1985), 78.

47. Ibid., 9, 18–19, 26, 31, 73, 100.

48. Sreten Vujovic, "An Uneasy View of the City," in Nebojsa Popov, *The Road to War in Serbia: Trauma and Catharsis* (Budapest, 2000), 123–45, 136, 132.

49. Cigar, *Genocide in Bosnia,* 83–85, 103.

50. Ibid., 105, 18; Serbian Academy of Arts and Sciences Memorandum, 1986, English translation at www.haverford.edu/relg/sells/reports/memorandumSANU.htm (accessed Oct. 21, 2003).

51. Vujovic, "Uneasy View of the City," 131.

52. Cigar, *Genocide in Bosnia,* 23, 40, 42, 63, 79.

53. Ibid., 105–6, 43–44; Vujovic, "Uneasy View of the City," 138.

54. Cigar, *Genocide in Bosnia,* 92ff.; Serbian Memorandum.

55. Cigar, *Genocide in Bosnia,* 78, 81.

56. John W. Miller, "Serbs Shrug Off Milosevic's Death," *Wall Street Journal,* Mar. 13, 2006, A4; Cigar, *Genocide in Bosnia,* 78, 74.

57. Serbian Memorandum.

58. Cigar, *Genocide in Bosnia,* 119; Vujovic, "Uneasy View of the City," 125–30.

59. Vujovic, "Uneasy View of the City," 134, 136–38.

60. Ibid., 132–36, 145n3.

61. Quoted in Heikelina Verrijn Stuart, "ICTY Grapples with Genocidal Intent for Srebrenica," *International Justice Tribune* (The Hague), July 11, 2005: www.justicetribune.com/index .php?page=v2_article&id=3103 (accessed Jan. 12, 2006).

62. Radovan Karadzic, March 1995 "Krivaja 95" order, quoted in Stuart, "ICTY Grapples with Genocidal Intent."

63. Norman Cigar and Paul Williams, *Indictment at The Hague: The Milosevic Regime and Crimes of the Balkan Wars* (New York, 2002), 257–87.

64. "Arab Gathering Letter," Oct. 1987, English translation from the Arabic original: www .aegistrust.org (accessed Dec. 12, 2005); Gérard Prunier, *Darfur: The Ambiguous Genocide* (Ithaca, 2005), x.

65. Eric Reeves, in Joyce Apsel, ed., *Darfur: Genocide Before Our Eyes* (New York, 2005), 31; "Arab Gathering Letter."

66. Quoted in Julie Flint and Alex de Waal, *Darfur: A Short History of a Long War* (London, 2005), 56.

67. See, for instance Apsel, *Darfur,* and the excellent reporting of Eric Reeves on Darfur: www.sudanreeves.org; "Darfur: New Attacks in Chad Documented," Human Rights Watch, New York, Feb. 5, 2006: http://hrw.org/english/docs/2006/02/03/chad12601_txt.htm (accessed Feb. 11, 2006).

68. Nicholas D. Kristof, "A Village Waiting for Rape and Murder," *New York Times,* Mar. 12, 2006; Kristof's columns of March 7, 14, 19, Apr. 16, Oct. 29, Nov. 12, 14, and 19, 2006; editorial, "Spreading Genocide to Chad," *New York Times,* Mar. 20, 2006.

69. "Raiders from Sudan Killed 118 in Chad, Rights Watch Reports," *New York Times,* May 26, 2006, A7; Amnesty Intenational, "Chad: Thousands Flee Janjawid Attacks," Oct. 20, 2006, AI index: AFR 20/012/2006, cited in Eric Reeves, "Khartoum Expels Kofi Annan's Special Representative," Oct. 26, 2006: www.sudanreeves.org (accessed Nov. 3, 2006); "Chad: Ethnic Attacks Kill up to 220," *New York Times,* Nov. 10, 2006, A8; Nicholas D. Kristof, "Boy's Wish: Kill Them All," *New York Times,* Nov. 21, 2006, A29. See also *New York Times,* Apr. 2, 2007, A3.

70. See Chalmers Johnson, *Blowback* (New York, 2000), 13; Johnson, *The Sorrows of Empire* (New York, 2004), 139; Peter Bergen, *Holy War, Inc.* (New York, 2001), 68; and Bergen, *The Osama bin Laden I Know* (New York, 2006), 60–61, 106.

71. Bergen, *The Osama bin Laden I Know,* 74–82; Assem Akram, *Histoire de la guerre d'Afghanistan* (Paris, 1996), 276–77.

72. Bruce Lawrence, ed., *Messages to the World: The Statements of Osama bin Laden* (London, 2005), xiii.

73. B. Raman, "Jamaat-e-Islami, Hizbul Mujahideen, and Al Qaeda" (South Asia Analysis Group paper no. 699, May 29, 2003): www.saag.org/papers7/paper699.html (accessed Oct. 31, 2006); Suba Chandran, "War in Iraq: Implications for Pakistan," Institute of Peace and Conflict Studies *Issue Brief* 6 (Apr. 2003): www.ipcs.org/newIpcsPublications.jsp?status=publications& status1=issue&mod=d&check=9&try=true; "Pakistan—Politics": www.globalsecurity.org/military/ world/pakistan/politics.htm, and Aqil Shah, "Musharraf's Democratic Talk, Military Walk," *World Leaders Forum,* Columbia University: http://ccnmtl.columbia.edu/projects/wlf/shah.html (all accessed Nov. 21, 2006); *New York Times,* Mar. 17, 2002, 1.

74. Statement of Sheikh Usamah Bin-Muhammad Bin-Ladin, Ayman al-Zawahiri, and three others, *Al-Quds al-'Arabi,* Feb. 23, 1998: www.ict.org.il/articles/fatwah.htm (accessed Jan. 15, 2006).

75. Anonymous letter, Sept. 26, 1998, translated in Alan Cullison, "Inside Al-Qaeda's Hard Drive," *Atlantic,* Sept. 2004, 60.

76. Jessica Stern, *Terror in the Name of God: Why Religious Militants Kill* (New York, 2003), 269.

77. Ramzi bin al-Shibh, "The Truth about the New Crusade: A Ruling on the Killing of Women and Children of the Non-Believers," translated in Cullison, "Inside Al-Qaeda's Hard Drive," 68.

78. David Bamber, "Bin Laden: Yes, I Did It," *London Daily Telegraph,* Nov. 11, 2001; Sheik Nasir bin Hamad al-Fahd, treatise quoted in Noah Feldman, "Islam, Terror and the Second Nuclear Age," *New York Times Magazine,* Oct. 29, 2006, 57.

79. Ayman al-Zawahiri to Abu Musab al-Zarqawi, "In the Name of God, Praise Be to God...," July 9, 2005: www.dni.gov/press_releases/letter_in_english.pdf (accessed Oct. 30, 2006).

80. Francis Deron, "Bloodshed in an Ancient Kingdom," *Guardian Weekly,* Dec. 23, 2005, 19; Chua, "JI School Grooming More Terrorists"; Lawrence, *Messages to the World,* 175.

81. Osama bin Laden to Mullah Omar, Oct. 3, 2001, translation in Cullison, "Inside Al-Qaeda's Hard Drive," 70.

82. Abdel Bari Atwan, *The Secret History of Al-Qaida* [2006], quoted in Charles Glass, "Cyber-Jihad," *London Review of Books,* Mar. 9, 2006, 16.

83. Transcript of bin Laden videotape, mid-Nov., 2001: www.msnbc.com/news/672063.asp (accessed Dec. 13, 2001).

84. Osama bin Laden, "To the Allies of America," Nov. 12, 2002, in Lawrence, *Messages to the World,* 174.

85. Elaine Sciolino, "From Tapes, a Chilling Voice of Islamic Radicalism in Europe," *New York Times,* Nov. 18, 2005, A1, A10.

86. Zawahiri to Zarqawi, "In the Name of God, Praise Be to God."

87. Statement of Bin-Ladin, al-Zawahiri, and three others.

88. Ayman al-Zawahiri, May 3, 2001, letter translated in Cullison, "Inside Al-Qaeda's Hard Drive," 65–67.

89. Unknown member of Islamic Jihad to Ayman al-Zawahiri, summer 2001, translation in Cullison, "Inside Al-Qaeda's Hard Drive," 67.

90. "Mending the Hearts of the Believers: The Link between the Campaigns in Makaleh, Fhilcha, and Bali," Yoni Fighel and Yoram Kehati, Institute of Counter-Terrorism, Nov. 28, 2002: www.ict.org.il (accessed Jan. 15, 2006).

91. Abu Musab al-Zarqawi, "In the Name of God, the Merciful, the Compassionate...," Feb. 2004, English translation at www.iraqcoalition.org/transcripts/20040212_zarqawi_full.html (accessed June 27, 2004).

92. Ibid.

93. Ibid.

94. Bin Laden to Mullah Omar, Oct. 3, 2001, letter translated in Cullison, "Inside Al-Qaeda's Hard Drive," 70; 58.

95. Transcript of bin Laden videotape.

96. Quoted in L. Paul Bremer, "In Iraq, Wrongs Made a Right," *New York Times,* Jan. 13, 2006, A21.

97. Zarqawi, "In the Name of God, the Merciful, the Compassionate."

98. Zarqawi, Apr. 6, 2004, doc. 13 in *What Does Al-Qaeda Want? Unedited Communiqués,* with commentary by Robert O. Marlin IV (Berkeley, 2004), 78–79.

99. "A Speech by Abu Musab al-Zarqawi from the Information Department of al-Qaeda Organization in the Land of Two Rivers," tr. SITE Institute, May 18, 2005: http://siteinstitute.org (accessed May 25, 2005).

100. Ibid.

101. Ayatollah Ali Al-Sistani, quoted in Georg Mascolo and Berhnard Zand, "Crumbling Iraq," *Der Spiegel,* July 25, 2005: http://service.spiegel.de/cache/international/spiegel/0,1518,druck-366834,00.html (accessed Jan. 6, 2006).

102. Zawahiri to Zarqawi, "In the Name of God, Praise Be to God."

103. "U.S. Uses Iraq Insurgent's Own Video to Mock Him," *New York Times,* May 5, 2006, A1, A12.

104. "Bin Laden Says West Is Waging War against Islam, and Urges Supporters to Go to Sudan," *New York Times,* Apr. 24, 2006, A8.

105. Jorge Cañizares Esguerra, "New World, New Stars: Patriotic Astrology and the Invention of Indian and Creole Bodies in Colonial Latin America, 1600–1650," *American Historical Review* 104:1 (1999): 47–49. See also chapters 1 and 3.

106. Adolf Hitler, *Mein Kampf* (New York, 1999), 423, 668.

107. Esguerra, "New World, New Stars," 34; Keith Thomas, *Man and the Natural World: Changing Attitudes in England, 1500–1800* (Oxford, 1983), 255–56; Wendy Lower, *Nazi Empire-Building and the Holocaust in Ukraine* (Chapel Hill, 2005), 99–101ff.; "Mending the Hearts of the Believers."

108. Alfred Rosenberg, Reich minister of the Occupied Eastern Territories, "Deutsche Siedler in südrussische Steppen gerufen als Pionere und vorbildliche Bauern," a summary of Rosenberg's planned lecture to Volksdeutsche, summer 1943 (I thank Wendy Lower for this citation; see also her *Nazi Empire-Building and the Holocaust in Ukraine,* 28); *Litzmannstädter Zeitung,* May 30, 1940; Ben Kiernan, *The Pol Pot Regime* (New Haven, 2002), 237; Schirmer, *Guatemalan Military Project,* 24, 70; Beatriz Manz, *Refugees of a Hidden War: The Aftermath of Counterinsurgency in Guatemala* (Albany, 1988), 111; CEH, *Guatemala: Memory of Silence,* 1:361, 3030; Defert, *Timor-Est,* 182; Joseph Ntamahungiro, "Eloge du Paysan Rwandais," *Dialogue* 130 (Sept.–Oct. 1988): 8; Charles Mironko, personal communication, Jan. 7, 2006. For "model villages" in Ireland in 1580, see p. 184 above.

109. Arthur Grey de Wilton, lord deputy of Ireland, to queen, Dec. 22, 1580, in Felix Pryor, *Elizabeth I: Her Life in Letters* (Berkeley, 2003), 77.

110. Sean O'Callaghan, *To Hell or Barbados: The Ethnic Cleansing of Ireland* (Dingle, 2000), 45; James Scott Wheeler, *Cromwell in Ireland* (Dublin, 1999), 5, 46; Nicholas Canny, *Making Ireland British, 1580–1660* (Oxford, 2001), 572; Tom Reilly, *Cromwell: An Honorable Enemy* (London, 1999), 20–22.

111. Reilly, *Cromwell,* 22.

112. Geoffrey Blomfield, *Baal Belbora: The End of the Dancing* (Sydney, 1981), 34; Katie Kane, "Nits Make Lice: Drogheda, Sand Creek, and the Poetics of Colonial Extermination," *Cultural Critique* 42 (1999): 81–103; Benjamin Madley, "California's Yuki," and "Killing the Yana" (both forthcoming). Madley cites Jeremiah Curtin's 1884 interviews with killers of Yana people, who stated, "We must kill them, big and little. Nits will be lice." Curtin, *Creation Myths of Primitive America . . .* (Boston, 1898), 517–18.

Acknowledgments

This book is a result of myriad conversations with people too numerous to name, but they all deserve my thanks.

My colleagues in the Genocide Studies Program at Yale University have been an inspiration for many years; I wish to thank in particular Johanna Bodenstab, Susan E. Cook, Kai Erikson, Geoffrey Hartman, Ethel Higonnet, Henry Huttenbach, Frederick J. Iseman, Helen Jarvis, Adam Jones, Edward Kissi, Dori Laub, Charles Mironko, Octovianus Mote, Barbara Papacoda, Niti Pawakapan, Thavro Phim, Toni Samantha Phim, Puangthong Rungswasdisab, Laura Saldivia, Russell Schimmer, and Philip Verwimp. Onetime graduate students affiliated with the program, including Jasmina Besirevic Regan, Soner Cagaptay, Frank Dhont, Heng Samnang, Curtis W. Lambrecht, Benjamin Madley, Kanika Mak, Charles Mironko, Jonathan Padwe, Lorraine Paterson, Steve Rhee, Miranda Sissons, Jessica Thorpe, and Charles Wheeler, have all taught me much. So have stimulating discussions with other colleagues at Yale, including Ivo Banac, Lydia Breckon, Nayan Chanda, Katherine Charron, Haydon Cherry, Harold C. Conklin, Tony Day, Michael Dove, Daniel Fineman, Kevin Fogg, Eugene Ford, Harvey Goldblatt, Valerie Hansen, Mette Bastholm Jensen, Charles Keith, Paul M. Kennedy, Christian Lentz, Adriane Lentz-Smith, Christian W. McMillen, Gustav Ranis, James C. Scott, Ian Shapiro, James Silk, Gaddis Smith, Eric Tagliacozzo, George R. Trumbull IV, Karl Turekian, Joanna Waley-Cohen, Sarah Weiss, and especially the late Robin W. Winks.

For their generous assistance in providing documents and suggestions for further research, I am very grateful to Doron Ben-Atar, Daniel Botsman, Kennon Breazeale, Daniel Chirot, Jason Cons, Nola Cooke, Vahakn N. Dadrian, Alison Des Forges, Brian W. Dippie, George Dutton, Peter Gay, the late Ruth Gay, Greg Grandin, Erik Grimmer-Solem, Nam-lin Hur, Simon Kim, Victor Lieberman, Wendy Lower,

Terry Martin, Ann McGrath, Linda Melvern, Sarah Shields, Kate Smith, Li Tana, C. Michele Thompson, Keng Vannsak, Stephen Vlastos, Elliott West, Charles Wheeler, and John K. Whitmore.

Daniel Botsman, Nam-lin Hur, and Simon Kim kindly supplied translations from Japanese; U Khin Maung Gyi from Burmese; Thavro Phim from Khmer; Puangthong Rungswasdisab and Chalong Soontravanich from Thai; Vy Vu and Mai Bui Dieu Linh from Vietnamese; Philippe Hunt from Dutch; and Ruth Hein from German. Unless otherwise noted, translations from French and Khmer are mine. Mark Beyersdorf, Denise Bossy, Brendan Brown, Alyce Hong Van, Kendra Mack, Nano Nagle, Van Nguyen, Don Phan, Rory Rapple, David A. Smith, and Vy Vu furnished valuable research assistance.

Michael Adas and Kai Erikson generously read drafts of the whole book and offered many helpful suggestions for which I am most grateful. Rolena Adorno, Doron Ben-Atar, Bain Attwood, Morten Bergsmo, R. Howard Bloch, Shayne Breen, Nicholas Canny, Vincent Carey, Paul Cartledge, Alfred A. Cave, Frank Chalk, Ian D. Clark, Juan R. I. Cole, Marcia Colish, Nola Cooke, Jan Critchett, Ann Curthoys, John Demos, John Mack Faragher, Sheila Fitzpatrick, Nancy Florida, Paul Freedman, Robert Gellately, Glenda E. Gilmore, Stephen L. Goldwater, Valerie Hansen, Manfred Henningsen, Richard Hovannisian, Nam-lin Hur, Peter B. Kiernan, Howard R. Lamar, Bill Leadbetter, Victor Lieberman, Ramsay MacMullen, Benjamin Madley, Robert Melson, John Merriman, Susanna Morton Braund, A. Dirk Moses, Stephen F. Nagle, Val Noone, Kevin Repp, Henry Reynolds, Merle C. Ricklefs, Lyndall Ryan, Timothy Snyder, Jonathan D. Spence, Gregory H. Stanton, Yuki Tanaka, Frank M. Turner, Henry A. Turner, Stephen G. Wheatcroft, John K. Whitmore, and Jay Winter all kindly read drafts of various parts of this book and provided helpful criticisms and feedback. None of them, however, should be held responsible for my views or for any errors remaining in the book.

This book could not have been written without the extraordinary research resources of Yale University's Sterling Memorial Library, including the Southeast Asia Collection and its hardworking curator, Rich Richie. I am also grateful to Chip Long and to the Whitney and Betty MacMillan Center for International and Area Studies at Yale for research support, to the Harry Frank Guggenheim Foundation for a grant that enabled me to write much of the book, and to the National Humanities Center for a grant that facilitated its completion. My editors at Yale University Press, Larisa Heimert and Chris Rogers, assistant editors Eleanor Goldberg and Laura Davulis, production editor Jessie Hunnicutt, copyeditor Robin DuBlanc, and my literary agent, Lisa Adams, have all been unfailingly supportive.

This book is dedicated to my wife, Glenda Elizabeth Gilmore, who made it happen, and to our family: Mia-lia, Derry, and Miles.

Index